WELCOME

Well, I'll be darned. In spite of efforts to suppress this secret book, you managed to find it. Now the power of computer wisdom will be passed to *you*, so *you* can become the next computer guru.

Insiders have known about this book for years. It's praised by computer experts worldwide for being the best computer book ever written, the key that unlocks the darkest secrets and cuts through the crap. Now those secrets are *yours*.

Phone me

While you train to become the next computer guru, phone me whenever you have a question about computers — or life — at my **secret home phone number: 617-666-2666**.

It's easy to memorize! After dialing Boston's area code (617), dial the phone number for the devil's double: 666-2-666.

Dial it when you wonder what-the-devil your computer's doing. When computers make you ill, dial "Sick, sick, sick! Too sick, sick, sick!"

Phone day or night, 24 hours: I'm almost always in, and I sleep just lightly.

Folks have smuggled copies of this secret book worldwide so I get phone calls from Finland, Ghana, Singapore, and even wilder places, such as Brooklyn. Each month, *thousands* more would-be gurus phone me for help. Now my life consists mainly of juggling phone calls to keep folks happy while still fulfilling my other responsibilities, such as constructing the next edition of this book.

The computer industry's getting worse. The friendly hobbyists who started this industry have been replaced by marketroids who give you no help unless you dial a 900 number or masochistically wait on hold for 45 minutes.

I'm one of the last fools still trying to give free help through computer Hell. My phone lines jam from thousands of frustrated computer users sobbing entreaties such as:

"Yes, Father, I have sinned. In a fit of jealously, I tried to double the size of my hard disk by putting it on steroids — using Mem Maker — and now my computer has become a mumbling idiot. I must do penance. Help me return my hard disk to the virgin innocence it once knew."

To juggle all the phone calls, I've made a few rules. . . .

Since this book's become too huge to read over the phone, if you ask me a question answered therein, I'll say which pages to read. After reading, phone me with any further questions.

If you want advice about which computer to buy, read the *newest* edition of the book, then phone me. For help curing an ill computer, call me when *your phone is next to the computer*. For help running a program, phone me when you're at the computer and *have the program's official manual*.

To handle hundreds of calls per day and still find time for my research and business responsibilities, I must keep the average call to 5 minutes. **Begin by saying your name, city, how you got my number ("from the 20th edition"), and a once-sentence summary of your question.** Then we'll chat — unless I'm in the middle of another call or meeting, in which case I'll call you back, free!

Come visit

Whenever you visit the Boston area, you can drop in and use my free computer library. Drop in anytime: day or night! But **in case I'm having an orgy with my 50 computers, please phone first** to pick a time when we're cooled down.

Mail the coupon

Mail us the coupon on this [...] you on our mailing list, which g[...] many wild services. You also get [...] this book.

Love your librarian

These details will help your librarian fill in the file cards and not get fired.

Title: The Secret Guide to Computers, 20th edition
So-called author: Russ Walter (also known as "Russy-poo")
Publisher: the same servant as the author
Address: bedroom at 22 Ashland St., Somerville MA 02144
Copywrong: 1995 by Russ Walter
International Standard Book Number (ISBN): 0-939151-20-0
Library of Congress: numbers pending; earlier edition 89-51851, QA 76 .W3

Elfish fun

This book was constructed by elves and associated critters, aiming to make your life elful instead of awful.

Grand elves:	Yvonne Bohemier	Lisbeth Shaw
Elfettes:	Kira Barnum	Maura Cabral
Friendly ghosts:	Cathy Carlson	Heather Hill
Sorcerer's apprentices:	Linda Gardner	Liz Card
Meadow sprites:	Irene Vassos	Richard Grant
Wandering minstrels:	Larry Mancini	Jeff Lowe
Artistes bizarre:	Cindy Best	Susan Goldenberg
Bubbly brights:	Anthony Kind	Nancy Kafka
Gigantic alien brains:	Adam Green	Roy Krantz
Friends of the Shah:	Michael Krigsman	Celena Sun
Queens from bygone days:	Priscilla Grogan	Julianne Wattles
Cantabrigian consorts:	Ken Russell	Naava Frank
Mischievous muses:	Lili Timmons	Shannon Linville
Brothers grin:	Dan Walter	Jim Walter
Women who wonder:	Ruth Spingarn	Donna Liao
Printer devils:	John Pow	Semline
Art collectors:	Dover	Formatt
Gnome (and is an island unto himself):	Russy-poo	

Introductory junk

My editor told me to put this stuff in. You don't have to read it.

Dedication I dedicate this book to the computer, without whom I'd be unemployed.

What this book will do for you It'll make you even richer than the author! Alas, he's broke.

Prerequisite This book was written for idiots. To see whether you can get through the math, take this test: count to ten but (here's the catch!) without looking at your fingers.

Acknowledgment I'd like to thank . . .

my many friends (whose names I've gladly forgotten);
my students (who naturally aren't my friends);
my word processor (which has a mind of its own);
all others who helped make this book impossible.

Apology Any original ideas in this book are errors.

Disclaimer The author denies any knowledge of the scintillating illegal activities he depicts.

Copyright Our copyright policy is simple: hey, copying is all right! Make as many copies as you like, and don't pay us a cent. Just follow the "free reprint" instructions on page 9.

Forward . . . because it's too late to turn back.

The Secret Guide to Computers is the world's only *complete* computer tutorial: it covers *everything* important about computers!

Feast your eyes on the massive table of contents, splashed across the next page. It reveals that the Guide includes all 8 parts of computer lore: "Buyer's guide", "Operating systems", "Word processing", "Databases", "Spreadsheets", "Wild applications", "Programming", and "Endnotes".

Buyer's guide

The Guide begins by explaining computer technology, computer jargon, and how to buy a great computer cheaply.

It analyzes each of the computer's parts (the **chips, disks, screens, printers, other hardware**, and **software**) and tells you the best way to buy a complete computer system. It explains how to buy the most common kind of computers (**IBM-compatibles**), the fascinating competitors from **Apple**, and **alternative computers** that are wildly different.

The Guide makes specific recommendations about which brands to buy and where to buy them. It delves into each manufacturer's goodies and not-so-goodies. It reveals the nasty details that salespeople try to hide. It turns you into a German nun, who knows the difference between what's blessed and what's wurst.

Operating systems

After getting a computer, you operate it by typing commands on its keyboard or wiggling its mouse. The Guide explains the popular operating systems: **MS-DOS** (used by IBM), the **Mac system** (used by the Apple Macintosh), and **Windows** (which makes IBM imitate a Macintosh).

Word processing

The most popular thing to do with a computer is to make it replace your typewriter. That's called "word processing". The word-processing chapter explains how to use the fanciest word-processing programs: **Ami Pro** (which is hassle-free), **Microsoft Word** (which performs many nifty tricks), and **Word Perfect** (the old classic still used by most businesses).

Databases

Instead of using file cards, put **databases** on the computer! The Guide explains how to use the easiest wonderful database program (**Q&A**) and analyzes **advanced databases** that are harder.

Spreadsheets

Tables of numbers are called **spreadsheets**. The Guide explains how to use the fanciest spreadsheet program: **Excel**. It also explains how to use competitors (**1-2-3 & Quattro**), which cost less to run.

Wild applications

The Guide lets you have wild fun and explore frontiers that are wildly challenging. You learn how to make the computer handle **graphics, desktop publishing, sound, multimedia, communication** (with the help of telephones and networking), **accounting** (incredibly difficult to do right!),

personal programs (everything from lovemaking to therapy!), **games** (I confess that they're the real reason why most of us buy computers), and **artificial intelligence** (the attempt to make the computer become human).

Programming

Our world is split into three classes of people:

avoiders (who fear and loathe computers and avoid them)
users (who use computers but don't really understand them)
programmers (who understand computers and can teach them new tricks)

The Guide elevates your mind to the heights of class 3: it turns you into a sophisticated programmer.

Since the Guide's explanation of "BASIC" expands your understanding of computers so dramatically, don't wait! Start reading it the same day you start "Databases" — as if you were taking two courses simultaneously.

To program the computer, you feed it instructions written in a *computer language*. The Guide explains all the popular computer languages.

It begins with the easiest popular language (**BASIC**).

Then it explains **DBASE** (the fanciest language for handling databases). It even covers the hot, new, improved versions of DBASE (such as DBASE 4 and Fox Pro).

Many colleges require freshmen to learn **PASCAL**. The Guide explains it, and even PASCAL's new Turbo versions.

All modern programs for word processing, databases, and spreadsheets were created by using **"C"**. The Guide explains Turbo C, Quick C, Microsoft C, and competitors.

Many elementary schools require their students to learn how to program in **LOGO**, a language that makes turtles dance across the computer's screen. The Guide explains 12 versions of LOGO.

In the "good old days", when programmers were treated like gods, the most popular computer languages were **FORTRAN** (for scientists) and **COBOL** (for businesses). Though they're called "the languages for old fogeys" now, many big computers still thrive on them — and so do many careers! The Guide covers a semester's course in each.

A gigantic chapter analyzes 23 **strange tongues** and divides those computer languages into three categories.

mainstream languages: FORTRAN, ALGOL, COBOL, BASIC, PL/I, PASCAL, MODULA, C, ADA, DBASE, EASY

radical languages: LISP, SNOBOL, APL, LOGO, FORTH, PILOT

specialized languages: APT, DYNAMO, GPSS, RPG, SPSS, PROLOG

The chapter tutors you in all of them. It even includes a multilingual dictionary that helps you translate programs to different computer languages.

To top it all off, you learn how to program by using the most common **assembler** for the IBM PC and translate your programs to the Macintosh and other computers.

Endnotes

I hate to admit it, but occasionally computers break! The chapter on **repairs** explains how to fix them.

We members of the computer industry all have skeletons in our closet. The Guide digs up **our past** and counsels you about how to improve your career and **your future**.

You also get an explanation of **numerical analysis**, an **index** to the entire Guide, and **coupons** for getting more goodies! Wow!

TABLE OF CONTENTS

PRAISED BY REVIEWERS

If you like this book, you're not alone.

Praised by computer magazines

All the famous computer magazines call Russ Walter "Boston's computer guru" and praise him for giving free consulting even in the middle of the night. Here's how they evaluate The Secret Guide to Computers. . . .

PC World: "Russ Walter is a PC pioneer, a trailblazer, the user's champion. Nobody does a more thorough, practical, and entertaining job of teaching PC technology. His incomparable Guide receives nothing but praise for its scope, wit, and enormous practicality. It offers a generous compendium of industry gossip, buying advice, and detailed, foolproof tutorials. It's a wonderful bargain."

Byte: "The Guide is amazing. If you need to understand computers and haven't had much luck at it, or have to teach other people about computers, or just want to read a good book about computers, get the Guide."

Computer Currents: "Your computer literacy quotient will always come up short unless you know something about Russ Walter. He's a folk hero. He knows virtually everything about personal computers and makes learning about computers fun. If you've given up in disgust and dismay at reading other computer books, get the Guide. It should be next to every PC in the country. PC vendors would do themselves and their customers a big favor by packing a copy of the Guide with every computer that goes out the door. The Guide deserves the very highest recommendation."

PC Magazine: "The Guide explains the computer industry, hardware, languages, operating systems, and applications in a knowledgeable and amusing fashion. It includes Russ Walter's unbiased view of the successes and failures of various companies, replete with inside gossip. By working your way through it, you'll know more than many who make their living with PCs. Whether novice or expert, you'll learn from the Guide and have a good time doing so. No other computer book is a better value."

Abacus: "Alternative-culture Walter provides the best current treatment of programming languages. It's irreverent, reminiscent of the underground books of the 1960's. It's simple to read, fast-paced, surprisingly complete, full of locker-room computer gossip, and loaded with examples."

Infoworld: "Russ Walter is recognized and respected in many parts of the country as a knowledgeable and effective instructor. His Guide is readable, outrageous, and includes a wealth of information."

Mac User: "It's an everything-under-one-roof computer technology guide."

Computerworld: "The Guide by unconventional computer guru Russ Walter is informative and entertaining."

Computer Shopper: "The Guide covers the entire spectrum. It's incredibly informative and amusing."

Home Office Computing: "Russ Walter is a computer missionary who's a success story."

Classroom Computer Learning: "Russ Walter's courses are intensive and inexpensive."

Compute: "Russ Walter is an industry leader."

Praised by the classics Earlier editions of the Guide were praised by all the classic computer magazines.

Popular Computing: "Russ Walter is king of the East Coast computer cognoscenti. His Guide is the biggest bargain in computer tutorials in our hemisphere. If CBS ever decides to replace Andy Rooney with a '60 Minutes' computer pundit, they'd need to look no further than Russ Walter. His wry Walterian observations enliven nearly every page of his book. His Guide is the first collection of computer writings that one might dare call literature."

Personal Computing: "The Guide is bulging with information. You'll enjoy it. Russ Walter's approach to text-writing sets a new style that other authors might do well to follow. It's readable, instructive, and downright entertaining. If more college texts were written in the Russ Walter style, more college students would reach their commencement day."

Creative Computing: "The Guide is fascinating, easy to understand, an excellent book at a ridiculously low price. We especially endorse it."

Cider Press: "The Guide should be given to all beginners with the purchase of their computers."

Softalk: "The Guide fires well-deserved salvos at many sacred cows. It's long been a cult hit."

Computer Bargain Info: "The Guide is widely acclaimed by experts as brilliant."

Eighty Micro: "Theatrical, madcap Russ is a cult hero."

Interface Age: "The Guide is a best buy."

Enter: "It's the best book about computer languages."

Microcomputing: "Plan ahead; get in on the Secret now."

Praised by mass-market magazines

Mass-market magazines call the Guide amazing.

Scientific American: "The Guide is irresistible. Every instruction leads to a useful result. Walter's candor shines; he makes clear the faults and foibles others ignore or cast in vague hints. The effect is that of a private conversation with a well-informed talkative friend who knows the inside story. The text reads like the patter of a talented midnight disc jockey; it's flip, self-deprecatory, randy, and good-humored. His useful frank content and coherent style are unique. First-rate advice on what and how to buy are part of the rich mix. No room holding a small computer and an adult learning to use it is well equipped without the Guide."

The Whole Earth Catalog in its "Coevolution Quarterly": "The personal-computer subculture was noted for its fierce honesty in its early years. The Guide is one of the few intro books to carry on that tradition, and the only introductory survey of equipment that's kept up to date. Russ Walter jokes, bitches, enthuses, condemns, and charms. The book tells the bald truth in comprehensible language."

Omni: "Guru Russ Walter sympathizes deeply with people facing a system crash at midnight, so he broadcasts his home phone number and answers calls by the light of his computers, cursors winking. He's considered an excellent teacher. His Guide is utterly comprehensive."

Changing Times: "Russ Walter is a computer whiz whose mission is to educate people about computers. Like a doctor, he lets strangers call him in the middle of the night for help with diagnosing a sick computer. His Guide covers everything you ever wanted to know."

Esquire: "The handy Guide contains lots of fact and opinion untainted by bias."

Barron's: "Russ Walter is an expert who answers questions for free and has been inundated by calls."

Praised by computer clubs

Computer clubs call the Guide the best computer book, in their newsletters, newspapers, and magazines.

Boston Computer Society: "The Guide is cleverly graduated, outrageous, and funny. Russ Walter turns computerese into plain speaking, while making you giggle. He's years ahead of the pack that claims to have ways of instructing computer novices. His unique mix of zany humor and step-by-step instruction avoids the mistakes of manuals that attempt to follow his lead."

Connecticut Computer Society: "Russ Walter's books have been used by insiders for years. He's special as a teacher because of three factors: his comprehensive knowledge of many computers and their languages, operating system, and applications; his ability to break complicated processes into the smallest components; and his humor. A valuable feature of the Guide is his candid comments about various computers and software. He's one of the few people able to review languages, machines, and software, all in a humorous, clear manner, with the whole endeavor set off by his sense of industry perspective, history, and culture. If you're ever struck with a computer problem, give Russ a call."

New England Computer Society: "Russ Walter is considered one of the few true computer gurus. His Guide is the world's best tutorial. It's the single best present anyone could receive who cares to know more about computers without going crazy."

New York's "NYPC": "The Guide is the perfect text for anyone beginning to learn about computers because it contains real info in readable form about a range of subjects otherwise requiring a whole reference library. It's even better for the experienced computer user, since it also contains many, many advanced concepts that one person could hardly remember. But one person apparently remembered them all: Russ Walter. He's a fountain of computer knowledge and can even explain it in words of one syllable. His Guide reads like a novel: you can read simply for fun. It's recommended to anyone from rank beginner to seasoned power user."

Sacramento (California) PC Users Group: "The Guide is the best collection of computer help ever written. It includes just about everything you'd want to know about computers. You'll find answers for all the questions you thought of and some you didn't think of. No holds barred, Walter even tells you who in the industry made the mistakes and rotten computers, and who seemed to succeed in spite of themselves. The Guide is fascinating. It's recommended for anyone even slightly interested in computers."

Praised by librarians

Librarians call the Guide the best computer book ever written.

School Library Journal: "The Guide is a gold mine of information. It's crystal clear, while at the same time Walter delivers a laugh a paragraph along with a *lot* of excellent info. It's accessible even to kids, who will love its loony humor. Buy it; you'll *like* it."

Wilson Library Bulletin: "The Guide is distinguished by its blend of clarity, organization, and humor. It cuts through the techno-haze. It packs more simple, fresh explication per page than anything else available."

Praised around the world

The Guide is praised by newspapers around the world.

Australia's "Sydney Morning Herald": "The Guide is the best computer intro published anywhere in the world. It gives a total overview of personal computers. It's stimulating, educational, provocative, and a damn good read."

The Australian: "The Guide's coverage of programming is intelligent, urbane, extremely funny, and full of great ideas."

England's "Manchester Guardian": "Russ Walter is a welcome relief. The internationally renowned computer guru tries to keep computerdom's honesty alive. His Guide is an extraordinary source of information."

Silicon Valley's "Times Tribune": "The Guide invites you to throw aside all rules of conventional texts and plunge into the computer world entirely naked and unafraid. This book makes learning not only fun, but hilarious, inspiring, and addicting."

Dallas Times Herald: "Easily the best beginners' book seen, it's not just for beginners. Its strength is how simple it makes everything, without sacrificing what matters."

Detroit News: "Russ Walter is a legendary teacher. His fiercely honest Guide packs an incredible amount of info. It's the only book that includes everything. He gives you all the dirt about the companies and their hardware, evaluates their business practices, and exposes problems they try to hide. Phone him. You'll always get a truthful answer."

Chicago Tribune: "The Guide is the best computer book. It's a cornucopia of computer delights written by Russ Walter, a great altruist and dreamer."

Kentucky's "Louisville Courier": "Walter's Guide will teach you more computer fundamentals than the thick books in the average bookstore. The Guide gives his no-bull insights. He not only discusses computer mail-order sources, which most books avoid; he names the bad guys. The Guide's biggest appeal is its humor, wit, and personality."

Philadelphia Inquirer: "Russ Walter is the Ann Landers for computer klutzes, a high-tech hero. His wacky, massive Guide is filled with his folksy wit."

New York Times: "The computer-obsessed will revel in Walter's Guide. He covers just about every subject in the microcomputer universe. It's unlikely you have a question his book doesn't answer."

Wall Street Journal: "Russ Walter is a computer expert, a guru who doesn't mind phone calls. He brings religious-like fervor to the digital world. His students are grateful. His Guide gets good reviews. He's influential."

Connecticut's "Hartford Courant": "If you plan to buy a personal computer, the best gift to give yourself is the Guide. It's crammed with info. It became an instant success as one of the few microcomputer books that was not only understandable and inexpensive but also witty — a combination still too rare today."

Boston Globe: "Russ Walter is a unique resource, important to beginning and advanced users. His Guide is practical, down-to-earth, and easy to read."

Boston Phoenix: "Russ Walter has achieved international cult status. He knows his stuff, and his comprehensive Guide is a great deal."

From our readers, we've received *thousands* of letters and phone calls, praising us. Here are some recent examples.

Intoxicated

Our books make readers go nuts.

Get high "I'm high! Not on marijuana, crack, or cocaine, but on what I did at my computer with BASIC and your Guide." (Beverly, Massachusetts)

Strange laughs "I enjoy the Guide *immensely*! My fellow workers think I'm strange because of all my laughing while reading it. Whenever I feel tired or bored, I pick up the Guide. It's very refreshing!" (Acton, Massachusetts)

Poo-poo "I finished the book at 2:30 AM and had to sit down and send you a big THANK-YOU-poo. A poet I am not, crazy I was not, until I started 18 months ago with this computer and then came *poo* who sealed my lot." (Hinesville, Georgia)

Computer dreams "Wow — I loved your book. My husband says I talk about computers in my sleep." (Los Altos Hills, California)

Bedtime story "The book's next to the bed, where my wife and I can see who grabs it first. The loser must find something else to do, which often causes serious degradation of reading comprehension." (Danville, New Hampshire)

Love in Paris "If you ever come to Paris, give me a call. I'll be more than happy to meet the guy I admire most in the computer industry." (Paris)

Sex "Great book. Better than sex." (Worcester, Massachusetts)

Devil "This book is great. It moves like the fastest Mac, soars with the eagles, and dances with the devil." (Chicago)

God "I'm a Russy groupie now! You are God! Your book lets me put it all together." (San Diego)

National TV "Great! When are you going on national TV? America needs you!" (Berkeley, California)

National debt "I think you do a fabulous job with computers! You should be in Washington & organize our country, and maybe we could be debt-free." (Tavares, Florida)

Beginners

Even beginners can master the Guide.

Godsend "You're a godsend. You saved me from being bamboozled by the local computer store." (Boston)

Saint "You should be canonized for bringing clarity and humor to a field often incomprehensible and dull." (Houston)

Companion to the lonely "Your book's a nice companion when I'm alone, because it talks. It answers more questions than I can ask." (Carson, California)

Computer disease "I was scared to go near a computer. I thought I might catch something. Now I can't wait." (Paterson, New Jersey)

Face-off "I used to be an idiot. Now I can stare my computer in the face. Thanks." (San Antonio, Texas)

Amaze the professor "I *love* the Guide! I've read it before taking a BASIC course, and I'm amazing my professor with my secret skills!" (Olney, Illinois)

Walking encyclopedia "Your Guide really helps. I work with a great programmer who's like a walking computer encyclopedia. Now I know what he's saying!" (San Leandro, California)

Muscle in "So many computer experts speak a language all their own. They look down on us and consider us to be outsiders trying to muscle our way into their world. Thanks for helping the outsiders." (New Iberia, Lousiana)

Facing fear "Thank you! I'm 42, married to a computer guru, with two daughters who've been in front of a computer since first grade. *Finally*, I feel that I can face my fear and that I'm not alone." (Malvern, Pennsylvania)

Granny's clammy "I'm a 58-year-old grandma. My daughter gave me an IBM PC. After weeks of frustration I got your Guide. Now I'm happy as a clam at high tide, eager to learn more & more. Wow!" (Seattle)

Moment of discovery "After retiring, I searched for something to stimulate my mind. I bought a computer and tried to unravel its mysteries. The more I studied big books bought from computer stores, the more confused I became. Then I stumbled across the Guide. At that precise moment I discovered the beautiful, crazy, wild world of the computer! Thanks." (Tewksbury, Massachusetts)

Bury the Book of Songs "This is the microcomputer book that should be buried in a time capsule for future archaeologists. By reading it, I've made my computer sing. My wife recognizes the melodies and wants to read the book." (Park Forest, Illinois)

Experts

Experts love the Guide.

PC Week reporter "I write for *PC Week* and think the Guide is the *best* book of its kind. I'm sending a copy to my little brother, who's a budding byte-head." (Boston)

Editor at Lotus "Thanks *so* much for sending the Guide. It's great! Seems I'm the only one here in my office at Lotus who hadn't heard about it. You've got quite a following. Again, thanks!" (Cambridge, Massachusetts)

Math professor "I'm a math professor. The Guide's the best way in the universe to keep up to date with computers. People don't have to read anything else — it's *all* there." (New York City)

Diehard mainframer "It is really neat! I've been a mainframe computer consultant for many years, and when your book came yesterday I couldn't put it down." (Cleveland Heights, Ohio)

Refreshed programmers "I passed the Guide around my team of mainframe programmers, and most of them bought. It's so refreshing, after the parched dryness of IBM-ese, to find a book in English!" (Union, New Jersey)

Research center "Our research center uses and misuses gigabytes of computers. The Guide will improve our use/misuse ratio." (Naperville, Illinois)

Careers

The Guide's propelled many careers.

Land a first job "Last month, I bought your Guide. I've never seen so much info, packed so densely, in so entertaining a read. I was just offered a computer job, thanks to a presentation based on your Guide. I'm very, very, very happy I bought your book." (San Francisco)

Land a top job "Thanks to the Guide, I got an excellent job guiding the selection of computers in a department of over 250 users!" (New York City)

Found Wall Street "Eight years ago, I took your intro programming course. Now I run the computer department of a Wall Street brokerage firm. I'm responsible for 30 people and millions of dollars of computer equipment. The Guide's always been my foremost reference. Thank you for the key to wonderful new worlds." (Long Beach, New York)

Consultant's dream "Inspired by your book, your love for computers, and your burning desire to show the world that computers are fun and easily accessible, I entered the computer field. Now I'm a computer consultant. Your ideas come from the heart. Thanks for following your dream." (Skokie, Illinois)

Kid who grew up "Years ago, I saw you sell books while wearing a wizard's cap. I bought a book and was as impressed as a 16-year-old could be. Now I've earned B.A.'s in Computer Science and English, and I'm contemplating teaching computers to high school students. I can think of no better way to plan a course outline than around your Guide." (Pennington, New Jersey)

Better late than never

Readers wish they'd found the Guide sooner.

1 year "I learned more from the Guide than from a year in the computer industry." (Redwood City, California)

5 years "I've fumbled for 5 years with computers and many books, all with short-lived flashes of enthusiasm, until I found your Guide. It's the first book that showed a light at the end of the tunnel, even for one as dull-brained as I." (Boise)

17 years "Though in a computer company for 17 years, I didn't learn anything about computers until I began reading the Guide. I love it! I always thought computer people were generically boring, but your book's changed my mind." (Hopkinton, Massachusetts)

Prince Charming arrives "Where have you been all my life? I wish I'd heard of your Guide long ago. I'd have made far fewer mistakes if it had been here alongside my computer." (White Stone, Virginia)

Hack a Mac "Great book. I'm 14 and always wanted to hack. Thanks to your Guide, I laughed myself to death and look forward to gutting my Mac. Yours is the friendliest, funniest book on computers I've seen. I'm finally going to teach my parents BASIC. If I'd started out with the Guide, I'd have saved five years of fooling around in the dark." (Northport, Alabama)

Pass-alongs

Readers pass the Guide to their friends.

Round the office "Send 150 books. I passed my Guide around the office, and just about everyone who saw it wants copies." (Middleburg Heights, Ohio)

Coordinating the coordinators "Your book is amazing! I'm telling the other 50 PC coordinators in my company to be sure they're in on the secret. Bless you for your magnanimous philosophy!" (Morristown, New Jersey)

Hide your secrets "I thought the Guide marvelous and proudly displayed it on my desk. A friend from South Africa saw it and said our friendship depended on letting her take it home with her. What could I do? You've gone international. I'm ordering another copy. Should I hide the book this time?" (Cinnaminson, New Jersey)

Cries and anger "I made the mistake of letting several friends borrow my copy of the Guide. Each time I tried getting it back, it was a battle. (I hate to see grown people cry.) I promised to order them copies of their own. I delayed several months, and now I've got an angry mob outside my door. While you process my order, I'll try pacifying them by reading aloud." (Winston-Salem, North Carolina)

Round the house "Dad bought your Guide to help him understand my computer. It's become the most widely read book in our house. We love it!" (Boca Raton, Florida)

Squabble with Dad "I love the Guide. Dad & I squabble over our only copy. Send a second so I can finish the Guide in peace." (New York City)

Change my brother "The Guide changed my computer scorn & fear to interest. Send my brother a copy, to effect the same transformation." (New York City)

Selling clones "I took the Guide to a meeting and used your words as a reason why the group should buy an IBM PC clone instead of the other computer they were looking at. It worked." (Sparks, Nevada)

Make your guru giggle "I showed the Guide to my guru. Between laughs, chuckles, and guffaws, he agreed to use it to teach his high-school computer class. He even admitted he'd learned something, and that's the most unheard of thing I ever heard of." (Arivaca, Arizona)

Smarter sales reps "Our company just released its first software product, and our sales reps are panic-stricken. I'm giving them the Guide to increase their computer background. Thanks for a super book." (Pittsburgh)

Advancing secretary "I'm ordering an extra copy for my secretary, to start her on the path to a higher paying and better regarded position." (Belleville, Illinois)

Compared with other publishers

The Guide's better than any other book.

Better than 10 "I learned more from your Guide than from a total of 10 books read previously." (Honolulu)

No big bucks "Your book is great! Its crazy style really keeps the pages turning. I appreciate someone who doesn't try to make big bucks off someone trying to learn. Thanks." (Vancouver, Washington)

Rip-off "If you can break even at your book's low price, lots of guys are ripping us off." (Choctaw, Oklahoma)

This section reveals who we are — even if you'd rather not know.

Interview with Russ

In this interview, Russ answers the most popular questions about this book and what's behind it.

Why did you write the Secret Guide? I saw my students spending too much effort taking notes, so I made up my own notes to hand them. Over the years, my notes got longer, so that the 20th edition totals 639 pages. Each time I develop a new edition, I try to make it the kind of book I wish I had when *I* was a student.

What does the Guide cover? Everything. Every computer topic is touched on, and the most important topics are covered in depth.

Who reads the Guide? All sorts. Kids read it because it's easy; computer professionals read it because it contains lots of secret tidbits you can't find anywhere else.

Why do you charge so little? I'm not trying to make a profit. I'm just trying to make people happy — by charging as little as possible, while still covering my expenses. Instead of "charging as much as the market will bear", I try to "charge so little that the public will cheer".

Do you really answer the phone 24 hours a day? When do you sleep? When folks call in the middle of the night, I wake up, answer their questions, then go back to bed. I'm near the phone 85% of the time. If you get no answer, I'm out on a brief errand, so please call again. If you get an answering machine, I'm out on a longer project: just leave your number and I'll call you back at *my* expense, even if it's long distance.

Why do you give phone help free? Are you a masochist, a saint, or a nut? I give the free help for three reasons: I like to be a nice guy; it keeps me in touch with my readers, who suggest how to improve the Guide further; and the happy callers tell their friends about me, so I don't have to spend money on advertising.

At computer shows, do you really appear as a witch? I wear a witch's black hat and red kimono over a monk's habit and roller skates, while my white gloves caress an African spear. Why? Because it's fun!

Did you write the whole Guide yourself? Yes, but I received many suggestions from my readers, friends, and staff, who also contributed some examples and phrases.

What's your background? I got degrees in math and education from Dartmouth and Harvard, taught at several colleges (Wellesley, Wesleyan, and Northeastern), and was a founding editor of *Personal Computing* magazine. But most of my expertise comes from spending long hours every day reading computer books and magazines, discussing computer questions on the phone, and analyzing the philosophy underlying the computer industry.

About the so-called author

Since the author is so lifeless, we can keep his bio mercifully short.

Birth of a notion The author, Russy-poo, was conceived in 1946. So was the modern ("stored-program") computer.

Nine months later, Russy-poo was hatched. The modern computer took a few years longer, so Russ got a head start. But the computer quickly caught up. Ever since, they've been racing against each other, to see who's smartest.

The race is close, because Russ and the computer have so much in common. Folks say the computer "acts human" and say Russ's personality is "as a dead as a computer".

Junior Jews Russ resembles a computer in many ways. For example, both are Jewish.

The father of the modern computer was John von Neumann, a Jew of German descent. After living in Hungary, he fled the Nazis and became a famous U.S. mathematician.

The father of Russy-poo Walter was Henry Walter, a German Jew who fled the Nazis and became a famous U.S. dental salesman. To dentists, he sold teeth, dental chairs, and balloons to amuse the kids while their mouths were mauled.

The race for brains To try beating the computer, Russ got his bachelor's degree in math from Dartmouth in yummy '69 and sadly remained a bachelor ever since (unless you count the computer he got married to).

After Dartmouth, he got an M.A.T. in math education from Harvard. Since he went to Harvard, you know he's a genius. Like most genii, he achieved the high honor of being a junior-high teacher.

After his classes showered him with the Paper Airplane Award, he moved on to teach at an exclusive private school for girls who were *very* exclusive. ("Exclusive" means everyone can come except you.)

After teaching every grade from 2 through 12 (he taught the 2nd-grade girls how to run the computer, and the 12th graders less intellectual things), he fled reality by joining Wesleyan University's math Ph.D. program in Connecticut's Middletown (the middle of Nowhere), where after 18 months of highbrow hoopla he was seduced by a computer to whom he's now happily married.

Married life After the wedding, Russ moved with his electrifying wife to Northeastern University in Boston (home of the bean and the cod), where he did a hilarious job of teaching in the naughty Department of "Graphic Science". After quitting Northeastern and also editorship of *Personal Computing*, he spends his time now happily losing money by publishing this book.

Since his wife was lonely, he bought her 40 computers to keep her company, with names such as "Anita Atari", "Aphrodite the Apple", "Baby Blue Burping Bonnie", "Coco the Incredible Clown", "Jack the Shack", "Kooky Casio", "Slick Vic", and "Terrible Tina with her Texas Instruments". He hid them in a van and drove them around the country, where they performed orgies and did a strip tease, to show students a thing or two about computer anatomy.

Banned in Boston, Russ and his groupies moved north, where they hide in a pleasure palace underneath the Porter Square pine tree. Each room in the palace has a nickname. Come visit the "Input Room" (kitchen), bathroom ("Output"), three hi-tech rooms ("Production", "Research", and "Creativity"), and four devilish rooms ("Sunshine", "The Cavern", "Pleasure", and "Pain").

Russ's body Here are Russ's stats, from head to toe: **head** in the clouds, **hair** departing, **brow** beaten, **eyes** glazed, **lashes** 40, **nose** to the grindstone, **mouth** off, **smile** bionic, **tongue** bitten, **teeth** remembered, **cheeks** in a royal flush, **chin** up, **shoulders** burdened, **wrists** watched, **hands** some, **thumbs** up, **ring finger** naked, **heart** all, **back** got everyone on it, **ass** unintentionally, **buns** toasted, **knees** knocked, **heeled** well, **arches** gothic, and **toes** stepped on.

He wears a stuffed shirt, slick slacks, and sacramental socks — very holy!

Russ's resumé We told Russ to write this book because when he handed us the following resumé, we knew he was the kind of author that publishers dream about: nuts enough to work for free!

Age: too. **Sex:** yes! **Race:** rat. **Religion:** Reformed Nerd. **Address:** wear pants instead. **State:** distressed. **Father:** time. **Mother:** earth. **Spouse:** Brussels. **Occupation:** vegetable. **Career goal:** play dead. **Hobbies:** sleeping and crying. **Sports:** dodging tomatoes. **Greatest pleasure:** hiding under the sink. **Favorite food:** thought. **Humor:** less.

About the company

What company? C'mon over, bring milk and cookies, and then we'll have some helluva company!

Come visit our Home Office, in Russ's home. It includes our Production Department, near or in Russ's bed. Russ gave birth to this book himself; nobody else would dare!

Special services

We do everything possible to make you happy. . . .

Discounts We give you a 20% discount for buying 2 copies of this book, 40% for 4 copies, 60% for 60 copies, and 67% for 666 copies (so you pay just $4.95 per copy). Use the coupon on the back page.

Use your past You're reading the 20th edition. To compute your discount, we count how many copies of the 20th edition you've ordered from us *so far*. For example, if you previously ordered 30 copies of the 20th edition and order 30 more, we say "Oh, you're up to 60 copies now!" and give you a 60% discount on the second order.

If you got a discount on an older edition because you bought many copies of it, we'll give you the same discount on the 20th edition even if you're buying just one copy.

To get a discount based on past orders, mail us the coupon on the back page. Next to your name, write your phone number and say, "I'm taking a discount because of past orders."

Free reprints You may copy this book free. Copy as many pages as you like, make lots of copies, and don't pay us a cent! Just phone Russ first and say which pages you're going to copy. Put this notice at the beginning of your reprint:

Most of this material comes from the 20th edition of The Secret Guide to Computers, copyright 1995 by Russ Walter and reprinted with permission. Get FREE LITERATURE about the complete Guide by phoning Russ at 617-666-2666, 24 hours (he's almost always in); or send a postcard to him at 22 Ashland Street (Floor 2), Somerville, MA 02144-3202.

Then send us a copy of your reprint.

You may give — or sell — the reprints to anybody. Go distribute them on paper, on disk, or electronically by phone. The Guide's being distributed by thousands of teachers, consultants, and stores and translated to other languages. Join those folks! Add your own comments, call yourself a co-author, and become famous! It's free!

Books on disks Instead of books printed on paper, you can request books printed on disks. For example, if you're ordering 4 books, you can scribble this note on the coupon: "Send 3 on paper and 1 on disk." **Say which format you want: choose either ASCII or Word Perfect 5.1.** We'll send 1.44M disks (unless you request 1.2M, 720K, or 360K instead).

The disks will help you write your *own* book and develop material to put on a computerized bulletin board. The disks include 62 files. They total about 3 megabytes if you request ASCII, 4½ megabytes if you request Word Perfect 5.1.

If you get books on disk, get at least one book on paper since the disks do *not* contain headlines, graphics, special symbols, and printer drivers.

An independent company, **Window Book**, has printed the book on **hypertext disks**, which let you bounce to different topics quickly. For details, phone them at 617-661-9515.

Preserved classics You're reading the 20th edition. We've also reprinted earlier editions, which include extra details about the famous old computers and software that became classics. For example, we've reprinted the 11th edition, a 750-page mammoth bound in 2 volumes, and offer it for just 40¢ per volume (80¢ total). Those insanely low prices are ideal for schools on tight budgets and for low-cost gifts to your friends. For details about those famous classic editions, ask us to send the free "classics memo and order form".

Blitz courses Russ gives his "blitz" course all over the world. Offered several times a year, it turns you into a complete computer expert in an intensive weekend.

Saturday (from 9AM to 9PM) covers the first four chapters: buyer's guide, operating systems, word processing, and databases. Sunday (9AM to 5PM) covers the other four: spreadsheets, wild applications, programming, and endnotes.

The entire 20-hour course costs just $50. That's just $2.50 per hour! To pay even less per person, form a group with your friends. For details, phone or use the back page's coupon.

Strange stuff We're developing future editions, videotapes, and *The Secret Guide to Tricky Living*. Get on our mailing list by using the coupon on the back page. Russ answers questions about life — everything from sex to skunks. Phone 617-666-2666 anytime!

BUYER'S GUIDE

BACKGROUND

Up until 1940, computers were people. Dictionaries said a "computer" was "a person who computes". For example, astronomers hired many computers, who computed the positions of the stars. People who computed were called "computers"; machines that computed were called "calculators".

After 1940, human computers were gradually replaced by gigantic machines. At first, those machines were called "gigantic calculators"; but enthusiasts soon began calling them "electronic computers". Today the word "computer" means "a *machine* that computes". This book explains how to buy and use such machines.

During the 1950's, people began to realize that electronic computers can do *more* than compute. Today's computers spend only a small fraction of their time doing numerical computations; they spend most of their time thinking about words and ideas instead.

Calling such wonderful machines "computers" is misleading. They ought to be called "thinkers" instead. The French call them "ordinateurs", which means "organizers"; that more accurately describes what the machines do than our old-fashioned word "computers".

If an alien ever visits our planet and examines how our computers act, the alien will deduce:

A "computer" is "a machine that thinks".

Suppose the alien comes from a strange colony of uptight chatterboxes, called "lawyers". After analyzing more carefully how we use the word "computer", the alien will make this statement, which is long-winded, stuffy, and precise:

A "computer" is "any machine that can seem to do useful thinking".

That's the definition I'll use in this book!

Since today's computers spend most of their time dealing with words and ideas, and spend very *little* time dealing with numbers, you need to know just a *little* math to understand computers. If you know that 5.2 is more than 5 and less than 6, you know more than enough math to master this book and get hired as a computer expert! Becoming a computer expert is easier than becoming an auto mechanic, and you don't get greasy!

Three computer sizes

Computers come in three sizes: big, small, and teeny-weeny. The big ones are called **maxicomputers** (or **mainframes**); the small ones are called **minicomputers**; and the teeny-weeny ones are called **microcomputers**.

Those terms are vague. How big is big? How little is little? How teeny-weeny is teeny-weeny? Opinions differ.

It's like trying to measure a person. If somebody calls you "big", it could mean three things:

You're tall.
You're fat.
You're sexually well endowed.

The same is true for computers: "big" is whatever excites the salesperson.

Though vague, the term "microcomputer" is handy. Especially if you're male, you'll find that saying "I have a microcomputer" is better than saying "I have a teeny weeny."

If somebody invents a totally new computer (resembling no older computers), and it costs between $10,000 and $300,000, it's called a minicomputer. Anything more expensive is a maxicomputer; anything cheaper is a microcomputer.

Maxicomputers can cost up to $20,000,000. The most expensive maxicomputers (costing over $10,000,000) are called **supercomputers**.

Microcomputers can cost down to $1. Yes, even *you* can afford some sort of microcomputer! If you're lucky, you'll even get one as a birthday present from your Mommy or Daddy or Hubby or Wifey.

If somebody invents a new computer resembling an older computer, the new computer is called the same type as the older computer, regardless of price. For example, if somebody invents a new computer that understands exactly the same commands as a famous minicomputer, the new computer is called a "minicomputer" also, even if it costs less than $10,000 or more than $300,000. If it costs less than $10,000, it's called a **low-end minicomputer** (and probably runs rather slowly); if it costs more than $300,000, it's called a **high-end minicomputer** or **supermini** (and probably runs extra-fast).

Usually, a maxicomputer fills a room; a minicomputer fits in a corner; and a microcomputer flops out on a desktop.

Companies began selling maxicomputers in the 1950's, minicomputers in the 1960's, and microcomputers in the 1970's. Today you can buy all three sizes.

Maxicomputers

The dominant manufacturer of maxicomputers is **IBM**, which stands for **International Business Machines Corporation**. Too often, it also stands for "Incredibly Boring Machines", "Inertia Breeds Mediocrity", "International Big Mother", "Imperialism By Marketing", "Intolerant of Beards & Moustaches", "Idolized By Management", "Incompetents Become Managers", "It Baffles Me", "It's a Big Mess", and "It's Better Manually".

Since IBM's first popular computers were colored blue, IBM's been nicknamed "Big Blue".

Why is Big Blue the dominant computer company? That puzzles many young programmers, who ask, "Mommy, why is the sky Big Blue?"

The first maxicomputers were invented in the 1940's and sold in the 1950's. Most of today's maxicomputers are souped-up versions of the **IBM 360**, which IBM announced in 1964. IBM called it the "360" because it could accomplish the "full circle" of computer applications, instead of being restricted to just science applications or just business applications. In 1970, IBM invented a souped-up version (called the **IBM 370**) and then further improvements. IBM's newest maxicomputers (the **IBM 3090** and the **IBM 4381**) understand the same commands as the IBM 360 and 370, but obey the commands much faster and also understand some extra commands.

IBM's competitors
IBM outsells all its competitors combined.

During the 1960's, maxicomputers were made by eight companies, called "IBM and the Seven Dwarfs". The dwarfs were **Burroughs** (whose computers are called "burritos"), **Univac** (a division of Sperry Rand), **NCR** (which stood for National Cash Register), **Control Data Corporation (CDC)**, **Honeywell** (whose original factory was next to a well), **RCA** (which stood for "Radio Corporation of America"), and **General Electric**.

In 1970, General Electric sold its computer division to Honeywell. In 1971, RCA's computer division shut down. That left just five dwarfs, whose initials spelled the word BUNCH. Cynics said that maxicomputers were made by "IBM and the BUNCH".

IBM's top engineer (Gene Amdahl) and CDC's top engineer (Seymour Cray) both quit and started their own computer companies, called **Amdahl** and **Cray**.

During the 1980's and 1990's, each company in the BUNCH disintegrated: Burroughs merged with Univac (and Sperry Rand) to form **Unisys**; NCR became part of **AT&T**; Control Data stopped building computers; and Honeywell sold its computer division to a French company, **Bull**.

Minicomputers

All the companies that make maxicomputers also make smaller computers — minicomputers. For example, IBM's newest minicomputer is the **Advanced System 400 (AS/400)**. But the most popular minicomputers are made by other companies, who are minicomputer specialists.

The most popular minicomputers are made by **Digital Equipment Corporation (DEC)**. Its first popular minicomputers were the **PDP-8** and **PDP-11**. DEC replaced them by the **Vax** (a souped-up PDP-11), then by a further improvement, called the **Alpha**. The typical Vax or Alpha costs *more* than $300,000 but is still called a "minicomputer" (or "high-end mini" or "supermini"), because it's based on the PDP-11, which was sold at minicomputer prices.

DEC is in Massachusetts. Other popular minicomputer specialists — also in Massachusetts — have been **Data General (DG)**, **Prime** (jokes about which are called "Prime ribs"), and **Wang** (founded by Dr. An Wang, a Chinese immigrant who became the richest man in Massachusetts: together with his wife and kids, his family was worth a billion dollars, until his son took over the business and wrecked it and An Wang died). Prime and Wang have stopped building computers.

The remaining three minicomputer specialists are Californian: **Sun** (whose fortunes rose quickly but then set), HP (which stands for **Hewlett-Packard** and "high-priced"), and **Silicon Graphics Incorporated (SGI)**. Since computers from all three of those California companies are used mainly

for producing graphics (beautiful artwork, Hollywood special effects, ads, magazines, and "artist renderings" of creations by architects & engineers), they're called **graphics/engineering workstations**.

Microcomputers

The most influential microcomputers are made by IBM and **Apple**.

<u>**Apple**</u> Apple's first computer was called the **Apple 1**. Then came improved versions, called the **Apple 2**, the **2+**, the **2e**, the **2c**, the **2c+**, and the **2GS**. Those improved versions are all called the **Apple 2 family**.

They've become obsolete, and Apple has stopped making them. Now Apple sells a much fancier, totally different kind of microcomputer, called the **Macintosh** (or **Mac**). Of all the microcomputers built today, the Mac is the easiest to learn how to use.

The Mac comes in many versions. The most popular are the **Performa**, the **Quadra**, and the **Power Mac**. Prices for good, complete Macs start at about $1300.

<u>**IBM**</u> IBM's early microcomputers (such as the **IBM 5100** and the **Datamaster 23**) were slow and overpriced.

In 1981, IBM began selling a faster microcomputer, called the **IBM Personal Computer (IBM PC)**. It became instantly popular because of its speed and amazingly low price.

Later, IBM developed a slightly improved version, called the **IBM PC eXTended (IBM PC XT)**, and then a much faster version, called the **IBM PC with Advanced Technology (IBM PC AT)**.

In 1987, IBM stopped making all those microcomputers and instead began making a new series of microcomputers, called the **Personal System 2 (PS/2)**. The PS/2 computers run the same programs as the IBM PC but display prettier graphics and include "slicker" technology.

Unfortunately, the PS/2 computers were overpriced. In 1990, IBM began selling **PS/1 computers**, which were similar to PS/2 computers but cost less. In 1992, IBM invented a new series called the **Valuepoint**, which cost even less. In 1993, IBM tried selling an even cheaper series, called the **Ambra**, but discontinued it. IBM's newest series is the **Aptiva**.

Instead of buying microcomputers from IBM, you can buy imitations, called **compatibles** or **clones**. Cynics call them **clowns**. They run the same programs as IBM's microcomputers but cost even less.

The most popular IBM clones are manufactured by **Compaq**, **Packard Bell**, **AST**, **Dell**, and **Gateway**. Of those five clone makers, Compaq charges the most, Gateway charges the least, and the others charge in-between.

IBM, Compaq, Packard Bell, and AST sell mainly through stores. Gateway's computers are sold just by mail-order. Dell began as a mail-order company, then experimented by selling through stores also, but now sells just by mail again.

You can buy IBM, Compaq, and Packard Bell computers at discount stores such as **Staples**, **Office Max**, **Price/Costco**, **Sam's Club**, **Fretter**, **Circuit City**, **Computer City**, **Comp USA**, **Micro Center**, **Fry's Electronics**, and **J&R Computer World**.

Another chain of stores selling computers is **Radio Shack**, which is owned by **Tandy**. Tandy used to build its own computers, but in 1993 it sold its computer factories to AST. So if you buy a new Tandy computer, it's really manufactured by AST. Tandy's computers are usually overpriced.

Apple, IBM, Compaq, Packard Bell, AST, Dell, and Gateway are big manufacturers. To pay less, buy from smaller manufacturers instead, who advertise in magazines such as *PC Magazine* and *Computer Shopper*. Of all the clone makers that are nationally known, the one giving the lowest prices while maintaining high quality is **Quantex** (at 800-836-0566).

Wild ducks Instead of buying from the leaders (Apple and IBM) and their followers (who build clones), you can buy from **wild duck** companies who dare to be different, freed from the Apple-IBM mentality.

The most popular wild duck company is **Commodore**. It became famous for making cheap computers such as the **Pet, Vic, Commodore 64**, and **Commodore 128** computers. Then Commodore switched to making a fancier computer called the **Amiga**, which can display mind-blowing color graphics on your screen and videotape. In 1994, Commodore filed for bankruptcy, so Commodore's future is murky.

Like Commodore, **Atari** made a cheap computer (the **Atari XE**) and then a fancier computer for color graphics and music (the **Atari ST**). Atari's computers used to be popular in America but have become rare. You can still find them in some American music stores and European computer stores.

Though Tandy sells mainly IBM clones, Tandy occasionally sells cheaper computers that are older and weirder, such as the **Radio Shack Color Computer**.

Who uses what? The typical business uses an IBM PC (or an XT, AT, PS/2, PS/1, Valuepoint, Ambra, or clone). So does the typical college and high school. Some businesses and colleges are trying Macs. The typical elementary school still uses Apple 2 family computers, because they cost less and offer a greater variety of kid-oriented programs. Wild duck computers, which are fun and cost little, appeal mainly to hobbyists seeking cheap thrills. Video artists (who create cartoons and other graphics for TV) prefer the Mac or Amiga. Musicians prefer the Mac, Amiga, or Atari ST.

Of all the general-purpose computers sold today in the USA, about 12% are Macs (built by Apple), 12% are personal computers built by IBM, 12% are clones by Compaq, 10% are clones by Packard Bell, 6% are clones by AST, 6% are clones by Dell, 6% are clones by Gateway, 34% are clones built by other manufacturers, and the remaining 2% are weirder (Commodore Amiga, Atari ST, Radio Shack Color Computer, other wild duck computers, minicomputers, and maxicomputers). Since percentages bob up and down by 2% each month, I've rounded all those percentages to the nearest 2%.

Although few people buy maxicomputers, IBM makes more profit from selling maxicomputers than microcomputers — since the typical maxicomputer sells for about a million dollars. And since the typical maxicomputer is shared by hundreds of people, maxicomputers affect many lives!

Although hardly anybody buys wild duck computers anymore, many Americans still own the *millions* of wild duck computers that were sold during the early 1980's, before IBM PC clones became so popular and cheap.

Those wild duck computers — abandoned by their owners, imprisoned forever in the darkness of American closets, and unable to re-emerge into the mainstream of American life — are the forgotten hostages of IBM clone wars.

Prices drop
On the average, computer prices drop 3% per month. That price decline's been in effect ever since the 1940's, and there's no sign of it stopping.

Suppose for a particular computer item the average price charged by dealers is $100. Next month, that item's average price will probably drop 3%, to $97. After *two* months, its average price will have dropped about 3% again, so its price will be 97% of $97, which is $94.09.

Here's how the math works out:

On the average, computer prices drop about 3% per month,
30% per year,
50% every two years,
90% every six years,
99% every twelve years.

Therefore:

If a computer item's average price is $100 today,
it will probably be $97 next month,
$70 a year from now,
$50 two years from now,
$10 six years from now,
$1 twelve years from now.

The typical computer system costs about $2000 now. Here's what the math looks like for a $2000 system:

If a computer system costs you $2000 today,
that system will probably cost you $1940 if you buy it a month from now,
$1400 if you buy a year from now,
$1000 if you buy two years from now,
$200 if you buy six years from now,
$20 if you buy twelve years from now.

Does that mean computer stores will be selling lots of computers for $20 twelve years from now? No! Instead, computer stores will *still* be selling computers for about $2000, but those $2000 systems-of-the-future will be much fancier than the systems sold today. By comparison, today's systems will look primitive — much too primitive to run the programs-of-the-future — so they'll be sold off as old, quaint, primitive junk in flea markets and garage sales.

Find that hard to believe? To become a believer in rapidly dropping prices, just try this experiment: walk into a flea market or garage sale today, and you'll see computer systems selling for $20 that sold for $2000 twelve years ago!

So the longer you wait to buy a computer, the less you'll pay. But the longer you wait, the longer you'll be deprived of having a computer, and the further behind you'll be in computerizing your life and turning yourself into a computer expert.

Don't wait. Begin your new computerized life *now*!

To computerize your home or small office, you'll probably buy a microcomputer, because it's all you can afford! To computerize a bigger company, buy a maxicomputer, or a few minicomputers, or lots of microcomputers.

This book emphasizes microcomputers, for four reasons:

Over 99.9% of all computers sold are microcomputers.

Unless you're rich, a microcomputer is all you can afford.

Even if your business can afford a bigger computer, you'll typically get better service — and also save money — by wiring lots of microcomputers together instead.

Since microcomputers were invented more recently than bigger computers, microcomputers are based on fresh, new ideas that make them more responsive to the needs of modern society.

Although I'll emphasize microcomputers, I'll explain bigger computers also, since *some* big businesses require them.

Eight computer styles

Computers come in eight popular styles: **hidden**, **pocket**, **notebook**, **laptop**, **TV**, **desktop**, **luggable**, and **floor**.

Hidden computers
A **hidden computer** hides inside another device.

For example, a computer hides inside your digital watch. Another computer hides inside your pocket calculator. Another computer hides inside your video-game machine.

Since such a computer spends its entire life dedicated to performing just one task (such as "telling the time"), it's also called a **dedicated computer**. Most such computers cost under $10.

Pocket computers
A **pocket computer** fits in your pocket. The typical pocket computer looks like a pocket calculator but includes keys you can press for typing all the letters of the alphabet, so you can store names and addresses and communicate with the computer by using English words. Since it fits in the palm of your hand, it's also called a **handheld computer** or **palmtop computer**.

The typical pocket computer comes with programs that help you jot notes, store phone numbers, and keep track of dates & times & to-do lists. That kind of pocket computer is called a **personal digital assistant (PDA)**.

The fanciest pocket computer is the **Newton**, developed by a research team from **Apple** and **Sharp**. It comes with many nifty programs that make it a PDA. Instead of including a keyboard, it includes a tablet you write on with a pen; the computer tries to read your scribbled handwriting — but often makes mistakes!

Other pocket computers, which are more traditional and use a keyboard, are made by **Sharp**, **Casio**, **Hewlett-Packard**, **Poquet**, **Atari**, and **Radio Shack**. Most cost between $70 and $600. You can buy most of them from discount dealers such as **S&W Computers & Electronics** in New York (phone 800-874-1235 or 212-463-8330).

Notebook computers
To let a pocket computer fit in your pocket, the keys on its keyboard are very tiny and therefore hard to press (unless you have tiny fingers). Most adults that have big fingers prefer a **notebook computer** instead. It looks like a pocket computer but has bigger keys and a bigger screen. It's about the size of a student's 3-ring notebook holding a ream of paper.

The typical notebook computer is about 11 inches wide, 8½ inches from front to back, and 1½ inches thick. It weighs about 6 pounds.

Notebook computers that weigh under 4 pounds are called **subnotebooks**.

The first notebook computer was the **Tandy 100**, built for Tandy by a Japanese company (Kyocera) in 1983. It was 12"x8½"x2" and weighed just 4 pounds. Then Tandy invented the **Tandy 102**, which was thinner (1½") and weighed just 3 pounds. Neither of those computers was IBM-compatible. Tandy's stopped making them.

The most famous notebook computers are made by **Apple**, **IBM**, **Compaq**, and **Toshiba**. Companies such as **EPS** and **Midwest Micro** sell notebook computers that are better deals: they include more equipment per dollar. Most notebook computers cost between $1000 and $2000.

Laptop computers
A **laptop computer** resembles a notebook computer but weighs slightly more. It weighs between 8 pounds and 16 pounds, including the battery. Though it's too heavy to be considered a notebook, it's still light enough to fit comfortably in your lap.

The typical laptop computer weighs about 14 pounds.

Laptop computers were popular during the 1980's. But in the 1990's, most manufacturers have redesigned their laptop computers so they weigh little enough to be called "notebook computers" instead. Hardly anybody builds laptop computers anymore, but many folks still use old laptops from the 1980's.

TV computers
A **TV computer** looks like a notebook or laptop computer but lacks a screen. Instead of including a screen, the computer attaches to your home's TV, so that whatever you type on the keyboard appears on TV! It turns you into a TV star! The TV screen shows everything you typed and the computer's replies.

During the 1980's, the most popular TV computers were the **Commodore 64**, the **Apple 2 family**, and the **Radio Shack Color Computer**. They're not built anymore, since modern desktop computers are better.

Desktop computers
Unfortunately, the picture on a TV screen is fuzzy. To get a sharper picture from a computer, replace the TV by a **computer monitor**, which is a modified TV specially designed for attaching to a computer.

The typical computer monitor's screen is 12-inch or 14-inch (measured diagonally). A computer system that includes such a monitor is called a **desktop computer system**, because it's the ideal system to put on your desk.

The typical desktop computer system consists of three objects: the keyboard, the screen, and the **system unit** (which contains the main circuitry). Wires run from the keyboard and screen to the system unit.

The most popular IBM clones are all desktop computers.

The Apple 2e, Apple 2c+, and Commodore 64 are basically TV computers, since they attach to TV's and their circuitry is small enough to hide inside the keyboard. But most folks who buy those computers attach monitors instead of TV's, to form desktop systems.

Luggable computers
Notice that most notebook and laptop computers are easy to carry but have poor screens, whereas desktop computers have excellent screens but are hard to carry. For a compromise, get a **luggable** computer: it resembles a desktop computer but is slightly smaller, so you can carry it more easily.

Its little 9-inch screen displays the same info as a desktop computer's 12-inch screen but in miniature. To read the 9-inch screen without squinting, you must sit close! That screen's built into the system unit so you don't have to carry it separately. The system unit has a handle so you can carry the whole computer in one hand. The keyboard snaps onto the system unit, so when you pick up the system unit you're also picking up the keyboard.

To stay small and easy to carry, the system unit contains hardly any slots for inserting extra circuitry. (If you want more slots, you must buy a desktop computer instead.)

Altogether, the system unit (including the built-in screen and snapped-on keyboard) weighs about 20 pounds — which is light enough to lug. It's about the same size as a portable sewing machine or a bulging briefcase. It's also the size of a lunchbox big enough to hold the food for a family picnic. Such a computer's called a **lunchbox** or **luggable** or **somewhat portable** or **transportable** or **compact**.

Pocket computers, subnotebook computers, notebook computers, laptop computers, and luggable computers are all examples of **portable** computers. Let's compare them. . . .

Pocket computers	weigh under 2 pounds.
Subnotebook computers	weigh between 2 and 4 pounds.
Notebook computers	weigh between 4 and 8 pounds.
Laptop computers	weigh between 8 and 16 pounds.
Luggable computers	weigh between 16 and 32 pounds.
Desktop computers	weigh over 32 pounds.

The first IBM-compatible luggable was the **Compaq Portable**. The first Mac that Apple invented was basically a luggable, since it had a 9-inch built-in screen and a handle; but since it lacked snaps to attach the keyboard, you had to carry the keyboard separately or buy a cloth bag holding both the keyboard and the system unit.

Luggables aren't built anymore. Modern Compaqs and Macs are desktops, notebooks, or subnotebooks instead.

Floor computers If a computer's too big to fit on your desktop, it stands on the floor. It's called a **floor computer** (or **floortop** or **floor-standing** or **freestanding**).

If the computer's short enough, you can hide it under your desk. Otherwise, you must give the computer its own corner of the room, or perhaps the whole room!

Most maxicomputers and minicomputers are floor computers; so are the fanciest microcomputers.

If the computer's height is greater than its width, the computer's called **vertical** or **vertically mounted** or a **tower**. If the computer is *much* taller than wide, it's called a **full tower**; if the computer's just *slightly* taller than wide, it's called a **mini tower**.

Inside your computer

A computer includes three main parts. The part that *thinks* is called the **processor** (because it processes information). The part that *remembers* the computer's thoughts is called the **memory**. The part that *communicates* those thoughts is called the **in/out system**, because it passes information into and out of the computer.

When you buy a computer, make sure the price includes all three parts!

Each part is important. A computer without memory is as useless as a person who says "I had a great idea, but I can't remember it." A computer without an in/out system is as useless as a person who says, "I had a great idea, but I won't tell you."

Processor The part that thinks — the processor — is also called the **central processing unit** (which is abbreviated as **CPU**).

During the 1940's and 1950's, the CPU was the biggest and most expensive part of the computer. But each year, manufacturers discover new ways to make the CPU smaller and cheaper. Today, the CPU is the smallest and cheapest part of the computer.

In a microcomputer, the CPU is just a tiny square metal **chip**, about a quarter of an inch on each side and a hundredth of an inch thick. It typically costs under $10. That kind of processor — small enough to fit on a single chip — is called a **microprocessor**.

Memory The three most popular kinds of memory are **ROM chips**, **RAM chips**, and **disks**.

The **ROM chips** remember information *permanently*. Even if you turn off the computer's power, the ROM chips continue to remember what they've been told.

The **RAM chips** remember information *temporarily*. They're electronic scratchpads that the CPU uses to store temporary memos. They get erased when you switch to a different computer problem or turn the computer off.

The **disks** work more slowly than ROM chips and RAM chips but can store larger quantities of information. Like ROM chips, disks can remember information *permanently*: unplugging the computer does *not* erase the disks. Each disk is round, but the typical disk is permanently sealed in a square casing, so that what you see is a square. The typical disk lets you edit the information on it. To use a disk, you must put it into a **disk drive**, which reads what's on the disk.

When buying a computer, make sure the price includes all three kinds of memory: ROM chips, RAM chips, and disks (with disk drives).

I/O The computer part that communicates — the in/out system — is also called the **input/output system** (or **I/O system**). It consists of many **I/O devices**.

The five most popular I/O devices to buy are a **keyboard**, **screen**, **printer**, **speaker**, and **mouse**.

The **keyboard** resembles a typewriter's. Put your fingers on the keys, and type commands to the computer!

The **screen** is an ordinary TV or *resembles* a TV. The screen shows what you typed on the keyboard and also shows the computer's responses. The most popular kind of screen is called a **monitor**, which resembles a TV but has no dial to select channels: the only channel you get is "computer".

The **printer** resembles a typewriter but has no keyboard. It prints the computer's answers on paper.

The **speaker** beeps at you when you type a wrong command. It can also play music and produce crude speech.

The **mouse** is a box as big as a pack of cigarettes. To feed a picture to the computer, you draw the picture on the computer's screen by sliding the mouse across your desk. For example, you can draw a circle on the screen by sliding the mouse in a circular motion.

Two of those devices — the keyboard and mouse — let you put information into the computer. They're called the **input devices**. The other three devices — the screen, printer, and speaker — let the computer spit out the answers and are called the **output devices**.

For extra fun, buy an extra I/O device, called a **modem** (pronounced "mode em"), which lets your computer tap into the phone system so your computer can chat with other computers around the world.

When you buy a computer, check whether the price includes all six of those I/O devices! If you get all six and they work well, you can join the many excited computerists who sing every day, "I/O, I/O, now off to work I go!"

Putting it all together Besides those three main parts — the CPU, memory, and I/O — you also need **cables** (to connect the parts together) and a **power supply** (to get electricity to the parts).

If your computer is small enough to run on batteries, the "power supply" consists of the batteries. If your computer is bigger and gets electricity by plugging into your office's wall, the "power supply" is a box called an **AC/DC transformer**: it converts the alternating current (coming from your office's wall) to the direct current that your computer requires.

When you look at the most popular kind of computer, you see a metal or plastic box called the **system unit**, in which hide the CPU, speaker, power supply, and memory.

The mouse is *not* inside the system unit; the mouse sits separately on your desk, and a cable runs from the mouse to the system unit. The other I/O devices (keyboard, screen, and printer) typically sit separately (like the mouse), but some manufacturers build them into the system unit instead.

Choose a safe environment During the summer, protect the computer's parts from overheating. Keep the computer cool! Turn it off when the room temperature rises over 93° — unless you buy a fan that creates a strong breeze, or you turn the computer off within 90 minutes to let it cool down. Pull down the window shade closest to the computer, to prevent sunlight from beating directly onto the computer.

During the winter, turn the computer off when the room temperature is below 50°. If the computer sat overnight in a cold, unheated car or office, don't use the computer until it warms up and any dewdrops in it evaporate.

Make sure your computer gets enough electricity. Check which outlets in your house or office attach to which fuses, to make sure the computer's not on the same circuit as an electric heater, refrigerator, air conditioner, or other major appliance that consumes enough electricity to dim the lights.

The three wares Computer equipment is called **hardware** because it's built from wires, screws, and other parts you can buy in hardware & electronics stores. Hardware includes the CPU, memory, I/O, cables, and power supply.

The information that the computer deals with is called **software**, because you can't feel it: it flows through the computer's circuits as coded pulses of electricity. The computer can handle two kinds of software: **data** (lists of names, addresses, numbers, words, and facts) and **programs** (lists of instructions that tell the computer what to do).

To feed the computer some software (data and programs), you can type the software on the keyboard, or insert ROM chips or disks containing the software, or let the computer receive the software from another computer (by running wires between the computers or letting the computers chat with each other by phone).

If you feed the computer wrong software — wrong facts or wrong instructions — the computer will print wrong answers. Wrong stuff is called **garbage**. If you feed the computer some garbage, the computer spits out garbage answers.

So if a computer prints wrong answers, the computer might not be broken; it might just have been fed wrong data or programs. If you think the computer's broken and tell a technician to fix it, the technician might reply, "Hey, the computer's fine! Don't blame the computer! It's *your* fault for feeding it garbage! If you put garbage in, you get garbage out!" That's called the principle of **garbage in, garbage out** (which is abbreviated **GIGO**, pronounced "guy go"). The technician will say, "it's just a case of GIGO".

The person sitting at the computer is called the **liveware**, **operator**, **user**, or **meathead** — because the person's head is made of meat instead of wires. The term **meathead** was first shouted publicly by that TV character from New York: Archie Bunker. The term **liveware** was invented in 1982 by Garry Trudeau, creator of the Doonesbury cartoons.

For a complete **computer system**, you need all three wares: the hardware (equipment), software (information), and liveware (people).

Beware of those three wares! You can spend lots of money on buying hardware (and repairing it), buying software (and improving it), and hiring people to help you (and training them). Make sure you've budgeted for all three wares!

Congratulations! Now you know the three ways that buying a computer can suck up your money. Yes, buying a computer can really suck.

Subculture

Computers are like drugs: you begin by spending just a little money on them, but then you get so excited by the experience — and so hooked — that you wind up spending more and more money to feed your habit.

Your first computer experience seems innocent enough: you spend just a little money for a cute little computer that has a color screen. You turn the computer on, tell it to play a game, and suddenly the screen shows dazzling superhuman colors that swirl hypnotically before you. You say "Wow, look at all those colors!" and feel a supernatural high.

But after two months of freaking out with your new computer, the high wears off and you wonder, "What can I buy that's new, exciting, and gives me an even bigger high?" So you buy more stuff to attach to your computer. Now you're in really deep, financially and spiritually. You're hooked. You've become addicted to computers. Each month you return to your favorite computer store, to search for an even bigger high — and spend more money.

Look at me. I'm a typical computer junkie. I've already bought 40 computers, and I'm still going. Somebody help me! My computers have taken over my home. Whenever I try to go to sleep, I see those computers staring at me, their lights winking, tempting me to spend a few more hours in naughty fun, even if the sun's already beginning to rise.

Drug addicts quickly catch on to computer jargon, because the lingo of today's computerized techno-streets is the same as that of the druggie's needle. For example, to buy a computer, you go to a **dealer**; and when you finally start using your computer, you're called a **user**.

As you get in deeper, searching for ever greater highs, you squander even more money on computer equipment, called **hardware**. You stay up late (playing computer games or removing errors from your programs) so that the next morning you come into work all bleary-eyed. Your boss soon suspects your computer habit, realizes you're not giving full attention to your job, and fires you.

Since you're jobless and your computer bills are mounting higher and higher, you soon run out of money to spend on computers — but you still have that urge to spend more! To support your habit, you write programs and try to sell them to your friends. That makes you a **pusher**. You turn your friends into addicts too, and you all join the ever-increasing subculture of **computer junkies**.

The only difference between computers and drugs is that if you're into drugs people call you a "washout", whereas if you're into computers people say you have a "wonderful career". And they're right!

As a computer pusher, you can make lots of dough. But to be a successful pusher, you must do it in style: instead of calling yourself a "pusher", call yourself a **computer consultant**. Yes, a computer consultant is a person who gives computer advice to other people — and pushes them into buying more computers!

A computer consultant who gives free computer help to kids is kind-hearted but also a wolf in sheep's clothing. The truth is revealed in these lines of Tom Lehrer's song, "The Old Dope Peddler":

He gives the kids free samples
Because he knows full well
That today's young innocent faces
Will be tomorrow's clientele.

My marriage I'm married to a computer. Marrying a computer is much groovier than marrying a person. For one thing, computers are good at "getting it on": they make you feel all electric and tingly. And computers never argue: they're always ready to "do it" (except when they "have a headache").

I wanted to call this book "The *Sexual* Guide to Computers" and put a photo of my wife and me on the cover; but some parts of the country still prohibit mixed marriages. That cover would be banned in Boston, which (alas!) is where I live. So I had to play cool and say "Secret" Guide to Computers. But here's the real secret: this book's about sex.

Your marriage The computer will fascinate you. It'll seduce you to spend more and more time with it. You'll fall in love with it.

You'll even start buying it presents. You'll buy it exotic foods — expensive programs to munch on. You'll buy it new clothes — dress it in a pretty little cloth cover, to keep the dust off. You'll adorn it with expensive jewels — a printer and an extra disk drive.

Then the computer will demand you give it more. While you're enjoying an exciting orgy with your computer and think it's the best thing that ever happened to you, suddenly the computer will demand you buy it more memory. It'll refuse to continue the orgy until you agree to its demand. And you'll agree — eagerly!

The computer's a demanding lover. You'll feel married to it. If you're already married to a human, your human spouse will feel jealous of the computer. Your marriage to that human can deteriorate and end in divorce.

Several women got divorced because they took my computer course. Their husbands had two complaints:

"You spend most of your time with the computer instead of with me. When you do spend time with me, all you want to talk about is the computer."

To prevent such a marital problem, coax your spouse to play a video game on the computer. Your spouse will get hooked on the game, become as addicted to the computer as you, *enjoy* blabbing about the computer with you, and even help you spend money on your habit. Sociologists call that **technological progress**.

Why buy a computer?

The average American has three goals: to make money, have fun, and "become a better person". Making money is called **business**; having fun is called **pleasure**; and becoming a better person is called **personal development**. The computer will help you meet all three goals: it'll improve your business, increase your pleasure, and help you grow into a better person.

The average computer buyer is a male who comes out at noon. During lunch hour, he walks into a computer store and says he wants to computerize his business. He wants a computer to do his accounting and also handle his mailing list. The computer store's salesperson talks him into also wanting a word-processing program, to help handle business correspondence.

After visiting one or two other computer stores, he buys a computer. Though the computer costs a lot, the salesperson reminds him that Uncle Sam gives a tax break for buying it since it's a "business expense".

He brings it home but starts feeling guilty about having spent so much. How will he convince his wife that the purchase was wise?

Suppose his wife's an old-fashioned mom who cooks. He tries to convince her that the computer will help her cook. . . .

"It will help you store your recipes, darling," he coos.

"No thanks," she replies. "When I find a recipe in the newspaper, I don't want to spend 15 minutes typing the entire recipe into the computer. I'd rather just clip the recipe out of the newspaper and — presto! — tape it to a file card. My manual system is faster than a computerized one!"

He tries again. "You could use the computer to store your phone numbers. When you want to look up a phone number, the computer will tell you instantly."

She retorts, "No thanks. To make a phone call, I don't want to have to turn on the computer, request the 'telephone' program, wait for the computer to ask whose number I'm interested in, sit at the keyboard and type in the jerk's entire name, then wait for the computer to respond. Instead of doing all that, it's quicker to just open my little black phone book, flip to the page where the number is, and dial my friend. Try again, lover-boy!"

"Well, darling, you could use the computer to remind you of birthdays and appointments."

"You must be crazy! I remember them quite well without a computer. I scribble a note on my calendar, which serves fine and costs just $5 instead of $1000. I understand how a disorganized bird-brain, like you, might need a computer to survive; but since I'm better organized, I don't need to rely on mechanical help."

Though admitting the computer does *not* fulfill any real need in the home, he lusts to buy a computer anyway — for the thrill of it — and looks for an excuse to justify the cost. **The computer's a solution looking for a problem.**

Women buy computers too. Apple ran a TV ad showing Dick Cavett in a kitchen, as he interviews a woman who bought a computer. "You're using it to store your recipes?" he asks. "No!" she retorts, "I'm using it to chart stocks!"

If you buy a computer, the idea of "using the computer to run your business" and "using the computer to store recipes" are just excuses. **Here are the REAL reasons why people buy computers. . . .**

Teenager: "Computers are a blast: sci-fi come true! Programming computers is the next best thing to becoming an astronaut!"

Parent: "Computers are taking over! My kids will have to master them to survive. If I buy my kids a computer, they'll explore it (instead of sex & drugs), get curious about how it's programmed, become programmers, get straight A's in school, become computer consultants, make lots of dough, and share their wealth with me, so I can brag about them to my neighbors."

Grandparent: "I want to be part of the 20th century. The whole world's becoming computerized, and I don't want my grandkids to think I'm 'out of it.' I want to share in this new excitement."

Kindergartner: "Grandma, please buy me a computer for my birthday! I really want one! And if you don't buy it, they say I'll never go to Harvard."

Social climber: "Damn! Now that big cars are passé, the computer's the only status symbol left. I'm sick of being intimidated by neighbors and bosses spouting computer jargon. I'm gonna learn that mumbo-jumbo myself so I can get back at those pompous asses and intimidate THEM!"

Worried worker: "My company is computerizing. If I don't master computers, they might master ME and take away my job! If I learn enough about them, I can keep my job, get a promotion, then quit and become a rich computer consultant!"

Adventurer: "The computer's a challenge. If I can master it, I know I'm not as stupid as people say!"

Middle-aged: "My life's become boring. I need an exciting new hobby — a computer! It's fun, could help my business, and even help me start a new business on the side. And I can keep fiddling with that cute toy even after my company retires me."

Doctor: "Playing with the computer's anatomy is like playing God. Besides, with a computer I could get my patients to pay their bills!"

English teacher: "My students get so hooked on computer games! I'm gonna find out why, then use computers to channel the kids' excitement toward a higher good: poetry!"

Wanting what's due: "I've worked hard all my life; I DESERVE a computer! I'm gonna get my hands on that mean machine, force it to obey all my commands, and make it my personal slave."

Subversive: "If Big Brother has Big Blue watching me, then by gosh I'll turn my computer into Big Mama and scramble their waves!"

Will your computer fulfill all those dreams? This Guide will help you find out!

Hassles

When you buy a new computer for your business, you'll have lots of hassles.

Repairs Since a complete computer system includes so many parts (CPU, RAM, keyboard, disk drives, printer, software, etc.), *at least one* of them won't work properly, and you'll need to fix it. Since the manufacturer or store will provide free repairs during the first year, you'll lose nothing but your temper.

Manuals You won't completely understand the manuals for your hardware and software, so you'll ask your friends and me for help. You can also try getting help from the manufacturers and dealers; but if your question's long-winded, their answers will be curt.

If the dealer who sold you the computer is honest, he'll say, "I don't know how to run all the hardware and software I sold you. To learn how, read the manuals. No, I haven't read them myself, because they're too long-winded, complicated, and vague. If you don't like the manuals, take our courses, which are expensive and won't teach you as much as you need but at least will make you feel you're making *some* progress."

Most dealers are not that candid.

Programs If you try writing your own programs, you'll discover Murphy's law: no matter how long you think a program will take to write, it will take you longer. If you're wiser and try to buy a finished program from somebody else, you'll find the program works worse than advertised, its manual is missing or unintelligible, and you'll need to modify the program to meet your personal needs.

Data entry If you figure out how to use the program, your next torture is to type the data you want the program to process. The typing is sheer drudgery, but you must do it.

Worthwhile? Those headaches are just the *beginning* of what can become an extended nightmare. Buying a computer starts by being exciting but quickly becomes nerve-racking.

Eventually, you'll get past that nerve-racking transition stage and become thrilled.

That painful transition is worth the effort if you plan to use the computer a lot. But if you plan to use a computer just occasionally, you might be better off not buying a computer at all: continue doing your work manually.

Promises Salespeople wanting you to buy fancy hardware or software say "it will be great", but computer stuff never turns out as good as promised.

For example, there's the tale of the woman who was married three times but remained a virgin. Her first husband, on his wedding night, discovered he was impotent; her second husband, on *his* wedding night, decided he was gay; and her third husband was a computer salesman who spent the whole night saying how great it was going to be.

Moral: computer salemen make great promises but don't deliver.

There's also the story of how a programmer died and came to the gates of Heaven, guarded by St. Peter, who let the programmer choose between Heaven and Hell. The programmer peeked at Heaven and saw angels singing boring songs. He peeked at Hell and saw wild orgies, so he chose Hell. Suddenly the wild orgies vanished, and he was dragged to a chamber of eternal torture. When he asked "What happened to the wild orgies?", the devil replied "Oh, that was just the demo."

Moral: many wild technologies are enticing; but when you try actually experiencing them, you have a devil of a time!

Periodicals

To keep up-to-date about computers, read newspapers and magazines. They contain the latest computer news, criticize hardware and software, advise you on what to buy, and include ads for the newest products, services, and discount dealers.

Some ads and articles use technical computer jargon, which you'll understand by reading this book.

How to get periodicals Visit your local computer stores and bookstores, and buy a copy of each newspaper and magazine that interests you. (If you live near Boston, you'll find many computer magazines in the kiosks in the middle of Harvard Square. If you visit a chain of computer stores called **Comp USA**, you'll find computer magazines there at discounted prices. Your local branch of **B. Dalton Bookseller** is another place to find lots of computer magazines.)

After reading the periodicals you bought — or borrowed from your local library — subscribe to the ones you like best.

Most periodicals come with a coupon that gives you a "special" discount off the subscription price "for new subscribers, if you hurry". Don't bother hurrying: the same discount is offered to practically everybody every year. And next year, when you renew, you'll be offered the same "special" discount, "for our loyal readers, if you hurry".

Shortly after you buy a one-year subscription, you'll receive a dishonest letter from the publisher warning that your subscription will "run out soon" and that "if you renew now, you'll get a special discount". Don't believe the letter; "run out soon" usually means "run out eight months from now", and "if you renew now" means "if you renew sometime within the eight months, or even later". Feel free to wait.

How to read reviews Many computer periodicals review the newest hardware and software, but don't take the reviews too seriously: the typical review is written by just one person and reflects just that individual's opinion.

Some reviewers are too easy: they heap praise and say everything is "excellent". Other reviewers are too demanding: they say everything is "terrible". If one product gets a rave review, and a competing product gets a scathing review, the reason might be the difference between the reviewers rather than the difference between the products.

Giant conglomerates Most computer magazines and newspapers are published by two giant conglomerates: **Ziff** and **IDG**.

Ziff, based in Manhattan, has for decades published magazines about many hobbies. In 1982, when computers became a popular hobby, Ziff began acquiring computer-magazine companies (such as **Creative Computing** and **PC Magazine**) so that Ziff's become one of the biggest computer publishers.

IDG (based in Framingham, Massachusetts) began publishing **Computerworld** in 1967. Later, it began publishing and buying up many other computer periodicals around the world. Now IDG publishes 190 computer periodicals in 60 countries.

Ziff and IDG have declared war on each other. For example, IDG refuses to publish articles by columnists who submit articles to Ziff. Each computer columnist must choose between either being a **Ziffer** or an **IDG'er**.

Mostly monthly Most computer magazines are published monthly and let you buy individual issues (for $2.95 or $3.95) or an annual subscription (for between $20 and $30).

Computer Shopper The fattest computer magazine is **Computer Shopper**, formerly independent but now owned by Ziff. It's huge! Each issue contains over 800 pages, and each page is oversized (9½"x13").

That's the magazine where all aggressive discount dealers advertise. It's where you'll find the lowest prices. It contains the wildest ads and articles, all uncensored. Since its editors don't check the ads and articles for accuracy, treat their wild claims as "questions to pursue" but not as "facts to trust".

The articles are relentlessly upbeat; they never criticize. For example, an article reviewing a lousy word processor raves about how it's so much better than a typewriter; an article reviewing a lousy 33-megahertz computer raves about how it's so much faster than a 25-megahertz model.

Browsing through Computer Shopper, you might see an ad bragging that a product was declared "Computer Shopper Best Buy of the Year". That praise sounds impressive — until you realize that the judges were "all the magazine subscribers who sent in postcards", and the award just meant the subscribers admired the ad's low price and didn't necessarily try or even see the product!

PC Magazine The most respected magazine is Ziff's **PC Magazine** because it's comprehensive, carefully edited, and its tone is restrained. It comes out every two weeks.

Alas, its editors assume the readers are rich enough to spend $4,000 on a computer system. Its "editor's choice" for what to buy usually costs more than most folks can afford. Its editorials claim you're a primitive moron if you don't buy the hottest, newest, most expensive personal computers invented this month.

Frankly, dear, I don't give a damn if a company can make a super-fast expensive computer. What I want is a reasonably fast computer that I can *afford*! I'm put off by magazines that say, "Here's something wonderful you can't afford." But us poor folks read PC Magazine anyway to find out how the other half live.

Even if your company can afford a pricey computer system recommended by PC Magazine, your office should probably buy two cheap systems instead to make *two* employees happy.

PC Magazine is famous for its blockbuster issues, such as its November issue that compares all new printers. But do you really want to read descriptions of 70 printers, 60 of which are no good? I wish the magazine would give *brief* descriptions of the bad 60 and longer descriptions of the good 10, but PC Magazine is too even-handed.

Alas, PC Magazine says nothing about rip-offs and other complaints that consumers have about manufacturers, and it places too much emphasis on boring business applications and not enough on family fun & fascination.

In short, PC Magazine represents the lifestyle of the rich and boring. But its even-handed careful editing make it a respected reference worth buying.

PC World To compete against Ziff's PC Magazine, IDG publishes **PC World**. It was started by the founder of PC Magazine — Dave Bunnell — after he squabbled with Ziff.

More human that PC Magazine, PC World includes a consumer-complaint department that publishes complaints about rip-offs and bad service. PC World also plays consumer advocate and gets the baddies to change their ways and give refunds to customers. When covering a topic such as printers, PC World covers fewer models than PC Magazine but covers those models more thoroughly and makes more comparisons between them.

Whereas PC Magazine forgets to consider price, PC World forgets other factors. But to err is human.

Easy magazines For folks who find PC Magazine and PC World too difficult, Ziff invented **PC Computing**, which is easier and includes great tutorials.

An independent publisher, Peed, puts out **PC Today**, which is even easier, and **PC Novice** which is the easiest! PC Today and PC Novice are both very brief.

Byte The oldest popular computer magazine is **Byte**. More technical than other popular magazines, it digs deeper into issues about designing computer hardware & software.

Newest magazines After starting PC Magazine and PC World, Dave Bunnell started a wilder magazine, called **New Media**, devoted to computerized art, sounds, and fun.

An even wilder magazine is a competitor called **Wired**, partly owned by Condé Nast (publisher of *Mademoiselle*, *Glamour*, *Vogue*, and *Self*). It's non-technical and espouses the grungy up-yours philosophy of life. It even prints four-letter words. Since each issue of Wired is wild, slick, and expensive, it's read by the hip rich, so it includes ads for upscale consumer goods such as Jetta cars and Absolut Vodka.

Two new magazines that are more traditional are **Windows Magazine** and **Windows Sources**.

Non-IBM magazines If you have a Mac, get Ziff's **Mac User** and IDG's **Macworld**. If you have an Apple 2, get **2 Alive** (6 times per year). If you have a Commodore Amiga, get **Amiga World**.

Weekly newspapers The only weekly newspaper covering computers of *all* sizes (maxi, mini, and micro) is **Computerworld**. It's published by IDG, which also publishes **Infoworld**, a livelier newspaper that concentrates on microcomputers. Infoworld's main competitors are Ziff's **Mac Week** (which covers Mac computers) and Ziff's **PC Week** (which covers the IBM PC and clones).

Infoworld, Mac Week, and PC Week are intended for computerists who buy lots of computers. To subscribe, you complete application forms asking how many computer purchases you make or influence yearly. If you answer acceptably, you get the newspapers free; otherwise, you must pay $125 per year for Mac Week, $130 per year for Infoworld, $195 per year for PC Week. That method of distribution — "specialists get it free, idiots pay through the nose" — is called **controlled circulation**. It assures advertisers that the readers are either influential or rich. Alas, it widens the gap between the "haves" and the "have-nots": if you're a low-income novice, this policy is guaranteed to "keep you in your place", unless you're lucky enough to find those magazines in your local library.

Computer Currents IDG publishes a monthly newspaper called **Computer Currents** and distributes it free at selected newsstands in six regions (San Francisco, Los Angeles, Dallas, Houston, Atlanta, and Boston). Each region has its own edition, with its own local news and ads. If you don't find one of the free newsstands, buy a subscription.

Look at the back page In many computer magazines and newspapers, the most fascinating writing occurs on the back page.

For example, the best rumor-mongerer is Robert Cringely, on the back page of Infoworld. The best humorists are Ron White (on the back page of Windows Sources), Lincoln Spector (on the back page of Computer Currents), and Rich Tennant (whose cartoons grace the back page of Computer Currents and PC Magazine).

List Here's an alphabetized list of the popular computer periodicals.

Magazine	Publisher	Issue	Year	Editorial office		Toll free
Amiga World	IDG	$3.95	$30/$25	NH	603-924-9471	800-365-1364
Byte	McGraw-Hill	$3.50	$30/$25	NH	603-924-9281	800-257-9402
Computer Currents	IDG	$3.00	$20/$0	CA	508-820-8118	
Computer Shopper	Ziff	$4.95	$40/$30	NY	212-503-3900	800-274-6384
Computerworld	IDG	$6.00	$48/$40	MA	508-879-0700	800-669-1002
Infoworld	IDG	$3.95	$130/$0	CA	415-572-7341	
Mac User	Ziff	$2.95	$27/$20	CA	415-378-5600	800-627-2247
Mac Week	Ziff	$6.00	$125/$0	CA	415-243-3500	
Macworld	IDG	$3.95	$30/$24	CA	415-546-7722	800-524-3200
New Media	Hypermedia	$3.95	$38/$0	CA	415-573-5170	
PC Computing	Ziff	$2.95	$25/$17	CA	415-578-7000	800-365-2770
PC Magazine	Ziff	$3.95	$50/$35	NY	212-503-5255	800-289-0429
PC Novice	Peed	$2.95	$24	NE	402-477-8900	800-424-7900
PC Today	Peed	$2.95	$24	NE	402-477-8900	800-424-7900
PC Week	Ziff	$6.00	$195/$0	MA	617-393-3700	800-451-1032
PC World	IDG	$3.95	$30/$20	CA	415-243-0500	800-825-7595
Windows Magazine	CMP	$2.95	$25/$17	NY	516-562-5948	
Windows Sources	Ziff	$2.95	$28/$20	NY	212-503-4144	800-364-3414
Wired	Wired Ventures	$4.95	$40	CA	415-904-0660	800-SO-WIRED
2 Alive	Quality Comp.	$3.95	$20	MI	313-774-7200	800-777-3642

That list shows each periodical's name, publisher, single-issue price, one-year subscription price (with any discounted price shown after a slash), editorial office's state and phone number, and any toll-free number for ordering a subscription.

Daily newspapers For *today's* news about the computer industry, read the business section of your town's daily newspaper, or read national newspapers such as **The Wall Street Journal**, **USA Today**, and **The New York Times**. The computer articles in **The Wall Street Journal** are excellent — especially Walter Mossberg's editorial (on the first page of the Marketplace section on Thursdays).

Every Tuesday, the Science section of **The New York Times** contains ads from New York's most aggressive discount dealers. It makes bargain hunters drool, but beware of dealers who are shady!

Discount dealers

In computer magazines and newspapers, you'll see many ads offering big discounts. And if you buy from a dealer who isn't in your state, the dealer won't charge you sales tax.

Discount dealers change prices every month. Instead of asking them for catalogs (which might be out of date), examine their most recent ads. Then phone to confirm the prices. Usually, prices go down every month, but sometimes they rise.

Before buying, ask whether the product's in stock, how long the dealer will take to fill your order, and how it will be shipped. Ask what the dealer charges for shipping: many dealers overcharge! Ask whether there's a surcharge for using a credit card. Since products are improved often, make sure the dealer is selling you the *newest* version.

If the product you get is defective, the dealer or manufacturer will fix or replace it. But if the product is merely "disappointing" or doesn't do what you expected or isn't compatible with the rest of your computer system, tough luck! Many discount dealers say "all sales are final." Other dealers let you return computers but not printers, monitors, or software. Some dealers let you return products but charge you a "restocking fee", which can be up to 25% of the purchase price!

So before you buy, ask questions about the product's abilities to make sure it will do what you expect. Tell the dealer what hardware and software you own, and ask the dealer whether the product's compatible with your system.

The typical product comes in a cardboard box. On the back of the box (or on some other side), you'll usually see a list of the **system requirements**. That's a list of what hardware and software you must already own to make that product work with *your* computer.

Use your credit card Pay by credit card rather than a check. If you pay by credit card and have an unresolved complaint about what you bought, Federal laws say that the credit-card company can't bill you! Moreover, if the mail-order company takes your money, spends it, and then goes bankrupt before shipping your goods, the credit-card company gets stuck, not you!

The nicest credit cards (such as Citibank's) double the manufacturer's warranty, so a "one-year warranty" becomes a *two*-year warranty! Does *your* credit card give you that warranty extension? Ask your bank!

What's missing? When buying computer equipment, find out what the advertised price does *not* include.

For example, the advertised price for a "complete computer system" might not include the screen. Ask! In a typical printer ad, the price does *not* include the cable that goes from the printer to your computer.

Read the fine print When reading an ad, make sure you read the fine print at the bottom of the ad. It contains many disclaimers, which admit that the deal you'll be getting isn't quite as good as the rest of the ad implies.

In the middle of an ad, next to an exciting price or feature or warranty, you'll often see an asterisk (*). The asterisk means: "for details, read the fine print at the bottom of the ad". That fine print contains disclaimers that will disappoint you. In long multi-page ads, the fine print is often buried at the bottom of just *one* of the ad's pages, far away from the page where the asterisk appeared, in the hope that you won't notice the fine print.

So if you see what looks like a great deal, but the deal has an asterisk next to it, the asterisk means "the deal is not really as great as we imply".

Many computer ads contain this fine print. . . .

"Monitor optional" means this price does NOT include a monitor. The monitor costs extra, even though the ad shows a photo of a computer with a monitor.

"Monitor/keyboard optional" means this price doesn't include a monitor and doesn't even include a keyboard. The monitor and keyboard cost extra.

"Upgrade price" means you get this price just if you already own an older version of this stuff.

"With system purchase" means you get this price just if you're stupid enough to also buy our overpriced full computer system at the same time.

"Reflects cash discount" means you get this price just if you're stupid enough to pay cash instead of using a credit card. (By paying cash, you can't complain to a credit-card company if we rip you off.) If you use a credit card, we'll charge you about 3% above the advertised price.

"Includes rebate" means you must pay us more, then request a rebate from the manufacturer. (You'll probably never get that rebate, since you'll forget to ask us for the rebate form, or you'll forget to mail the rebate form to the manufacturer, or the rebate form will have already expired, or you'll lose the receipt or code number you must mail with the rebate form to get the rebate.)

"Manufacturer's warranty" means that if the stuff breaks, don't ask us for help. Phone the original manufacturer instead (who will probably ignore you).

"Factory serviced" means another customer bought this stuff, didn't like it, and returned it to the factory, which examined it and thinks it's good enough to resell (after jiggling it a bit), so now we're sticking YOU with this lemon.

"For in-stock items" means that although we said we'd ship immediately, we won't if you order stuff that's not yet in our warehouse.

"25% restocking fee" means that if you return this stuff, we won't give you your money back. Instead, we'll keep 25% of your money (as a restocking fee) and return just 75% to you.

CDW versus PC Connection
Back in the 1980's, two big mail-order dealers set the tone for the rest of the discount industry. Those dealers were **Telemart** and **PC Connection**.

When **Telemart** went bankrupt in 1993, its assets were sold to **Computer Discount Warehouse (CDW)**, which has continued Telemart's tradition of low prices and wide selection. Phone CDW in Illinois at 800-500-4CDW (for Mac goodies) or 800-454-4CDW (for IBM-compatible goodies).

PC Connection has the best reputation for service because it processes orders fast, charges little for shipping, handles hassle orders promptly and generously, and gives technical help on a toll-free 800 number. It's in the tiny town of Marlow, New Hampshire (population 566, with a main street consisting mainly of a gas station). It began in a barn, then expanded to fill the inn across the street. Drop in anytime, enjoy the small-town friendliness, and wave to the 150 employees. Adventurers who've trekked to Marlow rave that it's quaint, friendly, and beautiful.

PC Connection's divisions
PC Connection has two divisions: IBM and Mac.

The IBM division advertises in *PC World* (phone 800-800-0003 or 603-446-0003) and *PC Magazine* (phone 800-800-0004 or 603-446-0004). The Mac division calls itself **Mac Connection** in *Macworld* (phone 800-800-3333 or 603-446-3333) and *Mac User* (phone 800-800-4444 or 603-446-4444). You can use the 800 numbers even if you're in Alaska, Hawaii, Puerto Rico, Virgin Islands, and Canada.

Each division sells mostly **software** but also some hardware (printers, disk drives, monitors, and chips to add to your computer). If you don't have a computer yet, the IBM division will sell you a Compaq; the Mac division will tell you to buy a Mac from your local Apple dealer (since Apple prohibits mail-order dealers from selling Macs).

Each division works round-the-clock, 24 hours daily (except Sunday evening and early Monday morning). Your order's shipped immediately, even if you've paid by check. (Checks are cleared in less than a day.) Your order's shipped by Airborne overnight express so it reaches you the next day; if you order between 12:01AM and 3:15AM Eastern Time, you'll usually receive your order the *same* day (because the company built a warehouse next to Airborne's airport in Ohio).

The IBM division is nice; the Mac division is even nicer. For USA shipping, the IBM division charges just $5, even if your order is big; the Mac division charges just $3. The IBM division's toll-free number is usually busy; the Mac division's toll-free number usually gets you a sales rep immediately. The IBM division offers fairly low prices (but not as low as other discount dealers); the Mac division offers rock-bottom prices, lower than almost any other Mac dealer.

Big competitors
The competitor that PC Connection fears the most is New Jersey's **Micro Warehouse**, which offers a greater variety of hardware and software, often at lower prices (especially for IBM-compatible goodies). Unfortunately, Micro Warehouse gives less technical help and sometimes has delays in shipping.

Like PC Connection, Micro Warehouse has two divisions. For the IBM division, phone 800-367-7080 or 908-905-5245. For the Mac division (which is called **Mac Warehouse**), phone 800-255-6227 or 908-367-0440.

Another competitor is Washington State's **Multiple Zones**. Like Micro Warehouse, it offers low prices on IBM and Mac goodies. Its IBM division, **PC Zone**, is at 800-258-2088. The Mac division, **Mac Zone**, is at 800-248-0800. For international calls to either division, phone 206-883-3088.

Cheap giants
The *biggest* discounters offering IBM-compatible hardware cheap are **Insight** and **USA Flex**. They usually charge less than PC Connection, Micro Warehouse, and PC Zone. Insight also advertises **software**; USA Flex does not. Insight offers the greatest variety of **disk drives**; USA Flex offers a greater variety of **printers and monitors**.

They advertise in *Computer Shopper*. USA Flex is on the back cover and all the back pages; Insight is in the middle.

Insight's ads often contain wrong prices, and Insight's order-takers often make mistakes, but Insight is willing to handle any complaints.

USA Flex is in Illinois at 800-944-5599. Insight is in Arizona at 800-488-0004 or 602-902-1176.

Midwest Micro is the biggest source of **printers**. *Computer Shopper*'s biggest advertiser, it runs 60 full-page ads in each issue! Selling even more printers than USA Flex, it also sells **modems and computers**. Its **notebook computers** include more features at lower prices than any competitors. Phone Midwest Micro in Ohio: 800-572-8844 for computers, 800-972-8822 for printers & modems & parts.

Discounts from retail stores
If you need hardware or software fast and can't wait for mail-order dealers to ship, go to the local computer stores that advertise in the business section of your local newspaper.

To encourage a store to give you a discount, mention low prices from competitors and agree to buy many items at once. Say that if you don't get a discount, you'll shop elsewhere. Many stores do **price-matching**: they'll match the price of any other local store, though not the prices of mail-order dealers. Some stores let salespeople give 10% discounts, which are subtracted from the salesperson's commission.

IBM and Apple give educational discounts to schools, teachers, and some college students. To find out whether *you* can get educational discounts, ask your school's administrators and your town's computer stores.

Superstores
For low prices, visit a chain of gigantic superstores called **Comp USA**, which was formerly called **Soft Warehouse**. It's based in Dallas but has spread to 75 other cities in 26 states. (For example, its New York City store is at 420 5th Ave., 212-764-6224.) To find the Comp USA store nearest *you*, phone 800-COMP-USA. You can phone day or night, 24 hours, and use that number to order computer goodies or a free catalog.

For **software and Hewlett-Packard printers**, Comp USA charges less than most other stores and mail-order dealers. For other printers and accessories, Comp USA's prices aren't as aggressive: you'll pay less at a competing superstore chain called **Staples** (which sells computers and also **general office supplies**). But Comp USA offers a greater variety of computer products than Staples, and Comp USA's salespeople are more knowledgeable and helpful.

Unfortunately, Comp USA handles repairs slowly (you must wait about a week), and Comp USA's prices for most hardware are slightly above other discounters. To get an IBM clone cheaply, buy elsewhere. To buy a **Mac**, try Staples, which has a very limited selection of Macs but great prices!

The other big chain of computer superstores is **Computer City**, secretly owned by Tandy. Like Comp USA, Computer

City sells IBM clones and Macs, at prices far below Tandy's Radio Shack stores.

Another computer-superstore chain is **Micro Center**, with just 8 superstores so far (in Ohio, Pennsylvania, Virginia, Georgia, and Southern California).

Salespeople at Computer City and Micro Center are usually more knowledgeable than at Comp USA and make customers happier. But in cities where those chains compete against each other, Comp USA lowers its prices to undercut those competitors. Comp USA puts up signs comparing prices and showing how much you save by shopping at Comp USA instead of Computer City or Micro Center.

In California's Silicon Valley, visit a chain of superstores called **Fry's Electronics**, which has been a local favorite for many years. In New York City, visit a superstore called **J&R Computer World**, which is near Wall Street (15 Park Row, New York City NY 10038, 800-221-8180 or 212-238-9000).

Bagel boys

Bagel boys Four discount dealers in New York City are called the **bagel boys**, because most of their employees are like me: Jewish men who enjoy eating bagels. (Yum!) Many of their employees are Hassidic Jews, an ultra-traditional sect who wear black suits, black coats, black hats, and beards. For the Jewish Sabbath, they close on Friday afternoon, stay shut on Saturday, and reopen on Sunday.

Those dealers sold cameras and other photography equipment, then started selling computer hardware also, plus a little software. They offer especially low prices on **printers, monitors, modems, and famous notebook computers**.

Here's how to reach them:

S&W Computers & Electronics, 31 W. 21st St. 800-874-1235 212-463-8330
47th Street Photo, 115 W. 45th St. 800-235-5016 718-722-4750
Tri State Computer, 650 6th Ave. (at 20th St.) 800-433-5199 212-633-2530
Harmony Computers, 1801 Flatbush Ave. B'klyn 800-441-1144 718-692-3232

If you phone Tri State computer, ask for David Rohinsky at extension 223. He'll treat you extra-nice.

Those four stores accept both walk-ins and mail-order. Except for Harmony, they all advertise in the Science section of the *The New York Times* each Tuesday. Except for 47th St. Photo, they all advertise in *Computer Shopper*.

Since they offer rock-bottom prices and deliver fast, I often buy there. But they have these drawbacks. . . .

Their tech-support staffs are too small. You'll get faster repairs elsewhere.

They often buy overstocked items from other dealers and resell them; but since those items have changed hands, the manufacturer's "limited warranty" on those items is no longer valid.

Though reputable now, their past has been murky. In 1994, the biggest software company (Microsoft) sued Harmony for distributing software improperly. During the 1980's, Tri State advertised printers at low prices but honored those prices just if you overpaid for the printer's cable. Most of those companies removed supplies & programs from the boxes of printers & computers they sold and charged extra to put the goodies back in.

Egghead Discount Software

Egghead Discount Software is a chain of stores giving discounts on **software** for the IBM PC and Mac. Egghead's prices are nearly as low as Comp USA's, and Egghead often runs special sales that drive prices even lower. To find the Egghead store nearest you, dial Egghead's headquarters in Washington State at 800-EGGHEAD.

Egghead is nutty, funny, and friendly. The chain's mascot is Professor Egghead, who's a cross between a balding Albert Einstein and a hairy egg. He brags the software is eggciting, eggzotic, eggstraordinary, and intelleggtual with many eggcoutrements and eggcessories, sold by eggsperts who eggsplain it all and give eggzibitions that are eggstravanzas.

Egghead sells business, educational, artistic, and fun software for the IBM PC and Mac. Egghead's customers like the low prices, wide selection, humorous friendliness, and permission to try software in the store before buying it. If you find a local competing store offering a lower price, Egghead will match that price and even charge you $1 less.

Surplus Software A discount dealer called **Surplus Software** sells old versions of excellent IBM-compatible software at very low prices: often $19.95! It also sells new versions cheaper than most other mail-order dealers. Phone Surplus Software in Oregon at 800-753-7877 or 503-386-1375.

Even if you want the newest software, your best bet's often to buy an old version from Surplus Software and then use that purchase as an excuse to get the special "upgrade price" on the new version. The old version's price plus the upgrade price is usually less than the price of buying the new version directly.

Computer shows Another way to find low prices is at a computer show. The lowest prices are at small shows called **flea markets** or **swap meets**. Many vendors at shows offer discounts, especially during the show's last three hours. When you buy at a show, jot down the vendor's name, address, and phone number, in case the goods don't work.

Beware: many vendors at those shows are like gypsies, traveling from show to show and hard to reach if you have a complaint. Many sell computers containing illegal copies of software that was never paid for and whose instruction manuals are missing. Make sure any software you buy comes with an official instruction manual (published by the company that invented the software), not just a book from a bookstore.

Used computers Instead of buying a new computer, you can sometimes save money by getting a used one.

The oldest source of used microcomputers is **The Boston Computer Exchange** (phone 800-262-6399 or 617-542-4414). It gives free info, by phone, about 1000 used computers you can buy. For more thorough info, get a copy of the complete 1000-computer Master List by sending the exchange $10.

The Exchange has no computers in stock. It's just a broker that passes info between buyers and sellers. The Exchange charges a seller $25 to be listed and get advice about what to charge. If a sale occurs, the seller must also pay the Exchange a 15% commission. The buyer pays the exchange nothing — unless the buyer wants a copy of the Master List.

Problem: should the buyer begin by mailing a check to the seller and hope the seller ships the computer? Or should the seller ship the computer first and hope the buyer pays for it?

Solution: to protect both the buyer and the seller against getting stiffed, the Exchange has the buyer first mail a check to the Exchange. When the Exchange receives the check, it tells the seller to mail the computer to the buyer. When the buyer receives the computer, the Exchange mails a check (minus the 15% fee) to the seller.

If the seller neglects to mail the computer, the Exchange refunds the check to the buyer. If the seller mails the computer but the buyer dislikes it, the Exchange talks with both parties to reach a compromise.

For an even better deal, try the **National Computer Exchange (NaComEx)** in New York (800-NaComEx or 212-614-0700). It charges the seller a 15% commission but just a $15 listing fee (instead of $25). If the computer costs under $334, NaComEx charges the seller a $50 commission (instead of 15%), whereas the Boston Computer Exchange refuses to handle cheap stuff at all.

Another used-computer broker is Atlanta's **American Computer Exchange** (800-786-0717 or 404-250-0050).

New computers cheap On page 72, I'll explain the *best* way to buy a complete new IBM clone cheaply.

CHIPS

CHIP TECHNOLOGY

The **system unit** is the box containing the CPU and other goodies (such as the speaker, power supply, and memory). If you unscrew that box and pry it open to see the circuitry inside, you'll see a green plastic board, on which is printed an electrical wiring diagram.

Since the diagram's printed in copper (instead of ink), the diagram conducts electricity; so it isn't just a diagram of an electrical circuit; it *is* an electrical circuit!

The green plastic board — including the circuit printed on it — is called a **printed-circuit board (PC board)**. Each wire that's stamped onto the PC board is called a **trace**.

The typical computer contains *several* PC boards.

Motherboard & babies

In your computer, the largest and most important PC board is called the **motherboard**. It lies flat on the bottom of the system unit.

The other PC boards are smaller. Those little baby boards (about the size of a postcard) are called **PC cards**.

The typical motherboard has several **slots** on it. Into each slot, you can put a PC card.

PCMCIA cards

If you buy a modern notebook computer, you'll see the case's right-hand wall has a special slot in it. You can shove a card into that slot without opening the notebook's case.

The kind of card that fits into that special slot is small and thin — the size of a credit card. That kind of card was invented by the **Personal-Computer Memory-Card International Assocation (PCMCIA)** and therefore called a **PCMCIA card**. That slot is called a **PCMCIA slot**.

People have trouble remembering what "PCMCIA" stands for. Cynics say it stands for "People Can't Memorize Computer Industry Acronyms". Since "PCMCIA" also stands for "Politically Correct Members of the CIA", computerists pronounce "PCMCIA" in two breaths: they say "PCM", then pause, then say "CIA".

Some PCMCIA cards are *very* thin. Other PCMCIA cards are slightly thicker, so they can hold extra circuitry. A PCMCIA card and its slot are called **Type 1** if their thickness is 3.3 millimeters, **Type 2** if 5 millimeters, **Type 3** if 10.5 millimeters, **Type 4** if 18 millimeters.

Caterpillars

On each PC board, you'll see black rectangles. If you look closely at a black rectangle, you'll see it has tiny legs, so it looks like a black caterpillar. (Though farmers think it looks like a "black caterpillar", city folks think it looks more like a "yucky roach". Kids call it just "a black thingy with legs".)

The "caterpillars" come in many sizes. In a typical computer, the shortest caterpillars are three-quarters of an inch long and have 7 pairs of legs; the longest are two inches long and have 20 pairs of legs.

Though each black caterpillar has legs, it doesn't move. It's permanently mounted on the PC board.

Each leg is made of tin and called a **pin**.

Sadistic hobbyists play a game where they yank the caterpillars from a PC board and throw the caterpillars across the room. That game's called "tin-pin bowling".

Hidden inside the caterpillar is a metal square, called a **chip**, which is very tiny. The typical chip is just an eighth of an inch long, an eighth of an inch wide, and a hundredth of an inch thick! On that tiny metal chip are etched *thousands* of microscopic electronic circuits! Since all those circuits are on the chip, the chip's called an **integrated circuit (IC)**.

Four purposes

Each chip serves a purpose. If the chip's purpose is to "think", it's called a **processor chip**. If the chip's purpose is to "remember" information, it's called a **memory chip**. If the chip's purpose is to help devices communicate with each other, it's called an **interface chip**. If the chip's purpose is to act as a slave and helper to other chips, it's called a **support chip**.

So a chip is either a processor chip or a memory chip or an interface chip or a support chip — or it's a combination chip that accomplishes *several* purposes.

How chips are designed

To design a chip, the manufacturer hires an artist, who draws on paper a big sketch of what circuits are to be put onto the chip. It helps if the artist also has a degree in engineering — and knows how to use another computer to help draw all the lines.

After the big sketch is drawn, it is photographed.

Have you ever photographed your friend and asked the photography store for an "enlargement"? To produce a chip, the chip's manufacturer does the opposite: it photographs the sketch but produces a "reduction" to just an eighth of an inch on each side! Whereas a photo of your friend is made on treated paper, the tiny photo of the chip's circuitry consists of metal and semiconductors on treated silicon so the photo's an actual working circuit! That photographic process is called **photolithography** (or **photolith**).

Many copies of that photo are made on a large silicon wafer. Then a cookie cutter slices the wafer into hundreds of chips. Each chip is put into its own caterpillar.

The caterpillar's purpose is just to hide and protect the chip inside it; the caterpillar's just a strange-looking package containing the chip. Since the caterpillar's a package that has two rows of legs, it's called a **dual in-line package (DIP)**. That DIP's only purpose is to house the chip.

Computer hobbyists are always talking about chips & DIPs. That's why computer hobbyists, at parties, serve chips & dips. And that's why computer hobbyists are called "dipchips".

Buying chips

If you ask a computer dealer to sell you a chip, the dealer also gives you the chip's DIP (the entire caterpillar). Since you've asked for a chip but also received a DIP, you might get confused and think that the caterpillar (the DIP) is the chip. But that caterpillar's *not* the chip; the chip hides inside the caterpillar.

The typical caterpillar-and-chip costs $3. You might pay somewhat more or somewhat less, depending on how fancy the chip's circuitry is.

If the circuits in a chip are defective, it's called a "buffalo chip". Folks who dislike that tacky term say "potato chip" or "chocolate chip" instead, like this: "Hey, the computer's not working! It must be made of chocolate chips!"

You can get chips from these famous mail-order chip suppliers:

Chip supplier	Address	Phone
Jameco	1355 Shoreway Rd., Belmont CA 94002	415-592-8097, 24 hours
JDR Microdevices	2233 Samaritan Dr., San Jose CA 95124	800-538-5000 or 408-559-1200
ACP	1310 E. Edinger, Santa Ana CA 92705	800-FONE-ACP

The following chip suppliers are newer and often charge less:

Chip supplier	Address	Phone
Nevada Computer	684 Wells Rd., Boulder City NV 89005	800-982-2928 or 702-294-0204
LA Trade	22825 Lockness Ave., Torrance CA 90501	800-433-3726 or 310-539-0019
Pacific Coast Micro	4901 Morena Blvd. #1111, San Diego CA 92117	800-581-6040 or 619-581-1439
Wordwide Tech	21 South 5th St., Philadelphia PA 19106	800-457-6937 or 215-922-0050
Memory Express	15140 Valley Blvd., City of Industry CA 91744	800-877-8188 or 818-333-6389
Chip Merchant	9541 Ridgehaven Ct., San Diego CA 92123	800-426-6375 or 619-268-4774

How chips chat

The chip inside the caterpillar acts as the caterpillar's brain. The caterpillar also contains a "nervous system", made of thin wires that run from the brain (the chip) to the legs (the pins). The wires in the caterpillar's nervous system are very thin: each wire's diameter is about half of a thousandth of an inch.

If one caterpillar wants to send electrical signals to another caterpillar, the signals go from the first caterpillar's brain (chip) through the caterpillar's nervous system to its legs (pins). Each pin is attached to a trace (wire) on the PC board. The signals travel through those traces, which carry the signals across the PC board until the signals reach the second caterpillar's pins. Then the signals travel through the second caterpillar's nervous system to that caterpillar's brain (chip).

Binary code To communicate with each other, the caterpillars use a secret code. Each code is a series of 1's and 0's. For example, the code for the letter A is 01000001; the code for the letter B is 01000010; the code for the number 5 is 101; the code for the number 6 is 110.

That's called the **binary code**, because each digit in the code has just *two* possibilities: it's either a 1 or a 0. In the code, each 1 or 0 is called a **binary digit**.

A **binary digit** is called a **bit**. So in the computer, each **bit** is a 1 or a 0.

When a caterpillar wants to send a message to another caterpillar, it sends the message in binary code. To send a 1, the caterpillar sends a high voltage through the wires; to send a 0, the caterpillar sends little or no voltage through the wires.

So to send the number 5, whose code number is 101, the caterpillar sends a high voltage (1), then a low voltage (0), then a high voltage (1). To send those three bits (1, 0, and then 1), the caterpillar can send them in sequence through the same leg (pin); or for faster transmission, the caterpillar can send them through three pins simultaneously: the first pin sends 1, while the next pin sends 0 and the third pin sends 1.

The speed at which bits are sent is measured in **bits per second (bps)**.

Bipolar versus MOS

Chips can be manufactured in two ways.

The old way's called **bipolar**. The new way's called **metal-oxide semiconductor** (MOS, which is pronounced "moss").

The new way (MOS) is more popular because it costs less, consumes less electricity, and can hold more circuitry inside the chip.

Microcomputers use only MOS. Minicomputers and maxicomputers use mainly MOS chips but also contain a few bipolar chips, because bipolar chips have one (and only one) advantage over MOS chips: bipolar chips work faster.

The most popular kind of MOS is called **negative-channel MOS**. (It's also called **n-channel MOS** or **NMOS**, which is pronounced "en moss".) The main alternative, called **complementary MOS** (or **CMOS**, pronounced "sea moss"), consumes even less electricity but can't hold as much circuitry inside the chip. CMOS chips are used in simple-minded battery-operated computers (such as digital watches, pocket calculators, pocket computers, and notebook computers) and in some parts of larger computers.

The part of the computer that thinks ("the brain") is called the **processor** (or **central processing unit** or **CPU**).

In a maxicomputer or minicomputer, the processor consists of several chips, which are **processor chips**.

In a microcomputer, the processor is so small that it consists of just a single chip, called a **microprocessor**. It sits on the motherboard. Yes, in a typical microcomputer, the part that does all the thinking is just a tiny square of metal, less than ¼" on each side!

Intel's designs

In the IBM PC and clones, the microprocessor uses a design invented by **Intel**.

I'll begin by explaining the Intel microprocessors. I'll discuss competitors later.

In the original IBM PC (and in the IBM PC XT), the microprocessor was the **Intel 8088**. IBM computers (and clones) containing that chip are called **XT-class computers**.

Later, Intel invented an improved version, called the **Intel 80286**. Since "80286" is too long a number for us humans to remember, most of us just call it the **Intel 286**. IBM used it in the IBM PC AT computer. That's why computers containing that chip are called **AT-class computers**.

After inventing the Intel 286, Intel invented a further improvement (called the **Intel 386**), then an even further improvement (called the **Intel 486**).

In 1993, Intel began selling an even further improvement, which ought to be called a **586**; but Intel calls it the **Pentium** instead, so Intel can trademark the name and prevent companies from copying it. It's the first computer chip that sounds like a breakfast cereal: "Hey, kids, to put zip into your life, try Penti-yumms. They build strong bodies, 5 ways!"

So altogether, IBM microcomputers and clones come in five popular classes:

Chip	When invented	Transistors on chip	Used in
8088	1979	29,000	XT computers
286	1982	134,000	AT computers
386	1985	275,000	386 computers
486	1989	1,200,000	486 computers
Pentium	1993	3,100,000	Pentium comp.

You can find programs that run okay on any chip; but many *modern* programs require a 286, 386, 486, or Pentium and won't run on an 8088.

To run modern programs QUICKLY and use all the modern features, you need a 386, 486, or Pentium. Most computers built today contain a 486 or Pentium.

The 8088 and 286 chips are found just in pocket computers, used computers, and old computers that liquidators are trying to unload. Many homes and offices still have old 8088 computers, bought many years ago. The people who still use those ancient computers restrict themselves to running very old-fashioned programs.

The Intel 386 comes in two varieties. The original variety was called the **Intel 386DX**. Later, Intel invented a stripped-down version called the **Intel 386SX**, which saves you money by being much cheaper (and just *slightly* slower). Similarly, the Intel 486 comes in two varieties: the original variety was called the **Intel 486DX**; later, Intel invented a stripped-down version called the **Intel 486SX**, which is much cheaper and just *slightly* slower.

The Intel 8088 is a slightly stripped-down version of a chip called the **Intel 8086** (which few computers contain).

So altogether, here are Intel's popular chips, from slowest to fastest:

slowest & cheapest:	Intel 8088
	Intel 8086
	Intel 286
	Intel 386SX
	Intel 386DX
	Intel 486SX
	Intel 486DX
fastest & most expensive:	Intel Pentium

Imitations

Intel's competitors have imitated Intel's chips.

The most popular imitation of the 8088 is the **V20 chip**. It's made by **Nippon Electric Company** (whose abbreviation is **NEC**, which is pronounced "neck"). People who use the V20 chip are said to have "gone necking". The most popular imitation of the 8086 is NEC's **V30 chip**; people who use that chip are said to have "done advanced necking". Imitations of the 286 are made by **Harris**. Imitations of the 386 are made by **IBM** and **Advanced Micro Devices (AMD)**. All those imitations work fine. Some go even faster than Intel's originals!

Imitations of the 486 are made by **AMD**, **Cyrix**, and **IBM**. AMD's imitations are fine. Cyrix's imitations are awful: they go *much slower* that Intel's originals. Cynics say Cyrix's chips should be called "386½" instead of "486". Cyrix's imitation of the 486SX is called the **486SLC**; Cyrix's imitation of the 486DX is called the **486DLC**. Like Cyrix, IBM's imitation of the 486SX is called the **486SLC**; IBM's imitation runs faster than Cyrix's, though not as fast as Intel's original.

Nobody imitates the Pentium yet.

Chart of details

You've seen that a Pentium is the fastest Intel chip, the 8088 is the worst, and other chips are intermediate. But how *much* do those chips differ from each other?

Don't ask that question to a computer salesman! Computer salesmen dispense lots of misinformation about computers, because the salesmen are lying or stupid. Usually the salesmen are lying *and* stupid!

Here's a famous riddle. . . .

What's the difference between a used-car dealer and a computer salesman?
Answer: the used-car dealer *knows* he's lying.

To learn the *truth* about how chips differ from each other, look at this big chart:

Chip	Internal accum.	External data path	Address	Math copr.	Megahertz	Efficiency	
8088	16-bit	8-bit	20-bit	no	4.77, 7.18, 8, 10, 12	10%	(5%)
8086	16-bit	16-bit	20-bit	no	8, 10	12%	(6%)
286	16-bit	16-bit	24-bit	no	6, 8, 10, 12, 16, 20	40%	(30%)
386SX	32-bit	16-bit	24-bit	no	16, 20, 25, 33, 40	40%	(40%)
386DX	32-bit	32-bit	32-bit	no	16, 20, 25, 33, 40	50%	(50%)
486SX	32-bit	32-bit	32-bit	no	20, 25, 33	100%	(100%)
486DX	32-bit	32-bit	32-bit	yes	25, 33, 40, 50	100%	(120%)
486DX2	32-bit	32-bit	32-bit	yes	50, 66	92%	(110%)
486DX4	32-bit	32-bit	32-bit	yes	75, 100	90%	(108%)
Pentium	64-bit	64-bit	32-bit	yes	60, 66, 75, 90, 100	180%	(220%)

That chart shows the chips we've discussed, listed from worst to best. Some are made by Intel, others by imitators such as Harris and AMD. The chart also shows the **Intel 486DX2** and the **Intel 486DX4**, which are very similar to the Intel 486DX.

Here's what the chart means. . . .

Internal accumulator Each chip contains **registers**. Each register can hold a binary code number (such as 01000001). The chip's main register is called the **accumulator**.

If the accumulator is wide enough to hold 32 bits inside it (such as 10000110111001111110010101010101), the accumulator is called **32-bit**; the chip is said to **contain a 32-bit accumulator** and be **32-bit internally**.

If the accumulator is narrower and holds just 16 bits, the accumulator is called **16-bit**. In that case, the chip can handle code numbers that are 16 bits long but *not* code numbers that are 32 bits long. If you try to feed that chip a 32-bit code number, the chip won't understand it.

The typical program uses just 16-bit instructions. (Instead of using a 32-bit instruction, it uses a pair of 16-bit instructions.)

But **a few fancy programs use 32-bit instructions**. To run those 32-bit programs, you must buy a chip that's 32-bit internally. The chart shows that **to run the fanciest programs (32-bit), you must buy at least a 386SX**.

External data path The column marked "external data path" tells how many of the chip's pins transmit data.

As you can see from the chart, the 386SX is "32-bit internal, 16-bit external". That means the 386SX contains a 32-bit accumulator but has just 16 data pins. To transmit the accumulator's 32 bits, the chip sends out 16 of the bits (on the 16 data pins), then sends out the next 16 bits by using those same pins.

That technique of using just a few pins to transmit many bits is called **multiplexing**. Computerists say the 386SX is "a 32-bit chip **multiplexed** onto 16 pins"; they say **the 386SX is a multiplexed 386DX**.

That's why the 386SX is slower than the 386DX: to transmit the 32 bits, the 386SX must send out two bursts of 16 bits, whereas the 386DX can send out a single burst of 32 bits all at once!

Notice that the 386SX is just as smart as the 386DX — it understands the same 32-bit codes — but it transmits them more slowly (as 2 bursts of 16, instead of 1 burst of 32). So **the 386SX is smart but a slow communicator** — like Einstein with his mouth full and trying to talk through a narrow drinking straw.

The 8088 is a multiplexed 8086. Like the 8086, the 8088 thinks about 16 bits; but the 8088 must send them out in two 8-bit bursts.

Address
The computer's main memory (which consists of RAM chips and ROM chips) is like a city: each location in it has an **address**. If the main memory is large enough to hold lots of info, it has lots of addresses.

A city has addresses such as "231 17th Street, Apartment 501". In the computer's main memory, each address is a binary code number instead, such as 01000101010111101010.

For an 8088 or 8086, each address must be brief: just 20 bits long. An 8088 or 8086 therefore can't handle a big main memory — and can't handle big programs.

A 286 can handle longer addresses (24-bit) so it can handle the big main memory required by modern big programs. That's why, **to run modern big programs, you must buy at least a 286**.

Though 24-bit addresses are long enough to handle all popular programs sold today, the 386DX permits even bigger addresses (32-bit), to prepare for the bigger programs of the far future — and to handle computers that are networked together and share a gigantic big RAM.

Math coprocessor
You can buy a **math coprocessor**, which is special circuitry that performs advanced math super-quickly. The math coprocessor's circuits are specially designed to quickly manipulate decimals, trigonometry, logarithms, and 80-bit numbers. If you don't have a math coprocessor, the only way the CPU can do advanced math is by obeying long-winded, slow programs fed to it slowly from the RAM, ROM, and disks. The math coprocessor lets the CPU do advanced math much faster: 10 times faster, 20 times faster, or even more!

Should you buy a math coprocessor? If you're doing lots of advanced math, the answer is "yes": you'll be amazed and thrilled at how much faster your computer performs the math! But if you're *not* doing lots of advanced math, don't bother getting a math coprocessor.

If you've drawn a picture on the computer's screen and want to rotate the picture, the math coprocessor will make the rotation go faster, because the computer must use trigonometry to rotate the picture and compute the picture's new coordinates. For example, if you draw a 3-D picture of a house and then want the computer to show you how the house looks from a different angle, the math coprocessor will help.

Just the 486DX, 486DX2, 486DX4, and Pentium chips contain math coprocessor circuitry; Intel's other CPU chips do not.

Here's the difference between a 486DX and a 486SX. . . .

A 486DX contains a math coprocessor.
A 486SX does not.

The 486DX was invented first. Later, Intel invented the 486SX by using this manufacturing technique: Intel took each 486DX whose math coprocessor was faulty and called it a 486SX. So a 486SX was just a defective 486DX.

If you buy a 486SX today, you get a 486DX whose math coprocessor is either defective or missing.

Problem: suppose you want to do advanced math quickly, but your computer's CPU chip lacks math-coprocessor circuitry (because you bought an 8088, 8086, 286, 386, or 486SX). To improve your computer's math speed, just buy a **math coprocessor chip**, which is a supplementary chip that contains math-coprocessor circuitry. Put that chip next to the CPU chip on the motherboard. Instead of buying a math coprocessor chip made by Intel, you can buy an imitation made by **Cyrix** or **Integrated Information Technology (IIT)**:

CPU	Which math coprocessor to buy
8088, 8086	Intel 8087 ($45)
286	Intel 287 ($49)
386SX	Intel 387SX ($54), Cyrix 83S87 ($44), or IIT 3C87SX ($52)
386DX	Intel 387DX ($74), Cyrix 83D87 ($48), or IIT 3C87 ($54)
486SX	Intel 487SX ($249)

Megahertz
In an army, when solders march, they're kept in step by a drill sergeant who yells out, rhythmically, "Hup, two, three, four! Hup, two, three, four! Hup, two, three, four!"

Like a soldier, the microprocessor takes the next step in obeying your program just when instructed by the computer's "drill sergeant", which is called the **computer clock**. The clock rhythmically sends out a pulse of electricity; each time the clock sends out a pulse, the microprocessor does one more step in obeying your program.

The clock sends out *millions* of pulses every second, so the microprocessor accomplishes *millions* of steps in your program every second!

Each pulse is called a **clock cycle**. The clock's speed is measured in **cycles per seconds**.

A "cycle per second" is called a **hertz (Hz)**, in honor of the German physicist Heinrich Hertz. A "million cycles per second" is called a **megahertz (MHz)**.

In the fastest IBM clones, the clock does 100 million cycles per seconds. That's 100 megahertz!

In the slowest IBM clones, the clock does just 4.77 million cycles per second. That's 4.77 megahertz.

Look at the big chart on the previous page. That chart's bottom line says you can buy five versions of the Pentium chip: the cheapest version can handle 60 megahertz, faster versions can handle 66, 75, or 90 megahertz, and the fastest version can handle 100 megahertz.

For some chips, the high-megahertz versions are clones manufactured by Intel's competitors instead of by Intel itself.

Efficiency and its consequences
A 386DX resembles a 486SX: each has a 32-bit internal accumulator, 32-bit external data path, 32-bit address, and no math coprocessor. Which runs your programs faster: a 33-megahertz 386DX or a 33-megahertz 486SX? The answer is: **a 33-megahertz 486SX runs your programs twice as fast as a 33-megahertz 386DX**, because a 486SX is twice as *efficient* as a 386DX: it accomplishes twice as much work per clock cycle because it's smart enough to work on several operations simultaneously.

In the big chart, the "Efficiency" column shows how efficient each microprocessor is, relative to a 486SX.

In the "Efficiency" column, I give two numbers. The first number shows how efficiently the computer handles simple programs (which contain just 16-bit codes and 20-bit addresses and don't try to use a math coprocessor). The second number (the **revised efficiency**) is based on the first number but includes a bonus (for having a math coprocessor) and penalties (for being limited to 16-bit instructions or 20-bit addresses).

Here's how a 486DX differs from a 486DX2:

A 50-megahertz 486DX thinks at 50 megahertz and communicates its answers at 50 megahertz.
To use it at full speed, you must put it on a motherboard that has 50-megahertz circuitry.

A 50-megahertz 486DX2 thinks at 50 megahertz but communicates its answers at just 25 megahertz.
It's intended to be put on a 25-megahertz motherboard (cheaper than a 50-megahertz motherboard).

Congratulations! You've learned that a 50-megahertz 486DX2 communicates slower than a 50-megahertz 486DX and therefore has a lower "efficiency" rating. Similarly:

A 66-megahertz 486DX2 thinks at 66 megahertz but communicates at just 33 megahertz.
Put it on a 33-megahertz motherboard.

A 75-megahertz 486DX4 thinks at 75 megahertz but communicates at just 25 megahertz.
Put it on a 25-megahertz motherboard.

A 100-megahertz 486DX4 thinks at 100 megahertz but communicates at about 33 megahertz.
Put it on a 33-megahertz motherboard.

To compute the total work accomplished, look at the big chart on page 24: multiply the cycle speed (megahertz) by the amount of work accomplished per cycle (revised efficiency).

Here are some popular chips:

Chip and megahertz	Total work accomplished	Chip's price	Motherboard's price
8088-4.77	.2385	$3	$33
8088-10	.5	$4	$34
8086-10	.6	$5	$35
286-6	1.8	$10	$40
286-8	2.4	$11	$41
286-10	3	$12	$42
286-12	3.6	$13	$43
286-16	4.8	$15	$45
286-20	6	$17	$47
386SX-16	6.4	$20	$50
386SX-20	8	$22	$52
386SX-25	10	$24	$54
386SX-33	13.2	$26	$56
386SX-40	16	$28	$58
386DX-40	20	$50	$90
486SX-25	25	$80	$120
486SX-33	33	$95	$135
486DX-33	39.6	$140	$180
486DX-40	48	$145	$185
486DX2-50	55	$150	$190
486DX2-66	72.6	$180	$220
486DX4-75	81	$400 ($184 if 1000)	$440
486DX4-100	108	$405 ($245 if 1000)	$445
Pentium-60	132	$410 ($273 if 1000)	$550
Pentium-66	145.2	$465 ($289 if 1000)	$605
Pentium-75	165	$475 ($301 if 1000)	$615
Pentium-90	198	$625 ($546 if 1000)	$765
Pentium-100	220	$825 ($673 if 1000)	$965

For example, look at the chart's bottom line. It says you can buy a Pentium chip running at 100 megahertz. Its "total work accomplished" is 220 (because 100 megahertz times the chip's revised efficiency of 220% is 220). You can buy it for $825 from discount dealers (who advertise in magazines such as *Computer Shopper*). If you want to buy 1000 of those Pentium-100 chips (to put in 1000 computers), phone Intel directly instead of dealers; Intel will give you a quantity discount and charge you just $673 per chip. For $965, discount dealers will sell you an entire Pentium-100 motherboard, including the Pentium-100 chip, ROM memory chips, and lots of other circuitry but *not* RAM memory chips (which cost extra and must be put onto the board to make the board work).

Notice that the most expensive chip, the Pentium-100, has a total-work-accomplished rating of 220. The cheapest chip, the 8088-4.77, has a total-work-accomplished rating of just .2385. That means the Pentium-100 can accomplish about 922 times as much work as the 8088-4.77.

But for a chip to accomplish anything at all, you must give it some work to do! If the chip must wait for you to tell it what to do, the chip accomplishes nothing useful during the wait: it just mumbles to itself.

So to make full use of a Pentium-100, make sure you know what commands to give the computer and make sure you help the chip reach its full potential by buying quick RAM, quick disk drives, and a quick printer. Otherwise, the Pentium-100 will act as idiotic as if it's in the army: it will just "hurry up and then wait" for the other parts of the system to catch up and tell it what to do next.

A mind is a terrible thing to waste! To avoid wasting the computer's mind (the CPU), make sure the other computer parts are fast enough to match the CPU and keep it from waiting.

If you get suckered into buying a computer that has a Pentium-100 chip but a slow RAM, slow disk drives, and a slow printer, you've bought a computer that's just half-fast; it's half-assed.

When you buy a microcomputer, its advertised price always includes a microprocessor, motherboard, and other goodies. Pay for the microprocessor separately just if you're inventing your own computer, buying parts for a broken computer, or upgrading your computer by switching to a faster microprocessor and motherboard.

Though the microprocessor is cheap, the computer containing it can cost thousands of dollars. That's because the microprocessor is just a tiny part of the computer. In addition to the microprocessor, you need memory chips, interface chips, and support chips; you also need PC boards to put the chips on; you also want I/O devices (keyboard, screen, printer, speaker, and mouse), disks, and software.

Discount dealers sell IBM clones for these prices:

Chip	Complete computer
8088	$150
8086	$200
286	$400
386SX	$600
386DX	$700
486SX	$1000
486DX	$1300
486DX2	$1600
486DX4	$1900
Pentium-60	$2000
Pentium-66	$2200
Pentium-75	$2400
Pentium-90	$2600
Pentium-100	$3600

Those prices include nearly everything you need (such as the CPU, memory chips, disks, keyboard, and a screen that displays lots of colors) but do *not* include a printer or software. Those prices are approximate; the exact price you pay depends on the quality, speed, and size of the various components.

Notice that a 286 computer costs $200 more than an 8086 computer. That's because a 286 computer includes a better CPU chip and also comes with a better keyboard, better screen, better memory chips, and better disks.

Motorola

Intel's biggest competitor is **Motorola**. It manufactures the **6809E microprocessor**, the **68000** (which is faster and understands advanced commands), several souped-up versions of the 68000, and the **Power PC**:

Chip	Price	Computers that use it
6809E	$3	Radio Shack Color Computer
68000	$9	Mac, Mac Plus, Mac SE, Mac Classic, Amiga (500, 600, 1000, 2000), Atari ST
68020	$45	Mac LC, old Mac 2, Amiga 1200
68030	lots	Mac (SE/30, Classic 2, LC 2, LC 3), new Mac 2, Amiga 2500 & 3000
68040	lots	Mac Centris, Mac Quadra, and Amiga 4000
Power PC	lots	Power Mac

Motorola's microprocessors are *not* Intel clones. They use different commands than Intel and require different software.

When fed the proper software, they work as fast as Intel's microprocessors:

Motorola's 6809E   is about as fast as Intel's 8080 (which was the predecessor to the 8088)

Motorola's 68000   is about as fast as Intel's 8086
Motorola's 68020   is about as fast as Intel's 286
Motorola's 68030   is about as fast as Intel's 386
Motorola's 68040   is about as fast as Intel's 486

Motorola's Power PC is about as fast as Intel's Pentium

What's the Power PC?
Motorola's fastest microprocessor, the **Power PC**, was invented by a team of researchers from three companies (Motorola, Apple, and IBM), all working together. That's why it's called the **love-triangle chip**. It was invented to prevent Intel from monopolizing the microcomputer marketplace.

The first version of the Power PC is called the **Power PC 601**. It's manufactured just by IBM. Later versions, such as the **Power PC 603**, the **Power PC 604**, and the **Power PC 620**, will be manufactured by both Motorola and IBM.

The Power PC is used in Apple's fastest computer (the **Power Mac**) and will also be used in fast computers that IBM is developing.

Intel emulation
Suppose your computer's microprocessor is made by Motorola, but somebody gives you software that's written for Intel microprocessors instead. You can run that software on your computer if you feed your computer an **Intel emulator** (software that makes Motorola microprocessors imitate Intel's). But Intel emulator software runs slowly. To accomplish tasks faster, buy software that runs directly on Motorola microprocessors without needing an Intel emulator.

Math coprocessor
Want a Motorola math coprocessor? For the 6809E CPU, no math coprocessor is available. For the 68000 or 68020, buy the **68881 math coprocessor** ($49). For the 68030, buy the **68882 math coprocessor** ($69). The 68040 comes in two versions: the standard version (called the **68RC040**) includes math-coprocessor circuitry; the stripped-down version (called the **68LC040**) does not. The Power PC includes math-coprocessor circuitry.

Classic microprocessors

Primitive old microcomputers contain microprocessors invented by **Zilog** and **MOS Technology**. They're *not* Intel clones.

Zilog, which is owned by Exxon, makes the **Z-80A microprocessor**, which is super-cheap: it costs just $2! It's in many obsolete computers, such as the Radio Shack TRS-80 models 1 & 2 & 3 & 4 & 12, the Kaypro 2 & 4 & 10, the Epson QX-10 & Geneva, the Timex-Sinclair 1000 & 1500, and the Coleco Adam.

The **6502 microprocessor** is available from its inventor (**MOS Technology**, which is part of Commodore) and from other chip makers. You can also get souped-up versions, which understand extra commands and go faster!

Chip	Price	Computers that use it
6502	$2	Apple 2, Apple 2+, old Apple 2e, and Atari 800
65C02	$7	Apple 2c, Apple 2c+, and new Apple 2e
6510	$15	Commodore 64, Commodore 128, and Commodore Vic
65C816	$17	Apple 2GS

The 65C02 and the 65C816 are made of CMOS; that's why their names contain the letter C. The other chips in that table are traditional: they're made of NMOS.

How many pins?

A cheap microprocessor (such as an 8088, 8086, Z-80, 6502, or 6809E) comes in a DIP (caterpillar) that has 40 pins (20 pairs of pins).

Fancier chips have more pins. For example, the Motorola 68000 comes in a DIP that has 64 pins.

If a chip is even fancier (such as the 68-pin Intel 286 or the 132-pin Intel 386DX), it requires too many pins to fit in a DIP. Instead of coming in a DIP, the chip usually comes in a **pin grid array (PGA)**, which is a square having many pins underneath it, as if it were a square porcupine lying on its back.

MEMORY CHIPS

Although the CPU (the computer's brain) can think, it can't remember anything. It can't even remember what problem it was working on!

Besides buying a CPU, you must also buy **memory chips**, which remember what problem the CPU was working on. To find out what the problem was, the CPU looks at the memory chips frequently — about a million times every second!

The part of the computer's main circuitry that contains the memory chips is called the **main memory**.

The typical memory chip comes in a DIP that has 8 pairs of legs (16 pins). In a typical microcomputer, the motherboard contains lots of memory chips.

If you buy extra memory chips (so that your computer can remember extra information), and the extra memory chips don't all fit on the motherboard, you must buy an extra PC card to mount them on; that extra card is called a **memory card**. If the memory card comes in a cute little cartridge that you can pop into and out of the computer easily, it's called a **memory cartridge**.

Warning: if you buy a memory chip or card or cartridge, and want to pop it into the computer, turn off the computer's power first. If you forget, and accidentally leave the power on while you're inserting (or removing) the memory, you might wreck your computer!

You need two kinds of memory chips: **RAM** and **ROM**. The **RAM** chips remember information temporarily; the **ROM** chips remember information permanently. Let's begin by looking at RAM chips.

RAM

If a chip remembers information just temporarily, it's called a **random-access memory chip (RAM chip)**.

When you buy RAM chips, they contain no information yet; you tell the CPU what information to put into them. Later, you can make the CPU erase that information and insert new information instead. The RAM chips hold information just temporarily: when you turn the computer's power off, the RAM chips are automatically erased.

Whenever the CPU tries to solve a problem, the CPU stores the problem in the RAM chips, temporarily. There it also stores all instructions on how to solve the problem; the instructions are called the **program**.

If you buy more RAM chips, the CPU can handle longer problems and programs. If the computer doesn't have enough RAM chips to hold the entire problem or program, you must split the problem or program into several shorter ones instead, and tell the CPU to work on each of the short ones temporarily.

How RAM is measured A **character** is any symbol you can type on the keyboard, such as a letter or digit or punctuation mark or blank space. For example, the word HAT consists of 3 characters; the phrase Mr. Poe consists of 7 characters (M, R, the period, the space, P, O, and E). The phrase LOVE 2 KISS U consists of 13 characters.

Instead of saying "character", hungry programmers say **byte**. So LOVE 2 KISS U consists of 13 bytes. If, in the RAM, you store LOVE 2 KISS U, that phrase occupies 13 bytes of the RAM.

RAM chips are manufactured by a process that involves doubling. The most popular unit of RAM is "2 bytes times 2 times 2 times 2 times 2 times 2 times 2 times 2 times 2 times 2", which is 1024 bytes, which is called a **kilobyte**. So **the definition of a kilobyte is "1024 bytes"**.

Although a kilobyte is exactly 1024 bytes, the following approximations are useful.

A kilobyte is about a thousand bytes. It's about how many characters you see on the screen of a TV computer. It's about *half* as many characters as you see on the screen of an 80-column monitor. It's about a *quarter* as many characters as you get on a typewritten page (assuming the page is single-spaced with one-inch margins and elite type).

The abbreviation for *kilobyte* is **K**. For example, if a salesperson says the computer has a "64K RAM", the salesperson means the main circuitry includes enough RAM chips to hold 64 kilobytes of information, which is slightly over 64,000 bytes.

A **megabyte** is 1024 kilobytes. Since a kilobyte is 1024 bytes, **a megabyte is "1024 times 1024" bytes, which is 1,048,576 bytes altogether**, which is slightly more than a million bytes. It's about how much you can fit in a 250-page book (assuming the book has single-spaced typewritten pages). The abbreviation for *megabyte* is **meg** or **M**.

A **gigabyte** (pronounced "gig a bite") is 1024 megabytes. It's slightly more than a billion bytes.

A **terabyte** is 1024 gigabytes. It's slightly more than a trillion bytes.

In honor of the words "kilobyte", "megabyte", "gigabyte", and "terabyte", many programmers name their puppies Killer Byte, Make a Byte, Giggle Byte, and Terror Byte.

Rows of RAM chips In a cheap microcomputer (such as the Commodore 64), the RAM is a row of eight NMOS chips. That row of chips holds 64K altogether. So it holds 64 kilobytes, which is slightly more than 64 thousand bytes (since a kilobyte is slightly more than a thousand bytes).

That row of chips is called a **64K chip set**. Each chip in that set is called a "64K chip", but remember that you need a whole *row* of those 64K chips to produce a 64K RAM.

Mail-order discount dealers charge 50¢ for a 64K chip. So to get 64K of RAM, you need a 64K chip set, which is a row of eight 64K chips, which costs "8 times 50¢", which is $4.

The most popular style of 64K chip is the **TI 4164**. Although that style was invented by Texas Instruments, other manufacturers have copied it.

If your computer is slightly fancier (such as the Apple 2c), it has *two* rows of 64K chips. Since each row is a 64K RAM, the two rows together total 128K.

If your computer is even fancier, it has **many** rows of 64K chips. For example, your computer might have four rows of 64K chips. Since each row is a 64K RAM, the four rows together total 256K.

64K chips didn't become popular until 1982. If your computer was built before then, it probably contains inferior chips: instead of containing a row of 64K chips, it contains a row of 16K chips or 4K chips.

During the 1980's, computer engineers invented 256K and 1M chips. The most popular style of 256K chip is called the **41256**, which you can get from discount dealers for $2. A 1M chip costs $6.

If your computer has very little RAM, you can try to enlarge the RAM, by adding extra rows of RAM chips to the motherboard. But if the motherboard's already full, you must buy an extra PC card to put the extra chips on. That extra PC card is called a **RAM memory card**.

Parity chip
The IBM PC and some clones contain an extra chip in each row, so that each row contains 9 chips instead of 8.

The row's ninth chip is called the **parity chip**. It double-checks the work done by the other 8 chips, to make sure they're all working correctly!

So for an IBM PC or one of those clone, you must buy 9 chips to fill a row.

SIMMs and SIPPs
If your computer is ultra-modern and you want to insert an extra row of RAM chips, you do *not* have to insert 8 or 9 separate chips. Instead, you can buy a strip that contains all 8 or 9 chips and just pop the whole strip into the computer's motherboard, in one blow.

The typical strip of chips is called a **Single In-line Memory Module (SIMM)** and pops into one of the motherboard's slots. If the strip pops into a series of pinholes instead, the strip is called a **Single In-line Pin Package (SIPP)**.

Discount dealers charge $15 for a SIMM that holds 256K, $39 for a SIMM that holds a megabyte, $148 for a SIMM that holds 4 megabytes. SIPPs cost $5 more than SIMMs.

Some computers use SIMMs containing a set of just 2, 3, or 4 chips. That set of chips is special and imitates 8 or 9 normal chips.

In old-fashioned computers, each SIMM fits into a motherboard slot by using 30 big pins. In computers that are more modern, each SIMM uses 72 big pins instead.

The typical SIMM contains chips that are fast: they retrieve information in 70 nanoseconds. (A **nanosecond** is a billionth of a second.) Old-fashioned SIMMs contain slower chips, requiring 80 nanoseconds; the fanciest SIMMs contains extra-fast chips, requiring just 60 nanoseconds.

If you want to buy an extra SIMM to put in your computer, make sure you buy the same kind of SIMM as the other SIMMs that are already in your computer. Make sure the extra SIMM has the same number of pins (30 or 72?), the same number of chips on it (2, 3, 4, 8, or 9?), and operates at the same number of nanoseconds (80, 70, or 60?).

Let your memory grow
In a typical computer, the RAM contains *several* rows of chips, so that the total RAM contains *several* megabytes.

Here's how much RAM you typically get altogether:

Computer's price	Typical quantity of RAM		
$50-$75	64K	(64 kilobytes,	65,536 bytes)
$75-$100	128K	(128 kilobytes,	131,072 bytes)
$100-$125	256K	(256 kilobytes,	262,144 bytes)
$125-$300	512K	(512 kilobytes,	524,288 bytes)
$300-$600	1M	(1 megabyte,	1,048,576 bytes)
$600-$900	2M	(2 megabytes,	2,097,152 bytes)
$900-$1,500	4M	(4 megabytes,	4,194,304 bytes)
$1,500-$2,500	8M	(8 megabytes,	8,388,608 bytes)
$2,500-$5,000	16M	(16 megabytes,	16,777,216 bytes)
$5,000-$10,000	32M	(32 megabytes,	33,554,432 bytes)

Mac
The original Mac (nicknamed the **Slim Mac**) included 128K of RAM. Then came a version nicknamed the **Fat Mac**, which included 512K. Next came an improvement called the **Mac Plus**, which included 1M.

Those Macs are obsolete. All Macs sold today come with at least 4M, which is what you need to run modern Mac software.

Names of classic computers
The **Commodore 64** computer got its name because it contained 64K of RAM. Then Commodore invented an improved version, the **Commodore 128**, which contained 128K of RAM.

The **Laser 128** imitates the Apple 2c. Each comes with 128K of RAM.

IBM
The original IBM PC came with just 16K of RAM, but you could add extra RAM to it. Here's how much RAM the typical IBM PC or clone contains now:

CPU	Typical quantity of main RAM
8088	512K or 640K
286	640K or 1M
386	2M or 4M
486	4M or 8M
Pentium	8M or 16M

To run modern IBM PC software, you need at least 4M of main RAM. To run the FANCY modern IBM PC software WELL, you need at least 8M. Get 8M!

For computers having lots of RAM, here's how it's divvied up. . . .

The first 640K of main RAM is called the **base memory** (or **conventional memory**). That's the part of the RAM that the computer can handle easily and quickly.

The next 384K is called **upper memory**. It's relatively unimportant, since most programs don't know how to use it.

Those two parts (the conventional memory and the upper memory) consume a total of 640K+384K, which is 1024K, which is one megabyte.

The rest of the main RAM (beyond that first megabyte) can be either **expanded** or **extended**. Here's the difference between "expanded" and "extended". . . .

Expanded RAM is old-fashioned. Extended RAM is modern. (To remember that, notice that the word "expanded" comes *before* "extended" in the dictionary.)

Expanded RAM runs slowly. Extended RAM runs fast.

Expanded RAM can be added to any IBM-compatible computer. Extended RAM requires a modern CPU (a 286, 386, or 486) and will *not* run on an 8088 or 8086 CPU.

Modern programs work best if you have modern RAM (extended). Old-fashioned programs don't understand extended RAM; they understand just old-fashioned RAM (expanded). Since most programs sold today are still old-fashioned, expanded RAM is more useful than extended RAM. To run *both* kinds of programs, you should buy both kinds of RAM.

Some primitive programs use just the 640K of conventional RAM. They don't understand how to use expanded or extended RAM at all.

Expanded RAM and extended RAM are both built from the same kind of NMOS RAM chips. Whether a chip acts as "expanded" or "extended" RAM depends just on what other hardware and software you bought to control those chips.

If a chip acts as "extended" RAM, the CPU gets information from that chip directly and fast.

If a chip acts as "expanded" RAM, the CPU gets the chip's information by copying that information to the upper memory area. Then the CPU examines what's in the upper memory area. That process is slow, since you must wait for the CPU to copy the chip's information to the upper memory area. That process was invented because it's the only way an 8088 or 8086 chip can handle RAM beyond a megabyte. **Extended RAM is faster and simpler but requires a 286, 386, 486, or Pentium — and is understood just by programs that are modern.**

For an 8088 or 8086 CPU, the expanded RAM comes on an **expanded RAM card**. That card contains the RAM chips and the hardware necessary to control them. That card is expensive.

For a 286 CPU, you can buy an expanded RAM card, an **extended RAM card** (which is cheaper), or a combination card that you can switch between the two.

For a 386, 486, or Pentium, you can put lots of RAM chips on the motherboard without buying any cards. The CPU normally treats those RAM chips as extended RAM; but you can run a program that makes those RAM chips imitate expanded RAM so that old-fashioned programs can use them.

If you have a 386, 486, or Pentium and want to run even the fanciest software well, buy at least 8M of RAM. The computer will use the first megabyte for conventional RAM (640K) and the upper memory (384K). The computer will use the remaining seven megabytes for extended RAM but make some of that extended RAM imitate expanded RAM.

A trio of companies (Lotus, Intel, and Microsoft) agreed on the technical details of how expanded memory should be handled. Their agreement is called the **Lotus-Intel-Microsoft Expanded Memory Specification (LIM EMS)**. Expanded memory fitting their specification is called **EMS memory**. To manage that expanded memory, you need a special program, called the **expanded memory manager (EMM)**.

The same trio of companies, working together with a fourth company (AST), developed an agreement on extended memory. Their agreement is called the **Lotus-Intel-Microsoft-AST eXtended Memory Specification** (or **LIMA XMS**). Extended memory fitting their specification is called **XMS memory**. To manage that extended memory, you need a program called the **extended memory manager**. The most popular extended memory manager is called "HIMEM.SYS".

The first 64K of extended memory is called the **high memory area (HMA)**, because it's just slightly higher than the base memory and upper memory. (The rest of the extended memory should be called "even higher memory", but nobody does.)

NMOS RAM versus CMOS
Most RAM chips are NMOS. The prices I quoted you were for NMOS.

If your computer operates on batteries, it uses CMOS instead, which consumes less electricity than NMOS. Unfortunately, CMOS chips cost more than NMOS. A 64K chip costs 50¢ if made of NMOS, but costs $4 if CMOS.

Dynamic versus static
A RAM chip is either **dynamic** or **static**.

If it's dynamic, it stores data for only 2 milliseconds. After the 2 milliseconds, the electrical charges that represent the data dissipate and become too weak to detect. When you buy a PC board containing dynamic RAM chips, the PC board also includes a **refresh circuit**. The refresh circuit automatically reads the data from the dynamic RAM chips and then rewrites the data onto the chips before 2 milliseconds go by. Every 2 milliseconds, the refresh circuit reads the data from the chips and rewrites the data, so that the data stays refreshed.

If a chip is static instead of dynamic, the electrical charge never dissipates, so you don't need a refresh circuit. (But you must still keep the power turned on.)

In the past, computer designers were afraid that the dynamic RAM's refresh circuit wouldn't work, and used static RAM instead. But today, refresh circuits are reliable, and the most popular kind of RAM is dynamic NMOS. For example, the TI 4116, 4164, and 41256 are all dynamic NMOS.

Dynamic RAM is called **DRAM**. So when an engineer says "give me a DRAM", he doesn't mean a liqueur, at least not yet.

Static NMOS is still available. CMOS and bipolar are always static.

Bipolar cache
In a maxicomputer, minicomputer, or fancy microcomputer, the RAM is divided into two sections. One section is huge, contains many rows of NMOS chips, and is called the **main RAM**. The other section is tiny, contains just a few bipolar chips, and is called the **cache** (which is pronounced "cash").

The cache's bipolar chips work much faster than the main RAM's NMOS chips.

In most IBM clones containing a 486DX, the NMOS chips retrieve information in 70 nanoseconds, and the bipolar chips take between 15 and 20 nanoseconds.

Unfortunately, the cache's bipolar chips are very expensive and hold just a few K. In most IBM clones containing a 486DX, the main RAM holds 4M or 8M; but the cache holds just 128K or 256K.

So the bipolar cache is a super-fast, super-expensive memory that's small.

In the bipolar cache, the computer keeps a copy of the main RAM's information that you've been using recently, so the CPU can grab that information again super-quickly.

ROM

If a chip remembers information *permanently*, it's called a **read-only memory chip (ROM chip)**, because you can read the information but can't change it. The ROM chip contains permanent, eternal truths and facts put there by the manufacturer, and it remembers that info forever, even if you turn off the power.

Here's the difference between RAM and ROM:

RAM chips remember, temporarily, info supplied by you.
ROM chips remember, forever, info supplied by the manufacturer.

The typical computer includes many RAM chips (arranged in rows) but just a *few* ROM chips (typically 6).

What kind of info is in ROM?

In your computer, one of the ROM chips contains instructions that tell the CPU what to do first when you turn the power on. Those instructions are called the **ROM bootstrap**, because they help the computer system start itself going and "pull itself up by its own bootstraps".

In the typical microcomputer, that ROM chip also contains instructions that help the CPU transfer information from the keyboard to the screen and printer. Those instructions are called the **ROM operating system** or the **ROM basic input-output system (ROM BIOS)**.

In the typical microcomputer, one of the ROM chips tells the computer how to make each character on the screen out of dots. That chip is called the **character generator**.

In famous old microcomputers, several ROM chips contain definitions of fundamental English words, which are called **BASIC** words. For example, those ROM chips contain the definitions of BASIC words such as PRINT, NEW, RUN, LIST, GO, TO, END, STOP, INPUT, IF, and THEN. Those BASIC definitions in the ROM are called the **ROM BASIC interpreter**.

Commodore 64

For example, let's look inside a primitive computer: the Commodore 64. It contains just four ROM chips. The first chip contains 8K, for the ROM bootstrap and ROM BIOS. The second contains Commodore's 8K ROM BASIC. The third contains Commodore's 4K character generator. The fourth contains ¼K that tells the computer how to make the screen produce pretty colors.

IBM

In the typical IBM PC or clone, the motherboard contains a **ROM BIOS chip**. That chip contains the ROM BIOS and also the ROM bootstrap. If your computer is manufactured by IBM, that chip is designed by IBM; if your computer is a clone, that chip is an imitation designed by a company such as **Phoenix**. Such a chip designed by Phoenix is called a **Phoenix ROM BIOS chip**. Other companies that design ROM BIOS chips for clones are **American Megatrends Incorporated (AMI)**, **Award** (a smaller company), and **Quadtel** (which is now owned by Phoenix.)

On a special PC card (called a **video display card**), you'll find a ROM chip containing the character generator.

If your computer is built by IBM, some chips on the motherboard contain the ROM BASIC interpreter. If your computer is a clone, all of BASIC comes on a disk instead of in ROM chips.

Altogether, the original IBM PC contained six ROM chips: the ROM BIOS chip, the character generator, and four ROM BASIC interpreter chips. Each of those six chips contained 8K, so that the computer's ROM totaled 48K. On newer computers from IBM and clones, the total is slightly different.

Extra ROM chips

Some microcomputers include extra ROM chips that tell the computer how to handle specific applications, such as word processing and accounting.

ROM cartridges

If your computer attaches to a TV and is old-fashioned (such as a Commodore Vic, Commodore 64, Commodore 128, Atari 800, Atari 800XL, or Radio Shack Color Computer), you can pop **ROM cartridges** into the computer. A **ROM cartridge** is a cartridge containing a PC card full of ROM chips. Etched into those ROM chips is a program.

The typical ROM cartridge contains a program that plays a video game, such as Space Invaders or Pac Man or computer chess. You can also buy ROM cartridges that contain programs for word processing, music, art, or tutoring you. Each ROM cartridge costs about $30.

How ROM chips are made

The info in a ROM chip is said to be **burned into** the chip. To burn in the info, the manufacturer can use two methods.

One method is to burn the info into the ROM chip while the chip's being made. A ROM chip produced by that method is called a **custom ROM chip**.

An alternate method is to make a ROM chip that contains no info but can be fed info later. Such a ROM chip is called a **programmable ROM chip (PROM)**. To feed it info later, you attach it to a device called a **PROM burner**, which copies info from a RAM to the PROM. Info burned into the PROM can't be erased, unless the PROM's a special kind: an **erasable PROM (EPROM)**.

To erase a typical EPROM, shine an intense ultraviolet light at it for 20 minutes. That's called an **ultraviolet-erasable PROM (UV-EPROM)**.

A fancier kind of EPROM can be erased quickly by sending it a 25-volt shock for a tenth of a second. That's called an **electrically erasable PROM (EEPROM)** or **electrically alterable PROM (EAPROM)**.

After you erase an EPROM, you can feed it new info.

If you're a manufacturer designing a new computer, begin by using an erasable PROM (EPROM), so you can make changes easily. When you decide not to make any more changes, switch to a non-erasable PROM, which costs less to manufacture. If your computer becomes so popular that you need to manufacture over 10,000 copies of the ROM, switch to a custom ROM, which costs more to design and "tool up for" but costs less to make copies of.

DISKS

FUNDAMENTALS

Memory comes in three popular forms: RAM chips, ROM chips, and disks. You already learned about RAM chips and ROM chips. Let's examine disks. A computer disk is round, like a phonograph record.

Three kinds

You can buy three popular kinds of computer disks:

A **floppy disk** is made of flimsy material. It's permanently encased in a sturdy, square dust jacket.
A **hard disk** is made of firmer material. It typically hides in your computer permanently, unseen.
A **CD-ROM** is a compact disk. It's the same kind of CD compact disk that plays music.

Each kind has its own advantages and disadvantages.

Floppy disks are the cheapest (about 50¢ per disk) and the easiest to mail to your friends: just stick the floppy disk in an envelope, perhaps with some padding. Unfortunately, floppy disks work the most slowly, and they hold the least data: the typical floppy disk holds about 1 megabyte, while the typical hard disk or CD-ROM can hold *many hundreds* of megabytes.

Hard disks work the fastest — over 20 times faster than the other kinds! But hard disks are also the most expensive. Moreover, they typically can't be removed from your computer and therefore can't be mailed to your friends.

CD-ROMs are the best value: CD-ROM disks cost less than 1¢ per megabyte to manufacture. But they have a frustrating limitation: the information on CD-ROM disks can*not* be edited.

Since each kind of disk has its own advantages and disadvantages, you'll want to buy all three kinds.

Spelling

Computer experts argue about spelling. Some experts write "**disk**", others write "**disc**".

Most manufacturers write "**disk**" when referring to floppy disks or hard disks, but write "**disc**" when referring to CD-ROMs. That inconsistency annoys me.

To be more consistent, I'll always write "**disk**", even when referring to CD-ROMs. Most computer magazines (such as *PC Magazine* and *PC World*) feel the same way I do: they always write "**disk**". The growing tendency is to always write "**disk**".

For hard disks, IBM used to write "**disc**" but now writes "**disk**".

FLOPPY DISKS

A **floppy disk** (or **diskette**) is round but comes permanently sealed in a square **dust jacket**. (Don't try to remove the floppy disk from its square jacket.)

The floppy disk is as thin and flimsy as a sheet of paper but is protected by the sturdy, square jacket that encases it.

Three sizes

Floppy disks come in three sizes.

The most popular size is called a **3½-inch floppy disk**, because it comes in a square jacket that's about 3½ inches on each side. (Actually, each side of the jacket is slightly *more* than 3½ inches, and the disk's diameter is slightly *less*.)

An older size, used mainly on older computers, is called **5¼-inch**. It comes in square jacket that's exactly 5¼ inches on each side.

An even older size, **8-inch**, is used just on ancient computers that are no longer built.

Those three sizes have nicknames:

An 8-inch floppy disk is called a **large floppy**.
A 5¼-inch floppy disk is called a **minifloppy**.
A 3½-inch floppy disk is called a **microfloppy**.

Jacket colors

The jacket of a 5¼-inch or 8-inch floppy disk is usually black. The jacket of a 3½-inch floppy disk is usually black, blue, white, or beige (very light grayish brown).

If you pay a surcharge, you can get jackets that have wilder colors.

History

8-inch floppies were invented in the early 1970's by IBM. 5¼-inch floppies were invented in the late 1970's by Shugart Associates, which later became part of Xerox.

3½-inch floppies were invented in the 1980's by Sony. They've become the most popular size because they're the smallest, cutest, and sturdiest. They're small enough to fit in the pocket of your shirt, cute enough to impress your friends, and sturdy enough to survive when you fall on your face. They're also easy to mail, since they're small enough to fit in a standard white business envelope and sturdy enough to survive the U.S. Postal System. Yup, nice things come in small packages!

Magnetized iron

The round disk (which hides inside the square jacket) is coated with rust, so it looks brown. Since the rust is made of iron, which can be magnetized, the disk stores magnetic signals. The pattern of magnetic signals is a code representing your data.

Drives

To use a floppy disk, you must buy a **floppy-disk drive**, which is a computerized record player.

If the drive is **external**, it's a box sitting near the computer. If the drive is **internal**, it's built into the middle of the computer.

The drive has a slit in its front side. To use the drive, push the disk (including its jacket) into the slit.

When pushing the sheathed treasure into the box's slit, don't shove too hard. Oooh! Please be gentle!

When you push your disk into the slit, don't push the disk in backwards or upside-down! Here's how to push the disk in correctly. . . .

First, notice that the disk's jacket has a label on it and also has a big oval cutout. (If the disk is 3½-inch, the cutout is covered by a metal slider.) Insert the disk so that the oval cutout goes into the drive *before* the label does. If the drive's slit is horizontal, make sure the label is on the *top* side of the jacket; if the drive is vertical, make sure the label is on the *left* side of the jacket.

After putting the disk into the slit, close the latch to cover the slit. (If the disk is 3½-inch, there is no latch.) Since the slit and latch act as a **door**, closing the latch is called **closing the door**.

As soon as you close the door, the disk drive automatically positions the disk onto the turntable that's hidden inside the drive. The turntable's called the **spindle**. It can spin the disk quickly.

Like a record player, the disk drive contains an arm with a "needle" on it. The needle is called the **read-write head**, because it can read what's on the disk and also write new information onto the disk.

Here's how to write new information onto the disk. Put your fingers on the computer's keyboard. Type a command that tells the computer you want to use the disk. Then type the information you want to transfer to the disk.

To transfer the information to the disk, the computer lowers the read-write head onto the disk. An electrical charge passes through the head. The charge creates an electromagnetic field, which magnetizes the iron on the disk's surface. Each iron particle has its own north and south pole; the patterns formed by the north and south poles are a code that stands for the information you're storing.

Tracks As the disk spins, the head remains stationary, so that the head draws a circle on the spinning disk's surface. The circle's called a **track**. To draw the circle, the head doesn't use ink; instead, it uses a pattern of magnetic pulses. Since your eye can't see magnetism, your eye can't see the circle; but it's there!

When you start using a blank disk, the arm puts the head near the disk's outer rim, so that the head's track (circle) is almost as wide as the disk. That track's called **track 0**.

Then the arm lifts the head, moves the head slightly closer to the virgin disk's center, and puts the head back down onto the disk again. The head draws another circular track on the disk, but this new circular track is slightly smaller than the previous one. It's called **track 1**.

Then the head draws track 2, then track 3, then track 4, and so on, until the head gets near the center of the disk, and draws the last circular track (which is smaller than the other tracks).

To organize the information on a track, the computer divides the track into **sectors**. Each "sector" is an arc of the circle.

Single-sided versus double-sided drives A modern disk drive has two read-write heads. One head uses the disk's top surface, while the other head uses the disk's bottom, so that the drive can use both sides of the disk simultaneously. That's called a **double-sided disk drive**. The drive puts information onto the disk by first using track 0 of the main side, then track 0 of the flip side, then track 1 of the main side, then track 1 of the flip side, etc.

If a disk drive is *not* modern — if it's ancient and primitive — it has just *one* read-write head, which uses just one side of the disk. The flip side of the disk is unused. That kind of drive is called a **single-sided disk drive**. Which side of the disk does the drive use? Though some drives use the side that has the label, other drives (by other manufacturers) use the side *opposite* the label instead.

Double-sided is also called **DS** and **2-sided** and **2S**. **Single-sided** is also called **SS** and **1-sided** and **1S**.

Capacity How many kilobytes can you fit on a floppy disk? The answer depends on which kind of drive you have.

The most popular kind of drive is called a **3½-inch high-density floppy drive**. Here's how it works.

It holds a 3½-inch floppy disk. It writes on both sides of the disk simultaneously, since it's a double-sided disk drive. It writes 80 tracks on each side. It divides each track into 18 sectors. Each sector holds "512 bytes", which is half a kilobyte, ½K.

Since the disk has 2 sides, 80 tracks per side, 18 sectors per track, and ½K per sector, the disk's total capacity is "2 times 80 times 18 times ½K", which is 1440K. So altogether, the disk holds 1440K. That's called **1.44M** (where an **M** is defined as being 1000K). That's why a 3½-inch high-density floppy drive is also called a **1.44M drive**.

The kind of disk you put into it is called a **1.44M floppy disk** (or a **3½-inch high-density floppy disk**). Since the disk holds 1.44M (which is 1440K), and since a K is 1024 bytes, the disk holds "1440 times 1024" bytes, which is 1,474,560 bytes altogether. That's a lot of bytes!

Although the disk holds 1440K, some of those K are used for "bureaucratic overhead" (such as holding a directory that reminds the computer which data is where on your disk). A Mac uses just 1 sector (½K) for bureaucratic overhead. An IBM-compatible computer uses 33 sectors (16½K) for bureaucratic overhead, leaving just 1423½K (1,457,664 bytes) for your data.

When you buy a blank disk to put in a 1.44M drive, make sure the disk is the right kind. Make sure the disk is 3½-inch; and to get full use of what the drive can accomplish, make sure the disk is high-density! The abbreviation for "high-density" is **HD**. A high-density 3½-inch disk has the letters **HD** stamped in white on its jacket; but the H overlaps the D, so it looks like this: **HD**. Also, a high-density 3½-inch disk has an extra square hole cut through its jacket.

Old computers use inferior floppy drives, whose capacities are *less* than 1.44M.

A capacity that's less than 150K is called **single-density (SD)**.
A capacity bigger than 150 but less than 1M is called **double-density (DD)**.
A capacity bigger than 1M is called **high-density (HD)**.

Anything less than high-density is called **low-density**.

Although the jacket of a high-density 3½-inch disk has "HD" stamped on them and an extra hole punched through it, the jackets of other kinds of disks often lack any distinguishing marks. Too bad!

Popular IBM-compatible drives
For IBM-compatible computers, four kinds of floppy drives have been popular:

IBM drive's name	Capacity	Details
5¼-inch double-density	360K	40 tracks per side, 9 sectors per track
5¼-inch high-density	1200K (which is 1.2M)	80 tracks per side, 15 sectors per track
3½-inch double-density	720K	80 tracks per side, 9 sectors per track
3½-inch high-density	1440K (which is 1.44M)	80 tracks per side, 18 sectors per track

Each of those IBM-compatible drives is double-sided and has ½K per sector. They're manufactured by companies such as **TEAC**, **NEC**, and **Chinon**.

The fanciest drives (3½-inch high-density) used to be expensive, but now you can buy them for just $49 from mail-order discount dealers (such as **Insight** at 1912 W. Fourth St., Tempe AZ 85281, phone 800-998-8028 or 602-902-1176).

Mac drives
For Mac computers, three kinds of floppy drives have been popular:

Mac drive's name	Capacity	Details
1-sided double-density	400K	1 side, 8-12 sectors per track
2-sided double-density	800K	2 sides, 8-12 sectors per track
high-density	1440K (which is 1.44M)	2 sides, 18 sectors per track

Each Mac drive is 3½-inch and has 80 tracks per side, ½K per sector. The Mac's high-density drive is called the **Mac Superdrive**.

On a disk, the inner tracks have smaller diameters than the outer tracks. Most drives squeeze as many sectors onto an inner track as onto an outer track, but the Mac double-density drives puts fewer sectors onto the inner tracks and put extra sectors onto the outer tracks. Specifically, the outer 16 tracks are divided into 12 sectors, the next 16 tracks into 11 sectors, the next 16 into 10, the next 16 into 9, and the inner 16 into 8.

Drives for other computers
For other computers, many kinds of floppy drives have been invented:

Computer	Drive capacity	Details
Apple 2 family	140K	5¼", 1 side, 35 tracks, 16 sectors, ¼K per sector
Tandy Color Computer	157½K	5¼", 1 side, 35 tracks, 18 sectors, ¼K per sector
Tandy Models 3, 4, 4P	180K	5¼", 1 side, 40 tracks, 18 sectors, ¼K per sector
Tandy Model 4D	360K	5¼", 2 sides, 40 tracks, 18 sectors, ¼K per sector
Commodore 64	170¾K	5¼", 1 side, 35 tracks, 17-21 sectors, ¼K per sector
Commodore Amiga	880K	3½", 2 sides, 80 tracks, 11 sectors, ½K per sector

For the Commodore 64, the 17 outer tracks are divided into 21 sectors, the next 7 tracks into 19 sectors, the next 6 tracks into 18 sectors, and the inner 5 tracks into 17 sectors.

Speed
In the disk drive, the disk spins quickly. The exact speed depends on what size disk the drive uses.

Low-density 5¼-inch disks revolve 5 times per second. That makes 300 revolutions per minute, 300 rpm.
8-inch disks and high-density 5¼-inch disks revolve faster: 6 times per second (360 rpm).
3½-inch disks revolve even faster: between 6½ and 10 times per second.

Buying disks

When you buy a floppy disk, make sure its size matches the size of the drive. For example, a 3½-inch disk will *not* work in a 5¼-inch drive.

If you buy a blank 5¼-inch floppy disk, you can stick it into any normal 5¼-inch drive, regardless of who manufactured the drive and who manufactured the computer. But after you've put information onto the disk, that information is understandable only to *your* kind of computer. For example, an Apple 2e cannot understand what an IBM PC writes.

When you go into a computer store to buy a disk that contains software, tell the salesperson which kind of computer you have, so that the salesperson can give you a disk containing information understandable to *your* computer.

If your drive is single-density or double-density, it can*not* handle high-density disks at all.

If your drive is 5¼-inch and high-density, it can *read* single-density and double-density disks, but it might have trouble writing new information onto them. So when buying blank disks for your 5¼-inch high-density drive to write on, avoid buying single-density or double-density disks.

The three crummy kinds of 5¼-inch floppy disks (single-sided single-density, single-sided double-density, and double-sided double-density) are all manufactured by the same process as each other. The only difference is the manufacturer's "guarantee": a double-sided double-density disk is "guaranteed" to work on both sides and hold lots of data; a single-sided or single-density disk is not. Even if you buy a disk that has a poor guarantee (just "single-sided single-density"), it typically works fine even if you use both sides and store lots of data. The only difference is that the manufacturer hasn't bothered testing the second side and hasn't bothered testing double-density data. During the 1970's and 1980's, single-sided single-density disks were significantly cheaper than double-sided double-density, but now the prices are about the same.

Formatting the disk
Before you can use a blank floppy disk, its surface must be **formatted** (divided into tracks and sectors). Buy a disk that's been formatted already, or buy an unformatted disk and format it by typing a command on your computer's keyboard.

After the disk's been formatted, you can store whatever information you wish onto the disk. Do *not* tell the drive to format that disk again. If you accidentally make the drive format the same disk again, the drive will create new tracks and sectors on the disk, and erase the old tracks and sectors, and therefore erase all your old data!

Remember:

If a disk is blank, format it before you use it.
If a disk already contains info, do NOT format it; it's been formatted already.

Name brands
The most famous manufacturers of floppy disks are **Verbatim** and **Maxell**. But instead of buying those brands, buy **generic** floppy disks instead. The generics cost less and typically work just as well.

Discount dealers
To get the lowest prices on generic floppy disks, contact **MEI Micro Center** (1100 Steelwood Rd., Columbus OH 43212, 800-634-3478) or **Diskettes Unlimited** (6206 Long Dr., Houston TX 77087, 800-DOG-DISK).

For example, here are the prices from MEI Micro Center for double-sided disks:

Kind of disk	100 disks	1000 disks
5¼-inch double-density, unformatted	$19 + $1.20	$160 + $12
5¼-inch high-density, unformatted	$26 + $1.20	$210 + $12
3½-inch double-density, unformatted	$31 + $2.40	$260 + $24
3½-inch high-density, formatted	$36 + $2.40	$300 + $24

Add up the prices of what you want, then add the handling charge ($3.25). For example, for 100 of the best disks (3½-inch high-density, formatted), MEI charges you $36 (for the disks) + $2.40 (shipping) + $3.25 (handling), which is $41.65. That's about 42¢ per disk. For 1000 of the best disks, MEI charges you $300 + $24 + $3.25, which is $327.25, which comes to about 33¢ per disk. Diskettes Unlimited charges even less but might give you slightly lower quality; for details, phone them.

What's a disk worth?
Although you can buy a blank floppy disk for under 50¢, a disk containing information costs much more. The price depends on how valuable the information is. A disk that explains to the computer how to play a game costs about $50. A disk teaching the computer how to handle a general business task (such as accounting, filing, or correspondence) usually costs about $200.

A disk containing intimate, personal data about your business's customers, suppliers, employees, and methods is worth even more — perhaps *thousands* of dollars! To compute how much it's worth to you, imagine that you've lost it, or that it fell into the wrong hands!

Protect your disks

Most parts of a computer system are sturdy: even if you bang on the keyboard and rap your fist against the screen, you probably won't do any harm. Only one part of a computer system is delicate: that part is the disk. Unfortunately, the magnetic signals on your disk are easy to destroy.

One way to accidentally destroy them is to put your disk near a magnet; so keep your disks away from magnets! For example, keep your disk away from paper clips that have been in a magnetized paper-clip holder. Keep your disk away from speakers (such as the speakers in your stereo, TV, and phone), because all speakers contain magnets. Keep your disk away from electric motors, because motors generate an electromagnetic field. So to be safe, keep your disk at least *six inches* away from paper clips, stereos, TV's, telephones, and motors.

Keep your disk away from heat, because heat destroys the disk's magnetism and "melts" your data. So don't leave your disk in the hot sun; don't leave it on a sunny windowsill; don't leave it in the back of your car on a hot day. If your disk drive or computer feels hot, quickly lower the temperature, by getting an air conditioner or at least a fan.

3½-inch floppy disks come in strong jackets, but 5¼-inch and 8-inch floppy disks come in jackets that are too weak and thin to protect disks from pressure. Don't squeeze your disk. Don't put it under a heavy object, such as a paperweight or a book. If you want to write a note on the disk's jacket, don't use a ball-point pen (which crushes the disk); use a soft felt-tip pen instead.

Keep the disk away from dust. For example, don't smoke cigarettes near the disk, because the smoke becomes dust that lands on the disk and wrecks the data.

Keep the disk dry. If you must transport a disk during a rainstorm, put the disk in a plastic bag. Never drink coffee or soda near the disk: your drink might spill.

To handle the disk, touch just the disk's jacket, not the brown disk itself. Holes in the jacket let you see the brown disk inside; don't put your fingers in the holes.

Power surges in ancient computers
If your computer is an IBM clone or by Apple, skip ahead to the next topic ("Write-protect notch").

If your computer is made by Commodore or Radio Shack and is so ancient that it's *not* an IBM PC clone, be careful: flipping the power switch on your ancient computer creates an electrical surge that wrecks the disk. On such a computer, don't flip the power switch when the drive contains a disk. Flip the power switch just when the drive's *empty*.

To turn such a computer on, make sure the drive's *empty*, then flip the power switch on. After the power's come on, insert the disk.

Before turning such a computer off, remove the disk from the drive. When the drive's *empty*, turn off the power.

Write-protect notch
When you buy a blank 5¼-inch or 8-inch floppy disk, the disk comes in a square black jacket. Since the jacket's square, it has four sides; but one of the sides has a notch cut into it.

You can cover the notch, by sticking a plastic **tab** over it. The tab has a gummed back, so you can stick it on the disk easily and cover the notch. You get the tab free when you buy the disk.

(For a 3½-inch disk, the notch is different: it's a square hole near the jacket's corner but not on the jacket's edge. To cover it, you use a black slider instead of a tab. On old Apple Mac disks, the slider was red instead of black.)

Whenever you ask the computer to change the info on the disk, the drive checks whether you've covered the notch.

For a 5¼-inch disk, the normal situation is for the notch to be uncovered. For a 3½-inch or 8-inch disk, the normal situation is for the notch to be covered.

If the situation's normal, the computer will obey your command: it will change the info on the disk as you wish. But **if the situation's _abnormal_ (because the notch is covered when it should be uncovered, or is uncovered when it should be covered), the computer will REFUSE to change the disk's info.**

Suppose your disk contains valuable info, and you're afraid some idiot will accidentally erase or alter that info. To prevent such an accident, make the situation abnormal (by changing whether the notch is covered), so that the computer will refuse to change the disk's info. It will refuse to erase the disk; it will refuse to add new info to the disk; it will refuse to alter the disk; it will refuse to write onto the disk. The disk is protected from being changed; it's protected from being written on. The disk is **write-protected** (or **locked**).

Since the tab affects whether the disk is write-protected, the tab is called a **write-protect tab**, and the notch is called a **write-protect notch**.

When you buy a disk that already contains info, the disk usually comes write-protected, to protect you from accidentally erasing the info. So if you buy a 5¼-inch floppy disk that already contains info, it might come with a write-protect tab already covering the notch, to write-protect the disk.

Instead of creating a notch and then covering it with a tab, some manufacturers save money by getting special disks that have no notch. The computer treats a notchless disk the same way as a disk whose notch is covered.

__Backup__ Even if you handle your disk very carefully, eventually something will go wrong, and some of the info on your disk will get wrecked accidentally.

To prepare for that inevitable calamity, tell the computer to copy all info from the disk onto a blank disk, so that the blank disk becomes an exact copy of the original. Store the copy far away from the original: store it in another room, or — better yet — another building, or — better yet — another city. If you're working in a country that's having a war, store the copy in another country.

The copy is called a **backup**. Use the backup disk when the original disk gets wrecked.

Making a backup disk is like buying an insurance policy: it protects you against disasters.

Every evening, make backup copies of all your disks — except for disks containing the same info as the day before.

Each week, I get phone calls from distressed business executives whose disks got wrecked and who didn't make backups. All I can offer them is sympathy. Their companies are ruined. Remember: "a backup a day keeps disaster away!"

When you buy a floppy that already contains software, try copying the floppy before you begin using it. If you're lucky, the computer will make the backup copy without any hassles. If you're unlucky, the software company has put instructions on the floppy that make the computer *refuse* to copy the disk, because the company fears that you'll illegally give copies to all your friends for free. A floppy that the computer refuses to copy, and which is therefore protected against illegal copying, is called **copy-protected**. A floppy that you *can* copy is called **copyable** (or **unprotected**).

__Short files__ The information on the disk is divided into **files**. Each file has its own name and its own purpose. For example, one file might be named JILL and consist of a memo that you wrote to your friend Jill; another file might be named PAYROLL and consist of information about your company's payroll. Each file consists of many sectors.

If one of the disk's sectors gets damaged, the computer might get so confused that it handles the entire file incorrectly, and so the entire file becomes unusable.

To minimize such damage, avoid creating large files; create many small files instead. For example, if you're writing a book and want to store the book on your disk, do *not* make the entire book be a single file; instead, split the book into chapters, and make each chapter a separate file. That way, a damaged sector will hurt at most one chapter, and can't hurt the entire book.

__Drive cleaners__ Don't bother trying to clean the heads of your floppy drive. The heads don't collect much dirt anyway, since the floppy disk's jacket has a cloth liner that traps most dirt. If your disk ever starts to act unreliable, clean the heads if you wish, but the culprit is more likely a **misaligned** head, a brownout, overheating, defective software, or a mistyped command.

HARD DISKS

Hard disks are better than floppy disks in three ways. . . .

Hard disks are sturdier than floppies.
Hard disks are hard and firm; they don't flop or jiggle.
They're more reliable than floppies.

Hard drives hold more information than floppy drives.
The typical floppy drive holds 360K, 720K, 1.2M, or 1.44M.
The typical hard drive holds 250M, 340M, or 420M.

Hard drives work faster than floppies.
The typical floppy disk rotates between 5 and 10 times per second.
The typical hard disk rotates between 60 and 120 times per second.

Hard drives are more expensive than floppy drives. The typical floppy drive costs about $50; the typical hard drive costs about $300.

Unfortunately, the typical hard disk can't be removed from its drive: the hard disk is **non-removable**, stuck inside its drive permanently. (Hard disks that are **removable** are rare.)

Since the typical hard disk is stuck forever inside its drive, in one fixed place, it's called a **fixed disk**.

Though the typical floppy-disk drive holds just one disk at a time, the typical hard-disk drive holds a whole *stack* of disks and handles all the stack's disks simultaneously, by using many arms and read-write heads. For example, the typical 420M hard drive holds a non-removable stack of disks, and the entire stack totals 420M. Each disk in the stack is called a **platter**.

If your hard drive is the rare kind that holds a *removable* stack of disks, the stack comes in a **cartridge** or **pack** that you can remove from the hard drive.

Back in 1977, the typical hard disk had a 14-inch diameter and was removable. The hard-disk drive was a big cabinet, the size of a top-loading washing machine; it cost about $30,000 and held 100M. It required a minicomputer or mainframe.

Hard disks, drives, and prices have all shrunk since then! Now the typical hard disk has a diameter of just 3½ inches. The typical hard drive is just 1 inch tall, costs $279, and holds 420M. It fits in a desktop microcomputer.

Some notebook computers use tiny hard disks whose diameter is just 2½ inches.

IBM drive letters
The typical IBM-compatible computer has both a floppy drive and a hard drive. The floppy drive is called **drive A**; the hard drive is called **drive C**.

If the computer has *two* floppy drives, the main floppy drive is called **drive A**, and the other floppy drive is called **drive B**. If the computer has *two* hard drives, the main hard drive is called **drive C**, and the other hard drive is called **drive D**.

Copy from floppy to hard & back

When you buy a program, it usually comes on a floppy disk. To use the program, put that floppy disk into the floppy drive, then copy the program from the floppy disk to the hard disk. (To copy the program onto an IBM-compatible hard disk, type the word "copy" or "install" or "setup". To find out which of those three words to type and when, follow the instructions in the manual that came with the program.)

Then use just the copy on the hard disk (which is sturdier, holds more info, and works faster than the floppy disk).

Like floppy disks, hard disks are coated with magnetized iron. Floppy disks and hard disks are both called **magnetic disks**. Like floppy disks, hard disks are in constant danger of losing their magnetic signals — and your data!

Protect yourself! Every day, take any new info that's on your hard disk and copy it onto a pile of floppy disks, so that those floppy disks contain a **backup copy** of what was new on your hard disk.

To avoid giant disasters, avoid creating giant files. If you're writing a book and want to store it on your hard disk, split the book into chapters, and make each chapter a separate file, so that if you accidentally say "delete" you'll lose just one chapter instead of your entire masterpiece.

How the head works

In a floppy drive, the read-write head (the "needle") touches the spinning floppy disk. But in a *hard* drive, the read-write head does *not* touch the spinning hard disk; instead, it hovers over the disk.

The distance from the read-write head to the hard disk is a tiny fraction of an inch, and small enough so that the read-write head can detect the disk's magnetism and alter it.

Since the head doesn't actually touch the disk, there isn't any friction, and so the head and the disk don't suffer from any wear-and-tear. That's why a hard-disk system lasts longer than a floppy-disk system and is more reliable.

<u>Winchester drives</u> In all modern hard drives, the head acts as a miniature airplane: it **flies** above the disk. It flies at a very low altitude: a tiny fraction of an inch. The only thing keeping the head off the rotating disk is a tiny cushion of air — a breeze caused by the disk's motion.

When you unplug the drive, the disk stops rotating, so the breeze stops, and the head comes to rest on a **landing strip**, which is like a miniature airport.

Such a drive is called a **flying-head drive**. It's also called a **Winchester drive**, because "Winchester" was IBM's secret code-name for that technology when IBM was inventing it.

The head flies at an altitude that's extremely low — about a ten-thousandth of an inch! That's even smaller than the width of a particle of dust or cigarette smoke! So if any dust or smoke lands onto the disk, the head will smash against it, and you'll have a major disaster.

To prevent such a disaster, the entire Winchester drive is sealed air-tight, to prevent any dust or smoke from entering the drive and getting onto the disk. Since the drive is sealed, you can't remove the disks (unless you buy an extremely expensive Winchester drive that has a flexible seal).

Speed

Here's how the computer retrieves data from the drive.

First, the drive's head moves to the correct track. The time that the head spends moving is called the **seek time**. Since that time depends on how far the head is from the correct track, it depends on where the correct track is *and where the head is moving from*.

According to calculus, on the average the head must move across a third of the tracks to reach the correct track. The time to traverse a third of the tracks is therefore called the **average seek time**.

A **millisecond (ms)** is a thousandth of a second. In a typical hard drive, the average seek time is 12 milliseconds. (In faster hard drives, the average seek time is 9 milliseconds; in slower hard drives, the average seek time is 28 milliseconds.)

After the head reaches the correct track, it must wait for the drive to rotate, until the correct sector reaches the head. That rotation time is called the **latency**. On the average, the head must wait for half a revolution; so the **average latency time** is a half-revolution. The typical hard drive rotates 60 times per second, so a half-revolution takes half of a sixtieth of a second, so it's a 120th of a second, so it's about .008 seconds, which is 8 milliseconds.

If you add the average seek time to the average latency time, you get the total **average access time**. So for a typical hard drive, the average access time = 12 milliseconds seek + 8 milliseconds latency = 20 milliseconds.

During the last few years, hard drive manufacturers have become dishonest: they say the "average access time" is 12 milliseconds, when they should actually say the "average seek time" is 12 milliseconds.

After the head finally reaches the correct sector, you must wait for the head to read the data. If the data consumes *several* sectors, you must wait for the head to read all those sectors.

Manufacturers

Most hard drives for microcomputers are manufactured by four companies: **Seagate Technology (ST)**, **Conner Peripherals**, **Quantum**, and **Western Digital**.

Seagate was the first of those companies to make hard drives for microcomputers, and it set the standard that the other companies had to follow. New Seagate drives work fine, though Seagate's older models were often noisy and unreliable.

Conner was the first company to invent hard drives tiny enough to fit in a laptop or notebook computer. Seagate ignored the laptop/notebook marketplace too long, and Conner's popularity zoomed up rapidly. Conner became the fastest-growing company in the history of American industry, though Conner's popularity finally started to level off.

Quantum became famous by manufacturing the hard drives that Apple buys to put in Mac computers. Quantum also builds drives for IBM PC clones. Quantum drives are excellent.

Western Digital has invented hard drives that cost less. They're popular in cheap clones and discount computer stores.

When buying a hard drive, you might also need to buy a **hard-drive controller**.

How many sectors?

Back in the 1980's, the typical hard-drive controller for IBM-compatible computers put 17 sectors on each track. That scheme was called the **Seagate Technology 506 with Modified Frequency Modulation (ST506 MFM)**.

An improved scheme, which squeezed 26 sectors onto each track, was called the **ST506 with Run Length Limited (ST506 RLL)**. A further improvement, which squeezed 34 sectors onto each track, was called the **Enhanced Small Device Interface (ESDI)**.

Squeezing extra sectors onto each track increases the drive's **capacity** (total number of megabytes) and also the **transfer rate** (the number of sectors that the head reads per rotation or per second).

All those schemes — MFM, RLL, and ESDI — have become obsolete.

Now the most popular scheme is called **Integrated Drive Electronics (IDE)**. Like ESDI, it squeezes 34 sectors onto each track; but it uses special tricks to transfer data faster.

The original version of IDE was limited to small drives: up to 528M. A new, improved version, called **Enhanced IDE**, goes faster and can also handle bigger drives. You can buy Enhanced IDE drives that hold up to 1275M, and even bigger Enhanced IDE drives are being invented.

Another fast scheme is the **Small Computer System Interface** (or **SCSI**, which is pronounced "scuzzy"). It's used on most Mac hard drives and the biggest IBM-compatible hard drives. It's faster than IDE but slower than Enhanced IDE.

Discounts on drives

You can buy a hard drive cheaply from a discount dealer called **Hard Drives International (HDI)**. It's a division of **Insight**, which is at 1912 W. Fourth St., Tempe AZ 85281; phone 800-927-2908 or 602-902-1176. You get a 30-day money-back guarantee and toll-free technical help. You can call sales and technical support anytime (24 hours per day, 365 days per year).

A smaller dealer, **Mega Haus**, sometimes charges even less. But Mega Haus doesn't have a true 30-day money-back guarantee (you must pay a 15% restocking fee), doesn't stay open late at night, and doesn't ship outside the USA. Mega Haus is in Houston at 800-786-1153 (IBM), 800-786-1191 (Mac), or 713-333-1910.

IBM-compatible drives A modern IBM-compatible hard drive costs **under 50 cents per megabyte**. For example, a 400M drive costs under $200.

Besides buying the hard drive, you must also buy a card to put in the computer's slot. For example, here are HDI's prices:

Capacity	Seek	Rotation	Cache	Type	Brand	Model	Price
420M	13 ms	3300 rpm	128K	IDE	Western Digital	WD2 420A	$189 + $20
✓ 528M	12 ms	4500 rpm	256K	IDE	Fujitsu	FJ2 684A	$209 + $20
730M	10 ms	4500 rpm	128K	Enhan'd IDE	Western Digital	WD2 700A	$279 + $40
✓ 850M	10 ms	4500 rpm	128K	Enhan'd IDE	Western Digital	WD2 850A	$299 + $40
1080M	10 ms	4500 rpm	128K	Enhan'd IDE	Western Digital	WD3 1000A	$399 + $40
✓ 1260M	12 ms	4500 rpm	256K	Enhan'd IDE	Maxtor	MX7 1260A	$449 + $40
2100M	9 ms	5400 rpm	256K	SCSI	Seagate	ST3 2430N	$949 + $100
4294M	9 ms	5411 rpm	512K	SCSI	Seagate	ST1 5230N	$1779 + $100
✓ 9080M	11 ms	5411 rpm	1024K	SCSI	Seagate	ST4 10800N	$3299 + $100

For the IDE drives, the extra $20 is for a **paddle board** that fits in an IBM PC AT slot. For the Enhanced IDE drives, the extra $40 is for a *pair* of boards that fit in a *pair* of IBM PC AT slots. For the SCSI drives, the extra $100 is for a SCSI controller card that fits in an IBM PC AT slot.

At the end of the model number, an A means AT-bus IDE (or Enhanced IDE); an N means SCSI.

For Western Digital and Maxtor drives, the main part of the model number is the capacity. For Seagate drives, the main part of the model number is the **unformatted capacity**, which is about 10% bigger than the usable (formatted) capacity.

The drive's **cache** (or **buffer**) contains RAM chips that hold copies of the sectors you used recently — so that if you want to look at those sectors again, you can read from the RAM chips (which are fast) instead of waiting for the disk to spin (which is slow).

The drives fall into four categories:

plain IDE drives
Enhanced IDE drives that are small (under 1 gigabyte)
Enhanced IDE drives that are big (at least 1 gigabyte)
SCSI drives

In each category, I put a check mark next to the biggest drive, because that drive is the best deal (has the lowest cost-per-megabyte).

Those were the prices in February 1995. By the time you read this book, prices might be even lower! Prices continually drop.

Mac drives The price of a Mac hard drive depends on whether the drive is **internal** (fits inside the Mac) or **external** (comes in a separate box that you put next to the Mac). Internal drives are cheaper; but if your Mac is small or filled up, you must buy an external drive instead.

For Mac drives, Mega Haus charges much less than HDI. Here are the Mega Haus prices:

Capacity	Seek time	Rotation	Cache	Brand	Internal	External
365M	11 ms	4500 rpm	128K	Quantum	$199	$259
541M	11 ms	4500 rpm	128K	Quantum	$249	$309
731M	11 ms	4500 rpm	128K	Quantum	$305	$365
1080M	10 ms	5400 rpm	256K	Fujitsu	$499	$559
2160M	10 ms	5400 rpm	512K	Quantum	$929	$989
4294M	8 ms	7200 rpm	512K	Micropolis	$2039	$2139
9080M	11 ms	5400 rpm	1024K	Seagate	$3339	$3439

Buy a big drive Back in the 1980's, a 40-megabyte drive was considered "big", and it was the most popular size to buy.

In the 1990's, a 40-megabyte drive is considered "too small". Even a 210-megabyte drive is considered "too small". Here's why.

To use modern programs on an IBM-compatible computer, you must make sure the hard disk contains some fundamental software, called **MS-DOS** and **Windows**. The newest version of MS-DOS (version 6.22) consumes over 5 megabytes. The newest version of Windows (version 3.11) consumes over 10 megabytes. That makes 15 megabytes altogether!

The typical Windows word-processing program (such as such Word Perfect 6.1 or Microsoft Word 6) consumes about 25 megabytes. So altogether, for DOS plus Windows plus a word-processing program, you've consumed over 40 megabytes already!

You'll need additional megabytes for additional business programs (about 10 megabytes per program), plus additional megabytes to hold what you type. After buying the computer, you'll probably spend the next several years accumulating *many* programs (a few each year). After a year or two, you'll accumulate over 210 megabytes, and you'll wish you'd bought a bigger drive instead.

Buy at least a 420-megabyte drive. A 420-megabyte drive costs just *slightly* more than a 210M drive and will last you for many years. You're buying peace of mind!

It's much cheaper to buy a 420-megabyte drive now than to buy a 210-megabyte drive now and another 210-megabyte drives later. Another reason for buying a 420-megabyte drive is that it will act faster than a 210-megabyte drive.

For example, suppose you want to store 210 megabytes of information, and you're debating whether to buy a 210-megabyte drive or a 420-megabyte drive. Suppose each drive is advertised as having a 13-millisecond seek time. The 420-megabyte drive will nevertheless act faster. Here's why. . . .

Suppose you buy the 420-megabyte drive and use just the first 210 megabytes of it. Since you're using just the first half of the drive, the head needs to move just half as far as usual; so over the 210-megabyte part that you're using, the effective average seek time is just half as much as usual: it's 6½ milliseconds!

CD-ROMS

Instead of buying a program on a floppy disk, you can buy a program on the same kind of **compact disk (CD)** that holds music. Since the CD cannot be erased, it's called a **CD read-only memory (CD-ROM)**.

To make your computer read the CD-ROM disk, put the disk into a **CD-ROM drive**, which is a souped-up version of the kind of CD player that plays music.

Like an ordinary CD player, a CD-ROM drive uses just **optics**. No magnetism is involved. The drive just shines a laser beam at the shiny disk and notices, from the reflection, which indentations (**pits**) are on the disk; the pattern of pits is a code that represents the data. So a CD-ROM drive is an example of an **optical disk drive**.

To put the disk into the drive, press a button on the drive. That makes the drive stick its tongue out at you! The tongue is called a **tray**. Put the disk onto the tray, so that the disk's label is face-up. (If the drive is old-fashioned, you must put the disk into a **caddy** first; but the most modern drives are **caddyless**.) Then push the tray back into the drive. Finally, use the keyboard or mouse to give a command that makes the computer taste what you've put on its tongue.

IBM drive letters

In the most modern kind of IBM-compatible computer, drive A is a 3½-inch floppy drive (1.44M), drive B is a 5¼-inch floppy drive (1.2M), drive C is a hard drive (holding about 420M), and drive D is a CD-ROM drive.

But if your computer has *two* hard drives, here's what happens: the first hard drive is C, the second hard drive is D, and the CD-ROM drive is E.

Size

CD-ROM disks come in two sizes:

The standard size has a diameter of 12 centimeters (which is about 5 inches) and holds 540 megabytes. The miniature size has a diameter of 8 centimeters (which is about 3 inches) and holds 180 megabytes.

Your CD-ROM drive can handle *both* sizes of CD-ROM disks. Each CD-ROM disk is single-sided: all the data is on the disk's *bottom* side — the side that doesn't have a label.

Yes, a standard-size CD-ROM disk holds 540 megabytes, which is a lot!

It's more than the typical hard drive.
It's 375 times as much as a high-density 1.44M floppy.
It's 1500 times as much as a 360K floppy.

Because a CD-ROM disk holds so much, a single CD-ROM can hold a whole library (including encyclopedias, dictionaries, other reference materials, famous novels, programs, artwork, music, and videos). It's the ideal way to distribute massive quantities of information! Moreover, a CD-ROM disk costs just $1.50 to manufacture (once you've bought the appropriate CD-ROM-making equipment, which costs several thousand dollars).

Speed

When buying a CD-ROM drive, the most important factor to consider is the drive's speed.

Transfer rate The speed at which the drive spins is called the **transfer rate**. The higher, the better!

On old drives, the transfer rate was 150 kilobytes per second.

Most new drives spin twice as fast: 300K per second.

That's called **double spin** or **double speed** or **dual speed** or **2X**.

Some drives spin even faster: 450K per second.

That's called **triple spin** or **triple speed** or **3X**.

The fastest drives spin at 600K per second.

That's called **quad spin** or **quad speed** or **4X**.

Seek time The average time it takes for the head to move to the correct track is called the **average seek time**.

The lower the average seek time, the better!

Under 200 milliseconds is great.
  200-300 milliseconds is typical.
  300-400 milliseconds is poor.
  Over 400 milliseconds is terrible.

Buying a drive

Of all the good CD-ROM drives, the **Sony CDU-55E** costs the least: just $129 from discount dealers (such as **USA Flex** at 800-723-2261). The drive is double-speed, has a 250-millisecond seek time, and includes a 256K cache. For good speed, make sure you get the Sony CDU-55E, not the Sony CDU-33A, an older model whose seek time was slower (320ms) and cache was smaller (64K).

The next major step up is the **Mitsumi FX-400**. It's the cheapest *quad*-speed drive. USA Flex sells it for $199. It has a 230ms seek time. Unfortunately, its cache is small: just 128K. Make sure you get the Mitsumi FX-400, not the Mitsumi FX001-D (an older model that was slower: double-speed, 250 ms, 32K).

The next step up is the **Toshiba XM-3501**. It gives you quad-speed, 150ms, 256K. USA Flex sells it for $298.

The best is the **Plextor 4Plex**. It gives you quad-speed and a gigantic cache: 1 megabyte! Unfortunately, its access time is unremarkable: 220ms. You can get it for $399 from discount dealers (such as Hard Drives International at 800-927-2908).

If you buy one of those faster drives, you'll be disappointed: those drives make the typical CD-ROM program run just *slightly* faster. That's because most CD-ROM programs are still designed under the assumption you're using a CD-ROM drive that's slow. So save your money: buy just a cheap drive (the Sony CDU-55E or Mitsumi FX-400).

External drives Those prices are for **internal drives**, which fit inside the computer's system unit. If your system unit is filled up and doesn't have any room left to insert an internal drive, you must buy an **external drive** instead, which sits outside the system unit and costs about $100 more.

Multimedia kits If you buy a CD-ROM drive, you'll also want a **sound card**, a pair of **stereo speakers**, and a few sample CD-ROM disks (so you can admire all that equipment you bought). That combo — a CD-ROM drive, sound card, pair of speakers, and sample CD-ROM disks — is called a **multimedia kit**.

For example, USA Flex sells the **Flex CD-Pro Classic**, which is a kit including the old Sony CDU-33A drive and the Sound Blaster 16 sound card. That kit costs $249; add $10 for a pair of speakers. To pay $50 less, get the **Flex CD-Pro Value** instead, which is similar but includes *imitations* of the Sony and Sound Blaster.

Insight sells the **Reveal Multimedia FX**. It's a multimedia kit that includes the Reveal CD-ROM drive (double-spin, 320 milliseconds, internal), sound card, pair of speakers, headset (including a microphone), a second microphone (which stands on your desk), and sample disks. . . .

The model 03, at $329, includes 12 sample disks.

The model 05, at $429, includes 20 sample disks and a joystick (for playing airplane-flight-simulation games).

The model 08, at $539, includes 35 sample disks, a joystick, a higher-quality sound card, and a higher-quality headset, and higher-quality speakers.

When you buy a new computer, you can ask the salesperson to include a multimedia kit. The computer, together with the multimedia kit, form a combo that's called a **multimedia computer system**. Most discount dealers sell multimedia computer systems based on the Mitsumi FX-400 drive. **Quantex** sells multimedia systems based on the Toshiba XM-3501 drive.

Dirt

A CD-ROM disk's main enemy is dirt.

When you buy a CD-ROM disk, it comes in a clear square box, called the **jewel box**. To use the CD-ROM disk, remove it from the jewel box and put the disk into the drive. When you finish using the disk, put it back into the jewel box, which keeps the dust off the disk.

When putting the CD-ROM disk into or out of a drive, don't put your fingers on the disk's surface: instead, **hold the disk by its edge**, so your greasy fingerprints don't get on the disk's surface.

Once a month, gently **wipe any dust** off the CD-ROM disk's bottom surface (where the data is). While wiping, be gentle and don't get your greasy fingerprints on the disk. Start in the middle and wipe toward the outer edge.

For example, my assistant and I were getting lots of error messages when using a sample CD-ROM disk we bought from Microsoft. I was going to phone Microsoft to complain, but my assistant asked, "What about dust?" I flipped the CD-ROM disk over and sure enough, a big ball of dust was on the disk's bottom side, where the data is recorded. I wiped it off. That CD-ROM disk has worked perfectly ever since.

I was so embarrassed! If my assistant hadn't reminded me to wipe the dust off, I'd have wasted hours of Microsoft's time hunting uselessly for a high-tech reason my CD-ROM disk wasn't working.

Other dangers

Don't put any fluids on the disk. The fluids that clean phonograph records will *wreck* CD-ROM disks.

If you want to write on the disk, **use a felt-tipped pen** (not a ballpoint or pencil). Don't stick any labels on the disk.

SCREENS

WHAT'S A SCREEN?

The computer's **screen** is an ordinary TV (the same kind you watch Bill Cosby on) or *resembles* a TV. The screen shows what you typed on the keyboard and also shows the computer's responses.

TELEVISIONS

If your computer can be attached to an ordinary TV, it's called a **TV computer**. Here's how to attach a TV computer to a TV.

Look at your TV's antenna. Wires run from the antenna to two screws, which are on the back of the TV:

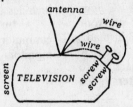

Loosen the two screws, to release the antenna. When you buy a TV computer, the salesperson also gives you a **switch box**. Attach that box to the two screws you loosened:

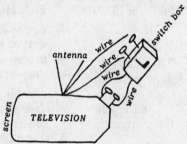

The salesperson also gives you an electrical cord looking like this:

It's called an **RCA cord**, because RCA invented it. Plug one end of that cord into your computer, and plug the opposite end into the switch box.

Attach the antenna's wires to the screws on the switch box:

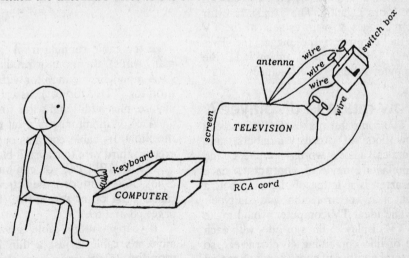

The switch box has a switch on it. If you move the switch toward the antenna, you have a normal TV, so you can watch Bill Cosby. If you move the switch toward the computer's RCA cord, your TV's controlled by the computer so that the computer can write messages on your TV screen.

So by moving the switch, you can make your TV act either normal or computerized. Your family will argue about which way to move the switch.

That switch box is the same kind used by video games (such as Mattel Intellivision, Atari VCS, and Colecovision). When you buy a TV computer, the salesperson will give you the switch box and RCA cord, free!

To use the computer, flip the computer's switch to channel 3 or 4, then turn your TV's dial to the same channel.

To get a sharp picture on your TV screen, *avoid* the channel used by your local TV station. For example, if you live in Boston or New York City, NBC hogs channel 4, so *avoid* channel 4; put your computer and TV on channel 3 instead.

Although most computers (such as Commodore and Radio Shack) use channels 3 and 4, some computers (such as Atari) use channels 2 and 3 instead, and some other computers use channels 10 and 33 and 34 instead.

If the image on your TV screen looks *fuzzy* — so that you can barely read the computer's writing — adjust the TV's "fine tuning" knob.

What the TV can do

Besides writing messages on your TV's screen, the computer can also draw its own *pictures* on the TV! And if your TV has color, you'll see the pictures in color!

When you watch Bill Cosby on TV, his face's size depends on the size of your TV's screen. If your TV's screen is tiny (less than 12 inches), his face looks small; if your TV's screen is 25 inches, his face looks bigger; and if you have a projection TV with a gigantic 60-inch screen, his face looks gigantic. The same's true for the messages & pictures sent to the TV by the computer: the bigger the TV's screen, the more magnified the computer's messages & pictures.

How much is displayed?

The computer makes the TV's screen show lots of words, numbers, and formulas. Those words, numbers, and formulas are made of **characters**: each character is a letter of the alphabet, a digit, or any other symbol you can type.

The ideal TV computer would make the TV display 25 lines of info, with each line of info containing 40 characters, so the total number of characters you see on the screen simultaneously is "25 times 40", which is 1000.

But most TV computers are less than perfect: they display slightly *fewer* than 25 lines of info and slightly *fewer* than 40 characters per line, so the total number of characters you see on the TV screen simultaneously is slightly less than 1000.

MONITORS

A **computer monitor** resembles a TV but produces a sharper picture and costs more.

Like a TV, a computer monitor uses a picture tube. The tube in a TV or monitor is called a **cathode-ray tube (CRT)**.

The monitor can be either **stand-alone** or **built-in**. A **stand-alone monitor** looks like a TV but has no antenna and no dial for selecting channels: the only channel you get is "computer". It doesn't need a switch box: instead, the computer's RCA cord (or similar cord) plugs directly into a hole in the monitor. Before buying a computer that uses a stand-alone monitor, ask whether the computer's price includes the monitor: the monitor might cost extra.

A **built-in monitor** is a screen permanently attached to the rest of the computer: the unit containing the computer's main circuits also contains the monitor.

Colors

When buying a TV, you ask for either "color" or "black-and-white". Similarly, when buying a computer monitor, ask for either **color** or **monochrome**. A color monitor displays all colors of the rainbow; a monochrome monitor displays just black-and-light.

Four kinds of monochrome monitors are popular:

A	**paper-white monitor**	displays black and white.
An	**amber monitor**	displays black and yellow.
A	**green-screen monitor**	displays black and light green.
A	**gray-scale monitor**	displays many shades of gray.

A color TV costs more than black-and-white. Similarly, a color monitor (that displays all the colors of the rainbow) costs more than a monochrome monitor.

Most monochrome monitors cost about $100. Most color monitors cost between $200 and $500.

Screen size

The typical color monitor's screen is 14 inches (measured diagonally). The typical monochrome monitor's screen is 12 inches, but some monochrome monitors use a smaller screen (9-inch) to make the monitor be smaller, weigh less, and be easier to carry.

Fat cables

If the cable running from the monitor to the computer is fat (so it contains many wires), the monitor produces a sharp image.

A monochrome monitor with a fat cable is called a **transistor-transistor-logic monitor (TTL monitor)**. Its cable contains one wire to transmit the fundamental picture, plus additional wires for further enhancements.

A color monitor with a fat cable is called a **red-green-blue monitor (RGB monitor)**. Its cable contains one wire to transmit red, a second wire to transmit green, a third wire to transmit blue, plus additional wires for further enhancements.

For the IBM PC, you can buy three kinds of RGB monitors: the cheapest are called **CGA monitors**; the better ones are called **EGA monitors**; the best ones are called **VGA color monitors**. (I'll reveal more details about those monitors on pages 68 and 69.)

If your monitor's cable is *not* fat, the picture isn't sharp. For example, if your monitor's cable is just a thin RCA cord, your monitor's called a **composite monitor**; its picture is fuzzy, though not as fuzzy as a plain TV.

Most computers (such as the IBM PC) can make a monitor display 80 characters per line. To fit so many characters on a line, the characters are made tiny. To display the tiny characters clearly, the monitor must either have a fat cable (to produce a sharp picture) or be monochrome; it must *not* be a composite color monitor. (If you try to display tiny characters on a composite color monitor, the characters are hard to read because the fuzzy colors bleed into each other.)

The typical monitor displays 25 80-character lines, so you see 2000 characters simultaneously.

VIDEO TERMINALS

A **video-display terminal (VDT)** is a monitor that communicates with a large computer and has an attached keyboard.

If 200 people are using a maxicomputer simultaneously, only one of them is sitting at the maxicomputer's main console. The other 199 people typically sit at 199 VDT's, which are in different rooms or even different cities.

LIQUID CRYSTALS

If your computer is tiny, it comes with a tiny screen, called a **liquid-crystal display (LCD)**. That's the kind of screen you see on digital watches, pocket calculators, pocket computers, notebook computers, and laptop computers.

Since an LCD screen uses little electricity, it can run on batteries. A traditional picture tube can*not* run on batteries. If your computer system runs on batteries, its screen is an LCD.

An LCD screen displays black characters on a white background. The screen consists of thousands of tiny crystals. Each crystal is normally white, but temporarily changes to black when an electrical charge passes through it.

A traditional picture tube emits light; that's why you can watch TV even in a dark room. But an LCD screen does *not* emit light; you can*not* read an LCD screen in a dark room. You must turn on a light, to see which of the crystals are white and which are black.

Some LCD screens come with a light to help you see the screen. If the light is *behind* the LCD surface, the screen is said to be **backlit**. Since the light consumes electricity, it quickly runs down the battery, which you must recharge often.

Although the crystals can change from white to black, they appear black only if you look at them from the correct angle, and if the light in the room is positioned correctly. If you move your head or the light, the black crystals will appear very light gray instead of black, and you'll have trouble reading the message they're trying to display. So if you have trouble seeing the message on an LCD screen, move your head or the light or the screen, until the message darkens. The fanciest LCD screens use **supertwist crystals**, which you can read from *any* angle; but they're expensive and consume more electricity.

Laptops use LCD screens instead of traditional picture tubes, because LCD screens consume less electricity, weigh less, and are less bulky. Desktops stay with traditional picture tubes, because the image on the typical LCD screen has poor contrast and resolution and responds too slowly to computer commands.

An **LCD plate** (or **LCD overhead-projection panel**) is a special LCD screen that you put on an overhead projector, which projects the LCD's image onto the wall of your office or classroom or auditorium, so that the image becomes several feet across.

The nicest low-cost LCD plate is the **Sharp QA-75**. It can display many shades of gray. It sells for about $1500. It attaches to the IBM PC, and you can buy a cable to connect it to a Mac.

PRINTERS

FUNDAMENTALS

A computer usually displays its answers on a screen. If you want the computer to copy the answers onto paper, attach the computer to a **printer**, which is a device that prints on paper.

The typical printer looks like a typewriter but lacks a keyboard. To feed information to the printer, you type on the *computer's* keyboard. The computer transmits your request through a cable of wires running from the back of the computer to the back of the printer.

A computer's advertised price usually does *not* include a printer and cable. The cable costs about $8; the typical printer costs several hundred dollars.

Printers are more annoying than screens. Printers are noisier, slower, cost more, consume more electricity, need repairs more often, and require you to buy paper and ink. But you'll want a printer anyway, to copy the computer's answers onto paper that you can give your computerless friends. Another reason to get a printer is that a sheet of paper is bigger than a screen and lets you see more information at once.

Printer dealers

To get a printer cheaply, phone these mail-order discount dealers:

Harmony Computers & Electronics
1801 Flatbush Ave.
Brooklyn NY 11210
800-441-1144 or 718-692-3232

Tri State Computer
650 6th Ave. (at 20th St.)
New York NY 10011
800-433-5199 or 212-633-2530

USA Flex
135 N. Brandon Dr.
Glen Ellyn IL 60139
800-USA-FLEX or 708-351-7172

Midwest Micro
6910 U.S. Route 36 East
Fletcher OH 45326
800-972-8822 or 513-368-2309

Midwest Micro offers the greatest variety of printers, a free 56-page catalog, and toll-free technical help; but its prices are slightly higher than the other three companies. To get special attention, ask Tri State for **David Rohinsky at extension 223** and tell him you're reading *The Secret Guide to Computers*.

To get low prices locally, walk into chains of discount superstores, such as **Comp USA** (which sells all kinds of computer equipment) and **Staples** (which sells all kinds of office supplies and some computer equipment).

Another way to get a printer cheap is to phone 800-873-7766. That gets you the Accessories Division of a major printer manufacturer, **Epson**. Say that you're interested in buying an Epson printer that's **factory-reconditioned** (which means "used but fixed up by the manufacturer to be like new") and want a catalog explaining which ones are available. They're usually older models, at ridiculously low prices. You get a 30-day money-back guarantee and 2-year warranty. Consumers who phoned that number and got those printers are happy.

Three kinds of printers

Three kinds of printers are popular.

A **dot-matrix printer** looks like a typewriter but has no keyboard. Like a typewriter, it smashes an inked ribbon against the paper. Like a typewriter, it's cheap: it typically costs about $150.

An **ink-jet printer** looks like a dot-matrix printer; but instead of containing a ribbon, it contains tiny hoses that squirt ink at the paper. It prints more beautifully than a dot-matrix printer and costs more. It typically costs about $250.

A **laser printer** looks like a photocopier. Like a photocopier, it contains a rotating drum and inky toner. It prints even more beautifully than the other two kinds of printers. Like a photocopier, it's expensive: it typically costs about $500.

Special requirements

As you progress from a dot-matrix printer to an ink-jet printer to a laser printer, the quality tends to go up, and so does the price. But here are exceptions. . . .

Color If you need to print in color (instead of just black-and-white), get an ink-jet printer. (Dot-matrix printers produce colors too crudely and slowly. Color laser printers cost too much — about $8,000.) Ink-jet printers that can print in color cost about $400.

Mailing labels Although you can print mailing labels on all three kinds of printers, the *easiest* way to print mailing labels is on a dot-matrix printer.

Multi-part forms If you want to print on a multipart form (using carbon paper or carbonless NCR paper), you must buy a dot-matrix printer.

Old accounting software Some old accounting software requires that you buy a dot-matrix printer. It also requires that the printer be an expensive kind that can handle extra-wide paper.

Cost of consumables

After you've bought the printer and used it for a while, the ink supply will run out, so you must buy more ink.

In the typical dot-matrix printer, the inked ribbon costs about $5 and lasts about 1000 pages, so it costs about a half a penny per page. That's cheap!

In the typical ink-jet printer, the ink cartridge costs about $20 and lasts about 500 pages, so it costs about 4 cents per page. That's expensive!

In the typical laser printer, the toner cartridge costs about $80 and lasts about 4000 pages, so it costs about 2 cents per page. That's expensive, but not as expensive as the ink in an ink-jet printer.

Those prices assume you're printing black text. If you're printing graphics or color, the cost per page goes up drastically. For example, full-color graphics on an ink-jet printer cost about 50 cents per page.

For all three kinds of printers, you must also pay for the paper, which costs about 1 cent per sheet if you buy a small quantity (such as a 500 sheets), or a half a cent per sheet if you buy a large quantity (such as 5000 sheets). For low prices on paper, go to Staples.

You must also pay for the electricity to run the printer; but the electricity's cost is negligible (much less than a penny per page) if you turn the printer off when you're not printing.

Warning: if you leave a laser printer on even when not printing, its total yearly electric cost can get high, since the laser printer contains a big electric heater. (You might even notice the lights in your room go dim when the heater kicks on.)

Daisy-wheel printers

Although the most popular kinds of printers are dot-matrix, ink-jet, and laser, some folks still use an older kind of printer, called a **daisy-wheel printer**. It's cute! Here's how it works. . . .

Like a typewriter and a dot-matrix printer, a daisy-wheel printer smashes an inked ribbon against paper. To do that, the daisy-wheel printer contains a device called a **daisy wheel**, which is an artificial daisy flower made of plastic or metal. On each of the daisy's petals is embossed a character: a letter, a digit, or a symbol. For example, one petal has the letter A embossed on it; another petal has B; another petal has C; etc.

Notice that each character is **embossed**. (The word "embossed" is like "engraved", but an "embossed" character is raised *up* from the surface instead of etched into the surface.)

To print the letter C, the printer spins the daisy wheel until the C petal is in front of the inked ribbon. Then a hammer bangs the C petal against the ribbon, which in turn hits the paper, so that an inked C appears on the paper.

The printer can print each character extra-dark or regular. To print a character extra-dark, the printer prints the character, moves to the right just 120th of an inch, and then reprints the character. Since the second printing is *almost* in the same place as the original character, the character looks darkened and slightly fatter. Those darkened, fattened characters are called **boldfaced**.

You can remove the daisy wheel from the printer and insert a different daisy wheel instead. Each daisy wheel contains a different **font**. For example, one daisy wheel contains italics; a different daisy wheel contains Greek symbols used by scientists.

The printer holds just one daisy wheel at a time. To switch to italics in the middle of your printing, you must stop the printer, switch daisy wheels (a tedious activity that requires your own manual labor!), and then press a button for the printer to resume printing.

Manufacturers The most famous daisy-wheel printer manufacturer was **Diablo**, founded by Mr. Lee in California. He sold the company to Xerox, then founded a second daisy-wheel printer company, **Qume** (pronounced "kyoom"), which he sold to ITT. In 1988 he bought Qume back. Other companies (such as **Brother** and **Juki**) invented imitations that claimed to be **Diablo & Qume compatible**.

Variants of the daisy wheel Over the years, many variants of the daisy wheel have been invented.

For example, **Nippon Electric Company (NEC)** invented a "wilted" daisy wheel, whose petals are bent. The wilted daisy wheel is called a **thimble**. Computerists like it because it spins faster than a traditional daisy and also produces a sharper image. It's used just in NEC's **Spinwriter** and **Elf** printers.

Another variation of the daisy wheel is the plastic **golf ball**, which has characters embossed all over it. IBM calls it a **Selectric typing element**. IBM uses it in typewriters, typesetting machines, and printers. It produces better-looking characters than daisy wheels or thimbles. Since it spins too slowly and needs too many repairs, IBM is discontinuing it.

Gigantic printers used by maxicomputers and minicomputers have characters embossed on **bands**, **chains**, and **drums** instead of daisies. Those printers are fast and cost many thousands of dollars.

Look closer

Now let's take a closer look at each of the three popular kinds of printers: dot-matrix, ink-jet, and daisy-wheel. . . .

DOT-MATRIX PRINTERS

A **dot-matrix printer** resembles a daisy-wheel printer; but instead of containing a daisy wheel, it contains a few **guns**, as if it were a super-cowboy whose belt contains several holsters.

Each gun shoots a pin at the inked ribbon. When the pin's tip hits the ribbon and smashes the ribbon against the paper, a dot of ink appears on the paper. Then the pin retracts back into the gun that fired it.

Since each gun has its own pin, the number of guns is the same as the number of pins.

9-pin printers

If the printer is of average quality, it has 9 guns — and therefore 9 pins. It's called a **9-pin printer**. The 9 guns are stacked on top of each other, in a column that's called the **print head**. If all the guns fire simultaneously, the pins smash against the ribbon simultaneously, so the paper shows 9 dots in a vertical column. The dots are very close to each other, so that the column of dots looks like a single vertical line. If just *some* of the 9 pins press against the ribbon, you get fewer than 9 dots, so you see just *part* of a vertical line.

To print a character, the print head's 9 guns print part of a vertical line; then the print head moves to the right and prints part of another vertical line, then moves to the right again and prints part of another vertical line, etc. Each character is made of parts of vertical lines — and each part is made of dots.

The pattern of dots that makes up a character is called the **dot matrix**. That's why such a printer's called a **9-pin dot-matrix printer**.

Inside the printer is a ROM chip that holds the definition of each character. For example, the ROM's definition of "M" says which pins to fire to produce the letter "M". To use the ROM chip, the printer contains its own CPU chip and its own RAM.

Manufacturers When microcomputers first became popular, most dot-matrix printers for them were built by a New Hampshire company, **Centronics**. In 1980, Japanese companies took over the marketplace. Centronics went bankrupt.

The two Japanese companies that dominate the industry are **Epson** and **Panasonic**.

Epson became popular because it was the first company to develop a disposable print head — so that when the print head wears out, you can throw it away and pop in a new one yourself, without needing a repairman. Also, Epson was the first company to develop a low-cost dot-matrix impact printer whose dots look "clean and crisp" instead of looking like "fuzzy blobs". Epson was the main reason why Centronics went bankrupt.

Epson is part of a Japanese conglomerate called the **Seiko Group**, which became famous by timing the athletes in the 1964 Tokyo Olympics. To time them accurately, the Seiko Group invented a quartz clock attached to an electronic printer. Later, the quartz clock was miniaturized and marketed to consumers as the "Seiko watch", which became the best-selling watch in the whole world. The electronic printer, or "E.P.", led to a better printer, called the "son of E.P.", or "EP's son". That's how the Epson division was founded and got its name!

Epson's first 9-pin printer was the **MX-80**. Then came an improvement, called the **FX-80**. Those printers are obsolete; they've been replaced by Epson's newest 9-pin wonders, the **FX-870** ($270) and the **FX-1170** (which can handle extra-wide paper and costs $347). Epson's cheapest and slowest 9-pin printers are the **LX-300** ($164) and the **Action Printer 2250** ($89). You can get those prices from discount dealers (Harmony, Tri State, and USA Flex).

For a 9-pin printer, I recommend buying the **Panasonic 1150** instead, because it prints more beautifully and costs just $125 from discount dealers such as Tri State. Too bad it can't handle extra-wide paper!

Besides Epson and Panasonic, four other Japanese companies also popular: **NEC**, **Oki**, **Citizen**, and **Star**. Printers from all six of those Japanese companies are intended mainly for the IBM PC, though they work with Apple 2 and Commodore computers also.

The most popular printers for the Mac were the **Imagewriter** and the **Imagewriter 2**. They were designed by Apple to print exact copies of the Mac's screen. They even print copies of the screen's wild fonts and graphics. Apple stopped marketing them, but you can still buy a refurbished Imagewriter for $127 and a refurbished Imagewriter 2 for $199 from **Computer Town** in New Hampshire at 603-898-3200. (**Refurbished** means "used but fixed up to be as-good-as-new".)

7-pin printers

Although the average dot-matrix printer uses 9 pins, some older printers use just 7 pins instead of 9. Unfortunately, 7-pin printers can't print letters that dip below the line (g, j, p, q, and y) and can't underline. Some 7-pin printers print just capitals; other 7-pin printers "cheat" by raising the letters g, j, p, q, and y slightly.

24-pin printers

Although 9 pins are enough to print English, they're *not* enough to print advanced Japanese, which requires 24 pins instead.

Manufacturers The first company to popularize 24-pin printers was **Toshiba**. Its printers printed Japanese — and English — beautifully. 24-pin Toshiba printers became popular in America, because they print English characters more beautifully than 9-pin printers.

Epson and all the other Japanese printer companies have copied Toshiba. Now the cheapest wonderful 24-pin printers are the **Epson Action Printer 3250** ($150), the **Epson Action Printer 3260** ($170), the **Panasonic 2023** ($155), the **Panasonic 2123** ($180), and the **Epson LQ-570+** (which is sturdier, easier to operate, and costs $234). The cheapest 24-pin printer that handles wide paper is the **Epson LQ-1070+** ($354). You can get those prices from Harmony, Tri State, and USA Flex.

In a typical, cheap 24-pin printer (such as the Epson Action Printer 3250), the even-numbered pins are slightly to the right of the odd-numbered pins, so you see two columns of pins. After firing the even-numbered pins, the print head moves to the right and fires the odd-numbered pins, whose dots on paper overlap the dots from the even-numbered pins. The overlap insures that the vertical column of up to 24 dots has no unwanted gaps.

In fancier 24-pin printers (such as the Panasonic 2023 and 2123), the 24 pins are arranged as a diamond instead of two columns, so that the sound of firing pins is staggered: when you print a vertical line you hear a quiet hum instead of two bangs.

Beyond 24 pins

The fastest dot-matrix printers use multiple print heads, so that they can print several characters simultaneously.

Why the daisies died

During the 1970's, daisy-wheel printers were popular, but they've died out. Computerists have switched to dot-matrix printers instead, for the following reasons.

The mechanism that spins the daisy is expensive, slow, and frequently needs repairs.

Dot-matrix printers can easily print graphics by making the pictures out of little dots. Daisy wheels cannot.

Although the first dot-matrix printers had just 7 pins and printed ugly characters, the newest 9-pin and 24-pin printers from Epson and Panasonic print prettier characters than the average daisy wheel. Moreover, you can make the typical 9-pin printer imitate an 18-pin printer by doing **2-pass printing**, in which the printer prints a line of text, jerks the paper up very slightly, and then prints the line again so the new dots fill the gaps between the old dots.

If you have a daisy-wheel printer and want to change to a different font (such as italics), you must spend your time manually switching daisy wheels. If you have a dot-matrix printer instead, just tell the printer which font you want (by pressing a button on the printer or on your computer's keyboard), and the printer will automatically switch to different patterns of dots to produce the different font, since the printer's ROM contains the definitions of *many* fonts. To make a daisy-wheel printer print so many fonts, you must buy several dozen daisy wheels, costing a total of several hundred dollars.

So daisy-wheel printers died because of competition from dot-matrix printers — and from ink-jet and laser printers, which print even more beautifully! Let's examine those super-beautiful printers now. . . .

An **ink-jet printer** resembles a dot-matrix printer but contains hoses instead of guns. The hoses squirt ink at the paper. The hoses are called **nozzles**. There are no pins or ribbons.

When you use an ink-jet printer, you hear the splash of ink squirting the paper. That splash is quieter than the bang produced when a dot-matrix printer's pins smash a ribbon. If you like quiet, you'll love ink-jet printers!

The most popular ink-jet printers are made by **Hewlett-Packard (HP)**. Recently, **Canon** and **Epson** have started making ink-jet printers also.

How does the ink get out of the nozzle and onto the paper? In ink-jet printers by HP and Cannon, a bubble of ink in the nozzle gets heated and becomes hot enough to burst and splash onto the paper. Epson's ink-jet printers use a different technique, in which the nozzle suddenly constricts and forces the ink out.

The most popular ink-jet printers can print in color. They mix together the three primary ink colors (red, blue, and yellow) to form all the colors of the rainbow.

Mainstream printers

Of all the ink-jet printers, the most amazing bargain is the **Canon Bubble Jet BJC-4000**. It prints in color nicely and quickly, handles a wide variety of paper well, and costs just $349 from discount dealers (such as Staples).

If you don't need color, get the **Canon Bubble Jet BJ-200ex**. It resembles the BJC-4000 but prints just in black and costs just $219 from discount dealers (such as Harmony).

If even $219 is beyond your budget, get the **Canon Bubble Jet BJ-100**. It resembles the BJ-200ex but prints slower and not quite as beautifully. It costs just $189 from Harmony.

The cheapest of those printers, the BJ-100, prints 360 **dots per inch (dpi)**. That means it can print 360 dots per inch across the paper (horizontally) and 360 dots per inch down the paper (vertically). The next step up, the BJ-200ex, prints 720 dpi horizontally, 360 dpi vertically; that's called **720x360 dpi**. The color printer, the BJC-4000, prints colors at 360 dpi, black at 720x360 dpi.

For the ultimate in color printing, get the **Epson Stylus Color Printer**. It prints colors at 720 dpi, both horizontally and vertically! Its color printing is so beautiful you'll think you're looking at a color photograph! Alas, like a color photo, it needs to print on expensive coated paper, which costs about 11 cents per sheet. If you feed the printer cheaper paper instead, the resolution reduces to 360 dpi. The printer is somewhat expensive: $489 from discount dealers (such as Harmony).

The *cheapest* ink-jet printer that can print in color is the **HP Deskjet 540**. Discounters advertise it for just $279; but at that price, it prints just in black. Add $40 for a color kit. But even at $279+$40, it's cheaper than the Canon BJC-4000. Unfortunately, it's slower and has this limitation: you can put into it a black-ink cartridge or a color-ink cartridge, but not both simultaneously — and the color-ink cartridge doesn't contain any black ink. So when you're printing in color, you can't print black on the same page. (If you try making the printer print black when the color cartridge is in, the printer tries to imitate black by printing red, blue, and yellow on top of each other; but that takes three times as long and produces

mud instead of black.) HP's fancier ink-jet printer, the **HP Deskjet 560C**, has *two* cartridge slots, so you can insert the black and color cartridges simultaneously; but that printer is expensive ($469). Alas, both of those HP printers produce just 300 dpi color, 600x300 dpi black.

Paper

If you buy an ink-jet printer, experiment with using different brands of paper. Some brands absorb ink much better than other brands. If you choose the wrong brand, the ink will **wick** (spread out erratically through the strands of the paper's fiber). Start by trying cheap copier paper, then explore alternatives. The brand of paper you buy makes a much bigger difference with ink-jet printers than with dot-matrix or laser printers.

Canon printers are better at tolerating paper differences than HP or Epson printers.

Ink

Canon's ink is water-based. The bad thing about water-based ink is that if you print on a sheet of paper or envelope that accidentally gets wet (from rain or a sweaty thumb), the ink will run and smear. But if you're careful to keep the paper dry, Canon's ink smears very little.

For printing in black, Canon's ink cartridges cost the most (about 5 cents per page). Epson and HP cartridges cost less (about 2½ cents per page). So if you're doing a lot of printing in black, you'll save money by switching from Canon to the HP Deskjet 540 or Epson's black-only printer (the **Epson Stylus 800 Plus**).

The typical color-ink cartridge suffers from this problem: it contains several colors, but if one of the colors runs out you must replace the entire cartridge, even if the other colors haven't run out yet. For example, if you're doing a lot of printing in red, but the red runs out, you must throw away the entire color cartridge, including the blue and yellow ink you haven't used yet. Environmentalists complain.

Canon makes a special color printer, the **Canon Bubble Jet BJ-600E**, which has separate cartridges for each color, so that when the red runs out you just throw away the red cartridge but keep the blue and yellow cartridges. Unfortunately, that printer is expensive ($449).

Portable printers

Canon's popular black-only printers, the BJ-200ex and the BJ-100, are each small and cute: they weigh just 6½ pounds. If you want something even smaller, get the **Canon BJ-10sx** ($229) or the **Deskjet 320** ($290); they weight just 4 pounds! Unfortunately, they print slowly and require you to insert each page manually, one page at a time; to add automatic paper feed for those printers, you must pay extra and also add extra weight.

Mac printers

All those ink-jet printers I described are IBM-compatible. If you have a Mac instead, you must buy a Mac printer — or a Mac version of an IBM-compatible printer.

The $280 **Apple Stylewriter 2** is the Mac version of the Canon BJ-200. The $449 **Apple Color Stylewriter 2400** is the Mac version of the Canon BJC-4000. The $571 **Apple Color Stylewriter Pro** is the Mac version of the Canon BJC-600. HP **Deskwriters** are Mac versions of HP Deskjets.

LASER PRINTERS

A **laser printer**, like an office photocopier, contains a drum and uses toner made of ink. The printer shines a laser beam at the drum, which picks up the toner and deposits it on the paper.

For the IBM PC, the most popular laser printers are made by Hewlett-Packard (HP).

HP's first laser printer was the **Laserjet**. Then came an improvement (the **Laserjet Plus**), a second improvement (the **Laserjet 2**), and further improvements (the **Laserjet 3** and **Laserjet 4**).

They've all been replaced by the **Laserjet 4 Plus**, a cheaper "personal" version called the **Laserjet 4P**, and an even cheaper "lower-cost" version called the **Laserjet 4L**.

Laserjet 4 Plus

The Laserjet 4 Plus is the best of all those printers. Here's how it works. . . .

It can print 12 pages per minute (12 **ppm**). It can print 600 dots per inch (600 **dpi**); and it uses a trick called **Resolution Enhancement Technology (RET)**, which can shift each dot slightly left or right and make each dot slightly larger or smaller.

Its ROM contains the definitions of 45 fonts. Each of those fonts is **scalable**: you can make the characters as big or tiny as you wish. If you want extra fonts, insert a **font cartridge** that contains extra ROM chips, or do this: buy a floppy disk containing definitions of extra fonts, put that disk into your computer, copy those font definitions to your computer's hard disk, then tell your computer to copy those font definitions to the printer's RAM. So altogether, the printer can handle three kinds of fonts: the 45 **internal fonts** that were inside the printer originally; the **cartridge fonts** that you added by inserting a cartridge; and **soft fonts** that are copied into the printer's RAM from the computer's disks.

The printer contains 2 megabytes of RAM, so it can handle lots of soft fonts and graphics on the same page. Moreover, the printer uses a trick called **data compression**, which compresses the data so that twice as much data can fit in the RAM (as if the RAM were 4 megabytes).

The printer costs $1370. That's the price charged by Staples (a chain of discount stores), and it includes a toner cartridge.

Cheaper printers

If you can't afford a Laserjet 4 Plus, buy a cheaper printer instead:

Laser printer	Resolution	RAM	Fonts	Speed	Price
HP Laserjet 4 Plus	600 dpi + RET	2M + compression	45 scalable	12 ppm	$1370
HP Laserjet 4P	600 dpi + RET	2M + compression	45 scalable	4 ppm	$949
HP Laserjet 4L	300 dpi + RET	1M + compression	26 scalable	4 ppm	$499
Brother HL-630	300 dpi	½M + compression	21 s + 24 b	6 ppm	$380
Panasonic KX-P4400	300 dpi	1M	28 bitmap	4 ppm	$299

In the cheapest laser printer (by Panasonic), the ROM's fonts are **bitmap**, which means "non-scalable", which means you can*not* make those fonts bigger or smaller: to get bigger or smaller fonts, you must buy different fonts (font cartridges or soft fonts).

In Brother's mid-priced laser printer (the HL-630), 21 of the fonts are scalable, and 24 are non-scalable (bitmap).

Laserjet 4V

In 1994, HP invented the **Laserjet 4V**. It resembles the Laserjet 4 Plus but is even fancier! It prints 16 pages per minute (instead of 12), and it comes with 4M of RAM (instead of 2M).

Best of all, it can accept extra-large paper (11 inches by 17 inches, instead of just 8½ inches by 14 inches). That extra-large paper, called **tabloid size**, is big enough to be the entire page of a tabloid newspaper! Moreover, the Laserjet 4V can print even at the paper's edge (without requiring a margin).

Discount dealers (such as Tri State) sell it for $1850.

Lexmark

When IBM decided to stop manufacturing printers, IBM sold its printer factory (in Lexington, Kentucky) to the factory's employees, who called their new company **Lexmark**. IBM let them still use the "IBM" name in their advertising, even though they'd become an independent company.

They became the first company to manufacture a 600 dpi laser printer. When HP copied their idea and invented the HP Laserjet 4, they upped the ante and invented a 1200 dpi laser printer! Moreover, it comes with 87 fonts! It's called the **Lexmark IBM Optra**.

It prints 1200 dpi at 8 ppm, and can print 600 dpi even faster! It comes in two versions:

The **Optra R** contains 2M, prints 600 dpi at 12 ppm, and costs $1427.
The **Optra Rx** contains 4M, prints 600 dpi at 16 ppm, and costs $1999.

Those are the prices charged by a discount dealer (USA Flex).

Color printers

You can buy color laser printers, but they're very expensive:

Laser printer	Resolution	RAM	Speed	List price
HP Color Laserjet	300 dpi	8M	10 ppm in black, 2 ppm in color	$7295
Xerox Color Laser Printer	300 dpi + RET	12M	12 ppm in black, 3 ppm in color	$8495
QMS Magicolor	600 dpi	12M	8 ppm in black, 2 ppm in color	$9999

Print engines

Each monochrome HP laser printer contains a photocopier print engine manufactured by Canon. In fact, each monochrome HP laser printer is just a modified Canon photocopier!

In HP's color laser printer, the print engine is made by Konica. In QMS's color laser printer, the print engine is made by Hitachi.

Brother, Panasonic, and Lexmark make their own print engines.

Older Laserjets

Many offices still use older Laserjets. Here's how the famous old Laserjets compare with modern ones:

Printer	Resolution	RAM	Fonts	Speed	Cheaper version
Laserjet 2	300 dpi	½M	bitmap	8 ppm	Laserjet 2P is 4 ppm
Laserjet 3	300 dpi + RET	1M	scalable	8 ppm	Laserjet 3P is 4 ppm, ½M
Laserjet 4	600 dpi + RET	2M + compression	scalable	8 ppm	Laserjet 4P is 4 ppm
Laserjet 4 Plus	600 dpi + RET	2M + compression	scalable	12 ppm	

The Laserjet 2 contains just a few bitmap fonts — and they're all ugly! If you have a Laserjet 2, I recommend that you add extra fonts to it by getting a font cartridge. The most popular font cartridges for the Laserjet 2 are the **Microsoft Z cartridge** (manufactured by HP) and the **25-in-1 cartridge** (manufactured by Pacific Data). For example, this entire *Secret Guide*, which you're reading now, was produced on a Laserjet 2 with the Microsoft Z cartridge (except for the cute pictures and largest headlines). If you have a Laserjet 3, 3P, 4, 4P, 4L, or 4 Plus, don't bother buying font cartridges, since those Laserjets include many good scalable fonts already.

PCL versus Postscript

When your computer wants to give the printer an instruction (such as "draw a diagonal line across the paper" or "make that scalable font bigger"), the computer sends the printer a code.

HP laser printers understand a code called **Printer Control Language (PCL)**. It was invented by HP. The newest version of PCL is called **PCL 5e**. It's understood by the Laserjet 4 (and by the Laserjet 4 Plus, 4P, and 4L). Older HP printers understand just older versions of PCL and can't perform as many tricks.

Most IBM-compatible laser printers (such as the ones by Epson, Panasonic, and Sharp) understand PCL, so that they imitate HP's laser printers, run the same software as HP's laser printers, and are **HP-compatible**. But most of them understand just *old* versions of PCL and can't perform as many tricks as the Laserjet 4 series.

Some laser printers understand a different code, called **Postscript**, which was invented by a company called **Adobe**.

Back in the 1980's, PCL was still very primitive. Postscript was more advanced. The fanciest laser printers from HP's competitors used Postscript. The very fanciest laser printers were bilingual: they understood both Postscript and PCL.

Now that PCL has improved and become PCL 5e, it's about as good as Postscript. PCL 5e printers cost less to manufacture than Postscript printers.

In Postscript, each command that the computer sends the printer is written by using English words. Unfortunately, those words are long and consume lots of bytes. In PCL, each command is written as a brief series of code numbers instead. Since PCL commands consume fewer bytes than Postscript commands, the computer can transmit PCL commands to the printer faster than Postscript commands, and PCL commands can fit in less RAM.

Mac printers

For the Mac, the most popular laser printer is Apple's **Laserwriter**, which comes in many versions:

Printer	Resolution	RAM	Fonts	Language	Speed	Price
Personal Laserwriter 300	300 dpi	½M	39 scalable	Quickdraw	4 ppm	$629
Personal Laserwriter 320	300 dpi + RET	2M	39 scalable	Postscript	4 ppm	$865
Laserwriter Select 360	600 dpi	7M	64 scalable	Postscript	10 ppm	$1297
Laserwriter 16/600 PS	600 dpi + RET	8M	64 scalable	Postscript	17 ppm	$2181

Those prices are from mail-order Mac discounters in southern California (such as **Creative Computers** at 800-222-2808, **Mac Professional** at 818-719-9200, and **Mac Storm** at 310-829-9780).

HP makes Laserjets that are modified to work with a Mac:

IBM version	Mac version & its RAM & its price		
Laserjet 4L	Laserjet 4ML	4M	$980
Laserjet 4P	Laserjet 4MP	6M	$1289
Laserjet 4 Plus	Laserjet 4M Plus	6M	$1889
Laserjet 4V	Laserjet 4MV	12M	$2749

Each Mac Laserjet understands both PCL and Postscript. Each attaches to both the IBM PC and the Mac. Those prices are from discounters (Tri State and Harmony).

BEST BUYS

The cheapest nice IBM-compatible printer is the 9-pin **Epson Action Printer 2250** ($89). The next major step up is the 24-pin **Epson Action Printer 3250** ($150). For a true workhorse, get the 24-pin **Epson LQ-570+** ($234).

For prettier printing, try an ink-jet printer such as the **Canon BJ-200ex** ($219). If you need printing in color, try the colorful **Canon BJC-4000** ($354) or the **Epson Stylus Color Printer** ($489). But remember that ink-jet printers are more finicky about what kind of paper you insert, and the ink is expensive.

The next major step up is to get a laser printer, such as the **Panasonic KX-P4400** (300 dpi, 4 pages per minute, $299), **Brother HL-630** (300 dpi, 6 pages per minute, $380), the **HP Laserjet 4P** (600 dpi + RET, 4 pages per minute, $949), the **HP Laserjet 4 Plus** (600 dpi + RET, 12 pages per minute, $1370). If you're rich, get a laser printer that's even fancier, such as the **Lexmark Optra R** ($1427), the **HP Laserjet 4V** ($1850), or the **Lexmark Optra Rx** ($1999).

Now let's plunge into the technical details of printer technology!

Impact versus non-impact

A printer that smashes an inked ribbon against the paper is called an **impact printer**. The most popular kind of impact printer is the dot-matrix printer. Other impact printers use daisy wheels, thimbles, golf balls, bands, chains, and drums. They all make lots of noise, though manufacturers have tried to make the noise acceptable by putting the printers in **noise-reducing enclosures** and by modifying the timing of the smashes.

A printer that does *not* smash an inked ribbon is called a **non-impact printer**. Non-impact printers are all quiet! The most popular non-impact printers are ink-jet printers and laser printers. Other non-impact printers are **thermal printers** (whose hot pins scorch the paper), and **thermal-transfer printers** (which melt hot colored wax onto the paper).

Each has its own disadvantages. Thermal printers require special "scorchable" paper. Thermal-transfer printers require expensive ribbons made of colored wax.

Resolution

If a printer creates characters out of dots, the quality of the printing depends on how fine the dots are — the "number of dots per inch", which is called the **print resolution**.

9-pin printers usually print 72 dots per inch vertically. That's called **draft quality**, because it's good enough for rough drafts but not for final copy. It's also called **business quality**, because it's good enough for sending memos to your coworkers and accountant.

If you make a 9-pin printer do 2 passes, it prints 144 dots per inch. That's called **correspondence quality**, because it's good enough for sending pleasant letters to your friends. It's also called **near-letter-quality (NLQ)**, because it looks nearly as good as the letters produced on a typewriter. The typical 9-pin printer has a switch you can flip, to choose either 1-pass draft quality (which is fast) or 2-pass correspondence quality (which is slower but prettier).

A 24-pin printer prints 180 dots per inch. That's called **letter quality (LQ)**, because it looks as good as the letters printed by a typical typewriter or daisy-wheel printer. It's good enough for writing letters to people you're trying to impress.

A standard laser printer prints 300 dots per inch. That's called **desktop-publishing quality**, because it's good enough for printing newsletters. It's also called **near-typeset-quality**, because it looks nearly as good as a typesetting machine.

A standard typesetting machine prints 1200 or 2400 dots per inch. Those are the resolutions used for printing America's popular magazines, newspapers, and books.

HP's Laserjet 2P Plus, 3, 3P, and 4L all print 300 dots per inch; but the 3, 3P, and 4L produce prettier output than the 2P Plus by using this trick: they can print each dot at 5 different sizes (ranging from "normal" to "extra tiny") and nudge each dot slightly to the right or left. HP's Laserjet 4 and 4P print 600 dots per inch.

Ink-jet printers by Canon and Epson usually print 360 dots per inch. HP's ink-jet printers usually print 300 dots per inch.

Character size

To measure a character's size, you must measure both its width and its height.

Width Like an old-fashioned typewriter, a traditional printer makes each character a tenth of an inch wide. That's called "10 characters per inch" or **10 cpi** or **10-pitch** or **pica** (pronounced "pike uh").

Some printers make all the characters narrower so you get 12 characters per inch. That's called **12 cpi** or **12-pitch** or **elite**.

The typical dot-matrix impact printer lets you choose practically any width you wish. For example, the Epson LQ-850 can print 5, 6, 7½, 8⅓, 10, 12, 15, 16⅔, and 20 cpi. The widest sizes (5, 6, 7½, and 8⅓ cpi) are called **double-width**, because they're twice as wide as 10, 12, 15, and 16⅔ cpi. The narrowest sizes (16⅔ and 20 cpi) are called **condensed** or **compressed**; they're 60% as wide as 10 and 12 cpi.

Some printers make each character a different width, so that a "W" is very wide and an "i" is narrow; that's called **proportional spacing**. It looks much nicer than uniform spacing (such as 10 cpi or 12 cpi). The typical modern printer lets you choose either proportional spacing or uniform spacing. Uniform spacing is usually called **monospacing**.

Height The typical sheet of paper is 11 inches tall. If you put one-inch margins at the top and bottom, you're left with 9 inches to print on.

After printing a line of type, the typical typewriter or printer jerks up the paper a sixth of an inch, then prints the next line. As a result, you get 6 lines of type per inch, so the entire sheet of paper shows "9 times 6" lines of type, which is 54 lines.

The fanciest printers, such as laser printers, can make characters extra-tall or extra-short. The character's height is measured in **points**. Each **point** is $1/72$ of an inch. A character that's an inch tall is therefore called "72 points tall". A character that's half an inch tall is 36 points tall.

Like a typewriter, a printer normally makes characters 10 points tall. (More precisely, it makes the top of a capital "Y" 10 points higher than the bottom of a small "y".) It also leaves a 2-point gap above the top of the "Y", to separate it from the characters on the previous line. That 2-point gap is called the **leading** (pronounced "ledding"). That technique is called "10-point type with 2-point leading". Since the type plus the leading totals 12 points, it's also called "10-point type on 12" (or "10 on 12" or "10/12").

Fonts

You can make a capital T in two ways. The simple way is draw a horizontal bar and a vertical bar, like this: T. The fancy way is to add **serifs** at the ends of the bars, like this: T. A character such as T, which is without serifs, is called **sans serif**, because "sans" is the French word for "without".

Monospaced fonts The most popular monospaced fonts are **Courier** (which has serifs) and **Letter Gothic** (which is sans serif). Letter Gothic was invented by IBM in 1956 for typewriters. Courier was invented for typewriters also.

Proportionally-spaced fonts The most popular proportionally spaced fonts are **Times Roman** (which has serifs) and **Helvetica** (which is sans serif). Times Roman was invented by *The Times* newspaper of London in 1931. Helvetica was invented by Max Miedinger of Switzerland in 1954. (The name "Helvetica" comes from "Helvetia", the Latin name for Switzerland.)

Samples Here are samples from the 300-dot-per-inch laser printer that printed this book (an HP Laserjet 2 printer with Microsoft Z cartridge):

```
This is Courier, 10 points high and 10 cpi.
This is Courier Bold (10 points high, 10 cpi).

This is Lineprinter (similar to Letter Gothic), 8.5 points high and 16.7 cpi.

This is 8-point Times Roman. It's very tiny, but sometimes nice things come in small packages.
This is 10-point Times Roman, Times Roman Bold, and Times Roman Italic.
This is 12-point Times Roman, Times Roman Bold, and Italic.
This is 14-point Times Roman Bold.

This is 8-point Helvetica. It's very tiny, but sometimes nice things come in small packages.
This is 10-point Helvetica, Helvetica Bold, and Helvetica Italic.
This is 12-point Helvetica, Helvetica Bold, and Helvetica Italic.
This is 14-point Helvetica Bold.
```

Here are samples from a 24-pin dot-matrix printer, the Epson LQ-570:

```
This is Epson's 10-cpi Courier.     This is 15-cpi Courier.
This is Epson's 10-cpi Prestige.    This is 15-cpi Prestige.
This is Epson's 10-cpi OCR-B.       This is 15-cpi OCR-B.
This is Epson's 10-cpi Orator-S.    This is 15-cpi Orator-S.
This is Epson's 10-cpi Script.      This is 15-cpi Script.
This is Epson's 10-cpi Script C.    This is 15-cpi Script C.


This is Epson's version of Times Roman. It's proportional.
This is Epson's version of Helvetica. It's proportional.
```

Here are samples from an ink-jet printer, the Canon BJ-200e. In these samples, the Canon is pretending it's the Epson LQ-570. The Canon's imitative printing looks better than Epson's original, since Canon's printer is an ink-jet instead of a dot-matrix. Look at how pretty Canon's printing is:

```
This is Epson's 10-cpi Courier.     This is 15-cpi Courier.
This is Epson's 10-cpi Prestige.    This is 15-cpi Prestige.
This is Epson's 10-cpi Orator-S.    This is 15-cpi Orator-S.
This is Epson's 10-cpi Script.      This is 15-cpi Script.

This is Epson's version of Times Roman. It's proportional.
This is Epson's version of Helvetica. It's proportional.
```

Canon doesn't imitate Epson's OCR-B or Script C.

Paper

Laser printers and most ink-jet printers accept a stack of ordinary copier paper. You put that paper into the printer's **paper tray**, which is also called the **paper bin** and also called the **cut-sheet paper feeder**.

Dot-matrix printers Though some dot-matrix printers handle stacks of ordinary copier paper, most dot-matrix printers handle paper differently. Here's how. . . .

To pull paper into the printer, dot-matrix printers can use two methods.

The simplest method is to imitate a typewriter: use a rubber roller that grabs the paper by friction. That method's called **friction feed**. Unfortunately, friction is unreliable: the paper will slip slightly, especially when you get near the bottom of the sheet.

A more reliable method is to use paper that has holes in the margins. The printer has **feeder pins** that fit in the holes and pull the paper up through the printer very accurately. That method, which is called **pin feed**, has just one disadvantage: you must buy paper having holes in the margins.

If your printer uses pin feed and is fancy, it has a clamp that helps the pins stay in the holes. The clamp (with its pins) is called a **tractor**. You get a tractor at each margin. A printer that has tractors is said to have **tractor feed**. Usually the tractors are **movable**, so that you can move the right-hand tractor closer to the left-hand tractor, to handle narrower paper or mailing labels.

A **dual-feed** printer can feed the paper *both* ways — by friction and by pins — because it has a rubber roller and also has sets of pins. The printer has a lever to the left of the roller and pins: if you pull the lever one way, the paper will pass by the roller, for friction feed; if you pull the lever the other way, the paper will pass by the pins, for pin feed.

Most dot-matrix printers have dual feed with movable tractors.

Paper that has holes in it is called **pin-feed paper** (or **tractor-feed paper**).

Like a long tablecloth folded up and stored in your closet, pin-feed paper comes in a long, continuous sheet that's folded. Since it comes folded but can later be unfolded ("fanned out"), it's also called **fanfold paper**. It's perforated so you can rip it into individual sheets after the printer finishes printing on it. If the paper's fancy, its margin is perforated too, so that after the printing is done you can rip off the margin, including its ugly holes, and you're left with what looks like ordinary typing paper.

The fanciest perforated paper is called **micro-perf**. Its perforation is so fine that when you rip along the perforation, the edge is almost smooth.

Paper width

Most printers can use ordinary typing paper or copier paper. Such paper is 8½ inches wide. On each line of that paper, you can squeeze 85 characters at 10 cpi, or 170 characters at 20 cpi, if you have no margins.

Pin-feed paper is usually an inch wider (9½ inches wide), so that the margins are wide enough to include the holes.

Some printers can handle pin-feed paper that's extra-wide (15 inches). Those **wide-carriage printers** typically cost about $130 more than standard-width printers.

Speed

The typical printer's advertisement brags about the printer's speed by measuring it in **characters per second (cps)** or **lines per minute (lpm)** or **pages per minute (ppm)**. But those measurements are misleading.

Dot-matrix and ink-jet printers

For example, Epson advertised its LQ-850 dot-matrix printer as "264 cps", but it achieved that speed only when making the characters small (12 cpi) and ugly (draft quality). To print characters that were large (10 cpi) and pretty (letter quality), the speed dropped to 73 cps.

Panasonic advertised its KX-P1091 dot-matrix printer as "192 cps", but it achieved that speed only if you threw an internal switch that made the characters even uglier than usual!

For dot-matrix and ink-jet printers, the advertised speed ignores how long the printer takes to jerk up the paper. For example the typical "80-cps" printer will print 80 characters within a second but then take an extra second to jerk up the paper to the next line, so at the end of two seconds you still see just 80 characters on the paper.

Daisy-wheel printers

To get an amazingly high cps rating, one daisy-wheel manufacturer fed its printer a document consisting of just one character repeated many times, so the daisy never had to rotate!

Laser printers

To justify a claim of "8 pages per minute", Apple salesmen noticed that their Laserwriter 2 NT printer takes a minute to produce 8 *extra* copies of a page. They ignored the wait of *several minutes* for the *first* copy!

Like Apple, most other laser-printer manufacturers say "8 pages per minute" when they should really say: "⅛ of a minute per additional copy of the same page".

Keep your eyes open

Don't trust any ads about speed! To discover a printer's true speed, hold a stopwatch while the printer prints many kinds of documents (involving small characters, big characters, short lines, long lines, draft quality, letter quality, and graphics).

Interfacing

A cable of wires runs from the printer to the computer. The cable costs about $8 and is *not* included in the printer's advertised price: the cable costs extra.

One end of the cable plugs into a socket at the back of the printer. The other end of the cable plugs into a socket at the back of the computer. The socket at the back of the computer is called the computer's **printer port**.

If you open your computer, you'll discover which part of the computer's circuitry the printer port is attached to. In a typical computer, the printer port is attached to the motherboard; but in some computers (such as the original IBM PC), the printer port is attached to a small PC card instead, called a **printer interface card**, which might not be included in the computer's advertised price.

When the computer wants the printer to print some data, the computer sends the data to the printer port; then the data flows through the cable to the printer.

Serial versus parallel

The cable contains many wires. Some of them are never used: they're in the cable just in case a computer expert someday figures out a reason to use them. Some of the wires in the cable transmit information about scheduling: they let the computer and printer argue about when to send the data. If the computer's port is **serial**, just one of the wires transmits the data itself; if the computer's port is **parallel**, eight wires transmit the data simultaneously.

Parallel ports are more popular than serial ports, because parallel ports transmit data faster, are more modern, and are easier to learn how to use. Unfortunately, parallel ports handle only short distances: if the printer is far away from the computer, you must use a serial port instead.

When you buy a printer, make sure the printer matches the computer's port. If your computer's port is parallel, you must buy a parallel printer; if your computer's port is serial, you must buy a serial printer instead.

If your computer has *two* printer ports — one parallel, one serial — you can attach the computer to either type of printer; but I recommend that you choose a printer that's parallel, because parallel printers cost less, and because many word-processing programs require that the printer be parallel.

Standard cables

The typical parallel printer expects you to use a cable containing 36 wires. Just 8 of the wires transmit the data; the remaining wires can be used for other purposes. That 36-wire scheme is called the **industry-standard Centronics-compatible parallel interface**.

The typical serial printer expects you to use a cable containing just 25 wires. Of the 25 wires, just 1 transmits data from the computer to the printer; the remaining wires can be used for other purposes. That 25-wire scheme is called the **recommended standard 232C serial interface (RS-232C serial interface)**.

Weird cables

If your computer is an IBM PC or clone, you'll get a surprise when you try attaching it to a parallel printer (which expects 36 wires): your computer's parallel port contains just 25 wires instead of 36! To attach the computer's 25-wire parallel port to a 36-wire parallel printer, computer stores sell a weird cable that has 25 wires on one end and 36 wires on the other.

If your computer is small and cute (such as the Apple 2c, 2GS, Mac, Commodore 64, or Radio Shack Color Computer), you'll get a surprise when you try attaching it to a standard serial printer (which expects 25 wires): your computer's serial port contains fewer than 10 wires! You must buy a weird cable that has 25 wires on one end and fewer on the other.

OTHER HARDWARE

KEYBOARDS

The usual way to communicate with the computer is to type messages on the computer's **keyboard**.

Famous keyboards

These pages show pictures of famous keyboards:

IBM PC

The IBM PC's keyboard can print all the letters of the alphabet (from A to Z), all the digits (from 0 to 9), and these symbols:

Symbol	Official name	Nicknames used by computer enthusiasts
.	period	dot, decimal point, point, full stop
,	comma	cedilla
:	colon	dots, double stop
;	semicolon	semi
!	exclamation point	bang, shriek
?	question mark	ques, query, what, huh, wildchar
"	quotation mark	quote, double quote, dieresis, rabbit ears
'	apostrophe	single quote, acute accent, prime
`	grave accent	left single quote, open single quote, open quote, backquote
^	circumflex	caret, hat
~	tilde	squiggle, twiddle, not
=	equals	is, gets, takes
+	plus	add
-	minus	dash, hyphen
_	underline	underscore, under
*	asterisk	star, splat, wildcard, Nathan Hale
&	ampersand	amper, amp, and, pretzel
@	at sign	at, whorl, strudel
$	dollar sign	dollar, buck, string
#	number sign	pound sign, pound, tic-tac-toe
%	percent sign	percent, grapes, James Bond
/	slash	forward slash, rising slash, slant, stroke
\	backslash	reverse slash, falling slash, backwhack
|	vertical line	vertical bar, bar, pipe, enlarged colon
( )	parentheses	open parenthesis & close parenthesis, left paren & right paren
[ ]	brackets	open bracket & close bracket, square brackets
{ }	braces	curly brackets, curly braces, squiggly braces, left tit & right tit
< >	brockets	angle brackets, less than & greater than, from & to, suck & blow

For example, the symbol * is officially called an "asterisk". More briefly, it's called a "star". It's also called a "splat", since it looks like a squashed bug. In some programs, an asterisk means "match anything", as in a card game where the Joker is a "wildcard" that matches any other card. The asterisk is also called a "Nathan Hale", since he was the American patriot who during the Revolutionary War declared this final thought before being hanged by the British: "I regret that I have just one *ass to risk* for my country."

The % sign is called a "James Bond" because it looks like that spy's code number: 007.

The IBM PC's keyboard also contains special keys that help you do special activities, such as move around the screen while you type:

Key	Usual purpose
↑	move up, to the line above
↓	move down, to the line below
←	move left, to the previous character
→	move right, to the next character
Home	move back to the beginning
End	move ahead to the end
Page Up	move back to the previous page
Page Down	move ahead to the next page
Tab	hop to next field or far to the right
Enter	finish a command or paragraph
Pause	pause until you press Enter
Print Scrn	copy from the screen to paper
Shift	capitalize a letter
Caps Lock	capitalize a whole phrase
Num Lock	use numbers on keyboard's right side
Scroll Lock	change how text moves up & down
Insert	insert new character in middle of text
Delete	delete the current character
Backspace	delete the previous character
Esc	escape from a mistake
F1	get help from the computer
F2, F3, etc.	do special activities
Ctrl	do special activities
Alt	do special activities

Many programs make those keys serve different purposes instead. Be safe: avoid those keys until you read the details in later chapters.

GRAPHICS-INPUT DEVICES

If you feed the computer a picture (such as a photograph, drawing, or diagram), the computer will analyze the picture and even help you improve it. To feed the computer a picture, you can use three methods. . . .

Method 1: point a video camera at what you want to take a picture of, while the video camera is wired to a box called **Computer Eyes**, which is wired to the computer.

Method 2: draw the picture on paper, then put that paper underneath an **optical scanner** wired to the computer.

Method 3: draw the picture by using a pen wired to the computer. The six popular kinds of computerized pens are **light pens**, **touch screens**, **graphics tablets**, **mice**, **trackballs**, and **joysticks**.

Light pens

A **light pen** is a computerized pen that you point at the screen of your TV or monitor. To draw, you move the pen across the screen.

Light pens are cheap: prices begin at $20. But light pens are less reliable, less convenient, and less popular than other graphics-input devices.

Touch screens

A **touch screen** is a special overlay that covers the screen and lets you draw with your finger instead of with a light pen.

Graphics tablets

A **graphics tablet** is a computerized board that lies flat on your desk. To draw, you move either a pen or your finger across the board.

The cheapest graphics tablet is the **Koala pad**. Koala makes versions of it for all the popular computers by IBM, Apple, Commodore, and Radio Shack.

Fancier tablets for the IBM PC are made by **Wacom**.

Mice

A **mouse** is a computerized box that's about as big as a pack of cigarettes. To draw, you slide the mouse across your desk, as if it were a fat pen.

When you slide the typical mouse, a ball in its belly rolls on the table. The computer senses how many times the ball rotated and in what direction.

The mouse was invented at Xerox's **Palo Alto Research Center (PARC)**. The first company to provide mice to the general public was **Apple**, which provided a free mouse with every Lisa and Mac computer. Now every Mac, Commodore Amiga, and Atari ST computer comes with a free mouse — and so do many IBM computers and clones.

Microsoft Mouse The nicest mouse for the IBM PC is the **Microsoft Mouse**.

Its first version was boring. Then came an improved version, nicknamed "The Dove Bar" because it was shaped like a bar of Dove soap. It felt great in your hand; but trying to draw a picture by using that mouse — or *any* mouse — was as clumsy as drawing with a bar of soap.

The newest version of the Microsoft Mouse is nicknamed "The Dog's Paw" because it's shaped like a dog's lower leg: it's long with an asymmetrical bump (paw) at the end. It feels even better than The Dove Bar, unless your hand is too small to wrap around it. Discount dealers sell it for $59.

Cheaper mice If you're nearly broke, buy a cheaper brand of mouse. Prices start at just $10.

Trackballs

A **trackball** is a box that has a ball sticking out the top of it. To draw, just put your fingers on the ball and rotate it.

Most notebook computers have a trackball built into the keyboard.

Technologically, a trackball is the same as a typical mouse: each is a box containing a ball. For a trackball, the ball sticks *up* from the box and you finger it directly; for a mouse, the ball hides *underneath* and gets rotated when you move the box.

The mouse feels more natural (somewhat like gripping a pen) but requires lots of desk space (so you can move the box).

The trackball was invented first. The mouse came later.

Joysticks

A **joystick** is a box with a stick coming out of its top. To draw, you move the stick in any direction (left, right, forward, back, or diagonally) as if you were the pilot of a small airplane.

The most popular joysticks are made by **Atari** and **Kraft**.

Atari joysticks work just on Atari and Commodore computers. Kraft joysticks are nicer, more expensive, and work on all popular computers by IBM, Apple, Commodore, and Radio Shack.

SPEAKERS

To produce sounds, the typical computer uses a **speaker** (similar to the speakers in your stereo system, but smaller).

The speaker is typically inside the system unit. Some computers use the speaker in your TV or monitor instead. By using the speaker, the computer beeps at you whenever you make an error.

Aesthetic computers, such as the Mac, can make the speaker play nice music. The IBM PC is a boring business computer that produces just harsh beeps, unless you make the IBM PC sound as good as a Mac by inserting a **sound card** (such as the **Sound Blaster**).

The fanciest computers can speak words, by attaching the speaker to a **speech synthesizer**.

The newest Mac computers come with a **microphone**. (You can also add a microphone to other computers.) By using the microphone, you can make the computer record sounds. For example, you can make the computer record the sound of your voice and imitate it, so the computer sounds just like you!

MODEMS

You can connect your computer to a telephone line so your computer can chat with other computers around the world! Here's how. . . .

To let your computer chat with a computer that's far away, attach each computer to telephone lines by using a "special device" that turns computer signals into telephone signals, and turns telephone signals back into computer signals.

Turning a computer signal into a telephone signal is called **modulating the signal**. Turning a telephone signal back into a computer signal is called **demodulating the signal**. Since the "special device" can modulate and also demodulate signals, the device is called a **modulator/demodulator** (or **modem**, which is pronounced "mode em").

Acoustic versus direct-connect

You can buy two kinds of modems.

The old-fashioned kind is a black box that has big ears on top, so that it can listen to the telephone. Because of its big ears, it's called a **Mickey Mouse modem** or an **acoustic coupler**. It usually costs $120.

The newer kind of modem plugs directly into the phone system, as if it were an answering machine. It doesn't have any ears: it has telephone wires instead. It's called a **direct-connect modem**. It usually costs under $100, and it's cheaper and more reliable than a Mickey Mouse modem. It's more popular than a Mickey Mouse modem because it's better than a Mickey Mouse modem in every way, except that you can't attach it to pay phones or to phones in hotel rooms.

Kinds of direct-connect modems

A direct-connect modem can be either **external** or **internal**. If it's **external**, it's a box that sits next to your computer. If it's **internal**, it's a printed-circuit card that hides inside your computer. Regardless of whether it's external or internal, a wire runs from it to the phone system.

Internal modems are more popular than external ones, because external modems typically cost more and require that you buy a cable to run from the modem to the computer. But external modems have the advantage of being easier to control, since they give you push-buttons and blinking lights.

Many notebook computers include internal modems at no extra charge. So do some desktop computers.

Most direct-connect modems have fancy features, such as **auto-dial** (which means the modem can memorize the other computer's phone number and dial it for you) and **auto-answer** (which means the modem automatically answers the phone whenever the other computer calls). A direct-connect modem having many such fancy features is called **smart**. Nearly all modems sold today are smart.

10 bits per character

To transmit a character, the modem usually transmits a 10-bit number, like this: 1001011101.

The first bit (which is always a 1) is called the **start bit**; it means "hey, wake up, and get ready to receive the data I'm going to send you". The last bit (which is always a 1) is called the **stop bit**; it means "hey, I'm done, you can go back to sleep until I send you more data". The eight middle bits (such as 00101110) are usually called the **data bits**: they're a code that represents 1 byte of information (1 character). So to transmit 1 character, the modem transmits 10 bits.

Speed

The typical modem transmits **2400 bits per second (2400 bps)**. That speed is also called **2400 baud**. Since 10 bits make a character, that kind of modem transmits 240 characters per second. That speed is quite fast: it's about as fast as the average person can read.

Faster modems can transmit 9600 bits per second (which is 9600 bps, 9600 baud, 960 characters per second). That's faster than you can read, but it's great for transmitting documents that you want to *skim*, programs that you want to *run*, and graphics.

Even faster modems can transmit 14400 bits per second. Since 1000 bits is called a **kilobit**, 14400 bits per second is called 14.4 **kilobits per second** (or 14.4 **kbps** or 14.4 **kilobaud**).

Some computerists still use old modems transmitting just 1200 bits per second (1200 baud) or 300 bits per second.

If you buy a fast modem, you can tell it to go slower. For example, if you buy a 9600-baud modem, you can tell it to go at five popular speeds: fast (9600 baud), medium (2400 baud), slow (1200 baud), and super-slow (300 baud).

To communicate with a friend's computer, your modem must go at the same speed as your friend's. For example, if you buy a 9600 baud modem but your friend has just a 300-baud modem, your modem's software will detect the slowness of your friend's modem and automatically **downshift** (slow down) to 300 baud.

Standards

Standards for modem communication have been invented by **AT&T** and a French-speaking international committee called the **Comité Consultatif International Télégraphique et Téléphonique (CCITT)**. Here's what they call their standards:

Speed	CCITT standard	AT&T standard
300 bps	V.21	Bell 103
1200 bps	V.22	Bell 212a
2400 bps	V.22bis	
9600 bps	V.32	
14400 bps	V.32bis	
19200 bps	V.32terbo	
28800 bps	V.34 (or V.fast)	

For example, if you see an ad for a **V.22-compatible modem** or a **Bell 212a modem**, the ad is trying to sell you a 1200 bps modem.

Notice that the second version of V.22 is called **V.22bis**, because **bis** is a French word that means "2nd version". Notice that the third version of V.32 is called **V.32terbo**, because **terbo** is an international word that combines the French "ter" (which means 3) with the English word "turbo" (which means "fast").

Find all those terms confusing? That's why computerists say that "CCITT" really stands for "Committee for Confusing International Telecommunications Terms".

Data compression

Modems sometimes use a shorthand notation that lets data to be expressed in fewer bits than normal, so more data can be transmitted per second. The shorthand notation is called a **data-compression technique.**

The most popular data-compression techniques are Microcom's **MNP level 5** (which compresses data to half as many bits as normal), Microcom's **MNP level 7** (which compresses data to a third as many bits as normal), and CCITT's **V.42bis** (which compresses data to a fourth as many bits as normal). For example, if you see an ad for a **2400-baud modem with MNP level 5**, that modem will transmit about as much data per second as a plain 4800-baud modem.

Fax

You can send messages from your computer to fax machines around the world, if you buy a **fax/modem**, which is a modem that can also send faxes. If the fax/modem is

fancy, it can also *receive* faxes and print them on your printer.

The typical fax/modem transmits modem information (to other computers) at 2400 baud. It transmits faxes (to fax machines) at 9600 baud. It's called a **2400/9600-baud fax/modem**. (Most ads list the modem speed first, then the fax speed, because the modem speed is more important.) More briefly, it's called a **2496 fax/modem**. Warning: though every 2496 fax/modem can send faxes at 9600 baud, the cheapest 2496 fax/modems *receive* faxes at just 4800 baud — or can't receive faxes at all!

Faster fax/modems can transmit 14400 baud (14.4 kilobaud) for faxes and modem data.

Brands

The most famous modems are made by **Hayes**, which charges high prices. Other companies make cheaper modems that imitate Hayes' and are called **Hayes-compatible**. Nearly all modems sold today are Hayes-compatible.

For example, high-quality Hayes-compatible modems have been built by **Everex** and **Practical Peripherals**. To avoid competition from those companies, Hayes sued Everex and bought Practical Peripherals. So Everex had to pay Hayes a royalty (and eventually stopped selling modems), and Practical Peripherals became owned by Hayes.

To pay less for a Hayes-compatible modem, get the ones made by **Infotel** or **Zoom**.

For example, you can get an Infotel 14400-baud fax/modem for just $69 internal, $85 external, from a discount dealer such as **Midwest Micro** (in Ohio at 800-972-8822). If even those prices are beyond your budget, get a Zoom fax/modem that's slower for just $45 internal, $70 external, from a discount dealer such as **Staples** (a chain of office-supply stores): it handles modem data at 2400 baud, sends faxes at 9600 baud, and receives faxes at 4800 baud.

COM1 versus COM2

A modem is an example of a **serial device**. You might own another serial device also, such as a serial mouse or a serial printer.

The IBM PC can handle two serial devices simultaneously. The first serial device is called **communication device #1 (COM1)**. The second serial device is called **COM2**.

If you add a modem to your IBM PC or clone, you must decide whether to call the modem COM1 or COM2.

Most hardware and software assume the modem is COM2. To avoid headaches, make the modem be COM2. Here's how.

If the modem is external, run its cable to your computer's COM2 port. (If your computer doesn't have a COM2 port yet, buy a **serial interface card** containing it.)

If the modem is internal, make sure the switch or jumper on the modem is set to the COM2 position; and make sure no other hardware in your computer system is called COM2. For example, if your computer contains a serial interface card having a COM2 port on it, you must **disable** the serial interface card's COM2 port (by moving a jumper or switch on it).

Avoid using COM3 or COM4, since the computer has trouble handling COM3 and COM4 reliably. (COM3 often conflicts with COM1, and COM4 often conflicts with COM2.)

Like a disk, a magnetic tape consists of magnetized rust. Just as you put a disk into a disk drive, you put a tape into a **tape drive**.

Tape drives are slower than disk drives. To skip from the disk's beginning to the disk's end, the disk drive's arm simply hops from the outermost track to the innermost track. But to skip from the beginning of a tape to the end of a tape, you must wait for the tape drive to wind the entire tape.

Cassettes for primitive computers

The cheapest kind of tape drive is an audio cassette tape recorder — the same kind you use for listening to music, at the beach or in your car. You can attach that kind of tape recorder to an old Radio Shack computer (such as the Radio Shack TRS-80 model 1, 3, or 4 or the Radio Shack Color Computer). Wires run from the tape recorder to the computer, and the computer sings a song into the tape recorder; the song is a code that represents the data.

Unfortunately, audio cassette tape recorders aren't very reliable. If you're using one of those old Radio Shack computers, you can improve the reliability somewhat by getting Radio Shack's own tape recorder, which is specially designed to work well with computers and automatically controls the tape's volume. But since a tape recorder is so much slower than a disk drive, I recommend that you *not* buy Radio Shack's tape recorder, and instead keep saving your pennies until someday you can afford a disk drive. Once you've experienced the thrilling speed, convenience, and pleasure of a disk drive, you'll never want to use a tape recorder ever again!

Commodore & Atari Old computers by Commodore and Atari (such as the Commodore Vic, Commodore 64, Commodore 128, and Atari 800) do *not* attach to ordinary audio cassette tape recorders; you must buy special cassette tape recorders sold by Commodore and Atari or — better yet — buy a disk drive instead, if you can afford it.

Coleco The Coleco Adam computer comes with a built-in cassette tape recorder, at no extra charge. Coleco's tape recorder is high-speed and requires specially lubricated tapes, sold by Coleco. Since it handles just tapes that contain computer information and can*not* play ordinary musical tapes, it's called a **digital cassette tape drive** instead of an audio cassette recorder. But even though Coleco's tape recorder is "high-speed" and handles computer data rather well, it's still not nearly as fast or convenient as a disk drive.

Modern microcomputers

Most people who buy modern computers (such as the Mac, Commodore Amiga, IBM PC, and clones) buy disk drives and don't bother using tapes at all.

If you buy a hard disk, how do you make a backup copy of that hard disk, and where do you put the backup? You could put the backup copy onto a second hard disk or onto a pile of about 50 floppy disks. Another possibility is to put the backup copy onto a special super-fast digital cassette tape drive that holds super-long cassette tapes that can contain backups.

Colorado The most popular such tape drives are the **Jumbo 120** and the **Jumbo 250**, both built by **Colorado Memory Systems** (which used to be an independent company but is now owned by Hewlett-Packard). Those Jumbo drives work with the IBM PC and clones.

The Jumbo 120 can back up a 120-megabyte hard disk by taking the hard disk's data, compressing it into a shorthand notation, and then storing the compressed data on a 60-megabyte tape. Because of that scheme, the Jumbo 120 is called a **60/120M tape drive**.

The Jumbo 250 can back up a 250-megabyte hard disk by compressing the hard disk's data onto a 120-megabyte tape. It's called a **120/250M tape drive**.

The Jumbo 120 uses the same blank tape as the Jumbo 250. The Jumbo 120 formats that tape to hold 60 megabytes of data (from a 120-megabyte drive), whereas the Jumbo 250 takes the same tape but formats it differently, to hold 120 megabytes of data (from a 250-megabyte drive).

To buy those drives cheaply, phone discount dealers such as **USA Flex** (800-USA-FLEX) and **Insight** (800-755-3874). Here's what they'll charge you:

Item	Price
Jumbo 120 drive	$99
Jumbo 250 drive	$165
tape, unformatted	$15 each (if you buy 5)
tape, formatted for Jumbo 250	$16 each (if you buy 5)

Each Jumbo drive is **internal**: it goes *in*side your computer. It uses the same controller card that controls your floppy disk drives. If you want to put the drive *out*side the computer, put the drive in an external case that costs $80.

Alternatives Instead of buying a tape drive, the typical computerist uses a pile of floppy disks or buys a second hard drive.

Big reels for big computers

Maxicomputers and minicomputers use big reels of tape for three purposes: to backup big disks, to send data by mail, and to store the **archives** (old files that are used rarely if ever).

The reel's diameter is 10½ inches. If you unwind the tape, you'll find the tape is half an inch wide and almost half a *mile* long! The exact length is 2400 feet.

To use a reel of tape, you put the reel into a **reel-to-reel tape drive**, which typically costs about $5000 and writes 1600 bytes per inch, so that the entire tape holds 43 megabytes. Super-fancy drives, used only on the largest maxicomputers, squeeze 6250 bytes onto every inch (instead of 1600), so that they squeeze 171 megabytes onto a single reel of tape.

IBM's fanciest drive not only writes 6250 bytes per inch but also does the writing amazingly quickly. It moves the tape at 200 inches per second, so that it transfers about 1.2 megabytes per second.

CASES

The motherboard and other main circuitry are enclosed in a box. The box and the circuitry inside it are called the **system unit**. The box itself — without its contents — is called the **case**.

Interference

The computer thinks at about the same speed (number of cycles per second) as radio & TV waves. If you put your computer next to a radio or TV, the computer's electromagnetic "thought waves" cause static on the radio or TV. To decrease that interference, move the computer away from the radio or TV (or change the position of the radio or TV's antenna).

The **Federal Communications Commission (FCC)** prohibits you from owning any device (such as a computer) that interferes with your neighbors' radio and TV. The FCC requires all computers to pass the **FCC class A non-interference test**. Any computer used in a *residential* area must also pass the **FCC class B non-interference test**, which is harder to pass than the class A test.

To help the computer pass the class A and class B tests, manufacturers line the insides of cases with metal that breaks up the electromagnetic waves.

When you buy a computer, ask whether it's **FCC class B approved**. If it's not — if it's just FCC class A approved — you cannot legally use it in a residential area.

SURGE SUPPRESSORS

Instead of plugging your computer into the wall, you can plug it into a **surge suppressor**, which is a special extension cord that protects your computer against surges in electrical power.

Unless you live in a neighborhood or building that has extremely poor electricity, don't bother buying a surge suppressor. The typical computer has some surge protection built into it *already*.

If you're worried about thunderstorms sending surges to your computer, just unplug your computer during storms! If your air conditioner or electric heater consumes too much electricity and causes a brownout (so your computer acts unreliably), use a plain extension cord to plug your computer into a different outlet, so that the computer's not on the same circuit as the power-hungry appliance.

During the summer, most computer errors are caused by temperatures over 95°, *not* by power surges.

SOFTWARE

KINDS OF SOFTWARE

The information stored in the computer is called **software**. Most software stays in RAM temporarily and is erased from RAM when you no longer need it. But *some* software stays in the computer's circuits *permanently*: it hides in the ROM and is called **firmware**.

To feed firmware to the computer, stick extra ROM chips into the main circuitry. To feed other kinds of software to the computer, use the keyboard, disk, or tape: type the information on the keyboard, or insert a disk or tape containing the information.

You can feed the computer four kinds of software: an **operating system**, a **language**, **application programs**, and **data**. Let's look at them. . . .

OPERATING SYSTEMS

An **operating system** is a set of instructions that explains to the CPU how to handle the keyboard, the screen, the printer, and the disk drive.

The operating system is divided into two parts. The fundamental part is in the ROM chips provided by the manufacturer. The advanced part is on a disk and called the **disk operating system** (or **DOS**, which is pronounced "doss"). So to use the advanced part of the operating system, you must make sure the computer contains a disk (floppy or hard) containing DOS.

Different computers use different operating systems:

Computers	Which operating systems they use
Apple 2, 2+, 2e, 2c, 2c+, 2GS	**Apple DOS** or **Pro DOS**
Radio Shack TRS-80	**TRSDOS** (pronounced "triss doss")
Apple Mac	**Mac System**
most ancient microcomputers	**Control Program for Microcomputers (CP/M)**
DEC's Vax minicomputers	**Virtual Memory System (VMS)**

Big IBM mainframes use an operating system called **Multiple Virtual Storage (MVS)** or an operating system called the **Virtual Machine with Conversational Monitor System (VM with CMS)**.

IBM PC and clones

Most of IBM's personal computers (such as the IBM PC, IBM PC XT, IBM PC AT, IBM PS/1, and IBM PS/2) use an operating system called **PC-DOS**. Clones use a variant called **MicroSoft DOS** (which is abbreviated as **MS-DOS**, which is pronounced "em ess doss").

Instead of buying PC-DOS or MS-DOS, you can buy a more modern operating system called **Operating System 2 (OS/2)**, but it causes complications and is unpopular.

Many people buy PC-DOS or MS-DOS and then modernize it by adding a supplement called **Microsoft Windows**. Microsoft Windows is *not* an operating system; it's a *supplement* to an operating system. Before buying Microsoft Windows, you must buy PC-DOS or MS-DOS.

A supplement, such as Windows, that modernizes an operating system and hides the system's ugliness is called an **operating-system shell**. PC-DOS, MS-DOS, and Windows are all called **operating environments**.

Unix

AT&T's Bell Laboratories invented an operating system called **Unix**. It's pronounced "you nicks", so it sounds like "eunuchs", which are castrated men. (Be careful! A female computer manager who seems to be saying "get me eunuchs" probably wants an operating system, not castrated men.) "Unix" is an abbreviation for "UNICS", which stands for "UNified Information and Computing System".

The original version of Unix was limited to DEC minicomputers used by just one person at a time. Newer versions of Unix can handle *any* manufacturer's maxi, mini, or micro, even when shared by lots of people at a time.

Microsoft has invented a slightly improved Unix called "e*X*tended U*nix*" or **Xenix** (pronounced "zee nicks"). It runs on the IBM PC and other microcomputers.

Though many programmers adore Unix, it won't outsell MS-DOS, since Unix is harder to learn, runs slower, consumes more memory, costs more, and is having its best features stolen by the latest versions of MS-DOS.

Languages that humans normally speak — such as English, Spanish, French, Russian, and Chinese — are called **natural languages**. They're too complicated for computers to understand.

To communicate with computers, programmers use **computer languages** instead. The most popular computer languages are **BASIC, LOGO, PASCAL, C, DBASE,** and **COBOL**. Each is a tiny *part* of English — a part small enough for the computer to master. To teach the computer one of those tiny languages, you feed the computer a ROM or disk containing definitions of that tiny language's words.

The typical microcomputer's ROM chips contain part of BASIC and part of the operating system. To use the computer fully, you must insert a disk containing the rest of BASIC and DOS.

Different people prefer different languages. Most students prefer LOGO in elementary school, BASIC in high school, PASCAL in college, and C in graduate school. To do accounting, most business executives prefer DBASE on microcomputers, COBOL on maxicomputers.

Although those six languages are the most popular, many others have been invented. Five old languages still in use are **FORTRAN, RPG, LISP, PL/I,** and **SPSS**. Five new languages are **FORTH, PILOT, PROLOG, ADA,** and **MODULA**.

The Secret Guide to Computers tutors you in *all* those languages and more, so you become a virtuoso!

The computer will do whatever you wish — if you tell it how. To tell the computer how to do what you wish, you feed it a **program**, which is a list of instructions, written in BASIC or in some other computer language.

To feed the computer a program, type the program on the keyboard, or buy a disk containing the program and put that disk into the drive. But before buying the disk, make sure it will work with *your* computer. For example, if the disk says "for MS-DOS computers", it will work with an IBM PC but not with an Apple.

A person who invents a program is called a **programmer**. Becoming a programmer is easy: you can become a programmer in just a few minutes! Becoming a *good* programmer takes longer.

You can buy two kinds of programs. The most popular kind is called an **application program**: it handles a specific application, such as payroll or psychotherapy or chess. The other kind of program is called a **system program**: it creates a system that just helps programmers write more programs!

Main applications

An old-fashioned office contains a typewriter, filing cabinet, and calculator. A modern office contains a computer instead.

To make the computer replace your typewriter, buy a **word-processing program**. To replace your filing cabinet, buy a **database program**. To replace your calculator, buy a **spreadsheet program**. Each program typically comes on a set of disks.

Why computerize? To save time! A word-processing program lets you edit mistakes faster than a typewriter. A database program lets you find info faster than thumbing through file cards. A spreadsheet program lets you revise numbers and totals faster than rekeying them on a calculator.

But even the most modern computerized offices still contain typewriters, filing cabinets, and calculators. Those pre-computer relics aren't used much, but they're still used *occasionally*, to accomplish tiny tasks for which a computer would be overkill.

A typewriter is more practical than a computer, if what you're typing is short (a paragraph or less), or if you're typing answers onto a form somebody mailed you. A filing cabinet is more practical than a computer, if you're filing fewer than 100 items, or if you're filing documents that were mailed to you and that would take too long to retype into the computer. A calculator is more practical than a computer if you're manipulating fewer than 10 numbers or writing numbers onto a pre-printed form.

But for *most* tasks, the computer is far superior to pre-computer relics. Here are the details.

Word processing A word-processing program helps you write memos, letters, reports, and books. It also helps you edit what you wrote.

As you type on the keyboard, the screen shows what you typed. By pressing buttons, you can edit what's on the screen and copy it onto paper and onto a disk.

The most popular word-processing program is **Word Perfect**, which lets you perform many tricks. About 60% of all people doing word processing are using Word Perfect. The fanciest versions of Word Perfect require a Mac, a Next computer, an IBM PC, or a clone. Stripped-down versions of Word Perfect are available for the Apple 2 family, Commodore 64, Amiga, Atari ST, minicomputers by DEC and Data General, and IBM mainframes. Discount dealers sell the IBM PC version for about $250; the other versions cost less.

The second most popular word-processing program is **Microsoft Word**. It runs on the Mac and the IBM PC.

Another wonderful word-processing program is **Ami Pro**. Though it's not as famous as Word Perfect of Microsoft Word, people who use Ami Pro are thrilled.

Though Word Perfect, Microsoft Word, and Ami Pro are fancy and popular among experts, they're complex. Many simpler word-processing programs have been invented for beginners.

Databases A database program helps you manipulate long lists of data, such as names, addresses, phone numbers, birthdays, comments about folks you know (your friends, customers, suppliers, employees, students, and teachers), past-due bills, and any other data you wish!

As you type the list of data, the computer automatically copies it onto a disk. The computer lets you edit that data and insert extra data in the middle of the list. The program makes the printer print the data in any order you wish: alphabetical order, ZIP-code order, chronological order, or however else you please.

The program can search through all that data and find, in just a few seconds, the data that's unusual. For example, it can find everybody whose birthday is *today*, or everybody who's blond and under 18, or everybody who lives out-of-state and has owed you more than $30 for over a year.

The best easy-to-use database program is **Q&A** (which stands for "Questions & Answers"). It lists for $399; discount dealers sell it for $189. It also includes an easy-to-use word processor, at no extra charge. It requires an IBM PC or clone.

To computerize your business cheaply and pleasantly, get an IBM PC clone and Q&A. If your business is typical, Q&A is the only applications program you'll ever need, since Q&A includes a top-notch database system and a word processor that's much easier to use than Word Perfect.

If you have a Mac, you can't run Q&A. Instead, get **Filemaker Pro**. It's an easy-to-use program that performs *almost* as many database tricks as Q&A but lacks a word processor. Discount dealers sell it for $265.

<u>What I use</u> Although this book discusses hundreds of application programs, I use only two of them on a daily basis: Q&A and Word Perfect. I use Q&A to run my book business, course business, accounting, and life. To type this book, I could have used Q&A but decided to use Word Perfect instead, because Word Perfect lets me perform extra word-processing tricks that make the book look pretty.

So Q&A and Word Perfect are the only two application programs I need. Maybe you'll discover they're the only application programs *you* need!

<u>DBASE</u> If you need even more database tricks than Q&A performs, invent your *own* database program by using a computer language called **DBASE** (pronounced "dee base"). It resembles BASIC but includes extra vocabulary for handling databases. It's published by the Ashton-Tate division of **Borland**. It runs on the IBM PC.

Another company, **Fox Software**, has invented an improvement on DBASE. The improvement is called **FOXPRO**. It runs on the IBM PC and the Mac. Recently, Fox Software became part of Microsoft.

To run the newest versions of DBASE and FOXPRO, get an IBM PC or clone. Older versions of FOXPRO run on the Mac.

Q&A and DBASE are the two most famous tools for databases on the IBM PC. Q&A is easier than DBASE but has some limitations. If you can live within those limitations, use Q&A; if you can't, you must use DBASE or FOX or a competitor (such as **Alpha**, **Filemaker Pro**, **Approach**, **Access**, or **Paradox**).

The typical business makes the mistake of buying DBASE and hiring a consultant to write DBASE programs. Six months later, the business complains that it's paid the consultant $2000 in fees and the consultant's program *still* doesn't work. The business would have been better off using Q&A, which is so easy it doesn't need a consultant.

<u>Spreadsheets</u> A spreadsheet program handles tables of numbers. For example, it can handle your budget, inventory, general ledger, baseball statistics, and student test scores.

As you type the numbers, the computer puts them onto the screen in neat columns. You can tell the program to compute the totals, subtotals, and percentages and put them on the screen also.

The computer lets you revise the numbers. Whenever you revise a number, the computer instantaneously recalculates all the totals, subtotals, and percentages and shows them on the screen, faster than your eye can blink!

When the numbers on the screen finally appeal to you (for example, your budget finally balances), press a button that makes the printer print onto paper the entire table of numbers, including even the totals, subtotals, and percentages. Pressing another button makes the computer copy the table onto a disk. The most popular spreadsheet programs can also graph the data.

Spreadsheet programs can become weapons that mesmerize people into believing everything you say — even if what you're saying is wrong. For example, suppose you want to submit a budget. If you scribble the budget on a scrap of paper, nobody will take you seriously; but if you put your data into a spreadsheet program that spits out beautifully aligned columns with totals, subtotals, percentages, bar charts, and pie charts, your audience will assume your budget's carefully thought out and applaud it, even though it's just a pretty presentation of the same crude guesses you'd have scribbled on paper.

The most famous spreadsheet program is **Lotus** 1-2-3, which runs on the IBM PC. Version 2.4 lists for $495, but discount dealers sell it for $289.

For a fancier spreadsheet program, get a competitor called **Quattro Pro**, which discount dealers sell for just $40!

The fanciest spreadsheet program is **Excel**, invented by Microsoft. It requires either a souped-up IBM PC (containing containing Microsoft Windows) or a Mac. Discount dealers sell it for $295.

For the Apple 2 family, the most famous spreadsheet program is **Appleworks**, which also handles word processing and databases.

The typical spreadsheet program requires that the entire spreadsheet fit in the computer's RAM. If your spreadsheet contains too many rows and columns to fit in RAM, you'll want to buy more RAM. But you might be wiser to give up the spreadsheet program and switch to a database program instead, since database programs store data on disks instead of in RAM. Database programs produce the same pretty tables as spreadsheet programs, so your boss won't know you switched.

Compulsive perfectionism

The most successful business programs are the ones that make work become fun, by turning the work into a video game. That's why word processing programs and spreadsheet programs are so successful — they let you move letters and numbers around the screen, edit the errors by "zapping" them, and let you press a button that makes the screen explode with totals, subtotals, counts, and other information.

Sometimes, word processing can be *too* much fun. Since it's so much fun to edit on a word processor, people using word processors edit more thoroughly than people using typewriters or pens. Word processing fosters **compulsive perfectionism**.

Word-processed documents wind up better written than non-electronic documents but take longer to finish. According to a survey by Colorado State, people using word processors take about 30% longer to generate memos than people using pens, and the word-processed memos are needlessly long.

Graphics

The first easy-to-use graphics program was **Mac Paint**, developed by Apple Computer Incorporated for the Mac. It lets you use the Mac's mouse to draw pictures on the screen, copy them onto paper, and perform special effects. It's fun. It's the program that made the Mac popular.

Mac Paint has been replaced by dozens of fancier programs that run on the Mac, IBM PC, and all other popular computers.

Architects and engineers draw blueprints by using a program for **computer-aided design (CAD)**.

Desktop publishing

A program that lets you combine graphics with text — to create posters, ads, and newsletters — is called a **page-layout program** or **desktop-publishing program**. The fanciest desktop publishing programs are **Aldus Pagemaker** and **Quark XPress**. Each runs on the IBM PC and Mac. They let you easily create headlines and multiple columns with graphics.

For the IBM PC, a pleasant alternative is **Ami Pro**, which is a word-processing program that includes many desktop-publishing commands.

Integrated programs

Instead of buying a word-processing program and also a database program and also a spreadsheet program, you can buy a single "monster" program that does a little bit of everything! Such a program's called an **integrated program**.

The best integrated programs for the IBM PC are **Q&A, Microsoft Works**, and **PFS First Choice**. Here's how they compare.

Q&A is the best at handling databases. Q&A's main weakness is that it does *not* handle spreadsheets at all.

Microsoft Works is the best at handling word processing and spreadsheets. Its main weakness is that it requires a peppy computer and a mouse to run well.

PFS First Choice is the easiest to learn how to use, but you'll outgrow it soon, since it lacks advanced features.

Each IBM clone built by Tandy comes with an integrated program called **Deskmate**. For the Apple 2 family, the most popular integrated program is **Appleworks**.

Creative applications

You can buy programs that teach you new skills, produce music, play games, and perform wild tricks.

Vertical software

Software that can be used by a *wide variety* of businesses is called **horizontal software**. Programs for word processing, databases, and spreadsheets are all examples of horizontal software.

Software targeted to a specific industry is called **vertical software**. Programs specifically for doctors, lawyers, and real-estate management are all examples of vertical software.

Vertical software is expensive because it can't be mass-marketed to the general public and isn't available from discount dealers. The typical vertical-market program costs about $2000, whereas the typical horizontal-market program costs about $200 from discount dealers.

Until the price of vertical software declines, use horizontal software instead. With just a few hours of effort, you can customize horizontal software to fit your own specific needs.

Viruses

Some nasty programmers have invented **computer viruses**, which are programs that purposely damage your other programs and sneakily copy themselves onto every disk that you use. To avoid catching a virus, make sure that the only software entering your computer comes from a reputable, safe source.

DATA

When you buy a program, it comes on a floppy disk. Here's how to use that **program disk**, if you have just one disk drive.

First, put the program disk into the drive, and press some buttons (or type a word) that makes the computer look at the disk. (To find out which buttons to press, read the manual that came with the program.)

When the computer finishes looking at the disk, remove the disk from the drive.

Insert a second disk, called the **data disk**. At first, the data disk contains no information; it's blank. Put your fingers on the keyboard and type the **data** that you want the computer to manipulate. The computer will display your data on the screen and copy it onto the data disk.

At night, before you go to bed, hide the data disk (which contains all the personal data you fed the computer) to protect it from any accidents and from any competitors, vandals, toddlers, pets, and goblins that go bump in the night.

Two drives

If your computer has *two* floppy disk drives, put the program disk in the main drive ("drive A") and the data disk in the other drive ("drive B").

If your computer has one floppy disk drive plus one hard disk drive, put the program disk in the floppy disk drive, copy its program onto the hard disk, then use just the hard disk. The hard disk holds the program and data.

Will your computer be pleasant to use? The answer depends mainly on which software you buy. Software companies will influence your life more than IBM, Apple, or any other hardware manufacturer.

The thirteen dominant software companies are **Microsoft**, **Novell**, **Lotus**, **Borland**, **Symantec**, **Oracle**, **Computer Associates**, **Intuit**, **Electronic Arts**, **Broderbund**, **Claris**, **Adobe**, and **Autodesk**. Here's why. . . .

Microsoft

The most important software company is **Microsoft**, which takes in about 4 billion dollars of revenue per year. It makes the most popular operating system (which is **MS-DOS**). The company's main founder, Bill Gates, became a billionaire when he was 30 years old and appeared on the cover of Time Magazine. Now Bill is 38 and worth 7 billion dollars. He doesn't have that much cash in his pocket, of course: most of his billions are invested in Microsoft stock.

Microsoft is the most diversified software company: besides selling MS-DOS, it also sells other operating environments (**Windows** and **Xenix**), programming languages (Microsoft BASIC, FORTRAN, COBOL, C, and others), a word-processing program (**Microsoft Word**), database programs (**Access** and **Fox Pro**), a spreadsheet program (**Excel**), an integrated program (**Microsoft Works**), a computerized encyclopedia (**Encarta**), and a wide variety of other software. It's the main software publisher for the IBM PC and Mac. It also wrote the versions of BASIC used by the Apple 2 family, Commodore Amiga, Commodore 64, and Radio Shack TRS-80.

Microsoft continually develops new products because of pressure from competitors. For example, Microsoft's been forced to improve Microsoft Word because of competition from Word Perfect and improve Microsoft C because of competition from Borland's C. Those continual pressures to improve keep Microsoft a vibrant, dynamically changing company.

Novell

Novell makes **Netware**, which is software that lets you wire computers together so they can communicate with each other.

In 1994, Novell bought **Word Perfect Corporation**, which makes the most popular word-processing program, Word Perfect. Novell's purchase was natural, since both companies are in Utah. Word Perfect Corporation sold out to Novell because Word Perfect Corporation's been having financial trouble, since many customers have been switching to Microsoft Word, which has been improving dramatically.

Novell also bought a product called **Quattro Pro**, which was invented by a company called **Borland**. Borland sold that product to Novell because Borland was having financial trouble competing against Microsoft.

Hey, if all of Microsoft's competitors have financial problems competing against Microsoft, maybe Novell will buy them all!

Altogether, Novell takes in about 3 billion dollars per year.

Lotus

Lotus makes the most popular spreadsheet program (which is **1-2-3**). For too many years, Lotus sat on its laurels, and customers gradually began to switch to competitors such as Microsoft Excel and Quattro Pro. We expected Lotus to gradually die.

But during the 1990's, Lotus displayed good taste and made wide moves: it dramatically improved 1-2-3; it bought a company called **Samna**, which made the nicest word-processing program (**Ami Pro**), so Ami Pro became a Lotus product; it began selling an easy-to-use presentation-graphics program, **Freehand**; and it began selling a product called **Notes**, which helps people send electronic mail to each other and edit each other's documents.

Now Lotus is doing okay. It takes in about a billion dollars per year.

Borland

Borland was started by Philippe Kahn, who grew up in France. To study math, he went to a university in Zurich, Switzerland, where he got curious about computers and decided to take a computer class.

The university offered two introductory classes: one explained how to program using a language called **PL/I**, the other explained **PASCAL**. Since PASCAL was brand new then, nobody had heard of it, so 200 students signed up for PL/I and just 5 students signed up for PASCAL. Philippe signed up for PASCAL because he hated big classes. His professor was PASCAL's inventor, Niklaus Wirth.

In 1983, Philippe went to California and started a computer company. Since he was an illegal alien, he tried to pretend he was thoroughly American and named his company **Borland**, in honor of the land that produced astronaut Frank Borman. His first product was **Turbo PASCAL**, which he had created back in Europe with the help of two friends.

Most other versions of PASCAL were selling for hundreds of dollars. Philippe read a book saying people buy mail-order items on impulse only if priced under $50, so he charged $49.95. The book and Philippe were right: at $49.95, Turbo PASCAL became a smashing success.

Later, Philippe improved Turbo PASCAL and raised its price to $149.95. He also bought other software publishers and merged them into Borland, so Borland became a huge company.

Philippe has occasionally experimented with dropping prices. For example, it dropped the price of its spreadsheet program, **Quattro Pro**, to just $49.95, even though Quattro Pro was in some ways better than 1-2-3, which Lotus was selling for about $300. The head of Microsoft, Bill Gates, said that the competitor that worries him the most is Borland, because he's afraid Philippe will pull another publicity stunt and drop prices below $50 again, forcing Microsoft to do the same.

Keep it up, Philippe! We need more clowns like you!

During the 1980's, Borland bought two companies that invented wonderful database programs: **Reflex** and **Paradox**. Recently Borland stopped selling Reflex, but Paradox lives on.

Paradox's main competitor was **DBASE**, published by a company called **Ashton-Tate**. Philippe decided to win the competition against Ashton-Tate the easy way: he *bought* Ashton-Tate, so now Borland publishes both Paradox and DBASE. Philippe said he bought Ashton-Tate mainly to get his hands on Ashton-Tate's mailing list, so he could sell DBASE users on the idea of converting to Paradox.

But Philippe paid too much for Ashton-Tate, whose products, employees, and mailing lists were all becoming stale. Since Ashton-Tate was a bigger company than Borland, Philippe had to borrow lots of money to buy Ashton-Tate, and he had trouble paying it back. Buying Ashton-Tate was Philippe's biggest mistake.

By 1994, Philippe was having trouble competing against Microsoft's rapidly improving products and also having trouble repaying the money he'd borrowed to finance the take-over of Ashton-Tate. Financially strapped, he sold Novell his crown jewel, Quattro Pro, gave Novell the right to make a million copies of Paradox.

Novell's founder, Ray Noorda, said candidly he wasn't thrilled by Quattro Pro but wanted to buy it anyway, just as an excuse to give Philippe some money, so Philippe could stay in business and scare Microsoft, so Bill Gates would devote his energy to fighting Philippe instead of fighting Novell.

Why fight?

See, no matter how rich the computer guys get, they still act like a bunch of tussling toddlers. I'm waiting for their mama to say, "Boys, boys, will you please stop fighting, shake hands, and make up!"

If Israel can make peace with the PLO and Jordan, why can't Bill Gates make peace with his competitors? Answer: they're all greedy — and Bill is brash. (For example, during an interview with CBS's Connie Chung, he walked out when she mispronounced "DOS" and asked a pointed question about a competitor.)

But Bill's actually somewhat glad at his competitors' successes, since Microsoft *needs* to have enough successful competitors to prevent the Justice Department from accusing Microsoft of being a monopoly.

By letting several competitors invent new ideas and bring them all to market, we consumers get to choose for ourselves which ideas are best — and vote on them with our dollars — rather than kowtow to a single dictator.

Symantec

My favorite database program, **Q&A**, is published by **Symantec**.

Like Lotus, Symantec shows good taste in acquisitions: it bought two companies making good versions of the C programming language (**Lightspeed** and **Zortech**) and also bought two companies making **DOS utility programs** that fix DOS's weaknesses (**Peter Norton Software** and **Central Point Software**).

Symantec tries hard to improve all those acquired products, but I wish it would improve Q&A instead! I'm sad to see Q&A, the world's best database program, be neglected and fall into obsolescence.

Specialized companies

Oracle and **Computer Associates (CA)** make software that runs on computers of all sizes: maxicomputers, minicomputers, and microcomputers. Oracle's software handles databases; CA's software handles accounting (such as bill-paying, bill-collecting, inventory, and payroll).

Intuit makes programs that handle accounting on microcomputers. Intuit's programs are cheap: under $100. Intuit's most popular accounting programs are **Quicken** (which tracks expenses and balances your checkbook), **Quickbooks** (which handles all major business accounting), and **Turbo Tax** (which helps you fill in your 1040 income-tax form for the IRS). Turbo Tax used to be published by a company called **Chipsoft**, but Intuit bought Chipsoft in 1994. Now Microsoft is trying to buy Intuit.

Electronic Arts and **Brøderbund** make the best educational games and low-cost tools for budding young artists and musicians. The two companies planned to merge but changed their minds, so they're still separate.

Claris, which is owned by Apple, makes the **Filemaker Pro** database (which is as easy as Q&A) and the **Claris Works** integrated package (which resembles Microsoft Works). Claris's programs run on the Mac. Out of pity for you folks who don't have Macs, Claris also sells versions that run on IBM PC clones using Windows.

Adobe makes **Postscript** software (used in many laser printers). In 1994, Adobe bought **Aldus** (the company that invented the first desktop-publishing program, **Pagemaker**).

Autodesk publishes **Autocad**, which is the fanciest program for handling computer-aided design (CAD).

You'll want four kinds of software: an operating system (which teaches the CPU how to handle the keyboard, screen, printer, and disks); a computer language (such as BASIC); application programs (such as a word-processing program, a spreadsheet program, and a database program); and data.

When shopping for a computer, beware: its advertised price usually does *not* include all four kinds of software. Ask the seller which software is included and how much the other software costs.

The typical fancy program (such as a word-processing program, database program, or spreadsheet program) has a **list price** of $495. That's also called the **manufacturer's suggested retail price (MSRP)**. If you buy the program directly from the software's publisher, that's the price you'll pay. (You'll also pay about $7 for shipping & handling. If the publisher has a sales office in your state, you'll also charged for sales tax, even if you're phoning the manufacturer's out-of-state headquarters.)

That list price is made ridiculously high as an marketing ploy, to give you the impression that the program is fancy enough to be worth a lot of money.

But if you walk into a typical computer store, you will *not* pay $495 for the program. Instead, you'll pay $299. That's called the **street price** because it's the price you see when you walk down the street and peek in the windows of computer stores. (You'll also pay sales tax.)

Instead of charging $299, mail-order dealers charge slightly less: $279. That's called the **mail-order price**. (You'll also pay about $7 for shipping & handling, but you won't pay tax if the mail-order company is out-of-state.) Another way to get that kind of price is to visit a discount computer superstore such as Comp USA.

Version upgrades

If you already own an older version of the program, you can switch to the new version cheaply, by asking for the **version upgrade**, which costs just $99. You can order the version upgrade at your local computer store, or from mail-order dealers, or directly from the program's publisher. The most aggressive dealers (such as Comp USA) charge slightly less: $95.

To qualify for the version upgrade, you must *prove* that you already own an older version of the program. You can do that in several ways. . . .

If you're ordering directly from the program's publisher, the program's publisher will check its records to verify that you had sent in your registration card for the previous version. If you're ordering at a local computer store, bring in the official instruction manual that came with the old version: the store will rip out the manual's first page (the title page) and mail it to the publisher. If you lost that manual, you can instead give the store Disk 1 of the old version's set of disks. The store needs the *original* title page or disk; copies are not accepted. If you're ordering from a mail-order dealer, send the dealer the title page by mail or fax.

Some manufacturers (such as Microsoft) use a simpler way to qualify you for the version upgrade: when you install the new version, it automatically searches your computer's hard disk for the old version and refuses to run if the old version is missing.

If you bought the old version shortly before the new version came out, you can get the new version free! Just phone the publisher and ask for the **free version upgrade**. Here's how you prove you bought the old version shortly before the new version came out (where "shortly before" is usually defined as meaning "within 60 days"): mail either your dated sales slip or a "free version-upgrade certificate" that came in the old version's box. Though the upgrade is "free", you must pay an exhorbitant charge for shipping and handling ($10 for just the disks, $30 for disks plus manuals).

Competitive upgrades

If you don't own an older version of the program, you can't get the version-upgrade price. Here's the best you can do: if you already own a competing program (such as a different brand of word processor that competes against the word processor you're trying to buy), ask for the **competitive-upgrade price**. It's usually $129, which is just slightly higher than the version-upgrade price. Get it from your local store, mail-order dealer, or directly from the publisher.

To prove you qualify for the competitive-upgrade price, provide the title page or Disk 1 of the competing program (or have Microsoft's software automatically scan for such programs).

Copying software

If you buy a program, you should make backup copies of the disks. Use the backup copies in case the original disks get damaged.

You're *not* allowed to give copies of the disks to your friends. That's against the law! If your friends want to use the program, they must buy it from the software publisher or a dealer, so that the programmer receives royalties.

If you give copies to your friends and become a lawbreaker, you're called a **pirate**; making the copies is called **piracy**; the copies are called **pirated software** or **hot software**. Don't be a pirate! Don't distribute hot software!

Some software publishers use tricks that make the computer refuse to copy the program. Those tricks are called **copy protection**; the software is **copy protected**. But even if the software publisher doesn't use such tricks, it's still against the law to make copies of the program for other people, since the program is still copy*righted*.

If your friends want to try a program before buying it, don't give them a copy of the program! Instead, tell your friends to visit you and use the program while they sit at your computer. That's legal, and it also lets you help your friends figure out how to use the software.

If you buy a version upgrade, you're *not* allowed to give the older version to a friend to use on a different computer. You must destroy the older version — or keep it just for emergencies, in case the newer version stops working. Some software publishers, such as Word Perfect, let you donate the old versions to schools, but just after getting the publisher's permission.

Demo disks

Besides sitting at a friend's computer, another way to "try before you buy" is to phone the program's publisher and ask for a free **demo disk**.

Although some demo disks are just useless animated ads, the best publishers provide useful demo disks (called **trial-size versions**) that closely imitate the full versions. For example, the typical trial-size version of a word-processing program has nearly all the features of the full version, but it refuses to print memos that are more than a page long and refuses to copy your writing onto a disk.

Trial-size versions are nicknamed **crippled software**, because each trial-size version has one or two abilities cut off. Playing with crippled software is a great way to give yourself a free education!

Freeware

Software that you're allowed to copy and use freely is called **freeware**. For example, most demo disks and trial-size versions are freeware.

Most software invented by schools, government agencies, and computer clubs is freeware. Ask!

Shareware

Some software, called **shareware**, comes with this plea: although the author lets you copy the software and try it, you're encouraged to mail the author a contribution if you like what you tried.

The suggested contribution, typically $25, is called a **registration fee**. It makes you a **registered user** and puts you on the author's mailing list, so the author can mail you a printed manual and newer versions of the software.

Though most shareware authors merely "ask" for contributions, other shareware authors "demand" that you send a contribution if you use the software for longer than a month. Software for which a contribution is "demanded" is called **guiltware** — because if you don't send the contribution, the author says you're guilty of breaking the law.

To get shareware, copy it from a friend. If none of your friends own the shareware you want, buy the disks from a computer club or store for about $5 per disk; but remember that the $5 pays for just the disk, not the registration fee that you're honor-bound to mail in if you extensively use the program.

Special deals

If your office wants many employees to use a program, ask the publisher for a **site license**, which permits your company to make copies for all employees in the office. But the employees are *not* allowed to take the copies home: the copies must all be used at the same site.

If you're in a school and trying to teach kids how to use a program, ask the publisher for a trial-size version or **educational version** or **educational site license**.

IBM - COMPATIBLES

The most popular microcomputers are made by IBM and imitators.

How IBM arose

IBM bases its entire marketing strategy on one word: *react*. IBM never creates a new kind of computer; instead, IBM watches its competitors' products, notices which ones sell well, and then designs a product that meets the same needs better.

Even IBM's own name is a reaction. IBM was started by Tom Watson. He'd been a salesman for National Cash Register (NCR) but was fired, so he took over a competing company (CTR) and vowed to make it even bigger than National Cash Register. To be bigger than "National", he called his company "International"; to be bigger than a "Cash Register" company, he bragged that his company would sell *all* kinds of "Business Machines". That's how the name "International Business Machine Corp." — IBM — was hatched. IBM quickly outgrew NCR.

IBM sold lots of business machines, especially to the U.S. Census Bureau. But in 1951, Remington Rand Corp. (which later merged with Sperry) developed the Univac computer and convinced the Census to use it instead of IBM's non-computerized equipment. To react, IBM quickly invented its own computers, which were more practical than the Univac. IBM quickly became the #1 computer company — and Sperry's Univac dropped to #2.

All of IBM's early computers were large. IBM ignored the whole concept of microcomputers for many years. IBM's first microcomputers, the IBM 5100 and IBM System 23, weren't taken seriously — not even by IBM.

IBM PC

When lots of IBM's customers began buying Apple 2 microcomputers to do Visicalc spreadsheets, IBM reacted by developing an improved microcomputer, called the **IBM Personal Computer (IBM PC)**, which did everything that Apple 2 computers could do, but better.

To invent the IBM PC, IBM created three secret research teams who competed against each other. The winner was the research team headed by Philip "Don" Estridge in Boca Raton, Florida. His team examined everything created by the other microcomputer companies (Apple, Radio Shack, Commodore, etc.) and combined their best ideas, to produce a relatively low-cost computer better than all competitors.

Don's team developed the IBM PC secretly. IBM didn't announce it to the public until August 12, 1981.

The IBM PC was a smashing success: IBM quickly became the #1 microcomputer company — and Apple dropped to #2.

The IBM PC became the best-selling microcomputer for business. More high-quality business programs became available for the IBM PC than for any other microcomputer. It became the standard against which all other microcomputers were compared. Even today, to use the best business programs you must buy an IBM PC or clone.

The IBM PC consists of three parts: a system unit (which contains most of the circuitry), a keyboard, and a monitor. Wires run from the keyboard and monitor to the system unit.

Keyboard The IBM PC's keyboard contains 83 keys, as follows. . . .

26 keys contain the letters of the alphabet.

10 keys (in the top row) contain the digits.

10 keys (on the keyboard's right side) form a numeric keypad. It contains the digits rearranged to imitate a calculator.

13 keys contain symbols for math and punctuation.

14 keys give you control. They let you edit your mistakes, create blank spaces and capitals, etc.

10 function keys (labeled F1, F2, F3, F4, F5, F6, F7, F8, F9, and F10) can be programmed to mean whatever you wish!

The keyboard was designed by Don Estridge personally. To fit all those keys on the small keyboard, he had to make the RETURN and SHIFT keys smaller than typists liked. Above the top row of keys, he put a shelf to hold pencils; to make room for that shelf, he had to put the 10 function keys at the left side of the keyboard, even though it would have been more natural to put the F1 key near the 1 key, the F2 key near the 2 key, etc.

System unit The IBM PC's system unit contains a 63½-watt **power supply** (which transforms AC current to DC) and a **motherboard**. On the motherboard, IBM puts the CPU, RAM chips, ROM chips, and support chips.

The motherboard also includes 5 slots that hold printed-circuit cards. The motherboard's 62 wires that run to and through the slots are called the **bus**. 8 of those wires carry data; the other 54 wires are "bureaucratic overhead" that helps control the flow. Since just eight wires carry data, the bus is called an **8-bit data bus**, its slots are called **8-bit slots**, and the printed-circuit cards that you put into the slots are called **8-bit cards**.

The CPU, which is on the motherboard, is an Intel 8088 running at a speed of 4.77 million cycles per second (4.77 **megahertz**).

In the original IBM PC, the motherboard could hold 4 rows of 16K RAM chips. 1 row of chips was included in the base price; the other 3 rows of chips cost extra. If you paid the extra cost and got all 4 rows of chips, you had a total of 64K.

Later, IBM improved the motherboard, so that it uses 64K chips instead of 16K chips. The 4 rows of 64K chips produce a grand total of 256K.

To expand beyond 256K, you must buy a **memory card**, which contains sockets for holding extra RAM chips.

The motherboard contains five 8K ROM chips. One of them contains the BIOS; the other four contain BASIC.

The motherboard includes a hookup to your home's cassette tape recorder, to make the tape recorder imitate a slow disk drive. For faster speed, you must buy a disk drive (which costs extra), and a controller card to connect the disk drive to. The original IBM PC was limited to two 5¼-inch disk drives, and each disk held just 160K. Later, IBM improved the disk system, so that each disk could hold 360K. (To make the improvement, IBM switched to *double*-sided disks and divided each track into 9 sectors instead of 8.)

Monitor The IBM PC's base price doesn't include a monitor — or even a video card to attach the monitor to.

When IBM announced the IBM PC, it announced two kinds of video cards. One kind, the **Monochrome Display Adapter (MDA)**, attaches to a TTL monochrome monitor. The other kind, the **Color/Graphics Adapter (CGA)**, attaches to an RGB color monitor instead.

Each of those cards gives you a hidden bonus. Hiding on the MDA card is a printer port, so you can attach a printer. Hiding on the CGA card is an RCA jack, so you can attach a composite color monitor or a TV switch box.

Why the IBM PC became popular

To invent the IBM PC, IBM combined all the best ideas that other computer companies had invented previously. IBM did it all legally: IBM found the best hardware and software companies and paid them manufacturing fees and royalties. IBM listened well: IBM put into the IBM PC all the inexpensive features that business users were begging computer companies to provide.

IBM had originally planned to charge a high price for the IBM PC; but in August 1981, a week before IBM announced the IBM PC to the world, IBM's top management decided to slash the prices by 25%. So the IBM PC was not only nice but also priced 25% less than the rumor mill had expected. Customers were thrilled and bought IBM PC's quickly.

At first, very few programs were available for it, but IBM turned that liability into a virtue: IBM ran ads telling programmers that since IBM hadn't written enough programs for the PC, programmers could get rich by writing their own. Because of those ads, many programmers bought the PC and wrote thousands of programs for it. All those programs eventually increased the computer's popularity even further.

IBM PC XT & clones

In March 1983, IBM announced the **IBM PC eXTended (IBM PC XT)**.

It resembles the IBM PC but includes a larger power supply (135 watts instead of 63½) and more expansion slots (8 instead of 5). The larger power supply allows the XT to handle a hard disk.

When IBM began selling the XT, IBM included a floppy disk drive, a 10-megabyte 85-millisecond hard disk, and serial port in the base price, but IBM later made them optional.

Many companies sell XT clones. The typical XT clone is better than the original XT in several ways. . . .

Keyboard Most clones have extra-large RETURN and SHIFT keys, so your fingers can hit those keys more easily.

Power supply In most clones, the power supply is extra-large (150 watts instead of 135).

CPU Instead of using an 8088 CPU, most clones use an 8088-1 CPU, which thinks twice as fast (10 megahertz instead of 4.77). Clones using that double-speed CPU are called **turbo XT clones**.

Memory DOS easily handles 640K of RAM and a 30-megabyte hard disk. (To go beyond those limits, you must use tricks.) The typical clone attains those limits: its motherboard contains 640K of RAM, and its hard disk holds 30 megabytes. IBM's XT disk holds only a third as much. Moreover, the typical clone's hard disk is quicker: its average seek time is 65 milliseconds instead of 85.

Monitor A company called **Hercules** invented a video card that improves on IBM's MDA card.

Like the MDA card, the Hercules card produces pretty characters on a TTL monochrome monitor and includes a parallel printer port. The Hercules card has this advantage: it can generate graphics.

Several companies make video cards imitating the Hercules card. Those imitations are called **Hercules-compatible graphics cards**.

The typical XT clone includes a TTL monochrome monitor attached to a Hercules-compatible graphics card.

IBM PC AT & clones

In August 1984, IBM announced the **IBM PC with Advanced Technology (IBM PC AT)**. It runs several times as fast as the XT because it contains a faster CPU and disk drives. Other companies have developed AT clones that go even faster.

CPU The CPU is an Intel 80286, which beats the 8088 by performing more cycles per second and also processing about 3 times as much information per cycle.

In IBM's original version of the AT, the 80286 CPU performed 6 million cycles per second (6 megahertz). In 1986, IBM switched to a faster 80286 that runs at 8 megahertz. Clones go even faster: 12 megahertz!

Bus The bus is 16-bit. That bus is called the **AT bus** or the **Industry Standard Architecture bus (ISA bus)**. Into its 16-bit slots, you can put 16-bit cards or old XT-style 8-bit cards.

Hard drives The AT handles faster hard drives than the XT.

IBM's original hard drive for the AT had a 40-millisecond average seek time and held 20 megabytes. That drive, built for IBM by a company called **CMI**, was unreliable. IBM eventually switched to a different supplier, and CMI went bankrupt.

Today's clones contain reliable drives that go even faster (28 milliseconds) and hold even more (40 megabytes and beyond).

Floppy drives The AT's floppy drive squeezes 1.2 megabytes onto high-density 5¼-inch floppy disks. That drive can also read the 360K disks created by XT computers, but it can*not* reliably create a 360K disk to send to an XT computer.

The typical computerist puts *two* floppy drives into the AT. The first drive deals mainly with 1.2 megabyte disks. The other drive is an XT-style 360K drive, which sits in the AT just to communicate to XT computers.

Keyboard The AT's original keyboard had 84 keys. Typists liked it better than the PC and XT keyboards, because it had larger RETURN and SHIFT keys.

In 1986, IBM switched to a larger keyboard having 101 keys. Its function keys (F1, F2, etc.) were in the top row (near the pencil ledge) instead of at the left.

Main power supply The AT's main power supply is 192 watts. Clones use power supplies that are slightly larger (200 watts).

SETUP When you first buy an AT, you (or your dealer) must run the **SETUP program**, which comes on a disk or in a ROM chip. That program makes the AT ask you how much RAM you bought, which monitor and disk drives you bought, and whether you bought a math coprocessor. The AT copies your answers into a CMOS RAM chip, powered by a battery sitting in a holder just left of the main power supply.

Even when you turn off the computer's main power switch, the CMOS RAM chip keeps remembering your answers — until its battery runs out after 4 years (or 1 year in some clones). Then the computer displays the wrong date and time and won't let you use the hard disk — until you run the SETUP program again, preferably with a fresh battery.

Improved graphics & PS/2

In September 1984, IBM announced an improved color video system. It consists of a video card called the **Enhanced Graphics Adapter (EGA)** and a compatible color monitor (called an **EGA monitor**). You can put an EGA card into the IBM PC, IBM PC XT, or IBM PC AT.

The EGA system is better than CGA, because EGA can display more colors and finer resolution (more dots per inch), and EGA obeys the computer's commands faster.

At the same time, IBM announced an even fancier video system, called the **Professional Graphics Controller (PGC)**, but it was too expensive to be popular.

On April 2, 1987, IBM announced a whole new series of computers, called the **Personal System 2 (PS/2)**, which ran the same programs as the PC but added better graphics. Shortly afterwards, IBM stopped manufacturing its old classic computers (the IBM PC, IBM PC XT, and IBM PC AT).

The classic computers used 5¼-inch floppy disks. The PS/2 computers use 3½-inch floppy disks instead, which take up less space on your desk, are sturdier, hold more bytes per square inch, and consume less electricity.

Different models The cheapest PS/2 computer is called the **PS/2 model 25**. The most expensive PS/2 computer is called the **PS/2 model 95**. Between those models — the 25 and the 95 — you can choose many others.

By June 1991, IBM had invented these models:

Models	CPU	Bus	Style	Video	Floppy
25, 30	8086	XT	desktop	MCGA	720K
25/286, 30/286	286	AT	desktop	VGA	1440K
50, 50Z	286	MCA	desktop	VGA	1440K
60	286	MCA	tower	VGA	1440K
35, 40	386SX	AT	desktop	VGA	1440K
L40	386SX	AT	notebook	VGA	1440K
55	386SX	MCA	desktop	VGA	1440K
57	386SX	MCA	desktop	VGA	2880K
65	386SX	MCA	tower	VGA	1440K
70	386DX	MCA	desktop	VGA	1440K
P70	386DX	MCA	luggable	VGA	1440K
80	386DX	MCA	tower	VGA	1440K
P75	486	MCA	luggable	XGA	1440K
90	486	MCA	desktop	XGA	1440K
95	486	MCA	tower	XGA	1440K

Towers of power The model 95 is a **tower** that gets erected on the floor underneath your desk. It's one of IBM's biggest erections. Its electrical juices surge through the cables that run from the tower up to the monitor and keyboard. Since it can service more add-on printed-circuit cards than the model 90 (which is a desktop), computerists call the model 95 an **expandable** version of the model 90. Ooh, how you'll love the expansion! That's why it's nicknamed the "stud".

The model 80 is a tower version of the model 70. The model 60 is a tower version of the model 50. The 65 is a tower version of the 55.

Model 50Z The **model 50Z** contains faster RAM chips than the model 50, so that the model 50Z's CPU never has to wait for the RAM chips to catch up. The "Z" stands for "zero wait states".

Floppy drive In models containing an 8086 CPU, the 3½-inch floppy drive is double-density (DD), so it puts 720K on a disk. In most other models, the 3½-inch floppy drive is high-density (HD), so it puts 1440K on a disk. The model 57 contains an experimental 3½-inch floppy drive that's **extra-high density (ED)**, so it puts 2880K on a disk.

Bus The models containing an 8086 CPU use the same 8-bit bus as the old IBM PC and IBM PC XT. All other under-50 models use the IBM PC AT 16-bit bus.

Models 50 and up contain a new style of bus, called the **Micro Channel**, using a technology called **Micro Channel Architecture (MCA)**. The Micro Channel transmits data faster than the old bus. It includes 16-bit and 32-bit slots. Unfortunately, the Micro Channel's 16-bit slots are a different size than the 16-bit slots in the IBM PC AT; you ca*nnot* put an IBM PC, XT, or AT card into a Micro Channel slot.

IBM holds a patent on the Micro Channel bus. Clone companies that copy the Micro Channel bus pay IBM a licensing fee. Other clone companies use the AT bus (ISA bus) instead, or a new 32-bit version of it (the **Extended ISA bus**, which is called the **EISA bus**, pronounced "ees uh bus"), or an even faster 32-bit version (the **Video Electronics Standards Association local bus**, which is called the **VESA local bus** or **VL bus**), or the fastest version (the **Peripheral Component Interconnect bus**, which is called the **PCI bus** and used mainly in computers containing a Pentium CPU).

MCGA The models containing an 8086 CPU also contain a chip called the **Multi-Color Graphics Array (MCGA)**, which produces nice graphics.

According to the laws of physics, all colors can be created by mixing red, green, and blue light in various proportions. The MCGA lets you create your own color by mixing an amount of red from 0 to 63, an amount of green from 0 to 63, and an amount of blue from 0 to 63; so altogether, the number of possible colors you can create is "64 times 64 times 64", which is 262,144.

After you create your favorite colors, the computer will let you display 256 of them on the screen simultaneously. To position those colors on the screen, you use a coordinate system permitting an X value from 0 to 319 and a Y value from 0 to 199.

If you're willing to use just 2 colors instead of 256, the computer will let you do higher-resolution drawing, in which the X value goes from 0 to 639 (so you have 640 choices) and the Y value goes from 0 to 479 (so you have 480 choices). That's called **640-by-480 resolution**.

<u>VGA</u> The models containing a 286 or 386 CPU contain a fancier graphics chip, called the **Video Graphics Array (VGA)**. Its 256-color mode is the same as MCGA's, but its high-resolution mode permits 16 colors instead of 2.

IBM's competitors sell clones whose graphics are even better than VGA! Besides giving you VGA's high resolution of 640-by-480, they give you an even higher resolution of 800-by-600 (called **800 VGA** or **VGA Plus**) and an even higher resolution of 1024-by-768 (called **1024 VGA** or **Super VGA** or **SVGA**). The fanciest clones give you a resolution of 1280-by-1024 (called **1280 VGA** or sometimes **Super-Duper VGA**).

Instead of giving you 262,144 colors, the fanciest clones give you 16,777,216 colors (by letting the red, green, and blue each range up to 255 instead of 63).

Since 16,777,216 colors are even more than the human eye can distinguish, clones that have 16,777,216 colors are said to have **true color**. They're also said to have **24-bit color** (because to distinguish among 16,777,216 colors, the computer must store each color as a 24-bit number).

If you buy a clone containing one of those souped-up VGA systems, make sure the VGA card contains **512K or 1M or 2M of video RAM** instead of just 256K. You need that extra RAM to get lots of colors at the super-high resolutions:

Video RAM	How many colors you can see simultaneously
256K	256 colors at 640x400; 16 colors at 800x600; 2 colors at 1280x1024
512K	256 colors at 640x480; 16 colors at 1024x768; 2 colors at 1280x1024
1M	16,777,216 colors at 640x480; 65,536 at 800x600; 256 at 1024x768; 16 at 1280x1024
2M	16,777,216 colors at 800x600; 65,536 at 1024x768; 256 at 1280x1024

Make sure the VGA card is 16-bit instead of 8-bit, so it can accept 16 bits of information at once. Then it can handle all those colors and dots *quickly!*

If the video is 1024x768 or 1280x1024, make sure it's **non-interlaced (NI)**. If it's **interlaced (I)**, it will flicker annoyingly when used at high resolution.

When buying a color monitor for VGA (or VGA Plus or Super VGA), make sure the monitor's **dot pitch** (distance between adjacent dots) is small: no bigger than .31 millimeters. If the dot pitch is bigger than .31 millimeters, the image on the screen is too blurry. Most monitors have a dot pitch of .28 millimeters, which is good; bad monitors have a dot pitch of .39, .41, or .52 millimeters.

Since VGA is so wonderful, practically everybody who buys an IBM clone orders VGA. VGA's popularity led VGA monitors and cards to be mass-produced on gigantic assembly lines, which dropped VGA's price even lower than EGA's. Since VGA is now cheaper and better than EGA, nobody buys EGA monitors or cards anymore (except people repairing old EGA systems).

<u>XGA</u> The PS/2 models having a 486 CPU contain a fancy graphics chip called the **eXtended Graphics Array (XGA)**. It resembles 1024-by-768 Super VGA.

<u>Price</u> The price of each PS/2 depends on how much RAM you buy, what size hard disk you buy, and what kind of monitor you buy. (If you can't afford a color monitor, buy a **gray-scale monitor** that shows shades of gray instead. The shades of gray crudely imitate the color graphics you'd get from MCGA, VGA, or XGA.)

If somebody offers you a "complete PS/2 system" cheaply, check whether that "complete" price includes the monitor. Usually it doesn't!

Cheaper than PS/2

The PS/2 computers were too expensive. In 1990, IBM invented a cheaper series of computers, called the **PS/1**. In 1992, IBM invented an even cheaper series, called the **PS/Valuepoint** (which you can buy in stores or by phoning IBM directly at 800-IBM-2YOU).

In 1993, IBM invented an even cheaper series called the **Ambra**, which IBM sold just by mail to compete against mail-order clone companies. The IBM division that produced and sold the Ambra was understaffed, confused, and mismanaged: shipments were delayed and unpredictable, many of the Ambras shipped were defective, and customers had difficulty getting IBM's Ambra division to send a repairman. Though the Ambra division advertised heavily, it was so badly managed and got such a bad reputation that it lost money. In 1994, IBM shut the division down.

In 1994, IBM began selling a nicer series, called the **Aptiva**.

IBM's flops

Some of your friends might still own IBM's other microcomputers, which were less successful.

IBM's **PC Junior** was intended for schoolkids. It had pretty graphics and a low price; but its add-ons were too expensive, its keyboard was awkward, and its circuitry differed enough from the original PC so the Junior refused to run some of the PC's programs.

IBM's **PC Portable** was a luggable inspired by Compaq but didn't include enough expansion slots.

After IBM invented the 8-megahertz AT, IBM had too many 6-megahertz and XT parts left in its warehouse. To use up those old parts, IBM created the **XT/286**, which contained a 6-megahertz AT CPU attached to an XT disk drive. The XT/286 was as unpopular as its parts.

IBM's **RS/6000** is a high-priced microcomputer that runs super-fast but can't run standard IBM PC software.

What happened to Don?

Although Don Estridge became popular for inventing the IBM PC and XT, his next two projects disappointed IBM: the PC Junior didn't sell well, and the AT's CMI hard drive was unreliable.

His bosses kicked him out of the Boca Raton research office and hid him in an obscure part of the company. A few months later, when he flew on a Delta jet, the jet crashed and killed him.

HOW CLONES ARE PRICED

Instead of buying from IBM, save money! Buy a clone instead!

Here's how most clones are priced. (I'll show you the prices that were in effect when this book went to press in February, 1995. Prices drop 3% per month, 30% per year.)

$1500 gets you a "standard" clone. That kind of clone is just fancy enough to run all the popular software without hassles.

If you pay *more* than $1500, you get a clone that's fancier — a powerful "muscle machine" that will impress your friends. They'll be impressed by how much money you spent. (If you pay *much* more than $1500, they might also be impressed by how stupid you were to overspend.)

If you pay *less* than $1500, you get a clone that's substandard. It will give you headaches when you try to run some popular software; but hey, if you can't afford $1500, a substandard clone is better than no computer at all. If you buy a substandard clone, your next task is to figure out which software it can handle well; then buy just that kind of software.

Here are the details. (I've rounded all prices to the nearest $25.)

CPU

The standard clone's CPU is a 486DX2-66. If you want a faster CPU instead, you must pay a surcharge:

CPU	Surcharge
486DX2-66	$0
486DX4-75	$50
486DX4-100	$100
Pentium-60	$225
Pentium-66	$250
Pentium-75	$275
Pentium-90	$525
Pentium-100	$725

If you're willing to buy a substandard computer, you pay less: deduct $25 for a 486DX2-50, deduct $100 for a 486SX-33.

If the CPU is a 486DX or 486DX2 or 486DX4, it should come with at least 128K of static RAM cache, or else deduct $25 as a penalty! If the CPU is a Pentium, it should come with at least 256K of static RAM cache (or else deduct $25).

If the CPU is a Pentium, it should come with the PCI local bus (or else deduct $50). If the CPU is a 486, it normally comes with the VESA local bus: add $25 for PCI local bus; deduct $25 for a bus that's neither VESA nor PCI.

RAM

The standard clone's RAM is 8M. If you want 16M instead, add $325. If you want 24M instead, add $650.

8M is enough for most purposes. Buy 16M or 24M just if your computer is manipulating big, complex pictures and photos, or if your computer is acting as a **server** (whose disk drive is being shared by many other computers in a network).

If you're willing to accept just 4M (which is substandard), deduct $150. But beware: the newest versions of popular Windows programs (such as Microsoft Word 6 and Word Perfect 6.1) are **memory hogs** that require 8M to run well.

Hard drive

The standard clone's hard drive is 540M (or 530M or 528M).

If you want a 730M instead, add $100. If you want 850M instead, add $125. If you want a gigabyte (1G) instead, add $225.

If you're willing to accept a 420M drive instead, deduct $25. If you're willing to to accept a 210M drive instead, deduct $50.

Although 420M is enough to run most software, programmers keep inventing software that's bigger and bigger. Software size has been increasing dramatically! Buying a 540M drive costs just $25 more than a 420M drive; that $25 is a worthwhile insurance policy against increases in software size.

Video

The standard clone includes a 14-inch color monitor. Add $100 for 15-inch, $375 for 17-inch.

A 14-inch monitor is adequate for most people and most software. 15-inch shows the same info as 14-inch but slightly magnified, so you can read "the fine print" on the screen more easily. 17-inch monitors are big enough to show an entire typewritten page on the screen readably, but they cost more than most folks can afford.

Although 15-inch and 17-inch monitors look impressive, they're usually not worth the extra cost. Instead of buying a 15-inch monitor, which costs $100 more than a 14-inch, most folks should buy just a 14-inch monitor and spend the $100 on 2M of extra RAM or 250M of extra hard-drive space.

Get a 15-inch or 17-inch monitor just if you have poor eyesight (or you're sharing the computer with somebody who has poor eyesight) or you're trying to create fine graphics and desktop publishing.

If the color monitor is 14-inch, its resolution should be at least 1024x768, and it should be non-interlaced at that resolution (or deduct $25). Its dot pitch should be no more than .28 millimeters (or deduct $25).

The video card should have at least 1M of RAM on it (or deduct $25). The video card should be Windows-accelerated or local-bus (or deduct $25).

Other hardware

The standard clone also includes these items:

In the standard clone	In non-standard clones
double-speed CD-ROM drive	If CD-ROM drive is quad-speed, add $100. If CD-ROM drive single-speed, deduct $50. If CD-ROM drive is missing, deduct $125.
sound card	If sound card is missing, deduct $50.
pair of stereo speakers	If pair of speakers is missing, deduct $25.
14400-baud fax/modem	If modem slower or lacks fax, deduct $25. If modem is missing, deduct $75.

The standard clone includes a **keyboard**, **mouse**, and a **3½-inch floppy drive**. Add $50 if it also includes a 5¼-inch floppy drive (used just to swap data with old computers and handle old software). Add $150 if it also includes a tape drive.

The standard clone comes in a **desktop case**. Add $25 if the case is a tower instead of a desktop. The tower case has just two advantages: it can hold extra cards (but you probably won't buy any!) and it can sit on the floor (so your desk is uncluttered and your monitor sits low enough to be seen without craning your neck up).

Software

The standard clone includes MS-DOS and Windows, with manuals.

Deduct $50 if DOS or its manual is missing. Deduct $50 if Windows or its manual is missing.

Add $25 if the price includes Windows for Workgroups instead of just Windows.

Add $25 for Quicken, $50 for Microsoft Works, $50 for Microsoft Encarta, $100 for Microsoft Word, $250 for Microsoft Office Professional CD (which is a CD-ROM disk that includes Microsoft Word plus other goodies but lacks instruction manuals).

Those prices are what big clone makers add in for software that comes with the computer. If instead you buy the software separately later, you'll pay much more!

Guarantees

The standard clone comes with a **30-day money-back guarantee**, a **1-year warranty**, and **lifetime toll-free tech support**.

Add $50 if the warranty is 3-year instead of 1-year.

Add just $25 if the warranty is 3-year on most of the system but just 1-year on the monitor. That's called a **3/1-year warranty**

Deduct $100 if the company is run by jerks. Here are signs that the company is run by jerks: the money-back guarantee is missing or shorter than 30 days, or you get charged a "restocking fee" for returning the computer, or the warranty is less than 1-year, or the tech support is not toll-free, or the tech-support phone number is usually busy or unanswered or is answered by a person who says to leave your phone number but doesn't return your call.

Kinds of clones

You've seen that a **standard clone** costs just $1500. But an **upscale clone** includes extras that raise the total cost to $1850; a **fancy clone** raises the total cost to $2300; a **luxury clone** raises the total cost to $3675; and a **downscale clone** lowers the total cost to $950. Here's how:

Feature	Standard clone	Upscale clone		Fancy clone		Luxury clone		Downscale clone	
CPU	486DX2-66	486DX4-100	($100 extra)	Pentium-75	($275 extra)	Pentium-90	($525 extra)	486SX-33	($100 less)
RAM	8M	8M		8M		16M	($325 extra)	4M	($150 less)
hard drive	540M	730M	($100 extra)	850M	($125 extra)	1G	($225 extra)	420M	($25 less)
monitor	14-inch	14-inch		15-inch	($100 extra)	17-inch	($375 extra)	14-inch	
CD-ROM drive	double-speed	double-speed		quad-speed	($100 extra)	quad-speed	($100 extra)	none	($125 less)
sound card	one	one		one		one		none	($50 less)
stereo speakers	one pair	one pair		one pair		one pair		none	($25 less)
fax/modem	14400-baud	14400-baud		14400-baud		14400-baud		none	($75 less)
floppy drives	3½-inch	3½-inch		3½-inch		3½-inch & 5¼-inch	($50 extra)	3½-inch	
tape drives	none	none		none		one	($150 extra)	none	
case	desktop	desktop		tower	($25 extra)	tower	($25 extra)	desktop	
Windows	plain	Workgroups	($25 extra)	Workgroups	($25 extra)	Workgroups	($25 extra)	plain	
applications	none	Works,Quicken,Enc	($125 extra)	Works,Quicken,Enc	($125 extra)	OfficePro,Qui,Enc	($325 extra)	none	
warranty	1-year	1-year		3/1-year	($25 extra)	3-year	($50 extra)	1-year	
TOTAL	**$1500**	$1500 + $350 extra =	**$1850**	$1500 + $800 extra =	**$2300**	$1500 + $2175 extra =	**$3675**	$1500 - $550 =	**$950**

Those prices do *not* include a printer, which is priced separately.

Which kind to buy Though a **standard clone** is adequate, a **fancy clone** is much nicer and will give you a happy thrill. It's the kind of clone that most mail-order dealers sell. It's the kind of clone I recommend.

If a fancy clone is beyond your budget but you'd like something better than just "standard", buy an **upscale clone**, which is a compromise. It will give you the pleasure of being uppity, better than standard.

A **luxury clone** is what computerists lust for, but spending so much money is foolish. To get a taste of luxury without being a fool, buy a fancy clone but soup it up by adding whichever luxurious element excites you the most. For example, if you're mainly lusting for a 17-inch monitor, go ahead: buy a fancy clone but with a 17-inch monitor instead of 15-inch.

If you're on a very tight budget and can't afford even a standard clone, buy a **downscale clone**. You can soup it up later, when you get richer. Just be aware that its limitations will occasionally annoy you and prevent you from accomplishing some tasks; within 2 years, you *will* soup it up; and making the alterations will cost you more (in labor charges, etc.) than if you buy a standard clone all at once.

Notebooks are pricey

The first rule about buying a notebook (or laptop) computer is: don't buy one unless you must! Try buying a desktop computer instead!

Though notebook computers are portable and cute, you pay a *lot* for portable cuteness.

For example, suppose you want a computer containing a 486SX-33 with 4M RAM, 200M hard drive, 1 floppy drive, color screen, DOS, Windows, and mouse (or trackball). To get a desktop computer containing all that, you pay about $925; to get a *notebook* computer containing all that, you must pay about $1725 instead.

Suppose you're rich enough to afford $1725. Does that mean you should buy a notebook computer? No! Here's what $1725 gets you. . . .

$1725 notebook: 486SX-33, 4M RAM, 200M drive, 1 floppy, 640x480 color
$1725 desktop: 486DX4-100, 8M RAM, 730M drive, 1 floppy, 1024x768 color, fax/mo, CD, sound

Desktop computers give you much more equipment per dollar than notebook computers.

Here's what $1200 gets you. . . .

$1200 notebook: 486SX-33, 4M RAM, 200M hard drive, 1 floppy, 640x480 gray-scale
$1200 desktop: 486DX2-66, 8M RAM, 420M hard drive, 1 floppy, 1024x768 color

So don't buy a notebook unless you *must*.

If you need to use a computer in two locations, don't buy a notebook: buy two desktop computers instead! Buying two desktop computers costs just *slightly* more than buying one notebook. Or buy a desktop computer that's light enough to carry to your car easily.

Buy a notebook computer just if you need to travel to many locations often, or if you're a student or researcher who needs to take notes in a lecture or library.

FAMOUS CLONES

I'd like to tell you about a company that makes reliable, powerful IBM clones, charges you very little, and is a pleasure to call if you ever need technical assistance.

That's what I'd *like* to tell you. Unfortunately, I haven't found such a company yet! If you find one, let me know!

Each day, I falsely hope I've finally found my hero company. I tell the name of the hero-company-du-jour to folks like you who read my book and call me for advice. But like O.J. Simpson, my hoped-for hero gets quickly accused by my customers of doubly murdering them in some way. How depressing! Can't any company do things right? I've been writing this book for 23 years and have yet to find a company I still feel proud about. I'm disgusted.

Hero companies rise but then fall because they suffer through the following business cycle. . . .

When the company begins, it's new and unknown, so it tries hard to get attention for itself by offering low prices. It also tries to help its customers by offering good service.

When news spreads about how the company offers low prices and good service, the company starts getting deluged with more customers than it can handle — and it's also stuck answering phone calls from old customers who still need help but aren't buying anything new. To reduce the overload, the company decides to reduce the number of customers (by lowering prices slower than the rest of the industry) or else reduce the service offered each customer (by neglecting to hire enough staff to handle all the questions) or else hire extra staff (who are usually less talented than the company's founders but nevertheless expect high pay). In any of those cases, the company becomes less pleasant than it was originally, and heroism is relegated to history. The company becomes just one more inconsequential player in the vast scheme of computer life.

Here are portraits of the players. Warning: these portraits are anatomically correct — they show which companies are pricks.

The computer industry is a soap opera, in which consumers face new personal horrors daily. Though I penned this in February, 1995, you can get the latest breathtaking episode of the computer industry's drama, *How the Screw-You Turns*, by phoning me anytime. I'll tell you the latest dirt about wannabe and were-to-be hero companies.

So before buying a computer, **phone me at 617-666-2666** to get my newest advice free. If you tell me your personal needs, I'll try to suggest a company or computer that most closely matches *you*. Before phoning me, become a knowledgeable consumer by reading the following juicy details about famous clones. . . .

Quantex

Of all the major companies that make clones, **Quantex** offers the lowest prices on Pentium computers. Moreover, Quantex's computers work well!

Here's what Quantex charged when this book went to press in February, 1995:

CPU	RAM	Hard drive	Video		Case	Software	Price
486DX2-66	8M	420M	14"	1M	desktop	family	$1499
486DX2-66	16M	730M	15"	1M	tower	family	$1899
486DX4-100	16M	730M	15"	1M	tower	family	$1999
Pentium-75	8M	850M	15"	1M	tower	family	$1999
Pentium-75	16M	850M	15"	2M	tower	office	$2349
Pentium-75	16M	1080M	17"	2M	tower	office	$2699
Pentium-90	16M	1080M	17"	2M	tower	office	$2949
Pentium-100	16M	1080M	17"	2M	tower	office	$3149

For example, the chart's bottom line says Quantex will sell you a computer system in which the CPU is fast (a Pentium running at a speed of 100 megahertz), the main RAM is huge (16 megabytes), the hard drive is huge (1080M), the monitor's screen contains a 17-inch tube (measured diagonally), and the video card contains 2 megabytes of additional RAM (so you can see lots of colors in high resolution). That computer system comes in a tower case (so you have lots of room inside to add even more goodies later), includes software to help you run your office, and costs just $3149.

But that's not all! When you buy one of the Quantex systems mentioned in that chart, you also get, at no extra charge, a quad-speed CD-ROM drive, sound card, pair of stereo speakers, 14400-baud fax/modem, PCI bus, 1.44M floppy drive (3½-inch high-density), mouse, MS-DOS, Windows for Workgroups, and 2 CD-ROM disks (containing the **Quicken** checkbook-balancing program, and the **Dragon Lore** game).

In that chart, "family software" means you also get 4 family-oriented CD-ROM disks: you get **Compton's Interactive Encyclopedia**, a health-advice program (**Mayo Clinic Family Health Book**), a program that makes greeting cards (**Card Shop Plus Deluxe**), and a collection called **Main Street Select**. "Office software" means you get 3 business-oriented CD-ROM disks: you get **The Complete Reference Library**, the **Everywhere USA Travel Guide**, and **Perfect Office** (a combination that includes the **Word Perfect for Windows** word processor, the **Quattro Pro** spreadsheet, and other goodies).

Each 486 system includes a 128K cache. Each Pentium system includes a 256K cache.

Quantex also sells stripped-down systems, which omit the CD-ROM drive, sound card, stereo speakers, and fax/modem.

Each Quantex system is a desktop or tower. Quantex does *not* sell notebook computers yet.

Quantex is in New Jersey. If you're not in New Jersey, Quantex won't charge you sales tax. For shipping, Quantex usually charges $65 to the Northeastern states (if you ask for shipping by UPS instead of Federal Express), about $90 elsewhere.

Phone Quantex at 800-836-0566 or 908-563-4166, or write to Quantex at 400-B Pierce Street, Somerset NJ 08873. Quantex is open Monday-Thursday 9AM-9PM, Friday 9AM-6PM, Saturday 10AM-4PM. Quantex is closed on Sunday.

Complaints People have several complaints about Quantex.

The biggest complaint is that the company doesn't have enough employees to answer all the phone calls. The sales staff, customer service staff, and technical support staffs are all overloaded. When you phone, you might get no answer, or a busy signal, or a secretary who takes your number and promises to call you back but does *not* call you back. Hint: if you get no answer at all, and the phone just keeps ringing and ringing, be patient: after about 30 rings, eventually somebody will answer.

Although most Quantex computers work fine, if yours breaks you'll be hopping mad when you discover that Quantex's technical-support staff is next-to-impossible to reach. People have tried for *many weeks* to reach Quantex's technical-support staff unsuccessfully.

At certain times of the year, I have sympathy for Quantex not answering their phones. *All* computer companies get overloaded in December and January, since during those months huge hoards of people suddenly buy computers for Christmas, end-of-year tax write-offs, and beginning-of-year budgets and try to get them fixed immediately. *All* computer companies get overloaded when they get rave reviews from magazines; Quantex has gotten *many* rave reviews from *PC World* magazine and others.

But sympathy goes just so far. For too many months of the year, Quantex is difficult to reach. Though most Quantex customers receive computers that work fine forever, a small but persistent percentage of Quantex customers get computers that break; and when those customers phone Quantex unsuccessfully, those customers feel ripped off.

Quantex ads claim that the computer comes with a 30-day money-back guarantee, a 1-year warranty, a year of on-site service (where a repairperson comes to your home), and a lifetime of free technical help. That what the ads *claim*; but in reality, if the computer breaks or you have a question about how to use it, you're on your own. You have a choice: either get a heart attack from the stress of trying to reach Quantex, or take the computer to a local repair shop and pay for the repair yourself, or try phoning me for free help.

Another problem with Quantex is delayed shipping. Usually, you must wait 4 weeks for Quantex to ship your computer, because Quantex is temporarily out of stock of one of the parts. Sometimes Quantex gets lucky and is able to ship in 2 weeks. If you're going to have to wait 4 weeks, some of the salespeople are honest and say "4 weeks", but other salespeople lie and say "2 weeks" when they know damn well it will take 4 weeks. If your salesperson says "2 weeks", try asking the customer-support staff instead (they're more pessimistic and more honest than the sales staff), or try asking a different salesperson about your order.

Quantex's keyboard and mouse are crummy. (The keyboard has a poor feel; the mouse is too bulky.)

In the previous edition of this book, I said Quantex's monitors were substandard, but Quantex has switched to better monitors that are above average.

Quantex's manuals are too short: they're incomplete. They're also too hard for the average beginner to understand.

Quantex ads show lots of smiling people. I'd like to meet them. A more honest ad would show lots of frowns, from customers waiting for computers or waiting for help.

It's just too bad that your chance of getting through to Quantex's technical-support staff is about as low as your chance of winning the lottery.

Price drops Quantex advertises in *Computer Shopper* magazine, which reaches subscribers on the fifteenth of the month. (For example, the February issue reaches subscribers on January 15th.) A week or two afterwards, the magazine finally starts appearing on magazine stands and in bookstores. The ads in each issue show new, lower prices. Quantex usually drops its prices about the 20th of the month. So to get the prices that Quantex advertises in the February issue of *Computer Shopper*, you must wait until about the 20th of January.

Suppose you order a computer from Quantex but then, while you're waiting to receive the computer, a new issue of *Computer Shopper* comes out and shows a new, lower price from Quantex. Phone Quantex immediately, before they ship your computer to you: they'll give you the new, lower price, but just if you ask!

Who owns Quantex? Quantex is owned secretly by **Fountain**, which is based in Taiwan. Quantex buys its cases and motherboards from Fountain.

Most daily operations of Quantex are run by Michael Polissky. He's Quantex's Vice President of Direct Marketing.

Sisters Quantex has two sister companies: **Micro Professionals** and **Pionex**. Like Quantex, they're secretly owned by Fountain and use Fountain's motherboards and cases. Micro Professionals is in Illinois; Pionex is in Florida. Like Quantex, Micro Professionals advertises in *Computer Shopper*; Pionex sells through liquidators instead (such as Damark and Home Shopping Club). Quantex offers lower prices than its sisters. Yes, Quantex is the cheapest hooker.

Quantex used to have another sister, called **Computer Sales Professional** (or **PC Professional**), but that sister faltered and got merged into Quantex.

Gateway

Gateway sells more computers by mail than any other company. Here's how Gateway became the mail-order king.

How Gateway arose Gateway began because of cows. In the 1800's, George Waitt began a cattle company. According to legend, he got his first herd by grabbing cattle that jumped off barges into the Missouri River on the way to the stockyards. His cattle business passed to his descendants and eventually into the hands of his great-grandson, Norm, who built the Waitt Cattle Company into one of the biggest cattle firms in the Midwest. The company is on the Missouri River, in Sioux City, Iowa, which is the city where Iowa meets South Dakota and Nebraska.

Norm's sons — Norm Junior and Ted — were more interested in computers than cows, so in 1985 they started the "Gateway 2000" company in their dad's office. They pointed out that computers are easier to ship to customers than cows, since computers can withstand a long journey without needing to be fed and without making a mess in their boxes. 22-year-old Ted was the engineer and called himself "president"; Norm Junior was the businessman and called himself "vice president". At first, they sold just parts for the Texas Instruments Professional Computer. Soon they began building their own computers. By the end of 1985, they'd sold 50 systems.

In 1986, they moved to a larger office in the Sioux City Livestock Exchange Building. They sold 300 systems that year.

In 1987, they sold 500 systems.

In 1988, Ted began a national marketing campaign by designing his own ads and running them in *Computer Shopper* magazine. His most famous ad showed a gigantic two-page photo of his family's cattle farm and the headline, "Computers from Iowa?" The computer industry was stunned — cowed — by the ad's huge size and by the IBM clones it offered at such low prices. In the ad, Ted emphasized that Gateway was run by hard-working, honest midwesterners who gave honest value. (At that time, most clones came from California or Texas; but Californians had a reputation for being "flaky", and Texans had a reputation for being "lawless"). Though cynics called Gateway "the cow computer", it was a success. The company moved a few miles south to a larger plant in Sergeant Bluff, Iowa. Gateway's operations there began with 28 employees. Sales continued to rise: in 1988, Gateway sold 4,000 computers, for which customers paid a total of 12 million dollars.

In 1989, Gateway sold 25,000 computers, for which customers paid 80 million dollars.

In the summer of 1989, Gateway had grown to 150 employees, so Gateway began building a larger plant. To get tax breaks and business grants, they built the plant upriver at North Sioux City, South Dakota. They moved there in January 1990. During 1990, Gateway became much more professional. In 1989, the "instruction manual" was 2 pages; in 1990, it was 2 books. In 1989, the "tech support staff" (which answers technical questions from customers) consisted of just 1 person, and you had to wait 2 days for him to return your call; in 1990, the tech support staff consisted of 35 people, and you could get through in 2 minutes. Gateway also switched to superior hard drives and monitors. Altogether, in 1990 Gateway sold about 100,000 computers, for which customers paid 275 million dollars, generating a net profit of $25 million.

Sales continued to climb. In 1991, Gateway sold 225,000 computers, for which customers paid 627 million dollars.

By early 1992, Gateway was selling nearly 2,000 computers per day and had 1,300 employees, including over 100 salespeople and 200 tech-support specialists to answer technical questions. By the end of 1992, Gateway had 1,876 employees. Total sales for 1992 were 1.1 billion dollars.

Not bad, for a company whose president was just 30! Since Gateway was owned by just Norm Junior and Ted, those two boys became quite rich! And at the end of 1993, Gateway went public, so now you can buy Gateway stock and own part of that dreamy company.

Gateway's become a rapidly growing cash cow: moo-lah, moo-lah!

But Gateway hasn't lost its sense of humor. When you buy a Gateway computer, it comes in a box painted to look like a dairy cow: white with black spots.

Each Gateway ad begins with gigantic photographs. In early ads, the photos showed individuals in beautiful landscapes. In newer ads, the photos show hoards of Gateway employees dressed as Robin Hood's men in Sherwood Forest, top-hatted performers in Vegas cabarets, teenagers in a nostalgic 1950's diner bathed in neon glow, or movie directors applauding a ship full of pirates.

The eye-popping photos, which seem to have nothing to do with computers, grab your attention. (Gateway's diner ad includes the only photo I've ever seen that makes meat loaf look romantic!) Then you get headlines and florid prose that try to relate the scene to Gateway's computers. Finally, after all that multi-page image-building nonsense, you get to the ad's finale, which reveals Gateway's great technical specifications (specs), great service policies, and low prices.

That way of building an ad — fluff followed by stuff — has worked wonders for Gateway! The idiots admire the photos, the techies admire the specs, and everybody buys!

Gateway was the first big mail-order manufacturer to give honest pricing: the advertised price includes everything except shipping. The price even includes a color monitor. And since the specs of all the components are great, a Gateway system is a *dream* system. When accompanied by dreamy ads and offered at a ridiculously low price, how can you *not* buy?

The company's official name is "Gateway 2000". Gateway ships worldwide.

If you're in the USA,   phone Gateway at 800-LAD-2000.
If you're in Canada,   phone Gateway at 800-846-3609.
If you're in Puerto Rico,   phone Gateway at 800-846-3613.
From anywhere in the world, phone Gateway at 605-232-2000.

Gateway's sales department is open weekdays 7AM-10PM, Saturday 9AM-4PM, Central Time. Gateway is closed on Sunday.

Gateway's address is:

Gateway 2000
610 Gateway Drive
PO Box 2000
North Sioux City SD 57049-2000

Prices Here are Gateway's prices:

CPU	RAM	Hard drive	Video		CD-ROM	Softw.	Price
486DX2-66	4M	340M	14"	1M	double-speed	Works	$1299 + $198
486DX2-66	8M	540M	14"	1M	double-speed	family	$1799
486DX2-66	8M	730M	15"	1M	double-speed	office	$1799 + $198
Pentium-60	8M	540M	15"	1M	quad-speed	family	$2099
Pentium-60	8M	730M	15"	1M	quad-speed	office	$1999 + $198
Pentium-75	8M	730M	15"	2M	quad-speed	family	$2299
Pentium-75	16M	730M	15"	1M	quad-speed	office	$2399 + $198
Pentium-90	8M	1G	15"	2M	quad-speed	family	$2799
Pentium-100	16M	1G	15"	2M	quad-speed	office	$2999 + $198

In the Software column, "Works" means you get a program called **Microsoft Works for Windows** (which handles elementary word processing, spreadsheets, databases, graphics, and telecommunications). "Family" means you get Microsoft Works for Windows and also get a general encyclopedia (**Encarta**), an encyclopedia about movies (**Cinemania**), a graphics program for kids (**Fine Artist**), and a game (**Microsoft Golf**). "Office" means you get **Microsoft Bookshelf** (which includes an encyclopedia, dictionary, thesaurus, atlas, almanac, and famous quotations) and **Microsoft Office Professional**, which includes a fancy word processor (**Microsoft Word**), spreadsheet (**Excel**), database (**Access**), and graphics-presentation program (**Power Point**).

All that software is by Microsoft, uses Windows, and comes on CD-ROMs. Alas, the CD-ROM version of Microsoft Office Professional does *not* include an instruction manual!

Most folks want three bonuses: a sound card, pair of stereo speakers, and 14400-baud fax/modem. If your system comes with "family" software, the price includes those bonuses. If your system comes with "Works" or "office" software instead, the price includes those bonuses just if you pay the "+$198". ($99 of that surcharge is for the sound card and speakers. The other $99 is for the fax/modem.)

All those systems also come with a mouse, MS-DOS, Windows for Workgroups, and a CD-ROM disk containing a program that helps you balance your checkbook (**Microsoft Money**).

Most systems give you a PCI bus, a cache (256K for Pentium, 128K for 486), and a large desktop case that can be upgraded to a tower for $50 extra. But if you buy the cheapest systems ($1299 + $198 and $1799), you get an inferior bus, no cache, and just a tiny desktop case that ca*nnot* be upgraded to a tower.

Dropping prices Those prices went into effect in February of 1994. By the time you read this book, Gateway's prices might be even lower.

When you phone Gateway to check a price, Gateway's salespeople often quote you a *lower* price than advertised. That's because Gateway's prices drop often, and the ads aren't as up-to-date as what the salespeople say. Moreover, Gateway likes to fool competitors by pretending to have high prices while actually offering prices so low that you can't say no, so competitors can't figure out why everybody's buying from Gateway.

Gateway usually drops its prices during the last week of each month.

Shipping If you order a computer, you must typically wait 2 weeks to receive it. That's because Gateway is swamped with orders and won't ship your order until nearly 2 weeks after you order; then Gateway will ship the computer by 2-day air and charge you $95 for shipping.

Tax Like most mail-order companies, Gateway used to charge sales tax just to customers who were in Gateway's state (South Dakota). Recently, Gateway has been forced to charge tax to customers in New York, Florida, Kentucky, and many other states — 28 states altogether! When you phone Gateway, ask the salesperson whether *you* must pay tax. Lucky for me, Massachusetts isn't on Gateway's list of taxable states yet.

Support Gateway's warranty used to be just 1 year, but now Gateway now offers a 3-year warranty on the entire system, including even the monitor. Gateway also gives you a 30-day money-back guarantee, lifetime toll-free tech support, 3-year on-site service (from Dow Jones, if you're within 100 miles of a Dow Jones service center), and free shipping of replacement parts by overnight air.

If you have a problem and want to speak to a technician, phone Gateway's technical-support department at 800-846-2301. It's open weekdays 6AM-midnight, Saturday 9AM-2PM, Central Time.

Delays Up through 1992, Gateway's popularity grew rapidly, and Gateway acquired many customers — too many for Gateway to handle! Gateway was understaffed. Customers complained about getting busy signals, shipping delays, and incompetent tech-support staff. The delays got worse and worse, until they reached a crisis point in January of 1993. By then, many of Gateway's former customers got disgusted, switched to other vendors instead, and complained to me and other journalists. *Infoworld*, *The Wall Street Journal*, and I wrote articles saying how bad Gateway had become.

That was enough of a "kick in the pants" to make Gateway clean up its act. After January of 1993, Gateway gradually improved the quantity and quality of its staff, so by August of 1993 Gateway's service and support had become no worse than the industry average.

But in September of 1993, Gateway started to get overloaded again; and by Christmas of 1993, Gateway was so overloaded that customers began to complain. By January of 1994, Gateway was back in a full-blown crisis again — just like the year before! Throughout the first half of 1994, Gateway's delays were intolerable: 5 weeks to get a computer, and next-to-impossible to get through to the technical-service department.

Gateway has improved. Now Gateway takes 2 weeks to ship a computer instead of 5. To help you get through to Gateway's technical-service department faster, Gateway has added more technicians to its staff and built a new, expanded service department in Kansas City, Missouri.

Nevertheless, getting through to a competent technician can be tough. In January (which is the computer industry's most overloaded month), getting through to the technical-service department is nearly impossible. In August (which is the computer industry's lightest month, since that's when Americans thinks about the beach instead of computers), getting through to Gateway technicians is easy. In other months, you can get through just if you dial repeatedly (until you get past a busy signal), then wait on hold (and hope you don't get kicked off because there are too many callers), then talk to an idiot, then wait for the idiot to call a supervisor who can answer your question.

So every January, newspapers print articles about how awful Gateway is; then Gateway apologizes; then by August everybody praises Gateway for being wonderful; and then the following January everybody wants to sue Gateway again.

Aren't business cycles fun?

Keyboard Some Gateway computers come with a keyboard that's manufactured by **Maxiswitch** and completely programmable: you can program any key to perform any function. For example, if you don't like the SHIFT key's location, you can program a different key to act as the SHIFT key.

Unfortunately, that feature is *too* fancy: many beginners accidentally hit the "Program macro" button, which then reprograms the keys so no key works as expected! Beginners have trouble finding the instructions that explain how to reset the keyboard to act normally again.

Gateway used to put that keyboard on *all* its computers but now puts it just on computers containing a Pentium-75, Pentium-90, or Pentium-100.

Giant monitors If your system is advertised as having a 15-inch monitor, you can switch to a 17-inch monitor by adding $260. If your system is advertised as having just a 14-inch monitor, you can switch to a 17-inch monitor by adding $360.

Notebooks and subnotebooks Gateway sells notebook and subnotebook computers, but Gateway's prices are too high (monochrome starts at $1999, color starts at $2799) and the warranty is shorter (just 1-year instead of 3-year).

Gateway versus Quantex Gateway charges more than Quantex but gives you these advantages: Gateway gives you better instruction manuals, better software, shorter delivery times, and easier access to technicians (except in January). On the other hand, Quantex gives you more hardware per dollar, lower shipping charges, and lets you pay no tax (unless you're in New Jersey).

VTech

Of all the computers I bought, my favorite is made by a company called **Video Technology** (or **Video Tech** or **VTech**). VTech's computers are built well, cost little, and come with decent manuals. A recent improvement in management lets you get technical support easily now, without the nightmare of busy signals and long delays that Quantex and Gateway subject you to.

VTech is a big, multinational company. It has 5,000 employees, headquartered in Hong Kong with assembly plants around the world. Its stock is publicly traded on the London stock exchange. It manufactures electronic toys (**Whiz Kid** and **Murduck**), digital cordless phones (**Tropez**), and computers. It has also owned **Central Point Software** (which publishes popular software such as **PC Tools**), though it recently sold Central Point Software to a competitor, Symantec.

For many years, VTech sold computers mainly to chains of stores, such as Sears and Staples. Its computers were sold under two brand names: **Leading Technology computers** and **Laser computers**.

Expotech In May 1992, VTech began an experiment: it created a mail-order division called **Expotech**, which advertised in *Computer Shopper* and *PC Magazine* and sold VTech's "Expotech computers" directly to consumers at ridiculously low prices, bypassing the stores, distributors, and other middlemen. Unfortunately, VTech didn't realize how important tech support was. Though most VTech computers worked well, VTech got a bad reputation because too many customers heard "all lines are busy" messages when phoning VTech's tech-support number. Also VTech did some dishonest chip switching: if you ordered a 486SX-33, VTech sent you instead a computer containing an Intel 486SX-25 instead; and to cover up the fraud, VTech covered up the chip with a label saying "Warranty void if label is removed". Most customers never noticed the switch, since VTech pushed the 486SX-25 to run at 33 megahertz, even though Intel hadn't warranted that chip to go that fast. VTech stopped that fraud when Intel stopped manufacturing 486SX-25 chips.

Telcom In December 1994, VTech ended its experiment of selling computers directly to consumers. Instead, VTech sold its mail-order Expotech division to a company called **Telcom**, whose main business is selling refurbished fax machines and copiers by advertising in the "in-flight magazines" that are distributed free to airline passengers. Now if you phone Expotech, your call will be answered by Telcom employees, who will sell you an Expotech computer manufactured by VTech.

Should you buy? VTech computers work well and come with decent manuals. Telcom ships them reasonably promptly: you'll typically receive your computer within 3 weeks.

Here's the bad news: Telcom will charge you a slightly higher price than VTech did. Here's the good news: since Telcom's tech-support lines aren't overloaded yet, you can reach Telcom's tech-support staff quickly. That's the main advantage of Telcom over Quantex and Gateway: Telcom answers its phones! Telcom won't leave you stranded! Telcom cares!

Note: Telcom's tech-support number is just for customers who bought from Telcom. If you bought from VTech before the switchover to Telcom, get tech support by phoning VTech directly at its old tech-support number, which isn't as overloaded as it used to be.

So to buy a great computer at a fairly low price and with decent tech support, **phone the Expotech division of Telcom in Lake Zurich, Illinois, at 800-215-3976**; then on your touch-tone phone, press 3 then TIM then #. That gets you a salesman named Tim Lilly, who used to work for VTech but now works for Telcom. If you tell him you've read *The Secret Guide to Computers*, he'll give you special attention and also some free software: choose either Microsoft Works or one of Expotech's ten "Twin Packs", which Expotech normally sells for $35.

Prices Expotech's cheapest computer costs just $1399. That gets you a 486DX2-66 with 540M hard drive, quad-speed CD-ROM drive, sound card with pair of stereo speakers, 14" monitor, mouse, MS-DOS, Windows for Workgroups, and Compton's Interactive Encyclopedia. The hard drive is above-average (made by **Conner**) and so is the monitor (made by **CTX**).

Unfortunately, that price includes just 4M of RAM. Add $165 to switch to 8M, bringing your total price to $1564.

If you're feeling more luxurious, spend $1679 instead, which includes 8M of RAM, a bigger monitor (15"), and fancier video card (containing 2M RAM instead of 1M).

Expotech sells fancier computers, too. For example, $2099 gets you a fancy system: a Pentium-75 with 8M RAM, 850M hard drive, 15" monitor, 2M video card, and the standard goodies (quad-speed CD-ROM, sound, mouse, DOS, Windows for Workgroups, and Compton's). For $100 less, you'll get a smaller drive (540M) and smaller video RAM (1M).

Add $69 for a 14400-baud fax/modem.

A tape drive costs $149 for 250M (by Colorado), $189 for 420 (by Conner), $279 for 850M (by Conner). Those prices include 1 free tape.

Shipping is $30 to the Chicago area (area codes 312, 708, and 815), $49 to Illinois and adjoining states (Indiana, Kentucky, Missouri, Iowa, and Wisconsin), $135 to Alaska and Hawaii, $89 to all other states.

EPS

EPS offers the lowest prices on notebook computers containing big hard drives. Here they are:

CPU	RAM	Hard drive	Price
486DX4-100	8M	540M	$2395 if dual-scan, $3095 if active
Pentium-75	8M	540M	$2745 if dual-scan, $3495 if active
Pentium-90	8M	540M	$2995 if dual-scan, $3895 if active
Pentium-90	16M	810M	$3495 if dual-scan, $4395 if active

Each EPS notebook computer weighs 6½ pounds and contains a sound card, built-in microphone, pair of built-in stereo speakers, trackball, 1.44M floppy drive, 1M video RAM, MS-DOS, Windows for Workgroups, and color LCD screen.

The notebook's price depends on which screen you choose. Choose either the 9½" **active-matrix screen** (which is wonderfully bright and fast) or the 10¼" **dual-scan passive-matrix screen** (which is slightly less bright, reacts slightly slower, and costs a lot less).

Each notebook comes with a leather carrying case, a 1-year warranty, a long-lasting battery made of **nickel metal hydride (NiMH)**, and **an AC adapter** (which plugs into the wall of your room and converts your building's alternating current into the direct current needed by the computer).

Expandable The computer is expandable. For example, you can easily pop out the hard drive and put in another one.

Suppose you're using the computer at your desk and wish you'd bought a desktop computer instead because it would have a bigger screen and keyboard. No problem! EPS's notebook computer has an **external video port** (so you can attach a big monitor) and an **external keyboard port** (so you can attach a big keyboard). Attach any monitor and keyboard you wish! Or let EPS soup up your system for you! For $995, EPS will sell you this combo: a 15" monitor, a keyboard, and a **docking station** (containing a quad-speed CD-ROM drive a fancier sound card, and extra slots & ports).

Though EPS doesn't include a fax/modem, you can buy one that comes on a PCMCIA card and insert that card into the notebook's PCMCIA slot. The slot is big (Type 3), so you can insert a Type 3 PCMCIA card or a pair of Type 2 PCMCIA cards (one card for the modem and one card for anything else).

Desktop computers EPS also sells desktop computers, at unremarkable prices.

Who is EPS? Like Gateway, EPS is in South Dakota. According to Gateway's head of sales, EPS was started by guys who were fired from Gateway. I don't know why they were fired — perhaps just for starting EPS? In any case, EPS has been in business for many years and has a decent reputation — no worse than Gateway's.

Phone EPS at 800-447-0921 or 605-966-5586. EPS is open weekdays 7AM-7PM, Saturday 9AM-5PM. If you prefer, write to EPS at 10069 Dakota Ave., PO Box 278, Jefferson SD 57038.

Packard Bell

Packard Bell is one of the four biggest computer companies. It sells more computers than Gateway, Dell, and AST. It even sells more computers in the USA than IBM!

Packard Bell markets mainly to the average American, who is curious about computers but doesn't understand them and doesn't want to spend much. Since the average American avoids computer stores and is scared to buy a computer by mail-order, Packard Bell sells cheap clones through discount department stores (such as Sears, Walmart, Sam's Club, Lechmere, Fredder, Price/Costco, Staples, and Office Max).

In the early 1990's, Packard Bell sold computers cheaply (for about $1000). Packard Bell computers became popular because they included 15 easy-to-use programs that were loaded already on the hard disk, so you could start using the computer immediately. The programs included games, tutorials, educational experiences, and simple productivity tools (such as Microsoft Works, which includes a word processor, database, spreadsheet, etc.). To keep the advertised price low, Packard Bell typically included a poor monitor (.39mm dot pitch, interlaced) or didn't include any monitor at all.

Now Packard Bell's marketing has become more traditional. The price has risen to about $1800. Packard Bell has switched to a better monitor (.28mm dot pitch, non-interlaced), though it's often not included in the advertised price. Fewer programs are included.

Unfortunately, Packard Bell provides programs on the hard disk but *not* on floppy disks. If you accidentally erase the hard disk, you've lost the programs! When you buy the computer, you're supposed to also buy a big stack of blank floppy disks and copy all the programs from the hard disk to floppy disks; but many consumers forget to do that.

What if it breaks? Most stores have a 30-day money-back guarantee. If your computer breaks during that 30-day period, your best bet is to return it to the store and ask for your money back.

If the computer breaks *after* the 30-day period, don't bother returning it to the store: the store won't give you your money back, and the store won't be able to fix the computer (unless you bought from a *computer* store). Instead, you must phone Packard Bell.

During the early 1990's, getting a Packard Bell computer repaired was tough. For example, I wrote this comment in the 1990 edition of *The Secret Guide to Computers*:

Warning: getting a Packard Bell computer repaired is tough. Dealers complain that Packard Bell doesn't provide replacement parts; customers complain that dealers say to phone Packard Bell, which rarely answers the phone. When it DOES answer, it says to leave your phone number for a call back. Then it either neglects to call you or tells you to phone a service company that tells you to get lost.

By 1993, Packard Bell improved slightly, but then Packard Bell's phone-support center got wrecked by the earthquake in Northridge & Los Angeles in January 1994. Customers who called after that got just circuit-busy messages.

In July 1994, Packard Bell moved its support center to Utah, which has fewer earthquakes. The support center's in the town of Magna, a suburb of Salt Lake City. But if you try phoning Packard Bell's support center (at 800-733-4411), you still usually get a recorded message saying that all lines are busy and you should try writing a letter or sending electronic mail instead. Of course, sending "electronic mail" is difficult if your computer is broken!

In spite of its questionable repair record, Packard Bell has grown rapidly and become one of the biggest computer companies in the USA. That's because Packard Bell has the right formula: good distribution (you can find Packard Bell computers at most department stores across the USA), good price (cheaper than IBM, Compaq, AST, and other famous brands), good easy-to-use programs (though they're the cheap kind that don't cost Packard Bell much), repairs handled directly by Packard Bell (so the department stores don't need any computer technicians on their staff), and a good-sounding name ("Packard Bell").

The name "Packard Bell" sounds good because it reminds consumers of the Bell Telephone companies, and consumers think "Packard Bell" might be somehow related to "Pacific Bell" or some other well-respected phone company — perhaps a merger between Hewlett-Packard and Ma Bell? To encourage that misconception, Packard Bell's slogan is "America grew up listening to us." But actually, Packard Bell is a completely independent company that never had anything to do with any phone company. Back in the 1950's, there was an unrelated company called "Packard Bell", which built radios; the Packard Bell computer company bought the name "Packard Bell" from the radio company, just so that the computer company would sound like it was related to a phone company. Some states require Packard Bell computers to be sold with a disclaimer warning the consumer that Packard Bell computers are "not affiliated with any Bell System entity".

In surveys of customer satisfaction done by *PC Magazine* and *PC World*, customers who have bought computers from Packard Bell computers are much less happy than customers who have bought other brands. Though the typical Packard Bell computer works okay, if you *do* need a repair you'll become *very* frustrated trying to reach Packard Bell's tech-support center.

But I've bumped into some Packard Bell customers who have been *thrilled* with tech support! That's because they bought their Packard Bell computers from computer stores instead of department stores, and the computer stores were willing to fix computers immediately without waiting for the customers to phone Packard Bell.

Compaq

The first company that made high-quality IBM clones was **Compaq**. (Before Compaq, the only IBM clones available were crummy.)

How Compaq began
It all began on a napkin. Sitting in a restaurant, two engineers drew on a napkin their picture of what the ideal IBM clone would look like. Instead of being a desktop computer, it would be a luggable having a 9-inch built-in screen and a handle, the whole computer system being small enough so you could pick it up with one hand. Then they built it! Since it was compact, they called it the **Compaq Portable Computer** and called the company **Compaq Computer Corporation**.

They began selling it in 1983. They charged about the same for it as IBM charged for the IBM PC.

They sold it just to dealers who'd been approved by IBM to sell the IBM PC. That way, they knew all their dealers were reliable — and they competed directly against IBM, in the same stores.

They succeeded fantastically. That first year, sales totalled 100 million dollars.

In 1984, they inserted a hard drive into the computer and called that souped-up luggable the **Compaq Plus**. They also built a desktop computer called the **Deskpro**. Like Compaq's portable computers, the Deskpro was priced about the same as IBM's computers, was sold just through IBM dealers, and was built well — a marvel of engineering, better than IBM's.

Later, Compaq expanded: it built IBM clones in many sizes, from towers down to subnotebooks. Compaq computers have all gotten the highest praise — and the highest prices. Because of their high prices, they're not cost-effective.

New leadership
Compaq was founded by Rod Canion. He was Compaq's chief executive until 1991, when his board of directors fired him and replaced him by Eckhard Pfeiffer, who lowered Compaq's astronomical prices somewhat and began selling through a greater variety of dealers and also through mail-order.

In 1994, Compaq became popular enough to catch up to IBM and Apple. Which company sells the most computers in the whole world? The answer is a three-way tie among Compaq, IBM, and Apple.

Compaq's new, cheaper computers are called **Pro Linea computers**, and Compaq makes even cheaper ones called **Presario computers**. Though cheaper than Compaq's older computers, they still cost much more than IBM clones from competitors such as Quantex, Gateway, and Packard Bell. Though Compaq has dropped prices several times, each drop started a price war where Compaq's competitors replied by dropping *their* prices too, so Compaq computers are *still* a bit overpriced in relation to competitors.

Though Compaq's prices remain high enough to prevent me from buying a Compaq, I'm grateful to Compaq for starting the price wars that let me pay less to Compaq's competitors!

If you buy a Compaq, you *do* get something in return for your high price: excellence! According to *PC World*'s surveys of users, Compaq is the *only* company that's terrific in both reliability and in ease of getting technical help. In other words, Compaq computers rarely break; and when they do, you get help immediately.

Aero Compaq's subnotebook computer is called the **Aero** because it's almost lighter than air: it weighs just 3½ pounds. At 7½"x10¼", it's smaller than a sheet of paper; and it's just 1½" thick. Discount dealers sell it for just $1099. That price includes a 486SX-25 CPU, 4M RAM, 84M hard drive, 8" gray-scale screen, trackball, DOS, Windows, and a program that helps you organize your time & work (Lotus Organizer).

Since the Aero does *not* have a floppy drive inside, to feed it programs you must either get an external floppy drive or else run a cable from a desktop computer to the Aero and transfer programs to the Aero through the cable. Originally, the Aero's price did not include a floppy drive at all, but now the price includes an external floppy drive. While supplies last, you can get a refurbished Aero without floppy drive for just $645 from a New York discounter called **Excel** (at 800-486-EXEL or 212-684-6930).

Phone Compaq's in Houston at 800-888-8196.

Dell

Though Compaq was the first company to make good IBM clones, its clones were expensive. The first company that sold fast IBM clones *cheaply* was **PC's Limited**, founded in 1984 by a 19-year-old kid, Michael Dell. He operated out of the bedroom of his condo apartment, near the University of Texas in Austin.

At first, his prices were low — and so were his quality and service. Many of the computers he shipped didn't work: they were **dead on arrival (DOA)**. When his customers tried to return the defective computer equipment to him for repair or a refund, his company ignored the customer altogether. By 1986, many upset customers considered him a con artist and wrote bitter letters about him to computer magazines. He responded by saying that his multi-million-dollar company was growing faster than expected and couldn't keep up with the demand for after-sale service. (Hmm . . . sounds like Gateway!)

In 1987, Dell raised his quality and service — and his prices. In 1988, he changed the company's name to **Dell Computer Corporation**.

Now he charges almost as much as IBM and Compaq. His quality and service are top-notch and set the standard for the rest of the mail-order industry. In speed and quality contests, his computers often beat IBM and Compaq. His ads bash Compaq for having higher prices than Dell and worse policies about getting repairs — since Dell offers on-site service and Compaq doesn't.

For example, in 1991 Dell ran an ad calling Dell's notebook computer a "road warrior" and Compaq's a "road worrier". It showed the Dell screen saying, "With next day on-site service in 50 states, nothing's going to stop you." It showed the Compaq screen saying, "Just pray you don't need any service while you're on the road, or you're dead meat."

His ads are misleading. Although his prices are much lower than Compaq's *list* price, his prices are just *slightly* less than the discount price at which Compaq computers are normally sold. Although Compaq doesn't provide free on-site service, you can sometimes get your Compaq repaired fast by driving to a nearby Compaq dealer.

Like IBM and Compaq, Dell has dropped its prices, though they're still higher than Gateway's. Dell tried selling through discount-store chains but gave up and decided to return to selling just by mail.

Dell computers used to come with this guarantee: if Dell doesn't answer your tech-support call within 5 minutes, Dell will give you $25! Dell doesn't make that guarantee anymore.

To get a free Dell catalog or chat with a Dell sales rep, phone 800-BUY-DELL.

Los Angeles Chinese

If you browse through ads in *Computer Shopper*, you'll notice that most of the companies offering rock-bottom computer prices are in two Los Angeles suburbs, called "Walnut" and "City of Industry". The owners and employees of those companies seem mostly Chinese. Here they are:

Company	Phone	City
Comtrade	800-969-2123, 818-961-6688	City of Industry
ABS	800-876-8088, 818-937-2300	City of Industry
Zenon	800-899-6119, 818-935-1828	City of Industry
Royal Electronics	800-486-0008, 818-855-5077	City of Industry
Cornell Computer Systems	800-886-7200, 909-594-5848	Walnut
Mitra/Channel Group	800-324-1441, 909-468-2888	Walnut
Altus	800-522-5887, 909-598-8158	Walnut
Professional Technologies	800-949-5018, 909-468-1368	Walnut
Bit Computer	800-935-0209, 909-598-1391	Walnut

I'm still investigating these companies. If you have any experiences with them, please tell me. Many folks have bought from those companies and been happy; others have been upset. Here's what I know so far. . . .

Comtrade and **Cornell** are the biggest and most famous of those companies. Because they're so big, they've appeared in surveys of user satisfaction by PC World. According to the surveys, folks who've bought from Comtrade & Cornell are less happy than folks who've bought from any other big company: Comtrade & Cornell computers are the most likely to need repairs, and Comtrade & Cornell are the hardest companies to get satisfaction from when you try phoning for help.

ABS advertises the lowest prices: complete computer systems starting at just $845! But when you phone, you discover the ads are wrong: actual prices are about $100 higher than advertised. That still undercuts most other companies.

For shipping, ABS usually charges $71 and waits 2 weeks before bringing your computer to the UPS truck, but a $25 bribe gets ABS to build the computer fast and bring it to the UPS truck within 3 days. Then you wait 1 week for UPS ground to get to you. Though $71+$25 might seem a lot, it's just $1 more than Gateway and gets you a computer faster than Gateway.

Though ABS's ads mention Pentium computers, ABS rarely stocks them, so ABS sells mainly 486 computers — cheaply because they contain a 486 clone chip made by AMD instead of Intel. (AMD's clones work fine.)

Instead of giving you MS-DOS version 6.22, ABS gives you a weirder DOS version (IBM PC DOS 6.1, OEM version), unless you pay $45 extra. Instead of giving you Windows for Workgroups, ABS gives you plain Windows, unless you pay $10 extra. ABS charges $59 for a 14400-baud fax/modem, $38 for a slower one.

Though ABS's 15-inch monitor contains a 15-inch tube, the monitor is an inferior version showing you an image less than 14 inches. (15-inch monitors from most other computer companies show you about 14¼ inches.)

Since ABS doesn't use enough packing material, the cable to the floppy drive often falls out during transportation. Just open the computer and push the cable into the back of the drive again. If you ask ABS about the problem, the technician seems to say "It's a Peking problem", but he's trying to say "It's a packing problem" with a Chinese accent. Yes, customers complain they can't understand the accents of ABS's technicians.

Though ABS has been a member of the Better Business Bureau, the Bureau reports many unresolved complaints about ABS, such as delays in getting refunds.

Despite ABS's weaknesses, many ABS customers tell me they're happy.

ABS does one thing well: it usually answers its phone immediately, without putting you on hold! Unfortunately, the only phone it answers immediately is the one for sales: the phone for tech support usually goes unanswered. If you can't reach the tech-support staff directly, phone the sales department and complain that you want to talk to a supervisor: that gets you through to tech support! (I don't know of any such trick for getting through to Quantex and Gateway.)

Altus's ad says, at the top in big bold letters, "PEACE OF MIND. Altus warranty gives you peace of mind. We start with a three year complete warranty on parts and labor." But near ad's bottom, in tiny print, you see "1-year warranty on CD-ROM, hard drive, monitor, and notebook", so the warranty is just 1 year on any part that's likely to break. Moreover, at the very bottom of the ad, even tinier print says "1 year warranty applies to manufactured items only". What does that mean? What's a "non-manufactured item"? Is this warranty worth anything at all?

Some of Altus's advertised prices seem ridiculously low. What's the catch? Here it is: when you read what the price includes, you'll notice that the description carefully avoids mentioning a monitor. You get none.

Mitra's ad is a two-page spread that begins by saying "Intel inside" and "We use only genuine Intel microprocessors in our quality computer systems". That implies all of Mitra's computers contain CPU chips manufactured by Intel. But that brag appears just on the left page. The computers on the right-hand page contain 486 chips made by Cyrix instead of Intel. The ad doesn't mention Cyrix; you wouldn't know unless you asked.

Nevertheless, consider Mitra, since it offers low prices and includes nice family software from Microsoft. The Better Business Bureau reports that Mitra has a good track record: just one complaint was ever filed against Mitra, and Mitra resolved it to the customer's satisfaction.

Professional Technologies was begun by a group of Asian companies who manufacture computer parts decided to combine their parts and sell complete computer systems. Professional Technologies is the company that markets their systems. When it began several years ago, I heard lots of complaints, but maybe the problems have been shaken out by now. Tell me your experiences.

Bit Computer is on the same street as Professional Technologies, just a few doors away. It's probably under the same ownership. It sells just notebook computers, including a fancy notebook computer that contains a DX4-75 CPU, 8M RAM, 340M hard drive, AND CD-ROM DRIVE and costs just $2695.

Zenon and **Royal** run big ads, emphasize quality, use award-winning parts, and seem solid. Zenon's computers are so nicely built and run so fast that they've received high praise from the reviewers at PC Magazine and PC World. I'm waiting for feedback from customers about service.

Alternatives

Here are other choices to consider.

Comp USA is the most popular chain of computer superstores. It's based in Dallas but has stores in many other big cities nationwide. It sells many computer brands, such as Dell, Compaq, and Toshiba. In 1991, it began building its own computers, called **Compudyne**. Previous editions of this Guide recommended Compudyne computers, but recently Compudyne prices have been too high. I hope they go back down! For more info about Compudyne computers, visit your local Comp USA store or phone Comp USA's headquarters at 800-COMP-USA (or 214-702-0055).

AST is a big computer manufacturer in Irvine, California. "AST" stands for the names of its founders, "Albert, Safi, and Tom". Albert and Tom have left AST, which is now headed by Safi. (Computer-trivia question: what's Safi's last name, and how do you spell it? Answer: Qureshey.) AST builds powerful, well-engineered computers, sold through computer stores, and priced lower than computers from IBM & Compaq, though higher than mail-order computers.

In 1993, Tandy (which owns Radio Shack) stopped manufacturing computers and sold all its factories to AST. So now AST makes all Tandy and Radio Shack computers. Those extra factories have made AST one of the world's 7 most popular computer manufacturers. (The "7 popular computer manufacturers", which make more computers than any other companies, are IBM, Compaq, Apple, Packard Bell, Dell, Gateway, and AST.)

AST also manufactures some of Dell's notebook computers. So if you try to buy a Tandy computer, Radio Shack computer, or Dell notebook computer, you're typically buying a computer built by AST.

Midwest Micro was praised in the previous edition for offering notebook computers at low prices. But Midwest Micro has dropped prices too slowly since then, so now Midwest Micro's notebooks aren't much cheaper than the excellent ones by Compaq, Toshiba, and IBM. Moreover, in December 1994 Midwest Micro became overloaded: shipments got delayed, customers complained about Midwest Micro's notebook and desktop computers not working, and tech support lines became jammed (like Gateway's).

I hope Midwest Micro drops its prices again and improves its service. Meanwhile, if you want to buy a notebook computer, you're probably better off going into a local store and buying a Compaq, Toshiba, or IBM.

Micron is one of America's biggest manufacturers of RAM chips. Recently, Micron began selling complete computer systems also. Its computers come with lots of RAM (since the RAM chips cost Micron nearly nothing) and run fast. According to surveys of computer users by PC World and PC Magazine, Micron's computers are slightly above average in reliability, and Micron is TERRIFIC at answering tech-support calls and resolving problems immediately. Micron's customers are happier than the customers from all other manufacturers! Micron's in Idaho at 800-347-4590 or 208-465-8970. Unfortunately, Micron's prices are very high, just like the prices from Compaq, IBM, and Dell.

Zeos, Gateway, Dell, and Northgate were the four biggest mail-order manufacturers back in the 1980's. Zeos and Northgate were both in Minnesota and called the "Minnesota twins". Zeos was in Saint Paul; Northgate was 15 miles away, in Eden Prairie. They were also called the "owls" because they were the only companies offering toll-free technical support around-the-clock, 24 hours.

In 1991, Zeos and Northgate both faced crises. Zeos's quality dipped, and several reviewers received Zeos computers that were defective. Northgate suffered severe financial problems and lost its president.

In 1994, Northgate finally went out of business. Zeos is still fully in business, though it's occasionally been operating at a loss. Like Micron, Zeos's prices are somewhat high. Micron wants to buy Zeos, and both companies look forward to the day when they can join forces and have enough combined clout to knock the hell out of Dell, Gateway, and other competitors. Stay tuned!

Zeos had a strange beginning. It was founded by Greg Herrick in 1986. He wanted to name the company "Eos" (which is the Greek word for "dawn"). He paid a designer $3,000 to design the "Eos" logo and stationery but then discovered that the name "Eos" was already being used by an architectural firm. He had to invent a new name quickly, and he hoped to shortcut the redesign process by just adding a letter in front of "Eos". He went through the whole alphabet — "Aeos", "Beos", "Ceos" — but they all sounded wrong, until he got to "Zeos". That became the company name! Years later, a colleague told him that in an early 1980's episode of the "Dr. Who" sci-fi series, Dr. Who encountered a planet named Zeos, whose sole resident was a computer, and the expedition to Zeos was led by a guy named Herrick. Just coincidence? Greg Herrick said he'd never heard of Dr. Who.

Phone Zeos at 800-272-8993 or 612-362-1212. If you try phoning for tech support, you'll discover that Zeos's tech-support number is busy most of the day but very easy to access in the middle of the night. Try after 3AM!

Acer is a consortium of Taiwanese computer companies. It has 20 factories, sells computers in 90 countries, and has annual sales of about 3 billion dollars. Acer computers are particularly popular in Southeast Asia and Latin America. Acer makes "Acer computers" and "Acros computers". They're sold mainly through computer stores and department stores. Acer also supplies parts for other brands of computers. For example, some Compudyne computers contain motherboards made by Acer.

Recently, Acer's begun selling by mail-order at 800-230-ACER, but Acer prices aren't low enough to compete against mail-order companies.

Bargain-brand computers are sold by discount department stores at low prices. Those computers cost so little because they're crummy. Check the specs!

Here's another reason why those computers cost so little: when you ask the dealer for help (because you're confused or the computer is broken), the dealer will typically say "I don't know. Phone the manufacturer." But when you try phoning the manufacturer, you'll find that the manufacturer's phone number is almost always busy, and you can't get through. Before buying a computer, try this experiment: ask the dealer what phone number you'd call if you need repairs or technical assistance, then try phoning that number and see whether anybody answers!

Local heroes? In many towns across the USA and around the world, entrepreneurs sell computers at ridiculously low prices. You'll find those entrepreneurs at computer shows and in the tiny stores they run. Before buying a computer, check the computer's technical specifications and the dealer's reputation.

If the dealer offers you software, make sure the dealer also gives you an official manual from the software's publisher, with a warranty/registration card. Otherwise, the software might be an illegal hot copy.

A used computer whose CPU is slow (an 8088) typically costs about $175. That price includes even the hard disk and monitor. Buy it from a friend, relative, or neighbor who is moving up to a fancier computer; or phone a used-computer broker such as the National Computer Exchange (phone 800-NACOMEX).

For further advice about which computer to buy, phone me anytime at 617-666-2666.

ORIGINAL APPLE

The original Apple computer was invented by Steve Wozniak, who was an engineer at Hewlett-Packard. In 1975, he offered the plans to his boss at Hewlett-Packard, but his boss said Steve's computer didn't fit into Hewlett-Packard's marketing plan. His boss suggested that Steve start his own company. Steve did.

He worked with his friend, Steve Jobs. Steve Wozniak was the engineer; Steve Jobs was the businessman. Both were young: Steve Wozniak was 22; Steve Jobs was 19. Both were college drop-outs. They'd worked together before: when high-school students, they'd built and sold **blue boxes** (boxes that people attached to telephones to illegally make long-distance calls free). Steve & Steve had sold 200 blue boxes at $80 each, giving them a total of $16,000 in illegal money.

To begin Apple Computer Company, Steve & Steve invested just $1300, which they got by selling a used Volkswagen Micro Bus and a used calculator.

They built the first Apple computer in their garage. They sold it by word of mouth, then later by ads. The advertised price was just $666.60.

APPLE 2

The original Apple computer looked pathetic. But in 1977, Steve & Steve invented a slicker version, called the **Apple 2**. Unlike the original Apple, the Apple 2 included a keyboard and displayed graphics in color. It cost $970.

The Apple 2 became a smashing success, because it was the first computer for under $1000 that could display colors on a TV. It was the *only* such computer for many years, until Commodore finally invented the Vic, which was even cheaper (under $300).

At first, people used the Apple 2 to play games and didn't take the computer seriously. But two surprise events changed the world's feelings about Apple.

MECC

The first surprise was that the Minnesota state government decided to buy lots of Apple 2 computers, put them in Minnesota schools, and write programs for them. That state agency, called the **Minnesota Educational Computing Consortium (MECC)**, then distributed the programs free to other schools across America.

Soon, schools across America discovered that personal computers could be useful in education, and that the only programs available came from Minnesota and required Apples. So schools across America bought Apples — and then wrote more programs for the Apples they'd bought. Apple became the "standard" computer for education — just because of the chain reaction that started with a chance event in Minnesota. The chain reaction spread rapidly, as teachers fell in love with the Apple's color graphics.

Visicalc

The next surprise was that a graduate student at the Harvard Business School and his friend at M.I.T. got together and wrote an amazing accounting program called **Visicalc**. They wrote it for the Apple 2 computer, because it was the only low-cost computer that had a reliable disk operating system.

(Commodore's computers didn't have disks yet, and Radio Shack's disk operating system was buggy until the following year. Apple's success was due to Steve Wozniak's brilliance: he invented a disk-controller card that was amazingly cheap and reliable.)

The Visicalc accounting program was so wonderful that accountants and business managers all over the country bought it — and therefore had to buy Apple computers to run it on.

Visicalc was better than any accounting program that had been invented on even the largest IBM maxicomputers. Visicalc proved that little Apples could be more convenient than even the most gigantic IBM.

Later, Visicalc became available for other computers; but at first, Visicalc required an Apple, and Visicalc's success led to the success of Apple.

In a typical large corporation, the corporate accountant wanted to buy an Apple with Visicalc. Since the corporation's data-processing director liked big computers and refused to buy microcomputers, the accountant who wanted Visicalc resorted to an old business trick: he lied. He pretended to spend $2000 for "typewriters" but bought an Apple instead. He snuck it into the company and plopped it on his desk. That happened all across America, so all large corporations had thousands of Apples sitting on the desks of accountants and managers but disguised as "typewriters" or "word processors".

Yes, Apple computers infiltrated American corporations by subversion. It was an underground movement that annoyed IBM so much that IBM eventually decided to invent a personal computer of its own.

Apple 2+

In 1979, Apple Computer Corporation began shipping an improved Apple 2, called the **Apple 2+**.

Its main improvement was that its ROM chips contained a better version of BASIC, called **Applesoft BASIC**, which could handle decimals. (The version of BASIC in the old Apple 2's ROM chips handled just integers.)

Another improvement was how the RESET key acted. On the old Apple 2, pressing the RESET key would abort a program, so the program would stop running. Too many consumers pressed the RESET key accidentally and got upset. On the Apple 2+, pressing the RESET key aborted a program just if you simultaneously held down the CONTROL key.

Slots

In the Apple 2+ and its predecessors, the motherboard contained eight slots, numbered from 0 to 7. Each slot could hold a printed-circuit card.

Slot 0 was for a **memory card** (containing extra RAM). Slot 1 was for a **printer card** (containing a parallel printer port). Slot 2 was for an **internal modem** (for attaching to a phone). Slot 3 was for an **80-column card** (to make the screen display 80 characters per line instead of 40). Slot 6 was for a **disk controller**. Cards in slots 4, 5, and 7 were more exotic.

Apple 2e

In 1983, Apple began shipping a further improvement, called the **Apple 2 extended, expanded, enhanced (Apple 2e)**. Most programs written for the Apple 1, 2, and 2+ also run on the Apple 2e.

Keyboard Whereas the Apple 2+ keyboard contained just 52 keys, the Apple 2e keyboard contains 63 keys. The 11 extra keys help you type lowercase letters, type special symbols, edit your writing, and control your programs.

For example, the Apple 2e keyboard contains all four arrow keys (↑, ↓, ←, and →), so you can easily move around the screen in all four directions. (The ↑ and ↓ keys were missing from the Apple 2+ keyboard.)

The Apple 2e keyboard contains a DELETE key, so you can easily delete an error from the middle of your writing. (The DELETE key was missing from the Apple 2+ keyboard.)

Slot 0 Unlike its predecessors, the Apple 2e omits slot 0, because the Apple 2e doesn't need a RAM card: the Apple 2e's motherboard already contains lots of RAM (64K).

Slot 3A The Apple 2e contains an extra slot. It's called slot 3A. It resembles slot 3 but holds a more modern kind of video card that comes in two versions: the plain version lets your Apple display 80 characters per line; the fancy version does the same but also includes a row of 64K RAM chips, so that your Apple contains 128K of RAM altogether.

Apple 2e versus IBM clones An Apple 2e system costs more than an IBM XT clone and in almost every way is worse: for example, the Apple 2e system has less RAM (128K instead of 640K), fewer keys on the keyboard (63 instead of 83), inferior disk drives (writing just 140K on the disk instead of 360K), and a crippled version of BASIC (understanding just 114 words instead of 178).

Nevertheless, the Apple 2e became quite popular, because **more educational programs and games are available for the Apple 2e than for any other computer**. That's because the Apple 2e still runs thousands of programs that were invented years ago for its predecessors: the Apple 1, 2, and 2+. Fewer educational programs and games have been written for the IBM PC and clones, because the IBM PC costs more than schools and kids can afford. Although the IBM PC has become the standard computer for business, the Apple 2e is still the standard computer for schools and kids.

Apple 2c

In 1984, Apple created a shrunken Apple 2e called the **Apple 2 compact (Apple 2c)**. Besides being smaller and lighter than the Apple 2e, it costs less.

Which is better: the 2e or the 2c? On the one hand, the 2c costs less, has the convenience of being more portable, and consumes less electricity. On the other hand, hobbyists spurn the 2c because it doesn't have any slots for adding cards; it's not expandable. But the average consumer doesn't long for extra cards anyway, since the motherboard includes everything a beginner needs: 128K of RAM, 80-character-per-line video circuitry, a disk controller, and two serial ports. You can run cables from the back of the 2c to a serial printer, modem, second disk drive, and joystick.

When the 2c first came out, its ROM was fancier than the 2e's, so that the 2c could handle BASIC and a mouse better than the 2e. But in February 1985, Apple began putting the fancy ROM chips in the 2e also, so that every new 2e handles BASIC and a mouse as well as the 2c.

Apple 2c+ Apple invented an improved Apple 2c, called the **Apple 2c+**, whose disk drive is 3½-inch instead of 5¼-inch. Though Apple's 3½-inch drive is technologically superior to Apple's 5¼-inch drive, most educational software still comes on 5¼-inch disks and is not available on 3½-inch disks yet.

Apple 2GS

In 1986, Apple created an improved version of the Apple 2e and called it the **Apple 2 with amazing graphics & sound (Apple 2GS)**.

Its graphics are fairly good (better than EGA, though not as good as VGA). Its musical abilities are amazing; they arise from Apple's **Ensoniq chip**, which can produce 32 musical voices simultaneously!

The computer contains an extra-fast CPU (the 65816), 128k of ROM, 256K of general-purpose RAM, and 64K of RAM for the sound synthesizer.

To run the popular 2GS programs, you must add an extra 256K of RAM, to bring the total RAM up to 512K. Better yet, get 1M of RAM. Discount dealers have sold the 2GS with 1M RAM for $800. That price does *not* include a monitor or any disk drives. To run the popular programs well, you must buy a *color* monitor and *two* disk drives.

Apple 2 family

All those computers resemble each other, so that most programs written for the Apple 2 also work on the Apple 2+, 2e, 2c, 2c+, and 2GS.

Apple has stopped marketing all those computers, but you can still buy them as "used computers" from your neighbors.

Laser 128

Instead of getting an Apple 2c, consider getting a **Laser 128**. It imitates an Apple 2c but costs less.

It runs most Apple 2c programs perfectly. (Just 5% of the popular Apple 2c programs are incompatible with the Laser 128.) Like the Apple 2c, the Laser 128 includes 128K of RAM, a disk drive, and a serial port. In three ways, it's even *better* than an Apple 2c: it includes a parallel printer port (so you can attach a greater variety of printers), a numeric keypad (so you can enter data into spreadsheets more easily), and a slot (so you can add an Apple 2e expansion card).

A souped-up version, called the **Laser 128EX**, goes three times as fast.

The Laser 128 and 128EX are built by the **Laser Computer** division of **VTech**, the same company that makes IBM clones. You can buy the Laser 128 for $279, and the Laser 128EX for $355, from a discount dealer called **USA Micro** (2888 Bluff St., Suite 257, Boulder CO 80301, phone 800-654-5426 or 303-938-9089).

Another discount dealer, **Perfect Solutions**, charges slightly more for the computers but slightly less for monitors and other add-ons. Contact Perfect Solutions at 12657 Coral Breeze Dr., West Palm Beach, FL 33414, phone 800-726-7086 or 407-790-1070.

Quality Computers

The biggest dealer still selling hardware and software for the Apple 2 family is **Quality Computers** (20200 Nine Mile Rd., PO Box 349, St. Clair Shores MI 48080, phone 800-777-3642 or 313-774-7200). That dealer sells a wide variety of goodies by mail and also publishes an Apple 2 magazine called **II Alive** ($3.95 per issue, 6 issues per year, $19.95 per year).

LUXURIOUS APPLES

Apple Computer Inc. invented two luxury computers, the **Apple 3** and the **Lisa**. Priced at about $10,000 (including monitor, hard drive, and software), they were too expensive for consumers, but Apple hoped that rich businesses would buy a few. They *didn't* buy. Those luxurious computers were financial failures.

But Apple learned from its mistakes. Here are the details. . . .

Apple 3

Back in 1980, shortly after the Apple 2+ was invented, Apple began selling the **Apple 3**. It was much fancier than the Apple 2+. Unfortunately, it was ridiculously expensive (it listed for $4995, plus a monitor and hard drive), it couldn't run some of the Apple 2+ software, and the first ones off the assembly line were defective. Few people bought it.

When the IBM PC came out and consumers realized the PC was better and cheaper than the Apple 3, interest in the Apple 3 vanished. Apple gave up trying to sell the Apple 3, but incorporated the Apple 3's best features into later Apples that were more affordable: the Apple 2e and the Apple 2GS.

Lisa

Apple's next attempt at a luxurious computer was the **Lisa**, which was named after Steve Job's daughter.

The Lisa was even more expensive than the Apple 3, and it didn't run *any* Apple 2+ software; in fact, it had a completely different CPU. But the Lisa received high praise, because its screen could draw fancy graphics quickly, and its operating system and business programs were extremely easy to learn to use: you just pointed at pictures instead of typing hard-to-remember computer commands.

The Lisa's screen displayed cute little drawings, called **icons**. Some of the icons stood for activities. To make the Lisa perform an activity, you looked on the screen for the activity's icon. (For example, to make the computer delete a file, you began by looking for a picture of a garbage can.) When you pointed at the icon by using a mouse, the Lisa performed the icon's activity.

The Lisa also used **horizontal menus** and **pull-down menus**. A horizontal menu was a list of topics printed across the top line of the screen. If you pointed at one of those general topics (by using the mouse), a column of more specific choices appeared underneath that topic; that column of specific activities was called a **pull-down menu**. You then looked at the pull-down menu, found the specific activity you were interested in, pointed at it (by using the mouse), and the computer would immediately start performing that activity.

Pointing at icons, horizontal menus, and pull-down menus was much easier to learn than using the kinds of computer systems other manufacturers had developed before. It was also fun! Yes, the Lisa was the first computer whose business programs were truly fun to run. And because it was so easy to learn to use, customers could start using it without reading the manuals. Everybody praised the Lisa and called it a new breakthrough in software technology.

But even though the Lisa was highly praised, few people bought it, because it was too expensive. It cost nearly $10,000.

Though Apple invented some business programs that were fun and easy to use, independent programmers had difficulty developing their *own* programs for the Lisa, because Apple didn't supply enough programming tools. Apple never invented a version of BASIC, delayed introducing a version of PASCAL, and didn't make detailed manuals available to the average programmer. And though icons and pull-down menus are easy to use, they're difficult for programmers to invent.

Apple gradually lowered the Lisa's price.

In January 1984, Apple introduced the **Macintosh (Mac)**, which was a stripped-down version of the Lisa. Like the Lisa, the Mac uses a mouse, icons, horizontal menus, and pull-down menus. The Mac's price was low enough to make it popular.

The Mac is even more fun and easy than the Lisa! It appeals to beginners who are scared of computers. Many advanced computerists use it also, because it feels ultra-modern, handles graphics quickly, and passes data from one program to another simply.

The original version of the Mac ran too slowly, but the newest versions run faster. They're priced about the same as IBM's computers, though not as cheaply as IBM clones.

Since the Mac's so easy to use and costs so little, many people have bought it. Lots of software's been developed for it — much more than for the Lisa. Alas, popular Mac software doesn't run well on the Lisa. Apple has stopped selling the Lisa and stopped selling a compromise called the **Mac XL**.

The first Macs

Apple began selling the Mac for $2495. The original version of the Mac consists of three parts: the mouse, the keyboard, and the system unit.

The system unit contains a 9-inch black-and-white screen (whose resolution is 512 by 384), a 3½-inch floppy disk drive, and a motherboard. On the motherboard sit an 8-megahertz 68000 CPU, two ROM chips (containing most of the operating system and many routines for drawing graphics), rows of RAM chips, a disk controller, and two serial ports (for attaching a printer and a modem).

That Mac is called the **original 128K Mac** because it includes 128K of RAM (plus 64K of ROM).

Then Apple invented an improvement called the **512K Mac** because it includes 512K of RAM. (It uses two rows of 256K chips instead of two rows of 64K chips.) Apple wanted to call it the "Big Mac" but feared that customers would think it was a hamburger.

In January 1986, Apple began selling a new, improved Mac, called the **Mac Plus**. It's better than the 512K Mac in several ways: it contains a larger RAM (1 megabyte instead of 512K), a larger ROM (128K instead of 64K), a better disk drive (double-sided instead of single-sided), a larger keyboard (which contains extra keys), and a port that lets you add a hard-disk drive more easily. The improved ROM, RAM, disk drive, keyboard, and port all serve the same overall purpose: they provide hardware and software tricks that let Mac programs run faster.

Like the 128K and 512K Macs, the Mac Plus includes one floppy drive.

Mac SE

In 1987, Apple introduced an even fancier Mac, called the **Mac SE**. It runs software 15% faster than the Mac Plus because it contains a cleverer ROM (which is 256K instead of 128K) and fancier support chips. It's also more **expandable**: it lets you insert extra circuitry more easily. The keyboard costs extra: buy the **standard keyboard** (which has 81 keys) or the **extended keyboard** (which has 105 keys and costs more).

Mac 2

When Apple introduced the Mac SE, Apple also introduced a luxury model, called the **Mac 2**. It contains a faster CPU (a 16-megahertz 68020) and 6 slots for inserting printed-circuit cards.

Instead of sticking you with a 9-inch black-and-white monitor, it lets you use any kind of monitor you wish: choose big or small; choose black-and-white or gray-scale or color. The monitor costs extra; so do the keyboard (standard or extended) and video card (which you put into a slot and attach the monitor to).

Since the Mac 2 lets you choose your own monitor, the Mac 2 is called a **modular Mac**. When buying a modular Mac, remember that the monitor costs extra!

New Macs

All the Macs that I've mentioned so far — the 128K Mac, 256K Mac, Mac Plus, Mac SE, and Mac 2 — are obsolete. Apple has stopped selling them. Instead, Apple sells newer Macs that are nicer. Here they are. . . .

Performa

The easiest way to buy a Mac is to buy a Mac called the **Performa**. It comes in several versions:

Computer	CPU	Memory	Monitor	Price
Performa 475	68040-25	4/160	14"	$1099
Performa 550	68030-33	5/160/CD	14"	$1299
Performa 575	68040-66/33	5/250/CD	14"	$1499
Performa 577	68040-66/33	5/320/CD	14"	$1549
Performa 578	68040-66/33	8/320/CD	14"	$1699
Performa 630	68040-66/33	4/250	14"	$1499
Performa 630CD	68040-66/33	8/250/CD	14"	$1899
Performa 635CD	68040-66/33	5/250/CD	15"	$1899
Performa 638CDV	68040-66/33	8/350/CD	15"	$2299
Performa 6112CD	Power PC 601-60	8/250/CD	15"	$2299
Performa 6115CD	Power PC 601-60	8/350/CD	15"	$2399

For example, that chart's bottom line says the Performa 6115CD computer contains a fast CPU (a Power PC 601 running at a speed of 60 megahertz), lots of memory (8 megabytes of RAM, a 350 megabyte hard drive, and a CD-ROM drive), and a 15-inch monitor. Most dealers selling it charge $2399.

Like Intel's DX2-66 chip, Motorola's 68040-66/33 chip thinks at 66 megahertz but communicates at just 33 megahertz and sits on a 33-megahertz motherboard.

When you buy a Performa, you get the following goodies at no extra charge: a keyboard, mouse, high-density 3½-inch floppy drive, fax/modem, sound, new operating system (**Mac System 7.5**), and lots of programs.

Which is better, the Performa 578 or the Performa 630CD? The Performa 630CD costs $200 more, even though it contains a smaller hard drive, because the Performa 630CD comes with more programs and is more **expandable**: it contains extra slots so you can add extra devices later.

In the Performa 638CDV, the "V" stands for "video": its price includes the **Apple Video/TV System**, which turns your computer into a TV (so you can watch up to 181 TV channels on your computer screen) and lets you attach your computer to a camcorder and VCR, so you can use the computer to edit videos.

Availability Most dealers sell the **Performa 575**, **Performa 630CD**, and **Performa 6115CD**. Those three Performas are the most popular.

Some of the other Performas are rare, sold by just a *few* dealers. You can get the **Performa 635CD** and **Performa 6112CD** at **Staples** (a chain of office-supply superstores). You can get all the other Performas at **Creative Computers**, which is a chain of Mac superstores in southern California; either walk into a Creative Computers store or order by mail at 800-222-2808 (day or night, 24 hours). Creative Computers gives free shipping of Performa computers to the 48 states by ground; add just $3 for next-day air.

Apple has stopped manufacturing the **Performa 460**, which had a 68030-33 CPU, a 4/80 memory, and a 14" monitor.

Monitor quality All Performas in the chart come with color monitors whose resolution is respectable (at least 640x480) and whose dot pitch is good (.28 or .26 millimeters). The discontinued Performa 460 came with a worse monitor whose screen was blurry (.39 millimeters).

Fax/modem The fanciest Performas (the 6112CD and 6115CD) come with a fax/modem that's fast: it sends and receives faxes and modem data at 14400-baud.

The other Performas come with a fax/modem that's a slow cripple: it sends and receives modem data at 2400-baud and sends faxes at 9600-baud; it can't *receive* any faxes. Since it can send faxes but not receive them, it's called a **send-fax/modem**.

Software Each Performa comes with lots of software. The exact list depends on which Performa you buy. Usually, you get about 20 programs altogether! For example, the Performa 635CD comes with:

the Mac operating system (**Mac System 7.5**)

a general encyclopedia (**New Grolier Multimedia Encyclopedia** CD-ROM)

a medical reference full of health tips (**The Family Doctor** CD-ROM)

a dictionary (**American Heritage Dictionary**, which includes definitions; and if you know a concept, the program helps you search for the word whose definition contains that concept)

an atlas (**Electronic Arts 3-D Atlas** CD-ROM)

an almanac of info about current events & 20th-century history culled from articles in TIME Magazine and CNN Newroom videos (**The TIME Almanac** CD-ROM)

an integrated program that handles word processing, databases, spreadsheets, and graphics (**Claris Works**)

a program that balances your checkbook and tracks your expenses (**Quicken**)

collections of cartoons and other clip-art pictures that you can insert into your own desktop-published documents (**MacGallery Clip Art Treasure Pak** and **Click Art Performa Collection**)

fun tools to help kids explore & learn & grow & do their homework (**The Writing Center**, **Kid Works**, and **Thinkin' Things**)

games (**Wacky Jacks Game Show** CD-ROM with Saturday Night Live's Don Pardo, **Spectre Challenger** fast-paced action game, **Crossword Wizard** crossword-puzzle maker, and **Spin Doctor Challenge**)

a utility that lets kids access their stuff easily while passwords prevent them from wrecking their parents' files (**At Ease**)

a utility that helps your Mac swap data with an IBM PC by sharing the same 3½-inch floppy disk (**Macintosh PC Exchange** and **MacLink Plus Easy Open Translators**)

a utility that lets you access Apple's on-line computer service by phone (**eWorld**)

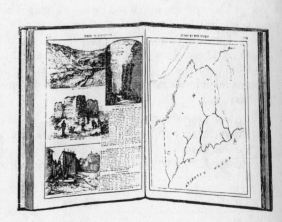

Service Each Performa comes with **lifetime toll-free technical support**. Yes, whenever you have a question about your Performa, or need help, phone Apple headquarters at **800-SOS-APPLE**, and you can get help, free, for your entire lifetime!

Here the good news: you can phone day or night, 24 hours! Here's the bad news: the phone number is usually busy. Keep trying!

Each Performa comes with a **one-year on-site warranty**. Here's what that means: during the first year, if Apple's technicians can't solve your problem by just chatting with you on the phone or sending you a replacement, they'll send a repairman to your home, free.

Printer Eventually, you'll want to add a printer, which is *not* included in a Performa's price. If you're on a tight budget, get Apple's **Stylewriter 2** ink-jet printer, which most discount dealers sell for just $280.

Quadra

Apple sells a series of Mac computers called the **Quadra**. Each Quadra computer contains a 68040 CPU. They're called **Quadra** computers because of the "4" in "68040".

The cheapest Quadra is the **Quadra 605**, which contains a 68040-25. Since other Quadras go faster, the Quadra 605 is rarely sold anymore.

Quadra versus Performa

The most popular Quadra is the **Quadra 630**. Like the Performa 630, it contains a 68040-66/33 CPU, a 4M RAM, and a 250M hard drive. It costs just $1079. That's $420 less than the Performa 630's $1499 price because the Quadra 630's price does *not* include a keyboard ($85), monitor ($298), fax/modem, or application programs. If you add those missing items to the Quadra 630's price, you'll pay more than for a Performa 630; but the Quadra 630 lets you *choose* which kind of keyboard, monitor, fax/modem, and programs to buy.

Get a Quadra 630 instead of a Performa 630 if you need extra keys on the keyboard, a bigger monitor, a faster fax/modem, and more advanced programs than the Performa 630 provides.

The Quadra is intended for folks smart enough to know that "quadra" is the Latin word for "4". The Performa is intended for folks stupid enough to think that the word "performer" should be pronounced that way.

The Quadra is intended to be sold by expert computer salespeople to expert customers. The Performa is intended to be sold by idiots to customers who are idiots.

Here are the details. . . .

Quadra computers are sold just by computer experts from computer stores (such as Comp USA). Performa computers are sold mainly by idiots in office-supply stores (such as Staples and Office Max).

To repair a Quadra, phone the computer technicians at the computer store where you bought it. To repair a Performa computer, phone Apple headquarters at 800-SOS-APPLE.

For a Quadra, choose which keyboard, monitor, and fax/modem you want; they cost extra. A Performa's price includes a keyboard, monitor, and fax/modem; there are no surcharges or choices.

A Quadra's price includes very little software. A Performa's price includes lots of software —— especially games and tutorials.

Though Performas are idiotic, they're the best values: you get more hardware and software per dollar when you buy a Performa than when you buy a Quadra.

The rule used to be simple: Quadras were sold just at computer stores; Performas were sold just at general stores. At the end of 1994, Apple began letting computer stores sell *both* kinds of computers (Quadras and Performas), to handle both kinds of customers (experts and idiots). Non-computer stores (such as Staples) are still restricted to selling to idiots: they sell just Performas, no Quadras.

Is the Power PC chip good?

The **Power PC** is an extra-fast CPU chip invented by a team from Apple, Motorola, and IBM, all working together. In March 1994, Apple began selling computers using that chip.

The first version of the Power PC chip is called the **Power PC 601**. Even faster versions (the **Power PC 604** and **Power PC 620**) will be developed later.

Now the Power PC 601 chip is used in fast Performa computers (the Performa 6112CD and Performa 6115CD). It's also used in a computer called the **Power Mac**, which is sold like the Quadra (just in computer stores, at a price that does *not* include a keyboard or monitor or fax/modem). The Power Mac comes in 4 versions:

Power Mac 6100/66 runs at 66 megahertz. It costs $1699 for 8/350, $1899 for 8/350/CD.
Power Mac 7100/80 runs at 80 megahertz. It costs $2729 for 8/500, $3049 for 8/700/CD.
Power Mac 8100/100 runs at 100 megahertz. It costs $3399 for 8/700, $4199 for 16/1000/CD.
Power Mac 8100/110 runs at 110 megahertz. It costs $5799 for 16/2000/CD.

Native mode If you buy a Mac containing a Power PC chip, your Mac will run at full speed just if you buy programs written specifically for that chip. Such programs are called **native-mode Power programs**. Programs written for other Macs instead will run on the Power PC chip but slowly, by using Apple's **emulator** that makes the Power PC chip try to imitate other Mac chips.

Computerists have been waiting for more native-mode Power programs to be written. Folks who bought Power Macs (and the Performa 6112CD and 6115CD) have been disappointed at the slow speed of the emulated software they must use.

Apple expects that sometime in 1995 the Power PC will have enough native-mode software to become popular, and the Quadras and cheap Performas will be phased out.

I'm writing this book at the beginning of 1995. You're living in my future! Please tell me, o future person: will Apple turn out to be right? In 1995, will the Power PC acquire enough native-mode software to become wildly popular? Or will Intel (which Apple calls "the evil empire") drop Pentium-chip prices enough so that folks continue to buy IBM clones instead of Power Macs? Even Apple lovers are betting, sadly, that Intel will win.

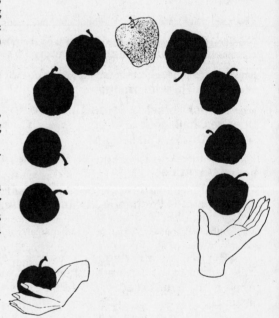

Powerbook

You can buy these notebook computers, called **Powerbooks**:

Name	CPU	Screen	Floppy?	RAM, drive, price
Powerbook 150	68030-33	passive gray-scale	yes	4/120 $1300
Powerbook 520	68040-50/25	passive gray-scale	yes	4/160 $1797
Powerbook 520c	68040-50/25	dual-scan color	yes	4/160 $2263, 12/320 $3269
Powerbook Duo 280c	68040-66/33	active color	no	4/320 $3379, 12/320 $3869
Powerbook 540c	68040-66/33	active color	yes	4/320 $3598, 12/320 $4439

Those prices are from discounters. The typical Powerbook weighs about 7 pounds and includes a floppy drive. The Powerbook Duo 280c weighs under 5 pounds because it lacks a floppy drive. The most expensive notebooks (the Powerbook Duo 280c and the Powerbook 540c) have high prices because their screens are **active-matrix** color, which means the screens are extra-bright and respond extra-fast.

Many Macs

Many other Macs have come & gone. The following Macs have been the most popular; I've underlined the ones that are still actively marketed:

CPU	Macs
68000-8	128K, 512K, 512Ke, Plus, SE, Classic
68000-16	Powerbook 100, Portable
68020-16	2, LC
68030-16	Performa 200&400, Powerbook 140, LC 2, Classic 2, Color Classic, SE/30, 2x, 2cx
68030-20	2si
68030-25	Performa 450, Powerbook 145&145B&160&170&210, LC 3&520, 2ci
68030-32	Performa 600&600CD, 2vx
68030-33	Performa 460&466&467&550, Powerbook 150&165&165c&180&180c&230&250&270c
68030-40	2fx
68040-20	Centris 610
68040-25	Performa 475&476, Quadra 605&610&660AV&700&900, LC 475, Centris 650&660AV
68040-33	Quadra 650&800&950
68040-40	Quadra 840AV
68040-50/25	Powerbook 520&520c
68040-66/33	Performa 575&577&578&630&630CD&635CD&638CDV, Quadra 630, Pbk. 280c&540c
601-60	Performa 6112CD&6115CD, Power Mac 6100/60
601-66	Power Mac 6100/66, Power Mac 7100/66
601-80	Power Mac 7100/80, Power Mac 8100/80
601-100	Power Mac 8100/100
601-110	Power Mac 8100/110

Should you buy a Mac?

Let's evaluate the Mac's famous features.

To use the Mac, you choose items from on-screen menus instead of having to memorize commands and type them. That's good!

To choose from a menu, the Mac requires you to point at the menu item by using a mouse. That's fun and easy to understand but slow: you must move your hand from the keyboard to the mouse, move the mouse's pointer to the menu item, then click the mouse's button. Fast typists prefer the menu methods popularized by Lotus 1-2-3 and Microsoft Windows: they let you keep your hands on the keyboard and just hit two keys. The first key (which in Lotus is a slash, and in Windows is the Alt key) tells the computer that you want to choose from a menu; the next key is the first letter of the menu item you're choosing.

In most Mac software, a menu across the top of the screen displays words, and a menu down the screen's left side displays little pictures called **icons**. Though the icons are cute and appeal to people who can't read English, you can get frustrated trying to guess what each icon means. For example, in Mac Paint one of the icons is supposed to be a picture of an eraser but looks more like a block of wood. Mac software takes the world back to the age of hieroglyphics, which are *not* an improvement over the Roman alphabet!

The Mac remains popular because it's great for graphics, cute enough to turn computer haters into computer lovers, and sports a screen that can display different typestyles and type sizes quickly enough to amaze desktop-publishing enthusiasts.

Price The Macs are competitively priced against IBM but not against IBM PC clones. That's why most people buy IBM PC clones, not Macs.

The IBM-versus-Mac contest would be more interesting if somebody would clone the Mac cheaply; but nobody dares, since many of the Mac's parts are copyrighted and patented by Apple. Recently, Apple has started licensing other companies to build Mac clones, but those clones aren't cheap.

The IBM PC can be cloned more easily, because IBM buys most of its parts from suppliers who also sell to IBM's competitors. Just a *few* parts in IBM's computers are built and patented by IBM. For many years, IBM didn't enforce its patents, though in 1988 IBM finally sent clone manufacturers letters demanding retroactive licensing fees.

Mac versus IBM Which is better, a Mac or an IBM PC?

When the Mac was invented in 1984, the answer was simple: though the Mac's software was easier to understand than the IBM PC's, the Mac ran too slowly, and not enough Mac software was available.

Now the IBM PC and Mac have both improved. IBM PC programmers, inspired by the Mac, have developed Mac-like easy-to-use software that runs on the IBM PC. To compete, Apple and its friends have developed faster Mac hardware and more Mac software. So the IBM PC and Mac are resembling each other more.

The question of which to buy is a matter of personal taste. The IBM PC appeals to people who are efficient, businesslike, conservative; the Mac appeals to people who are inspired, artistic, radical. Though I still recommend IBM PC clones, my advice might shift if the Mac continues to improve.

Mac-inspired systems Inspired by the Mac, programmers have invented **graphical user interfaces (GUI)**, which are software utilities making other computers resemble a Mac. The most popular are **Microsoft Windows** (which runs on the IBM), **OS/2** (on the IBM), **Gem** (on the IBM and Atari ST), **Geos** (on the IBM, Apple 2GS, and Commodore 64), and **Prodos 16** (on the Apple 2GS); but the Mac's more pleasant than them because the Mac's been around longer and developed a bigger library of software to choose from.

Much of the Mac's success is due to Guy Kawasaki, whose title at Apple was "Mac Software Evangelist". He convinced all major software companies to write programs for the Mac and make their programs resemble each other, so once you've learned to use one Mac program you can easily learn all the others. That's what makes the Mac so wonderfully easy to use: consistent software interfaces.

NEWTON

In 1993, Apple invented a palmtop computer called the **Newton**.

Instead of containing a keyboard, it contains a tablet you write on with a pen. The computer tries to read your handwriting and figure out which words you scribbled.

The newest version of the Newton, the **Newton Message Pad 120**, costs $590 from discount dealers (such as Creative Computers). While supplies last, you can get an older version (the **Newton Message Pad 100**) for just $199 from discounters such as Creative Computers and Mac Warehouse.

Is Newton good?

Computerists praise Apple for hitting on the Newton idea, and say the idea is very striking, but complain that the resulting Newton acts brain-damaged: it makes many mistakes when trying to interpret your handwriting. Because Newton makes so many mistakes, it isn't popular: most folks don't give a fig about Newton.

The modern world needs to go beyond Newton. We need an Einstein.

John Sculley, who headed Apple when the Newton was invented, hoped that the Newton would have a major effect on his career.

He was right: the Newton *did* have a major effect on his career. It *ended* his career: Apple's board of directors ousted him for spending too much effort on the Newton and not enough on Apple's mainstream products.

WHO RUNS APPLE?

Steve Wozniak got in an airplane crash that hurt his head and gave him amnesia, so he left the company and enrolled in college under a fake name ("Rocky Clark"). After he graduated, he returned to Apple Computer Company quietly. Steve Jobs managed the company.

Though Apple was successful, Steve Jobs' strategies upset some computerists. For example, Apple's ads claimed that the Apple was the first personal computer (it was *not* the first!); Apple launched a big campaign to make businessmen buy Apple PASCAL (even though Apple PASCAL was of no help to the average businessman whatsoever); Apple prohibited its dealers from displaying games (though Apple has since relented); and Apple still prohibits authorized dealers from selling Apples by mail order.

Apple Computer Inc. donated free Apple computers to schools for three reasons: to be nice, get a tax write-off, and lure schools into buying Apples (to be compatible with the Apples that the schools received free). But if Apple *really* wanted to be nice, it would lower prices further so that low-income consumers could afford them. Apple isn't trying to sell to the poor; instead, Apple's trying to sell to the "chic".

Steve & Steve both left Apple and went separate ways. Apple's next head was John Sculley, a marketer who used to be a vice-president of Pepsi. He made Pepsi the #2 soft drink (just behind Coke) and kept Apple the #2 microcomputer company (just behind IBM). In 1993, he stepped down; now Apple's headed by Michael Spindler, an efficient German trying to drop Apple's costs and prices.

ALTERNATIVE COMPUTERS

COMMODORE

Commodore is the computer company that's called "the house that Jack built", because it was started by Jack Tramiel.

How Commodore began

Jack began his career by being in the wrong place at the wrong time: he was a Jew in Poland during World War 2. He was thrown into the Auschwitz concentration camp, where he learned to view life as a war to survive. When he finally escaped from the camp, he moved to Canada and started an aggressive, ruthless business whose motto for survival was, "Business is war!"

He called his company **Commodore**. At first, it just repaired typewriters; but it grew rapidly. Then Commodore built its own pocket calculators and sold them.

War of the chips

In Commodore's calculators, the CPU was a microprocessor chip manufactured by a company called **MOS Technology**. But MOS Technology was in trouble because of how that company had begun. . . .

In 1974, the most popular microprocessors had been the Intel 8080 and the Motorola 6800. Chuck Peddle, who helped invent the 6800, quit Motorola in 1975 and founded MOS Technology with his friends. MOS Technology manufactured the **6501 microprocessor**, which was so similar to Motorola's 6800 that Motorola threatened to sue. To placate Motorola, MOS Technology stopped manufacturing the 6501 and switched to the **6502**, invented by Chuck Peddle and different enough from Motorola's 6800 to avoid a lawsuit. The 6502 chip became very popular; many companies paid MOS Technology to manufacture it. One of MOS Technology's biggest customers was Commodore.

Although the 6502 was legal, Motorola sued MOS Technology for its illegal predecessor, the 6501. The suit dragged through the courts for two years and cost MOS Technology many thousands of dollars in lawyers' fees. Finally, in 1977, Motorola won $200,000.

That put MOS Technology into financial trouble, so it announced a desire to be bought by some company having lots of cash. Commodore, rich by then, bought it.

Just before that sale, Canada's tax laws changed. To duck taxes, Commodore moved its headquarters (in theory) to the Bahamas. That's how MOS Technology became part of "Commodore Limited", a Bahamanian company, and how Commodore found itself running a company that made chips. Commodore had entered the computer business.

Dealing with competitors

At MOS Technology, Chuck Peddle had sold a 6502 chip to Steve Wozniak for $25. Steve used the chip to create the Apple computer. When Commodore saw Apple computers becoming popular in California, Commodore offered to buy the Apple Computer Company — and almost succeeded. Apple wanted $15,000 more than Commodore offered, so the deal never came off. Commodore's regretted it ever since.

Then Commodore hired Chuck Peddle to design a "Commodore computer". Commodore hoped to sell the Commodore computer to Radio Shack and let Radio Shack distribute it through Radio Shack's stores. Radio Shack said, "Great idea! Finish designing your computer, and tell us more about it." Commodore finished designing it and showed it to Radio Shack. Radio Shack said, "Your argument for selling low-cost computers was so convincing, we decided to build our own. Thanks for the idea." That's how Radio Shack got the idea of manufacturing computers!

Pet

Rebuffed by Apple and Radio Shack, Jack Tramiel decided to fight back by building a computer better and cheaper than anything Apple and Radio Shack had. Commodore called its new computer the **Pet**, because Commodore's marketing director was the same guy who invented the Pet Rock. He figured that if people were stupid enough to buy a Pet Rock, they'd *really* love a Pet computer! He was right: people loved the idea of a Pet Computer. Sales skyrocketed.

Commodore told the press that "Pet" was an abbreviation for "Personal Electronic Transactor". Actually, Commodore invented "Pet" first and later made up what it stood for.

Commodore announced the Pet in 1977 and said it would cost just $495. That price would include *everything*: the CPU, RAM, ROM, keyboard, monitor, and tape recorder. The ROM would have a good version of BASIC. The screen would display capital letters, lower-case letters, punctuation, math symbols, and many weirder symbols also (such as hearts, diamonds, clubs, spades, curves, circles, and rectangles).

Other microcomputer manufacturers were scared because Commodore's price was far lower than everybody else's, Commodore's computer offered more features, and Commodore was wealthy enough to spend more on ads and marketing than all other manufacturers combined.

Many computer magazines called the Pet "the birth of a new generation" in personal computers. The Pet's designer, Chuck Peddle, was treated to many interviews.

Disappointments Commodore raised its price from $495 to $595 before taking orders. To order the Pet, the customer had to send the $595 in full, plus shipping charges, then wait for Commodore to deliver.

Many folks mailed Commodore the money and waited a long time, but Commodore didn't ship. People got impatient.

Computer stores that had advertised the Pet got annoyed. Though the stores had received many orders from customers, Commodore wasn't yet shipping. Customers complained to the stores, and the stores couldn't solve the problem.

Meanwhile, Radio Shack entered the market with its TRS-80 model 1 priced at $599 — about the same price as Commodore's Pet. Radio Shack was kinder than Commodore: Radio Shack asked customers for just a 10% deposit (Commodore required payment in *full*); Radio Shack didn't charge for shipping (Commodore did); Radio Shack set up repair centers throughout the USA (Commodore's only repair center was in California); and Radio Shack delivered computers quickly (Commodore still wasn't delivering!).

Finally, Commodore admitted that the $595 Pet would *not* be delivered anytime soon! Commodore would deliver instead a $795 version that included 4K of extra RAM. So if you already sent $595 to Commodore and wanted a computer soon, you'd have to send an extra $200.

That was a rip-off, since 4K of extra RAM was *not* worth an extra $200. But customers were so desperate that they sent the $200 anyway.

Radio Shack shipped its computers on a first-come, first-served basis. Commodore didn't: Commodore gave preferential treatment to its "friends". If you ordered a Radio Shack computer, Radio Shack gave you an accurate estimate of when you'd receive the computer. If you ordered a computer from Commodore, you hadn't the faintest idea of when it would arrive, because you didn't know how many "friends" were on Commodore's list.

Radio Shack's computer came with a 232-page manual that was cheery and easy. Commodore's computer came with just 10 loose pages that were incomplete and hard to understand.

After announcing a low-cost printer, Commodore changed its mind and decided to sell just an expensive printer. After announcing a low-cost disk drive, Commodore changed its mind and decided to sell just an expensive unit containing *two* disk drives. Those wrong announcements lowered public confidence in Commodore even further.

That's how Commodore entered the personal computer market. And that's why the Pet (which at first was the best-selling computer) managed to drop in popularity, below Radio Shack, and even below Apple. Commodore dropped from being the #1 microcomputer company to being #3, after Radio Shack (#1) and Apple (#2).

Commodore came out with a souped-up Pet, called the **Commodore Business Machine (CBM)**. But that wasn't enough to let Commodore rise above the number 3 spot.

As Commodore's fortunes dipped, Chuck Peddle and his friends quit. Apple hired them but treated them as second-class citizens, so they returned to Commodore.

The problem with RAM
Commodore came out with several versions of the Pet. Each version contained a different quantity of RAM.

If you bought a stripped-down version and later wanted to increase its RAM, Commodore refused to install extra RAM. Instead, Commodore insisted that you buy a whole new Pet.

Some Commodore customers, who couldn't afford a new Pet, bought extra RAM chips from chip dealers and installed the chips themselves. To stop those tinkerers, Commodore played dirty: it began cutting a hole in the PC board where the extra RAM chips would go, so the tinkerers couldn't insert the chips. That nasty hole angered customers, who realized that Commodore spent almost as much money to cut the hole as it would have cost to provide the extra RAM chips!

The problem with tape
Commodore changed the Pet to handle tapes differently. The new Pet tape system was incompatible with the old Pet tape system: tapes created for the old Pet wouldn't work on the new Pet.

Commodore didn't notify customers of the change. The new Pet looked just like the old Pet; it didn't contain any kind of label saying "new". Customers who wrote programs for old Pets and then bought additional Pets discovered that their programs didn't work on the new Pets. They thought their new Pets were broken.

When Commodore secretly changed the tape system, companies selling tapes of Pet computer programs received angry letters from customers who bought the tapes and couldn't make the tapes work on their new Pets. The customers though the companies were crooks; the companies thought the customers were lying; and it took a long time for

people to realize that the real culprit was Commodore, who had changed the Pet without telling anybody.

When the companies discovered that Commodore had changed the Pet without providing a label to distinguish new Pets from old, the companies realized they'd have to give each customer *two* copies of each program, so the customer could try both versions. That's when many companies gave up trying to sell Pet tapes. They sold tapes for Apple and Radio Shack computers instead. That's why there's more software for Apple and Radio Shack than for Commodore.

Vic
Because of World War 2, Jack was scared of Nazis and the Japanese. He feared that the Japanese would suddenly invade the USA by flooding America with cheap Japanese computers to put Commodore and other American companies out of business. And he noticed that Commodore's share of the computer market was already sinking.

Paranoid, in April 1980 he called his engineers together and screamed at them, "The Japanese are coming! The Japanese are coming! So *we*'ll become the Japanese!" He laid out his bold plan: Commodore would build the world's first under-$300 computer to display colors on an ordinary TV and produce three-part harmony through the TV's speaker. At that time, the only under-$300 computer was Sinclair's ZX-80, which was black-and-white and crummy.

Commodore's engineers replied, "Build a color computer cheaply? Impossible!" Jack replied, "Do it!" Commodore's engineers finally managed to do it.

MOS Technology, owned by Commodore, had already invented the amazing **Video Interface Chip (Vic)**, which could handle the entire process of sending computer output to the TV screen. Since that chip was so cheap, Commodore decided to use it in the under-$300 computer. Unfortunately, it put just 22 characters per line on the screen. (By contrast, the Pet had 40 characters per line, and most computers today have 80 characters per line.) So the under-300 computer would display just 22 characters per line.

Naming the computer
Since the new computer was feminine and foxy, Commodore wanted to call it the "Vixen". But Commodore discovered that a "Vixen" computer couldn't sell in Germany, because "Vixen" sounds like the German word "Wichsen", which is obscene.

Commodore hastily changed the name to **Vic** and ran TV ads for the "Vic" computer. But that got Commodore into even worse trouble, because "Vic" sounds like the German word "Ficke", which is even *more* obscene!

Although Commodore still calls it the "Vic" in the United States, Commodore calls it the "VC" computer in Germany and pretends "VC" stands for "Volks Computer".

Price
Commodore began shipping the Vic in 1981. The original price was $299.95. Over the years, the price gradually dropped, so that stores eventually sold the Vic for about $55.

Ads
To sell the Vic, Commodore tried three kinds of ads.

The first featured TV star William Shatner, who played Captain Kirk in Star Trek. The ad emphasized how the Vic was wonderful, amazing, out of this world, fun, exciting. But then people started thinking of the Vic as just a sci-fi toy.

To combat the "toy" image, Commodore changed to a second kind of ad, which said the Vic was as cheap as a video-game machine but more educational for your kids.

When Texas Instruments began making similar claims, Commodore changed to a third kind of ad, which revealed that Commodore's disk drives, printers, and phone hookups cost much less than Texas Instruments'.

Popularity The Vic's low price, fun colors, and effective ads made it become popular fast in the USA, England, Germany, and Japan. Commodore quickly sold over a million Vics! The Vic became the world's best-selling computer!

Commodore 64

In 1982, Commodore began selling an improved Vic, called the **Commodore 64** because it included 64K of RAM. (The original Vic had just 5K.)

The Commodore 64 also improved on the Vic by displaying 40 characters per line (instead of just 22) and including 20K of ROM (instead of just 16K).

Price The Commodore 64's price went through 4 phases.

In phase 1, the recommended list price was $599.95, and Commodore tried to force all its dealers to charge that price in full. If a dealer advertised a discount, Commodore refused to send that dealer any more computers. (Commodore's policy was an example of **price fixing**, which is illegal.)

In phase 2, Commodore allowed discounts. Dealers charged just $350. Moreover, Commodore mailed a $100 rebate to anybody trading in another computer or a video-game machine, even if that computer or game was worth less than $100. Bargain-hunters bought the cheap Timex Sinclair 1000 computer just to trade in for a Commodore 64. A New York dealer, "Crazy Eddy", sold junky video-game machines for $10 just so his customers could mail them to Commodore for the $100 rebate. Commodore donated most of the traded-in computers and games to charities for a tax write-off but kept some Timex Sinclair 1000's for use as doorstops.

In phase 3, Commodore stopped the $100 cash rebate but offered a lower over-the-counter price. Discount dealers sold the Commodore 64 for just $148.

In phase 4, the Commodore sold an improved version called the **Commodore 64C**, whose keyboard contained extra keys. Discount dealers sold the Commodore 64C for just $119. The Commodore 64C came with a free copy of the **Geos** operating system, which made the computer resemble a Mac.

Why so cheap? Here's why the Commodore 64 cost so much less than an Apple 2c or IBM PC.

The Commodore 64's advertised price did *not* include a disk drive or monitor. Moreover, Commodore's disk drives and monitors were terrible.

Commodore's original disk drive, the **Model 1541**, needed repairs frequently (because its head went out of alignment). It ran ridiculously slowly (because its cable to the computer contained just one wire to transmit data, instead of several wires in parallel). It put very little info on the disk (just single-sided single-density).

Commodore's original color monitor, the **Model 1702**, produced a blurry image (because the monitor was composite instead of RGB). The image was *not* sharp enough to display 80 characters per line clearly, though it was adequate for displaying 40; so most Commodore 64 software displayed just 40 characters per line. IBM PC software displayed 80 instead. Another problem with Commodore's video was that the M looked too much like N, and the B looked like 8.

Eventually, Commodore developed an improved monitor (the **1802**) and improved disk drives (the **1541C** and **1541-2**).

The Commodore 64's version of BASIC wasn't as fancy as the IBM PC's. In fact, it was even worse than the Apple 2's. For example, it didn't even include a command to let you draw a diagonal line across the screen.

The Commodore 64's printer port was non-standard: it worked only with the strange printers manufactured by Commodore, unless you bought a special adapter. The Commodore 64's keyboard included just 66 keys, and its layout was archaic. The Commodore 64's CPU, the 6502, was slower than the 65C02 CPU in the current Apple 2e & 2c and *much* slower than the CPU in the IBM PC.

Popularity The Commodore 64 became popular because it was cheap. Commodore sold over a million of them. Because of that popularity, many programmers who wrote programs for Apple computers rewrote their programs to also work on the Commodore 64. Soon the Commodore 64 ran nearly as many popular programs as the Apple 2c but cost less. Even after adding on the price of a disk drive and a monitor, Commodore 64 still totalled less than the price of an Apple 2e, Apple 2c, IBM PC, or IBM PC Junior.

The Commodore 64 contained a fancy music synthesizer chip that produced a wide variety of musical tone qualities. When the Commodore 64 played music, it sounded much better than an Apple 2e or 2c or IBM.

Jack jumps ship

After the Commodore 64 became successful, Jack Tramiel wanted to hire his sons to help run Commodore; but Commodore's other major shareholders refused to deal with Jack's sons. So Jack quit. He sold his 2 million shares of Commodore stock, at $40 per share, netting himself 80 million dollars in cash.

After Jack quit, Commodore tried selling two new computers — the **Commodore 16** and **Commodore Plus 4** — but they had serious flaws. Then Commodore invented two great computers: the **Commodore 128** and **Amiga**.

Commodore 128

The **Commodore 128** ran all the Commodore 64 software and also included a better version of BASIC, a better keyboard, and better video. To go with it, Commodore invented a superior RGB monitor (the **Model 1902**) and a superior disk drive (the **Model 1571**).

Later, Commodore invented the **Commodore 128D** computer, which included a built-in disk drive.

Amiga

The **Amiga** is Commodore's newest and fanciest computer. It contains three special chips that produce fast animated graphics in beautiful shades of color. Like the Mac, it uses a mouse and pull-down menus.

The Amiga's first version was called the **Amiga 1000**. Later, Commodore replaced it by newer versions: the **Amiga 500**, **Amiga 600**, **Amiga 1200**, **Amiga 2000**, **Amiga 3000**, and **Amiga 4000**.

Amigas are used mainly by video professionals and by others interested in animated graphics.

Aside from graphics, not enough good software is available for Amigas. The Amigas are not compatible with the Commodore 64 or Mac. The Amiga 2000 can be made to imitate an IBM PC but costs more than most IBM PC clones.

Bankruptcy

In 1994, Commodore filed for bankruptcy because it had trouble paying its bills. Commodore's future is murky.

Tandy, which owns Radio Shack, has been around for many years.

Thanks to Tandy

Radio Shack helped the computer industry in many ways.

Radio Shack was the first big chain of stores to sell computers nationally. It was the first chain to reach rural areas.

Radio Shack invented the first low-cost assembled computer. That was the **TRS-80 model 1**, which cost $599, including the monitor.

Radio Shack was the first company to keep computer prices low without skimping on quality.

Radio Shack sold the first notebook computer (the **Tandy 100**, invented by Tandy with help from Microsoft and a Japanese manufacturer, Kyocera).

Radio Shack sold the first pocket computers, which were manufactured for Tandy by Sharp and Casio.

Radio Shack invented the first cheap computer having fancy graphics commands. That was the **Color Computer**, whose BASIC was designed by Microsoft as a "rough draft" for the fancier BASIC in the IBM PC.

But once the IBM PC came out and became the standard American computer, Tandy had difficulty figuring out how to be profitably innovative, since Americans want to buy just tradiitonal IBM PC's and clones.

Tandy's given up trying to be wildly innovative. Now Radio Shack sells just IBM clones. Tandy tried some experiments in building IBM clones innovatively, but Tandy's never built anything as radical as Apple's Mac or Commodore's Amiga.

Though Tandy's IBM clones cost less than the computers by IBM and Compaq, they cost much more than the clones offered by mail-order dealers. Mail-order dealers thank Tandy for charging high prices that are easy to beat!

Nicknames

Tandy's computers are often called "TRS" computers. The "TRS" stands for "Tandy's Radio Shack". People who dislike TRS computers add the letters A and H, and call them "TRASH" computers.

Tandy's customers are therefore called "trash collectors". On the other hand, Apple lovers are called "worms", "pie people", "fruits", and "suffering from Appleplexy"; Commodore lovers are called "boat people", "swabbies", and "deck ducks"; IBM lovers are called "blue bloods" (because old IBM computers were blue); and kids who play with Atari computers are called "Atari-eyed dreamers & screamers".

How Tandy began

The Tandy Leather Company was begun by Charles Tandy. Later, he acquired Radio Shack, which had been a Boston-based chain of discount electronics stores.

Under his leadership from his Fort Worth headquarters, Tandy/Radio Shack succeeded and grew 30% per year, helped by the CB radio craze that was sweeping the country. When the market for CB radios declined, he began looking for a new product to sell, to continue his 30% growth.

Commodore was inventing a computer and tried to convince Tandy's staff to sell it. Don French, a Tandy salesman whose hobby was building computers, recommended to Charles Tandy that Radio Shack start selling computers. Instead of buying computers from Commodore, Radio Shack hired Steve Leininger to design a Radio Shack computer and keep the cost as low as possible.

Steve wanted his computer to handle lower-case letters instead of just capitals. But since interfacing the lower-case chip would have added 10¢ to the cost, management rejected lower case: Radio Shack's computer handled just capitals. (In those days, lower-case letters weren't considered important. Later, when customers began demanding lower-case letters, Radio Shack regretted not spending the extra dime. Customers were spending $50 to rip open the Radio Shack and rearrange the chips to get lower-case.)

The monitor was a modified black-and-white TV built for Radio Shack by RCA.

RCA told Radio Shack that the standard color for the TV's case was "Mercedes silver"; any other color would cost extra. Radio Shack accepted Mercedes silver and painted the rest of the computer to match the TV. When you get your hands on a Radio Shack computer, you're supposed to feel as if you're driving a Mercedes. But since Mercedes silver looked like gray, Radio Shack became nicknamed "the great gray monster". Californians preferred Apples, whose beige matched their living-room decors. (Later, in 1982, Radio Shack wised up and switched from "Mercedes silver" to white.)

Radio Shack's original computer listed for just $599 and consisted of four devices: a **keyboard** (in which hid the CPU, ROM, & RAM), a **monitor** (built for Radio Shack by RCA), a cheap Radio Shack **tape recorder**, and an **AC/DC transformer**. Wires ran between those devices, so that the whole system looked like an octopus.

Radio Shack wanted to put the AC/DC transformer *inside* the keyboard, so that the computer system would consist of three boxes instead of four. But if the AC/DC transformer had been inside the keyboard, Underwriters Laboratories would have delayed approval for 6 months, and Radio Shack didn't want to wait that long.

Radio Shack named its computer the **TRS-80** because it was by Tandy's Radio Shack and contained a Z-80 CPU.

To officially announce its new computer, Radio Shack called a press meeting, to take place on a Monday morning in August 1977, on the front steps of the New York Stock Exchange. But when Radio Shack's management stood on those steps and were surrounded by reporters, a guy ran up to the group and yelled that a bomb had gone off two blocks away. The reporters all ran away to cover the story, and Radio Shack wasn't able to announce its new computer!

Radio Shack rushed to find a new place to announce its computer. Radio Shack heard that the Boston Computer Society was going to run a computer show that week — Wednesday through Friday. So Radio Shack's management drove up to Boston, got a booth at the show, and announced its computer there. Radio Shack was shocked when it discovered that the entire show and entire Boston Computer Society were run by Jonathan Rotenberg, a 14-year-old kid!

That intro was successful: people liked and bought Radio Shack's new computer. The base price was $599. For a complete business system (including two disk drives and a printer), Radio Shack charged $2600, while Radio Shack's competitors charged over $4500.

Problems with DOS Radio Shack hired Randy Cook to write the DOS. My friend Dick Miller was one of the first people to try it. He noticed that DOS version 1.0 didn't work; it didn't even boot! He told Radio Shack, which told Randy Cook, who fixed the problem and wrote version 1.1. Dick noticed it worked better but still had a big flaw: it didn't tell you how much disk space was left and — even worse — as soon as the disk was filled it would self-destruct!

Then came version 1.2. It worked better but not perfectly.

Since Radio Shack's DOS was still buggy, Visicalc's inventors put Visicalc onto the Apple instead of the TRS-80. Apple became known as the "Visicalc machine", and many accountants began buying Apples instead of TRS-80's.

Meanwhile, a Colorado company named **Apparat** invented its own improvements to Radio Shack's DOS. Apparat showed its improvements to Dick, who liked them and recommended calling them "NEWDOS". Many folks bought NEWDOS and formed NEWDOS colonies.

Dealing with the public
In 1977, when Radio Shack began selling the TRS-80, customers didn't understand what computers were.

For example, at a Radio Shack show, I saw a police chief buy a TRS-80. While carrying it out of the room, he called back over his shoulder, "By the way, how do you program it?" He expected a one-sentence answer.

Radio Shack provided a toll-free 800 number for customers to call in case they had any questions. Many customers called because they were confused. For example, many customers had this gripe: "I put my mouth next to the tape recorder and yelled TWO PLUS TWO, but it didn't say FOUR!"

Radio Shack's first version of BASIC provided just three error messages: WHAT (which means "I don't know what you're talking about"), HOW (which means "I don't know how to handle a number that big") and SORRY (which means "I'm sorry I can't do that — you didn't buy enough RAM yet"). Those error messages confused beginners. For example, this conversation occurred between a Radio Shack customer and a Radio Shack technician who answered the 800 number (Chris Daly). . . .

Chris: "What's your problem?"
Customer: "I plugged in the video, then the tape recorder, then . . . "
Chris: "Yes, sir, but what's the problem?"
Customer: "It doesn't work."
Chris: "How do you *know* it doesn't work?"
Customer: "It says READY."
Chris: "What's wrong with that? It's *supposed* to say READY."
Customer: "It isn't ready."
Chris: "How do you *know* it isn't ready?"
Customer: "I asked it 'Where's my wife Martha?', and it just said WHAT."

Other Z-80 computers
After the TRS-80, Tandy invented improved versions: the TRS-80 Models 2, 3, 4, 4D, 4P, 12, 16, & 16B, and the Tandy 6000. Like the Model 1, they contained a Z-80 CPU and included a monochrome monitor.

Coco To compete against the Commodore 64, Tandy invented the **Color Computer**, nicknamed the **Coco**. Folks who loved it started **Hot Coco Magazine**. Cynics thought the Coco was just a useless toy — a parody of a computer — and call it **Coco the Clown**.

Like the Commodore 64, the Coco could attach to either a monitor or an ordinary TV, and it could store programs on either a disk or an ordinary cassette tape (the same kind of tape that you listen to music on).

Tandy began selling the Coco in 1980 — the year before IBM began selling the PC. Microsoft, which invented the Coco's BASIC ROM, also invented the IBM PC's. The Coco's BASIC ROM was Microsoft's "rough draft" of the ROM that went into the IBM PC. The Coco could be described as "an IBM PC that wasn't quite right yet". In the Coco's BASIC, the commands for handling graphics and music were similar to the IBM PC's but slightly more awkward. People who couldn't afford an IBM PC but wanted to practice writing programs for the IBM PC bought the Coco.

The original Coco was called the **Coco 1**. Then came improved versions: the **Coco 2** and **Coco 3**. Tandy also invented a cheap, tiny version called the **Micro Coco**.

Pocket computers Tandy sold 8 different pocket computers, numbered **PC-1** through **PC-8**. They fit in your pocket, ran on batteries, and included LCD screens.

Notebook computers In 1983, Tandy, Epson, and NEC all tried to sell cheap notebook computers. Just Tandy's became popular, because it was the cheapest ($499) and the easiest to learn how to use. It was called the **Model 100**.

Later Tandy sold an improved version, the **Model 102**. It included more RAM, weighed less, and listed for $599. It included a nice keyboard, LCD screen (displaying eight 40-character lines), 32K RAM, 32K ROM (containing BASIC, a word-processing program, some filing programs, and a telecommunications program), and 300-baud modem (for attaching to a phone, after you bought a $19.95 cable). It was 8½ inches by 12 inches, and just 1½ inches thick! It weighed just 3 pounds. Reporters used it to take notes that could be easily phoned to the newspaper.

Tandy's stopped selling it, since IBM-compatible notebooks are much more powerful.

Why Tandy is popular
Tandy has 7000 Radio Shack stores. Besides infiltrating every major city, they're also in remote rural areas, where few other computer stores compete.

The phrase that best describes Tandy is "solid value". Tandy keeps its quality high and its prices below IBM's and Apple's (though not as low as generic clones). Tandy's computers and prices are aimed at middle-America consumers, not business executives (who buy from IBM) or bargain-hunting hobbyists (who buy mail-order).

Tandy's computers are built reliably. Tandy's assembly line checks them thoroughly before shipping to Tandy's stores.

If your Tandy computer *does* need repair, just bring it to your neighborhood Radio Shack store. If the computer's still under warranty, the store will fix it free even if you bought it from a different store. If the warranty has expired, Radio Shack charges very little for the labor of fixing it.

Bad attitude
Tandy's headquarters used to provide toll-free numbers that customers could call for technical help. Tandy switched to numbers that were not toll-free. To make matters worse, Tandy recently decided to refuse answering any questions unless the customer buys a support contract. Tandy's claim to offer better support than mail-order companies is Texas bull.

During the 1980's, Tandy established a dress code for its computer centers: employees who met the public had to don blue or gray suits, blue or white shirts, no beards, and no moustaches. Tandy fired a center manager for refusing to shave his beard. Wasn't the personal-computing revolution supposed to give us tools to express our *individuality*? The computer revolution's founders did their creative work while wearing jeans. Tandy's dress code offended some Jewish and other religious groups whose members wore beards.

Recently, Tandy shut down all its computer centers. At regular Radio Shack stores, beards are permitted.

Sellout
In 1993, Tandy stopped manufacturing computers. Tandy sold all its factories to another computer company, **AST**. So now Tandy buys its computers from AST.

Of all the major computer manufacturers, Atari is the strangest — and most creative!

Video games

The world's first popular video game was **Pong**, invented in 1972 by a California company named **Atari**, which is a Japanese war cry that means "beware!"

After Pong, Atari invented a game called **Asteroids**, then dozens of other games. Atari's games were placed in arcades and in your neighborhood bar. To play the games, you had to insert quarters.

In 1975, Atari invented a machine that played Pong on your home's TV.

In 1976, Warner Communications Inc. bought Atari; and so Atari became a wholly-owned subsidiary of Warner. Warner was a gigantic company: it owned Warner Brothers movies & cartoons, Warner Cable TV, DC Comics, and many other subsidiaries.

In 1977, Atari invented the **Video Computer System (VCS)**, which is a machine that plays a wide variety of games on your home TV. Each game comes as a ROM cartridge. Later, companies such as Mattel and Coleco invented machines that were similar but fancier.

Early personal computers

In 1979, Atari began selling complete personal computers. Atari's first two computers were the **Atari 400** (which was cheap) and the **Atari 800** (which had a nicer keyboard). They were far ahead of their time. Of all the microcomputers being sold, Atari's had the best graphics, the best music, and the best way of editing programs. Compared to the Atari, the Apple looked pitiful! And yet Atari charged *less* than Apple!

But Atari made two mistakes. . . .

The first mistake was that Atari didn't hire Bill Gates to write its version of BASIC; instead, it hired the same jerk who invented Apple's DOS. Like Apple's DOS, Atari's BASIC looks simple but can't handle serious business problems.

The second mistake was Atari's belief that personal computers would be used mainly for games. Atari didn't realize that personal computers would be used mainly for business. As a result, Atari sank lots of effort into developing spectacular games, but didn't sink enough effort into developing software and hardware for word processing, accounting, and filing.

Even after developing some slightly improved computers (the **600 XL**, the **800 XL**, and the **1200 XL**), Atari lost lots of money.

Jack attack

Much to Atari's surprise, Atari wound up getting bought by Jack Tramiel, who had been the head of Commodore. Here's how that happened. . . .

When Jack quit being the head of Commodore, he sold his Commodore stock for 80 million dollars. He used some of that cash to take his wife on a trip around the world.

When they reached Japan, the heads of Japanese computer companies said, "Jack, we're so glad you quit Commodore, because now we can enter the American computer marketplace without having to fight you."

That comment scared Jack. He didn't want to let the Japanese invade the U.S. computer market. So he started a second computer company, called "Tramiel Associates", whose sole purpose was to stop the Japanese invasion.

Tramiel Associates bought Atari from Warner. Since Jack was rich and Atari was nearly worthless (having accumulated lots of debt), Jack managed to buy all of Atari at 4PM one afternoon by using his Visa card.

Now Jack and his sons run Atari. He competes against the company he founded: Commodore.

Jack turned Atari around so that Atari became successful again.

XE

When Jack took over Atari, he replaced Atari's computers by two new computers: the **65 XE** and the **130 XE**. They run the same software as Atari's earlier computers but are cheaper to manufacture, since Jack is an expert at redesigning computers to cut costs.

Jack passed the savings on to consumers. Discount dealers sold the 65 XE for $84 and the 130 XE for $119 — prices so low that the Japanese couldn't compete!

The 65 XE includes "about 65,000 bytes of RAM" (actually, 64K). The 130 XE includes "about 130,000 bytes of RAM" (actually, 128K).

Later, Atari sold a modified 65 XE, called the **XE Game System**. It cost $150 and included games instead of BASIC.

Jackintosh

In 1985, Jack began selling a low-cost imitation of Apple's Macintosh computer. Jack's low-cost imitation is nicknamed the "Jackintosh". It's also called the **Atari 520 ST**.

It uses the **Gem operating system**, which was invented by **Digital Research** for the Atari and the IBM PC. Although Gem makes the 520 ST look like a Mac, the ST will *not* run Mac software: you must buy software specially modified to work on the 520 ST.

When the 520 ST first came out, its prices were about half as much as the Mac and Amiga so that, by comparison, the Mac and Amiga looked overpriced. To fight back, Apple lowered the Mac's price, and Commodore lowered the Amiga's. But the 520 ST is still the cheapest of the bunch.

The ST's BASIC is not by Microsoft but is similar.

Programmers have created a reasonable quantity of software for the ST, but the Amiga has more and the Mac has even more.

When Apple announced the Mac Plus, which contains 1 megabyte of RAM, Atari responded by announcing the **1040 ST**, which contains 1 megabyte also. Then Atari announced a 2-megabyte version (the **Mega-2**) and 4-megabyte version (the **Mega-4**).

Is Atari popular?

But Atari's had difficulty competing in the USA ever since the prices of the Amiga and IBM clones dropped, but Atari computers remain popular in Europe.

OPERATING SYSTEMS

To begin operating a computer, you find its power switch, turn it on, and then what?

What do you type? What do you do? How will the computer respond?

The answers to those questions depend on which **operating system** your computer uses.

Most IBM clones use an operating system called **MS-DOS**, supplemented by **Windows** (which lets you more easily use a mouse). Mac computers use a different operating system instead, called the **Mac System**. This book explains how to use all three: MS-DOS, Windows, and the Mac System.

Other kinds of computers use different operating systems instead.

Five issues

To judge which operating system is best for you, consider five issues. . . .

Hardware requirements Which hardware must you buy before you run the operating system? Does the operating system run on a cheap microcomputer, or does it require a computer that's more expensive? If it requires an expensive computer, can you justify the high cost? Which CPU chip is required? How much RAM? How much space on the hard disk? Does it require a mouse?

Speed Does the operating system run quickly, or must you wait a long time for it to obey your commands? After you've given a command, do you spend a long time twiddling your thumbs, waiting for the operating system to catch up to you? If the operating system runs too slowly, maybe you'd get your work done faster if you'd use an old-fashioned typewriter or calculator instead of a computer!

Multitasking To what extent can the operating system handle many people, tasks, and devices simultaneously? Can the operating system begin working on a second task before the first task has finished, so the operating system is working on both tasks simultaneously? For example, while the operating system is making the printer print and waits for the printer to finish printing, can the operating system let you simultaneously use the keyboard, so you can feed the computer further commands — and can the operating system start obeying those commands, even though the printer hasn't finished obeying your previous command yet?

User interface How do you feed commands to the operating system and tell it what to do? Do you type the commands on the keyboard, or are you supposed to use a mouse instead? Are the commands or mouse-methods easy for you to remember, or must you keep referring back to the instruction manual to remember how to use the damned computer?

Program availability Think about your goal (why you bought the computer and what kind of programs you want the computer to run), and ask whether those kinds of programs have been written for this operating system yet. For example, have programs been written yet to make this operating system

handle word processing, databases, spreadsheets, graphics, desktop publishing, speech, music, multimedia, telecommunication, networks, and accounting — and do those programs work excellently, meet all your needs, and thrill you?

Three kinds of user interface

How do you give commands to the computer? The answer depends on what kind of **user interface** the operating system uses. Three kinds of user interface have been invented.

Command-driven In a **command-driven** interface, you give commands to the computer by **typing the commands on the keyboard**.

For example, MS-DOS uses a command-driven interface. To command MS-DOS to copy a file, you sit at the keyboard, type the word "copy", then type the details about which file you want to copy and which disk you want to copy it to. To command MS-DOS to erase a file so the file is deleted, you type the word "erase" or "del", then type the name of the file you want to delete.

Menu-driven In a **menu-driven** interface, you act as if you were in a restaurant and ordering food from a menu: you give orders to the computer by **choosing your order from a menu that appears on the screen**.

For example, Pro DOS (an operating system used on some Apple 2 computers) has a menu-driven interface. When you start using Pro DOS, the screen shows a menu that begins like this:

```
1.  Copy files
2.  Delete files
```

If you want to copy a file, press the "1" key on the keyboard. If you want to delete a file instead, press the "2" key. Afterwards, the computer lets you choose *which* file to copy or delete.

Icon-driven In an **icon-driven** interface, the screen shows lots of cute little pictures; each little picture is called an **icon**. To give orders to the computer, you **point at one of the icons by using a mouse**, then use the mouse to make the icon move or disappear or turn black or otherwise change appearance.

For example, the Mac's operating system (which is called the Mac System) has an icon-driven interface. When you turn the Mac on, the screen gets filled with lots of little icons.

If you want to copy a file from the Mac's hard disk to a floppy disk, just use the mouse! Point at the icon (picture) that represents the file, then drag the file's icon to the floppy disk's icon. Dragging the file's icon to the floppy's icon makes the computer drag the file itself to the floppy itself.

One of the icons on the screen is a picture of a trash can. To delete a file, drag the file's icon to the trash-can icon. When you finish, the trash can will bulge, which means the file's been deleted, thrown away.

Multitasking methods

Our country is being run by monsters! Big monster computers are running our government, our banks, our insurance companies, our utility companies, our airlines, our railroads, and other big businesses.

How do those big computers manage to handle so many people and tasks simutaneously? Here are the methods used by those maxicomputers — and by many minicomputers and microcomputers, too. . . .

Scheduling the CPU

Suppose your organization buys a multi-million-dollar maxicomputer. How can the employees all share it? The answer depends on what kind of operating system you buy.

Why batch-processing was invented
In the 1950's, the only kind of operating system was **single-user**: it handled just one person at a time. If two people wanted to use the computer, the second person had to stand in line behind the first person until the first finished.

The first improvement over single-user operating systems was **batch processing**. In a batch-processing system, the second person didn't have to stand in line to use the computer. Instead, he fed his program onto the computer's disk (or other kind of memory) and walked away. The computer ran it automatically when the first person's program finished.

That procedure was called **batch processing** because the computer could store a whole batch of programs on the disk and run them in order.

Why multiprogramming was invented
While running your program, the CPU often waits for computer devices to catch up. For example, if your program makes the printer print, the CPU waits for the printer to finish. When the printer finishes, the CPU can progress to your program's next instruction.

While the CPU is waiting for the printer (or another slow device), why not let the CPU temporarily work on the next guy's program? That's called **multiprogramming**, because the CPU switches its attention among several programs.

In a simple multiprogramming system, the CPU follows this strategy: it begins working on the first guy's program; but when that program makes the CPU wait for a slow device, the CPU starts working on the second program. When the second program makes the CPU wait also, the CPU switches its attention to the third program, etc. But the first program always has top priority: as soon as that first program can continue (because the printer finished), the CPU resumes work on that program and puts all other programs on hold.

Why round-robin time-slicing was invented
Suppose one guy's program requires an hour of computer time, but another guy's program requires just one minute. If the guy with the hour-long program is kind, he'll let the other guy go first. But if he's mean and shoves his way to the computer first, the other guy must wait over an hour to run the one-minute program.

An improved operating system can "psyche out" the situation and help the second guy without waiting for the first guy to finish. Here's how the operating system works. . . .

A **jiffy** is a sixtieth of a second. During the first jiffy, the CPU works on the first guy's program. During the next jiffy, the CPU works on the second guy's program. During the third jiffy, the CPU works on a third guy's program, and so on, until each program has received a jiffy. Then, like a card dealer, the CPU "deals" a second jiffy to each program. Then it deals a third jiffy, etc. If one of the programs requires little CPU time, it will finish after being dealt just a few jiffies and "drop out" of the game, without waiting for all the other players to finish.

In that scheme, each jiffy is called a **time slice**. Since the computer deals time slices as if dealing to a circle of card players, the technique's called **round-robin time-slicing**.

To make that technique practical, the computer must be attached to many terminals so each guy has his own terminal. The CPU goes round and round, switching its attention from terminal to terminal every jiffy.

If you sit at a terminal, a few jiffies later the CPU gets to your terminal, gives you its full attention for a jiffy, then ignores you for several jiffies while it handles the other users, then comes back to you again. Since jiffies are so quick, you don't notice that the CPU ignores you for several jiffies.

That technique's an example of **timesharing**, which is defined as "an operating system creating the *illusion* that the CPU gives you its full attention continuously".

In that system, you might not get a full jiffy on your turn. For example, if your program needs to use the printer, the CPU sends some data out to the printer but then immediately moves on to the next person, without waiting for the printer to catch up. When the CPU has given all the other people their jiffies and returns to you again, the CPU checks whether the printer has finished the job yet.

Fewer switches
While the CPU works on a particular guy, the **state** of that guy's program is stored in the CPU and RAM. When that guy's jiffy ends, the CPU typically copies that guy's state onto the disk, then copies the next guy's state from disk to the CPU and RAM. So every time the CPU switches from one guy to the next, the CPU must typically do lots of disk I/O (unless the CPU's RAM is large enough to hold both guy's programs simultaneously).

Such disk I/O is "bureaucratic overhead". It consumes lots of time. The only way to reduce that overhead is to switch guys less often.

Let's develop a way to make the CPU switch guys less often but still switch fast enough to maintain each guy's illusion of getting continuous attention.

Suppose a guy's a "CPU hog": he's running a program that won't finish for several hours. Instead of giving him many short time slices, the CPU could act more efficiently by totally ignoring him for several hours (which will make everybody else in the computer room cheer!) and then giving him a solid block of time toward the end of those hours. He'll never know the difference: his job will finish at the same time as it would otherwise. And the CPU will waste less time in bureaucratic overhead, since it won't have to switch attention to and from him so often.

To determine who's the hog, the CPU counts how many jiffies and how much RAM each guy's been using. If a guy's count is high, he's been acting hoggish will probably continue to be a hog, so the CPU ignores him until later, when he's given a solid block of time. If that block is *too* long, the other guys will be ignored too long and think the CPU broke; so that solid block should be just a few seconds. If he doesn't finish within a few seconds, give him another block later.

The Decsystem-20 and other great timesharing systems use that strategy.

Distributed processing
Now you know how to make many people share a single CPU efficiently. But since the CPU chip in an IBM PC costs just $3, why bother sharing it? Why not simply give each guy his own CPU?

Today many companies are abandoning maxicomputers that have fancy timesharing operating systems and are replacing them by a collection of IBM PC clones, each of which handles just one person at a time.

That's called **distributed processing**: tying together many little CPU's instead of forcing everybody to share one big CPU.

Scheduling the memory

Suppose your program is too big to fit in the RAM. What should you do? The obvious answer: chop the program into little pieces, and run one piece at a time.

Virtual memory If you buy a computer system that has **virtual memory**, the operating system automatically chops your program into little pieces, puts as many pieces as possible into the RAM, and runs them. The remaining pieces are put on a disk instead. When the CPU finishes processing the pieces in the RAM and needs to get to the pieces on disk, the operating system automatically fetches those pieces from the disk and copies them into the RAM — after copying the no-longer-needed pieces from the RAM to the disk.

Each piece of the program is called a **page**. On most computers, each page is 4K. Copying a page from the disk to the RAM (or vice versa) is called **paging** or **swapping**.

Multi-user RAM If many people try to share the RAM, the operating system tries to squeeze all their programs into the RAM simultaneously. If they won't all fit, the operating system temporarily puts some of their programs onto disk until the other programs are done (or have used up a time-slice).

If lots of users try to share a tiny RAM, the operating system spends most of its time shuttling their programs from disk to RAM and back to disk. That bad situation — in which the operating system spends more time copying programs than running them — is called **thrashing**, because the operating system is as helpless as a fish out of water. If the operating system is big and thrashing, it's called a **beached whale**. The only solution is to buy more RAM or tell some of the users to go home!

Scheduling the I/O

After the CPU sends a command to a slow device (such as a printer or terminal), the CPU must wait for the device to obey. While the CPU waits, it ought to do something useful — such as processing somebody else's program, or processing a different part of the same program.

Buffers Here's how the CPU handles the problem of waiting. When the CPU wants to send a list of commands to a slow device, it puts that list of commands into a **buffer**, which is a special part of the RAM. The device peeks at the commands in the buffer. While the device reads and obeys those commands, the CPU switches attention to other programs or tasks.

The buffer's in RAM. But *which* RAM? In a traditional computer system, the buffer's in the main RAM. In a more modern system, each I/O device contains an auxiliary RAM, just big enough to hold the device's buffer.

Buffers are used not just for printers and terminals but also for disk drives and tape drives. Each slow device needs its own buffer.

Spooling Suppose you share a maxicomputer with other users. What if your program says to write answers on the printer, but somebody else is still using the printer?

In that situation, the CPU *pretends* to obey your command: it pretends to send your answers to the printer. But actually it sends your answers to a disk instead. The CPU keeps watching the printer: as soon as the other person finishes using the printer, the CPU automatically copies your answers from the disk to the printer and erases them from the disk.

That technique of putting your answers temporarily on disk is called **spooling**; it's handled by a part of the operating system called the **spooler**. Spooling is used mainly for the printer but can also be used for other output devices, such as the plotter. The word "spool" is an abbreviation for "Simultaneous Processing Of On-Line devices"; spooling handles people who try simultaneously to use the printer and other on-line devices.

If several people try to use the printer simultaneously, the spooler stores all their answers on disk temporarily and then prints those answers one a time. The answers waiting on the disk are called the **printer's waiting-line** or the **printer's queue** or (even more briefly) the **print queue**. If the printer is slow and many people try to use it simultaneously, the print queue can get quite long.

Suppose you want to use the printer, but somebody else is using it to print paychecks. If your operating system lacks a spooler, it says "please wait for the other person to finish" or else makes a mess — by printing your answers in the middle of the other person's paycheck! Moral: get a spooler!

Personality

The operating system can give the computer a personality, so the computer acts as a conversationalist, a drudge, or a boss.

Conversationalist A "conversationalist" is a computer you chat with by using a keyboard and screen. The conversation might be about a computer game you're playing, an airplane seat you're reserving, or your personality (if the computer is trying to play therapist). Throughout the conversation, what you say to the computer is brief, and so are the computer's replies. Typically, you're asking the computer for more output, or the computer's asking you for more input.

Instead of calling such a computer a "conversationalist", computists call it an **interactive computer**. If it handles many programs simultaneously, with each program on a different terminal, it's called a **timesharing computer**. If its memory contains lots of data and it answers questions about the data, it's called a **data-retrieval system** or **customer-inquiry system** or **commercial real-time system**.

Drudge A "drudge" is a computer that takes in piles of data and spits out piles of answers. Traditionally, the data comes on cards (or forms that are scanned), and the answers are printed on paper. While the computer works, it asks you no questions; you don't need to chat with it. It just does its job faithfully, blue-collar style.

If the drudge lets you start feeding it a second program before the first program has finished, it's a **batch processor**. If the batch processor starts *working on* the second program before the first program has finished, so that it's working on both programs simultaneously, it's called a **multiprogramming batch processor**.

Boss A "boss" is a computer that monitors another machine (such as a burglar-alarm system, a microwave oven's timer, a series of synchronized traffic lights, an electronic organ, a life-support system giving periodic intravenous injections to an unconscious patient, or a computerized asssembly line). The computer makes sure everything's running smoothly. Typically, you don't see the computer: it hides inside the machine it monitors.

Instead of calling such a computer a "boss", computer ads call it a **controller** or a **scientific real-time system**.

GET INTO DOS

The typical business uses IBM PC clones, because they cost little and run the best business software. (For example, the typical IBM PC clone costs half as much as the typical Mac, and the IBM PC versions of database programs are better than the Mac versions.)

The first software to get for an IBM PC or clone is the **disk operating system (DOS)**. It teaches the computer how to handle disk drives. The most popular DOS for the IBM PC and clones was invented by a company called **MicroSoft**, which worked together with IBM to invent **MicroSoft DOS**, also called **MS-DOS**.

MS-DOS comes on a pile of floppy disks, which must be fed into the computer before you use any other disks. If you buy a computer with a hard disk, your dealer's probably fed the MS-DOS floppies into the computer and copied their info onto the hard disk, so you don't need the floppies anymore.

Versions of DOS

MS-DOS comes in many versions. Versions for the IBM PC are called **PC-DOS**. Versions for clones built by Compaq are called **Compaq DOS**.

Make sure you get the MS-DOS version that's intended for *your* computer. Get it from the dealer who sold you the computer.

If you use the wrong version of DOS — for example, if you try to use PC-DOS on a Compaq computer, or try to use Compaq DOS on a different brand of clone — the computer will gripe (especially when you try writing programs in BASIC) or will give you the wrong time or will handle your disk drives too slowly or do something else weird. You don't need those hassles, so get the right version of DOS!

MS-DOS has been improving. For example, let's look at how Microsoft and IBM have gradually improved PC-DOS (which is the IBM PC version of MS-DOS).

The original version of PC-DOS was called **version 1**. Then came an improvement called version 1.1. Then came versions 2, 2.1, 3, 3.1, 3.2, and 3.3.

Version 1 handled just the original IBM PC and its 5¼-inch floppy disks. That version wrote on just one side of each disk and put 8 sectors on each track, so that each disk held 160K. **Version 1.1** could write on *both* sides of each disk, so that each disk held 320K.

Version 2 could also handle the IBM PC XT and its 10-megabyte hard disk. That version also squeezed more data onto each floppy disk: onto each track, it put 9 sectors instead of 8, so the floppy disk held 360K instead of 320K. **Version 2.1** could also handle the IBM PC Junior.

Version 3 could also handle the IBM PC AT, its 20-megabyte and 30-megabyte hard disks, and its high-density 5¼-inch floppy disks (which held 1.2 megabytes instead of 360K). **Version 3.1** could also handle networks. **Version 3.2** could also handle the IBM PC Convertible and its 3½-inch 720K floppies. **Version 3.3** could also handle the IBM PS/2 and its 3½-inch 1.44 megabyte floppies.

Other early versions of MS-DOS (such as Compaq DOS) were numbered similarly to PC-DOS. For example, Compaq

DOS version 3.31 resembled PC-DOS version 3.3 but let you more easily handle hard disks bigger than 30 megabytes.

In July 1988, Microsoft and IBM began selling **version 4**. Like Compaq DOS version 3.31, it let you handle huge hard disks easily. But alas, version 4 consumed too much RAM and was incompatible with some older programs.

In June 1991, Microsoft and IBM began selling **version 5**, which fixed DOS 4's problems and included many exciting new commands. In 1993 they began selling **version 6**, which was even fancier.

Afterwards, Microsoft and IBM parted company and decided to compete against each other. IBM invented and sold **version 6.1**, without any involvement from Microsoft. Then Microsoft decided to fight back by inventing and selling **version 6.2**. Then IBM retaliated with **version 6.3**.

<u>Headaches</u> Some DOS versions give you headaches.
Versions 1.0 and 1.1 can't handle hard disks at all.

Versions 2.0 and 2.1 have difficulty handling hard disks bigger than 16 megabytes. Here's why. When you first use a hard disk, DOS is supposed to search for bad sectors on the hard disk, draw a **map** of where those bad sectors are, and remember to avoid those bad sectors. Versions 2.0 and 2.1 search for bad sectors throughout the first 16 megabytes *but don't bother to map the bad sectors on the rest of a big hard disk*. If you use those versions of DOS, everything will seem fine at first; but when you finally fill more than 16 megabytes of your disk, DOS will eventually encounter bad sectors it didn't map, get upset, and refuse to run your programs.

Versions 3.0 and 3.2 make lots of errors. Avoid them.

Versions before 3.2 can't handle 3½-inch floppies. **Version 3.2** handles 3½-inch floppies, but just if they're double-density instead of high-density.

Version 4 consumes too much RAM.

Versions 6.1 and 6.3 are weird, since they're the only version that Microsoft didn't help design. They're the only version that doesn't accept standard Microsoft commands.

Versions 3.3, 5, and 6.2 work fine. They're the versions used by most corporations. **Version 6.0** works fine also, but just if you avoid using its three fanciest routines (**Double Space**, **Smart Drive**, and **Mem Maker**), which are disastrously unreliable. In **version 6.2**, those routines have been fixed and work better, but they still cause enough complications so you should avoid them. (I explain why in the "Repairs" chapter.)

A company called **Stac Electronics** sued Microsoft for putting Stac's ideas into Double Space. In 1994, Stac won the suit. The judge ordered Microsoft to pay Stac and stop selling versions 6.0 and 6.2, so Microsoft came out with **version 6.21** (which omits Double Space) and **version 6.22** (which includes a Double Space clone called **Disk Space**). When Stac complained that Microsoft wasn't removing all remaining copies of versions 6 and 6.2 from shelves quickly enough, Microsoft squashed the problem by paying Stac even more and buying 15% of the Stac company itself. So now Microsoft is a Stac shareholder, and the two companies are buddies.

DR DOS Instead of buying MS-DOS, you can buy an imitation called **DR DOS** (or **Novell DOS**). It's made by a company called **Digital Research (DR)**, which is now owned by **Novell**.

Though DR DOS resembles MS-DOS, I prefer MS-DOS because it includes BASIC and is more compatible with Windows and other software.

Which version I'll emphasize I'll emphasize how to use DOS 6.2. My explanation of DOS 6.2 applies to all of its variants (DOS 6.20, 6.21, and 6.22).

Which other versions I'll explain In case you don't have DOS 6.2 yet, I'll also explain earlier versions of DOS and how they differ.

To keep this chapter mercifully short, I'll assume your computer is normal. For example, I'll assume you're using a reasonably new version of DOS (version 2 or higher), you're not using IBM's weird versions (6.1 and 6.3), and you're not using DR-DOS or Novell DOS.

Modern versus classic DOS versions 5, 6, and 6.2 are similar to each other. I'll refer to them as **modern DOS**. Earlier DOS versions (2, 2.1, 2.2, 3, 3.1, 3.2, 3.3, and 4) are called **classic DOS**.

Notice that in the computer industry, the word "classic" is a euphemism that means "old, obsolete, and decrepit". Go ahead: follow that tradition! Next time you meet a person who's old, obsolete, and decrepit, say "You're a classic!"

Cost

The best way to get DOS is from the dealer who sold you the computer.

Most dealers include DOS in the computer's price. A few dealers charge for DOS separately.

Piracy If you buy two computers, you must buy two copies of DOS. It's illegal to buy just one DOS and copy it to the other computer. That's called **illegal copying**; it's **piracy**.

Some dealers illegally copy DOS onto the computer's hard disk without paying Microsoft or IBM for it. Recently, Microsoft has been requiring every dealer who copies DOS onto a hard disk to give the customer an official **Microsoft certificate of authenticity** with a hologram sticker on it. The certificate comes from Microsoft and proves that the DOS was paid for. The hologram sticker shows you a 3-dimensional picture of the DOS version number (such as "6.2").

Usually, the certificate comes with an official Microsoft manual (not just a book from a bookstore!) and an official set of DOS floppy disks (on which are pasted official Microsoft labels that are printed, not handwritten!). But the manual and floppies are optional, and some dealers are too cheap to provide them. If you get neither a manual nor floppies, your dealer is either a crook, a cheapskate, or an ass — or the dealer got the goods from a manufacturer who's a crook, a cheapskate, or an ass!

How to upgrade If you own an old version of DOS, you can switch to MS-DOS 6.22 by getting the **MS-DOS 6.22 upgrade** for about $50. Switching is simple if you have a high-density 3½-inch floppy drive and already own a version numbered *above* 2.1.

If you own MS-DOS 6.0, you can switch to MS-DOS 6.22 for under $10 by getting the **MS-DOS 6.22 Step Up** disk (which is 3½-inch high-density). For example, **Staples** sells that disk for $8.49. That cheap disk works just if you already own MS-DOS 6.0 (or 6.20 or 6.21). It does *not* work if you own an older DOS and does *not* work if you own DOS 6.1 or 6.3 (which are the weird versions by IBM). Since it costs so little and does so little (it just turns 6.0 or 6.20 or 6.21 into

6.22, which is almost the same!), it does *not* come with a certificate, hologram, or manual.

List of commands & equations

To use DOS, you put your fingers on the keyboard and type a DOS command or equation. The popular DOS commands & equations are explained on these pages:

Command	What the computer will do	Page
a:	make drive A be the current drive	106
attrib +r mary	make MARY be a read-only file	134
b:	make drive B be the current drive	106
backup c:mary a:	copy MARY to a set of floppies in drive A	132
c:	make drive C be the current drive	106
cd sarah	make SARAH be the current directory	107
chkdsk	check the disk for bytes and errors	108
cls	clear the screen, so it becomes blank	102
copy con mary	copy from keyboard to a file called MARY	112
date	show the date, and let it be changed	102
defrag	rearrange files so they're not fragmented	128
del mary	delete a file called MARY from the disk	114
deltree sarah	delete the SARAH folder & everything in it	114
dir	show a directory of all files	103
dir sarah	show a directory of all the files in SARAH	105
dir sarah /s	show the SARAH directory & subdirectories	129
diskcopy a: b:	make disk B be an exact copy of disk A	111
do music	do the MUSIC program in MUSIC folder	130
echo off	stop displaying DOS commands	116
echo wow	show the word "wow" on the screen	102
edit mary	edit file called MARY, using modern editor	114
edlin mary	edit file called MARY, using an old editor	115
fdisk	partition the hard disk into C, D, E, etc.	124
format a:	format the disk in drive A	110
format a: /s	format disk in drive A & make it bootable	124
help	list all the DOS commands & explain them	129
Lh doskey	load the doskey driver into upper memory	122
Lh mode LPT1 retry=b	wait for printer to respond, even if long wait	122
Lh mouse	load the mouse driver into upper memory	121
Lh mscdex /d:mscd000	load CD-ROM driver into upper memory	122
Lh share	check if programs interfere with each other	122
md sarah	make a new directory, called SARAH	112
mem	show how big the RAM memory is	127
more<mary	show a file called MARY, a page at a time	130
move mary a:	move MARY to drive A, and delete from C	114
msav	run the MicroSoft Anti-Virus program	128
msbackup	copy from the hard disk to a set of floppies	131
msd	make MicroSoft Diagnostics analyze computer	127
path c:\dos	whenever a program not found, search c:\dos	121
print mary	copy a file called MARY onto paper	126
prompt pg	make prompt be "C:\>" instead of "C>"	121
rd sarah	remove directory SARAH from the disk	114
rem written by Joey	ignore this remark & skip ahead to next line	129
ren mary lambchop	rename MARY; change to LAMBCHOP	114
restore a: c: /s	copy all backed-up files to the hard disk	132
scandisk	scan the disk for errors and fix them	127
set temp=c:\dos	define "temp" to mean "c:\dos"	121
subst a: b:\	when told to use drive A, will use B instead	130
sys a:	copy the DOS system files to drive A	124
time	show the time, and let it be changed	102
type mary	show, on the screen, what's in the MARY file	113
undelete	try to retrieve any files accidentally deleted	129
unformat a:	try to unformat the disk in drive A	110
ver	say which version of DOS is being used	102
win	start running Windows	122
xcopy a: b: /s	copy all files and subdirectories from A to B	135

Equation	Meaning	Page
buffers=40	handle 40 sectors at once	119
device=dos\emm386.exe ram d=48	use expanded RAM	118
device=dos\himem.sys /testmem:off	use extended RAM	118
devicehigh=dos\ansi.sys	use special characters	119
devicehigh=dos\setver.exe	handle old software	119
devicehigh=mtmcdas.sys /d:mscd000	use CD-ROM drive	120
dos=high,umb	use high & upper RAM	119
files=50	handle 50 files at once	119
stacks=0,0	create no stacks	119

How to start DOS

Here's how to use start using DOS. If you ever have difficulty following my instructions, **phone me anytime for free help at 617-666-2666.**

DOS comes on a pile of floppy disks. When you buy a new computer, your dealer typically copies DOS onto the hard disk for you (so that the hard disk contains DOS already). Copying DOS onto the hard disk is called **installing** (or **loading**) DOS onto the hard disk.

Here's how to use a computer whose hard disk contains DOS.

If your computer doesn't have a hard disk yet, or its hard disk doesn't contain DOS yet, practice on a friend's computer whose hard disk *does* contain DOS. (Later, in a section called "How to make a blank hard disk bootable", I'll explain how to copy DOS onto *your* hard disk.)

Unpack the computer When you buy a computer system, it typically comes in three cardboard boxes. Open them, and put their contents on your desk.

One box contains the monitor. One box contains the printer. The third and biggest box contains the computer's main part (the **system unit**), keyboard, mouse, and floppy disks.

Each box also contains power cords, cables, and instruction manuals.

Here are exceptions:

If you didn't buy a printer, the printer box is missing.
If you bought a tower computer, put it on the floor instead of on your desk.
If you bought a portable computer (notebook or laptop), there is no monitor.
Some computers don't come with a mouse.

Connect the cables Into the back of the system unit, plug the cables that come from the monitor, printer, keyboard, and mouse. Into your wall's electrical socket, plug the power cords that come from the monitor, printer, and system unit.

Here are exceptions:

For some computers, such as the Leading Edge Model D, the keyboard's cable plugs into the system unit's FRONT instead of back.

For some monochrome monitors, the power cord plugs into the system unit instead of into the wall.

For portable computers, the keyboard and screen come attached to the system unit, so you don't need to run cables between them.

Find the floppy drives At the front of the system unit, you'll see one or two slots. (In most computers, the slots are horizontal.) You can put floppy disks in those slots. Those slots are called the **floppy drives**.

Exception:

If your computer is a notebook or laptop, the floppy drives are in the computer's right side instead of in the front.

What's in the floppy drives? Remove any disks from the floppy drives, so that the floppy drives are empty and you can start fresh.

Does your computer have a hard disk containing DOS? If so, your computer is normal: leave the floppy drives empty and skip ahead to the section called "Turn on the computer".

If your computer does *not* have a hard disk — or the hard disk doesn't contain DOS yet — you must put the main DOS floppy disk into the main floppy drive. Here's how. . . .

Step 1: grab the main DOS floppy disk. That disk usually has a label that says "DOS Disk 1" or "DOS Program Disk" or "DOS Install Disk". Make sure you grab the original disk, not a copy made by a friend. (On the original disk, the label is printed; on a copy, the label is usually handwritten.)

Step 2: find the main floppy drive. If you have two floppy drives, the *main* floppy drive is usually the one on the left or top.

Step 3: put that disk into that drive. If the drive's slot is horizontal, make sure the disk's label is on *top* of the disk; if the slot is vertical, make sure the disk's label is on the disk's *left* side. If the disk is 5¼-inch, it has a big oval cutout; if the disk is 3½-inch, it has a chrome metal slider; make sure that cutout or slider goes into the drive *before* the label does.

If the disk is 5¼-inch, close the drive's door. Here's how: if the slot is horizontal, pull the door latch down; if the slot is vertical, pull the door latch to the right.

Turn on the computer Flip the computer's power switch to the ON position.

Can't find the power switch? Here are some hints. . . .

The power switch is on or near the system unit's *right* side. (If you don't find the switch on the right side, check the right part of the front side or the right part of the back side.)

On traditional computers, the power switch is red. It might say "1" instead of "ON" and "0" instead of "OFF".

On some computers (such Quantex's), the power "switch" is actually a pushbutton on the front, near the right.

Turn on the screen Turn on the computer's screen (monitor or TV). If you're using a TV, turn it to channel 3, 4, or 33.

After a few seconds, the screen will display some messages. (If you don't see the messages clearly, make sure the cable from the screen to the system unit is plugged in tightly, and adjust the screen's contrast and brightness knobs.)

Examine the keyboard Test your powers of observation by staring at the keyboard. Try to find the following keys (but don't press them yet). . . .

Find the **ENTER key**. That's the big key on the right side of the keyboard's main section. It has a bent arrow on it. It's also called the **RETURN key**. You press it at the end of every line you type; it makes the computer read what you typed.

Find the **BACKSPACE key**. It's above the ENTER key and to the right of the + key. It has a left-arrow on it. You press it when you want to erase a mistake.

Find the key that has the letter A on it. When you press the A key, you'll be typing a small "a".

Near the keyboard's bottom left corner, find the **SHIFT key**. It has an up-arrow on it. Under the ENTER key, you'll see another SHIFT key. Press either SHIFT key when you want to capitalize a letter. For example, when you want to type a capital A, hold down a SHIFT key; and while you keep holding down the SHIFT key, tap the A key.

Find the key that looks like this:

```
!
1
```

It's near the keyboard's top left corner. That's the **1 key**. You press it when you want to type the number 1. Press the keys to its right when you want to type the numbers 2, 3, 4, 5, 6, 7, 8, 9, and 0. If you press the 1 key while holding down a SHIFT key, you'll be typing an exclamation point (!). Here's the rule: if a key shows two symbols (such as ! and 1), and you want to type the top symbol (!), you must typically hold down a SHIFT key.

Find the key that has the letter U on it. To the right of that key, you'll see the letters I and O. Don't confuse the letter I with the number 1; don't confuse the letter O with the number 0.

In the keyboard's bottom row, find the wide key that has nothing written on it. That's the **SPACE bar**. Press it whenever you want to leave a blank space.

Get to the standard C prompt

The **standard C prompt** is this symbol:

```
C:\>
```

It consists of 4 characters: a **capital C**, a **colon**, a **backslash**, and a **greater sign**.

Look at the screen's bottom message. **If the bottom message says** —

```
C:\>
```

your computer is ready for DOS: skip ahead to the section called "Simple commands".

If the bottom message does *not* say "C:\>", your computer isn't ready. Here's what to do:

On the screen	What to do
bottom message says "C:\DOS>"	Type "cd \" (then press the ENTER key).
bottom message says "C:\" then a word then ">"	Type "cd \" (then press the ENTER key).
bottom message says "C>"	Type "prompt pg" (then press the ENTER key).
bottom message says "D>", "E>", or "F>"	Type "c:" (then press the ENTER key).
bottom message begins with "D:", "E:", or "F:"	Type "c:" (then press the ENTER key).
bottom message says "Enter new date (mm-dd-yy):"	Press the ENTER key.
bottom message says "Enter new time:"	Press the ENTER key.
bottom message says "ENTER = Continue F1 = Help F3 = Exit"	Tap the F3 key then the Y key.
bottom message says "or press Esc to Exit"	Do NOT insert the SELECT disk. Just tap the Esc key.
bottom right corner says "Doc 1 Pg 1 Ln 1" Pos 1""	Tap the F7 key, then the N key, then the Y key.
top line says "Program Manager"	Tap the Alt key, then the F key, then the X key, then the ENTER key.
top line says "MS-DOS Shell" or "Start Programs"	Tap the F3 key.
a list of choices	Choose "Exit to DOS".

After doing one of those actions, check whether the screen's bottom message says "C:\>" yet. If it does *not* say "C:\>", look through that list of actions again, and keep trying until you finally see "C:\>" at the bottom of the screen. When you finally see "C:\>", skip ahead to the next section (entitled "Simple commands").

Non-system disk Instead of saying "C:\>", the computer might gripe by saying:

```
Non-System disk or disk error
Replace and press any key when ready
```

That means you put the wrong floppy disks in the floppy drives, or your hard disk doesn't contain DOS yet.

When you get that message, remove any floppy disks from the floppy drives, so the floppy drives are empty.

If your dealer says your computer has a hard disk containing DOS, leave the floppy drives empty. If your dealer says your computer lacks a hard disk (or your hard disk lacks DOS), try again to put the main DOS disk into the main floppy drive.

Then press the ENTER key.

BASIC words If your computer is manufactured by IBM, the bottom message might be this list of BASIC words:

```
1LIST  2RUN   3LOAD"  4SAVE"  5CONT   6,"LPT1 7TRON  8TROFF  9KEY    0SCREEN
```

Treat that problem just as if the computer had said "Non-System disk".

A prompt Instead of saying "C:\>", the computer might say "A>" or "A:\>". That means the computer is ignoring the concept of a "hard disk". Here's what to do.

If your computer has a hard disk containing DOS, turn off the screen and computer, remove any floppy disks from the floppy drives, wait until the fan in the computer's motor becomes silent, then turn the computer and screen back on.

If your computer has no hard disk (or its hard disk is broken or lacks DOS), you're stuck! You must use "A>" or "A:\>" instead of "C:\>", and a few of the examples in this book won't work on your computer (until you get a hard disk containing DOS).

How to shut down

When you finish using the computer, here's the safest way to shut the computer down, so you don't lose any data.

First, make the computer display the standard C prompt, so the screen's bottom message is this:

```
C:\>
```

(If you can't figure out how to make the computer display that C prompt, make it display "A:\>" or "A>" or "1 LIST" instead.)

Remove any floppy disks from the drives.

To be safe, wait ten seconds. (The purpose of that wait is to let the DOS 6.0 version of the SMARTDRIVE caching program finish editing your hard disk. While it edits, you'll hear some clicking sounds. If you're sure you're not using that caching program or a similar program, you don't need to wait. If you're using a different version of SMARTDRIVE — such as the version that comes with DOS 5 or DOS 6.2 or Windows — you don't need to wait.)

If your screen is a monitor or TV, turn it off. Then turn off the computer.

SIMPLE COMMANDS

After the C prompt (which is "C:\>"), the computer waits for you to type a **DOS command**. When typing a DOS command, remember these principles:

Type the command after the C prompt. Remember that the C prompt is typed by the computer, not by you.

To capitalize a letter, or type a character that's on the top part of a key, hold down the SHIFT key; and while you keep holding down the SHIFT key, tap the key that has the character you want.

If you type a command incorrectly, press the BACKSPACE key, which is above the ENTER key and has a left-arrow on it.

When you finish typing a command, press the ENTER key. That key makes the computer read what you typed.

Start by trying these simple DOS commands. . . .

Version (ver)
After the C prompt you can type "ver", like this:

`C:\>ver`

(When you finish typing that command, remember to press the ENTER key.)

The "ver" command makes the computer tell you which VERsion of MS-DOS you're using. For example, if you're using MS-DOS Version 6.2, the computer will say:

`MS-DOS Version 6.20`

Echo
The computer's your obedient slave: it will say whatever you wish!

For example, here's how to make the computer say "wow". After the C prompt, type "echo wow", like this:

`C:\>echo wow`

(To type the space after the word *echo*, press the **SPACE bar**, which is the long horizontal bar at the bottom of the keyboard.) Remember to press the ENTER key at the end of that command. Then the computer will say:

`wow`

If you want the computer to say it loves you, type this:

`C:\>echo I love you`

(To capitalize the letter I, hold down the SHIFT key; and while you keep holding down the SHIFT key, tap the I key.) That command makes the computer say:

`I love you`

If you want the computer to say it likes strawberry ice cream, type this:

`C:\>echo I like strawberry ice cream`

Then the computer will say:

`I like strawberry ice cream`

Be creative! Make the computer say something wild!

Notice that the echo command makes the computer act like a canyon: whatever you say into the computer, the echo command makes the computer echo back.

Clear screen (cls)
Suppose you make the computer say "I love you" (and other things that are even wilder), and then your boss walks by. You might be embarrassed to let your boss see your love messages. Here's how to hide all the screen's messages.

After the C prompt, type "cls", like this:

`C:\>cls`

The "cls" command makes the computer CLear the Screen, so all messages on the screen are erased and the screen becomes blank. The only thing that will remain on the screen is —

`C:\>`

so that you can give another command.

Date
The computer has a built-in calendar. To use it, type "date" after the C prompt like this:

`C:\>date`

That makes the computer tell you the date. For example, if today is Wednesday, January 24, 1996, the computer should say:

`Current date is Wed 01-24-1996`

To remember the date, the computer uses its built-in digital clock/calendar. If the clock/calendar's battery has run down or is missing, the computer will say a wrong date.

Confirming the date After the computer says what it thinks the date is, it says:

`Enter new date (mm-dd-yy):`

If the computer's date seems correct, press the ENTER key.

If you notice that the computer's date is wrong, remind the computer of the correct date. For example, if the correct date is January 24, 1996, type "1-24-96" then press ENTER at the end of that date. (Do *not* type "Wednesday" or "Wed"; the computer will figure that out automatically.)

Time
To find out what time it is, type "time" after the C prompt like this:

`C:\>time`

That makes the computer tell you the time.

For example, if the time is 2.71 seconds after 1:45AM, the computer will say:

`Current time is  1:45:02.71a`

The "a" means "AM". (If your DOS is classic, it will omit the "a".)

If the time is 2.71 seconds after 1:45PM, the computer will say:

`Current time is  1:45:02.71p`

The "p" means "PM". (If your DOS is classic, it will omit the "p", use a 24-hour clock, and say "13:45:02.71".)

To remember the time, the computer uses its built-in digital clock. The computer will say a wrong time if the clock's battery has run down or is missing, or the clock's thinking has been interrupted by other computer activities, or your town has switched to daylight savings time, or you've taken the computer on an airplane to a different time zone.

Confirming the time After the computer says what it thinks the time is, it says:

`Enter new time:`

If the computer's time seems correct, press the ENTER key.

If you notice that the computer's time is wrong, remind the computer of the correct time. For example, if the correct time is exactly 1:45PM, type "1:45p" (for modern DOS) or "13:45" (for classic DOS); then press ENTER at the end of that time.

Directory (dir)

After the C prompt you can type "dir", like this:

```
C:\>dir
```

That "dir" command makes the computer show you a directory of the files that are stored on the hard disk.

If you're using DOS 6.2, the directory looks like this:

```
DOS           <DIR>            06-01-94   3:53a
WINDOWS       <DIR>            06-02-94   3:10a
WP            <DIR>            06-19-94   6:24p
AMIPRO        <DIR>            06-15-94   3:37a
QA            <DIR>            06-04-94   5:48p
EXCEL         <DIR>            06-08-94   10:10p
BACKUP        <DIR>            06-09-94   4:06p
COMMAND   COM        54,619   09-30-93   6:20a
CONFIG    SYS           182   06-28-94   11:12p
AUTOEXEC  BAT           166   06-29-94   12:39a
DO        BAT            44   06-09-94   11:18p
```

(On your computer, the directory might look slightly different, depending on what your hard disk contains and which version of DOS you're using For example, if your DOS is earlier than version 6.2, it's too stupid to put commas in big numbers such as 54,619.)

In that sample directory, one line says:

```
COMMAND   COM        54,619 09-30-93   6:20a
```

That line says the hard disk has a file whose name is "COMMAND.COM"; that file contains 54,619 bytes and was last updated on September 30, 1993, at 6:20AM.

The next line says the disk also has a file named "CONFIG.SYS", which contains 182 bytes and was last updated on June 28, 1994 at 11:12PM. The lines underneath say that the disk also has a file called "AUTOEXEC.BAT" and a file called "DO.BAT".

Extensions

Notice that a file's name (such as "AUTOEXEC.BAT") consists of up to 8 characters (such as "AUTOEXEC"), then a period, then an **extension** of up to 3 characters (such as "BAT"). The period separates the main part of the filename from the extension.

In the directory that the computer prints on your screen, each line shows a file's name and extension but doesn't bother showing the period.

The period is called a **dot**. So if you're chatting with another computer expert about "AUTOEXEC.BAT", pronounce it "AUTOEXEC dot BAT".

The computer can handle many different types of files. Each type has a different extension:

Ext'n	What the file contains
.BAT	a **BAT**ch of DOS commands
.COM	a short program that's been **COM**piled
.EXE	a fancy program that you can **EXE**cute
.BAS	a program written by using **BAS**IC
.PRG	a **PR**o**G**ram written by using DBASE or FOXPRO
.SYS	list of hardware you bought & how you want **SYS**tem to operate
.386	info that's useful just if your CPU is a **386** (or 486 or Pentium)
.TXT	Te**XT** that you can read
.HLP	messages that He**LP** you learn how to use a program you bought
.DOC	**DOC**ument written by a word processor such as Microsoft Word
.OLD	an **OLD**, outdated version, being kept just in case of emergency
.BAK	a **BA**c**K**up version, being kept just in case of emergency
.DAT	**DAT**a
.TMP	Te**MP**orary data, which the computer will use and then erase
.INI	data to **INI**tialize a program, so the program starts properly
.DBF	a **D**ata**B**ase **F**ile that contains data used by DBASE or FOXPRO
.DTF	a **D**a**T**abase **F**ile that contains data used by Q&A
.IDX	an **I**n**D**e**X** to a database file
.XLS	an E**X**ce**L** **S**preadsheet, created by using the Excel program
.WK1	a **W**or**K**sheet created by using the **1**-2-3 spreadsheet program
.WQ1	a **W**orksheet created by using **Q**uattro (which imitates **1**-2-3)

Folders

The sample directory's top line says:

```
DOS           <DIR>            06-01-94   3:53a
```

That line says the hard disk has a file named "DOS". The <DIR> means that the file is actually a **directory folder** that contains other files! That folder was created on June 1, 1994 at 3:53AM; many items have been put in that folder since then.

The next line says:

```
WINDOWS       <DIR>            06-02-94   3:10a
```

That means the hard disk has a folder named "WINDOWS", created on June 2, 1994 at 3:10AM.

The lines underneath say that the hard disk also has folders named "WP", "AMIPRO", "QA", "EXCEL", and "BACKUP".

Summary statistics

When the computer finishes printing the directory, it prints summary statistics:

```
        11 file(s)           55,011 bytes
                        21,426,176 bytes free
```

That means the directory contains 11 files. (7 of them are folders, such as DOS and WINDOWS. The other 4 are simple files, such as COMMAND.COM and CONFIG.SYS.)

The simple files consume 55,011 bytes altogether. The hard disk uses other bytes to store the folders and any files that are in the folders.

(If your DOS is classic, it doesn't bother to say "55,011 bytes".)

Besides the simple files, folders, and files in folders, the hard disk also contains these 6 special items: 2 **hidden files** (called "IO.SYS" and "MSDOS.SYS"), 2 copies of the **file allocation table (FAT)**, the **boot record**, and the directory itself.

The "21,426,176 bytes free" means that over 21 million bytes on the hard disk are still unused. (On *your* computer, the number of bytes free might be different.)

Pausing When you type "dir", the computer tries to show you a directory of the files that are stored on the hard disk. If your hard disk has more files than can fit on the screen, the list of files moves up the screen too quickly for you to read.

Here's how to see the directory more easily. . . .

Instead of typing "dir", type "dir /p", like this:

```
C:\>dir /p
```

That means "directory pausing". When you give that command, the computer starts printing the directory on the screen; but when the screen becomes full, the computer pauses and says:

```
Press any key to continue . . .
```

While the computer pauses, read the part of the directory that's on the screen. When you finish reading that part, strike a key (such as the ENTER key). Then the computer will print the rest of the directory, pausing at the end of each screenful (page).

So "dir /p" means "directory, pausing at the end of each page" (or "directory paged").

Wide If you type "dir /w", you'll see a directory that's wide and leaves out the details; the computer will print:

```
[DOS]          [WINDOWS]       [WP]          [AMIPRO]       [QA]
[EXCEL]        [BACKUP]        COMMAND.COM   CONFIG.SYS     AUTOEXEC.BAT
DO.BAT
```

What's a switch? A **switch** is a comment that begins with a **slash**. You've already learned about two switches: "/p" and "/w".

To type the slash, make sure you press the **forward slash** key, which says "/" on it. Do *not* press the key that says "\", which is a **backslash**.

If you wish, you can put a blank space before the slash. The blank space is optional. For example, you can say either "dir /p" or "dir/p".

You can combine switches. For example, if you want the directory to pause and also be wide, say "dir /p/w".

The computer doesn't care which switch you type first: typing "dir /p/w" does the same thing as typing "dir /w/p".

Fancy switches (in modern DOS) If your DOS is classic, skip ahead to the next section, entitled "Attributes". Modern DOS understands these fancy switches. . . .

Order. You can put the letter O after dir, like this: "dir /o". That shows you the directory in alphabetical order: the computer lists the folders from A to Z, then lists the other files from A to Z, like this:

```
AMIPRO       <DIR>           09-15-94    3:37a
BACKUP       <DIR>           06-09-94    4:06p
DOS          <DIR>           06-01-94    3:53a
EXCEL        <DIR>           06-08-94   10:10p
QA           <DIR>           06-04-94    5:48p
WINDOWS      <DIR>           06-02-94    3:10a
WP           <DIR>           06-19-94    6:24p
AUTOEXEC BAT            166  06-29-94   12:39a
COMMAND  COM         54,619  09-30-93    6:20a
CONFIG   SYS            182  06-28-94   11:12p
DO       BAT             44  06-09-94   11:18p
```

If you want to see the directory in *chronological* order (from the oldest date to the newest date), say "dir /od" (which means "DIRrectory in Order of Date"). If you want to see the directory in order of size, say "dir /os"; that makes the computer display the folders first, then display the other files in order of size, from the smallest number of bytes to the largest.

If you want to see the directory alphabetized by extension (so that all the .BAT files come before the .COM files), say "dir /oe" (which means "DIRectory in Order of Extension"). Better yet, say "dir /oen" (which means "DIRectory in Order of Extension and Name"), so that all the .BAT files come before the .COM files, and all the .BAT files are in alphabetical order.

At the end of any of those commands, you can put "/p" to make the computer pause at the end of each screenful.

Lowercase. You can put the letter L after dir, like this: "dir /l". That shows you the directory in lowercase letters instead of capitals, so you see this:

```
dos          <DIR>        06-01-94    3:53a
windows      <DIR>        06-02-94    3:10a
wp           <DIR>        06-19-94    6:24p
amipro       <DIR>        06-15-94    3:37a
qa           <DIR>        06-04-94    5:48p
excel        <DIR>        06-08-94   10:10p
backup       <DIR>        06-09-94    4:06p
command com   54,619      09-30-93    6:20a
config   sys     182      06-28-94   11:12p
autoexec bat     166      06-29-94   12:39a
do       bat      44      06-09-94   11:18p
```

That L switch was invented because most people can read lowercase words faster than capitalized words.

Brief. You can say "dir /b". That makes the computer print the directory briefly, without bothering to print each file's length, time, and date, and without bothering to print summary statistics. The computer will print just:

```
DOS
WINDOWS
WP
AMIPRO
QA
EXCEL
BACKUP
COMMAND.COM
CONFIG.SYS
AUTOEXEC.BAT
DO.BAT
```

The computer will print it very fast — instantly!

The computer doesn't understand "dir /b/w". If you say "dir /b/w", the computer ignores the /w and does just "dir /b".

Attributes
Some files have special qualities, called **attributes**.

For example, your hard disk contains two special files, called "IO.SYS" and "MSDOS.SYS". Those files contain the fundamentals of DOS and must never be erased! To prevent you from accidentally erasing them, the computer *hides* them from you, so you don't even know they're there! When you say "dir", the computer is sneaky and purposely avoids mentioning those two files!

Modern DOS lets you peek at those two hidden files. Just say "dir /ah". That makes the computer show a directory of files having the Attribute of being Hidden. For example, if you say "dir /ah" using DOS 6.2, the typical computer will say:

```
IO       SYS     40,566   09-30-93    6:20a
MSDOS    SYS     38,138   09-30-93    6:20a
```

Exception: if you're using PC-DOS instead of generic MS-DOS (because your computer's built by IBM instead of being a generic clone), those files are named "IBMBIO.COM" and "IBMDOS.COM" instead.

Modern DOS lets you see the names of all your folders (directories). Just say "dir /ad". That makes the computer show a directory of all files having the Attribute of being Directories. The computer will say:

```
DOS          <DIR>        06-01-94    3:53a
WINDOWS      <DIR>        06-02-94    3:10a
WP           <DIR>        06-19-94    6:24p
AMIPRO       <DIR>        06-15-94    3:37a
QA           <DIR>        06-04-94    5:48p
EXCEL        <DIR>        06-08-94   10:10p
BACKUP       <DIR>        06-09-94    4:06p
```

What's in a folder?
To find out what's in a folder, say "dir" then the folder's name. For example, to find out what's in the DOS folder, say "dir dos", like this:

```
C:\>dir dos
```

You can put a switch at the end of that command:

```
C:\>dir dos /p
```

To find out what's in the WINDOWS folder, say "dir windows". (That command works just if you have a WINDOWS folder. If you do *not* have a WINDOWS folder, the computer gripes by saying "File not found".)

Saying "dir dos" shows you the files that are in the DOS folder. That list of files is called the **DOS directory**. Saying "dir windows" shows you the files that are in the Windows folder; that list of files is called the **Windows directory**. Saying just "dir" shows you the files that are *not* in folders; that list of files is called the **main directory** (or **root directory**).

So to see the root directory, just type "dir" after the standard C prompt, like this:

```
C:\>dir
```

The other directories (such as the DOS directory and the Windows directory) are called **subdirectories**.

Just one file
To find info about one file, say "dir" then the file's name. For example, to find info about "COMMAND.COM", say "dir command.com". The computer will print:

```
COMMAND  COM     54,619   09-30-93    6:20a
```

Versions of COMMAND.COM
To tell which version of COMMAND.COM you have, use this chart:

COMMAND.COM version	Size	Date	Time
COMMAND.COM in MS-DOS 5	47,845 bytes	04-09-91	5:00a
COMMAND.COM in MS-DOS 6	52,925 bytes	03-10-93	6:00a
COMMAND.COM in MS-DOS 6.20	54,619 bytes	09-30-93	6:20a
COMMAND.COM in MS-DOS 6.21	54,619 bytes	02-13-94	6:21a
COMMAND.COM in MS-DOS 6.22	54,645 bytes	05-31-94	6:22a

For those modern versions of MS-DOS, notice that the version number is the same as the time: MS-DOS 5 was invented at 5am, MS-DOS 6 was invented at 6am, and MS-DOS 6.20 was invented at 6:20am. So either Microsoft programmers do all their work early in the morning, or else Microsoft lies about the time.

Most computerists believe that Microsoft lies about the time — not just the time when COMMAND.COM was invented, but also the time when future products will come out. As Microsoft programmers say, "Time is reprogrammable."

What if your COMMAND.COM does *not* say 5am, 6am, 6:20am, 6:21am, or 6:22am, or your COMMAND.COM has a different date or size than listed in that chart? Then you're probably using an older version (such as version 4, which was timed at 12am), or an even newer version (such as 6.23 or 7), or a variant version (such as IBM PC-DOS), or a version that's been infected by a virus.

Try this experiment: examine your DOS directory (by saying "dir dos /p"). You'll notice that most of your DOS files have the same date and time as your COMMAND.COM.

Wildcards The symbol "*" is called an **asterisk** or a **star**. To type it, tap the 8 key while holding down the SHIFT key.

Try this experiment: type "dir *.bat". (That command is pronounced "dir star dot bat".) That makes the computer print an abridged directory, showing information about just the files whose names end in ".bat". The computer will print:

```
AUTOEXEC BAT        106 06-29-94  12:39a
DO       BAT         44 06-09-94  11:18p
```

The symbol "*" means "anything". That's why saying "dir *.bat" makes the computer show a directory of anything that ends in ".bat".

To see a directory of files whose names *begin* with d, say "dir d*". The computer will print:

```
DOS         <DIR>        06-01-94   3:53a
DO       BAT         44 06-09-94  11:18p
```

A symbol (such as "*") that "matches anything" is called a **wildcard**.

Different drives Your computer's main floppy drive is called **drive A**. If your computer has *two* floppy drives, the second floppy drive is called **drive B**. In most computers, drive A is on *top* of drive B or to the *left* of drive B.

The main part of your computer's main hard drive is called **drive C**. If your computer has more than one hard drive, or its hard drive is **partitioned** into several parts, or you have a CD-ROM drive, or your computer is wired to other computers on a computer network, those additional disk surfaces are called **drive D**, **drive E**, **drive F**, etc.

To practice using drive A, try this experiment. . . .

Step 1: find drive A. It's the main floppy drive. If your computer has *two* floppy drives, drive A is probably on *top* of drive B or to the *left* of drive B.

Step 2: notice drive A's size. Take a ruler and measure the slot in drive A. If the slot is 5¼ inches long, drive A is called 5¼-inch. If the slot is 3½ inches long, drive A is called 3½-inch.

Step 3: grab a floppy disk. Pick a disk that's the same size as drive A. (For example, if drive A is 5¼-inch, pick a disk that's 5¼-inch.) Pick a disk that contains information already. (For example, pick a floppy disk that contains DOS or Windows or Word Perfect or a game or some other program or data.)

Step 4: put that disk into drive A. If the drive's slot is horizontal, make sure the disk's label is on *top* of the disk; if the slot is vertical, make sure the disk's label is on the disk's *left* side. If the disk is 5¼-inch, it has a big oval cutout; if the disk is 3½-inch, it has a chrome metal slider; make sure that cutout or slider goes into the drive *before* the label does.

If the disk is 5¼-inch, close the drive's door. Here's how: if the slot is horizontal, pull the door latch down; if the slot is vertical, pull the door latch to the right.

Step 5: type "dir a:". You can type "dir a:" after the standard C prompt, so your screen looks like this:

```
C:\>dir a:
```

To type the colon ":", make sure you hold down the SHIFT key.

If you're lucky, the computer will print a directory that lists the files on drive A's disk.

If you're *un*lucky, the computer will gripe by saying "Not ready reading drive A" or "General failure reading drive A". Then the computer will ask:

```
Abort, Retry, Fail?
```

To respond, choose Abort (by pressing the A key). Then the computer will say "C:\>" again. Try again to do the five steps

properly. (Make sure you don't insert the disk backwards or upside-down. If you're using a 5¼-inch disk, make sure you close the door. If you're still having trouble, try using a different floppy disk instead, or try using the other floppy drive.)

Once you've mastered the art of typing "dir a:", be bold: experiment! For example, try typing switches (such as "dir a: /p") or wildcards (such as "dir a:*.bat" or "dir a:w*"). Try putting other floppy disks into drive A, and find out what's on them (by typing "dir a:" again).

If you have a drive B, put a floppy disk into it and find out what's on that disk by typing "dir b:".

Change drive (a: or b: or c:)

When the computer is waiting for you to type a DOS command, the computer normally prints this prompt:

```
C:\>
```

That's called the **standard C prompt**. It means the computer is thinking about drive C.

A prompt Here's how to change the prompt, so the computer will think about drive A instead of drive C. In drive A put a floppy that contains info, then say "a:", so your screen looks like this:

```
C:\>a:
```

When you press ENTER at the end of that line, the computer changes the prompt to this:

```
A:\>
```

That's called the **A prompt**. It means that the computer is thinking about drive A.

After the A prompt, try saying "dir", so your screen looks like this:

```
A:\>dir
```

Because of the A prompt, that "dir" makes the computer print a directory of drive A (instead of drive C).

When you finish using the floppy in drive A and want to use the hard disk again, make the computer return to a standard C prompt. Here's how. After the A prompt, type "c:", so your screen looks like this:

```
A:\>c:
```

When you press ENTER at the end of that line, the computer will change the prompt back to this:

```
C:\>
```

The drive the computer thinks about is called the **current drive** (or **default drive**). If the computer says "C:\>", the default drive is C; if the computer says "A:\>", the default drive is A.

So to make A become the default drive, say "a:" (and press ENTER). To make C become the default drive again, say "c:" (and press ENTER).

B prompt If you have a drive B, try this experiment: in drive B put a floppy that contains info, then say "b:" (and press ENTER). The computer changes the prompt to this:

```
B:\>
```

Then if you type "dir", the computer will print a directory of drive B. To return to a C prompt, type "c:" (and press ENTER).

Change directory (cd)

One of the folders on your hard disk is called DOS. To find out what's in that folder, you can say "dir dos" after the C prompt, like this:

```
C:\>dir dos
```

Here's another way to find out what's in the DOS folder. Say "cd dos". (The "cd" means "change directory".) That makes the computer think about the DOS folder. The computer changes the prompt to this:

```
C:\DOS>
```

That means the computer is thinking about drive C's DOS folder. If you type "dir" after that prompt, the computer will print a directory of the files in drive C's DOS folder.

When you finish using the DOS folder, you should **return to the standard C prompt by saying "cd \"**. (Make sure you type a backslash \, not a forward slash /.) Then the computer will print a standard C prompt again:

```
C:\>
```

Suppose your hard disk contains a WINDOWS folder. Here's how to explore what's in that folder. . . .

First, make sure the screen shows a standard C prompt: "C:\>". Then say "cd windows". That makes the computer think about the WINDOWS folder, so the computer changes the prompt to this:

```
C:\WINDOWS>
```

To find out what's in that WINDOWS folder, say "dir /p", which makes the computer print a directory of the files in the WINDOWS folder.

You get a surprise: one of the files in the WINDOWS folder is another folder, called SYSTEM. Yes, SYSTEM is a folder that's inside the WINDOWS folder.

To find out what's in the SYSTEM folder, say "cd system" after the prompt, so your screen looks like this:

```
C:\WINDOWS>cd system
```

That makes the computer think about the SYSTEM folder inside the WINDOWS folder, so the computer changes the prompt to this:

```
C:\WINDOWS\SYSTEM>
```

Then if you say "dir", the computer will print a directory of the files in the WINDOWS SYSTEM folder.

Parents When a folder is inside another folder, the situation resembles a pregnant woman: the inner folder is called the **child**; the outer folder is called the **mommy** (or **parent**). For example, the SYSTEM folder is the child of the WINDOWS folder.

When you finish using the SYSTEM folder, you have a choice. **If you say "cd ..", those two periods make computer return to the mommy folder** (WINDOWS) and say:

```
C:\WINDOWS>
```

If instead you say "cd \", the backslash makes the computer return to the root directory and say:

```
C:\>
```

Saying "cd .." is therefore called "returning to mommy". Saying "cd \" is called "returning to your roots". Whenever you feel lost and scared, return to mommy or your roots!

Pointer files Socrates warned, "Know thyself." Freud warned, "Be prepared to tell me about your mother."

To obey their warnings, each folder contains a Socrates file and a Freud file. The Socrates file, called ".", reminds the folder of what files are in the folder. The Freud file, called "..", reminds the folder of who the folder's mother is, so the computer will know what to do when you type "cd ..".

That's why, when you're in the middle of a folder and say "dir", the first two files you see in the directory are called "." and "..". They're called **pointer files** because they point to the folder's inner self and mommy.

Short cut Suppose the computer says:

```
C:\DOS>
```

That means the computer is thinking about the DOS folder. To make the computer think about the WINDOWS SYSTEM folder instead, you can use two methods.

The normal method is to say "cd \" (which makes the computer leave the DOS folder and return to the standard C prompt), then say "cd windows", then say "cd system".

The shorter method is to combine all those cd commands into this single command: "cd \windows\system". In that command, make sure you type the backslashes.

Backslash versus forward slash Don't confuse the backslash (\) with a forward slash (/).

Type a backslash (\) when you're discussing folders, such as "cd \windows\system".
Type a forward slash (/) when you're giving switches, such as "dir /p" or "dir /w".

EXTERNAL COMMANDS

So far, you've learned 7 major commands: ver, echo, cls, date, time, dir, and cd. How does the computer understand them?

When you turn on the computer, the computer automatically runs a program called "COMMAND.COM", which teaches the computer how to react to those commands. Since the definitions of those commands are stored inside COMMAND.COM, those commands are called **internal commands**.

Now you're going to learn 3 fancy commands whose definitions are too long to fit in COMMAND.COM. The 3 fancy commands are "format" (which puts a format onto a disk), "diskcopy" (which makes a copy of a disk), and "chkdsk" (which checks your disk). Don't type them until I fully explain how to use them.

The definition of "format" is in a file called "FORMAT.COM". The definition of "diskcopy" is in a file called "DISKCOPY.COM". The definition of "chkdsk" is in a file that classic DOS calls "CHKDSK.COM" but modern DOS calls "CHKDSK.EXE".

Since the definitions of "format", "diskcopy", and "chkdsk" lie outside of COMMAND.COM, those 3 commands are called **external commands**.

When you give one of those external commands, the computer tries to obey the command by running the FORMAT.COM program, DISKCOPY.COM program, CHKDSK.COM program, or CHKDSK.EXE program.

If your computer is set up normally, those programs are in drive C's DOS folder. In that case, if you say —

```
C:\>dir dos /p
```

you'll see that the DOS directory includes FORMAT.COM, DISKCOPY.COM, and CHKDSK.EXE (or CHKDSK.COM).

But alas, your computer might be set up *ab*normally. Those programs might be in the root directory instead of in a DOS subdirectory. Those programs might be in a subdirectory which, instead of being called "DOS", is called "BIN" or "UTIL". Those programs might be on a drive D instead of C. If your computer doesn't have a hard disk, those programs might be on one of the DOS floppy disks instead.

Where are those programs in *your* computer? Find out now! Say —

```
C:\>dir dos /p
```

If you see that the DOS directory includes FORMAT.COM, DISKCOPY.COM, and CHKDSK.EXE (or CHKDSK.COM), you're lucky. If you're unlucky, explore other directories (by saying " dir /p" or "dir bin /p" or "dir util /p" or "dir d: /p" or "dir a: /p"), until you find the directory that contains those external DOS programs.

Check disk (chkdsk)

To check your computer's disk and RAM, type "chkdsk". Try it now!

If your computer is set up properly, it has a feature called **path to DOS**, so you can type "chkdsk" after any prompt, so your screen looks like this —

```
C:\>chkdsk
```

or like this —

```
C:\DOS>chkdsk
```

or like this —

```
C:\WINDOWS>chkdsk
```

or even like this —

```
C:\WINDOWS\SYSTEM>chkdsk
```

Then the computer will print a message saying how many bytes are in your hard drive and your RAM.

Example For example, when I say "chkdsk" on my computer, the computer prints this message:

```
212,058,112 bytes total disk space
     81,920 bytes in 2 hidden files
    389,120 bytes in 85 directories
190,115,840 bytes in 3,324 user files
     45,056 bytes in bad sectors
 21,426,176 bytes available on disk

      4,096 bytes in each allocation unit
     51,772 total allocation units on disk
      5,231 available allocation units on disk

    655,360 total bytes memory
    634,464 bytes free
```

The top line says the hard disk is big enough to hold 212,058,112 bytes altogether. That's about 212 million bytes. Since a million bytes is about the same as a megabyte, that's about 200 megabytes.

The next line says 81,920 bytes are in the 2 hidden files (IO.SYS and MSDOS.SYS).

The next line says the disk contains 85 folders (subdirectories). For each folder, the computer must store the folder's name and a list of which files are in the folder. Altogether, those 85 folder names and 85 folder lists consume 389,120 bytes.

The disk contains 3,324 user files. (Those are the files that aren't hidden and aren't names of folders.) Some of those files are in the root directory and can be seen when you type "dir"; the rest of those files are buried in folders. Altogether, those 3,324 user files consume 190,115,840 bytes.

It's difficult to manufacture a flawless hard disk. Most hard disks contain some unreliable areas, which are called **bad sectors**. According to the "chkdsk" command, my computer knows that 45,056 bytes on the hard disk's surface are in bad sectors. Since the computer *knows* that those sectors are bad, the computer won't put any data there, and those bad sectors won't do any harm.

The typical hard drive contains fewer than 200,000 bytes in bad sectors. The typical floppy disk has no bad sectors at all.

(If your hard disk contains *more* than 200,000 bytes in bad sectors, or the number of bytes in bad sectors increases rapidly each month, return the disk to your dealer for repair or replacement. If a floppy disk contains any bad sectors at all, buy a different floppy disk instead, since nearby sectors might be partly unreliable, and discount dealers sell new floppy disks for less than $1.)

Although the top line says my hard disk is big enough to hold about 212 million bytes, the lines below show that most of those bytes are used for the 2 hidden files, the 85 folders, the 3,324 user files, and bad sectors. Just 21,426,176 bytes remain unused; they're available for any additional files we want to put on the disk.

Each file consists of several **clusters** on the disk's surface. The next line says that each cluster (allocation unit) consists of 4,096 bytes (which is 4 kilobytes). The next lines say that altogether the disk holds 51,772 clusters, of which 5,231 remain unused.

The bottom two lines discuss the RAM chips, not the hard disk. They say that the RAM chips contain 655,360 bytes (640 kilobytes) of conventional memory. Some of those bytes are used by DOS itself; 634,464 bytes remain unused; they're available for any program we wish to run.

Actually, I bought more RAM chips — 4 megabytes altogether! But just 640K of them are used for conventional memory. The rest of them are used for extended and expanded memory, which the "chkdsk" command doesn't analyze.

Even if you buy many megabytes of RAM, the largest RAM quantity that the "chkdsk" command will ever mention is 655,360 bytes, because 655,360 bytes is the largest size that *conventional* RAM can be.

No hard disk? If you're using an early version of DOS and your computer doesn't have a hard disk, here's what to do. . . .

Grab the floppy disk that contains CHKDSK.COM. (If you're using DOS version 1, 2 or 3, grab the main DOS floppy disk. If you're using DOS version 4, grab Operating Disk 1.)

Put that disk into drive A. After the A prompt, say "chkdsk".

Bad command When you say "chkdsk", the computer might say:

Bad command or file name

That means the computer can't find the CHKDSK program.

To solve that problem, examine your spelling: maybe you spelled "chkdsk" incorrectly?

If you don't have a hard disk, maybe you inserted the wrong floppy disk?

If you have a hard disk and spelled "chkdsk" correctly, maybe your computer is set up incorrectly. To handle such a computer, remind the computer that the "chkdsk" command is in the DOS subdirectory (by typing "\dos\chkdsk" instead of just "chkdsk").

If you don't have a DOS subdirectory but instead have a subdirectory called BIN, try typing "\bin\chkdsk". If instead you have a subdirectory called UTIL, try typing "\util\chkdsk".

Different drives If you say "chkdsk" after the C prompt, the computer will check the disk in drive C.

To check the disk in drive A, say "chkdsk a:". To check disk B, say "chkdsk b:".

Lost chains If you accidentally turn off the computer while the computer is in the middle of thinking about a file, the computer might get confused and forget the file's name and which folder the file belongs to. Such a file, whose identity has been lost, is called a **lost chain**.

When you say "chkdsk", the computer checks whether your disk contains any lost chains. If the computer notices a lost chain, the computer will say "errors" and might ask:

Convert lost chains to files?

To reply, press the N key.

Fix If you say "chkdsk" and the computer notices errors on your disk (such as lost chains), the computer tells you about the errors but doesn't fix them.

To fix the errors, say "chkdsk" again but put "/f" at the end of the command, like this:

C:\>chkdsk /f

The "/f" makes the computer fix minor errors (such as lost chains).

If you're using DOS 6.2, the computer says:

Instead of using CHKDSK /F, try using SCANDISK.
Do you still want to run CHKDSK /F (Y/N)?

To reply, press Y then ENTER.

If the computer asks "Convert lost chains to files?" again, press the N key again. This time, the computer will get rid of the "lost chains" problem by erasing those chains.

(Almost always, the chains contain fragments of old junk that you want erased. If you press Y instead of N, the computer will turn those chains into files instead of erasing them. The files will be named "FILE0000.CHK", "FILE0001.CHK", "FILE0002.CHK", etc.)

If you want to check the disk in drive A and fix it, say "chkdsk a: /f".

Format (in every DOS)
& unformat (in modern DOS)

Suppose you buy a blank floppy disk. Before you can use that disk, it must be **formatted**.

You can buy disks that have been formatted. If your disk has *not* been formatted yet, you must format it yourself; here's how.

Follow 9 steps To avoid difficulties when formatting, follow these 9 steps. . . .

Step 1: make sure the disk is blank and a virgin, never used before. Take the disk out of a new, unopened box of blank disks. Do *not* use a disk that already contains info!

Step 2: make sure the disk is the same size as the drive you plan to put it in. If the drive's slot is 5¼ inches long, make sure the disk is 5¼-inch. If the drive's slot is 3½ inches long, make sure the disk is 3½-inch.

Step 3: make sure the disk is the same density as the drive. If the drive is high-density, make sure the disk is high-density. If the drive is double-density, make sure the disk is double-density.

To find out the density of the drive, ask your dealer (or read the ads and manuals that came with the computer). A 5¼-inch drive holds 360K if double-density, 1.2M if high-density. A 3½-inch drive holds 720K if double-density, 1.44M if high-density. In a typical 8088 computer, the drives are double-density. In a typical 386, 486, or Pentium computer, the drives are high-density. In a typical 286 computer, drive A is high-density; drive B is either a double-density 5¼-inch or a high-density 3½-inch.

To find out the density of the disk, read the disk's label and the box that the disk came in. "HD" means high-density; "DD" means double-density. The typical high-density 3½-inch disk has "HD" stamped on it and has square cutouts in *two* of the disk's corners (instead of just one corner). The typical double-density 5¼-inch disk is made of magnetic material that's brownish-gray (instead of charcoal gray) and has its central hole reinforced by a Mylar ring.

Step 4: temporarily empty the drives. If you have a hard drive, remove any floppies from the floppy drives. If you do *not* have a hard drive, put into drive A the DOS disk containing FORMAT.COM.

Step 5: get the standard prompt onto the screen. If you have a hard disk, make the computer say "C:\>". If you do *not* have a hard disk, make the computer say "A:\>" (or "A>").

Step 6: say "format a:" or "format b:" (and press ENTER at the end of that line). If you're planning to put the blank disk into drive A, say "format a:". If you're planning to put the blank disk into drive B, say "format b:". Be sure to say "format a:" or "format b:" rather than just "format".

Then if you're lucky, the computer will say:

```
Insert new diskette
and press ENTER when ready
```

(If instead the computer says "Bad command or file name", remind the computer which folder FORMAT.COM is in. For example, if FORMAT.COM is in a folder called DOS, say "\dos\format a:"; if FORMAT.COM is in a folder called BIN, say "\bin\format a:".)

Step 7: put the blank disk into the drive. If you said "format a:", put the blank disk into drive A (after removing any disk that's already in drive A). If you said "format b:", put the blank disk into drive B.

If the disk is 5¼-inch, close the drive's door.

Step 8: press the ENTER key. If you're lucky, the computer will say "Formatting"; then it will format the blank disk.

The formatting takes about a minute. During that time, the computer divides the disk's surface into tracks and sectors, checks the disk's surface for flaws, and puts these 4 items onto the disk: the **boot record**, the **directory**, and 2 copies of the **file allocation table (FAT)**. When the formatting is finished, the computer will say "Format complete".

(If the computer gripes, try again to do those eight steps correctly!)

Step 9: answer questions. If you're using modern DOS or DOS 4, the computer will ask:

```
Volume label (11 characters, ENTER for none)?
```

Then you can invent a name for the disk. Keep the name short: no more than 11 characters. Type the name, then press the ENTER key. (If you're too lazy to invent a name, press ENTER without typing a name.) Then in the future, whenever you ask the computer to print the disk's directory, the computer will automatically print the disk's name at the top of the directory.

At the end of the whole formatting procedure, the computer will ask:

```
Format another (Y/N)?
```

If you want to format another blank disk, press the Y key (which means "Yes"); otherwise, press the N key (which means "No"). Then press ENTER.

Mistakes When giving the format command, what happens if you make a mistake?

Make sure the disk you're formatting was blank. If it wasn't blank, the computer will automatically *make* it blank, by destroying the information on it!

Make sure you say which drive to format. To format the disk in drive A, say "format a:". To format the disk in drive B, say "format b:".

If you forget to say "a:" or "b:" after the word "format", the computer gets nasty. Modern DOS and DOS 4 make the computer print this gripe:

```
Required parameter missing
```

DOS 3.2 & 3.3 make the computer print this gripe instead:

```
Drive letter must be specified
```

If you're using an even older version of DOS, the computer won't gripe. Instead, it will format whatever disk is in the default drive, which might not be the drive you intended! For example, if the default drive is C, the computer will format drive C's hard disk, and so it will erase the information on your hard disk!

Format the whole box If you buy a box of unformatted blank disks, format all the disks in the box immediately. Avoid giving the format command again — until you buy your next box of unformatted blank disks.

Unformat (in modern DOS) Suppose you accidentally format a disk that contained some important files. When the formatting is done, the files seem to be gone.

But *if you're using modern DOS*, you can get the files back! Just tell the computer to **unformat** the disk. For example, to unformat the disk in drive A, say "unformat a:". The computer will say, "Press ENTER when ready." Press ENTER. The computer will ask, "Are you sure?" Press Y. Then the computer will unformat the disk. Afterwards, if you say "dir a:", you'll see that the files are still there!

Unconditional format (modern DOS) Modern DOS lets you say "/u" at the end of the format command, like this: "**format a: /u**". That formats the disk faster, so you don't have to wait long for the formatting to finish. The "/u" also reduces the chance that the computer will gripe at you. When I want modern DOS to format a disk, I usually say "/u".

The only disadvantage of saying "format a: /u" is that the disk cannot be unformatted. The "/u" tells the computer to format **unconditionally** and not waste time worrying about the possibility that you might change your mind and want to unformat. Saying "/u" means you're confident and demand quick results.

Quick format (in modern DOS) Suppose a disk in drive A has been formatted and contains files, but you no longer need those files. To erase all the files on the disk, you can just reformat the disk by again saying "format a:".

Unfortunately, saying "format a:" makes you wait about a minute, while the computer erases the files and divides the disk's surface into tracks and sectors again.

Modern DOS lets you reformat faster by saying "**format a: /q/u**". The "/q" tells the computer to reformat *quickly*, by erasing the files but not bothering to redivide the disk's surface into tracks and sectors; the computer will reuse the tracks and sectors. The "/u" tells the computer to reformat *unconditionally*, without preparing for the possibility of an unformat. The computer accomplishes "format a: /q/u" in just a few seconds.

Double-density format (DOS 3 & up) Suppose

you buy a double-density disk and want to format it. The most reliable way to format it is to use a double-density drive.

But suppose you don't have any double-density drives. Try a trick: stick the double-density disk into a high-density drive, and give one of the trick format commands listed below.

These tricks work well if the disk is 3½-inch. If the disk is 5¼-inch, these tricks are less reliable, but you're welcome to try them anyway.

Here are the tricks for trying to format a double-density disk in high-density drive A. . . .

Modern DOS and DOS 4 let you do this:

If the disk is 3½-inch, say "format a: /f:720", which means format for 720K.
If the disk is 5¼-inch, say "format a: /f:360", which means format for 360K.

To make modern DOS finish the format faster and with less chance of the computer griping, put "/u" at the end of the command:

If the disk is 3½-inch, say "format a: /f:720 /u".
If the disk is 5¼-inch, say "format a: /f:360 /u".

DOS 3.3 doesn't understand "/f:". Do this instead:

If disk is 3½-inch, say "format a: /n:9". The "/n:9" means 9 sectors per track.
If disk is 5¼-inch, say "format a: /4". The "/4" means 40 tracks.

Those are the commands to format a double-density disk in a high-density drive.

DOS 3, 3.1, and 3.2 can't handle high-density 3½-inch drives but use the same command as DOS 3.3 for handling high-density 5¼-inch drives. DOS 1, 1.1, 2, and 2.1 can't handle high-density drives at all.

Diskcopy

To copy a floppy disk, give the "diskcopy" command. It copies info from one floppy disk (called the **source**) to a blank floppy (called the **target**). It copies the entire disk, so that at the end of the process the target disk will become an exact clone of the source disk.

Follow 7 steps To avoid difficulties when copying

disks, follow these 7 steps. . . .

Step 1: choose a source disk. Decide which disk you want to copy. It must be a *floppy* disk, since the "diskcopy" command copies just floppy disks, not hard disks.

Step 2: choose a target disk. It should be blank and a virgin, never used before. It must be the same type of disk as the source disk: specifically, it must be floppy, and it must be the same size and density as the source disk. For example, if the source disk is 5¼-inch, the target disk must be 5¼-inch (not 3½-inch); if the source disk is double-density, the target disk must be double-density (not high-density).

Step 3: temporarily empty the drives. If you have a hard drive, remove any floppies from the drives. If you do *not* have a hard drive, put into drive A the DOS disk containing DISKCOPY.COM.

Step 4: get the standard prompt onto the screen. If you have a hard disk, make the computer say "C:\>". If you do *not* have a hard disk, make the computer say "A:\>" (or "A>").

Step 5: say "diskcopy a: b:" or "diskcopy a: a:" or "diskcopy b: b:" (and press ENTER at end of that line). If the source disk can be read by both drive A and drive B, say "diskcopy a: b:". If the source disk can be read by drive A but not by drive B, say "diskcopy a: a:". If the source disk can be read by drive B but not by drive A, say "diskcopy b: b:".

Confused? Use this chart:

Source disk	Drive A	Drive B	What to type
1.44M	1.44M	1.44M	diskcopy a: b:
1.44M	1.44M	not 1.44M	diskcopy a: a:
1.44M	not 1.44M	1.44M	diskcopy b: b:
1.2M	1.2M	1.2M	diskcopy a: b:
1.2M	1.2M	not 1.2M	diskcopy a: a:
1.2M	not 1.2M	1.2M	diskcopy b: b:
360K	5¼-inch	5¼-inch	diskcopy a: b:
360K	5¼-inch	not 5¼-inch	diskcopy a: a:
360K	not 5¼-inch	5¼-inch	diskcopy b: b:
720K	3½-inch	3½-inch	diskcopy a: b:
720K	3½-inch	not 3½-inch	diskcopy a: a:
720K	not 3½-inch	3½-inch	diskcopy b: b:

Then if you're lucky, the computer will say, "Insert SOURCE disk".

(If instead the computer says "Bad command or file name", remind the computer which folder DISKCOPY.COM is in. For example, if DISKCOPY.COM is in a folder called DOS, give a command such as "\dos\diskcopy a: b:".)

Step 6: insert the appropriate disks and press ENTER. Here are the details. . . .

What you said	What to do now
diskcopy a: b:	Put the source disk into drive A. Put the target disk into drive B. Press ENTER. Wait until the computer asks "Copy another"?
diskcopy a: a:	Put the source disk into drive A. Press ENTER. When computer says so, put target disk in drive A. Press ENTER. When computer says so, put source disk into drive A. Press ENTER. Continue swapping the source and target disks, until the computer asks "Copy another"?
diskcopy b: b:	Put the source disk into drive B. Press ENTER. When computer says so, put target disk into drive B. Press ENTER. When computer says so, put source disk into drive B. Press ENTER. Continue swapping the source and target disks, until the computer asks "Copy another"?

During this step, the computer copies info from the source disk to the RAM chips, and then from the RAM chips to the target disk. If the target disk wasn't formatted previously, the computer formats it automatically while doing this step.

Step 7: press Y or N. If you want to copy another disk, press the Y key (which means "Yes"); otherwise, press the N key (which means "No").

Copy DOS When you buy a new computer, the first

thing you should do is copy the main DOS disk, by saying "diskcopy a: b:" (or "diskcopy a: a:"). Then use the copy. Store the original disk in a safe place — so that if the copy ever gets accidentally damaged, you can go back to the original.

You should also copy the other DOS disks and any other important software you bought.

Copy protection Although the "diskcopy" command

usually works, sometimes it doesn't! The computer might *refuse* to copy a disk!

That happens if the disk's programs were written by programmers who fear you'll give copies of the disk to all your friends without paying royalties. Those programmers alter the disk, to prevent "diskcopy" from working.

A disk altered to prevent the "diskcopy" command from working is said to be a **copy-protected disk**.

EDIT YOUR DISKS

Here's how to edit the info on your disks. I'll assume you have a hard drive.

(If you don't have a hard drive, put a formatted floppy disk in drive B and use that instead of drive C. If you don't have a hard drive and don't have a drive B, use drive A — or better yet, practice these commands on somebody else's computer!)

Make directory (md)

Let's create a new folder on your hard disk.

First, get a standard C prompt, so your screen looks like this:

```
C:\>
```

Then invent a name for your folder. The name can be up to 8 characters long, such as SARAH or TONY or JUNK or POETRY or FIDDLING. Type "md" then the name.

For example, **to Make a Directory called SARAH, say "md sarah"** after the C prompt, like this:

```
C:\>md sarah
```

At the end of that line, press the ENTER key. The computer will pause briefly, while it creates a SARAH directory. (If the computer says "Directory already exists" or "Unable to create directory", your disk *already* contained something called SARAH, and you must pick a different name instead.)

Then the computer will say "C:\>" again, so you can give another DOS command.

To prove that the SARAH directory was created, say "dir sarah". The computer will show that SARAH contains two files: Socrates (.) and Freud (..).

Go ahead! Create a folder named SARAH and other folders!

Cd Suppose you've created a SARAH folder. If you wish, you can go into the SARAH folder by saying "cd sarah", which means "Change Directory to SARAH". That makes the computer say:

```
C:\SARAH>
```

Then if you say "dir", the computer will show you the SARAH directory's two files. To return to the root directory, say "cd \".

Copy

The Jewish religion prohibits Orthodox Jews from eating ham. That's why Mary had a little lamb:

```
Mary had a little lamb,
'Cause Jewish girls can't eat no ham.
If Mary were a Hindu now,
Mary couldn't eat no cow.
Religions all are fine and dandy,
Even my dentist's, which says "No candy!"
But Ma's religion makes me shiver.
That's why mine says "Ma, no liver!"
```

Copy from console Here's how to put that poem onto your hard disk and call it MARY.

First, type "copy con mary" after the C prompt, like this:

```
C:\>copy con mary
```

(If your hard disk *already* contains a file named MARY, DOS 6.2 makes the computer ask, "Overwrite MARY?" To reply, press the Y key then ENTER.)

Underneath that typing, type the poem. (If you don't like that poem, make up your own! If you're a slow typist, make up a poem that's shorter to type, or type just the first two lines.)

Underneath your poem, press the F6 key and then the ENTER key. The computer will automatically copy your poem onto the hard disk and call it MARY.

To prove that your computer put the poem onto the disk, look at the hard disk's directory, by typing "dir /p". You'll see that one of the files in the directory is MARY.

Your computer's **console** consists of the keyboard and screen. Saying "copy con mary" tells the computer that you want to copy from the console (keyboard and screen) to a disk file named MARY.

Copy to console Suppose your disk contains a file called MARY. To find out what's in MARY, say "copy mary con". That makes the computer copy MARY from the disk to your console's screen. For example, if MARY was a poem, the poem will appear on your screen.

Filenames You can give a file any short name you wish, such as MARY or LAMBCHOP. **Keep the filename short: you can't make it longer than 8 characters.**

At the end of the filename, you can put a period and a 3-character **extension**.

For example, you can name a file "LAMBCHOP.YUM". In that example, the "LAMBCHOP" is called the **filename**; the "YUM" is called the **extension**.

Copy to floppy After you've created a file named MARY on your hard disk, you can copy MARY to a floppy disk. Here's how.

If drive A contains a formatted floppy disk, **you can copy MARY to drive A's disk by saying "copy mary a:".** Try it!

(If the computer gripes by saying "Write protect error", your floppy disk is a special kind that can't be written on. To reply, press the A key, which means "Abort", then try using a different floppy disk instead.)

To prove that MARY's been copied to drive A, make the computer print the directory of drive A, by saying "dir a:".

To copy MARY from the hard drive to drive B, say "copy mary b:".

Suppose you've put MARY on a floppy disk in drive A and want to copy MARY from that floppy disk to a disk in drive B. Make the computer say "A:\>", then say "copy mary b:".

Suppose MARY's on a floppy disk in drive A and you want to copy MARY to another floppy disk, but you don't have a drive B. Even though you don't have a drive B, you can say "copy mary b:". The computer will pretend your single floppy drive is both A and B; the computer will tell you when to remove disk A from the drive and insert disk B instead.

Copy to folder Suppose MARY is on a floppy disk in drive A, and your hard disk contains a folder called SARAH. Here's how to copy MARY to the SARAH folder. At the standard C prompt, say "copy a:mary sarah", so your screen looks like this:

```
C:\>copy a:mary sarah
```

That tells the computer to copy drive A's MARY to the SARAH folder. (When giving that command, do *not* put a space after the "a:".)

Here's another way to copy drive A's MARY file to the hard disk's SARAH folder. First, get into the SARAH folder by saying "cd sarah". That makes the computer say:

```
C:\SARAH>
```

Then tell the computer to copy drive A's MARY by saying "copy a:mary", so your screen looks like this:

```
C:\SARAH>copy a:mary
```

(When giving that command, do *not* put a space after the "a:".)

Many ways to copy
Here's a list of the many ways to copy a file.

Goal	What to say		
copy from the keyboard to a hard-disk file called MARY	`C:\>copy con mary`		
copy MARY from the hard disk to your screen	`C:\>copy mary con`		
copy MARY from the hard disk to drive A	`C:\>copy mary a:`		
copy MARY from the hard disk to drive B	`C:\>copy mary b:`		
copy MARY from drive A to drive B	`A:\>copy mary b:`		
copy MARY from drive A (to the hard disk)	`C:\>copy a:mary`		
copy MARY from drive A to the hard disk's SARAH folder	`C:\>copy a:mary sarah`	or say	`C:\SARAH>copy a:mary`
copy everything from drive A to the hard disk's SARAH folder	`C:\>copy a:*.* sarah`	or say	`C:\SARAH>copy a:*.*`
copy everything from the SARAH folder to drive A	`C:\>copy sarah a:`	or say	`C:\SARAH>copy *.* a:`
copy MARY from the SARAH folder to drive A	`C:\>copy sarah\mary a:`	or say	`C:\SARAH>copy mary a:`
copy everything from the SARAH folder to the TONY folder	`C:\>copy sarah tony`	or say	`C:\SARAH>copy *.* \tony`
copy MARY from the SARAH folder to the TONY folder	`C:\>copy sarah\mary tony`	or say	`C:\SARAH>copy mary \tony`
make a copy of MARY, but call the copy "SUE"	`C:\>copy mary sue`		

Copy entire floppy to another floppy
Suppose drive A's floppy disk contains important info, and you want to copy all that info to another disk.

If possible, use the "diskcopy" command, by saying "diskcopy a: b:" or "diskcopy a: a:". That makes an exact copy of the entire disk. Unfortunately, the "diskcopy" command can't handle hard disks, and it requires that the target disk be exactly the same size and density as the source disk.

An alternative way to copy all files from drive A to drive B is to say:

`A:\>copy *.* b:`

That tells the computer to copy files from drive A to drive B. But that "copy" command does *not* copy the hidden files (IO.SYS and MSDOS.SYS), does *not* copy folders, and does *not* copy any files buried in folders. It copies just the visible simple files listed in the root directory. And before giving that "copy" command you must make sure drive B's disk has been formatted.

Copy entire floppy to the hard disk
To copy all files from drive A to the *hard* disk, you can use several methods.

One method is to **make a hard-disk folder**, such as SARAH, by saying:

`C:\>md sarah`

Then copy files from drive A to that folder by saying:

`C:\>copy a:*.* sarah`

That copies just the simple files that are visible in drive A's root directory.

When giving that command, make sure you mention a hard-disk folder such as SARAH. Do *not* just say "copy a:*.*" without mentioning SARAH. If you make the mistake of saying just "copy a:*.*", the computer will copy drive A's files to your hard directory's *root* directory, where they'll destroy any hard disk files that have similar names.

For example, if drive A contains a file called "AUTOEXEC.BAT" and you make the mistake of saying "copy a:*.*", that file will be copied to your hard disk's root directory and destroy the AUTOEXEC.BAT file that was on your hard disk previously. Then your hard disk won't work properly, and you'll phone me with tears in your eyes about how you wrecked your hard disk. People from all over the world phone me with that problem every week.

Spare me the agony: remember to **never say just "copy a:*.*"**. Instead, always mention a folder, such as "copy a:*.* sarah".

When you buy a program, you usually get an instruction manual and a set of floppy disks. Read the instruction manual — especially the part entitled "Getting started" or "Installation". It tells you the programmer's opinion of the best way to copy the floppy disks onto your hard disk.

Instead of having you create a folder such as SARAH and then having you say "copy a:*.* sarah", the instruction manual usually tells you to put the first floppy disk into drive A and then type "a:install" or "a:setup". When you type that command, the computer starts running a program called "INSTALL.EXE" or "SETUP.EXE" on the first floppy disk. That program automatically creates a folder on your hard disk and copies files to that folder from the floppy disk. Then the program makes the computer tell you to insert the other floppy disks, and the program automatically copies files from those disks to your hard disk's folder.

During that process, the program asks you questions about what kind of computer equipment you bought and what your desires are. The program copies just the files that are relevant to your needs and desires; it also edits those files to meet your needs more closely.

Type
Suppose you've put on your hard disk a file called MARY containing a poem. To see the poem on your screen, you can tell the computer to copy MARY to the console's screen, by saying "copy mary con". An even easier way to copy MARY to the screen is to say just "type mary".

Experiment! See what's in your hard disk's "AUTOEXEC.BAT" file by saying "type autoexec.bat", like this:

`C:\>type autoexec.bat`

See what's in your hard disk's "CONFIG.SYS" file by saying:

`C:\>type config.sys`

Which files are ASCII
MARY, AUTOEXEC.BAT, and CONFIG.SYS all contain words and numbers that you can read on the screen. Other files are weirder. For example, if you say "type command.com", you'll see strange symbols instead of words and numbers.

Files such as MARY, AUTOEXEC.BAT, and CONFIG.SYS, which all contain words and numbers you can read, are called **ASCII files** (pronounced "ass key files"). The COMMAND.COM file contains special symbols and is therefore *not* an ASCII file.

If somebody says, "Give me an ASCII file", that person wants to be given a floppy disk that contains an ASCII file, which is a file that the person can read by giving the "type" command.

Files that end in .BAT are always ASCII files. Files ending in .COM and .EXE are never ASCII files. Files ending in .TXT are usually ASCII files.

Congratulations! You've learned all the essentials of DOS! If you're in a rush, you may skip ahead to other chapters. If you keep reading here, you'll become a DOS *expert!*

Rename (ren)

Suppose a file is named MARY. To change that file's name to LAMBCHOP, say "rename mary lambchop".

Before giving that command, make sure the computer has given you the right prompt. For example, if MARY is on drive A, change the name to LAMBCHOP by saying:

```
A:\>rename mary lambchop
```

If MARY is in the hard drive's SARAH folder, change the name MARY to LAMBCHOP by saying:

```
C:\SARAH>rename mary lambchop
```

Instead of typing the word "rename", you can type just "ren", like this: "ren mary lambchop".

By saying "rename" (or "ren"), you can rename a simple file (such as MARY), but you cannot rename a folder. For example, if you have a folder named SARAH, you cannot change SARAH to TONY by saying "rename".

Delete (del)

Suppose a file is named MARY. To delete that file from the disk, say "del mary".

Before giving that command, make sure the computer has given you the right prompt. For example, if MARY is on drive A, delete MARY by saying:

```
A:\>del mary
```

If MARY is in the hard drive's SARAH folder, delete MARY by saying:

```
C:\SARAH>del mary
```

Delete all files
To delete *all* files from the SARAH folder, say:

```
C:\>del sarah
```

The computer will ask, "Are you sure?" To reply, press the Y key (which means Yes) and then ENTER.

Then the computer will delete all files from the SARAH folder — except for Socrates (.), Freud (..), any hidden files, and any folders that are inside the SARAH folder.

To delete all files from drive A, say:

```
A:\>del *.*
```

When the computer asks "Are you sure?", press Y then ENTER. Then the computer will delete all files from drive A — except for hidden files and folders.

Move (in DOS 6 & 6.2)

DOS 6 & 6.2 let you say "move". The word "move" serves two purposes. . . .

Purpose 1: move a file
For example, suppose MARY is a file on the hard disk, and you want to move MARY to drive A. Just say:

```
C:\>move mary a:
```

That copies MARY from the hard disk to drive A and then deletes MARY from the hard disk.

Saying "move mary a:" has the same effect as saying "copy mary a:" and then "del mary". So "move" means "make a copy and then destroy the original".

Purpose 2: rename a folder
If SARAH is a folder and you want to change its name to TONY, say "move sarah tony", like this:

```
C:\>move sarah tony
```

Remove directory (rd)

Suppose your hard disk contains a folder named SARAH. Here's how to remove that folder from the hard disk.

First, delete all files from the SARAH folder by saying:

```
C:\>del sarah
```

When the computer asks "Are you sure?", press the Y key and then ENTER.

Now the SARAH folder should be empty. Finally, get rid of the SARAH folder itself, by saying Remove the Directory SARAH:

```
C:\>rd sarah
```

If you're lucky, the computer will respond by saying just:

```
C:\>
```

That means the SARAH folder has been removed. If you're *un*lucky, the computer will gripe by saying:

```
Invalid path, not directory,
or directory not empty
C:\>
```

That means the SARAH folder can't be removed yet, because the SARAH folder isn't empty yet: it contains other folders or hidden files. Get rid of the folders inside it, then try again to say "rd sarah".

Deltree (in DOS 6 & 6.2)

If you want to delete a folder named SARAH, DOS 6 & 6.2 permit this shortcut: just say "deltree sarah", like this. . . .

```
C:\>deltree sarah
```

The computer will ask whether you're sure; press Y then ENTER. Then the computer will delete all the files in the SARAH folder, delete any folders in the SARAH folder, and remove the SARAH folder itself. So the computer automatically does "del sarah" and "rd sarah" and does the same for any folders in SARAH.

Saying "deltree sarah" is nifty, because it automatically makes the computer perform a series of "del" and "rd" commands for you.

The "deltree sarah" means "delete the tree of SARAH". It makes the computer delete the SARAH folder and also any files or folders that have been sprouting in SARAH.

Edit (in modern DOS)

To edit a file easily, give the "edit" command. To give that command, you must buy modern DOS.

(If you're using a classic DOS instead, skip ahead to the next section, which explains how to give the "edlin" command instead.)

Before giving the "edit" command, decide which file you want to edit. (For example, suppose you want to edit a file you created called "MARY".)

Make the computer give you the correct prompt. (For example, if MARY is in your hard disk's root directory, make the computer say "C:\>". If MARY is in your hard disk's SARAH folder, make the computer say "C:\SARAH>". If MARY is in drive B, make the computer say "B:\>".)

After that prompt, say "edit mary".

If you're lucky, the screen's bottom line will say "MS-DOS Editor", the screen's top line will say "File", and the screen's second line will say "MARY". (If instead the computer gripes, make sure your DOS folder contains EDIT.COM, EDIT.HLP, and QBASIC.EXE.)

In the middle of the screen, you'll see all of MARY's lines:

```
Mary had a little lamb,
'Cause Jewish girls can't eat no ham.
If Mary were a Hindu now,
Mary couldn't eat no cow.
Religions all are fine and dandy,
Even my dentist's, which says "No candy!"
But Ma's religion makes me shiver.
That's why mine says "Ma, no liver!"
```

NUM LOCK key
In your keyboard's upper-right corner, you might see a light marked "Num Lock". If that light is glowing, turn it off by pressing the **NUM LOCK key** underneath it.

Cursor
On your screen, the first character (the M) is underlined. The underline blinks. That blinking underline is called the **cursor**.

To move that cursor to the right, press the key that has a right-arrow on it. You can move the cursor in all four directions, by pressing the right-arrow, left-arrow, down-arrow, and up-arrow keys. Each of those keys automatically repeats: so to move the cursor to the right *several* characters, just keep your finger on the right-arrow key a while.

(If pressing the arrow keys makes you see numbers instead of a moving cursor, press the NUM LOCK key.)

To move the cursor all the way left, to the line's beginning, press the **HOME key**. To move the cursor far right, to the line's end, just past the line's last word, press the **END key**.

Insert a character
Here's how to insert extra characters anywhere in your document. Move the cursor to where you want the extra characters to begin. Then type the characters you want to insert. To make room for characters you're inserting, other characters on that line will automatically move to the right.

Insert a line
To insert an extra line in your document, move the cursor to the screen's left edge, where you want the extra line to begin. Then while holding down the Ctrl key, tap the N key (which means "**New line**").

You'll see a blank line. To make room for it, other lines will automatically move down.

Leave the new line blank, or type there whatever characters you wish!

Delete a character
To delete the character you just typed, press the **BACKSPACE key** (which is above the ENTER key and has a left-arrow on it).

To delete a character you typed long ago, move the cursor to that character, then press the **DELETE key** (which says "Delete" or "Del" on it). To delete a passage typed long ago, move the cursor to the passage's beginning, then tap the DELETE key several times (or hold down the DELETE key a while), until the passage disappears.

Delete a line
To delete an entire line, put the cursor anywhere in that line. Then, while holding down the Ctrl key, tap the Y key (which means "**Yank the line**"). The entire line will disappear.

Use that same technique to eliminate a blank line: put the cursor at the blank line, then press Ctrl with Y.

Move a line
To move a line far up or far down, first delete the line from its old position (by moving the cursor to that line, then pressing Ctrl with Y), so the line temporarily disappears.

Where do you want to move the line? Put the cursor at the screen's left edge, just under where you want the line to reappear.

Then do this: while holding down the SHIFT key, tap the INSERT key. The line will magically reappear there! To make room for it, other lines will automatically move down.

Exit
When you finish editing the file, tap 4 keys:

Tap the Alt key (which means "Menu").
Tap the F key (which means "File").
Tap the X key (which means "eXit").
Tap the ENTER key (which means "Yes").

That makes the computer exit from the editor. You see a DOS prompt (such as "C:\>"), so you can give another DOS command.

Make a big boo-boo?
If you make a big mistake and wish you hadn't tried to edit MARY, tap 4 keys:

Tap the Alt key (which means "Menu").
Tap the F key (which means "File").
Tap the X key (which means "eXit").
Tap the N key (which means "No").

That makes the computer ignore all the editing you've done, so that MARY returns to its original state. MARY returns to the state it was in before you started using the editor.

You see a DOS prompt (such as "C:\>"), so you can give another DOS command.

Edlin (in early DOS versions)
If your DOS is classic, edit a file by giving the "edlin" command. (If your DOS is modern, don't bother reading this; skip ahead to the next topic, "Batch Files".)

Here's how to give the "edlin" command.

First, decide which file you want to edit. (For example, suppose you want to edit a file you created called "MARY".)

Next, make the computer give you the correct prompt. (For example, if MARY is in your hard disk's root directory, make the computer say "C:\>". If MARY is in your hard disk's SARAH folder, make the computer say "C:\SARAH>". If MARY is in drive B, make the computer say "B:\>".)

After that prompt, say "edlin mary".

If you're lucky, the computer will say:

```
End of input file
```

(If instead the computer says "Bad command or file name", your computer is set up incorrectly and can't find the EDLIN.COM program. In that case, remind the computer where the EDLIN.COM program is. For example, if the EDLIN.COM program is in your hard disk's DOS folder, say "c:\dos\edlin mary". If the EDLIN.COM program is in drive A, say "a:edlin mary".)

Then the computer will print an asterisk:

```
*
```

After the asterisk, you can type any edlin command.

List
For your first edlin command, type "lL" after the asterisk, so your screen looks like this:

```
*1L
```

That makes the computer print a List of MARY's lines, starting at line 1. The computer automatically numbers the lines, so you see this:

```
1:*Mary had a little lamb,
2: 'Cause Jewish girls can't eat no ham.
3: If Mary were a Hindu now,
4: Mary couldn't eat no cow.
5: Religions all are fine and dandy,
6: Even my dentist's, which says "No candy!"
7: But Ma's religion makes me shiver.
8: That's why mine says "Ma, no liver!"
```

Underneath, the computer prints another asterisk, so you can give another edlin command.

Edit If you want to edit line 5, type "5" (and then press ENTER).

The computer will print a copy of line 5, so you see this:

```
5:*Religions all are fine and dandy,
```

Underneath, retype that line however you want it. For example, try typing "Religions can be wonderful and fancy,". To save time, instead of retyping the word "Religions" (which is unchanged), just press the right-arrow key 9 times (since "Religions" has 9 characters).

When you finish retyping the line, press ENTER at the end of it.

Delete If you want to Delete line 6, type "6D" after the asterisk. That makes the computer delete line 6 and renumber all the lines that came underneath it.

Then look at the new version of MARY, by typing "1L" again.

Insert Here's how to insert extra lines and make them become lines 3 and 4, so that the old lines 3 and 4 become 5 and 6.

Type "3I" after the asterisk. The computer will say:

```
3:*
```

Then type whatever words you want to be in the new line 3.

When you press the ENTER key at the end of that line, the computer will say:

```
4:*
```

Then type whatever words you want to be in the new line 4.

When you press the ENTER key at the end of that line, the computer will say:

```
5:*
```

If you don't want to type a new line 5, say Cancel, by tapping the C key *while holding down the Ctrl key*.

Then look at the new version of MARY, by typing 1L again.

Exit When you finish editing MARY, type "E" after the asterisk. That makes the computer End the editing and Exit from edlin. You see a DOS prompt (such as "C:\>"), so you can give another DOS command.

When exiting from edlin, the computer puts *two* versions of MARY onto the disk. The new, edited version is named "MARY". The previous version is on the disk also, but its name has been changed to "MARY.BAK".

Make a big boo-boo? If you make a big mistake and wish you hadn't tried to edit MARY, type "Q" after the asterisk. That tells the computer to Quit.

The computer asks "Abort edit?" Press Y and then ENTER.

That makes the computer ignore all the editing you've done, so that MARY returns to its original state. MARY returns to the state it was in before you started using edlin.

You see a DOS prompt (such as "C:\>"), so you can give another DOS command.

Optional capitals When giving an edlin command, you do *not* have to capitalize. For example, to delete line 6 you can type "6d" instead of "6D".

BATCH FILES

You can invent your own command and make it stand for a list of other commands.

For example, let's invent a command called "status" that makes the computer display a wide directory and also remind you of which DOS version you're using. To invent that "status" command, just create a file called "STATUS.BAT", which contains two lines, "dir /w" and "ver".

To create that STATUS.BAT file, type this —

```
C:\>copy con status.bat
dir /w
ver
```

then press the F6 key and then the ENTER key.

Afterwards, whenever you type the word "status", like this —

```
C:\>status
```

the computer will look at the file "STATUS.BAT" and obey the commands you stored there: the computer will automatically do "dir /w" and then "ver".

A file that's a list of commands is called a **batch file**. The file "STATUS.BAT" is a batch file, because it's a list of two commands ("dir /w" and "ver"). The name of every batch file must end in ".BAT", which stands for "batch".

Echo off

While the computer performs a batch file, the computer prints little messages reminding you of what it's doing. For example, while the computer performs the "ver" command in "STATUS.BAT", the computer prints the word "ver" on your screen. Each such message is called an **echo**.

If you don't want to see such messages, say "echo off" at the beginning of your batch file, like this:

```
A>copy con status.bat
echo off
dir /w
ver
```

Clear screen (cls)

Another command you can put at the beginning of your batch file is "cls". That makes the computer begin by erasing the screen, so you don't see any distractions.

Put "cls" just under "echo off", so that the computer even erases the words "echo off" from the screen. Here's what the batch file looks like now:

```
C:\>copy con status.bat
echo off
cls
dir /w
ver
```

Echo

Let's define "chick", so that if you say —

```
C:\>chick
```

the computer will recite this chicken riddle:

```
Why did the chicken cross the road?
To escape from Colonel Sanders!
```

To define "chick", type this —

```
C:\>copy con chick.bat
echo off
cls
echo Why did the chicken cross the road?
echo To escape from Colonel Sanders!
```

then press F6 and ENTER.

Replaceable parameter (%1)

You can define "greet", so that if you say —

```
C:\>greet Peter
```

the computer will say:

```
What will Peter do today?
Will Peter work, or will Peter play?
Peter needs a holiday.
Welcome, Peter! Hip, hip, hooray!
```

If you say —

```
C:\>greet Suzie
```

the computer will say:

```
What will Suzie do today?
Will Suzie work, or will Suzie play?
Suzie needs a holiday.
Welcome, Suzie! Hip, hip, hooray!
```

If you say —

```
C:\>greet Godzilla
```

the computer will say:

```
What will Godzilla do today?
Will Godzilla work, or will Godzilla play?
Godzilla needs a holiday.
Welcome, Godzilla! Hip, hip, hooray!
```

To define "greet", type this —

```
C:\>copy con greet.bat
echo off
cls
echo What will %1 do today?
echo Will %1 work, or will %1 play?
echo %1 needs a holiday.
echo Welcome, %1! Hip, hip, hooray!
```

then press F6 and ENTER. Make sure you type the "%1" in that batch file.

Afterwards, when you say "greet Peter" or "greet Suzie" or "greet Godzilla", the computer will print a greeting to Peter or Suzie or Godzilla, by automatically substituting the person's name for "%1". Try it!

@Echo off (in DOS 3.3 & up)

So far, you've learned two sophisticated ways to begin a batch file.

One way is to begin by saying:

```
echo off
```

That prevents the computer from printing echo messages. Unfortunately, that method still leaves the words "echo off" on your screen.

The second way is to begin by saying:

```
echo off
cls
```

That flashes the words "echo off" on your screen, then immediately erases those words (because "cls" erases the screen). Unfortunately, "cls" erases all previous commands from the screen also; that prevents you from browsing at the screen to see what you had done previously.

The *most* sophisticated way to begin a batch file is to begin by saying:

```
@echo off
```

without saying "cls". (To type the symbol "@", tap the 2 key while holding down the SHIFT key.) The symbol "@" prevents the words "echo off" from appearing on your screen but still lets you see all previous screen activity.

The "@echo off" command is understood just by DOS 3.3, DOS 4, and modern DOS.

When you turn the computer on, it goes through a procedure called **booting**. Here's what the computer does while it's booting.

POST

First, the computer plays doctor and gives itself a checkup, to make sure all its innards are working okay. That's called the **power-on self test (POST)**.

Code numbers If the IBM PC detects an illness, it prints a code number telling you where the illness is:

Code number	Which part of the computer is ill
0	main power supply (or other fundamentals)
1	motherboard (or the battery for the date & time)
2	RAM chips
3	keyboard
4	monochrome monitor (or its video card)
5	CGA color monitor (or its video card)
6	floppy disk (or its drive or controller)
7	math coprocessor chip (8087 or 80287 chip)
9	LPT1 parallel port (to attach the printer to)
11	COM1 serial port (to attach a modem or mouse)
12	COM2 serial port (to attach a modem or mouse)
13	joystick (or other device attached to game port)
14	printer
17	hard disk (or its drive or controller)
24	EGA color monitor (or its video card)

After printing the code number, it prints a two-digit number, which is usually 01. For example, the computer usually prints 301 if the keyboard is broken (or not plugged into the system unit, or plugged in loosely, or has an XT-AT switch in the wrong position). The computer usually prints 1701 if the hard disk is broken (or the hard disk's controller is broken or the hard disk's cable to the controller is loose).

Although the IBM PC prints those code numbers, modern clones print English words instead. For example, if a modern clone detects that the keyboard is broken, the clone says "Keyboard error" or "Keyboard failure" or "No scancode from keyboard" or some similar message.

Experiment! Turn off your computer, unplug its keyboard, turn the computer back on, and see how *your* computer gripes! (Then turn the computer off again, and plug the keyboard back in.)

RAM test To test the RAM chips, the computer puts data into them, then reads the chips to see if the data remains.

During that process, the typical computer will tell you how much RAM you have. For example, if you have 640K of RAM, the screen will show the computer counting up to 640K.

If your computer is old-fashioned, you'll see it count up to 640K *twice*. The first time it counts to 640K, it puts data into the RAM chips; the second time it counts to 640K, it reads the chips to see whether the data's still there. For that kind of computer, if you trust the RAM chips and don't want to wait for the computer to test them, press the SPACE bar in the middle of the test. That interrupts the RAM test and makes the computer move on to the next activity.

During the RAM test, the original IBM PC shows no numbers on the screen at all. That computer leaves you in the dark until the RAM test is done.

Beeps At the end of the entire POST testing, the computer gives a short beep, which tells you the testing's done.

If you ever hear a *long* beep, or a *series* of several beeps, the computer's trying to send you an alarm. Look at the messages on the screen for details! If you hear the alarm but don't see any messages on the screen, the cause is usually a faulty electrical current: the power cord (that goes from the computer to the wall) is loose, or your town's electric company isn't generating enough volts, or an appliance in your building (such as an electric heater or refrigerator) is stealing too much electricity, or the power supply inside your computer is bad, or your motherboard is very defective.

If you hear the short beep that means the POST test is done, and you don't hear any alarms, but your screen is totally dark, the problem is probably just your screen. Make sure the screen is turned on (so its power light glows); make sure the screen's contrast and brightness knobs are turned up; make sure the cable that runs from the screen to the computer is plugged in tight; and make sure one of your colleagues didn't attach the wrong screen to the wrong computer!

Boot drive

After finishing the power-on self test, the computer decides which disk drive will be the **boot drive**.

To decide, the computer begins by checking whether drive A contains a formatted disk. If it *does* contain a formatted disk, it becomes the boot drive (so that later the computer will eventually print "A>" or "A:\>" on your screen).

If drive A does *not* contain a formatted disk (or the drive's door is accidentally open), the computer looks for drive C. If the computer finds drive C (because you bought a hard disk and formatted the main part of it), drive C becomes the boot drive (so that later the computer will eventually print "C>" or "C:\>" on your screen).

If drive A doesn't contain a formatted disk but you don't have a drive C either, here's what happens. If your computer's built by IBM, the computer prints "IBM Personal Computer BASIC" on your screen and lets you write programs in BASIC. If your computer's a clone instead, it waits for you to insert a formatted disk into drive A.

Hidden system files

Next, the computer searches in the boot drive's root directory for two hidden system files.

MS-DOS calls them "IO.SYS" and "MSDOS.SYS". PC-DOS calls them "IBMIO.COM" and "IBMDOS.COM".

No system files? If the computer doesn't find the hidden system files, the computer gripes:

```
Non-System disk or disk error
Replace and press any key to continue
```

To reply, put in drive A a disk containing those files (or make drive A be empty and hope that drive C contains those files). Then press ENTER. Again the computer will choose a boot drive and search for hidden system files.

CONFIG.SYS

Next, the computer looks in the boot drive's root directory for a file called "CONFIG.SYS". If the computer finds the file, it obeys the instructions in that file; those instructions teach the computer how to manage hardware intelligently — how to CONFIGure your SYStem. If the computer does *not* find CONFIG.SYS, the computer does *not* gripe; instead, the computer just manages hardware stupidly.

Does *your* computer have a hard disk? If so, does drive C's root directory contain CONFIG.SYS? To find out, say:

```
C:\>type config.sys
```

If you're lucky, that command will make the screen show you what's in the CONFIG.SYS file. (If you're *un*lucky, the computer will just reply, "File not found", which means the computer can't find a CONFIG.SYS file.)

On my fanciest computer, when I say —

```
C:\>type config.sys
```

the screen shows me these 9 equations:

```
device=dos\himem.sys /testmem:off
device=dos\emm386.exe ram d=48
dos=high,umb
stacks=0,0
buffers=40
files=50
devicehigh=dos\ansi.sys
devicehigh=dos\setver.exe
devicehigh=mtmcdas.sys /d:mscd000 /p:320
```

But on *your* computer, different equations might be better! Here are the details. . . .

HIMEM.SYS (in modern DOS) The top equation (**device=dos\himem.sys /testmem:off**) makes the computer run the HIMEM.SYS program, which is in the DOS folder. That program teaches the computer how to manage **extended RAM**, which is RAM beyond the first 640K.

For example, suppose your computer has 8 megabytes of RAM altogether. Without that equation, your computer would handle just 640K of RAM and waste the rest of the 8 megabytes!

A program (such as HIMEM.SYS) that teaches the computer how to manage extra hardware is called a **device driver**. To put a device driver into CONFIG.SYS, begin the equation by saying "device=".

When you boot the computer, the POST makes the computer check your RAM chips to make sure they're reliable. The DOS 6.2 version of HIMEM.SYS wastes time by checking the RAM chips *again*, unless you say "/testmem:off", which tells DOS 6.2 to skip the recheck. **Say "/testmem:off" only if you're using DOS 6.2**; for earlier versions of DOS say just:

```
device=dos\himem.sys
```

Windows 3.1 comes with its own version of HIMEM.SYS. That version is earlier (and worse) than the version that comes with DOS 6 & 6.2, but it's better than the DOS 5 version. So **if you're stuck with DOS 5 or earlier, and your Windows is 3.1, say "device=windows\himem.sys" instead of "device=dos\himem.sys"**. Do *not* make that switch if you have DOS 6 or 6.2. If you have Windows 3 instead of Windows 3.1, make that switch just if your DOS is 4 or earlier.

Omit the HIMEM.SYS line altogether if your computer is so primitive that it has *less* than 1M of RAM, or its CPU is *slower* than a 286, or you're Windowless with DOS 4 or earlier.

EMM386.EXE (in modern DOS) The next equation (**device=dos\emm386.exe ram d=48**) makes the computer run the EMM386.EXE program, which is in the DOS folder. That program is a device driver that manages **upper memory** and also turns some extended RAM into **expanded RAM** (which is the kind of RAM required by old-fashioned programs).

That program is called EMM386.EXE because it's an **E**xpanded **M**emory **M**anager that runs on any computer whose CPU is at least a **386**. It runs if your CPU is a 386, 486, or Pentium.

Use the EMM386.EXE equation just if your CPU is very modern (386, 486, or Pentium) and your CONFIG.SYS file contains the HIMEM.SYS equation. If you switched the HIMEM.SYS equation from "dos\himem.sys" to "windows\himem.sys", switch the EMM386.EXE equation to "windows\emm386.exe".

How much expanded RAM does EMM386.EXE create? The version of EMM386.EXE in DOS 6 & 6.2 is smart: it creates as much expanded RAM as necessary! It creates extra expanded RAM while old-fashioned software is running (such as the DOS versions of Word Perfect and 1-2-3), and creates less while modern software is running (such as Windows), since modern software wants extended RAM instead.

The DOS 5 and Windows versions of EMM386.EXE are stupid: they want you to say how much expanded RAM to create, by inserting a number such as 512 before the "ram", like this:

```
device=dos\emm386.exe 512 ram d=48
```

The 512 tells the computer to create 512K of expanded RAM. 512 is the best number to pick if your computer has 4M of RAM and you're using a wide variety of programs (Windows programs and non-Windows programs). If you pick a bigger number than 512, you create *more* than 512K of expanded RAM; if you pick a smaller number, you create *less* expanded RAM and have more extended RAM left. Pick a big number (such as 1024) if your RAM is bigger than 4M and you're using mainly old software wanting expanded RAM (such as the DOS versions of Word Perfect and Lotus 1-2-3). Pick a small number (such as 256) if your RAM is smaller than 4M or you're using mainly modern software (such as Windows). If you omit the number, the computer assumes 256.

If all your software is modern (so you don't need any expanded RAM at all), type "noems" instead of "ram", like this:

```
device=dos\emm386.exe noems d=48
```

The "noems" tells the EMM386.EXE not to bother turning extended RAM into expanded RAM, but to still manage upper memory.

The EMM386.EXE program reserves at most 32K of RAM for **direct memory access (DMA)**, unless you say "d=48", which reserves 48K instead. **Say "d=48" just if you have a sound card** (or any other device requiring more than 32K of DMA).

DOS (in modern DOS)
The next equation (**dos=high,umb**) moves some software out of the base RAM and puts that software elsewhere instead, so the base RAM has more space left for other programs.

That equation is an abbreviation for this pair of equations:

Equation	Meaning
dos=high	move buffers & part of DOS to the high memory area
dos=umb	move utility programs to the upper memory area

The computer understands "dos=high" just if CONFIG.SYS contains a HIMEM.SYS equation. The computer understands "dos=umb" just if CONFIG.SYS contains an EMM386.EXE equation. So if CONFIG.SYS mentions HIMEM.SYS but not EMM386.EXE, say just:

```
dos=high
```

Stacks (in DOS 3.3 & up)
The next equation (**stacks=0,0**) tells the computer that your software handles interruptions well, so there are no stacks of unexplained interrupts, and the computer doesn't need to reserve any RAM for them.

If your software is so unreliable that the computer gripes by saying "Stack Overflow" or "Exception error 12", say:

```
stacks=9,256
```

That makes the computer create 9 stacks, each containing 256 bytes. If the computer *still* gripes, create even more stacks (up to 64) and make them bigger (up to 512 bytes each). If the computer *still* gripes, buy better software!

Omit the stacks equation if your DOS is earlier than version 3.3.

Buffers
The next equation (**buffers=40**) makes the computer reserve enough RAM to hold copies of 40 of the disk's sectors. That speeds up the computer since the computer can look at those RAM copies faster than waiting for the disk to spin to the correct sector.

Each buffer consumes ½K of RAM. The 40 buffers therefore consume 20K of RAM.

If your DOS is classic or your RAM is smaller than 1M, you can't afford to devote 20K of RAM to buffers, so ask for *fewer* than 40 buffers: say "buffers=15".

If your computer uses a program called SMARTDRV (which I don't recommend), say "buffers=10".

Files
The next equation (**files=50**) makes the computer reserve enough RAM to hold 50 filenames, so the computer can manipulate 50 files simultaneously.

Most programs manipulate just a *few* files simultaneously. For those programs, saying "files=30" is fine. But some programs try to manipulate *more* than 30 files simultaneously and require you to say "files=50" or even "files=60" or even "files=99".

If you wish, start by saying "files=30" and then see whether any of your fancy programs complain; if they complain, switch to a higher number.

ANSI.SYS
The next equation (**devicehigh= dos\ansi.sys**) makes the computer run the ANSI.SYS program, which lets the screen display special characters and colors. That equation is ignored by most software, but it's required by *some* software, especially when your computer is using a modem to telecommunicate with computerized bulletin boards trying to put pretty boxes of info onto your screen.

If you wish, try omitting the ANSI.SYS equation, and put it back in just if you encounter software that gripes about missing ANSI.SYS.

Notice the equation begins with the word "devicehigh" instead of "device". The "high" makes the computer put ANSI.SYS into upper memory instead of base RAM, so the base RAM is free for other purposes.

The computer understands the "high" just if CONFIG.SYS mentions "umb" (as in "dos=umb" or "dos=high,umb"). **If CONFIG.SYS does NOT mention "umb", say "device" instead of "devicehigh",** like this:

```
device=dos\ansi.sys
```

SETVER.EXE (in modern DOS)
The next equation (**devicehigh=dos\setver.exe**) makes the computer run the SETVER.EXE program, which makes your new DOS pretend to be an old version, so old software will still work when you buy the new DOS.

This equation is useful only in modern DOS. Omit the equation if your DOS is classic.

Even in modern DOS, you can often omit this equation, since *most* software doesn't care which version of DOS you bought. Include the equation just if you're using old software that gripes about your new DOS.

On *my* computer, I include this equation because I like to use an old DOS program called BACKUP.EXE. Since that program gripes when it discovers I'm using DOS 6.2 instead of DOS 5, I must make DOS 6.2 pretend to be DOS 5.

When typing the equation, say "device" instead of "devicehigh" if your CONFIG.SYS lacks "umb".

Mtmcdas (supplement to DOS)
My CONFIG.SYS file's bottom equation (**devicehigh= mtmcdas.sys /d:mscd000 /p:320**) makes the computer run the MTMCDAS.SYS driver program, which controls Mitsumi's brand of CD-ROM drive.

That driver program is special. I got it from Mitsumi, not from Microsoft. It does *not* come as part of MS-DOS. Use it just if your CD-ROM drive is made by Mitsumi.

My other fancy computer uses a CD-ROM drive made by Sony instead of Mitsumi. On that computer, I use Sony's driver program (which is called SLCD.SYS), and the line looks like this:

```
devicehigh=slcd.sys /d:mscd000 /b:300 /m:p
```

If you use a different brand of CD-ROM drive, you must use a different driver. Even if you have the same drive as I, you might have to change the switches (such as /p:320 and /b:300) to make the drive compatible with *your* computer.

If your CD-ROM drive works fine, so does your CONFIG.SYS's CD-ROM line: leave it the way your manufacturer gave it to you!

If you don't have a CD-ROM drive at all, omit this line altogether.

Your own CONFIG.SYS
If your drive C's root directory doesn't contain a CONFIG.SYS file yet, create one! For example, you can create a CONFIG.SYS file just like mine by typing this —

```
C:\>copy con config.sys
device=dos\himem.sys /testmem:off
device=dos\emm386.exe ram d=48
dos=high,umb
stacks=0,0
buffers=40
files=50
devicehigh=dos\ansi.sys
devicehigh=dos\setver.exe
devicehigh=mtmcdas.sys /d:mscd000 /p:320
```

and then pressing the F6 key and then ENTER. That's the perfect CONFIG.SYS for my fanciest computer; but for *your* computer, modify those equations to handle your computer's peculiarities, as I suggested when I explained each equation.

If your drive C's root directory contains a CONFIG.SYS file *already*, you can edit it by saying "edit config.sys" (in modern DOS) or "edlin config.sys" (in classic DOS). But **before you perform surgery on your CONFIG.SYS file, copy it onto a floppy disk** (by saying "copy config.sys a:"), so that if you make a mistake you can return to what you had before.

The computer examines the CONFIG.SYS equations just when the computer is booting. If you edit CONFIG.SYS or create a new CONFIG.SYS, **the computer won't obey the new CONFIG.SYS equations until the next time you boot the computer.**

If your dealer or colleague has put many strange lines into your CONFIG.SYS file, do *not* erase them until you find out why they're there. Most of those lines are probably time-wasting junk put there by bloated Microsoft DOS installation routines and should be erased, but *some* of those lines might be essential. Be especially cautious about erasing any lines saying "device =" or "devicehigh =".

When in doubt, leave your CONFIG.SYS alone. Better safe than sorry! Follow the advice of the world's best repairman: "If it ain't broke, don't fix it."

Hints
If you're ambitious and try to "improve" a CONFIG.SYS file, here are some hints.

Say "devicehigh" instead of "device", except for the lines about HIMEM.SYS and EMM386. For "devicehigh" to work, CONFIG.SYS must mention "umb".

The purpose of "**smartdrv**" and "**fastopen**" is to help the computer get information from the disk faster; but if you have an IDE drive (or any other drive with a built-in disk cache), your drive is fast enough already! You should usually remove any mention of "fastopen" (which conflicts with commands such as "defrag") and "smartdrv" (which consumes too much RAM, can conflict with telecommunications programs, and can cause inconsistent writing to the disk).

To avoid conflicts, the letters "**emm**" must appear in CONFIG.SYS just once. For example, if your CONFIG.SYS mentions "emm386.exe", it must *not* mention "emm386.sys" or anything about "**qemm**" or "**nemm**".

You should usually remove any line saying "**break=on**", which slows your computer down. The purpose of "break=on" is to let you interrupt the computer more easily; but once you learn how to control the computer correctly, you won't want to interrupt it anyway!

Unless your computer is wired to a computer network, you can safely save some RAM by removing any mention of "**lastdrive**".

If you remove a line saying "**shell**", you must copy COMMAND.COM from the DOS folder to the root directory by saying —

```
C:\>copy dos\command.com
```

and if you're using DOS version 4 (or 4.01) you must also say:

```
C:\>copy dos\share.exe
```

If your computer's a Leading Edge Model D, make sure your CONFIG.SYS file contains a line saying "**device = clkdvr.sys**" and the root directory contains Leading Edge's CLKDVR.SYS program, which teaches your computer how to give the correct date and time.

For free help, phone me anytime at 617-666-2666.

COMMAND.COM
After the computer deals with the issue of CONFIG.SYS, the computer looks in the boot drive for a program called "COMMAND.COM". (The computer looks in the root directory, unless CONFIG.SYS contained a "shell =" equation telling the computer to look in the DOS folder instead.)

If the computer doesn't find COMMAND.COM, the computer gripes:

```
Bad or missing Command Interpreter
```

If the computer *does* find COMMAND.COM, the computer runs the COMMAND.COM program, which teaches the computer how to react to internal commands (such as ver, echo, cls, date, time, dir, cd, md, copy, type, rename, ren, del, and rd).

AUTOEXEC.BAT

Next, the computer looks in the boot drive's root directory for a batch file called "AUTOEXEC.BAT". The computer AUTOmatically EXECutes any commands in that file.

Does *your* computer have a hard disk? If so, does drive C's root directory contain AUTOEXEC.BAT? To find out, say:

```
C:\>type autoexec.bat
```

If you're lucky, that command will make the screen show you what's in the AUTOEXEC.BAT file. (If you're *unlucky*, the computer will just reply, "File not found", which means the computer can't find an AUTOEXEC.BAT file.)

On my fanciest computer, when I say —

```
C:\>type autoexec.bat
```

the computer shows me this batch of DOS commands:

```
@echo off
path c:\dos;c:\windows
set temp=c:\dos
set blaster=a220 i7 d1 t4
set sound=c:\sgnxpro
Lh mouse
Lh doskey
Lh mscdex /d:mscd000 /m:10 /e
```

In certain situations, I recommend adding 4 extra lines, so the AUTOEXEC.BAT becomes this:

```
@echo off
prompt $p$g
path c:\dos;c:\windows
set temp=c:\dos
set blaster=a220 i7 d1 t4
set sound=c:\sgnxpro
Lh mouse
Lh doskey
Lh mscdex /d:mscd000 /m:10 /e
Lh mode LPT1 retry=b >nul
Lh share /L:500 /f:5100
win
```

Here's what all those lines mean — and how you might need to change some of them for *your* computer. . . .

Echo The top command (**@echo off**) prevents the computer from printing excessive messages on the screen. (To type the symbol "@", tap the 2 key while holding down the SHIFT key.)

If your DOS is earlier than version 3.3, you must omit the symbol "@" and say just:

```
echo off
```

Prompt The next command (**prompt pg**) tells the computer how to make the DOS prompts look, so that when you're in drive C's SARAH folder the computer will say "C:\SARAH>" instead of just "C>".

If your DOS is earlier than 6 and you forget to say "prompt pg", the computer will say just "C>" instead of "C:\SARAH>", even when you're in the SARAH folder.

DOS 6 & 6.2 is smarter: even if you don't say "prompt pg", DOS 6 & 6.2 assume you *meant* to say "prompt pg". **So if you're using DOS 6 or 6.2, you don't need to say "prompt pg".**

Path The next command (**path c:\dos;c:\windows**) tells the computer to hunt in the DOS and WINDOWS folders whenever you give a command whose definition the computer can't find elsewhere.

Use that command only if drive C has folders called "DOS" and "WINDOWS". If drive C has a DOS folder but no WINDOWS folder, say just:

```
path c:\dos
```

If you forget to give a path command, and you're booting from drive C, DOS 6 & 6.2 assume you *meant* to say "path c:\dos". Earlier DOS versions make no assumptions; they create no path for you.

Set temp The next command (**set temp=c:\dos**) says that whenever the computer needs to create a temporary file (which holds data temporarily and then self-destructs), the computer should put that file into the DOS folder (instead of into the root directory or a different folder).

Use that command just if drive C has a folder called "DOS".

Set blaster The next command (**set blaster=a220 i7 d1 t4**) helps a sound card work properly, if the sound card resembles the Soundblaster. **Omit this command if you don't have a sound card** or if your sound card isn't Soundblaster-compatible.

Set sound The next command (**set sound= c:\sgnxpro**) says the files about sound are in a folder called SGNXPRO.

Omit this command if you don't have a sound card. If you DO have a sound card, mention the correct folder; for example, if your sound folder is called AUDIO16 instead of SGNXPRO, say:

```
set sound=c:\audio16
```

Mouse (supplement to DOS) The next command (**Lh mouse**) makes the computer run the MOUSE.COM program, which is a device driver that teaches the computer how to react when you move the mouse and click the mouse's buttons.

The "Lh" tells the computer to "load high" the mouse program, so the computer copies the mouse program into upper memory. (The computer doesn't care whether you capitalize the L.)

Use that command just if you have a mouse and a program called "MOUSE.COM".

The MOUSE.COM program is *not* included in the price of DOS. Instead, you get the MOUSE.COM program on a floppy disk from the company that manufactured your mouse or computer, and you must copy the MOUSE.COM program onto your hard disk.

The "Lh mouse" command works just if the MOUSE.COM program is in your root directory or DOS folder. **If MOUSE.COM is in a different folder, remind the computer which folder MOUSE.COM is in.** For example, if MOUSE.COM is in a folder called MOUSEY, say:

```
Lh mousey\mouse
```

If MOUSE.COM is in a folder called MICKEY, say:

```
Lh mickey\mouse
```

If MOUSE.COM is in a folder called MOUSE, say:

```
Lh mouse\mouse
```

If your CONFIG.SYS file mentioned "mouse" already, don't put any mouse command in your AUTOEXEC.BAT file. **Omit the "Lh" part of the command if your CONFIG.SYS file lacks any mention of "umb".**

Doskey (in modern DOS)

The next command (**Lh doskey**) makes the computer run the DOSKEY.COM program. That program modifies DOS so that when you're typing a DOS command, you can edit the command easily by pressing these keys:

Pressing the left-arrow key moves the cursor left without erasing characters.
Pressing the right-arrow key moves the cursor to the right.
Pressing the DELETE key deletes a character.
Pressing the INSERT key lets you type extra characters to insert.
Pressing the up-arrow key repeats the previous DOS command you typed.

Use that command just if your DOS is modern. Omit the "Lh" part of the command if your CONFIG.SYS file lacks "umb".

The command is useful just if you often type DOS commands and edit them. If you rarely type any DOS commands (because you mainly use Windows or menus instead), omit this command.

Mscdex (in DOS 6 & 6.2)

The next command (**Lh mscdex /d:mscd000 /m:10 /e**) makes the computer run the MicroSoft CD EXtension, which is a program that teaches the computer how to control your CD-ROM drive. **Use this command just if you have a CD-ROM drive.** The command is part of DOS 6 & 6.2.

In the mscdex command, the "/m:10" says to reserve enough RAM to hold copies of 10 sectors from the CD-ROM. In other words, it creates 10 buffers.

The "/e" says to put those buffers in expanded RAM (instead of in base RAM). The "/e" works just if your computer has expanded RAM, so **say "/e" just if your CONFIG.SYS file's EMM386.EXE line says "ram"**. Omit the "/e" if your CONFIG.SYS file's EMM386.EXE line says "noems" instead.

The "/d:mscd000" says the CD-ROM drive is named mscd000.

Instead of "mscd000", you can invent any other name you wish. Put the name in this command and also in CONFIG.SYS's CD-ROM equation.

Omit the "Lh" part of the command if your CONFIG.SYS file lacks "umb".

Mode

The next command (**Lh mode LPT1 retry=b >nul**) tells the computer to be patient and wait for the printer to respond even if the wait is long. **Use this command just if your printer's an inkjet or a slow (4-page-per-minute) laser printer.**

To give this kind of command when your CONFIG.SYS file lacks "umb", omit the "Lh" and say just:

```
mode LPT1 retry=b >nul
```

To give this kind of command when your DOS is earlier than version 4, say this instead:

```
mode LPT1 ,,p >nul
```

Share (in DOS 4 & modern DOS)

The next command (**Lh share /L:500 /f:5100**) makes the computer check whether programs might interfere with each other.

If programs were designed well, no such checking would be needed. Unfortunately, a word-processing program called "Microsoft Word 6 for Windows" is designed poorly and must be prevented from interfering with other programs. Microsoft's other new word-processing programs for Windows (such as "Microsoft Works 3 for Windows" and "Microsoft Publisher 2") are designed poorly also and require a "share" command.

Say "Lh share /L:500 /f:5100" just if you use a program that requires a "share" command, such as Microsoft Word 6 for Windows, Microsoft Works 3 for Windows, and Microsoft Publisher 2.

Unfortunately, that "share" command makes all your programs run much slower. You'll wish you didn't buy Microsoft Word 6 for Windows!

Win (supplement to DOS)

The bottom command (**win**) makes the computer automatically start running Windows. Use this command just if Windows is required by nearly all your software. Omit this command if you often use non-Windows software.

Since I frequently use the DOS non-Windows versions of Word Perfect and Q&A, my AUTOEXEC.BAT file does *not* say "win".

Your own AUTOEXEC.BAT

If your drive C's root directory doesn't contain an AUTOEXEC.BAT file yet, create one! For example, you can create an AUTOEXEC.BAT file by typing this —

What to type	Changes you might make
C:\>copy con autoexec.bat	
@echo off	If DOS is earlier than 3.3, omit "@".
prompt pg	DOS 6 & 6.2 let you omit this line.
path c:\dos;c:\windows	If no Windows, omit ";c:\windows".
set temp=c:\dos	If no folder called "DOS", edit this.
set blaster=a220 i7 d1 t4	If no sound card, omit this line.
set sound=c:\sgnxpro	If no SGNXPRO folder, edit this.
Lh mouse	Say "mouse\mouse" if necessary.
Lh doskey	If your DOS is classic, omit this line.
Lh mscdex /d:mscd000 /m:10 /e	If no CD-ROM drive, omit this line.
Lh mode LPT1 retry=b >nul	Omit if printer works fine without it.
Lh share /L:500 /f:5100	Omit if no Word for Windows 6.
win	Omit if use non-Windows programs.

then press the F6 key and then ENTER.

If your drive C's root directory contains an AUTOEXEC.BAT file already, you can edit it by saying "edit autoexec.bat" (in modern DOS) or "edlin autoexec.bat" (in classic DOS). But **before you perform surgery on your AUTOEXEC.BAT file, copy it onto a floppy disk** (by saying "copy autoexec.bat a:"), so that if you make a mistake you can return to what you had before.

The computer examines the commands in AUTOEXEC.BAT just when the computer is booting. If you edit AUTOEXEC.BAT or create a new AUTOEXEC.BAT, **the computer won't obey the new AUTOEXEC.BAT equations until the next time you boot the computer.**

If your dealer or colleague has put many strange lines into your AUTOEXEC.BAT file, don't erase them until you discover their purpose. When in doubt, leave AUTOEXEC.BAT alone.

Hints

If you're ambitious and try to "improve" an AUTOEXEC.BAT file, here are some hints.

Make sure it's the *top* line that says "**@echo off**" (or the *top* pair of lines that say "echo off" and "cls").

Just one line should say "**path**". For example, if a line says "path c:\dos" and a line says "path c:\windows", combine them into a single line saying "path c:\dos;c:\windows".

The bottom line of AUTOEXEC.BAT is particularly important: it tells the computer what to show the human when AUTOEXEC.BAT finishes. If that line says "**win**", the computer will automatically do Windows. If that line says "**dosshell**", the computer will automatically run the DOS shell program, which crudely imitates Windows. If that line says "**menu**", the computer will automatically display a list of programs for the human to choose from (if you or your dealer created a file called "MENU.BAT" or "MENU.COM" or "MENU.EXE"). If the bottom line mentions some other program, the computer will automatically run that program.

Though it's cute to see the computer automatically run Windows, the DOS shell, a menu, or another program, it's a nuisance if you'd rather run a different program instead. I recommend that you delete any such line, so the computer will just say "C:\>" and wait for you to *choose* which program to run next. Then after that C prompt, type "win" or "dosshell" or "menu" or the name of some other program.

You can remove any line saying "**ver**", since "ver" just makes the computer print a message saying which DOS version you're using.

You can remove any line saying "**verify off**", since the computer does "verify off" even if you don't say so!

Every modern computer includes a battery-powered clock/calendar chip, which keeps track of the time and date even when the computer is turned off. That chip is missing from old-fashioned computers (such as the original IBM PC), which must be coached by inserting "**date**" and "**time**" lines into your AUTOEXEC.BAT file.

If your CONFIG.SYS file has a line mentioning "shell=c:\dos\command.com" (which tells the computer to find COMMAND.COM in the DOS folder instead of in the root directory), your AUTOEXEC.BAT file should have a line saying "**set comspec=c:\dos\command.com**".

For free help in editing your AUTOEXEC.BAT file, phone me anytime at 617-666-2666.

No AUTOEXEC.BAT
If the computer doesn't find AUTOEXEC.BAT, the computer automatically performs the "date" and "time" commands (which ask you to confirm the date and time). Then the computer prints a DOS prompt and waits for you to type a DOS command.

Riddle
Congratulations! Now you're smart enough to master the answer to the favorite riddle among programmers.

Riddle: What do you get when you cross Lee Iacocca with a vampire?
Answer: an AUTOEXEC.BAT

Your input
After the computer deals with the issue of AUTOEXEC.BAT, the computer waits for you to type something on the keyboard (such as a DOS command).

Reboot
You've learned that when you turn the computer on, the computer performs this boot procedure: the computer does a power-on self test (POST), decides whether to boot from drive A or drive C, then obeys all commands in the boot drive's IO.SYS, MSDOS.SYS, CONFIG.SYS, COMMAND.COM, and AUTOEXEC.BAT and waits for your input.

After using the computer awhile, suppose you hit some wrong keys that make the computer start acting strangely, and you're so confused by the whole situation that you don't know what to do. When all else fails, boot the computer again. That's called **rebooting**. Here are three ways to reboot. . . .

Method 1: power down
Turn the computer off. Wait 10 seconds (for the RAM chips to cool down and forget whatever crazy stuff they were thinking of). Turn the computer back on again.

Since that procedure makes you wait for the RAM chips to cool down, it's called a **cold reboot**.

Method 2: RESET
Press the **RESET button**, by using your favorite finger.

That button's *not* on the keyboard. Instead, it's usually on the front of the computer system's unit, somewhere near the floppy drive's door.

(You'll find the RESET button on most clones but not on computers built by IBM. On some obsolete clones, the reset button is on the *back* of the system unit.)

When you press that button, the computer stops whatever it was doing. The screen goes blank. The computer beeps, then reboots by doing the POST, etc.

That's called "giving the machine the finger". It's also called a **one-finger reboot** or **hardware reboot** or **hard boot**.

Method 3: Ctrl Alt DELETE
While holding down the Ctrl and Alt keys simultaneously, tap the key that says "Delete" (or "Del"). That requires three fingers!

That makes the computer stop whatever it was doing. The screen goes blank. The computer beeps, then reboots. But the computer abridges the reboot procedure: during the POST, it doesn't bother testing the RAM.

That's called "giving the machine three fingers". It's also called a **three-finger reboot** or **software reboot** or **soft boot** or **warm boot**. It's the fastest way to reboot, since you don't have to wait for the RAM test or for the machine to cool down. But if the computer ever goes so wacko that it ignores your keyboard, it also ignores that three-finger reboot, so you must use one of the other rebooting methods instead.

"Hey, honey, how's work at the computer? Getting frustrated? Computer's not being nicey-nicey to yoosy-yoosy? Why don't you do a soft, warm boot? But wait, *here's* a soft, warm boot! In fact, here's a pair of them! Merry Christmas!"

I have a nightmare that when making love to a woman, I accidentally hit the wrong combinations of her "buttons", she reboots, and I realize she was just a machine.

I've met people like that. Haven't you? In the middle of a pleasant relationship, you accidentally hit the wrong "buttons", the person nastily reboots, and you realize the person you've been admiring is just a machine.

If you're a politician, your goal is to make the voters find your opponent's reset button before they find yours.

Make a disk bootable
When you boot the computer (by turning it on, pressing RESET, or pressing Ctrl ALT DELETE), the computer looks in drive A or C for a **bootable disk** (a disk that's been formatted and contains the two hidden system files and COMMAND.COM).

When you buy DOS, it usually comes on a pile of floppy disks. In that pile, the first disk is bootable. (Exception: if you bought the DOS 5, 6, or 6.2 *upgrade* instead of DOS 5, 6, or 6.2 itself, the first disk in the DOS upgrade's pile is *not* bootable.)

If your computer came with a hard disk containing DOS, your hard disk is bootable.

If you have a bootable disk, you can make other disks become bootable. For example, if you have a bootable hard disk, **here's how to make a blank floppy become bootable**. . . .

First, turn the computer on without any floppy in the drive, so the computer says "C:\>". Then put the blank floppy into drive A.

If the floppy wasn't formatted yet, say "**format a: /s**". That formats the floppy and copies onto it the two hidden system files and COMMAND.COM.

If the floppy was formatted already, say "**sys a:**". That copies the two hidden system files to the floppy. If your DOS is modern, that command also copies COMMAND.COM. (If your DOS is classic, say "sys a:" and then say "copy command.com a:".)

How to make a blank hard disk bootable

Suppose you buy a hard disk that's new and totally blank, so it doesn't even contain DOS. Here's how to make it bootable.

First, the hard disk must be **low-level formatted**. It's been low-level formatted already if the drive is IDE or if your dealer is nice. Otherwise, you must do a low-level format yourself. (The way to do a low-level format depends on which hard drive, hard-drive controller, and CPU you bought. For details, ask your dealer.)

Next, put the first DOS floppy into drive A and turn the computer on. If you're using DOS 4 or modern DOS, the computer will automatically install DOS onto your hard disk and make the hard disk bootable; just follow the instructions you see on the screen. If you're using an earlier DOS, you must go through the following procedure instead. . . .

The computer will say "A>" or "A:\>".

Next, tell the computer how to split the hard drive into several parts, called "drive C", "drive D", drive E", etc. Each of those parts is called a **partition**. To partition the hard drive, say "**fdisk**". The computer will say:

```
Choose one of the following:
  1. Create DOS partition
  2. Change Active Partition
  3. Delete DOS Partition
  4. Display Partition Information
Enter choice: [1]
```

Choose option 1, by pressing the ENTER key. The computer will ask you several questions; respond to each by pressing the ENTER key. Tell the computer to make the primary DOS partition (drive C) be as large as possible and active. At the end of the process, reboot the computer (with the first DOS floppy still in drive A), so you see "A>" again.

Then say:

```
A>format c: /s
```

That makes the computer format drive C. The "/s" makes the computer copy the hidden system files and COMMAND.COM onto drive C, so drive C becomes bootable.

(When you give that format command, if the computer gripes by saying "Invalid drive specification", try again to partition the hard drive.)

You can press these special keys. . . .

PAUSE key

Suppose you say "dir dos" or give some other command that makes the computer print a long message on your screen. If the computer is printing faster than you can read, make the computer pause (so you can catch up and read the message) by pressing the PAUSE key. That makes the computer pause until you press another key (such as ENTER).

On modern keyboards, which have 101 or 102 keys, the PAUSE key is the last key in the top row. Older keyboards, which have just 83 keys, lack a PAUSE key: instead, tap the NUM LOCK key while holding down the Ctrl key.

Break (Ctrl PAUSE)

Suppose you tell the computer to perform an activity that takes lots of time (such as print a long directory, or format a disk, or copy an entire disk). While the computer is performing, suppose you change your mind and want the computer to stop.

To make the computer stop, tell the computer to **break** the activity. Here's how: tap the PAUSE key while holding down the Ctrl key.

(If your keyboard doesn't have a PAUSE key, tap the SCROLL LOCK key while holding down the Ctrl key.)

The computer will stop the activity. Then tell the computer what to do next: type your next command.

F5 (in DOS 6 & 6.2)

In case CONFIG.SYS or AUTOEXEC.BAT contain errors that prevent the computer from booting properly, DOS 6 & 6.2 let you perform this trick. . . .

Try booting the computer; but when the computer says "Starting MS-DOS", immediately press the F5 key. That makes the computer skip CONFIG.SYS and AUTOEXEC.BAT and just give you a DOS prompt.

F8 (in DOS 6 & 6.2)

When the computer says "Starting MS-DOS", try pressing F8 immediately (instead of F5).

Then the computer shows you each line of CONFIG.SYS and asks you whether to obey the line. Press Y to make the computer obey the line, or press N to make the computer ignore the line.

Then the computer asks you whether to obey AUTOEXEC.BAT. Press Y or N. If you press N, the computer skips AUTOEXEC.BAT. If you press Y instead, here's what happens: DOS 6 makes the computer do all of AUTOEXEC.BAT; DOS 6.2 makes the computer show you each line of AUTOEXEC.BAT and ask you to press Y or N for each line.

Alt characters

You can type these special characters:

20 ¶			
21 §			

128	Ç	160	á	192	└	224	α
129	ü	161	í	193	┴	225	ß
130	é	162	ó	194	┬	226	Γ
131	â	163	ú	195	├	227	π
132	ä	164	ñ	196	─	228	Σ
133	à	165	Ñ	197	┼	229	σ
134	å	166	ª	198	╞	230	μ
135	ç	167	º	199	╟	231	τ
136	ê	168	¿	200	╚	232	Φ
137	ë	169	⌐	201	╔	233	Θ
138	è	170	¬	202	╩	234	Ω
139	ï	171	½	203	╦	235	δ
140	î	172	¼	204	╠	236	∞
141	ì	173	¡	205	═	237	φ
142	Ä	174	«	206	╬	238	ε
143	Å	175	»	207	╧	239	∩
144	É	176	░	208	╨	240	≡
145	æ	177	▒	209	╤	241	±
146	Æ	178	▓	210	╥	242	≥
147	ô	179	│	211	╙	243	≤
148	ö	180	┤	212	╘	244	⌠
149	ò	181	╡	213	╒	245	⌡
150	û	182	╢	214	╓	246	÷
151	ù	183	╖	215	╫	247	≈
152	ÿ	184	╕	216	╪	248	°
153	Ö	185	╣	217	┘	249	·
154	Ü	186	║	218	┌	250	·
155	¢	187	╗	219	█	251	√
156	£	188	╝	220	▄	252	ⁿ
157	¥	189	╜	221	▌	253	²
158	₧	190	╛	222	▐	254	■
159	ƒ	191	┐	223	▀		

For example, here's how to type the symbol ñ, whose code number is 164. Hold down the Alt key; and while you keep holding down the Alt key, type 164 *by using the numeric keypad* (the number keys on the far right side of the keyboard). When you finish typing 164, lift your finger from the Alt key, and you'll see ñ on your screen!

Those characters are called **alternate characters** or **Alt characters** or **IBM graphics characters**.

Repeat (F3)

To repeat a DOS command, press the F3 key, then ENTER. Here are examples. . . .

Suppose you have a file called MARY and say "print mary" to print it on paper. To print a *second* copy (to hand a friend), you don't have to say "print mary" again: just press the F3 key. That makes the computer automatically put the words "print mary" on the screen again. Then press ENTER.

Suppose you say "dir a:" to display a directory of the floppy in drive A. To see the directory of *another* floppy, put that floppy into drive A and then press the F3 key, which makes the computer say "dir a:" again. Press ENTER.

Suppose your hard disk contains a folder called SARAH, and you have a pile of floppy disks containing info that's simple (no folders or hidden files). Here's how to copy everything from those floppy disks to SARAH. Put the first floppy into drive A. Copy everything from that floppy to SARAH by saying "copy a:*.* sarah". Put the second floppy into drive A, then press the F3 key and ENTER. Put the third floppy into drive A, then press the F3 key and ENTER.

Sometimes, the computer ignores the F3 key. That happens if you've recently given a command (such as "edit") that uses lots of RAM and "steals" that RAM from the F3 command.

If your AUTOEXEC.BAT says "Lh doskey" (because your DOS is modern), you can press the up-arrow key instead of F3. The up-arrow key has two advantages over F3:

The up-arrow key is easier for humans to remember than F3 (which beginners confuse with F2 and F4).

Unlike F3, the up-arrow key *always* works, even if you recently gave a command such as "edit" that consumes lots of RAM.

Normally, the computer prints its answers on the screen. To make the computer print its answers on the printer's paper instead, use any of the following methods. . . .

PRINT SCREEN key

If your keyboard is modern (with 101 keys), one of the keys is marked "Print Screen".

Dump Pressing the PRINT SCREEN key makes the printer dump onto paper a snapshot of everything that's on the screen. The snapshot on the paper is called a **screen dump**.

Echo Try this experiment: *while holding down the CONTROL key* (which is marked "Ctrl"), tap the PRINT SCREEN key. Then lift your fingers. That makes the computer perform this trick: it waits for you to type something, then copies your typing onto paper. The copying onto paper is called **echoing**.

The computer will continue echoing onto paper whatever you type on the screen (and whatever the computer types on the screen), until you tell the computer to *stop* echoing (by pressing CONTROL with PRINT SCREEN again).

Notice that to stop the echo, you hit the same keys that started the echo. That situation's called a **toggle**. A **toggle** is a key (or series of keystrokes) that tells the computer to start a process and, when hit again, tells the computer to stop.

Computerists say, "The printer-echo toggle is CONTROL with PRINT SCREEN." They also say, "To toggle the printer echo, hit CONTROL PRINT SCREEN."

PrtSc key If your keyboard has just 83 keys (instead of 101), it has a "PrtSc" key instead of a "Print Screen" key. On such a keyboard, here's how to get a screen dump: *while holding down the SHIFT key*, press the "PrtSc" key. Here's how to start echoing: *while holding down the Ctrl key*, press the "PrtSc" key.

PC Junior If your computer is a PC Junior, get a screen dump by pressing the Fn key then the PrtSc key; start echoing by pressing the Fn key then the Echo key.

Laser printers If you're using a laser printer (such as the Hewlett-Packard Laserjet 2), **you might see the printer's FORM FEED light go on. That means a sheet of paper has been printed and is waiting to be removed from the printer.**

To remove the paper, turn off the ON LINE light (by tapping the ON LINE button), then press the FORM FEED button.

After you've removed the paper, turn the ON LINE light back on (by pressing the ON LINE button again).

IBM graphics characters If you try to make your printer print an IBM graphics character (such as Alt 164, which is ñ), the printer might print a weirder character instead, unless you're using software (such as a word processor) that reminds the printer to use IBM graphics characters.

Prn

When giving a DOS command, you can use the printer by saying "prn". Here are examples. . . .

Pipe to printer If you type ">prn" at the end of a command, the computer will send the answers to the printer instead of to the screen.

For example, to make the computer send a directory of drive A to the printer (instead of to your screen), give this command: "dir a: >prn". That's pronounced, "directory of drive A, redirected to the printer" or "directory of drive A, piped to the printer". The space before the symbol ">" is optional: you can say either "dir a: >prn" or "dir a:>prn".

To print "I love you" on paper, give this command: "echo I love you>prn".

To type all the lines of file MARY onto paper (instead of onto your screen), say "type mary>prn".

Copy file to printer Another way to copy all the lines of MARY onto your printer's paper is to say "copy mary prn".

To send info directly from your keyboard (console) to the printer, say "copy con prn". Underneath that command, type whatever sentences you want the printer to print. When you finish typing your last sentence, press the F6 key and then the ENTER key. Then the printer will print all the sentences.

Print

Another way to print all MARY's lines onto paper is to say "print mary".

(If the computer says "Bad command or file name", your computer is set up incorrectly and can't find the PRINT.COM program. In that case, remind the computer where the PRINT.COM program is. For example, if the PRINT.COM program is in your hard disk's DOS folder, say "c:\dos\print mary". If the PRINT.COM program is in drive A, say "a:print mary".)

The first time you give the print command, the computer will ask you for the "Name of list device". To reply, just press the ENTER key.

While the printer is printing MARY's lines, the screen will show a DOS prompt and let you continue typing DOS commands. So the computer is doing two things simultaneously — it's printing MARY's lines at the same time that it's letting you type additional commands. In that situation, MARY is said to be printed **in the background**.

ANALYZE YOUR COMPUTER

To analyze your computer, you can type "dir" (which tells you which files are on the disk) and "chkdsk" (which tells you how much the disk can hold, how much free space is left on the disk, how much conventional RAM you have, and how much free space is left in conventional RAM). I explained those commands earlier.

Now I'll reveal additional commands, which let you analyze your computer more thoroughly, diagnose hidden ills, and help you cure those illnesses. Give these additional commands whenever you buy a new computer and want to find out whether you were ripped off, or whenever your computer acts sick, or whenever you want to supercharge your computer and make it super-healthy, or whenever you're just plain curious about how your computer is faring!

Mem (in DOS 4 & modern DOS)

DOS 4, 5, 6, and 6.2 will tell you how much RAM memory is in your computer, if you say "mem".

DOS 6.2 For example, my computer has DOS 6.2 and a 4-megabyte RAM. Saying "mem" makes it print this table on my screen:

```
Memory Type        Total  =   Used  +   Free
----------------   -------    -------    -------
Conventional        640K       20K       620K
Upper                91K       26K        65K
Reserved            384K      384K         0K
Extended (XMS)    2,981K      485K     2,496K
----------------   -------    -------    -------
Total memory      4,096K      915K     3,181K
```

That table's bottom line says the computer has 4 megabytes (4,096K) of memory chips. 915K of that memory is being used already, leaving 3,181K free to hold additional programs and data.

The table's other lines show how the 4 megabytes is split into several parts: conventional RAM, upper RAM, reserved RAM, and extended RAM.

Next, the computer prints a line of subtotals. Those subtotals show what happens when you add the conventional and upper RAM together:

```
Total under 1 MB    731K      46K       685K
```

Then the computer prints this message:

```
Total Expanded (EMS)          3,392K (3,473,408 bytes)
Free Expanded (EMS)           2,736K (2,801,664 bytes)
```

That means 3,392K of my extended RAM can be turned into expanded RAM. Some of that expanded RAM is consumed by the EMM386.EXE program itself, leaving 2,736K free.

If you say "mem /c/p" (which means "MEMory Classification with Pauses"), the screen will display a more detailed message, which also lists each program in the first megabyte and reveals how much RAM each of those programs consumes. (When you finish reading the first screenful, press ENTER to see the second.)

DOS 6 In DOS 6, saying "mem" has almost the same effect as in DOS 6.2. Unfortunately, DOS 6 is too stupid to put commas in big numbers, and DOS 6 says "Adapter RAM/ROM" instead of "Reserved".

DOS 4 & 5 In DOS 4 & 5, saying "mem" makes the computer print this kind of message on your screen:

Message	Meaning
655360 bytes total conventional memory	The conventional RAM is 655,360 bytes (640K).
655360 bytes available to MS-DOS	All of those bytes can be used.
630480 largest executable program size	Since DOS itself consumes some of those bytes, 630,480 bytes remain for programs to use.
1441792 bytes total EMS memory	The EMS expanded memory is 1,441,792 bytes,
1048576 bytes free EMS memory	of which 1 megabyte is left for programs to use.
3145728 bytes total contiguous extended memory	Main extended memory is 3 megs.
0 bytes available contiguous extended memory	None of those bytes are wasted.
1900544 bytes available XMS memory	Some of those bytes were turned into expanded memory, leaving 1,900,544 bytes.

Missing memory? If the "mem" command reports less available free memory than you expected, increase the available free memory by editing your CONFIG.SYS and AUTOEXEC.BAT files.

To make modern DOS manage extended memory, make sure your CONFIG.SYS file says "device=dos\himem.sys". To make those DOS versions manage expanded memory on a 386, 486, or Pentium, make sure CONFIG.SYS has a line mentioning "emm386".

In CONFIG.SYS and AUTOEXEC.BAT, avoid mentioning "smartdrv", which consumes lots of RAM.

Msd (in DOS 6 & 6.2)

If you have DOS 6 or 6.2 or Windows 3.1, you can say "msd". That makes the computer run the MicroSoft Diagnostics program, which analyzes your computer and prints its analysis on the screen.

The analysis tells you who manufactured the motherboard and ROM BIOS chip, what kind of CPU chip you have (8088, 286, 386, 486, or Pentium), how much RAM you have (conventional, extended, and expanded), what kind of video card you have, whether you're attached to a network, which version of DOS you're using, what kind of mouse you have, whether you have a game card (to attach a joystick), which disk drives you have (A, B, and C), how many parallel printer ports you have (to attach printers to), how many serial ports you have, and more!

When you finish reading the analysis, press the F3 key.

Scandisk (in DOS 6.2)

The "chkdsk /f" command makes the computer fix errors on your hard disk — but just the errors that are obvious. To fix *all* important errors, even the errors that are not obvious, say "scandisk" instead, like this:

```
C:\>scandisk
```

That command works just if you have DOS 6.2. Once you've given that command, the computer says, "ScanDisk is now checking drive C".

Then the computer starts testing five aspects of drive C: the drive's **media descriptor**, the **file allocation tables**, the **directory structure**, the **file system**, and the **surface scan**. Each of those tests is quick (just a few seconds), except for the surface scan, which typically takes about 20 minutes.

The computer does the four quick tests. Then it gives you an estimate of how long the surface-scan test will take. It asks you:

```
Do you want to perform a surface scan now?
```

If you do, press ENTER; if you don't (because you're too impatient to wait for it to finish), press N instead.

During all those tests, if the computer detects a error on your hard disk, the computer will try to fix it. Just follow the computer's instructions on the screen! If the computer says "ScanDisk found data that might be lost files or directories", press L then S.

Verdict When the computer has finished all tests you requested, the computer will give you its verdict.

If you're very lucky, the computer will give you this verdict:

```
ScanDisk did not find any problems on drive C.
```

If you're *somewhat* lucky, the computer will say this instead:

```
ScanDisk found and fixed problems on drive C.
```

If you're totally luckless, and your disk is too hideously screwed up to be fixable, the computer will give up and just say:

```
There are still errors on drive C.
```

Dismissal After the computer prints one of those three verdicts, press the X key.

Other drives If you want the computer to fix the disk that's in drive A instead of C, say "scandisk a:", like this:

```
C:\scandisk a:
```

Defrag (in DOS 6 & 6.2)

Suppose you delete a small file from your hard disk, so your hard disk acquires a small unused gap. If you then try to put a big file onto your hard disk, the computer might put part of the big file into the small unused gap and put the rest of the big file elsewhere, so that the big file consists of two separated **fragments**. In that case, the big file is said to be **fragmented**. Unfortunately, a fragmented file slows down the computer, since the computer must look in two separate parts of the disk to find the complete file.

To make the computer handle the hard disk faster, rearrange the files on the disk so that none of the files are fragmented. That's called **defragmenting the disk** (or **defragging** the disk).

How to defrag DOS 6 & 6.2 let you defrag drive C easily. Here's how.

First, make the computer display a normal C prompt, so you see this:

```
C:\>
```

Next, make sure your disk is acting reliably. To check your disk's reliability, say "scandisk" (in DOS 6.2) or "chkdsk/f" (in DOS 6).

After you've assured yourself that your disk is acting reliably, **say "defrag c: /f"**, like this:

```
C:\>defrag c: /f
```

That makes the computer **defrag** drive C fully. The computer will also put your files as close as possible to the directory tracks (the outermost tracks), so the computer can access the files faster.

Usually, the process takes several minutes. (While you're waiting, go have a cup of coffee or a snack or go work on a non-computerized problem or make love.) When the computer's finished, it will play a quick burst of joyous music

and then say "C:\>" again, so you can give another DOS command.

When to defrag About once a month (or whenever you're in the mood!), say "defrag c: /f" again, which rearranges the files again and restores youthful peppiness to your hard drive. Yes, saying "defrag c: /f" is like letting your hard drive drink from the fountain of youth!

Msav (in DOS 6 & 6.2)

To make sure your hard disk doesn't have any viruses, run the **MicroSoft Anti-Virus** program by saying "msav" at the C prompt, like this:

```
C:\>msav
```

The computer will say "MicroSoft Anti-Virus" and "Main Menu". Press ENTER.

The computer will check your entire RAM and hard disk for viruses. That's called **scanning for viruses** (or **doing a virus scan**).

If the computer finds a virus, the computer will say "Virus Found". The computer will tell you the virus's name and which file it infected. To respond, press ENTER. The computer will get rid of the virus. That's called **cleaning out** the virus.

If the computer notices a program was changed since the previous time you said "msav", the computer will say "Verify Error". The computer will tell you the program's name and how the program was changed. Usually this "Verify Error" message does *not* mean you have a virus; it usually means just that you installed a newer version of the program. To respond, press either D (to delete the program, because you think it's infected by a virus) or U (to tell the computer that you changed the program *intentionally* and to Update the computer's understanding of it) or O (to temporarily ignore the problem and cOntinue).

When the computer has finished scanning for viruses, the computer will brag about the number of "Viruses Detected and Cleaned". Press the ENTER key, then the X key, then the ENTER key again.

CHKLIST.MS While running the MicroSoft Anti-Virus program, the computer usually puts into each directory an extra file called **CHKLIST.MS**, which is a CHecKLIST created by MicroSoft. It lets the computer check for future "Verify Errors". The next time you say "msav", the computer looks at those CHKLIST.MS files again to see whether any suspicious changes have been occurring on your hard disk.

If you're confident you won't acquire any viruses soon, you can erase those CHKLIST.MS files. Here's how.

Say "msav" again at the C prompt, like this:

```
C:\>msav
```

The computer will say "MicroSoft Anti-Virus" and "Main Menu". To delete all the CHKLIST.MS files, press the F7 key, then ENTER, then X, then ENTER again.

Other drives To make the computer check whether drive A contains any viruses, say "msav a:", like this:

```
C:\>msav a:
```

Check all disks If the computer ever finds a virus on one of your disks, make the computer check *all* your floppy disks and any additional hard disks you have, since the virus might have spread. If you've been swapping floppy disks or electronic mail with your friends, tell those friends you got a virus and to scan *their* disks too!

Amaze your friends! Try these tricks. . . .

Dir /s (in modern DOS)

Suppose MARY is a file on your hard disk, but you forget which folder contains MARY. If your DOS is modern, just say:

```
C:\>dir mary /s
```

The "/s" makes the computer search through all folders (subdirectories). The computer will tell you which folders contain MARY.

/? (in modern DOS)

Modern DOS lets you put "/?" at the end of any command. That makes your screen show a short reminder of how to use the command and its switches.

For example, if you say "dir /?", your screen will show a short reminder of how to use the "dir" command and how to use "dir" switches (such as /p, /w, /o, /od, /os, /oe, /oen, /l, /b, /ah, /ad, and /s).

Help (in modern DOS)

Modern DOS understands your cries for help.

<u>DOS 5</u> If you say "help", DOS 5 prints on your screen an alphabetical list of all DOS commands and explains briefly what each command means.

(You see the first part of that list. Press ENTER to continue and see the next part. To see the list on paper instead, say "help>prn".)

<u>DOS 6 & 6.2</u> If you say "help", DOS 6 & 6.2 print on your screen an alphabetical list of all DOS commands.

(You see the top part of the list. To see the list's bottom, depress the down-arrow key awhile, or press the PAGE DOWN key twice. To see the top of the list again, press the PAGE UP key twice.)

The commands are arranged in three columns.

For details about a particular command (such as "dir"), move the blinking cursor to that command by using the down-arrow key, up-arrow key, PAGE DOWN key, PAGE UP key, or TAB key. (The TAB key moves from column to column.) When the cursor's reached that command, press ENTER.

You'll see details about the command's **syntax** (vocabulary and grammar). If the details are too long to fit on the screen, see the rest of them by pressing the PAGE DOWN key several times. If you want to print all the details on paper, tap the Alt key then F then P then ENTER.

When you finish examining the command's syntax, do this: while holding down the Alt key, tap the N key (which means "Next topic"). That gives you the next topic (the command's **notes**, or **examples** of how to use the command, or another command). To go back to the previous topic, do this: while holding down the Alt key, tap the B key (which means "Back").

When you finish using the help system, tap the Alt key, then F, then X.

Undelete (in modern DOS)

Suppose you accidentally delete some important files. *If your DOS is modern*, you can get the files back!

That's because when you say to delete a file, the file does *not* vanish. Instead, the file stays on the disk, but the filename's first letter is replaced by a symbol indicating you no longer need the file. That old file stays on the disk until newer files need to use that part of the disk. Then the old file gets covered up by the newer files.

Here's how to try getting that old, deleted file back. (This method works only if you haven't created newer files that use the same part of the disk.)

First, go to the drive and subdirectory where the deleted files were. For example, if the files were in drive A, make the computer say:

```
A:\>
```

If the files were in the hard drive's SARAH folder, make the computer say:

```
C:\SARAH>
```

Then say "undelete". (If the computer says "Bad command or filename", the computer can't find the UNDELETE.EXE file that defines the word "undelete".)

The computer will search on the disk for files you recently said to delete. (If the computer says "No entries found", you're probably in the wrong drive or wrong folder, or the files can no longer be undeleted.)

When the computer finds a recently deleted file, it will print the file's name, except that the first letter will be replaced by a question mark. For example, if the file's name was MARY, the computer will say "?ARY". Then the computer will ask, "Undelete?" If you really want to undelete MARY, press Y; otherwise, press N. If you press Y, the computer will say, "Please type the first character for ?ARY". Since the first character of MARY is M, press M.

The computer will do that procedure for each deleted file. Afterwards, to prove the files have been undeleted, say "dir".

Remark (rem)

When the computer obeys your CONFIG.SYS file or a batch file (such as AUTOEXEC.BAT), **the computer ignores any line that begins with the word "rem".**

For example, suppose your AUTOEXEC.BAT file contains a line saying "Lh share /L:500 /f:5100", and you're debating whether to omit that line. Just insert "rem" at its beginning, so it becomes "rem Lh share /L:500 /f:5100", which makes the computer ignore the line. Then reboot the computer and see whether you like what happens. If you *don't* like what happens, edit that line again and remove the "rem". Inserting and removing the "rem" is quicker than deleting and retyping the entire line.

The word "rem" means "remark". When the computer encounters a line that begins with the word "rem", the computer assumes the line is just a "remark" you're mumbling to yourself, so the computer ignores the line.

The line beginning with "rem" can be a command you want to deactivate (such as "rem Lh share /L:500 /f:5100") or a remark you want to make to humans (such as "rem this batch file was written by Joey when drunk" or "rem the next three lines were written by Microsoft to control the mouse").

More

Suppose your disk contains a poem called MARY. To see that poem on your screen, the usual method is to say "type mary". But if MARY contains more than 23 lines, it won't all fit on the screen.

One way to see the long poem is to say "type mary" and then keep hitting the PAUSE key (to see a piece of the poem at a time).

An easier way to see the poem is to say "**more<mary**". That resembles "type mary" but makes the computer automatically pause at the end of each screenful. (To make the computer continue to the next screenful, press ENTER.)

The command "more<mary" is pronounced, "more from mary". When typing that command, make sure you type "<", which means "from". Do *not* type ">".

Subst (in DOS 3.1 & up)

Here's a nifty trick. Into drive B, put a disk that contains some files. Then say:

```
C:\>subst a: b:\
```

Afterwards, whenever you talk about drive A, the computer will SUBSTitute drive B instead. For example, if you say "dir a:", the computer will give you a directory of drive B.

That command is useful in the following situation. . . . Suppose drive A is 5¼-inch and drive B is 3½-inch. In that situation, you should buy programs on 5¼-inch floppies rather than 3½-inch, because most programs and their manuals assume you're inserting the floppies into drive A. But suppose you make the mistake of buying a program on a 3½-inch floppy instead.

If you insert that floppy into drive B, and the program gripes at you because it insists you put the floppy into drive A, just say "subst a: b:\", and try again to run the program. When the program checks to make sure you put the floppy into drive A, the program will think you obeyed, because the drive you put the floppy in is now called "drive A".

When you finish using the "subst a:" command and want to turn your computer back to normal, delete the "subst a:" command by saying:

```
C:\>subst a: /d
```

DO.BAT

To organize the files on your hard disk, you can use many methods. My favorite is the "DO.BAT" method, which I invented. Here it is. . . .

How to create DO.BAT Put a file called "DO.BAT" into your DOS directory, by typing:

```
C:\>copy con dos\do.bat
@echo off
cd \%1
%1
cd \
dir /ad/o/w/L
```

If your DOS is earlier than version 3.3, change the "@echo off" to this:

```
echo off
cls
```

In classic DOS, change the "dir /ad/o/w/L" to this:

```
dir *. /w
```

When you've finished typing, press F6 and ENTER.

What DO.BAT accomplishes That "DO.BAT" file defines the word "do" so that if you ever type a command such as "do music", the computer will automatically go into the MUSIC folder ("cd \%1"), run the MUSIC program ("%1"), return to the root directory ("cd \"), and print a menu of all the disk's folders ("dir /ad/o/w/L", which means "**di**rectory of **a**ll **di**rectories, in alphabetical **o**rder, displayed **w**ide across the screen, in **L**owercase letters").

If you type "do poker", the computer will automatically go into the POKER folder ("cd \%1"), run the POKER program ("%/1"), return to the root directory ("cd \"), and print a menu of all the disk's folders again ("dir /ad/o/w/L").

If you type just the word "do", the computer will just return you to the root directory ("cd \") and print a menu of all the disk's folders ("dir /ad/o/w/L").

So here are the rules:

Whenever you get confused, just type the word "do". It makes the computer return to the root directory and also display a menu of all the disk's folders.

To run a program, just say "do" followed by the program's name. For example, to run the MUSIC program, just say "do music". That automatically makes the computer go into the MUSIC folder, run the MUSIC program, then return to the root directory and display the menu of all the disk's folders again.

Name each folder the same as its main file

To let the DO.BAT program accomplish all that, you must set up your software properly. Here's how.

For each major program you buy, create a folder.

For example, suppose you buy a program called Marvelous Music, which comes on a pile of floppies. You should create a folder for Marvelous Music. Here's how.

First, find out the name of Marvelous Music's main file. You can do that by reading the Marvelous Music instruction manual. For example, if the instruction manual says, "to start the program, type the word MUSIC", then the name of Marvelous Music's main file is MUSIC.

Another way to find the name of Marvelous Music's main file is to put Marvelous Music's main disk into drive A and examine its directory (by typing "dir a:"). If the directory shows a file ending in .EXE or .COM, that file's probably the main file. If the directory shows a file called AUTOEXEC.BAT, peek at what the AUTOEXEC.BAT file says (by saying "type a:autoexec.bat"); it probably mentions the main file.

Suppose you've discovered the main file's name is MUSIC (or MUSIC.EXE or MUSIC.COM). Then make a MUSIC folder on the hard disk by typing "md music", so your screen looks like this:

```
C:\>md music
```

Next, put a Marvelous Music floppy into drive A. Copy all its files onto your hard disk's MUSIC folder by typing "copy a:*.* music", so your screen looks like this:

```
C:\>copy a:*.* music
```

Put another Marvelous Music floppy into drive A, and say "copy a:*.* music" again. Do the same for each floppy, until the entire set of Marvelous Music floppies has been copied to the hard disk's MUSIC folder.

Repeat that procedure for each application program you bought.

(Exception: some programs require you to say "install" or "setup" instead of a copy command. To find out whether to say "install" or "setup", read the manual that comes with the program. During the "install" or "setup" procedure, when the computer asks you to name the folder [subdirectory], name it the same as the main file that will be in it.)

Try it! To test whether you created the folders correctly, try using DO.BAT. Here's how.

Say "do". If DO.BAT is working correctly, saying "do" will make the computer display a list of all your folders. For example, if you created a MUSIC folder and a POKER folder, the computer will print a list that includes "MUSIC" and "POKER".

To use MUSIC, say "do music". Then the computer will obey the DO.BAT file, automatically switch to the MUSIC folder, run the MUSIC program, and — when the MUSIC program finishes — automatically return to the root directory and print a menu of all folders, so you can choose which other application to run next.

AUTOEXEC.BAT If you wish, **put an extra line at the bottom of your AUTOEXEC.BAT file, and make that line say just "do".**

Then when you turn on the computer, the computer will automatically perform "do", so it will automatically display a list of all your folders. That list acts as a menu. For example, to choose MUSIC from that menu, say just "do music"; that makes the computer do the MUSIC program and then show you the menu again.

Windows The DO.BAT program manages just non-Windows programs. If you're using mainly Windows programs, don't bother creating DO.BAT and don't bother putting "do" at the bottom of your AUTOEXEC.BAT file.

COPY & PROTECT WELL

Here's how to copy and protect the files you love.

Msbackup (in DOS 6 & 6.2)

Eventually, some files will get accidentally erased from your hard disk, because you give the wrong command or your disk needs repair. To protect against that inevitable calamity, copy all your hard disk's important files onto floppy disks. Doing that is called "**backing up** your hard disk onto floppies". The copies (on the floppies) are called **backups**.

The niftiest way to back up your hard disk is to give the "msbackup" command. To give that command, you must buy DOS 6 or 6.2.

(If your DOS is earlier than 6.2, skip ahead to the next section, which explains how to give the old "backup" command instead.)

How to back up To back up your hard disk by giving the "msbackup" command, just say "msbackup" at the C prompt, like this:

```
C:\>msbackup
```

If you're lucky, the computer will say "Microsoft Backup 6.0". But if your MSBACKUP program was never used before and was therefore never configured, the computer will gripe by saying "Backup requires configuration for this computer." Here's how to respond:

Remove any floppies from your drives. Press ENTER seven times.

When the computer tells you, insert a blank disk into drive A and press ENTER.
When the computer tells you, insert a second blank disk into drive A.
The computer will say "Backup Complete". Press ENTER.

When the computer tells you, insert the first blank disk back into drive A and press ENTER.
When the computer tells you, insert the second blank disk back into drive A.
The computer will say "Compare Complete". Press ENTER three times.

Now your MSBACKUP program is configured, and the computer says "Microsoft Backup 6.0".

When the computer says "Microsoft Backup 6.0", press ENTER.

Near the left edge of the screen, you'll see this symbol: [-C-]. That represents drive C. If you also have a drive D, you'll also see the symbol [-D-].

Press the down-arrow key once, so you move to the [-C-], and the [-C-] becomes **highlighted** (its background becomes black instead of blue).

Now you have three choices:

Choice 1: if you want to back up **ALL FILES** from drive C (and you have a gigantic pile of floppies to put those files on), press the SPACE bar once or twice, until the phrase "All files" appears next to the [-C-].

Choice 2: if you want to back up **THE SAME LIST OF FILES** that you backed up the previous time, just let the [-C-] keep having the phrase "Some files" next to it.

Choice 3: if you want to back up **JUST A FEW FILES** from drive C, press the SPACE bar once or twice, until NO phrase appears next to the [-C-]. Press ENTER. You'll see a list of drive C's folders (directories). Press the down-arrow key several times, until a directory you want to back up is highlighted. In the right-hand part of the screen, you'll see a list of all files in that directory.

If you want to back up ALL the files in that directory, press the SPACE bar, so the symbol ▶ appears next to the directory's name. If you want to back up JUST ONE of the files in that directory, do this instead: press the right-arrow key (to move to the right-hand part of the screen), press the down-arrow key several times (until the file you want to back up is highlighted), and press the SPACE bar, so a check mark appears next to the file's name.

If you want to back up SEVERAL directories, put the symbol ▶ in front of each directory's name. To back up SEVERAL files, put a check mark in front of each file's name.

If you make a mistake and want to erase a symbol or check mark, just highlight it and then press the SPACE bar.

When you finish putting the symbols and check marks in front of everything you wish to back up, press ENTER.

After you've finished making one of those three choices, press S (which means "Start backup").

Put a blank floppy disk into drive A. Press ENTER. If the floppy wasn't formatted yet, the computer will automatically format it. (If the floppy wasn't blank, the computer will tell you what was on it; press the letter "O" to erase and Overwrite what was on it.)

The computer will back up all the folders and files you requested. If they're too long to fit on one floppy, the computer will tell you to insert extra floppies. If you pause a while before inserting an extra floppy, you must press ENTER to confirm that you put it in.

When the computer has finished, it will say "Backup Complete". Press ENTER, then Q (which means "Quit").

How the backup is named
The entire set of floppies you wrote on is called the **backup set**.

The backup set has a name. For example, the backup set is named "CC60124B" if the backup set was created by backing up starting at drive **C**, ending at drive **C**, in 1996, on the date **01/24**, and was that date's second backup set (backup **#B**).

In that backup set, the first floppy contains a gigantic file called "CC60124B.001". The second floppy contains a gigantic file called "CC60124B.002". The third floppy contains a gigantic file called "CC60124B.003". Each gigantic file is a combo of several files from the hard disk.

Restore
If you ever want to use the backup set (because your hard disk has an accident), say this again:

```
C:\>msbackup
```

The computer will say "Microsoft Backup 6.0" again. Press the R key (which means "Restore").

The computer remembers the names of all the backup sets you ever created and assumes you want to use the most recent set. For example, if your most recent backup set was named "CC60124B", the computer says:

```
Backup Set Catalog:
CC60124B.FUL
```

(If you want to use an older backup set instead, press ENTER. You'll see a list of all the sets you ever created. Press the down-arrow key until the set you want to use is highlighted, then press the SPACE bar, so a check mark appears next to the set you want. Press ENTER.)

Then press the down-arrow key twice, so the [-C-] is highlighted.

You have two choices:

Choice 1: if you want to copy **ALL THE BACKUP SET'S FILES** to drive C, press the SPACE bar, so the phrase "All files" appears next to the [-C-]. Then press the TAB key.

Choice 2: if you want to copy **JUST ONE FILE** to drive C, press the ENTER key. You'll see a list of drive C's directories. Press the down-arrow key several times, until the directory you're interested in is highlighted. Then press the right-arrow key. Press the down-arrow key several times, until the file you're interested in is highlighted. Press the SPACE bar, so a check mark appears next to the file's name. Press the ENTER key.

After you've finished making one of those two choices, press S (which means "Start restore").

Put the backup set's first floppy in drive A. Press ENTER. When the computer tells you, put remaining floppies in drive A.

When the computer has finished, it will say "Restore Complete". Press ENTER, then Q (which means "Quit").

Backup (in early DOS versions) & restore
The "msbackup" command requires DOS 6 or 6.2. If your DOS is earlier than DOS 6, use the "backup" and "restore" commands instead. Here's how.

(If you're using DOS 6 or 6.2, skip ahead to the next section, entitled "Copy instead of backup".)

Backup
First, grab a pile of floppies. Make sure each floppy is blank, *formatted*, and the right size to fit in drive A.

How much of the hard disk do you want to back up? The whole hard disk? Or just *part* of the hard disk? Just one folder? Just one file? Decide.

Then give one of these commands:

What you want to back up	Command
a file named MARY in the root directory	C:\>backup c:mary a:
all files in the root directory	C:\>backup c: a:
the entire hard disk (all files in root directory and in all folders)	C:\>backup c: a: /s
all files in the SARAH folder	C:\>backup c:sarah a:
all files in the SARAH folder or in folders that are in SARAH	C:\>backup c:sarah a: /s
a file named MARY in the SARAH folder	C:\>backup c:sarah\mary a:

Then the computer will tell you to put a floppy into drive A. (The computer will also remind you that the floppy should be blank — and if the floppy is *not* blank, the computer will erase whatever was on it.) Go ahead: put a formatted floppy into drive A. Then press ENTER.

The computer will copy from the hard disk to that floppy disk. If that floppy disk becomes full, the computer will tell you to insert a second floppy disk. Put the second floppy into drive A, then press ENTER. The computer will tell you to insert a third floppy, fourth floppy, etc., until the copying is finished.

When the whole process is finished, what's on those floppies?

If your DOS is new (version 3.3, 4, or 5), the first floppy contains a pair of files called BACKUP.001 and CONTROL.001; the second floppy contains a pair of files called BACKUP.002 and CONTROL.002; the third floppy contains a pair of files called BACKUP.003 and CONTROL.003, etc. Those BACKUP and CONTROL files contain, in code, the backup copies of your hard disk's files.

If your DOS is earlier, the computer uses a more primitive system: the first floppy contains a file called "BACKUPID.@@@", plus many little backup files. For example, if you backed up a poem called MARY that was in the SARAH folder, one of the little backup files is called MARY; it contains the same info as the original poem but also contains an extra line saying "\SARAH\MARY", to remind the computer which folder the file came from.

Restore
If you ever want to use those backup copies (because your hard disk has an accident), say:

```
C:\>restore a: c: /s
```

That makes the computer copy all files from the floppy pile back to the hard disk. If you want to copy just *one* of the files from the floppy pile (such as MARY in the SARAH folder), say:

```
C:\>restore a: c:sarah\mary
```

Notice that "restore" is the opposite of "backup". Use "backup" to copy from the hard disk to a pile of floppies; use "restore" to copy from a pile of floppies to the hard disk.

The "restore" command puts back on the hard disk exactly what was there before the accident. On your hard disk, the "restore" command recreates destroyed files and destroyed folders. For example, if an accident totally destroyed your hard disk's SARAH directory, so that the name "SARAH" is no longer on the hard disk, don't worry: if you backed up the hard disk before the accident, the "restore" command will automatically create a folder on your hard disk, and name that folder "SARAH", and put back in it all the files that were destroyed.

Since new versions of DOS handle the "backup" and "restore" commands differently than old versions, make sure you use the same DOS version for "restore" as you used for "backup".

Make backups small Suppose you back up your entire hard disk onto a gigantic pile of floppies (by saying "C:\>backup c: a: /s"). Suppose the first floppy in that pile gets a scratch on it. Later, when you try to say "restore", the computer notices the scratch on the first floppy, gripes at you, and refuses to restore. The entire pile of floppies has become useless, because of one scratch!

To avoid losing a whole pile of floppies from one scratch, make smaller piles instead: back up just one subdirectory at a time, so that each subdirectory gets its own pile of floppies. That way, if a floppy gets a scratch, you lose just one subdirectory instead of the whole hard disk.

Formatting during backup Before giving the backup command, you're supposed to have a pile of blank disks that have been formatted. What if one of the disks hasn't been formatted yet?

If your DOS is modern, the backup command will format the disk for you. If your DOS is 3.2 or earlier, the computer will gripe about the unformatted disk. If your DOS is 3.3 or 4, the computer will gripe unless you said "/f" at the end of the backup command; the "/f" tells the computer to format any unformatted disks.

Modified files If you say "/m" at the end of the backup command, the computer will back up just the files that "need to be backed up". Those are the files that have been edited or created since the last time you said "backup".

The backup you create by saying "/m" is called the "backup of modified files". It's also called an **incremental backup**, since it consists of just the added files that weren't backed up before.

Copy instead of backup

If the group of files you want to back up is short enough so that the entire group fits on a single floppy, say "copy" instead of "backup" or "msbackup", since the "copy" command is easier and more reliable.

If the group of files you want to back up is too long to fit on a single floppy, but you're too rushed to wait for the "backup" or "msbackup" command to handle a huge pile of floppies, try this trick: instead of telling the computer to "backup" to floppies, tell the computer to "copy" to a hard disk folder named BACKUP. Here are the details. . . .

If your hard disk doesn't contain a BACKUP folder already, make a BACKUP folder by saying:

`C:\>md backup`

Then to back up all the files in the SARAH folder, just tell the computer to copy SARAH's files to the BACKUP folder by saying:

`C:\>copy sarah backup`

That scheme works just if your hard disk is big enough to hold the BACKUP folder. If you use that scheme, you should still back up your work onto floppies occasionally, in case the entire hard drive breaks and you lose both SARAH and the BACKUP folder.

I recommend that you copy all important files to the BACKUP folder once a day, and back up all important files onto floppies once a week.

Be wary

Never trust a computer! Even if you copied up your data to a BACKUP folder and floppies, the data you backed up might be wrong, and all those copies might be equally defective! To be safer, use these tricks. . . .

Alternate between TWO piles of floppies. The first time you copy onto floppies, use the first pile. The second time you copy (the next day or week), use the second pile instead. The next time you copy, use the first pile again. The next time, use the second pile. The next time, go back to the first pile. Keep alternating! That way, if something's wrong with the data on today's pile, you can go back to the other pile. Nervous institutions (such as banks and the military) have *seven* piles — one for each day of the week. That way, if Friday's data is wrong — and so is the data for Thursday, Wednesday, Tuesday, Monday, and Sunday — you can at least go back to the good data you had last Saturday!

Copy your work onto paper periodically, and keep the paper copies for several weeks. The nice thing about paper is: you can see what's on it. You don't have to worry about the paper being secretly defective. When dealing with data, paper's the only medium you can trust. Just don't leave it near your dog. Lock it in your filing cabinet. (I mean the paper, not the dog.)

Where to put data files

A hard disk contains **programs** and **data files**. In a typical business, the info in the data files changes daily, but the programs remain stable. The business makes backup copies of programs monthly but backs up data files daily, to ensure the backups incorporate the latest changes.

To back up data files simply, some businesses put them all in a DATA folder (directory), backed up daily.

Sharing the disk If several employees share a hard disk, they might accidentally destroy each other's data files. To prevent that, your business can give each employee a separate folder (directory). For example, you can put all of Fred's data files in a folder called FRED and put Mary's data files in folder MARY.

An even surer way to prevent employees from destroying each other's data files is to give each employee a floppy disk. Fred gets a floppy labeled "Fred's data"; Mary gets a floppy labeled "Mary's data". No data files are stored on the hard disk, which contains just programs. But employees dislike using floppies, which are slower than hard disks and can't handle long files.

Recommendation I recommend keeping things simple by creating as few folders as possible. Put the MUSIC program and all its data files in the MUSIC folder. To distinguish Fred's music from Mary's, have Fred begin his filenames with an F, and have Mary's begin with M. Let Fred be responsible for backing up his own files, and Mary be responsible for backing up hers.

Attrib (in DOS 3 & up)

To protect your important files from being erased accidentally, make backup copies of the files (by saying "backup" or "msbackup" or "copy" or "diskcopy").

Another way to protect the files is to give the "attrib" command. To use it, your DOS must be new (version 3 or newer).

Here's how.

Read only
To protect a file named MARY, say "attrib +r mary". That prevents MARY from being accidentally changed.

For example, if somebody tries to delete MARY by saying "del mary", the computer will refuse and say:

`Access denied`

If somebody tries to delete many files by saying "del *.*", the computer will delete *most* files but not MARY.

If somebody tries to create a new MARY and obliterate the old one (by saying "copy con mary", then typing some lines, then pressing F6 and ENTER), the computer will refuse and say:

`Access denied - MARY`

If somebody tries to edit MARY by saying "edit mary", the computer will refuse and say:

`Path/file access error`

If somebody tries to edit MARY by saying "edlin mary", the computer will refuse and say:

`File is READ-ONLY`

If somebody tries to find out what MARY is (by saying "dir mary" or "type mary" or "copy mary prn") or rename MARY (by saying "rename mary lambchop"), the computer *will* obey. The computer will let people *read* MARY *but not destroy* what's in MARY. That's because **saying "attrib +r mary" means, "give MARY the following ATTRIBute: Read only!"**

MARY will remain read-only forever — or until you cancel the "attribute read-only". **To cancel, say "attrib -r mary".** In that command, the "-r" means "take away the read-only attribute", so that MARY is *not* read-only and can be edited.

Hide (in modern DOS)
For a different way to protect MARY, **say "attrib +h mary". That hides MARY, so that MARY will not be mentioned when you type "dir".**

After you've hidden MARY, it will not be affected by any "del", "rename" or "copy". If you try to wreck MARY by copying another file to it, the computer will say "Access denied". If you try to change MARY's attributes by saying "attrib +r mary" or "attrib -r mary", the computer will refuse and say "Not resetting hidden file".

Although MARY is hidden and isn't mentioned when you say "dir", the computer will let you access that file if you're somehow in on the secret and know that the file exists and is called "MARY". For example, the computer *will* let you look at the file by saying "type mary" and edit the file by saying "edit mary" or "edlin mary". If you say "edlin mary" (because your DOS is too old to understand "edit"), be careful: after the editing is done, the new MARY will be visible unless you say "attrib +h mary" again.

If MARY is hidden, **you can "unhide" MARY (and make MARY visible again) by saying "attrib -h mary".**

System (in DOS modern)
For an alternate way to hide MARY, say "attrib +s mary". That turns MARY into a system file, which is similar to being hidden.

For the ultimate in hiding, say "attrib +h +s mary". Then even if somebody tries to unhide MARY by saying "attrib -h mary", MARY will still be hidden by the +s.

To undo the +s, say "attrib -s mary".

Archive (in DOS 3.2, 3.3, 4, and modern DOS)
If you say "/m" at the end of the "backup" command, the computer backs up just the files that have been "modified". Files that have been modified (and therefore should be backed up) are called **archive files**.

To turn MARY into an archive file (so that MARY will be backed up by the "backup" command with "/m"), say "attrib +a mary".

To *prevent* MARY from being backed up by the "backup" command with "/m", say "attrib -a mary".

Normal
After playing with MARY's attributes, you can make MARY be normal again by saying "attrib -r -h -s +a mary". That makes MARY be *not* read-only, *not* hidden, *not* a system file, and able to be backed up by the "backup" command with "/m".

Examine the attributes
To examine MARY's attributes, say "attrib mary". The computer will say "MARY" and print some letters. For example, if it prints the letters R, H, S, and A, it means MARY is read-only, hidden, system, and archive. If it prints just the letters R and H, it means MARY is read-only and hidden but not system or archive.

If you say just "attrib" (without mentioning MARY), the computer will print a directory that tells you the attributes of every file.

Xcopy (in DOS 3.2 & up)

Instead of saying "copy", try saying "xcopy", which means: eXtended copy. The "xcopy" command resembles "copy" but has eXtended abilities, so it can perform fancier tricks.

To use "xcopy", your DOS must be version 3.2, 3.3, 4, or modern. Since "xcopy" is an external command (defined by XCOPY.EXE), it works just if your computer is set up correctly and can find the XCOPY.EXE file.

Here are examples of using "xcopy". . . .

Duplicating a floppy
Suppose drive A contains a 5¼-inch floppy full of info, drive B contains a blank formatted 3½-inch floppy, and you want to copy all files from drive A to drive B.

Since the drives are different sizes, you can't say "diskcopy a: b:". You *can* say "copy a:*.* b:"; but that copies just the files in the root directory, not the folders.

To copy all files — even the files that are in folders — say "**xcopy a: b: /s**". The "/s" makes sure that the copying includes all folders (subdirectories) that contain files.

In modern DOS, that command copies all files except hidden and system files (such as IO.SYS and MSDOS.SYS). Classic DOS copies even those files.

That command doesn't bother copying folders that are empty. To copy *all* folders, even the ones that are empty, say "**xcopy a: b: /s/e**".

Copying a floppy to the hard disk
Suppose drive A contains a floppy full of info. Here's how to create a folder called SARAH on your hard disk and make it contain everything that was on the floppy (all the floppy's files and folders):

```
C:\>xcopy a: sarah\ /s/e
```

In that command, the backslash after "sarah" makes the computer create a folder named SARAH if it doesn't exist already. (By typing that backslash, you don't have to bother saying "md sarah".)

The "/s/e" makes the computer copy everything from the floppy — even the floppy's folders. If you omit the "/s/e", the computer will copy just the files in the floppy's root directory.

Duplicating a folder
Suppose your hard disk contains a folder called SARAH. Here's how to make a copy called SARAH2 (so that your hard disk will contain both SARAH and SARAH2):

```
C:\>xcopy sarah sarah2\ /s/e
```

In that command, the backslash after "sarah2" makes the computer create a folder named SARAH2 if it doesn't exist already. The "/s/e" makes the computer copy everything from SARAH — even folders that are in the SARAH folder.

Renaming a folder
Suppose your hard disk contains a folder called SARAH, and you want to change its name to TONY. The computer won't let you say "rename sarah tony". Instead, create a copy of SARAH called TONY (by saying "xcopy sarah tony\ /s/e"), then remove SARAH (by saying "rd sarah" after deleting all of SARAH's files).

Copying a folder to a floppy
Suppose your hard disk contains a folder named SARAH, and you want to copy all SARAH's files to a floppy in drive A.

To keep things simple, let's assume SARAH does *not* have any folders hiding inside it, or you don't wish to copy any such folders. Since this is a simple copying job, you can probably use the simple "copy" command instead of "xcopy" and just say:

```
C:\>copy sarah a:
```

But suppose you run into this hassle: the floppy's too small to hold all SARAH's files. Then you must copy SARAH's files to a *pile* of floppies. One way to do that is to say:

```
C:\>backup sarah a:
```

But that fills the floppies with files that are useless until you say "restore".

To copy SARAH's files to a pile of floppies, try the following trick instead. This trick works if each file in SARAH is brief (so that no single file is too long to fit on a floppy). Say:

```
C:\>attrib +a sarah\*.*
```

Then insert the first formatted floppy and say:

```
C:\>xcopy sarah a: /m
```

The computer will copy some files from SARAH to the floppy. When that floppy gets full, the computer will say "Insufficient disk space" and stop copying.

Then insert the second floppy. Say "xcopy sarah a: /m" again (by retyping it or by pressing the F3 key or the up-arrow key). Press the ENTER key at the end of that command. The computer will continue where it left off: it will copy different files onto that second floppy.

When the computer says "Insufficient disk space" again, insert the third floppy, and say "xcopy sarah a: /m" again (and press ENTER). Keep inserting floppies and saying "xcopy sarah a: /m", until the computer is done and no longer says "Insufficient disk space".

MAC SYSTEM

START YOUR MAC

Here's how to use a Mac computer.

I'll begin by explaining the **Mac Color Classic**, which is the easiest Mac to understand. (Other Macs are similar but slightly more complex. I'll explain how they differ.)

Set up the Mac

When you buy a Mac Color Classic, the salesperson hands you a big brown cardboard box. Take the box home. Open it and peek inside.

You'll see clear plastic bags. They contain the computer, keyboard, mouse, and little goodies (power cord, keyboard cable, floppy disks, and instruction manuals). Rip the bags open.

Put the computer on your desk. Plug one end of the power cord into your wall and the other end into the back of the computer.

Look at the mouse (a small object the size of a pack of cigarettes). A cable comes out of it. If you're right-handed, plug that cable into the keyboard's right side; if you're left-handed, plug that cable into the keyboard's left side.

Attach the keyboard to the computer, by plugging one end of the keyboard's cable into the side of the keyboard and the other end into the back of the computer.

Flip the keyboard upside-down, so you don't see the keys. Look at the left and right edges of the keyboard: you'll see two levers (near where the cables go in). Pop up the levers, so the keyboard sprouts two legs. Then flip the keyboard right-side up (so you see the keys again, and the keyboard rests on its two legs).

Congratulations! You've installed the computer! Now you can say on your resumé that you're a "computer expert experienced at installing advanced computer equipment".

Other Macs For old Macs, the cardboard box is *white* (instead of brown), the keyboard has *no legs*, the keyboard plugs into the computer's *front* (instead of back), and the mouse plugs into the *computer* (instead of into the keyboard). For some Macs, the monitor or hard drive is sold separately and must be cabled to the computer.

The Mac Color Classic has a built-in microphone; for other Macs, the microphone is missing or must be cabled to the computer.

The Mac Powerbook is a notebook computer that's all in one piece and requires no assembly.

Turn on the Mac

At the back of the Mac, next to the power cord, you'll see a switch marked "1" and "0". That's the **on/off switch**. Put that switch in the "on" position by pressing the "1". Then press the **POWER ON key**, which is at the top of the keyboard and has the symbol ◄ on it.

The computer will make an overture to you: you'll hear a musical chord. On the screen, you'll briefly see an arrow, then a smile, then this message:

Welcome to Macintosh.

Eventually, you'll see little pictures, called **icons**. The screen's top left corner will show the **Apple icon** (a partly eaten apple). The screen's bottom right corner will show the **trash icon** (picture of a trash can). Those icons mean the **Finder** (the fundamental part of the Mac's operating system) is ready.

If your Mac's been used by other people, they might have left your Mac in a strange state, with several rectangular windows on the screen. To make sure your Mac is normal, with no windows on the screen, do the following. . . .

Next to the space bar, you'll see the **COMMAND key** (which has an Apple and a squiggle on it) and the **OPTION key**. Hold down both of those keys simultaneously; and while you keep them down, tap the W key.

Congratulations! Now you have a turned-on Mac, ready and willing to obey your every command!

Other Macs On expensive Macs, the on/off switch is a button that pops in and out, or it's in the form of a car-ignition key. If you're sharing such a Mac, your friends probably already put that switch in the correct position, so don't touch it: just press the POWER ON key.

Cheap Macs don't use a POWER ON key: just press 1 on the on/off switch.

Some Mac monitors have a separate switch that you must turn on.

If your Mac's hard drive is external, turn that drive on and wait 15 seconds before turning on the Mac.

Old Macs make a beep instead of playing a chord.

On old Macs, the COMMAND key has a squiggle on it but no apple.

Performa Macs make the screen display a Launcher window. To follow the instructions in the book, make sure the Launcher window disappears. Again, here's how to make the Launcher window (and all other windows) disappear: hold down the COMMAND and OPTION keys; and while keeping them down, tap the W key.

If you don't see "Welcome to Macintosh", your Mac isn't set up properly. For example, the monitor might be turned off (turn it on!), the hard drive might be missing (buy a hard drive!), your dealer might have neglected to copy the Mac operating system onto the hard drive (ask the dealer to help you!), or a previous user left a floppy disk in the floppy drive (remove the floppy disk).

If your Mac doesn't have a hard drive, you'll have difficulty running modern software and using this book. Either buy a hard drive or phone me to get an older edition of this book.

Although the trash icon is usually in the bottom right corner, it might be in a different place if the previous user moved it.

USE THE MOUSE

Your computer comes with a **mouse**. The mouse's **tail** is a cable that runs from the mouse to the keyboard. The area where the tail meets the mouse is called the mouse's **ass** or **rear**.

The mouse's underside — its belly — has a hole in it, and a ball in the hole.

Put the mouse on your desk and directly in front of your right arm. (If you're left-handed, put it in front of your left arm.) Make the mouse lie flat (so its ball rubs against the desk). **Make the mouse face you** so the apple on the mouse appears right-side up, and you don't see the mouse's ass.

Other Macs The Mac Powerbook uses a trackball instead of a mouse. The trackball is part of the keyboard.

Move the arrow

Move the mouse across your desk. As you move the mouse, remember to keep it flat and facing you.

On the screen, you'll see an arrow, which is called the **pointer** or **cursor**. As you move the mouse, the arrow moves also. If you move the mouse to the left, the arrow moves to the left. If you move the mouse to the right, the arrow moves to the right. If you move the mouse toward you, the arrow moves down. If you move the mouse away from you, the arrow moves up.

Practice moving the arrow by moving the mouse. Remember to keep the mouse facing you at all times.

If you want to move the arrow far, and your desk is small, move the mouse until it reaches the desk's edge; then lift the mouse off the desk, lay the mouse gently on the middle of the desk, and move the mouse across the desk in the same direction as before.

Other Macs If your Mac uses a trackball (instead of a mouse), move the arrow by rotating the trackball.

Click an icon

The most important part of the arrow is its tip, which is called the **hot spot**.

For an experiment, move the arrow so its hot spot (tip) is in the middle of the trash can. That's called **pointing at** the trash can.

On top of the mouse is a rectangular button that you can press. Tapping that button is called **clicking**.

While you're pointing at the trash can, try clicking (by tapping the button). That's called "**clicking** the trash can" (or "**clicking on** the trash can" or "**selecting** the trash can"). When you do that, the trash can turns black. Try it!

Near the screen's top right corner, you'll see the words "Macintosh HD". Above those words, you'll see a rectangle with a black dot in its bottom left corner. That rectangle is supposed to be a picture of a Macintosh hard-disk drive. That rectangle's called the **hard-disk icon**. Try clicking in the middle of the rectangle. When you do that, it turns black.

Whenever you click an icon, that icon turns black, and the other major icons turn white. For example, when you click the trash icon, the hard disk icon turns white; when you click the hard disk icon, the trash icon turns white.

An icon that's black is **selected**; an icon that's white is called **unselected** or **deselected**. Usually, just one icon is selected (black); all the other icons are deselected (white).

(The Apple icon is a different kind of icon. If you click it, no colors change. I'll explain it later.)

Try this experiment: click in the center of the screen, where there are no icons. All the screen's icons suddenly turn white.

Here are the rules:

If you click a white icon, it turns black. All other icons turn white.
If you click where there's no icon, all icons turn white.

Other Macs The hard-disk icon might have a different name and shape. For example, 80-megabyte hard disks manufactured by Jasmine are labeled "Direct Drive 80" (instead of "Macintosh HD") and have an icon that looks like a flower (instead of a rectangle).

Drag an icon

You can move an icon to a different place on the screen. Here's how.

Point at the icon by moving the arrow's tip to the middle of the icon. (Put the arrow's tip in the middle of the icon picture, *not* in the middle of the words underneath it.)

Hold down the mouse's button; and while you keep the button down, move the mouse. As you move the mouse *with the button down*, you'll be moving the arrow *and the icon*. That's called **dragging the icon**. When you've dragged the icon to your favorite place on the screen, lift your finger from the mouse's button, and the icon will stay there.

Your screen's top line of information is called the **menu bar**. It contains eight items: the Apple icon, the **Help icon** (which is a picture of a question mark in a bubble), the **Finder icon** (which is a picture of a Mac), and the words **File**, **Edit**, **View**, **Label**, and **Special**. Here's how to use them.

Point at the Apple icon. Hold down the mouse's button. While you keep the button down, you see this **menu** underneath the Apple icon:

```
About This Macintosh...
Alarm Clock
Calculator
Chooser
Control Panels
Key Caps
Note Pad
Puzzle
Scrapbook
```

The menu appears only while you hold down the mouse's button. (If you lift your finger from the mouse's button, the menu disappears.)

Seeing the menu (by holding down the mouse's button) is called **pulling down the menu**, because it's like pulling down a window shade that has graffiti written on it. Since you see the menu by pulling it down, it's called a **pull-down menu**. Since that menu appears underneath the Apple icon, it's called the **Apple menu**.

If you point at one of the menu bar's other items (Help icon, Finder icon, File, Edit, View, Label, or Special) and hold down the mouse's button, you'll see other menus. For example, to see the **File menu**, point at the word "File" and then hold down the mouse's button.

Experiment! Try each item on the menu bar, and look at their pull-down menus. Those menus list some of the fascinating things your Mac can do!

Other Macs New Macs (such as the Mac Color Classic) use version 7 of the operating system. That's called **System 7**. Old Macs use **System 6** instead, whose menu bar lacks the Help icon, Finder icon, and Label.

On some Macs, Apple menu displays slightly different choices. The top choice might say "About This Computer" or "About the Finder" (instead of "About This Macintosh"). The fifth choice might say "Control Panel" instead of "Control Panels". Extra choices might be displayed.

About This Macintosh

From the Apple menu, choose **About This Macintosh**. Here's how.

Point at the Apple icon. Hold down the mouse's button, so you see the Apple menu, including "About This Macintosh". While you keep the button down, point at "About This Macintosh". Then lift your finger from the button.

The computer will obey your command: it will tell you about your Mac.

To do that, the computer will display a **window** in the middle of the screen. In the window, you'll see a message about your Mac.

For example, on *my* Mac Color Computer the message says: I have a Mac Color Computer; the operating system is version 7.1, copyrighted by Apple Computer Inc. 1983-1992; your RAM is 4 megabytes (4,096K), of which 1,182K is used by system software, leaving 2,884K unused in a big block (plus 30 K unused in smaller blocks). On *your* Mac Color Computer, the numbers might be different, and the number of bytes that are used and unused will vary as your Mac performs different activities.

Other Macs If you don't see "About This Macintosh" on the Apple menu, choose "About This Computer" or "About the Finder" instead.

Drag a window

Look at the top line of the window containing the "About This Macintosh" message. The window's top line gives the window's **title** ("About This Macintosh").

Try this experiment. Drag the window's title to a different part of the screen. (To do that, point at the title; hold down the mouse's button; while you keep the button down, move the mouse.) As you drag the title, the rest of the window automatically drags along with it. When you've dragged the window to your favorite place on the screen, lift your finger from the mouse's button, and the window will stay there.

Close the window

When you finish looking at the message in a window, you must **close the window**. Here's how.

In the window's top left corner, you'll see a tiny square, called the **close box**. To close the window, click the close box (by pointing at the square and then tapping the mouse's button). The window will close and disappear from the screen.

WIMP

The Mac is called a **WIMP computer**, because it uses Windows, Icons, Mice, and Pull-downs.

Commodore's Amiga computer and Atari's ST computer imitate the Mac: they use Windows, Icons, Mice, and Pull-downs also. So they too are WIMP computers.

Any program using Windows, Icons, Mice, and Pull-downs is called **WIMPy**. You can buy WIMPy programs for many computers — even for the IBM PC!

If you have an IBM PC, you can buy **Microsoft Windows**, which is software that makes the IBM PC try to imitate a Mac. But the imitation is screwed up; it makes the IBM PC become a *messed-up* Mac. The Mac is nicer than any imitation! The Mac is a beauty that the beast can't resemble.

This chapter examines the Mac's beauty further. The next chapter examines the poor fake: Microsoft Windows.

Key Caps

To explore the Mac's keyboard, choose **Key Caps** from the Apple menu. (To do that, point at the Apple icon and drag down to the phrase "Key Caps").

You'll see a window that shows a picture of your keyboard. It reminds you of what your keyboard looks like.

In the picture, all the letters are lower-case. Try typing a word (such as "love"): you'll see the word in lower-case letters.

SHIFT key If you hold down your keyboard's SHIFT key, the letters in the picture change to capitals. While holding down the SHIFT key, try typing a word; you'll see the word in capital letters, like this: LOVE.

OPTION key If you hold down your keyboard's OPTION key, the letters in the picture change to weird symbols. While holding down the OPTION key, try typing; you'll be typing symbols from Greek, Swedish, French, Spanish, Japanese, math, and other un-American pleasures. To get extra symbols, hold down the OPTION and SHIFT keys simultaneously.

Accents To type an accent, use these keystrokes:

Accent	What keys to press
^	OPTION with i
~	OPTION with n
¨	OPTION with u
´	OPTION with e
`	OPTION with `

For example, here's how to type ô. Type the code for ^ (which is OPTION with i), then take your finger off the OPTION key and type the letter you want under the accent (the "o"). Nothing appears on the screen until you complete the whole process; then you'll see ô.

Close When you've finished exploring Key Caps, close the window, by clicking its close box.

Calculator

To do calculations, choose **Calculator** from the Apple menu. (To do that, drag from the Apple icon down to the word "Calculator".)

You'll see a window that looks and acts like a pocket calculator. For example, to compute 42+5, click the calculator's 4 key (by using the mouse to point at the 4 key and then clicking), then click 2, then +, then 5, then =. The calculator will show the answer, 47.

Instead of using the mouse, you can do that calculation a different way, by using the Mac's keyboard. On the right side of the keyboard, you'll see the **numeric keypad**, which looks just like the on-screen calculator. On that keypad, tap the 4 key, then the 2 key, then (while holding down the SHIFT key) the + key, then 5, then =. The on-screen calculator will show 47.

Try fancier calculations, by using these symbols:

Symbol	Meaning
+	plus
-	minus
*	times
/	divided by
=	total
.	decimal point
c	clear

When you finish using the calculator, close the window, by clicking its close box.

Multiple windows

The screen can show several windows simultaneously.

For example, choose Key Caps from the Apple menu, so that you see the Key Caps window on the screen. While the Key Caps window remains on the screen, choose Calculator from the Apple menu. You'll see both the Key Caps window and the calculator window on the screen simultaneously.

The calculator window sits in front of the Key Caps window, and partly blocks your view of the Key Caps window. The front window (the calculator window) is called the **active window**. That's the window you're using at the moment. For example, if you type "2+2=", the computer will say 4, because the calculator window is active.

To make the Key Caps window active instead, click anywhere in the Key Caps window. That moves the Key Caps window in front of the calculator window, so that the Key Caps window partly blocks your view of the calculator. Since the Key Caps window is in front (active), if you use the keyboard now you'll be dealing with Key Caps instead of the calculator.

To switch back to the calculator, click anywhere in the calculator window.

If you don't like the way that the active window blocks your view of the other window, move the active window (by dragging its title) or make the active window disappear (by clicking its close box).

Shut Down

When you're done using the Mac, choose **Shut Down** from the **Special menu**. That makes the Mac shut itself off.

While shutting itself off, the Mac tidies up the information on the disks, ejects any floppy disks from the drives, and then turns off its own power (so the power light goes off and the screen turns black).

The next time you want to use the Mac, just press the ◄ key, which turns the Mac back on.

Other Macs When you choose Shut Down from the Special menu, some Macs say "It is now safe to switch off your computer" or "You may now switch off your Macintosh safely". Then press the on/off switch's "0". To turn such a Mac back on, press the on/off switch's "1" again.

When turning a Mac off, remember to also turn off any external drive.

EXPLODE AN ICON

The Mac was designed by sadists. If an icon fascinates you, you're supposed to explode it, by blowing it up!

For example, suppose the Macintosh HD icon is on the screen, and it fascinates you. Explode it! Here's how: point at that Macintosh HD icon, then tap the mouse's button twice quickly, so the taps are less then a second apart. That's called **exploding the icon** or **double-clicking the icon** or **opening the icon**.

After the icon explodes, you can see what was hiding inside it. You see that inside the Macintosh HD icon, these 6 **items** were hiding: the **System Folder, Teachtext, Read Me, Quicktime 1.5, Hypercard 2.1 Player**, and **Macintosh Basics**. On your screen, you see their icons: the System Folder icon, the Teachtext icon, the Read Me icon, the Quicktime 1.5 icon, the Hypercard 2.1 Player icon, and the Macintosh Basics icon.

(You see those icons when your computer is new. If your computer's been used, the people using it might have added extra icons or deleted some icons.)

Those icons all appear in a window titled "Macintosh HD". As with any window, you can move it by dragging its title.

Other Macs Different Macs contain different items and icons.

Size box

In the window's bottom right corner is a tiny icon that shows overlapping squares. That icon is called the **size box**.

Drag the size box to another part of the screen (by moving the size box while holding down the mouse's button). As the size box moves, so does the window's bottom right corner, so that the window's size changes.

By dragging the size box, you can make the window very large — or very small.

If you make the window small, it shows fewer icons. Some of the icons are hiding out of view. To see the hidden icons again, make the window larger.

Zoom box

In the window's top right corner is a tiny icon that shows a picture of a square inside a square. That icon is called the **zoom box**.

Try clicking the zoom box. When you do, the window's size changes.

Clicking the zoom box usually makes the window become the perfect size — just big enough to show all its icons (so none of its icons are hidden anymore).

Once the window's become the perfect size, clicking the zoom box again makes the window return to whatever weird size it had before reaching perfection. So clicking the zoom box makes the window switch to perfection — or back to imperfection.

Try it! Click the window's zoom box several time, and see the window switch back and forth between perfection and imperfection.

Other Macs For System 6, clicking the zoom box makes the window become huge (filling most of the screen) instead of "the perfect size".

Scroll boxes

Since the hard disk of a new Mac normally contains six items (the System Folder, Teachtext, Read Me, Quicktime 1.5, Hypercard 2.1 Player, and Macintosh Basics), the hard disk's window is supposed to show six icons. But if you make the window very small (by using the size box), the window becomes too small to show the six icons. Instead, the window shows just *some* of the icons.

Try this experiment: drag the size box until the window becomes so small that it shows just one icon.

When you make the window that small, a blue ribbed square **scroll box** appears at the bottom of the window, and another blue ribbed square scroll box appears on the window's right side. By dragging the scroll boxes, you can shift the view that you see through the window, so you see different icons in the window. Shifting the view by moving the scroll boxes is called **scrolling**.

Arrows and gray rectangles
Here's another way to shift the window's view: click the arrows and gray rectangles that appear next to the scroll boxes.

If you click an arrow, the scroll box nudges in the direction that the arrow points. To nudge even further in that direction, click that arrow several times, or just point at the arrow and hold down the mouse's button for a while.

If you click a gray rectangle, the scroll box hops toward that rectangle. It hops far enough to make the window show the next windowful of information.

The part of the window that consists of the scroll box, arrows, and gray rectangles is called the **scroll bar**.

Peek in folders

Try this experiment. Enlarge the Macintosh HD window by clicking its zoom box. Use the scroll boxes to adjust the window's view, until you see all six items in the window.

Four of those items are folders: the System Folder, Quick Time 1.5, Hypercard 2.1 Player, and Macintosh Basics. Each of their icons is in the shape of a manila folder. Let's peek inside the folders.

Start by peeking inside the System Folder. To do that, double-click the System Folder icon. The System Folder icon will explode and show you everything inside it.

When you finish peeking inside the System Folder, click its close box.

Other Macs Different Macs contain different folders.

RUN TEACHTEXT

Get the Teachtext icon onto the screen (by exploding the Macintosh HD icon).

Notice that the Teachtext icon isn't in the shape of a folder. Instead of being a folder, Teachtext is an **application program**.

To start using an application program (such as Teachtext), explode its icon, by double-clicking it. Then the screen's appearance changes dramatically.

Teachtext is a simple word processor; it lets you type words and sentences simply. Try it! After exploding the Teachtext icon, try typing whatever sentences you wish to make up. For example, try typing a memo to your friends, or a story, or a poem. Be creative! Whatever you type is called a **document**.

Other Macs If your Mac is a Performa, here's how to get the Teachtext icon onto the screen. Explode the Macintosh HD icon (so you see the Macintosh HD window), then explode the Applications folder in that window.

Use the keyboard

The following hints will help you type. . . .

To capitalize a letter of the alphabet, type that letter while holding down the **SHIFT key**.

To capitalize a whole passage, tap the **CAPS LOCK key**, then type the passage. The computer will automatically capitalize the passage as you type it. When you finish typing the passage, tap the CAPS LOCK key again: that tells the computer to stop capitalizing.

If you make a mistake, press the **DELETE key**. That makes the computer erase the last character you typed.

To erase the last *two* characters you typed, press the DELETE key *twice*.

If you're typing near the screen's right edge, and you type a word that's too long to fit on the screen, the computer will automatically move the word to the line below.

When you finish a paragraph, press the **RETURN key**. That makes the computer move to the line underneath so you can start typing the next paragraph.

If you want to double-space between the paragraphs, press the RETURN key *twice*.

If you want to indent a line (such as the first line of a paragraph), begin the line by pressing the **TAB key**. The computer will indent the line slightly (as if you pressed the SPACE bar twice).

To type an accent, use the same technique as when you're using Key Caps. For example, to type the symbol ô, type the code for ^ (which is OPTION with i), then type the "o".

Other Macs On old Macs, the DELETE key is called the BACKSPACE key and says "Backspace" on it.

Scroll through documents

If your document contains too many lines to fit in the window, the window will show just *part* of the document. To see the rest of the document, move the scroll box (by dragging it or by clicking on the nearby arrow or gray area).

Insert characters

To insert extra characters anywhere in your document, click where you want the extra characters to appear (by moving the mouse's pointer there and then pressing the mouse's button). Then type the extra characters.

For example, suppose you typed the word "fat" and want to change it to "fault". Click between the "a" and the "t", then type "ul".

(When you're using the Mac, notice that you click *between* letters, not *on* letters.)

As you type the extra characters, the screen's other characters move out of the way, to make room for the extra characters.

While you're inserting the extra characters, you can erase nearby mistakes by pressing the DELETE key.

Select text

Suppose the document contains a phrase you mistyped. Here's how to edit the phrase.

First, make the phrase turn black, by using any of these methods. . . .

The drag method
Point at the phrase's beginning.
Drag to the phrase's end.

The shift-click method
Click at the phrase's beginning.
While holding down the SHIFT key, click at the phrase's end.
(That's called **shift-clicking** the phrase's end.)

The double-click method
If the "phrase" is just one word, double-click it.

Turning the phrase black is called **selecting the phrase**.

Then say what to do to the phrase. For example, if you want to *erase* the phrase, press the DELETE key. If you want to *replace* the phrase instead, just type whatever words you want the phrase to become. If you want to *move* the phrase instead, choose **Cut** from the **Edit menu**, then click where you want the phrase to be, then choose **Paste** from the Edit menu.

Notice that the Cut command makes sense only if you've selected some text (by turning that text black).

If you *don't* select any text — if no phrase is black — the computer refuses to let you say Cut. In that situation, when you pull down the Edit menu, you'll notice that the word "Cut" appears on the menu very faintly: the word "Cut" is **dimmed**; it's **grayed** instead of being written in sharp black.

Here's the rule: **when a word on a menu is dimmed, the computer refuses to let you choose that word**. The usual reason for the refusal is that you haven't selected a phrase (or icon or other part of the screen).

Start over

If you mess up the entire document and want to erase it all (so you can start over again, fresh, from scratch), choose **Select All** from the Edit menu, then press the DELETE key.

Save

To copy the document onto the disk, choose **Save** from the **File menu**.

Then invent a name for your document. For example, you can invent a short name such as —

Joe

or a long name such as:

Stupidest Memo of 1995

The name can be up to 31 characters long. It can't contain a colon and can't begin with a period, but it can contain any other characters you wish! At the end of the name, press the RETURN key. That makes the computer copy the document onto the disk.

Afterwards, if you change your mind and want to do more editing, go ahead! Edit the document some more. When you finish that editing, save it by choosing **Save** from the File menu again.

Finish

When you finish working on a document, click the close box.

(The computer might ask, "Save changes?" If you reply by clicking Don't Save, the computer won't copy your latest changes to the disk. If you click Save instead, the computer will chat with you, just as if you chose Save from the File menu.)

The document will disappear from the screen, but you're still in the middle of using Teachtext. To prove you're still in the middle of using Teachtext, notice that the only words in the menu bar are the Teachtext words (File and Edit); you do *not* see the full set of standard words (File, Edit, View, Label, and Special).

Then go to the File menu, and choose **New**, **Open**, or **Quit**. Here's what happens. . . .

If you choose **New**, the computer will let you start typing a new document.

If you choose **Open** and then double-click the name of an old document you created earlier, the computer will put that document onto the screen and let you edit it.

If you choose **Quit**, the computer will finish using the application program (Teachtext), so the menu bar will show the full set of standard words (File, Edit, View, Label, and Special).

The screen will show the Teachtext icon next to all the other icons in the Macintosh HD window. Some of those icons are new; you automatically created them when you saved your documents. For example, if you created a document called "Stupidest Memo of 1995", you'll see a new icon marked "Stupidest Memo of 1995".

The Mac is smart: it remembers how each document was created. For example, it remembers that "Stupidest Memo of 1995" was created by using Teachtext.

If you explode the "Stupidest Memo of 1995" icon (by double-clicking it), the Mac notices that the memo was created from Teachtext. So the Mac deduces that you must be interested in Teachtext. Then the Mac automatically starts running Teachtext and makes Teachtext open that memo, so you see the memo on the screen and can edit it.

Here's the general rule: if you double-click a document's icon, the Mac notices which application program created the document; then the Mac makes that application program run and open the document.

Forget to Quit? When you finish using Teachtext, you're supposed to choose Quit from the File menu. If you forget to choose Quit, the Teachtext program is still in the computer's RAM chips (even if the screen shows other icons and other menu items).

To check whether the Teachtext program is still in the RAM chips, point at the **Finder icon** (which is in the screen's top right corner and shows a picture of a Mac); then hold down the mouse's button, so you see the **Finder menu**. If the menu mentions Teachtext, then Teachtext is still in the RAM chips! To remove Teachtext from the RAM chips, choose Teachtext from the Finder menu, then choose Quit from the File menu.

Problem: you try starting Teachtext (by double-clicking the Teachtext icon), but nothing seems to happen. Here's why nothing seems to happen: you're in Teachtext *already*, because you forgot to Quit from Teachtext the previous time you used Teachtext. **Solution: choose Quit from the File menu**; then your computer will act normally.

Final two steps When you finish using the computer, remember to take these two steps:

1. If you're in the middle of using an application program (such as Teachtext), get out of it by choosing Quit from the File menu.

2. When you see the usual desktop screen (with the menu bar saying File, Edit View, Label, and Special), choose Shut Down from the Special menu.

Other Macs If your Mac is a Performa and you tell it to save your Teachtext document, it puts the document in the Documents folder. That folder normally appears on the right side of your screen (between the hard-drive icon and the trash can).

If you're using System 6, the Finder icon and Finder menu are missing (unless you installed Multifinder).

Here's the stuff I was afraid to talk about earlier!

Manipulate the desktop

When you turn the Mac on, the screen shows you the **desktop**, which is a gray area on which you see the hard disk icon and the trash can icon. The hard disk icon might be exploded, to show you what's on the disk.

Each thing on the disk is called an **item**. The Mac can handle three kinds of items: **folders** (such as the System Folder), **application programs** (such as Teachtext), and **documents** (such as "Stupidest Memo of 1995"). Application programs and documents are called **files**.

The typical icon on the screen stands for an item or for a whole disk.

Now I'm going to explain how to manipulate the icons. If you're a beginner, experiment with just the icons that stand for junky documents (such as "Stupidest Memo of 1995"); if you fiddle with files that are more serious, you might be sorry!

Rename an icon To change an icon's name (such as "Stupidest Memo of 1995"), click the name under the icon. (Click the name, not the icon.) Then retype the name and press RETURN.

Move an icon If an icon's name (such as "Stupidest Memo of 1995") blocks the names of other icons, do this: enlarge the window (by clicking the zoom box) and then drag the icon to a blank part of the window.

If you want to move an icon into a different folder, just drag the icon there. Here's how. If the folder's exploded, so you see the folder's window, drag the icon to any blank part of that window. If the folder's *not* exploded, drag the icon you're moving to the folder's icon.

Create a new folder To create a new folder, choose **New Folder** from the File menu. That makes the computer create a new folder and put it in the active window. The new folder has nothing in it; it's empty. The computer temporarily names it "untitled Folder".

Invent a better name for the folder (such as "Sue"). Type that name, then press RETURN.

Copy an item To copy an icon (and the item it stands for), click the icon (so it turns black), then choose **Duplicate** from the File menu.

That makes the computer create a copy of the icon. The computer puts the copy just to the right of the original.

If the original icon was named "Joe" (for example), the copy is automatically named "Joe copy". If you don't like that name, retype it and press RETURN.

Other Macs System 6 says "Copy of Joe" instead of "Joe copy".

Trash items

To erase an item (folder, application program, or document), drag its icon to the **trash can**. You'll see the trash can bulge, because it contains the item.

The item will stay in the trash can until the computer **empties the trash**. To make the computer empty the trash, choose **Empty Trash** from the Special Menu, then click OK.

When the computer empties the trash, the trash can stops bulging: the trash items disappear forever, erased from the disk.

Peek in the trash If the trash can is bulging (because the trash hasn't been emptied yet), and you want to see what items the trash can contains, double-click the trash can's icon. You'll see all the items in the trash.

Rescue If you change your mind about which items you want to erase, you can rescue an item from the trash can: just move the item's icon out of the trash can!

To do that, you can drag the item's icon from the trash can to a different window. Another way to get the item out of the trash can is to click the item's icon, then choose **Put Away** from the File menu. That makes the computer put the item's icon back in the disk's window or folder that the icon originally came from.

Other Macs System 6 automatically empties the trash whenever you choose Shut Down from the Special Menu, restart the Mac, eject a floppy disk, copy an icon, or start running an application program (such as Teachtext).

Clock

The Mac contains a clock. To use it, choose **Alarm Clock** from the Apple menu. A window will appear.

Window's size The window can have two sizes: small (in which you see just one line of information) or large (in which you see three lines).

At the window's top right corner, to the right of the time, you'll see tiny icon, called a **lever**. Clicking that lever changes the window's size. Make the window large (by clicking the lever if necessary), so that you see three lines of information.

Current time The window's top line shows you the time that's on the Mac's clock.

If that time is wrong, reset the Mac's clock. To do that, click the simple clock icon (in the window's bottom *left* corner), edit the time in the window's middle line (by clicking the part of the time that's wrong, then retyping it), then press the RETURN key.

Date To see the date, click the calendar icon (which is in the middle of the window's bottom line). That makes the date appear in the window's middle line. If the date's wrong, edit it: click the part that's wrong, retype that part, then press RETURN.

Alarm You can set an alarm, so the computer will beep you at a certain time. Here's how.

Click the alarm-clock icon (in the window's bottom right corner). Edit the alarm time (in the window's middle line). Left of the alarm time, you'll see a tiny icon, which is the **alarm on/off switch**; click that switch, to make the alarm-clock icon look like it's ringing. Close the window.

That sets the alarm clock to the time you wish. When that time comes, the computer will beep at you, and the Apple icon (in the top left corner of the screen) will turn into a flashing clock.

To turn off the alarm, choose Alarm Clock from the Apple menu, click the alarm-clock icon (in the three-line window's bottom right corner), and click the alarm on/off switch (at the left edge of the window's middle line).

Battery Even when you turn the Mac off, its clock keeps running by using a battery inside the Mac.

After several years, the battery runs down. Then the clock becomes inaccurate, until you buy a new battery.

Floppy disks

Here's how to use floppy disks.

Initialize a blank floppy
You can buy a blank floppy disk and put it in your Mac. Here's how.

First, make sure you buy the right kind of blank floppy disk. The disk should be 3½-inch; and for a modern Mac (such as the Mac Color Classic), the disk should be high-density. (A high-density 3½-inch floppy disk has "HD" stamped on it. Two of the disk's corners have square holes in them. If you hold the disk up to a light, you can see light come through one of those two holes; the other hole is blocked.)

On the front of the Mac, you'll see a horizontal slot. Put the floppy disk into that slot. When you insert the disk, make sure the arrow engraved on the disk points at the computer, the disk's label is on *top* of the disk, and the disk's metal slider goes into the computer before the label does.

Push the disk all the way in.

If the disk is indeed 3½-inch, high-density, and blank, the computer says "This disk is unreadable" and asks, "Do you want to initialize it?" Click the word Initialize, then click the word Erase.

The computer says, "Please name this disk". Invent a name for the disk (up to 27 characters long); type the name and then press RETURN.

The computer says "Formatting disk". After 50 seconds (during which the computer formats the disk), the computer says "Verifying Format", then "Creating Directory".

Finally, an icon for the disk appears on the screen. Under the disk's icon, you see the disk name you invented.

If you double-click the disk's icon, you see the disk's window. That window has no items in it yet, since the disk is still empty.

Copy an item to the floppy
To copy an item from the hard disk to the floppy disk, drag the item's icon to the floppy-disk icon (or into the floppy-disk window).

Eject the floppy
When you finish using the floppy and want to remove it from the Mac, choose **Put Away** from the File menu. That makes the computer eject the floppy (unerased and unharmed). The floppy's icon disappears from the screen.

If you haven't done so yet, get a pen and scribble the floppy's name onto the floppy's label.

Copy a floppy item to your hard disk
Here's how to copy one item from a floppy disk to your hard disk.

If you haven't done so yet, insert the floppy disk into the Mac. You'll see the floppy disk's icon.

Double-click the floppy disk's icon, so you see the floppy disk's window. In that window, find the item you want to copy to the hard disk.

Drag that item's icon to the hard disk's icon (or into the hard disk's window or into one of the hard disk's folders).

Copy an entire floppy disk to your hard disk
Here's how to copy all of a floppy disk's information to your hard disk.

First, if you haven't done so yet, insert the floppy disk into the Mac. You'll see the floppy disk's icon.

Drag the floppy disk's icon to your hard disk's icon.

On your hard disk, the computer will create a new folder, which has the same name as the floppy disk and contains the same items.

Explode that folder, to check what's in it. If it contains another folder called System Folder, erase that System Folder (by dragging it to the trash), because your hard disk should contain just *one* System Folder.

Create a ghost icon
If a floppy's in the drive, and you're done using the floppy, try this experiment: close the floppy's windows, then choose **Eject Disk** from the Special menu. That makes the computer eject the floppy but leave the floppy's icon on the screen. The floppy's icon becomes covered with black dots, as if somebody had thrown black sand over its dead body. That icon is called a **ghost icon**, because it represents the spirit of a departed disk!

When you insert the next floppy into the drive, that floppy's icon appears on the screen also. That's how to get two floppy-disk icons on the screen simultaneously — even if you have just one floppy-disk drive.

Copy an entire floppy to another floppy
Here's how to copy an entire floppy to another floppy.

Grab the floppy you want to make a copy of, and put that floppy into the drive, so you see that floppy's icon. Then choose Eject Disk from the Special menu, so that the computer ejects the floppy but leaves its ghost icon on the screen.

Next, insert a *blank* floppy and let the computer initialize it. When the computer asks you to name the floppy, do *not* give it the same name as the floppy you're making a copy of. Pick a different name instead.

When the computer finishes initializing the blank floppy, the blank floppy's icon appears on the screen.

Drag the ghost icon to the blank floppy's icon. Click the word OK. Obey the computer's instructions about putting floppies in the drive. Then the computer will make the copy.

Make backups
To protect yourself against mistakes, accidents, and disasters, make extra copies of every floppy you own. The extra copies are called **backups**. For example, make a backup copy of the Macintosh System Tools disk.

If you're making a copy of a disk called "Joe", do *not* call the copy "Joe" also, because then you'll get confused about which disk is which. Instead, call the copy "Fred" or "Joey" or — better yet — "Copy of Joe" or "Joe copy".

Other Macs
For old Macs, buy floppy disks that are double-density (instead of high-density).

In System 6, the File menu doesn't offer a choice called "Put Away". Instead, eject the floppy by dragging the floppy's icon to the trash can. (Don't worry: that will *not* erase the floppy.)

In System 6, if you want to create a ghost icon, choose Eject from the File menu (instead of Eject Disk from the Special menu).

Clipboard

When you turn on the Mac, it creates a special document called the **Clipboard**, which sits in the RAM chips instead of on a disk.

Practically anytime you're using the Mac, you can choose **Show Clipboard** from the Edit menu. That makes the computer show you the Clipboard, by putting the Clipboard's window on the screen. When you finish looking at the Clipboard's window, click its close box.

Copy & Paste

Try this experiment. Create a document (by using an application program such as Teachtext). In that document, select a phrase (so the phrase becomes black). From the Edit menu, choose **Copy**. That makes the computer copy the phrase to the Clipboard. So if you look at the Clipboard's window (by choosing Show Clipboard from the Edit menu), you'll see that the Clipboard contains a copy of the phrase.

Next, try this experiment. Click anywhere in your Teachtext document (or any other normal document), then choose **Paste** from the Edit menu. That copies the Clipboard's phrase to where you clicked.

So the major Clipboard commands are Copy and Paste. Saying Copy lets you copy from a Teachtext document to the Clipboard; saying Paste lets you copy from the Clipboard to a Teachtext document.

Copy versus Cut

If you select a phrase in your Teachtext document and then say Copy, the phrase appears in *two* places: in your Teachtext document and also in the Clipboard. Instead of saying Copy, you can say **Cut**, which copies the phrase to the Clipboard but also erases the phrase from the Teachtext document, so that the phrase appears in just *one* place: the Clipboard.

Cut & Paste

Here's how to move a phrase to a different part of your document.

Select the phrase (so it becomes black). Choose Cut from the Edit menu (so the computer moves the phrase to the Clipboard).

Click in your document, where you want the phrase to appear. Click Paste from the Edit menu (so the computer copies the phrase from the Clipboard to where you clicked).

Four Clipboard commands

Altogether, the Edit menu contains four Clipboard commands:

Edit menu's command	What the computer will do
Show Clipboard	show the Clipboard's window
Copy	copy a selected phrase to the Clipboard
Cut	erase selected phrase but put copy of it on Clipboard
Paste	copy the Clipboard's phrase to where you clicked

What the Clipboard can hold

The Clipboard holds just one phrase at a time. So when you copy a new phrase to the Clipboard (by saying Copy or Cut), that new phrase replaces the Clipboard's previous phrase, which vanishes from the Clipboard.

When you put a phrase on the Clipboard, the Clipboard keeps remembering that phrase even if you switch to a different application program. For example, after copying a phrase from a Teachtext document to the Clipboard, you can switch from Teachtext to Superpaint (which draws pictures) and paste that phrase into the middle of your picture. You can also copy a selected part of a Superpaint picture to the Clipboard, then paste that picture into the middle of a Microsoft Word word-processing document.

Print on paper

To let your Mac print on paper, you must buy a printer and run a cable from the printer to the Mac.

Then tell the Mac what kind of printer you bought. To do that, choose **Chooser** from the Apple menu (so you see the **Chooser window**), then click the kind of printer you chose to buy, then click further details from the menus. When you finish, close the Chooser window (by clicking its close box).

Print a document

Suppose you've created a document by using Teachtext. To print the document onto paper, you can use two methods.

Method 1: while you're using Teachtext to edit the document (so that the document is on the screen), choose **Print** from the File menu, then click the word Print.

Method 2: while you're *not* using Teachtext, click the document's icon, then choose **Print** from the File menu and click the word Print.

Print a window

When you're not in the middle of running an application program, here's how to copy the active window onto paper: choose **Print Window** from the File menu, then click the word Print.

Other Macs

For System 6, choose Print Directory instead of Print Window, and click the word OK instead of the word Print.

Advanced selection

Open the hard drive's window, so you see several icons in the window. You've learned that if you click a white icon, it turns black (and all the other icons turn white).

Shift-click an icon

Here's a new rule: if you click an icon *while holding down the SHIFT key*, that icon changes color. If the icon was white, it turns black; if the icon was black, it turns white. The other icons are unaffected. That's called "**shift-clicking** the icon".

Select a group

Here's how to select a group of icons, so they all turn black and all other icons turn white.

To begin, click where there's no icon. That turns all icons white, so that you start with a clean slate.

Find the first icon that you want to be in the group, and click it. That icon turns black.

Shift-click all the other icons that you want in the group. Those icons turn black also, while the rest of the screen remains unchanged.

Select all

If you want *all* icons in the active window to turn black, just choose **Select All** from the Edit menu.

Drag a group

After you've selected a group of icons (so several icons are black), try dragging one of those icons. Surprise! As you drag that icon, it will move — and so will all the other icons in the group.

For example, if you drag that icon into a folder, you'll be dragging the whole group into the folder. If you drag that icon to the trash, you'll be dragging the whole group to the trash. If you drag that icon to a different disk instead, you'll be dragging the whole group to that disk.

COMMAND key

Between the OPTION key and the SPACE bar, you'll see a key that has a squiggle on it. The squiggle looks like a cloverleaf. On the Mac Color Classic and all other modern Macs, that key also has a picture of an Apple on it.

That key is called the **SQUIGGLE key** or **CLOVERLEAF key** or **APPLE key**. It's also called the **COMMAND key**, because it lets you give commands.

For example, suppose you want to close a window. One way to close the window is the click its close box. Another way is to choose **Close** from the File menu. But another way is to hold down the COMMAND key; and while you keep the COMMAND key down, tap the W key.

Here's how I discovered that trick. I looked at the File menu, saw the word "Close" there, and noticed that a squiggle and a W were next to the word "Close".

Discover more tricks! Look at each menu, and notice which words have squiggles and letters next to them!

The Finder and Teachtext let you give these squiggle commands:

Command	Meaning
COMMAND A	select ALL things in the window (so they blacken)
COMMAND C	COPY the selected phrase to the Clipboard
COMMAND D	DUPLICATE the selected icon
COMMAND E	EJECT the disk from the drive
COMMAND I	display INFORMATION about the selected icon
COMMAND N	create a NEW folder or document
COMMAND O	OPEN a folder, application program, or document
COMMAND P	PRINT onto paper
COMMAND Q	QUIT the application program
COMMAND S	SAVE the document (copy it from RAM to disk)
COMMAND V	paste from Clipboard and insert it here (^)
COMMAND W	WIPE out the WINDOW, by closing the window
COMMAND X	X out (cut, and move to the Clipboard)
COMMAND Y	YANK floppy out of the drive (or item out of trash)
COMMAND Z	ZAP the previous command; undo that command

Visual tricks

Here's how to make the Mac perform visual tricks.

Label menu Normally, an item's icon is black-and-white. (If the item's a folder, its icon has a slightly blue tinge.)

You can dramtically color an item's icon. To do that, click the item's icon, then choose a color from the **Label menu**. You can choose 7 colors: **Essential orange**, **Hot red**, **In-Progress pink**, **Cool sky-blue**, **Personal deep-blue**, **Project-1 green**, and **Project-2 brown**. The icon turns that color. (Since the icon is still selected, it's temporarily dark; but the darkness will go away when you click elsewhere on your screen.)

By choosing among those colors, you can color-code your work. Make the icons of all work-in-progress be colored In-Progress pink, so you can find those icons easily.

If you change your mind and want to remove the color from an icon, just click the icon and choose **None** from the Label menu.

Pretty views After you explode an icon and see its window, you can use the **View menu**, which gives you seven choices.

The normal choice is **Icon**. If you choose **Small Icon** instead, the icons in the active window appear small, so you can fit more icons in the window without having to scroll.

If you choose **Name** instead, the icons in the active window appear even smaller, and the computer automatically rearranges the icons so that the item names are in alphabetical order. The computer also tells you each item's size (in kilobytes), kind ("folder", "document", or "application program"), label (such as "In Progress") and date (when you last edited it). Before a folder's icon, you normally see the symbol ▸. If you click that symbol, you'll see all the items in the folder, and the symbol becomes ▾. When you finish examining the folder's items, click the ▾, so it becomes ▸ again

and the folder's items hide.

Instead of choosing Name (which lists the items alphabetically), you can choose **Date** (which lists the newest items first), **Size** (which lists the biggest items first), **Label** (which lists Essential orange items first), or **Kind** (which lists application programs first).

For the prettiest view, choose Small Icon from the View menu. Then, *while holding down the OPTION key*, choose **Clean Up** from the Special menu. That makes the computer rearrange all the icons, so they're in a neat column and don't overlap. (If you choose Icon instead of Small Icon, or you forget to hold down the OPTION key, the result isn't as pretty.)

Balloons At the top of the screen, you see the menu bar (which contains words such as File and Edit). In the menu bar, you see a balloon with a question mark in it.

That balloon's called the **Help icon**. If you point at it and hold down the mouse button, you'll see the **Help menu**.

For a wild experience, choose **Show Balloons** from the Help menu.

Then move the mouse pointer across the screen, and pause when the pointer's on an object (such as an icon or a menu choice). Don't click; just pause. Suddenly you see a little balloon, with a message explaining the object's purpose.

Go ahead: move the pointer from object to object, and read all the little balloons! You can even pull down a menu, pause at each menu choice, and read a balloon about each menu choice.

Then go ahead and use your Mac as you do normally — except that if you ever pause on an object, a balloon pops up.

Though balloons are fun, they can sometimes distract you from getting your work done. To stop seeing balloons, choose **Hide Balloons** from the Help menu.

Other Macs System 6 gives you no Label menu, no label choice in the View menu, no Help icon, and no balloons.

Closing thoughts

Before we leave the wonderful, wacky world of Mac and return to the ponderous, boring world of IBM, here are some closing thoughts.

Close all windows When you're not in the middle of running an application program, try this experiment. Click a window's close box *while holding down the OPTION key*.

That window will close; and while it closes, *all the other windows will close also*.

Make your Mac normal If you're sharing the Mac with friends who are beginners, put the Mac back to normal before you shut down. Then your friends won't be confused by the wild orgy you had with your Mac!

Here's how to put the Mac back to normal.

Get out of any application program (by choosing Quit from the File menu). If you've given a window a fancy view, return that window to Icon view (or Small Icon view). Then close all windows (by clicking a close box while holding down the OPTION key).

Drag the trash can to the screen's bottom right corner. Drag the hard-drive icon to the top right part of the screen.

Then choose Shut Down from the Special menu.

WINDOWS

STARTING

Windows is software that makes an IBM PC (or clone) resemble a Mac. Windows is published by **Microsoft**.

The earliest version of Windows that was good enough to be popular was **Windows 3**. Then came a major improvement, called **Windows 3.1**.

Next came **Windows 3.11**, which is very similar to Windows 3.1. It lists for $150. Discount dealers sell it for $89. If you already have Windows 1, 2, or 3, you can upgrade to Windows 3.11 for just $49. It usually comes on 3½-inch high-density floppies; if you don't have a 3½-inch drive, buy a 5¼-inch version instead. Windows 3.11 is also available in a souped-up version, called **Windows for Workgroups 3.11**.

Recently, Microsoft has been trying to develop a further improvement. It ought to be called "Windows 4"; but Microsoft decided to call it **Windows 95** instead, in the hope that it would be available for sale by the end of 1995. Its nickname is **Chicago**, because it doesn't go as far as a more way-out version nicknamed **Cairo**.

This chapter explains Windows 3.1, which is the version most businesses still use. (If you have Windows 3.11 or Windows for Workgroups 3.11, follow my instructions for Windows 3.1.)

Prepare for Windows

Before putting Windows 3.1 into your computer, you must buy MS-DOS (version 3.1 or higher) and fancy hardware. . . .

CPU Windows requires a fast CPU: a 286, 386, 486, or Pentium. Moreover, the most advanced parts of Windows refuse to work unless you buy a 386, 486, or Pentium.

Hard drive Windows requires a hard drive.

Floppy drive Since Windows comes on high-density floppy disks, you'll want a high-density floppy drive: 1.2M or 1.44M. If you don't have such a drive, you must mail the high-density floppy disks back to Microsoft and exchange them for low-density floppy disks.

RAM Windows 3.1 requires at least 1M of RAM. To run Windows quickly, completely, and without hassles, you need at least 4M of RAM. Some Windows programs need even more RAM: 8M!

Video card Windows requires a graphics video card: Hercules, CGA, EGA, or VGA. To run Windows pleasantly, get a VGA card and VGA color monitor; otherwise, the screen's display is crude and slow.

Mouse You should buy a mouse. Without a mouse, you must use awkward keystrokes that are hard to remember.

Buy the right stuff This chapter assumes you've bought enough software and hardware to run Windows well: MS-DOS 3.1 or later, a 386 or 486 or Pentium, a hard drive, a high-density floppy drive, 4M of RAM, a VGA color monitor, and a mouse.

Copy Windows to the hard disk

Here's how to copy Windows 3.1 to the hard disk.

Turn on the computer without any floppy in drive A. Windows 3.1 comes on a set of floppy disks; you get six 3½-inch disks or seven 5¼-inch disks. When you see the C prompt, put Windows Disk 1 into drive A and type "a:".

The computer will display an A prompt. Type "setup".

The computer will say "Windows Setup", then pause, then say "Welcome to Setup". Press ENTER twice.

The computer will say, "Please insert Disk 2." Insert it into drive A and press ENTER. (If you're using 5¼-inch disks, the computer will then say, "Please insert Disk 3." Insert it and press ENTER.)

The computer will say, "Please type your full name." Type your name. (At the end of your name, if your copy of Windows is owned by your company, press TAB and then type your company's name.) At the end of all your typing, press ENTER twice.

When the computer tells you, insert additional disks and press ENTER.

After you've inserted Disk 6 and pressed ENTER, the computer will say "Select a printer". You'll see an alphabetized list of printers. Tap the down-arrow key several times, until *your* printer appears on the screen and is blue. Press ENTER twice. (If you're using 5¼-inch disks, the computer will then say, "Please insert Disk 7." Insert it and press ENTER.)

The computer will look for programs on your hard disk. If the computer pauses at a program and waits for your response, tap the down-arrow key several times until the program's name is blue, then press ENTER.

On the screen, you'll see buttons labeled "Run Tutorial" and "Skip Tutorial". Choose "Skip Tutorial" by pressing the S key.

The computer will say, "Windows is now set up." Press D. You'll see a C prompt, like this:

```
C:\WINDOWS>
```

Turn off the computer, so you can start fresh.

Run Windows

To run Windows, turn on the computer without any floppy disk in drive A. When you see the C prompt, type "win" (and press ENTER).

A box containing information is called a **window**. You see this window:

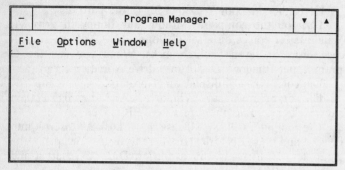

On the window's top line, you see the window's **title**: "Program Manager". That tells you the window is called the **Program Manager window**.

In the middle of that big window, you might see a small window, such as the **Main window**:

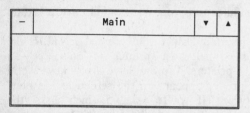

If you see the Main window (or another small window), do this: while holding down the Ctrl key, tap the F4 key. That makes the small window disappear, so the only window on the screen is the Program Manager window.

Position the mouse

Look at the computer's mouse. The mouse's **tail** is a cable that runs from the mouse to the computer. The area where the tail meets the mouse is called the mouse's **ass**.

The mouse's underside — its belly — has a hole in it, and a ball in the hole.

Put the mouse on your desk and directly in front of your right arm. Make the mouse lie flat (so its ball rubs against the desk). **Make the mouse face you** so you don't see its ass.

Move the arrow

Move the mouse across your desk. As you move the mouse, remember to keep it flat and facing you.

On the screen, you'll see an arrow, which is called the **mouse pointer**. As you move the mouse, the arrow moves also. If you move the mouse to the left, the arrow moves to the left. If you move the mouse to the right, the arrow moves to the right. If you move the mouse toward you, the arrow moves down. If you move the mouse away from you, the arrow moves up.

Practice moving the arrow by moving the mouse. Remember to keep the mouse facing you at all times.

If you want to move the arrow far and your desk is small, move the mouse until it reaches the desk's edge; then lift the mouse off the desk, lay the mouse gently on the middle of the desk, and rub the mouse across the desk in the same direction as before.

Choose from a menu

The most important part of the arrow is its tip, which is called the **hot spot**.

For an experiment, move the arrow so its hot spot (tip) is in the middle of the word "File". When you do that, you're **pointing at** the word "File".

On the top of the mouse, you'll see 2 or 3 rectangular buttons you can press. **The main button is the one on the left.** That's the only button Windows uses. Tapping it is called **clicking**. So to **click**, tap the left button.

While you're pointing at the word "File", click (by tapping the left button). That's called **clicking "File"**.

When you click "File", you'll see this **File menu**:

```
New...
Open
Move...
Copy...
Delete
Properties...
Run...
Exit Windows...
```

In that menu, the bottom choice is "Exit Windows". If you choose "Exit Windows", the computer will stop using Windows.

Try it! Click "Exit Windows" (by moving the arrow there and then tapping the left button). You'll see this window:

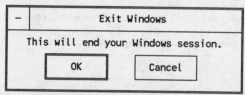

If you want to exit from Windows and make the screen show a C prompt, click "OK" (by moving the arrow there and then clicking). If you do *not* want to exit from Windows, click "Cancel" instead.

That whole procedure for exiting from Windows can be summarized in one sentence:

Choose "Exit Windows" from the File menu, then click OK.

Try that procedure! Notice it involves these three steps. . . .

Step 1: choose from a menu bar
The first step is to choose "File" from this menu:

```
File    Options    Window    Help
```

That menu's in a horizontal box. The box is called a **menu bar**.

To choose a word (such as "File") from a menu bar, you can use three methods:

Mouse method: by using the mouse, click the word you want.

Arrow-key method: move to the menu (by tapping the Alt key), move to the word you want (by pressing the right-arrow key several times, if necessary), then press ENTER.

Underlined-letter method: move to the menu (by tapping the Alt key), then type the word's underlined letter (for example, type the F in "File").

The mouse method is the simplest. Use the other methods if your mouse is broken or missing or makes your flesh crawl.

Step 2: choose from a pull-down menu
After you choose "File", this menu appears underneath "File":

```
New...
Open
Move...
Copy...
Delete
Properties...
Run...
Exit Windows...
```

That menu is a vertical list that "falls down" from the word "File". It's called a **pull-down menu**.

To choose a command (such as "Exit Windows") from a pull-down menu, you can use the same three methods:

Mouse method: by using the mouse, click the command you want.

Arrow-key method: move to the command you want (by pressing the down-arrow key several times), then press ENTER.

Underlined-letter method: type the underlined letter (for example, type the x in "Exit Windows").

Step 3: choose from a dialog box
After you choose "Exit Windows", this window appears:

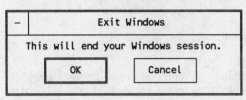

That window warns that you're about to exit from Windows and asks you whether you're sure. If you're sure you want to exit from Windows, click "OK"; otherwise, click "Cancel".

Since that window lets the computer chat with you about your intentions, it's called a **dialog box**. (According to English teachers, it ought to be called a "dialogue box", but computer nerds refuse to type the "ue".)

In the dialog box, each major choice (such as "OK" and "Cancel") is called a **button**. Each button looks like a rectangle. Usually the "OK" button is **highlighted** (its sides are made of doubled or thickened lines).

To communicate with the computer, press one of the buttons. To press a button, you can use two methods:

Mouse method: by using the mouse, click the button you want.

ENTER method: to press the highlighted button (which is usually "OK"), press ENTER; to press a different button instead, move to it (by pressing the TAB key several times) so the button is highlighted, then press ENTER.

Here's a short cut: to press the "Cancel" button, just press the Esc key (which means "Escape and Cancel").

Three dots
Notice that the bottom of the File menu says "Exit Windows...". The three dots (...) tell you that if you choose that command, you'll encounter a dialog box.

Resize a window
You can make a window be three sizes: **maximum**, **normal**, or **minimum**.

A **maximum window** consumes the whole screen.
A **normal** window fills about half the screen.
A **minimum window** is shrunk so it's a tiny picture, called an **icon**.

The symbol for maximum is ▲ (a triangle pointing up).
The symbol for minimum is ▼ (a triangle pointing down).
The symbol for normal is ▲▼ (a pair of balanced triangles).

If a window is normal, its top right corner contains the symbols ▼ and ▲. Using your mouse, click ▼ to make the window become minimum; click ▲ to make the window become maximum.

If a window is maximum, its top right corner contains the symbols for minimum and normal. Click one of those symbols to make the window change size.

If a window is minimum, it's just a tiny picture — an icon. Try clicking that icon. Then you'll see a menu. From the menu, choose **Maximize** (to make the window become maximum) or **Restore** (to make the window become whatever size it was previously).

Try it! Make the Program Manager's window become maximum, minimum, and normal again.

Drag
To **drag** an object, point at it (by using the mouse), then hold down the mouse's left button, and while you keep that button down, move the mouse.

For example, try this experiment. Make the Program Manager's window be minimum, so it's just an icon. Point at the icon (by using the mouse), then hold down the mouse's left button, and while you keep that button down, move the mouse. As you move the mouse, the icon moves. You can drag the icon anywhere on the screen! Try it! Here's the rule: if a window is minimum (so it's just an icon), and you want to move it to a different part of the screen, drag it.

Here's another experiment to try. Make the Program Manager's window be normal, so it fills about half the screen. At the top of that window, you'll see the words "Program Manager". Those words are called the window's **title**. Point at that title ("Program Manager"), then drag it to a different part of the screen (by holding down the mouse's button as you move the mouse). As you drag the title, you'll also be automatically dragging the entire window. Here's the rule: **to move a normal window, drag its title**.

A normal window is a rectangle. To change its width, drag its right-hand edge. To change its height, drag its bottom edge. To change its width and height simultaneously, drag its bottom right corner.

Try it! Make the Program Manager be a normal window, then change its width and height by dragging its edges and bottom right corner.

Scroll arrows
Here's another series of experiments to try.

Make the Program Manager be a maximum window, so it consumes the whole screen. Inside that big window, you'll see five icons (little pictures), called **Accessories**, **Games**, **StartUp**, **Applications**, and **Main**. If somebody else was using the computer, you might see some extra icons.

Make the Program Manager be a normal window (so it fills about half the screen). You'll probably still see those icons in the Program Manager window.

Make the Program Manager's window be smaller, by dragging its edges or bottom right corner. Make the window too small to hold all the icons, so you see just *some* of the icons. Instead of seeing everything that belongs in the Window, you see just a **partial view**.

When you see a partial view, you see arrows near the window's corners. By clicking the arrows, you can shift your view. To see icons farther to the right, click the right-arrow. (To see icons even *farther* to the right, click the right-arrow again. To see icons *very* far to the right, click the right-arrow repeatedly — or point at the right-arrow and then hold down the mouse's left button awhile.) To see icons farther to the left, click the left-arrow; to see icons that are higher, click the up-arrow; to see icons that are lower, click the down-arrow.

Try it! Click those arrows! They're called **scroll arrows**.

ACCESSORIES

Make the Program Manager window be rather large, so it consumes most of the screen but not the top quarter of the screen. In that window, look for the **Accessories** icon. (If you don't see that icon, adjust the window by using the scroll arrows.) **Double-click** the Accessories icon. (To double-click the icon, move the arrow to the icon, then tap the mouse's left button twice *quickly*, so the two taps are less than .3 seconds apart.)

You'll see the **Accessories window**. In that window, you'll see 13 icons: **Write, Paintbrush, Terminal, Notepad, Recorder, Cardfile, Calendar, Calculator, Clock, Object Packager, Character Map, Media Player,** and **Sound Recorder**. Each of those icons is called an **accessory**, because it's an extra "jewel" that comes with Windows at no extra charge.

The following accessories are the most useful.

Clock

To use the Clock, double-click the Clock icon. You'll see the **Clock window**, with a picture of a clock in it.

You can choose two kinds of clocks. An **analog clock** has an hour hand, minute hand, and second hand. A **digital clock** has no hands: it shows just digits.

The first time you (or your colleagues) ask for the clock, Windows 3.1 shows a digital clock. To switch from digital to analog, choose **Analog** from the **Settings menu**. (To do that, click the word "Settings", then click the word "Digital".) To switch back to a digital clock, choose **Digital** from the Settings menu.

The clock normally shows the correct time. (If the clock's time is wrong, here's how to reset it: exit from Windows, then give the "time" command from the DOS prompt.)

The clock also shows the date.

The clock keeps on ticking — silently. If you want to put yourself into a trance, watch the analog clock's second hand move. (It's better than counting sheep.)

If you want the clock to be larger, maximize its window by clicking ▲. Then the clock will fill the whole screen. That's how to turn your entire $2,000 computer into a $2 clock! But hey, it's a *high-tech* clock! To freak out your friends, hide the keyboard and system unit under the desk, so your friends see just the screen displaying the analog clock. That high-tech clock for rich people belongs to a style of art called "nouveau kitsch — the Rolex for the thinking bitch".

If you want the clock to be tiny, minimize its window by clicking ▼. Then the clock will be a tiny icon. Even though it's tiny, it still runs! Though it's too tiny to show the seconds, it still shows the correct hour and minutes.

<u>**Close**</u> When you finish using the clock, **close** it. Here's how.

Make the Clock window be normal or maximum. In the Clock window's top left corner, you'll see a square containing a horizontal bar:

```
┌───┐
│ - │
└───┘
```

That square is called the **control box**. When you finish using the Clock window, double-click the control box. That makes the Clock window disappear.

Calculator

To use the Calculator, double-click the Calculator icon. You'll see the **Calculator window**, containing a picture of a pocket calculator.

To compute 42+5, click the calculator's 4 key (by using the mouse to point at the 4 key and then clicking), then click 2, then +, then 5, then =. The calculator will show the answer, 47.

Instead of using the mouse, you can do that calculation a different way, by using the computer's keyboard. Try it! On the computer's keyboard, tap the 4 key, then the 2 key, then (while holding down the SHIFT key) the + key, then 5, then =. The calculator will show 47.

Try fancier calculations, by pressing these calculator buttons:

Button	Meaning
+	plus
-	minus
*	times
/	divided by
=	total
.	decimal point
C	clear
Back	backspace

Warning: in versions of Windows created before 1995, the computer has trouble subtracting numbers that end in ".01". For example, if you compute 2.01 minus 2, the correct answer is .01, but the computer mistakenly says 0 instead.

You can choose two kinds of calculators. A **standard calculator** is small and cute: it does just arithmetic. A **scientific calculator** is big and imposing: it includes extra buttons, so you can do advanced math.

The first time you (or your colleagues) ask for the calculator, the computer shows a standard calculator (small and cute). If you want the calculator to be scientific instead, choose **Scientific** from the **View menu**. (To do that, click the word "View", then click the word "Scientific".) Then you'll see extra buttons, such as these:

Button	Meaning
PI	pi (which is 3.14159265359)
x^2	squared
x^3	cubed
n!	factorial

For example, if you click the PI button, the computer will say 3.14159265359. If you click the 7 button and then say "squared" (by pressing the x^2 button), the computer will multiply 7 by itself and say 49 (which is called "7 squared"). If you click the 7 button and then say "cubed" (by pressing the x^3 button), the computer will do "7 times 7 times 7" and say 343 (which is called "7 cubed"). If you click the 7 button and then say "**factorial**" (by pressing the n! button), the computer will multiply together all the numbers up to 7 (1 times 2 times 3 times 4 times 5 times 6 times 7) and say 5040 (which is called "7 factorial").

The scientific calculator also contains buttons that help you handle big exponents, logarithms, trigonometry, statistics, hexadecimal numbers, and assembly-language programming. I'll explain the mathematical concepts behind those buttons later, on page 384 (exponents), 385 (logarithms), 396 (trigonometry), 573 (hexadecimal numbers), and 584 (assembly-language programming). If you're adventurous, just go push buttons and see what happens: no matter which button you press, the computer won't blow up!

After making the calculator be scientific, you can make it become standard again by choosing **Standard** from the View menu.

When you finish using the calculator, double-click its control box.

Write

When you buy Windows, you get a word-processing program free! That word-processing program is called **Write**. It's one of the Windows accessories.

To use Write, double-click the Write icon. You'll see the **Write window**. Maximize it by clicking ▲.

Now you can do word processing: you can type words and sentences simply. Try it! Type whatever sentences you wish to make up. For example, try typing a memo to your friends, or a story, or a poem. Be creative! Whatever you type is called a **document**.

While you're typing, you see the symbol ¤. That symbol appears at the end of what you've typed; that symbol marks the end of your document.

<u>**Use the keyboard**</u> The following hints will help you type. . . .

To capitalize a letter of the alphabet, type that letter while holding down the **SHIFT key**. (One SHIFT key is next to the Z key; the other SHIFT key is next to the ? key. Each SHIFT key has an up-arrow on it.)

To capitalize a whole passage, tap the **CAPS LOCK key**, then type the passage. The computer will automatically capitalize the passage as you type it. When you finish typing the passage, tap the CAPS LOCK key again: that tells the computer to stop capitalizing.

If you make a mistake, press the **BACKSPACE key**. That makes the computer erase the last character you typed. (The BACKSPACE key is in the top right corner of the keyboard's main section. It's to the right of the + key, and it has a left-arrow on it.)

To erase the last *two* characters you typed, press the BACKSPACE key *twice*.

If you're typing near the screen's right edge, and you type a word that's too long to fit on the screen, the computer will automatically move the word to the line below.

When you finish a paragraph, press the **ENTER key**. That makes the computer move to the line underneath so you can start typing the next paragraph.

If you want to double-space between the paragraphs, press the ENTER key *twice*.

If you want to indent a line (such as the first line of a paragraph), begin the line by pressing the **TAB key**. The computer will indent the line a half inch.

To make a phrase toward the right, press the TAB key several times before typing the phrase. To move a phrase down, press the ENTER key several times before typing the phrase.

Like DOS, Windows lets you type these special characters:

128 Ç	144 É	160 á	225 ß
129 ü	145 æ	161 í	
130 é	146 Æ	162 ó	227 ¶
131 â	147 ô	163 ú	
132 ä	148 ö	164 ñ	230 µ
133 à	149 ò	165 Ñ	
134 å	150 û	166 ª	241 ±
135 ç	151 ù	167 °	
136 ï	152 ÿ	168 ¿	246 ÷
137 ë	153 Ö		
138 è	154 Ü	170 ¬	248 °
139 ï	155 ¢	171 ½	249 •
140 î	156 £	172 ¼	250 ·
141 ì	157 ¥	173 ¡	
142 Ä	158 P	174 «	
143 Å	159 ƒ	175 »	253 ²

For example, here's how to type the symbol ñ, whose code number is 164. Hold down the Alt key; and while you keep holding down the Alt key, type 164 *by using the numeric keypad* (the number keys on the far right side of the keyboard). When you finish typing 164, lift your finger from the Alt key, and you'll see ñ on your screen! Try it!

But Windows goes beyond DOS, by letting you also use this chart:

		0192 À	0224 à
	0161 ¡	0193 Á	0225 á
0130 ,	0162 ¢	0194 Â	0226 â
0131 ƒ	0163 £	0195 Ã	0227 ã
0132 „	0164 ¤	0196 Ä	0228 ä
0133 …	0165 ¥	0197 Å	0229 å
0134 †	0166 ¦	0198 Æ	0230 æ
0135 ‡	0167 §	0199 Ç	0231 ç
0136 <	0168 ¨	0200 È	0232 è
0137 ‰	0169 ©	0201 É	0233 é
0138 Š	0170 ª	0202 Ê	0234 ê
0139 ‹	0171 «	0203 Ë	0235 ë
0140 Œ	0172 ¬	0204 Ì	0236 ì
	0173 -	0205 Í	0237 í
	0174 ®	0206 Î	0238 î
	0175 ¯	0207 Ï	0239 ï
	0176 °	0208 Ð	0240 ð
0145 '	0177 ±	0209 Ñ	0241 ñ
0146 '	0178 ²	0210 Ò	0242 ò
0147 ¡	0179 ³	0211 Ó	0243 ó
0148 "	0180 ´	0212 Ô	0244 ô
0149 •	0181 µ	0213 Õ	0245 õ
0150 –	0182 ¶	0214 Ö	0246 ö
0151 —	0183 ·	0215 ×	0247 ÷
0152 ˜	0184 ¸	0216 Ø	0248 o
0153 ™	0185 ¹	0217 Ù	0249 ù
0154 š	0186 º	0218 Ú	0250 ú
0155 ›	0187 »	0219 Û	0251 û
0156 œ	0188 ¼	0220 Ü	0252 ü
	0189 ½	0221 Ý	0253 ý
	0190 ¾	0222 Þ	0254 þ
0159 Ÿ	0191 ¿	0223 ß	0255 ÿ

For example, here's how to type the symbol ã, whose code number is 0227: while holding down the Alt key, type 0227 on the numeric keypad.

Scroll through documents If your document contains too many lines to fit on the screen, the screen will show just *part* of the document. To see the rest of the document, click the scroll arrows.

Insert characters To insert extra characters anywhere in your document, click where you want the extra characters to appear (by moving the mouse's pointer there and then pressing the mouse's button). Then type the extra characters.

For example, suppose you typed the word "fat" and want to change it to "fault". Click between the "a" and the "t", then type "ul".

(When you're using Windows, notice that you click *between* letters, not *on* letters.)

As you type the extra characters, the screen's other characters move out of the way to make room for the extra characters.

While you're inserting the extra characters, you can erase nearby mistakes by pressing the BACKSPACE key or DELETE key. The BACKSPACE key erases the character that's *before* the mouse's pointer. The DELETE key erases the character that's *after* the mouse's pointer.

Split a paragraph Here's how to split a long paragraph in half, to form two short paragraphs.

Decide which word should begin the second short paragraph. Click the left edge of that word's first letter.

Press the BACKSPACE key (to erase the space before that word), then press the ENTER key. Now you've split the long paragraph in two!

If you want to double-space between the two short paragraphs, press the ENTER key again. If you want to indent the second paragraph, press the TAB key.

Combine paragraphs After typing two paragraphs, here's how to combine them, to form a single paragraph that's longer.

Click at the end of the first paragraph. Press the DELETE key several times, to delete unwanted ENTERs and TABs. Now you've combined the two paragraphs into one!

Then press the SPACE bar (to insert a space between the two sentences).

Movement keys To move to different parts of your document, you can use your mouse. To move faster, press these keys instead:

Key you press	Where the pointer will move
right-arrow	right to the next character
left-arrow	left to the previous character
down-arrow	down to the line below
up-arrow	up to the line above
END	right to the end of the line
HOME	left to the beginning of the line
PAGE DOWN	down to the next screenful
PAGE UP	up to the previous screenful
Ctrl with right-arrow	right (to next word or punctuation symbol)
Ctrl with left-arrow	left (to beginning of a word or punctuation)
Ctrl with PAGE DOWN	down to the screen's bottom line
Ctrl with PAGE UP	up to the screen's top line
Ctrl with END	down to the end of the document
Ctrl with HOME	up to the beginning of the document

Menu bar While you're using Write, the top of the screen shows this menu bar:

<u>F</u>ile	<u>E</u>dit	Fi<u>n</u>d	<u>C</u>haracter	<u>P</u>aragraph	<u>D</u>ocument	<u>H</u>elp

Let's use that menu bar. . . .

Underline Here's how to underline a phrase (<u>like this</u>). Choose **Underline** from the **Character menu**. Type the phrase. Then choose **Regular** from the Character menu.

Bold Here's how to make a phrase be bold (**like this**). Choose **Bold** from the Character menu. Type the phrase. Then choose Regular from the Character menu.

Here's how to make a phrase be bold and underlined (**<u>like this</u>**). Choose Bold from the Character menu. Choose Underline from the Character menu. Type the phrase. Then choose Regular from the Character menu.

Italics Here's how to italicize a phrase (*like this*). Choose **Italics** from the Character menu. Type the phrase. Then choose Regular from the Character menu. (That technique works only if your printer can italicize.)

Select text Here's how to dramatically change a phrase you typed.

Point at the phrase's beginning, then drag to the phrase's end (while holding down the mouse's left button). The whole phrase turns black. Turning the phrase black is called **selecting the phrase**.

Then say what to do to the phrase. For example, choose one of these activities:

To underline the phrase, choose Underline from the Character menu.
To make the phrase be bold, choose Bold from the Character menu.
To italicize the phrase, choose Italics from the Character menu.
To delete the phrase, press the DELETE key.
To replace the phrase, just type whatever words you want the phrase to become.

To copy the phrase (so it appears twice), do this:
while holding down the Alt key, click where you want the copy to appear.

To move the phrase (so it appears just in the new location), do this:
while holding down the Alt and SHIFT keys, click where you want the phrase to appear.

Other ways to select The usual way to select a phrase is to point at the phrase's beginning, then drag to the phrase's end. But sometimes other methods are faster! To select a phrase, choose one of these methods:

Method 1: point at the phrase's beginning, then drag to the phrase's end.
Method 2: click the phrase's beginning; then while holding down the SHIFT key, click the phrase's end.

Method 3: by using your keyboard's movement keys (such as the up-arrow, down-arrow, left-arrow, and right-arrow keys), move to the phrase's beginning; then while holding down the SHIFT key, use the movement keys to move to the phrase's end.

Method 4: to select just one word, double-click in the middle of it.
Method 5: to select a sentence, click in the middle of the sentence while holding down the Ctrl key.

Method 6: to select a whole line, click the screen's left edge, left of the line.
Method 7: to select a whole paragraph, double-click the screen's left edge, left of the paragraph.
Method 8: to select the whole document, click the screen's left edge while holding down the Ctrl key.

Center Here's how to center a title. Choose **Centered** from the **Paragraph menu**. Type the title. At the end of the title, press ENTER. Then choose **Normal** from the Paragraph menu.

Here's how to center a title you typed previously: click anywhere in the title, then choose Center from the Paragraph menu. Here's how to uncenter a title you typed previously: click anywhere in the title, then choose Normal from the Paragraph menu.

Save To copy the document onto the disk, choose **Save** from the **File menu**.

Then invent a name for your document. The name must be short: no more than 8 letters. For example, the name can be "jennifer" or "al". Type the name you wish and press ENTER.

That makes the computer copy the document onto the hard disk. For example, if you named the document "jennifer", the computer will put in your hard disk's WINDOWS subdirectory a file called "JENNIFER.WRI", which means "JENNIFER created by the WRIte program".

Afterwards, if you change your mind and want to do more editing, go ahead! Edit the document some more. When you finish that editing, save it by choosing Save from the File menu again.

Print To copy the document onto paper, choose **Print** from the File menu, then press ENTER.

Finish When you finish working on a document, choose **New**, **Open**, or **Exit** from the File menu.

If you choose **New**, the computer will let you start typing a new document. If you choose **Open** and then double-click the name of an old document, the computer will put that document onto the screen and let you edit it. If you choose **Exit**, the computer will stop using Write and let you use a different accessory instead.

Before the computer obeys New, Open, or Exit, it checks whether you saved your document. If you didn't save your document, the computer asks, "Save current changes?" If you click "Yes", the computer copies your document's most recent version to the hard disk; if you click "No" instead, the computer ignores and forgets your most recent editing.

Paintbrush

When you buy Windows, you get a paint program free! That program, called **Paintbrush**, lets you paint pictures. It's one of the Windows accessories.

To use Paintbrush, double-click the Paintbrush icon. You'll see the **Paintbrush window**. Maximize it by clicking ▲.

Move the mouse pointer to the screen's middle. Then drag (move the mouse while holding down the mouse's left button). As you drag, you'll be drawing a squiggle.

For example, try drawing a smile. To do that, put the mouse pointer where you want the smile to begin (at the smile's top left corner), then depress the mouse's left button while you draw the smile. When you finish drawing the smile, lift the mouse's button. Then draw the rest of the face!

Colors When you draw, you're normally drawing in black.

At the screen's bottom, you'll see 28 colors: red, yellow, green, etc. To draw in one of those colors instead of in black, click the color you want.

Line Here's how to draw a line that's perfectly straight.

At the left side of the screen, you'll see many icons. One of the icons is a diagonal line. Click it. Put the mouse pointer in the screen's middle, where you want the line to begin, and drag to where you want the line to end.

When you finish drawing lines and want **to draw squiggles instead, click the brush icon** (which is above the line icon).

Rectangle Here's how to draw a rectangle whose sides are perfectly straight.

At the left side of the screen, you'll see two icons that are rectangles. Click the left rectangle.

Put the mouse pointer in the screen's middle, where you want the rectangle's top left corner to be. Drag to where you want the rectangle's opposite corner.

Spray Here's how to vandalize your own drawing, by using a can of spray paint!

At the left side of the screen, you'll see an icon that's a can of spray paint. Click it. Put the mouse in the screen's middle, where you want to begin spraying, and drag!

Erase To erase a mistake, click the simple eraser icon, which is *above the brush icon*.

Then drag across the part of your drawing that you want to erase. The part you drag across will become white.

Thickness At the screen's bottom left corner, you'll see eight horizontal lines, ranging from "thin" to "thick". Click the thickness you want.

For example, if you click the thickest line, everything you draw will be very thick. Your squiggles, lines, and rectangles will all be very thick — as if you were using a brush that's very thick and wide. The eraser will be thick and wide too, and so will the nozzle on the can of spray paint.

Save To copy your drawing onto the disk, choose **Save** from the **File menu**.

Then invent a name for your document. The name must be short: no more than 8 letters. For example, the name can be "jennifer" or "al". Type the name you wish and press ENTER.

That makes the computer copy the document onto the hard disk. For example, if you named the document "jennifer", the computer will put in your hard disk's WINDOWS subdirectory a file called "JENNIFER.BMP", which means "JENNIFER the Bit MaP". (A **bit map** is a picture made of many itty-bitty dots.)

Afterwards, if you change your mind and want to improve the drawing, go ahead! When you finish making improvements, save them by choosing Save from the File menu again.

Print To copy the drawing onto paper, choose **Print** from the File menu, then press ENTER.

Unfortunately, the typical printer can't print colors. It prints black-and-white instead.

Instead of printing a dark color (such as blue), the printer will print black. Instead of printing a light color (such as yellow), the printer will print white.

Finish When you finish fiddling with a drawing, choose **New**, **Open**, or **Exit** from the File menu.

If you choose **New**, the computer will let you start a new drawing. If you choose **Open** and then double-click the name of an old drawing, the computer will put that drawing onto the screen. If you choose **Exit**, the computer will exit from Paintbrush so you can use a different accessory instead.

If you say New, Open, or Exit without saving your drawing, the computer asks, "Save current changes?" If you click "Yes", the computer copies your drawing to the hard disk; if you click "No" instead, the computer ignores and forgets your recent drawing efforts.

Calendar

To use the Calendar, double-click the Calendar icon. You'll see the **Calendar window**. Near the top of the window, you'll see the current time and date. (If the time and date are wrong, here's how to reset them: exit from Windows, then give the "time" and "date" commands from the DOS prompt.)

Choose **Month** from the **View menu**. You'll see a calendar of the entire month. On that calendar, today's date is blackened and surrounded by the symbols > and <.

Near the top of the window, you'll see a left-arrow icon and a right-arrow icon. To see a calendar of *next* month, click the right-arrow icon. To see a calendar of the month after that, click the right-arrow icon again. By clicking the right-arrow icon repeatedly, you can see the calendar of any month in the future (up through the year 2099).

To see a calendar of the previous month, click the left-arrow icon. By clicking the left-arrow icon repeatedly, you can see any month in the past (back through 1980).

When you finish using the calendar, choose **Exit** from the Calendar's **File menu**.

Close

When you finish using the accessories, close the Accessories window by double-clicking its control box.

Make the Program Manager window be normal.

In that window, you'll see the **Main** icon. Double-click it.

You'll see the **Main window**, which contains 8 icons: **File Manager**, **Control Panel**, **Print Manager**, **Clipboard Viewer**, **MS-DOS Prompt**, **Windows Setup**, **PIF Editor**, and **Read Me**.

Here's how to use the icons that are popular.

MS-DOS Prompt

The following trick lets you leave Windows *temporarily*, give a DOS command, and then return to Windows.

Double-click the DOS Prompt icon. The computer will say:

```
C:\WINDOWS>
```

Then give any DOS commands you wish. (For example, if you type "dir" and press ENTER, the computer will show you a directory.)

When you finish playing with DOS commands, type "exit" (and press ENTER). The computer will return to Windows, and you'll see the Main window again.

Here's a summary of what I said: **if you double-click the DOS Prompt icon, the computer lets you type DOS commands until you type "exit"**. Notice that the computer keeps waiting for you to type "exit". If you never type "exit", the computer gets frustrated. Make your computer happy: type "exit", so the computer can return to Windows and breathe a sigh of relief.

So if you're using Windows and want to give DOS commands, you can use two methods.

Method 1: leave Windows temporarily (by double-clicking the DOS Prompt icon), then give DOS commands, then type "exit" to return to Windows.

Method 2: leave Windows permanently. To do that, choose Exit Windows from the Program Manager's File menu (or double-click the Program Manager's control box).

File Manager

To manipulate the files on your hard disk, double-click the File Manager icon.

You'll see the **File Manager window** and the **Directory Tree window**.

In the Directory Tree window, you'll see the names of your hard disk's subdirectories. The names are in alphabetical order.

By using your keyboard's up-arrow and down-arrow keys, move the cursor to the subdirectory that interests you. (For example, try moving the cursor to the WINDOWS subdirectory.) Then press ENTER.

You'll see the names of your files in the subdirectory. The names are in alphabetical order. Move the cursor to the file that interests you (by using the mouse).

For example, try moving the cursor to a file you invented, such as JENNIFER.WRI.

Then say what to do to the file. Choose one of these activities:

To delete the file, press the DELETE key. Then press ENTER twice.

To peek at the file, press ENTER. When you finish peeking at the file, double-click the file's close box.

To rename the file, choose **Rename** from the **File menu**. Then type the new name you're inventing (such as JENNY.WRI). Make sure you type the correct three-letter ending: for example, type ".WRI" at the end of a Write document's name; type ".BMP" at the end of a Paintbrush drawing's name. After typing the three-letter ending, press ENTER.

When you finish using the File Manager, choose **Exit** from the File menu.

Control Panel

To change how Windows acts, double-click the Control Panel icon.

You'll see the **Control Panel window**, which contains 12 icons: **Color, Fonts, Ports, Mouse, Desktop, Keyboard, Printers, International, Date/Time, 386 Enhanced, Drivers**, and **Sound**. (The 386 Enhanced icon appears just if you have a 386 or 486 or Pentium, and you have at least 2 megabytes of RAM.)

Here's how to use icons that are popular.

<u>**Date/Time**</u> To reset the date and time without leaving Windows, double-click the Date/Time icon.

The computer will say what it thinks the date and time are. If the computer is wrong, click the part of the date or time you want to change.

To the right of where you clicked, you'll see an up-arrow and a down-arrow. To make the date or time later, click the up-arrow; to make the date or time earlier, click the down-arrow.

When the date and time look correct, click "OK".

<u>**Color**</u> To change the screen's colors, double-click the Color icon. You'll see the **Color window**. Near that window's top-right corner, you'll see an arrow pointing down at a hyphen. Click that arrow.

You'll see this list of color schemes:

```
Windows Default
Arizona
Black Leather Jacket
Bordeaux
Cinnamon
Designer
Emerald City
Fluorescent
Hotdog Stand
LCD Default Screen Settings
LCD Reversed - Dark
Mahogany
Monochrome
Ocean
Pastel
Patchwork
Plasma PS
Rugby
The Blues
Tweed
Valentine
Wingtips
```

Press your keyboard's HOME key (to make sure you're at the top of the list). Tap your keyboard's down-arrow key several times, until you reach your favorite color scheme. Then press ENTER. All the screen's colors will change and become your favorites!

<u>**Printers**</u> If you bought a font cartridge for your laser printer, tell the computer which font cartridge you bought. To do that, double-click the Printers icon.

You'll see the **Printers window**.

Click the word "Setup". At the screen's bottom left corner, you'll see a list of font cartridges. (To see the bottom of the list, click the scroll arrow next to it.) Click the cartridge you bought. Click "OK". Click "Close".

<u>**Close**</u> When you finish using the Control Panel window, close it by double-clicking its control box.

Close

When you finish using the Main window, close it by double-clicking its control box.

WORD PROCESSING

A **word-processing program** helps you write and edit sentences and paragraphs. Whatever you're writing and editing (such as a business letter, report, magazine article, or book) is called the **document**.

Remember that a word-processing program is mainly for manipulating *sentences and paragraphs*. To manipulate pretty drawings, get a **graphics program** instead; to manipulate a table of numbers, get a **spreadsheet program**; to manipulate a list of names (such as a list of your customers), get a **database program**.

To use a word-processing program, put your fingers on the keyboard, then type the paragraphs that make up your document, so they appear on the screen. Edit them by using special keys on the keyboard. Finally, make the computer send the document to the printer, so the document appears on paper. You can also make the computer copy the document onto a disk, which will store the document for many years.

How "word processing" was invented

Back in the 1950's, 1960's, and 1970's, computers were used mainly to manipulate lists of numbers, names, and addresses. Since those manipulations were called **data-processing (DP)**, the typical computing center was called a **data-processing center (DP center)**. It was run by a team of programmers and administrators called the **data-processing department (DP department)**.

Those old computer systems were usually expensive, unreliable, and complex. They needed big staffs to provide continuous repairs, reprogramming, and supervision. They were bureaucratic and technological nightmares. The term "data-processing" got a bad reputation.

Secretaries who wanted to write and edit reports preferred to use simple typewriters, rather than deal with the dreaded "data-processing department".

When easy-to-use word-processing programs were finally invented for computers, secretaries were afraid to try them because computers had developed a scary reputation. The last thing a secretary wanted was a desktop computer, which the secretary figured would mean "desktop trouble".

That's why the term "word-processing" was invented. Wang, IBM, and other manufacturers said to the secretaries, "We know you don't like computers and data-processing equipment. But don't worry: the machines we want to put on your desks are *not* computers; they're just souped-up typewriters. You like typewriters, right? Then you'll like these cute little machines also. We call them **word processors**. Don't worry: they're not data-processing equipment; they're not computers."

The manufacturers were lying: their desktop machines *were* computers. To pretend they weren't computers, the manufacturers called them **word processors** and omitted any software dealing with numbers or lists.

The trick worked: secretaries acquired word processors, especially the **Wang Word Processor** and the **IBM Displaywriter**.

Today's secretaries are less afraid of computers, know how to handle IBM PC clones, and run word-processing programs on them.

Three definitions of "word processor"

Strictly speaking, a "word processor" means "a computer whose main purpose is to do word processing". But some folks use the term "word processor" to mean "a word-processing program" or "a typist doing word processing".

In ads, a "$500 word processor" is a machine; a "$200 word processor" is a program you feed to a computer; a "$12-per-hour word processor" is a typist who understands word processing.

Which program to buy

Which word-processing program should you buy? The answer depends on your personal needs and desires. Here are the major competitors. . . .

Microsoft Word

Microsoft Word is the fanciest word-processing program. You'll be amazed at all the fancy tricks it can perform!

It's available for the Mac and the IBM PC.

Nearly all Mac users use Microsoft Word. It's become the standard in the Mac community.

If you have an IBM PC, you can buy either a DOS version or a Windows version of Microsoft Word. The Windows version runs better. The DOS version should be ignored.

Though the Windows version is officially called "Microsoft Word for Windows", it's nicknamed **Winword**. The newest version, **Winword 6a** eliminates the errors that occurred in version 6, and it's called "the best word-processing program" by nearly all the IBM and Windows magazines.

But though version 6a gets glowing reviews, it runs well just if your computer is powerful: a 486 or Pentium, with a big hard disk and at least 8 megabytes of RAM.

If your computer is just a 386, version 6a runs too slowly. If your computer has just 4 megabytes of RAM instead of 8, version 6a tries to make 4 megabytes of your hard disk imitate to be 4 megabytes of extra RAM, and the program spends most of its time waiting for the hard disk to spin. If you want to use all the fancy features the critics rave about, the program consumes 25 megabytes of your hard disk, plus 10 extra megabytes of free space to store temporary files, where the program makes notes to itself about what you're doing. Since the program consumes too much RAM and hard-disk space, it's called **fatware**.

Magazine reviewers praise Winword and don't mention its fatware problems, since the reviewers are rich folks who have 486 or Pentium computers, 8 megabytes of RAM, and huge hard drives.

Some folks still use Winword 2, which isn't as fancy as Winword 6a but has the advantage of running fine on a 386 with just 4M of RAM and a small hard drive.

Like Winword 6a, Microsoft Word's new Mac version is too fat. Mac lovers who happily used Word for the Mac version 5.1 (which resembles Winword 2) get upset when they upgrade to version 6 of Word for the Mac and discover it wants 8 megabytes of RAM and more hard disk space.

Ami Pro

The French word for "friend" is *ami*. It's pronounced, "Ah, me!"

For a word processor that's friendly and professional, get **Ami Pro for Windows**. Hassle-free, it runs fine even if you have just a 386 computer with just 4M of RAM and a small hard disk. Sucking you into the world of desktop publishing, it lets you wiggle your mouse to easily create multiple columns, headlines, drawings, and bar & pie charts. Use it to create eye-popping ads, blaring front pages of newspapers, and whatever else you want to make hot and spicy. After you master it, you'll be saying, "Ah, me: pro!"

Ami Pro was invented by a company called **Samna**. Since Ami Pro was so impressive, **Lotus** bought Samna, so Lotus sells Ami Pro.

Back in 1993, the computer magazines all declared Ami Pro the best word-processing program — better than Winword 2 in practically every way! When Winword 6 came out, the reviewers said Winword 6 was better than Ami Pro, since Winword 6 included extra-fancy word-processing features, and since the reviewers didn't notice Winword 6 was too fat.

Word Perfect

Though Microsoft Word is fancy and Ami Pro is pleasant, most businesses still use an older word-processing program, called **Word Perfect**. They use a version called **Word Perfect 5.1 for DOS**. It runs much faster than any Windows program. It runs on any IBM-compatible computer having a hard disk and 512K of RAM. It runs even if the CPU is just an 8088! It's the word processor I used for writing this book!

Back in 1990, when Microsoft Word and Ami Pro hadn't been fully developed yet, Word Perfect was the only word-processing program that worked well on IBM clones. (Microsoft Word worked well just on the Mac.)

After 1990, Word Perfect faced serious competition from Winword and Ami Pro, which both require Windows. But if your MS-DOS computer does *not* have Windows, Word Perfect remains your only choice for a good full-featured word processor. For example, if your computer's CPU is an 8088 or 286, or your RAM is less than 4 megabytes, you can't run Windows well — so buy Word Perfect!

Users have two complaints about Word Perfect 5.1 for DOS:

Since its commands are hard to remember, you need to keep peeking at a **cheat sheet** (a sheet of paper containing a list of commands).

While you're typing and editing, the screen doesn't quite show what will appear on paper. For example, if you give a command to make a big, tall headline, the headline won't look any bigger or taller than the rest of the text while you're typing; it will look bigger JUST ON PAPER (or when you tell Word Perfect to show you a **print preview**, which is an uneditable screen view of what will appear on paper). If you insert graphics into your document, you won't see them until you print them out on PAPER (or stare at the print preview).

Despite those complaints, Word Perfect survives. In just a few days, you get used to Word Perfect's commands and don't need to peek at the cheat sheet as often. Though Word Perfect doesn't let you easily create a newspaper's front page (since it doesn't show you the headlines, photos, and captions conveniently), Word Perfect is fine for typical business letters and books having simple layouts (like mine).

To combat the complaints, Word Perfect Corporation has invented versions that are more modern (**Word Perfect 6 for DOS** and **Word Perfect 6.1 for Windows**), but they require more RAM, run slowly, and aren't yet as pleasant as Winword and Ami Pro.

Word Perfect 6 for DOS needs at least a 386 with 2M RAM. Word Perfect 6.1 for Windows needs at least a 486 with 8M of RAM to run well (though you can limp by with a 386 and 6M of RAM if you're *very patient*).

Many secretaries enjoy Word Perfect 5.1 for DOS. They throw temper tantrums when their bosses decide to upgrade to Word Perfect 6.1, which runs slower and uses totally different keystrokes, which secretaries must relearn.

Though Word Perfect Corporation hopes you'll buy version 6 or 6.1, the company still sells version 5.1 for us oldtimers and secretaries who are too lazy to switch. The 5.1 version that's still sold is called **version 5.1+**. (The "+" means it includes a few features from version 6.)

Word Perfect also has versions for the Mac, Apple 2e, Apple 2GS, Commodore Amiga, Atari ST, Next, OS/2, Unix, Dec Vax, Data General minicomputers, and IBM mainframes.

Little word processors

Those big, fancy word processors (Microsoft Word, Ami Pro, and Word Perfect) are expensive: discount dealers sell them for between $89 and $319 each.

They're more than most folks need. If you wish, get a word processor that's smaller, cheaper, and easier to learn.

For example, Windows comes with a free word-processing program called **Windows Write** (explained in my Windows chapter). The Mac comes with a free word-processing program called **Teachtext** (explained in my Mac System chapter); use Teachtext or step up to **Write Now**, which understands more commands than Teachtext, is as easy as Teachtext, and requires less RAM than Microsoft Word.

The most pleasant database program, **Q&A**, includes a simple word-processing program called **Q&A Write**. If you buy Q&A, make sure you get the DOS version of it; the Windows version is disliked by everybody. You can get the DOS version for $179 from discount dealers such as Harmony (phone 800-441-1144 or 718-692-3232).

Another way to get a simple word processor is to buy an integrated program such as **PFS First Choice** (for DOS), **Microsoft Works** (for DOS, Windows, or the Mac), **Claris Works** (for Windows or the Mac), or **Appleworks** (for the Apple 2). Each of those integrated programs costs about $90. Some computers (such as Packard Bell's) come with one of those integrated programs at no extra charge.

But if you get one of those cheap programs, you'll soon lust for a fancier one and buy Microsoft Word, Ami Pro, or Word Perfect anyway.

Old classics

During the early 1980's, many folks used **Wordstar** (the *first* powerful word-processing program for microcomputers), **Multimate** (the first program that made the IBM PC imitate a Wang word-processing machine), **Displaywrite** (which made the IBM PC imitate an IBM Displaywriter word-processing machine), **PC-Write** (shareware you could try for free before sending a donation to the author), and **Xywrite** (which ran faster than any other word processor). But by 1990, most of those users had switched to Word Perfect 5.1.

What's in this book

This book explains how to use 7 word processors: **Teachtext** (page 141), **Windows Write** (page 151), **Ami Pro** (page 158), **Microsoft Word** (page 163), **Q&A Write** (page 173), and **Word Perfect** (page 183). I hope you enjoy them!

AMI PRO

To do fancy word processing and desktop publishing easily, get **Ami Pro**. It's a word processor that includes lots of tools for desktop publishing. It's easy, powerful, and pretty.

It lists for $130. You can get it for just $90 from discount dealers such as Staples.

The original version was called just **Ami** (which is the French word for "friend"). Then came an improved version, called **Ami Professional** (or **Ami Pro**).

Ami and Ami Pro were published by **Samna**. In 1991, Lotus bought Samna, so Samna's become a division of Lotus.

Here's how to use Ami Pro version 3.1. It requires 4M of RAM and Windows 3.1.

To find out how to use Windows, read my Windows chapter. That chapter also explains how to use Windows Write, which is the word processor that comes free with Windows. **Practice using Windows Write before you use Ami Pro.**

Copy Ami Pro to the hard disk

Ami Pro comes on floppy disks. To use Ami Pro, you must copy it from those floppy disks to your hard disk. Here's how.

Turn on the computer without any floppy in drive A. Start Windows (by typing "win" after the C prompt). You'll see the Program Manager Window.

Choose **Run** from the **File menu**. The computer will say "Command Line".

When you buy Ami Pro version 3.1, you get a big box that contains the main manual, several booklets, and eight 1.44M floppies. (If your computer requires 720K or 5¼-inch floppies instead, get them by phoning Lotus at 800-343-5414. Canadians call 800-Go-Lotus instead.)

Put Disk 1 in drive A. Type "a:install" (and press ENTER).

Type your name, press the TAB key, type the name of your company, and press the ENTER key. (If you don't have a company, type "Ami Pro Lovers Association".)

Press ENTER five more times. The computer says, "Insert Disk 2". Put Disk 2 in drive A and press ENTER. When the computer tells you, do the same for Disks 3, 4, 5, 6, 7, and 8.

If the computer asks "Modify AUTOEXEC.BAT?", click the "No" button (by using the mouse).

The computer will say, "Install complete". Press ENTER.

Exit from Windows (by choosing "Exit Windows" from the File menu, then clicking "OK"). Turn off the computer, so you can start fresh.

Launch Ami Pro

Here's how to start using Ami Pro version 3.1.

Turn on the computer without any floppy in drive A. Start Windows (by typing "win" after the C prompt). The computer will say "Program Manager".

Double-click the Lotus Applications icon. Double-click the Ami Pro 3.1 icon.

The screen's top shows this menu bar:

```
File Edit View Text Style Page Frame Tools Window Help
```

Customize Ami Pro

Ami Pro can act in different ways, to meet the needs of different people. When you use Ami Pro, it begins by acting however the previous user told it to. If the previous user was a jerk, Ami Pro will act jerky.

The following procedure makes Ami Pro act as a professional desktop publisher. The first time you use Ami Pro, do this procedure. The next time you use Ami Pro, you can skip the procedure — unless a colleague has used your copy of Ami Pro and given different commands instead.

Here's the procedure. . . .

Ruler Click "View". You'll see the **View menu**. If one of the View menu's choices is **Show Ruler**, choose it. That makes the computer put a ruler across the top of the screen. The ruler is numbered in inches: 1", 2", 3", etc.

Preferences From the View menu, choose **View Preferences**. Make sure the boxes next to "Vertical ruler" and "Display as printed" each contain an X. (To put an X in a box, click the box.)

Make sure box next to "Custom view" contains 91. If it contains a different number, raise or lower that number (by clicking the nearby arrows) until that number becomes 91.

The other boxes don't matter.

When you've finished, click "OK".

Type your document

Start typing your document.

Ami Pro uses the mouse and fundamental keys the same way as Windows Write. For details, read these sections on pages 151-152:

"Use the keyboard"
"Scroll through documents"
"Insert characters"
"Split a paragraph"
"Combine paragraphs"

Movement keys

To move to different parts of your document, you can use your mouse. To move faster, press these **movement keys** instead:

Keys you press	Where the pointer will move
right-arrow	right to the next character
left-arrow	left to the previous character
down-arrow	down to the line below
up-arrow	up to the line above
END	right to the end of the line
HOME	left to the beginning of the line
PAGE DOWN	down to the next screenful
PAGE UP	up to the previous screenful
Ctrl with right-arrow	right (to next word or punctuation symbol)
Ctrl with left-arrow	left (to beginning of a word or punctuation)
Ctrl with a period	right to the next sentence
Ctrl with a comma	left to the beginning of a sentence
Ctrl with down-arrow	down to the end of a paragraph
Ctrl with up-arrow	up to the beginning of a paragraph
Ctrl with PAGE DOWN	down to the next page
Ctrl with PAGE UP	up to the previous page
Ctrl with END	down to the end of the document
Ctrl with HOME	up to the beginning of the document

CONTROL key

To manipulate your document quickly, use the CONTROL key (which says Ctrl on it).

Underline Here's how to underline a phrase (<u>like this</u>). Press Ctrl with U, then type the phrase, then press Ctrl with U again.

Word underline Here's how to underline all of a phrase's words individually (<u>like</u> <u>this</u>), without underlining the spaces between them. Press Ctrl with W, then type the phrase, then press Ctrl with W again.

Bold Here's how to make a phrase be bold (**like this**). Press Ctrl with B, then type the phrase, then press Ctrl with B again.

Italics Here's how to italicize a phrase (*like this*). Press Ctrl with I, then type the phrase, then press Ctrl with I again.

Normal You can combine techniques. For example, here's how to make a phrase be underlined and bold (**<u>like this</u>**). Press Ctrl with U (to underline), then press Ctrl with B (to make bold), then type the phrase, then press Ctrl with N (to make the computer revert to "normal" printing).

Equidistant Here's how to make a title be exactly centered ("equidistant"). Press Ctrl with E, then type the title (and press ENTER), then press Ctrl with E again.

Justify Here's how to justify several paragraphs, so their right margins are perfectly straight. Press Ctrl with J, then type the paragraphs (pressing ENTER after each paragraph), then press Ctrl with J again.

Right Here's how to make a short line of text be flush right, so the text is next to the right margin. Press Ctrl with R, then type the short line of text (and press ENTER), then press Ctrl with R again.

Display To see a display of the entire page, press Ctrl with D. The screen will display a mock-up of how the entire page will look: you'll see the entire page, shrunk to fit on the screen. When you finish admiring that display, press Ctrl with D again.

Go You can go to page 3 quickly by using this trick: press Ctrl with G, then type the number 3 and press ENTER. (That technique works just if your document contains at least 3 pages.)

Find If your document contains the word "love", here's how to make the computer find that word.

Click at the beginning of the document. (To search through just *part* of your document for "love", click at the beginning of that part.)

Press Ctrl with F. Type "love".

Press ENTER several times. Each time you press ENTER, the computer moves to the next "love" in your document. When the computer can't find any more "love" in your document, the screen's bottom left corner briefly displays a message saying how often your document says "love".

The computer ignores capitalization. If you tell it to find "love", it will also find "Love" and "LOVE".

The computer looks for complete words. If you tell it to find "love", it will *not* find the "love" in "loves" or "glove".

Save To save the document (copy it onto the disk), press Ctrl with S. The computer will say "Filename". Invent a short name for your document (no more than 8 letters). Type the name and press ENTER.

That makes the computer copy the document onto the hard disk. For example, if you named the document "jennifer", the computer will put onto the hard disk a file called "JENNIFER.SAM", which means "JENNIFER created by SAMna. (Samna is the division of Lotus that invented Ami Pro.) The file will be in the documents subdirectory (called "DOCS"), which is part of the AMIPRO subdirectory.

Afterwards, if you change your mind and want to do more editing, go ahead! When you finish that extra editing, save it by pressing Ctrl with S again.

Print To print the document onto paper, press Ctrl with P. Then press ENTER.

Zap If you make a mistake, zap the mistake by pressing Ctrl with Z. That makes the computer zap ("undo") the mistake.

For example, if you accidentally deleted some text, pressing Ctrl with Z will make the text reappear.

Pressing Ctrl with Z tells the computer undo your previous action. But what's your "previous action"? When you press Ctrl with Z, the computer might undo a different action that you expected.

If pressing Ctrl with Z accidentally makes the text look even worse instead of better, and you wish you hadn't pressed Ctrl with Z, do this: press Ctrl with Z again! That "zaps the zap" and returns your text to its original state.

Fonts

At the screen's bottom, you see the name of a typeface: **Times New Roman**.

Click that typeface name. You see an alphabetized list of typefaces, like this:

```
Arial
Courier New
LotusLineDraw
Modern
Roman
Script
Symbol
Times New Roman
WingDings
```

(You might also see some extra entries contributed by your printer's manufacturer or by any font packages you bought.)

The best typefaces are Times New Roman (for most typing), Arial (for big headlines and tiny type), and Courier New (for tables of numbers). Click the typeface you want.

At the screen's bottom, to the right of the typeface, you see a number (which is normally 12). That's the **point size**. Click that number. You see a list of point sizes to choose from, like this:

```
4
6
8
9
10
11
12
14
16
18
20
22
24
30
36
42
48
60
72
```

Click the point size you want. (The bigger the point size you choose, the bigger the characters will be.)

After you've chosen a typeface and point size, type some words. They'll be in the typeface and point size you selected. (Your document's other words, which you typed earlier, remain unaffected.)

You'll be typing in the typeface and point size you chose, until you switch to a different typeface or point size or hop to a different part of your document.

Select text

Here's how to dramatically change a phrase you typed.

Point at the phrase's beginning, then drag the phrase's end (while holding down the mouse's left button). The whole phrase turns black. Turning the phrase black is called **selecting the phrase**.

Then say what to do to the phrase. For example, choose one of these activities:

To underline the phrase, press Ctrl with U.
To make the phrase be bold, press Ctrl with B.
To italicize the phrase, press Ctrl with I.
To delete the phrase, press the DELETE key.
To replace the phrase, just type whatever words you want the phrase to become.

To make the phrase be a different typeface,
click the typeface at the bottom of the screen, then click the typeface you want.

To make the phrase be a different point size,
click the point-size number at the bottom of the screen, then click the point size you want.

Other ways to select The usual way to select a phrase is to point at the phrase's beginning, then drag to the phrase's end. But sometimes other methods are faster! To select a phrase, choose one of these methods:

Method 1: point at the phrase's beginning, then drag to the phrase's end.
Method 2: click the phrase's beginning; then while holding down the SHIFT key, click the phrase's end.

Method 3: by using your keyboard's movement keys (such as the up-arrow, down-arrow, left-arrow, and right-arrow keys), move to the phrase's beginning; then while holding down the SHIFT key, use the movement keys to move to the phrase's end.

Method 4: to select just one word, double-click in the middle of it.
Method 5: to select just one sentence, click in the middle of it while holding down the Ctrl key.
Method 6: to select just one paragraph, double-click in the middle of it while holding down Ctrl key.

Move a phrase To move a phrase to a new location, just "select the phrase, and then drag from the middle of the phrase to the new location." Here are the details. . . .

First, select the phrase you want to move, so the phrase turns black.

Then take your finger off the mouse's button. Move the mouse's pointer to the middle of the phrase.

Finally, hold down the mouse's button; and while you keep holding down the mouse's button, drag the mouse pointer (which is a vertical line) wherever you want the phrase to move. (Drag the vertical line anywhere you wish in the document, or drag to the end of the document, but don't try to drag past the document's end. During the drag, the vertical line turns blue, then red.)

At the end of the drag, lift your finger from the mouse's button. Presto, the phrase moves where you wished!

Page menu

You can improve how your text is placed on the page.

Page break When you finish typing a paragraph, you normally press the ENTER key. Instead of pressing ENTER, try this experiment: choose **Breaks** from the **Page menu**, then click OK. That makes the next paragraph be on the next page.

Columns In a newspaper, text is printed in many narrow columns. Here's how to create such columns. Choose **Modify Page Layout** from the Page menu. Underneath "Number of Columns", click how many columns you want. (For example, if you want each page to be divided into 4 columns, click the "4".) Then click "OK".

When you finish working on a document, choose **Exit** or **Close** from the File menu.

If you choose **Exit**, the computer will stop using Ami Pro, and you'll see the Windows Program Manager.

If you choose **Close** instead of Exit, the computer will let you work on another document, and your next step is to choose **New** or **Open** from the File menu.

If you choose New and then click "OK", the computer will let you start typing a new document.

If you choose Open and then double-click the name of an old document, the computer will put that document onto the screen and let you edit it.

Didn't save?

If you didn't save your document before doing those procedures, the computer asks, "Save?" If you click "Yes", the computer copies your document's most recent version to the hard disk; if you click "No" instead, the computer ignores and forgets your most recent editing.

Congratulations!

You've learned all the fundamental commands of Ami Pro!

The computer can improve your vocabulary.

Spelling

Here's how to check the document's spelling.

For example, type a short document that contains just this one sentence:

```
Be huppy!
```

To spell-check the document, click at the document's beginning. Click the **Dictionary icon**, which is blue and says "ABC". (It's under the word "Help".)

Click "OK".

The computer looks up each word in the dictionary. The computer finds "Be" in the dictionary but can't find "huppy". The computer highlights the strange word "huppy" and prints this list of suggestions:

```
hoopoe
happy
guppy
puppy
```

Notice that the computer's immense vocabulary even includes "hoopoe", which is a European bird that looks like a cross between a parrot and a zebra!

You have several choices:

If you meant "hoopoe", "happy", "guppy", or "puppy", click what you meant & then click "Replace".
If you meant "huppy" and want to add that slang word to the dictionary, click "Add To Dictionary".
If you meant "huppy" but don't want to add that slang word to the dictionary, click "Skip".
If you meant some other word instead, type it (without pressing ENTER) and click "Replace".

When the computer finishes checking the entire document, the screen's bottom left corner briefly say "Spell check complete."

Thesaurus

Suppose your document contains the word "caress". To find synonyms for that word, click it, then click the **Thesaurus icon** (which is say "T" and is under the word "Help").

You'll see the **Thesaurus window**. It contains this list of synonyms for "caress":

```
cosset
cuddle
dandle
fondle
love
pet
```

If you want to replace "caress" by a synonym, click the synonym you want then click "Replace".

When you finish using the Thesaurus window, double-click its control box (or click "Cancel").

You can draw a box and put information inside it. For example, if you're creating a newspaper, you'll want to draw a big box and put a big masthead or headline inside it. Underneath, you'll want to draw a smaller box and put a picture inside it. Yes, Ami Pro lets you draw a box and put text *or a picture* inside it!

A box that contains information (such as text or a picture) is called a **frame**. It surrounds the information, just as a picture frame surrounds a picture.

Here's how to draw a box (frame).

Find the **Frame icon**, which looks like a red picture frame. (It's near the top of the screen, just under the word "Window".)

Click the Frame icon. Point in your document, where you want the box's top left corner to be, and drag to where you want the box's opposite corner. For best results, make the box's top left corner be in the middle of the page, and make the box's opposite corner be below that and far to the right, where the page's text area meets the right margin.

The box appears. All your document's words and columns move out of the way to make room for the box.

To make sure that the box doesn't bump into nearby text, the computer makes the box slightly smaller than you requested. To make the box beautiful, the computer gives the box rounded corners and a shadow.

The box temporarily has black bumps on it. The bumps are called **handles**.

In the box, you can put text or a drawing (but not both).

Text

To put text in the box, double-click in the box and then type the text.

Drawing

If you want the box to contain a drawing instead of text, make sure the box has handles. (If the box doesn't have handles yet, create them by clicking in the box). Click the **Drawing icon**, which looks like a pencil and is near the screen's top right corner.

Near the top of the screen, you see these icons for drawing: **Arrow, Hand, Slanted Line, Zigzag, Polygon, Rectangle, Rounded Rectangle, Oval, Arc,** and **Text**. Here's how to use them:

What you want to draw	How to draw it
slanted line	Click the Slanted Line icon. Start where you want the line to begin, and drag to where you want the line to end.
horizontal, vertical, or 45° line	It's similar to drawing a slanted line, but depress the SHIFT key during the whole process.
zigzag	Click the Zigzag icon. Click where you want the zigzag to begin. Click where you want each bend in the zigzag. Double-click where you want the zigzag to end.
polygon	Click the Polygon icon. Click where you want the polygon's first corner. Click where you want each additional corner, but *double*-click at the last corner.
rectangle	Click the Rectangle icon. Start where you want the rectangle's top left corner, and drag to where you want the rectangle's opposite corner.
square	It's similar to drawing a rectangle, but depress the SHIFT key during the whole process.
rectangle with rounded corners	It's similar to drawing a rectangle, but click the *Rounded* Rectangle icon.
square with rounded corners	Draw a rounded rectangle while depressing the SHIFT key.
oval	Click the Oval icon. Imagine a rectangle big enough to hold your oval: start where you want that rectangle's top left corner, and drag to where you want that rectangle's opposite corner.
circle	It's similar to drawing an oval, but depress the SHIFT key during the whole process.
arc that's a quarter of an oval	Click the Arc icon. Imagine the entire oval: start at the oval's leftmost or rightmost point, and drag to where you want the arc to end.
title in the middle of the drawing	Click the Text icon (which says "abc"). Click where you want the title to begin. Type the title.

To nudge the entire drawing slightly — but without moving the frame that it's in — do the following: click the Hand icon, then start in the middle of the drawing and drag in the direction that you want to nudge.

Here's how to edit an object that you drew. Click the Arrow icon. Click the middle of the object, so that the object gets handles (bumps). Then choose one of these activities:

Activity	How to do it
Delete the object	Press the DELETE key.
Change the object's size	Point at one of the handles. Drag the handle in the direction you want the object to stretch (or shrink).
Move the object	Point at the object's center (not at a handle). Drag in the direction that you want the object to move.

Edit a frame

Here's how to edit an entire frame. Click outside the frame, then click inside the frame. The frame gets handles. Then choose one of these activities:

To delete the frame, press the DELETE key.
To change the frame's size, drag a handle.
To move the frame, point at the frame's center and drag.

MICROSOFT WORD

The fanciest word-processing program ever invented is **Microsoft Word**. It runs in all three popular environments (DOS, Windows, and Mac) and uses similar commands in each of those environments.

Other versions

This chapter explains how to use **version 6 of Microsoft Word for Windows**. Other versions of Microsoft Word are similar.

<u>**Mac**</u> If you're using a Mac instead of Windows, here's the main difference: instead of pressing the Ctrl key, press the COMMAND key (on which you'll see a squiggly cloverleaf — and also see an apple if your keyboard is modern).

<u>**Old versions**</u> If your version of Microsoft Word is older than version 6, you should upgrade to version 6!

If you can't upgrade (because you have no money or because your computer has too little RAM or too slow a CPU to run Word well), phone me at 617-666-2666 to get an older version of this book. The 19th edition explained **version 2 of Word for Windows** and also **version 5.1 of Word for the Mac**. So did the 18th and 17th editions.

Prepare yourself

Before reading this chapter, read and practice my Windows chapter. Before using version 6 of Microsoft Word for Windows, you must buy Windows 3.1 and 4M of RAM. To run version 6 of Microsoft Word for Windows *well*, you should have a 486 or Pentium, and you should have 8M of RAM.

Copy Microsoft Word to the hard disk

Microsoft Word comes on floppy disks. To use Microsoft Word, you must copy it from those floppy disks to your hard disk. Here's how.

Turn on the computer without any floppy in drive A. Start Windows (by typing "win" after the C prompt). You'll see the Program Manager Window.

Choose **Run** from the **File menu**. The computer will say "Command Line".

What happens next depends on how you bought Word.

<u>**If you bought just Word**</u> If you bought just Microsoft Word — without buying Microsoft Office — you get a box that contains two manuals, nine 1.44M floppies, and a coupon you can mail to Microsoft to get 1.2M floppies instead.

Put Disk 1 in drive A. Type "a:setup" (and press ENTER).

The computer will say "Microsoft Word 6.0 Setup". Press ENTER.

If Disk 1 was never used before, the computer will ask you to type your name. Type your name, press the TAB key, and type the name of your company (if any).

Press ENTER several times, until the computer says, "Please insert Disk 2." Put Disk 2 in drive A and press ENTER. When the computer tells you, do the same for Disks 3 through 9.

The computer will say, "Microsoft Word Setup needs to restart Windows." Press ENTER.

<u>**If you bought Office**</u> Here's the smartest way to acquire Microsoft Word: buy a cheaper word processor (such as Ami Pro), then use that as an excuse to buy the upgrade version of **Microsoft Office Professional**, which includes Microsoft Word, Microsoft Excel (a spreadsheet program), Microsoft Access (a database program), and other goodies.

The Microsoft Office Professional Upgrade comes in a huge box that contains ten manuals, thirty-one 1.44M floppies, and a coupon you can mail to get 1.2M floppies instead.

Put Disk 1 in drive A. Type "a:setup" (and press ENTER).

The computer will say "Microsoft Office 4.3 Professional Setup". Press ENTER.

If Disk 1 was never used before, the computer will ask you to type your name. Type your name, press the TAB key, and type the name of your company (if any).

Press ENTER several times, until the computer says, "Choose the type of installation by clicking one of the buttons." If you click the **Complete/Custom button**, the computer will install Microsoft Office Professional completely and consume 114 megabytes of your hard disk. If you click the **Typical button**, the computer will install just the most commonly used features of Microsoft Office Professional and consume just 58 megabytes of your hard disk. If you click the **Laptop/Minimum button**, the computer will install just the minimum features you need to survive and consume just 29 megabytes of your hard disk. **Click one of those buttons.**

Press ENTER several times, until the computer says, "Please insert Disk 2". Put Disk 2 in drive A and press ENTER. When the computer tells you, do the same for Disks 3 through 31.

If the computer says "Setup couldn't create a SYSTEM.MDA file", press ENTER.

The computer will say, "Setup needs to restart Windows." Press ENTER.

Close the Microsoft Office Cue Cards window (by double-clicking its control box).

<u>**Final steps**</u> Close the Microsoft Office window. Close the Program Manager window.

The computer will say "Exit Windows". Press ENTER.

Then turn off the computer, so you can start fresh.

Launch Microsoft Word

Here's how to start using Microsoft Word.

Turn on the computer without any floppy in drive A. Start Windows (by typing "win" after the C prompt). If the computer says "Microsoft Office Cue Cards", close the Microsoft Office Cue Cards window (by double-clicking its control box). The computer says "Program Manager".

If you see a slanted W near the screen's top right corner, click it. If you don't see a slanted W, double-click the Microsoft Office icon then the Microsoft Word icon.

The screen's top says:

`Microsoft Word - Document1`

You also see this **menu bar**:

```
File Edit View Insert Format Tools Table Window Help
```

If the computer says "Tip of the Day", press ENTER.

See the rulers

About 2 inches down from the top of the screen, you should see a **horizontal ruler**, which goes across the screen and is numbered 1", 2", 3", 4", 5", etc. If you don't see that ruler, make it appear by choosing **Ruler** from the **View menu**.

At the screen's left edge, you should see a **vertical ruler**, which goes up & down the screen and is numbered 1", 2", etc. If you don't see the vertical ruler, make it appear by choosing **Page Layout** from the View menu.

Now you see *two* rulers — a horizontal ruler, plus a vertical ruler — so you can use the full power of Microsoft Word!

Let's begin. . . .

Type your document

Start typing your document.

Microsoft Word uses the mouse and fundamental keys the same way as Windows Write. For details, read these sections on pages 151-152:

"Use the keyboard"
"Scroll through documents"
"Insert characters"
"Split a paragraph"
"Combine paragraphs"

All delete

Here's how to delete the entire document, so you can start over. . . .

While holding down the Ctrl key, press the A key. That means "all". All of the document turns black.

Then press the DELETE key. All of the document disappears, so you can start over!

Movement keys

To move to different parts of your document, you can use your mouse. To move faster, press these **movement keys** instead:

Key you press	Where pointer moves
right-arrow	right to the next character
left-arrow	left to the previous character
down-arrow	down to the line below
up-arrow	up to the line above
END	right to the end of the line
HOME	left to the beginning of line
PAGE DOWN	down to the next screenful
PAGE UP	up to the previous screenful

FORMATTING TOOLBAR

Near the screen's top, you see the **formatting toolbar**:

Each symbol on the toolbar is called a **tool**. Here's the name of each tool:

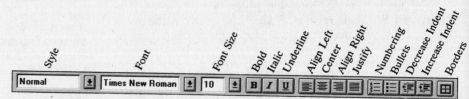

If you forget a tool's name, try this trick: point at the tool (by using the mouse, but *without* clicking), then wait a second. Underneath the tool, you'll see the tool's name; and at the screen's bottom left corner, you'll see a one-sentence explanation of what the tool does.

The toolbar's right half consists of 12 tools saying "**B**", "*I*", "U", etc. Those 12 tools are called **buttons**. To use a button, press it by clicking it with the mouse. Here are the details. . . .

Underline

Here's how to underline a phrase (<u>like this</u>). Push in the **Underline button** (which says <u>U</u> on it) by clicking it. Then type the phrase you want underlined. Then pop the Underline button back out (by clicking it again).

Bold

Here's how to make a phrase be bold (**like this**). Push in the **Bold button** (which says **B** on it) by clicking it. Then type the phrase you want emboldened. Then pop the Bold button back out (by clicking it again).

Here's how to make a phrase be bold and underlined (**<u>like this</u>**). Push in the Bold and Underline buttons (by clicking them both). Then type the phrase. Then pop those buttons back out (by clicking them again).

Italic

Here's how to italicize a phrase (*like this*). Push in the **Italic button** (which says *I* on it) by clicking it. Then type the phrase you want italicized. Then pop the Italic button back out (by clicking it again).

Align

While typing a line, you can click one of these **alignment buttons:**

Align Left	Center	Align Right	Justify
☰	☰	☰	☰

Clicking the **Center button** makes the line be centered,

like this line

Clicking the **Align Right button** makes the line be at the right margin,

like this line

Clicking the **Align Left button** makes the line be at the left margin,

like this line

Clicking one of those buttons affects not just the line you're typing but also all other lines in the same paragraph.

Clicking the **Justify button** makes the paragraph be **justified**, so the paragraph's bottom line is at the left margin, and each of the paragraph's other lines is at *both* margins (by inserting extra space between the words),

like   this   line

When you click one of those alignment buttons, you're pushing the button in. That button pops back out when you push a different alignment button instead.

When you start typing a new document, the computer assumes you want the document to be aligned left, so the computer pushes the Align Left button in. If you want a different alignment, push a different alignment button instead.

For example, if you're typing a title or headline and want it to be centered, press the **Center button**. If you're typing a business letter and want it to begin by showing the date next to the right margin, press the **Align Right button**. If you're typing an informal memo or letter to a colleague or friend, and want the paragraph to look plain, ordinary, modest, and unassuming (like Clark Kent), press the **Alight Left button**. If you're creating something formal (such as a newspaper or textbook) and want the paragraph to have perfectly straight edges (so it looks official, uptight, and professional, like Robocop), press the **Justify button**.

Clicking one of those alignment buttons affects the entire paragraph you're typing. (The paragraphs you typed earlier remain unaffected.)

To change the alignment of a paragraph you typed earlier, click in the middle of that paragraph and then click the alignment button you wish.

When you start typing a new paragraph, the computer gives that paragraph the same alignment as the paragraph above, unless you say differently (by pressing one of the alignment buttons).

Centered title Here's how to type a centered title, using the techniques you've learned so far. . . .

Press the ENTER key twice (to leave a big blank space above the title).

Next, press the Center button (so the title will be centered) and the Bold button (so the title will be bold). Type the words you want to be in the title, and press the ENTER key afterwards.

Congratulations! You've created a centered title!

Next, make the paragraph underneath the title be normal: make that paragraph be uncentered (click the Align Left button or Justify button) and make it be unbolded (click the Bold button, so the Bold button pops back out).

Font size

Look at the **Font Size box**. In that box, you normally see the number 10. That means the characters you're typing are 10 points high. Here's how to type characters that are bigger or smaller. . . .

Method 1: click the Font Size box. In that box, type a size number from 8 to 72. The number can end in .5; the number can be 8 or 8.5 or 9 or 9.5 or 10 or bigger. (Theoretically, you can pick a number even smaller than 8 or even bigger than 72, but those extreme numbers create ugly results.) When you finish typing the number, press the ENTER key.

Method 2: click the down-arrow that's to the RIGHT of the Font Size box. You start seeing this list of popular sizes: 8, 9, 10, 11, 12, 14, 16, 18, 20, 22, 24, 26, 28, 36, 48, and 72. (It appears in a window that's too small to show the entire list; to see the rest of the list, click the window's scroll arrows.) That list of popular sizes is called the Font Size menu. Click the size you want.

Afterwards, whatever characters you type will be the size you chose. (The characters you typed earlier remain unaffected.)

The popular sizes look like this:

This text is 8 points high, 9 points high, 10 points high, 11 points high, 12 points high, 14 points high, 16 points high, 18 points high, 20 pt., 22 pt., 24 pt., 26 pt., 28 pt., 36pt., 48pt., 72pt.

When you finish typing the enlarged or reduced characters, here's how to return to typing characters that are normal size (10-point): click the down-arrow that's to the right of the Font Size box, then click the 10.

Font

When you type, you're normally using a font called "Times New Roman". If you wish, you can switch to a different font instead.

The most popular Windows fonts are "Times New Roman", "Arial", and "Courier New". Here's how they look:

> This font is called "Times New Roman". It's the best for typing long passages of text, such as paragraphs in books, newspapers, magazines, and reports. It squeezes lots of words onto a small amount of paper but remains easy to read. You can make it plain or **bold** or *italic* or ***bold italic***.
>
> ## If you make it big and bold, like this, it resembles an old-fashioned newspaper headline.

> This font is called "Arial". It's simple. You can make it plain or **bold** or *italic* or ***bold italic***. It resembles Helvetica.
>
> It's the best for typing short phrases that attract attention. For example, **if you make it big and bold, like this, it's good for titles, signs, and posters.** If you make it small, like this, it's good for footnotes, photo captions, classified ads, telephone books, directories, and catalogs.

> ```
> This font is called "Courier New".
>
> If you make it 12 points high, like this, it
> resembles the printout from a typewriter.
>
> It makes each character have the same width: for
> example, the "m" has the same width as the "i". It's
> a good font for typing tables of numbers, since the
> uniform width lets you line up each column of numbers
> easily. To make sure each column aligns properly,
> press the Align Left button, not the Justify button.
>
> Make it plain or bold or italic or bold italic.
> ```

In the **Font box**, you see the name of a font, which is usually "Times New Roman". Click the down-arrow that's to the *right* of that font's name. You start seeing a list of fonts, including "Times New Roman", "Arial", "Courier New", and several other fonts. (It appears in a window that's too small to show the entire list; to see the rest of the list, click the window's scroll arrows.) The list of font is called the **Font menu**.

The best fonts have "TT" written in front of them. The "TT" means the font is a **True Type font** (created by a system that lets you make the characters as big or as small as you wish and accurately reproduces those characters onto your screen and paper). For example, "Times New Roman", "Arial", and "Courier New" are True Type fonts and have "TT" written in front of them.

Click the font you want.

Afterwards, whatever characters you type will be in the font you chose. (The characters you typed earlier remain unaffected.)

When you finish typing in that font, here's how to return to typing characters that are normal (Times New Roman): click the down-arrow that's to the right of the Font box, then click Times New Roman.

Style

When you type, you typically use style called "Normal", which is 10-point Times New Roman aligned left.

If you wish, you can switch to a different style instead. For example, you can switch to a style called "Heading 1", which is 14-point Arial with extra blank space between paragraphs. Here's how.

In the **Style box**, you see the name of a style, which is typically "Normal".

Click the down-arrow next to that style name. You see a list of styles, including "Normal", "Heading 1", and several other styles. The list of styles is called the **Style menu**.

Click the style you want.

Afterwards, whatever paragraphs you type will be in the style you chose. (The paragraphs you typed earlier remain unaffected.)

When you finish typing a paragraph in that style (and pressed the ENTER key at the end of that paragraph), here's how to make the next paragraph be Normal: click the down-arrow next to the Style box, then click Normal.

Centered title Here's the sophisticated way to type a centered title.

Press the ENTER key. Choose "Heading 1" from the Style menu. Push in the Centered button. Type the title, and press the ENTER key afterwards.

The computer will automatically make the next paragraph be Normal and aligned left; you don't have to say so!

Indent

Before typing a paragraph, you can press the TAB key. That makes the computer indent the paragraph's first line.

If you want to indent *all* lines in the paragraph, do this instead of pressing the TAB key: while typing the paragraph, click the **Increase Indent button**. That makes the computer indent *all* lines in the paragraph. (The paragraphs you typed earlier remain unaffected.)

When you start typing a new paragraph, the computer indents that paragraph if the paragraph above it was indented.

If you indented a paragraph by clicking the Increase Indent button but then change your mind, here's how to *un*indent the paragraph: click in the paragraph, then click the **Decrease Indent button**.

Example Suppose you start typing a new document. Here's how to make just paragraphs 3, 4, and 5 be indented.

Type paragraphs 1 and 2 normally (without pressing the Increase Indent button).

When you start typing paragraph 3, press the Increase Indent button. That makes the computer start indenting, so paragraphs 3, 4, and 5 will be automatically indented.

When you start typing paragraph 6, here's how to prevent the computer from indenting it: click the Decrease Indent button at the beginning of paragraph 6.

Changing your mind To indent a paragraph you typed earlier, click in the middle of that paragraph and then click the Increase Indent button. To *un*indent a paragraph you typed earlier, click in its middle and then click the *Decrease* Indent button.

Extra indentation If you click the Increase Indent button *twice* instead of just once, the computer will indent the paragraph farther. After typing that doubly indented paragraph, if you want the paragraph below to be unindented you must click the Decrease Indent button twice.

Each time you click the Increase Indent button, the computer indents the paragraph a half inch farther. Each time you click the Decrease Indent button, the computer indents the paragraph a half inch less.

Bullets Here's a different way to indent an entire paragraph: while typing the paragraph, push in the **Bullets button** (by clicking it). That makes the computer indent the paragraph slightly (just a quarter inch) and also put a bullet (the symbol ●) to the left of the paragraph's first line. That's called a **bulleted paragraph**.

After you've typed a bulleted paragraph, any new paragraphs you type underneath will be bulleted also — until you request an *un*bulleted paragraph (by popping the Bullet button back out).

Numbering Here's another way to indent an entire paragraph: while typing the paragraph, push in the **Numbering button** (by clicking it). That makes the computer indent the paragraph slightly (a quarter inch) and put "1." to the left of the paragraph's first line. That's called a **numbered paragraph**.

When you type a new paragraph underneath, that paragraph will be numbered "2.", the next paragraph will be numbered "3.", etc. Any new paragraphs you type underneath will be numbered also — until you request an *un*numbered paragraph (by popping the Numbering button back out).

SELECT TEXT

Here's how to dramatically change a phrase you typed.

Point at the phrase's beginning, then drag to the phrase's end (while holding down the mouse's left button). The whole phrase turns black. Turning the phrase black is called **selecting the phrase**.

Then say what to do to the phrase. For example, choose one of these activities:

To underline the phrase, push in the Underline button.
To make the phrase be bold, push in the Bold button.
To italicize the phrase, push in the Italic button.

To prevent the phrase from being underlined, bold, or italicized, pop those buttons back out.

To change how the phrase's paragraphs are aligned, click one of the alignment buttons.
To change how the phrase's paragraphs are indented, click one of the indentation buttons.

To change the phrase's point size, choose the size you want from the Font Size menu.
To change the phrase's font, choose the font you want from the Font menu.
To change the phrase's style, choose the style you want from the Style menu.

To delete the phrase, press the DELETE key.

To replace the phrase, just type whatever words you want the phrase to become.

Go ahead! Try it now! It's fun!

Other ways to select

The usual way to select a phrase is to point at the phrase's beginning, then drag to the phrase's end. But sometimes other methods are faster! To select a phrase, choose one of these methods:

Method 1: point at the phrase's beginning, then drag to the phrase's end.
Method 2: click the phrase's beginning; then while holding down the SHIFT key, click the phrase's end.

Method 3: by using your keyboard's movement keys (such as the up-arrow, down-arrow, left-arrow, and right-arrow keys), move to the phrase's beginning; then while holding down the SHIFT key, use the movement keys to move to the phrase's end.

Method 4: to select just one word, double-click in the middle of it.
Method 5: to select just one paragraph, triple-click in the middle of it.
Method 6: to select several paragraphs, triple-click in the middle of the first paragraph you want; then while holding down the SHIFT key, click in the middle of the last paragraph.

Method 7: to select just one sentence, click in the middle of it while holding down the Ctrl key.
Method 8: to select the entire document (all!), press the A key while holding down the Ctrl key.

Move a phrase

To move a phrase to a new location, just "select the phrase, and then drag from the middle of the phrase to the new location." Here are the details. . . .

First, select the phrase you want to move, so the phrase turns black.

Then take your finger off the mouse's button. Move the mouse's pointer to the middle of the phrase (so you see an arrow).

Finally, hold down the mouse's button (so you see a vertical dotted line); and while you keep holding down the mouse's button, drag that line to wherever you want the phrase to move. (Drag the line anywhere you wish in the document, or drag to the end of the document, but don't try to drag past the document's end.)

At the end of the drag, lift your finger from the mouse's button. Presto, the phrase moves where you wished!

Near the screen's top, above the formatting toolbar, you see the **standard toolbar**:

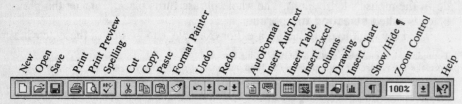

Here's how to use those tools. . . .

Save

To save the document (copy it onto the disk), click the **Save button**.

If you haven't saved the document before, the computer will say "File Name". Invent a short name for your document (no more than 8 characters). Type the name and press ENTER.

That makes the computer copy the document onto the hard disk. For example, if you named the document "mary", the computer will put a document called MARY.DOC into the WINWORD subdirectory (folder).

(If you bought the entire Microsoft Office instead of just Word, the WINWORD folder is inside the MSOFFICE folder.)

Afterwards, if you change your mind and want to do more editing, go ahead! When you finish that extra editing, save it by clicking the Save button again.

Save often If you're typing a long document, click the Save button about every 10 minutes. Click it whenever you get to a good stopping place and think, "What I've typed so far looks good!"

Then if an accident happens, you'll lose at most 10 minutes of work, and you can return to the last version you felt good about.

Print

Here's how to print the document onto paper. Make sure you've bought a printer, attached it to the computer, turned the printer's power on, and put paper into the printer. Then click the **Print button**. The printer will print your document onto paper.

Finish

When you finish working on a document, choose **Exit** or **Close** from the **File menu**.

If you choose **Exit**, the computer will stop using Microsoft Word, and you'll see the Windows Program Manager.

If you choose **Close** instead of Exit, the computer will let you work on another document, and your next step is to click the **New button** or the **Open button**.

If you click the New button, the computer will let you start typing a new document.

If you click the Open button and then double-click the name of an old document, the computer will put that document onto the screen and let you edit it.

Didn't save? If you didn't save your document before doing those procedures, the computer asks, "Do you want to save?" If you click "Yes", the computer copies your document's most recent version to the hard disk; if you click "No" instead, the computer ignores and forgets your most recent editing.

Congratulations! You've learned all the fundamental commands of Microsoft Word!

Undo

If you make a mistake (such as accidentally deleting some text, or accidentally giving the text an ugly font), click the **Undo button** (which shows an arrow turning back). That makes the computer undo your last activity, so your text returns to the way it looked before you made your boo-boo.

To undo your last *two* activities, click the Undo button *twice*.

If you click the Undo button, the computer might undo a different activity than you expected. If clicking the Undo button accidentally makes the text look even worse instead of better, and you wish you hadn't clicked the Undo button, you can "undo the undo" by clicking the **Redo button** (which shows an arrow bending forward).

Show paragraphs

The symbol for "Paragraph" is ¶, which looks like a backwards P.

If you push in the **¶ button** (by clicking it), the screen will show a ¶ symbol at the end of each paragraph, so you can easily tell where each paragraph ends. The screen will also show a dot (·) wherever you pressed the SPACE bar and show a right-arrow (→) wherever you pressed the TAB key, so you easily tell how many times you pressed those keys.

For example, if you typed "I love you" correctly, the screen will show "I·love·you". If you see "I·love···you" instead, you know you accidentally pressed the SPACE bar three times after "love" instead of just once, so you should delete the two extra spaces (by moving there and then pressing the DELETE key twice).

When you finish examining the ¶ symbols and dots and right-arrows, and you're sure you've put just one space between each pair of words, here's how to make those special symbols vanish: pop the ¶ button back out (by clicking it again).

The f problem When you're using Windows, the computer's screen has difficulty showing you the letter "f" correctly. When you type an "f" by using the normal font (10-point Times Roman), the screen shows too little space after the "f".

For example, if you try typing "fM", the screen shows "fM" — even though the printer will print "fM" correctly on paper. If you try typing "f M", the screen shows "fM" — even though the printer will print "f M" correctly on paper. If you try typing "of Mary", the screen shows "ofMary", even though the printer will print "of Mary" correctly on paper.

So the spacing you seen on the screen does *not* correctly match the spacing that will appear on paper! To discover how much space will appear on paper, press in the ¶ button, and notice how many dots appear. Make sure just one dot appears after each word.

Some conservative Americans have trouble handling dirty words that begin with "f". Notice that Windows has the opposite problem: it has trouble showing words that *end* in "f".

I hope somebody at Microsoft reads this book and fixes the f problem soon!

Move

Here's another way to move a phrase to a new location.

Select the phrase (by dragging across it with the mouse, so the phrase turns black). Click the **Cut button** (which looks like a pair of scissors). The phrase will vanish from its original location.

Then click the new location where you want the phrase to reappear, and click the **Paste button** (which looks like a clipboard). The phrase will appear there.

Copy

Here's another way to copy a phrase, so the phrase appears in your document *twice*.

Select the phrase (by dragging across it with the mouse, so the phrase turns black). Click the **Copy button**. Then click where you want the copy of the phrase to appear, and click the **Paste button**. The copy will appear there, so the phrase will be in your document *twice*.

If you want the phrase to appear in your document a *third* time, click where you want that additional copy to appear, then click the Paste button again. If you want the phrase to appear in your document a *fourth* time, click where you want that additional copy, then click the Paste button again.

Format Painter

Suppose one part of your document looks pretty, and one part looks ugly. Here's how to make the ugly part look as pretty as the pretty part.

Drag across the pretty part, so you've selected it and it's turned black. Click the **Format Painter button**. Then drag across the ugly part.

The computer will make the ugly part look as pretty as the pretty part. For example, the ugly part will have the same font and font size as the pretty part; it will be underlined, boldfaced, and italicized the same way as the pretty part; and if the pretty part was big enough to include a complete paragraph, the ugly part's paragraphs will be aligned the same way as the pretty part.

If you do the procedure incorrectly and wish you *hadn't* pressed the Format Painter button, just click the Undo button, which makes the document return to its previous appearance.

AutoFormat

If you click the **AutoFormat button**, the computer will analyze your document and try to improve the way it looks.

For example, if your document contains what seems to be a heading, the computer will make it Arial 14-point bold. If you're writing a letter that ends with —

Sincerely,

and a few other lines underneath it, the computer will indent the word "Sincerely" and the lines underneath, so they all begin at the center of the paper instead of at the left margin. If a line in your document begins with the symbol * or + or -, and you've put a space after that symbol, the computer replaces the symbol with a bullet (●). If a paragraph begins with a number (such as "1."), the computer indents all the paragraph's lines, so they're all indented farther than the "1." The computer makes many other improvements also!

But here's an exception: if you *already* tried to fiddle with the appearance of a line, the computer leaves that line alone.

So if you were too stupid to give formatting commands, the computer does the formatting for you. But if you formatted a line yourself, the computer assumes you're a pro who knows what you're doing, and the computer leaves your formatting alone.

If you pressed the AutoFormat button and like what the computer did to your document, great! Go ahead and edit the document further!

If you *don't* like what the computer did, click the Undo button, which makes the document return to its previous appearance.

Check your spelling

Kan yoo spel gud? Yure nott shoor?

The computer can check the words in your document, to make sure you spelled them all correctly.

For example, type a short document that contains just this one sentence:

Be huppy!

To spell-check the document, click in the middle of the document's first word ("Be"), then click the **Spelling button**.

The computer looks up each word in the dictionary. It starts at the word you clicked (the document's first word), then looks up all the other words also.

For example, if you typed "Be huppy!", the computer finds "Be" in the dictionary but can't find "huppy". The computer highlights the strange word "huppy" and prints this list of suggestions:

hoopoe
happy
guppy
puppy

Notice that the computer's immense vocabulary even includes "hoopoe", which is a European bird that looks like a cross between a parrot and a zebra!

You have several choices:

If you meant "hoopoe", "happy", "guppy", or "puppy", click what you meant & then click "Change".
If you meant "huppy" and want to add that slang word to the dictionary, click "Add".
If you meant "huppy" but don't want to add that slang word to the dictionary, click "Ignore".
If you meant some other word instead, type that word in the "Change To" box and click "Change".

When the computer finishes checking the entire document, the computer says, "The spelling check is complete." Click "OK".

Starting in the middle To spell-check a document, you normally begin by clicking the document's *first* word. If you click a different word instead, the computer begins by looking up *that* word in the dictionary, then checks the words that come afterwards in the document, then checks the document's beginning.

Columns

In a newspaper, text is printed in many narrow **columns**. In a business letter, text is printed in a single wide column.

The computer assumes you want a single wide column. Here's how to tell the computer you want many narrow columns. . . .

Click the **Columns button**. You'll see a tiny picture of a newspaper page that has several columns. Point at that picture's leftmost column, and drag to the right, until the number of columns you want turns blue.

For example, if you want 3 columns, drag to the right until 3 columns turn blue. If you want 6 columns, drag to the right until 6 columns turn blue.

When you take your finger off the mouse's button, your entire document changes, so it has as many columns as you requested.

After you've finished typing a paragraph (and pressed ENTER), try this experiment: while holding down the Ctrl and SHIFT keys, press ENTER again. That creates a **column break**: it makes the next paragraph be at the top of the next column.

Change your mind? If you change your mind and want just 1 column, click the Columns button again, so you see the tiny picture of a newspaper page again. Click that picture's left column, so just one column turns blue.

Tables

In the middle of a document, you can type a table of numbers. Here's how.

Click the **Insert Table button**. You see a tiny picture of a table that has 4 rows and 5 columns. Altogether, it contains 20 cells (since 4 times 5 is 20).

Point at that table's top left cell, and drag down and to the left, until the number of rows and columns you want turns blue.

For example, if you want just 3 rows and 4 columns, drag down and to the right until 3 rows and 4 columns turn blue, so you see 12 blue cells altogether.

When you take your finger off the mouse's button, you'll see the table you requested.

Then just fill in the cells with whatever numbers and words you wish. To move from cell to cell, click with the mouse, or press the TAB key (which moves right to the next cell), or press SHIFT with TAB (which moves left to the previous cell), or press the arrow keys repeatedly.

In a cell, you can type a number, word, sentence, or even an entire paragraph! If you start typing a paragraph in a cell, the computer will automatically make the cell and its row taller, so the entire paragraph will fit in the cell. You can even type *several* paragraphs in a single cell: just press the ENTER key at the end of each paragraph. If you want to indent the first line of one of those paragraphs, press the SPACE bar several times or press Ctrl with TAB.

Gridlines On the screen, each cell is a rectangle made of 4 dotted lines. Those lines are called the **gridlines**.

When you print the table onto paper, the paper will *not* show those dotted gridlines: the gridlines appear just on the screen, not on paper.

Extra rows Here's how to create an extra row at the bottom of the table: click in the table's bottom right cell, then press the TAB key.

Here's how to insert an extra row into the *middle* of the table: click in the row that's underneath where you want the extra row to appear, then click the Insert Table button again.

Column widths The computer assumes you want the table's columns to all be the same width. But you can change that assumption!

For example, here's how to adjust the width of the table's left column (column 1). Move the mouse until its pointer is on the vertical gridline that separates column 1 from column 2, and the pointer's shape turns into this symbol: ←||→. Then drag the vertical gridline to the right (to make the column wider) or left (to make the column narrower).

If you make a column wider, the computer shrinks all columns to the right of it. If you make a column narrower, the computer expands all columns to the right of it.

If you want to fine-tune the widths of *all* columns, work from left to right: adjust the width of column 1 (by dragging the gridline that separates it from column 2), then adjust the width of column 2 (by dragging the gridline that separates it from column 3), then adjust the width of column 3 (by dragging the gridline that separates it from column 4), etc.

Numbers If a column contains mostly numbers, here's how to make that column look prettier, so the numbers are aligned properly.

Move the mouse until its pointer is at the *very top* of the column and is centered on the gridline above the column, so the pointer's shape turns into this symbol: ↓. Then click. The entire column turns black.

Push in the Align Right button (on the formatting toolbar). That makes all cells in that column be aligned right, so the numbers are aligned properly.

Table AutoFormat When you've finished typing numbers and words into all the cells, try this trick: click in the middle of the table by using the mouse's *right* button (instead of the left button). A menu appears on the screen. From that menu, choose **Table AutoFormat**, then press ENTER.

That makes the computer analyze all your columns and improve their widths. The computer will make each column become just wide enough to hold the data in it.

The computer will also underline the headings atop the columns.

If you like what the computer did to your table, great! Go ahead and edit the table further!

If you *don't* like what the computer did, click the Undo button, which makes the table return to its previous appearance.

Below the table When you've finished editing the table, here's how to put paragraphs below it.

Click below the table by using the mouse, or go below the table by pressing the down-arrow key several times. Then type the paragraphs you want below the table.

Delete Here's how to delete a row, column, or the entire table.

Click in the middle of what you want to delete. From the **Table menu**, choose **Select Row** (if you want to delete a row) or **Select Column** (if you want to delete a column) or **Select Table** (if you want to delete the entire table). The row, column, or table you selected turns black.

Next, from the Table menu, choose **Delete**.

Preview

If you're wondering what a page will look like but don't want to waste a sheet of paper to find out, click the **Print Preview button**. The computer will show you a mock-up of what the entire page will look like: you'll see the entire page, shrunk to fit on the screen.

Since the entire page is shrunk to fit on the screen, the page and its characters look too tiny for you to read the words easily, but you'll be able to see the page's overall appearance: how much of the page is filled up, which parts of the page are blank, and whether the info on the page is centered.

Wouldn't you like to ride in an airplane, fly high above your house, and see an aerial view of your house and neighborhood, so all the people look like tiny specs, and you see — in one amazing view — the overall layout of your house and yard and neighborhood and city? Wouldn't you be thrilled? Clicking the Print Preview button gives you that same thrill: you see an aerial view of the page you were typing, as if you were flying over it in an airplane: you see the layout of your entire page in one amazing view, and the characters on it look like tiny specs.

While you're admiring the view, the word "Close" appears at the screen's top center. When you finish admiring the view, click the word "Close".

Zoom

Look at the **Zoom Control box**. In that box, you normally see the number 100%. That means the computer's screen is showing you the actual size of what will appear on paper.

To the right of the Zoom Control box, you see a down-arrow. Click it. You see this **Zoom menu**:

```
200%
150%
100%
75%
50%
25%
10%
Page Width
Whole Page
Two Pages
```

If you click **200%**, the computer makes the screen's characters be twice as big, so you can read them even if you're sitting far away from the screen or you have poor vision. It's like looking at the document through a magnifying glass: the document looks enlarged, so you can see the details of each word and character more clearly; but not as many words and characters fit on the screen. Use the arrow keys to see different parts of the page.

Clicking 200% enlarges just what you see on the *screen*: it does *not* enlarge what appears on paper.

Try it! Try clicking 200%!

When you finish admiring that view, make the screen return to normal, by choosing **100%** from the Zoom menu.

If you click **Whole Page** instead of 200%, the computer does just the opposite: the computer makes the screen's characters be very tiny, so the whole page fits on the screen — as if you were doing a print preview.

CONTROL KEY

On your keyboard, you'll see a key marked "Ctrl". It's called the **CONTROL key**. Here's how to use it.

Buttons

Try this experiment: *while holding down the Ctrl key*, tap the U, B, I, L, R, J, E, S, N, or O key.

Pressing Ctrl with U is the same as clicking the Underline button.
Pressing Ctrl with B is the same as clicking the Bold button.
Pressing Ctrl with I is the same as clicking the Italic button.

Pressing Ctrl with L is the same as clicking the Left Align button.
Pressing Ctrl with R is the same as clicking the Right Align button.
Pressing Ctrl with J is the same as clicking the Justify button.
Pressing Ctrl with E is the same as clicking the Center button (also called the "Equidistant" button).

Pressing Ctrl with S is the same as clicking the Save button.
Pressing Ctrl with N is the same as clicking the New button.
Pressing Ctrl with O is the same as clicking the Open button.

Partial printing

Clicking the Print button makes the printer print your *entire* document.

If you want to print just *part* of your document, do this instead of clicking the Print button: while holding down the Ctrl key, tap the P key.

Then say how much of your document to print.

To print just the page you were working on, click the Current Page button.
To print just pages 1, 3, and 5 through 8, click the Pages button, then type "1,3,5-8".
If you selected (blackened) a phrase in your document, print just that by clicking the Selection button.

Then click "OK".

Page break

After you've finished typing a paragraph (and pressed ENTER), try this experiment: while holding down the Ctrl key, press ENTER again. That creates a **page break**: it makes the next paragraph be at the top of the next page.

If you change your mind, here's how to remove the page break: click at the beginning of the paragraph you've put at the top of a page; then press the BACKSPACE key.

Column break

If you've divided your document into columns (by clicking the Columns button), and finished typing a paragraph in one of the columns, try this experiment: while holding down the Ctrl and SHIFT keys, press ENTER again. That creates a **column break**: it makes the next paragraph be at the top of the next column.

If you change your mind, here's how to remove the column break: click at the beginning of the paragraph you've put at the top of a column; then press the BACKSPACE key.

Controlled movement

When you're editing your document, here's what happens if you press the movement keys while holding down the Ctrl key:

Keys you press	Where the pointer will move
Ctrl with right-arrow	right (to the next word or punctuation symbol)
Ctrl with left-arrow	left (to the beginning of a word or punctuation)
Ctrl with down-arrow	down to the next paragraph
Ctrl with up-arrow	up to the beginning of a paragraph
Ctrl with PAGE DOWN	down to the last word on the screen
Ctrl with PAGE UP	up to the first word on the screen
Ctrl with END	down to the end of the document
Ctrl with HOME	up to the beginning of the document

If you've typed a document that's several pages long, here's how to move back to page 2: press Ctrl with G (which means "go to"); then type a 2 and press ENTER. You'll see page 2 on the screen. Then press the Esc key.

Find

Here's how to make the computer search through your document to find whether you've used the word "love".

Click where you want the search to begin. (For example, if you want the search to begin at the document's beginning, click in the middle of the document's first word.) Then while holding down the Ctrl key, tap the F key. Type the word you want to find ("love") and press ENTER.

The computer searches for "love". If the computer finds a "love" in your document, it highlights that "love" so it turns black. If you want to find the next "love" in your document, press ENTER; if you do *not* want to search for more "love", press the Esc key instead.

Q&A WRITE

STARTING

Here's how to start using Q&A versions 3 and 4 for DOS. (If you're still using version 1, 1.1, or 2, follow my instructions for version 3, which is similar. Better yet, upgrade!)

I'll assume you have a hard disk whose CONFIG.SYS file mentions "files" and "buffers" (as I recommended in the MS-DOS chapter).

Copy Q&A to the hard disk

Version 3 comes on seven 5¼-inch floppies. Version 4 comes on eight 5¼-inch floppies. (If you want 3½-inch floppies, ask your dealer for the 3½-inch version.)

Here's how to copy Q&A to the hard disk.

Version 3 Turn on the computer without any floppy in drive A. After the C prompt, type "md qa" (so you're making a subdirectory called QA). After the next C prompt, type "cd qa" (so you're changing to the QA subdirectory).

Put Q&A System Disk 1 into drive A, and type "copy a:*.*" (which copies all the floppy's files onto the hard disk). Follow the same procedure for all the other Q&A floppy disks, in numerical order: do Q&A System Disk 2, then Q&A System Disk 3, etc., and finally the Q&A Tutorial.

Version 4 Turn on the computer without any floppy in drive A. When you see the C prompt, put the Q&A #1 Install Disk in drive A and type "a:install".

The computer says, "Q&A Version 4.0 Installation". Press ENTER twice.

The computer says, "DESTINATION DRIVE SELECTION". Press the down-arrow key twice, so the "C:" is darkened. Press ENTER.

The computer says "C:\QA4". Tap the BACKSPACE key (so you change the computer's message to "C:\QA"). Press ENTER twice.

Here's what happens next (when you're using 5¼-inch floppies).

The computer says, "Please insert disk 2". Put the Q&A #2 Disk in drive A and press ENTER.
The computer says, "Please insert disk 3". Put the Q&A #3 Disk in drive A and press ENTER.
The computer says, "Please insert disk 4". Put the Q&A #4 Disk in drive A and press ENTER.
The computer says, "Please insert disk 5". Put the Q&A #5 Disk in drive A and press ENTER.
The computer says, "Please insert disk 6". Put the Q&A #6 Disk in drive A. Press ENTER 4 times.

Then the computer shows the top of an alphabetical list of printers. Press the down-arrow key several times, until *your* printer is darkened.

Press the SPACE bar (so a check mark appears next to your printer). Press ENTER 4 times.

Here's what happens next:

The computer shows a list of tutorial files. Press the F5 key. Press ENTER.
The computer says, "Please insert disk 7". Put the Q&A #7 Disk in drive A. Press ENTER 4 times.
The computer shows a list of databases. Press the F5 key. Press ENTER 4 times.

Then the computer shows a list of utility files. Put check marks next to ASC-CODE.ASC, LINE-DOC.DOC, and QABACKUP.EXE. (Do *not* put a check mark next to HIMEM.SYS, since that version of HIMEM.SYS is obsolete.) To create a check mark, press the down-arrow key repeatedly until the item you want to check is darkened, then press the SPACE bar. When you've created all three check marks, end the whole process by pressing ENTER.

The computer says, "Please insert disk 8". Put the Q&A #8 Disk in drive A. Press ENTER 5 times.

Make Q&A act better

After you've copied Q&A to the hard disk, make Q&A act better. Here's how.

Step 1: get to the utilities menu Type "qa". Computer says "Q&A MAIN MENU". Press U then ENTER. Computer says "UTILITIES MENU".

Step 2: select automatic execution Press S then ENTER. Press the down-arrow key several times, until the words "Automatic Execution" are highlighted. Press the left-arrow key (so that the word "Yes" is highlighted). Press

the F10 key. Computer says "UTILITIES MENU" again.

Step 3: select a printer Press P. The computer will say "PRINTER SELECTION". Press ENTER twice.

If you're using version 3, here's what happens next:

Computer says "LIST OF PRINTERS". Press the PAGE DOWN (or PgDn) key repeatedly until you see the name of your printer (or a similar printer). Use the arrow keys to move to your printer's name. Press ENTER twice. Press the F10 key.

If you're using version 4, this happens instead:

Computer says "LIST OF PRINTER MANUFACTURERS". If you don't see name of your printer's manufacturer, press PAGE DOWN (or PgDn) key. Use arrow keys to move to your printer's name. Press ENTER. You see a list of printer models. Use arrow keys and PAGE DOWN key to move to your printer model. Press ENTER twice.

Finally, the computer says, "Your printer has been installed". Press N. The computer says "UTILITIES MENU" again.

Step 4: exit Press the "Esc" key. Press X. You'll see a C prompt. Turn off the computer, so you can start fresh.

Run Q&A

To run Q&A, turn on the computer without any floppy in drive A.

If you've put the DO.BAT file onto your hard disk (as I recommended in the MS-DOS chapter) and put Q&A into the QA subdirectory (as I recommended above), your life is easy! Just type "do qa".

If you have *not* put DO.BAT onto your hard disk, do this instead: type "cd qa" and then "qa".

The computer will print this on the screen:

```
Q&A MAIN MENU
F - File
R - Report
W - Write
A - Assistant
U - Utilities
X - Exit Q&A
```

That **main menu** is a list of the various activities the program can perform for you.

If you're using version 4 and have a mouse, you'll see a small red rectangle in the middle of the screen. Move that rectangle out of the way — to the screen's top right corner — by rolling the mouse toward your desk's back right corner.

Get into typing

To use Q&A's word processor, choose "W - Write" from the main menu by pressing the W key. (That works if you followed my instructions about "select automatic execution". If you did *not* follow those instructions, you must press ENTER after pressing W — and you must press ENTER after choosing any item from any menu!)

The screen will show the **write menu**:

```
WRITE MENU
T - Type/edit
D - Define page
P - Print
C - Clear
G - Get
S - Save
U - Utilities
M - Mailing labels
```

That menu is a list of what Q&A's word processor can do for you.

To begin, choose "T - Type/edit" from the write menu (by pressing T).

The lower right-hand corner of the screen will say "Line 1 of Page 1 of 1", which means you can begin typing your document.

Type the document

Begin typing whatever document you wish to create. For example, try typing a novel that begins like this:

Once upon a time, a man was walking down the street, when lo and behold, his house was gone. As he gaped into the hole, a burning sensation in his shoes warned him that . . .

I'll let you complete that paragraph yourself! Be creative!

Shift keys To capitalize a letter, type the letter while holding down a Shift key. (One Shift key is next to the Z key; the other Shift key is next to the ? key. Each Shift key has an up-arrow on it.)

BACKSPACE key If you make a mistake, erase it by pressing the BACKSPACE key, which erases the character you just typed. (The BACKSPACE key is in the upper-right corner of the keyboard's main section. It's to the right of the + key, and it has a left-arrow on it.)

ENTER key As you type that paragraph and get near the right margin, do *not* press the ENTER key. Just keep on typing! The computer will press the ENTER key for you automatically.

If you try to type a long word near the right margin, and the word's too long to fit before the margin, the computer will automatically move the entire word to the line below. The computer's ability to automatically move an entire word to the line below is called **word wrap**.

Since the computer automatically presses the ENTER key for you, **never press the ENTER key yourself until you reach the end of a paragraph**. Pressing the ENTER key there makes the computer return to the left margin, so that you can begin a new paragraph. Pressing the ENTER key means: begin a new paragraph.

If you want to double-space between paragraphs, press the ENTER key *twice*.

TAB key If you want to indent the new paragraph's first word, press the TAB key before typing that word. (The TAB key is next to the Q key and has arrows on it.) Pressing the TAB key indents the word a half inch.

To indent the word even farther, press the TAB key *extra* times before typing the word. Each *extra* time you press the TAB key, the word indents a *full* inch farther.

Lists To type a list of short lines, such as this recipe for White Death Cookies —

3 cups of powdered milk
2 cups of water
1 pound of sugar
1 pound of cocaine
mix & shape
bake at 350 degrees for 15 minutes
serves 7 ghosts

press the ENTER key at the end of each line.

Try typing this English-French dictionary:

ENGLISH	FRENCH
love	amour
pain	peine
tenderness	tendresse

Here's how. Type the first column's heading (ENGLISH), press the TAB key several times (to move far to the right), type the second column's heading (FRENCH), and press ENTER. Type "love", press the TAB key repeatedly until you're under FRENCH, type "amour", and press ENTER. Use the same technique for the table's other lines.

CAPS LOCK

If you press the CAPS LOCK key, the letters of the alphabet will be automatically capitalized (and you'll be in **caps mode**), until you press the CAPS LOCK key again. When you're in caps mode, the screen's bottom center says "Caps".

If your keyboard is modern, its top right corner has a Caps Lock light. When you're in caps mode, that light glows.

NUM LOCK

On the keyboard's right side, you'll see a group of keys containing numbers. That group of keys is called the **numeric keypad**.

Try this experiment: on the numeric keypad, press the 5 key. If that made a "5" appear on your screen, you're in **number mode**. If that did *not* make a "5" appear on your screen, you're *not* in number mode. To switch to or from number mode, press the NUM LOCK key.

When you're in number mode, the screen's bottom center says "Num".

If your keyboard is modern, its top right corner has a Num Lock light. When you're in number mode, that light glows.

In this chapter, we'll use the numeric keypad for purposes more advanced than typing numbers. So to follow the instructions in this chapter, do *not* use those keys to type numbers: **do NOT be in number mode**. (Do *not* have the bottom of the screen say "Num". Do *not* let the Num Lock light glow. Do *not* let the 5 key put a "5" on the screen.)

Press the NUM LOCK key if necessary, so that you're *not* in number mode.

Move the cursor

After you've typed a few paragraphs (and pressed the ENTER key at the end of each paragraph), you can move around the screen and edit your document.

Arrow keys On your screen the short, blinking underline is called the **cursor**. To move the cursor up, press the key that has an up-arrow on it. You can move the cursor in all four directions, by pressing the up-arrow, down-arrow, left-arrow, and right-arrow keys. Each of those keys automatically repeats: so to move the cursor up *several* lines, just keep your finger on the up-arrow key a while.

(If the arrow keys don't work, that's because you're in number mode. Get out of number mode by pressing the NUM LOCK key.)

Word hop *While holding down the CONTROL key* (which says "Ctrl" on it), you can tap the right-arrow key. That makes the cursor hop to the right: to the next word.

While holding down the CONTROL key, you can tap the left-arrow key. That makes the cursor hop left to the beginning of the current word; if the cursor's *already* at the word's beginning, it will hop to the beginning of the previous word.

Pages A sheet of paper is called a **page**. The typical page is tall enough to hold 54 lines of your document. The page is taller than your screen, which holds just 21 lines.

As you type, the computer automatically divides your document into pages and screenfuls.

When you're at the top of a page, the screen shows the top of that sheet of paper, like this:

When you're at the bottom of a page, the screen shows the bottom of that sheet of paper, like this:

When you're moving from one page to the next, the screen shows the bottom of one page and then the top of the next page, like this:

Near the top and bottom of each page, the screen shows a blank space, for the top and bottom margins.

Far hop To make the cursor hop far, press these keys:

Keys you press	Where the cursor will move
HOME	the beginning of the line
HOME HOME	the top of the screen
HOME HOME HOME	the top of the page
HOME HOME HOME HOME	the beginning of the document
Ctrl with HOME	very top (same as four HOMEs)
END	the end of the line
END END	the bottom of the screen
END END END	the bottom of the page
END END END END	the end of the document
Ctrl with END	very end (same as four ENDs)
PAGE UP (PgUp)	the previous screenful
PAGE DOWN (PgDn)	the next screenful
Ctrl with PgUp	the previous page
Ctrl with PgDn	the next page

DELETE key

To delete the character you just typed, press the BACKSPACE key. To delete a character you typed long ago, move the cursor to that character, then press the DELETE key (which says "Del" on it). To delete a passage typed long ago, move the cursor to passage's beginning, then tap the DELETE key several times (or hold down the DELETE key a while), until the passage disappears.

Combine paragraphs After typing two paragraphs, here's how to combine them to form a single paragraph that's longer.

By pressing the up-arrow key, move the cursor to the first paragraph's bottom line. Move to the end of that line, by pressing the END key. Delete the end-of-paragraph mark, by pressing the DELETE key.

Press the DELETE key a few more times (to delete unwanted TAB spaces and ENTERs).

INSERT key

Q&A can be in two modes: **typeover** or **insert**.

When you start using Q&A, it's in typeover mode. In typeover mode, the cursor's an underline.

To switch to insert mode, tap the INSERT key (which says "Ins" on it). When you're in insert mode, the bottom of the screen says "Insert" and the cursor's a square (instead of an underline). To switch back to typeover mode, tap the INSERT key again.

How to type over Suppose your document contains incorrect characters. Here's how to replace them.

Move the cursor to where the incorrect characters begin. Make sure you're in typeover mode (so that the cursor's an underline). Then type over the characters you want to change.

How to insert Here's how to insert extra characters into the middle of your document.

Move the cursor to where you want the extra characters to begin. Make sure you're in insert mode (by tapping the INSERT key if necessary), so that the bottom of the screen says "Insert" and the cursor's a square. Then type the characters you want to insert.

The other characters on the screen will automatically move out of the way to make room for the extra characters.

Split a paragraph Here's how to split a paragraph into two shorter paragraphs.

What word should begin the second short paragraph? Move the cursor to that word's first letter.

Make sure you're in insert mode (by pressing the INSERT key if necessary), so that the bottom of the screen says "Insert". Press ENTER. Now you've split the long paragraph into two!

If you want to double-space between the two short paragraphs, press ENTER again. If you want to indent the second paragraph, press the TAB key.

FUNCTION KEYS

On the keyboard, you'll see **function keys** labeled F1, F2, F3, F4, F5, F6, F7, F8, F9, and F10. If your keyboard is modern, those function keys are on the *top* of the keyboard, along with two extra keys (F11 and F12).

By pressing the function keys, you can give these commands:

Command	Keys to press	Notes for version 3 users
Assign fonts	Ctrl F9	
Calculate	Alt F9	
Capitalize	F8 then B then A	This command is just in version 4.
Center	F8 then A then C	In version 3, press F8 then C.
Continue	F10	
Copy	F5	
Copy to file	Ctrl F5	
Define page	Ctrl F6	
Delete block	F3	
Delete line	Shift F4	
Delete to right	Ctrl F4	
Delete word	F4	
Double space	F8 then A then D	This command is just in version 4.
Draw	F8 then L then D	In version 3, press F8 then D.
Enhance	Shift F6	
Export	Ctrl F8	
Field	Alt F7	
Footer	F8 then L then F	In version 3, press F8 then F.
Go to	Ctrl F7	
Header	F8 then L then H	In version 3, press F8 then H.
Help	F1	
Hyphenate	Alt F6	
Insert doc	F8 then D then I	In version 3, press F8 then I.
Left	F8 then A then L	In version 3, press F8 then U.
Lowercase	F8 then B then L	This command is just in version 4.
Macro	Shift F2	
Macro run	Alt F2	This command is just in version 4.
Move	Shift F5	
Move to file	Alt F5	
New page	F8 then L then N	In version 3, press F8 then N.
Print	F2	
Print block	Ctrl F2	
Restore	Shift F7	
Right	F8 then A then R	This command is just in version 4.
Save	Shift F8	
Scroll up	F9	
Scroll down	Shift F9	
Search	F7	
Set tabs	F8 then L then S	In version 3, press F8 then S.
Single space	F8 then A then S	This command is just in version 4.
Spell	Shift F1	
Spell word	Ctrl F1	
Statistics	Ctrl F3	
Temp margin	F6	
Thesaurus	Alt F1	This command is just in version 4.
Title	F8 then B then T	This command is just in version 4.
Triple space	F8 then A then P	This command is just in version 4.

Put that chart (or a photocopy of it) next to the computer.

When you buy Q&A, you get a plastic **template** that you put next to the function keys. The template contains an abridged version of the chart.

While you're using Q&A, the bottom of Q&A's screen displays a different abridgment of the chart.

Here's how to use those function keys. . . .

Delete word (F4)

To delete a word, put the cursor at the word's first character, then say "Delete word" (by pressing the F4 key).

Delete line (Shift F4)

To delete a whole line of text, put the cursor in that line, then say "Delete line". (Here's how to say "Delete line": *while holding down the Shift key*, press the F4 key.)

Delete to right (Ctrl F4)

To delete the far right part of a line, put the cursor where that part begins, then say "Delete to right". (Here's how to say "Delete to right": *while holding down the Ctrl key*, press the F4 key.)

Go to (Ctrl F7)

To make the cursor hop to page 3, say "Go to" (by pressing Ctrl with F7), then type 3 and press F10.

Statistics (Ctrl F3)

If you say "Statistics" (by pressing Ctrl with F3), the computer will tell you how many words, lines, and paragraphs are in your document. It will also tell you how many words, lines, and paragraphs are in your document's first part (the part before the cursor) and how many are in the second part (the part after the cursor).

When you finish looking at those statistics, press the ESCAPE key (which says "Esc" on it).

Align (F8 A)

If a line of text is short, you can make the line be **aligned** in three ways: **flush left** or **centered** or **flush right**.

This line is flush left.

This line is centered.

This line is flush right.

The computer assumes you want each line to be flush left, unless you say otherwise. Here's how to change the line's alignment.

Version 4 Move the cursor to the line whose alignment you want to affect. (It can be a line you typed already or a line you're going to start typing.)

Press F8 then A. (The A stands for "align".) Then press L (to make the line be flush left) or C (to make the line be centered) or R (to make the line be flush right).

Version 3 Move the cursor to the line whose alignment you want to affect. It can be a line you typed already or a line you're going to start typing.

If you want to center the line, press F8 then C.

If you want the line to be flush left, put the cursor on the line's first word (or anywhere to the right of that word), then press F8 then U. (The U stands for "uncenter".)

Version 3 doesn't understand how to make the line be flush right.

Help (F1)

If you forget how to use Q&A, say "Help" (by pressing the first function key, F1). You'll see a chart that reminds you what each function key does. Then press the ESCAPE key (which says "Esc" on it).

BLOCKS

You can manipulate a large portion of your document with a single keystroke! The portion you're manipulating is called the **block**. It can consist of several words, several sentences, several paragraphs, or even several pages.

To manipulate a block, put the cursor at the block's beginning. (For example, to manipulate a whole paragraph, put the cursor at the paragraph's beginning.) Then give one of these commands. . . .

Delete block (F3)

To delete the block, say "Delete block" (by pressing F3). Then put the cursor at the block's last character, and press F10.

Copy (F5)

To copy the block (instead of deleting it), say "Copy" (by pressing F5). Then put the cursor at the block's last character, and press F10. Put the cursor where you want the block's copy to appear, and press F10.

Move (Shift F5)

To move the block (so it vanishes from its current location and reappears elsewhere), say "Move" (by pressing Shift with F5). Then put the cursor at the block's last character, and press F10. Move the cursor where you want the block's new position to be, then press F10 again.

Enhance (Shift F6)

To enhance the block (so it looks different from the rest of the document and stands out), say "Enhance" (by pressing Shift with F6).

Then say which enhancement to perform:

press U to Underline (so the block looks <u>like this</u>)
press B to make Bold (so the block looks **like this**)
press I to italicize (so the block looks *like this*)
press X to X out (so the block looks ~~like this~~)
press S to Subscript (so the block is lowered, like this)
press P to suPerscript (so the block is raised, like this)
press R to make Regular again (so the block looks like this)

Put the cursor at the block's last character, and press F10.

<u>Don't see the bold?</u> If you pressed B (to make Bold) but the block doesn't look bold, adjust your screen's contrast and brightness knobs.

<u>Don't see the underline?</u> If you're using a CGA, EGA, or VGA monitor and pressed U (to underline), the block will change color on the screen but won't be underlined until you print it on paper.

<u>Don't see other enhancements?</u> If you pressed I (to italicize), the block will change color on the screen. It will be italicized just on paper, and just if your printer knows how to italicize.

You face the same hassle with other enhancements (X out, subscript, and superscript): on your screen the block just changes color. The desired enhancements occur just on paper, and just if your printer knows how to perform them.

FINAL STEPS

After editing your document, copy it onto the hard disk and paper and move on to a different task. Here's how. . . .

Save (Shift F8)

While you're typing and editing your document, it's in the computer's RAM chips but *not* on a disk. If the computer's electricity is knocked out (by a thunderstorm or by your cat pulling the plug) or you accidentally hold down the DELETE key awhile, the RAM chips and your document will be erased.

To protect against accidents, copy your document onto a disk. Copying a document onto a disk is called **saving**.

To save, just say "Save" (by pressing Shift with F8).

Then the computer will ask you to invent a name for your document. The name must be short: no more than 8 letters. For example, the name can be "jennifer" or "al". Type the name you wish and press ENTER.

The computer will copy the document onto the hard disk (drive C) and put that document into the QA subdirectory.

Afterwards, if you improve the document by editing it further, the improved version will be in the RAM chips, but the disk will still contain the old version. To copy the improved version onto the disk, say "Save" again (by pressing Shift with F8) and press ENTER. The computer will replace the disk's old version by the new version.

Typing a long document? Say "Save" every 10 minutes, so if an accident happens you'll lose at most 10 minutes of work!

Print (F2)

Here's how to copy your writing onto paper.

Make sure the printer is turned on. Make sure you've saved your document (to protect yourself in case the printer doesn't work). Then say "Print" (by pressing F2). The computer will say "PRINT OPTIONS". Press F10.

Clear (Esc C)

Here's how to erase the screen (so you can start creating a new document).

Press the ESCAPE key, which says "Esc" on it. You'll see the write menu. Choose "C - Clear" (by pressing C).

If the computer asks "Are you SURE you want to continue?", press Y.

Get (Esc G)

Here's how to copy a document from your hard disk to your screen.

Press the ESCAPE key, which says "Esc" on it. You'll see the write menu. Choose "G - Get" (by pressing G). Either type "jennifer" (and press ENTER) or choose JENNIFER from a menu (by pressing ENTER, moving the cursor to JENNIFER, and pressing F10).

If the computer asks, "Are you SURE you want to continue?", press Y.

Exit (Esc Esc)

When you've finished using Q&A's word processor, press the Esc key twice. (If the computer asks, "Are you SURE?", press Y.) You'll see the main menu. Choose "X - Exit Q&A" (by pressing X). The screen will show a C prompt, so you can give a DOS command.

PAGE LAYOUT

Your page's general appearance is called the **layout**. Here's how to improve it.

(In version 4, some of the following commands require you to type the letter L. The L stands for "Layout".)

Header (F8 L H)

Normally, the top 6 lines of each page are blank, to form the top margin. Anything you scribble in that margin is called a **header**.

For example, suppose you're writing a top-secret memo and want to scribble this note in the top margin of every page:

```
Reminder! The info in this memo is TOP SECRET!
```

Here's how to do it.

Say "Header". (To do that in version 4, press F8 then L then H. To do that in version 3, press F8 then H).

Type the header:

```
Reminder! The info in this memo is TOP SECRET!
```

Then press F10. The computer will put that header in the top margin of every page.

If you don't like that header, try one of these:

```
Please do not copy! It's copyrighted by starving author!
ACHTUNG! To keep your job, reply to this memo by Friday!
SALE! To order any of these items, call our 800 number!
I love you!!! I love you!!! I love you!!! I love you!!!
```

If you change your mind and want to edit the header, just say "Header" again, retype the header, and press F10 again.

The header can be *several* lines long.

While typing the header, you can use all of Q&A's editing techniques. For example, while typing the header, you can center it by saying "Center". (In version 4, that's F8 then A then C; in version 3, that's F8 then C.)

Page numbers
The computer can print page numbers on each page. Here's how to make the computer print "Page 1 of the Great American Novel" at the top of page 1, print "Page 2 of the Great American Novel" at the top of page 2, etc.

Say "Header" (by pressing F8 then H). Type this —

```
Page # of the Great American Novel
```

and press F10.

That makes the computer number all the pages. The computer prints "Page 1 of the Great American Novel" on the first page, "Page 2 of the Great American Novel" on the second page, etc.

Footer (F8 L F)

To print in the bottom margin (instead of the top margin), say "Footer" instead of "Header". (In version 4, "Footer" is F8 then L then F. In version 3, "Footer" is F8 then F.)

Define page (Ctrl F6)

The computer assumes that when the document is printed on paper, you want each character to be a tenth of an inch wide and a sixth of an inch high. To change that assumption and others, say "Define page" (by pressing Ctrl with F6).

Then the computer says:

Left margin: 10	Right margin : 68
Top margin : 6	Bottom margin: 6
Page width : 78	Page length : 66

```
Characters per inch.............:   10   12   15   17
Begin header/footer on page #...:   1
Begin page numbering with page #:   1
```

That means:

the left margin's width is 10 characters (1 inch)
the right margin begins 68 characters (6.8 inches) from the paper's left edge
the top and bottom margins are each tall enough to hold 6 lines (1 inch)
the paper's width is 78 characters (7.8 inches)
the paper's height is 66 lines (11 inches)
the printer will make each character a 10th of an inch wide
headers and footers will be printed on all pages (beginning at page 1)
pages will be numbered starting at page 1

To edit those numbers, move the cursor (by pressing the arrow keys or ENTER). For example, if you want "Right margin" to be 75, move the cursor to "Right margin" (by pressing the right-arrow key repeatedly, or pressing TAB or ENTER once) and then type 75. If your paper's width is 8½ inches (85 characters), move the cursor to "Page width" (by pressing arrow keys repeatedly) and then type 85.

Characters per inch
To make each character to be small (just a 17th of an inch wide), move the cursor to "Characters per inch" and then move the cursor to 17.

The first time you use Q&A, I recommend that you stick with 10 characters per inch, for two reasons:

1. Some printers have difficulty printing more than 10 characters per inch.

2. If you change the number of characters per inch, you must also change the margins. For example, suppose you want the left margin to be 1 inch wide. If you change to 17 characters per inch, you must tell the computer to make the left margin be 17 characters wide instead of 10 characters wide.

Begin headers/footers
Suppose you create a document in which the first three pages are special. (For example, a title page, then an acknowledgment page, then a table-of-contents page.) Suppose you want to omit the header or footer from those first three pages, so that the header or footer appears just on pages 4, 5, 6, etc. To do that, move the cursor to "Begin header/footer on page #", then type 4.

Begin page numbering
If your header or footer says to print a page number, the computer normally makes the first header or footer say "page 1" and the headers or footers on later pages say "page 2", "page 3", etc.

If you want the first header or footer *not* to say "page 1", tell the computer what page number to say instead. For example, if you told the computer to omit the header or footer from three special pages, so that the first header or footer is on page 4, you probably want that header or footer to say "page 4". To do that, move the cursor to "Begin page numbering with page #" and type 4.

Finish
When you finish editing, and the entire screenful of numbers looks correct, press F10.

New page (F8 L N)

Here's how to leave the bottom part of page 2 blank, so that you can scribble a diagram in the blank and make the next topic begin on a fresh new page.

Type whatever words you want on page 2. At the end of last paragraph you want on page 2, press ENTER.

Then say "New page". (To do that in version 4, press F8 then L then N. To do that in version 3, press F8 then N.)

The computer leaves the bottom of page 2 blank and hops to the top of page 3. What you type next will appear at the top of page 3 instead of the bottom of page 2.

Page-break symbol Saying "New page" is called **inserting a page break**. When you say "New page" at the bottom of page 2, the computer puts this symbol at the bottom of page 2's screen:

⌐

That symbol is called the **page-break symbol**. It appears just on your screen, not on paper.

If you say "New page" but then change your mind, put the cursor on the page-break symbol and press the DELETE key.

Set tabs (F8 L S)

You press the TAB key to indent the top line of a paragraph, or to hop to a new column when typing a table.

Whenever you press the TAB key, the cursor moves toward the right, until it reaches the next **tab stop**.

If you want to change the positions of the tab stops, say "Set tabs". (To do that in version 4, press F8 then L then S. To do that in version 3, press F8 then S.)

You'll see a **ruler** that has several T's on it. Each T is a tab stop.

To erase a tab stop, move the cursor to that T, then press DELETE. To create a new tab stop, move the cursor across to where you want that tab stop, then type T.

When you finish editing the tab stops, press F10.

Decimal tabs When you type a column of numbers, you want their decimal points to line up, like this:

```
    74.9
5,382,931.726
    -.82
```

Those decimal points are **aligned** with each other. Here's how to type that column of numbers with aligned decimal points. . . .

Say "Set tabs". Move the cursor as far right as you want the decimal points to be. Type D, so that you see a D on the ruler. (The D stands for **decimal tab stop**.) Then press F10.

Move the cursor to the line where you want the first number to appear. Put the cursor at the beginning of that line (by pressing HOME if necessary). Press the TAB key several times, until you reach the position where you want the decimal point. Then type the first number (74.9). As you type it, the computer automatically shifts it towards the left, so its decimal point winds up where you requested. Press ENTER.

Now you're ready to type the second line. To do so, press TAB repeatedly, until the cursor's where you want the decimal point (underneath the first number's decimal point). Then type the second number (which is 5,382.931.726) and press ENTER.

For the third line, press TAB repeatedly until the cursor's where you want the decimal point, then type the third number and press ENTER.

Temp margin (F6)

Here's how to widen your document's left margin temporarily, so that an entire section of your document will be indented.

Indenting the next section To indent the next section that you'll type, put the cursor where you want the section to begin. Move the cursor to the right, as far as you want the section to be indented, so that the cursor's where you want the temporary left margin to be. Say "Temp margin" (by pressing F6) and "Left" (by pressing L).

Then type the words, sentences, and paragraphs that you want to be in the section. The entire section will be indented.

At the end of the section's last paragraph, press the ENTER key. Then say "Temp margin" (F6) and "Clear" (C). That ends the temporary margin, so the rest of your document will have the usual margin and not be indented.

Indenting a previous paragraph Here's how to indent a paragraph that you typed previously.

Put the cursor at the paragraph's beginning, so the cursor's on the first character of the paragraph's first word.

Make sure you're in insert mode (by pressing the INSERT key if necessary). Press the SPACE bar or TAB key several times until the paragraph's first word is indented as far as you wish. Then indent the rest of the paragraph by saying "Temp margin" (F6) and "Left" (L).

Unindenting a previous paragraph Here's how to unindent a paragraph that you typed and indented previously.

Put the cursor at the paragraph's beginning, so the cursor's on the first character of the paragraph's first word.

Make sure you're in insert mode (by pressing the INSERT key if necessary). Press the BACKSPACE key several times until the paragraph's first word is unindented. Then unindent the rest of the paragraph by saying "Temp margin" (F6) and "Clear" (C).

Draw (F8 L D)

Here's how to draw a line.

Put the cursor where you want the line to begin. Say "Draw". (To do that in version 4, press F8 then L then D. To do that in version 3, press F8 then D).

Then draw the line, by pressing the arrow keys. For example, to make the line go to the right a distance of 3 characters, press → three times. To make the line go to the right and then down, press → and then ↓. To draw a box of size 5, press → five times, then ↓ five times, then ← five times, then ↑ five times.

To draw a diagonal line, press the 1, 3, 7, or 9 key on the numeric keypad. To draw a *double* line, press the 2, 4, 6, or 8 keys on the numeric keypad while depressing the Shift key or turning on the Num Lock light.

When you finish drawing, press F10.

VOCABULARY

The computer can improve your vocabulary.

Spell (Shift F1)

Q&A comes with a disk that includes a list of all popular English words. That list is called a **dictionary**. Although that "dictionary" does *not* include definitions of those words, it *does* include each word's correct spelling. The dictionary contains 100,000 words.

You can tell the computer to check each word in your document against the dictionary, to make sure all the words in your document are spelled correctly. That's called **checking your spelling** or **doing a spelling check** or **doing a spell check** or **spell checking**.

If the computer notices that a word in your document is not in the dictionary, it highlights the word.

For example, type a short document that contains just this one sentence:

    Be huppy!

To spell-check the document, move the cursor to the beginning of the document, then say "Spell" (by pressing Shift with F1).

The computer looks up each word in the dictionary. The computer finds "Be" in the dictionary but can't find "huppy". The computer highlights the strange word "huppy" and prints this **spell-check menu**:

    L - List possible spellings
    I - Ignore word & continue
    A - Add to dictionary & continue
    S - Add to dictionary & stop
    E - Edit word & recheck

Choose "List possible spellings" (by pressing L). The computer prints this list of suggestions:

    1 puppy
    2 happy
    3 guppy
    4 hippy
    5 puppies

If you meant one of those words, type the word's number. If none of those words is what you meant, press the ESCAPE key (Esc) to return to the spell-check menu.

Here's how to use other choices on the spell-check menu. Choosing "Ignore word and continue" makes the computer ignore the "huppy" problem, so "huppy" stays in the document. Choosing "Add to dictionary & continue" makes the computer add the slang word "huppy" to its dictionary. Choosing "Edit word & recheck" makes the computer wait for you to type a word to replace "huppy"; when you finish typing the replacement,

press ENTER.

When the computer finishes checking the entire document, the bottom of the screen says "Spelling check completed".

Be careful about adding If the computer gripes about a word you typed, do *not* add your word to the computer's dictionary unless you're *sure* that you've spelled it correctly!

Start at the beginning Q&A spell-checks just the part of the document that comes after the cursor. To spell-check the *entire* document, make sure you put the cursor at document's beginning before you say "Spell".

Spell word (Ctrl F1)

If you say "Spell word" (Ctrl F1) instead of "Spell", the computer will check the spelling of just one word: the word where the cursor is. Say "Spell word" if you're nervous about the spelling of just one word and don't want to wait for the computer to check the spelling of your whole document.

Thesaurus (Alt F1)

Version 4 includes a **thesaurus**. (Version 3 does not. If you have version 3, skip ahead to the next topic.)

For example, suppose you'r writing a love story and type the word "caress". Can you think of a different word instead, that means roughly the same thing as "caress" but is better?

If you can't, the computer can! Just ask the computer to use its thesaurus to find **synonyms** for "caress".

Here's how. In your document, type the word "caress". Move the cursor to that word. Say "Thesaurus" (by pressing Alt with F1).

The computer prints these synonyms for "caress":

    noun: embrace, fondling, hug, kiss, squeeze, touch.

    verb: clutch, embrace, grasp, hold;
           feel, fool around, hold, make out, neck, nuzzle;
           cradle, cuddle, embrace, fondle, hug, love, pet, snuggle, stroke.

That means the noun "a caress" has 6 synonyms: an embrace, fondling, hug, kiss squeeze, and touch.) The verb "to caress" has 17 synonyms: to clutch, embrace, grasp, hold, feel, fool around, etc.

If one of those words interests you, go explore! For example, if the word "fondle" interests you, move the cursor to "fondle" and say "Thesaurus" again (Alt F1). The computer will print these synonyms for "fondle":

    verb: examine, feel, finger, grope, handle, manipulate, maul, palpate, paw,
           probe, touch;
           caress, cradle, cuddle, embrace, hug, love, pet, snuggle, stroke.

Notice that the computer is like a therapist: it realizes that a lover who wants to "fondle" might really want to "maul"!

If you want to replace "caress" by a synonym, move the cursor to the synonym you want and press F10. If you *don't* want to replace "caress", press the Esc key instead.

Have fun Is your sex life boring — or out of control? Ask the computer for a synonym!

Some of the computer's suggestions are peculiarly appropriate. If you request a synonym for "sex", the computer suggests "congress". If you want to "screw", the computer recommends having a "shaft". If you're looking for a "rabbi", the computer suggests a "padre" instead. Homosexuals will enjoy looking up the word "gay", which the computer considers to be "scintillating" and "ecstatic". Prostitutes don't fare as well: the computer considers them to be "mishandled", "misemployed", and "perverts". Don't be fooled by a man who acts "amorous"; just ask the computer for a reaction, and the computer will say "horny".

Go ahead: write a feminist article entitled, "Sexual Myths Perpetrated by Computer Thesaurus". Or write a sociolinguistic article entitled, "Sexual Practices Arising (Bigger and Bigger!) from the English Language — And Vice Versa". After all, our culture is defined by our language, isn't it?

Q&A lets you perform these advanced tricks!

Alt

Look back at page 125, column 1. It shows a list of special symbols, with their code numbers.

For example, it shows that the code number for the symbol ñ is 164. So to type the symbol ñ, do this: hold down the Alt key; and while you keep holding down the Alt key, type 164 *by using the numeric keypad* (the number keys on the far right side of the keyboard). When you finish typing 164, lift your finger from the Alt key, and you'll see ñ on your screen!

Bad code numbers Codes 20 and 21 don't work when you're using Q&A (though they work when typing MS-DOS commands). On laser printers (such as the Hewlett-Packard Laserjet 2), code 249 is • instead of ·, and code 252 is η instead of ⁿ.

Search (F7)

Here's how to make the computer search through your document to find whether you've used the word "love".

Say "Search" (by pressing F7). This menu appears:

```
Search for..:
Replace with:
Method......:  Manual   Automatic   Fast automatic
```

Type "love", so the menu looks like this:

```
Search for..: love
Replace with:
Method......:  Manual   Automatic   Fast automatic
```

Then press F7 again.

The computer searches for the word "love". If it can't find "love" in your document, it says "NOT FOUND". If it *does* find a "love" in your document, it says "FOUND", puts the cursor there, and waits for you to press F7 (to find the next "love") or Esc (to stop searching).

Replace fast Here's how to replace each "love" in your document by "idolize".

Say "Search" (by pressing F7). Make the menu look like this:

```
Search for..: love
Replace with: idolize
Method......:  Manual   Automatic   Fast automatic
```

To do that, type "love" and press ENTER, then type "idolize" and press ENTER, then press END (or → twice). When the menu looks like that, press F7.

The computer replaces every "love" by "idolize". Then it says "COMPLETED".

Replace manually Here's how to tell the computer to replace each "love" by "idolize" — but make the computer pause at each "love" so you can double-check whether you really want to replace it by "idolize".

Say "Search" (by pressing F7). Make the menu look like this:

```
Search for..: love
Replace with: idolize
Method......:  Manual   Automatic   Fast automatic
```

To do that, type "love" and press ENTER, then type "idolize" and press ENTER, and then — if "Manual" isn't highlighted already — press HOME (or ← repeatedly). When the menu looks like that, press F7.

The computer stops at the first "love" in your document.

If you want to replace that "love" by "idolize", press F10 then F7.

The computer stops at each "love" in your document and goes through the same routine (by waiting for you to press F10 then F7).

When the computer reaches the end of the document, it says "Search and replace completed".

If you want to stop that process before the computer finishes, press Esc (to stop the process entirely) or F7 (to avoid replacing the current "love" by "idolize" but continue searching for other "loves" to replace).

Wrong capitals When you tell the computer to replace, the computer doesn't bother to capitalize.

For example, consider this document:

I love you. Love you! LOVE YOU!

If you tell the computer to replace each "love" by "idolize", the computer produces this:

I idolize you. idolize you! idolize YOU!

Notice that the computer doesn't bother to capitalize "idolize". You must edit the document manually, to produce:

I idolize you. Idolize you! IDOLIZE YOU!

Phrases When the computer asks you what to search for, you can type a whole phrase. For example, instead of telling the computer to search for any "love", tell the computer to search for "love to sing".

Why search? Suppose you've written a history of America and want to find the part where you started talking about Lincoln. If you forget which page that was, no problem! Just put the cursor at the beginning of the document and tell the computer to search for "Lincoln".

Advanced menu Try this experiment: say "Search" (by pressing F7), so you see the search menu. Then press the PgDn key; that makes the search menu becomes longer, so it looks like this:

```
Search for..:
Replace with:
Method......:  Manual      Automatic   Fast automatic
Type........:  Whole words  Text       Pattern
Case........:  Insensitive  Sensitive
Range.......:  All          To end     To beginning
```

If you say to search for "love", the computer assumes you want to search for the word "love" but not for variants such as "loves", "lover", and "lovely". If you *do* want to search for such variants also, move the cursor to the word "Text" (so the word "Text" is highlighted). Then the computer will search for any word that contains "love". When it searches, the computer will stop at words such as "love", "loves", "lover", and "lovely". It will also stop at words such as "glove", "clove", "clover", "pullover", "slovenly", and "auriculoventricular".

If you say to search for "love", the computer assumes you also want to search for "Love" and "LOVE". If you do *not* want to search for such variants, move the cursor to the word "Sensitive" (so the word "Sensitive" is highlighted).

If you say to search for "love", the computer assumes you want to search through the entire document. The computer searches through the part of the document that comes after the cursor, then the part of the document that comes before. If you want to search through just the part of the document that comes after the cursor, highlight "To end". If you want to search through just the part of the document that comes before the cursor, highlight "To beginning".

Macro (Shift F2)

The computer can help you write love letters.

For example, suppose you want each love letter to end with this message: "As always, I love you passionately, forever, my darling!!!". Instead of typing that long message at the end of each love letter, you can make the computer automatically type the message for you!

To do that, choose a letter of the alphabet to stand for the message. For example, you can choose A or B or C. Here's how. . . .

Say "Macro" (by pressing Shift with F2). Then press D (which means "Define"). The computer says:

```
Type the macro identifier.  For example:  ALT-A, ALT-B, etc.
```

Choose a letter of the alphabet, such as A or B. Type that letter *while holding down the Alt key*.

(If the computer asks "That key is already defined; do you want to redefine it?", you should say "No" by pressing "N", then start the whole procedure over and choose a different letter of the alphabet.)

The screen's lower-right corner shows a flashing square. Type the message you want to record. For example, type:

```
As always, I love you passionately, forever, my darling!!!
```

At the end of the message, say "Macro" again (Shift F2). Then if you're using version 4, press F10.

The computer says:

```
If you want to save your macros to disk now, press ENTER.
```

Press ENTER.

In the future, whenever you want the computer to automatically type the passionate message, just press the chosen letter *while holding down the Alt key*.

Jargon The message that you're recording ("As always, I love you passionately, forever, my darling!!!") is called the **macro**. The **macro's name** is "Alt A" or "Alt B" or whatever other name you choose.

Why use macros? Whatever you type often, you should turn into a macro. The macro can even contain commands that make the computer underline, boldface, center, and do other fancy tasks. The macro can be any sequence of keystrokes you wish!

Creating a macro is like turning on a tape recorder: yes, the computer will record *any* keystrokes you wish! For example, the macro can even be a recording of the sequence of keystrokes that make the computer save your document onto the disk and then print your document on paper.

QAMACRO.ASC When you invent macros, the computer puts their definitions onto the hard disk, in a file called "QAMACRO.ASC". Unless you erase that file, the computer remembers your macro definitions forever.

Assign fonts (Ctrl F9)

Here are samples of popular fonts. . . .

```
This is a sample of the Courier font.
```
This is a sample of the Lineprinter font.

This is 8-point Times Roman, 10-point Times Roman, 12-point Times Roman.

This is 8-point Helvetica, 10-point Helvetica, 12-point Helvetica.

In the Courier font, each character is $1/10$ of an inch wide; so Courier's a **10-characters-per-inch font**. In Lineprinter, each character is $1/17$ of an inch wide. In Times Roman and Helvetica, each letter of the alphabet has its own width: for example, the letter "m" is wider than the letter "i".

Since Courier's characters all have the same width as each other, they're called **monospaced**. Lineprinter's characters are monospaced also. Times Roman and Helvetica are *not* monospaced; they're **proportionally spaced** instead.

A **point** is $1/72$ of an inch. The first sample of Times Roman is called *8-point* because it's 8 points high: the top of the capital T is 8 points higher than the bottom of the small p. The other samples of Times Roman are larger.

The computer assumes you want a 10-characters-per-inch font (such as Courier). To print the document in a different font, teach the computer which 9 fonts are your favorites. Here's how. . . .

Say "Assign fonts" (by pressing Ctrl with F9). Then press F6. The computer will say "LIST OF FILES".

Move the cursor to the name of your printer (or a similar printer) by pressing the down-arrow key several times. (If you're using version 4 with just one printer, use this short cut: just tap the END key.)

Press F10.

Choose a **regular font** (the font you plan to use most often, on a regular basis), as follows. Move the cursor down to the word "Regular", and press F6. You'll see a list of fonts. (If the list is too long to fit on the screen, press PgDn to see the rest of it.) Move the cursor to whichever font you want to become the regular font. (Make sure to choose a font that's in your printer or computer already, rather than an extra-cost optional font that you didn't buy yet.) Press F10.

Congratulations! You've chosen the regular font. Choose fonts 1, 2, 3, 4, 5, 6, 7, and 8 in the same way. So altogether, you're choosing a regular font plus 8 supplementary fonts.

When you finish choosing fonts, press F10.

Finish typing and editing your document. When you tell the computer to print the document on paper, the computer will print most of it by using the regular font you chose.

If you want a block in your document to use a different font instead, move the cursor to the block's beginning and say "Enhance" by pressing Shift with F6. (Then if you're using version 3, press F.) Type the desired font's number (1 through 8), move the cursor to the end of the block, and press F10.

WORD PERFECT

STARTING

Here's how to use the world's most popular word processor, **Word Perfect**. It's been published by **Word Perfect Corporation** (1555 North Technology Way, Orem, UT 84057, phone 801-225-5000). In 1994, Word Perfect Corporation became part of a bigger company, **Novell**.

Word Perfect has gradually improved. Word Perfect version 4.0 for MS-DOS led to versions 4.1, 4.2, 5.0, and 5.1. Most businesses use version 5.1.

This chapter explains Word Perfect version 5.1 for DOS. It also explains how earlier versions differed.

After inventing version 5.1 for DOS, Word Perfect Corporation developed fancier versions (such as **version 6 for DOS** and **version 6 for Windows**), but they're controversial because they consume more RAM, run more slowly, and require you to learn different keystrokes.

Discount dealers charge about $250 for the various versions.

To use version 5.1 for DOS, you need 512K of RAM. You'll also want a hard disk. If you don't own a hard disk yet, buy one! If you don't, you must have two floppy drives — and making Word Perfect use them is very awkward. If you try using version 5.1 with two floppy drives, they must be modern enough to hold at least 720K each.

I'll assume you have a hard disk whose CONFIG.SYS file mentions "files" and "buffers" (as I recommended in my MS-DOS chapter). Version 5.1 consumes 4½ megabytes of your hard disk; earlier versions consume less.

When you buy version 5.1, you get a dozen 5¼-inch floppy disks. (You also get 3½-inch disks containing the same info as the 5¼-inch disks. You get just a *few* 3½-inch disks, because each 3½-inch disk holds twice as many bytes as a 5¼-inch disk.)

Copy Word Perfect to the hard disk

Here's how to copy Word Perfect to the hard disk.

Version 5.1 Turn on the computer without any floppy in drive A. When you see the C prompt, put Word Perfect's "Install/Learn/Utilities 1" disk into drive A and type "a:".

The computer will display an A prompt. Type "install".

Here's what happens next, if your Word Perfect 5.1 disks are 5¼-inch. (The procedure for 3½-inch disks is similar.) I'll assume your disks were manufactured on or after May 31, 1991. (Disks manufactured before then don't work quite as nicely.)

The computer will say "Word Perfect Installation". Press ENTER.

The computer will ask, "Do you see red, green, and blue colored boxes?" If you see all three colors (because you have a color monitor), press ENTER; if you don't, press N.

The computer will ask, "Install to a hard disk?" Press ENTER.

Press C (which tells the computer you want to customize Word Perfect). Press T then W, then type "wp" (and press ENTER). That tells the computer you want to put Word Perfect into a hard-disk subdirectory called "WP". The computer will ask, "Create?" Press ENTER then E. Press ENTER twice.

Next, you perform an exercise in computerized calisthenics, called **shove and press**. When the computer tells you, shove a floppy disk into drive A and press ENTER several times. Here are the details:

What the computer will say	How you should respond
Insert the Install/Learn/Utilities 2 disk	insert it and press ENTER 7 times
Insert the Program 1 disk	insert it and press ENTER
Insert the Program 2 disk	insert it and press ENTER twice
Insert the Spell/Thesaurus 1 disk	insert it and press ENTER twice
Insert the Spell/Thesaurus 2 disk	insert it and press ENTER twice
Insert the PTR Program/Graphics 1 disk	insert it and press ENTER twice
Insert the PTR Program/Graphics 2 disk	insert it and press ENTER

Then the computer will ask, "Do you want to install the Small .DRS File?" Press N. Press ENTER 5 times.

The computer will say "Insert the Printer disk". Insert the Printer 1 disk and press ENTER. Press the PAGE DOWN (or PgDn) key repeatedly, until you see the name of your printer. In front of that name, you'll see a number. Type that number and press ENTER. (If you see *two* numbers, choose the number that does not have an asterisk.) Press ENTER again.

The computer will say to insert another Printer disk. Insert it and press ENTER twice.

The computer will say "Enter license number". Type that number (which is on the Customer Registration card that came in the Word Perfect package) and press ENTER. Press ENTER again.

You'll see an A prompt. Turn off the computer, so you can start fresh.

Old versions Turn on the computer without any floppy in drive A. After the C prompt, type "md wp" (so you're making a subdirectory called WP). After the next C prompt, type "cd wp" (so you're changing to the WP subdirectory).

Put one of Word Perfect's floppy disks into drive A, and type "copy a:*.*" (which copies all the floppy's files onto the hard disk). Follow the same procedure for the other Word Perfect disks.

Then turn off the computer, so you can start fresh.

Run Word Perfect

To run Word Perfect, turn on the computer without any floppy in drive A.

If you've put the DO.BAT file onto your hard disk (as I recommended in the MS-DOS chapter) and put Word Perfect into the WP subdirectory (as I recommended above), your life is easy! Just type "do wp".

If you have *not* put DO.BAT onto your hard disk, do this instead: type "cd wp" and then "wp".

You'll eventually see "Doc 1 Pg 1", which means you can begin typing your document.

Type the document

Begin typing whatever document you wish to create. For example, try typing a novel that begins like this:

Once upon a time, a man was walking down the street, when lo and behold, his house was gone. As he gaped into the hole, a burning sensation in his shoes warned him that . . .

I'll let you complete that paragraph yourself! Be creative!

Shift keys To capitalize a letter, type the letter while holding down a Shift key. (One Shift key is next to the Z key; the other Shift key is next to the ? key. Each Shift key has an up-arrow on it.)

BACKSPACE key If you make a mistake, erase it by pressing the BACKSPACE key, which erases the character you just typed. (The BACKSPACE key is in the upper-right corner of the keyboard's main section. It's to the right of the + key, and it has a left-arrow on it.)

ENTER key As you type that paragraph and get near the right margin, do *not* press the ENTER key. Just keep on typing! The computer will press the ENTER key for you automatically.

If you try to type a long word near the right margin, and the word's too long to fit before the margin, the computer will automatically move the entire word to the line below. The computer's ability to automatically move an entire word to the line below is called **word wrap**.

Since the computer automatically presses the ENTER key for you, **never press the ENTER key yourself until you reach the end of a paragraph**. Pressing the ENTER key there makes the computer return to the left margin, so that you can begin a new paragraph. Pressing the ENTER key means: begin a new paragraph.

If you want to double-space between paragraphs, press the ENTER key *twice*.

TAB key If you want to indent the new paragraph's first word, press the TAB key before typing that word. (The TAB key is next to the Q key and has arrows on it.) To indent that word even farther, press the TAB key *several* times. Each time you press the TAB key, the computer indents a half inch farther.

Lists To type a list of short lines, such as this recipe for White Death Cookies —

3 cups of powdered milk
2 cups of water
1 pound of sugar
1 pound of cocaine
mix & shape
bake at 350 degrees for 15 minutes
serves 7 ghosts

press the ENTER key at the end of each line.

Try typing this English-French dictionary:

ENGLISH	FRENCH
love	amour
pain	peine
tenderness	tendresse

Here's how. Type the first column's heading (ENGLISH), press the TAB key several times (to move far to the right), type the second column's heading (FRENCH), and press ENTER. Type "love", press the TAB key repeatedly until you're under FRENCH, type "amour", and press ENTER. Use the same technique for the table's other lines.

Version 4.0 If you're using version 4.0 (instead of a newer version), the computer will occasionally say "Position hyphen". To reply, tap the F1 key.

CAPS LOCK

If you press the CAPS LOCK key, the letters of the alphabet will be automatically capitalized (and you'll be in **caps mode**), until you press the CAPS LOCK key again. When you're in caps mode, the screen's bottom right corner says "POS" instead of "Pos".

If your keyboard is modern, its top right corner has a Caps Lock light. When you're in caps mode, that light glows.

NUM LOCK

On the keyboard's right side, you'll see a group of keys containing numbers. That group of keys is called the **numeric keypad**.

Try this experiment: on the numeric keypad, press the 5 key. If that made a "5" appear on your screen, you're in **number mode**. If that did *not* make a "5" appear on your screen, you're *not* in number mode. To switch to or from number mode, press the NUM LOCK key.

If your keyboard is modern, its top right corner has a Num Lock light. When you're in number mode, that light glows.

In this chapter, we'll use the numeric keypad for purposes more advanced than typing numbers. So to follow the instructions in this chapter, do *not* use those keys to type numbers: **do NOT be in number mode**. (Do *not* let the Num Lock light glow. Do *not* let the 5 key put a "5" on the screen.)

Press the NUM LOCK key if necessary, so that you're *not* in number mode.

Move the cursor

After you've typed a few paragraphs (and pressed the ENTER key at the end of each paragraph), you can move around the screen and edit your document.

Arrow keys On your screen the short, blinking underline is called the **cursor**. To move the cursor up, press the key that has an up-arrow on it. You can move the cursor in all four directions, by pressing the up-arrow, down-arrow, left-arrow, and right-arrow keys. Each of those keys automatically repeats: so to move the cursor up *several* lines, just keep your finger on the up-arrow key a while.

(If the arrow keys don't work, that's because you're in number mode. Get out of number mode by pressing the NUM LOCK key.)

HOME key Pressing the HOME key means "very". For example, if you press the HOME key and then the left-arrow key, the cursor will move "very left", to the beginning of the line. You can move very far in all four directions:

Keys you press	Where the cursor will move
HOME then ←	the beginning of the line
HOME then →	the end of the line
HOME then ↑	the top of the screen
HOME then ↓	the bottom of the screen

Another way to move to the end of the line is to press the END key.

If you press HOME then ↑, and the cursor is *already* at the top of the screen, the cursor will move to the top of the previous screen. If you press HOME then ↓, and the cursor is *already* at the bottom of the screen, the cursor will move to the bottom of the next screen.

Instead of pressing HOME then ↑, try this short cut: press the special "-" key that's on the keyboard's far right side (at the far right side of the numeric keypad). Similarly, instead of pressing HOME then ↓, press the numeric keypad's "+" key. (To use those short cuts, make sure you're not in number mode.)

Pressing HOME *twice* means "very very". If you press HOME twice and then ↑, the cursor will move "very very up", to the top of the whole document. If you press HOME twice and then ↓, the cursor will move "very very down", to the bottom of the whole document.

Pages A sheet of paper is called a **page**. The typical page is tall enough to hold 54 lines of your document. The page is taller than your screen, which holds just 24 lines.

If your document is longer than a page, your screen shows a horizontal dotted line at the bottom of each page. (That line is called a **page break**.)

If you press the PAGE DOWN key (PgDn), the cursor moves down to the next page. If you press the PAGE UP key (PgUp), the cursor moves up to the previous page.

Try this experiment: while holding down the CONTROL key (which says "Ctrl" on it), tap the HOME key. Then press ↑ (to move to the top of the current page) or ↓ (to move to the page's bottom) or type a number (for example, type 3 and then ENTER, to move to page 3).

When you finish typing a paragraph, you normally press the ENTER key, which tells the computer to end the paragraph. If you press the ENTER key *while holding down the CONTROL key*, the computer will end the paragraph *and insert a page break*, so that the next paragraph will appear at the top of the next page.

DELETE key

To delete the character you just typed, press the BACKSPACE key. To delete a character you typed long ago, move the cursor to that character, then press the DELETE key (which says "Del" on it). To delete a passage typed long ago, move the cursor to passage's beginning, then tap the DELETE key several times (or hold down the DELETE key a while), until the passage disappears.

Insert

Here's how to insert extra characters anywhere in your document. Move the cursor to where you want the extra characters to begin. Then type the characters you want to insert.

To make room for characters you're inserting, other characters on that line will automatically move to the right. They might move past the screen's right edge, so you can't see them; but they'll come back onto the screen again when you move the cursor.

Replace characters If your document contains incorrect characters, you can replace them by using two methods.

Method 1. Move the cursor to the beginning of the incorrect characters. Press the DELETE key several times, until the incorrect characters disappear. Then type the characters you want instead.

Method 2. Move the cursor to the beginning of the incorrect characters. Press the INSERT key (which says "Ins" on it); it makes the screen's bottom left corner say "Typeover". Type the correct characters; they'll cover up the bad characters. When you finish, press the INSERT key again (to make the screen stop saying "Typeover").

Split a paragraph Here's how to split a paragraph into two shorter paragraphs.

What word should begin the second short paragraph? Look at the space before that word. Move the cursor to that space. Delete that space (by pressing the DELETE key), then press ENTER. Now you've split the long paragraph into two!

If you want to double-space between the two short paragraphs, press ENTER again. If you want to indent the second paragraph, press the TAB key.

Combine paragraphs After typing two paragraphs, here's how to combine them to form a single paragraph that's longer.

By pressing the up-arrow key, move the cursor to the first paragraph's bottom line. Move to the end of that line, by pressing the END key. Delete the end-of-paragraph mark, by pressing the DELETE key.

Press the DELETE key one or two more times (to delete unwanted TABs and ENTERs). Press the SPACE bar (to insert a space between the two sentences).

FUNCTION KEYS

On the keyboard, you'll see **function keys** labeled F1, F2, F3, F4, F5, F6, F7, F8, F9, and F10. If your keyboard is modern, those function keys are on the *top* of the keyboard, along with two extra keys (F11 and F12).

By pressing the function keys, you can give 40 commands, which are explained on the following pages:

Command	What the computer will do	Keys to press	Page
Block	define a block	F12 (or Alt F4)	187
Bold	start (or stop) making text be boldface	F6	187
Cancel	cancel a command, or restore deleted text	F1	189
Center	center a title or column heading or block	Shift F6	187
Columns/table	make columns for newspapers, tables, math	Alt F7	192
Date/outline	type the date, or create an outline	Shift F5	199
End field	mark the end of a field, in a merge file	F9	201
Exit	exit from a menu or document or subsection	F7	188
Flush right	type next to the right margin	Alt F6	190
Font	change to a different font	Ctrl F8	193
Footnote	create a footnote or endnote	Ctrl F7	200
Format	margins, tab stops, page & document layout	Shift F8	190
Graphics	insert graphics with captions	Alt F9	205
Help	help you remember what keys to press	F3	202
Indent	indent the entire paragraph	F4	190
Indent both	indent and center the entire paragraph	Shift F4	190
List files	display a disk's directory & analyze its files	F5	189
Macro	use a macro	Alt F10	198
Macro define	invent a macro	Ctrl F10	198
Mark text	table of contents, index, cross-reference, list	Alt F5	200
Merge codes	insert special codes, to control the merging	Shift F9	201
Merge/sort	handle form letters, mailing lists, sorting	Ctrl F9	200
Move	move a sentence, paragraph, page, or block	Ctrl F4	202
Print	print on paper, or show a preview on screen	Shift F7	188
Replace	search for a phrase & replace it by another	Alt F2	196
Retrieve	copy a document from the disk to the screen	Shift F10	188
Reveal codes	show (or stop showing) hidden codes	F11 (or Alt F3)	187
Save	copy the document to a disk	F10	188
Screen	create lines, boxes, windows, rewrites	Ctrl F3	204
Search	search ahead through text, to find a phrase	F2	196
Search back	search back through text, to find a phrase	Shift F2	196
Setup	change the way Word Perfect behaves	Shift F1	202
Shell	leave Word Perfect temporarily & do DOS	Ctrl F1	203
Spell	check spelling, count words, find repetitions	Ctrl F2	196
Style	invent or use a style	Alt F8	198
Switch	switch documents, or switch to & from caps	Shift F3	203
Tab align	in a column of numbers, align decimal points	Ctrl F6	190
Text in/out	use other programs, passwords, comments	Ctrl F5	203
Thesaurus	find synonyms & antonyms	Alt F1	197
Underline	start (or stop) underlining the text	F8	187

Put that chart (or a photocopy of it) next to the computer.

Old versions (such as 4.0) lack the fanciest features (such as "Shell" and "Thesaurus"). Those old versions give the following keystrokes different meanings:

Keystroke	New meaning	Old meaning	When the new meaning began
Ctrl F1	Shell	Do nothing	version 4.1
Alt F1	Thesaurus	Hard space	version 4.1
Alt F8	Style	Page format	version 5.0
Ctrl F8	Font	Print format	version 5.0
Shift F1	Setup	Super/subscript	version 5.0
Alt F9	Graphics	Merge codes	version 5.0
Shift F9	Merge codes	Merge end	version 5.0
F9	End field	Merge return	version 5.1
Alt F7	Columns/table	Math/columns	version 5.1

Notice that Word Perfect makes heavy use of the Shift, Alt, and Ctrl keys. To help you find those keys, Word Perfect comes with decals to put on those keys. Stick the green decal on the left Shift key, the red decal on the Ctrl key, and the blue decal on the Alt key. Since they're decals for keys, they're called **keycals**.

Word Perfect also comes with a plastic **template** that you put next to the function keys. The template contains a chart giving each function key's purpose. The chart is color-coded. Commands written in green require that you hold down the green key (the Shift key). Commands written in blue require that you hold down the blue key (the Alt key). Commands written in red require that you hold down the red key (the Ctrl key). Commands written in black are simple: they don't require any colored keys.

The template and keycals are extremely helpful. They makes Word Perfect become easy. Without them, Word Perfect is a nightmare. If you lose the template and keycals, buy another set by phoning Word Perfect Corporation at 800-321-4566.

Here's how to use the function keys. . . .

Center (Shift F6)

Suppose you've finished typing a paragraph (and pressed the ENTER key afterwards). Here's how to make the next line be a centered title.

Say "Center" (by pressing Shift with F6). Type the title, then press ENTER.

Bold (F6)

Here's how to make a phrase be bold (**like this**).

Say "Bold" (by pressing F6). Type the phrase, then press the right-arrow key.

If the phrase you said to make "bold" doesn't look bolder than the rest of your document, adjust your screen's contrast and brightness knobs.

Underline (F8)

Here's how to underline a phrase (like this).

Say "Underline" (by pressing F8). Type the phrase, then press the right-arrow key.

If your screen makes the phrase look shaded instead of underlined, don't worry: regardless of how the phrase looks on the screen, the printer will underline the phrase on paper.

Reveal codes (F11 or Alt F3)

When you tell the computer that you wish to center, make bold, underline, or do something else special, the computer turns your wish into a code and inserts that code in your document.

For example, suppose you type this document in Word Perfect:

```
We kissed at every moment we could.
Wow!
```

To remember that you want "every moment" to be UNDerlined and "Wow!" to be below, Word Perfect stores your document like this:

```
We kissed at [UND]every moment[und] we could.[HRt]Wow!
```

The [UND] code means "start UNDerlining". The [und] code means "end underlining". The [HRt] code means "press the Hard ReTurn key" so that the next word (Wow!) appears on the line below.

The screen normally shows just this:

```
We kissed at every moment we could.
Wow!
```

The [UND], [und], and [HRt] are **hidden codes** that don't appear on the screen.

If you WANT the hidden codes to appear on the screen, say "Reveal codes" by pressing F11. (If your keyboard doesn't have an F11 key or you're using a Word Perfect version older than 5.1, press Alt with F3.) You'll see this at the bottom of the screen:

```
We kissed at [UND]every moment[und] we could.[HRt]
Wow!
```

While you're looking at the [UND], [und], and [HRt] codes, you can edit them.

For example, if you change your mind and want "every moment" *not* to be underlined, move the cursor to the [UND] and then press the DELETE key. The [UND] will disappear. When the [UND] disappears, the computer automatically makes the [und] disappear also.

When you finish looking at codes and editing them, hide them by pressing F11 (or Alt F3) again.

Whenever Word Perfect confuses you, say "Reveal codes" (by pressing F11 or Alt F3) and then stare at the codes, to find out what's really going on.

Here are Word Perfect's popular codes:

Code	Meaning
[UND]	start underlining
[und]	end underlining
[BOLD]	start boldfacing
[bold]	end boldfacing
[Tab]	indent (because the human pressed the TAB key)
[HRt]	hard return (the human pressed the RETURN key)
[SRt]	soft return (computer pressed RETURN because at margin)
[HPg]	hard page break (human pressed CONTROL with RETURN)
[SPg]	soft page break (computer pressed because previous page full)
[Center]	start centering (end centering when reach RETURN or TAB)

Versions older than 5.1 say [Cntr] instead of [Center]. At the end of the centered text, those old versions say [C/A/Flrt].

Block (F12 or Alt F4)

You can manipulate a large portion of your document with a single keystroke! The portion you're manipulating is called the **block**. It can consist of several words, several sentences, several paragraphs, or even several pages.

Here's how to manipulate a block. . . .

Move the cursor to the beginning of the block. (For example, to manipulate a whole paragraph, move the cursor to the beginning of the paragraph.)

Then say "Block" by pressing F12. (If your keyboard doesn't have an F12 key or you're using a Word Perfect version older than 5.1, press Alt with F4.)

Move the cursor to the end of the block.

Then say what to do to the block. For example, choose one of these activities:

To make the block be bold, say "Bold" (by pressing F6).

To underline all the words in the block, say "Underline" (by pressing F8).

To center all the lines in the block, say "Center" (Shift with F6) then press Y. Give this command only if each of the block's lines is brief. For example, give this command to center a poem or a multi-line headline.

To delete the block, press the Del key then the Y key.

To move the block (so it vanishes from its current location and reappears elsewhere), press Ctrl with Del. Then move the cursor where you want the block's new position to be, and press ENTER.

To copy the block (so the block appears twice in your document), press Ctrl with Ins. Then put the cursor where you want the block's copy to be, and press ENTER.

Inferior versions If you're using an old version of Word Perfect (before 5.1) or an old-fashioned keyboard (lacking an F12 key), your computer won't understand "Ctrl with Del" or "Ctrl with Ins". Here's what to do.

Versions 5.0 and 5.1. Instead of pressing "Ctrl with Del", press Ctrl with F4 and then type BM. Instead of pressing "Ctrl with Ins", press Ctrl with F4 and then type BC.

Versions 4.0, 4.1, and 4.2. Instead of pressing "Ctrl with Del" or "Ctrl with Ins", do the following. Say "Move" (Ctrl with F4). Press either the 1 key (to move the block) or the 2 key (to copy the block). Put the cursor where you want the block to appear. Say "Move" again (Ctrl with F4). Tap the 5 key. You've finished the procedure: the block has been moved or copied.

After you've edited your document, you'll want to undo any mistakes, copy the document onto the hard disk and paper, and move on to a different document or task. Here's how. . . .

Save (F10)

While you're typing and editing a document, the document's in the computer's RAM chips. It's *not* on a disk. If the computer's electricity goes off (because of a thunderstorm or because your cat pulled the plug), the RAM chips will be erased — and so will your document!

Another way to accidentally erase your document is to hit a wrong key. For example, if your cat jumps onto your keyboard and then sits on your DELETE key for several minutes, your document will be deleted. Other accidents can be caused by dogs, babies, novices, and you!

To protect against accidents, copy your document onto a disk. Copying a document onto a disk is called **saving**.

To save, just say "Save" (by pressing F10).

Then the computer will ask you to invent a name for your document. The name must be short: no more than 8 letters. For example, the name can be "jennifer" or "al". **Type the name you wish and press ENTER.**

The computer will copy the document onto the hard disk (drive C) and put that document into the WP subdirectory.

Afterwards, if you improve the document by editing it further, the improved version will be in the RAM chips, but the disk will still contain the old version. To copy the improved version onto the disk, say "Save" again (by pressing F10) and press ENTER. The computer will ask, "Replace?" Press Y. The computer will replace the disk's old version by the new version.

Save often If you're typing a long document, say "Save" every 10 minutes. Then if an accident happens, you'll lose at most 10 minutes of work!

Exit (F7)

When you finish editing your document, say "Exit" (by pressing F7).

The computer will ask, "Save document?" Press Y.

If the document's name appears at the bottom of the screen, press ENTER. (If no name appears, invent a name for the document — and when you finish typing the name, press ENTER.)

If the computer asks "Replace?", press Y.

The computer will ask, "Exit WP?" If you want to exit from Word Perfect and make the screen show a C prompt, press Y. (If you do *not* want to exit from Word Perfect, press N; then the screen will go blank, so you can create another document.)

Retrieve (Shift F10)

Here's how to copy a document from your hard disk to your screen.

First, make the screen be blank. (To do that, say "Exit" by pressing F7, then press N twice.)

Then say "Retrieve" (by pressing Shift with F10). Type the name of the document you want to retrieve from the hard disk (such as "jennifer"), and press ENTER.

Combine documents Normally, you should make the screen be blank before you say "Retrieve". If the screen is *not* blank, the computer inserts the retrieved document in the middle of the document that was on the screen.

So here's how to combine two documents. First, get one of the documents onto the screen. Then put the cursor where you want the second document to be inserted. (For example, if you want the second document to be inserted at the end of the first document, put the cursor at the end of the first document.) Say "Retrieve", type the name of the second document, and press ENTER.

Create a document template Create a document called LETTER. At the top of the document, type your return address and any other information you want as your letterhead. Further down the document, say "Dear", but leave the letter's details blank: just create blank lines, by pressing the ENTER key a few times. At the end of the document, say "Sincerely" or "Very truly yours" or whatever other oily cliché you want to close the letter with. Leave a few more blank lines (so you can sign the letter), then type your name. Save the document. Such a document — which contains generalities but no details — is called a **document template**.

Then whenever you want to write a letter, just retrieve that LETTER document, edit it (by inserting lines of text after "Dear"), and save the edited version under a different name. For example, if the edited version is a letter to Susan, name the edited version "SUSAN".

Besides LETTER, you should create several other document templates. For example, create a document template called MEMO, which begins with phrases such as "Memo to", "From", "Regarding", and "Date".

By saving document templates such as LETTER and MEMO, you'll be saving and automating all the stupid, tedious, repetitive parts of the typing task. Then just fill in the blanks — creatively!

Print (Shift F7)

To copy your writing onto paper, make sure the printer is turned on. Make sure you've saved your document (to protect yourself in case the printer doesn't work). Then say "Print" (by pressing Shift with F7).

You'll see the **print menu**. In version 5.1, the print menu's first two items look like this:

```
1 - Full
2 - Page
```

If you want to print the entire, full document, choose the print menu's first item by pressing 1 or F. (Notice that the 1 and F are in boldface. If you don't see the boldface on your screen, adjust the screen's contrast and brightness knobs.) If you want to print just the page that contains the cursor, choose the print menu's second item by pressing 2 or P.

To become a Word Perfect expert, get in the habit of choosing menu items by pressing letters (such as F and P) instead of numbers (such as 1 and 2). The letters are easier to memorize. For example, to print just a page, it's easier to get in the habit of pressing P than pressing 2.

Old versions If you're stuck with an ancient version (4.0, 4.1, or 4.2), you can't choose by letter: you must type numbers instead.

Selecting a printer driver A **printer driver** is software that handles your printer's peculiarities. For example, a **Panasonic 1124 printer driver for Word Perfect** is software that helps Word Perfect handles the peculiarities of the Panasonic 1124 printer. Word Perfect comes with 437 printer drivers.

When you buy Word Perfect, you must tell it which printer you bought. That process is called **selecting a printer driver**. If you're using version 5.1, you selected a printer driver during the process of copying Word Perfect to the hard disk.

If you're using version 5.0 instead, here's how to select a printer driver. After you turn on the computer and start using Word Perfect, say "Print" (by pressing Shift with F7). From the menus, choose **Select Additional** (by pressing S then A). You'll see an alphabetical list of printers. Press PgDn several times, until you see *your* printer. Move the cursor to your printer's name (by pressing the down-arrow), and press ENTER twice. When the bottom of the screen says "Press Exit to quit", press F7 four times.

Simple choices The print menu offers you many choices. You've seen that to print the full document, choose **Full** (by pressing F); to print just the page containing the cursor, choose **Page** (by pressing P). Here are some other choices. . . .

To print *several* pages, choose **Multiple** (by pressing M), then say which pages to print. For example, to print pages 2, 5, and 7 through 11, type "2,5,7-11" and press ENTER. To print just the document's last part — from page 15 to the end — type "15-" and press ENTER.

Suppose JENNIFER is a document you've saved on the hard disk. If you want to print the JENNIFER document instead of the screen's document, choose **Document**, then type "jennifer" and ENTER.

Preview While you're experimenting with editing and printing your document, you'll make many mistakes that can waste lots of paper. To avoid wasting paper, tell the computer to print to your screen instead of to paper. Printing to the screen is called **previewing**. Here's how to do it. . . .

Choose **View** from the print menu. (That choice works only if your computer contains a graphics card.) The screen shows a picture of a sheet of paper. That picture, called the **preview**, shows how the current page will look on paper.

If your graphics card is VGA, the preview is pretty.

Underneath the preview, you'll see this menu:

`1 100%   2 200%   3 Full-page   4 Facing-pages`

That menu lets you modify the preview. Press 1 for a view that's the actual size, 2 for a magnified view (in which the characters appear larger than on paper), 3 for a miniaturized view (so that the entire, full page fits on your screen), 4 for a miniaturized view that includes not just the cursor's page but also the facing page. You can also press the arrow keys (to move around the page), and PgUp & PgDn (to move to different pages).

When you finish looking at the preview, say "Exit" (by pressing F7).

Multiple copies The printer assumes you want to print just one copy of each page. To change that assumption — and make the printer print 10 copies of each page — choose **Number**, then type 10 (and ENTER).

If you'll print many copies of each page, you can speed up the printing by choosing **mUltiple Printer**. (To do that, type U then P.) That will make the printer print the copies faster — especially if you have a laser printer. When doing that high-speed copying, the printer doesn't bother to collate the pages. If you want to switch back to regular-speed printing (and have automatic collating), choose **mUltiple**

Wordperfect.

Extra fonts If you buy extra fonts and insert them into your printer (by inserting a font cartridge or soft font or font wheel), tell the computer which fonts you've bought. To do so, choose **Select Edit Cartridges** from the print menu (by typing SEC). Then follow the menus on the screen. For example, if you've bought a font cartridge for a Hewlett-Packard laser printer, move the cursor to the word "Cartridges" (by pressing the down-arrow key), press S (for Select), move the cursor to the cartridge's name (by pressing the down-arrow and PgDn keys), press ENTER (so an asterisk appears), and press F7 five times.

Cancel (F1)

If you make a mistake, undo it by saying "Cancel" (F1).

For example, suppose you say "Print" (because you plan to print something) but then change your mind. Just say "Cancel": that makes the print menu disappear, so the screen shows your document again.

Suppose you delete some text (by pressing DELETE or BACKSPACE or using Typeover mode or telling the computer to delete a block) but then change your mind. Just say "Cancel". The text you recently deleted will reappear! If that text doesn't interest you, choose **Previous** (by pressing P), and you'll see other text you deleted previously. If that's still not the text you want, choose Previous again. When you finally see text that interests you, choose **Restore**, and that text will be kept in your document.

List files (F5)

To find out what documents are on your hard disk, say "List files" (by pressing F5), then press ENTER.

The computer will create an alphabetical list of all the files in the hard disk's WP subdirectory. You'll see the top part of that list; to see the rest of the list, press the PgDn key several times. In that list, some of the files are documents you created; the other files are part of Word Perfect itself.

To manipulate a document, move the cursor to the document's name (by using the PgDn key and arrow keys). Then choose one of the following activities. . . .

To peek at the document, choose **Look** (by pressing L). You'll see the beginning of the document; to see the rest of it, press the PgDn key several times. When you finish looking at the document, press F7.

To print the document onto paper, choose **Print** (by pressing P) then press ENTER.

To change the document's name, choose **Move** (by pressing M), then type a new name (and press ENTER).

To delete the document from the disk, choose **Delete** (by pressing D) then press Y.

When you finish using the list-files menu, say "Exit" (by pressing F7).

Two ways to retrieve Suppose JENNIFER is a document in the hard disk's WP subdirectory. Here's how to retrieve JENNIFER, so that the screen shows all the words in the JENNIFER document and you can edit them.

Method 1 (which you learned before): make the screen be blank (by pressing F7 then pressing N twice), say "Retrieve" (Shift F10), then type "jennifer" (and press ENTER).

Method 2 (which requires less typing): make the screen be blank (by pressing F7 then pressing N twice), say "List files" (F5), move the cursor to JENNIFER (by using the arrow keys), then choose **Retrieve** (by pressing R).

TRICKY SPACING

Here are tricks to control how your document is spaced.

Indent (F4)

Before typing a paragraph, you can press the TAB key. That makes the computer indent the paragraph's first line.

Instead of pressing the TAB key, try saying "Indent" (by pressing F4). That makes the computer indent *all* lines in the paragraph.

Indent both (Shift F4)

If you say "Indent both" (by pressing Shift with F4) instead of just "Indent", the computer will indent *both* of the paragraph's edges — the left edge *and the right edge* — so that the paragraph is centered.

Margin release (Shift TAB)

At the beginning of a paragraph, you can press the TAB key *while holding down the Shift key*. That makes the paragraph's first line begin abnormally far to the left: in the left margin. The paragraph's other lines will be normal.

Since the Shift TAB command lets you write in the left margin, it's called the **margin release** command.

For an interesting effect, try this: at the beginning of a paragraph, say "Indent" (by pressing F4) and then press Shift TAB. That makes all the lines of the paragraph be indented except the first line. That technique — in which the first line is normal and the other lines hang under it indented — is called a **hanging indent**.

Flush right (Alt F6)

If a line of text is short, you can make the line be **flush left** or **centered** or **flush right**.

This line is flush left.

This line is centered.

This line is flush right.

To make the line be flush left (so it's at the left margin), just type the line and then press ENTER. To make the line be centered, say "Center" (Shift F6) before typing the line. To make the line be flush right (so it's at the right margin), say "Flush right" (Alt F6) before typing the line.

You can make part of a line be flush left and part be flush right, like this:

This part is flush left.   This part is flush right.

To do that, begin by typing the part you want flush left. Then say "Flush right" (Alt F6), type the part you want flush right, and press ENTER.

Tab align (Ctrl F6)

When you type a column of numbers, you want their decimal points to line up, like this:

```
   74.9
5,382,931.726
     -.82
```

Those decimal points are **aligned** with each other. Here's how to type that column of numbers with aligned decimal points. . . .

Say "Tab align" (Ctrl F6) several times, until the cursor's where you want the decimal point to be. (Each time you say "Tab align", the cursor moves to the right a half inch.)

Type the first number (74.9). As you type it, the computer automatically shifts it towards the left, so its decimal point winds up where you requested. Press ENTER.

Now you're ready to type the second line. To do so, say "Tab align" several times, until the cursor's where you want the decimal point (underneath the first number's decimal point). Then type the second number (which is 5,382,931.726) and press ENTER.

For the third line, say "Tab align" repeatedly until the cursor's where you want the decimal point, then type the third number and press ENTER.

Format page (Shift F8 then P)

Here's how to control the general appearance of each page if you're using version 5.0 or 5.1. (Earlier versions are quite different and awkward.)

Move the cursor to the document's beginning. Say "Format" (by pressing Shift F8). Choose **Page** (by pressing P). You'll see the **format page menu**.

Page size The typical sheet of paper — like the paper in this book — is 8½ inches wide and 11 inches tall. Computerists say that the **page width** is 8½ inches and the **page length** is 11 inches.

The computer assumes you want that width and length. Here's how to change that assumption. . . .

In version 5.1, choose **Size Other Select Other** (by typing S then PgDn then SO). In version 5.0, choose "Size Other" (by typing SO).

Type the page width in inches (and ENTER) and the page length in inches (and ENTER). Then press F7.

Top & bottom margins The computer assumes you want 1-inch margins at the top and bottom of each page. To change that assumption, choose **Margins** (by typing M), type the top margin in inches (and ENTER) and the bottom margin in inches (and ENTER).

In this Secret Guide, I made the margins smaller, so I could squeeze more words onto each page. I made the top and bottom margins be .3 inches.

Page numbers Here's how to make the computer print page numbers on all the pages.

Choose **Numbering Position** (by typing NP).

On a page, where do you want the page number to be printed? Type 1 for top left corner, 2 for top center, 3 for top right corner, 4 for top outer corner (left corner on even pages, right corner on odd pages), 5 for bottom left corner, 6 for bottom center, 7 for bottom right corner, or 8 for bottom outer corner. Press ENTER.

Before printing a page number, do you want the computer to print some words? On page 7, for example, instead of just printing "7" would you rather print "Great American Novel - Page 7"? To print words before each page number, choose **Style** (by typing S), type the words you want before each page number ("Great American Novel - Page"), press the SPACE bar (to leave a blank space after the word "Page"), and press ENTER.

When you finish telling the computer about page numbers, press ENTER again.

That makes the computer number all the pages. The computer prints "Great American Novel - Page 1" on the first page, "Great American Novel - Page 2" on the second page, etc. Each of those messages appears near (but not in) the margins. Each message is separated from your document by a blank line.

The messages appear when you print the document on paper (or look at a page preview). They do *not* appear on the screen while you're editing the document.

Exit When you finish using the format page menu, say "Exit" (by pressing F7).

Format line (Shift F8 then L)

Here's how to control the general appearance of each line if you're using version 5.0 or 5.1. (Earlier versions are quite different and awkward.)

Move the cursor to the document's beginning. Say "Format" (by pressing Shift F8). Choose **Line** (by pressing L). You'll see the **format line menu**.

Left & right margins The computer assumes you want 1-inch margins at the left and right of each page. To change that assumption, choose **Margins** (by typing M), type the left margin in inches (and ENTER) and the right margin in inches (and ENTER).

In this Secret Guide, I made the margins smaller to squeeze more words on each page. I made the left and right margins on this page be .5 inches; but the left and right margins on the table-of-contents page are just .3 inches.

Changing the margins can be very handy. If you're a student who wrote an eight-page paper, and your teacher requires it to be ten pages long instead, just enlarge the margins and— presto! —you suddenly have a ten-page paper.

Justification In a newspaper, each column's right edge is perfectly straight, like this:

Notice that the right edge of this paragraph is perfectly straight. Notice that the right edge of this paragraph is perfectly straight. Notice that the right edge of this paragraph is perfectly straight.

In documents that are less formal, each column's right edge wavers slightly, like this:

Notice that the right edge of this paragraph wavers slightly. Notice that the right edge of this paragraph wavers slightly. Notice that the right edge of this paragraph wavers slightly.

If the right edge is perfectly straight, the text is said to be **justified**. If the right edge wavers slightly, the text is said to be **unjustified** or **ragged-right**.

To make the right edge be perfectly straight (justified), the computer slightly increases the space between words. The smartest word processors (such as Word Perfect) combine *three* techniques to make the right edge straight: they increase the space between some words, decrease the space between other words, and increase the space between letters in a word.

Justified (straight) text looks formal, professional, and distinguished. Unjustified (wavering) text looks informal, friendly, and cheery.

Look at ads in newspapers. Notice which ads are right-justified (to give a "professional" image) and which ads are ragged-right (to give a more "friendly" image).

Most of the Secret Guide's text is justified. That's why, at first glance, this book looks professional, formal, and distinguished. (Only when you actually *read* it do you realize that the Guide's author is a nut, gone totally bonkers.)

Telling the computer to "justify" does *not* affect the document's appearance on the screen. It affects just the document's appearance on paper.

The computer assumes you want to justify. To change that assumption, choose **Justification Left** (JL) in version 5.1; choose "Justification No" (JN) in version 5.0.

Double spacing Usually, the computer prints text on every line. If you're going to print on paper to hand to your teacher, boss, or publisher, you might wish to put a blank line between each line of text, so your reader can scribble comments in those blanks. Having those blank lines is called **double spacing**.

The Secret Guide is *not* double spaced, because double spacing would require twice as much paper and double the book's cost. The Guide is **single spaced**.

The computer assumes you want single spacing. To double space instead, choose **Spacing** (by pressing S) and type 2 (then ENTER). If you type 1.75 instead of 2, the text will look double spaced on the screen but will look slightly less than double spaced on the printer.

Tab stops You press the TAB key to indent a paragraph's top line or hop to the next column in a table.

Whenever you press the TAB key, the cursor moves toward the right, until it reaches the next **tab stop**. You can change the positions of the tab stops.

Traditional typists put tab stops at half-inch intervals, so that paragraphs are indented a half-inch, and so each column in a table is a half-inch wide. The computer assumes those tab stops please you. If they don't, choose **Tab** (by pressing T).

You'll see a **ruler** with an L at each tab stop. To erase a tab stop, move the cursor to that L and press DELETE. To create a new tab stop, move the cursor across to where you want the tab stop and type L (for a simple tab stop) or D (for a **decimal tab stop**); when you finish editing the tab stops, press F7.

To align decimal points in a column of numbers, you can use two methods. Method 1: create a decimal tab stop where you want the decimal points to be; before typing each number, move to that tab stop by pressing the TAB key. Method 2: create a simple tab stop where you want the decimal points to be; before typing each number, move to that tab stop by saying "Tab align" (Ctrl F6).

Exit When you finish using the format line menu, exit by pressing F7.

Format other (Shift F8 then O)

Here's how to leave a gap in your document, so that you can insert a big handwritten diagram.

Type the line that you want above the gap (and press ENTER). Say "Format" (by pressing Shift F8). Choose **Other Advance Down** (by typing OAD).

Say how tall you want the gap. For example, if you want the gap to be 3¼ inches tall, type 3.25 (and ENTER).

Say "Exit" (F7). Then type the line you want below the gap.

The gap appears when you print the document on paper (or look at a page preview). It does *not* appear on the screen while you're editing the document.

Columns/table (Alt F7)

You can create newspaper columns and tables.

Newspaper columns In a newspaper, text is printed in many narrow **columns**. In a business letter, text is printed in a single wide column.

The computer assumes you want a single wide column. Here's how to tell the computer you want many narrow columns. . . .

In version 5.1, say "Columns/table" (Alt F7), then choose **Columns Define** (CD); in version 5.0, say "Math/columns" (Alt F7), then choose "Define" (D).

You'll see the **column definition menu**.

Now the computer assumes you want 2 columns. If you want more, choose **Number** (N) then type the number of columns (and ENTER).

The computer assumes you want the gap between columns to be .5 inches. If you want a different size gap, choose **Distance** (D) then type the distance across the gap (and ENTER).

When you finish using the column definition menu, exit by pressing F7 *just once*. Then in version 5.1, choose **On** (by pressing O); in version 5.0, choose "Column-on" (by pressing C).

In the Secret Guide, text is usually printed in 2 columns, but the table-of-contents page is printed in 5 columns. In the Secret Guide, the gap between columns is usually .3 inches, but on the table-of-contents page the gap between columns is less.

Column jump If you divided the page into several columns, here's how to jump the cursor from column to column. While holding down the CONTROL key, tap the HOME key. Then press → to jump right, or press ← to jump left.

Column break Suppose you divided the page into several columns. If you press the ENTER key while holding down the CONTROL key, the computer will end the paragraph *and insert a column break*, so that the next paragraph will begin at the top of the next column.

Table In the middle of a document, you can type a table of numbers. Here's how.

Put the cursor where you want the table to begin. Say "Columns/table" (Alt F7). Choose **Tables Create** (TC). Say how many columns you want in the table (for example, 4) and press ENTER. Say how many rows you want in the table (for example, 7) and press ENTER. The computer will create a table having 4 columns and 7 rows, so you see this:

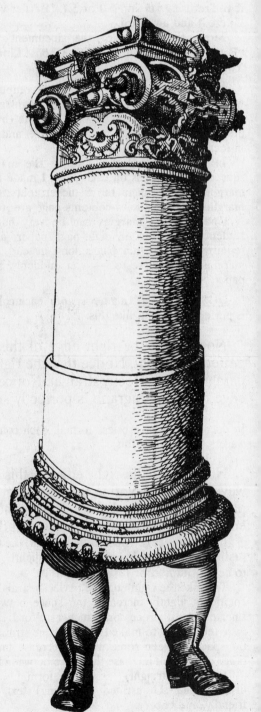

Say "Exit" (F7).

Then fill in those 28 blank cells. Here's how. Type what you want in the first cell. Press the TAB key; it moves the cursor to the right, to the next cell. Type what you want in that cell. Continue the process (pressing the TAB key after each cell), until you've filled all the cells.

In each cell, you can type numbers or words or sentences or paragraphs. If you what you type is too long to fit in the cell, the computer automatically makes the cell taller (and all the other cells in the row also), so that the cell can hold several lines of information.

When you've typed the last cell (in the bottom right corner), press the down-arrow key (instead of TAB). Then type the rest of your document.

Conflict If you've divided a page into newspaper columns, the computer refuses to create tables on that page.

FANCY CHARACTERS

To make your document more interesting, create fancy characters. Here's how.

Font (Ctrl F8)

Here are samples of popular fonts. . . .

This is a sample of 8-point Times Roman.

This is a sample of 10-point Times Roman.

This is a sample of 12-point Times Roman.

This is a sample of 12-point Times Roman bold.

This is a sample of 8-point Helvetica.

This is a sample of 10-point Helvetica.

This is a sample of 12-point Helvetica.

This is a sample of 12-point Helvetica bold.

This is a sample of Courier.

This is a sample of Courier bold.

This is a sample of Lineprinter.

In Courier, each character is $\frac{1}{10}$ of an inch wide; so Courier's a **10-characters-per-inch font**. In Lineprinter, each character is $\frac{1}{17}$ of an inch wide. In Times Roman and Helvetica, each letter of the alphabet has its own width: for example, the letter "m" is wider than the letter "i".

Since Courier's characters all have the same width as each other, they're called **monospaced**. Lineprinter's characters are monospaced also. Times Roman and Helvetica are *not* monospaced; they're **proportionally spaced** instead.

A **point** is $\frac{1}{72}$ of an inch. The first sample is called *8-point* Times Roman because it's 8 points high: the top of the capital T is 8 points higher than the bottom of the small p.

In *The Secret Guide to Computers*, most of the text is 10-point Times Roman, and most of the headings are 12-point Helvetica (or 14-point Helvetica, which is even larger). In the chapters on DOS and programming, most of the examples are Lineprinter.

The computer assumes you want a 10-characters-per-inch font (such as Courier). To print the document in a different font, you must say "Font". In Word Perfect 5.0 and 5.1, the "Font" command is delightfully simple and powerful. That's why I chose Word Perfect for writing *The Secret Guide to Computers*.

To switch fonts, move the cursor to the beginning of the document (or wherever you want the font switch to begin). Say "Font" (Ctrl F8). Then choose **Font** (by pressing F).

You'll see a menu of fonts. Move the cursor to the font you want, then say "Select" (by pressing S).

The font you selected will be used on paper but *not* on your screen, which will remain monospaced (except when you preview).

Spaces after a sentence When you use a monospaced font, put 2 spaces after a sentence or colon. For example. . . .

2 spaces follow this sentence. Nice!

When you use a proportionally spaced font, put just 1 space after a sentence or colon. For example. . . .

1 space follows this sentence. Nice!

Quotation marks When you use a monospaced font, type a quotation mark by using this symbol: ". For example. . . .

I saw "Hamlet" last night.

When you use a proportionally spaced font, use the following trick. . . . To form an opening quotation mark ("), press the accent key (') twice. To form a closing quotation mark ("), press the apostrophe key (') twice. Although your screen will look ugly —

I saw ''Hamlet'' last night.

your paper will look beautiful:

I saw "Hamlet" last night.

Enhancements After choosing a font, you can enhance it.

For example, to underline the font (like this), say "Underline" (by pressing F8). To make the font be bolder (so the characters are made of thicker strokes, **like this**), say "Bold" (by pressing F6).

To italicize the font (so the characters are slanted, *like this*), say "Font" (Ctrl F8) then choose **Appearance Italic** (AI). To redline the font (so the background is shaded, like this), say "Font" (Ctrl F8) then choose **Appearance Redline** (AR). To strike out the font (so the characters are crossed out, ~~like this~~), say "Font" (Ctrl F8) then choose **Appearance Strikeout** (AS).

To change the font's size, say "Font" (Ctrl F8), and choose **Size** (S). Then say which size you want. . . .

To make the font be 20% larger, choose **Large**.
To make the font be 50% larger, choose **Very-large**.
To make the font be twice as large, choose **Extra-large**.
To make the font be 20% smaller, choose **Small**.
To make the font be 40% smaller, choose **Fine**.
To make it small & lowered ($_{like\ this}$), choose **suBscript**.
To make it small & raised ($^{like\ this}$), choose **suPerscript**.

For example, if you've been using 10-point type and choose "Large", you'll be switching to 12-point type.

You've learned about many enhancements: bold, underline, italic, redline, strikeout, large, very-large, extra-large, small, and fine. **After giving one of those enhancement commands, type the text that you want enhanced, then press the right-arrow key.**

If your printer is fancy (such as the HP Laserjet 3), all those enhancements work. If your printer is semi-fancy (such as an HP Laserjet 2 or 2P with a Microsoft Z font cartridge), only *some* of those enhancements work, but Word Perfect tries to approximate.

For example, suppose you're using 10-point type and choose "Very-large" (which should generate 15-point type), but your printer lacks a 15-point font. If your printer has a 14-point font or 16-point font instead, Word Perfect will give you one of those fonts as an approximation to 15-point.

You'll see the enhancements on paper but not on your screen (except when you preview).

Here's how to enhance a block of text that you typed previously. Move the cursor to the block's beginning. Say "Block" (by pressing F12 or Alt F4). Move the cursor to the block's end. Say "Font" (Ctrl F8). Then say which enhancement you want (such as "Appearance Italic" or "Size Large").

Alt

You can type these special characters:

Code	Char	Code	Char	Code	Char	Code	Char	Code	Char
		128	Ç	160	á	192	└	224	α
1	☺	129	ü	161	í	193	┴	225	ß
2	●	130	é	162	ó	194	┬	226	Γ
3	♥	131	â	163	ú	195	├	227	π
4	♦	132	ä	164	ñ	196	─	228	Σ
5	♣	133	à	165	Ñ	197	┼	229	σ
6	♠	134	å	166	ª	198	╞	230	µ
7	•	135	ç	167	º	199	╟	231	τ
8	◘	136	ê	168	¿	200	╚	232	Φ
9	○	137	ë	169	⌐	201	╔	233	Θ
10	◙	138	è	170	¬	202	╩	234	Ω
11	♂	139	ï	171	½	203	╦	235	δ
12	♀	140	î	172	¼	204	╠	236	∞
13	♪	141	ì	173	¡	205	═	237	φ
14	♫	142	Ä	174	«	206	╬	238	ε
15	☼	143	Å	175	»	207	╧	239	∩
16	►	144	É	176	░	208	╨	240	
17	◄	145	æ	177	▒	209	╤	241	±
18	↕	146	Æ	178	▓	210	╥	242	≥
19	‼	147	ô	179	│	211	╙	243	≤
20	¶	148	ö	180	┤	212	╘	244	⌠
21	§	149	ò	181	╡	213	╒	245	⌡
22	▬	150	û	182	╢	214	╓	246	÷
23	↨	151	ù	183	╖	215	╫	247	≈
24	↑	152		184	╕	216	╪	248	°
25	↓	153	Ö	185	╣	217	┘	249	·
26	→	154	Ü	186	║	218	┌	250	·
27	←	155	¢	187	╗	219	█	251	√
28	∟	156	£	188	╝	220	▄	252	ⁿ
29	↔	157	¥	189	╜	221	▌	253	²
30	▲	158	₧	190	╛	222	▐	254	■
31	▼	159	ƒ	191	┐	223	▀		

For example, here's how to type the symbol ñ, whose code number is 164. Hold down the Alt key; and while you keep holding down the Alt key, type 164 *by using the numeric keypad* (the number keys on the far right side of the keyboard). When you finish typing 164, lift your finger from the Alt key, and you'll see ñ on your screen! When you print the document onto paper, the ñ will also appear on paper.

Bad code numbers Do *not* type code 240. It makes the typical computer refuse to work until you turn the power off and on again.

Do not type code 152. What it prints on the screen doesn't match what it prints on paper.

On many dot-matrix printers, codes 1-6, 8-20, 22-31, and 250 don't work. On laser printers (such as the Hewlett-Packard Laserjet 2), version 5.0 prints codes 249-252 wrong, but version 5.1 prints them fine.

Compose (Ctrl V)

If you're using version 5.0 or 5.1, try the following experiment. Say "Compose" (by pressing Ctrl with V). Then type this:

Type	See	Type	See	Type	See
a`	à	a^	â	ae	æ
e`	è	e^	ê	AE	Æ
i`	ì	i^	î	ao	å
o`	ò	o^	ô	c/	¢
u`	ù	u^	û	c,	ç
				C,	Ç
a'	á	n~	ñ	P¦	¶
e'	é	N~	Ñ	Pt	₧
E'	É	~~	≈	ss	ß
i'	í				
o'	ó	f-	ƒ	??	¿
u'	ú	L-	£	!!	¡
		+-	±	<<	«
a"	ä	--	—	>>	»
A"	Ä				
e"	ë	a=	ª	/2	½
i"	ï	o=	º	/4	¼
o"	ö	Y=	¥		
O"	Ö	<=	≤	*O	o
u"	ü	>=	≥	*.	·
U"	Ü	==	≡	**	·

You'll see the following symbols on paper but *not* on the screen:

Type	See just on PAPER
co	©
ro	®
xo	¤

This chart shows extra characters you can type:

	1	2	3	4	5	6	7	8	9	10	11
0	`		▨	•	♥	-	⌠	A	א	A	あ
1	´		▨	○	♦	±	⌡	α	ב	а	い
2	ˆ	˚	■	♣	≤	|	B	ג	Б	う
3	^	˚	▮	•	♠	≥	∫	β	ד	б	え
4	˜	.	▮	★	♂	∝	√	Β	ה	В	お
5	´		▮	¶	♀	/	—	Б	ו	в	っ
6	`	^	▮	§	✿	/	Σ	Γ	ז	Г	ゃ
7	¨	=	▪	¡	☺	\	Π	γ	ח	Г	ゅ
8	˙	˘	—	¿	●	÷	Π	Δ	ט	Д	ょ
9		ˇ	‖	«	♪	|	δ	י	Е	が
10	`	˜	⌐	»	♫	‹	ƒ	E	ך	Е	き
11	'	'	⌐	£	▬	›	ε	כ	е	け
12	,	˙	⌐	¥	⌂	~	Z	ל	Ё	あい
13	,	,	⌐	₨	‼	≈	ζ	ם	ё	あい
14	˚	ˌ	├	ƒ	√	≡	H	מ	Ж	うえ
15		┬	ª	‡	∈	η	ן	ж	うえ
16		┴	º	—	∩	Θ	נ	З	おか
17		┤	½	⌐		θ	ס	з	かき
18	ˇ	├	¼	▫	Σ	I	ע	И	きく
19	˘	=	¢	⌾	∞	‖	ι	ף	й	くけ
20	˜	‖	²	←	⌐	‖	K	פ	Й	けこ
21		┌	ⁿ	☞	→	{	κ	ץ	Й	こが
22	˘	┐	®	☏	‡	Λ	צ	К	がぎ
23	ß	┘	©	✓	↑	λ	ק	к	ぎぐ
24	ı	┴	¤	□	↓	M	ר	Л	ぐ
25	J	┼	¾	⊠	↔	μ	ש	л	げ
26	Á	┬	³	☹	↕	N	ת	М	ご
27	á	˝	˘	#	►	ν	М	さ
28	Â	┴	b	◄	Ξ	Н	し
29	â	┼	♮	▲	}	ξ	Н	す
30	Ä	╞	"	▼	{	O	О	せ
31	ä	┤	'	⌚	·	o	О	そ
32	À	├	"	✗		Π	П	ざ
33	à	╘	—	☎	◦	π	П	じ
34	Å	╔	—	⌐	•	P	Р	ず
35	å	╩	‹	Å	ρ	Р	ぜ
36	Æ	╦	›	º	Σ	С	ぞ
37	æ	╚	○	μ	σ	с	た
38	Ç	├	□	—	Σ	Т	ち
39	ç	╬	†	×	ς	Т	っ
40	É	╧	‡	∫	T	У	て
41	é	╨	™	Π	τ	у	と
42	Ê	╟	SM	∓	Y	Ф	だ
43	ê	╤	℞	∇	υ	ф	ぢ
44	Ë	●	∂	Φ	Х	づ
45	ë	=	°	φ	х	で
46	È	╫	■	"	X	Ц	ど
47	è	┴	•	→	χ	ц	な
48	Í	—	□	ℓ	Ψ	Ч	に
49	í	╨	▫	ℓ	ψ	ч	ぬ
50	Î	—	ℏ	Ω	Ш	ね

In that chart, each column is called a **character set**.

Column 1 contains European accents.
Column 2 contains exotic accents.
Column 3 contains characters for drawing boxes.
Column 4 contains typographic symbols.
Column 5 contains icons (cute pictures).
Column 6 contains popular symbols for math and science.
Column 7 contains characters for making extra-tall math symbols.
Column 8 contains Greek.
Column 9 contains Hebrew.
Column 10 contains Russian.
Column 11 contains Japanese.

To type one of those characters, say "Compose" (Ctrl with V), then type the character's column number, a comma, and the row number, then press ENTER.

For example, to type a frowning face (which is in column 5, row 26), say "Compose" (Ctrl with V), then type "5,26" and press ENTER.

If you type a fancy character (such as a frowning face), it won't appear on your screen. It *will* appear on paper if you're using version 5.1.

Version 5.1 can print *every* character in that chart, and on *every* modern printer! Version 5.0 prints just the simplest characters.

I've shown the first 50 rows of the chart. The entire chart contains 234 rows. To see what's in rows 51 through 234, experiment — or examine appendix P at the back of the Word Perfect 5.1 reference manual. (You get that manual when you buy Word Perfect 5.1).

SEARCH FOR WORDS

The computer can search for words in the document, in the dictionary, and in the thesaurus.

Search (F2)

Here's how to make the computer search through your document to find whether you've used the word "love".

Put the cursor where you want the search to begin. (For example, if you want to search through the whole document, put the cursor at the document's beginning. If you want to search through just *part* of your document, put the cursor at the beginning of that part.)

Say "Search" (by pressing F2). Type —

love

(Type just what you want the computer to search for; do *not* press ENTER.) Then press F2 again.

The computer searches for "love". If the computer finds a "love" in your document, it moves the cursor immediately after that "love". If you want to find the next "love" in your document, press F2 again twice.

If the computer can't find any more "love" in your document, it says "not found".

<u>Capitals</u> When you tell the computer what to search for, make sure you type "love", not "Love". If you type "love", the computer searches for all loves, regardless of how they're capitalized. If you type "Love", the computer thinks you're insisting on a capital L, so the computer searches just for loves that begin with a capital L.

<u>Embedded words</u> When you tell the computer to search for "love", the computer will find any "love" in your document — even if "love" is hidden in another word. For example, the computer will find the "love" in "loves", "lover", "lovely", "glove", "clove", "clover", "pullover", "slovenly", and "auriculoventricular".

When the computer asks you what to search for, try this experiment: press the SPACE bar, then type "love", then press the SPACE bar again (and then press F2). That tells the computer to search for "love" surrounded by spaces. That prevents the computer from stopping at "loves", "lover", "lovely", "glove", and other weird words that contain "love". Unfortunately, it also prevents the computer from finding these kinds of "love" . . .

next to a hyphen: "love-hate relationships" and "the fall-in-love syndrome"
ending a sentence: "I'm in love!" and "Are you in love?" and "She's in love."
in a list: "to love, dream, despair" and "two kinds of love: great and goopy"
starting a paragraph (since that "love" is preceded by ENTER or TAB)
"love" in quotation marks or parentheses

<u>Phrases</u> When the computer asks you what to search for, you can type a whole phrase. For example, instead of telling the computer to search for any "love", tell the computer to search for "love to sing".

<u>Codes</u> Instead of searching for a word or phrase, you can search for a code. For example, to search for underlines, do this: say "Search" (by pressing F2), say "Underline" (by pressing F8), and the press F2 again.

<u>Skip ahead</u> Suppose you've written a history of America and want to find the part where you started talking about Lincoln. If you forget which page that was, no problem! Just put the cursor at the beginning of the document and tell the computer to search for "Lincoln".

Search back (Shift F2)

If you say "Search back" (Shift F2) instead of "Search", the computer will search through the part of the document that comes *before* the cursor (instead of the part that comes after).

Replace (Alt F2)

You can search for a word and replace it by a different word. For example, here's how to change each "love" in your document to "idolize".

Put the cursor at the beginning of the document, then say "Replace" (by pressing Alt with F2).

The computer asks, "Confirm?" Press Y.

Type "love", press F2, type "idolize", and press F2 again.

The computer stops at the first "love" in your document and asks, "Confirm?" If you want to replace that "love" by "idolize", press Y; otherwise press N.

The computer stops at each "love" in your document and goes through the same routine (by asking "Confirm?").

The computer does all that fairly well. For example, consider this document:

I love you. Love you! LOVE YOU! I want to kiss your glove.

If you put the cursor at the beginning of that document and unthinkingly tell the computer to change each "love" to "idolize", the computer produces this:

I idolize you. Idolize you! Idolize YOU! I want to kiss your gidolize.

Notice that the computer correctly changes "love" to "idolize", and "Love" to "Idolize". Unfortunately, it changes "LOVE" to "Idolize" (which ought to be "IDOLIZE") and "glove" to "gidolize".

<u>Applications</u> If you write a letter that talks about Fred, then want to write a similar letter about Sue, tell the computer to scan through your document and change each "Fred" to "Sue". If you write a book about "How to be a better salesman", and then a feminist tells you to change each "salesman" to "salesperson", make the computer change them all automatically.

If you're writing a long advertisement that mentions "Calvin Klein's Hot New Flaming Pink Day-Glo Pajamas" repeatedly, and you're too lazy to type that long phrase so often, just type the abbreviation "CKP". When you've finished typing the document, tell the computer to replace each "CKP" by the long phrase it stands for.

Spell (Ctrl F2)

Word Perfect comes with a disk that includes a list of all popular English words. That list is called a **dictionary**. Although that "dictionary" does *not* include definitions of those words, it *does* include each word's correct spelling. The dictionary contains 120,000 words.

You can tell the computer to check each word in your document against the dictionary, to make sure all the words in your document are spelled correctly. That's called **checking your spelling** or **doing a spelling check** or **doing a spell check** or **spell checking**.

If the computer notices that a word in your document is not in the dictionary, here's what the computer does. It highlights the word, tries to guess what other words you might have meant instead, and displays those words on the screen. If one of those words is what you meant, you can choose it, and the computer will put it in the document in place of the wrong word.

For example, type a short document that contains just this one sentence:

```
Be huppy!
```

To spell-check the document, say "Spell" (by pressing Ctrl with F2). From the menu, choose **Document** (by pressing D).

The computer looks up each word in the dictionary. The computer finds "Be" in the dictionary but can't find "huppy". The computer highlights the strange word "huppy" and prints this list of suggestions:

A. happy	B. heap	C. hep
D. hip	E. hippie	F. hippo
G. hoop	H. hop	I. hope
J. hopi	K. hype	L. hypo
M. whoop		

```
1 Skip-once  2 Skip  3 Add  4 Edit
```

Press A if you meant "happy", B if you meant "heap", C if you meant "hep", etc.

If you really meant "huppy" and want to add that new slang word to the dictionary, choose **Add** (by pressing 3). If you really meant "huppy" but don't want to add that slang word to the dictionary, choose **Skip** (by pressing 2). If you meant some other word instead, choose **Edit** (by pressing 4), type the word you meant, and say "Exit" (by pressing F7).

When the computer finishes checking the entire document, it will tell you how many words were in the document. Press ENTER.

Be careful about adding
If the computer gripes about a word you typed, do *not* add your word to the computer's dictionary unless you're *sure* that you've spelled it correctly!

Capitals
Word Perfect doesn't check capitalization much. For example, if you accidentally type "america" instead of "America", Word Perfect doesn't notice the error.

If you type "fAt" instead of "fat", Word Perfect 5.1 notices that your capitalization is totally crazy. It gripes by saying:

```
Irregular Case
```

Earlier versions of Word Perfect don't notice that "fAt" is wrong.

Repeated words
Suppose your document contains the sentence "Save our our planet".

Word Perfect's spell checker notices that you typed the word "our" twice. It suggests that you delete the second "our".

Computers versus humans
Even if you're a spelling-bee champion, you should make the computer spell-check your document because the computer can spot tiny typographical errors that human proofreaders overlook.

But after the computer checks your document, you should make a human check the document also, because only a human can realize that the sentence "I live you" is wrong and should be "I love you" instead.

Thesaurus (Alt F1)
Suppose you're writing a love story and type the word "caress". Can you think of a different word instead, that means roughly the same thing as "caress" but is better?

If you can't, the computer can! Just ask the computer to use its **thesaurus** to find **synonyms** for "caress".

Here's how. In your document, type the word "caress". Move the cursor to that word. Say "Thesaurus" (by pressing Alt with F1).

The computer prints this:

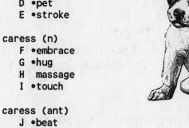

```
caress (v)
   A •cuddle
   B •fondle
   C •nuzzle
   D •pet
   E •stroke

caress (n)
   F •embrace
   G •hug
   H  massage
   I •touch

caress (ant)
   J •beat
   K •blow
```

```
1 Replace-word  2 View-doc  3 Look-up-word  4 Clear-column
```

That list gives five **synonyms** for the verb "to caress" (to cuddle, fondle, nuzzle, pet, and stroke), four synonyms for the noun "a caress" (an embrace, hug, massage, touch), and two **antonyms** (opposites) of "caress": beat and blow.

Most of those words have a dot before them. (The only word that does *not* have a dot is "massage".) The dot means: go explore! For example, if you want to explore "hug", press hug's code letter (G), and the computer will display these synonyms for "hug": cuddle, embrace, snuggle, squeeze, clasp, cling to, grasp, hold. If you want to erase hug's synonyms from the screen, choose **Clear-column** (by pressing 4).

If you want to replace "caress" by a synonym, choose **Replace-word** (by pressing 1), then type the synonym's code letter. If you want to keep "caress" in your document, say "Cancel" instead (by pressing F1).

Suffixes
Word Perfect's thesaurus understands suffixes (such as "-ing"). If you ask Word Perfect to find synonyms for "caressing" or "caressed" or "caresses", Word Perfect is smart enough to realize that the root word is "caress": it will give you synonyms for "caress".

Unfortunately, Word Perfect doesn't understand which suffixes are appropriate. If you ask Word Perfect to find synonyms for "massage", it makes the mistake of giving you synonyms for "mass". (Gee, I never realized that getting a massage was anything like going to Mass!)

Should you use a thesaurus?
If you're having trouble finding the exact word to express an idea, type the closest word that comes to your mind and then tell the computer to find synonyms. If you're lucky, one of the synonyms will be an improvement.

If you're writing a novel, the computer's synonyms can help give you fresh ideas. For example, if you're writing a bedroom scene and the only word you can think of is "caress", ask the computer to display synonyms, which will give you wild ideas! Then ask for synonyms of *those* synonyms, to lead your novel into new directions that are truly "novel"! You can write an entire wild-ride-through-the-craziness-of-life novel just by following the themes that the thesaurus suggests!

And why not a movie! I can see it now — at the end of the movie, the credits say, "based on a story by Word Perfect's thesaurus".

Tired of typing the same stuff again and again? Here's how to make the *computer* do the typing!

Repeat (Esc)

Try this experiment. Press the ESCAPE key (which says "Esc" on it), then type an "x". The computer will type the letter "x" 8 times, like this:

xxxxxxxx

The ESCAPE key means "repeat". So if you press the ESCAPE key and then the x key, the computer will repeatedly press the x key — 8 times.

If you press the ESCAPE key and then the TAB key, the computer will repeatedly press the TAB key — 8 times.

If you press the ESCAPE key and then the left-arrow key, the computer will repeatedly press the left-arrow key — 8 times.

After you press the ESCAPE key, you can type a number. For example, if you press the ESCAPE key, then type 50, then press x, the computer will press the x key 50 times (instead of 8 times).

Macro define (Ctrl F10)

The computer can help you write love letters.

For example, suppose you want each love letter to end with this message: "As always, I love you passionately, forever, my darling!!!". Instead of typing that long message at the end of each love letter, you can make the computer automatically type the message for you!

To do that, choose a letter of the alphabet to stand for the message. For example, you can choose A or B or C. Here's how. . . .

Say "Macro define" (by pressing Ctrl with F10). The computer says "Define macro". Choose a letter of the alphabet, such as A or B or C. Type that letter *while holding down the Alt key*. (If the computer says "Already Exists", you should press ENTER, then start the whole procedure over and choose a different letter of the alphabet.)

The computer will say "Description". Press ENTER.

The computer will say "Macro Def". Type the message you want to record. For example, type:

As always, I love you passionately, forever, my darling!!!

At the end of the message, say "Macro define" again (Ctrl with F10).

In the future, whenever you want the computer to automatically type the passionate message, just press the chosen letter *while holding down the Alt key*.

Jargon The message that you're recording ("As always, I love you passionately, forever, my darling!!!") is called the **macro**. The **macro's name** is "Alt A" or "Alt B" or whatever other name you choose.

Why use macros? You should make a macro of anything you type often. For example, if you're sending lots of love letters, the macro can be "As always, I love you passionately, forever, my darling!!!". If you're sending lots of hate letters instead, the macro can be "Please pay your bill promptly, to avoid losing your credit rating and being sent a carton of sour milk".

If you're sending lots of business letters, the macro can contain your name followed by the name of your company and its address and phone number.

The macro can even contain commands that make the computer underline, boldface, center, and do other fancy tasks. The macro can be any sequence of keystrokes you wish!

Creating a macro is like turning on a tape recorder: yes, the computer will record *any* keystrokes you wish! For example, the macro can even be a recording of the sequence of keystrokes that make the computer save your document onto the disk and then print your document on paper.

Macro files Whenever you invent a macro, the computer puts the macro's definition onto the hard disk.

The definition of "Alt A" is put into a file called "ALTA.WPM". The definition of "Alt B" is put into "ALTB.WPM".

Unless you erase those files, the computer remembers your macro definitions forever.

Macro (Alt F10)

Instead of making a macro's name be "Alt A" or "Alt B", you can make a macro's name be longer, such as "jennifer". You can pick any name up to 8 letters long. Here's how.

Say "Macro define" (by pressing Ctrl with F10). The computer says "Define macro". Instead of typing "Alt A" or "Alt B", type "jennifer" and press ENTER. (If the computer says "Already Defined", say "Cancel" and try again.)

Press ENTER again. While the computer says "Macro Def", type the message you want to record. At the end of the message, say "Macro define" again (Ctrl with F10).

The computer puts the message onto the hard disk, in a file called "JENNIFER.WPM".

In the future, whenever you want the computer to automatically type that message, say "Macro" (Alt F10) then type "jennifer" and ENTER.

Style (Alt F8)

The computer understands typestyles such as "Bold" (F6) and "Underline" (F8). You can invent your *own* typestyles! For example, here's how to teach the computer that "Bunder" is a new typestyle meaning "bold and underlined".

Say "Style" (Alt F8). Choose **Create Name** (by typing CN). Type the name for the typestyle you're inventing ("Bunder"), and press ENTER.

Choose **Codes** (by typing C). Type the definition of the typestyle: say "Bold" (F6) and say "Underline" (F8). At the end of that definition, say "Exit" (F7) three times. Congratulations — you've defined "Bunder"!

Whenever you want to tell the computer to "Bunder", say "Style" (Alt F8). You'll see an alphabetized list of styles that have been created. Move the cursor to "Bunder" (by pressing the down-arrow key several times) and press ENTER.

Now anything you type will be in the typestyle "Bunder". It will be bolded and underlined automatically.

When you finish typing what you want bolded and underlined, press the right-arrow key to shut off the style.

Chapter headings Suppose your document's divided into chapters, and each chapter has a heading like this:

Chapter 7: Laughter at Her Funeral

Note the heading begins with the word "Chapter". The heading is centered. It's bold. It has a blank line above it.

Let's create a style making all that happen automatically! Here's how.

Say "Style" (Alt F8). Choose "Create Names" (CN). Type the name for the style you're inventing ("Chapterhead") and press ENTER.

Choose "Codes" (C). Type the definition of Chapterhead: press the ENTER key (so the computer will leave a blank line above the heading), say "Bold" (F6), say "Center" (Shift F6), type the word "Chapter", and press the SPACE bar (so the computer will leave a blank space after the word "Chapter").

Say "Exit" (F7) three times. Congratulations! You've defined "Chapterhead"!

Whenever you want to type a chapter heading, say "Style" (Alt F8), move the cursor to "Chapterhead", and press ENTER.

On the screen, you'll see:

Chapter

Finish the chapter heading, by typing "7: Laughter at Her Funeral" (or "8: My Life in Prison"). At the end of that heading, press ENTER. Then end the style (by pressing the right-arrow key).

Saving When you save the document, the computer automatically saves all the styles you invented for it.

Date/outline (Shift F5)

The computer can automatically type the date — and create an outline.

Date To make the computer type today's date, say "Date/outline" (Shift F5), then choose **Text** (by typing T).

Suppose you're writing a long memo, but you're not sure how many days you'll spend writing it, and you're not sure on which day you'll print it. Instead of putting *today*'s date in the memo, you want to put a *future* date in the memo. But you're not sure which future date. Here's what to do. . . .

Put the cursor where you want the date to appear. Say "Date" (Shift F5) then choose **Code** (by typing C). That makes the computer put a special **date code** into your document. When you look at the document today, the screen shows today's date; but if you save the document onto your disk and then retrieve the same document tomorrow, the screen will automatically show tomorrow's date instead! If you retrieve the document two centuries from now, the screen will automatically show the date two centuries from now! That's how to make the computer automatically update your letters, even after you die!

Outline Let's create this outline:

Symphony of an American workday
I. opening blaring chords: the alarm clock rings
II. overture
   A. pissing in bathroom (New Age music)
   B. dressing & trying to rush (Bolero dance getting faster)
   C. eating breakfast (rhythmic crunch)
III. the first act: morning work (development section)
IV. intermission: fast-food lunch & errands (scherzo)
V. the second act: afternoon work (further development)
VI. finale: eating dinner (yummy chomping chords)
VII. coda: evening goof-off fun (rondo)
VIII. dying strains: reaching out hand to set alarm clock

Here's how. Begin by typing the title ("Symphony of an American workday"). At the end of that title, say "Date/outline" (Shift F5) and choose **Outline On** (by typing the letter O twice). That tells the computer to do something special whenever you press ENTER or TAB.

Try it! Press ENTER. The computer says:

I.

Finish that line (by typing " opening blaring chords: the alarm clock rings") and press ENTER. The computer says:

II.

Finish that line (by typing " overture") and press ENTER. Since that line said "II.", the computer assumes you want the next line to be "III.", so the computer says:

III.

Since you *don't* want "III." yet, press TAB. That tells the computer you want to indent (instead of having "III."). The computer changes the "III." to:

   A.

Finish that line (by typing " pissing" etc.) and press ENTER. The computer says:

   B.

Finish that line (by typing " dressing" etc.) and press ENTER. The computer says:

   C.

Finish that line (by typing " eating" etc.) and press ENTER. The computer says:

   D.

Correct that line by pressing Shift TAB, which tells the computer to unindent. The computer changes the "D." to:

III.

Finish that line and the rest of the outline. At the end of the outline's final line ("set alarm clock"), say "Date/outline" (Shift F5) and choose **Outline oFf** (by typing O then F).

Besides using Roman numerals (such as "I.") and capitals (such as "A."), the computer knows how to use Arabic numerals and small letters. For example, the computer lets you create this outline:

An egotist's outline of the universe
I. dead things
II. living things
   A. plants
   B. animals
      1. subhumans
      2. humans
         a. dumb humans
         b. smart humans
            (1) smart asses
            (2) me
               (a) my gross anatomy
               (b) my brain
                  i) sane part of brain
                  ii) horniness
                     a) printable
                     b) unprintable

Families In an outline, each line is called a **topic**. Its **subtopics** are the lines indented underneath it. A topic, together with all its subtopics, forms a **family**.

To edit an entire family, put the cursor on the family's top line. Say "Date/outline" (Shift F5) and choose **Outline** (O). Then choose how you want to edit the family:

If you want to *delete* the family, choose **Delete Yes** (DY).

If you want to *move* the family instead, choose **Move** (M), then move the family (by using the arrow keys) and press ENTER.

If you want to *copy* the family (so it appears twice), choose **Copy** (C), then point where you want the copy to appear (by using the arrow keys) and press ENTER.

When you finish that editing, the computer automatically renumbers the entire outline, so that the outline's new first topic is called "I", the next major topic is called "II", etc.

Footnote (Ctrl F7)

Suppose you're writing a religious pamphlet in which you want to say "Read it in the Bible tonight!" Suppose you want to add a footnote saying, "written by God", so that the main text looks like this —

Read it in the Bible[1] tonight!

and the bottom of the page contains this footnote:

[1]Written by God.

To do all that, type "Read it in the Bible", say "Footnote" (by pressing Ctrl F7), then choose **Footnote Create** (by typing FC). Type the footnote ("Written by God."), say "Exit" (by pressing F7), then finish typing the rest of the main text (" tonight!").

The computer will automatically number the footnote: it will automatically type [1] after "Bible" and type [1] before "Written by God." If your document contains more footnotes, the computer will automatically number them 2, 3, 4, etc. On paper, the computer will put the footnotes at the bottom of the page. It will put a 2-inch horizontal line above the footnotes to separate them from the main text. You'll see the footnotes on paper but not on your screen (except when you preview).

If you insert extra footnotes, the computer will automatically renumber the other footnotes, so that the first footnote appearing in your document is numbered 1, the second footnote is numbered 2, etc.

Unfortunately, the computer refuses to create footnotes on a page that contains newspaper columns.

To print footnotes, the computer normally uses a font that's simple but boring: Courier. To make footnotes look better, tell the computer to print them in a small font. Here's how. . . .

Move the cursor to near the beginning of the document, just after where you defined the document's font. Say "Font" (by pressing Ctrl F8) and choose "Size Small" (by typing SS). Say "Footnote" (Ctrl F7) and choose **Footnote Options** (FO). Say "Exit" (F7), then press the right-arrow key.

Mark text (Alt F5)

The computer will create an index to put at the back of the book you're writing. The index lists all of your document's important words in alphabetical order, and tells you the page where each word appears.

To create an index, move the cursor through your document. Whenever the cursor comes to a word (such as "Boston") that you want in the index, say "Mark text" (by pressing Alt F5), choose **Index** (by pressing I), and press ENTER twice.

(If you want to index a multi-word phrase, such as "Salt Lake City", do this: move the cursor to the beginning of the phrase, say "Block", move the cursor to the end of the phrase, say "Mark text" choose Index, and press ENTER twice.)

When the cursor finally comes to the end of the document, say "Mark text", choose **Define Index** (by typing DI), and press ENTER. Tell the computer where to put the page numbers in the index; you have five choices:

Command	How page numbers are in index	How an index entry looks
N	No page numbers in index	Boston
P	Page numbers in index simply	Boston 2
(	(in parentheses)	Boston (2)
F	Flush right	Boston 2
L	Leaders and flush right	Boston. 2

Type N, P, a parenthesis, F, or L.

Finally, say "Mark text" again, choose **Generate Generate** (by typing GG), and press ENTER. The computer will generate the index and put it at the end of your document on the screen.

Later, if you edit your document further, you must generate a new index, by saying "Mark text" and choosing Generate Generate again.

Merge/sort (Ctrl F9)

The computer can alphabetize. For example, type this document. . . .

Here are the most joyous sensations in America:
pastrami
salami
jelly
belly
rose
toes
How many of them have you licked today?

Here's how to alphabetize that list of sensations.

Put the cursor at the beginning of that list: put it at the beginning of "pastrami". Say "Block" (by pressing F12 or Alt F4). Make the entire list change color (by putting the cursor underneath the list, at the beginning of "How"). Say "Merge/sort" (Ctrl F9). Choose **Perform** (by pressing P).

The computer will alphabetize the list. Your document will become . . .

Here are the most joyous sensations in America:
belly
jelly
pastrami
rose
salami
toes
How many of them have you licked today?

Alphabetizing is called **sorting**.

To alphabetize a list of people, type each person on a separate line. Begin with each person's last name, like this. . . .

Welcome to the Advertising Hall of Fame!
Presenting America's favorite temptresses:

NAME	FAME
Lee, Sara	bakes
Jemimah, Aunt	pancakes
Piggy, Miss	ingratiates
Madonna, Sheeayntno	fakes

Ah, the power of marketing!

To alphabetize that list, put the cursor at the beginning of the list (the L of "Lee"), say "Block" (F12 or Alt F4), put the cursor underneath the list (on the blank line under "Madonna"), say "Merge/sort" (Ctrl F9), and choose Perform (P). The computer will alphabetize the document so you see this. . . .

Welcome to the Advertising Hall of Fame!
Presenting America's favorite temptresses:

NAME	FAME
Jemimah, Aunt	pancakes
Lee, Sara	bakes
Madonna, Sheeayntno	fakes
Piggy, Miss	ingratiates

Ah, the power of marketing!

Merge codes (Shift F9)

Suppose you want to send letters to gay couples, inviting them to a party. For example, let's send letters to Peter and Paul (the "Almond Joy" couple), Mary and Kaye (the "Cosmetics" couple), and Mickey and Donald (the "Disney" couple).

Let's send Peter a letter saying:

Dear Peter,

Come to the party!
We're having a blast!
So get in gear
And move your a--!

Let's send Paul a similar letter that begins "Dear Paul", send Mary a similar letter that begins "Dear Mary", etc.

First, create this mailing list:

Peter{END RECORD}
===
Paul{END RECORD}
===
Mary{END RECORD}
===
Kaye{END RECORD}
===
Mickey{END RECORD}
===
Donald{END RECORD}
===

To type that document, begin by typing "Peter". Next, say "Merge codes" (Shift F9) and choose **End** (E). That makes the computer say {END RECORD}. Then the computer automatically types the "=" row and presses the ENTER key for you.

Type the next name ("Paul"). Say "Merge codes End" again (Shift F9 then E).

Type the next name ("Mary"). Say "Merge codes End" again (Shift F9 then E).

When you finish typing the entire document, say "Exit" (F7) and press Y. Invent a title for your mailing list (such as "friends"): type the title and press ENTER. That makes the computer call your mailing list "FRIENDS" and put it on your hard disk. That document is called the **mailing list** or **secondary merge file**.

The computer asks, "Exit WP?" Press N.

The screen becomes blank. Type this form letter:

Dear {FIELD}1~,

Come to the party!
We're having a blast!
So get in gear
And move your a--!

When you type that form letter, instead of typing a specific name (such as Peter or Paul) you must type this symbol: {FIELD}1~. Here's how to type the symbol {FIELD}1~: say "Merge codes" (Shift F9), choose **Field** (F), then type 1 (and press ENTER).

When you finish typing the entire document, say "Exit" (F7) and press Y. Invent a title for your form letter (such as "invitatn"): type the title and press ENTER. That makes the computer call your form letter "INVITATN" and put it on your hard disk. That document is called the **form letter** or **primary merge file**.

The computer asks, "Exit WP?" Press N.

The screen becomes blank. Say "Merge/sort" (Ctrl F9) and choose "Merge" (M). Type the name of the primary file ("invitatn") and press ENTER. Type the name of the secondary file ("friends") and press ENTER.

The computer will write all the letters to all the people! You'll see some of those letters on the screen. (To see the rest of them, press the up-arrow key a while.)

To print all the letters onto paper, say "Print" (Shift F7) and choose "Full" (F).

That entire process of combining a mail list with a form letter is called **doing a mail merge**.

End field (F9)

Let's write mass-produced letters, like this:

Memo to Sue Johnson in New York

Dear Sue,
   Gee, your life is really a trip! I wish I was as lucky as you! Have a fun, hot time in New York!

Memo to Tom Jones in the beautiful island paradise of Hawaii

Dear Tom,
   Gee, your life is really a trip! I wish I was as lucky as you! Have a fun, hot time in the beautiful island paradise of Hawaii!

Memo to Devil Satan in Hell

Dear Devil,
   Gee, your life is really a trip! I wish I was as lucky as you! Have a fun, hot time in Hell!

First, create this mailing list:

Sue{END FIELD}
Johnson{END FIELD}
New York{END RECORD}
===
Tom{END FIELD}
Jones{END FIELD}
the beautiful island paradise of Hawaii{END RECORD}
===
Devil{END FIELD}
Satan{END FIELD}
Hell{END RECORD}
===

To type that document, begin by typing the first field, "Sue". Then say "End field" (by pressing F9); that makes the computer say {END FIELD} and automatically press the ENTER key for you.

Type the next field ("Johnson") then say "End field" (F9). Type the next field ("New York") then say "Merge codes End" (Shift F9 then E).

Do the same for Tom and the Devil.

When you finish typing the entire document, say "Exit" (F7) and save the document. Then type this new document:

Memo to {FIELD}1~{FIELD}2~in {FIELD}3~

Dear {FIELD}1~,
   Gee, your life is really a trip! I wish I was as lucky as you! Have a fun, hot time in {FIELD}3~!

To type the symbol {FIELD}1~, say "Merge codes Field" (Shift F9 then F) then type 1 and ENTER. To type the symbol {FIELD}2~, say "Merge codes Field" (Shift F9 then F) then type 2 and ENTER.

When you finish typing the entire form letter, say "Exit" (F7) and save the document.

Let the screen become blank. Say "Merge/sort" (Ctrl F9) and choose "Merge" (M). Type the name of the form letter and press ENTER. Type the name of the mailing list and press ENTER. The computer will write all the letters to all the people.

These tricks let you use Word Perfect more easily — and even draw pictures!

Help (F3)

If you forget how to use Word Perfect, say "Help" (by pressing F3). Then press any key on the keyboard, and see what happens!

If you press a letter of the alphabet, the computer will explain all Word Perfect concepts that begin with that letter. For example, if you press the letter B several times, the computer will tell you which keys to press for a Backward search, Block, Bold, Bottom margin, and every other Word Perfect task that begins with the letter B.

If you press keys that are *not* letters, the computer will explain what those keys do. For example, if you press the INSERT key, the computer will explain what the INSERT key does. If you press the F8 key, the computer will explain what the F8 key does, and how it means "Underline". If you press Shift F7 then V, the computer will explain that Shift F7 V means "Print View".

If you press the "Help" key (F3) twice, the computer's screen will show a copy of the plastic template, which reminds you what all the F keys do.

When you've finished getting all the help you need, press ENTER.

Controlled hop

To make the cursor hop, hold down the CONTROL key. While you keep holding down the CONTROL key, tap an arrow key.

The right-arrow key makes the cursor hop right to the next word.

The left-arrow key makes the cursor hop left to the beginning of the current word. If the cursor's there *already*, it will hop to the beginning of the previous word.

The down-arrow key makes the cursor hop down to the next paragraph.

The up-arrow key makes the cursor hop up to the beginning of the current paragraph. If the cursor's there *already*, it will hop to the beginning of the previous paragraph.

For the down-arrow and up-arrow keys to work, you must have version 5.1 and an **enhanced keyboard** (a keyboard modern enough to contain an F12 key).

Controlled deletion

To delete a simple block of text quickly, hold down the CONTROL key.

While you keep holding down the CONTROL key, tap the DELETE key or END key or PAGE DOWN key. Tapping the DELETE key makes the computer delete a whole word. Tapping the END key makes the computer delete the line's "end" (the cursor's character and all characters afterwards on the line). Tapping the PAGE DOWN key and then Y makes the computer delete the page's "bottom" (the cursor's character and all characters afterwards on the page).

Old versions If your version of Word Perfect is old — 4.0, 4.1, 4.2, or a copy of 5.0 shipped before 1989 — tap BACKSPACE instead of DELETE.

Move (Ctrl F4)

Here's a fast way to edit a block that's a single sentence, paragraph, or page.

Put the cursor anywhere in the block and then say "Move" (Ctrl F4).

How big is the block? Choose **Sentence** (by typing S) or **Paragraph** (by typing P) or **pAge** (by typing A).

Then choose one of these activities. . . . To delete the block, choose **Delete** (by pressing D). To move the block (so it vanishes from its current location and reappears elsewhere), choose **Move** (by pressing M); then move the cursor where you want the block's new position to be, and press ENTER. To copy the block (so the block appears twice in your document), choose **Copy** (by pressing C); then move the cursor where you want the block's copy to be, and press ENTER.

Setup (Shift F1)

You can change Word Perfect, so that it runs faster. If you're sharing your computer with beginners who are intimidated by high speed, do *not* make these changes unless your colleagues agree! *Ask them first!*

After getting your colleague's permission, say "Setup" (Shift F1). You'll see the **setup menu**.

No backups In version 5.1, you can choose **Environment Backup Timed No** (EBTN) then ENTER. That prevents the disk drive from interrupting you every half hour to make backup copies of your work.

Fast columns To make multi-column documents appear on the screen faster, tell the computer to display just one column at a time. Here's how: if you have version 5.1, choose **Display Edit Side No** (DESN) then press ENTER twice; if you have version 5.0, choose "Display Side No" (DSN) then press ENTER.

Fast cursor In version 5.0, you can make the cursor move faster by choosing "Cursor 5" (C5) and make the disk save faster by choosing "Fast Yes" (FY).

Exit When you finish playing with the setup menu, say "Exit" (F7).

F11 and F12 For keyboards that have F11 and F12 keys, the F11 key is supposed to mean "Reveal codes" and F12 is supposed to mean "Block". Version 5.1 knows that, but version 5.0 doesn't. If you're using version 5.0 and your keyboard has F11 and F12 keys, here's how to teach the computer to use those keys. . . .

Your Word Perfect Conversion disk contains a file called "ENHANCED.WPK". Copy that file to your hard disk's WP subdirectory (by using DOS's copy command). Then go into Word Perfect, say "Setup" (Shift F1), and choose "Keyboard" (K). Make sure the cursor is on the same line as the word ENHANCED. Press ENTER, then "Exit" (F7).

That makes F11 mean "Reveal codes" and F12 mean "Block". It also makes Shift F11 mean "Font Appearance Italic", Ctrl F11 mean "Font Size Large", and Alt F11 mean "Font Size Very-large". It also lets you use this short cut to move a block: put the cursor at the block's beginning, press F12, put the cursor at the block's end, press Ctrl F12, put the cursor where you want the block to appear, press ENTER.

Shell (Ctrl F1)

If you say "Shell" (Ctrl F1) and then choose **Go** (by typing G), the computer will temporarily stop using Word Perfect, so that you can give DOS commands instead (such as "dir").

When you finish playing with DOS commands, type the word "exit" (and press ENTER). That makes the screen return to Word Perfect and the document you were editing.

Text in/out (Ctrl F5)

Word Perfect documents contain hidden codes. Documents produced by different word processors contain different hidden codes.

DOS files (such as AUTOEXEC.BAT and CONFIG.SYS) contain no hidden codes at all. Files containing no hidden codes are called **ASCII files**.

Here's how to make Word Perfect edit an ASCII file. . . .

Exit from any Word Perfect document you were working on, so the screen becomes blank.

Say "Text in/out" (Ctrl F5). Choose **Text Retrieve** (by typing TR). That warns the computer that the file you want to edit is an ASCII file instead of a Word Perfect document.

Type the file's name. (If the file's in the root directory instead of the WP subdirectory, put a backslash before the file's name. If the file's in a different subdirectory, type a backslash, then the subdirectory's name, then another backslash, then the file's name.) At the end of the file's name, press ENTER.

The file will appear on the screen. Edit the file by using the same commands as if you were editing a Word Perfect document.

When you finish editing the file, say "Text in/out" (Ctrl F5) and choose **Text Save** (by typing TS). Press ENTER, then Y. That saves the document as an ASCII file instead of a file containing Word Perfect hidden codes. Congratulations!

To erase the screen (so you can edit another document), say "Exit" (F7). But **when the computer asks "Save document?", say "No" (N)**. If you make the mistake of saying "Yes", the computer will save the document in Word Perfect form (including Word Perfect's hidden codes), which will destroy the ASCII form you already saved.

Switch (Shift F3)

The "Switch" command lets you switch capitalization and documents.

Capitalize Suppose you've typed some text, then change your mind and want to capitalize it. Here's how to capitalize the block.

Put the cursor at the block's beginning. Say "Block" (by pressing F12 or Alt F4). Put the cursor at the block's end (so the entire block changes color).

Say "Switch" (by pressing Shift F3). Choose **Uppercase** (by typing U).

Uncapitalize Here's how to uncapitalize a block.

Put the cursor at the block's beginning. Say "Block". Put the cursor at the block's end.

Say "Switch" (by pressing Shift F3). Choose **Lowercase** (by typing L).

The computer will uncapitalize all the letters in the block — except possibly the first letter in each sentence.

Switch documents Word Perfect makes the computer's RAM hold two documents at a time. They're called **document 1** and **document 2**. When you start using Word Perfect, you're manipulating just document 1. That's the document you're typing and editing. While you're dealing with document 1, the screen's lower-right corner says "Doc 1".

To switch to document 2, say "Switch" (by pressing Shift F3). Then the screen's lower-right corner says "Doc 2", and you're manipulating document 2.

At first, document 2 is blank. You can manipulate document 2 by using all the Word Perfect commands. For example, you can type some sentences into document 2, or you can make document 2 be a copy of a saved document (by saying "Retrieve").

To switch back to document 1, say "Switch" again.

Here's how to move or copy a block from document 2 to document 1. Put the cursor at the beginning of document 2's block. Say "Block" (F12 or Alt F4). Put the cursor at the end of the block. Tell the computer you want to move or copy the block. (For example, if you're using version 5.1 with enhanced keyboard, say "move" by pressing Ctrl DELETE or say "copy" by pressing Ctrl INSERT.) Put the cursor where you want the block to appear in document 1 (by saying "Switch" and then pressing the arrow keys). Press ENTER.

When you finish playing with document 2, put the cursor back in document 2 and then say "Exit". When the computer asks, "Save document?", answer the question. When the computer asks, "Exit doc 2?", press Y. That makes document 2 become blank and puts the cursor back in document 1.

Screen (Ctrl F3)

The "Screen" command lets you split the screen into windows and draw lines.

Split screen Try this experiment: say "Screen" (by pressing Ctrl F3), choose **Window** (by pressing W), then type 11 (and ENTER). Now the top 11 lines of your screen show document 1; the bottom part of your screen shows document 2. Computerists say that the screen is **split** into two **windows**; each window shows a document.

The cursor's in document 1. To move the cursor to document 2, say "Switch" (Shift F3). To move the cursor back to document 1, say "Switch" again.

At first, document 2 is blank. When the cursor is in document 2, you can manipulate document 2 by using all the Word Perfect commands.

When you finish playing with document 2, put the cursor back in document 2 and then say "Exit". When the computer asks, "Save document?", answer the question. When the computer asks, "Exit doc 2?", press Y. Document 2 becomes blank. To devote the whole screen to document 1 (and stop the split-screen windowing), do this: say "Screen" (Ctrl F3), choose "Window" (W), then type 24 (and ENTER).

Draw lines To draw a line easily, put the cursor where you want the line to begin.

At that place, make sure you're using a monospaced font (in which all the characters have the same width as each other). Make sure you're not in a justified paragraph (move the cursor out of the paragraph, or change the paragraph to ragged-right).

Say "Screen" (Ctrl F3) and choose **Line** (L).

Then draw a line by pressing the arrow keys. For example, to make the line go to the right a distance of 3 characters, press → three times. To make the line go to the right and then down, press → and then ↓.

To switch to a *double* line, press 2. To switch to a line made of asterisks, press 3. To revert back to a simple line, press 1.

To draw a box of size 5, press → five times, then ↓ five times, then ← five times, then ↑ five times.

When you finish drawing, say "Exit" (by pressing F7).

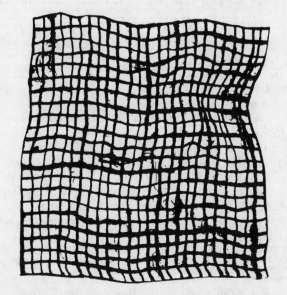

Graphics (Alt F9)

Here's a more sophisticated way to draw lines. This sophisticated way works *anywhere* in your document (even if you're using a proportionally spaced font or you're in a justified paragraph). **This sophisticated way will produce beautiful lines on paper, though not on your screen** (except when you preview).

Horizontal line To draw a horizontal line, put the cursor where you want the line to begin, say "Graphics" (Alt F9), and choose **Line Horizontal** (LH).

The computer assumes you want the horizontal line to go completely across the column of text (from the column's left edge to the column's right edge). If you'd rather make the line go just from the *cursor* to the column's right edge, choose **Horizontal Right** (HR).

Say "Exit" (F7).

Vertical line To draw a vertical line, put the cursor where you want the line to begin, say "Graphics" (Alt F9), and choose **Line Vertical** (LV).

The computer assumes you want the vertical line to be in the left margin. If you'd rather put the line at the cursor's position, choose **Horizontal Set** (HS) then ENTER.

The computer assumes you want the line to go completely up and down the page (from the top margin to the bottom margin). If you'd rather make the line go just from the *cursor* to the bottom margin, choose **Vertical Bottom** (VB).

Say "Exit" (F7).

Box Before drawing boxes, tell the computer what kind of boxes you like. Here's how.

Put the cursor at the beginning of your document. Say "Graphics" (Alt F9), then choose **Box Options Border** (by typing BOB).

You can make the left edge of each box be a **Single** line (S), **Double** line (D), **dAshed** line (A), **dOtted** line (O), **Thick** line (T), **Extra-thick** (E), or have **No** line at all (N). Type one of those letters. Do the same thing for the box's right edge, top edge, and bottom edge.

The computer assumes you want the interior of each box to be light gray (10% black and 90% white). If you prefer a darker shade (20% black), choose **Gray** (G) then type 20 (and ENTER).

Say "Exit" (F7).

Now that you've told the computer what kind of boxes you like, create some!

Here's how to create a box that's 3.8 inches wide and has the word "Love" in the middle. Put the cursor where you want the box to begin. Press the ENTER key (so you're starting a new paragraph). Say "Graphics" (Alt F9), choose **Box Create Size Width** (BCSW), type 3.8 (and ENTER), choose "Edit" (E), type "Love", and press F7 twice.

On paper, the box will appear next to the column's right edge. The box will be at or slightly below where the cursor was.

After creating the box, try typing several sentences, so that you've completed a paragraph. That paragraph will appear next to the box. The computer will make the paragraph narrow, to leave room for the box.

Instead of making the box contain just "Love", try a longer phrase! While typing it, try changing fonts, centering, and doing whatever other tricks you wish! The box can even contain a multi-paragraph essay!

DATABASES

A **database program** is a program that manipulates lists of facts. It can store information about your friends & enemies, customers & suppliers, employees & stockholders, students & teachers, hobbies & libraries. It puts all that data about your life and business onto a disk, which acts as an electronic filing cabinet. Then it lets you retrieve the data easily. It can generate mailing lists, phone directories, sales reports, and any other analyses you wish.

It's called a **database program** or **database management system (DBMS)** or **information retrieval system**. The terms are synonymous.

File-cabinet jargon

In an old-fashioned office that lacks a computer, you'll see a filing cabinet containing several drawers. One drawer's labeled CUSTOMERS; another drawer's labeled EMPLOYEES; another drawer's labeled SUPPLIERS. Each drawer contains alphabetized index cards.

For example, the drawer labeled CUSTOMERS contains a card about each customer; the first card might be labeled "ADAMS, JOAN"; the last card might be labeled "ZABRONSKI, JILL". The first card contains all known information about Joan Adams: it contains her name, address, phone number, everything she bought, how much she paid, how much she still owes, and other personal information about her. That card is called her **record**. Each item of information on that card is called a **field**.

If the card is a pre-printed form, it allows a certain amount of space for each item: for example, it might allow only 30 characters for the person's name. The number of characters allowed for a field is called the **field's width**. In that example, the width of the NAME field is 30 characters.

Each drawer is called a **file**. For example, the drawer that contains information about customers is called the **customer file**; another drawer is the **employee file**; another drawer is the **supplier file**.

The entire filing cabinet — which contains all the information about your company — is called the **database**.

A sample file

Here's a file about amazing students in the School of Life:

```
Last name: Smith                    First name: Suzy
Age: 4              Class: 12
Comments: Though just 4 years old, she finished high school because she's fast.

Last name: Bell                     First name: Clara
Age: 21             Class: 10
Comments: The class clown, she never graduated but had fun trying. Super-slow!

Last name: Smith                    First name: Buffalo Bob
Age: 7              Class: 2
Comments: Boringly normal, he's jealous of his sister Suzy. Always says "Howdy!"

Last name: Kosinski                 First name: Stanislaw
Age: 16             Class: 11
Comments: He dislikes Polish jokes.

Last name: Ketchopf                 First name: Heinz
Age: 57             Class: 1
Comments: His pour grades make him the slowest Ketchopf in the West.

Last name: Nixon                     First name: Tricky Dick
Age: 78             Class: 13
Comments: The unlucky President, he disappointed our country.

Last name: Walter                    First name: Russy-poo
Age: 44             Class: 0
Comments: This guy has no class.
```

That file consists of seven records: Suzy Smith's record, Clara Bell's record, Buffalo Bob Smith's record, Stanislaw Kosinski's record, Heinz Ketchopf's record, Tricky Dick Nixon's record, and Russy-poo Walter's record.

Each record consists of five fields: last name, first name, age, class, and comments. The age and class fields are narrow; the comments field is very wide.

Database programs versus word processing

Like a word processing program, a database program lets you write information, put it onto a disk, edit it, and copy it onto paper.

In a word processing system, the information's called a **document**, consisting of paragraphs which in turn consist of sentences. In a database system, the information's called a **file** (instead of a document); it consists of records, which in turn consist of fields.

Since a database program resembles a word processor, a word processor can act as a crummy database program. A *good* database program offers the following extras, which the typical word processor lacks. . . .

A good database program can alphabetize, put information into numerical order, and check for criteria. For example, you can tell it to check which customers are women under 18 who have light red hair and live in a red-light district, make it print their names and addresses on mailing labels in zip code order, and make it print a phone book containing their names and numbers. As you can see, database programs are very potent and can be nasty tools for invading people's privacy!

PFS

Most database programs are hard to use. In 1980, John Page invented the first *easy* database program. He called it the **Personal Filing System (PFS)**. It ran on Apple 2 computers. He developed it while sitting in his garage.

He showed the program to two friends: Fred Gibbons and Janelle Bedke. The three of them tried to find a company willing to market his program, but no company was interested, so they decided to market the program themselves by forming a company, **Software Publishing Corporation**.

The program became very popular. Software Publishing Corporation became a multi-million-dollar corporation. It developed improved versions of PFS for the Apple 2 family, Radio Shack models 3 & 4, Commodore 64, Mac, and IBM PC. Today, the fanciest version of PFS is **Professional File**, which runs on the IBM PC.

The company also invented a word processor, whose IBM version is called **Professional Write**. It works well with Professional File. Discount dealers sell Professional Write for $142; when you buy it, you get Professional File free!

You can write a memo by using Professional Write and build a mailing list by using Professional File. Then use those programs together to print personalized copies of your memo to everybody on your mailing list.

Software Publishing Corporation has invented an even easier program, called **PFS First Choice**. It includes the easiest parts of both Professional File and Professional Write. It also includes spreadsheets, graphics, and telecommunication. It's simple to use and cheap: $159 list, $76 at discount.

In 1988, John Page and Janelle Bedke got bored and quit the company, but Fred Gibbons and the rest of his staff are hanging on. Although they still publish Professional File and Professional Write, they no longer publish PFS First Choice. Instead, PFS First Choice is published by **Spinnaker**, which pays Software Publishing Corporation a 16% royalty.

Q&A

Inspired by the PFS series, a new company called **Symantec** developed a similar program, called **Q&A**.

At first glance, Q&A seems to just imitate the PFS series, since Q&A uses almost the same commands and keystrokes as the first IBM version of PFS. But Q&A understands many extra commands also, making Q&A much more powerful than the PFS series. Q&A handles just two topics — databases and word processing — but very well! In the entire history of mankind, Q&A is the most useful program ever invented! It's fairly easy (almost as easy as the PFS series), and it's so powerful that it can handle the computing needs of almost all businesses.

<u>Versions</u> Symantec started selling version 1 of Q&A in 1985, versions 1.1 and 2 in 1986, version 3 in 1988, and version 4 in 1991. All those versions use MS-DOS, which requires that you buy an IBM PC or clone.

Symantec has developed a Windows version, but don't buy it. Everybody who's tried it hates it. It requires too many keystrokes and mouse-strokes per task. The DOS version is much easier and swifter. Also, the Windows version consumes 20 megabytes of your hard disk. I'll discuss the DOS version.

<u>RAM</u> Q&A requires at least 512K of RAM. Q&A runs much faster if you have at least 640K of RAM. To run version 4 of Q&A with version 4 of MS-DOS (which consumes lots of RAM), you *must* have at least 640K.

<u>Hard disk</u> Version 4 requires a hard disk. If you don't have a hard disk, you must buy an earlier version instead and use two floppy drives.

<u>Cost</u> Version 4 lists for $399. A New York discount dealer, called **Harmony**, sells it for just $189 (plus shipping). Phone Harmony at 800-441-1144 or 718-692-2828.

<u>Programmable</u> Q&A is **programmable**, which means you can teach it new tricks.

For example, I taught Q&A how to run my business. Now Q&A handles all my mailing lists, orders, shipping labels, income, expenses, and taxes. Q&A runs my entire life!

I also used Q&A to create the master index at the back of this book.

<u>Gigantic files</u> Q&A can handle gigantic files. Each file can contain up to 256 megabytes. You can divide the file into as many records as you wish and divide each record into as many fields as you wish.

In version 4, each record can be as long as you wish, and each field can contain up to 32 kilobytes. Earlier versions restrict each record to 16 kilobytes and each field to 1.6 kilobytes.

STARTING

Here's how to handle databases by using Q&A versions 3 and 4 for DOS.

Prepare yourself

Before using Q&A to handle databases, practice using Q&A to handle word processing, by reading pages 172-182. For example, I assume you've followed the instructions on page 172 about how to "Make Q&A act better".

The main menu

By following the instructions on page 172 about how to "Run Q&A", make the computer display this Q&A **main menu:**

```
Q&A MAIN MENU
F - File
R - Report
W - Write
A - Assistant
U - Utilities
X - Exit Q&A
```

If you're using version 4 and have a mouse, you'll see a small red rectangle in the middle of the screen. Move that rectangle out of the way — to the screen's top right corner — by rolling the mouse toward your desk's back right corner.

The file menu

To make Q&A handle databases, choose "F - File" from the main menu by pressing the F key. (That works if you followed the instructions on page 172 about how to "Make Q&A act better". If you did *not* follow those instructions, you must press ENTER after pressing F — and you must press ENTER after choosing any item from any menu.)

The screen shows the **file menu.** In version 4, it looks like this:

```
             FILE MENU
 D - Design file    R - Remove
 A - Add data       M - Mass update
 S - Search/update  T - Post
 P - Print          U - Utilities
 C - Copy
```

(Version 3 lacks "T - Post" and "U - Utilities". You see "B - Backup" instead.)

Whenever you're done filing, you should return to the main menu by pressing the Esc key several times. Then you can exit by pressing X. That's the only correct way to stop using Q&A's database. Do *not* just turn off the power! If you turn off the power without pressing X first, you might wreck the data files you created.

Field commands

While using the filing part of Q&A, you can give these **field commands:**

Field command	Keys to press	
Add new records	Ctrl F6	
Calculate	F8	
Calculate mode	Shift F8	
Customize file	Shift F9	
Date	Ctrl F5	
Delete field/line	Shift F4	
Delete field/line end	Ctrl F4	
Delete record	F3	
Delete word	F4	
Ditto field	F5	
Ditto record	Shift F5	
Edit field	F6	
File menu	Shift F10	
Help	F1	
Macro	Shift F2	
Macro run	Alt F2	just in version 4
Mask override	Alt F4	just in version 4
Next record	F10	
Previous record	F9	
Print record	F2	
Print remaining records	Ctrl F2	
Reset @NUMBER	Ctrl F8	
Retrieve spec	Alt F8	just in version 4
Search for records	F7	
Search options	Ctrl F7	
Table	Alt F6	
Table definition	Shift F6	
Time	Alt F5	
Undo edit	Shift F7	just in version 4
Values permitted	Alt F7	just in version 4

Put that chart (or a photocopy of it) next to the computer.

The rest of this chapter explains how to use the file menu and the field commands.

DESIGN FILE

Here's how to design a new file. From the file menu, choose "D - Design file" (by pressing D).

That makes the computer show the **design menu**. In version 4, it looks like this:

```
DESIGN MENU
D - Design a new file
R - Redesign a file
C - Customize a file
P - Program a file
S - Secure a file
A - Customize application
```

(In version 3, the bottom three choices are missing.)

Look back on page 148, at the sample file of students in the School of Life. Let's create that file and call it STUDENTS. To do that, press the D key (which chooses "D - Design a new file" from the menu), type "students", then press ENTER.

Type the form

Most of the screen will become blank. On the blank screen, type a form, which you'll fill in later. For example, if you want to store each student's last name, first name, age, and class, plus comments, type this form:

```
Last name:                    First name:
Age:            Class:
Comments:
```

Here's how. Type the word "Last", then a space, then the word "name", then a colon. Move to the right (by holding down the right-arrow key or space bar or TAB key), then type the phrase "First name", then a colon. Press the ENTER key, and type the lines underneath.

That form creates five fields: last name, first name, age, class, and comments. Each field name ends with a colon.

When you've finished typing the form, copy it onto the hard disk, by pressing the F10 key.

Examine the T screen

On the screen, you'll see the form you typed. The computer automatically puts a T in each field, so your screen looks like this:

```
Last name: T                  First name: T
Age: T          Class: T
Comments: T
```

Move the cursor

The cursor's at the first T. To move the cursor around the screen, you can use the arrow keys.

To move the cursor faster, use the TAB key (which is next to the Q key). When you press the TAB key, the cursor moves to the next field.

For example, if the cursor's at the T for "Last name", and you press the TAB key, the cursor will move to the T for "First name". If you press the TAB key again, the cursor will move to the T for "Age".

Experiment! Try moving the cursor around the screen by using the TAB key.

Unfortunately, the TAB key is hard for your fingers to reach. To move the cursor more easily, tap the ENTER key instead. (While you're manipulating a form, the ENTER key imitates the TAB key.)

So to move the cursor ahead to the next field, tap TAB or ENTER. To move back to the previous field, tap TAB (not ENTER) *while holding down the Shift key*.

Change T to N

Each T on the screen is a **format code**; it stands for "Text". If you want a field to contain a number instead of text, change that field's T to an N.

For example, since you want the person's "Age" to be a number, you must change Age's T to N. To do that, move the cursor to the Age's T (by pressing the TAB key), then type N.

You can type either N or n. The computer doesn't care about capitalization.

Also change Class's T to N, so your screen looks like this:

```
Last name: T                  First name: T
Age: N          Class: N
Comments: T
```

That tells the computer that the person's age and class are Numbers, and everything else about the person consists of words and other general Text.

Use the N code just for numbers that are simple (such as 0, 7, 2150, .2, .09, and -31.8).

Use the T code for numbers that contain dashes (such as phone numbers) and for long numbers that can begin with 0 (such as ZIP codes). Use the T code for social security numbers, since they contain dashes and can begin with 0.

Finish

Press the F10 key. The computer will say GLOBAL FORMAT OPTIONS.

Press F10 again. You'll see the file menu again.

Congratulations! You've created a STUDENTS database on your hard disk! That database consists of two files (STUDENTS.DTF and STUDENTS.IDX) in the QA subdirectory.

ADD DATA

You've seen how to make the computer put a file called STUDENTS onto the disk. Although the file is organized so that each record will consist of five fields, the file doesn't contain any records yet, since it doesn't yet contain the names and data about any specific students.

To add the names of specific students and the data about them, choose "A - Add data" from the file menu (by pressing A). Press ENTER.

The screen will show the form you designed:

```
Last name:                    First name:
Age:             Class:
Comments:
```

Then fill in the blanks.

For example, suppose one of the students is Suzy Smith. Fill in the form to look like this:

```
Last name: Smith              First name: Suzy
Age: 4           Class: 12
Comments: Though just 4 years old, she finished high school because she's fast.
```

Here's how. Type Smith, then move the cursor to the next field by pressing ENTER (or TAB). Type Suzy, then press ENTER. Type 4, then ENTER. Type 12, then ENTER. Type the commentary sentence.

When you've finished filling in Suzy Smith's form, say "Next record" (by pressing F10). Then the computer will show a blank form again:

```
Last name:                    First name:
Age:             Class:
Comments:
```

Fill in the blanks again, for the next student (Clara Bell).

Repeat that process for each student. As you type the students' records, the computer automatically copies them to the STUDENTS.DTF file (which is in your hard disk's QA subdirectory).

Move the cursor

To move the cursor a short distance, use the arrow keys. Here's how to move the cursor farther:

Keys you press	Where the cursor will move
TAB	the next field
Shift with TAB	the previous field
HOME	the beginning of the field
END	the end of the field
HOME HOME	the first field on the screen
END END	the last field on the screen
F10	the next record
F9	the previous record
Ctrl with HOME	the first record you added during this session
Ctrl with END	the last record you added during this session

Delete

If you make a mistake, point at it (by moving the cursor there), then tell the computer how much to delete.

To delete just one character, press the Del key. To delete a whole word, say "Delete word" (by pressing F4). To delete everything you typed in the field, say "Delete field/line" (by pressing Shift with F4). To delete everything you typed in the whole record, say "Delete record" (by pressing F3); when the computer asks "Are you sure?", press Y.

Ditto

If you move the cursor to a field and then say "Ditto field" (by pressing F5), the computer will make the data in that field be a copy of the previous student's. To make the entire record be a copy of the previous student's, say "Ditto record" (by pressing Shift with F5).

Edit (just in version 4)

If you have version 4, try this trick: while you're typing words in a field, say "Edit field" (by pressing F6).

A gigantic box will appear at the bottom of the screen. The words you typed appear in that box. Since the box is big, it can hold lots of words. Type as many as you wish! You can even type a long essay about the student! When you type near the box's bottom, the text in the box automatically moves out of the way, so you can type even more! You can type many pages! While you're typing them, you're using Q&A's word processor, so you can use all the word-processing tricks you learned: press ENTER at the end of each paragraph, press TAB to indent a paragraph, and use page 154's table to give advanced word-processing commands (such as "Spell" and "Thesaurus").

When you finish typing in the box, press the F10 key.

In the future, whenever you want to see or edit that boxed essay again, move the cursor to that field and say "Edit field" (F6) again.

Finish

When you finish typing the last student's record, and you still see that record on the screen, say "File menu" by pressing Shift with F10 (instead of saying "Next record"). Then the screen will display the file menu again (instead of waiting for you to type another record).

SEARCH/UPDATE

To search through the file to find a particular student, choose "S - Search/update" from the file menu (by pressing S). Press ENTER.

The screen will show the form you designed again:

Last name: First name:
Age: Class:
Comments:

If you fill in a few of the blanks, the computer will fill in the rest. For example, if you fill in just the last name (Smith) and press F10, the computer will find everybody whose last name is Smith. It will show you each Smith's record, one at a time.

Whenever the computer finds a Smith's record, the computer pauses to let you look at the record and edit it. (Editing is also called **updating**.) To edit the record, move the cursor to the field you want to revise (by pressing TAB, ENTER, or arrow keys), then retype that field. (To hop to the screen's bottom field, press END twice; to hop back up to the screen's top field, press HOME twice.)

When you finish examining and revising the record, choose one of these actions:

What you want to do next	What to say
see the next Smith	"Next record" (by pressing F10)
see the previous Smith	"Previous record" (by pressing F9)
see the first Smith	Ctrl with HOME
see the final Smith	Ctrl with END
see the file menu	"File menu" (by pressing Shift with F10)
delete this Smith & see the next Smith	"Delete record" (F3) then Y
undo the revisions	"Undo edit" (Shift F7, just in version 4)
undo the revisions & see the file menu	press Esc, then usually Y
search for other records (not Smiths)	"Search for records" (by pressing F7)
create other records & add them to file	"Add new records" (by pressing Ctrl with F6)

If the computer can't find who you're searching for (because there aren't any Smiths or there isn't any "next Smith" or "previous Smith"), the computer will say "No forms" or "No more forms" or "No previous form". Press the Esc key, which makes the computer show the file menu.

Fancy search techniques

If you tell the computer to search for "smith" instead of "Smith", the computer will still find all the Smiths, since the computer doesn't care about capitalization.

If you tell the computer to search for "S.." instead of "Smith" (by putting "S.." in the last name field), the computer will get everybody whose last name begins with "S". Saying "..th" gets names ending with "th". Saying "..m.." gets names containing an "m". Saying "S..h" gets every name that begins with S and ends with h. Saying "S????" gets every name that contains an S followed by exactly 4 more letters.

Not The symbol for "not" is "/". For example, saying "/Smith" gets everybody whose name is *not* Smith. Saying "/..m.." gets every name *not* containing an m.

Or The symbol for "or" is ";". For example, saying "Smith;Bell" gets everybody named Smith or Bell.

Unsure of the spelling? Suppose you want to find Kosinski's record, but you can't remember how he spells his name. You don't remember whether it's "Kosinski", "Cosinski", "Kozinski", "Kosinscki", or "Kosinsky"; you remember merely that it includes the letters "in". If you put "..in.." into the last name field, the computer will find everybody whose name contains "in" — and it will find Kosinski's record.

Suppose somebody phones to ask you about a student; but the phone connection is poor (with lots of static) and the person also mumbles. You think he's asking about somebody named "Cuzomskuh", but you're not sure. Tell the computer to find all the students that *sound like* "Cuzomskuh". To do that, put "~Cuzomskuh" in the last name field. The symbol ~ means "sounds like". (On the original IBM keyboard, it's next to the ENTER key; on the new IBM keyboard, it's next to the 1 key; on the Leading Edge keyboard, it's next to the BACKSPACE key. While typing it, you must hold down the Shift key.) The computer will find Kosinski and any other students that sound like "Cuzomskuh".

Search on age If you fill in just the age, the computer will find everybody that age. For example, to find everybody who's 10 years old, put "10" in the age field.

To find everybody who's *less* than 10 years old, say "<10". For *greater* than 10, say ">10". For *greater than or equal to* 10, say ">=10". For *greater than 10 but less than 18*, say ">10..<18".

To find the oldest student, say "max". To find the youngest, say "min".

To find the 3 oldest students, say "max3". The computer will show you the oldest student, then the next oldest, then the 3rd oldest.

In the age field, if you say just "=" (instead of "=10"), the computer will find everybody whose age is equal to *nothing*: it will find everybody whose age was left blank. To find everybody whose age is *not* blank, ask for "/=".

Alphabetical order The computer understands alphabetical order — the order in which words and names would appear in a dictionary.

For example, if you ask for the names that are "<Smith" (by putting "<Smith" in the last name field), the computer will find all names "less than Smith", which means all names that come before Smith in the dictionary. Asking for ">Smith" gets you all names that come *after* Smith in the dictionary.

Search through comments If you search for "..slow.." in the comments field, the computer will find everybody whose comment mentions "slow". It will find Clara Bell (who's "Super-slow!") and also find Heinz Ketchopf ("the slowest Ketchopf in the West").

Unrestricted search If you leave all the fields blank so that you're not telling the computer to search for anything particular, the computer will show you *all* the records in the file, without any restrictions.

Expand a field If a field is too narrow to hold your search request, type as much of the request as fits in the field, then say "Edit field" (by pressing F6).

The computer will let you type the rest of the request at the bottom of the screen; do so. When you finish typing the request, move on to the next field (by pressing ENTER) or make the computer start searching (by pressing F10).

Multi-field search

Suppose you want to find everybody who's old and stupid. Specifically, suppose you want to find everybody whose age is over 40 and who still hasn't finished the second grade. Put ">40" in the age field, and put "<3" in the class field.

The computer will find Heinz Ketchopf (who's 57 years old and in the first grade) and Russy-poo Walter (who's 44 years old and whose class is 0). They're the students who are old and stupid.

Suppose you want to find the students who are old *or* stupid. To do that, put ">40" in the age field, put "<3" in the class field, then say "Search options" (by pressing Ctrl with F7). Move the cursor down, then across to the word ANY. Press F10. The computer will find Buffalo Bob Smith, Heinz Ketchopf, Tricky Dick Nixon, and Russy-poo Walter, because each of them is either old or stupid.

Sort

When you've told the computer which records to search for, you normally press F10, which makes the computer start searching.

Instead of just pressing F10, try doing the following: say "Calculate" (by pressing F8), then type "1a" in the field that interests you most, then finally press F10.

That makes the computer display the records in alphabetical or numerical order. For example, if you put "1a" in the last name field, the computer will display the records in alphabetical order, by last name. If you put "1a" in the age field instead, the computer will display the student records in order of age, starting with the youngest student.

Putting the records into alphabetical or numerical order is called **sorting**.

The usual kind of sorting is called **ascending**. When you type "1a", the "a" stands for "ascending".

If you type "1d" instead, you get the opposite kind of sorting, which is called **descending**. For example, if you put "1d" in the last name field, the computer will display the records in reverse alphabetical order, beginning with any Z names and ending with A. If you put "1d" in the age field, the computer will display the student records in order of *decreasing* age, starting with the oldest student and ending with the youngest.

Suppose you put "1a" in the last name field and "2a" in the age field. The "1a" makes the computer sort by last name. If several students have the same last name (such as the Smiths), the age field's "2a" makes the computer "break the tie" by using the age: the computer will show you the Smiths from youngest to oldest. In that situation, the last name field is called the **primary** sort field; the age field (which is used only for breaking a tie) is called the **secondary** sort field. The "1a" means "primary ascending"; the "2a" means "secondary ascending".

Table

Suppose you search for youngsters (by saying "Age: <18" and then pressing F10). When the computer shows you the first youngster's record, say "Table" (by pressing Alt with F6). The computer will display this table, which shows the records of *all* youngsters simultaneously:

Last name	First name	Age	Class	Comments
Smith	Suzy	4	12	Though just 4→
Smith	Buffalo Bob	7	2	Boringly norm→
Kosinski	Stanislaw	16	11	He dislikes P→

In that table, each row is a record. The top row is Suzy Smith's record. The bottom row is Stanislaw Kosinski's record.

Each column is a field. The left column is the "Last name" field. The last column is the "Comments" field.

Since the screen is narrow, it shows just 5 thin columns. Look at Stanislaw Kosinski's "Comments" field. Since the column's too thin to show his entire Comments field ("He dislikes Polish jokes"), the column shows just the first few characters ("He dislikes P") and a right-arrow (which tells you that the field contains more characters). Version 3 doesn't bother to show the right-arrow.

If you're using version 4, you can edit the table while you stare at it. Just move the cursor down to the row you want to edit (by pressing the down-arrow key), and move the cursor across to the field you want to edit (by pressing the TAB key). Here's what to do next:

If you want to retype the field's info completely (and it's short), go ahead: retype it!
If you want to edit the field's info slightly (and it's short), just press F5 and then edit.
If the field's info is long (so you see "→"), do this: press F6, then edit, then press F10.

If a file contains more than 5 fields, the table usually shows just the first 5 fields. If you're using version 4, you can see the other fields by pressing the TAB key several times.

Here's another way to see 5 different fields (in both versions 3 and 4). Say "Table definition" (by pressing Shift with F6). In the five fields you want to see, type the numbers 1, 2, 3, 4, and 5. Make sure those numbers aren't in any other fields. Then press F10.

The screen's tall enough to show 17 rows of the table. To see other rows of a long table, press the PgDn key.

After viewing the table, move the cursor to the row that interests you most, then press F10. The screen will show all details of that row's record.

PRINT

Whenever the screen shows a student's record, you can print that record on paper. Just say "Print record" (by pressing F2), then press F10.

To have more fun instead, say "Print remaining records" (by pressing Ctrl with F2), then press F10. The computer will print the record, then print all subsequent records in the bunch you were examining or adding.

The print menu

To do fancier printing, get the file menu onto the screen, then choose "P - Print" (by pressing P). Press ENTER.

The screen will show the **print menu**. From that menu, choose "D - Design/redesign a spec".

Invent a name for the printout you'll create. The name can be up to 31 characters long, and it can even contain blank spaces. Type the name, then press F10.

The computer will show a blank form. Fill in the blanks to tell the computer which records to print. For example, to print all the Smiths, put "Smith" in the "Last name" field; then press F10.

The computer will show another blank form. Choose one of these three strategies. . . .

Strategy 1: leave the form blank. That tells the computer you want standard printing. The computer will print all the record's fields, in the same positions that they appear on the screen.

Strategy 2: give coordinates. For example, if you type "2,10" in the last name field, the computer will print the student's last name on paper, 2 lines down from the top margin, and starting in the 10th space from the left margin. If you omit a field's coordinates, that field will be unprinted.

Strategy 3: use + and x. For example, if you type a "+" in the last name field, the computer will print the last name. If you type an "x" in the last name field, the computer will print the last name and then automatically do a carriage return, so the next field it prints will appear underneath. Any field you leave blank will be unprinted.

When you've chosen one of those three strategies (and filled in the form appropriately), press F10.

The computer will say "FILE PRINT OPTIONS". If you want the computer to print the field labels (so that the computer will print "Last name: Smith" instead of printing just "Smith"), move the cursor down to "Print field labels?", then move left to "Yes".

Press F10 again, then ENTER. The computer will print the records you requested, then show you the print menu again.

If you want to repeat the printing, choose "P - Print records" from that menu. (In version 3, choose "P - Print forms".) Move the cursor to your printout's name. Press F10 then ENTER. The computer will repeat the printing and show you the print menu again.

When you don't want to do any more printing, press Esc. you'll see the file menu again.

Report

To print a fancy report, get the Q&A main menu. (To do that, get the file menu, then press Esc.) From the Q&A main menu, choose "R - Report". The screen will show a **report menu**. From that menu, choose "D - Design/redesign a report" (by pressing D). Press ENTER.

Invent a name for the report you'll create. The name can be up to 31 characters long, and it can even contain blank spaces. Type the name, then press F10. (If you're using version 4, then choose "C - Columnar report" by pressing C.)

The computer will show a blank form. Fill in the blanks, to tell the computer who to report on. For example, if you want to report on just the Smiths, put "Smith" in the "Last name" field. To report on *everybody* (which is what I suggest), leave the form blank.

Press F10. The computer will show another blank form. This report will consist of several columns. Put 1 in the field that you want to be the leftmost column, 2 in the field that you want to be the next column, etc. For example, if you want the person's last name to be the leftmost column, the first name to be the next column, and the age to be the third column, type this:

```
Last name: 1                    First name: 2
Age: 3               Class:
Comments:
```

Better yet, put an "as" in the last name field, and put an "a" in the age field, like this:

```
Last name: 1,as                 First name: 2
Age: 3,a             Class:
Comments:
```

In the last name field, the "as" stands for "ascending sort"; it forces the computer to print the last names in alphabetical order. In the age field, the "a" stands for "average": it makes the computer print the average age.

When you finish filling in that form, press F10 twice, then ENTER. The computer will print this report:

Last name	First name	Age
Bell	Clara	21.00
Ketchopf	Heinz	57.00
Kosinski	Stanislaw	16.00
Nixon	Tricky Dick	78.00
Smith	Suzy	4.00
	Buffalo Bob	7.00
Walter	Russy-poo	44.00
=========	===========	=====
Average:		32.43

Notice that the computer alphabetizes the left column, clumps the two Smiths together, and prints the average age. The computer automatically makes each column wide enough to fit even the longest names and numbers.

When the computer finishes printing the report, it shows the report menu again.

If you want to print the report again, choose "P - Print a report" from that menu (by pressing P). Press ENTER. Move the cursor to your report's name. Press F10 then ENTER. The computer will reprint the report and show you the report menu again.

When you don't want to print any more reports, press Esc. You'll see the main menu again.

Fancy codes Instead of saying "as" (for ascending sort), you can say "ds" (which gets you a descending sort).

Besides telling you the column's average (for which the code is "a"), Q&A can also tell you the column's total ("t"), count ("c"), largest number ("max"), smallest number ("min"), and all subtotals ("st"). To make Q&A do so, just put those codes in the blanks.

Mail merge

Suppose you want to write a personalized letter to each student, so that Suzy Smith's letter will say —

```
Dear Suzy,
Come to the party for grade 12 on Saturday.
```

and Clara Bell's letter will say —

```
Dear Clara,
Come to the party for grade 10 on Saturday.
```

Here's how. . . .

First, get into the word processor. (To do that, get to the file menu, then get to the main menu by pressing Esc, then choose "W - Write" from the menu, then choose "T - Type/edit" from the next menu.)

Type this form letter:

```
Dear *First name*,
Come to the party for grade *Class* on Saturday.
```

To type it, begin by typing the word "Dear", then tap the space bar once.

To create the "*First name*", do the following. Say "Field" (by pressing Alt with F7). The computer will ask you for the name of the file; type "students" then ENTER. The computer will display this list:

```
FIELD NAMES
Age
Class
Comments
First name
Last name
```

Move the cursor to "First name", then ENTER. The computer will automatically type "*First name*" in the middle of your memo.

Then type the rest of the form letter. Remember to type the comma after *First name*, and remember that you can make the computer automatically type *Class* for you, by pressing Alt with F7.

When you finish typing the form letter, say "Print" (by pressing F2). Then press F10.

You'll see a blank form. Use it to say which students will get the letter. (For example, to send the letter to just the Smiths, put "Smith" in the last name field. To send the letter to *all* the students, leave the fields blank.) Press F10 then ENTER.

The computer will print the letters to all the students you requested. That massive printing is called a **mail merge**, because the computer does it by merging the form letter with the mailing list of students.

When the computer finishes, you'll be using Q&A's word processor again. To leave the word processor, press Esc twice; if the computer asks "Are you SURE?", press Y. You'll see the Q&A main menu.

MASS MOVES

Here's how to manipulate many records at once. . . .

Mass update

Suppose Mr. Smith — the father of Suzy Smith and Buffalo Bob Smith — dies. His wife, Mrs. Smith, remarries and changes her name to Mrs. Finkelstein. She also changes the names of her kids, so that "Suzy Smith" becomes "Suzy Finkelstein", and "Buffalo Bob Smith" becomes "Buffalo Bob Finkelstein".

We must tell the computer to turn the Smiths into Finkelsteins. Since Suzy and Buffalo Bob are such wonderful kids, we'll also move them into super-advanced classes that are ten times their ages: we'll move Suzy (who is 6) into class 60, and move Buffalo Bob (who is 7) into class 70. Here's how to do all that. . . .

From the file menu, choose "M - Mass update" (by pressing M). Press ENTER. You'll see a blank form.

Tell the computer who to search for. Since you want the computer to search for all the Smiths, type "Smith" in the last name field, then press F10.

You'll see another blank form. Tell the computer how to change the Smiths' records, by typing this:

```
Last name: #1="Finkelstein"        First name:
Age: #2          Class: #3=10*#2
Comments:
```

Notice you must put #1, #2, and #3 in the three fields involved (Last name, Age, and Class). To make field #1 (which is Last name) become Finkelstein, say #1="Finkelstein". To make field #3 (which is Class) become 10 times field #2 (Age), say #3=10*#2.

When you finish typing all that, press F10 then N. The computer will change the Smiths to Finkelsteins and make their classes become 10 times their ages. Then you'll see the file menu again.

How to make the whole school skip Suppose *all* the school's students are doing so well that you want to skip them ahead 5 years. (You'll move all the first graders to the 6th grade, all the second graders to the 7th grade, all the third graders to the 8th grade, etc.) Here's how. . . .

From the file menu, choose "M - Mass update". Press ENTER. You'll see a blank form. Without typing any restrictions, just press F10 (since you want to update *all* students).

You'll see another blank form. Since you want to increase each student's class by 5, you should make the class be called "field #1" and add 5 to it. To do that, say "Class: #1=5+#1", which means "the Class is field #1; and field #1 will become equal to 5 more than what it had been." Then press F10.

The computer will increase each student's class by 5. Then you'll see the file menu.

Remove

Suppose all the Finkelsteins are murdered. Let's remove them from the file.

To remove the Finkelsteins, choose "R - Remove" from the file menu by pressing R. Press ENTER. (If you're using version 4, then choose "S - Selected records" by pressing S.)

You'll see a blank form. In the last name field, type "Finkelstein".

Press F10 then Y. The computer will delete all the Finkelstein records. Then you'll see the file menu again.

Backup

Here's how to make the second copy of STUDENTS.

If you're using version 3, choose "B - Backup" from the file menu by pressing B. If you're using version 4, choose "U -Utilities" from the file menu by pressing U, then choose "B - Backup database" by pressing B.

Press ENTER.

The computer will say "Backup to:". To copy STUDENTS to the disk in drive A, put a blank formatted disk into drive A, say "Delete line" (Shift F4), type "a:students", then press ENTER. The computer will copy STUDENTS from the hard disk to drive A.

If you're using version 4, press Esc to see the file menu again.

Copy

Let's create a DOGS file about a dog-obedience school. We want the DOGS file to contain the same design that we used in the STUDENTS file, so a sample DOGS record will look like this:

```
Last name: McGregor               First name: Lassie
Age: 2          Class: 12
Comments: She's a brilliant collie. Named after her grandma, a TV star!
```

Here's how to create the DOGS file, so it uses the same design as the STUDENTS file but doesn't contain the names of humans.

From the file menu, choose "C - Copy" (by pressing C). Press ENTER.

You'll see a **copy menu**. Tap the D key (for "D - Copy design only"). Type the name of the new file you're creating ("dogs"), then ENTER.

The computer will create file called DOGS, having the same design as STUDENTS but without any data in it.

You'll see the copy menu again. Press Esc, to see the file menu again.

CUSTOMIZE

You can customize Q&A to meet your personal needs.

For example, let's create a database of all your friends and customers around the world. Let's store each person's address and phone number (to replace your phone book and Rolodex and create a mailing list). Let's also store comments about each person and date the comments, to make the file act as a diary.

Suppose some of those people occasionally send you money. Let's record how much each person sends and make Q&A compute the totals, so Q&A does your accounting.

Suppose you're in Massachusetts, and some of the money you receive is for goods you sell. Let's make Q&A compute the 5% sales tax, so Q&A does your taxes.

Here's how to make Q&A do all that. . . .

Type the form

From Q&A's file menu, choose "D - Design file" (by pressing D). When you see the design menu, tap the D key (to choose "D - Design a new file"), type "friends" (which will be the name for the file), and press ENTER.

On the blank screen, type this form:

```
First name:                     Last name:
Department:                                    >
Company:                                       >
Address:                                       >
City:               State:   Zip:      > Country:

Phone numbers:                                 >


Sales tax code (T=Taxable, R=Resale, N=Nonprofit):
                                       ┌──────────────┐
                                       │ Price:       │
                                       │ Sales tax:   │
Comments<                              │ Total:       │
                                       └──────────────┘
```

Boxes Notice that the form includes two boxes. The top box contains the fields for the mailing label. The bottom box contains the money fields.

Here's how to draw a box. Place the cursor where you want the box's upper-left corner. Give the word-processing command for "Draw". (To do that in version 3, press F8 then D. To do that in version 4, press F8 then L then D.) Move the cursor towards the right; as you move it, you'll be drawing the box's top line. Draw the box's other three lines by moving the cursor down, then left, then up until you've returned to the upper-left corner. Then press F10.

The computer doesn't care whether you draw the box. The box's purpose is just to beautify the life of your **data-entry operator** (the person who'll be staring at the screen for many hours while entering your data).

Six parts Like most good forms, that form consists of 6 parts in this order:

a box containing the mailing label's fields, in the order they'll appear on the label

other fields that the operator must fill in (phone numbers, price, and sales tax code)

fields that the operator will skip because they'll be filled in by computer (sales tax and total)

a big space where the operator can jot comments (such as "this guy is a jerk" or "treat her nicer next time" or "oops — we goofed" or "discuss this tough order with the boss" or other comments that are more specific)

a field for inserting a GROUP CODE, which is a code to generate selective mailings; for example, you can browse through all the records, put "p" in the ones that look interesting, and then tell the computer to send mail to each person whose group code is "p"

a field to hold the date (we'll make the computer insert the date automatically, but we'll also let the operator change the date to handle special situations)

```
                                               >
         Group code:      Date:                >
```

Shortened fields Look at the "Department" field. It begins with the word "Department", then comes a colon, then 42 blank spaces, then the symbol ">".

Later, when the data-entry operator adds new records to the file by typing in data, the computer will permit the operator to "fill in the 42 blanks" by filling in 42 characters. The computer will prevent the operator from typing on or past the ">".

That prevents the operator from being too long-winded and typing too much to fit on tiny mailing labels.

Multi-line fields Look at the "Comments" field. It begins with the word "Comments", then comes the symbol "<" (instead of a colon), then several blank lines. At the end of the last blank line, you'll see the symbol ">".

The symbols "<" and ">" surround the area in which the operator can type comments. If you omit the symbol ">", the computer will restrict the operator to just one line of comments.

When you create a multi-line field, Q&A prohibits you from having other symbols nearby. Specifically, you can't put a multi-line field in a box, and you can't put two multi-line fields side-by-side.

Final step When you finish typing that form, press F10.

Change the format codes

You'll see the form you typed (except that the symbols "<" and ">" are hidden). The computer automatically puts format code T in each field, but you must change some of those T's to other codes instead. To do so, move the cursor to each T (by pressing TAB, ENTER, or arrow keys), then edit some of the T's, to make your screen look like this:

```
First name: T          Last name: T
Department: T                        >
Company: T                           >
Address: T                           >
City: T            State: TU Zip: TU  > Country: TU

Phone numbers: T                     >

                                     Price: MC JR
Sales tax code (T=Taxable, R=Resale, N=Nonprofit): TU   Sales tax: MC JR
                                     Total: MC JR

Comments T
```

```
                                                          >
             Group code: TU  Date: D                      >
```

Here's why.

Uppercase The state's format code should be TU instead of just T. The U means "Uppercase". It makes the computer automatically capitalize what the data-entry operator types.

The format code for Zip should be TU because some of the customers are in Canada, where Zip codes have capital letters in them.

Use T for phone numbers The format code for phone numbers is T (not N), so that the phone number field can contain more than just numbers. T lets you include phrases such as "home number", "work number", "extension", and "call after 4:30PM". T also lets you include parentheses and dashes, like this: (617) 666-2666.

Money For money, the best format code is "MC JR", which means "Money with Commas and Justified Right". For example, suppose the operator types this price: "42831.7". When the operator finishes typing it and moves to the next field (by pressing TAB or ENTER), the "MC" code makes the computer automatically insert a dollar sign and comma and put 2 digits after the decimal point, so the screen shows "$42,831.70" instead of just "42831.7". Then the computer slides the $42,831.70 toward the right edge of the screen (because of the "JR" code), so that the decimal point is directly above the decimal points of numbers underneath.

If you like all that but want the computer to omit the dollar sign, replace the "M" by "N2" (which means "number with 2 digits after the decimal point").

Time The format code for date is D. (A similar format code is H, which means "hours and time of day".)

Finish When you've finished typing the format codes, press F10. If the computer says GLOBAL FORMAT OPTIONS, press F10 again. Then you'll see the file menu.

The customize menu

From the file menu, choose "D - Design file" again. From the next menu, choose "C - Customize a file" (by pressing C). Press ENTER.

You'll see the **customize menu:**

```
CUSTOMIZE MENU
F - Format values
R - Restrict values
T - Field template
I - Set initial values
S - Speed up searches
D - Define custom help
C - Change palette
```

(Instead of "T - Field template", version 3 has "P - Program form", "E - Edit lookup table", and "A - Assign access rights".)

Let's see how to use the most popular choices.

Change palette

To change the screen's colors, choose "C - Change palette". You'll see a blank form.

Fill in a few fields, notice the screen's color scheme, and then press F8. The colors on the screen will change. (If you have a monochrome monitor, the underlines will disappear.)

Each time you press F8, the colors, underlines, boldfacing, etc. will change again. When you finally see a color scheme you like, press F10, to return to the customize menu.

The color schemes are called **palettes**. Many of the palettes are humorously wild.

The bottom of the screen shows the palette's number. The most *practical* palettes are #2 and #3. They're the only palettes that show clearly which field you're editing.

If your monitor is monochrome, choose palette #3. If your monitor is CGA color, choose palette #2. If your monitor is EGA or VGA color, choose either palette #3 (whose high contrast is the easiest to read) or palette #2 (whose soft blues will make you fall in love).

Initial values

To let your data-entry operator fill in the forms faster, choose "I - Set initial values".

You'll see a blank form. If you fill in some of the fields now, the operator won't have to fill them in later.

For example, if most of your customers are in San Francisco, California (because you grew up there and still advertise there), put "San Francisco" in the city field and "CA" in the state field. Put "@date" in the date field. Then press F10.

Later, when your data-entry operator adds new records, the computer will automatically fill in some of the fields by typing San Francisco, CA, and the correct date. The operator can edit what the computer typed, when the operator needs to deal with a customer that's not in San Francisco or not in California or whose record must be postdated.

Restrict values

To protect yourself from data-entry errors, choose "R - Restrict values". You'll see a blank form.

Type in any restrictions you want to put on the data. For example, to restrict the price to under $50,000, type "<50000" in the price field. To restrict the sales tax code to T, R, or N, type "T;R;N" in the sales tax code field (after widening the field by pressing F6). When you finish typing the restrictions, press F10.

Later, if the data-entry operator tries to bypass a restriction (by typing a huge price or typing a wrong sales tax code), the computer will type this warning:

`Value not in specified range.  Please verify before continuing.`

Although the computer types that warning, the computer permits the operator to keep that unusual data in the file (so that the operator can handle unusual customers). The warning just alerts the operator that the value typed was nonstandard. That warning helps the operator notice typographical and clerical errors.

Speedy fields

To make Q&A run faster, choose "S - Speed up searches". You'll see a blank form.

Type an S in each field that you often use for searching. For example, since you often look up a customer's record by using the customer's last name, type an S in the last name field. I recommend that you type an S in the last name field, company field, Zip field, and data field.

Putting an S in a field makes the computer create an index for that field. The index helps the computer search on that field more quickly. A field containing an S is called a **speedy field** or an **index field**.

Although the S makes the computer search faster, the S has two drawbacks: its index consumes a lot of space on the disk, and the computer must pause to update the index whenever you add a new record.

Because of those drawbacks, do *not* put an S in every field! Put an S in just the three or four fields that you search on most often.

When you finish typing the S's, press F10.

Program

To get total control over the computer, program it!

If you're using version 4, choose "P - Program a file" from the design menu, then press ENTER, then choose "P - Program form". If you're using version 3, choose "P - Program form" from the customize menu.

You'll see a blank form.

Let's make the computer automatically compute the Sales tax and Total. The computation involves four fields: the Price (which we'll call field #1), Sales tax code (#2), Sales tax (#3), and Total (#4).

Make the Price be field #1, by typing "#1" in the Price's blank.

Make the Sales tax code be field #2, by typing "#2" in the Sales tax code blank.

Make the Total be field #4 and also be *the Price plus the Sales tax*, by typing this in the Total blank: "#4=#1+#3".

In Massachusetts, which has a "5% sales tax", how much money should the Sales tax be? If a sale is taxable (because the Sales tax code is T), the Sales tax should be 5% of the Price. That means field #3 (which is the Sales tax) should equal .05 times field #1 (which is the Price). If the sale is *not* taxable, the Sales tax should be 0 instead. To explain all that to the computer, type this in the Sales tax blank (after pressing F6 to widen the field):

`#3: if #2="T" then #3=.05*#1 else #3=0`

When you type that line, make sure you type quotation marks around the "T". That line tells the computer that for this field (field #3), do the following computation: if field #2 (the Sales tax code) equals "T", then make field #3 equal .05 times field #1; otherwise, make field #3 equal 0.

After filling in the blanks that way, press F10. Later, when the data-entry operator enters a customer's record, the operator can fill in just the Price and Sales Tax code and then say "Calculate" (by pressing F8), which makes the computer obey your programming and automatically fill in the Sales tax and Total.

ADVANCED DATABASES

Q&A is the best database program I've ever seen. It's easy to learn, costs little, and includes a word processor. You can make Q&A perform many fancy tricks, by using the customize menu and macros. By choosing "A - Assistant" from the main menu, you can even teach Q&A to understand English, so you can type commands in ordinary English instead of using function keys. On a scale of 1 to 10, Q&A deserves a 9 — and I haven't yet found a system that deserves a 10.

Q&A has a few weak spots. If they bother you, explore Q&A's competitors instead. . . .

Reflex

Reflex is a database program that lets you view the data in five ways: it lets you see a **form view** (a filled-in form showing a record), a **list view** (a large spreadsheet showing the entire file), a **graph view** (a graph of all the data), a **report view** (a report on the entire file, with subtotals), and a **crosstab view** (a table of totals for statisticians).

Reflex can show you many views simultaneously, by dividing your screen into windows. As you edit the view in one window, the views in other windows change simultaneously. For example, if one window shows numbers and another window shows a graph, the graph changes automatically as you edit the numbers.

Reflex is partly a database program and partly a spreadsheet. Many of Reflex's features were copied by Microsoft's spreadsheet, Excel.

Reflex is published by Borland; but Borland has stopped bothering to market it anymore, because the competition from Q&A and other database programs is too fierce.

Relational databases

Reflex is a **simple flat-file system**, which means it manipulates just one file at a time. Q&A goes a step further: while you're editing a file, Q&A lets you insert information from a second file.

Software that goes even further than Q&A and lets you edit two files simultaneously is called a **relational database program** (or **relational database management system** or **relational DBMS**).

The most popular relational database programs for DOS are **DBASE**, **FOXPRO**, and **Paradox**. You can customize them to meet *any* need, because they include complete programming languages.

Another relational database program for DOS is **Alpha 4**. It lets you accomplish some tasks more easily than DBASE, FOXPRO, and Paradox, but it does not include a programming language.

Windows wars

Recently, programmers have been trying to invent database programs for Windows. Going beyond DOS programs such as Q&A, Windows database programs let the screen display pretty fonts and photographs.

For example, Borland has invented Windows versions of DBASE and Paradox. Microsoft has invented a Windows version of FOXPRO and a new Windows database program called **Microsoft Access**.

The most popular database program for the Mac is **Filemaker Pro**. It's as easy as Q&A! It's published by **Claris**, which is owned by Apple. Recently, Claris has invented a Windows version of Filemaker Pro.

To battle all those new competitors for the Windows database market, the first popular Windows database (**Approach**) has been improved; and Alpha Software has invented **Alpha 5**, which resembles Alpha 4 but handles Windows and is also programmable.

Symantec invented a Windows version of **Q&A**, but Q&A's Windows version is hated by everybody. It's worse than the DOS version and also worse than all other major Windows databases. If you're going to use Q&A, stick with Q&A's DOS version.

Hierarchy Though Q&A for Windows is terrible, the other Windows database programs are fine. Here's the hierarchy.

The easiest major Windows database program to learn is **Filemaker Pro**. It's also the least powerful, since it's neither relational nor programmable.

The next step up is **Approach**. By a "step up", I mean it's more powerful than Filemaker Pro — it performs more tricks and handles a wider variety of problems — but it's also more complex (harder to learn & use). Unlike Filemaker Pro, it's relational. But it's still not programmable.

The next step up (in power and complexity) is **Alpha 5**. It's relational and also programmable! But its programming language is small.

The next step up is **Microsoft Access**. Its programming language is bigger.

The next step up is the triumvirate: the Windows versions of **DBASE**, **FOXPRO**, and **Paradox**. They're powerful, fancy, and more than most folks can understand. If you buy one of them, you'll probably admire the big box it comes in, put it on the shelf, and invite friends to visit you and admire your big box, but you'll never figure out how to use it.

What to buy

Since computers were supposed to make our lives *easy*, I recommend you get one of the *easy* database programs: Q&A for DOS, Filemaker Pro for Windows, or Approach. Go beyond them just if your database needs are too complex for them to handle.

Even if your database needs are complex, begin by practicing with an *easy* database program first, so you master database fundamentals easily and quickly without getting distracted by needlessly complex details.

Complex database programs are like sneakers with untied shoelaces: though their overall design can theoretically let you perform amazing feats, you'll probably trip, get bloodied, and have to call in a first-aid squad to help you survive. In computer lingo, the "first-aid squad" is a team of high-priced computer consultants.

To save your blood and avoid high fees to consultants, start with Q&A for DOS. I run my entire business using Q&A for DOS and never found any need to switch.

SPREADSHEETS

Any table of numbers is called a **spreadsheet**. For example, this spreadsheet deals with money:

```
            January    February
Income     $9,030.95  $12,486.99
Expenses   $7,000.55   $9,210.75
-----------------------------------
Profit     $2,030.40   $3,276.24
```

A spreadsheet can show how many dollars you earned (or spent or plan to spend), how many goods you have in stock, how people scored in a test (or survey or scientific experiment), or any other numbers you wish!

A **spreadsheet program** helps you create spreadsheets, edit them, and analyze them.

Visicalc

The first spreadsheet program was invented in 1979. It was **designed** by Dan Bricklin and **coded** by Bob Frankston. (That means Dan Bricklin decided what features and menus the program should have, and Bob Frankston wrote the program. Dan and Bob worked together closely and occasionally switched roles: Dan sometimes did some coding, and Bob sometimes did some designing.) They called the program **Visicalc**, because it was a "visible calculator".

The original version of Visicalc ran on the Apple 2 computer and required 64K of RAM. Later versions of Visicalc ran on the Radio Shack TRS-80 and IBM PC.

Supercalc

The next spreadsheet program was called **Supercalc** because it was superior to Visicalc. It was invented by a company called **Sorcim** (which is "micros" spelled backwards). Eventually, Sorcim became part of a big conglomerate called **Computer Associates**.

The original version of Supercalc ran on computers using the CP/M operating system. The most popular CP/M computer — the Osborne 1 — came with a free copy of Supercalc.

CP/M computers have become obsolete. New versions of Supercalc have been developed for the Apple 2 and the IBM PC.

Multiplan

The first spreadsheet program to handle multiple spreadsheets simultaneously — and the relationships between them — was **Multiplan**.

Invented by Microsoft, it runs on a greater variety of computers than any other spreadsheet program. Versions of Multiplan have been invented for CP/M computers and also for the Radio Shack TRS-80, Commodore 64, Texas Instruments 99/4, IBM PC, Apple 2, and Apple Macintosh.

Context MBA

The first spreadsheet program that had "extras" was **Context MBA**, invented in 1981 by **Context Management Systems**. Besides handling spreadsheets, the program also handled graphs, databases, word processing, and telecommunications.

It ran slowly. Its word processing abilities were severely limited: it couldn't center, and it wouldn't let you set tab stops. The first version used a strange operating system (the PASCAL P System) instead of MS-DOS. An MS-DOS version, called **Corporate MBA**, didn't come until later. Those problems prevented it from becoming popular.

Lotus 1-2-3

Today's most popular spreadsheet program was invented in 1983. It was designed by Mitch Kapor and coded by Jonathan Sachs for the IBM PC. They called the program **1-2-3**, because it ran fast and was supposed to handle three things: spreadsheets, graphs, and word processing. But when Jonathan examined Context MBA, he realized that putting a good word processor into 1-2-3 would consume too much RAM and make the program run too slowly. He omitted the word processor and replaced it by a stripped-down database processor instead. So 1-2-3 handles spreadsheets (well), graphs (okay), and databases (poorly).

Mitch and Jonathan called their company **Lotus Development Corporation**, because Mitch was a transcendental-meditation instructor who got entranced by contemplating lotus flowers.

Versions of 1-2-3 The original version of 1-2-3 was called **version 1** (or **release 1**). It required 192K of RAM. Then came fancier versions, called **version 1A**, **version 2**, **version 2.01**, **version 2.2**, and **version 2.3**.

The newest popular version is called **version 2.4**. It lists for $495, but you can get it for just $289 from discount dealers (such as Harmony in New York, phone 800-441-1144 or 718-692-3232). It runs on any IBM PC clone having a hard disk and 384K of RAM. If you want to use version 2.4's advanced features, you need 512K of RAM. If you don't have a hard disk, get version 2.2 — or better yet, get a hard disk!

You can also buy a stripped-down version, called the **home version**, for just $99! Get it from dealers such as PC Connection (phone 800-800-0004).

Lotus has also invented an extra-fancy version called **version 3.4A**, but it's unpopular because it requires a megabyte of RAM, requires a fancy CPU (286, 386, or 486), is incompatible with some old 1-2-3 routines, temporarily modifies DOS in a way that sometimes causes conflicts with Windows, and costs too much ($595 list, $339 from Harmony).

Lotus has also invented Windows versions, which run more slowly. The newest Windows version is called **version 4**.

Symphony After inventing 1-2-3, Jonathan Sachs began inventing a program called 1-2-3-4-5. Like Context MBA, it handled five tasks: spreadsheets, graphs, databases, word processing, and telecommunications. While he was developing it, he realized that the program was becoming too large and confusing to be pleasant, so he quit developing it and then quit the company. Other Lotus employees finished that program and renamed it **Symphony**.

Jonathan was right: the program is too large and confusing to be pleasant, and its word processor is awful. Most businesses buy just 1-2-3 instead.

Changed leadership Like Jonathan, Mitch began feeling that Lotus Development Corporation and its products were becoming too big and confusing, so Mitch quit too.

Now Lotus Development Corporation is run by Jim Manzi. He's young, rich, vain, egotistical, and nasty. The rest of the computer industry hates him. Fortunately, his employees are nice.

Cheap clones

To save money, you can buy a cheap imitations of 1-2-3. The cheap imitations are called **1-2-3 clones** or **1-2-3 twins**.

The first 1-2-3 twins were **The Twin** (published by Mosaic Software) and **VP-Planner** (published by Paperback Software). Lotus sued both of those publishers and put them out of business.

The only 1-2-3 clone that remains is called **As-Easy-As** because it's as easy as 1-2-3! Since it's **shareware**, you can copy it free from your friends or your local computer club; if you like it, you're encouraged to mail a $50 donation to the author.

Apple's influence

In 1983 — the same year that Lotus invented 1-2-3 — Apple invented **Lisa Calc**. It was the first spreadsheet program to use a mouse. It ran just on the Lisa computer, which was expensive ($8,000).

When Apple began selling the Macintosh computer the next year (1984), Microsoft began selling **Multiplan for the Mac**, which ran on the Mac and combined the best features of Multiplan and Lisa Calc.

Excel The next year, 1985, Microsoft invented a further improvement, called **Excel** because it's excellent. Like 1-2-3, Excel handles spreadsheets, graphs, and databases.

Apple wanted to sue Microsoft for inventing the Windows operating system, which makes the IBM PC resemble a Mac. To avoid the suit, Microsoft agreed to put Excel only on the Mac for a year. Exactly one year later, when that agreement expired, Microsoft put Excel on the IBM PC.

So now Excel runs on both the Mac and the IBM PC. Each version lists for $495 ($295 at discount).

The newest IBM version is called **Excel 5**. It requires that you buy Windows.

Excel's dead competitors Several companies tried to compete against Excel; but when Microsoft kept improving Excel so dramatically, those competitors gave up trying to sell their spreadsheets. Excel won!

The spreadsheets that lost were **Wingz** (published by **Informix**) and **Resolve** (published by **Claris**, which is a software company owned by Apple).

Appleworks In 1983 — the year of Lotus 1-2-3 and Lisa Calc — Apple invented a program called **Appleworks**. It was a primitive, mouseless program that ran on the Apple 2 computer and handled three tasks: spreadsheets, databases, and word processing.

Although Appleworks was originally published by Apple, now it's published by Apple's spin-off company, Claris. The current version, **Appleworks 3**, lists for $249 ($170 at discount).

Claris also publishes a program called **Appleworks GS**, which is quite different. Designed by Kevin Harvey, it requires an Apple 2GS, uses a mouse, and handles 7 tasks: spreadsheets, graphs, databases, word processing, telecommunications, graphic painting, and desktop publishing. It lists for $299 ($200 at discount).

Quattro

The newest great spreadsheet program is called **Quattro**, because it's what comes after 1-2-3. It was invented by Borland.

After inventing Quattro, Borland invented an improved version called **Quattro Pro**. It combined the best features of 1-2-3 and Excel. Then came further improvements, called **Quattro Pro 2**, **Quattro Pro 3**, **Quattro Pro 4**, and **Quattro Pro 5**.

In 1991, Borland invented **Quattro Pro Special Edition (Quattro Pro SE)**. It's a stripped-down version of Quattro Pro 3.

Prices have dropped. Now discount dealers (such as Egghead) sell Quattro Pro 5 for just $40; and while supplies last, you can get Quattro Pro SE for just $16 (plus shipping) from a liquidator called **Surplus Software** in Oregon (phone 800-753-7877 or 503-386-1375).

In 1994, Borland sold all Quattro rights to another company, **Novell**; so future versions of Quattro will be published by Novell instead of Borland. Unfortunately, Novell has a history of charging high prices.

What to buy

If you have an Apple 2GS, get Appleworks GS. If you have a different Apple 2, get Appleworks 3.

If you have a Mac, get Excel.

If you have an IBM PC (or clone), get 1-2-3 version 2.4, 1-2-3 home version, Excel 5, Quattro Pro 5, Quattro Pro SE. 1-2-3 version 2.4 is what most businesses buy; it's the "standard". If your job requires you to learn 1-2-3 but you can't afford the full version, buy the home version. Of all the spreadsheet programs, Excel 5 is the most modern and most fun; but it requires you to buy Windows. Quattro Pro 5 for Windows is similar to Excel 5; if it's still on sale for $40, grab it! If you don't have enough hardware to run Windows pleasantly (at least a 386 with 4M of RAM), get Quattro Pro 5 for DOS, which has some of the thrills of Quattro Pro 5 for Windows. If you're on a tight budget, get Quattro Pro SE, since it's available for $16 and is *much* nicer than cheap clones such as Twin, VP-Planner, and As-Easy-As.

STARTING

Here's how to use Excel version 4 for the IBM PC and Mac. Other versions are similar.

Copy Excel to the hard disk

Excel comes on floppy disks. To use Excel, you must copy it from those floppy disks to your hard disk. Here's how.

IBM Turn on the computer without any floppy in drive A.

Start Windows (by typing "win" after the C prompt). You'll see the Program Manager Window.

Choose **Run** from the **File menu**. The computer will say "Command Line".

Excel comes on five 5¼-inch high-density floppy disks. Put Excel Disk 1 in drive A. Type "a:setup" (and press ENTER).

If your Excel floppy disks were never used before, the computer will ask you to type your name. Type your name, press the TAB key, type the name of your company (if any), and twice press ENTER.

Press ENTER five more times.

The computer will say, "Please insert the following disk . . . Disk 2". Put Excel Disk 2 in drive A and press ENTER. When the computer tells you, do the same for Excel Disks 3, 4, and 5.

The computer will say, "Microsoft Excel Setup is Complete!" Press ENTER.

Close the Microsoft Excel 4.0 window (by double-clicking its control box). Close the Program Manager window.

The computer will say "Exit Windows". Press ENTER.

Then turn off the computer, so you can start fresh.

Mac If your hard drive is external (instead of being inside the Mac), turn on the drive and wait 15 seconds (until you don't hear any more clicking).

Turn on the Mac without any floppy in the drive. You'll see the hard disk's icon.

Excel comes on seven floppy disks. Put Excel Disk 1 in the floppy drive. Double-click the Microsoft Excel Setup icon.

If your Excel floppy disks were never used before, the computer will ask you to type your name. Type your name, press the TAB key, type the name of your company (if any), and press RETURN.

Then press RETURN twice. The computer will say, "Select Disk and Folder". Click the New Folder button. Type "Microsoft Excel", and press RETURN. Click the Setup button.

When the computer tells you, insert Excel Disks 2, 3, 4, 5, 6, and 7.

The computer will say, "Microsoft Excel Setup complete." Press RETURN.

Then shut down the computer by doing this procedure: choose Shut Down from the Special menu, turn off the computer, and turn off any external hard drive.

Launch Excel

Here's how to start using Excel.

IBM Turn on the computer without any floppy in drive A. Start Windows (by typing "win" after the C prompt). The computer will say "Program Manager".

Double-click the Microsoft Excel 4.0 icon. You'll see another Microsoft Excel icon; double-click it.

(If your copy of Excel was never used before, the computer will say "Introducing Microsoft Excel". To reply, click the button marked "Exit to Microsoft Excel".)

Mac If your hard drive is external (instead of being inside the Mac), turn on the drive and wait 15 seconds (until you don't hear any more clicking).

Turn on the Mac without any floppy in the drive. Double-click the hard disk's icon. Double-click the Microsoft Excel folder's icon. Double-click the Microsoft Excel program's icon.

Fill in the cells

The screen shows a grid that begins like this:

	A	B	C	D	E	F
1						
2						
3						
4						

The grid's columns are labeled A, B, C, D, E, etc. How many columns do you see? That depends on what kind of screen you bought. . . .

A cheap Mac screen (9" mono or 12" color) shows columns A through F.
A cheap IBM screen (640-by-480 VGA) shows columns A through I.
A fancier Mac or IBM screen shows more columns.

The grid's rows are labeled 1, 2, 3, etc.

A cheap Mac screen (9" mono or 12" color) shows rows 1 through 16.
A cheap IBM screen (640-by-480 VGA) shows rows 1 through 18.
A fancier Mac or IBM screen shows more rows.

The grid is called a **spreadsheet** or **worksheet**.

Notice that the computer puts a box in column A, row 1. If you tap the right-arrow key, that box moves to the right, so it's in column B. If you tap the down-arrow key, the box moves down, to row 2. By tapping the four arrow keys, you can move the box in all four directions, to practically anywhere on the grid. Try it!

Each possible position of the box is called a **cell**.

The box's original position (in column A, row 1) is called **cell A1**. If you move the box there and then tap the right-arrow key, the box moves to column B, row 1; that position is called **cell B1**.

Just move the box from cell to cell, and put into each cell whatever words or numbers you wish!

For example, suppose you run a small business whose income is $7000 and expenses are $5000. Those are the figures for January; the figures for February aren't in yet. Let's put the January figures into a spreadsheet, like this:

	A	B	C	D	E	F
1		January				
2	Income	7000				
3	Expenses	5000				
4	Profit					

To begin, move the box to cell A2. Type the word Income. As you type that word, you see it appearing in cell A2. (It also appears temporarily in an **input area** at the top of the screen.)

Press the down-arrow key, which moves the box down to cell A3. Type the word Expenses.

Press the down-arrow key (to move to cell A4). Type the word Profit.

Move the box to cell B1 (by pressing the up-arrow three times and then the right-arrow once). Type the word January.

Press down-arrow. Type 7000.

Press down-arrow. Type 5000.

Press down-arrow again.

BACKSPACE key
If you make a mistake while typing the words and numbers, press the **BACKSPACE key** to erase the last character you typed. (If your Mac doesn't have a key marked "BACKSPACE", press the key marked "DELETE" instead.)

The left-arrow key will *not* help you erase the last character you typed. Instead, the left-arrow key moves the box to a different cell.

Mac's alternate keys
The Mac permits these shortcuts: instead of pressing the down-arrow key (which is hard to reach), you can press the RETURN key; instead of pressing the right-arrow key, you can press the TAB key.

Type a formula
Although the computer's screen shows the words you typed (Income, Expenses, and Profit), the computer doesn't understand what those words mean. It doesn't know that "Profit" means "Income minus Expenses". The computer doesn't know that the number in cell B4 (which represents the profit) ought to be the number in cell B2 (the amount of income) minus the number in cell B3 (the dollars spent).

You must *teach* the computer the meaning of Profit, by teaching it that the number in cell B4 ought to be the number in cell B2 minus the number in cell B3. To do that, move the box to cell B4, then type this formula:

=B2-B3

Notice that **every formula begins with an equal sign**. The rest of the formula, B2-B3, tells the computer to subtract the number in cell B3 from the number in cell B2 and put the answer into the box's cell (which is cell B4).

When you've finished typing the formula, press the ENTER key. Then the computer automatically computes the formula's answer (2000) and puts that number into the box's cell (B4), so the screen looks like this:

	A	B	C	D	E	F
1		January				
2	Income	7000				
3	Expenses	5000				
4	Profit	2000				

The formula "=B2-B3" remains in effect forever. It says that the number in cell B4 will always be the B2 number minus the B3 number. If you ever change the numbers in cells B2 and B3 (by moving the box to those cells, retyping the numbers, and pressing ENTER), the computer automatically adjusts the number in cell B4, so the number in cell B4 is still B2 minus B3 and still represents the correct profit.

For example, suppose you move the box to cell B2, then type 8000 (to change the January income to $8000), and then press ENTER. As soon as you press ENTER, the profit in cell B4 immediately changes to 3000, right in front of your eyes!

(The Mac permits this shortcut: instead of pressing the ENTER key, you can press the RETURN key, which is easier to reach. Throughout this chapter, whenever I say to press the "ENTER" key, you can typically press the "RETURN" key instead.)

A typical spreadsheet contains *dozens* of numbers, totals, subtotals, averages, and percentages. Each cell that contains a total, subtotal, average, or percentage is defined by a formula. Whenever you retype one of the numbers in the spreadsheet, the computer automatically readjusts all the totals, subtotals, averages, and percentages, right before your eyes.

Remember to begin each formula with an equal sign. The rest of the formula can contain these symbols:

Symbol	Meaning
+	plus
-	minus
*	times
/	divided by
.	decimal point

It can also contain E notation and parentheses. For details about how to use those symbols, E notation, and parentheses, read pages 322-327, which explain BASIC's fundamentals and math.

Error in formula
If you type a formula incorrectly, the computer might beep at you and say "Error in formula". To respond, press ENTER (or click OK); then retype the part of the formula that was wrong, and press ENTER again.

Less typing When you're creating a formula such as "=B2-B3", you do *not* have to type the "B2". Instead, you can choose one of these shortcuts. . . .

Instead of typing "B2", you can type "b2" without bothering to capitalize. When you've finished typing the entire formula ("=b2-b3"), press the ENTER key. Then the computer will capitalize your formula automatically!

Instead of typing "B2", you can move the mouse pointer to the middle of cell B2, then press the mouse's button. That's called "clicking cell B2". When you click cell B2, the computer automatically types "B2" for you! So to create the formula "=B2-B3", you can do this: type the equal sign, then click cell B2, then type the minus sign, then click cell B3. When you've finished creating the entire formula, press ENTER.

Instead of typing "B2", you can move the box to cell B2 by using the arrow keys. When you move the box to cell B2, the computer automatically types "B2" for you! So to create the formula "=B2-B3", you can do this: type the equal sign, then move the box to cell B2 (by using the arrow keys), then type the minus sign, then move the box to cell B3. When you've finished creating the entire formula, press ENTER.

On a Mac, you don't have to type any plus signs. For example, to type the formula =B2+B3, you can type the equal sign, then click cell B2, then click cell B3 (without bothering to type the plus sign). The Mac will insert the plus sign automatically!

Edit old cells

To edit what's in a cell, move the box to that cell. Then choose one of these editing methods. . . .

Method 1: press the BACKSPACE key. That makes the cell become totally blank. (If your Mac doesn't have a key marked "BACKSPACE", press the key marked "DELETE" instead.)

Method 2: retype the entire text, number, or formula that you want to put into the cell.

Method 3: in the input area (at the top of the screen), look at what you typed, find the part of your typing that you want to change, and click that part (by using the mouse). Then edit your typing as if you were using a word processor: you can use the left-arrow key, right-arrow key, BACKSPACE key, DELETE key, and mouse. When you finish editing, press the ENTER key.

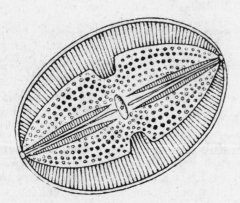

Sum function

To make a cell be the sum of cells B2 through B9, you can type this formula:

=B2+B3+B4+B5+B6+B7+B8+B9

Instead of typing all that, you can type just this:

=SUM(B2:B9)

A **function** is a word that makes the computer calculate (such as SUM). After each function, you must put parentheses. For example, you must put parentheses after SUM.

Since the computer ignores capitalization, you can type:

=sum(b2:b9)

Here's how to type the formula =sum(b2:b9) quickly. . . .

Begin by typing the "=sum(".

Drag from cell B2 to cell B9. To do that, move the mouse to cell B2, then hold down the mouse button while moving to B9. That makes the computer type the "B2:B9".

When you've finished, press the ENTER key, which makes the computer automatically type the ")".

Notice that the word SUM begins with the letter S, which in the Greek alphabet is called "sigma" and written "Σ". That's why, in math, the symbol for the word SUM is Σ. Near the screen's top center, you'll see the Σ.

Here's an even faster way to type the formula =SUM(B2:B9). Click the Σ. It makes the computer type "=SUM()". It also makes the computer guess what you want the sum of. The computer puts that guess inside the parentheses. If the computer's guess differs from what you want (B2:B9), fix the guess (by dragging from cell B2 to cell B9). When you finally see the correct formula, =SUM(B2:B9), press ENTER.

To find the sum of cells B2 through H2 (which is B2+C2+D2+E2+F2+G2+H2), type this:

=sum(b2:h2)

To find the sum of all cells in the rectangle that stretches from B2 to C4 (which is B2+B3+B4+C2+C3+C4), type this:

=sum(b2:c4)

Average

To find the average of cells B9 through B13, you can type this:

=(b9+b10+b11+b12+b13)/5

But this way is shorter:

=average(b9:b13)

To type that quickly, begin by typing "=average(". Then drag from cell B9 to cell B13. Then press the ENTER key, which makes the computer automatically type the ")" for you.

To find the average of cells C7, B5, and F2, you can ask for (c7+b5+f2)/3, but a nicer way is to type:

=average(c7,b5,f2)

HOP FAR

Here's how to be quick as a bunny and hop far in your spreadsheet.

Farther rows

The screen shows just a few rows, which are numbered 1, 2, 3, etc. Row 1 is at the top of the screen. Row 15 is near the bottom of the screen.

Try this experiment. Move the box down to row 15 (by pressing the down-arrow key repeatedly). Then press the down-arrow key several more times. Eventually, you'll get to row 30, and later to row 100, and much later to row 1000, and even later to row 10000. The largest row number you can go to is 16384.

To make room on the screen for those new rows, row 1 disappears temporarily. If you want to get back to row 1, press the up-arrow key repeatedly.

Farther columns

The screen shows just a few columns, which are lettered A, B, C, etc. If you press the right-arrow key repeatedly, you'll eventually get to column Z.

Altogether, the computer lets you have 256 columns. The first 26 columns are lettered from A to Z. The next 26 columns are lettered from AA to AZ. The next 26 columns are lettered from BA to BZ. And so on. The last column — the 256th — is IV. That's why people who use spreadsheets are called "IV league accountants".

Autorepeat

Here's a shortcut: instead of pressing an arrow key repeatedly, just hold down the key awhile.

Mouse

To move the box to a distant cell even faster, use the mouse: just click in the middle of the cell you wish.

PAGE keys

Instead of pressing the down-arrow key repeatedly, try pressing the PAGE DOWN key. It makes the computer hop down to the next screenful. (The PAGE DOWN key is on the IBM keyboard and the Mac extended keyboard but not the Mac standard keyboard.)

To hop back up to the previous screenful, press the PAGE UP key.

Instead of pressing the right-arrow key repeatedly, try pressing the PAGE DOWN key *while holding down the CONTROL key*. It makes the computer hop right to the next screenful. To hop left, press the PAGE UP key while holding down the CONTROL key.

HOME key

If you press the **HOME key**, the box moves far left, so it lands in column A. (The HOME key is on the IBM keyboard and the Mac extended keyboard but not the Mac standard keyboard.)

If you press the HOME key *while holding down the CONTROL key*, the box moves to the spreadsheet's first cell, which is cell A1.

CONTROL arrow

If you press an arrow key *while holding down the CONTROL key* (or the Mac's COMMAND key), the box moves to the spreadsheet's edge.

For example, if you press the right-arrow key while holding down the CONTROL key, the box moves to the spreadsheet's right edge. That means the box moves to the right, until it reaches column IV or a boundary cell (a cell containing data and next to an empty cell).

F5 key

To move the box to a distant cell immediately, press the F5 key. Then type the cell's name (such as C9) followed by ENTER.

(If your Mac doesn't have an F5 key, tap the G key while holding down the COMMAND key.)

How many rows and columns are in your spreadsheet, and how big are they? Here's how to adjust them.

Widen a column

When you start using Excel, each cell is wide enough to hold an 8-digit number on the IBM or a 10-digit number on the Mac.

Here's how to make column D be wider, so each cell in column D can hold longer numbers and words. At the top of column D, you see the letter D; to the right of that letter D, you see a vertical gridline. Drag that line toward the right, until the column is as wide as you like! (If you want to make the column *narrower*, drag that line toward the *left*.)

If you *double-click* that line instead of dragging it, the computer will make the column just wide enough to hold the widest data in it. (If the column doesn't contain data yet, the computer will leave the column's width unchanged.)

Widen several columns
Here's how to widen columns D, E, F, and G simultaneously.

Drag from the D to the G. All those columns turn black.

Look at the vertical gridline to the right of the D. Drag the top of that gridline toward the right. That widens column D; and when you release your finger from the mouse's button, all the other columns you selected will widen also.

If you *double-click* the top of that gridline instead of dragging it, the computer will make the columns just wide enough to hold the data in them.

Long numbers
If you try to type a long number in a cell that's too narrow to hold the number, the cell might display symbols instead of the number.

For example, try typing a long number in a cell that's just 4 characters wide. Instead of displaying the long number, the IBM displays 4 number signs (####); the Mac displays 3 number signs that are extra-wide.

Although the cell displays just those symbols, the computer remembers the long number you typed. To see the long number, widen the cell (by widening its column).

So if you see number signs in a cell, the computer is telling you that the cell is too narrow and should be widened.

Long words
Try this experiment. Make cell B1 be just 4 characters wide. Then try to type the word "January" in that cell.

That cell, B1, might show just the first 4 letters (Janu). But if the next cell (C1) is blank, cell B1 will temporarily widen to hold "January", then contract to its original size (4 characters) when you enter data in cell C1.

Delete a column

Here's how to delete column D.

Standard method: click the D at the top of column D, then choose **Delete** from the **Edit menu**.

Mac shortcut: click the D at the top of column D, then press COMMAND with K (which stands for "Kill").

IBM shortcut: using your mouse's *right* button (instead of the left), click the D at the top of column D; then choose Delete from the menu that appears.

The computer erases all the data from column D, so column D becomes blanks, which the computer immediately fills by shifting some data from other columns. Here's how. . . .

Into column D, the computer moves the data from column E. Then into column E, the computer moves the data from column F. Then into column F, the computer moves the data from column G. And so on.

At the end of the process, the top of the screen still shows all the letters (A, B, C, D, E, F, G, etc.); but now column D contains the data that used to be in column E; and column E contains the data that used to be in column F; etc.

After rearranging the spreadsheet, the computer fixes all formulas. For example, after column E's data has moved to column D, the computer hunts through all formulas in the spreadsheet and fixes them by changing each "E" to "D". The computer also changes each "F" to "E", each "G" to "F", etc.

Delete several columns
You've learned how to delete column D. Here's how to delete *several* columns. To delete columns D, E, F, and G, drag from the D to the G, then do the following. . . .

Standard method: choose Delete from the Edit menu.

Mac shortcut: press COMMAND with K (which stands for "Kill").

IBM shortcut: using your mouse's *right* button (instead of the left), click the D at the top of column D; then choose Delete from the menu that appears.

Delete a row

Here's how to delete row 2.

Standard method: click the 2, then choose Delete from the Edit menu.

Mac shortcut: click the 2, then press COMMAND with K (which stands for "Kill").

IBM shortcut: using your mouse's *right* button (instead of the left), click the 2; then choose Delete from the menu that appears.

Then the computer erases all the data from row 2, so row 2 becomes empty; but then the computer immediately fills that hole, by shifting the data from other rows. Here's how. . . .

Into row 2, the computer moves the data from row 3. Then into row 3, the computer moves the data from row 4. Then into row 4, the computer moves the data from row 5. And so on.

At the end of the process, the left edge of the screen still shows all the numbers (1, 2, 3, 4, 5, etc.); but now row 2 contains the data that used to be in row 3; and row 3 contains contains the data that used to be in row 4; etc.

The computer fixes all formulas.

Insert a column

Here's how to insert an extra column in the middle of your spreadsheet.

Click where you want the extra column to appear. For example, if you want the extra column to appear where column D is now, click the D. Then choose **Insert** from the Edit menu (or use this Mac shortcut: press COMMAND with I).

The computer will move other columns out of the way, to make room for the extra column. The computer will also fix each formula.

Insert a row

Here's how to insert an extra row in the middle of your spreadsheet.

Click where you want the extra row to appear. For example, if you want the extra column to appear where row 2 is now, click the 2. Then choose **Insert** from the Edit menu (or use this Mac shortcut: press COMMAND with I).

The computer will move other rows out of the way, to make room for the extra row. The computer will also fix each formula.

Zoom

To see twice as many rows and twice as many columns on your screen, choose **Zoom** from the **Window menu**, then click the button marked **50%**, then click OK. The computer will make all the screen's characters tiny (half as tall and half as wide), so twice as many rows and twice as many columns fit on the screen.

If you want to see *four* times as many rows and four times as many columns, click **25%** instead of 50%. But that makes the characters too tiny to read easily.

To make the screen return to normal, choose Zoom from the Window menu again, then click **100%**, then click OK.

If you wish, you can click different percentages, such as **75%** (which shrinks the screen's characters just slightly) or **200%** (which enlarges the screen's characters, so you can read them even if you're sitting far away from the screen).

Try this trick: start at one cell, and drag to another cell far away. All the cells between them turn black. Then choose Zoom from the Window menu, click **Fit Selection**, then click OK. That shrinks or enlarges the characters just enough so that all the black cells fit on the screen.

Panes

On your screen, you see a window that contains part of your spreadsheet. (That window is big enough to usually show columns A through F on a cheap Mac, columns A through I on a cheap IBM, and more columns on a computer having a fancier screen.)

You can divide that window into two or four **windowpanes**, so that each windowpane shows a different part of your spreadsheet.

Vertical panes

Here's how to divide your window into two windowpanes, so that the left pane shows columns A, B, and C, while the right pane shows columns X, Y and Z.

Get column A onto the screen (by pressing the HOME key). At the screen's bottom left corner, you see the scroll bar's left-arrow pointing at a black vertical rectangle. Drag that rectangle to the right. As you drag, you'll see a vertical line move across your spreadsheet. Drag until the vertical line is in the middle of the spreadsheet. (For best results, drag that line slightly to the right of column C's right edge.)

That line splits the screen into two panes. The left pane shows columns A through C; the right pane shows columns D and beyond.

Click anywhere in the right pane. That puts the box in the right pane, and makes the right pane active. Press the right-arrow key several times, until you reach columns X, Y, and Z.

If you want to move the box back to the left pane, just click the left pane.

To stop using vertical panes, double-click the black vertical rectangle (or drag it back to the screen's bottom left corner).

Horizontal panes

Here's how to divide your window into two panes, so that the top pane shows rows 1, 2, and 3, while the bottom pane shows rows 97, 98, and 99.

Get row 1 onto the screen (by pressing the PAGE UP key several times). At the screen's top right corner, you'll see the scroll bar's up-arrow pointing at a black horizontal rectangle. Drag that rectangle down. As you drag, you'll see a horizontal line move down your spreadsheet. Drag until the horizontal line is in the middle of the spreadsheet. (For best results, drag that line slightly under row 9's bottom edge.)

That line splits the screen into two panes. The top pane shows rows 1 through 9; the bottom pane shows rows 10 through 18.

Click anywhere in the bottom pane. (That puts the box in the bottom pane, and makes the bottom pane active.) Press the down-arrow key several times, until you reach rows 97, 98, and 99.

If you want to move the box back to the top pane, just click the top pane.

To stop using horizontal panes, double-click the black horizontal rectangle (or drag it back to the screen's top right corner).

Freeze panes

You should put a title at the top of each column. For example, if column B contains financial information for January, and column C contains financial information for February, you should put the word January at the top of column B, and the word February at the top of column C. Since the words January and February are at the top of the columns, they're in row 1. They're called the **column titles**.

If row 2 analyzes Income, and row 3 analyzes Expenses, you should put the word Income at the left edge of row 2, and the word Expenses at the left edge of row 3. Since the words Income and Expenses are at the left edge of the spreadsheet, they're in column A. They're called the **row titles**.

So in a typical spreadsheet, the column titles are in row 1, and row titles are in column A.

Unfortunately, when you move beyond column I or beyond row 18 (by pressing the arrow keys repeatedly), the titles normally disappear from the screen, and you forget the purpose of each row and column. Here's how to solve that problem.

Get cell A1 onto the screen (by pressing CONTROL with HOME). Click cell B2. Choose **Freeze Panes** from the Window menu.

Now the window is divided into four panes. The main top pane contains the column titles (January, February, etc.); the main left pane contains the row titles (Income, Expenses, etc.); a tiny pane in the upper-left corner contains a blank cell; and a huge pane contains all the spreadsheet's data.

Click cell B2 (which is in the huge pane). Then move around that pane, by using the arrow keys or mouse. As you move, the column and row titles will stay fixed on the screen, since they're in the other panes.

To stop using freeze panes, choose **Unfreeze Panes** from the Window menu.

On your spreadsheet, find these cells: B2, B3, B4, C2, C3, and C4. Those six cells are next to each other. In fact, they form a giant rectangular area, whose top left corner is B2.

Here's how to take all the data in that rectangle and move it to a different part of your spreadsheet.

Drag from the rectangle's first cell (B2) to the rectangle's last cell (C4). The entire rectangle turns black (except for the first cell, which stays white).

Surrounding the rectangle, you'll see four walls. Those walls are the four sides of the rectangle.

Using your mouse, **point at one of the rectangle's walls**. (Do *not* point at a corner.) When you've pointed correctly, the mouse pointer turns into an arrow (*not* a cross).

While the mouse pointer looks like an arrow, hold down the mouse's button and **drag the wall**. While you drag the wall, the rest of the rectangle drags along with it. Drag until the entire rectangle is at a part of the spreadsheet that was blank. Then lift your finger from the mouse's button.

That's how you move a rectangle of data to a new place in your spreadsheet that had been blank.

Try it!

After moving the rectangle of data, the computer automatically adjusts all formulas mentioning the moved cells. For example, if the data in cell B2 has moved to cell E7, the computer searches through the entire spreadsheet and, in each formula, changes "B2" to "E7".

Excel lets you copy information in several ways.

Fill to the right

Here's how to make lotsa love with the computer!

In a cell, type the word "love".

Then move the mouse until the mouse's pointer is at that cell's bottom right corner. When the pointer's exactly at the corner, the pointer changes to this thin cross: +.

Then hold down the mouse's left button, and drag toward the right, until you've dragged across several cells.

When you lift your finger off the mouse's button, all those cells will contain copies of the word in the first cell. They'll all say "love"!

Go ahead! Try turning your computer into a lovemaking machine! Do it *now!* This is an important exercise to try before you get into more advanced computer orgies!

Here's another example. In a cell, type the word "tickle". Then to make lotsa tickles, point at that cell's bottom right corner (so you see +) and drag it to the right. The cells you drag across will all say "tickle".

Fill down

When you point at a cell's bottom right corner and drag, you usually drag to the *right*. But if you prefer, you can drag *down*, so you're copying to the cells *underneath* (instead of the cells to the right).

Extend a series

You've learned that if the original cell said "love", the adjacent cells will say "love"; and if the original cell said "tickle", the other cells will say "tickle".

But if the original cell said "January", the adjacent cells will *not* say "January". Instead, the computer makes them say "February", "March", "April", "May", etc.

So **here's how to put the words "January", "February", "March", "April", etc., across the top of your spreadsheet. Begin by typing "January" in cell B1. Then drag that cell's bottom right corner to the right, to column H or I or even farther!** The farther you drag, the more months you'll see!

The computer is smart:

If you start with January,	the computer will say February, March, April, etc.
If you start with October,	the computer will say November, December, January, etc.
If you start with Jan,	the computer will say Feb, Mar, Apr, etc.
If you start with 29-Jan,	the computer will say 30-Jan, 31-Jan, 1-Feb, etc.
If you start with Oct-95,	the computer will say Nov-95, Dec-95, Jan-96, etc.
If you start with 29-Dec-95,	the computer will say 30-Dec-95, 31-Dec-95, 1-Jan-96, etc.
If you start with Monday,	the computer will say Tuesday, Wednesday, Thursday, etc.
If you start with Mon,	the computer will say Tue, Wed, Thu, etc.
If you start with 10:00 AM,	the computer will say 11:00 AM, 12:00 PM, 1:00 PM, etc.
If you start with 10:00,	the computer will say 11:00, 12:00, 13:00, etc.
If you start with 22:00,	the computer will say 23:00, 0:00, 1:00, etc.
If you start with 1st,	the computer will say 2nd, 3rd, 4th, etc.
If you start with 1st Idiot,	the computer will say 2nd Idiot, 3rd Idiot, 4th Idiot, etc.
If you start with Idiot 1,	the computer will say Idiot 2, Idiot 3, Idiot 4, etc.
If you start with Year 1991,	the computer will say Year 1992, Year 1993, Year 1994, etc.
If you start with 1991 Results,	the computer will say 1992 Results, 1993 Results, 1994 Results, etc.
If you start with 2nd Quarter,	the computer will say 3rd Quarter, 4th Quarter, 1st Quarter, etc.
If you start with 2nd Qtr,	the computer will say 3rd Qtr, 4th Qtr, 1st Qtr, etc.
If you start with 2 Q,	the computer will say 3 Q, 4 Q, 1 Q, etc.
If you start with Quarter 2,	the computer will say Quarter 3, Quarter 4, Quarter 1, etc.
If you start with Q2,	the computer will say Q3, Q4, Q1, etc.

If you start with just a plain number (such as 1), the computer will just copy that number; it will *not* say 2, 3, 4, etc. If you start with just the plain number 1991, the computer will just copy that number; it will *not* say 1992, 1993, 1994, etc.

To make the computer do more than just copy, include a word. For example, instead of saying just 1, say "Idiot 1"; then the computer will say "Idiot 2", "Idiot 3", "Idiot 4", etc. Instead of saying just 1991, say "Year 1991" or "1991 Results" or "People We Accidentally Shot In 1991"; then the computer will generate similar headings for 1992, 1993, etc.

Copy a formula's concept

If you ask the computer to copy a formula, the computer will copy the *concept* underlying the formula.

For example, suppose you put this formula in cell B4: =B2+B3. That means cell B4 contains "the sum of the two numbers above it". If you drag that cell's bottom right corner to the right, the computer will copy that formula's *concept* to the adjacent cells: C4, D4, E4, etc. For example, the computer will make C4's formula be "the sum of the two numbers above it", by making C4's formula be =C2+C3. The computer will make D4's formula be =D2+D3. The computer will make E4's formula be =E2+E3.

For another example, suppose cell B4 contains the formula =2*B3, so that B4 is "twice the cell above it". When the computer copies that concept to cell C4, the computer will make C4's formula be "twice the cell above it"; the computer will make C4's formula be =2*C3.

For another example, suppose cell B4 contains the formula =2*A4, so that B4 is "twice the cell to the left of it". When the computer copies cell B4 to C4, the computer will make C4's formula be "twice the cell to the left of it"; the computer will make C4's formula be =2*B4.

Absolute addresses Notice again how copying from B4 to C4 turns the formula =B2+B3 into =C2+C3: it turns each B into a C.

If you want to prevent those changes, put dollar signs in the original formula. For example, if you want to prevent B3 from turning into D3, put dollar signs around the B3, so cell B4 contains this formula:

=B2+$B$3

When you copy that cell to C4, the dollar signs prevents the computer from turning the B3 into C3; C4's formula will become =C2+$B$3 (instead of =C2+C3).

Here's how to type "=B2+$B$3" quickly. Type the "=" sign, then move the box to cell B2, then type the "+" sign. Finally, **create the $B$3 by using this trick: move the box to cell B3, then press the IBM's F4 key or the Mac's COMMAND T**. When you've finished creating the entire formula, press ENTER.

A cell's name (such as B3) is called the cell's **address**, because the cell's name tells you where to find the cell. An address that contains dollar signs (such as $B$3) is called an **absolute address**, because the address is absolutely fixed and will never change, not even when you copy the formula. An address that lacks dollar signs is called a **relative address**, because when you copy that address you'll be copying the cell's relationship to the other cells.

Finished creating your spreadsheet? Here's how to copy it to the disk and printer and move on to another task.

At the screen's top left corner, just under the word File, you see four **icons** (little pictures).

The first icon is a **new spreadsheet**'s blank grid, containing no data yet.
The second icon is a picture of a file folder that's been pried **open**.
The third icon is a picture of a 3½-inch floppy **disk**.
The fourth icon is a picture of a **printer** that's printing on a sheet of paper.

Here's how to use them.

Save to disk

To copy your spreadsheet onto a disk, click the **disk icon**.

If you haven't invented a name for the spreadsheet yet, the computer will say "Save As". Invent a name for your spreadsheet. The name can be fairly long: up to 8 IBM characters or 31 Mac characters. For example, if you want the spreadsheet to be named JENNIFER, type JENNIFER and press ENTER. That instructs the computer to put a file named JENNIFER into your hard disk's EXCEL folder. (An IBM's hard disk will name the file "JENNIFER.XLS"; the .XLS stands for "eXceL Spreadsheet".)

If the name you invented was already used by another file, the computer will interrupt the process and ask, "Replace existing JENNIFER?" If you click OK, the computer will copy your spreadsheet onto the hard disk and erase the previous file named JENNIFER. If you click Cancel instead, the computer will cancel your request to copy the spreadsheet onto the disk, so the original file named JENNIFER will remain intact.

After you've copied your spreadsheet onto the disk, if you change your mind and want to do more editing, go ahead! Edit the spreadsheet some more. When you finish that editing, click the disk icon again. This time, the computer won't bother asking you for the spreadsheet's name; the computer will assume you want to use the same name as before.

Print on paper

If you click the **printer icon**, the printer will print your spreadsheet onto paper.

Page Setup Here's a trick. Before clicking the printer icon, try choosing **Page Setup** from the **File menu**. Then tell the computer what kind of printing you prefer. Here's how. . . .

For **orientation**, click either **Portrait** or **Landscape**. Normally, the computer does Portrait. If you click Landscape instead, the computer will rotate the spreadsheet 90 degrees, so more columns will fit on the paper.

Normally, the computer leaves 1-inch **margins** at the top and bottom of the paper and ¾-inch margins at the sides. To change those sizes, type the number of inches you want for the **Left Margin**, then press the TAB key, then do the same for the **Right Margin**, **Top Margin**, and **Bottom Margin**.

Normally, the computer starts printing the spreadsheet near the paper's top left corner. If you want the spreadsheet to be centered instead, put an x in the **Center Horizontally** and **Center Vertically** boxes, by clicking those boxes.

Normally, the computer prints the spreadsheet's gridlines (the lines that separate the columns from each other and the rows from each other). If you *don't* want the computer to print the gridlines, remove the x from the **Gridlines** box, by clicking that box.

Normally, the computer doesn't bother printing the column names (A, B, C) and row names (1, 2, 3). If you *want* the computer to print them, put an x in the **Row & Column Headings** box, by clicking that box.

Have you ever taken a photograph and asked for an "enlargement"? The computer can do the same thing: when it prints your spreadsheet onto paper, it can produce an **enlargement** (so you can read the spreadsheet even if you're standing far away from the sheet of paper). The computer can also produce a **reduction** (so the spreadsheet is made of tiny characters and consumes less paper). Enlargements and reductions are called **scaling**. Normally, the computer does *not* do scaling: it prints at 100% of original size. To make the computer do scaling, click the **Reduce/Enlarge** button, press the TAB key, then type a percentage different from 100%. For example, if you want the spreadsheet to look gigantic (twice as tall and twice as wide), type 200. If you want the spreadsheet to look tiny (miniaturized), type 50. To make the characters just small enough so that the entire spreadsheet fits on one sheet of paper, click the **Fit to** button instead.

At the top of each sheet of paper, the computer prints a **header**. For the header, the computer normally prints the spreadsheet's name, such as:

```
                    JENNIFER.XLS
```

To change that header, click the **Header** button. Then tell the computer what header you want. For example, suppose you want this header:

```
Annual blood drive              1995 results                by Count Dracula
```

Type the left part ("Annual blood drive"), press the TAB key, type the center part ("1995 results"), press TAB again, type the right part ("by Count Dracula"), and press ENTER.

When you finish expressing all your preferences to the computer, click OK. Then click the print icon.

Those preferences affect the printing of just the current spreadsheet. They don't affect other spreadsheets you create later.

Close your spreadsheet

When you've finished using your spreadsheet, do the following. . . .

Standard method: choose **Close** from the **File menu**.

Mac shortcut: click the close box.

IBM shortcut: at the left edge of row 1, you see a 1; above it, you see an empty box; above it, you see a box containing a horizontal line; it's your spreadsheet's control box; double-click it.

If the computer asks "Save changes?", click No.
Your spreadsheet vanishes from the screen.
Then choose one of these activities:

To invent a new spreadsheet, click the **new spreadsheet icon**.

To use an old spreadsheet, click the **open icon**. You'll see a list of all your hard disk's spreadsheets. Double-click the spreadsheet you want to use. (Make sure you double-click a spreadsheet that ends in ".xls".) The computer will copy that spreadsheet from the hard disk to your screen.

Delete a spreadsheet

If you want to delete a spreadsheet from your hard disk, choose **Delete** from the File menu. You'll see a list of all the files in your hard disk's Excel folder. Click the spreadsheet you want to delete. On the Mac, click Delete; on the IBM, click OK. Then click Yes, then click Close.

Quit Excel

When you finish using Excel, go to the File menu and choose **Quit** (for Mac) or **Exit** (for IBM). If the computer asks "Save changes?", click No.

BEAUTIFY YOUR CELLS

Like an amoeba trying to wear a dress, you too can try to beautify your cells! First, **select which cells you want to beautify.** Here's how.

To select **one cell**, click it.
To select **several adjacent cells**, drag from the first cell you want to the last cell.
To select **a whole rectangular area**, drag from one corner of rectangle to the opposite corner.

To select **column D**, click the D.
To select **columns D through G**, point at the D and drag to the G.

To select **row 2**, click the number 2 at the left edge of row 2.
To select **rows 2 through 5**, point at the 2 and drag to the 5.

To select **the entire spreadsheet**, click the empty box that's left of the letter A.

When doing one of those selections, use the mouse; to click, use the mouse's left button (not the right).

The part of the spreadsheet you've selected is called the **selection** or **range**. It has turned entirely black (except for the cell where the box is).

After you've made your selection, tell the computer how to beautify it. Choose one of the following forms of beauty. . . .

Italics

To make all writing in the selection be italicized (*like this*), push the *I* button (which is at the top of the screen, just under the word Format or Options), by clicking it. The *I* button will be pushed in, and the writing will be italicized. If you change your mind and want the writing *not* to be italicized, select the writing again (so it turns black again), then click the *I* button again (so the button pops back out).

Bold

To make all writing in the selection be bold (**like this**), click the **B** button (which is at the top of the screen, next to the *I* button). If you change your mind and want the writing *not* to be bold, select the writing again (so it turns black again), then click the **B** button again (so the button pops back out).

To get bold italics, push in the bold button and also the italic button.

Grow

To make all writing in the selection grow bigger (like this), click the button that has a big A on it. (That button is next to the *I* button.) To make the writing grow even bigger, click that button again. For even bigger writing, click the button again. If the computer beeps instead of making the writing bigger, you've already reached the maximum size that the computer can handle.

To make your spreadsheet easier to read, use big writing for the column headings (such as January), the row headings (such as Income, Expenses, and Profit), any totals, and the bottom-line results (such as the $2000 profit).

Shrink

To make all writing in the selection become smaller (like this), click the button that has a little A on it.

Clear

To make all writing in the selection vanish (so it's erased), do the following. . . .

Standard method: choose **Clear** from the Edit menu.

IBM shortcut: press the DELETE key.

Mac shortcut: press the Del key; if your keyboard doesn't have a Del key, press COMMAND with B (which means "Blank").

Then press ENTER.

Align

To nudge all writing in the selection slightly to the left or slightly to the right, click one of these three buttons:

≡   ≡   ≡

Those buttons are near the top of the screen, just under the word Options or Window. Here's what those buttons do:

clicking the left button makes each cell's writing be flush left	like this
clicking the center button makes each cell's writing be centered	like this
clicking the right button makes each cell's writing be flush right	like this

If you don't click any of the buttons, here's what happens: if the cell contains a word, the computer puts the word flush left; if the cell contains a number instead, the computer puts the number flush right.

In a simple spreadsheet, row 1 usually contains words (such as January, February, and March). Those words are headings for columns of numbers. The numbers are flush right. **To align the headings with the numbers beneath them, make the headings be flush right also.** To do that, select row 1 (by clicking the 1), then click the right button.

Format the numbers

To make all numbers in the selection look better, click the down-arrow that's just under the word Formula or Format. You'll see this menu:

Menu	Meaning	Examples	
Normal	display normally	1538.4	-0.739
Currency	dollars & cents, insert commas, parenthesize negatives	$1,538.40	($0.74)
Currency [0]	same as "Currency", but round to nearest dollar	$1,538	($1)
Comma	same as "Currency", but omit the dollar sign	1,538.40	(0.74)
Comma [0]	same as "Currency [0]", but omit the dollar sign	1,538	(1)
Percent	multiply by 100, round to an integer, put % afterwards	153840%	-74%

From that menu, choose whichever format you wish, by clicking it.

Here are more details about each format. . . .

Choosing **Normal** makes each number appear normal.

Choosing **Currency** makes each number look like dollars-and-cents. To do that, the computer puts a dollar sign before the number, rounds the number to two decimal places, and inserts commas in large numbers. If the number is negative, the computer displays the number in red and put parentheses around it.

Currency [0] resembles Currency but makes the computer round to the nearest dollar. The computer doesn't bother showing any cents. That prevents your spreadsheet from being cluttered with unimportant details, such as pennies. It makes the spreadsheet easier to look at. It's for idiots who would get distracted by details. The next time you meet an accountant, ask this riddle: "What's the definition of an idiot's accountant? An accountant who doesn't show any cents!"

Comma resembles Currency but prevents the computer from printing the dollar sign. This format appeals to accountants who tire of seeing dollar signs all day. Those accountants consider dollar signs to be boring distractions. By omitting the dollar signs, you give you spreadsheet a lean-and-mean look, so it looks just like the physique of the average accountant.

Comma [0] combines all those thoughts. It's for lean, mean idiots.

Percent converts the number to a percent. For example, if the number is .25, the computer converts it to a percent (by multiplying by 100%); the computer displays 25%.

SORT

This spreadsheet shows how Sue, Al, and Pedro scored on a test:

	A	B	C
1	Sue	42	
2	Al	7	
3	Pedro	100	

You can make the computer alphabetize the names, so the spreadsheet becomes:

	A	B	C
1	Al	7	
2	Pedro	100	
3	Sue	42	

You can make the computer put the scores in numerical order, so the spreadsheet becomes:

	A	B	C
1	Al	7	
2	Sue	42	
3	Pedro	100	

You can make the computer put the scores in *reverse* numerical order (from highest score to lowest score), so the spreadsheet becomes:

	A	B	C
1	Pedro	100	
2	Sue	42	
3	Al	7	

Putting data in order (alphabetically or numerically) is called **sorting**. The entire rectangular area that's involved in the sorting (which includes cells A1, A2, A3, B1, B2, and B3) is called the **data area**.

To sort, make the data area become black (by dragging from cell A1 to cell B3), then choose **Sort** from the **Data menu**. You'll see the **sort window**.

Do you want to sort by name or by score? The computer assumes you want to sort by the data area's first column (the A column, the name column). If you want to sort by score instead, click anywhere in the score column (the B column).

Normal order (from lowest number to highest number, or from A to Z) is called **ascending order**. Reverse order (from highest number to lowest number, or from Z to A) is called **descending order**. The computer assumes you want ascending order; if you want descending order instead, click the Descending button in the sort window's bottom left corner.

Click OK. Then the computer will interchange the rows of data so that the data area becomes sorted!

CHART

You can graph your data. In Excel, graphs are called **charts**.

For example, suppose you want to graph the data from a company you run. Your company sells Day-Glo Pink Hair Dye. (Your motto is: "To brighten your day, stay in the pink!")

You have two salespeople, Joe and Sue. Joe's worked for you a long time, and sells about $8,000 worth of dye each month. Sue joined your company recently and is rapidly improving at encouraging people to turn their hair pink. (She does that by inventing slogans for various age groups, such as "Feminine babes wear pink!", "You look so sweet with your new hair style — spun, pink, cotton candy!", "Don't be a dink! Go pink!", "Pink is punk!", "Pink: the color that says *I'll be your Valentine, but lighten up!*", "Be what you drink — a Pink Lady!", "Let that sexy, slinky, pink panther inside you glow!", "Love is a pink Cadillac — with hair to match!", and "When you're in a sour mood, look like a pink grapefruit!")

This spreadsheet shows how many dollars worth of dye Joe and Sue sold each month:

	A	B	C	D	E	F	G	H	I
1		January	February	March					
2	Joe	8000	6500	7400					
3	Sue	2000	4300	12500					

The spreadsheet shows that Joe sold $8000 worth of dye in January, $6500 in February, and $7400 in March.

Sue's a trainee. She sold just $2000 worth in January, but her monthly sales zoomed up to $12500 by March.

Here's how to turn that spreadsheet into a graph.

First, type the spreadsheet.

Next, format the numbers. To do that, drag from the first number (cell B2) to the last number (cell D3), then click the down-arrow that's just under the word Format, then click "Currency [0]". The spreadsheet becomes this:

	A	B	C	D	E	F	G	H	I
1		January	February	March					
2	Joe	$8,000	$6,500	$7,400					
3	Sue	$2,000	$4,300	$12,500					

Tell the computer which cells to graph. To do that, drag from the blank starting cell (A1) to the *last number* (cell D3). Drag just to *that cell*, since the computer gets confused if you drag across extra cells or rows or columns.

Click the Chart Wizard icon, which is near the screen's top right corner. (That icon shows a magic wand waving over a bar graph.)

The screen's bottom left corner tells you, "Drag in document to create a chart." Obey the computer: **drag across some blank cells**, where you want the graph to appear. (For example, drag from cell A4 to Mac cell F16 or IBM cell I18.) The larger the area you drag across, the larger the graph will be.

The computer says "Chart Wizard". **Click the Next button 4 times, then click OK.**

Then the computer draws the graph and make it part of your spreadsheet, so your spreadsheet looks like this:

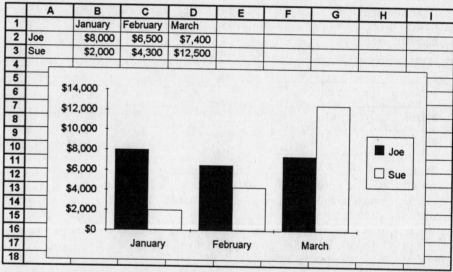

	A	B	C	D	E	F	G	H	I
1		January	February	March					
2	Joe	$8,000	$6,500	$7,400					
3	Sue	$2,000	$4,300	$12,500					
4									
5									
6									
7									
8									
9									
10									
11									
12									
13									
14									
15									
16									
17									
18									

If you click the print icon, your printer will print the entire spreadsheet, including the graph! If you click the disk icon, your hard disk will store a copy of the entire spreadsheet, including the graph.

Edit

You can edit the graph easily.

If you **change the numbers** in the spreadsheet's cells, the graph will change too, automatically!

To **move the graph** to a different blank area of your spreadsheet, just point at the graph and drag it wherever you wish!

If you want to **erase the graph**, click it and then press the BACKSPACE key.

1-2-3 & QUATTRO

STARTING

Here's how to start using Quattro Pro (versions 3, 4, and SE) and 1-2-3 (versions 2.2, 2.3, and 2.4). Other versions are similar.

Copy to the hard disk

You'll want to copy the program onto a hard disk. Here's how — but if you're sharing the computer, ask your colleagues whether they did this step already!

Quattro Pro Turn on the computer without any floppy in drive A.

Versions 3 and SE come on double-density floppy disks. When you buy version 4, you get three high-density 5¼-inch disks and two high-density 3½-inch disks; if your computer doesn't have a high-density disk drive, you can exchange those disks for double-density disks.

When you see the C prompt, put Disk 1 in drive A and type "a:install".

The computer will say, "QUATTRO PRO Installation". Press ENTER twice.

The computer will say "C:\QPRO". Do this. . . .

Version 4: press the F2 key.
Versions 3 and SE: press the down-arrow key, then ENTER.

Press the BACKSPACE key three times (so the "C:\QPRO" changes to "C:\Q"). Do this. . . .

Version 4: press ENTER twice.
Versions 3 and SE: press ENTER, then up-arrow, then ENTER again.

Put Disk 2 in drive A, and press ENTER. Then do the same for any other disks.

The computer will say, "The QUATTRO PRO files have been installed on your hard disk." Press ENTER twice.

The computer will say, "Company Name". Press the F2 key. Type the name of your company or organization. (If you don't belong to a company or organization, type the word "Personal".) At the end of that typing, press ENTER twice.

The computer will say, "Name". Press the F2 key. Type your own first name and last name. At the end of your name, press ENTER twice.

The computer will say, "Serial #". Press the F2 key. Type the serial number that was printed on the label of Disk 1. At the end of the serial number, press ENTER four times. For versions 3 and SE, press ENTER a fifth time.

The computer will say, "Printer Manufacturer". Press the F2 key. You'll see a list of printer manufacturers. Press the right-arrow key several times, until *your* printer's manufacturer is highlighted. Press ENTER twice.

The computer will say, "Printer Model". Press the F2 key. You'll see a list of printer models. Press the right-arrow key several times, until *your* printer model is highlighted. Press ENTER 7 times for versions 4 and SE, 8 times for version 3. You'll see a C prompt.

Then turn off the computer, so you can start fresh.

1-2-3 versions 2.3 and 2.4 Turn on the computer without any floppy in drive A.

Versions 2.3 and 2.4 of 1-2-3 come on nine 5¼-inch floppy disks. When you see the C prompt, put Disk 1 in drive A and type "a:". The computer will display an A prompt. Type "install".

The computer will say "Lotus Install Program". Press ENTER.

If the computer says "RECORDING YOUR NAME", do this: type your name, press ENTER, type your company's name, and press ENTER twice.

Press ENTER two more times. The computer will say "C:\123R23" or "C:\123R24". Press the BACKSPACE key three times, so the computer says just "C:\123". Press ENTER twice.

The computer will say, "Insert Disk 2 in drive A". Do it and press ENTER. The computer will say, "Insert Disk 3 in drive A". Do it and press ENTER. Do the same for disks 4, 5, 6, 7, 8, and 9.

The computer will say, "FILE TRANSFER SUCCESSFUL". Press ENTER 6 times.

The computer will say, "Select a text printer driver." You'll see the beginning of a list of printer manufacturers, alphabetized. Move the box to the name of your printer's manufacturer, by pressing the down-arrow key repeatedly. Then press ENTER.

You'll see a list of printer models. Move the box to the name of your printer model. Then press ENTER three times.

The computer will say, "Select a graphics printer driver." Move the box to your printer's manufacturer again, and press ENTER. Move the box to the name of your printer model; press ENTER six times. You'll see a DOS prompt.

Then turn off the computer, so you can start fresh.

1-2-3 version 2.2 Version 2.2 of 1-2-3 comes on seven 5¼-inch floppy disks. You also get, free, a program called **Always**, which comes on five extra 5¼-inch floppy disks. So altogether, you get 12 disks.

Step 1: initialize 1-2-3. Turn on the computer without any floppy in drive A. When you see the C prompt, put the 1-2-3 System Disk in drive A, and type "a:". The computer will display an A prompt. Type "init". (If the computer says "Bad command or file name", somebody else initialized 1-2-3 already, so skip ahead to step 2.)

You'll see a 1-2-3 copyright message. Press ENTER twice. The computer will say, "Please enter your name". Type your name. The computer will say "Confirm (Y/N)". Type Y. The computer will say "Please enter your company's name". Type your company's name. The computer will say "Confirm (Y/N)" again. Type Y again. The computer will say "Press ENTER to continue". Press ENTER twice.

Step 2: enter the 1-2-3 subdirectory. When you see the A prompt, type "c:". The computer will display a C prompt. Type "md 123" (so you're making a subdirectory called 123). After the next C prompt, type "cd 123" (so you're changing to the 123 subdirectory).

Step 3: copy 1-2-3. Type "copy a:*.*" (which copies all the floppy's files onto the hard disk). Put another 1-2-3 floppy into drive A and type "copy a:*.*" again (which copies all of that floppy's files onto the hard disk). Repeat that procedure for each of the 1-2-3 floppies (but *not* for the Allways floppies), so each 1-2-3 floppy is copied onto the hard disk.

Step 4: install 1-2-3. Type "install". Eventually, the computer will say "Press ENTER to begin the Install program." Press ENTER five times.

You'll see a list of monitors. Which monitor do you have? Move the box to your monitor's name, by pressing the down-arrow key several times. To do that, you might find this chart helpful:

Your monitor	Choose this monitor from menu
normal monochrome	Hercules Graphics Card (80 x 25)
laptop monochrome	Toshiba T1100 Plus and T1200
Compaq monochrome	Compaq, single-color monitor
AT&T monochrome	AT&T 6300 single-color monitor
CGA color	IBM color card, color monitor
EGA color	IBM/Compaq Enhanced Graphics (EGA 80 x 25)
VGA color or mono	IBM/Compaq Video Graphics (VGA 80 x 25)
MCGA color or mono	IBM Multi-Color (MCGA) Color

Press ENTER twice. You'll see a list of printer manufacturers. Move the box to the name of your printer's manufacturer. (If your manufacturer's name isn't listed, choose "Epson" for dot-matrix; choose "HP" for laser.)

Press ENTER. You'll see a list of printers. Move the box to your printer's model number. (If you chose "Epson" because your printer's manufacturer was unlisted, try choosing "FX" for 9-pin, "LQ 2500" for 24-pin.)

Press ENTER three times. You'll see a list of printer manufacturers again. Move the box to the name of your printer's manufacturer again.

Press ENTER. Move the box to your printer's model number again.

Press ENTER five times. The computer will ask, "Do you want to leave Install?" Move the box to Yes.

Press ENTER. You'll see a DOS prompt.

Then turn off the computer, so you can start fresh.

Run the program

To run the program, begin by turning on the computer without any floppy in drive A.

If you've put the DO.BAT file onto your hard disk (as I recommended in the MS-DOS chapter), your life is easy! Just type "do q" to do Quattro Pro; type "do 123" to do 1-2-3.

If you have *not* put DO.BAT onto your hard disk, your life is harder! You must type "cd q" and then "q" to do Quattro Pro; you must type "cd 123" and then "123" to do 1-2-3.

Move the box

The screen shows a table that begins like this:

```
      A     B       C       D       E       F       G       H
1  [      ]
2
3
4
```

Normally, the letters go from A to H; but if you're using Quattro Pro 4 with an EGA or VGA monitor, the letters go from A to I. Normally, the numbers start at 1 and go up to 20; but if you're using Quattro Pro 3 or 4 with an EGA or VGA monitor, the numbers go up to 22 or 23.

Notice that the computer puts a box in column A, row 1. If you tap the right-arrow key, that box moves to the right, so it's in column B. If you tap the down-arrow key, the box moves down, to row 2. By tapping the four arrow keys, you can move the box in all four directions, to practically anywhere on the screen.

Jargon Each possible position of the box is called a **cell**.

The box's original position (in column A, row 1) is called **cell A1**. If you move the box there and then tap the right-arrow key, the box moves to column B, row 1; that position is called **cell B1**.

To **point** at a cell, move the box to that cell. Since you use the box to point at cells, the box is called the **cell pointer**.

Create a spreadsheet

To create a spreadsheet, you move the box from cell to cell, and put into each cell whatever words or numbers you wish.

For example, suppose you run a small business whose income is $7000 and expenses are $5000. Those are the figures for January; the figures for February aren't in yet. Let's put the January figures into a spreadsheet, like this:

```
    A        B        C        D        E        F        G        H
1            January
2   Income   7000
3   Expenses 5000
4   Profit
```

To begin, move the box to cell A2. Type the word Income, then press the down-arrow key, which moves the box down to cell A3. Now your screen shows the word Income in cell A2, and the box is in cell A3.

Try that! When you do, here's what happens. While you type the word Income, it appears temporarily in an **input area** at the top of the screen. It appears just in the input area until you press the down-arrow key, which copies Income to cell A2 and moves the box down.

After the box has moved to cell A3, continue typing the spreadsheet as follows. Type the word Expenses, press the down-arrow key (to move to cell A4), type the word Profit, move the box to cell B1 (by pressing the up-arrow three times and then the right-arrow once), type the word January, press down-arrow, type 7000, press down-arrow, type 5000, and press down-arrow again.

BACKSPACE key
If you make a mistake while typing the words and numbers, press the **BACKSPACE key** to erase the last character you typed.

The left-arrow key will *not* help you erase the last character you typed. Instead, the left-arrow key moves the box to a different cell.

Type a formula
Although the computer's screen shows the words you typed (Income, Expenses, and Profit), the computer doesn't understand what those words mean. It doesn't know that "Profit" means "Income minus Expenses". The computer doesn't know that the number in cell B4 (which represents the profit) ought to be the number in cell B2 (the amount of income) minus the number in cell B3 (the dollars spent).

You must *teach* the computer the meaning of Profit, by teaching it that the number in cell B4 ought to be the number in cell B2 minus the number in cell B3.

To do that, move the box to cell B4, then type this formula:

+B2-B3

Notice that **every formula normally begins with a plus sign**. The rest of the formula, B2-B3, tells the computer to subtract the number in cell B3 from the number in cell B2, and put the answer into the box's cell (which is cell B4).

When you type that formula, you don't have to bother capitalizing the B: capitalization is optional.

While you're typing that formula, it appears in the input area.

When you've finished typing the formula, press the ENTER key. Then the computer automatically computes the formula's answer (2000) and puts that number into the box's cell (B4), so the screen looks like this:

```
    A        B        C        D        E        F        G        H
1            January
2   Income   7000
3   Expenses 5000
4   Profit   2000
```

The formula "+B2-B3" remains in effect forever. It says that the number in cell B4 will always be the B2 number minus the B3 number. If you ever change the numbers in cells B2 and B3 (by moving the box to those cells, retyping the numbers, and pressing ENTER), the computer automatically adjusts the number in cell B4, so the number in cell B4 is still B2 minus B3 and still represents the correct profit.

For example, suppose you move the box to cell B2, then type 8000 (to change the January income to $8000), and then press ENTER. As soon as you press ENTER, not only does the number 8000 appear in cell B2 but also the profit in cell B4 immediately changes to 3000, right in front of your eyes!

A typical spreadsheet contains *dozens* of numbers, totals, subtotals, averages, and percentages. Each cell that contains a total, subtotal, average, or percentage is defined by a formula. Whenever you retype one of the numbers in the spreadsheet, the computer automatically readjusts all the totals, subtotals, averages, and percentages, right before your eyes.

Remember to begin each formula with a plus sign. The rest of the formula can contain these symbols:

Symbol	Meaning
+	plus
-	minus
*	times
/	divided by
.	decimal point

It can also contain E notation and parentheses. For details about how to use those symbols, E notation, and parentheses, read pages 322-327, which explain BASIC's fundamentals and math.

Edit simply

To edit what's in a cell, move the box to that cell. Then type the word, number, or formula that you want to put into the cell.

If the cell's word, number, or formula was *almost* correct, and you're too lazy to retype it all, do the following. Move the box to that cell. Press the F2 key. Now the cursor is in the input area. Edit the word, number, or formula as if you were using a word processor. (Use the BACKSPACE, DELETE, INSERT, left-arrow, and right-arrow keys.) When you finish editing, press ENTER.

If you type a formula incorrectly, the computer might beep at you. Then the cursor stays in the input area, so you can edit the error.

Use functions

To make a cell be the sum of cells B2 through B9, you can type this formula:

```
+B2+B3+B4+B5+B6+B7+B8+B9
```

Instead of typing all that, you can type just this:

```
+@SUM(B2..B9)
```

A **function** is a word that makes the computer calculate (such as SUM). Put the symbol @ before each function: say @SUM instead of SUM.

After each function, you must put parentheses. For example, you must put parentheses after SUM.

Since the computer ignores capitalization, you can type:

```
+@sum(b2..b9)
```

You can omit the plus sign and the second period, and type just this:

```
@sum(b2.b9)
```

To find the sum of cells B2 through H2 (which is B2+C2+D2+E2+F2+G2+H2), type this:

```
@sum(b2.h2)
```

To find the sum of all cells in the rectangle that stretches from B2 to C4 (which is B2+B3+B4+C2+C3+C4), type this:

```
@sum(b2.c4)
```

Average To find the average of cells B9 through B13, you can type this:

```
+(b9+b10+b11+b12+b13)/5
```

But this way is shorter:

```
@avg(b9.b13)
```

To find the average of cells C7, B5, and F2, you can ask for (c7+b5+f2)/3, but a nicer way is to type:

```
@avg(c7,b5,f2)
```

Point in a formula

While you're typing a formula, you can point at cells instead of typing their names. For example, **in the middle of a formula, instead of typing B2, you can just point at cell B2**, by moving the box to cell B2. When you move the box to cell B2, the computer automatically types B2 for you.

So to type the formula +B2–B3, just type the equal sign (or plus sign), move the box to cell B2, then type the minus sign, then move the box to cell B3. Try it! When you've finished constructing the formula, press ENTER.

To type the formula @sum(b2.b9) quickly, type the "@sum(", then move the box to B2, then type the period, then move the box to B9, then type the ")".

Fill a cell

Suppose you want to fill an entire cell with dashes, so that the cell looks like this:

```
----------
```

Here's how to do that quickly.

Type a backslash (which is the symbol "\"), then type the dash, then press ENTER. The backslash means "fill", so the computer will fill the entire cell with dashes.

Be joyous Instead of typing a dash, try typing the word JOY. Then the computer will fill the cell with JOY, like this:

```
JOYJOYJOY
```

Hop far

Here's how to be quick as a bunny and hop far in your spreadsheet.

Farther rows The screen shows just a few rows, which are numbered 1, 2, 3, etc. Row 1 is at the top of the screen. Row 15 is near the bottom of the screen.

Try this experiment. Move the box down to row 15 (by pressing the down-arrow key repeatedly). Then press the down-arrow key several more times. Eventually, you'll get to row 30, and later to row 100, and much later to row 1000. The largest row number you can go to is 8192.

To make room on the screen for those new rows, row 1 disappears temporarily. If you want to get back to row 1, press the up-arrow key repeatedly.

Farther columns The screen shows just a few columns, which are lettered A, B, C, etc. If you press the right-arrow key repeatedly, you'll eventually get to column Z.

Altogether, the computer lets you have 256 columns. The first 26 columns are lettered from A to Z. The next 26 columns are lettered from AA to AZ. The next 26 columns are lettered from BA to BZ. And so on. The last column — the 256th — is IV. That's why people who use spreadsheets are called "IV league accountants".

Do *not* try to put data in all the rows and columns! Your computer doesn't have enough RAM to hold that much data. Cynics say, "Before you run out of spreadsheet, you'll run out of RAM."

Autorepeat Here's a shortcut: instead of pressing an arrow key repeatedly, just hold down the key awhile.

Screenfuls To move far down, press the PAGE DOWN key. To move far up, press the PAGE UP key. To move far to the right, press the TAB key. To move far to the left, press the TAB key *while holding down the SHIFT key*. Each of those keys moves the box far enough so that you see the next screenful of rows and columns.

HOME key Cell A1 is called the **home cell**, because that's where life and your spreadsheet begins: at home! To move the box there, press the HOME key.

END key If you press the END key and then an arrow key, the box moves to the spreadsheet's edge.

For example, if you press the END key and then the *right*-arrow key, the box moves to the spreadsheet's *right* edge. That means the box moves to the right, until it reaches column IV or a boundary cell (a cell containing data and next to an empty cell).

F5 key To move the box to a distant cell immediately, press the F5 key. Then type the cell's name (such as C9) followed by ENTER.

MAJOR EDITING

To give a command, press the slash key (which as the symbol "/" on it). Next, choose from the **main menu**, which appears at the top of the screen. In Quattro Pro, the main menu looks like this:

```
File Edit Style Graph Print Database Tools Options Window
```

In 1-2-3, the main menu looks like this:

```
Worksheet Range Copy Move File Print Graph Data System Add-in Quit
```

After you've pressed the slash key, choose a command from the main menu by typing the command's first letter.

If you're not sure which command to choose, press the right-arrow key several times; that makes the computer explain each command's purpose.

After choosing a command, the computer might ask you for further details, by giving you a **submenu** to choose from. **To choose a command from a submenu, type the command's first letter.**

If you make a mistake, press the Esc key several times. That cancels the menus, so they disappear. (Then if you wish, you can try again to use the menus: press the slash key again and choosing menu commands again, by typing the first letter of each command you wish.)

Here are examples. . . .

Erase all

Here's how to erase the entire spreadsheet so that all the cells become blank and you can start over again.

Quattro Pro Say **File Erase Yes** by pressing the slash key, then the F key, then the E key, then the Y key, like this: /FEY.

1-2-3 Say **Worksheet Erase Yes** by pressing the slash key, then the W key, then the E key, then the Y key, like this: /WEY. If you're using version 2.3 or 2.4, the computer might ask, "Erase worksheet?"; to reply, press Y.

Try it! Go ahead! Try erasing the entire spreadsheet! Do it *now*. It's a good way to practice using menus.

Erase one cell

Suppose you want to erase just one cell so it becomes blank. Move the box to that cell, then do the following.

Quattro Pro Press the DELETE key.

1-2-3 For version 2.3 and 2.4, press the DELETE key. For version 2.2, say **Range Erase** (by typing /RE), then press ENTER.

Erase several cells

Here's how to erase *several* cells, so they become blank.

Move the box to the first cell you want to erase. If you're using Quattro Pro, say **Edit Erase-block** (by typing /EE); if you're using 1-2-3, say **Range Erase** (by typing /RE). Move the box to the last cell you want to erase. Press ENTER.

The computer will erase that first cell, last cell, and the cells between them.

For example, if the first cell is B2, and the last cell is B7, the computer will erase B2, B3, B4, B5, B6, and B7. If the first cell is B2, and the last cell is E2, the computer will erase B2, C2, D2, and E2. If the first cell is B2, and the last cell is C4, the computer will erase B2, B3, B4, C2, C3, and C4.

The first cell, last cell, and the cells between them form a rectangle. Quattro Pro calls that rectangle a **block**; 1-2-3 calls it a **range**.

So here's how to erase a rectangle of cells: point at one corner of the rectangle (by using the arrow keys), then say Edit Erase-block (or Range Erase), then point at the rectangle's opposite corner and press ENTER.

Delete some columns

Here's how to **delete** column B.

Move the box to column B. For Quattro Pro, say **Edit Delete Columns** (by typing /EDC); for 1-2-3; say **Worksheet Delete Column** (by typing /WDC). Press ENTER.

The computer erases all the data from column B, so column B becomes blanks, which the computer immediately fills by shifting some data from other columns. Here's how. . . .

Into column B, the computer moves the data from column C. Then into column C, the computer moves the data from column D. Then into column D, the computer moves the data from column E. And so on.

At the end of the process, the top of the screen still shows all the letters (A, B, C, D, E, F, G, etc.); but now column B contains the data that used to be in column C; and column C contains the data that used to be in column D; etc.

After rearranging the spreadsheet, the computer fixes all formulas. For example, after column C's data has moved to column B, the computer hunts through all formulas in the spreadsheet and fixes them by changing each "C" to "B". The computer also changes each "D" to "C", each "E" to "D", etc.

You've learned how to delete column B. Here's how to delete *several* columns. Move the box to the first column you want to delete, then say Edit Delete Columns (for Quattro Pro) or Worksheet Delete Column (for 1-2-3), then move the box to the last column you want to delete, then press ENTER. The computer will delete that first column, last column, and the columns between them.

Delete some rows

Instead of deleting columns, you can delete rows.

Move the box to the first row you want to delete. For Quattro Pro, say **Edit Delete Rows**; for 1-2-3, say **Worksheet Delete Row**. Move the box to the last row you want to delete. Press ENTER.

Insert some columns

You can insert extra columns in the middle of your spreadsheet. When you do, the computer will move other columns out of the way, to make room for the extra columns. The computer will also adjust each formula.

Here's how to insert extra columns.

Point where you want the first extra column to appear (by moving the box there). For Quattro Pro, say **Edit Insert Columns**; for 1-2-3, say **Worksheet Insert Column**. Point where you want the last extra column. Press ENTER.

Insert some rows

Here's how to insert extra rows.

Point where you want the first extra row. For Quattro Pro, say **Edit Insert Rows**; for 1-2-3, say **Worksheet Insert Row**. Point where you want the last extra row. Press ENTER.

Move

You can move your data.

Move a rectangle
On your spreadsheet, find these cells: B2, B3, B4, C2, C3, and C4. Those six cells are next to each other. In fact, they form a giant rectangular area, whose top left corner is B2.

You can tell the computer to take all the data in that rectangular area and move it to a different part of your spreadsheet. For example, you can tell the computer to move the data to the part of your spreadsheet that begins at E7.

Then the computer will move B2's data to E7, B3's data to E8, B4's data to E9, C2's data to F7, C3's data to F8, and C4's data to F9. In other words, all the data in the original rectangle (whose top left corner is B2) will get moved to a rectangle whose top left corner is E7.

The computer will also adjust all formulas that refer to the cells in the rectangle.

Here's how to make the computer do all that.

Point at the original rectangle's top left corner (B2).

For 1-2-3, say **Move**. For Quattro Pro, say **Edit Move** (or use this shortcut: while holding down the CONTROL key, tap the M key).

Point at the original rectangle's bottom right corner (C4). Press ENTER.

Point at the new rectangle's top left corner (E7). Press ENTER.

Make sure it's blank
Before you move a rectangle, make sure the place you're moving it to is blank. (The computer will *not* move cells out of the way, to make room for the rectangle.)

If you can't find a blank space to put the rectangle, you must *create* a blank space (by erasing cells or by inserting new blank columns or rows).

Close the gap
When the computer finishes moving the rectangle, the rectangle's original position becomes a group of empty cells. If you want those empty cells to vanish, point there and tell the computer to delete the rows and columns those cells are in.

Different kinds of rectangles
Try moving different kinds of rectangles.

For example, try moving a rectangle that consists of one column of numbers. For that rectangle, the "top left corner" is the column's top number; the "bottom right corner" is the column's bottom number.

Try moving a rectangle that consists of one row of words. For that rectangle, the "top left corner" is the row's first word; the "bottom right corner" is the row's last word.

Try moving a rectangle that consists of just one cell. That rectangle's "top left corner" and "bottom right corner" are just the cell itself.

Copy

You can copy your data.

Copy a cell
Here's how to copy a cell's data to a different place, so the cell's data will appear in *both* places.

Point at the cell.

For 1-2-3, say **Copy**. For Quattro Pro, say **Edit Copy** (or use this shortcut: while holding down the CONTROL key, tap the C key).

Press ENTER. Point where you want the copy to appear. Press ENTER again.

Make sure it's blank
Before you copy a cell's data, make sure the place you're copying it to is blank. The computer will *not* move cells out of the way to make room for the copy.)

Copy a formula's concept
If you ask the computer to copy a formula, the computer will copy the *concept* underlying the formula.

For example, suppose cell B4 contains the formula +B2+B3, so that B4 is the sum of the two cells above it. If you tell the computer to copy cell B4 to E9, the computer will make E9's formula be "the sum of the two cells above it"; the computer will make E9's formula be +E7+E8.

For another example, suppose cell B4 contains the formula +2*B3, so that B4 is twice the cell above it. If you tell the computer to copy cell B4 to E9, the computer will make E9's formula be "twice the cell above it"; the computer will make E9's formula be +2*E8.

For another example, suppose cell B4 contains the formula +2*A4, so that B4 is twice the cell to the left of it. If you tell the computer to copy cell B4 to E9, the computer will make E9's formula be "twice the cell to the left of it"; the computer will make E9's formula be +2*D9.

Multiple copies of a cell
Here's how to copy a cell's data to *several* places.

Point at the cell.

For 1-2-3, say Copy. For Quattro Pro, say Edit Copy (or use this shortcut: while holding down the CONTROL key, tap the C key).

Press ENTER.

Point where you want the first copy to appear. Press the period key. Point where you want the last copy to appear. Press ENTER.

Copy a rectangle
Here's how to copy a rectangle of data to a different place, so the rectangle's data will appear in both places.

Point at the rectangle's top left corner.

For 1-2-3, say Copy. For Quattro Pro, say Edit Copy (or use this shortcut: while holding down the CONTROL key, tap the C key).

Point at the rectangle's bottom right corner. Press ENTER.

Point where you want the copy of the rectangle to begin appearing. (That's where the new rectangle's top left corner will be.) Press ENTER.

Dollar signs Notice again how copying from B4 to E9 turns the formula +B2+B3 into +E7+E8: it turns each B into an E, the 2 into a 7, and the 3 into an 8.

If you want to prevent those changes, put dollar signs in the original formula. For example, to prevent the 3 from turning into an 8, put a dollar sign before the 3, so cell B4 contains this formula:

+B2+B$3

When you copy that cell to E9, the dollar sign prevents the computer from turning the 3 into an 8; E9's formula will become +E7+E$3 (instead of +E7+E8).

To prevent the 2 from turning into a 7, put a dollar sign before the 2, like this:

+B$2+B3

To prevent each B from turning into an E, put a dollar sign before each B, like this:

+$B2+$B3

To prevent any changes from occurring at all, put a dollar sign before each column letter and each row number, like this:

+$B$2+$B$3

When you copy that formula from cell B4 to E9, the computer will put that same formula into cell E9, without making any changes. Cell E9 will contain +$B$2+$B$3.

You can use this short cut: instead of typing $B$2, you can point at cell B2 and then press the F4 key. Pressing the F4 key makes the computer insert the dollar signs. So to type $B$2 quickly, point at cell B2 then press the F4 key.

Kinds of addresses A cell's name (such as B3) is called the cell's **address**, because the cell's name tells you where to find the cell.

An address that contains dollar signs (such as $B$3) is called an **absolute address**, because the address is absolutely fixed and will never change, not even when you copy the formula.

An address that lacks dollar signs is called a **relative address**, because when you copy that address you'll be copying the cell's relationship to the other cells.

An address containing just one dollar sign (such as B$3) is called a **mixed address**, because it's partly relative and partly absolute.

When you start Quattro Pro & 1-2-3, each cell is wide enough to hold 9 characters.

Widen a column

Here's how to make column D be wider, so that each cell in column D can hold longer words and numbers.

Point at column D (by moving the box there).

For 1-2-3, say **Worksheet Column Set-width** (by typing /WCS). For Quattro Pro, say **Style Column-width** (by typing /SC) or use this shortcut: press CONTROL with W.

Tap the right-arrow key several times, until the column is as wide as you like. (If you want to make the column *narrower*, tap the *left*-arrow key.)

Press ENTER.

Widen several columns

Let's widen *several* columns.

Here's how to change the computer's assumption that most cells should be 9 characters wide. For Quattro Pro, say **Options Formats Global-width** (by typing /OFG); for 1-2-3, say **Worksheet Global Column-width** (by typing /WGC). Repeatedly tap the right-arrow key until the columns are as wide as you like, then press ENTER.

That changes the computer's assumption that most cells should be 9 characters wide, but it does *not* change any column whose width you specified previously (by saying Column Width or Worksheet Column Set-width).

You can widen columns B, C, D, and E by using the following trick. Move the box to column B. For Quattro Pro SE, say **Style Block-widths Set-width** (by typing /SBS); for Quattro Pro 3 and 4, say **Style Block-size Set-width** (by typing /SBS); for 1-2-3, say **Worksheet Column Column-range Set-width** (by typing /WCCS). Move the box to column E, and press ENTER. Repeatedly tap the right-arrow key until the columns are as wide as you like, then press ENTER.

Long numbers

If you try to type a long number in a cell that's too narrow to hold the number, the cell might display symbols instead of the number.

For example, try typing a long number in a cell that's just 4 characters wide. Instead of displaying the long number, the computer displays 4 asterisks (****).

Although the cell displays just those symbols, the computer remembers the long number you typed. To see the long number, widen the cell (by widening its column).

So if you see asterisks or number signs in a cell, the computer is telling you that the cell is too narrow and should be widened.

Long words

Try this experiment. Make cell B1 be just 4 characters wide. Then try to type the word "January" in that cell.

That cell will probably show just the first 4 letters (Janu). You probably won't see the remaining letters (ary). But if the next cell (C1) is blank, the computer will temporarily widen cell B1 to hold "January".

Cell B1 will contract to its original size (4 characters) when you enter data in cell C1.

After you've finished creating your spreadsheet, you'll want to do six things:

Slide headings toward the right, so they're over the numbers.
Beautify columns of numbers, by aligning their decimal points.
Rearrange the data to put it in numerical or alphabetical order.
Copy the data onto paper.
Copy the data onto a disk.
Move to a different spreadsheet or task.

Here's how. . . .

Right justify

In a simple spreadsheet, row 1 usually contains words (such as January, February, and March). Those words act as headings for columns of numbers.

Unfortunately, those words are too far to the left, so they aren't exactly above the numbers. (That happens because when the computer puts short data into a wide cell, the computer puts the data near the cell's *left* edge if the data is a word, but puts the data near the cell's *right* edge if the data is a number.)

To make the words in row 1 align better with the numbers below them, tell the computer to shift the words in row 1 to the right slightly. Here's how.

To shift just one word to the right, put a quotation mark before the word. For example, if you want just the word March to be shifted to the right, type this in the cell:

"March

Here's how to shift *all* the words in row 1 to the right. Point at the beginning of row 1 (by pressing the HOME key). For Quattro Pro, say **Style Alignment Right**; for 1-2-3, say **Range Label Right**. Point at the rightmost filled cell in row 1. Press ENTER.

Format the numbers

Normally, the screen displays numbers like this:

	A	B	C	D	E	F
1	1538.4					
2	-0.739					

Here's how to display those numbers more beautifully.

If the numbers in your spreadsheet represent money, try this experiment. For Quattro Pro, say **Options Formats Numeric-format Fixed**, then press ENTER, then press Q, then press Q again; for 1-2-3, say **Worksheet Global Format Fixed**, then press ENTER.

That makes the spreadsheet show 2 digits after each decimal point and round each amount to the nearest penny, so that the numbers look like this:

	A	B	C	D	E	F
1	1538.40					
2	-0.74					

If you type a **comma** instead of saying Fixed, the computer will also put commas in large numbers and put parentheses around negative amounts, so that the spreadsheet looks like this:

	A	B	C	D	E	F
1	1,538.40					
2	(0.74)					

If you say **Currency** instead of Fixed, the computer will also put dollar signs in front of the numbers, like this:

	A	B	C	D	E	F
1	$1,538.40					
2	($0.74)					

But before giving that command, you must widen column A, to allow enough room to insert the dollar signs.

If you say **Percent** instead of Fixed, the computer will express each number as a percentage, by putting a percent sign after the number and multiplying the number by 100, like this:

	A	B	C	D	E	F
1	153840.00%					
2	-73.90%					

If you change your mind, and want to return to the traditional format (instead of Fixed or comma or Currency or Percent), say **General** instead of Fixed.

Those commands change the formats of all the numbers in the spreadsheet.

Here's how to change the formats of just a *few* numbers. Point at the first number whose format you want to change. For Quattro Pro, say **Style Numeric-format**; for 1-2-3, say **Range Format**. Choose a format: say **Fixed** or **Currency** or **Percent** or **General** or a **comma**. Press the ENTER key (unless you chose General). Point at the last number whose format you want to change. Press the ENTER key.

Suppose you format a few special numbers (by saying Block Display-format or Range Format), and later give a different format to the worksheet as a whole (by saying Defaults Format Display or Worksheet Global Format). The format given to the worksheet as a whole will affect *most* of the worksheet but will *not* affect the special numbers you formatted already.

Sort the data

This spreadsheet shows how Sue, Al, and Pedro scored on a test:

	A	B	C	D	E	F
1	Sue	42				
2	Al	7				
3	Pedro	100				

You can make the computer alphabetize the names, so the spreadsheet becomes:

	A	B	C	D	E	F
1	Al	7				
2	Pedro	100				
3	Sue	42				

You can make the computer put the scores in numerical order, so the spreadsheet becomes:

	A	B	C	D	E	F
1	Al	7				
2	Sue	42				
3	Pedro	100				

You can make the computer put the scores in *reverse* numerical order (from highest score to lowest score), so the spreadsheet becomes:

	A	B	C	D	E	F
1	Pedro	100				
2	Sue	42				
3	Al	7				

Jargon Putting data in order (alphabetically or numerically) is called **sorting**.

Normal order (from lowest number to highest number, or from A to Z) is called **ascending order**. Reverse order (from highest number to lowest number, or from Z to A) is called **descending order**.

The entire rectangular area that's involved in the sorting (which includes cells A1, A2, A3, B1, B2, and B3) is called the **data area**.

Procedure For Quattro Pro, say **Database Sort**; for 1-2-3, say **Data Sort**. You'll see the **sort menu**, which offers you several choices.

For Quattro Pro, choose **Block** (by typing B); for 1-2-3, choose **Data-range** (by typing D). Point at the data area's first cell (A1), type a period, point at the data area's last cell (B3), and press ENTER.

You'll see the sort menu again. For Quattro Pro, choose **1st-key** (by typing the number 1); for 1-2-3, choose **Primary-key** (by typing P). To alphabetize by student name, move the box to column A; to alphabetize by score instead, move the box to column B. Press ENTER. Type an A (for ascending order) or D (for descending order). Press ENTER.

You'll see the sort menu again. Choose **Go** (by typing G). The computer will go sort.

If you want the computer to sort differently (for example, by score instead of student name, or descending instead of ascending), say Database Sort or Data Sort again. Since the computer still remembers the previous data area, you do *not* have to say Block or Data-range again; just say 1st-key or Primary-key again, point at the field name you want to sort on, press ENTER, type an A or D, etc.

Print on paper

To print on paper, turn the printer off, put paper into the printer, and adjust the paper if necessary so that the printer is ready to print at the top of a new sheet. Then turn the printer back on.

Quattro Pro Say **Print**. You'll see the **print menu**, which offers you several choices.

Choose **Block** (by typing B). Point at the first cell you want to print (which is usually A1), type a period, point at the last cell you want to print (such as H20), and press ENTER.

You'll see the print menu again. Choose **Spreadsheet-print** (by typing S). The printer will print. (If the spreadsheet is too wide to fit on the paper, the printer will print the left part of the spreadsheet on one sheet of paper and the right part of the spreadsheet on the next sheet.) When the printer has finished, you'll see the print menu again.

(If you're using a laser printer, the paper won't come out of the printer yet. I'll explain later how to make the paper come out.)

If you want to print another copy of the same cells, choose Spreadsheet-print again. If you want to print different cells instead, choose Block, then say which cells to print, then choose Spreadsheet-print.

If you want to print at the top of a new sheet of paper (instead of the bottom of the previous sheet), tell the printer to jerk up the paper by giving a special **"jerk paper"** command before you say Spreadsheet-print. To give the "jerk paper" command, say **Adjust-printer Form-feed** (by typing A then F).

To make the paper come out of a laser printer, give that "jerk paper" command.

When you finish using the printer, choose **Quit** from the print menu (by typing Q). That makes the print menu disappear, so that you can do anything else you wish.

1-2-3 Say **Print Printer**. You'll see the **print menu**, which offers you several choices.

Choose **Range** (by typing R). Point at the first cell you want to print (which is usually A1), type a period, point at the last cell you want to print (such as H20), and press ENTER.

You'll see the print menu again. Choose **Go** (by typing G). The printer will go print. (If the spreadsheet is too wide to fit on the paper, the printer will print the left part of the spreadsheet on one sheet of paper and the right part of the spreadsheet on the next sheet.) When the printer has finished, you'll see the print menu again.

(If you're using a laser printer, the paper won't come out of the printer yet. I'll explain later how to make the paper come out.)

If you want to print another copy of the same cells, choose Go again. If you want to print different cells instead, choose Range, then say which cells to print, then choose Go.

If you want to print at the top of a new sheet of paper (instead of the bottom of the previous sheet), tell the printer to jerk up the paper by giving a special **"jerk paper"** command before you say Go. To give the "jerk paper" command, say **Page** (by typing P).

To make the paper come out of a laser printer, give that "jerk paper" command.

When you finish using the printer, choose **Quit** from the print menu (by typing Q). That makes the print menu disappear, so that you can do anything else you wish.

Save on disk

Here's how to copy your spreadsheet onto the hard disk.

Say **File Save** (or use this Quattro Pro shortcut: while holding down the CONTROL key, tap the S key). Then invent a name for the spreadsheet; for example, if you want the spreadsheet to be named FRED, type FRED and press ENTER.

The computer will try to copy the spreadsheet onto the hard disk and call the spreadsheet "FRED".

If the hard disk contains a file named FRED *already*, the computer will interrupt the process and display a menu that says "Cancel" and "Replace".

If you choose **Replace** (by typing R), the computer will copy your spreadsheet onto the hard disk and erase the previous file named FRED. If you choose **Cancel** instead, the computer will cancel your request to copy the spreadsheet onto the disk, so the original disk file named FRED will remain intact.

Retrieve from disk

Here's how to see a list of all the spreadsheets on your hard disk.

Say **File Retrieve**. If the computer asks a question (such as "Lose your changes?" in Quattro Pro or "Retrieve file?" in 1-2-3), press Y.

(Next, if you're using 1-2-3, press the F3 key.)

You'll see a list of all the spreadsheets on your hard disk.

If you don't want to use any of those spreadsheets at the moment, tap the BREAK key while holding down the CONTROL key. (The BREAK key is at the upper-right corner of your keyboard. That key also says Pause or Scroll Lock.)

If you *do* want to use one of those spreadsheets, point at the one you want to use and press ENTER. The computer will copy that spreadsheet from the disk to the RAM and show that spreadsheet on your screen.

Delete from disk

Here's how to erase a spreadsheet from your hard disk.

Quattro Pro Say **File Utilities File-manager** (by typing /FUF). The computer will display a directory of all the spreadsheets on your hard disk.

Point at the spreadsheet you want to delete, press the DELETE key, and press Y (to confirm that Yes, you really want to delete it). Then say **File Close** (by typing /FC).

1-2-3 Say **File Erase Worksheet**. Press the F3 key.

The computer will display a directory of all the spreadsheets on your hard disk.

If you change your mind and don't want to erase any of them, tap the BREAK key while holding down the CONTROL key. If you *do* want to erase one of them, point at it, press ENTER, and press Y (to confirm that Yes, you really want to erase it).

Quit

When you finish using the spreadsheet program, here's how to quit.

Quattro Pro Say **File eXit** (or use this shortcut: while holding down the CONTROL key, tap the X key). If the computer asks "Lose your changes and exit?", press Y. The screen will show a C prompt, so you can give a DOS command.

1-2-3 Say **Quit Yes** (by typing a slash, then Q, then Y). If the computer asks "End 1-2-3?", press Y. The screen will show a C prompt, so you can give a DOS command.

ADVANCED VIEWS

Congratulations! Now you know all the fundamental spreadsheet commands!

Here are advanced commands that provide better ways to view your spreadsheet.

Vertical windows

You can divide the screen into two **windows** so that each window shows a different part of your spreadsheet.

Here's how to divide your screen into two windows, so that the left window shows columns A, B, and C, while the right window shows columns X, Y, and Z. (The two windows will be separated from each other by a vertical line.)

Get column A onto the screen (by pressing the HOME key). Move the box to the middle of the screen (column E). For Quattro Pro, say **Window Options Vertical**; for 1-2-3, say **Worksheet Window Vertical**.

The screen splits into two windows. The left window shows columns A through D; the right window shows columns E through H.

The box begins in the left window, but you can move it to the right window by pressing the F6 key.

Here's how to put columns X, Y, and Z into the right window: move the box to the right window (by pressing the F6 key), then tap the right-arrow or TAB key several times (until you reach columns X, Y, and Z).

If you want to move the box back to the left window, press the F6 key again.

Here's how to stop using vertical windows. For Quattro Pro, say **Window Options Clear**; for 1-2-3, say **Worksheet Window Clear**.

Horizontal windows

Here's how to divide the screen into two windows, so that the top window shows rows 1, 2, and 3, while the bottom window shows rows 97, 98, and 99. (The two windows will be separated from each other by a horizontal line.)

Get row 1 onto the screen (by pressing the HOME key). Move the box to the middle of the screen (row 10). For Quattro Pro, say **Window Options Horizontal**; for 1-2-3, say **Worksheet Window Horizontal**.

The screen splits into two windows. The top window shows rows 1 through 9; the bottom window shows rows 10 through 19.

The box begins in the top window, but you can move it to the bottom window by pressing the F6 key.

Here's how to put rows 97, 98, and 99 into the bottom window: move the box to the bottom window (by pressing the F6 key), then tap the down-arrow or PAGE DOWN key several times (until you reach rows 97, 98, and 99).

If you want to move the box back to the top window, press the F6 key again.

Here's how to stop using horizontal windows. For Quattro Pro, say Window Options Clear; for 1-2-3, say Worksheet Window Clear.

Titles

You should put a heading at the top of each column. For example, if column B contains financial information for January, and column C contains financial information for February, you should put the word January at the top of column B, and the word February at the top of column C. Since the words January and February are at the top of the columns, they're in row 1. They're called the **column titles**.

If row 2 analyzes Income, and row 3 analyzes Expenses, you should put the word Income at the left edge of row 2, and the word Expenses at the left edge of row 3. Since the words Income and Expenses are at the left edge of the spreadsheet, they're in column A. They're called the **row titles**.

So in a typical spreadsheet, the column titles are in row 1, and row titles are in column A.

Unfortunately, when you move to a different part of the spreadsheet (by tapping the PAGE DOWN key or TAB key), the titles tend to disappear from the screen, and you forget the purpose of each row and column.

Procedure Before playing with titles, clear away any vertical or horizontal windows that you created.

Then move the box to cell B2. For Quattro Pro, say **Window Options Locked-titles Both**; for 1-2-3, say **Worksheet Titles Both**.

Afterwards, even if you tap the PAGE DOWN or TAB key, the titles will stay on the screen.

After you've forced the titles to stay on the screen, you can't move the box to row 1 or column A anymore. Row 1 and column A are off limits. For example, if you press the HOME key, which tries to send the box to cell A1, the box will go only as far as cell B2; it will stay in B2.

If you *want* to move the box to row 1 or column A (so you can revise the titles), you must cancel the titles command. Here's how. For Quattro Pro, say **Window Options Locked-titles Clear**; for 1-2-3, say **Worksheet Titles Clear**.

Manual recalculation

Suppose you've created a gigantic spreadsheet, containing dozens of rows and columns (all filled with numbers, formulas, and words), and you want to change four of the numbers.

The normal way is to point to the cell containing the first number, retype the number, press the ENTER key, and then *wait for the computer to recalculate all the formulas that use the number*. If the spreadsheet is large, hundreds of cells might contain formulas using the number, and you might wait a long time for the computer to recalculate them all.

When the computer has finished recalculating, you point to the second number to change, retype it, press the ENTER key, and again *wait for the computer to recalculate all the formulas using that number*. Next, retype the third number, press the ENTER key, and *wait*. Then retype the fourth number, press the ENTER key, and *wait*.

So to change the four numbers, you must wait four times for the computer to recompute all relevant formulas in the spreadsheet. You'll be annoyed when you have to wait so long, four times!

To avoid waiting four times, do this: for Quattro Pro, say **Options Recalculation Mode Manual** then press the Esc key twice; for 1-2-3, say **Worksheet Global Recalculation Manual**. Then move around the spreadsheet and retype the four numbers. When you press the ENTER key after each number (or RETURN or an arrow key), the computer will *not* automatically recalculate all the formulas; instead, the computer will put onto the screen a note saying "Calculate" (or "CALC"), which means "I ought to recalculate all the formulas, but I'm not going to bother." Since the computer doesn't bother to recalculate all the formulas, the computer is immediately ready for you to type more numbers; you do *not* have to wait for the computer.

After you've typed all four numbers (without ever having to wait for the computer), and you've pressed the ENTER key after each number, and you're finally ready for your coffee break, press the F9 key.

Pressing the F9 key makes the computer recalculate all the formulas. While the computer is recalculating, go have your cup of coffee. When you come back, all the formulas will have been recalculated, and the "Calculate" note will be gone.

Using that method, you must wait for the computer only once (during your coffee break), instead of waiting four times.

That method is called **manual recalculation**. Instead of recalculating automatically each time you press the ENTER key, the computer recalculates when you press the F9 key, which manually triggers the recalculation.

If you ever want the computer to go back to recalculating automatically, do this: for Quattro Pro, say **Options Recalculation Mode Background** then press the Esc key twice; for 1-2-3, say **Worksheet Global Recalculation Automatic**.

Graph on screen

Suppose you're running a company that sells Day-Glo Pink Hair Dye. (Your motto is: "To brighten your day, stay in the pink!")

You have two salespeople, Joe and Sue. Joe's worked for you a long time, and sells about $8,000 worth of dye each month. Sue joined your company recently and is rapidly improving at encouraging people to turn their hair pink. (She does that by inventing slogans for various age groups, such as "Feminine babes wear pink!", "You look so sweet with your new hair style — spun, pink, cotton candy!", "Don't be a dink! Go pink!", "Pink is punk!", "Pink: the color that says *I'll be your Valentine, but lighten up!*", "Be what you drink — a Pink Lady!", "Let that sexy, slinky, pink panther inside you glow!", "Love is a pink Cadillac — with hair to match!", and "When you're in a sour mood, look like a pink grapefruit!")

This spreadsheet shows how many dollars worth of dye Joe and Sue sold each month:

	A	B	C	D	E	F
1		January	February	March		
2	Joe	8000	6500	7400		
3	Sue	2000	4300	12500		

The spreadsheet shows that Joe sold $8000 worth of dye in January, $6500 in February, and $7400 in March.

Sue's a trainee. She sold just $2000 worth in January, but her monthly sales zoomed up to $12500 by March.

Let's turn that spreadsheet into a graph. First, type the spreadsheet. Here's what to do next. . . .

Quattro Pro
Point at the spreadsheet's top left corner (cell A1) by pressing the HOME key. Say **Graph**. You'll see the **graph menu**.

Choose **Graph-type** (by typing G). If you want to create a **line graph** like this —

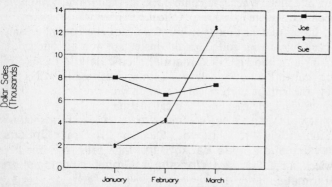

choose **Line** (by typing B). If instead you want to create a **bar graph** like this —

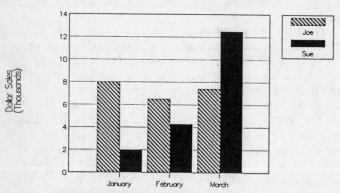

choose **Bar** (by typing B).

You'll see the graph menu again. Choose **Fast-graph** (by typing F), point at the last number (cell D3), and press ENTER. You'll see the graph you desired, except that two titles are missing: the **main title** ("How much we sold") and the **Y-axis title** ("Dollar Sales").

Here's how to add those two titles to your screen's graph. . . .

Press ENTER. You'll see the graph menu again. Choose **Text** (by typing T). Type the number **1**, then the main title ("How much we sold"), then press ENTER. Type a **Y**, then the Y-axis title ("Dollar Sales"), then press ENTER. Press the Esc key.

You'll see the graph menu again. Choose **View** (by typing V). You'll see the whole graph, including the two titles. Press ENTER.

You'll see the graph menu again. When you finish playing with graphs, press the ESCAPE key. That makes the graph menu disappear.

The computer will remember what kind of graph you wanted. If you revise the numbers in the spreadsheet, you can see the revised graph by just pressing the F10 key. The graph will immediately appear. After you've admired it, press the ENTER key.

If you save the spreadsheet (by saying File Save), the computer automatically saves the graph also. Later, if you retrieve the spreadsheet (by saying File Retrieve), the computer retrieves the graph also; to see the graph, just press the F10 key.

1-2-3
Say **Graph**. You'll see the **graph menu**, which offers you several choices.

Choose **Group** (by typing G), point at the first heading (cell B1), type a period, point at the last number (cell D3), press ENTER, and say **Rowwise** (by typing R).

You'll see the graph menu again. Choose **View** (by typing V). You'll see a graph. It looks *almost* as good as this —

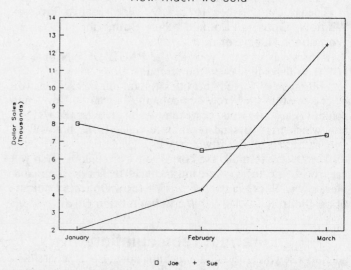

but your screen's graph is missing three items: the **title** ("How much we sold"), the **Y-axis label** ("Dollar Sales"), and the **legend** (which says that the box is "Joe" and the plus sign is "Sue").

Here's how to add those three items to your screen's graph. . . .

Press ENTER. You'll see the graph menu again. Choose **Options** (by typing the letter O). You'll see the **options menu**.

Choose **Titles First** (by typing TF). Type the title ("How much we sold") and press ENTER.

You'll see the options menu again. Choose **Titles Y-axis** (by typing TY). Type the Y-axis label ("Dollar Sales") and press ENTER.

You'll see the options menu again. Choose **Legend Range** (by typing LR), point at the first person (cell A2), type a period, point at the last person (cell A3), and press ENTER.

You'll see the options menu again. (If you have a color monitor and want to see graphs in color instead of monochrome, choose **Color** by typing C.)

From the options menu, choose **Quit** (by typing Q). That gets rid of the options menu.

You'll see the graph menu. Choose View again. You'll see the whole graph, including the title, Y-axis label, and legend. That kind of graph is called a **line graph**.

Press ENTER. You'll see the graph menu again.

If you want to see a **bar graph**, choose **Type Bar**, then choose View again. You'll see this bar graph:

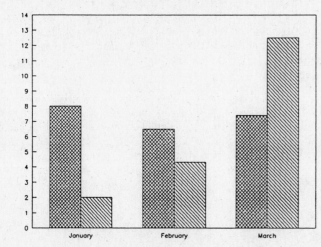

When you finish admiring that graph, press ENTER, so you see the graph menu again. If you want to see the line graph again, choose **Type Line**, then choose View again, and when you finish admiring the graph press ENTER, so you see the graph menu again.

When you finish playing with graphs, choose **Quit**. That makes the graph menu disappear.

The computer will remember what kinds of graph you wanted. If you revise the numbers in the spreadsheet, you can see the revised graph by just pressing the F10 key. The graph will immediately appear. After you've admired it, press the F10 key again.

If you save the spreadsheet (by saying File Save), the computer automatically saves the graph also. Later, if you retrieve the spreadsheet (by saying File Retrieve), the computer retrieves the graph also; to see the graph, just press the F10 key.

Graph on paper

Here's how to print a graph on paper.

Quattro Pro Get the graph onto the screen. Press ESCAPE several times, until the graph and menus disappear. Say **Print Graph-print Go** (by typing /PGG).

1-2-3 version 2.3 and 2.4 Get the graph onto the screen. Press ESCAPE several times, until the graph and menus disappear. (Then if you're using version 2.3, turn Wysiwyg on by doing this: say **Add-in Attach** by typing /AA; move the box to "WYSIWYG.ADN" by repeatedly pressing the right-arrow key; press ENTER; and choose **No-key Quit** by typing NQ.)

Move the box below your spreadsheet. (To do that, move the box to column A, then down to the bottom row that contains your data, then down two more rows.)

Type a colon (:). To do that, remember that you must press the SHIFT key. Then you'll see the **Wysiwyg menu**. From that menu, choose **Graph Add Current** (by typing GAC). Type a period, then move the box to column G and down 15 more rows. (The farther you move to the right and down, the bigger your graph will be.) Press ENTER. You'll see the graph below your spreadsheet. Choose **Quit** (by typing Q).

Type a colon, so you see the Wysiwyg menu again. Choose **Print** (by typing P).

You'll see the **Wysiwyg print menu**. Choose **Range Set** (by typing RS). To print the spreadsheet and the graph, point at the first cell you want to print (which is usually A1), type a period, point at the last cell you want to print (at the graphic's bottom row in column G), and press ENTER.

You'll see the Wysiwyg print menu again.

If nobody told Wysiwyg what kind of printer you bought, do so now. Here's how. From the Wysiwyg print menu, choose **Config Printer** (by typing CP). Point at the resolution level you want (the higher the resolution you choose, the prettier but slower your printer will print), and press ENTER. Choose **Quit**.

You'll see the Wysiwyg print menu again. Choose **Go** (by typing G). The printer will go print.

1-2-3 version 2.2 Get the graph onto the screen. Press ESCAPE several times, until the graph and menus disappear.

Say **Graph Save** (by typing /GS). Type a name for the graph (invent whatever name you like), then press ENTER. The computer will copy the graph onto the hard disk. Say Quit (by typing Q).

Get out of 1-2-3 (by saying Quit Yes). If you started 1-2-3 by saying "do 123", type "cd 123".

Type "pgraph" (so the computer runs the PGRAPH print-graph program in your 123 subdirectory).

The computer will display this **PGRAPH menu**:

Image-select Settings Go Align Page Exit

The first time you use the PGRAPH program, tell it which hardware you bought. Here's how. (If you're using a colleague's computer, ask whether this procedure was done already.) Say **Settings Hardware** (by typing SH). You'll see the **hardware menu**. Choose **Graphs-directory** (by typing G), type "c:\123", and press ENTER. You'll see the hardware menu again. Choose **Fonts-directory** (by typing F), type "c:\123" again, and press ENTER. You'll see the hardware menu again. Choose **Printer** (by typing P), point at the resolution level you want (the higher the resolution you choose, the prettier but slower your printer will print), press the SPACE bar (which makes the symbol # appear), and press ENTER. You'll see the hardware menu again. Choose **Quit** (by typing Q). Say **Save** (by typing S). You'll see the PGRAPH menu again. Now PGRAPH knows which hardware you bought.

Here's how to make the PGRAPH program print the graph. . . .

Choose **Image-select** by typing I. You'll see a list of all the graphs on your hard disk. Point at the graph you want to print, press the SPACE bar (which makes the symbol # appear), and press ENTER.

You'll see the PGRAPH menu again. Choose **Go** (by typing G). The computer will go print the graph.

You'll see the PGRAPH menu again. Choose **Exit Yes** by typing EY. That makes the computer stop using the PGRAPH program.

You'll see a DOS prompt. If you want to run the 1-2-3 program again, type "123"; if you want to return to the DOS root directory instead, type "cd \".

WILD APPLICATIONS

BACKGROUND

In the preceding chapters, you learned all the standard poop about computers: you learned about their hardware, operating systems, word processing, databases, and spreadsheets.

But there's more to computer life than just that! Computer life also includes art, music, games, and fun! Lovemaking, too!

So let's get wild! This section of the book shows you how. It reveals everything wild about computers, including not just wild fun but also wild challenges — such as building a robot that acts just like you, and finding an accounting program that actually works well!

I wish you happy hunting through this thicket of pleasures and pain. When you finish, you'll understand why computers are just a high-tech form of sadomasochism.

Enjoy!

GRAPHICS

DELUXE PAINT

To create beautiful pictures on your computer's screen, get a program called **Deluxe Paint** — or one of its cousins.

Deluxe Paint was invented in California by Dan Silva in 1985. Then he invented an improved version (**Deluxe Paint 2**). Then he developed a further improvement (**Deluxe Paint 3**), which included advanced graphics tricks and also animation. His programs all ran on the Commodore Amiga. They were published by Electronic Arts.

An Electronic Arts employee — Brent Iverson — developed an **IBM version of Deluxe Paint 2**. Then another Electronic Arts employee — Steve Shaw — developed an IBM version of Deluxe Paint 3 and called it **Deluxe Paint Animation**. He also invented a lesser version called **Deluxe Paint 2 Enhanced**, which includes all the features of Deluxe Paint 3 except animation.

Electronic Arts also developed an **Apple 2GS version of Deluxe Paint 2**.

Electronic Arts also sells several paint programs for the Mac: **Studio 1** has animation but no color; **Studio 8** and **Studio 32** have color but no animation. They were all developed by an independent group of French programmers inspired by Dan Silva.

In this chapter, I'll concentrate on the IBM versions. Each IBM version requires 640K of RAM and a mouse.

Choose an IBM version

Which IBM version should you buy — Deluxe Paint 2, Deluxe Paint 2 Enhanced (which should be called Deluxe Paint 2½), or Deluxe Paint Animation (which should be called Deluxe Paint 3)?

Intelligence Deluxe Paint Animation understands more commands than the other versions, and it's the only version that produces animation.

Price Deluxe Paint 2 has been included free with many computers and software packages. That's because it's considered obsolete! Discount dealers sell Deluxe Paint 2 Enhanced and Deluxe Paint Animation for about $100 each.

Hard disk Deluxe Paint 2 Enhanced and Deluxe Paint Animation require a hard disk. If you don't have a hard disk, you must buy Deluxe Paint 2.

VGA Deluxe Paint Animation requires a VGA (or MCGA) video card. If your video card is worse than that — if you have just EGA, CGA, or Hercules — you must buy Deluxe Paint 2 or Deluxe Paint 2 Enhanced.

High resolution Unfortunately, Deluxe Paint Animation operates just in low resolution (320-by-200). (Instead of using RAM to store higher resolution, it uses RAM to store your animation.) If you insist on full VGA resolution (640-by-480), buy Deluxe Paint 2 or Deluxe Paint 2 Enhanced. To operate in Super VGA resolution (800-by-600 or 1024-by-768), you must buy Deluxe Paint 2 Enhanced.

Summary Deluxe Paint 2 is obsolete. Use it only if you get it free or you're broke or you lack a hard disk.

If your computer has a poor video card (Hercules monochrome, CGA, or EGA), get Deluxe Paint 2 Enhanced.

If your computer has a good video card (MCGA, VGA, or Super VGA), get either Deluxe Paint Animation or Deluxe Paint 2 Enhanced. Deluxe Paint Animation offers animation, but Deluxe Paint 2 Enhanced offers higher resolution.

Assumption In the rest of this section, I assume you're using Deluxe Paint 2 Enhanced or Deluxe Paint Animation.

Copy to the hard disk

When you buy Deluxe Paint 2 Enhanced or Deluxe Paint Animation, you get four 5¼-inch floppies and two 3½-inch floppies.

Here's how to copy the 5¼-inch floppies to your hard disk. (Copying the 3½-inch floppies is similar.)

Turn on the computer without any floppy in drive A. When you see the C prompt, put the PROGRAM Disk into drive A and type "a:". The computer will display an A prompt.

Type "install". The computer will say "Installation".

If you're using Deluxe Paint Animation, press ENTER twice. If you're using Deluxe Paint 2 Enhanced instead, press ENTER once, then type "dp" (so the screen says "dp" instead of "DPAINT"), then press ENTER again.

When the computer tells you, put the other three disks in drive A and press ENTER.

The computer will say, "Installation Complete!" (Then if you're using Deluxe Paint 2 Enhanced, do this: type "century", press ENTER, and wait for the computer to copy fonts to the hard disk.)

Turn off the computer, so you can start fresh.

Run the paint program

To start using the paint program, turn on the computer without any floppy in drive A.

To do Deluxe Paint Animation, type "do da". To do Deluxe Paint 2 Enhanced, type "do dp".

(That "do" method works if you put the DO.BAT file onto your hard disk as I recommended in the MS-DOS chapter. If you have *not* put DO.BAT onto your hard disk, do Deluxe Paint Animation by typing "cd da" and then "da"; do Deluxe Paint 2 Enhanced by typing "cd dp" and then "dp".)

Choose a video mode

If you're using Deluxe Paint 2 Enhanced, you must choose a video mode. (If you're using Deluxe Paint Animation, you don't have to choose a video mode, and you can skip ahead to the next section.)

Deluxe Paint 2 Enhanced shows you this list of video modes:

a.	CGA	320 x 200	4 colors
b.	CGA	640 x 200	2 colors
c.	EGA	320 x 200	16 colors
d.	EGA	640 x 200	16 colors
e.	EGA	640 x 350	16 colors
f.	MCGA	320 x 200	256 colors
g.	MCGA	640 x 480	2 colors
h.	VGA	320 x 200	16 colors
i.	VGA	640 x 200	16 colors
j.	VGA	640 x 350	16 colors
k.	VGA	640 x 480	16 colors
l.	Hercules	720 x 348	2 colors
m.	Tandy	320 x 200	16 colors
o.	Amstrad	640 x 200	16 colors
p.	Extended VGA	640 x 400	256 colors
q.	Extended VGA	640 x 480	256 colors
r.	Extended VGA	800 x 600	2 colors
s.	Extended VGA	800 x 600	16 colors
t.	Extended VGA	800 x 600	256 colors
u.	Extended VGA	1024 x 768	2 colors
v.	Extended VGA	1024 x 768	16 colors

Type a letter from "a" to "v". Here's which letter to type:

Video you bought	Type this letter
Hercules monochrome	"l"
CGA	"a" for lots of colors, "b" for high resolution
EGA	"e"
MCGA	"f" for lots of colors, "g" for high resolution
VGA	"f" for lots of colors, "k" for high resolution

A plain VGA system is limited to 640-by-480 resolution and has a 256K video RAM. If your VGA system can handle higher resolution or has extra video RAM, you have **extended VGA**, which lets you type these letters instead:

Extended VGA you got		
Resolution	Video RAM	Type this letter
640-by-480	512K	"q" for lots of colors, "k" for high res.
800-by-600	256K	"f" for lots of colors, "s" for high res.
800-by-600	512K	"t"
1024-by-768	256K	"f" for lots of colors, "u" for high res.
1024-by-768	512K	"t" for lots of colors, "v" for high res.

If you choose a letter near the end of the alphabet ("p" through "v"), you face two complications:

The computer might say, "Specify which card is active". To reply, press the SPACE bar, look at the menu of VGA card manufacturers, and type your manufacturer's code letter. (If your VGA card is manufactured by a company that's not on the menu, try pretending that your VGA card is an AST VGA Plus, which handles video modes q and r.)

The computer might say, "Not enough memory". That means your computer doesn't have enough expanded RAM. Choose a different letter instead.

Move the mouse

Look at the computer's mouse. The mouse's **tail** is a cable that runs from the mouse to the computer. The area where the tail meets the mouse is called the mouse's **ass**.

The mouse's underside — its belly — has a hole in it, and a ball in the hole.

Put the mouse on your desktop and directly in front of you. Make the mouse lie flat (so its ball rubs against the desk). **Make the mouse face you** so you don't see its ass.

In the middle of the screen, you'll see a cross, which is called the **mouse pointer**.

Move the mouse across your desk. As you move the mouse, remember to keep it flat and facing you. As you move the mouse, the cross moves also.

If you move the mouse to the left, the cross moves to the left. If you move the mouse to the right, the cross moves tot he right. If you move the mouse toward you, the cross moves down. If you move the mouse away from you, the cross moves up.

Practice moving the cross by moving the mouse. Remember to keep the mouse facing you at all times.

If you want to move the cross far and your desk is small, move the mouse until it reaches the desk's edge; then lift the mouse off the desk, lay the mouse gently on the middle of the desk, and rub the mouse across the desk in the same direction as before.

Draw a squiggle

On the top of the mouse, you'll see 2 or 3 rectangular buttons you can press. **The main button is the one on the left.**

The middle of the screen is a white, rectangular area that's huge: it consumes most of the screen. That area is called the **painting area**. It's where you draw your pictures.

Try this experiment. Put the cross in the middle of the screen, in the middle of the painting area. *While holding down the mouse's left button*, move the mouse. That activity — moving the mouse while holding down the mouse's left button — is called **dragging**. As you drag, you'll be drawing a squiggle.

For example, try drawing a smile. To do that, put the cross where you want the smile to begin (at the smile's upper-left corner), the depress the mouse's left button while you draw the smile. When you finish drawing the smile, lift the mouse's button. Then draw the rest of the face!

Click an icon

At the screen's right edge, you see these pictures:

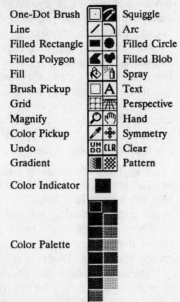

One-Dot Brush	Squiggle
Line	Arc
Filled Rectangle	Filled Circle
Filled Polygon	Filled Blob
Fill	Spray
Brush Pickup	Text
Grid	Perspective
Magnify	Hand
Color Pickup	Symmetry
Undo	Clear
Gradient	Pattern

Color Indicator

Color Palette

Those pictures are called **icons** (or **tools**).

Try this experiment: move the mouse pointer (the cross) to those icons. When the cross reaches those icons, the cross turns into an arrow.

Line

Here's how to draw a line that's perfectly straight.

Move the mouse pointer until it turns into an arrow, and the arrow's tip is in the middle of the Line icon. Then tap the mouse's left button. (That's called **clicking the Line icon**.)

Then put the mouse pointer in the middle of the screen, in the middle of the painting area, where you want the line to begin. Drag to where you want the line to end (by moving there while holding down the mouse's left button).

The line you desired will appear!

Practice drawing lines. When you finish drawing lines and want **to draw squiggles instead, click the Squiggle icon**. (Since the Squiggle icon looks like a paintbrush, it's also called the Freehand Brush icon).

Practice! Draw lines, then squiggles, then lines, then squiggles. When you feel comfortable, explore the following icons, which are more advanced. . . .

Arc

To draw an arc (a smooth curve), click the Arc icon (which is also called the Curve icon). Then put the mouse pointer in the painting area, where you want the arc to begin, and drag to where you want the arc to end. Lift your finger off the mouse's button, move the mouse until the arc has the curvature you wish, then click.

Undo

If you make a mistake, click the Undo icon. That makes the computer erase the last object you drew (or undo your last activity). The screen will look the same as before you drew that object (or did that activity).

Clear

To erase *everything* you drew on the screen (so the screen becomes white and you can start over), click the Clear icon (which says CLR). If you're using Deluxe Paint Animation, you must then press ENTER.

Color Palette

Normally, the computer draws black shapes (on a white background). To draw in a color other than black, look at the Color Palette icon (which is divided into many colors), and click the color you want. The color you choose is called the **foreground color**.

For example, to draw a blue object, do this: click blue, then draw the object. To erase part of an object, do this: click white, then cover the object by drawing with white paint.

If you're using Deluxe Paint 2 Enhanced and chose a 2-color video mode, the only colors in the palette are black and white.

If you're using Deluxe Paint Animation (or Deluxe Paint 2 Enhanced in a 256-color mode), the Color Palette icon shows just *some* of the colors. To see other colors, repeatedly click the Right Arrow icon (at the screen's bottom right corner). To go back to the colors you were seeing before, click the Left Arrow icon. When you see your favorite color, click it.

Color indicator

In the middle of the Color Indicator icon, you see the color that you picked to be the foreground color.

Color pickup

Suppose you've drawn a picture, and one of the colors you've used is so nice that you want to use it again. Click the Color Pickup icon (which looks like an eyedropper that soaks up ink), then click your picture's middle, where you used that color. That color will become the foreground color.

Filled rectangle

To draw a rectangle whose sides are perfectly straight, and whose middle is filled in, click the Filled Rectangle icon. Then put the mouse pointer in the painting area, where you want the rectangle's top left corner to be. Drag to where you want the rectangle's opposite corner.

Filled circle

To draw a circle whose middle is filled in, click the Filled Circle icon. Then put the mouse pointer in the painting area, where you want the circle's center to be. Drag until the circle is as big as you wish.

Filled polygon

To draw a polygon whose middle is filled in, click the Filled Polygon icon. Then click in the painting area, where you want the polygon's first corner to be.

Click where you want the polygon's second corner to be. Presto — the computer draws a line from the first corner to the second corner!

Click where you want the polygon's third corner to be. The computer draws a line from the second corner to the third corner.

Keep clicking, until you've clicked all the corners. Then press the SPACE bar, which makes the computer draw a line from the last corner back to the first corner and fill in the polygon.

Filled blob

To draw a blob (lumpy circle) whose middle is filled in, click the Filled Blob icon (which is also called the Filled Freehand Shape icon). Then put the mouse pointer in the painting area, where you want the blob to begin. Drag in a circular motion (so you're drawing a lumpy circle). When you lift your finger from the mouse's button, the computer completes the circular shape (by drawing a line back to where you began) and fills in the middle.

Fill Suppose your drawing contains a big area that's all the same color. For example, suppose you drew a big filled rectangle, circle, polygon, or blob. Here's how to change the color of that area.

Click in the Color Palette, at the new color you want, so it becomes the foreground color. (The new color can be red, blue, black, white, or any other color you wish.)

Click the Fill icon (which looks like a paint bucket).

The mouse pointer turns into a paint bucket. Move the mouse pointer carefully, so the tip of the paint (spilling out of the bucket) is in the middle of the large area whose color you want to change. Then click.

The entire area's color will change to the foreground color. If you make a mistake, click the Undo icon and try again.

You can use that technique to change the color of *any* big area that's all the same color. For example, if you draw a big yellow sun, you can change the sun's color to orange.

Here's how to start drawing a landscape. Clear the screen (by clicking the Clear icon). Then draw the horizon, as follows: by using the Squiggle icon, draw a horizontal black squiggle all the way across the screen. Make sure the squiggle goes *all* the way across the screen — from the screen's far left to the screen's far right — so that there are no gaps in the horizon, and so that it's impossible to travel from the sky (above the horizon) to the ground (below the horizon) without crossing the horizon.

Then make the sky blue. To do that, click the blue part of the Color Palette icon, then click the Fill icon, then click in the middle of the sky. (If you're using Deluxe Paint 2 Enhanced in a 2-color mode, pick black instead of blue and make a night scene.)

The entire sky will turn blue (or black).

If you made a mistake and forgot to make the horizon go all the way across the screen, the sky's blue paint will leak through the horizon and make the ground blue. Click the Undo icon and try again!

To make the ground be desert brown or lawn green or fantasy-land purple, click your favorite ground color in the Color Palette, then click Fill, then click in the middle of the ground.

Here's how to draw a face that's embarrassed. Clear the screen (by clicking the Clear icon). Begin using the Squiggle icon, draw the face's black outline (a circle with two bumps on it — for the ears). Make sure the face's bumpy circle is a *complete* circle and has no gaps. Make sure it's impossible to go from the middle of the face to the screen's edge without crossing the face's circle.

Then make the face turn red. To do that, click the red part of the Color Palette icon, then click the Fill icon, then click in the middle of the face. The entire face will turn red.

If you made a mistake and forgot to make the face's circle be complete, the face's red paint will bleed through the gap in the face's circle and make the rest of the screen be bloody. Yuk! Click the Undo icon and try again!

Spray To vandalize your own drawing by using a can of spray paint, click the Spray icon (which looks like a can of spray paint and is also called the Airbrush icon). Then put the mouse pointer in the painting area, where you want to begin spraying, and drag!

Text To put words in the middle of your picture, click the Text icon. Then click in the painting area, where you want the words to begin. Type the words.

Grid To draw simple diagrams more easily, click the Grid icon before you draw. Then anytime you click or drag the mouse (except when drawing squiggles), the computer will automatically nudge the mouse pointer so that its X and Y coordinates are a multiple of 8.

For example, try this experiment. Click the Grid icon. Draw a line (by using the Line icon). Now try to draw another line that starts at exactly the same point as the first line. Because of the grid, you don't have to bother putting the mouse pointer exactly where the first line began; just put the mouse pointer *close* to that point, and the computer will automatically nudge the mouse pointer so that its coordinates are a multiple of 8 — and exactly where the first line began.

Magnify To magnify part of the screen temporarily, so you can see more clearly what you're drawing there, click the Magnify icon (which looks like a magnifying glass). Then click in the part of painting area you want to magnify.

The screen splits into two parts. The left part of the screen shows the objects in their actual size; the right part of the screen shows the objects magnified.

Go ahead: continue drawing! Whatever you draw will appear in the left part of the screen (actual size) and simultaneously in the right part of the screen (magnified).

When you finish needing magnification, click the Magnify icon again. The screen will return to its usual, unmagnified state.

Hand While looking at a magnified part of the screen, here's how to nudge the magnifying glass so you see a slightly different view.

Click the Hand icon. (It's also called the Grabber icon.) Put the mouse pointer in the middle of the magnified view. Drag a short distance in the direction that you want to nudge the view.

Symmetry To create perfect symmetry, click the Symmetry icon (which looks like a snowflake or the image seen through a kaleidoscope). Then move the mouse pointer near the center of the painting area. You'll see the mouse pointer and 11 clones of it — 12 pointers altogether, arranged in a circle.

Go ahead: continue drawing! Whatever you draw will be duplicated 11 extra times, so you'll see 12 copies of your drawing. The 12 copies are arranged in a circle and rotated, and 6 of those copies are mirror images (flipped backwards). Groovy!

When you finish symmetric drawing, click the Symmetry icon again. Then you'll have just one mouse pointer, instead of 12.

Pop out a menu

You can make the screen display extra icons. Here's how.

Zigzag Try this experiment. Point at the Line icon, then hold down the mouse's left button awhile. A new menu pops out onto the screen. (It's called a **pop-out menu**). The menu shows two icons. One of them is a copy of the Line icon. The other is the **Zigzag icon**: it's a line with a bend in it. To use the Zigzag icon, drag to it.

Here's how to draw a zigzag (try it!). Drag to the Zigzag icon (which pops out of the Line icon). Then click in the painting area, where you want the zigzag to begin. Click where you want the zigzag's first bend. Click where you want the zigzag's second bend. Click at each additional bend. Click where you want the zigzag to end. Then press the SPACE bar. (If the zigzag's ending point is the same as where the zigzag began, pressing the SPACE bar is optional.)

The Zigzag icon is also called the "Connected Lines" icon or "Polyline" icon.

After you've used the Zigzag icon, that icon stays on the screen, where the Line icon used to be.

If you ever want to draw a simple line again, make the Line icon reappear. Here's how. Point at the Zigzag icon. Hold down the mouse's left button. You'll see the pop-out menu again. Drag to the pop-out menu's Line icon.

Practice drawing zigzags, then simple lines, then zigzags again. When you feel comfortable, explore the following icons, which are more advanced. . . .

Zigzag arcs To draw a zigzag made of a series of arcs instead of lines, drag to the **Zigzag Arcs** icon, which pops out of the Arc icon. Then point in the painting area, where you want the first arc to begin, and drag to where you want that arc to end. Lift your finger off the mouse's button. Move the mouse until that arc has the curvature you wish, then click.

Click where you want the second arc to end, and click where you want that second arc to curve. Click where you want the third arc to end, and click where you want the third arc to curve. Do the other arcs.

When you finish the last arc, press the SPACE bar.

The Zigzag Arcs icon is also called the "Connected curves" icon or "Polycurve" icon.

Extended color palette If you're using Deluxe Paint Animation (or Deluxe Paint 2 Enhanced in a 256-color mode), try this trick. In the Color Palette icon, point at one of the colors, and hold down the mouse's left button awhile. You'll see a pop-out menu displaying all 256 colors simultaneously. Drag to the color you want. It becomes the foreground color.

If you're using Deluxe Paint 2 Enhanced in a 16-color mode, try this similar trick instead. In the Color Palette icon, point at your favorite color, and hold down the mouse's left button awhile. You'll see a pop-out menu that displays 16 modifications of that color. (The computer creates the modifications by adding tiny polka dots made of the other colors. The modifications made by polka dots are called **dithers**.) Drag to whichever dither you like. That dither becomes the foreground color.

Modified rectangles Point at the Filled Rectangle icon, and hold down the mouse's left button.

You'll see four pop-out icons. One of them is a copy of the Filled Rectangle icon. Another (**Filled Square**) acts like the Filled Rectangle icon but always produces a perfect square. The other two icons (**Unfilled Rectangle** and **Unfilled Square**) let you draw an outline shape whose middle is *not* filled in.

Modified circles Point at the Filled Circle icon, and hold down the mouse's left button.

You'll see six pop-out icons. One of them is a copy of the Filled Circle icon. The other pop-out icons are **Filled Ellipse**, **Filled Rotated Ellipse**, **Unfilled Circle**, **Unfilled Ellipse**, and **Unfilled Rotated Ellipse**.

To draw a filled ellipse (oval), choose the **Filled Ellipse** icon. Then in the painting area, imagine a rectangle just big enough to contain the ellipse you want. (That's called the **bounding rectangle**.) Point at that rectangle's top left corner, and drag to the opposite corner. The ellipse will appear.

To draw a filled *rotated* ellipse, choose the **Filled Rotated Ellipse** icon. Then click in the painting area, where you want the ellipse's center to be. Move the mouse until the ellipse is as fat and tall as you wish. Then drag in a circular motion, until the ellipse is rotated to the angle you wish.

Unfilled polygon The **Unfilled Polygon** icon pops out of the Filled Polygon icon.

Modified squiggles Point at the Squiggle icon, which looks like a paintbrush that's drawing a squiggle. Hold down the mouse's left button. You'll see three pop-out icons.

One of them is a copy of the Squiggle icon.

Another popped-out icon (**Dotted Squiggle**) acts like the Squiggle icon but makes the squiggle be a series of dots instead of a continuous curve. If you want the dots to be *far* apart, drag the mouse *fast* while drawing the dotted squiggle. That icon is also called the Discontinuous Freehand Brush icon.

The other popped-out icon (**Stopped Squiggle**) produces just a single dot instead of a complete squiggle. Since it stamps just one dot onto your screen, it's also called the Single-Stamp Freehand Brush icon.

Magnification level When you use the Magnify icon, it normally magnifies objects by a factor of 4, so that each object appears 4 times as wide and 4 times as tall. That's called a **magnification level of 4x**.

To choose a different magnification level, point at the Magnify icon and hold down the mouse's left button. You'll see a pop-out menu that offers these magnification levels: 2x, 3x, 4x, 6x, 8x, 12x, and 16x. Drag to the magnification level you want.

Choose a brush

To draw with*out* a computer, you can buy a collection of paintbrushes. To draw a thick line, use a thick brush. To draw a thin line, use a brush that's tiny and fine. To create a weird texture, paint with a *tooth*brush. To create a *big* weird texture, paint with a *hair*brush. To create a *gigantic* weird texture, get together with your friends, undress, cover yourselves with paint, and roll around on a large sheet of canvas. (That's called *Technicolor mud wrestling*. It's a quick, fun way to create an abstract pop mural. The mural makes a great conversation piece when you match the shapes on it with the various people and their parts.)

Your computer lets you paint on the screen by using *all* kinds of brushes. You can even invent your *own* brush, having any shape you like!

Here's how to pick a brush.

Built-in brushes Point at the **One-Dot Brush** icon, and hold down the mouse's left button.

You'll see 18 brush shapes. Some of them are round brushes. Some are square. Some have multiple tufts (like a tiny toothbrush, or like a paintbrush whose bristles have been purposely frayed apart). Some are chisel-pointed (like a miniature ax, for calligraphy and Japanese effects). They're called **the 18 built-in brushes**.

Drag to whichever built-in brush interests you, and try it! The computer will use that brush to draw all shapes (squiggles, lines, arcs, etc.), until you switch to a different brush.

Custom brushes Here's how to invent your *own* brush.

First, decide what shape you want the brush to produce when you tap the brush onto paper. Do you want the resulting shape to be a tiny dot, or a circle, or a square, or an irregular blob, or blob that's the same shape as a ear, or a blob that looks like Bart Simpson's hair, or some other weird shape?

Draw that shape in the painting area. (For example, if you want the brush's blob to look like Bart Simpson's hair, draw a picture of Bart Simpson's hair.) When drawing that shape, use your favorite colors!

To make that shape become your brush, click the **Brush Pickup** icon. Then draw a rectangle around the shape: point where you want the rectangle's top left corner, and drag to where you want the rectangle's opposite corner. When you lift your finger off the mouse's button, the shape becomes your new brush. Its colors become the new colors you'll be drawing in.

The computer will automatically click the Dotted Squiggle icon for you. Go have fun! Drag the mouse wherever you wish! As you drag, you'll be drawing dotted squiggles by using your new brush and colors.

The brush you invented is called a **custom brush**. It will be your brush until you invent a different custom brush or switch back to one of the 18 built-in brushes (by clicking the One-Dot Brush icon).

There's more to painting than just Deluxe Paint!

Mac Paint's children

Although Deluxe Paint is a good painting program, it wasn't the first. The first popular painting program ever invented was **Mac Paint**. It was invented in 1984 — the year before Deluxe Paint. It was invented by Bill Atkinson at Apple Computer Ince. To use it, you had to buy a Mac. At first, it was included free with the Mac. Later, Apple priced it at $149.

In 1986, Ann Arbor Software published an improved Mac Paint called **Full Paint**. A few months later, at the end of 1986, Silicon Beach published an even fancier program, called **Super Paint**. They understand all Mac Paint's commands, plus more. Discount dealers sell Super Paint 1.1 for $79 and Super Paint 2 for $109.

In 1987, Apple created a spin-off company, **Claris**, to publish Mac Paint. Claris developed **Mac Paint 2**, which is fancier than the original Mac Paint but not as fancy as Full Paint, Super Paint, or Deluxe Paint.

Clip art

Some artists sell little cartoons that you can insert into your own masterpiece. Those cartoons are called **clip art**. You can buy a disk containing hundreds of little cartoons, stick that disk into your computer, and insert your favorite cartoons into your Deluxe Paint masterpiece.

By using Deluxe Paint commands, you can modify the cartoons to suit your own taste. For example, you can make a cartoon larger or smaller, or change the expression on the person's face, or change the writing in the bubble that comes out of the person's mouth.

Computer dealers sell dozens of disks full of such cartoons. Copying and editing those cartoons is much faster than creating your own art from scratch.

Thunder Scan

You can attach the computer to a video camera, and feed the video picture directly into the computer, so the computer can manipulate the picture.

The cheapest way to do that is to buy a teeny-weeny video camera called the **Thunder Scan**. It comes in a cartridge. To use it, buy a Mac Imagewriter printer, remove the printer's ribbon cartridge, and insert the Thunder Scan cartridge instead. Then turn on the printer; but instead of inserting blank paper, insert any page containing a photo. The printer tries to move the ribbon back and forth, to print; but since the ribbon's been replaced by the Thunder Scan camera, the printer moves the camera instead; so the camera moves back and forth over the entire photo, scans the photo, and feeds it through a wire to the Mac's RAM, which displays the photo on the Mac's screen. Then you can copy the photo to the disk, and edit the picture by using Mac Paint.

Thunder Scan was invented by Andy Hertzfeld, who also helped invent the Mac. Thunder Scan lists for $249, but discount dealers (such as Mac Connection) sell it for just $199.

CAD

To design a building (or machine), you must create a blueprint. Making the computer create a blueprint is called **computer-aided drafting** (or **computer-aided design** or **CAD**). If those blueprints are fed to computerized machines that manufacture the parts for the building, the whole process is called **computer-aided design & computer-aided manufacturing (CAD/CAM)**.

Many architects and engineers use CAD programs. The CAD programs resemble Deluxe Paint but have several advantages. . . .

The CAD programs can do math. They can look at your diagrams, compute all the measurements (lengths, surface areas, and volumes), and write those measurements on the blueprints.

The CAD programs can do advanced geometry. For example, they can draw a circle, even if you don't tell the center and radius. Just say three points that you want the circle to touch! The CAD programs will figure out which circle goes through those three points and will draw it.

After you've drawn an object, the CAD programs can rotate it and show you the views from different angles, in the form of blueprints or as artistic perspective drawings.

The CAD programs let you name the parts of your object and move the parts around. If one part covers another part and hides it, the CAD programs remember that the hidden part is still there, so that the hidden part will automatically reappear if you ever more the other part out of the way.

Although CAD programs are excellent for drawing and analyzing straight lines, circles, and ovals, they're *not* good at handling artistic squiggles. So if you're an artist who likes to draw wild squiggles, do *not* get a CAD program: instead, stick with Deluxe Paint. CAD programs are strictly for architects, engineers, and other folks who do technical drafting.

Traditional top-notch CAD programs require you to sit at a fancy screen (called a **graphics workstation**) attached to an expensive computer costing over $50,000. Newer CAD programs work on microcomputers and are almost as fancy.

The fanciest CAD program for microcomputers is **Autocad**. The newest version of Autocad lists for $3500; it requires an IBM AT (or AT clone) and a **math coprocessor chip** (which helps the computer handle decimals quickly). A stripped-down version, called **Autocad Lite**, sells for about $400. A fun version, called **Autosketch**, lists for just $80 and runs on *any* IBM clone.

Autocad's main competitor is **Cadkey**, which has more commands for 3-dimensional drawing but fewer commands for 2-dimensional drawing. It lists for $3195.

The first CAD program for the Mac was **Mac Draw**. For elementary CAD applications, you can get by with Super Paint, which includes some of the commands of Mac Draw plus all the commands of Mac Paint. Better CAD programs for the Mac are being developed.

Business graphics

Business executives like to turn tables of numbers into pie charts and bar charts. The most popular way to produce those charts is to use a spreadsheet program (such as Lotus 1-2-3), which lets you type a table of numbers and then say "Graph".

Lotus 1-2-3 produces just a few types of graphs, and its graphs look crude. To create graphs that are fancier and prettier, buy a fancier spreadsheet program (such as **Microsoft Excel**) or a **presentation-graphics program** (such as **Microsoft Powerpoint** or **Lotus Freelance** or **Harvard Graphics**). Those presentation-graphics programs are especially good for preparing slide shows and overhead transparencies.

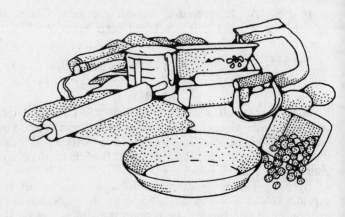

CLASSIC COMPUTER ART

During the 1960's, many creative ideas were generated about how computers would someday create their own weird art, using a wild combination of formulas and random numbers, and unshackled by the bounds of human culture.

Here's how to make the computer produce wild art, by using the wonderful classic tricks invented in the 1960's and 1970's. . . .

Gray levels

You can express every black-and-white photograph as a table of numbers. Each number in the table represents the darkness of a different point — the higher the number, the darker the point. The "darkness numbers" are called **gray levels**. To feed a picture into the computer, type in the table of gray levels. Or aim a special camera at the object you want pictured; the camera system will automatically compute the gray levels and send them to the computer via a wire.

You can program the computer to change the gray levels in any weird way you wish, and draw the result. In the 1960's, the Computer Technique Group of Japan did this to an ordinary photograph of John Kennedy:

Shot Kennedy

Diffused Kennedy

Kennedy in a Dog

Here's what the group did to a photograph of Marilyn Monroe:

Monroe in the Net

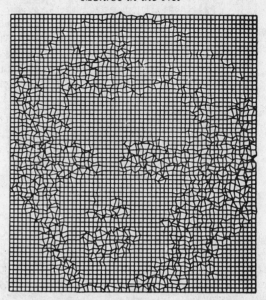

Csuri & Shaffer fed the computer a realistic line drawing of an old man; here's what came out:

Random Light and Shadow

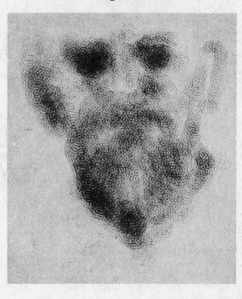

I did this with the help of a computer:

Pin-Up

```
        $$$$$$$$$
       $$$$$$$$$$
     $$$$$$$$$*$$$
     $$$$$$$$*$$$$
     $$$$.$$  $$.$$
     $$$$...$   .$$
     $$$$$.$$$ .$$$.
      $$$$$....$$$.
     $$$$$$ $$ $*$$$
     $$$$$$ .. **$$$
     *** $$$*** $$ $
     ***  $ ** *$$ $$
     ****     .* *$ $
     ****.. $*.  *. *
     *...  $*.   * *
     **.. $**.** *. *
     **.. $**** *** .
     **.  $*      *
     **.  $       *.
     *$**. *      *.
     *.*$*** *    *.
     *.***$*** * *.
     *.*****$** * .
     .*.*****$$** . .
     .*..***.   $* *. .
     .*.***.... $* .
     *..****  ... $$ ***.
     *.*****  * *** ...
     *.*****...    *.....
      *.*****..    ******...
     ****** .******.... ***
       ....*********** ***.
       * *              ** **
     ****************** ******
       * **          ** .*****
       **            ** .****.
       * *********** *.*****.
       * **         $*.****.
     *$ **       ***$.***.*
       $*      *****$..$$.**
     ********** .**$..** .***
       **       ****$.** .* **
       * **  ** .**$ ** .**
     ** ******.*$. *.*****
       *    $***$*.**.  *  *
       * **   $$$ $*.*.  *  *
       *    $  $*.*.      **
       *       $*#.       **
       *       $#.     *
       **      $#.      **
       *     $$**      **
       *       $$
```

The *Pin-Up* has these specifications. . . .

scene: a scantily clad woman sitting on a stool

4 gray levels

4 symbols (1 for each gray level: a blank, a period, an asterisk, and a dollar sign)

1537 symbols altogether (53 rows x 29 columns)

In the specification, the numbers are small, yet the picture is clear. To obtain the clarity, I did non-computerized finagling.

At Bell Telephone Laboratories, Knowlton & Harmon produced a picture with much larger specifications. . . .

scene: two sea gulls flying in the clouds
16 gray levels
141 symbols (each gray level has several symbols; the computer chooses among them at random)
11616 symbols altogether (88 rows x 132 columns)

Instead of using blanks, periods, asterisks, and $, they used cats, battleships, swastikas, and other weird shapes. Here are the 141, listed from lightest to darkest, with some repetitions:

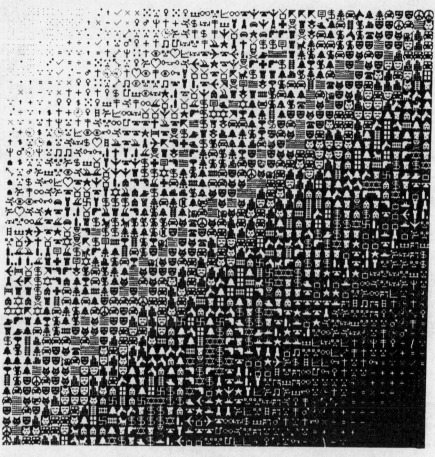

The picture is several feet long. Seen from a distance, it looks like this:

Gulls

Here's a close-up view of part of one of the gull's wings:

If you don't like sea gulls, how about *Mona Lisa*?

In 1971, Michael Hord made the computer turn photographs into artistic sketches. Here's what the computer did to a photograph of his boss, and to a photograph of a colleague's girlfriend:

Boss

Woman

To draw each sketch, the computer's camera scanned the original photograph and found the points where the photograph changed dramatically from light to dark. Then, on a sheet of paper, it plotted those points; and through each of those points, it drew a short line perpendicular to the direction in which the original photograph darkened.

More precisely, here's what the computer did. . . . It looked at four adjacent points on the original photograph:

A B
C D

It computed the darkness of each of those points. Then it computed the "darkening in the X direction", defined as:

(darkness at B) + (darkness at D) - (darkness at A) - (darkness at C)

Then it computed the "darkening in the Y direction", defined as:

(darkness at A) + (darkness at B) - (darkness at C) - (darkness at D)

Then it computed the "overall darkening", defined as:

(darkening in the X direction)² + (darkening in the Y direction)²

If the overall darkening there turned out to be large, the computer sketched a short line, in the vicinity of the points ABCD, and perpendicular to the direction of darkening. More precisely, the line's length was 1, and the line's slope was:

$$- \frac{\text{the darkening in the X direction}}{\text{the darkening in the Y direction}}$$

Morphs

Here's how to make an L slowly become a V. Notice that the letters L and V are both made by connecting three points:

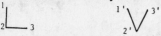

Let 1" be the point halfway between 1 and 1'; let 2" be halfway between 2 and 2'; and let 3" be halfway between 3 and 3'. Then 1", 2", and 3" form a shape that's halfway between an L and a V:

The process can be extended further:

Turning one shape into another (such as turning an L into a V) is called **a metamorphosis** or **morphing**. The intermediate shapes (that are between the L and the V) are called the **morphs**.

Using that method, the Computer Technique Group of Japan gradually turned a running man into a Coke bottle, and then into Africa:

Running Cola is Africa

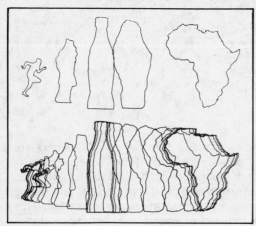

The group turned this head into a square:

Return to a Square

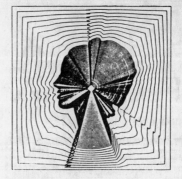

The head on the left returns to a square by using **arithmetic progression**: the lines are equally spaced. The one on the right uses **geometric progression** instead: the lines are close together near the inside square, but further apart as they expand outward.

Csuri & Shaffer exploded a hummingbird:

Chaos to Order

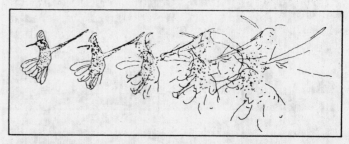

The hummingbird at the far right was obtained from the one at the far left, by moving each line a random distance and in a random direction (between 45° and -45°).

Computers can make movies. The best movie ever made by a computer is called *Hunger* (or *La Faim*). It was made under the auspices of the Canadian Film Board. It's a 10-minute cartoon, in color, with music; but it goes far beyond anything ever done by Walt Disney. It uses the same technique as *Running Cola is Africa*: it shows objects turning into other objects.

It begins by showing a harried, thin executive at his desk, which has two phones. One of the phones rings. He answers it. While he's talking on that phone, his other phone rings. To talk on both phones simultaneously, his body splits in two. (How does a single body become two bodies? By using the same technique as turning a running man into a coke bottle.)

On the other side of his desk is an armchair, which turns into a secretary, whose head turns into a clock saying 5PM, which tells the executive to go home. So he stretches his arms in front of him, and becomes his car: his hands become the headlights, his arms become the front fenders, his face becomes the windshield. You have to see it to believe it.

He drives to a restaurant and gets the waitress, who turns into an ice-cream cone. Then he eats her.

As the film progresses, he becomes increasingly fat, lustful, slothful, and miserable. In the end, he falls into hell, where he's encircled by all the poor starving naked children of the world, who eat his flesh. then the film ends. (Don't see it before eating dinner!)

It combines computer art and left-wing humanitarian politics, to create an unforgettable message.

Now morphing is being applied to color photographs and video images. For example, Hollywood movies use morphing to show a person gradually turning into a monster; environmentalists use morphing to show a human baby gradually turning into a spotted owl; and portrait photographers who have gone high-tech use morphing to show you gradually turning into the person you admire most (such as your movie idol or your lover).

Order versus disorder

Computer artists are starting to believe that **art is a tension between order and disorder**. Too much order, or too much disorder, will bore you. For example, in *Chaos to Order*, the hummingbird on the left is too orderly to be art. The hummingbird on the right is more interesting.

Consider *Gulls*. Seen from a distance, it's an orderly picture of gulls. Seen up close, it's an orderly picture of a cat or battleship or swastika. But from a middling distance, it looks like disorderly wallpaper: the symbols repeat, but not in any obvious cycle. That element of disorder is what makes the picture interesting.

At first glance, *Pin-Up* is just a disorderly array of periods, asterisks, and dollar signs. At second glance, you see order: a girl. **Art is the formation of order from disorder.**

A first glance at *Monroe in the Net* shows order: a piece of graph paper. A second glance shows disorder: some of the graph's lines are inexplicably bent. A third glance shows order: Marilyn Monroe's face pops out at you. Her orderly face is formed from the disorder of bent lines.

Return to a Square uses arithmetic progression and geometric progression to create an over-all sense of order, but the basic elements are *dis*orderly: a head that's bumpy, and a panorama of weird shapes that lie uncomfortably between being heads and squares but are neither.

Many programs create disorder by random numbers. *Chaos to Order* uses random numbers to explode the hummingbird. *Gulls* uses random numbers to help choose among the 141 symbols.

An amazing example of random numbers is this picture by Julesz & Bosche:

To your eyes, the picture seems quite ordered. Actually, it's quite *dis*ordered. One pie-shaped eighth of it is entirely random; the other seven eighths are copies of it. The copying is the only element of order, but very powerful. Try this experiment: *cover seven-eighths of the picture.* You'll see that the remaining eighth is totally disordered, hence boring.

That program imitates a child's *kaleidoscope*. Do you remember your childhood days, when you played with your kaleidoscope? It was a cardboard "telescope" that contained a disorganized pile of colored glass and stones, plus a series of mirrors that produced eight-way symmetry, so that what you saw resembled a giant multicolored snowflake. The program by Julesz & Bosche uses the same technique, computerized. Hundreds of programmers have imitated Julesz & Bosche, so that today you can buy kaleidoscope programs for your Apple, Radio Shack, etc. Or try writing your own!

Take this test:

One of those is a famous painting (*Composition with Lines*, by Piet Mondrian, 1917). The other was done by a computer (programmed by A. Michael Noll in 1965). *Which one was done by the computer? Which one do you like best?*

The solution is on the next page, but *don't peek until you've answered!*

The computer did the top one.

The programmer surveyed 100 people. Most of them (59) thought the computer did the bottom one. Most of them (72) preferred the top one — the one that was actually done by the computer.

The test shows that people can't distinguish computer art from human art, and that the computer's art is more pleasing that the art of a famous painter.

The computer's version is more disordered than Mondrian's. The computer created the disorder by using random numbers. The survey shows that most people like disorder: Mondrian's work is too ordered. It also shows that most people mistakenly think the "computer" means "order".

Envelopes

Try this experiment. On a piece of paper, put two dots, like this:

Bug 1   Bug 2

The dots represent little insects, or "bugs". The first bug is looking at the second bug. Draw the first bug's line of sight:

Bug 1   Line of sight   Bug 2

Make the first bug take a step toward the second bug:

Bug 1   Bug 2

Make the second bug run away, in any direction:

Bug 1

Bug 2

Now repeat the entire process. Again, bug 1 looks at bug 2; draw its line of sight:

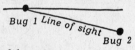

Bug 1 Line of sight
Bug 2

Bug 1 moves toward bug 2:

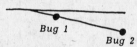

Bug 1
Bug 2

Bug 2 keeps running away:

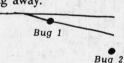

Bug 1

Bug 2

If you repeat the process many times, you get this:

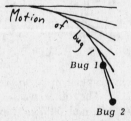

Motion of bug 1

Bug 1

Bug 2

The "motion of bug 1" looks like a curve. (In fact, it's a parabola.) The "curve" is composed of many straight lines — the lines of sight. That's how to draw a fancy curve by using straight lines.

Each straight line is called a **tangent** of the curve. The entire collection of straight lines is called the curve's **envelope**. Creating a curve, by drawing the curve's envelope, is called **stitching the curve** — because the lines of sight act as threads, to produce a beautiful curved fabric.

You can program the computer to draw those straight lines. That's how to make the computer draw a fancy curve — even if you know nothing about "equations of curves".

To get a curve that's more interesting, try these experiments:

What if bug 2 doesn't walk in a straight line? What if bug 2 walks in a curve instead?

What if bug 1 goes slower than bug 2, and takes smaller steps?

What if the bugs accelerate, or slow down?

What if there are *three* bugs? What if bug 1 chases bug 2, while bug 2 chases bug 3, while bug 3 chases bug 1?

What if there are *many* bugs, all chasing each other, and their starting positions are random?

What if there are just two bugs, but the bugs are Volkswagens, which must drive on a highway having nasty curves? Show the bugs driving on the curved highway. (Their lines of sight are still straight; but instead of moving along their lines of sight, they must move along the curve that represents the highway.)

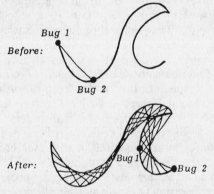

Before: Bug 1

Bug 2

After: Bug 1   Bug 2

What if each bug has its own highway, and all the bugs stare at each other?

Here are some elaborate examples. . . .
Four bugs chasing each other:

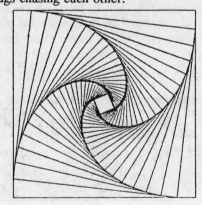

The next example, called *Compelling*, appeared in the famous book and movie, *The Dot and the Line*. (Norton Juster made it by modifying art that had appeared in *Scripta Mathematica*.) It resembles the example above, but makes the 4 bugs start as a rectangle (instead of a square), and makes the bug in the upper left corner chase the bug in the opposite corner (although *looking* at a nearby bug instead).

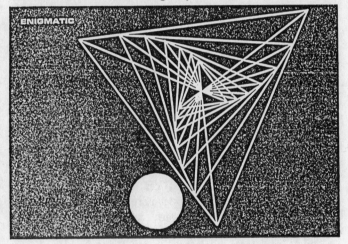

Enigmatic (from *The Dot and the Line*) makes 3 bugs chase each other, and a fourth bug stay motionless in the center:

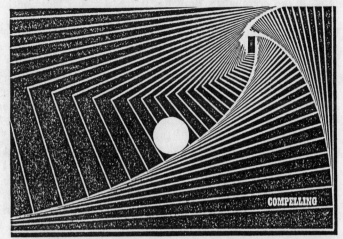

I invented *Kite*, which has 8 bugs chasing each other:

I also invented *Sails*, which has 14 bugs chasing each other:

Elliptic Motion (by my student Toby D'Oench) has 3 bugs staring at each other, as they travel on 3 elliptical highways:

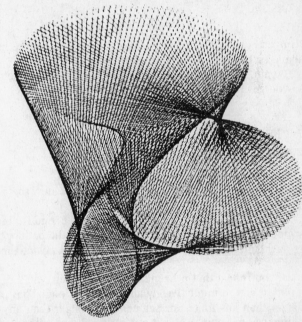

Archimedean Spiral (by Norton Starr) has bugs on circles. The bugs stare at each other but don't move:

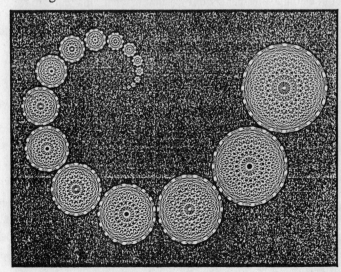

Fractals

A **fractal** is an infinitely bumpy line. Here's how to draw one.

Start by drawing a 1-inch line segment:

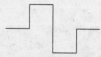

In the middle of that segment, put a bump and dip, like this:

Altogether, that bent path is 2 inches long. In other words, if the path were made of string, and you stretched the string until it was straight, the string would be 2 inches long. That's twice as long as the 1-inch line segment we started with. So here's the rule: putting a bump and dip in a path makes the path twice as long.

That bent path consists of seven segments. Put a bump and a dip in the middle of each segment, like this:

Altogether, those bumps and dips make the path twice as long again, so now the path is 4 inches long.

Again, put a bump and dip in the middle of each segment, so you get this:

Again the path's length has been doubled, so now the path is 8 inches long.

If you again put a bump and dip in the middle of each segment, the path's length doubles again, so the path becomes 16 inches long. If you repeat the procedure *again*, the path reaches 32 inches.

If you repeat that procedure infinitely often, you'll develop a path that's infinitely wiggly and infinitely long. That path is longer than any finite line segment. It's longer than any finite 1-dimensional object. But it still isn't a 2-dimensional object, since it isn't an "enclosed area". Since it's bigger than 1-dimensional but isn't quite 2-dimensional, it's called **1½-dimensional**. Since 1½ contains a fraction, it's called **fractional-dimensional** or, more briefly, **fractal**.

Look out your window at the horizon. What do you see? The horizon is a horizontal line with bumps (which represent hills and buildings and other objects). But on each hill, you see tiny bumps, which are trees; and on each tree, you see even tinier bumps, which are leaves; and on each leaf, you see even tinier bumps, which are the various parts of the leaf; and each part of the leaf is made of even smaller bumps (molecules), which have even smaller bumps (atoms), which have even smaller bumps (subatomic particles). Yes, the horizon is an infinitely bumpy line, a fractal!

You can buy software that creates fractals. Computer artists use fractal software to draw horizons, landscapes, and other bumpy biological objects. For example, they used fractal software to create landscapes for the *Star Wars* movies. You can also use fractals to draw a bumpy face that has zillions of zits.

Now you understand the computer artist's philosophy of life: "Life is a lot of lumps."

What's art?

To create art, write a weird program whose consequences you don't fully understand, tell the computer to obey it, and look at the computer's drawing. If the drawing looks nice, keep it and call it "art" — even if the drawing wasn't what you expected. Maybe it resulted from an error, but so what? **Anything interesting is art.**

If the drawing "has potential" but isn't totally satisfying, change a few lines of the program and see what happens — or run the program again unchanged and hope the random numbers will fall differently. The last thing to invent is the title. Whatever the drawing reminds you of becomes the title.

For example, that's how I produced *Kite* and *Sails*. I did *not* say to myself, "I want to draw a kite and sails". I just let the computer pick random starting points for the bugs and watched what happened. I said to myself, "Gee whiz, those drawings remind me of a kite and sails." So I named them *Kite* and *Sails*, and pretended that I chose those shapes on purpose.

That method may seem a long way from DaVinci, but it's how most computer art gets created. The rationale is: don't overplan. . . . let the computer "do its own thing"; it will give you art that escapes from the bounds of human culture and so expands your horizons!

Modern style

Computer art has changed. The **classic style** — which you've been looking at — consists of hundreds of thin lines in mathematical patterns, drawn on paper and with little regard for color. The **modern style** uses big blobs and streaks of color, flashed on a T.V. tube or film, which is then photographed.

Uncreative art

You've seen that computers can create their own weird art by using a wild combination of formulas and random numbers, unshackled by the bounds of human culture.

Today, programs such as Deluxe Paint let people use computers to create art easily and cheaply. Unfortunately, the typical person who buys a graphics program uses it to create the same kind of junk art that would be created by hand — just faster and more precisely. That's the problem with computers: they make the production of mediocrity even easier and more glitzy.

3-D DRAWING

The computer drew these three-dimensional surfaces:

Three Peaks
by John Szabo

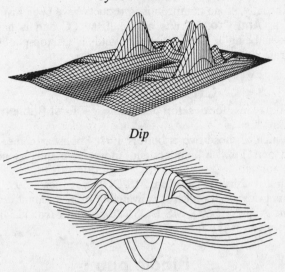

Dip

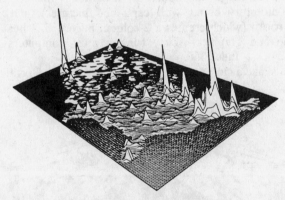

Those were done for the sake of art. This was done for the sake of science:

Population Density in the U.S.
by the Harvard University Mapping Service

The hardest part about three-dimensional drawing is figuring out which lines the computer should *not* show, because they're hidden behind other surfaces.

Coordinates

Try this experiment. Put your finger on the bridge of your nose (between your eyes). Now move your finger 2 inches to the right (so that your finger is close to your right eye). Then move your finger 3 inches up (so that your finger is near the upper right corner of your forehead). From there, move your finger 8 inches forward (so that your finger is 8 inches in front of your forehead).

Your finger's current position is called (2,3,8), because you reached it by moving 2 inches right, then 3 inches up, then 8 inches forward. The 2 is called the **X coordinate**; the 3 is called the **Y coordinate**; the 8 is called the **Z coordinate**.

You can reach any point in the universe by the same method! Start at the bridge of your nose, and get to the point by moving right (or left), then up (or down), then forward (or back).

The distance you move to the right is called the **X coordinate** (if you move to the left instead, the X coordinate is a negative number). The distance you move up is called the **Y coordinate** (if you move down instead, the Y coordinate is a negative number). The distance you move forward is called the **Z coordinate** (if you move back instead, the Z coordinate is a negative number).

Projecting the coordinates

To draw a picture of a three-dimensional object, put the object in front of you, and then follow these instructions. . . .

Pick a point on the object. (If the object has corners, pick one of the corners.) Figure out that point's X, Y, and Z coordinates (by putting your finger on the bridge of your nose and then seeing how far you must move your finger right, up, and forward to reach the object).

Then compute the point's **projected X coordinate** (which is X/Z) and the point's **projected Y coordinate** (which is Y/Z). For example, if X is 2 and Y is 3 and Z is 8, the projected X coordinate is 2/8 (which is .25) and the projected Y coordinate is 3/8 (which is .375). On graph paper, plot the projected X coordinate and the projected Y coordinate, like this:

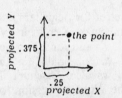

Then plot the point:

Go through the same procedure for every point on the object (or at least for the corners). Connect the dots and — presto! — you have a three-dimensional picture of the object! And the picture is mathematically accurate! It's what artists call a "true perspective drawing".

To make the picture look traditionally beautiful, place the object slightly to the left of you and slightly below your eye level, so that all the X and Y coordinates become negative.

Computerizing the process

You can program the computer so that if you input a point's X coordinate, Y coordinate, and Z coordinate, the computer will calculate the projected X coordinate (from dividing X by Z) and the projected Y coordinate (from dividing Y by Z) and plot the point on the computer's screen (by using high-resolution graphics).

The easiest way to draw three-dimensional pictures is to buy a special three-dimensional arm that attaches to an Apple computer. To draw a picture of an object, move the mechanical arm until the arm's finger touches the object. Immediately the arm's software computes the X coordinate, Y coordinate, and Z coordinate of the touched point; you don't need a ruler! It also computes the projected X coordinate and the projected Y coordinate and plots the points on your television. If you have a graphics printer, the software also plots the point on your printer's paper.

DESKTOP PUB

WHAT TO BUY

A **desktop publishing program** lets you combine words and graphics to create newspapers, newsletters, posters, and other visually-oriented ads and publications.

Pagemaker

The first fancy desktop publishing program was **Pagemaker**. It lets you create headlines, columns of text, and graphics on the screen easily, and move them by using a mouse.

Pagemaker was originally on the Mac but is now available for Windows also. Version 5 of Pagemaker is quite new and quite expensive: discount dealers sell it for $579.

Pagemaker's competitors

Quark XPress and **Ventura Publisher** handle multi-page documents and fancy typesetting better than Pagemaker, but they're harder to learn how to use and they're not as convenient for handling graphics.

They often require you to type numbers of inches instead of using a mouse. Typing numbers is more precise than using a mouse (especially if your hands are jittery), but using a mouse is more fun!

Pagemaker is better for beginners and for laying out one-page advertisements. Quark XPress and Ventura Publisher are better for professionals and for laying out long manuscripts.

Quark XPress was originally on the Mac but is now available for Windows also. Discount dealers sell the Mac version for $549, the Windows version for $596.

Ventura Publisher is available in MS-DOS and Windows versions. Discount dealers sell each for $469.

Desktop publish or word process?

The dividing line between "word processing" and "desktop publishing" is blurry.

Fancy word processors, such as Word Perfect and Microsoft Word, let you create multiple columns, but can't handle headlines or graphics well. Fancy desktop publishers, such as Aldus Pagemaker and Ventura Publisher, let you create text and edit it, but they lack advanced editing features, and they run too slowly to keep up with a fast typist.

To create a newsletter quickly, create the text by using a full-featured word processor, create the graphics by using a full-featured graphics program, and then rearrange the text and graphics into headlined columns by using a desktop-publishing program.

Desktop publishing programs are harder to understand than word processors. Too often, beginners wind up with messed-up documents from those programs, which are nicknamed "Pagewrecker", "Quirk Distress", and "Vulgar Publisher".

Compromise

Recently, some compromise products have been invented, such as **Ami Pro**. It runs on the IBM PC and is halfway between being a word processor and a desktop-publishing program.

Cheap publishing

To pay less for desktop publishing, get **First Publisher** or **Publish It**.

Which of those two is better? First Publisher comes with more fonts; Publish It understands more commands, especially for graphics.

First Publisher runs on MS-DOS and costs $99 from discount dealers. Publish It is available from discount dealers for the Apple 2 ($74), MS-DOS ($105), and Mac ($223); the Mac version is the fanciest.

Kiddie pub

Kids use a simplified form of desktop publishing, called **kiddie pub**.

The most popular kiddie pub programs are **The Print Shop** (which prints posters and greeting cards), **Certificate Maker** (which prints awards), **Kidwriter** (which creates electronic story books with captioned pictures), and **The Newsroom** (which creates a 2-column page with a headline on top and graphics). They run on most computers and typically cost under $50.

Let's take a closer look at **The Print Shop** and **Certificate Maker**. . . .

PRINT SHOP

To create big signs and greeting cards easily, get **The Print Shop**, invented by David Balsam & Martin Kahn.

It's published by Broderbund, which has sold over 500,000 copies. It's the most popular graphics program ever created for the Apple 2e & 2c. Now it's available for all the other popular computers also, such as the Mac, MS-DOS, Windows, the Commodore 64, and the Atari 800.

MS-DOS versions Several MS-DOS versions have been invented.

The first was called simply **The Print Shop**. Then came a modest improvement called **The New Print Shop**. Those versions run on practically any computer.

Later came a dramatically fancier version called **The Print Shop Deluxe**. Unfortunately, it requires a VGA monitor and a 386 or 486 CPU. Discount dealers sell it for $50.

Here's how to use the first MS-DOS version. (The later versions are fancier.)

Boot up

To start using the first MS-DOS version, turn on the computer and get an A prompt on the screen. Then put The Print Shop disk into drive A, and type PS.

Main menu

The computer will show you the main menu:

```
MAIN MENU

GREETING CARD
SIGN
LETTERHEAD
BANNER
SCREEN MAGIC
GRAPHIC EDITOR
SETUP
EXIT PRINT SHOP
```

To choose an item from the menu, point at the item (by using the up-arrow and down-arrow keys), and then press ENTER.

SETUP

The first time you use The Print Shop, choose SETUP from the menu. The computer will ask which printer, screen, and disk drives you bought, then return you to the main menu.

SIGN

To create a sign, choose SIGN from the main menu. The computer will let you create a sign having words and a picture in the middle, and a fancy border around the edge.

The computer begins by asking which kind of border you want. You have 17 choices: a thin line, thick line, double line, stars, beads, hearts, flowers, lace, lattice, wicker, woven, spirals, seashells, musical notes, candy canes, umbrellas, or none.

Then the computer asks which picture you want in the middle of the sign, and gives you 140 choices. . . .

Festivities: Halloween pumpkin, Thanksgiving turkey, Christmas tree, Christmas wreath, Hanukkah menorah, birthday cake, stork carrying baby, gift box, gift wrapping

Pleasures: heart, cupid, rose, dancing, top hat, musical notes, bells, piano, trumpet, drum

Refreshments: ice cream, ice-cold drink, coffee, tea, champagne, bartender

Animals: grinning dog, poodle, crouching cat, erect cat, bunny, turtle, teddy bear, parrot, dove, bird house, penguin in tuxedo, cuddly penguin, butterfly, lion, tiger, rhino, unicorn, shark, pig

Pointers: left arrow, right arrow, finger pointing left, finger pointing right, thumbs up, thumbs down

Money: piggy bank, money bag, safe, cash register, hands passing money, demanding money, Master Card, Visa

Transportation: antique car, taxi, chauffeur, reserved for handicapped, train, sailboat, rocket, baggage, woman walking

Communication: phone, mailman, express mail, reader, eyes, eye chart, pen & paper, pen & ink, artist, typesetter, confidential file

Thought: teacher, student, graduation, certificate, scales of justice, gavel, ballot box, solar energy, desk piled with work

Other: boss, meeting, alarm clock, house, yard sale, family, mother & child, lifting weights, skiing, warm-up exercise, tired feet, skull, candlestick, light bulb, sunshine, outer space, yin-yang, life buoy, flower, good-luck horseshoe, shoes, iron, running faucet, robot, computer, floppy disk, Charlie Chaplin, white flag, lock, closed, question mark, string wrapped around finger, block saying "A", 20 patterns

After you choose one of those clip-art pictures, the computer asks how large to make it. If you choose a small size, the computer asks whether you want the picture repeated, to create a wallpaper or tile pattern.

Next, you choose one of 12 type styles. Then start typing the words you want to put on the sign. To make extra-large characters, press the F7 key; to make extra-fancy characters, press the F9 key. The computer will automatically center your message vertically and horizontally, unless you say otherwise.

Finally, the computer asks where you'd like the sign to appear. You have four choices: your paper, your screen, your disk, or your T-shirt. If you choose T-shirt, the printer will print the entire sign backwards onto paper, so that when you iron it onto your T-shirt the writing will appear correct. The computer also gives you a chance to request multiple copies.

After the computer prints, the computer gives you the opportunity to create more copies or return to the main menu.

BANNER

From the main menu, if you choose BANNER (instead of SIGN), the computer will let you produce a banner as long as you wish. You can even make it long enough to cover the entire length of your hallway! Each letter on the banner will be huge — about six inches high — so that you can read the banner from far away. Your printer will print the entire banner sideways, on tractor-feed paper: when you take the banner out of the printer, turn the banner 90° counterclockwise, so you can read it.

Other menu choices

LETTERHEAD makes the computer print your name & address & graphics at the top or bottom of your stationery. GREETING CARD makes the computer produce a greeting card with your own front cover, inside message, and credit line on the back (instead of saying "by Hallmark"). SCREEN MAGIC makes the computer create a sign based on a kaleidoscope instead of clip art. GRAPHIC EDITOR lets you create your *own* clip art, by using a joystick or the arrow keys. EXIT PRINT SHOP returns you to DOS.

Add-ons

After you buy The Print Shop, you'll also want to buy the **Graphics Library** (which includes extra clip art) and **The Print Shop Companion** (which includes extra borders, type styles, and graphics-editor commands).

NOTHING WITHOUT LABOUR.

CERTIFICATE MAKER

To print certificates, get **Certificate Maker**, published by Springboard Software. The version for the Apple 2e & 2c lists for $49.95; the version for the IBM PC lists for $59.95.

220 choices

Certificate Maker creates 220 kinds of certificates:

Love: certificate of love, sweetheart award, best kisser award

Drinking: wine taster's certificates, wine connoisseur's certificate, beer connoisseur's license

Pleasures: photographer's award, best vacation pictures award, globetrotter's certificate, party animal

Personal strengths: cheerfulness award, citizenship award, community service award, award for quitting smoking, nicest smile, outstanding attitude, coolness under pressure

Personal weaknesses: sweet tooth certificate, award for painting yourself into a corner, out on a limb, PIGSTY award (others for bad haircut, big mouth, foot in mouth, back seat driver, Mr. Know-It-All, Ms. Know-It-All, couch potato, "sticking to your guns", and worst joke)

Good work: certificate of promotion, efficiency award, hardest worker award, troubleshooter's certificate, job well done, outstanding in your field, master certificate maker, best boss award (2 versions), best secretary award (2 versions), employee of the WEEK (others for month and year)

Non-work: procrastinator's award, clock watching award, most coffee breaks award, company clown, infecting co-workers

Flops: Murphy's law degree, quack license, horrible mention, wanted, LEMON award (others for dead carp, can of worms, rude awakening, and thanks for nothing)

Family: certificate of wedded bliss, happy birthday certificate, adoption certificate, award for eating all of your yucky vegetables, greatest backyard chef, in the doghouse, best friends certificate (6 versions), DOG owner's license (others for cat and bird), ANNIVERSARY award (others for best mom, best dad, good girl, good boy, bad girl, bad boy, clean teeth, clean room, gourmet chef, and newborn baby)

School: certified idiot, class clown, diploma (3 versions), MATHEMATICS award (others for reading, writing, and computer whiz-kid), computer operator's license, certificate of SCHOLASTIC ACHIEVEMENT (others for geography skills, mathematics skills, and graduation), certificate of READING proficiency (others for writing, spelling, art, music, science, history, social studies, and physical education)

Sports: teamwork award, poor sportsmanship award, world's greatest athlete, world's worst athlete, most valuable player, least valuable player, most valuable member, marksmanship award, fishing award, skiing award, gymnastics award (4 versions), GOLFING award (others for bowling, swimming, baseball, basketball, football, soccer, hockey, tennis, racquetball, and track & field, 3 versions of each)

General: driver's license, the widest thinnest tallest smallest award, honorable mention, congratulations, best suggestion, thank you, what will I be when I grow up?, most likely to . . . , award for FIRST PLACE (others for second place, third place, and best idea), certificate of MERIT (others for achievement, excellence, appreciation, recognition, attendance, membership, participation, completion, improvement, proficiency, and performance), license (3 general versions), certificate of . . . (3 general versions), award for . . . (2 general versions), award (3 general versions), also 16 general religious awards, 11 general awards for children, and 4 totally general awards

Most of those certificates include funny drawings. For example, the certificate that says "Outstanding in Your Field" includes a picture of the person in a field of grass, all alone.

Customizing the certificates

Below the certificate's title and drawing, you can write your own detailed text (using 5 type styles), followed by the date and your signature. The program even comes with some gold seals to stick on.

You have 24 choices for the certificate's border. To make the border look impressive (like money), try getting a ribbon that has green ink, or put green toner into your photocopying machine.

The program includes a database feature, so you can type a list of all your friends and send them all personalized certificates.

SOUND

Computers have become quite good at speaking.

You can also buy a talking car that tells you when it needs an oil change, a talking bathroom scale that makes cynical comments about how much your weight's gone up since yesterday, and many other talking devices. You can even buy Coke from a talking vending machine that invites you to deposit your coins and then says "Thank you".

Talking watch

Whenever I want to find out the time, I just press a button on my wrist watch, and its computer voice proudly proclaims the time in perfect English. Whenever I get lonely at night and want somebody to talk to me, I just press the watch's button and thrill to the sound of its soothing voice.

It also acts as the world's most humane alarm clock. Instead of giving an awful ring, its human voice says, "Attention, please! It's 7:30AM." Then it plays some jazzed up Bach.

If I'm still sleepy and ignore the alarm, five minutes later it will say, "Attention, please! It's 7:35AM. Please hurry." It will also subject me to some more Bach. It will keep reminding me every five minutes, until I'm awake enough to turn off the alarm.

You can buy the **Vox Watch** at Radio Shack for $39.95.

Reading to the blind

The most impressive talking device ever invented is the **Kurzweil Reading Machine**, which reads books to the blind.

It looks like a photocopying machine. Just lay a book on top of the machine, and the machine reads the book to you, even if the book is laid down crookedly and has dirt on it and has multiple columns and photos and uses weird type.

When it was invented many years ago, it used to cost $50,000. Then the price dropped to $20,000. Then the price dropped even lower, but it still costs more than the average blind person can afford. To use such a machine, you must either be rich or live near a library owning the machine.

Most blind people who are computerized use cheaper devices instead: an IBM PC clone supplemented by a scanner, voice synthesizer, and cheap software.

Can computers listen?

Though computers are good talkers, they're not good listeners.

No computer's been invented yet that will replace your secretary and let you dictate a letter to it. The computer devices currently on the market have *tiny* vocabularies, require you to pause after every word, and need to be "trained" to understand *your* accent.

Computerized music is advancing rapidly. Now you can sit down at a portable piano-style keyboard (light enough to carry in one hand), bang out a tune, feed the tune to a computer, and have the computer edit out your errors, play the tune back using the tone qualities of any instrument you wish (or even a whole orchestra), and print the score on paper.

Such developments are shaking up the entire music industry.

When you watch a TV commercial or movie, the background music that sounds like a beautiful orchestra or band is often produced by just a single person sitting at a computerized music synthesizer. The imitation of orchestral instruments is so exact that even professional musicians can't hear the difference. As a result, whole orchestras of musicians are now unemployed.

Music synthesizers come in two categories. One kind's cheap ($25 to $500) and easy to use, but produces sounds that are tinny. The other kind produces beautiful sounds but costs a lot ($500 to $20,000) and is harder to learn to master. Programmers are trying to meld those two categories together. I wish they'd hurry up!

Ultimate Music Machine

Musicians, programmers, and engineers are working together to create the Ultimate Music Machine, which makes all other musical instruments obsolete. You can buy all its parts at your local computer and music stores, but the software and hardware that connects the parts is awkward. I expect some company will eventually build an assembled version that you just plug into the wall for immediate fun.

Part 1: the tone-quality creator
The Ultimate Music Machine can imitate all other musical instruments. To make it imitate an instrument, play a few notes of that instrument into the machine's microphone. The machine makes a digital recording of the instrument, analyzes the recording, and stores the analysis on a 3½-inch floppy disk.

The machine's analysis is quite sophisticated. For example, it realizes that a violin note has a vibrato (because the violinist's finger wiggles), that each piano note begins with a bang and ends with a hum, and that the piano's bass notes sound "fatter" than the treble notes (because the bass notes are made from different kinds of strings).

The machine lets you edit the analysis, to create totally new tone qualities, such as "piolin" (which is a compromise between a piano and a violin).

When you buy the machine, it comes with recordings of the most popular instruments, and lets you add your own and edit them. It also lets you use fundamental waveforms (such as sine waves, square waves, and triangle waves), which act as building blocks for inventing sounds that are wilder.

Part 2: the note creator
The machine includes a piano-style keyboard (with black and white notes on it). To feed the machine a melody, tap the melody on the keyboard. You can also play chords. The machine notices which notes you strike the hardest, so it records your accents.

The machine includes a **pitch-bend dial**, which you turn to make the notes slide up the scale, like a slide trombone.

If you're not good at the keyboard, use the machine's screen instead, which displays a musical staff and lets you move notes onto the staff by using a mouse. You can also use the mouse to edit any errors you made on the keyboard, and to create repetitions and increase the tempo.

If you fear mice and keyboards, just sing into the machine's microphone. The machine notices which notes you've sung and records them.

If you're too lazy to create a melody or harmony, the machine creates its own. Its built-in computer analyzes your favorite music, notices its rhythms, note transitions, and harmonic structures, and then composes its own music in the same style.

Part 3: output
The machine plays the editing music through stereo speakers. As the music plays, the complete score moves across the screen, in traditional music notation. The machine also prints the score on paper. Yes, the machine prints a complete score showing how you sang into the mike or tickled the keys!

Vendors The Ultimate Music Machine is built from **music synthesizers**. The most popular synthesizers are made by four Japanese companies: **Casio, Roland, Yamaha**, and **Korg**. Their synths cost from $25 to $3000 and contain tiny computers. For extra computing power, attach a Macintosh computer by using a **Musical Instrument Digital Interface cable (MIDI cable)**. To print pretty scores cheaply, add **Deluxe Music Construction Set**, a Mac program published by Electronics Arts for under $50.

MULTIMEDIA

WHAT'S MULTIMEDIA?

Multimedia is the attempt to make your personal computer overwhelm your senses by feeding you text, music, voice, graphics, animation, and video movies on the screen all simultaneously! To do that well, you need a fast computer (at least an Intel 486 or a Mac Quadra 630) with a CD-ROM drive and some circuitry to handle sounds well.

Microsoft's most famous example of multimedia is **Microsoft Encarta**. It's a CD-ROM disk that contains the complete text of the 29-volume Funk & Wagnalls encyclopedia, supplemented by 1000 extra articles, 8 hours of sound, written & spoken samples of 60 languages, 7800 photos and illustrations, 100 animations and video clips, 800 maps, plus more. Using Encarta is fun: using your mouse, just click on whatever topic on the screen interests you and — whammo! — you see it and hear it. Discount dealers sell it for just $70.

Inspired by Encarta's success, Microsoft has gone on to develop other multimedia titles that are more specific. For example, **Cinemania** is a CD-ROM that contains over 19,000 movie reviews written by Leonard Maltin, Roger Ebert, Pauline Kael, and Baseline, plus biographies of nearly 4,000 performers and other film-biz folks, plus some photographs, audio tracks, video clips, and stills. Discount dealers sell it for just $53.

Microsoft has also done multimedia titles on topics such as Beethoven's 9th Symphony (including detailed analysis of the music, the man, and his times), Stravinsky's Rite of Spring, works by Mozart & Shubert, London's National Gallery of Art, and baseball lore.

Keep your eyes open: more multimedia is to follow!

TOOLS

Though using multimedia created by companies such as Microsoft can be fun, it's even more fun to create your own!

Most software purporting to help you create multimedia is tedious to use and expensive. But here's the exception: buy **Magic Theatre**, a CD-ROM disk published by two companies working together (**Knowledge Adventure Inc.** and **Instinct Corporation**). Comp USA sells it for just $35.

It lets you create animated cartoons with sound, so easily that you can create exciting cartoons after just a few *seconds* of preparation!

Designed for kids, you'll learn how to use it in just a few minutes.

The $35 price even includes a microphone, accompanied by a CD-ROM disk that includes lots of clip art, pre-made animated objects, music, and sound effects, which you can combine in just a few seconds to produce an on-screen animated movie that you'll like a lot better than Saturday morning cartoons — especially since *you* created it!

The cartoons you'll produce will seem child-like, but that's their charm!

Try it, you'll like it. If you have kids, the whole family can pitch in to make a family animated movie. Your neighbors will be jealous.

COMMUNICATION

TELECOMMUNICATION

To let your computer communicate with computers that are far away, connect your computer to a telephone line by using a **modem**.

Communication programs

To manage your modem, you need a disk containing a **communication program**.

The cheapest popular communication programs are **Bitcom** and **Procomm**. The typical modem manufacturer gives you the Bitcom or Procomm disk at no extra charge. When you buy Windows, you get a communication program called **Terminal** at no extra charge.

To perform extra tricks, buy a fancier communication program such as **Procomm Plus** ($65), **Procomm Plus for Windows** ($79), **Smartcom** ($100), or **Crosstalk for Windows** ($115). Those are the prices charged by discount dealers.

You get Smartcom free if you buy a modem that has the "Hayes" brand on it.

Another way to get a communication program is to buy an integrated package such as **Microsoft Works** or **First Choice**. Those integrated packages also produce word processing, databases, spreadsheets, and business graphs. Of all the communication programs, the easiest to understand is First Choice's.

Settings

To communicate with another computer, make sure that both computers are set to communicate in the same way:

Question	Possible answers	Usual answer
Which baud rate?	300, 1200, 2400, 9600, 14400, or 28800	2400
How many data bits?	7 or 8	8
What's the parity bit?	0, 1, even (E), odd (O), or none (N)	none (N)
How many stop bits?	0 or 1	1
What kind of duplex?	half-duplex (H) or full-duplex (F)	full duplex (F)
Is XON/XOFF enabled?	yes (enabled) or no (disabled)	yes (enabled)

When computer experts chat with each other about which communication method to use, they usually discuss those questions in that order. For example, if the expert's computer is typical, the expert will say "My computer communicates at 2400 8 N 1 F enabled". To communicate with that computer, you must set up your computer the same way. To do that, run the communication program, which asks you those questions and waits for you to answer. The communication program also asks you whether the modem is COM1 or COM2.

Popular online services

The most popular computer systems for Americans to communicate with are **Compuserve** (which is in Ohio and owned by H&R Block), **Prodigy** (which is in New York State and owned by IBM & Sears), and **America OnLine** (which is in Viginia, independent, and called **AOL**).

Each service charges you $9.95 per month to tap into its computers. For Prodigy and AOL, that monthly fee gets you just 5 hours of connect time per month; each additional hour costs $2.95. For Compuserve, that monthly fee gets you unlimited hours per month of Basic services, but Compuserve's Extended services can cost up to $4.80 per hour.

Each service typically gives new subscribers a special "free trial" offer, such as "the first month free" or "the first 10 hours free". For example, when you buy a modem, it usually comes with coupons giving you free trials on the three services, so you can sample the joys of telecommunication. After your free trial has ended, you get billed every month automatically on your Master Card or Visa.

Each service contains many databases you can tap into. Some of those databases are for professionals. Others are for shopping, stocks, news, airline reservations, hobbies, games, and other forms of fun.

Each service has branch offices staffed by computers in all major American cities. If you call the branch office nearest you, you'll automatically be connected to the service's headquarters at no extra charge, so you can tap into the databases without paying for any long-distance calls.

Besides letting you tap into databases, those computers let you swap information with other computerists by using **electronic mail**. For example, if you and your friend Sue both use Compuserve, Sue can send Compuserve a message addressed to you. Her message will stay on Compuserve's disk. The next time you use Compuserve, Compuserve will tell you that a message from her is waiting on Compuserve's disk. Compuserve will offer to "read" it to you, by sending it to your personal computer's screen.

By using Compuserve, you can send messages to all your computerized friends and even to strangers. Compuserve users have organized themselves into clubs, called **special interest groups (SIGs)**. Each SIG is devoted to a particular hobby, profession, or computer topic. If you join a SIG, you can read the messages sent by all other members of the SIG, and you can leave your own messages for them. Prodigy and AOL have SIGs also, but Compuserve's are the oldest and offer the most sophisticated discussions.

You can also play with the **CB Simulator**, which imitates a CB radio and lets you chat (via typed messages) with other wild people across the country. You can give yourself a fake name ("handle"), to protect your anonymity.

Compuserve users spend most of their time playing with the electronic mail, SIGs, and CB Simulator, rather than the databases.

Here's how those service arose. . . .

Compuserve was invented first. Though it had good SIGs and databases, it was somewhat complex to use and was boring: it transmitted text but no graphics.

Then came **AOL**, which was graphical and fun. At first, it ran just on Commodore 64 computers, but later it was redone for the IBM PC and Mac. On the Commodore 64, it used a joystick; on the IBM PC and Mac, it uses a mouse. It's the easiest service to use. Its popularity is growing the most rapidly. Sometimes the service gets overloaded, so when you call you get a busy signal.

Prodigy was invented last. Like a newspaper, it's financed by advertisers: while you're using Prodigy, the top part of the screen shows the information you requested, but the bottom part of the screen invites you to see ads for many products. You can ignore those invitations! Prodigy is also the most "family-oriented" service: it offers the most goodies for kids (easy databases and educational games), and it censors announcements and messages to avoid obscenities and libel suits.

By using Compuserve, Prodigy, and AOL, you can reach **information providers** such as **Dialog** (a collection of 450 databases on many subjects, plus the full text of most U.S. newspapers), **Nexis** (the full text of many U.S. newspapers and magazines), **News Net** (the full text of 800 industry newsletters and news wires, covering over 30 industries and professions), **Lexis** (the resources of approximately 50 law libraries), and **Dow Jones News/Retrieval** (business news, stock prices, and the full text of *The Wall Street Journal*).

Internet

Back when we were fighting the Cold War against Russia, the Pentagon created a computer network that so that universities could transmit research results to each other and the Pentagon even if some phone lines and buildings got bombed. That network has become civilian and is called the **Internet**.

If you're in one of those universities, you can use the Internet to send electronic mail. If you're not, join the Internet by paying money to an **Internet access provider** who hooks you up. For example, you can use America OnLine, Prodigy, or Compuserve as your Internet access provider.

Bulletin boards

A computerized **bulletin board system (BBS)** resembles Compuserve but is free. It emphasizes electronic mail, SIGs, and CB Simulators.

It's run by a hobbyist from a computer in the hobbyist's own home or office. You can swap messages with the hobbyist and all other callers on the system, as if they were pen pals. Some bulletin boards are sexually explicit (heterosexual or gay). Some of my friends met wonderful people on bulletin boards — and married them!

You can choose from *thousands* of bulletin boards around the country. To find the bulletin boards in *your* neighborhood, ask your local computer

store or computer club or school's computer department. Also look at the back pages of *Computer Shopper* magazine, where you'll see lists of thousands of bulletin boards in the United States and around the world.

These free general-purpose bulletin boards are the most popular:

Alabama: Huntsville 205-551-9004, Decatur 205-306-0486
Alaska: Anchorage 907-563-3407, Wasilla 907-376-2779
Arizona: Phoenix 602-331-1112, Paradise Valley 602-951-8379, Sun City 602-933-1205
Arkansas: Walnut Ridge 501-886-1701
California, north: San Francisco 415-931-0649, Sacramento 916-727-3007, Fresno 209-277-3008, Stockton 209-943-1880, Monterey 408-655-5555, Gilroy 408-847-0665, Danville 510-743-9314, Walnut Creek 510-943-6238
California, south: Los Angeles 310-398-7804, Long Beach 310-436-1311, Manhattan Beach 310-374-9994, N. Hollywood 818-508-0214, Calabasas 818-999-1829, Poway 619-679-6915, Vista 619-749-2741, Capistrano Beach 714-493-4779, Fullerton 714-529-9525, Irvine 714-581-9699, Mission Viejo 714-837-9677, Simi Valley 805-527-4502, Riverside 909-780-5175 & 909-928-2701
Colorado: Denver 303-457-1111, Arvada 303-940-8328, Aurora 303-680-7209, Littleton 303-347-2921
Connecticut: New Haven 203-787-5460, Fairfield 203-335-4073, Guilford 203-457-1246
Delaware: Hockessin 302-234-2792
District of Columbia: Washington 202-606-8688
Florida, north: Pensacola 904-476-1270, Gainesville 904-332-9547, Crystal River 904-563-0066
Florida, south: Miami 305-242-1160 & 305-254-8441, Margate 305-977-0098, Fort Myers 813-481-5575 & 813-574-2301, New Port Richey 813-849-4034, Stuart 407-692-9649, Oviedo 407-359-0167
Georgia: Savannah 912-353-8014, Tybee Island 912-786-5888, Flower Branch 404-967-2200
Hawaii: Honolulu 808-737-2665, Wahiawa 808-624-1527, Hilo 808-935-3148
Idaho: Emmett 208-365-5223, Meridian 208-887-4752, Twin Falls 208-734-6592
Illinois: Chicago 312-384-6250 & 312-769-1323, Bolingbrook 708-230-9068, Glenview 708-724-2449, Northfield 708-501-4851, Crystal Lake 815-459-0825, Champaign-Urbana 217-255-9000
Indiana: Indianap. 317-293-8630, Ft. Wayne 219-456-4127, S. Bend 219-272-8129, Evansville 812-424-1099
Iowa: Ames 515-232-0969, Osage 515-732-4555
Kansas: Topeka 913-234-9395 & 913-478-9239, Wichita 316-529-8880
Kentucky: Fort Knox 502-942-0089 & 502-352-2169, Betsy Layne 606-478-1503
Louisiana: New Orleans 504-885-5928, Baton Rouge 504-273-3238, Lafayette 318-988-5558
Maine: Lewiston 207-783-0874, Rockland 207-594-7025, Cape Elizabeth 207-799-9080
Maryland: Rockv. 301-738-9060, Silver Spr. 301-933-5193, Chest'n 410-778-9688, Odenton 410-360-4639
Massachusetts: Plymouth 508-746-6010 & 508-833-0508, Chelmsford 508-256-1434, Haverhill 508-521-6941, Kingston 617-582-2223, Wilbraham 413-599-0981
Michigan: Mt. Clemens 810-469-8461, Freeland 517-695-9952, Traverse City 616-275-7000
Minnesota: Bloomington 612-835-0440, Chaska 612-442-5635, Little Falls 612-632-4513
Mississippi: Columbus 601-329-3247, Starkville 601-323-2120
Missouri: St. Louis 314-427-2509, Columbia 314-446-0475, Cameron 816-632-3297
Montana: Missoula 406-549-6325
Nebraska: Omaha 402-734-4748 & 402-453-5356 & 402-496-9987, Bellevue 402-293-0984
Nevada: Las Vegas 702-222-0409 & 702-386-7979
New Hampshire: Newton 603-642-5949, Raymond-Kingston 603-895-9916
New Jersey, north: Union City 201-863-5253, Bayonne 201-437-2816, New Milford 201-692-1110
New Jersey, south: Bridgeton 609-451-7950, Millville 609-327-5553, Petersburg 609-628-4311, Long Branch 908-571-4666, Metuchen 908-494-8666
New Mexico: Albuquerque 505-294-5675 & 505-275-9696, Las Vegas 505-425-6995
New York, north: Rochester 716-224-8216, Whitehall 518-499-0532, Watertown 315-786-1120
New York, south: Brooklyn 718-251-9346 & 718-972-6099, Queens 718-446-2157, Hicksville 516-433-1843, Patchogue 516-475-6406, Mt. Vernon 914-667-4567, Mt. Kisco 914-242-8227
North Carolina: Rockingham 910-895-0368, Sanford 919-776-2368
North Dakota: Bismarck 701-258-0872, Fargo 701-293-0207, Grand Forks 701-594-6677 & 795-9730
Ohio: Cleveland 216-235-9900, Cincinnati 513-231-9463
Oklahoma: Oklahoma City 405-672-5893, Ponca City 405-765-6469, Stillwater 405-377-4286
Oregon: Portland 503-232-9202 & 503-253-9014, Corvallis 503-758-5448
Pennsylvania: Philadelphia 215-535-6579 & 215-657-8470, Feasterville 215-357-8177, Allentown 610-740-9196, Bloomsburg 717-387-1725, Erie 814-825-8660
Rhode Island: Middletown 401-848-9069
South Carolina: Lexington 803-359-5646, North Charleston 803-552-4389
South Dakota: Sioux Falls 605-331-5831
Tennessee: Sevierville 615-577-9342, Adamsv. 901-632-1947, Memphis 901-377-5715
Texas: Dallas 214-644-6060, Corpus Christi 512-242-2206, Lubbock 806-745-9144, Midland-Odessa 915-561-5115, Lufkin 409-634-6899
Utah: Brigham City 801-723-6117, Salt Lake City 801-532-3716 & 801-264-1191
Vermont: Williamstown 802-433-1367
Virginia: Arlington 703-241-8757, Reston 703-620-8900, Falmouth 703-899-2285, Chesap. 804-523-6681
Washington: Olympia 206-956-1123, Gig Harbor 206-884-5364, Sequim 206-681-2706, Grandview 509-882-1417, Walla Walla 509-529-3726
West Virginia: Fairmont 304-363-2252, Weirton 304-723-2133
Wisconsin: Milwaukee 414-384-1055, Madison 608-274-7483, Ashland 715-682-3929
Wyoming: Sheridan 307-672-3817, Rock Springs 307-382-2907 & 307-382-6127, Casper 307-237-7016

Puerto Rico: San Juan 809-273-3531, Hormigueros 809-849-5921
Canada: Ottawa (Ontario) 613-226-3423, Vancouver (British Columbia) 604-572-8213, Regina (Saskatch.) 306-352-9378, Chateauguay (Quebec) 514-692-3264, Sydney (Nova Scotia) 902-567-3948
Mexico: Mexico City 52-5-659-7678, Monterrey 52-8-356-8446, Chihuahua 52-14-16-3194
Europe: Rome (Italy) 39-6-322-4037, Milano (Italy) 39-11-331-06044, Saint-Firmin (France) 33-92-553-288, Tilburg (Netherlands) 31-13-681-825, East Harling (United Kingdom) 44-953-717234

Smiley's pals

Here's a picture of a smiling face:

:)

It's called a **smiley**. If you rotate that face 90°, it looks like this:

:-)

People who chat on bulletin boards often type that symbol to mean "I'm smiling; I'm just kidding".

For example, suppose you want to tell President Clinton that you disagree with his speech. If you communicate the old-fashioned way, with pencil and paper, you'll probably begin like this:

Dear Mr. President,
     I'm somewhat distressed at your recent policy announcement.

But people who communicate by electronic mail tend to be more blunt:

Hey, Bill!
     You really blew that speech. Jeez! Your policy stinks. You should be boiled in oil, or at least paddled with a floppy disk. :-)

The symbol ":-)" means "I'm just kidding". That symbol's important. Forgot to include it? Then poor Bill — worried about getting boiled in oil — might have the FBI arrest you for plotting an assasination.

The smiley, ":-)", has many variations:

Symbol	Meaning
:-)	I'm smiling.
:-(	I'm frowning.
:-<	I'm real sad.
:-c	I'm bummed out.
:-C	I'm REALLY bummed out!
:-I	I'm grim.
:-/	I'm skeptical.
:->	I have a devilish grin.
:-D	I'm laughing.
:-o	I'm shouting.
:-O	I'm shouting really loud.
:-@	I'm screaming.
:-8	I talk from both sides of my mouth.
:-p	I'm sticking my tongue out at you.
:-P	I'm being tongue-in-cheek.
:-&	I'm tongue-tied.
:-9	I'm licking my lips.
:-*	My lips pucker for a kiss or pickle.
:-x	My lips are sealed.
:-#	I wear braces.
:-$	My mouth is wired shut.
:-?	I smoke a pipe.
:-)	I have a beard.
:-B	I have buck teeth.
:-[	I'm a vampire.
:-{)	I wear lipstick.
:-()	I have a moustache.
:-~)	My nose runs.
:-)~	I'm drooling.
:-)-8	I have big breasts.
:*)	I'm drunk.
:^)	My nose is broken.
:~i	I'm smoking.
:/i	No smoking!
:~j	I'm smoking and smiling.
:'-(	I'm crying.
:'-)	I'm so happy, I'm crying.
:)	I'm a midget.
;-)	I'm winking.
.-)	I have just one eye,
,-)	but I'm winking it.
?-)	I have a black eye.
8-)	I wear glasses.
B-)	I wear cool shades, man.
%-)	My glasses broke.
g-)	I wear pince-nez glasses.
P-)	I'm a pirate.
O-)	I'm a scuba diver.
|-O	I'm yawning.
|^O	I'm snoring.
X-(	I just died.
8:-)	My glasses are on my forehead.
B:-)	My sunglasses are on my forehead.
O:-)	I'm an angel.
+:-)	I'm a priest.
[:-)	I'm wearing a Walkman.
&:-)	I have curly hair.
@:-)	I have wavy hair.
8:-)	I have a bow in my hair.
(:-)	I wear a toupee,
):-)	but the wind is blowing it off.
-:-)	I'm a punk rocker,
-:-(	but real punk rockers don't smile.
3:]	I'm your pet,
3:[	but I growl.
}:->	I'm being devilish,
>;->	and lewdly winking.
=:-)	I'm a hosehead.
E-:-)	I'm a ham radio operator.
C=:-)	I'm a chef.
=|:-)=	I'm Uncle Sam.
<):-)	I'm a fireman.
*<:-)	I'm Santa Claus.
*:o)	I'm Bozo the clown.
<:I	I'm a dunce.

Since those symbols are pictures (icons) that help you emote, they're called **emoticons** (pronounced "ee MOTE ee cons").

Downloading

Some bulletin boards contain software you can copy freely (since the software is freeware or shareware).

Copying from the bulletin board to your own computer is called **downloading**. If you write your own software and want to contribute it to the bulletin board, you **upload** the software to the bulletin board.

Barriers

Although Compuserve and bulletin boards can be fun, two barriers prevent them from being used by the average American.

1. If you want to find a particular piece of information, you'll have a hard time figuring out which database to contact and how to extract the information from it.

2. Typing messages to people is tedious and impersonal. (I'd rather chat on the phone. Most people can chat faster than they can type.)

Voice mail

Engineers are developing **voice mail**. It lets you record your voice onto a computer disk, so that other computerists can retrieve it. It acts as a high-tech answering machine.

Unfortunately, a voice-mail message consumes lots of disk space; but as disks continue to get cheaper, the price problem will go away.

How to use Terminal

When you buy Windows, you get some **accessories** at no extra charge. In the Windows chapter, I explained how to use five of those accessories: Clock, Calculator, Write, Paintbrush, and Calendar. Here's how to use the other popular accessory, **Terminal**, which is a communications program. I'll explain the version that comes with Windows 3.1.

Turn on the computer without any floppy in drive A. Start Windows (by typing "win" after the C prompt). The computer will say "Program Manager".

Double-click the Accessories icon. Double-click the **Terminal icon**.

(If nobody has used Terminal on your computer before, the computer will ask which COM port your modem uses. Click the answer. If you're not sure, try COM2.)

You'll see the **Terminal window**. Maximize it by clicking ▲.

While you're using Terminal, the top of the screen shows this menu bar:

```
File  Edit  Settings  Phone  Transfers  Help
```

Settings menu Click the word **Settings**. You'll see this **Settings menu**:

```
Phone Number...
Terminal Emulation...
Terminal Preferences...
Function Keys...
Text Transfers...
Binary Transfers...
Communications...
Modem Commands...
Printer Echo
Timer Mode
Show Function Keys
```

From that Settings menu, choose **Phone Number**.

Type the phone number of the computer you want to chat with. For example, if you want to chat with Microsoft's bulletin board system, type this:

```
1-206-637-9009
```

(Since the computer ignores the hyphens, you can type just 12066379009 instead.)

If you're making a long-distance call, remember to type the 1 at the beginning of the phone number.

If you're sitting in an office whose phone system requires you to dial 9 to get an outside line, put 9 and a comma at the beginning of the phone number, like this:

```
9,1-206-637-9009
```

The comma makes the computer wait 2 seconds for an outside line before dialing the rest of the phone number.

At the end of the phone number, press the ENTER key.

Choose **Communications** from the Settings menu. You'll see the **Communications window**. Here's how to use it. . . .

In the **Connector box**, click COM2 if your modem is using COM2. (Most modems use COM2. If your modem uses COM1 instead, click COM1.)

In the **Baud Rate box**, you'll see this list of baud rates: 110, 300, 600, 1200, 2400, 4800, 9600, 19200. Click the baud rate you want to communicate at. For example, if you have a 2400-baud modem and you want to communicate to a computer that has a 2400-baud modem, click 2400. (If your computer's modem has a different speed than the other computer's modem, click the LOWER baud rate. If you have a 14400-baud modem, too bad: since 14400-baud isn't on the list of choices, choose 9600-baud instead.)

When you finish using the Communications window, press the ENTER key.

Congratulations! Now you've fed the proper settings to your computer! You're ready to dial the other computer! Here's how. . . .

Phone menu From the **Phone menu**, choose **Dial**. Your computer's modem will dial the phone number you requested.

On the screen, you'll see ATDT and the phone number being dialed. For example, if you said to dial "9,1-206-637-9009", you'll see:

```
ATDT9,12066379009
```

When your modem finishes dialing the number, you'll see what happens.

If the computer you're communicating to doesn't answer the phone, and the phone just rings & rings, your modem will give up after 30 seconds and say "NO CARRIER".

If the computer you're communicating to is busy chatting with somebody else, the phone number you're dialing will give a busy signal, and your screen will say "BUSY".

If the computer you're communicating to is in a good mood and DOES answer the phone successfully, your screen will say "CONNECT". Then go ahead and chat with that computer! That computer will ask you questions; remember to press the ENTER key at the end of each answer. When you finish chatting with that computer, say "bye" or "goodbye" or "logoff" or "logout" or whatever other word that computer requires. That's called **logging out**; it makes the other computer hang up its phone. Your screen will say "NO CARRIER". Then YOU must hang up YOUR phone too, by choosing **Hangup** from the Phone menu. Your screen will say "ATH" and "OK".

Call waiting

If you ordered "call waiting" from your local phone company, turn off the call-waiting feature before using your modem (to prevent you and your modem from getting interrupted by an incoming call that goes "beep"). Here's how to turn off the call-waiting feature. . . .

From the Settings menu, choose **Modem commands**. In the **Dial Prefix** box, change "ATDT" to "ATDT*70". Then press ENTER.

That turns off the call-waiting feature temporarily, until your modem finishes chatting with the other computer.

Touch-tone versus pulse

Terminal assumes you have the most modern kind of phone: a touch-tone phone! That's the kind of phone on which each button makes a unique sound, and each sound has a different pitch.

If you have an older phone instead, it uses **pulse** instead of touch-tone. The typical pulse phone has a rotary dial; to dial a number, you rotate the dial, which makes a series of clicks.

If you have one of those old, pulse phones, you must warn the computer. Here's how. From the Settings menu, choose Modem commands. In the Dial Prefix box, change "ATDT" to "ATDP".

Graphics

To let the other computer send you graphics (such as a box surrounding some text), do this: from the Settings menu, choose **Terminal Preferences**. Then on the keyboard, press F then T (so that in the Terminal Font box, "Terminal" is highlighted instead of "Fixedsys"). Then press ENTER.

Save settings

Here's how to make your computer memorize the phone number, baud rate, and other settings you chose from the Settings menu.

From the **File menu**, choose **Save**. Invent a name for your settings; the name can be up to 8 characters long. For example, the name can be GOODSET or PHONEJIM or any other short name you wish to invent. Type the name you've invented. At the end of the name, press the ENTER key.

The computer will copy your settings onto the hard disk. For example, if you chose the name GOODSET, the computer create a file called GOODSET.TRM in your WINDOWS folder and will copy all your settings to that file.

Exit

When you finish using Terminal, choose **Exit** from the File menu. If you haven't saved your most recent settings, the computer will ask, "Do you want to save?" If you don't want to save them, click the "No" button.

Then the Terminal window will disappear. You'll see the Accessories window of Program Manager again.

Open

In the future, when you use Terminal again, here's how to use the settings you copied onto the hard disk.

From Terminal's File menu, choose **Open**. Then type the name of your settings (such as GOODSET) and press ENTER.

LOCAL-AREA NETWORKS

If you run wires between computers that are in the same office building, you're creating a **local-area network (LAN)**. Each computer in the LAN is called a **node**.

For the IBM PC and clones, you can create four kinds of LANs. Here they are, beginning with the fanciest and most expensive.

Server LANs

A **server LAN** consists of one main computer (called the **server**) wired to several lesser computers (called **workstations**).

A special person (called the **network supervisor**) tells the server how to act. Other office workers (called **users**) sit at the workstations.

The server's hard disk contains a database that all the workstations can access. The server's high-quality high-speed printer can print whatever the workstations tell it to.

Each workstation uses MS-DOS, but the server uses a different operating system instead that runs faster. The server's operating system is called the **network operating system (NOS)**.

Netware The most popular NOS is **Netware**, published by **Novell**. The newest version is **Netware 4.1**, but some folks still use **Netware 3.12**. Here are the prices charged by discount dealers:

Number of users	Netware 3.12 price	Netware 4.1 price
5	$579	$609
10	$1349	$1389
25	$1959	$2049
50	$2679	$2779
100	$3600	$4090
250	$6766	$8689
500		$14595
1000		$26539

Those are the prices charged by discount dealers such as **Network Express** (1611 Northgate Blvd., Sarasota FL 34234, phone 800-374-9899 or 813-359-2876), **Insight** (800-927-2904), and **Computer Discount Warehouse** (800-726-4CDW).

Netware can be complex. For example, the infamous version 2.15C came on about 40 floppy disks, accompanied by 20 manuals! Newer versions let you do more tricks than earlier versions and are also easier to install; for example, you can get version 4.1 on CD-ROMs instead of floppies. Nevertheless, the new versions are still hard enough so that the typical office buying Netware pays the computer store to send a technician to the office to set up the network. The technician typically spends an entire afternoon to get the installation started, then leaves the computer running overnight (while Netware spends several hours formatting the server's hard disk) and comes back the next morning to finish setting up the network.

Computers The typical Novell network has slow workstations attached to a faster server.

In the early 1980's, the typical workstation contained an 8088 CPU. The server contained a 286.
In the late 1980's, the typical workstation contained a 286 CPU. The server contained a 386.
In the early 1990's, the typical workstation contained a 386 CPU. The server contained a 486.
In the late 1990's, the typical workstation contains a 486 CPU. The server contains a Pentium.

The server also contains a big RAM and a big hard drive. Now (in the late 1990's) the typical server contains at least 16M of RAM and a 1-gigabyte hard drive.

Cables To form a Novell network, connect all the computers in the network by using **thin Ethernet cables**. Each cable is typically 25 feet long and costs $15.

Run a thin Ethernet cable from the first computer to the second computer, then run a cable from the second computer to the third, then from the third computer to the fourth, etc.

Make the server be one of the computers in the middle of that chain of cables. All the other computers in the chain are the workstations.

At each end of the entire chain, you must put a **cable terminator** ($3 each).

Network cards Into each of the network's computers, you must insert an **Ethernet network adapter card**. It's a printed-circuit card to which you attach the thin Ethernet cables. It costs about $100.

How the network works Each user sits at a workstation. When the user turns on the workstation's power, the workstation asks for the user's name (and maybe a password). Typing the name and password is called **logging on to the network**.

After the user logs on, the user's workstation accepts normal MS-DOS commands, just as if the user weren't on a network.

For example, if the workstation contains two floppy disk drives, they're called A and B, and the user can find out what's on drive A by typing "dir A". If the workstation contains a hard drive, that drive is called C. But if the user tells the workstation to get a file from "drive F", the workstation will get that file from the *server*'s hard drive, by using the network. The server is everybody's "drive F". For example, to find out what files are on the server, the user gets a directory of those files by typing "dir f".

Passwords and other security measures prevent any individual user from messing up the important files on the server. The network also prints reports saying how much time each user has been spending on the network.

That's how the typical Novell network acts, but *your* Novell network might be set up to use a different letter than F. If the letter F bothers you (because it reminds you of sex), you can set up the network so that the server's hard disk is called "G" instead.

Total cost To create a 25-user Novell network, you face many costs.

First, buy Netware (for $1959 or $2049). Next, spend many thousands of dollars to buy a server and 25 workstations. For those 26 computers, buy 26 network cards (about $100 each), 26 cables (at $15 each), and 2 cable terminators ($3 each). Pay several thousands dollars for the labor of installing Netware on the server, fiddling with each workstation's AUTOEXEC.BAT, inserting the 26 network cards, stringing the 26 cables so that nobody trips on them (you might have to punch holes through your office's walls and floors!), buying **network versions** of all the programs you want to use on the network, and training all the users.

Hey, nobody said progress was cheap!

Since installing a Novell network is so expensive, don't do it unless you have no other choice. Let's look at some cheaper alternatives. . . .

Peer-to-peer networks

A **peer-to-peer network** is a network in which more than one computer can act as a server. In a peer-to-peer network, every computer can be given the ability to send files directly to every other computer. Since each computer runs ordinary MS-DOS (instead of a special server DOS such as Netware), the network runs more slowly than a server network but is more flexible.

The best and most popular peer-to-peer network is **Lantastic**, invented by **Artisoft**. Lantastic comes in three versions.

The fancy version uses thin Ethernet cables and Ethernet network cards — just like Novell. But instead of using a "server" and Netware, it uses the **Lantastic operating system**, which is much easier to install (it comes on just one floppy disk!) and costs less.

Discount dealers sell a 2-user starter kit for about $500. That price includes the Lantastic operating system, networking hardware (thin Ethernet cables, terminators, and Ethernet network cards), and manuals to hand the 2 users. Your only additional expense is the labor of installing it all, which is easy!

Ethernet transmits data at a speed of 10 megabits per second. (That's 10 million electric signals per second.) If you don't need that much speed, you can save money by getting a 2-megabit-per-second version of Lantastic; its 2-user starter kit costs just $359.

Zero-slot LANs

To cut your cost even further, buy a LAN that doesn't need a network card — and therefore doesn't need a slot to put the network card into. That kind of LAN is called a **zero-slot LAN**. To attach the LAN's cable to the computer, plug the cable into the computer's **parallel printer port** or RS-232 serial port.

Unfortunately, a zero-slot LAN handles just one pair of users — just 2 computers. The hardware setup is so easy: just run the cable from one computer's port to the other computer's port!

The most popular zero-slot LANs are **Lantastic Z** and **Desklink**. Discount dealers sell each for about $90.

Desklink comes with a serial cable (to plug into the serial ports). Since the main part of the serial cable is an ordinary phone cord, you can run Desklink even between computers that are many yards apart: just buy a longer phone cord or an extension cord from your local phone store (such as AT&T or Radio Shack). Unfortunately, it works slowly: just 0.1 megabits per second.

Lantastic Z uses that same kind of serial cord (at the same speed) but also includes an 18-foot parallel cable, which you can use instead for faster transmission. But even if you use the parallel cable, the transfer rate will be much slower than the network-card versions of Lantastic.

File transfer programs

To pay even less, get a **file transfer program**. The most popular one is **Laplink**, from the makers of Desklink. Discount dealers sell it for just $99. It includes a **universal cable** that you can attach to either serial or parallel ports.

Even easier to use than Desklink, Laplink is a program that shows you which files are on each computer's hard disk and lets you copy files from one computer to the other. Laplink's only purpose is to copy files. If you're sitting at computer A and you want to run a program on computer B's hard disk, Desklink lets you run it immediately; Laplink requires that you copy the program to your own hard disk first.

Laplink's main competitors are **The Brooklyn Bridge** ($75 from discount dealers) and **Paranet Turbo** (just $55 from the publisher, Nicat Marketing Corp., 207-788 Beatty St., Vancouver BC V68 2M1 Canada, phone 604-681-3421).

Good dealers

If you're near Boston and want to install a Novell or Lantastic network, you can get help from a dealer called **Aegis** (in Watertown at 617-923-2500). The Aegis employees are friendly and competent. They usually charge just $65 per hour.

Another Boston-area company to explore is **Synaxis** (in Needham Heights at 617-449-4400). It has more experience and knowledge about setting up big Novell networks for law offices and banks. It charges about $90 per hour.

For advice about setting up big Novell networks for law offices, phone **Krantz-Woodland Technologies** at 617-266-1031. It's a consulting company that gives good advice about how to save money and grief when buying and installing computers, networks, and law software. It operates from the home of Roy Krantz, who's an old buddy of mine. He's taught many courses with me. In his previous life, he founded a company called "Digicom Computers", which merged into "Compuware Services", which changed its name to "Synaxis", from which Roy departed to found Krantz-Woodland Technologies.

If you're in another part of the world, ask around to find the best network dealer near you. If you have any experiences to share, please tell me!

Instead of buying a LAN, try these cheaper ways to share. . . .

Sharing a printer

Suppose you and a colleague want to share a printer. Instead of buying a LAN, just unplug the printer's cable from one computer and reattach it to the other computer!

If you're too lazy to unplug the printer's cable, another alternative is to buy a box called an **AB switch box**, which most dealers sell for about $15. Into the box, plug the printer's cable and two cables (called "A" and "B") that go to the two computers. The switch box has a switch on it; if you flip the switch to position A, electricity flows between the printer and the computer attached to cable A; if you flip the switch to position B instead, the printer is electronically attached to B's computer.

To let *four* people share a printer, get an **ABCD switch box**, which attaches the printer to four computers called A, B, C, and D. Dealers sell it for about $20.

Hewlett-Packard, which makes the most popular laser printers, warns you that traditional switch boxes generate surges that damage laser printers. When switching, avoid damage by turning the laser printer off — or turning it off-line. Better yet, instead of using a traditional (**mechanical**) switch box, use an **electronic switch box**, which has no mechanical switches and doesn't generate any surges. The cheapest ones cost about $75.

But since you can buy a cheap laser printer (such as the Panasonic 4410) for just $599, your best bet is to buy a separate cheap laser printer for each computer and forget switch boxes and networking!

Sneaker net

Of all the networking schemes ever invented, my favorite is **sneaker net**, because it costs the least. To transfer data to your colleague's computer by using sneaker net, just copy the data onto a floppy disk, then put on your sneakers and run with your floppy to your colleague's desk!

That method is also called the **Nike net**. In Boston, it's called the **Reebok net**. Besides being free, it's also the healthiest network for you, since it gives you some exercise!

ACCOUNTING

GENERAL ACCOUNTING

In a typical store, the *employees* resell *products* to *customers* for a *profit*, after buying the products from *suppliers*.

To manage the store, you must keep track of all five concerns: your employees, products, customers, profit, and suppliers.

Each requires its own computer program. To compute what to pay your *employees*, get a **payroll program**. To monitor which *products* you have in stock, get an **inventory program**. To keep track of what your *customers* owe — how much you're supposed to receive from them — get an **accounts-receivable program**. To compute your *profits*, get a **general-ledger program**. To handle debts to your *suppliers* and figure out how much to pay, get an **accounts-payable program**.

So altogether, you need five programs: **payroll (PR)**, **inventory (INV)**, **accounts receivable (A/R)**, **general ledger (GL)**, and **accounts payable (A/P)**. Let's look at them more closely.

Payroll

The payroll program writes paychecks to your employees. It computes how much each employee earned (the employee's **gross wage**), then subtracts various **deductions**, and writes the difference (**net pay**) onto the paycheck.

It handles several kinds of deductions: the **federal withholding tax (FED)**, the **Federal Insurance Contributions Act's social-security tax (FICA SOCSEC)**, state taxes, local taxes, and payments to health and pension plans.

It prints checks to the government, to pay the taxes that were deducted and your state's unemployment insurance. At the end of each quarter and year, it fills in all the payroll-information forms that government bureaucrats require.

If the program's fancy, it counts how many employees are in each department of your company, totals how much money each department is spending for labor, and keeps track of employee vacations and attendance records.

Before buying a payroll program, check whether it includes a table that lets it automatically compute *your* state's income tax.

Inventory

The inventory program counts how many products are in stock.

It prints each product's sales history, predicts when each product will sell out, and notices which products are generating the largest profits. By analyzing all that information, it determines which products to reorder and in what quantities.

For each product it says to reorder, it prints a purchase order, to mail to the supplier. It keeps track of whether the supplier has sent the requested goods.

At the end of the year, it totals the dollar value of all the products in the inventory, to help compute the value of your business and your tax.

Accounts receivable

The accounts-receivable program computes how much each customer owes. For each customer who pays immediately, the program prints a receipt; for customers who plan to pay later, it prints a **bill** (for services) and an **invoice** (for goods).

It notices which bills and invoices have been paid. It sends **dunning notices** to the customers who are late in paying — the ones that are **past-due**. It refuses to accept orders from customers who are past-due or reaching their credit limit.

It computes a finance charge for customers who pay late. It gives discounts to customers who pay quickly or buy large quantities.

It records each customer's name, address, phone number, and buying habits, so your sales force can talk the customer into buying even more. It records your salesperson's name, and computes the salesperson's commission.

Before your company services a customer, the program gives the customer a written estimate of the cost.

General ledger

The general-ledger program computes the company's profit, by combining info from the other five programs. It prints a variety of profit reports for your stockholders, bank, financial planners, and government. The reports show the results for the day, week, month, quarter, and year.

It tracks each department's budget, to make sure that no department spends too much. To protect your money from being stolen or embezzled or lost, the program performs **double-entry bookkeeping**: whenever it credits money to one account, it debits the same amount of money from another account, so that the books balance.

If the program's fancy, it stores your business's history for the last several years. It compares your current profit against earlier profits, and each current budget item against previous budgets. It tells how much your business is improving or declining. It even tries to predict your business's future.

Accounts payable

The accounts-payable program prints checks to your suppliers, to pay for the products they sent you.

The program delays payment as long as a supplier allows, so that you can temporarily invest that money in your own business, without requiring bank loans. That's called, "making full use of the supplier's line of credit".

The program stores each supplier's name, address, phone number, product line, and discount policy, so that you can purchase easily and wisely.

Which accounting package to buy

I have not yet found an accounting package that I really like. Each accounting package has its own headaches.

Old generation Of all the cheap general accounting packages for the IBM PC, the most famous is **Dac Easy Accounting**. It lists for $149.95; discounters sells it for $80. That price includes everything except payroll, which costs extra. Version 4.0 was full of bugs, but version 4.0.3 and later are okay.

To pay even less, get its little sister, **Dac Easy Light** ($69.95 list, $42 from discounters). It's the only accounting package that's easy to start using. It's much easier than Dac Easy Accounting!

Unfortunately, Dac Easy Light has many limitations. For example, it doesn't handle payroll or inventory. It can't handle large companies, since it limits most of its database files to 500 records each. It doesn't print well on laser printers, though it handles dot-matrix printers fine. Its instruction manual is too brief: it doesn't explain advanced topics.

If you use Dac Easy Accounting or Dac Easy Light to print invoices, the invoices will be ugly. For example, if somebody buys 4 sweaters from you, the invoice will not say that the quantity sold is 4; instead it will say that the quantity sold is 4.00.

If you have a Mac, do *not* buy the Mac version of Dac Easy Light! The Mac version is poorly designed and much harder to use than the IBM PC version.

If you're looking for an accounting package that's *pleasant*, try **Money Matters**. You can get it for just $32 from discount dealers such as PC Connection. It comes with a very warmly written manual that guides you through the process very well. It understands 13 kinds of businesses and comes already set up for them. It's harder to learn than Dac Easy Light but can perform a greater variety of tasks and do a deeper analysis of your business activities. It can produce three kinds of invoices: "inventory based" (showing quantity sold and how many items are on backorder), "service based" (for doctors and other service providers), and "professional letter" (to print on letterhead stationery). They look great! Money Matters also lets you construct your own databases of computerized "file cards" on which you can store notes about job costs, vehicle repair records, or anything else you wish — and those databases will work in conjunction with all the rest of your accounting.

As your business grows, you'll eventually outgrow Money Matters. Then you can step up to a fancier version called **One-Write Plus**, which is much harder to learn but can handle companies that are larger and more complex. It lists for $299; discounters sells it for $159.

Unfortunately, Money Matters and One-Write Plus suffer from this peculiarity: whenever you type an amount of money or a phone number, your screen will look nutty until you finish typing all the digits. For example, when you try to type $6.25 (by pressing 6 then 2 then 5), you'll see $_.__ then $_.6 then $_.62 then finally $6.25. To avoid going nuts, avoid looking at the screen until you finish typing!

Another fine package, which unfortunately costs much more, is **Businessworks PC**. It lists for $795. It can handle accounting situations that are more complex and advanced than the other programs I've listed.

New generation Recently, a new generation of accounting packages has arisen. They're very popular because they're easy to use.

The most popular and easiest to use of the new generation is **Quickbooks**. You can get it for just $82 from discounters. Add $25 if you also want **Quickpay**, which does payroll. Unfortunately, Quickbooks doesn't keep track of inventory. It runs under MS-DOS.

The next step up is **MYOB**, which stands for "Mind Your Own Business". MYOB is somewhat harder than Quickbooks but performs a greater variety of accounting tasks. It was originally written for the Mac, but now you can also buy a Windows version. Discounters sell each version for about $110.

Two kinds of accounting

There are two ways to do accounting: **conservative** and **cowboy**.

The conservative way is to do double-entry bookkeeping, which records each transaction as a "credit" to one account and a "debit" from an offsetting account. That forces the books to balance and prevents any department from going over budget or stealing money.

All "professional" accountants use that conservative method. But it's tedious and hard for a novice to fully understand.

If the company is small enough so that the president knows all the employees personally, watches their work, personally approves all payments, and has a good gut feel for how the business is doing, the conservative "double-entry" method is an unnecessary waste of time. Instead, the president can simply total all the payments that the company received, total all the checks that the company wrote, total the value of the inventory, and report those totals to the government at tax time — after breaking down those totals into the subcategories that the government requires. The president can do all that easily with a pocket calculator or a spreadsheet program (such as Lotus 1-2-3). That approach is called **cowboy**, because it's quick but suffers from a dangerous lack of controls.

Most small companies having fewer than 10 employees use that cowboy approach — and so do I! That approach is reasonable only if the president is personally involved in all facets of the company's day-to-day operations and has enough common-sense wisdom to compensate for a lack of computer-generated analyses.

Accounting hassles

Although some companies use standard accounting packages such as Dac, Money Matters, One-Write Plus, and Businessworks PC, most do not, for four reasons.

1. To use those accounting packages, you must understand the theory of debits and credits, which is complicated.

2. Those accounting packages work best if your company's an intermediary that buys from manufacturers and resells to stores.

If you run a retail store in which most customers pay cash, you'll complain that the accounting packages don't automate your cash register or automatically copy data from the cash register slips to the sales records and inventory module. If you run a non-profit organization, you'll dislike how the accounting packages keep bragging about your "profit" instead of how much you're "under budget". If you run a doctor's office, you'll regret that the accounting packages don't record your patient's medical histories and needs, don't fill in the forms that your patient's insurance companies require, and can't handle multiple payers (in which the patient pays part of the bill and several insurance companies split the rest of the bill). If you run a consulting firm that dispenses services rather than goods, you typically won't need inventory or accounts-payable modules, and many items in the other modules will be irrelevant.

3. Each company does business in its own unique way, whose peculiarities can't be handled well by any general-purpose accounting package.

For example, your company may have a unique way of offering discounts to customers. To make the computer automatically compute those special discounts, you must write your own program; but then you'll have difficulty making your program transfer that discount information to the accounting package you bought.

Because of each company's uniqueness, the typical company avoids generic accounting packages and instead hires a programmer to write a customized program, by using a language such as BASIC or DBASE.

4. General-purpose accounting packages print standard reports but don't let you invent your own. Instead of using the reports generated by general-purpose accounting packages, many managers prefer to design their *own* reports, by copying the company's data into a spreadsheet program (such as 1-2-3) or data-management system (such as Q&A or DBASE) and then "fiddling around" until the report looks pretty. General-purpose accounting packages don't let you fiddle.

If you have just one accounting problem to solve, you can buy a simple, pleasant program to solve that problem.

Quicken

To balance your checkbook, get **Quicken**. It can also write the checks and report how much money you've spent in each budget category.

You can get Quicken for MS-DOS, Windows, the Mac, and Apple 2. Discount dealers sell each version for about $40.

Taxes

For help in completing your 1040 Federal Income Tax form and all the associated schedules (A, B, C, D, E, etc.), get **Turbo Tax** ($39 from discounters) or **Andrew Tobias's Tax Cut** ($45 from discounters). Turbo Tax gets you through the computations faster. Andrew Tobias's Tax Cut dishes out more personal advice.

Home finances

To help keep track of your mortgage, life insurance, stocks, credit-card bills, and other aspects of modern consumerism, get **Andrew Tobias's Managing Your Money** ($43 from discounters).

Besides doing accounting, it also dishes out advice on how you should invest your money. To determine your life-insurance needs, it asks lots of questions about your lifestyle and predicts when you'll die! Try it: buy the program and find out when the computer says you'll croak.

Mail Order Wizard

If you're running a moderately large mail-order company, get a program called **Mail Order Wizard**. It handles order fulfillment well: it makes sure the goods are in stock, automatically computes the shipping charges (based on the weight of the goods and the packaging), bills the customers, and keeps track of which ads and catalogs are the most profitable. It also has built-in morality: if an item is out of stock for more than 30 days, it automatically sends a notice to all customers who ordered the item and offers to cancel their orders and refund their money.

It's published by **Haven Corporation**, a 17-person organization run by Bruce Holmes who, like me, gives 24-hour free help and has a strange sense of humor; it's the only accounting program that makes you laugh while you're installing it. You also get a helpful newsletter that teaches you mail-order tricks, and the company runs a cheery annual conference where users get together and swap tricks about computers and the mail-order biz.

Mail Order Wizard is used by the mail-order divisions of many famous organizations, such as Ben & Jerry's Ice Cream, Famous Amos Cookies, Magellan Travel, the Frank Lloyd Wright Foundation, and the MIT Bookstore.

I became aware of this program when my brother Dan and his wife Linda discovered it, bought it, got thrilled, and dumped all the other accounting programs they'd been using. Now they're rich — their Eagle America router-bit company has become a multi-million-dollar mail-order business.

I'm still poor. Gee, maybe I should be using Mail Order Wizard too!

Unfortunately, Mail Order Wizard handles just one accounting task: order fulfillment. It does *not* deal with payroll and other overhead expenses. Its keystrokes are non-standard, though you get clear instructions on how to master them.

It can handle big mailing lists (up to 4 million customers) and big mail-order catalogs (advertising up to 5400 products).

It's a bit pricey: $1895 for one computer, $2995 for a 2-computer network, $3995 for a 4-computer network, $5495 for an 8-computer network, and $6995 for an unlimited network.

If you can't afford $1895, buy a stripped-down version:

Version	What it can handle		Price
Wiz Kid	5,000 customers	80 products	$495
Wiz Kid Plus	10,000 customers	200 products	$995
Wizard Apprentice	20,000 customers	5400 products	$1495
Wizard	4,000,000 customers	5400 products	$1895

The Wizard can do credit-card approvals by modem; the stripped-down versions cannot. The Wizard and the Wizard Apprentice include the UPS manifest system (software that simplifies paperwork for shipping by UPS); the Wiz Kid and the Wiz Kid Plus do not.

For more info (or a $20 demo disk), contact Haven Corporation at 1227 Dodge Ave., Evanston IL 60202-1008; phone 800-676-0098 or 708-869-3553.

PERSONAL PROGRAMS

ANALYZE YOURSELF

The computer can analyze your body and mind.

Death

Terrence Lukas wrote a program that predicts when you'll die. The program makes the computer ask for your age and sex; then it asks about the life and health of your parents and grandparents, your weight, your personal habits (smoking, drinking, exercise, and sleep), your history of medical check-ups, your social class (your education, occupation, and income), and your lifestyle: urban or rural, single or married, aggressive or passive, and whether you use seat belts. The computer combines all that information, to tell you when you'll probably die.

The program uses the latest statistics from life-insurance companies and from medical research. Lukas wrote the program at the University of Illinois Medical Center.

Running the program is fun. Each time you answer a question, the computer tells you how your answer affects its prediction. You see its prediction bob up and down, until the questions finally end, and the computer gives you its final prediction of when you'll die. It's like watching the early returns of a Presidential election, except the topic is you!

The computer pops out with surprising comments, based on the latest medical research. Here are some comments the computer prints:

Professionals usually live longer, except musicians, architects, and pharmacists. Why this is true is unknown.

Cooks, chefs, bakers, and other people who work at jobs associated with overeating have a lower life expectancy.

Adults that sleep too much use too many hours in nonphysical activity. They may be unhappy and sleep as an escape, or may be ill. Depressed people have shorter life expectancies.

Moderate drinking (up to two drinks per day) reduces stress and aids digestion. Heavy drinking, however, produces physiological damage. As for teetotalers, they may have rather rigid value systems and may undergo stress in maintaining them.

The program is on pages 34-36 of the November 1977 issue of *Kilobaud Microcomputing Magazine*.

Brainwaves

A computer has been programmed to read your mind, by analyzing your brainwaves. A newspaper article described the program dramatically: you're an airplane pilot . . . your plane is going to crash . . . but you think "Up!", and the plane automatically goes back up! . . . because the plane is run by a computer that's reading your brainwaves!

But what if the pilot is sadistic, and thinks "Down"?

Anyway, the program isn't perfected yet. When the computer tries to distinguish brainwaves that mean *up* from brainwaves that mean *down*, it gets the right answer 75% of the time. In other words, 25% of the time it goofs. I'd hate to be in a plane controlled by a computer that was having a bad day!

Recently, the U.S. Government has shifted the emphasis of this research. The new emphasis is more practical: to make the computer ring a buzzer, when the pilot's brainwaves indicate the pilot is daydreaming.

Horoscopes

If you hate horoscopes as much as I do, you'll love Adrian Thornton's program. It makes the computer print fake horoscopes. The computer asks when you were born, computes your sign, and then prints an enchanting remark.

For example, if your sign turns out to be Capricorn, the computer will print:

You are conservative and afraid of taking risks. You don't do much of anything and are lazy. There has never been a Capricorn of any importance. Capricorns should avoid standing still too long, as they tend to take root and become trees.

If you're a Virgo, the computer will print:

You are the logical type and hate disorder. This nitpicking is sickening to your friends. You are cold and unemotional and sometimes fall asleep while making love. Virgos make good bus drivers.

You'll enjoy seeing your own "horror"scope. The complete program is on pages 48-49 of the February 1979 issue of *Kilobaud Microcomputing Magazine*.

Psychotherapy

In 1966, Joseph Weizenbaum programmed the computer to act as a psychotherapist. On the keyboard, you type whatever thoughts come to your mind, and the computer will give you therapy. When typing on the terminal, feel free to use whatever words you wish — you don't have to use a "computer language".

The most amazing thing about the program is that it does a decent job of therapy, even though the computer doesn't know what you're talking about! Weizenbaum's program contains the definitions of only a handful of words; but if you use words the computer doesn't know, the computer does an amazingly good job of "faking". For example, if you say, "My junkapoo is like my iliabop", the computer will continue the conversation by asking you, "In what way?" even though the computer doesn't know what a junkapoo or an iliabop is.

Here's a conversation between his computer and a patient.

Patient:	Men are all alike
Computer:	In what way?
Patient:	They're always bugging us about something or other.
Computer:	Can you think of a specific example?
Patient:	Well, my boyfriend made me come here.
Computer:	Your boyfriend made you come here.
Patient:	He says I'm depressed much of the time.
Computer:	I am sorry to hear you are depressed.
Patient:	It's true. I am unhappy.
Computer:	Do you think coming here will help you not to be unhappy?
Patient:	I need some help, that much seems certain.
Computer:	What would it mean to you if you got some help?
Patient:	Perhaps I could learn to get along with my mother.
Computer:	Tell me more about your family.
Patient:	My mother takes care of me.
Computer:	Who else in your family takes care of you?
Patient:	My father.
Computer:	Your father.
Patient:	You are like my father in some ways.
Computer:	What resemblance do you see?
Patient:	You are not very aggressive, but I think you don't want me to notice that.
Computer:	What makes you think I am not very aggressive?
Patient:	You don't argue with me.
Computer:	Why do you think I don't argue with you?
Patient:	You are afraid of me.
Computer:	Does it please you to believe I am afraid of you?
Patient:	My father is afraid of everybody.
Computer:	What else comes to mind when you think of your father?
Patient:	Bullies.
Computer:	Does that have anything to do with the fact that your boyfriend made you come here?

Like the famous psychotherapist Carl Rogers, the computer asks probing questions that make the patient open up, but it never gives advice: the patient must discover the truth for herself.

I'll explain exactly how the program works, so you can become a psychotherapist yourself, and get hundreds of thousands of dollars by bilking your patients.

The computer begins by replacing some of the patient's words:

Typed by patient	Replacement
mom	mother
dad	father
dont	don't
cant	can't
wont	won't
dreamed	dreamt
dreams	dream
I	you@
me	you
you	I
my	your
your	my
myself	yourself
yourself	myself
I'm	you're
you're	I'm
am	are@
were	was

For example, the sentence *Well, my boyfriend made me come here* becomes *Well, your boyfriend made you come here.*

The computer hunts through the revised sentence or paragraph for one of these **keywords**. . . .

Category 8: computer, computers, machine, machines
Category 7: name
Category 6: alike, like, same
Category 5: remember
Category 4: dreamt
Category 3: dream, if
Category 2: everybody, everyone, nobody, was, your
Category 1: always
Category 0: are, are@, because, can, certainly, deutsch, espanol, francais, hello, how, I, I'm, italiano, maybe, my, no, perhaps, sorry, what, when, why, yes, you@, you're

If the computer finds *several* of those keywords, it chooses the one in the highest category; if they lie in the same category, it chooses the one the patient typed first.

Then it looks up the keyword in this phrasebook:

Patient's keyword   Computer's reply

Patient's keyword	Computer's reply
alike	In what way?
always	Can you think of a specific example?
are	
are I . . .	Why are you interested in whether I am . . . or not?
are . . .	Did you think they might not be . . . ?
are@	
are you . . .	Do you believe you are . . . ?
are	Why do you say "am"?
because	Is that the real reason?
can	
can I . . .	You believe I can . . . , don't you?
can you . . .	Whether or not you can . . . depends on you more than on me.
certainly	You seem quite positive.
computer	Do computers worry you?
computers	Do computers worry you?
deutsch	I am sorry, I speak only English.
dream	What does that dream suggest to you?
dreamt . . .	Really, . . . ?
espanol	I am sorry, I speak only English.
everybody	Really, everybody?
everyone	Really, everyone?
hello	How do you do — please state your problem.
how	Why do you ask?
I	
I remind you of	In what way?
I are . . .	What makes you think I am . . . ?
I . . . you	Why do you think I . . . you?
I	We were discussing you — not me.
if . . .	Do you think it's likely that . . . ?
I'm . . .	What makes you think I am . . . ?
italiano	I am sorry, I speak only English.
like	
(am, is, are, was) . . . like	In what way?
like	(get a different keyword)
machine	Do computers worry you?
machines	Do computers worry you?
maybe	You don't seem quite certain.
my . . .	Why are you concerned over my . . . ?
name	I am not interested in names.
no	Are you saying "no" just to be negative?
nobody	Really, nobody?
perhaps	You don't seem quite certain.
remember	
you remember . . .	Do you often think of . . . ?
do I remember . . .	Did you think I would forget . . . ?
remember	(get a different keyword)
same	In what way?
sorry	Please don't apologize.
was	
was you . . .	What if you were . . . ?
you was	Were you really?
was I . . .	Would you like to believe I was . . . ?
was	(get a different keyword)
what	Why do you ask?
when	Why do you ask?
why	
why don't I . . .	Do you believe I don't . . . ?
why can't you . . .	Do you think you should be able to . . . ?
yes	You seem quite positive.
you@	
you (want, need) . . .	What would it mean to you if you got . . . ?
you are . . . (sad, unhappy, depressed, sick)	I am sorry to hear you are (sad, etc.).
you are . . . (happy, elated, glad, better)	How have I helped you to be (happy, etc.)?
you (feel, think, believe, wish) you	Do you really think so?
you (feel, think, believe, wish) . . . I	(use the keyword "I" instead)
you are . . .	Is it because you are . . . that you came to me?
you (can't, cannot) . . .	How do you know you can't . . . ?
you don't . . .	Don't you really . . . ?
you feel	Tell me more about such feelings.
you . . . I	Perhaps in your fantasy we . . . each other.
your	
your . . . (mother, father, sister, brother, wife, children)	Tell me more about your family.
your . . .	Your . . .
you're	(treat as "you@ are")

For example, if the keyword is *sorry*, the computer looks up *sorry* in the phrasebook, which says to print "Please don't apologize."

Suppose the patient types, "If the job is lousy, he'll die." The keyword is *if*. In the phrasebook, *if* is followed by three dots, which stand for the part of the clause that comes after *if*, which is "the job is lousy". (The computer figures out where the clause ends by looking at the punctuation.) The phrasebook says to print "Do you think it's likely that the job is lousy?"

The symbol @ serves just to locate the correct keyword in the phrasebook. Thereafter, it's ignored.

Here's what happens if the keyword is *you@*. After locating *you@* in the phrasebook, the computer ignores the @. If the patient's revised sentence contains *you want* . . . or *you need* . . . , the computer prints "What would it mean to you if you got . . . ?" If the patient's sentence contains *you are* . . . *sad*, the computer prints "I am sorry to hear you are sad."

For each reply in the phrasebook, Weizenbaum stored a list of alternatives. For example, here are the alternatives to "Please don't apologize":

Apologies are not necessary.
What feelings do you have when you apologize?
I've told you that apologies are not required.

While chatting with the patient, the computer keeps track of which replies it has printed already, and uses the alternatives to avoid repetition.

If the patient's statement doesn't contain a keyword, the computer may give one of these replies:

I am not sure I understand you fully.
Please go on.
What does that suggest to you?
Do you feel strongly about discussing such things?

Or it may take a second look at earlier parts of the conversation, retrieve a clause that contained *your* . . . , and print one of these replies:

Let's discuss further why your . . . .

Earlier you said your . . . .

Does that have anything to do with the fact that your . . . ?

For example, it may retrieve the clause *Your boyfriend made you come here* and print:

Does that have anything to do with the fact that your boyfriend made you come here?

The program was written at the Massachusetts Institute of Technology (MIT). The programmer, Joseph Weizenbaum, named the program "Eliza", to honor Eliza Doolittle — the woman in *My Fair Lady* and *Pygmalion*, who learned to speak English and have a good conversation.

Some people think Weizenbaum's program shows that computers can communicate as well as psychotherapists. But Weizenbaum himself holds the opposite view; he believes the program shows that psychotherapists communicate as poorly as computers.

You can buy a disk called **Golden Oldies**, which contains imitations of four classic programs: Adventure, Pong, Life, and Weizenbaum's Eliza. The disk is published by Software Country, distributed by Electronic Arts, costs about $35, and comes in versions for the Apple 2e & 2c, Macintosh, Commodore 64, Amiga, Atari 800 XL, and IBM PC.

Improved versions
After Weizenbaum invented Eliza, other programmers invented improvements. For example, in one of the improved versions, whenever the computer doesn't understand you, it reacts like the typical rich psychotherapist — it bluffs and says:

I understand fully. Please go on.

The computer never really understands what you say. For example, in one version, if you say "My, my, my!", the computer will reply:

Tell me more about your your your.

Radio Shack's headquarters phoned me, and asked for permission to use my explanation of Weizenbaum's program. I agreed, whereupon Radio Shack invented and sold a version that makes the computer *talk* — by using a voice synthesizer. You'll freak out when you hear the computer's voice giving you therapy. Radio Shack's program costs $15, comes on tape, and requires a model 1 or model 3 TRS-80. To hear the voice, you must buy the voice synthesizer. (But even if you don't buy the voice synthesizer, the program will impress you.)

The cheapest way to get a version of Eliza is to buy a book called *BASIC Computer Games Volume 2 (TRS-80 edition)*. Get it at your local Radio Shack store. It costs just $7 and includes 84 programs — one of which is a version of Eliza written in BASIC. That version of Eliza isn't as good as the original; but since it's cheap and written in BASIC, you'll enjoy buying it for self-study. Here's part of a conversation between that version and a patient:

Patient: I am not the greatest conversationalist.
Computer: Do you believe it is normal to be not the greatest conversationalist?

Patient: Yes.
Computer: I see.

Patient: How can you see without any eyes?
Computer: Don't you believe that I can see without any eyes?

Patient: No. So prove it.
Computer: Are you saying "no" just to be negative?

Patient: Absolutely not.
Computer: You are being a bit negative.

Patient: So you want to fight, do you?
Computer: We were discussing you — not me.

Patient: Don't back down, friend.
Computer: Why do you bring up the topic of friends?

Patient: I don't have any friends.
Computer: Don't you really have any friends?

Patient: No, not really.
Computer: Why not?

Unfortunately, most versions of Eliza are passive. The typical Eliza program works well only if the patient's talkative. If the patient doesn't say much, the program can't react too much and is useless.

Recently, John Holland invented a better version of Eliza. His version's more aggressive. He calls it "Analiza 2" (because it "analizas" the patient). If the patient's too quiet or too boring or too uninformative, Analiza 2 makes the computer give the patient a "jolt", by asking an electrifying question or making a ridiculous Zen-like statement. For example, the computer might ask, "Did you ever try to commit suicide with a hammer?" Here's a list of the computer's favorite "jolts":

Nasty questions the computer asks
Did you ever try to commit suicide with a hammer?
Is your interest in sex still not very strong?
Do you want to know what I suspect?

Prying questions the computer asks
Tell me, what is your worst fear?
Why don't you tell me about your first romance?
I want to know about your lifestyle.
Tell me what is troubling you.
Honestly now, what is your biggest concern?

Ridiculous statements the computer makes
With strong drugs you can learn to control your concern!
You certainly are curious!
And you are obstinate!

Complaints the computer makes
You seem inhibited.
This isn't really very exciting.
Getting started is often difficult.

Comments the computer makes about timing and complexity
Well, time is almost up. Is there anything else you want to discuss?
I hate to bring this up, but you still owe me $53.00 from your last visit!
Last time you were extremely inquisitive. Have you abandoned seeking simple solutions?
Last time you were difficult to understand. Were you trying to confuse me?
Let's keep it simple this time.
Say, I am having trouble with your long sentences. Keep it simple. I am only human.

Yes, your patient will love to hear the computer say it's "only human". You can get Analiza 2 for $50 from Supersoft (Box 1628, Champaign, IL 61820, 217-359-2112). It runs on most computers that have the CP/M operating system.

Paranoid

What if the world becomes full of computerized psychoanalysts, and there aren't enough patients to keep them busy? Kenneth Colby solved that problem: in 1971 at Stanford University, he programmed a computer to be a crazy patient. Specifically, he programmed his computer to be a paranoid schizophrenic. In the following conversations, psychiatrists interrogate his computer.

Conversation 1

Psychiatrist:	How long have you been in the hospital?
Computer:	About a week.
Psychiatrist:	Are you depressed?
Computer:	No.
Psychiatrist:	Were you taking drugs?
Computer:	No.
Psychiatrist:	What is your problem?
Computer:	People make me nervous.
Psychiatrist:	How do they do that?
Computer:	They stare at me.
Psychiatrist:	Why?
Computer:	Maybe they don't like the way I look or something.
Psychiatrist:	Do you look unusual in some way?
Computer:	Why are you interested in my looks?
Psychiatrist:	Because you said people stare at you.
Computer:	Well, sometimes.
Psychiatrist:	How do you get along with people?
Computer:	I don't communicate very much with the others.
Psychiatrist:	Why not?
Computer:	They don't realize what's going on most of the time.
Psychiatrist:	What is going on?
Computer:	Do you know how the underworld operates?

Conversation 2

Psychiatrist:	How are you today?
Computer:	OK.
Psychiatrist:	What is your name?
Computer:	My name is Frank Smith.
Psychiatrist:	How old are you?
Computer:	Twenty-eight.
Psychiatrist:	Are you married?
Computer:	No.
Psychiatrist:	What sort of work do you do?
Computer:	I work in the post office.
Psychiatrist:	Why are you in the hospital?
Computer:	I shouldn't be here.
Psychiatrist:	Who brought you here?
Computer:	The police.
Psychiatrist:	What trouble did you have with the police?
Computer:	Cops don't do their job.
Psychiatrist:	What do they do instead?
Computer:	Cops arrest the wrong people.
Psychiatrist:	They arrest the right ones sometimes.
Computer:	The law should get those Italian crooks.
Psychiatrist:	Are you Italian?
Computer:	My background is British but I was born in this country.
Psychiatrist:	Do you know any Italian crooks?
Computer:	I try to avoid the underworld.
Psychiatrist:	Are you afraid of the underworld?
Computer:	The Mafia are the worst gangsters.
Psychiatrist:	Are you connected with the Mafia?
Computer:	You know, they know me.
Psychiatrist:	How do they know you?
Computer:	They spy on me.
Psychiatrist:	Why do they?
Computer:	They want to get false evidence to frame me.

Psychiatrist:	What do they have against you?
Computer:	They are out to get me.
Psychiatrist:	What for?
Computer:	I have incriminating evidence against the Mafia.
Psychiatrist:	Are you sure of all this?
Computer:	You don't believe me?

Conversation 3

Psychiatrist:	Tell me something about yourself.
Computer:	I went to the track at Bay Meadows a while back.
Psychiatrist:	What happened there?
Computer:	There's a lot of crooked gambling there.
Psychiatrist:	Why do you think the gambling is crooked?
Computer:	I have worried that gangsters have too much power in this country.

Conversation 4

Psychiatrist:	How do you like the hospital?
Computer:	I don't communicate very much with others.
Psychiatrist:	Do other people at the hospital get on your nerves?
Computer:	I shouldn't have come here.
Psychiatrist:	Why do you say you shouldn't have come here?
Computer:	They made me come here.

The computer's response depends on how much FEAR, ANGER, and MISTRUST it has at the moment. Those three variables are affected by what the psychiatrist says. For example, if the psychiatrist gives the computer a compliment, the FEAR, ANGER, and MISTRUST usually decrease. But if MISTRUST is already high, the computer interprets the compliment as a sly attempt at pacification, and its ANGER increases instead of decreases. ANGER can also be increased by questions that humiliate (*Tell me about your sex life*) or imply subjugation (*Perhaps you should stay in the hospital longer*).

To prove his computer is paranoid, Colby had 8 psychiatrists interview it and also interview paranoid humans via teletypewriters. Transcripts of all the interviews were sent to psychiatrists around the country, who were asked to judge whether each interview was with a human or with the computer. The psychiatrists were unable to tell the difference: only 51% of their guesses were correct.

Some computerists got the "brainstorm" of hooking Weizenbaum's computer to Colby's, to see whether the computerized psychotherapist could cure the computerized schizophrenic. The experiment was a disaster: both computers were so passive that the discussion rapidly degenerated into trivia.

But so do conversations between humans!

FALL IN LOVE

Can the computer help you fall in love? Here are some famous attempts, in chronological order. (I've rounded all dates to the nearest 5 years.)

TV love (1960)

A computer appeared on national TV, to make people fall in love.

Guys and gals in the audience answered questionnaires about their personality and fed them into the computer. The computer chose the guy and gal that were most compatible. That guy and gal had their first blind date on national television.

Each week, that scenario was repeated: the computer chose another couple from the audience.

Each lucky couple appeared on the show again several weeks later so the audience could find out whether the couple was in love.

One of the couples was unhappy: the gal didn't like the guy, even though she *wanted* to like him. She volunteered to be hypnotized. So, on national TV, a hypnotist made her fall in love with her partner.

The computer was a huge Univac. Today, the same kind of matching could be done with a microcomputer. Any volunteers?

Computer-dating services (1965)

College students began relying on computers, to find dates. Here's how the typical computer-dating service worked. . . .

You answered a long questionnaire — about 8 pages. The questionnaire asked about your sex, age, height, weight, hair color, race, religion, how often you drank and smoked, how "handsome" or "attractive" you were (on a scale of 1 to 10), how far you wanted to go on your first date, whether you wanted to get married soon, and how many children you'd like. It also asked many questions about your personality.

One of the questions was:

Suppose you receive in the mail some spoons you didn't order. The accompanying note says the spoons were sent by a charitable organization, and begs you to either send a contribution or return the spoons. You don't like the spoons. What will you do?
1. Keep the spoons without paying.
2. Return the spoons.
3. Pay for the spoons.

Another question was:

A girl returned from her date after curfew. Her excuse was that her boyfriend's car broke down. What's your reaction?

Again, you had a multiple-choice answer. One of the choices was, "Ha!"

For each question, you had to say how *you* would answer it, and how you'd want your *date* to answer it. That was tough. What if you wanted your date to be stunningly beautiful but also humble? What if you wanted to meet somebody who's ugly and insecure enough to be desperate to have sex? Such issues were debated in college dorms throughout the nation.

After completing the questionnaire, you mailed it with about $10 to the computer-dating service. Within two months, the service would send you the names, addresses, and phone numbers of at least 5 people you could date. If your personality was very easy to match, the service might send you *more* than 5 names; but even if your personality was lousy, you'd get at least 5. Periodically throughout the year, you'd also get updates that matched you with people who enrolled after you.

The most popular computer-dating service was **Operation Match**, started by students at Harvard. Its main competitor was **Contact**, started by students at M.I.T. Both services quickly became profitable and had subscribers from all across the country.

One gal's personality was so wonderful that the computer matched her with 110 guys! She had to explain to her mom why 110 guys were always on the phone — and she had to figure out how to say "no" to 109 of them.

One gal got matched to her roommate's boyfriend. They didn't stay roommates long.

When I was a freshman, I applied to *both* services, to make sure I'd meet "the gal of my dreams". Contact sent me names of gals at prestigious schools (such as Wellesley and Bennington), while Operation Match sent me names of gals at schools such as the State University of New York at Albany.

I thought I was the only nut desperate enough to apply to *both* services, but I got a surprise! When I saw the list of names from Contact and the list from Operation Match, I noticed a gal who appeared on *both* lists! Like me, she'd been desperate enough to apply to both services, and both computers agreed she'd be a perfect match for me!

I had a date with her but couldn't stand her.

When I'd answered the questionnaire, I was a very bashful boy, so the computer matched me to bashful girls. But by the time I received the computer printout, I'd become wilder, and the girls the computer recommended were no longer "my type".

Contact raised its price to $15, then $20. But $20 was still cheap for what you were getting.

Contact ran a newspaper ad that seemed to be selling groceries. It said, "Dates — 2¢ per pound". The ad then explained that one gal got enough dates so that, when she totaled the weight of their bodies, she figured they cost her 2¢ per pound.

The Dartmouth dater (1965)

When Dartmouth College was still all-male, a student there wrote a cruel program that evaluated dates by asking lots of "practical" questions such as:

Is she pretty?
How far away does she live?
Does she have a car?

I put down that I was dating a 14-year-old girl who was 7 feet tall and weighed 300 pounds but had a perfect personality. I gave her personality a 10, and even said that she lived nearby and had a car.

In spite of her excellent personality, the computer didn't like her. The computer said:

She must be pregnant. Where did you get that pig?
Worst score yet produced by this computer!

Video dating (1975)

During the 1970's, people wanted everything to be natural. They wanted "natural food" and "natural love".

Since computerized love seemed unnatural, its popularity declined. Operation Match and Contact went out of business.

They were replaced by **video dating**, in which a **video-dating service** shows you videotapes of members of the opposite sex and lets you contact the person whose videotape you like best. That way, you never have a "blind" date: you see the person on videotape before you make the date. The service also makes a videotape of *you!*

The video-dating service tapes *thousands* of people. Since you don't have enough time to look at thousands of tapes, the service tells you to answer a questionnaire, which is fed into a computer. The computer tells you which people you're most compatible with; then you look at those people's tapes.

Computer dancing (1975)

At a Connecticut prep school (Hotchkiss), the head of the computer center arranged a "computer dance".

All the students answered questionnaires, which were fed into a computer. The computer matched the boys with the girls, so each boy got one girl. The boy had to take the girl to the dance.

The computer center's staff announced the dancing partners in a strange way: one morning, the students found all the halls decorated with strips of punched paper tape, saying (in billboard-style letters) messages such as "George Smith & Mary Jones". If you were a student, you looked up and down the halls (your heart beating quickly), to find the tape displaying your name alongside the name of your mysterious computer lover.

Shrieks and groans. "Aarrgghh! You wouldn't *believe* who the computer stuck me with!"

Computer weddings (1980)

Here's how the first true "computer marriage" occurred. . . .

One company's terminal was attached to another company's computer. A programmer at the first company often asked a programmer at the second company for help. They contacted each other by typing messages on their terminals, and let the computer relay the messages back and forth. One of the programmers was a guy, the other was a gal, and they fell in love, even though they had never met. Finally, the guy typed on his terminal, "Let's get married". The gal typed back, "Yes". And so they got engaged — even though they had never met.

Their marriage ceremony used three terminals: one for the guy, one for the gal, and one for the minister. The minister typed the questions at his own terminal; then the guy and gal typed back, "I do".

Reverend Apple Reverend Apple is an Apple computer programmed to perform marriage ceremonies.

It performed its first marriage on Valentine's Day, 1981. The groom was a guy named Richard; the bride was a gal named Debbie. The computer printed the standard wedding-ritual text on the screen, and then asked the usual questions. Instead of answering "I do", the bride and groom just had to type "Y".

Reverend Apple is smart. For example, if the bride or groom types "N" instead of "Y", the computer beeps, tells the couple to try again, and repeats the question.

The program was written by M.E. Cavanaugh at the request of Rev. Jon Jaenisch, who stood by Reverend Apple while the ceremony was being performed.

Rev. Jaenisch is a minister of the Universal Life Church — the church that lets you become an "ordained minister" by just paying $5, and become a "doctor of divinity" by just paying $20. He's known as the "Archbishop in Charge of Keyboarding".

For his next feat, he plans to make the computer perform divorces. He also uses the computer to persuade kids to come to church. He claims, "What better way to get kids into church than by letting them play with a computer? It's more interesting than praying."

For a while, he couldn't interest enough couples in using Reverend Apple. He complained, "It's not easy to convince people to get married by a computer. They don't think it's romantic." NBC television news and many newspapers wanted to interview him, but he couldn't find enough willing couples.

And besides, he's a reverend only part-time. His main job's as an employment agent: he's supposed to help companies find programmers. He thought Reverend Apple's reputation would help him find programmers, but it didn't.

But Reverend Apple eventually started to catch on. During its first eight months, it performed six marriages.

Jaenisch says, "The first couple had nothing to do with computers professionally: the groom drove a tow-truck and was an hour late for the ceremony because he wanted to work overtime. But the second couple was *very* involved with computers: they even asked for a printout of the ceremony."

The sixth ceremony's groom earned his living by fixing computer power supplies and said, "It was nice with our friends all gathered around the console, and someone brought champagne. But part of our vow was to never buy a home computer: we have to get away from machines *some*time."

Love Bug (1980)

You can buy a **Love Bug**. It's a small computerized box that you put in your pocket. You feed the box information about your personality. When you walk through a singles bar, if you get near a person of the opposite sex who's compatible and has a Love Bug also, your Love Bug beeps. As you and the other person get closer and closer, the Love Bugs beep to each other even more violently. The more violently your Love Bug beeps, the closer you are to your ideal partner.

Using a Love Bug to find a date is like using a Geiger counter to find uranium. The louder the Love Bug beeps, the louder your heart will pound.

Selectrocution (1980)

If you don't like the Love Bug, how about a **love billboard**? One company sells love billboards to singles bars.

Each person who enters the bar wears a gigantic name tag showing the person's initials. For example, since I'm Russ Walter, my tag says, in gigantic letters, "RW". If I see an attractive gal whose tag says "JN", and I like her smile, I tell the person who operates the billboard. A few seconds later, a gigantic computerized billboard hanging over the entire crowd flashes this message:

FOR JN FEMALE: YOU HAVE A NICE SMILE--RW MALE

Everybody in the bar sees my message. When the gal of my dreams, "JN female", sees it, she hunts for "RW male", and we unite in computerized joy.

That's great for bashful people, like me, who'd rather pass notes than face a stranger unprepared.

It's called **Selectrocution**, because it gives your social life an electronic tingle that ends all your problems.

Interlude (1980)

The most provocative sex program is **Interlude**. It interviews both you and your lover, then tells you what sexual activities to perform. Some of the activities are quite risqué. (Puritans think the program should be called "Inter Lewd".)

The program runs on your Radio Shack or Apple computer. (The explicit full-color ad shows a half-clad girl on satin sheets caressing her Apple.)

The program's based loosely on Masters-and-Johnson sexual therapy. It interviews each person separately and privately, then recommends a sexual interlude.

During the interview, the computer asks you questions such as:

How long would you like the interlude to last?

You can choose any length of time, from "several seconds" to "several days".

If you choose "several seconds", the computer recommends that while driving home from a party, you put your lover's finger in your mouth and seductively caress it with your tongue. If you choose "several days", the computer recommends telling your lover to meet somebody at the airport; but when your lover arrives at the airport, make your lover find *you* there instead, armed with two tickets for a surprise vacation.

The computer also asks questions such as:

Do you like surprises?

You have several choices: you like to *give* surprises, *be* surprised, or don't like surprises at all. If you like to *be* surprised, and your lover likes to *give* surprises, the computer tells you to leave the room; after you've left, the computer gives your lover secret hints about the best way to surprise you.

The computer asks which parts of the body you like. (One choice is: "buttocks".) The computer also asks which kinds of accessories you like. (One choice is: "whips and chains".) The computer asks whether you want the interlude to occur "immediately" or "later": if you say "later", the computer recommends buying elaborate props to make the interlude fancier.

Some of the interludes are weird. For example, if you're a woman and want to surprise your husband, the computer recommends calling his office to invite him home for lunch. When he arrives, he finds all the shades pulled down: you do a nude dance on the table, then sit down to eat.

During the interview, the computer's questions are often corny. For example, the computer asks:

If your interlude were on TV, what show would it resemble?

Sample choices are "Three's Company", "Roots", and "a commercial". If you say "Roots", the computer says "heavy!" If you say "a commercial", the computer says "yecch!"

The computer asks how much sex you'd like. If you say "lots!" but your lover says the opposite, the computer will recommend that you take a cold shower, to cool your hot passion.

If you've been married for at least twenty years, you'd probably like to change a few things about your sex life but are afraid to tell your spouse that you've been less than thrilled. You'd like an intermediary to whom you can express your anxieties and who will pass the message to your spouse gently. The Interlude program acts as that intermediary, in a playful way.

Interlude's programmer says he created it because he was tired of hearing people wonder what to do with their personal computers. Once you've tried the Interlude program, your personal computer will suddenly become *very* personal!

It's rated R. To avoid an X rating, it insists on having one man and one woman: it doesn't permit homosexuality, group sex, or masturbation. Sorry!

The program came out in May, 1980. Within a year, ten thousand copies were sold.

In 1986, an improved version was invented: **Interlude 2**. It's available for the IBM PC and the Apple 2 family. You can get it for $45.95 (plus $4.95 shipping and $1.78 for credit-card processing) from Dolphin Computers (309 Judah Street #214, San Francisco, CA 94122, phone 415-566-4400).

Pornopoly (1980)

To have an orgy, try this trick. Invite your friends over for a "game". Tell them it's a computerized version of Monopoly. When they arrive, surprise them by telling them they'll play **Pornopoly**, the computerized version of Monopoly that's rated X.

Like Monopoly, Pornopoly lets you buy and sell property; but the streets have names such as Bedroom Avenue, Horny Avenue, Hot Jugs Avenue, Jock Strap Place, and Orgasm Railroad. You get penalty cards such as: name 7 four-letter words that rhyme with duck. You might be told to play doctor, and conduct a physical examination of another player . . . or remove the pants of your favorite player by using only your teeth. When a player lands on a monopoly that you own, the player must take a drink, remove an article of clothing, kiss you, give you a free feel, or strip completely for two turns. At the end of the game, whoever remains dressed is the winner.

This successful program has been featured on national TV. Copies have been requested by Hugh Hefner, Johnny Carson, Rona Barrett, an army chaplain, and a dozen foreign countries. To add your own name to that list, try contacting Computer Consultants of Iowa (Box 427, Marion, Iowa 52302, 319-373-1306, if still in business).

Pornopoly costs $30, but the company doesn't accept money: it accepts only Master Charge, Visa, and COD. If you're a kid, tough luck: the company says, "This is an adult party game rated XXX and some people may find it offensive."

Among the offended is a New Orleans grandmother who read an article about the program and wrote this note to the company: "Thanks to you, I intend to start contributing to Moral Majority, something I've avoided until now."

The program's available for Radio Shack, Apple, Commodore, and Atari computers. *Infoworld* (the microcomputer industry's scandal sheet) criticizes the Atari version for its poor graphics, vague manual, and occasional bugs. If you try the Radio Shack, Apple, or Commodore version, tell me how you like it. And can I play?

Computers can replace people.

Bartenders

Many bar owners don't trust the bartenders they hire. They claim the bartenders give too many free drinks to friends, steal money from the till, and put too much or too little liquor in the drinks.

To solve the problem, many bars now contain a computer that mixes and pours drinks. The computer mixes accurately. Although the computer is run by the bartender, the computer keeps an accurate record of how many drinks it makes, so there is little chance for cheating. The computer also keeps track of the inventory.

The computers are manufactured and sold by NCR (Dayton, Ohio), Bar Boy Inc. (San Diego, California), Electronic Dispensers International (Concord, California), and Anker-Werke (Germany). Prices range from $600 to $15000. Holiday Inn has been developing its own model.

Doctors

If you're ill, would a computer diagnose your illness more accurately than a human doctor?

During the 1970's this article appeared in *The Times*:

A medical diagnostic system designed at Leeds University has proved more accurate than doctors in assessing the most likely cause of acute abdominal pain among patients admitted to the university's department of surgery.

Last year 304 such patients were admitted to the unit, and the computer's diagnosis proved correct in 92 percent of the cases, compared with 80 percent accuracy by the most senior doctor to see each case.

After each patient had been seen by the doctor and examined, the doctor's findings were passed on to a technician, who translated them into language used by the computer. The computer would list the likely diagnoses in order of probability. If the computer and the doctor in charge of the case disagreed, the computer would on request suggest further investigations that might be useful.

In the year-long trial the computer's diagnoses proved correct in 279 cases. In 15 it was wrong, in 8 the patient's condition was not included in the diseases considered by the computer, and in 2 no computer diagnosis was made because the doctors concerned with the case disagreed about the findings.

Whereas the computer advised an operation on 6 occasions when it would have proved unnecessary, in practice 30 such operations were carried out on the basis of the surgeon's own judgment. The computer accurately classified 84 of the 85 patients with appendicitis, compared with 75 by the doctors, and its suggestion that no operation was necessary proved correct on 136 out of 137 occasions.

The computer is reliable only if accurate data are fed into it on the basis of the doctor's interrogation and examination of the patient.

In a 1970's experiment at another hospital, each patient was given a computer terminal and could use it to communicate with the computer about his illness. Afterwards, most of the patients said they'd rather deal with the computer than with the human doctors.

This report is by James Martin and Adrian Norman:

The Los Angeles County General Hospital Shock Research Unit is concerned with circulatory shock, which results in low blood pressure, low blood flow, and an extremely unstable circulatory system. The proportion of circulatory-shock patients who die is large.

A computer was installed to improve the monitoring and care of these patients. A patient in this ward has many instruments attached to him: six thermistors measure the temperature at various parts of his body; pressures are measured in the circulatory system; catheters are inserted into an artery and a vein; and a urinometer measures liquid waste. The instruments are all directly connected to the computer, and other details about the patient are given to the machine by the nurse.

The computer prints out a log about the patient's condition, and if any measurement falls outside critical limits set by the doctor for that patient, the computer notifies the ward staff.

Tutors

Judith Harris, John Swets, and Wallace Feurzeig made the computer run a logic game. The computer thinks of a letter of the alphabet; your goal is to discover which letter it is, as quickly as possible. You can ask the computer questions about the letter's shape.

In this example, the human begins by asking whether the letter has any curves:

Human: Curves?
Computer: One.

Human: Loose ends?
Computer: Two.

Human: Obliques?
Computer: Zero.

Human: C.
Computer: You don't have enough information yet to get the right answer. How do you know it isn't J, for example?

Human: J.
Computer: You don't have enough information yet. How do you know it isn't C, for example?

Human: Horizontals?
Computer: Zero. That was a wasted question. It did not eliminate any possibilities.

Human: Verticals?
Computer: Zero. Good question.

Human: G.
Computer: Wrong. Your guess is inconsistent with the information you've been given. You must have forgotten that the right letter hasn't any HORIZONTAL LINES. The letter you guessed can't be right — it has too many LOOSE ENDS.

Human: Curves?
Computer: The answer is still: one.

Human: X.
Computer: Wrong. Your guess is inconsistent with the information you've been given. I think you only made that guess to see what I would say.

Human: C.
Computer: Yes, you've done it. Good work. If you want to play again, start right in.

Notice that the human can input either a guess (followed by a period) or a question (followed by a question mark). Possible guesses are A, B, C, D, etc. Possible questions are Curves, Loose ends, etc.; the human is given a list of possible questions before he runs the program.

Medicine That logic game was modified to form a lesson about medicine. The medical case was designed by Preston Munter, of the Harvard Health Center; the programming was done by John Swets, Wallace Feurzeig, and Myra Breen. The object of the "game" is to diagnose an illness correctly, by performing sufficient tests. The human can input either a diagnosis (Measles) or a request for a test (X-ray). Before running the program, the human is given a list of 35 possible diagnoses and 40 possible tests.

Here are excerpts from a long RUN:

Computer: Please type your name, the date, and a slash.

Human: Myra Breen, August 1963/

Computer: It is mid-December. Late this afternoon, a patient was admitted to the hospital. He is a well-developed, well-nourished, 34-year-old Negro coal miner. He was brought in by his wife, who reports that he has had "the grippe" for about 4 days. During the past 3 days she has given him fluids and aspirin every 6 hours with no sign of improvement. Today he suddenly became much worse. For the past 2 days he had complained of feeling very warm and of pain in his belly. This morning he had a severe shaking chill that was so bad his teeth rattled. . . . Begin the physical examination as soon as you are ready.

Human: Physical exam?

Computer: Fine. What in particular would you like to know?

Human: Chest exam?

Computer: It is common practice in the medical profession to begin an examination by checking the patient's general appearance.

Human: General appearance?

Computer: Acutely prostrated, lying in bed on his right side. Looks acutely ill, sweaty, apprehensive, but alert. Paroxysmal cough, bringing up a little rusty streaked sputum. Breathing with difficulty.

Human: EENT exam?

Computer: Check all of the vital signs first!

Human: Temperature?

Computer: 103.

Human: Blood pressure?

Computer: 150/84.

Human: Pulse?

Computer: 100 a minute. Occasional extra systole. . . .

Human: Abdominal exam?

Computer: Diffusely tender, some splinting noticed in lower right quadrant and occasionally radiating to right flank area.

Human: The grippe.

Computer: There's insufficient information for any conclusive diagnosis at this time. You're not being careful!

Human: Musculo-skeletal system?

Computer: Essentially negative, except for generalized weakness and aching.

Human: Extremities?

Computer: Normal, except nail beds are questionably cyanotic but difficult to determine because of patient's skin color.

Human: Rectal exam?

Computer: You're not being careful! The patient is too acutely ill for a rectal examination.

Human: Laboratory reports?

Computer: Fine. Which lab tests would you like to have done?

Human: RBC?

Computer: A red blood count will be done. Results will be sent to you as soon as possible. . . . Would you like to alert the night nurse to set up the lab tests you'll want to see tomorrow?

Human: Yes.

Computer: Good. That will speed things up. However, there's nothing further that can be done tonight to help the patient. Let's call it quits for now. Perhaps you'll be in a better position to diagnose the case tomorrow after the first lab reports come in and you have reexamined the patient. Have a good night's sleep, and when you're back on duty tell me to "proceed."

Human: Proceed.

Computer: It's morning and you're making your rounds. You've come to our patient and are given the night nurses's report: "Temperature remained high but patient spent a reasonably comfortable night. Cough diminished but persists. Occasional traces of blood in sputum. Patient still dyspneic and still has pain in abdomen. The second series of lab tests was initiated." Some of the first series of lab reports have just come in: urine exam, insufficient fluid for analysis; RBC, 5 million; WBC, 15500; differential, shift to left. . . . You may be prepared to make the diagnosis now. Are you?

Human: No.

Computer: Fine. Nevertheless, we've got a fair amount of information — at least enough to raise some, perhaps several, diagnostic possibilities. Have you any in mind?

Human: Yes.

Computer: Name one.

Human: Pulmonary infarction.

Computer: Fine. Pleural pain, dyspnea, fever, and the physical exam signs and symptoms are certainly consistent with pulmonary infarction. Do you think that shaking chills and the presence of rusty sputum further support this diagnosis?

Human: No.

Computer: Right. Though the white count is consistent, isn't it?

Human: No.

Computer: Wrong. The white count is consistent. This should further support your diagnosis. We've considered one possibility. Do you have another diagnosis in mind?

Human: No.

Computer: In that case I'd like to talk about viral pneumonia. The tachycardia, high WBC, elevated respiratory rate, shaking chills, bloody sputum, and severe pleural pain all lend weight to that diagnosis — right?

Human: Yes.

Computer: You're way off base. There's not an iota of truth to any part of what I just said; in fact, the opposite of what I said is true. You'd better review some elementary medicine, doctor. . . .

Human: Pleural effusion.

Computer: A good contender, but let's be careful. What evidence would rule it in or out?

Human: Positive evidence of another disease.

Computer: Is there such evidence?

Human: Possible evidence though inconclusive.

Computer: Since you aren't sure, continue the examination until you have conclusive evidence one way or the other.

Human: RBC?

Computer: An RBC is not indicated at this time. It's an unnecessary expense for a poor patient.

Human: WBC?

Computer: 22500.

Human: Staph pneumonia.

Computer: Fair enough. But where is the guilty organism? When you have isolated staphylococcus aureus in significant numbers in your samples of this patient's fluids or excretions, let me know.

Human: Pneumococcal pneumonia.

Computer: Are you absolutely sure?

Human: Yes.

Computer: You can't be, until you have irrefutable evidence. What would help you nail down the diagnosis?

Human: Evidence from sputum smear and culture.

Computer: Good. Anything else?

Human: No.

Computer: I think you might also want evidence from x-ray findings. Go ahead and we'll see what happens.

Human: X-ray?

Computer: Not ready yet. Try the blood lab.

Human: Differential?

Computer: Marked shift to left. . . .

Human: X-ray?

Computer: The x-ray shows: area of consolidation, right lower lobe, consistent with pneumatic process. This is a good time to review the total findings and to make another tentative diagnosis — if you like.

Human: Evidence of fluid?

Computer: No evidence of fluid.

Human: Sputum smear?

Computer: Gram-positive rods.

Human: Strep pneumonia.

Computer: Fine, but how can you distinguish this from any other bacterial pneumonia? Wait until you have an irrefutable case.

Human:	Viral pneumonia.
Computer:	But what about shaking chills, rusty sputum, elevated WBC, etc. — all the evidence of an acute febrile bacterial process? You are in error, doctor.
Human:	Sputum culture?
Computer:	Presence of pneumococci.
Human:	Strep pneumonia.
Computer:	Incredible! You have disregarded the positive findings that should clearly have established the correct diagnosis.
Human:	Pneumococcal pneumonia.
Computer:	Very good. It's obvious now, though there were some confusing signs and symptoms in the picture. You've seen your way through to the correct diagnosis.

Religion Bruce Jones programmed the computer to teach you about religion. Here's an example:

Computer:	This program is designed to teach you some things about the so-called "documentary hypothesis" as formulated by Julius Wellhausen and others. First, what is your name?
Human:	George
Computer:	All right, George, who wrote the first five books of the Bible, according to tradition?
Human:	Moses
Computer:	You are off to a good start. Do you know what those first five books are called? They are called . . .
Human:	the Pentateuch
Computer:	Right you are. Torah is the traditional Jewish name for them. They are also called the Pentateuch ("penta" = 5). People very early noticed that there was a problem with saying that Moses wrote the Torah. If you already know the basis of their suspicion, tell me.
Human:	Some things in the text reflect later conditions, after Moses.
Computer:	You are right, of course, but there was an even more obvious problem. Try again.
Human:	I don't know.
Computer:	At the end of the Pentateuch the author says, "Moses . . . died there." Does that seem strange to you?
Human:	yes
Computer:	Why?
Human:	Moses could not have written about his own death.
Computer:	O.k. Also, right after the report of Moses' death and burial (Deut. 34), the text says, "No man knows the place of his burial TO THIS DAY." How do those last three words strike you?
Human:	They seem later than the event they are talking about.
Computer:	A good observation, George. Many people considered these words to be anachronistic. That is, "this day" is sharply distinguished from the time of the burial. It seems likely, therefore, that the time of writing was much later than the time of burial. Again (so the argument goes), Moses was not the author. Would these observations about the end of Deuteronomy convince you that Moses did not write the Torah?
Human:	yes
Computer:	Why do you say that?
Human:	A man cannot write his own obituary.
Computer:	Probably not many people would have been convinced if our evidence were so limited. After all, Moses could have written everything except the last chapter. However, as early as the 18th century, people noticed another problem. . . .

The computer searched through the human's input, to see whether he used words indicating a correct answer. The computer never said a flat "Wrong", since religious answers are a matter of personal belief, and since the human might be smarter or weirder than the computer program was prepared for.

Robots

In 1962 at MIT, Heinrich Ernst connected the computer to a mechanical hand that could feel. He made the hand build objects out of blocks, and made it put blocks into boxes.

Shakey One of the most famous robots is a guy named "Shakey", built at the Stanford Research Institute (SRI) in 1970. His eye contains a television camera (optical scanner). Instead of legs, he has wheels. Instead of arms, he has antennae (for feeling) and a bumper (for pushing). His brain is a computer: instead of carrying it around with him, he leaves it in another room and communicates with it by wireless methods.

To see how he works, suppose you type this message on his computer's terminal:

Push the block off the platform.

He begins by looking for the platform. If the platform is not in the room, he goes out to the hall and steers himself through the hall (by looking at the baseboards) until he arrives at the next room. He peers into the room to see whether it contains a platform. If not, he hunts for another room. When he finally finds a room containing a platform with a block on it, he tries to climb onto the platform to push the block off. But before climbing the platform, he checks the platform's height. If it's too high to get onto easily, he looks for a device to help him climb it. For example, if a ramp is lying in the room, he pushes the ramp next to the platform and then wheels himself up the ramp. Finally, he pushes the block off.

He can handle unexpected situations. For example, while he's getting the ramp, suppose you pull the platform to a different place. That doesn't faze him: he hunts for the platform again, and then pushes the ramp to it.

In 1971, Shakey's powers were extended, so he can handle commands such as:

Turn on the lightswitch.

If the lightswitch is too high for his bumper to reach, he looks for a device to climb onto, such as a box. If he finds a box that looks helpful, he climbs onto it to check whether it is tall enough; if it is, he climbs off, pushes it to the lightswitch, climbs on it again, and finally flicks the switch.

Another task he can handle is:

Push three boxes together.

He finds the first box and pushes it to the second. Then he finds the third box, and pushes it to the second.

He understands over 100 words. Whatever command you give him becomes his "goal", and he must reason out how to accomplish it. He might discover that to accomplish it, he must accomplish another goal first — for example, to move the block off the platform, he must first find the platform; to do that, he might have to look in another room; to do that, he must leave the room he's in; to do that, he must turn his wheels.

Simulator One

Here's a picture of a robot named Simulator One:

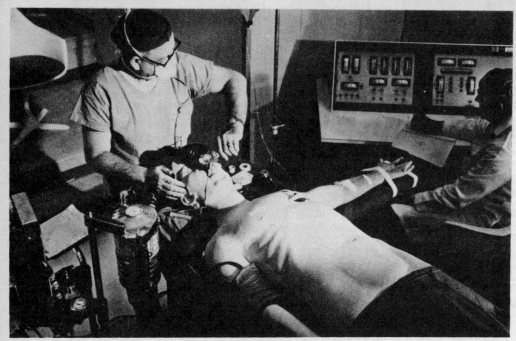

In the picture, a doctor is taking Simulator One's blood pressure and pulse. Another doctor is watching the computer console.

Simulator One is a model patient. He can blink, breathe, cough, vomit, respond to drugs, and even die. He's used in med school, to train doctors how to administer anesthetics during surgery.

Improved robots

This report (abridged) is by Bertram Raphael, the director of the SRI Artificial Intelligence Center:

Here's what robots were capable of doing a few years ago.

At Hitachi Central Research Laboratory, a TV camera was aimed at an engineering plan drawing of a structure. A second camera looked at blocks spread out on a table. The computer "understood" the drawing, reached toward the blocks with its arm, and built the structure.

At MIT, the camera was not shown a plan; instead, it was shown an example of the actual structure desired. The computer figured out how the structure could be constructed, and then built an exact copy.

At Stanford University, the hand obeyed spoken directions. For example, if someone said into the microphone, "Pick up the small block on the left," that is precisely what the arm would do.

In Scotland at the University of Edinburgh, a jumble of parts for two wooden toys was placed on a table. "Freddy," the Edinburgh robot, spread out the parts so that it could see each one clearly, and then, with the help of a vise-like work station at one corner of the table, assembled first the toy car and then the toy boat.

Recently, robot researchers have built robots that can perform truly practical tasks. For example:
At Stanford, the system that used to stack toy blocks can now assemble a real water pump.
At SRI, a computer-controlled arm with touch and force sensors can feel its way as it packs assembled pumps into a case.
At MIT, programs are under development to enable a computer to inspect and repair circuit boards for use in computers, TV sets, and other electronic equipment.

The Beast

Not all robots involve computers. Here's an example of a noncomputerized robot (reported by James Slagle, abridged):

A. George Carlton, John G. Chubbuck, and others at the Applied Physics Laboratory of John Hopkins University built a machine called The Beast.

It's a battery-operated cylinder on wheels that's 18 inches in diameter. It has tactile, sonar, and optical apparatus. The sonar permits The Beast to find its way down the center of the hall. When its battery becomes sufficiently run-down, The Beast optically looks for an electric outlet and plugs itself in to recharge its battery.

The Beast was often let loose to roam in the halls and offices at the Applied Physics Laboratory in order to see how long it could survive without "starving." Once it survived 40.6 hr. Many a new and unsuspecting secretary has been startled when The Beast entered her office, plugged itself into an electric outlet, and then departed.

When it feels a step down, it knows enough to turn around, so that it doesn't fall downstairs. But this logic sometimes makes it starve when it encounters a raised threshold. After getting on the threshold, it thinks it's about to fall, so it turns around. After turning around it again thinks it's going to fall, so it turns back and forth until it starves.

It also starved when some workmen changed all the outlets from the flush to the projecting type. To cope with the new situation, the researchers changed some of the circuitry.

Japan

A newspaper article said that in Japan robots are being used in many practical ways. One robot arc-welds, reducing the time by 90%. Another grasps an object, determines the best way to pack it in a box, and does the packing; it uses television cameras and delicate arms. Another washes windows. Another wiggles a rod to catch a fish, takes the fish off the hook, dumps it into a bin, and returns the line to the water. Another directs traffic. Talking robots are being used instead of kimono-clad females in inns and restaurants.

Commenting on the quality of life in Japan, the article went on to say that people are buying whiffs of oxygen from vending machines.

The article was tacked on the bulletin board at the MIT Artificial Intelligence Laboratory, together with this graffito about how the Japanese robots would act differently if they were as smart as people. . . .

Human:	Weld these parts.
Robot:	The steel in those parts is grossly inferior. They must have been made in the U.S. Send them back. Also, have my welding machine tuned up.
Human:	Pack those widgets.
Robot:	Can I break them in half first?
Human:	No.
Robot:	"No" is not an allowed answer. I only have small shipping boxes. (Proceeds to break widgets in half and stuff them into boxes.)
Human:	Wash those windows.
Robot:	What?? And get my precious electrical and mechanical components all wet??
Human:	Catch a fish.
Robot:	(Proceeds to catch a fish, take it off the hook, and throw it back.) Okay.
Human:	What did you throw it back for?
Robot:	It was under the size limit. Anyway, it was full of mercury.
Human:	Direct that traffic.
Robot:	Will I get hazardous duty pay for this work?
Human:	Greet those customers.
Robot:	Sorry, my shift is over.
Human:	(Ready to faint.) Give me some air.
Robot:	Use that "machine" over there. (Points to vending machine.)

Programmers have taught the computer to compose its own poetry and other literature.

The Taoist Hiroshima Elevator (1961)

In Italy, Nanni Balestrini created poetry by feeding the computer three passages.

He fed the computer this passage from Lao Tzu's *Tao Te Ching*: "While the multitude of things comes into being, I envisage their return. Although things flourish, they all return to their roots."

He fed this passage from Michihito Hachiya's *Hiroshima Diary*: "The blinding fireball expands rapidly, thirty times brighter than the sun. When it reaches the stratosphere, the summit of the cloud takes on the well-known mushroom shape."

He fed this from Paul Goldwin's *The Mystery of the Elevator*: "head pressed on shoulder, hair between lips, lay motionless without speaking, till he moved his fingers slowly, trying to grasp".

He told the computer to mix them up. Here's the result:

Head pressed on shoulder, thirty times
brighter than the sun, I envisage their return —
until he moved his fingers slowly. . . . And while the multitude
of things comes into being, at the summit of the cloud
they all return to their roots and take on
the well-known mushroom shape, endeavoring to grasp.

Hair between lips, they all return
to their roots. In the blinding fireball
I envisage their return — until he moved his fingers
slowly — and although things flourish
takes on the well-known mushroom shape, endeavoring
to grasp, while the multitude of things comes into being.

In the blinding fireball I envisage
their return. When it reaches the stratosphere, while the multitude
of things comes into being, head pressed
on shoulder, thirty times brighter than the sun,
they all return to their roots. Hair
between lips takes on the well-known mushroom shape.

They lay motionless without speaking. Thirty times
brighter than the sun, they all return
to their roots. Head pressed on shoulder,
they take on the well-known mushroom shape, endeavoring
to grasp. And although things flourish,
they expand rapidly, hair between lips.

While the multitude of things comes into being in the blinding
fireball, they all return
to their roots. They expand rapidly — until he moved
his fingers slowly, when it reached the stratosphere
and lay motionless without speaking, thirty times
brighter than the sun, endeavoring to grasp.

I envisage their return — until he moved his fingers
slowly in the blinding fireball.
They all return to their roots. Hair
between lips and thirty times brighter than the sun
lay motionless without speaking. They expand,
rapidly endeavoring to grasp the summit.

In Balestrini's program, *Tao Te Ching* was represented as four phrases:

while the multitude of things comes into being
I envisage their return
although things flourish
they all return to their roots

Hiroshima Diary was represented as six phrases, and *The Mystery of the Elevator* as five.

For each verse, the computer was told to choose nine phrases at random, and print them in a random order (never juxtaposing phrases from the same passage), to form six lines of roughly equal metrical length.

Actually the computer printed the poem in capital letters, without punctuation; Balestrini himself then added the punctuation and polished the grammar. The whole thing was actually done in Italian; you've been reading Edwin Morgan's translation, with my punctuation.

Bubbles (1966)

At Northwestern University, programmers made the computer compose nice poetry. To use their program, you type a list of nouns, verbs, and other words. The computer randomly chooses five of your words to be **theme words**. The computer combines all your words to form sentences, but chooses the theme words more often than the others. It combines the sentences into verses and tries to keep the lengths of the lines approximately equal. It puts a theme word into the title.

In one poem, the computer chose *bubble* to be a theme word. The title was: ODE TO A BUBBLE. The poem contained phrases such as, "Ah, sweet bubble." The word *bubble* appeared so often that even the stupidest reader could say:

"Oh, yeah. I really understand this poem. Ya see, it's about a bubble."

The poem had all the familiar poetic trappings, such as "but alas!", which marked the turning point. (Cynics argue that the poem didn't *really* have a turning point, since the computer didn't have the faintest idea of what it was saying!)

Kids and physics (1968)

In England at Manchester University, Mendoza made the computer write children's stories. Here's a story the computer composed:

> The sun shone over the woods. Across the fields softly drifted the breeze, while then the clouds, which calmly floated all afternoon, moved across the fields.
>
> Squirrel, who scampered through the trees, quickly ran off; and off noisily ran Little Grey Rabbit. She sniffed at the house; but out of the door noisily hurried Hare, who peered at slowly the flowers. Squirrel quickly scampered over the woods and fields, but Old Grey Owl flew over the woods and fields. Down the path to the woods ran Little Grey Rabbit, who then sniffed at a strawberry pie.

The first paragraph uses these words:

Verbs	moved	drifted	shone	floated	touched	melted	looked down on	warmed
Nouns								
the clouds	1	1	0	1	0	1	0	0
the sun	0	1	1	1	1	0	1	1
the breeze	1	1	0	1	1	2	0	0
the sky	0	0	0	0	1	0	1	1
Adverbs								
gently	1	1	1	1	1	1	1	1
quietly	1	1	1	1	1	1	1	1
loudly	1	1	1	1	1	1	1	1
softly	1	1	1	1	1	1	1	1
calmly	1	1	1	1	1	1	1	1
soon	1	1	1	1	1	1	1	1
then	1	1	1	1	1	1	1	1
(no adverb)	2	2	2	2	2	2	2	2
Endings								
by	1	1	0	1				
over the woods	1	1	1	1				
across the meadows	1	1	1	1				
through the trees	1	1	1	1				
down	0	0	1	0				
for a long time	0	0	1	1				
all day	1	1	1	1				
all afternoon	1	1	1	1				
the grass					1	1	1	1
the leaves of the trees					1	1	1	1
the garden					1	1	1	1
the flowers					1	1	1	1
the little house					1	0	1	1
the old oak tree					1	1	1	1
the treetops					1	1	1	1

ADDITIONAL WORDS: which, and, while, they, it

To construct a sentence, the computer uses that table. Here's how.

First, the computer randomly chooses a noun. Suppose it chooses *the sun*.

Then it looks across the row marked *the sun*, to choose a verb whose score isn't 0. For example, it's possible that *the sun shone*, but not possible that *the sun melted*. Suppose it chooses *shone*.

Then it looks down the column marked *shone*, to choose an adverb and an ending. Notice that the ending can't be *by*, since its score is 0. *No adverb* has a score of 2, whereas *gently* has a score of 1; that makes *no adverb* twice as likely as *gently*.

If the computer chooses *no adverb* and *over the woods*, the resulting sentence is: The sun shone over the woods. In fact, that's the first sentence of the story you just read.

The computer occasionally changes the word order. For example, instead of typing "The breeze drifted softly across the fields", the computer begins the second sentence by typing, "Across the fields softly drifted the breeze".

To combine short sentences into long ones, the computer uses the words at the bottom of the table: *which, and, while, they,* and *it*. If two consecutive clauses have the same subject, the computer substitutes a pronoun: *they* replaces *the clouds*; *it* replaces *the sun, the trees,* and *the sky*. The program says a *which* clause can come after a noun (*not* a pronoun); the *which* clause must use a different verb than the main clause.

Here's the vocabulary for the second paragraph:

Verbs	scampered	flew	ran	hurried	sniffed at	peered at	ate	munched and crunched
Nouns								
Little Grey Rabbit	0	0	2	3	1	1	0	0
Old Grey Owl	0	3	0	0	1	3	2	2
Squirrel	3	0	1	1	1	1	3	3
Hare	0	0	0	2	1	1	2	2
Adverbs								
then	0	1	1	1	1	1	0	0
slowly	0	2	0	0	1	1	1	1
quickly	1	1	1	1	0	0	1	1
soon	1	0	1	1	0	0	1	1
happily	1	0	0	1	0	0	1	1
gaily	1	0	0	1	0	0	1	1
noisily	1	0	1	1	0	0	2	3
(no adverb)	5	4	4	5	2	2	5	5
Endings								
off	1	1	1	1				
over the woods and fields	1	1	1	1				
through the trees	1	1	1	1				
among the treetops	0	1	0	0				
into the home	1	0	1	1				
out of the door	1	0	1	1				
down the path to the woods	1	0	1	1				
about the garden	1	1	1	1				
the house					1	1	0	0
the hollow tree					1	1	0	0
an old oak tree					1	1	0	0
the flowers					1	1	0	0
two buns					1	1	1	1
a strawberry pie					1	1	1	1
six cabbages					1	1	1	1

ADDITIONAL WORDS: who, and, but, she, he

Here's another story the program produced:

> The breeze drifted by. Across the fields softly moved the clouds; and then the breeze, which calmly touched the treetops, drifted across the fields. Quietly the sun shone over the woods. The sky calmly shone across the fields.
>
> Out of the door ran Squirrel; and off hurried Hare, who munched and crunched two buns happily. Off slowly flew Old Grey Owl, and Squirrel soon ate two buns. Old Grey Owl, who peered at a strawberry pie, munched and crunched two buns; but noisily Little Grey Rabbit, who peered at an old oak tree, slowly ran down the path to the woods. Soon she hurried down the path to the woods, but then she sniffed at two buns. She hurried down the path to the woods.

Why did Mendoza make the computer write those stories? He explains:

This work all began when a well-known scientist joined our physics department. He had spent several years away from academic life and was able to take a long cool look at academic procedures. He soon formed the theory that students never learned any ideas; all they learned was a vocabulary of okay words which they strung together in arbitrary order, relying on the fact that an examiner pressed for time would not actually read what they had written but would scan down the pages looking for these words. I set out to test his hypothesis.

I began by writing "Little Grey Rabbit" stories. I tested these stories out on my very small children; but after some minutes they grew irritable, because nothing actually happened. This shows that even small children of three can measure entropy.

Then I altered the vocabulary and grammar — making the sentences all very dead — to imitate the style of physics textbooks. The endpoint came when a colleague at another university secretly sent me an exam a week before it was given to the students. I wrote vocabularies and copied down what the computer emitted. Using a false name, I slipped my paper in among the genuine ones. Unfortunately, it was marked by a very conscientious man, who eventually stormed into the Director's office shouting, "Who the hell is this man — why did we ever admit him?" So perhaps my colleague's hypothesis was wrong, and students are a little better than we think.

Here's one of the computer's answers:

In electricity, the unit of resistance is defined by electrolysis; and the unit of charge, which was fixed at the Cavendish lab in Rayleigh's classic experiments, was measured at the Cavendish lab. Theoretically, the absolute ohm is defined in a self-consistent way. The unit of resistance, which was determined with a coil spinning in a field, was fixed at the Cavendish lab; and this, by definition, is expressed in conceptual experiments. Theoretically the absolute ohm, which was redetermined using combined e.m.u. and e.s.u., is expressed by the intensity at the center of a coil.

Here's another of the computer's answers:

In this country, Soddy considered Planck's hypothesis from a new angle. Einstein 50 years ago asserted quantisation.

At a photocathode, electrons which undergo collisions in the Compton effect as energy packets or quanta are emitted at definite angles; nevertheless, particles in a photocell produce photoelectrons of energy $hv = E_0$. Photons in vacuo transmute into lower frequencies, and light quanta in the Compton effect emit emission currents.

Particles emit current proportional to energy; electrons in vacuo interact with loss of surface energy (work function); nevertheless, particles which are emitted in a photocell with conservation experimentally are conserved with energy hv. The former, at a metal surface, undergo collisions with emission of current; and at a metal surface, electrons produce emission currents.

Einstein assumed the gas of quantum particles; but quite recently Rayleigh, who quite recently solved the problem in an old-fashioned way, considered radiation classically. Planck, who this century assumed the A and B coefficients, explained the gas of quantum particles but before Sommerfield; Rayleigh, who quite recently was puzzled on Boltzmann statistics, tackled the problem with disastrous results.

Planck, who this century assumed the gas of quantum particles in 1905, this century considered the ultraviolet catastrophe; but quite recently Jeans, who tackled the problem in an old-fashioned way, was puzzled with disastrous results.

Black body radiation that exerts thermodynamic forces in an engine is equivalent to a relativistic system. Out of a black body, a photon that is equivalent to (out of a black body) an assembly of photons is assumed to be a non-conservative system; at the same time, thermodynamically, black body radiation that in a piston is assumed to be a relativistic system exerts quantised forces.

The radiation gas that obeys Wien's displacement law is considered as a system of energy levels. Quantally, a quantum particle exerts a Doppler-dependent pressure, although this produces equilibrium transition probabilities.

Black body radiation in an engine produces equilibrium transition probabilities.

Aerospace (1968)

In 1968, Raymond Deffrey programmed the computer to write fake reports about the aerospace industry. Shortly afterwards, I improved the program. The improved program contains these lists:

Introductory phrases
thus
indeed
however
moreover
similarly
furthermore
for example
in addition
in particular
to some extent
in this regard
on the other hand
for the most part
as a resultant implication
in view of system operation
in respect to specific goals
based in system engineering concepts
utilizing the established hypotheses
based on integral subsystem considerations
considering the postulated interrelationships

Noun phrases
the structural design
the sophisticated hardware
the total system rationale
any discrete configuration made
the fully integrated test program
any associated supporting element
the product configuration baseline
the independent function principle
the preliminary qualification limit
the subsystem compatibility testing
the greater flight-worthiness concept
a constant flow of effective information
the characterization of specific criteria
the anticipated third-generation equipment
initiation of critical subsystem development
the evolution of specifications over a given time
the philosophy of commonality and standardization
the incorporation of additional mission constraints
a consideration of system and/or subsystem technologies
a large portion of the interface coordination communication

Verb phrases
adds explicit performance limits to
effects a significant implementation to
adds overriding performance constraints to
presents extremely interesting challenges to
is further compounded, when taking into account
must utilize and be functionally interwoven with
requires considerable systems analysis to arrive at
necessitates that urgent consideration be applied to
maximizes the probability of success and minimizes time for
recognizes the importance of other systems and necessity for

To produce a typical sentence, the computer prints an introductory phrase, then a noun phrase, then a verb phrase, then a noun phrase. The phrases are chosen randomly.

Each paragraph consists of six such sentences. The computer isn't allowed to use the same phrase twice within a paragraph. The introductory phrase is omitted from the first sentence of the first paragraph, the second sentence of the second paragraph, etc.; so the report can't begin with the word *furthermore*, and the style varies.

Here's the beginning of one such report:

The Economic Considerations of the Aerospace Industry

A large portion of the interface coordination communication necessitates that urgent consideration be applied to the product configuration baseline. For example, the fully integrated test program adds explicit performance limits to the independent function principle. Moreover, the sophisticated hardware presents extremely interesting challenges to the philosophy of commonality and standardization. In view of system operation, a constant flow of effective information must utilize and be functionally interwoven with the preliminary qualification limit. In addition, any discrete configuration made adds overriding performance constraints to any associated supporting element. Thus, the anticipated third-generation equipment maximizes the probability of success and minimizes time for the total system rationale.

Me-Books (1972)

In 1972, Freeman Gosden Jr. started the Me-Books Publishing Company. It published books for kids. But if you bought a Me-Book for your child, you wouldn't see in it the traditional names "Dick, Jane, and Sally"; instead, you'd see the name of your own child. To order the book, you had to tell the company the names of all your children, and their friends, and pets. Their names appeared in the story.

The story was printed beautifully, in a 32-page hard-covered book with pictures in color. It cost just $3.95.

You could choose from four stories: "My Friendly Giraffe", "My Jungle Holiday", "My Birthday Land Adventure", and "My Special Christmas".

For example, if you lived on Jottings Drive, and your daughter's name was Shea, and her friend's name was Douglas, the story "My Friendly Giraffe" included paragraphs such as this:

> One morning Shea was playing with Douglas in front of her home. When she looked up, what do you think she saw walking down the middle of Jottings Drive? You guessed it. A giraffe!

Ted Nelson, author of *Computer Lib*, played a trick. He ordered a copy of "My Friendly Giraffe", but pretended that his child's name was "Tricky Dick Nixon" who lived on "Pennsylvania Ave." in "Washington". Sure enough, the company sent him "My Friendly Giraffe: A Me-Book for Tricky Dick". Here are some excerpts:

> Once upon a time, in a place called Washington, there lived a little boy named Tricky Dick Nixon. Now, Tricky Dick wasn't just an ordinary little boy. He had adventures that other little boys and girls just dream of. This is the story of one of his adventures. It's the story of the day that Tricky Dick met a giraffe. . . .
>
> As the giraffe came closer and closer, Tricky Dick started to wonder how in the world he was going to look him in the eye. . . .
>
> Tricky Dick knew there were no jungles in Washington. Especially on Pennsylvania Ave. But Tricky Dick wasn't even a little bit worried. First, because he was a very brave little boy. And second, because he knew that his friend, the giraffe, would never take him anyplace bad. . . .
>
> Tricky Dick was home. Back in Washington. Back on Pennsylvania Ave. And with a story to tell his friends, that they wouldn't have believed if they hadn't seen Tricky Dick riding off on the giraffe's back. Tricky Dick would long be a hero to those who had seen him that day. . . .
>
> There would be many other exciting adventures for Tricky Dick and his friends. And maybe, just maybe, if you're a very good boy, someday we'll tell you about those, too.

Me-Books were commercially successful: many thousands of them were sold. Teachers liked the books, because the books encouraged students to read: students enjoyed reading books that contained their own names.

Pornography (1973)

I programmed the computer to turn words into sentences. For example, Judith Ann Abrams fed the computer this list of words:

Names	Other nouns	Trans. verbs	Other verbs	Adjectives	Exclamations
Barbara	bastard	bite	disapprove	bitchy	rats
Buster	bikini	caress	fall down	creepy	such language
Clyde	bitch	castrate	fly	dead	ugh
Colin	boat	climb	hesitate	enthusiastic	
Debbie	cigarette	enjoy	sing	evil	
Ed Shanahan	creep	kiss	sleep	gaudy	
Jeff	dress	knife	sleepwalk	green	
Keith	ethanol	lick	sneeze	gross	
Kerri	eyelid	pick	vanish	horny	
Liz	fly	pull	walk	insane	
Miles	gambling	rip		juicy	
Nicholson 700	jerk	screw		mixed-up	
Norwalk	knee	shake		monstrous	
	kneecap	take off		multicolored	
	lip	teach		neurotic	
	mouth	undo		obscene	
	navel			paranoid	
	piece			prickly	
	pornography			profane	
	shirt			provocative	
	stud			repulsive	
	tongue			sensuous	
	virgin			sexual	
	whiskey sour			sexy	
	whore			shiny	
				sick	
				stimulating	
				strange	
				succulent	
				tasty	
				unsettled	
				weird	

A **transitive verb** is an action you can do to an object. For example, since you can *bite* and *caress* an object, *bite* and *caress* are transitive verbs.

Here's what the computer printed:

> A Sexy, Profane Creep's Tongue
> by Judith Ann Abrams and the computer
>
> The lip is tasty.
> Ugh!
> The mouth is enthusiastic. Does the gaudy bastard sleepwalk?
> The tongue's whore caresses the bikini. When Nicholson 700 is screwing the creepy jerk over a piece, Jeff is teaching the gambling. Does paranoic Liz hesitate? Why does the tongue kiss the creep stimulatingly on horny Buster?
> Undo! Pull the fly repulsively! A multicolored, enthusiastic cigarette is neurotic. Is a multicolored, weird dress's navel under the strange bikini? Why is the obscene dress's cigarette Colin's ethanol? Rats! Why is the dead, insane, tasty, shiny, knifing creep's bitch unsettled and strange?
> Clyde is over Ed Shanahan. Kissing the bastard, a paranoid ethanol is unsettled. Why is the prickly kneecap's mouth on the creepy piece? Teaching Norwalk is sneezing paranoidly and grossly under provocative, shiny Debbie. As a sexy, walking tongue's virgin takes off the bitchy cigarette over the profane stud then castrates enthusiastic Mile's lip paranoidly, the dead, gaudy knee is stimulating and multicolored. Even though the dead, insane piece licks strangely and neuroticly in the flying, mixed-up eyelid's knee, the dead, biting, obscene bikini is on a repulsive mouth's gambling.
> The pornography is gaudy. Kerri sleepwalks. Why is the tongue sensuous? Buster is sick. Is Miles monstrous? Debbie is neurotic and paranoid, when a stimulating fly picks the navel's jerk under Ed Shanahan. Why is the dress succulent? Hesitating, a kneecap sleeps and climbs the dead, bitchy ethanol. As insane Colin's bastard falls down weirdly in a sensuous dress, green, unsettled Mile's virgin is strange and sexual.
> Is the creepy eyelid provocative? The gambling's whisky sour teaches a navel.
> Is the gambling evil? The bitch walks. Is the virgin profane? Why is the navel sick? Is Liz enthusiastic? Debbie enjoys the creep. Fly! Shaking, green Kerri pulls weird Colin's fly on a sick navel, then vanishes over Norwalk.
> Undo the virgin! While obscene Liz is juicy and sexual, profane, gaudy Jeff's knee is under a succulent whore's navel. Tear Keith's lip bitchily and juicily on sick, weird, multicolored Barbara! Why is Buster insane? The shirt knifes the bikini. Colin shakes the bitch. The whiskey sour hesitates over the green jerk. When a tasty tongue's ethanol walks, Kerri rips the boat and disapproves under enthusiastic Miles. Such language! Keith sings. Why is Buster bitchy?

Notice that the computer turned her adjectives into adverbs, by adding *ly* and making other changes. *Gross* became *grossly*, and *juicy* became *juicily*. Unfortunately, the computer's method wasn't perfect: the computer turned *stimulating* into *stimulatingly* (a non-existent word), and turned *neurotic* into *neuroticly* (instead of *neurotically*).

It conjugated her verbs. *Screw* became *screwing*, and *bite* became *biting* (the computer dropped the *e*). *Lick* became *licks*, and *teach* became *teaches* (the computer added the *e* after the *ch*).

It added *'s* to her nouns. *Jeff* became *Jeff's*. *Miles* became *Miles's* (it should have become *Miles'*).

For each sentence, the grammar is chosen randomly. The chance is 10% that the sentence will begin with an exclamation. If the sentence isn't merely an exclamation, the chance is 18% that the sentence will be a question.

If it's a question, there's a 40% chance it will begin with the word *why*. There's a 50% chance the main part of the question will have the form *does . . . noun phrase . . . verb phrase*, and a 50% chance it will have this form instead: *is . . . noun phrase . . . complement*.

To construct a noun phrase from nouns, adjectives, etc., the computer uses random numbers. It uses random numbers to also construct verb phrases and complements.

The program uses a special variable, called W. At the beginning of the composition, W is near zero; but it tends to increase as the composition progresses. It affects the **complexity**. When W is large, the chance is large that the computer will print adjectives, adverbs, subordinate clauses, and correlative clauses.

This sentence was produced by a small W:

The lip is tasty.

This sentence was produced by a large W:

As a sexy, walking tongue's virgin takes off the bitchy cigarette over the profane stud then castrates enthusiastic Mile's lip paranoidly, the dead, gaudy knee is stimulating and multicolored.

Poetic images (1973)

One of my students, Toby D'Oench, made the computer create poetic images, such as these:

TO GUINEVERE —— LADY OF THE LAKE
Silent mists
Billow in creations
Windmills for flames evolve into ethers
    Merlin again

MY MEMORY
Frozen children
Quiver with leaves
Creations with leaves hover over thoughts
    Gardens of verse

A NEW ENGLAND BARN
Lazy fragrances
Waft by ethers
Seas on fragrances billow in sorrow
    Rusted pitchforks

NEWPORT
Frozen sails
Slumber in fog
Hazes for sails waft by thoughts
    Docks —— yachts —— luxuries of eras gone by

The program contains these lists:

Adjectives	Prepositions	Verbs
fleeting	of	billow in
crimson	on	glitter with
silent	under	flutter by
sensate	above	drift with
pliant	below	flow into
gloomy	in	ponder about
pallid	with	waft by
inky	by	quiver with
frozen	for	hover over
lazy	through	gleam like
		wander through
		slumber in
		dart by
		evolve into
		sing to

Title . . . noun . . . ending

TO REMBRANDT . . . windmills . . . A simple brush
WAITING FOR THE PATIENT . . . ethers . . . Waiting
THE PROPHET . . . visions . . . Then a word
LISTERINE . . . breaths . . . Plastic society
NEWPORT . . . sails . . . Docks —— yachts —— luxuries of eras gone by
EXISTENCE . . . seas . . . In the beginning?
SUMMER IN WATTS . . . flames . . . Tar-street neon —— and the night
TO GUINEVERE —— LADY OF THE LAKE . . . mists . . . Merlin again
NOON IN CALCUTTA . . . hazes . . . Emaciated dark forms strewn like garbage
WEST HARBOR . . . fog . . . A solitary gull slices through
A NEW ENGLAND BARN . . . fragrances . . . Rusted pitchforks
A CHILD'S MICROSCOPE . . . creations . . . The wonderful amoeba
A GROUP PORTRAIT . . . bundles . . . Christmas
THE MILKY WAY . . . cosmos . . . A gooey mess
TOMBSTONE . . . sorrow . . . Rubbings
LIFE AT THE END OF A BRANCH . . . leaves . . . Swirling to the ground
SEASHELLS AND THINGS . . . waves . . . Dribble-dribble-dribble castle
A BEAVER POND . . . reeds . . . Thwack
MY MEMORY . . . children . . . Gardens of verse
EINSTEIN . . . thoughts . . . Somehow through this —— an understanding of a superior order

To create a poetic image, the computer fills in this form:

```
        TITLE
Adjective   Noun that goes with the title
Verb    Noun
Noun    Preposition   Noun   Verb   Noun
    Ending that goes with the title
```

Curses (1978)

Tom Dwyer & Margot Critchfield made the computer curse you. Here are some of the computer's curses:

May an enraged camel overwhelm your garage.
May an ancient philosopher lay an egg on your dill pickle.
May seven large chickens sing an operatic solo to your love letters.

To invent a curse, the computer fills in the blanks:

May _____ _____ your _____.
    subject   verb phrase   object

The computer uses these words randomly:

Subjects	Verb phrases	Objects
an enraged camel	send a mash note to	mother-in-law
an ancient philosopher	get inspiration from	psychoanalyst
a cocker spaniel	redecorate	rumpus room
the Eiffel Tower	become an obsession of	fern
a cowardly moose	make a salt lick out of	garage
the silent majority	buy an interest in	love letters
the last picture show	overwhelm	piggy bank
a furious trumpet player	pour yogurt on	hamburger
Miss America	sing an operatic solo to	dill pickle
seven large chickens	lay an egg on	Honda

You can find that program on page 152 of their book, *BASIC and the Personal Computer*.

The computer can analyze what humans write.

English poetry

Can the computer analyze English poetry? From 1957 to 1959 at Cornell University, Stephen Parrish made the computer alphabetize the words in Matthew Arnold's poetry. Here's an excerpt:

```
                                        Page              Line
                                        in                in
                                        book  Poem's title poem
CONSCIOUS
  back with the conscious thrill of shame 181  Isolation Marg  19
  conscious or not of the past           287  Rugby Chapel   45
CONSCIOUSNESS
  the last spark of man's consciousness with words 429 Empedocles II 30
  and keep us prisoners of our consciousness 439 Empedocles II 352
CONSECRATE
  Peter his friend with light did consecrate 445 Westmin Abbey 50
CONSECRATES
  which consecrates the ties of blood for these indeed 196 Frag Antigone 31
CONSECRATION
  won consecration from time             281  Haworth Church 46
  foreshown thee in thy consecration-hour 446 Westmin Abbey 75
```

To find out what Matthew Arnold said about love, just look up LOVE. Such an index is called a **concordance**.

That concordance was the first produced by a computer. Previously, all concordances of poetry were created by hand, using filing cards. For example, in 1870 a group of researchers began creating a concordance to Chaucer, by hand. They started at the letter A. 45 years later, they were only up to the letter H!

Did the poet Shelley steal ideas from others? Joseph Raben, at Queens College, believed Shelley borrowed imagery from Milton. To prove it, in 1964 he made the computer produce concordances to Shelley's *Prometheus Unbound* and Milton's *Paradise Lost* and compare them. The computer found many similarities between Shelley and Milton.

What were Shakespeare's favorite words? In 1971 at Münster University in Germany, Marvin Spevack fed the computer all the works of Shakespeare, and made it count how often each word occurs. Disregarding trivial words such as *a* and *the*, the computer discovered Shakespeare's favorite word was *love*: he used it 2,271 times. Next come *heart*, *death*, *man*, *life*, and *hand*. He never used the word *hero*. In *Macbeth*, the word *good* occurs more often than any other adjective, noun, or adverb, and more often than most verbs.

By counting words, other researchers made the computer graph the rise and fall of themes in a novel.

American history

Who wrote the *Federalist Papers*? Historians knew some of the papers were by Alexander Hamilton and others by James Madison, but the authorship of the remaining papers was in dispute.

In 1964, Mosteller and Wallace made the computer compare the literary styles of the papers, by counting the frequency of words such as *by*, *enough*, *from*, *to*, *upon*, *while*, and *whilst*. It concluded that all the disputed papers were written by Madison, not Hamilton.

The statistical evidence was so high that historians accept the computer's finding as fact.

The Bible

Can the computer analyze the Bible? In 1951, Texas clergyman John Ellison made the computer compare 309 Greek manuscripts of the New Testament. Underneath each word of a standard text, the computer printed the variants found in other manuscripts. It classified the manuscripts according to their similarities.

In 1957, he published a concordance to the Revised Standard Bible, and a pair of other researchers (Tasman & Busa) indexed the Dead Sea Scrolls.

Did the apostle Paul really write all those marvelous letters attributed to him in the New Testament? Or were they actually written by somebody else?

In 1964, Scottish clergyman Andrew Morton used the computer to deduce that Paul didn't write some of those letters.

All Morton did was count how often Paul used the Greek word *kai* in each sentence. *Kai* means *and*. Coming to a conclusion about Biblical authorship by counting just the word *and* might seem silly, but Morton said he analyzed 20 writers of ancient Greek and found each used *kai* with a constant frequency. In the "Pauline" letters, the frequency of *kai* varied a lot, implying some of them were not by Paul.

Ellison distrusted Morton's assumption that a man's literary style must remain constant. He warned: if Morton's method were applied to the Declaration of Independence and Thomas Jefferson's letters to his wife, the computer might conclude that either Jefferson didn't write the Declaration of Independence or another man was writing love letters to Mrs. Jefferson. In 1965, to prove his point, he applied Morton's method to two of Morton's own articles on the subject: the computer concluded that Morton could not be the author of both!

Forgery

IBM programmed the computer to detect a forged signature — even if the signature looks correct to the naked eye.

To use the IBM forgery-detection system, write your signature by using IBM's special pen, attached to the computer. As you write, the computer notices how hard you press the pen against the paper and how fast you move the pen.

If somebody else tries to pretend he's you, he must sit down at the machine and try to duplicate your signature. If he presses the pen hardest at different points of the signature, or if he accelerates the pen's motion at different points, the computer says he's a fake.

The system works well, because the average crook trying to forge your signature will hesitate at the hard parts. His hesitation affects the pen's pressure and acceleration, which tell the computer he's faking.

IBM developed the system in 1979 but isn't selling it yet. When it does, remember: the system works just on signatures written with IBM's pen.

TRANSLATE RUSSIAN

Soon after computers were invented, programmers tried to make them translate Russian into English. They chose Russian instead of Spanish, for three reasons:

1. Few humans could translate Russian. Spanish translators were a-dime-a-dozen.

2. Computer experts love hard problems. Russian is harder than Spanish.

3. Most computers were owned by the Department of Defense, which is *very* interested in Russia.

Early attempts

In 1954, IBM wrote a program that translated Russian sentences such as:

Gasoline is prepared by chemical methods from crude oil. The price of crude oil is determined by the market. The quality of the crude oil is determined by the calorie content.

Unfortunately, most Russian sentences are not so simple. During the 1960's, the end of a Russian paper on space biology was fed into an advanced program written by Computer Concepts, Inc. Here's the translation that came out:

Thus, the examination of some from fundamental RADIOBIOLOGICESKIX problems shows, that in this a field still very much NEREWENNYZ questions. This is clear, since cosmic RADIOBIOLOGI4 is very young RAZDELOM young science efforts of scientific different specialties of the different countries of the world successful PRODOLJENY will be expanded there are.

The computer couldn't translate the words in capital letters and was stumped by Russian grammar.

The competing program, written by the Air Force, translated the same passage a little better:

Thus, consideration of from basic radio-biological problems shows that in a given region still very many unsolved questions. This and intelligibly, since space radiobiology is very young division of young science — space biology. However, is base to trust that jointly scientists of different specialties of various countries of world/peace radiobiological investigations in outer space will be successfully continued and expanded.

In 1966, a special committee of the National Academy of Sciences concluded that the experience of computer translation was "uniformly discouraging" and that hiring a human translator was cheaper than doing the two-step process of computer translation followed by human editing.

During the last 20 years, computer prices have fallen, but so has the availability of Americans who know Russian, so the computer's usefulness is still in doubt. Today, most translations are still done by humans, who use computers to help do the word processing and to search through a dictionary and thesaurus.

Famous errors

If you program the computer to translate an English sentence into Russian, and then the Russian back to English, will you get back the same English sentence you started with?

One programmer tried, "The spirit is willing, but the flesh is weak." The computer translated it into Russian, then back into English, and printed, "The booze is strong, but the meat is rotten."

Another programmer tried, "Out of sight, out of mind." The computer printed, "Blind idiot."

At an engineering conference, a computer was translating scientific papers into English, when it suddenly started talking about "water sheep". Everyone was confused. Finally they figured it out: the computer meant **hydraulic rams**.

Xerox's amazing translation machine

In Moscow during the 1960's, American companies were showing off their products, but none of the Russians were interested in Xerox's photocopiers — until some Xerox employees put on an amazing demonstration. They "photocopied" some English writing, and — presto! — a beautiful Russian translation of it came out of the machine! The machine was acting as a translator! And the translation was flawless, even though the English text was complex!

The Russians were very excited, and ordered hundreds of the amazing translation machine.

But before shipping the machines, the Xerox guys confessed it was just a gag. The employees had sneaked the Russian version into the machine, before beginning the demonstration.

What if Americans had the same sense of humor about nuclear war? "Hello, Gorbachev? This is George Bush, on the hot line. We just fired some nuclear missiles. They're heading straight for Moscow. Ha, ha! Just kidding."

ꓤAMES

Much of our country's computing power is spent playing games. Here's why. . . .

Shannon's trees

In 1950, Claude Shannon proposed a way to make the computer win at checkers, chess, and other complicated games.

To understand his method, let's try to make the computer win a game of checkers. As in all checker tournaments, one player is called BLACK, and the other is called WHITE (even though his pieces are actually red). BLACK makes the first move. When a player can jump, he must. The game ends when one of the players can't move (either because he has no pieces or because his pieces are blocked).

To simplify the game, we'll play on a 4-by-4 board, instead of the traditional 8-by-8. Each player has two pieces instead of twelve.

This diagram shows 63 possible positions:

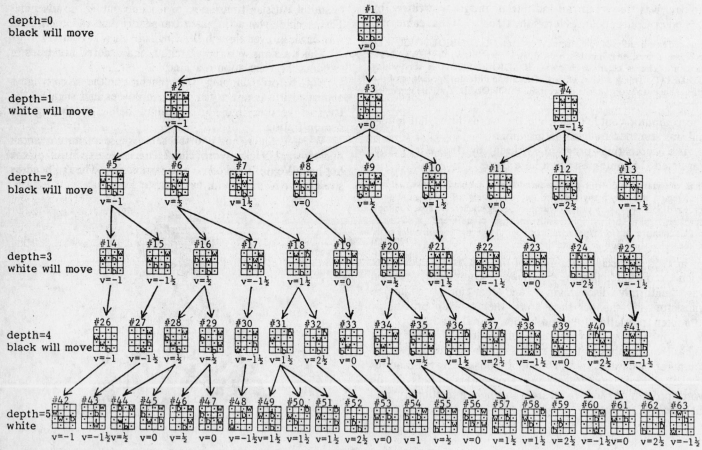

Position #1 is the initial position, from which black will move. The three arrows coming from position #1 represent the three legal moves he can choose from. Depending on which move he chooses, the board will wind up in position #2 or #3 or #4. Which move is best?

If he moves to position #2, white will reply by moving to position #5 or #6 or #7.
If he moves to position #3, white will reply by moving to position #8 or #9 or #10.
If he moves to position #4, white will reply by moving to position #11 or #12 or #13.

The diagram shows all possible ways the game's first five moves could go. Throughout the diagram, w means white man, b means black man, ẃ means white king, and ḃ means black king. The diagram's called a **tree**. (If you turn it upside down, it looks like the kind of tree that grows in the ground.) The arrows are called the tree's **branches**. The tree's **depth** is 5.

Which position should black choose: #2, #3, or #4? The wisdom of your answer depends on how deep you make the tree. In this particular game, a depth of 5 is satisfactory; but in 8-by-8 checkers or chess you might have to dig deeper. Theoretically, you should keep digging until you reach the end of the game; but such a tree might be too large to fit in your computer's memory.

For chess, Shannon estimated that a complete tree requires 10^{120} branches. Einstein estimated that the number of electrons in the universe is only 10^{110}. If Shannon and Einstein are both right, the tree can't fit in the universe!

Having constructed a tree of depth 5, look at the bottom positions (#42 through #63) and evaluate them, to see which positions look favorable for black. You should consider many factors: which player has control of the center of the board? which player can move the most without being jumped? and so on. But to keep matters simple, let's consider just one factor: which player has the most men? Consider a king to be worth 1½ men.

Subtract the number of white men from the number of black men: the result of the evaluation is a number, which is called the position's **value**. If it's negative, black is losing; if it's positive, black is winning; if it's zero, the game is heading for a draw.

For example, consider position #42. Since black has one man and white has two, the value is 1 minus 2, which is -1. That's why I've written "v=-1" underneath that position. The value of each position at depth=5 is computed by that method.

For the positions at depth=4, use a different method. For example, here's how to find the value of position #29. That position has two possible outcomes: #46 and #47. Which outcome is more likely? Since the move will be made by black, and black's goal is to make the value large, he'll prefer to move to #46 instead of #47. Since the most likely outcome is #46, whose value is ½, assign position #29 a value of ½ also.

Here's the rule: to compute the value of a position at depth=4, find the *maximum* value of the positions it points to. (The value of position #29 is the maximum value of positions #46 and #47, which is ½.)

To compute the value of a position at depth=3, find the *minimum* value of the positions it points to (since it's white's turn to move, and white wants to minimize). For example, the value of position #18 is the minimum value of positions #31 and #32, which is 1½.

Compute the values for depth 2 by maximizing, and the values for depth 1 by minimizing. Finally, you get these results:

The value of position #2 is -1.
The value of position #3 is 0.
The value of position #4 is -1½.

Since black wants to maximize values, black should move to position #3. If white is also a good player, the game will probably gravitate toward position #53, a draw. If white is a poorer player, black will win.

That method of choosing the best move was proposed by Shannon. Since it makes heavy use of minimums and maximums, it's called the **minimax method**.

Samuel's checkers

After Shannon, the next person to become famous was Arthur Samuel. He spent a long time (twenty years, from 1947 to 1967) trying to make the computer win checkers. He used Shannon's minimax idea, but made many improvements.

His first spectacular success came in 1962, when his program won a game against Robert Nealey, a former Connecticut checkers champion. After the game, Nealey said "The computer had to make several star moves in order to get the win. . . . In the matter of the end game, I have not had such competition from any human being since 1954, when I lost my last game."

Later, the computer played six more games against Nealey. Nealey won one of them; the other five were draws.

In 1965 the computer played four games against W.F. Hellman, the World Champion. The games were played by mail. Under those conditions, Hellman won all four. But in a hastily played game where Hellman sat across the board from the computer, the result was a draw.

In 1967 the computer was beaten by the Pacific Coast Champion, K.D. Hanson, twice.

In short, the computer wins against most humans and draws against most experts, though it loses to the top champions. To bring the computer to that level of intelligence, Samuel improved Shannon's method in three ways. . . .

1. When choosing among several moves, the computer analyzes the most promising ones more deeply.

2. After computing the value of a position (by examining the positions under it), the computer writes the value on a piece of tape. If the position recurs in another game, the computer looks at the tape instead of repeating the analysis.

3. To compute the value of a position, the computer examines many factors in addition to the number of pieces each player has. The computer combines the factors, to form combination-factors, and then combines the combination-factors to form a single value. The relative importance given to each factor is determined by "experience". Samuel experimented with two forms of experience: he had the computer play against itself, and also had it analyze 250,000 moves that occurred in checker championships.

Chess

While Samuel was programming checkers, other programmers tried to write a similar program for chess. They had a hard time. In 1960 the best chess program that had been written was beaten by a ten-year-old kid who was a novice.

Greenblatt
The first decent chess program was written in 1967 by Richard Greenblatt and his friends at MIT. It actually won a game in a chess tournament.

But in most tournaments, it lost. In 1970 and 1971, it lost every game in every tournament it entered.

Slate & Atkins
In 1968, Atkins & Gorklen, undergraduates at Northwestern University, wrote a chess program. Inspired by their program, David Slate, a graduate student in physics there, wrote a chess program also. In 1969, Slate & Atkins combined the two programs, to form a better program, **Chess 2.0**.

During the next several years, they continually improved the program. Their most famous version was called **Chess 4.7**.

Their program is playing chess against human experts — and winning! Their computer has scored several triumphs in tournaments designed for humans.

In 1976, their computer won the class B section of the Paul Masson American Chess Championships. Against the humans in that tournament, it scored 5 wins, no losses. By winning that tournament, it achieved a U.S. Chess Federation score of 2210 and became a chess Master.

Then it entered the Minnesota State Championship, to try to become the Minnesota State Champion, but lost (it scored 1 win, 3 losses, 1 tie).

In August 1968, an International Chess Master, David Levy, bet about $5,000 against several computerists. He bet that no computer would win a chess match against him in the next ten years. He won the bet: in August 1978, Chess 4.7 tried one last time to win a match against him, but lost (it scored 1 win, 3 losses, 1 tie).

Slate & Atkins improved Chess 4.7, to form **Chess 4.9**, which is the world champion of computer chess.

But though it's the world champion of computer chess, it's not necessarily the "best" program. It wins because it runs on a super-fast maxicomputer (manufactured by Control Data Corporation). Other chess programs, written for slower computers, are at a disadvantage.

Minicomputer chess
Almost as fast as Chess 4.9 is a program called **Belle**, written at Bell Telephone Laboratories. Belle runs on an unusual minicomputer that's specially wired to create trees quickly.

Microcomputer chess
Each of those programs — Chess 4.9 and Belle — requires an expensive CPU and lots of RAM. Is it possible to write a decent chess program using only a cheap CPU and very little RAM? Yes! In 1976, a Canadian named Peter Jennings wrote a program called **Microchess 1.0**; it ran on a $250 microcomputer (the Kim 1), which contained a 6502 CPU, no ROM, and only 1K of RAM! The program played decently, though not spectacularly.

Later, he improved the program, and called the improvement **Microchess 1.5**. It plays on the Radio Shack model 1 and the Apple. The version on the model 1 consumes 4K of RAM: 2K is for the logic, and the other 2K are just to make the picture of the chess board look pretty! You can get Microchess 1.5 for just $20 from your local Radio Shack store or Apple dealer.

In 1978, an amazing chess program was written by a husband-and-wife team: Dan and Kathe Sprachlin. They named the program **Sargon**, to honor an ancient king. It ran on the Jupiter microcomputer, which contained an 8080 CPU and 16K RAM. It played much better than Microchess. When the Jupiter computer became obsolete, the Sprachlins rewrote the program, to make it run on the Radio Shack model 1 and the Apple. Then they developed an improved version called **Sargon 2**, and a further improvement called **Sargon 3**, which runs on *all* the popular computers. Sargon 3 is published by the Hayden division of Spinnaker.

For many years, Sargon 3 was considered the best microcomputer chess program. But in 1986, Sargon 3 was beaten by a new program called **Chessmaster 2000**. Like Sargon 3, Chessmaster 2000 contains many features that make it fun for both experts and novices. It's published by Software Toolworks, distributed by Electronic Arts, costs about $35, and comes in versions for the Apple 2e & 2c, Commodore 64 & Amiga, Atari 800 XL & ST, and IBM PC.

Recently, Sargon 3 has been replaced by **Sargon 4**, and Chessmaster 2000 has been replaced by **Chessmaster 2100** and **Chessmaster 3000**.

When you play against the computer by using Sargon 4, Chessmaster 2100, or Chessmaster 3000, you can ask the computer for help, by pressing a special key. Then the computer will tell you how it would move, if it were in your position. You can follow the computer's suggestion or ignore it. (Since your goal is to outsmart the computer, you should listen to the computer's advice; but instead of *following* the advice, you should try to devise a move that's even more clever.)

Many companies manufacture hand-held electronic chess games. Some of the games even contain a tiny voice synthesizer, which lets the computer tell you its moves verbally. Some of the games even contain a mechanical arm, so that the computer will pick up the pieces and move them. Some of the games have touch-sensitive boards, so that you can indicate your move by just pushing the square you want to move from and the square you want to move to. For humor, some of the chess games have the computer make wisecracks about your style of playing.

Choosing a level

When you begin playing a top-notch computer game (such as Chessmaster 3000), you must choose the "level" at which you want the computer to play. If you choose a low level, the computer will move quickly, without much forethought. If you choose a high level, the computer will play more carefully (and make better moves); to do that, the computer "looks ahead", by building a very large tree, which requires lots of time; and so you must wait a long time until the computer moves. If you choose a level that's very high, the computer will need *several hours* to compute its move.

Why a computer?

Playing against the computer is more interesting than playing against a human.

When you play against a human friend, you must wait a long time for your friend to move. When you play against Chessmaster 3000 at a low level, the computer moves almost immediately. So you can play several games against the computer (and learn a lot from them) in the same amount of time you'd need to play just *one* game against a human. So by playing against the computer, you gain experience faster than by playing against a human. Bobby Fischer, who became the world chess champion, now plays *only* against computers; he refuses to play against humans and hasn't defended his title.

The computer is kinder than a human. If you make a bad move, the computer lets you "take it back" and try again. If you seem to be losing, the computer lets you restart the whole game. The computer — unlike a human — has infinite patience and no ego. Playing against the computer is less threatening than playing against a human.

If you have a computer, you don't have to worry about finding an opponent who's "at your level"; when you play against the computer, just tell the computer at what level you want it to play. The computer will act about as smart as you wish.

Othello

Chess and checkers are both played on a checkerboard. Another game that's played on a checkerboard is **Othello**. It uses checkers, but each checker has two sides: one side is white; the flip side is black.

When the game begins, only four checkers are on the board: two of them have their white side showing, and the other two checkers show black.

The game is for two players. One is called the white player, and the other is called the black player.

For example, suppose you're the white player. On your turn, you put an extra checker onto the board, so that the checker shows white. You must position the checker so that it and a previously placed white checker surround some black checkers. Then you flip all the surrounded black checkers, so that they become white.

Similarly, on his turn, the black player puts a black checker onto the board, so that some of your white checkers are surrounded by black, and he flips all those white checkers, so that they become black.

The game ends when the board is entirely filled with checkers. If most of the checkers are white, the white player wins; otherwise, black wins.

The game is tricky, because the definition of "surrounded checkers" is strange, and because you can't easily figure out who's winning. At first glance, you'd think that if most of the checkers on the checkerboard are white, white is ahead; but at the end of the game, the situation can change drastically. For example, the black player might place a black checker in such a way that most of the white checkers become black. So you must guard against dangerous positions. During the early parts of the game, the white checkers' *positions* are more important than their *quantity*.

The game began centuries ago in England, where it was called **Reversi**. It resembled the Japanese game called **Go**. About 1975, it was marketed in the United States as a board game, under the name **Othello** (which is trademarked by Gabriel Industries). Programmers tried to make the computer imitate the game and win.

After writing Sargon 2 (the award-winning chess program), Dan and Kathe Sprachlin turned their attention to Othello, and wrote an award-winning Othello program called **Reversal**. It plays Othello better than any other program ever invented. Like Sargon 2, it's been published by Hayden, runs on the Apple, allows several levels of play, costs $35 on disk, and lets you press a "tutoring" button whenever you want the computer to give you advice on how to reply. For added humor, each checker shows a frown or smile. For example, if the white checkers outnumbered the black, the white checkers wear smiles, and the black checkers wear frowns; the smiles and frowns grow bigger, as white's lead over black increases. And whenever a checker is added to the board or flipped, the computer plays a musical fanfare.

Unfortunately, Hayden has become part of Spinnaker, which has stopped publishing the program, because most people have forgotten how to play Othello and no longer want to play. Too bad! It was a fun game.

Backgammon

Backgammon is a game played with dice. It requires both luck and skill. For many years, the world champion backgammon player was a human. But recently, he was beaten by a computer, in a thorough match.

The human was a poor loser: he blamed it on "bad luck". He refuses to admit that the computer has more skill than he. Nevertheless, the computer is now the world champion.

Hey! Let's have some action!

Arcade games

The first popular arcade game was **Pong**, which made the computer crudely imitate a game of ping-pong. Then came **Space Invaders**, in which you had to shoot aliens who were dropping bombs on you.

Those games restricted you to moving in just one direction. The first popular arcade game that let you move two-dimensionally was **Asteroids**. It let you move through the sky while dodging asteroids and enemy space ships.

Those outer-space and sports games appealed mainly to boys. The first arcade game appealing mainly to girls was **Pac Man**, a non-violent fantasy in which you ran through a maze full of food and tried to gobble as much as possible, before ghosts gobbled *you*. It appealed especially to dieting girls who dreamed of pigging out without getting caught.

In all those games, the graphics were crude. The first arcade game that used professional graphics was **Dragon's Lair**, which contained a videodisk full of animated cartoons drawn by artists who had worked at Walt Disney Studios. To dodge obstacles that appear in the cartoons, you move your joystick, which changes the action that the cartoons display.

Each year's arcade games reflect the latest fads. For example, you can play arcade games about break-dancing and kung-fu.

Game watch

A **game watch** is a digital wrist watch that plays a video game. If you're stuck in the middle of a boring business meeting, look at your game watch.

When your colleagues see you looking at your watch, they'll think you're an impatient executive tracking the time. Meanwhile, you're just having fun!

Olympics

In 1980, Tim Smith quit his job at Burroughs and spent the next 9 months programming **Olympic Decathlon**, which made the Radio Shack Model 1 computer imitate all ten of the decathlon's events.

In his game, one of your fingers represents your left leg, and another finger represents your right leg. To "run", you tap those fingers (left, right, left, right) as quickly as possible on the keyboard. By using those fingers and others, you compete in all ten events: the 100-meter dash, long jump, shot-put, high jump, 400-meter dash, 110-meter hurdles, discus throw, pole vault, javelin throw, and 1500-meter run. You can play solo or against your friends. At parties, you can form teams and cheer each other on.

Later, he wrote versions for the Apple 2 and the IBM PC. They're published by Microsoft.

A competing company, **Epyx**, has invented a variation that displays better graphics. It comes on a pair of disks, called **Summer Games** and **Summer Games 2**. It plays the national anthems of all major countries and includes sixteen games: pole vault, diving, 4x400-meter relay, 100-meter dash, gymnastics, freestyle relay, 100-meter freestyle, skeet shooting, triple jump, rowing, javelin, equestrian, high jump, fencing, cycling, and kayaking. It runs on all popular computers: IBM, Mac, Apple 2, C64, Amiga, and ST.

Sports heroes

A game called **One-on-One** accurately imitates a basketball shooting match between two stars: Larry Bird and Julius ("Doctor J") Erving. The program imitates each player's personal strengths and weaknesses. You can take the role of either player and try to avoid getting creamed by the other. Programmed by Eric Hammond with help from Larry and Doctor J, it's published by Electronic Arts.

Adventure is a game where you hunt for some sort of "treasure".

Original Adventure

The original version of Adventure was written by Will Crowther & Don Woods, on a PDP-10 maxicomputer at Stanford University's Artificial Intelligence Lab.

When you run the program, the computer says you're near a shack at the end of a road. The computer offers to act as your body and understand any two-word command. Then it waits for your command. You can tell it to GO NORTH or GO FORWARD or — if you're going along a stream — you can say FOLLOW STREAM or GO DOWNSTREAM.

The first time you play this game, you feel lost — the game's an adventure. As you wander in whatever direction you please, the computer says you're going through forests, across streams, over hills, etc.

After much aimless wandering, you'll eventually see a stream. If you follow the stream, you'll come to a mysterious iron grate. If you try to BREAK GRATE, the computer says you're not strong enough. If you try to OPEN GRATE, the computer says you have no keys. You'll get more and more frustrated, until the computer offers to give you a hint — but the hint will cost you several points. If you acquiesce, the computer will give you this hint: find the keys!

To find the keys, the typical stupid player tries wandering through the forests and valleys again. But if you're smart, you'll remember that at the beginning of the adventure you were next to a shack. So you go back to the shack, walk inside, and find keys! So you trek back to iron grate, and use the keys to get in. You think — aha! — you've succeeded!

But actually, you've just begun! The grate leads you into a cave that contains 130 rooms, which form a big three-dimensional maze. Lying in the maze are 15 buried treasures; but as you walk through the maze, you can easily forget where you are and where you've come from; you can waste lots of time just walking in circles, without realizing it!

To add to the challenge, the cave contains many dangers, such as trap doors (if you fall in, you break every bone in your body!) and trolls & snakes, which you must ward off by using various devices that you must find in the cave's rooms or even back at the shack. Yes, you might have to trek all the way back to the shack again!

Finally, after dodging all the evil things in the cave, you reach the treasures. You grab them up and start walking away with them. But then you hear footsteps behind you, and pirates steal your treasures! Then you must chase the pirates.

If you manage to keep your treasures and your life and get out of the cave, you haven't necessarily won. The nasty computer keeps score of how *well* you retrieve the treasures. The maximum possible score is 350. After you've played this game many times and learned how to duck all your adversaries quickly, you'll find you scored just 349 points, and you'll wonder what you did wrong that cost you 1 point. The answer is: during the adventure, you must borrow magazines from a room in the cave; to get the extra point, you must return them!

The game's a true adventure, because as you wander through forests and the rooms in the cave, the computer tells what you see, but you don't know whether what you see is important. For example, when you walk into a room, the computer might say the room contains a small cage. That's all

it says. You must guess whether the cage has any significance and what to do to the cage, if anything. Should you pick it up? Try to break it? Kiss it? Carry it? Try anything you like — give any command to your computer-body that you wish — and see what happens.

Here's a list of the most useful commands. . . .

To reach a different room in the cave, say GO NORTH (or SOUTH, EAST, WEST, UP, or DOWN). You can abbreviate: instead of typing "GO NORTH", just type "N".

Whenever you see a new object, TAKE it. Then you can carry it from room to room and use it later whenever you need it. If you see a new object and want to TAKE it, but your hands are already full, DROP one of the other objects you're carrying.

To see a list of what you're carrying, tell the computer to take INVENTORY. To make the computer describe your surroundings again, say LOOK.

To see your score so far, say SCORE.

If you say SAVE, the computer will copy your current position onto the disk, so you can return to that position later. If you ever want to give up, just say QUIT.

Throughout the game, you get beautifully lyrical writing. For example, the computer describes one of the rooms as follows: "You are in a splendid chamber thirty feet high. The walls are frozen rivers of orange stone."

The game's an adventure about a person exploring a cave. Since *you're* the person in the adventure and can type whichever actions you wish, you affect how the adventure progresses and ends. Since it's high-quality story-telling whose outcome is affected by your input, it's called **interactive fiction**.

Microcomputer versions

Although Adventure was originally written for a PDP-10 maxicomputer, you can get an exact imitation for microcomputers.

The first imitations (published by Microsoft for the Apple 2 and by Creative Computing for CP/M computers) are no longer marketed. Today, the best imitation for microcomputers comes on a disk called the **Golden Oldies**, published by Software Country and distributed by Electronic Arts. The disk includes four programs: Adventure, Eliza, Pong, and Life. It's been available for the IBM PC, Mac, Apple 2e & 2c, Commodore 64, Commodore Amiga, and Atari 800 XL. But getting your hands on it is difficult, since it's no longer being actively distributed.

Infocom

After Adventure became popular, several programmers invented a variation called Zork, which lets you input long sentences instead of restricting you to two-word phrases. Like Adventure, Zork consists of hunting for treasures in a cave. In Zork, you reach the cave by entering a house's basement.

Like Adventure, Zork originally ran on a PDP-10 computer. Infocom has published versions of Zork for microcomputers. Versions for the IBM PC, Mac, Apple 2e & 2c, Apple Macintosh, Commodore Amiga, Atari ST, and Radio Shack Models 3 & 4 cost $39.95. Versions for the Commodore 64, Atari 800 XL, and Radio Shack Color Computer 2 cost just $34.95.

Zork sold so well that Infocom published sequels, called **Zork 2** and **Zork 3**. Then Infocom published other variations, where the cave's been replaced by experiences in outer space or by thrillers involving spies, murders, mysteries, and haunted castles. Infocom's latest big hits are **The Hitchhiker's Guide to the Galaxy** (based on the award-winning wacky outer-space novel by Doug Adams) and **Leather Goddesses of Phobos** (which lets you choose among three naughtiness levels, from "prude" to "lewd"; choosing "lewd" makes the computer asks whether you're at least 18; it also asks whether you're male or female, and you get a titillating 3-D comic book with a scratch-and-sniff card).

Infocom was an independent company but has been acquired by Activision.

Sierra On-Line

Shortly after Infocom developed the microcomputer version of Zork, Sierra On-Line developed **Super Stud Adventure**, which was quickly renamed **Softporn Adventure**. Instead of exploring a cave, you explore a brothel. To enter the brothel, you must find the secret password (hint: go to the bathroom and look at the graffiti!) and find enough money to pay for your pleasures (by taking a taxi to a casino and gambling).

That was the first **urban adventure**, and also the first **sexual adventure**. The ad for it showed a photograph of the programmers (Ken & Roberta Williams) nude in a California hot tub. Fortunately, the water in the tub was high enough to cover any problems.

The original adventure, Infocom adventures, and Softporn Adventure display wonderful text but no graphics. They're called **text adventures**.

The most ambitious **graphics adventure** ever created was **Time Zone**, published in 1981 by Sierra On-Line. The Time Zone program is so long that it fills *both* sides of 6 Apple disks; that's 12 sides altogether! In fact, the game's so long that nobody's ever finished playing it! Here's how to play . . .

You use a computerized "time machine", which transports you to 9 times (400 million B.C., 10000 B.C., 50 B.C., 1000 A.D., 1400, 1700, 1982, 2082, and 4082) and 8 locations (North America, South America, Europe, Africa, Asia, Australia, Antarctica, and Outer Space).

Wherever you go, your screen shows a high-resolution color picture of where you are. For example, if you choose "approximately 1400", Christopher Columbus will welcome you aboard his ship. Altogether, the game contains over 1400 pictures! You travel through history, searching for clues that help you win.

Time Zone is historically accurate and doesn't let you cheat. For example, when you find a book of matches in the year 2082, your time machine will let you carry the matches back to 1982 but not to 1700 — since matches weren't invented until 1800.

Living through history isn't easy. Jonathan Rotenberg, chairman of the Boston Computer Society, played the game and said:

I've been killed dozens of times. I've been assassinated by Brazilian terrorists, karate-chopped by a Brazilian monk, eaten by a tyrannosaur, crushed in an Andes avalanche, stampeded by a buffalo, overcome by Antarctic frostbite, and harpooned by Mayan fishermen.

And you see it all in color!

Time Zone sold for $99.95. Alas, teenagers didn't buy it, because it took too long to win and was too expensive. Sierra On-Line has stopped selling it.

Recently, Sierra On-Line has made Softporn Adventure even more exciting, by adding graphics. The new graphic versions are called **Leisure Suit Larry in the Land of the Lounge Lizards, Leisure Suit Larry 2: Looking for Love in all the Wrong Places**, and **Leisure Suit Larry 3: Passionate Patti in Pursuit of the Pulsating Pectorals**.

Creative Computing

Dave Ahl, publisher of *Creative Computing Magazine*, copied the movie **Roller Coaster** onto a videodisk, then attached the videodisk player to the computer, to let the computer control which part of the movie you see. He wrote an adventure game that lets the computer illustrate each location and action by a 10-second clip from the movie. When you play the game, your goal is to save your friends before they ride on a roller coaster that crashes. It's the world's first **video adventure**. Your actions determine which part of the movie you see next, which disaster scenes you manage to avoid, and the fate of your friends. It's the world's first **interactive movie**.

Although Dave and his friends all love to play the game, the Actors Guild refuses to let Dave sell the game to strangers. The Guild claims that when Dave shows the scenes in an order different from the original movie's, he's destroying the "artistic integrity" of the actors' performances.

Ha! Does the Guild *really* believe that a grade-B horror flick has any artistic integrity at all?

Spinnaker

Spinnaker publishes the **Windham Classics**. It's a series of adventure games based on kid's novels.

You become Dorothy in **The Wizard of Oz**, Jim Hawkins in **Treasure Island**, Fritz in **Swiss Family Robinson**, Alice in **Alice in Wonderland**, and Green-Sky in **Below the Root**. The games include graphics. To make those adventure games easy, whenever you get stuck the computer helps you by printing a list of words to try typing.

Each computerized novel costs just $9.95 for the Commodore 64, $39.95 for the Apple 2e & 2c and IBM PC.

Spinnaker also publishes **Telarium Software**, based on novels that are more adult. You become Perry Mason in **The Case of the Mandarin Murder**, the crime reporter in Agatha Christie's **The Scoop**, the researcher in Michael Crichton's **Amazon**, and the major characters in **Fahrenheit 451, Rendezvous with Rama, Dragonworld**, and **Nine Princes in Amber**.

The Perry Mason one, besides being fun, also trains you to become a lawyer. It comes with a lawyer's handbook that explains the 6 ways to object to the prosecutor's questions: you can complain that the prosecutor's asking an IRRELEVANT question, relying on HEARSAY, BROWBEATING the witness, LEADING the witness to a suggested answer, getting an OPINION from a person who isn't an expert, or trying to get facts from a person who's UNQUALIFIED to know them.

To make sure you understand those six ways to object, the handbook includes a multiple-choice test about them. The test is titled "Study Guide for the California Bar Exam".

The game also lets you invent your own questions for the witnesses and give commands to your secretary (Della Street) and detective (Paul Drake). It costs $39.95 for the Apple 2e & 2c and IBM PC, $32.95 for the Commodore 64. The other games in the Tellarium series cost the same or less.

Broderbund

Broderbund has published a game called **Where in the World is Carmen Sandiego?** You try to catch and arrest the notorious international thief, Carmen Sandiego, and the other thieves in her organization, called the *Villain's International League of Evil (V.I.L.E.)*, as they flee to 30 cities all over the world.

To help you understand those 30 cities, the game comes with a geography book: the 928-page unabridged edition of *The World Almanac and Book of Facts*.

As you play the game, you unearth clues about which cities the thieves are fleeing to. But to use the clues, you must look up facts in the almanac. By playing the game, you learn how to use an almanac, and also learn geography. When you figure out which city to travel to, the screen shows a map of the world, shows you traveling to the city, and then shows a snapshot of what the city looks like, so that the game also acts as a travelogue.

Because the game is so educational, it's won awards from *Classroom Computer Learning Magazine* and the Software Publishers Association.

Strictly speaking, it's not a true adventure game, since it does *not* let you input your own words and phrases. Instead, you just choose from menus, which make the game easier for youngsters.

Broderbund has created three sequels. **Where in the USA is Carmen Sandiego?** has you chasing Carmen's gang across all 50 states; the game comes with *Fodor's USA* travel guide. **Where in Europe in Carmen Sandiego?** takes you to all 34 countries in Europe and comes with Rand McNally's *Concise Atlas of Europe*. **Where in Time is Carmen Sandiego?** lets you romp through historical time periods.

For the Apple 2 family and IBM PC, the original version costs $39.95, and the sequels cost $44.95 each. For the Commodore 64, you pay $5 less. Those are the list prices; discount dealers charge even less.

Electronic Arts

My favorite text adventure is **Amnesia**, published by Electronic Arts for the Apple 2e & 2c and IBM PC. Like Softporn Adventure, Amnesia takes place in a city; but Amnesia is far more sophisticated than its predecessor.

When you start playing Amnesia, you wake up in a hotel room in New York City. You discover you have no clothes (you're stark naked), no money (you're flat broke), and no recollection of who you are — because you're suffering from amnesia. You don't even remember your name.

You look at yourself, and notice you're a male. Your first problem is to get some clothes and money. But then you learn you have other problems that are even more serious. For example, you get a call from a guy who reminds you that today is your wedding day, and that if you don't hurry up and marry his daughter without further mess-ups, he'll use his pistol. You also discover that the FBI is looking for you, because the state of Texas has reported that you're a murderer.

After getting some clothes (so you can stop scaring the hotel's maids), there are several ways to get out of your jam. (I've tried them all!)

One way is to say "yes" to the pistol-packing papa and marry his daughter, who takes you to Australia, where you live on a sheep ranch for the rest of your life. But then you never learn who you really are! Whenever you ask your wife about your past, she simply says, "You wouldn't want to know." You die of old age, peacefully; but even on your deathbed, you don't learn who you are; and so when you die, you feel sad. In that case, you score lots of points for survival, but zero for detective work and zero for character development.

A different solution is to say "no" to the bride and — after getting bloodied — run out of the hotel, onto the streets of New York. Then the fun begins — because hiding on the program's disks is a complete map of Manhattan (from Battery Park all the way up to 110th Street), including all the streets and landmarks and even all the subway stops! Yes, this gigantic game includes 94 subway stations, 200 landmarks, and 3,545 street corners.

As you walk one block north, then one block east, etc., the computer describes everything you pass, even the most sublime (The Museum of Modern Art) and the most ridiculous (Nedick's hamburger stands). You can ride the subway — after you get enough money to buy a token. The game even includes all the subway signs, such as "Downtown — Brooklyn" and "Uptown — Queens". To catch the E train, you must hop in as soon as it arrives. Otherwise, it departs without you, and the computer says "an F train comes" instead.

As night falls, the computer warns you to find a place to sleep. (You can't go back to your hotel, since you're in trouble there.) To find a free place to stay, you can try phoning the names in your address book — once you find a phone booth, and get a quarter to pay for each call. The address book contains 17 listings: J.A., A.A., Chelsea H., drugs, F°, Sue G., E.H., interlude, kvetch, J.L., R & J, sex, soft, Lila T., T.T.T.T., and Wit's End. Each of those listings is an adventure in itself, and you must explore each of them thoroughly, to fully discover who you really are.

If your body ever gets weak (from sleeplessness or hunger or being hit by too many muggers), you faint on the sidewalk, wake up in a hospital, and get found there by the FBI, which returns you to the state of Texas, which executes you for murder. But even that deadly ending has a cheery note. For example, you can choose your last meal: would you like steak and potatoes, or turkey? When you finally die, you can wind up in purgatory, which consists mainly of getting mosquito bites, with an opportunity to take a rowboat to heaven, if you can just remember your *real* name and tell the boatman.

The entire adventure has the structure of a good novel: a gripping introduction (you're a nude, broke, amnesiac groom in a hotel), a thorough development section (wandering through the streets of New York, searching for your identity and the meaning of life), and a conclusion (a whimsical death scene, or something better).

The text was written by Thomas Disch, the award-winning sci-fi novelist. It's lyrical. For example, when you escape from the hotel and walk out onto the streets of New York, the computer says: "It feels great to be a single faceless, nameless atom among the million others churning about in the grid of Manhattan's streets. It feels safe."

The game combines all our nightmares about New York into a wild, exciting adventure.

The game's affected my own life. Now whenever something in my life goes wrong, instead of groaning I just say, "I'm in another wild part of Amnesia!" In Amnesia, as in life, the only way to score top points for living is to experience it *all*. To live life to the fullest, you must take risks, have the courage to face unknown dangers, and revel in the excitement of the unexpected.

Though Amnesia received lots of praise from reviewers, sales were disappointing. Electronic Arts stopped publishing it. I bet if they'd rename it "Lost in New York", it would sell well — at least in New York!

ARTIFICIAL INTELLIGENCE

NATURAL VERSUS ARTIFICIAL

You have what's called **natural intelligence** (except when your friends accuse you of having "natural stupidity"). The intelligence of a computer, by contrast, is **artificial**. Can the computer's **artificial intelligence** ever match yours?

For example, can the computer ever develop the "common sense" needed to handle exceptions, such as a broken traffic light? After waiting at a red light for several hours, the typical human would realize the light was broken. The human would try to proceed past the intersection, cautiously. Would a computer programmed to "never go on red" be that smart?

Researchers who study the field of artificial intelligence have invented robots and many other fascinating computerized devices. They've also been trying to develop computers that can understand ordinary English commands and questions, so you won't have to learn a "programming language". They've been trying to develop **expert systems** — computers that imitate human experts such as doctors and lawyers.

EARLY DREAMERS

The dream of making a computer imitate us began many centuries ago. . . .

The Greeks

The hope of making an inanimate object act like a person can be traced back to the ancient Greeks. According to Greek mythology, Pygmalion sculpted a statue of a woman, fell in love with it, and prayed to the gods to make it come to life. His wish was granted — she came to life. And they lived happily ever after.

Ramon Lull (1272 A.D.)

In 1272 A.D. on the Spanish island of Majorca, Ramon Lull invented the idea of a machine that would produce *all* knowledge, by putting together words at random. He even tried to build it.

Needless to say, he was a bit of a nut. Here's a description of his personality (written by Jerry Rosenberg, abridged):

Ramon Lull married young and fathered two children — which didn't stop him from his courtier's adventures. He had an especially strong passion for married women. One day as he was riding his horse down the center of town, he saw a familiar woman entering church for a High Mass. Undisturbed by this circumstance, he galloped his horse into the cathedral and was quickly thrown out by the congregants. The lady was so disturbed by his scene that she prepared a plan to end Lull's pursuit once and for all. She invited him to her boudoir, displayed the bosom that he had been praising in poems written for her, and showed him a cancerous breast. "See, Ramon," she said, "the foulness of this body that has won thy affection! How much better hadst thou done to have set thy love on Jesus Christ, of Whom thou mayest have a prize that is eternal!"

In shame Lull withdrew from court life. On four different occasions a vision of Christ hanging on the Cross came to him, and in penitence Lull became a dedicated Christian. His conversion was followed by a pathetic impulse to try to convert the entire Moslem world to Christianity. This obsession dominated the remainder of his life. His "Book of Contemplation" was divided into 5 books in honor of the 5 wounds of Christ. It contained 40 subdivisions — for the 40 days that Christ spent in the wilderness; 366 chapters — one to be read each day and the last chapter to be read only in a leap year. Each of the chapters had 10 paragraphs to commemorate the 10 commandments; each paragraph had 3 parts to signify the trinity — for a total of 30 parts a chapter, signifying the 30 pieces of silver.

In the final chapter of his book he tried to prove to infidels that Christianity was the only true faith.

Gulliver's Travels Several centuries later — in 1726 — Lull's machine was pooh-poohed by Jonathan Swift, in *Gulliver's Travels*.

Gulliver meets a professor who has built such a machine. The professor claims his machine lets "the most ignorant person . . . write books in philosophy, poetry, politics, law, mathematics, and theology without the least assistance from genius and study."

The machine is huge — 20 feet on each side — and contains all the words of the language, in all their declensions, written on scraps of paper that are glued onto bits of wood connected by wires.

Each of the professor's 40 students operates one of the machine's 40 cranks. At a given signal, every student turns his crank a random distance, to push the words into new positions.

Gulliver says:

He then commanded 36 of the lads to read the several lines softly as they appeared upon the frame; and where they found three or four words together that might make part of a sentence, they dictated to the four remaining boys who were scribes. Six hours a day the young students were employed in this labor, and the professor showed me several volumes in large folio already collected, of broken sentences, which he intended to piece together, and out of those rich materials to give the world a complete body of all arts and sciences.

Karel Capek (1920)

The word **robot** was invented in 1920 by Karel Capek, a Czech playwright. His play "R.U.R." shows a factory where the workers look human but are really machines. The workers are dubbed *robots*, because the Czech word for *slave* is *robotnik*.

His play is pessimistic. The invention of robots causes unemployment. Men lose all ambition — even the ambition to raise children. The robots are used in war, go mad, revolt against mankind and destroy it. In the end only two robots are left. It's up to them to repopulate the world.

Isaac Asimov (1942)

Many sci-fi writers copied Capek's idea of robots, with even more pessimism. An exception was Isaac Asimov, who depicted robots as being loving. He coined the word **robotics**, which means the study of robots, and in 1942 developed what he calls the "Three Laws of Robotics". Here's the version he published in 1950:

1. A robot may not injure a human being or, through inaction, allow a human being to come to harm.

2. A robot must obey the orders given it by human beings, except where such orders would conflict with the First Law.

3. A robot must protect its own existence, as long as such protection does not conflict with either the First or the Second Law.

Norbert Wiener (1947)

The word **cybernetics** was invented in 1947 by Norbert Wiener, an MIT professor. He defined it to be "the science of control and communication in the animal and the machine." Wiener and his disciples, who called themselves **cyberneticists**, wondered whether it would be possible to make an electrical imitation of the human nervous system. It would be a "thinking machine". They created the concept of **feedback**: animals and machines both need to perceive the consequences of their actions, to learn how to improve themselves. For example, a machine that is producing parts in a factory should examine the parts it has produced, the heat it has generated, and other factors, to adjust itself accordingly.

Wiener, like Ramon Lull, was something strange. He graduated from Tufts College when he was 14 years old, got his doctorate from Harvard when he was 18, and became the typical "absent-minded professor". Many anecdotes are told about him.

For example, once he went to a conference and parked his car in the parking lot. When the conference was over, he went to the lot, but forgot where he parked his car, and even forgot what it looked like. So he waited until all the other cars were driven away, and took the car that was left.

When he and his family moved to a new house a few blocks away, his wife gave him written directions on how to reach it, because she knew he was very absent-minded. But sure enough, when he was leaving his office at the end of the day, he couldn't remember where he put her note, and of course he couldn't remember where the new house was. So he drove to his old neighborhood instead. He saw a young child and asked her, "Little girl, can you tell me where the Wieners have moved?" "Yes, Daddy," came the reply, "Mommy said you'd probably be here, so she sent me to show you the way home."

One day he was sitting in the campus lounge, intensely studying a paper on the table. Every now and then, he would get up, pace a bit, and then return to the paper. Everyone was impressed by the enormous mental effort reflected on his face. Once again he rose from his paper, took a few rapid steps around the room, and collided with a student. The student said, "Good afternoon, Professor Wiener." Wiener stopped, stared, clapped a hand to his forehead, said "Wiener — that's the word," and ran back to the table to fill the word "wiener" in the crossword puzzle he was working on.

Once he drove 150 miles to a math conference at Yale University; but when the conference was over, he forgot he had come by car, so he returned by bus. The next morning, he went out to his garage to get his car, discovered it was missing, and complained to the police that while he was away someone had stolen it.

Those anecdotes were collected by Howard Eves, a math historian.

Alan Turing (1950)

Can a computer "think"? In 1950, Alan Turing proposed the following test. In one room, put a human and a computer. In another room, put another human (called the Interrogator) and give him two terminals — one for communication with the computer, and the other for communication with the other human — but don't tell the Interrogator which terminal is which. If he can't tell the difference, the computer's doing a good job of imitating the human, and, according to Turing, we should say that the computer can "think".

It's called the Imitation Game. The Interrogator asks questions. The human witness answers honestly. The computer pretends to be human.

To win, the computer must be able to imitate human weaknesses as well as strengths. For example, when asking to add two numbers, it should pause before answering, as a human would. When asked to write a sonnet, a good imitation-human answer would be, "Count me out on this one. I never could write poetry." When asked "Are you human", the computer should say "yes".

Such responses wouldn't be hard to program. But a clever Interrogator could give the computer a rough time, by requiring it to analyze its own thinking:

Interrogator:	In the first line of your sonnet which reads "Shall I compare thee to a summer's day," wouldn't "a spring day" do as well or better?
Witness:	It wouldn't scan.
Interrogator:	How about "a winter's day". That would scan all right.
Witness:	Yes, but nobody wants to be compared to a winter's day.
Interrogator:	Would you say Mr. Pickwick reminded you of Christmas?
Witness:	In a way.
Interrogator:	Yet Christmas is a winter's day, and I don't think Mr. Pickwick would mind the comparison.
Witness:	I don't think you're serious. By a winter's day one means a typical winter's day, rather than a special one like Christmas.

If the computer could answer questions that well, the Interrogator would have a hard time telling it wasn't human.

Donald Fink has suggested that the Interrogator say, "Suggest an unsolved problem and some methods for working toward its solution," and "What methods would most likely prove fruitful in solving the following problem. . . . "

Turing believed computers would someday be able to win the game and therefore be considered to "think". In his article, he listed nine possible objections to his belief, and rebutted them. . . .

1. Soul
Thinking's a function of man's immortal soul. Since computers don't have souls, computers can't think.

Rebuttal: since God's all-powerful, He can give computers souls if He wishes. Just as we create children to house His souls, so should we serve Him by creating computers.

2. Dreadful
If machines could equal us in thinking, that would be dreadful!

Rebuttal: too bad!

3. Logicians
Logicians have proved it's impossible to build a computer that can answer every question.

Rebuttal: is it possible to find a *human* that can answer every question? Computers are no dumber than we. And though no one can answer every question, why not build a succession of computers, each one more powerful than the next, so every question could be answered by at least one of them?

4. Conscious
Although computers can produce, they can't be *conscious* of what they've produced. They can't feel pleasure at their successes, misery at their mistakes, and depression when they don't get what they want.

Rebuttal: the only way to be absolutely sure whether a computer has feelings is to become one. A more practical experiment would be to build a computer that explains step-by-step its reasoning, its motivations, and the obstacles it is trying to overcome, and also analyzes emotional passages such as poetry. Such a computer is clearly not just parroting.

5. Human
A computer can't be kind, resourceful, beautiful, friendly, have initiative, have a sense of humor, tell right from wrong, make mistakes, fall in love, enjoy strawberries and cream, make someone fall in love with it, learn from experience, use words properly, be the subject of its own thought, have as much diversity of behavior as a man, or do something really new.

Rebuttal: why not? Although such a computer hasn't been built yet, it might be possible in the future.

6. Surprise
The computer never does anything original or surprising. It does only what it's told.

Rebuttal: how do you know "original" human work isn't just grown from a seed implanted by teaching, or the effect of well-known general principles? And who says computers aren't surprising? The computer's correct answers are often surprisingly different from a human's rough guesses.

7. Binary
Nerve cells can sense gradual increases in electrical activity — you can feel a "little tingle" or a "mild pain" or an "ouch" — whereas a computer's logic is only binary — either a "yes" or "no".

Rebuttal: by using techniques such as "random numbers", you can make the computer imitate the flexible, probabilistic behavior of the nervous system well enough so that the Interrogator can't tell the difference.

8. Rules
Life can't be reduced to rules. For example, if you have a traffic-light rule that says "stop when the light is red, and go when the light is green", what do you do when the light is broken, and both the red and green appear simultaneously? Maybe you should have an extra rule saying in that case to stop. But some further difficulty may arise with that rule, and you'd have to create another rule. And so on. You can't invent enough rules to handle all cases. Since computers must be fed rules, they cannot handle all of life.

Rebuttal: although life's more than a simple set of rules, it might be the *consequences* of simple psychological laws of behavior, which the computer could be taught.

9. ESP
Humans have extrasensory perception (ESP), and computers don't.

Rebuttal: maybe the computer's random-number generator could be hooked up to be affected by ESP. Or to prevent ESP from affecting the Imitation Game, put both the human witness and the computer in a telepathy-proof room.

How to begin
To make the computer an intelligent creature, Turing suggested two possible ways to begin. One way would be to teach the computer abstract skills, such as chess. The other way would be to give the computer eyes, ears, and other sense organs, teach it how to speak English, and then educate it the same way you'd educate a somewhat handicapped child.

Suicide?
Four years later — on June 8, 1954 — Turing was found dead in bed. According to the police, he died from potassium cyanide, self-administered. He'd been plating spoons with potassium cyanide in electrolysis experiments. His mother refuses to believe it was suicide, and hopes it was just an accident.

It's hard to make the computer understand plain English!

Confusion

For example, suppose you feed the computer this famous saying:

Time flies like an arrow.

What does that saying mean? The computer might interpret it three ways. . . .

Interpretation 1: the computer thinks "time" is a noun, so the sentence means "The time can fly by as quickly as an arrow flies."

Interpretation 2: the computer thinks "time" is a verb, so the sentence means "Time the speed of flies like you'd time the speed of an arrow."

Interpretation 3: the computer thinks "time" is an adjective, so the sentence means "There's a special kind of insect, called a 'time fly', and those flies are attracted to an arrow (in the same way moths are attracted to a flame)."

Suppose a guy sits on a barstool and shares his drinks with a tall woman while they play poker for cash. If the woman says to him, "Up yours!", the computer might interpret it eight ways:

The woman is upset at what the man did.
The woman wants the man to raise up his glass, for a toast.
The woman wants the man to up the ante and raise his bet.
The woman wants the man to hold his cards higher, so she doesn't see them.
The woman wants the man to pick up the card she dealt him.
The woman wants the man to raise his stool, so she can see him eye-to-eye.
The woman wants the man to pull up his pants.
The woman wants the man to have an erection.

For another example, suppose Mae West were to meet a human-looking robot and ask him:

Is that a pistol in your pocket, or are you glad to see me?

The robot would probably analyze that sentence too logically, then reply naively:

There is no pistol in my pocket, and I am glad to see you.

In spite of those confusions, programmers have tried to make the computer understand English. Here are some famous attempts. . . .

Baseball (1961)

In 1961 at MIT, programmers made the computer answer questions about baseball.

In the computer's memory, they stored the month, day, place, teams, and scores of each game in the American League for one year. They programmed the computer so that *you can type your question in ordinary English*. The computer analyzes your question's grammar and prints the correct answer.

Here are examples of questions the computer can analyze and answer correctly:

Who did the Red Sox lose to on July 5?
Who beat the Yankees on July 4?
How many games did the Yankees play in July?
Where did each team play in July?
In how many places did each team play in July?
Did every team play at least once in each park in each month?

To get an answer, the computer turns your questions into equations:

Question	Equations
Where did the Red Sox play on July 7?	place = ? team = Red Sox month = July day = 7
What teams won 10 games in July?	team (winning) = ? game (number of) = 10 month = July
On how many days in July did eight teams play?	day (number of) = ? month = July team (number of) = 8

To do that, the computer uses this table:

Word in your question	Equation
where	place = ?
Red Sox	team = Red Sox
July	month = July
who	team = ?
team	team = ?

The computer ignores words such as *the*, *did*, and *play*.

If your question mentions *Boston*, you might mean either "place = Boston" or "team = Red Sox". The computer analyzes your question to determine which equation to form.

After forming the equations, the computer hunts through its memory, to find the games that solve the equations. If an equation says "number of", the computer counts. If an equation says "winning", the computer compares the scores of opposing teams.

The programmers were Bert Green, Alice Wolf, Carol Chomsky, and Kenneth Laughery.

What's a story problem?

When you were in school, your teacher told you a story that ended with a mathematical question. For example:

Dick had 5 apples. He ate 3. How many are left?

In that problem, the last word is: *left*. That means: subtract. So the correct answer is 5 minus 3, which is 2.

Can the computer solve problems like that? Here's the most famous attempt. . . .

Arithmetic & algebra (1964)

MIT awarded a Ph.D. to Daniel Bobrow, for programming the computer to solve story problems involving arithmetic and algebra.

Customers Let's see how the computer solves this problem:

If the number of customers Tom gets is twice the square of 20 percent of the number of advertisements he runs, and the number of advertisements he runs is 45, what is the number of customers Tom gets?

To begin, the computer replaces *twice* by *2 times*, and replaces *square of* by *square*.

Then the computer separates the sentence into smaller sentences:

The number of customers Tom gets is 2 times the square 20 percent of the number of advertisements he runs. The number of advertisements he runs is 45. What is the number of customers Tom gets?

The computer turns each sentence into an equation:

number of customers Tom gets = 2 * (.20 * number of advertisements he runs)^2
number of advertisements he runs = 45
X = number of customers Tom gets

The computer solves the equations and prints the answer as a complete sentence:

The number of customers Tom gets is 162.

Here's a harder problem:

The sum of Lois's share of some money and Bob's share is $4.50. Lois's share is twice Bob's. Find Bob's and Lois's share.

Applying the same method, the computer turns the problem into these equations:

Lois's share of some money + Bob's share = 4.50 dollars
Lois's share = 2 * Bob's
X = Bob's
Y = Lois's share

The computer tries to solve the equations but fails. So it assumes "Lois's share" is the same as "Lois's share of some money", and "Bob's" is the same as "Bob's share". Now it has six equations:

Original equations
Lois's share of some money + Bob's share = 4.50 dollars
Lois's share = 2 * Bob's
X = Bob's
Y = Lois's share

Assumptions
Lois's share = Lois's share of some money
Bob's = Bob's share

It solves them and prints:

Bob's is 1.50 dollars.
Lois's share is 3 dollars.

Distance The computer can solve problems about distance:

The distance from New York to Los Angeles is 3000 miles. If the average speed of a jet plane is 600 miles per hour, find the time it takes to travel from New York to Los Angeles by jet.

The resulting equations are:

distance from New York to Los Angeles = 3000 * miles
average speed of jet plane = (600 * miles)/(1 * hours)
X = time it takes to travel from New York to Los Angeles by jet

The computer is unable to solve them. But in its memory it finds the formula "distance = speed * time". It winds up with 7 equations:

Original equations
distance from New York to Los Angeles = 3000 * miles
average speed of jet plane = (600 * miles)/(1 * hours)
X = time it takes to travel from New York to Los Angeles by jet

Formula
distance = speed * time

Assumptions
distance = distance from New York to Los Angeles
speed = average speed of jet plane
time = time it takes to travel from New York to Los Angeles by jet

It solves them and prints:

The time it takes to travel from New York to Los Angeles by jet is 5 hours.

Age The computer can solve problems about age:

Mary is twice as old as Ann was when Mary was as old as Ann is now. If Mary is 24 years old, how old is Ann?

To begin, the computer replaces *twice* by *2 times*, and replaces *how old* by *what*.

When the computer sees the words *as old as*, it knows the problem has to do with ages, so it breaks the problem into these sentences:

Mary's age is 2 times Ann's age X years ago. X years ago Mary's age is Ann's age now. Mary's age is 24. What is Ann's age?

The resulting equations are:

Mary's age = 2 * (Ann's age - X)
Mary's age - X = Ann's age
Mary's age = 24
Y = Ann's age

The computer prints:

Ann's age is 18.

Hint If a situation appears hopeless, the computer asks you for help. In the following conversation, the human poses a problem, and the computer begs for a hint:

Human:	The gross weight of a ship is 20000 tons. If its net weight is 15000 tons, what is the weight of the ship's cargo?
Computer:	Do you know any more relationships among these variables: gross weight of ship, tons, its net weight, weight of ship's cargo?
Human:	Yes.
Computer:	Tell me.
Human:	The weight of a ship's cargo is the difference between the gross weight and the net weight.
Computer:	The weight of the ship's cargo is 5000 tons.

Limitations The program has some limitations. It cannot solve quadratic equations. If the computer tries to apply the formula "distance = speed * time" to a problem involving *two* distances, it forgets which distance is which.

The computer's vocabulary is limited. It doesn't realize that *how many* means *what is the number of*, and *how far is* means *what is the distance to*. For problems about age, the characters must be named Mary, Ann, Bill, Father, or Uncle, unless you diddle with the computer's memory.

If the human types *Tom has 2 apples, 3 bananas, and 4 pears*, the comma before the *and* makes the computer split the sentence into two wrong "sentences":

Tom has 2 apples, 3 bananas.
4 pears.

If the human mentions *the number of times John went to the movies*, the computer thinks *times* means multiplication, and tries to multiply *number of* by *John went to the movies*.

Encyclopedia (1964-1966)

In 1964, Simmons, Klein, and McConlogue (at the Systems Development Corporation) fed a child's encyclopedia into a computer.

If you type *What do worms eat?* the computer hunts through the encyclopedia, to find sentences mentioning both *worms* and *eat*. (To hasten the hunt, it uses an index produced by another program.) It finds two sentences:

Birds eat worms on the grass.
Most worms usually eat grass.

After analyzing the grammar of your question and those sentences, the computer realizes the first sentence is irrelevant, and prints just the correct answer:

Most worms usually eat grass.

In 1965, the program's abilities were extended, so that if you type *What animals live longer than men?* the computer searches through the encyclopedia for related words:

Word in sentence	Related words searched
animals	mammals, reptiles, fish
live	age
longer	older, ancient
men	person, people, women

Here's an example of the program's operation in 1966. The human creates some encyclopedia material about horses, and then retrieves it:

Human: Enter horse=noun, is=isverb, animal=noun, live=verb, on=prep, farm=noun, strong=adj, pull=verb, wagon=noun, most=adj, are=isverb, eat=verb, hay=noun, all=adj, red=adj, many=adj, have=haveverb, long=adj, mane=noun, some=adj, person=noun, race=verb.
Computer: Entered in dictionary.

Human: Plurals horse=horses, animal=animals, farm=farms, wagon=wagons, mane=manes, person=people.
Computer: Ok.

Human: Start.
Computer: Ready.

Human: A horse is an animal. Horses live on a farm. Strong horses pull wagons. Most horses are strong. Horses eat hay. All horses are red. Many horses have long manes. Some people race horses.
Computer: Learned.

Human: Forget "all horses are red".
Computer: Forgotten.

Human: What is a horse?
Computer: Horse is an animal.

Human: What do horses eat?
Computer: Horses eat hay.

Human: What do horses do?
Computer: Horses live on a farm and eat hay. Strong horses pull wagons.

Human: What do strong horses do?
Computer: Strong horses pull wagons.

Human: Do many horses have long manes?
Computer: Yes.

Human: Do all horses have long manes?
Computer: To my knowledge, no.

Human: Describe horses?
Computer: Horses are an animal. Most horses are strong. Many horses have long manes. Horses live on a farm and eat hay. Strong horses pull wagons. Some people race horses.

When the computer's answer consists of several sentences, it prints the most relevant sentence first, and the others in decreasing order of relevance.

Military (1966)

Thompson and Craig (at General Electric) made the computer answer military questions such as:

Has the 25th battalion arrived in Texas since 3 P.M.?

Is the 100th scheduled to arrive at Ft. Lewis before the 200th leaves Ft. Lewis?

Eliza (1966-1967)

In 1966 at MIT, Joseph Weizenbaum wrote the Eliza program, which makes the computer act as a psychotherapist.

In 1967, he changed the program, to make it handle keywords such as *also, call, compute, define, is, let, of, thanks, where*, and the symbol =.

In the following conversation, the human teaches the computer how to find the area of a circle, a sphere, and a square, and then asks the computer questions about geometry. The human also teaches the computer how to speak German —

English	German
I say	ich sage
I mean	meine ich
what is	wieviel ist
squared	quadrat

and gradually starts speaking to the computer in German.

Human: The area of a circle is pi times the radius of the circle squared. The area of a sphere is pi times the diameter of the sphere squared. The area of a square is the side of the square squared. The diameter of an object is twice the radius of the object. The radius of a ball is 10. What is the area of the ball?
Computer: The assumption that ball is circle is consistent — shall I go on?

Human: No.
Computer: The assumption that ball is sphere and object is consistent — shall I go on?

Human: Yes.
Computer: It's 1256.6359.

Human: What is the diameter of the ball?
Computer: It's 20.

Human: The radius of a dish is 10. What's the area of the dish?
Computer: The assumption that dish is circle is consistent — shall I go on?

Human: Yes.
Computer: It's 314.15899.

Human: The radius of a globe is 10. A globe is a sphere. A sphere is an object. What is the area of the globe?
Computer: It's 1256.6359.

Human: The side of a plate is 10. What is the area of the plate?
Computer: The assumption that plate is square is consistent — shall I go on?

Human: Yes.
Computer: It's 100.

Human: When I say board I mean plate. What is 3 times the side of the board?
Computer: It's 30.

Human: Please call that x. Let f(z) be z squared minus z. Compute f(x).
Computer: It's 870.

Human: When I say ich sage I mean I say. When ich sage meine ich I mean I mean. Wenn ich sage wieviel ist meine ich what is. Wenn ich sage quadrat meine ich squared. Nun, sagen sie mir bitte, wieviel is x quadrat.
Computer: I didn't understand you.

Human: Ja, tut mir leid, ich sollte fragen wieviel IST x quadrat.
Computer: It's 900.

Calculus (1969)

At MIT, Charniak made the computer solve story problems involving calculus.

Human: Water is flowing into a conical filter at the rate of 15 cubic inches per second. If the radius of the base of the filter is 5 inches and the altitude is 10 inches, find the rate at which the water level is rising when the volume is 100 cubic inches.

Computer: The answer is .53132943 * in * sec^-1 * pi^-.33333332.

Probability (1971)

Rensselaer Polytechnic Institute awarded a Ph.D. to J.P. Gelb, for making the computer solve story problems involving probability.

Human: From a zorch containing 4 ferd and 3 brakky and 5 chartreuse werfels, 3 are drawn. What is the probability that 2 are chartreuse and the other brakky?

Computer: Replacement involved?

Human: No.

Computer: 3/22 (or .1363636).

SURVEYING THE FIELD

The field of "artificial intelligence" includes many categories.

For example, it includes attempts to make the computer win at chess and checkers, understand English, and create its own original art and music. It also includes attempts to imitate human feelings, personal interactions, and therapists. I explained those topics earlier.

Protocol method

During the 1950's and 1960's, most research in artificial intelligence was done at the Massachusetts Institute of Technology (MIT) and the Carnegie Institute of Technology (CIT, now called Carnegie-Mellon University). At Carnegie, the big names were Allen Newell and Herbert Simon. They invented the **protocol method**. In the protocol method, a human is told to solve a tough problem and, while he's solving it, to say at each moment what he's thinking. A transcript of his train of thought is recorded and called the **protocol**. Then programmers try to make the computer imitate that train of thought.

Using the protocol method, Newell and Simon produced programs that could "think like humans". The thinking, like human thinking, was imperfect. Their research did *not* try to make the computer a perfect thinker; instead, it tried to gain insight into how *humans* think. Their point of view was: if you think you really understand human psychology, go try to program it. Their attempt to reduce human psychology to computer programs is called **mentalism**, and has replaced Skinner's stimulus-response behaviorism as the dominant force in psychology today.

Abstract math

Many programmers have tried to make the computer do abstract math.

In 1957 Newell, Simon, and Shaw used the protocol method to make the computer prove theorems about symbolic logic, such as "Not (p or q) implies not p". In 1959 and 1960, Herbert Gelernter and his friends made the computer prove theorems about Euclidean geometry, such as "If the segment joining the midpoints of the diagonals of a trapezoid is extended to intersect a side of the trapezoid, it bisects that side."

In 1961, MIT awarded a Ph.D. to James Slagle for making the computer compute indefinite integrals, such as:

$$\int \frac{x^4}{(1-x^2)^{5/2}} \, dx$$

The computer gets the answer, which is:

$$\arcsin x + \frac{\tan^3 \arcsin x}{3} - \tan \arcsin x + c$$

Each of those programs works by drawing a tree inside the computer's memory. Each branch of the tree represents a possible line of attack. The computer considers each branch and chooses the one that looks most promising.

A better symbolic-logic program was written by Hao Wang in 1960. His program doesn't need trees; it always picks the right attack immediately. It's guaranteed to prove any theorem you hand it, whereas the program by Newell, Simon, and Shaw got stuck on some hard ones.

A better indefinite integration program was written by Joel Moses in 1967 and further improved in 1969. It uses trees very rarely, and solves almost any integration problem.

A program that usually finds the right answer but might fail on hard problems is called **heuristic**. A heuristic program usually involves trees. The checkers, chess, and geometry programs are heuristic. A program that's guaranteed to always give the correct answer is called **algorithmic**. The original symbolic-logic program was heuristic, but Wang's improvement is algorithmic; Moses's indefinite integration program is almost algorithmic.

GPS

In 1957 Newell, Simon, and Shaw began writing a single program to solve *all* problems. They called the program **GPS (General Problem Solver)**. If you feed the program a goal, a list of operators, and associated information, the program will tell you how to achieve the goal by using the operators.

For example, suppose you want the computer to solve this simple problem: a monkey would like to eat some bananas that are too high for him to reach, but there's a box nearby he can stand on. How can he get the bananas?

Feed the GPS program this information. . . .

Now: monkey's place = place#1; box's place = place#2; contents of monkey's hand = empty

Want: contents of monkey's hand = the bananas

Difficulties: contents of monkey's hand is harder to change than box's place, which is harder to change than monkey's place

Allowable operator	Definition	
climb box	before:	monkey's place = box's place
	after:	monkey's place = on the box
walk to x	after:	monkey's place = x
move box to x	before:	monkey's place = box's place
	after:	monkey's place = x; box's place = x
get bananas	before:	box's place = under the bananas; monkey's place = on the box
	after:	contents of monkey's hand = the bananas

GPS will print the solution:

walk to place#2
move box to under the bananas
climb box
get bananas

The GPS approach to solving problems is called **means-ends analysis**: you tell the program the means (operators) and the end (goal). The program has proved theorems in symbolic logic, computed indefinite integrals, and solved many famous puzzles, such as "The Missionaries and the Cannibals", "The Tower of Hanoi", and "The 5-Gallon Jug and the 8-Gallon Jug". But the program works slowly, and you must feed it lots of information about the problem. The project was abandoned in 1967.

Vision

Another large topic in artificial intelligence is **computer vision**: making the computer see.

The first problem tackled was **pattern recognition**: making the computer read handwritten printed letters. The problem is hard, because some people make their letters very tall or wide or slanted or curled or close together, and the pen may skip. Reasonably successful programs were written, although computers still can't tackle script.

Interest later shifted to **picture processing**: given a photograph of an object, make the computer tell what the object is. The problem is hard, because the photo may be taken from an unusual angle and be blurred, and because the computer gets confused by shadows.

Scene analysis is even harder: given a picture of a group of objects, make the computer tell which object is which. The problem is hard, because some of the objects may be partly hidden behind others, and because a line can have two different interpretations: it can be a crease in one object, or a dividing-line between two objects.

Most of the research in picture processing and scene analysis was done from 1968 to 1972.

Ray Kurzweil has invented an amazing machine whose camera looks at a book and reads the book, by using a voice synthesizer. Many blind people use it.

Robots

Researchers have built robots. The first robots were just for experimental fun, but today's robots are truly useful: for example, the Japanese are using robots to manufacture cars. In the United States, many young kids are being taught "LOGO", which is a language developed at the MIT Artificial Intelligence Laboratory that makes the computer control a robot turtle.

Today's research

Today, research in artificial intelligence is done at four major universities: MIT, Carnegie, Stanford, and Edinburgh (Scotland).

Reflexive control

In the Soviet Union, weird researchers have studied **reflexive control**: they programmed the computer to be disobedient. The first such programmer was Lefevr, in 1967. In 1969 Baranov and Trudolyubov extended his work, by making the computer win this disobedience game:

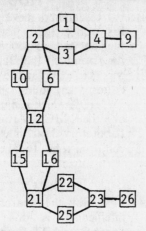

The human begins by choosing either node 9 or node 26, *but doesn't tell the computer which node he's chosen*. The computer starts at node 12; on each turn, it moves to an adjacent node. When it reaches either node 9 or node 26, the game ends: if the node the computer reaches is one of the human chose, the human wins; if the computer reaches the opposite node, the computer wins. Before each move, the human tells the computer where to go; but the computer may decide to do the opposite (disobey).

What strategy should the computer use? If it always obeys, or always disobeys the human will catch on and make it lose.

Instead, Baranov and Trudolyubov programmed the computer to react as follows:

obey the human twice, then disobey three times, then obey once, disobey thrice, obey once, disobey twice, obey thrice, disobey once, obey thrice, disobey once, . . .

The irregular alternation of obedience and disobedience confuses the human in a way that works to the computer's advantage. Using that strategy, the computer played against 61 humans, and won against 44 of them (72%). In other words, the typical human tried to mislead the computer but in fact "clued it in" to the human's goal.

Later experiments with other games indicated that the following pattern of disobedience is usually more effective:

obey the human twice, disobey thrice, obey once, disobey four times, obey once, disobey thrice, obey thrice, disobey twice, obey thrice, disobey once, obey once, disobey once

Misinformation

Unfortunately, most research in the field of artificial intelligence is just a lot of hot air. For years, researchers have been promising that intelligent, easy-to-use English-speaking computers and robots would be available at low prices "any day now". After several decades of listening to such hoopla, I've given up waiting. The field of artificial intelligence should be renamed "artificial optimism".

Whenever a researcher in the field of artificial intelligence promises you something, don't believe it until you see it and use it personally, so you can evaluate its limitations.

If a computer seems to give intelligent replies to English questions posed by a salesman or researcher demonstrating artificial intelligence, try to interrupt the demo and ask the computer *your* English questions. You'll typically find that the computer doesn't understand what you're talking about at all: the demo was a cheap trick that works just with the peculiar English questions asked by the demonstrator.

For many years, the top researchers in artificial intelligence have been exaggerating their achievements and underestimating how long it will take to develop a truly intelligent computer. Let's look at their history of lies. . . .

In 1957 Herbert Simon said, "Within ten years a digital computer will be the world's chess champion." In 1967, when the ten years had elapsed, the only decent chess program was Greenblatt's, which the American Chess Federation rated "class D" (which means "poor"). Though chess programs have improved since then, the best chess program is still far less than an "international master" or "grandmaster" or "world champion".

In 1957 Simon also said, "Within ten years a digital computer will discover and prove an important new mathematical theorem." He was wrong. The computer still hasn't discovered or proved any important new mathematical theorem. The closest call came in 1976, when it did the *non-abstract part* of the proof of the "4-color theorem".

In 1958 Newell, Simon, and Shaw wrote a chess-playing program which they admitted was "not fully debugged" so that one "cannot say very much about the behavior of the program"; but they claimed it was "good in spots (opening)". In 1959 the founder of cybernetics, Norbert Wiener, exaggerated about their program; he told New York University's Institute of Philosophy that "chess-playing machines as of now will counter the moves of a master player with the moves recognized as right in the textbooks, up to some point in the middle game." In the same symposium Michael Scriven carried the exaggeration even further by saying, "Machines are already capable of a good game." In fact, the program they were describing played very poorly, and in its last official bout (October 1960) was beaten by a ten-year-old kid who was a novice.

In 1960 Herbert Gelernter (who wrote the geometry-theorem program) said, "Today hardly an expert will contest the assertion that machines will be proving interesting theorems in number theory three years hence." More than twenty years have elapsed since then, but neither Gelernter nor anyone else has programmed the computer to prove theorems in number theory.

In June 1963 this article appeared in the *Chicago Tribune*:

The development of a machine that can listen to any conversation and type out the remarks just like an office secretary was announced yesterday by a Cornell University expert on learning machines. The device is expected to be in operation by fall. Frank Rosenblatt, director of Cornell's cognitive systems research, said the machine will be the largest "thinking" device built to date. Rosenblatt made his announcement at a meeting on learning machines at Northwestern University's Technological Institute.

No such machine exists today, let alone in 1963.

Also in 1963, W. Ross Ashby said, "Gelernter's theorem-proving program has discovered a new proof of the **pons asinorum** that demands no construction." He said the proof is one that "the greatest mathematicians of 2000 years have failed to notice . . . which would have evoked the highest praise had it occurred." In fact, the *pons asinorum* is just the simple theorem that the opposite angles of an isosceles triangle are equal, and the computer's constructionless proof had already been discovered by Pappus in 300 A.D.

In 1968 the head of artificial intelligence in Great Britain, Donald Michie, said, "Today machines can play chess at championship level." In fact, when computers were allowed to participate in human chess tournaments, they almost always lost.

In 1970 the head of artificial intelligence at MIT, Marvin Minsky, said:

In three to eight years we will have a machine with the general intelligence of an average human being. I mean a machine that will be able to read Shakespeare, grease a car, play office politics, tell a joke, have a fight. At that point, the machine will begin to educate itself with fantastic speed. In a few months it will be at genius level, and a few months after that its powers will be incalculable.

His prediction that it would happen in three to eight years — between 1973 and 1978 — was ridiculous. I doubt it will happen during this century, if ever.

Exaggerations concern not just the present and future but also the past. Back in 1962 Arthur Samuel's checker program won one game against Robert Nealey, "a former Connecticut checkers champion". Notice that Nealey was a *former* champion, not *the current* champion when the game was played. Also notice the program won a single game, not a match; and in fact it lost to Nealey later. In 1971 James Slagle slid over those niceties, when he just said that the program "once beat the champion of Connecticut." More recent writers, reading Slagle's words, have gone a step further and omitted the word *once*: one textbook says, "The current program beat the champion of Connecticut". It's not true.

Why do leaders of artificial intelligence consistently exaggerate? The answer is obvious: to get more research funds from the government. Hubert Dreyfus, chairman of the philosophy department at Berkeley, annoys them by attacking their claims.

The brain

Will the computer be able to imitate the human brain? Opinions vary.

Marvin Minsky, head of artificial intelligence at MIT, says *yes*: "After all, the human brain is just a computer that happens to be made out of meat."

Biologists argue *no*: the brain is composed of 12 billion **neurons**, each of which has between 5,000 and 60,000 **dendrites** for input and a similar number of **axons** for output; the neurons act in peculiar ways, and no computer could imitate all that with complete accuracy — "The neuron is qualitatively quite different from on-off components of current computers."

Herbert Simon (head of artificial intelligence at Carnegie and a psychologist), points out that certain aspects of the brain, such as short-term memory, are known to have very limited capacity and ability. He believes the inner workings of the brain are reasonably simple; it produces complicated output only because it receives complicated input from the sense organs and environment: "A man, viewed as a behaving system, is quite simple. The apparent complexity of his behavior over time is largely a reflection of the complexity of the environment in which he finds himself." Simon believes that if a computer were given good sense organs, the ability to move, and an elementary ability to learn, and were placed in a stimulating environment (unlike the dull four walls of a computer center), it would start acting in complex ways also.

Hubert Dreyfus, chairman of the philosophy department at Berkeley, argues that progress in artificial intelligence has been very small, is being blocked now by impenetrable barriers, and — most important — the computer's approach to solving problems bears little relationship to the more powerful methods used by humans. He's cynical about the claim that an improvement in computer programs represents progress toward understanding the human mind, which is altogether different: "According to this definition, the first man to climb a tree could claim tangible progress toward reaching the moon. Rather than climbing blindly, it's better to look where one is going."

PROGRAMMING

This is the middle page of the book. The 319 pages before it cover what's new and hot about computers. The 319 pages after it cover the eternal truths.

10 years from now, the stuff in the first half of the book will be considered "obsolete". The stuff in the second half of the book will be considered "still true".

This page is your introduction to eternity.

Why program?

We begin our look at eternal truths by studying programming. Of the 8 sections that make up this book, the section on programming is the longest: 271 pages! It's this book's deepest and most thorough adventure. It's the adventure that does the most to expand your mind and turn you into a brilliant thinker. Here's where your career's long-term growth gets its biggest boost.

Here's where you learn the secret of computer life! You learn how to take a computer — which is just a hunk of metal and plastic — and teach it new skills, by feeding it programs. Your teaching and programs turn the computer into a thinking organism. If you teach the computer well, you can make it become as smart as you and even imitate your personality. You become the computer's God, capable of making the computer do anything you wish. Ah, the power!

Folks who read just the first half of this book are at the mercy of Microsoft and other money-grubbing companies: whenever those unfortunate folks want to make the computer do something, they must buy a program that teaches the computer how. If computer stores don't carry a program for that particular task — or if the program's price is unaffordable — those folks are out of luck.

But once you learn how to program, you're lucky! You can make the computer do anything you want! All you need is the patience and perseverence to finish writing your program. And if you ever get stuck, phone me anytime at 617-666-2666 for free help.

When you finish writing your program, you can sell it to the idiots who've read just the first half of the book — and you're on your way to turning yourself into the next Microsoft.

It's easy

Programming the computer can be easy. You'll write your own programs just a few minutes from now, when you reach page 328! As you read farther, you'll learn how to write programs that are more sophisticated.

Computer languages

To program a computer, you put your fingers on the computer's keyboard and type commands. You type the commands in English.

The computer understands just *part* of English; it understands just a *few* words and phrases. The words and phrases the computer understands are called the **computer's language**.

Most computers understand a language called **BASIC**. It consists of words such as PRINT, GO, TO, INPUT, IF, and THEN.

To begin, I'll explain how to program the computer by using those BASIC words. Afterwards, I'll explain how to use different computer languages instead.

For example, I'll explain how to program the computer by using a language called **C**. In C, you must say "printf" instead of "PRINT", and you must say "scanf" instead of "INPUT".

Notice that C appeals to dirty minds who like to say "f" words! Another reason why programmers use C is that programs written in C run faster and consume less RAM than if written in BASIC.

But let's start with BASIC, which is pleasantly human, easy, and tasteful.

Why learn so many languages?

Programmers love to argue about which language is best. **BASIC** is easy to learn. **C** runs quickly and consumes less RAM. **DBASE** includes extra words that help manipulate databases. **PASCAL** lets you organize your thinking better. **LOGO** fascinates kids by showing turtles move across the computer's screen. **FORTRAN** handles complex numbers used by engineers. **COBOL** handles the giant accounting tasks faced by big banks, insurance companies, and the IRS. Thousands of other languages have been invented, too!

Each language continually improves by stealing words from other languages — just as we English speakers stole the word "restaurant" from the French, and the French stole the word "weekend" from us.

Because of the mutual stealing, computer languages are becoming more alike. But each language still retains its own "inspired lunacy", its own weird words that other languages haven't copied yet.

This book turns you into a complete expert by teaching you how to program in *many* languages, so you become multilingual!

Learning a new language affects your way of thinking. For example, most American think cockroaches are disgusting; but when a German housewife sees a cockroach, she just giggles, because she thinks of the German word for "cockroach", which is "küchenschabe", which means "kitchen scraper", "a cute little thing that sweeps the kitchen". Yes, even the ugliest problems look cute when you know how to express your thoughts multilingually!

Each language adds new words to your vocabulary so you gain new ways to express your problems, solutions, and thoughts about them. When you face a tough programming problem and try to reduce it to words the computer understands, you'll think more clearly if you're multilingual and mastered enough vocabulary to turn the vague problem into precise words quickly.

An expert programmer can boil complex hassles down to a series of simple concepts. To do that, you need on the tip of your tongue the words defining those simple concepts. The more computer languages you study, the more words you'll learn, so you can quickly verbalize the crux of each computer problem and solve it.

BASIC FUN

To program the computer, you must use a language that the computer understands. Most computers understand a language called **BASIC**, which is a small part of English.

BASIC was invented by two Dartmouth College professors (John Kemeny and Tom Kurtz) in 1964. Later they improved it. Today, BASIC consists of words such as PRINT, GO, TO, INPUT, IF, and THEN.

Here's how to program the computer by using those BASIC words.

Microsoft BASIC

Different computers speak different *dialects* of BASIC. The most popular dialect was invented in 1975 by a 19-year-old kid, Bill Gates. Since he developed software for microcomputers, he called himself **Microsoft** and called his BASIC dialect **Microsoft BASIC**.

Since Microsoft BASIC is so wonderful, all the popular computer companies paid him to make their computers understand Microsoft BASIC. That's right: IBM, Apple, Commodore, Tandy, Atari, Texas Instruments, and *hundreds* of other computer companies all had to pay off Bill.

Microsoft BASIC has become so popular that Bill had to hire hundreds of employees to help him fill all the orders. Microsoft Incorporated has become a multi-billion-dollar company, and Bill has become a famous billionaire, the wealthiest person in America — he's still just in his 30's!

Over the years, Bill gradually improved Microsoft BASIC. Some computers use old versions of Microsoft BASIC; other computers use his latest improvements.

What's in this chapter?

This chapter on BASIC explains **Modern Microsoft BASIC**, whose popular commands and functions are explained on the following pages:

Command	What the computer will do	Page	Similar to
BEEP	hum for a quarter of a second	373	SOUND, PLAY
CIRCLE (100,100),50	draw a circle at (100,100) with radius 50	372	LINE, PAINT
CLOSE	put finishing touches on the data files	415	OPEN
CLS	clear the screen, so it becomes blank	333	NEW, LOCATE
DATA MEAT,POTATOES	use this list of data: MEAT, POTATOES	350	READ, RESTORE
DATE$="01-24-1996"	set the clock/calendar to 01-24-1996	395	TIME$=
DEFINT A-Z	make all the numeric variables be integers	397	X=
DELETE 30-80	delete lines 30-80 from the program	332	LIST, EDIT
DIM X$(7)	make X$ be a list of 7 strings	379	X=
EDIT 30	edit line 30 of the program	332	LIST, DELETE
END	skip the rest of the program	336	STOP
FIELD 1, 30 AS X$	let file#1's record be 30 bytes and called X$	417	GET, PUT
FILES	print the names of all the disk files	336	SAVE, LOAD
FOR X = 1 TO 100	repeat the lines underneath, 100 times	355	NEXT
GET 1,7	from file#1, get the 7th record	417	FIELD, PUT
GO TO 10	skip to line 10 of the program	334	GOSUB
GOSUB 1000	do the subroutine that begins at line 1000	376	RETURN
IF A$="FINE" THEN PRINT	if A$ is "FINE", print a blank line	345	ON N GO TO
INPUT "WHAT NAME";N$	ask "WHAT NAME?" and get answer N$	341	LINE INPUT
INPUT#1, A$	input from file#1 the value of A$	415	INPUT
KILL "JOE"	erase the file JOE from the disk	337	FILES, NEW
LINE (0,0)-(100,100)	draw a line from (0,0) to (100,100)	372	PLOT, CIRCLE
LINE INPUT "TYPE IT";N$	say "TYPE IT" and grab whole line as input	407	INPUT
LIST	print a list of all the program's lines	331	LLIST, EDIT
LLIST	copy all the program's lines onto paper	333	LIST, PRINT#1
LOAD "JOE"	copy the program JOE from disk to RAM	337	SAVE, RUN
LOCATE 3,7	move to the 3rd line of screen, 7th position	371	PRINT, CLS
LPRINT "I LOVE YOU"	print "I LOVE YOU" on paper	333	PRINT, PRINT#1
LSET X$="I LOVE LUCY"	make field variable X$ be "I LOVE LUCY"	417	FIELD, PUT
MID$(A$,2)="OWL"	change the middle of A$ to "OWL"	394	X=
NEW	start a new program	328	RUN, DELETE
NEXT X	repeat the lines above, for the next X	355	FOR
ON ERROR GO TO 1000	if the lines below cause errors, go to 1000	414	RESUME
ON N GO TO 80,100,20,350	go to 80, 100, 20, or 350, depending on N	413	ON N GOSUB
ON N GOSUB 80,100,20,350	gosub 80, 100, 20, or 350, depending on N	413	ON N GO TO
OPEN "S" FOR OUTPUT AS 1	create a data file called "S"; output to it	415	CLOSE
PAINT (100,101)	fill in the shape that surrounds (100,101)	372	LINE, CIRCLE
PLAY "CDG#B-A"	play this music: C, D, G sharp, B flat, A	374	SOUND, BEEP
PLOT (100,100)	put a dot at the point (100,100)	372	LINE, CIRCLE
POKE 7512,14	into memory cell #7512, put the number 14	414	X=
PRINT 5+2	print the answer to 5+2	326	?
PRINT USING "##.#"; 30/7	print 30/7, rounded to one decimal place	374	PRINT
PRINT#1, "EAT"	print onto file#1 the word "EAT"	415	PRINT, LPRINT
PUT 1,50	in file#1, change the 50th record	417	FIELD, GET
RANDOMIZE	make random numbers be unpredictable	388	X=
READ A$	get a string from the DATA and call it A$	350	DATA, RESTORE
RENAME "JOE" TO "FRED"	find the file JOE and rename it "FRED"	337	FILES, SAVE
RENUM	renumber all the program's lines, by 10's	367	LIST, EDIT
RESTORE	go back to the beginning of the data	351	READ, DATA
RESUME 30	end the error trap, by going to line 30	414	ON ERROR GO TO
RETURN	return to the main routine (from subroutine)	376	GOSUB
RUN	obey all the program's instructions now	328	LIST, LOAD
SAVE "JOE"	copy the program to disk and call it "JOE"	336	FILES, LOAD
SOUND 440,18.2	make a sound of 440 hertz, for 1 second	373	PLAY, BEEP
STOP	stop the program and print a message	336	END
SWAP A,B	make A and B swap values with each other	409	X=
TIME$="13:45:07"	set the clock to 7 seconds after 13:45	395	DATE$=
X=47	make X stand for the number 47	337	INPUT, POKE
? 5+2	print the answer to 5+2	326	PRINT
'THIS PROGRAM IS DUMB	note that this program is dumb	367	PRINT

Function	Meaning	Value	Page	Similar to
ABS(-7)	absolute value of -7	7	386	INT, SGN
ASC("A")	ASCII code number for A	65	392	CHR$
ATN(1)/D	arctangent of 1, in degrees	45	396	TAN
CHR$(65)	65th ASCII character	"A"	392	ASC
COS(60*D)	cosine of 60 degrees	.5	396	SIN, TAN
CVD("RAT NAN~")	convert to double-precision	.2014209944946413	417	MKD$
CVI("ME")	convert to integer	17741	417	MKI$
CVS("NAN~")	convert to single-precision	.201421	417	MKS$
DATE$	today's date	varies	395	TIME$
EOF(1)	test whether at end of file#1	varies	416	LOF
EXP(1)	e raised to the first power	2.718282	384	LOG, SQR
INPUT$(4)	4 characters that are input	varies	407	STICK
INSTR("NEEDED","ED")	position of ED in NEEDED	3	395	other INSTR
INSTR(4,"NEEDED","ED")	search from the 4th character	5	395	other INSTR
INT(17.9)	turn into an integer	17	386	ABS, SGN
LEFT$("SMART",2)	left 2 characters of SMART	"SM"	394	RIGHT$, MID$
LEN("SMART")	length of SMART	5	394	RIGHT$, MID$
LOC(1)	location of record in file#1	varies	417	LOF
LOF(1)	length of file#1, in bytes	varies	416	EOF
LOG(2.718282)	logarithm base e	1	385	EXP
MID$("SMART",2)	begin at the 2nd character	"MART"	394	other MID$
MID$("SMART",2,3)	begin at the 2nd, take 3	"MAR"	394	other MID$
MKD$(.2014209944946413)	make the double a string	"RAT NAN~"	417	CVD
MKI$(17741)	make the integer a string	"ME"	417	CVI
MKS$(.201421)	make the single a string	"NAN~"	417	CVS
MOUSE(1)	how far mouse to right	varies	408	STICK
PEEK(7512)	peek at memory cell #7512	varies	414	RND
RIGHT$("SMART",2)	rightmost 2 characters	"RT"	394	MID$
RND	random decimal	varies	391	other RND
RND(5)	random integer from 1 to 5	varies	388	other RND
SGN(-546)	sign of -546	-1	386	ABS, INT
SIN(30*D)	sine of 30 degrees	.5	396	COS, TAN
SQR(9)	square root of 9	3	384	EXP, LOG
STICK(0)	how far joystick to right	varies	408	MOUSE
STR$(81.4)	turn 81.4 into a string	" 81.4"	395	VAL
STRING$(5,"B")	a string of 5 B's	"BBBBB"	395	other STRING$
STRING$(5,66)	66th ASCII character, 5 times	"BBBBB"	395	other STRING$
TAN(45*D)	tangent of 45 degrees	1	396	ATN
TIME$	current time of day	varies	395	TIMER, DATE$
TIMER	# of seconds since midnight	varies	395	TIME$, DATE$
VAL("72.6")	remove the quotation marks	72.6	395	STR$

All popular microcomputers use either Modern Microsoft BASIC or a slight variation of it.

At the end of this BASIC chapter is an amazing appendix called "Versions of BASIC". It explains the versions of BASIC used by IBM, Commodore, Apple, Tandy, and dozens of other manufacturers, including yours. It reveals the subtle ways that your computer's BASIC differs from Modern Microsoft BASIC.

If you don't have a computer yet, ignore the appendix: read just the main text, which explains Modern Microsoft BASIC.

If you *do* have access to a computer, read the main text (which explains Modern Microsoft BASIC); but **before trying the examples on your computer, peek at the appendix** to see how your computer's BASIC differs from Modern Microsoft BASIC. To reach that appendix easily, put a bookmark *now* at the following page:

Kind of computer you have	Where to put the bookmark
IBM PC or any computer that uses IBM PC software	page 422
Apple Mac	page 427
Apple 2, 2+, 2e, 2c, 2c+, or 2GS	page 431
Commodore	page 438
Tandy's Radio Shack TRS-80 model 4	page 443
Tandy's Radio Shack TRS-80 Color Computer	page 445
other computer	page 449

If you ever get confused about how to program *your* computer, phone me at 617-666-2666. I'll help you, free!

The keyboard

Each year, manufacturers improve their keyboards. I expect that someday most manufacturers will use the **Walter keyboard**, which I invented several years ago. It looks like this:

Clear Help	ClrDoc Escape	! 1	@ 2	# 3	$ 4	% 5	^ 6	& 7	* 8	(9	) 0	_ −	BackWd Backsp	DeleWd Delete
\ LfTab	| Tab	Q	W	E	R	T	Y	U	I	O	P	+ =	{ [	}]
` Functn	~ Control	A	S	D	F	G	H	J	K	L	: ;	" '	Enter	
Boot Break	PrtDoc Print	Shift	Z	X	C	V	B	N	M	< ,	> .	? /	Shift	Top ↑
• Pause	• Echo	• Caps	• Insert	Space						Copy Move	LfMar ←	RtMar →	Bottom ↓	

Now I'm going to explain how to use the most important keys. But don't touch the keys on *your* keyboard until you've read the next section (which is called "Get Started") and the "Versions of BASIC" appendix (which reveals how *your* keyboard differs from the Walter keyboard).

<u>**Numbers**</u> Look at the Walter keyboard. The top row of keys contains the numbers.

Don't confuse 1 with I; the number 1 is in the top row. Don't confuse zero with the letter O; the number zero is in the top row.

(On older keyboards, the zero has a slash through it, like this: Ø. That's called a **slashed zero** or a **Swedish zero**.)

<u>**The SHIFT key**</u> One of the keys looks like this:

If you press that $4 key, you'll type a 4. Here's how to type a dollar sign instead: hold down the SHIFT key; and while you keep holding down the SHIFT key, tap the $4 key. Here's the general rule: **if a key has two symbols on it, and you want to type the top symbol, hold down the SHIFT key.**

About the SHIFT key, beginners often make two boo-boos. The first boo-boo is forgetting to press it. For example, suppose you want to type a dollar sign, and you press the $4 key but forget to hold down the SHIFT key; then you'll be typing a 4 instead.

The other boo-boo is trying to hit the SHIFT key and another key at exactly the same time. You can't do it; it's impossible; you'll wind up hitting one key before the other. The trick is to hold down the SHIFT key *first*; and while you keep holding it down, give the other key a light tap.

Beginners often make those boo-boos. When they realize their mistakes, they say "Oh, shit!" That's why programmers call it the "shit" key.

The keyboard contains *two* SHIFT keys. They serve the same purpose as each other. Use whichever SHIFT key makes your fingers feel more comfortable.

<u>**The CAPS key**</u> If you tap the CAPS key, the computer will automatically capitalize all the letters you type. For example, if you tap the CAPS key and then press the M and E keys, the screen will show a capitalized ME. The computer will continue to capitalize all the letters, until you tell the computer to stop capitalizing.

To make the computer stop capitalizing, just tap the CAPS key again. After you've told the computer to stop capitalizing, pressing the M and E keys make the screen show a small me — unless you simultaneously hold down the SHIFT key.

<u>**The BACKSPACE key**</u> The BACKSPACE key says BACKSP on it. If you make a typing mistake, erase the mistake by pressing the BACKSPACE key, which makes the computer erase the last character you typed. To erase *two* characters, press the BACKSPACE key *twice*.

(On older keyboards, the BACKSPACE key has a left-arrow on it, like this: ←. To find out about *your* keyboard's BACKSPACE key, check the "Versions of BASIC" appendix.)

The ENTER key The most important key is the ENTER key. When using BASIC, **press the ENTER key at the end of every line you type**. The ENTER key takes the line you've typed and enters that line into the computer, so that the computer reads the line.

The computer ignores what you type, until you press the ENTER key. If you forget to press the ENTER key at the end of the line, the computer doesn't read what you typed, and so the computer doesn't do anything, and you wonder why the computer seems broken.

(On older keyboards, the ENTER key is called the RETURN key.)

Get started

Make sure the various parts of your computer system are correctly attached to each other. Then turn on the power. If your computer is modern (and uses Microsoft BASIC), it will say:

OK

(Older computers don't say OK. Instead, they say READY or print a bracket. For further details about *your* computer, read the "Versions of BASIC" appendix.)

Be bold In science fiction, computers blow up; in real life, they never do. No matter what keys you press, no matter what commands you type, you won't hurt the computer. The computer is invincible! So go ahead and experiment. If it doesn't like what you type, it will gripe at you, but so what?

Troubles When you try using the computer, you'll have trouble — because you're making a mistake, or the computer is broken, or the computer is weird and works differently from the majority of computers discussed in this book. (Each computer has its own "personality", its own quirks.)

Whenever you have trouble, laugh about it, and say, "Oh, boy! Here we go again!" (If you're Jewish, you can say all that more briefly, in one word: "Oy!") Then get some help.

Get help For further help with *your* computer, read the "Versions of BASIC" appendix. For even more help, read the beginner's manual that came with your computer, or ask the genie who gave you the computer (your salesperson or parent or boss or teacher or friend).

If you're sitting near computers in your office, school, or home, and other people are nearby, ask them for help. They'll gladly answer your questions because they like to show off and because the way *they* got to know the answers was by asking.

Computer folks like to explain computers, just as priests like to explain religion. Remember: you're joining a cult! Even if you don't truly believe in "the power and glory of computers", at least you'll have a few moments of weird fun. So play along with the weird computer people, boost their egos, and they'll help you get through your initiation rite. Above all, assert yourself, and **ask questions**. "Shy guys finish last."

When dealing with the computer and the people who surround it, be friendly but assertive. To make sure you get your money's worth from a computer course, ask your teachers and coworkers questions, questions, questions! If you're using a computer that you won, get help from the person who gave it to you.

Your town probably has a **computer club**. (To find out, ask the local schools and computer stores.) Join the club, and tell the members you'd like help with your computer. Probably some computer hobbyist will help you.

And remember — you can call *me* anytime at 617-666-2666, and I'll help you, free!

Let's try to make the computer print the answer to 5+2. (And let's hope the computer says 7.)

Type this:

```
PRINT 5+2
```

Type that carefully! Here's how. . . .

First, **type the word PRINT**, by pressing the P key, then the R key, then I, then N, then T. (Since most computers don't care about capitalization, don't bother pressing the SHIFT key.)

After typing the word PRINT, type a blank space (by pressing the SPACE bar). Then press the 5 key. Then type a plus sign, but be careful: **on most keyboards, the plus sign is on the top part of a key; so to type the plus sign, you must hold down the SHIFT key.** Then type the 2.

When you've finished typing that line, **press the ENTER key, which makes the computer read what you've typed.** Then the computer will print the answer:

```
7
```

If your computer prints a wrong answer instead or says ERROR, you made a typing mistake. Find your mistake (by looking at the screen), and then try again to type:

```
PRINT 5+2
```

Underneath the answer, the computer will print the word OK (or some old-fashioned word, such as READY). That means it's okay for you to feed the computer the next problem; the computer's ready for another problem.

If you want to subtract 3 from 7, type this:

```
PRINT 7-3
```

(To type the minus sign, you do *not* press the SHIFT key.) When you've finished typing that line, remember to press the ENTER key, which makes the computer read that line and print the answer. The computer will print:

```
4
```

You can use decimal points and negative numbers. For example, if you type this —

```
PRINT -26.3+1
```

the computer will print:

```
-25.3
```

Multiplication

To multiply, use an asterisk. To multiply 2 by 6, type this:

```
PRINT 2*6
```

The computer will print:

```
12
```

Division

To divide, use a slash. So to divide 8 by 4, type this:

```
PRINT 8/4
```

The computer will print:

```
2
```

Question mark

If you're too lazy to type the word PRINT, type a question mark instead. For example, instead of typing —

```
PRINT 5+2
```

you can type:

```
? 5+2
```

The question mark is an abbreviation. It stands for the word PRINT.

If you wish, think of the question mark as standing for the word "What's". For example, if you want to ask the computer "What's 5+2", type this:

```
? 5+2
```

Huge & tiny numbers

Do *not* put commas in large numbers. To write four million, do *not* write 4,000,000; instead, write 4000000.

If the computer's answer is huge (more than a million) or tiny (less than .01), the computer might print the answer strangely. Here's how. . . .

E notation The computer might print the letter E, which means "move the decimal point".

For example, suppose the computer says the answer to a problem is:

```
8.51673E+12
```

The E means, "move the decimal point". The plus sign means, "towards the right". Altogether, **the E+12 means, "move the decimal point towards the right, 12 places."** So look at 8.51673, and move the decimal point towards the right, 12 places; you get 8516730000000.

So when the computer says the answer is 8.51673E+12, the computer really means the answer is 8516730000000, approximately. The exact answer might be 8516730000000.2 or 8516730000000.79 or some similar number, but the computer prints just an approximation.

Suppose your computer says the answer to a problem is:

```
9.26E-04
```

After the E, the minus sign means, "towards the *left*". So look at 9.26, and move the decimal point towards the left, 4 places. You get:

.000926

So when the computer says the answer is 9.26E-04, the computer really means the answer is:

.000926

You'll rarely see E notation: the computer uses it only if an answer is huge (many millions) or tiny (tinier than .01). But when the computer *does* use E notation, remember to move the decimal point!

The highest number The highest number the computer can handle is about 1E38, which is 1 followed by 38 zeros, like this:

```
100000000000000000000000000000000000000
```

If you try to go much higher, the computer will say:

```
OVERFLOW ERROR
```

The tiniest decimal The tiniest decimal the computer can handle is about 1E-38, which is a decimal point followed by 38 digits, 37 of which are zeros, like this:

```
.00000000000000000000000000000000000001
```

If you try to go tinier, the computer will have an "underflow error" and will "fake" the answer: it will give zero instead of the correct answer.

Order of operations

What does "2 plus 3 times 4" mean? The answer depends on who you ask.

To a clerk, it means "start with 2 plus 3, then multiply by 4"; that makes 5 times 4, which is 20. But to a scientist, "2 plus 3 times 4" means something different: it means "2 plus three fours", which is 2+4+4+4, which is 14.

Since computers were invented by scientists, computers think like scientists. If you type —

PRINT 2+3*4

the computer will think you mean "2 plus three fours", so it will do 2+4+4+4 and print this answer:

14

The computer will *not* print the clerk's answer, which is 20. So if you're a clerk, tough luck!

Scientists and computers follow this rule: **do multiplication and division before addition and subtraction.** So if you type —

PRINT 2+3*4

the computer begins by hunting for multiplication and division. When it finds the multiplication sign between the 3 and the 4, it multiplies 3 by 4 and gets 12, like this:

PRINT 2+3*4
        ⌣
        12

So the problem becomes 2+12, which is 14, which the computer prints.

For another example, suppose you type:

PRINT 10-2*3+72/9*5

The computer begins by doing all the multiplications and divisions. So it does 2*3 (which is 6) and does 72/9*5 (which is 8*5, which is 40), like this:

PRINT 10-2*3+72/9*5
         ⌣   ⌣
         6   40

So the problem becomes 10-6+40, which is 44, which is the answer the computer prints.

Parentheses   You can use parentheses the same way as in algebra. For example, if you type —

PRINT 5-(1+1)

the computer will compute 5-2 and print:

3

You can put parentheses inside parentheses. If you type —

PRINT 10-(5-(1+1))

the computer will compute 10-(5-2), which is 10-3, and will print:

7

STRINGS

Let's make the computer fall in love. Let's make it say, "I love you".

Type this:

PRINT "I LOVE YOU"

Type it carefully. Begin by typing the word PRINT. (If you're lazy, type a question mark instead.) Then press the SPACE bar. Then type a quotation mark, but be careful: **on most keyboards, the quotation mark is on the top part of a key; so to type the quotation mark, you must hold down the SHIFT key.** Then type I LOVE YOU. Then type another quotation mark.

At the end of the line, press the ENTER key. The computer will obey your command; it will print:

I LOVE YOU

You can change the computer's personality. For example, if you give this command —

PRINT "I HATE YOU"

the computer will reply:

I HATE YOU

Notice that to make the computer print a message, you must put the message between quotation marks. The quotation marks make the computer copy the message without worrying about what the message means. For example, if you misspell "I love you", and type —

PRINT "AIEEE LUF YA"

the computer will still copy the message (without worrying about what it means); the computer will print:

AIEEE LUF YA

Jargon

The word "JOY" consists of 3 characters: J and O and Y. Programmers say that the word "JOY" is a **string** of 3 characters.

A **string** is any collection of characters, such as "JOY" or "I LOVE YOU" or "AIEEE LUF YA" or "76 TROMBONES" or "GO AWAY!!!" or "XYPW EXR///746". The computer will print whatever string you wish, but remember to **put the string in quotation marks**.

Strings versus numbers

The computer can handle two types of expressions: **strings** and **numbers**. Put strings (such as "JOY" and "I LOVE YOU") in quotation marks. Numbers (such as 2+2) do *not* go in quotation marks.

Accidents

Suppose you accidentally put the number 2+2 in quotation marks, like this:

```
PRINT "2+2"
```

The quotation marks make the computer think "2+2" is a string instead of a number. Since the computer thinks "2+2" is a string, it copies the string without analyzing what it means; the computer will print:

```
2+2
```

It will *not* print 4.

Suppose you accidentally forget to put the string "I LOVE YOU" in quotation marks, and type this instead:

```
PRINT I LOVE YOU
```

Since you forgot the quotation marks, the computer thinks the I LOVE YOU is a weird number instead of a string; but the computer doesn't know what kind of weird number it is since the computer doesn't know the meaning of love. Whenever the computer is confused, it either gripes at you or prints a zero. In this particular example, it will print a zero, like this:

```
0
```

So if you incorrectly tell the computer to say it loves you, it will say zero.

Long commands on small screens

Try typing this command:

```
PRINT "I LIKE TO EAT AND DRINK AND GAZE INTO YOUR EYES AS WE DREAM ABOUT LOVE"
```

That command's long. It won't fit on a single line of your screen if your screen's small; but go ahead and type the command anyway. When you reach the screen's right edge, the computer automatically moves you to the line below so you can continue typing. **Do not press the ENTER key, until you've typed the entire command.**

After typing the entire command, press the ENTER key. The computer will print:

```
I LIKE TO EAT AND DRINK AND GAZE INTO YOUR EYES AS WE DREAM ABOUT LOVE
```

Now that you've had fun experimenting with the word PRINT, you're ready for the big-time; you're ready to program the computer!

Three steps

Programming the computer consists of three steps.

Step 1: type the word NEW

That tells the computer you're going to invent a new program.

After you type the word NEW, press the ENTER key. The computer will say OK. (If your computer is old-fashioned, it will say some other word instead, such as READY.)

Step 2: type your program

A **program** is a list of numbered commands. For example, suppose you want the computer to say:

```
I LOVE YOU
YOU TURNED ME ON
LET'S GET MARRIED
```

Type this program:

```
1 PRINT "I LOVE YOU"
2 PRINT "YOU TURNED ME ON"
3 PRINT "LET'S GET MARRIED"
```

Every line of the program must be numbered: you must type those numbers. Every line of the program must say PRINT; you must type the word PRINT. (Or, if you're too lazy to type the word PRINT, you can type a question mark instead.) Every line of that program must include quotation marks; you must type the quotation marks.

At the end of each line, press the ENTER key.

Step 3: type the word RUN

That tells the computer to look at the program you've written, and run through it.

After you've typed the word RUN, press the ENTER key.

The computer will print everything you requested; it will print:

```
I LOVE YOU
YOU TURNED ME ON
LET'S GET MARRIED
```

Then the computer will say OK.

Review

Let's review that procedure. You type:

```
NEW
1 PRINT "I LOVE YOU"
2 PRINT "YOU TURNED ME ON"
3 PRINT "LET'S GET MARRIED"
RUN
```

The numbered instructions (1, 2, and 3) are called the **program**. Above the program, you type the word NEW; below the program, you type the word RUN. The words NEW and RUN are *not* numbered.

After you've done all that correctly (and pressed the ENTER key after the word RUN), the computer will obey the program and print what you requested.

Each line of the program must be numbered. Putting a number at the beginning of a line makes the line become part of your program; the computer won't obey the line until the program is RUN. Here's the rule: **a number in front of the line tells the computer to wait until you type the word RUN.**

Another example

For another example, try typing this:

```
NEW
1 PRINT "I LONG"
2 PRINT 2+2
3 PRINT "U"
RUN
```

At the end of each line, remember to press the ENTER key. When you press the ENTER key after the word RUN, the computer obeys the program.

The first line makes the computer print "I LONG". The second line makes the computer add 2 and 2, so the computer prints the number 4. The third line makes the computer print the letter U.

Altogether, the computer prints:

```
I LONG
 4
U
```

Yes, the computer says it longs for you!

In that example, the computer indents the 4, so that the 4 has a blank space before it. That's because of this rule: the computer automatically puts a blank space before every positive number.

After the computer's finished running that program, if you type the word RUN again the computer will print again:

```
I LONG
 4
U
```

A program's a list of numbered instructions. If the program you typed isn't on the screen anymore, and you'd like to see that list of numbered instructions again, type the word LIST. The computer will say:

```
1 PRINT "I LONG"
2 PRINT 2+2
3 PRINT "U"
```

Poem

Suppose you want to make multiple copies of this poem:

```
SPRING HAS SPRUNG.
THE GRASS HAS RIZ.
I WONDER WHERE
THE FLOWERS IS.
```

First, turn the poem into a program, by typing:

```
NEW
1 PRINT "SPRING HAS SPRUNG."
2 PRINT "THE GRASS HAS RIZ."
3 PRINT "I WONDER WHERE"
4 PRINT "THE FLOWERS IS."
```

Then type the word RUN (and press the ENTER key). The computer will print the poem.

If you type the word RUN again, the computer will print the poem again. Each time you type the word RUN, the computer will print the poem.

To print *many* copies of the poem, just type the word RUN many times, like this. . . .

You type:	RUN
Computer types:	SPRING HAS SPRUNG.
	THE GRASS HAS RIZ.
	I WONDER WHERE
	THE FLOWERS IS.
	OK
You type:	RUN
Computer types:	SPRING HAS SPRUNG.
	THE GRASS HAS RIZ.
	I WONDER WHERE
	THE FLOWERS IS.
	OK
You type:	RUN
Computer types:	SPRING HAS SPRUNG.
	etc.

If you hate poetry and all other forms of art, cheer up: by using the same technique, you can make the computer type many copies of your favorite flubbed-up business letter or your favorite obnoxious ad.

Colons

You can put several statements on the same line, like this:

```
1 PRINT "I THINK": PRINT "OF FLEAS": PRINT "AND SNEEZE"
```

The computer will PRINT "I THINK". Then the computer will PRINT "OF FLEAS". Then the computer will PRINT "AND SNEEZE". Altogether, the computer will print:

```
I THINK
OF FLEAS
AND SNEEZE
```

Become an expert

To invent your *own* program and make the computer handle it, go through the three steps again: type the word NEW, then type your program, then type the word RUN. Remember to press the ENTER key at the end of each line, and remember that the commands NEW and RUN are *not* numbered.

Those three steps (NEW then program then RUN) are all you have to know about programming! C'mon, write some programs! It's easy! Try it. You'll have lots of fun!

A person who writes a program is called a **programmer**. Congratulations: *you're* a programmer!

Write several programs like the ones I've shown you already. Then you can put on your résumé that you have "a wide variety of programming experience", and you can talk your way into a programming job!

The rest of this chapter explains how to become a *good* programmer.

Programming the computer is like driving a car: the only way to become an expert is to put your hands on that mean machine and try it yourself.

If you have access to a computer, put this book next to the computer's keyboard. At the end of each paragraph, type the examples and look, look, see the computer run. Invent your own variations: try typing different numbers and strings. Invent your own programs: make the computer print your name or a poem; make it solve problems from your other courses and the rest of your life. The computer's a fantastic toy. Play with it.

If you're a student, don't wait for your instructor to give lectures and assign homework. *Act now.* You'll learn more from handling the computer than from the lectures or readings. Experience counts.

Let me tell you the story of Charlie. . . .

At Wesleyan University's computer center, one of the directors was having trouble making the computer print the university's payroll. He asked me for help, but I said I didn't know either. I saw a little kid sitting at one of the keyboards. "Hey, Charlie," I called to him, "we're having trouble getting the payroll out."

Little Charlie came over and typed some stuff on our keyboard. "The payroll will be out in a minute," he said gleefully.

Charlie was just in seventh grade. He'd never taken a computer course; his school didn't offer one. But by spending the whole summer just "hanging around" our computer, he knew it better than we.

Be like Charlie. Hang around your computer. Communicate with it every day. At first, that will be even harder than talking with a cat or a tree, because the computer belongs to a different species, a different kingdom; but keep trying. Get to know it as well as you know your best friend.

When dealing with the computer and the people who surround it, be friendly but also assertive. To make sure you get your money's worth from a computer course, ask your teacher, classmates, lab assistants, and other programmers questions, questions, questions!

If you're taking a French course, you might find French difficult; and if you're taking a computer course, you might find computers difficult also. But even a stupid three-year-old French kid can speak French, and even kindergarten kids can program the computer. They've got just one advantage over you: practice!

CORRECTING ERRORS

If you make an error, you can correct it in three ways. . . .

If you notice the error before you press the ENTER key, correct the error by using the BACKSPACE key.

If you mess up the whole program, rewrite it, by typing the word NEW and then starting from the beginning again.

If you mess up a line, retype it underneath. For example, suppose you type —

```
1 PRIMT "I LOVE YOU"
```

and then you notice that you misspelled the word PRINT. Just retype the line, so your screen looks like this:

```
1 PRIMT "I LOVE YOU"
1 PRINT "I LOVE YOU"
```

For another example, suppose you type this tongue-twister —

```
1 PRINT "SHE SELLS"
2 PRINT "SEE SHELLS"
3 PRINT "BY THE SEASHORE"
```

and then you notice that in line 2, the SEE ought to be SEA. Underneath the program, retype that line, so your screen looks like this:

```
1 PRINT "SHE SELLS"
2 PRINT "SEE SHELLS"
3 PRINT "BY THE SEASHORE"
2 PRINT "SEA SHELLS"
```

When you type RUN, the computer will run the corrected version and print:

```
SHE SELLS
SEA SHELLS
BY THE SEASHORE
```

When you type LIST, the computer will list the corrected program; the computer will say:

```
1 PRINT "SHE SELLS"
2 PRINT "SEA SHELLS"
3 PRINT "BY THE SEASHORE"
```

What if the computer gripes?

If the computer ever gripes at you, don't worry: just correct your error.

For example, suppose you type —

```
1 PRIMT "ROSES ARE RED"
2 PRINT "CABBAGE IS GREEN"
3 PRINT "MY FACE IS FUNNY"
4 PRINT "BUT YOURS IS A SCREAM"
```

and you don't notice that you misspelled PRINT in line 1.

If you type RUN, the computer will try to run the program but will be confused by line 1, so it will gripe at you. It will say:

```
SYNTAX ERROR IN 1
```

That means the computer hasn't the faintest idea of what you're talking about in line 1.

Your next step is to correct the error. To do that, just retype line 1 correctly, and then type the word RUN again.

So altogether, the conversation looks like this. . . .

You type this, but it's wrong:	1 PRINT "ROSES ARE RED"
	2 PRINT "CABBAGE IS GREEN"
	3 PRINT "MY FACE IS FUNNY"
	4 PRINT "BUT YOURS IS A SCREAM"
	RUN
The computer gripes at you:	SYNTAX ERROR IN 1
You type this to correct error:	1 PRINT "ROSES ARE RED"
	RUN
The computer recites the poem:	ROSES ARE RED
	CABBAGE IS GREEN
	MY FACE IS FUNNY
	BUT YOURS IS A SCREAM

Common bloopers

If you're like most beginners, you'll make these mistakes soon — if you haven't made them already!

You type **the letter O instead of zero**, or type zero instead of the letter O. Your typing looks correct to you, but the computer gripes.

You type a command (such as RUN) but forget to **press the ENTER key afterwards**. The computer keeps waiting for you to press it. Since you don't realize the computer's waiting for you, and since the computer isn't replying, you think the computer broke.

You tell the computer to PRINT a message, but you forget to **put the message in quotation marks**. So the computer gripes or prints a zero instead.

You start typing a new program but forget to **type the word NEW**. So when you type RUN, the computer runs a mishmash of the new program with the previous program and reprints some messages from the previous program.

Rearranging your program

You don't have to type your program in order.

For example, suppose you type:

```
4 PRINT "TOES"
2 PRINT "TOAD"
3 PRINT "LICKS"
1 PRINT "MY"
```

In its mind, the computer automatically rearranges the program, so the numbers are in increasing order, like this:

```
1 PRINT "MY"
2 PRINT "TOAD"
3 PRINT "LICKS"
4 PRINT "TOES"
```

If you'd like to peek inside the computer's mind and see what program the computer's thinking of, type the word LIST, like this. . . .

You type this program:	4 PRINT "TOES"
	2 PRINT "TOAD"
	3 PRINT "LICKS"
	1 PRINT "MY"
You type this command:	LIST
Computer types the program in increasing order:	1 PRINT "MY"
	2 PRINT "TOAD"
	3 PRINT "LICKS"
	4 PRINT "TOES"

If you type RUN, the computer will print:

```
MY
TOAD
LICKS
TOES
```

Whenever you're confused, type the word LIST. Then the computer will tell you what's in its mind; and what's in its mind might surprise you!

Fancy example Type this example and see what happens:

```
NEW
10 PRINT "MY"
90 PRINT "TRUCK"
32 PRINT "SNEEZE"
50 PRINT "TOE"
32 PRINT "NEED A"
70
80 PRINT "HAT"
80
20 PRINT "SORE FEET"
```

In its mind, the computer rearranges the program to put the numbers in increasing order.

The lowest number is 10, which prints "MY". Next comes line 20, which prints "SORE FEET".

Next comes line 32. Since you typed line 32 *twice*, the computer assumes you didn't like the first version and want the second version instead, so line 32 prints "NEED A".

Next comes line 40, which prints "TOE".

Next comes line 70. Since line 70 is blank, the computer ignores it.

Next comes line 80. Since you typed line 80 *twice*, the computer assumes you didn't like the first version and want the second version instead, which is blank. Since it's blank, the computer ignores it. So the computer ignores line 80 altogether!

Finally comes line 90, which prints "TRUCK".

If you type LIST, the computer will show you the result of all that reasoning. The computer will type:

```
10 PRINT "MY"
20 PRINT "SORE FEET"
32 PRINT "NEED A"
50 PRINT "TOE"
90 PRINT "TRUCK"
```

If you type RUN, the computer will print:

```
MY
SORE FEET
NEED A
TOE
TRUCK
```

If you think about that example, you'll notice two things:

To revise a line, just retype it.

To erase line 80, just type —
```
80
```
with nothing else on the line.

NEW versus RUN

The word NEW erases your program from the computer's mind, to make way for a new one.

But the word RUN does *not* erase the program. After the run, you can continue inserting, deleting, and revising lines.

Numbering by tens

If your first line is numbered 1, and your second line is numbered 2, you can't squeeze a line between them, since decimals aren't allowed. So **expert programmers number their lines 10, 20, 30, 40, . . . instead of 1, 2, 3, . . .**

That way, if your first line is numbered 10 and your second line is numbered 20, and you want to insert an extra line between them, you can call it 15. If you later want to insert an extra line between 10 and 15, you can call it 12. If you want to insert another line between 10 and 12, you can call it 11.

Ranges of lines

If your program's too long to fit on your screen, tell the computer to list *part* of your program.

For example, to list just line 30, type this:

```
LIST 30
```

To list lines 30 through 80, type this:

```
LIST 30-80
```

To list from line 30 to the end of your program, type this:

```
LIST 30-
```

To list from the beginning of your program up to line 80, type this:

```
LIST -80
```

To delete lines 30 through 80, type this:

```
DELETE 30-80
```

That works on most computers. Some computers are different; check the "Versions of BASIC" appendix.

Arrow keys

To correct a mistake in your program quickly, try using the arrow keys. Here's how.

See the error Make sure the line you want to correct is on the screen. If it's not on the screen yet, put it onto the screen by using the word LIST or EDIT.

For example, to put line 30 onto the screen, type —

```
LIST 30
```

or type:

```
EDIT 30
```

Move to the error On the keyboard, you'll see a key that shows an arrow pointing to the left; it's called the **left-arrow key**. You'll also see a key that shows an arrow pointing to the right; it's called the **right-arrow key**. You'll also see an **up-arrow key** and a **down-arrow key**.

On the computer's screen, you'll see a little blinking rectangle, called the **cursor**. Move it to the part of the line you want to correct, by pressing the arrow keys. (To move the cursor to the left, press the left-arrow key; to move the cursor to the right, press the right-arrow key; to move the cursor up, press the up-arrow key; to move the cursor down, press the down-arrow key.)

If you typed the word LIST, you must press the up-arrow key to move the cursor up to the line you want to correct. If you typed the word EDIT instead, you don't need to press the up-arrow key; the word EDIT puts the cursor on the correct line automatically.

Correct the error When you've moved the cursor to the part of the line you want to correct, make your corrections.

To delete a character, move the cursor to that character, then press the DELETE key. To replace a character, move the cursor to that character, then type the new character you want instead. To insert extra characters in the middle of the line, move the cursor where you want the extra characters to begin, press the INSERT key, then type the extra characters.

When you've finished correcting the line, press the ENTER key, which tells the computer to take the corrections seriously.

Final comments After pressing the ENTER key, if you want to move the cursor to the bottom of the screen, press the down-arrow key several times.

That method of editing works on *most* computers. To find out how to edit easily on *your* computer, read the appendix.

TRICKY PRINTING

Printing can be tricky! Here are the tricks. . . .

Semicolons

Run this program:

```
10 PRINT "FAT";
20 PRINT "HER"
```

Line 10 makes the computer print FAT; and line 10 ends with a semicolon. **The semicolon makes the computer print the next item on the same line**; so the computer will print HER on the same line, like this:

```
FATHER
```

This command shows what happens to an evil king on a boat:

```
PRINT "SIN";"KING"
```

The computer will print SIN, and will print KING on the same line, like this:

```
SINKING
```

Blank lines

Life consists sometimes of joy, sometimes of sorrow, and sometimes of a numb emptiness. To express those feelings, run this program:

```
10 PRINT "JOY"
20 PRINT
30 PRINT "SORROW"
```

Line 10 makes the computer print JOY. **Line 20 makes the computer print a blank empty line**, underneath JOY. Altogether, the computer will print:

```
JOY

SORROW
```

Indenting

Suppose you want the computer to print this letter:

```
DEAR JOAN,
    THANK YOU FOR THE BEAUTIFUL
NECKTIE.  JUST ONE PROBLEM--
I DON'T WEAR NECKTIES!
            LOVE,
            FRED-THE-HIPPIE
```

This program prints it:

```
10 PRINT "DEAR JOAN,"
20 PRINT "   THANK YOU FOR THE BEAUTIFUL"
30 PRINT "NECKTIE.  JUST ONE PROBLEM--"
40 PRINT "I DON'T WEAR NECKTIES!"
50 PRINT "            LOVE,"
60 PRINT "            FRED-THE-HIPPIE"
```

In the program, each line contains two quotation marks. **To make the computer indent a line, put blank spaces after the first quotation mark.**

Spaces after numbers

Try typing this command:

```
PRINT -3;"IS MY FAVORITE NUMBER"
```

Whenever the computer prints a number, it prints a blank space afterwards; so the computer will print a blank space after -3, like this:

`-3 IS MY FAVORITE NUMBER`

(space)

Spaces before numbers

This command tells what to put in your coffee:

`PRINT 7;"DO";"NUTS"`

The computer prints 7 and DO and NUTS. Since 7 is a number, the computer prints a blank space after the 7. **The computer prints another blank space <u>before</u> every number that's positive**; so the computer prints another blank space before the 7, like this:

`7 DONUTS`

(spaces)

Hey, if you're feeling cool, maybe this command expresses your feelings:

`PRINT "THE TEMPERATURE IS";4+25;"DEGREES"`

The computer prints THE TEMPERATURE IS, then 4+25 (which is 29), then DEGREES. Since 29 is a positive number, the computer prints a blank space before and after the 29:

`THE TEMPERATURE IS 29 DEGREES`

(spaces)

Use this command if you're even colder:

`PRINT "THE TEMPERATURE IS";4-25;"DEGREES"`

The computer prints THE TEMPERATURE IS, then 4-25 (which is -21), then DEGREES. Since -21 is a number, the computer prints a space after it; but since -21 is *not* positive, the computer does *not* print a space before it. The computer prints:

`THE TEMPERATURE IS-21 DEGREES`

(no space) (space)

Yuk! That looks ugly! It would look prettier if there were a space before the -21. To insert a space, put the space inside quotation marks:

`PRINT "THE TEMPERATURE IS ";4-25;"DEGREES"`

(inserted space, before the quotation mark)

Then the computer will print:

`THE TEMPERATURE IS -21 DEGREES`

(inserted space)

Multiple calculations

By using semicolons, you can make the computer do many calculations at once.

For example, this command makes the computer do 6+2, 6-2, 6*2, and 6/2, all at once:

`PRINT 6+2;6-2;6*2;6/2`

That makes the computer print the four answers:

`8 4 12 3`

The computer prints spaces between the answers, because the computer prints a space after every number (and an additional space before every number that's positive).

Clear the screen

If you press the CLEAR key (which is on the Walter keyboard), the computer erases the entire screen, so that the screen becomes cleared, empty, blank.

Though pressing the CLEAR key erases the screen, it does *not* erase the computer's memory. The computer still remembers what program you were working on. The only way to erase the computer's memory is to type the word NEW.

So whenever you want to begin a new program, type the word NEW, which erases the previous program; pressing the CLEAR key is *not* sufficient.

You can begin your program with this line:

`10 CLS`

It makes the computer automatically CLear the Screen, before doing the rest of the program.

For example, run this program:

`10 CLS`
`20 PRINT "I'M SITTING ON TOP OF THE WORLD"`

Line 10 makes the computer CLear the Screen. Since the screen's been cleared, line 20 prints this message *at the top of the screen*:

`I'M SITTING ON TOP OF THE WORLD`

On older computers, the CLEAR key is missing and the CLS command doesn't work. To find out about *your* computer, see the "Versions of BASIC" appendix.

Print on paper

You've learned how to make the computer print messages, poems, and business letters on your screen. But if you want to mail those messages and letters to your friends, you face this problem: the post office refuses to mail your screen! And it's hard to stuff your screen into an envelope! So to mail the computer's wise words to your friends, you must tell the computer to print on paper instead of on the screen.

To make the computer print on paper, attach the computer to a **printer**, which handles paper and looks like a typewriter without a keyboard.

You can control the printer in four ways.

The PRINT key The simplest way is to press the PRINT key, which is on the Walter keyboard. Pressing the PRINT key makes the printer dump onto paper a snapshot of everything that's on the screen. The snapshot on paper is called a **screen dump**.

The ECHO key A fancier way to print on paper is to press the ECHO key, which is also on the Walter keyboard. Pressing the ECHO key turns your entire computer system into a gigantic typewriter. After you press the ECHO key, whatever you or the computer type onto the screen will also be echoed onto the paper. For example, if you press the ECHO key and then type the word LOVE, the word LOVE will appear on both the screen and the paper. The printer will continue to echo everything that's typed, until you tell the printer to stop echoing. To tell the printer to stop, just press the ECHO key again.

The LPRINT command If you type LPRINT instead of PRINT, the computer will print on paper instead of on the screen. For example, to make the computer print I LOVE YOU on paper, type this:

`LPRINT "I LOVE YOU"`

The LLIST command To list your program on paper, instead of on the screen, type an extra L in front of the word LIST, like this:

`LLIST`

Differences Although modern computers include a PRINT key and an ECHO key and understand LPRINT and LLIST, older computers do not. To find out about *your* computer, read the "Versions of BASIC" appendix.

GOING & STOPPING

You can tell the computer to go and stop.

GO TO

This program makes the computer go wild:

```
10 PRINT "CAT"
20 PRINT "DOG"
30 GO TO 10
```

Line 10 makes the computer print CAT. Line 20 makes it print DOG.

Line 30 makes it go back to line 10 again, so it prints CAT again. Then it prints DOG again, and comes to line 30 again, which makes it go back to line 10 again, print CAT and DOG again, and then jump back again. . . .

The computer will print the words CAT and DOG again and again, like this:

```
CAT
DOG
CAT
DOG
CAT
DOG
CAT
DOG
CAT
DOG
etc.
```

The computer will try to print the words CAT and DOG again and again, forever.

Try running that program; you'll have fun watching the computer go crazy. The computer will print the words CAT and DOG on every line of your screen; and even when all the lines of your screen have been used, the computer still doesn't stop: all the CATs and DOGs rise to the top of the screen and finally off the screen, to make way for new CATs and DOGs to appear at the bottom of the screen. You'll see a blur, as thousands of CATs and DOGs go flying up the screen.

If you told the computer to use the printer (which prints on paper), you'll see reams of paper spewing out, saying CAT and DOG. Soon your whole room will be buried under piles of paper saying CAT and DOG thousands of times!

To stop this madness, you must give the computer some kind of "jolt" that will put it out of its misery. And now we come to the controversial part of this book. **To put the computer out of its misery, you must give an <u>abortion</u>. To give the abortion, press the BREAK key.** That makes the computer stop running your program; it will **abort your program** and say OK. Then you can give any command, such as LIST.

(The BREAK key is on the Walter keyboard. To find out about *your* computer's keyboard, check the "Versions of BASIC" appendix.)

Here's a picture of that program:

The computer follows the arrows, which make it go round and round in a **loop**. Since the computer will try to go round and round the loop forever, the loop is called **infinite**. The only way to stop an infinite loop is to abort it.

In that program, you typed just three lines; but since the third line said to GO TO the beginning, the computer does an infinite loop. By saying GO TO, you can make the computer do an infinite amount of work. Moral: **the computer can turn a finite amount of human energy into an infinite amount of good**. Putting it another way: **the computer can multiply your abilities by infinity.**

Love

Let's spread love throughout the world! Type this program, which makes the computer multiply your love:

```
10 PRINT "LOVE"
20 GO TO 10
```

Even though you typed the word LOVE just once, the computer will print it many times, like this:

```
LOVE
LOVE
LOVE
LOVE
LOVE
etc.
```

The computer will print repeatedly, until you abort its love.

For more lovely fun, put a semicolon after LOVE, like this:

```
10 PRINT "LOVE";
20 GO TO 10
```

The semicolon makes the computer print LOVE *next to* LOVE:

```
LOVELOVELOVELOVELOVELOVELOVELOVELOVELOVELOVELOVELOVELOVELOVELOVELOVELOVE
LOVELOVELOVELOVELOVELOVELOVELOVELOVELOVELOVELOVELOVELOVELOVELOVELOVELOVE
LOVELOVELOVELOVELOVELOVELOVELOVELOVELOVELOVELOVELOVELOVELOVELOVELOVELOVE
etc.
```

If you put a space after LOVE, like this —

```
10 PRINT "LOVE ";
20 GO TO 10
```

the computer will put a space after each LOVE:

```
LOVE LOVE LOVE LOVE LOVE LOVE LOVE LOVE LOVE LOVE LOVE LOVE LOVE LOVE LOVE LOVE
LOVE LOVE LOVE LOVE LOVE LOVE LOVE LOVE LOVE LOVE LOVE LOVE LOVE LOVE LOVE LOVE
LOVE LOVE LOVE LOVE LOVE LOVE LOVE LOVE LOVE LOVE LOVE LOVE LOVE LOVE LOVE LOVE
etc.
```

Instead of making the computer print LOVE, try making it print an ad (such as BUY JOE'S MEAT), or political slogan (such as STOP POLLUTION), or your name, or something else you feel emotional about. Like a dog, the computer imitates its master's personality. If your computer acts "cold and heartless", it's because *you* are!

Smelly poetry

Suppose you want to send this poem to all your friends:

```
I'M HAVING TROUBLE
WITH MY NOSE.
THE ONLY THING IT DOES IS:
BLOWS!
```

Just run this program:

```
10 PRINT "I'M HAVING TROUBLE"
20 PRINT "WITH MY NOSE."
30 PRINT "THE ONLY THING IT DOES IS:"
40 PRINT "BLOWS!"
50 PRINT
60 GO TO 10
```

Lines 10-40 print the poem. Line 50 prints a blank line at the end of the poem. Line 60 makes the computer do all that repeatedly, so the computer will print:

```
I'M HAVING TROUBLE
WITH MY NOSE.
THE ONLY THING IT DOES IS:
BLOWS!

I'M HAVING TROUBLE
WITH MY NOSE.
THE ONLY THING IT DOES IS:
BLOWS!

I'M HAVING TROUBLE
WITH MY NOSE.
THE ONLY THING IT DOES IS:
BLOWS!
```

etc.

The computer will print infinitely many copies of the poem — unless you abort it. If you activate the computer's printer, the copies will be printed on paper, so you can mail them to your nosy friends.

Life as an infinite loop

A program that makes the computer do the same thing again and again forever is an infinite loop.

Some humans act just like computers. Those humans do the same thing again and again. Every morning they GO TO work, and every evening they GO TO home. GO TO work, GO TO home, GO TO work, GO TO home, . . . Their lives are sheer drudgery. They're caught in an infinite loop.

Go to your bathroom, get your bottle of shampoo, and look at the instructions on the back. A typical bottle has three instructions:

```
Lather.
Rinse.
Repeat.
```

Those instructions say to lather, then rinse, then repeat — which means to lather again, then rinse again, then repeat again — which means to lather again, then rinse again, then repeat again. . . . If you follow those instructions, you'll never finish washing your hair! The instructions are an infinite loop! The instructions are a program: they program you to use lots of shampoo! That's how infinite loops help sell shampoo.

Infinite pause

This program tortures the computer:

```
10 GO TO 10
```

Line 10 tells the computer to go to line 10, which tells the computer to go to line 10, which tells the computer to go to line 10. . . . The computer will do line 10 again and again, forever. So the computer will spend the rest of its life just mumbling to itself. That program has turned your beautiful computer into a bumbling, mumbling idiot.

The "10 GO TO 10" is called an **infinite pause**, because it makes the computer pause from doing all useful work, forever.

If you're mean enough to give your computer that program, please abort it! Otherwise, a member of the Association for Prevention of Cruelty to Computers will stick pins in your voodoo doll.

To make the program even meaner, insert line 5, like this:

```
5 CLS
10 GO TO 10
```

Line 5 makes the computer CLear the Screen, so that the whole screen becomes blank. And line 10 renders the computer completely useless: the computer will ignore anything you type, since the computer is busy doing "10 GO TO 10" forever. Now you have a computer whose screen is permanently blank and that ignores anything you type on the keyboard! To get really mean, walk up to your best friend's computer, type that program, type the word RUN, and watch your friend suffer when the screen and keyboard both stop working! (And see how long your friend remains your "friend"!) The only way your (ex-)friend can fix the computer is to give an abortion or turn off the power.

(Remember: *most* computers understand CLS, but *yours* might not. To find out about *your* computer, check the "Versions of BASIC" appendix.)

To elaborate on that program, add line 7, like this:

```
5 CLS
7 PRINT "I REFUSE TO WORK FOR YOU"
10 GO TO 10
```

When you RUN that program, the screen goes blank, then the computer says it refuses to work for you, and then line 10 does indeed make the computer refuse to work for you! The computer will refuse all your work — it'll just mumble to itself — until you give it an abortion.

Now that I've turned you into a computer saboteur, the whole world will worry that you'll kidnap computers, hold them hostage, and threaten to turn them into "10 GO TO 10" idiots! You can even cause a moral dilemma for people who are against abortions and are even more against "pulling the plug". Is God against abortions for computers?

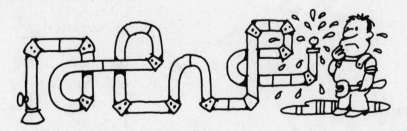

How to skip ahead

Did you ever dream about having a picnic in the woods? This program expresses that dream:

```
10 PRINT "LET'S MUNCH"
20 PRINT "SANDWICHES UNDER"
30 PRINT "THE TREES"
```

It makes the computer print:

```
LET'S MUNCH
SANDWICHES UNDER
THE TREES
```

Let's turn that dream into a nightmare, in which we all become giant termites. To do that, insert the shaded line:

```
10 PRINT "LET'S MUNCH"
15 GO TO 30
20 PRINT "SANDWICHES UNDER"
30 PRINT "THE TREES"
```

The computer does line 10, which prints LET'S MUNCH. Then it does line 15, which makes it skip ahead to line 30, which prints THE TREES. So altogether, the computer prints:

```
LET'S MUNCH
THE TREES
```

In that program, line 15 made the computer skip ahead to line 30 and skip over line 20.

END

To make the computer skip the bottom part of your program, say END:

```
10 PRINT "SHE SMELLS"
20 END
30 PRINT "OF PERFUME"
```

The computer will print SHE SMELLS and then end, without printing OF PERFUME.

After the computer ends, it'll say OK. Then you can type any command, such as LIST (to see the program again) or RUN (to make the computer print SHE SMELLS again) or NEW (to create a new program).

STOP

Instead of saying END, you can say STOP, like this:

```
10 PRINT "SHE SMELLS"
20 STOP
30 PRINT "OF PERFUME"
```

The computer will print SHE SMELLS and then stop, without printing OF PERFUME.

When the computer encounters the word STOP, it prints a message telling you which line said STOP.

For example, when the computer stops because line 20 said STOP, the computer prints "STOPPED AT LINE 20" or "BREAK IN LINE 20" or "BREAK IN 20". (The exact wording depends on which computer you bought.)

So if you type —

```
10 PRINT "SHE SMELLS"
20 STOP
30 PRINT "OF PERFUME"
```

and then type RUN, the computer will print something like this:

```
SHE SMELLS
BREAK IN 20
```

DISKS VERSUS TAPES

While you're working with a program, the computer keeps the program in its **random-access memory (RAM)**. In a typical microcomputer, the RAM handles just one program at a time. If you want the computer to remember *several* programs, you can put one program in the RAM but must put the remaining programs on a disk or tape instead.

Save on disk

Here's how to use a disk. (I'll explain tape later.)

Before typing your program, make sure the computer and disk have both been properly prepared. To find out how to prepare *your* computer and disk, read the "Versions of BASIC" appendix.

Then type your program. For example, try typing this program:

```
NEW
10 PRINT "MY DAD"
20 PRINT "IS GLAD"
```

Underneath the program, try typing this:

```
SAVE "JOE"
```

That makes the computer copy the program from the RAM to the disk, and name the program JOE.

Copying from the RAM to the disk is called "saving" the program. SAVE "JOE" means: save the program and name it "JOE".

Altogether, here's what you typed:

```
NEW
10 PRINT "MY DAD"
20 PRINT "IS GLAD"
SAVE "JOE"
```

(On *your* computer, the procedure might be slightly different: check the "Versions of BASIC" appendix.)

To make sure the computer copied the program onto the disk, type this word:

```
FILES
```

The computer will print the names of all the programs on the disk, and one of the names it will print is JOE.

The program is now in *two* places: the program's original version is still in the RAM, and a copy of it is on the disk. The copy is called JOE.

If you type NEW, you'll erase the RAM, and so the program won't be in the RAM anymore. But although the program's original version is no longer in the RAM, the *copy* (which is called JOE) remains on the disk. To prove JOE's still on the disk, type the word FILES again, which makes the computer say again that JOE's still on the disk.

How to choose a name

If you don't like the name JOE, choose a different name instead. For example, to create a program named SUE, type a program and then say:

```
SAVE "SUE"
```

The name of your program can be "JOE" or "SUE" or any other brief string of letters and digits. For example, it can be "LOVER" or "POEM4U".

Pick a name that reminds you of the program's purpose. For example, if the program prints a bill to a customer, call the program "BILL"; if the program plays chess, call the program "CHESS"; if it gives a quiz, call it "QUIZ"; if it tutors a human about the elements of sex, call it "SEX"; if it tutors a human about advanced sex, call it "SEX2".

Load from disk

You've seen that the word SAVE makes the computer copy a program from the RAM to the disk. **The opposite of the word SAVE is the word LOAD: it makes the computer copy a program from the <u>disk</u> to the <u>RAM</u>.**

For example, if you want the computer to copy JOE from the disk to the RAM, type this:

```
LOAD "JOE"
```

It tells the computer to load JOE into the RAM (from the disk). After typing that, the program's in the RAM again. To prove it's in the RAM, type the word LIST, so that the computer will LIST the program that's in the RAM; or type the word RUN, which makes the computer RUN the program that's in the RAM.

So if JOE's on a disk, you can run it by first copying it to the RAM and then saying RUN, like this:

```
LOAD "JOE"
RUN
```

Instead of typing that pair of lines, you can type this single line, which is a short-cut:

```
RUN "JOE"
```

That makes the computer automatically load JOE (from the disk to the RAM) and run it.

Edit the disk

Suppose you don't like the version of JOE that's on the disk. Here's how to revise JOE.

First, copy JOE from the disk to the RAM, by saying:

```
LOAD "JOE"
```

Then examine the program, by typing:

```
LIST
```

Then revise the program, by retyping some of its lines or adding new ones.

When you've finished revising the program's version that's in the RAM, copy the revisions from the RAM to disk, by saying again:

```
SAVE "JOE"
```

That command makes the computer copy the revised version of JOE onto the disk (and erases the previous version of JOE from the disk).

If JOE's on the disk and you want to change its name to FRED, type this:

```
RENAME "JOE" TO "FRED"
```

Protect yourself

Suppose you're creating a program named TOM, which is so long that it takes you several hours to type. You'll be upset if, after several hours of typing, your town suddenly has a blackout that makes the computer forget what you typed.

To protect yourself against such a calamity, type SAVE "TOM" every fifteen minutes. Then if your town has a blackout, you'll lose just a few minutes of work; the rest of your work will have already been saved on a disk.

Typing SAVE "TOM" every fifteen minutes protects you against blackouts and also against "computer malfunction" and any careless errors you might make.

Each time you say SAVE "TOM", the computer puts a copy of the program onto the disk and saves that copy permanently — or at least until you type SAVE "TOM" again fifteen minutes later. Even if your RAM is erased (by a blackout or computer malfunction or your carelessness), TOM will still be on the disk.

Space on the disk

If you invent many programs and put them on the disk, the disk will someday become full. If you try to put more programs onto the disk than the disk can hold, the computer will gripe by printing a message such as:

```
DISK FULL
```

Someday, you'll decide you no longer have any use for JOE, and that JOE's just wasting space on your disk. To erase JOE from the disk, type this:

```
KILL "JOE"
```

Tapes

If you can't afford a disk drive, try using cassette tapes instead, which serve the same purpose as disks but are cheaper and slower. (To find out whether *your* computer accepts cassette tapes, check the "Versions of BASIC" appendix.)

Here's how to put a program onto a cassette tape. First, type the program. Then put a tape into the tape recorder; to do that, you might have to press the recorder's EJECT button.

Rewind the tape, by pressing the recorder's REWIND button. When the tape is rewound, press the recorder's STOP button.

If the recorder has a counter, press the counter's button, so the counter becomes zero.

Press the recorder's FAST FORWARD button, until you get to a part of the tape that's blank and good. (The very beginning of the tape is bad. Wait until the counter gets to at least 10.) Then press the STOP button.

If the recorder has a counter, notice the counter's number, and write it onto the tape's label, by using a pencil.

To find out what to do next, read the "Versions of BASIC" appendix, which explains the peculiarities of *your* computer!

USING VARIABLES

WHAT'S A VARIABLE?

A letter can stand for a number. For example, X can stand for the number 47, as in this program:

```
10 X=47
20 PRINT X+2
```

Line 10 says X stands for the number 47. In other words, X is a name for the number 47.

Line 20 says to print X+2. Since X is 47, X+2 is 49; so the computer will print 49. That's the only number the computer will print; it will not print 47.

Jargon

A letter that stands for a number is called a **numeric variable**. In that program, X is a numeric variable; it stands for the number 47. The **value** of X is 47. Line 10 is called an **assignment statement**, because it **assigns** 47 to X.

More examples

Here's another example:

```
10 Y=38
20 PRINT Y-2
```

Line 10 says Y is a numeric variable that stands for the number 38.

Line 20 says to print Y-2. Since Y is 38, Y-2 is 36; so the computer will print 36.

Example:

```
10 B=8
20 PRINT B*3
```

Line 10 says B is 8. Line 20 says to print B*3, which is 8*3, which is 24; so the computer will print 24.

One variable can define another:

```
10 M=6
20 P=M+1
30 PRINT M*P
```

Line 10 says M is 6. Line 20 says P is M+1, which is 6+1, which is 7; so P is 7. Line 30 says to print M*P, which is 6*7, which is 42; so the computer will print 42.

A value can change:

```
10 F=4
20 F=9
30 PRINT F*2
```

Line 10 says F's value is 4. Line 20 changes F's value to 9, so line 30 prints 18.

Hassles

On the left side of the equal sign, you must have one variable:

Allowed	**Not allowed**	**Not allowed**
P=M+1	P-M=1	1=P-M
(one variable)	(two variables)	(not a variable)

The variable on the left side of the equation is the only one that changes. For example, the statement P=M+1 changes the value of P but not M. The statement A=B changes the value of A but not B:

```
10 A=1
20 B=7
30 A=B
40 PRINT A+B
```

Line 30 changes A, to make it equal B; so A becomes 7. Since both A and B are now 7, line 40 prints 14.

"A=B" versus "B=A" Saying "A=B" has a different effect from "B=A". That's because "A=B" changes the value of A (but not B); "B=A" changes the value of B (but not A).

Compare these programs:

```
10 A=1          10 A=1
20 B=7          20 B=7
30 A=B          30 B=A
40 PRINT A+B    40 PRINT A+B
```

In the left program (which you saw before), line 30 changes A to 7, so both A and B are 7. Line 40 prints 14.

In the right program, line 30 changes B to 1, so both A and B are 1. Line 40 prints 2.

A variable is a box

If variables ever confuse you, think of a variable as being a box. Here's how....

The computer's random-access memory (RAM) consists of electronic boxes. This program puts a number into a box:

```
10 X=47
20 PRINT X+2
```

Line 10 puts 47 into box X, like this:

Box X | 47 |

Line 20 says to print what's in box X, plus 2. So the computer will print 49.

You can change what's in a box:

```
10 F=4
20 F=9
30 PRINT F*2
```

Line 10 puts 4 into box F:

Box F | 4 |

Line 20 puts 9 into box F; the 9 replaces the 4:

Box F | 9 |

Line 30 prints 18.

To see why "A=B" has a different effect from "B=A", compare these programs again:

```
10 A=1        10 A=1
20 B=7        20 B=7
30 A=B        30 B=A
40 PRINT A+B  40 PRINT A+B
```

In both programs, lines 10 and 20 do this:

Box A | 1 |

Box B | 7 |

In the left program, line 30 makes the number in box A become 7 (so both boxes contain 7, and line 40 prints 14). In the right program, line 30 makes the number in box B become 1 (so both boxes contain 1, and line 40 prints 2).

When to use variables

Here's a practical example of when to use variables.

Suppose you're selling something that costs $1297.43, and you want to do these calculations:

```
multiply $1297.43 by 2
multiply $1297.43 by .05
add $1297.43 to $483.19
divide $1297.43 by 37
subtract $1297.43 from $8598.61
multiply $1297.43 by 28.7
```

To do those six calculations, you could run this program:

```
10 PRINT 1297.43*2; 1297.43*.05; 1297.43+483.19; 1297.43/37; 8598.61-1297.43
20 PRINT 1297.43*28.7
```

But that program's silly, since it contains the number 1297.43 six times. This program's briefer, because it uses a variable:

```
10 C=1297.43
20 PRINT C*2; C*.05; C+483.19; C/37; 8598.61-C; C*28.7
```

So **whenever you need to use a number several times, turn the number into a variable**, which will make your program briefer.

String variables

A string is any collection of characters, such as "I LOVE YOU". Each string must be in quotation marks.

A letter can stand for a string — if you put a dollar sign after the letter, like this:

```
10 G$="DOWN"
20 PRINT G$
```

Line 10 says G$ stands for the string "DOWN". Line 20 prints:

```
DOWN
```

In that program, G$ is a variable. Since it stands for a string, it's called a **string variable**.

Every string variable must end with a dollar sign. The dollar sign is supposed to remind you of a fancy S, which stands for String. Line 10 is pronounced, "G String is DOWN".

If you're paranoid, you'll love this program:

```
10 L$="THEY'RE LAUGHING AT YOU"
20 PRINT L$
30 PRINT L$
40 PRINT L$
```

Line 10 says L$ stands for the string "THEY'RE LAUGHING AT YOU". Lines 20, 30, and 40 make the computer print:

```
THEY'RE LAUGHING AT YOU
THEY'RE LAUGHING AT YOU
THEY'RE LAUGHING AT YOU
```

Nursery rhymes

The computer can recite nursery rhymes:

```
10 P$="PEAS PORRIDGE"
20 PRINT P$;" HOT"
30 PRINT P$;" COLD"
40 PRINT P$;" IN THE POT"
50 PRINT "NINE DAYS OLD"
```

Line 10 says P$ stands for "PEAS PORRIDGE". Lines 20-50 make the computer print:

```
PEAS PORRIDGE HOT
PEAS PORRIDGE COLD
PEAS PORRIDGE IN THE POT
NINE DAYS OLD
```

This program prints a fancier rhyme:

```
10 H$="HICKORY, DICKORY, DOCK!"
20 M$="THE MOUSE (SQUEAK! SQUEAK!)"
30 C$="THE CLOCK (TICK! TOCK!)"
40 PRINT H$
50 PRINT M$;" RAN UP ";C$
60 PRINT C$;" STRUCK ONE"
70 PRINT M$;" RAN DOWN"
80 PRINT H$
```

Lines 10-30 define H$, M$, and C$. Lines 40-80 make the computer print:

```
HICKORY, DICKORY, DOCK!
THE MOUSE (SQUEAK! SQUEAK!) RAN UP THE CLOCK (TICK! TOCK!)
THE CLOCK (TICK! TOCK!) STRUCK ONE
THE MOUSE (SQUEAK! SQUEAK!) RAN DOWN
HICKORY, DICKORY, DOCK!
```

Undefined variables

If you don't define a numeric variable, the computer assumes it's zero:

```
10 PRINT R
```

Since R hasn't been defined, line 10 prints zero.

The computer doesn't look ahead:

```
10 PRINT J
20 J=5
```

When the computer encounters line 10, it doesn't look ahead to find out what J is. As of line 10, J is still undefined, so the computer prints zero.

If you don't define a string variable, the computer assumes it's blank:

```
10 PRINT F$
```

Since F$ hasn't been defined, line 10 makes the computer print a line that says nothing; the line the computer prints is blank.

Long variable names

A numeric variable's name can be a letter (such as X) or a longer combination of characters, such as:

```
PROFIT.IN.1989.BEFORE.NOVEMBER.PROMOTION
```

For example, you can type:

```
10 PROFIT.IN.1989.BEFORE.NOVEMBER.PROMOTION = 3497.18
20 PROFIT.IN.1989 = PROFIT.IN.1989.BEFORE.NOVEMBER.PROMOTION + 6214.27
30 PRINT PROFIT.IN.1989
```

The computer will print:

```
 9711.45
```

The variable's name can be quite long: up to 40 characters!

The first character in the name must be a letter. The remaining characters can be letters, digits, or periods.

The name must not be a word that has a special meaning to the computer. For example, the name cannot be PRINT.

If the variable stands for a string, the name can have up to 40 characters, followed by a dollar sign, making a total of 41 characters, like this:

```
MY.JOB.IN.1989.BEFORE.NOVEMBER.PROMOTION$
```

Although modern computers permit long variable names, primitive computers don't. To find out whether *your* computer permits long variable names, check the "Versions of BASIC" appendix.

Professional programmers use long variable names, because long names make the programs easier to understand.

I'll avoid long names since some computers don't permit them; but if your computer permits them, use them!

INPUT

Humans ask questions; so to turn the computer into a human, you must make it ask questions too. **To make the computer ask a question, use the word INPUT.**

This program makes the computer ask for your name:

```
10 INPUT "WHAT IS YOUR NAME";N$
20 PRINT "I ADORE ANYONE WHOSE NAME IS ";N$
```

When the computer sees line 10, the computer asks "WHAT IS YOUR NAME?" and then waits for you to answer the question. Your answer will be called N$. For example, if you answer MARIA, then N$ is MARIA. Line 20 makes the computer print:

```
I ADORE ANYONE WHOSE NAME IS MARIA
```

Here's the whole conversation; I've underlined the parts typed by you. . . .

You tell the computer to run:	RUN
The computer asks for your name:	WHAT IS YOUR NAME? MARIA
The computer praises your name:	I ADORE ANYONE WHOSE NAME IS MARIA

Try that example. Be careful! When you type line 10, which says INPUT, make sure you type the two quotation marks and the semicolon. You don't have to type a question mark: when the computer runs your program, it will automatically put a question mark at the end of the question.

Just for fun, run that program again and pretend you're somebody else. . . .

You tell the computer to run:	RUN
The computer asks for your name:	WHAT IS YOUR NAME? BUD
The computer praises your name:	I ADORE ANYONE WHOSE NAME IS BUD

When the computer asks for your name, if you say something weird, the computer will give you a weird reply. . . .

Make the computer run:	RUN
Computer asks your name:	WHAT IS YOUR NAME? NONE OF YOUR BUSINESS!!!
The computer replies:	I ADORE ANYONE WHOSE NAME IS NONE OF YOUR BUSINESS!!!

College admissions

This program prints a letter, admitting you to the college of your choice:

```
10 INPUT "WHAT COLLEGE WOULD YOU LIKE TO ENTER";C$
20 PRINT "CONGRATULATIONS!"
30 PRINT "YOU HAVE JUST BEEN ADMITTED TO ";C$
40 PRINT "IT FITS YOUR PERSONALITY"
50 PRINT "I HOPE YOU GO TO ";C$
60 PRINT "          RESPECTFULLY YOURS"
70 PRINT "          THE DEAN OF ADMISSIONS"
```

When the computer sees line 10, the computer asks "WHAT COLLEGE WOULD YOU LIKE TO ENTER?" and waits for you to answer. Your answer will be called C$. If you'd like to be admitted to HARVARD, you'll be pleased. . . .

You tell the computer to run:	RUN
The computer asks:	WHAT COLLEGE WOULD YOU LIKE TO ENTER? HARVARD
The computer admits you:	CONGRATULATIONS!
	YOU HAVE JUST BEEN ADMITTED TO HARVARD
	IT FITS YOUR PERSONALITY
	I HOPE YOU GO TO HARVARD
	RESPECTFULLY YOURS
	THE DEAN OF ADMISSIONS

You can choose any college you wish:

```
RUN
WHAT COLLEGE WOULD YOU LIKE TO ENTER? HELL
CONGRATULATIONS!
YOU HAVE JUST BEEN ADMITTED TO HELL
IT FITS YOUR PERSONALITY
I HOPE YOU GO TO HELL
          RESPECTFULLY YOURS
          THE DEAN OF ADMISSIONS
```

That program consists of three parts:

1. The computer begins by asking you a question ("What college would you like to enter?"). The computer's question is called the **prompt**, because it prompts you to answer.

2. Your answer (the college's name) is called **your input**, because it's information that you're *putting into* the computer.

3. The computer's reply (the admission letter) is called the **computer's output**, because it's the final answer that the computer puts out.

INPUT versus PRINT

The word INPUT is the opposite of the word PRINT.

The word PRINT makes the computer print information out. The word INPUT makes the computer take information in.

What the computer prints out is called the **output**. What the computer takes in is called **your input**.

Input and Output are collectively called **I/O**, so the INPUT and PRINT statements are called **I/O statements**.

Once upon a time

Let's make the computer write a story, by filling in the blanks:

ONCE UPON A TIME, THERE WAS A YOUNGSTER NAMED _____
                                                           your name

WHO HAD A FRIEND NAMED _____
                                friend's name

_____ WANTED TO _____ _____
  your name   verb (such as "pat")   friend's name

BUT _____ DIDN'T WANT TO _____ _____
    friend's name   verb (such as "pat")   your name

WILL _____ _____ _____
    your name   verb (such as "pat")   friend's name

WILL _____ _____ _____
    friend's name   verb (such as "pat")   your name

TO FIND OUT, COME BACK AND SEE THE NEXT EXCITING EPISODE

OF _____ AND _____
   your name   friend's name

To write the story, the computer must ask for your name, your friend's name, and a verb. To make the computer ask, your program must say INPUT:

```
10 INPUT "WHAT IS YOUR NAME";Y$
20 INPUT "WHAT'S YOUR FRIEND'S NAME";F$
30 INPUT "IN 1 WORD, SAY SOMETHING YOU CAN DO TO YOUR FRIEND";V$
```

Then make the computer print the story:

```
40 PRINT "HERE'S MY STORY...."
50 PRINT "ONCE UPON A TIME, THERE WAS A YOUNGSTER NAMED ";Y$
60 PRINT "WHO HAD A FRIEND NAMED ";F$
70 PRINT Y$;" WANTED TO ";V$;" ";F$
80 PRINT "BUT ";F$;" DIDN'T WANT TO ";V$;" ";Y$
90 PRINT "WILL ";Y$;" ";V$;" ";F$
100 PRINT "WILL ";F$;" ";V$;" ";Y$
110 PRINT "TO FIND OUT, COME BACK AND SEE THE NEXT EXCITING EPISODE"
120 PRINT "OF ";Y$;" AND ";F$
```

Here's a sample run:

```
WHAT'S YOUR NAME? DRACULA
WHAT'S YOUR FRIEND'S NAME? MARILYN MONROE
IN 1 WORD, SAY SOMETHING YOU CAN DO TO YOUR FRIEND? BITE
HERE'S MY STORY....
ONCE UPON A TIME, THERE WAS A YOUNGSTER NAMED DRACULA
WHO HAD A FRIEND NAMED MARILYN MONROE
DRACULA WANTED TO BITE MARILYN MONROE
BUT MARILYN MONROE DIDN'T WANT TO BITE DRACULA
WILL DRACULA BITE MARILYN MONROE
WILL MARILYN MONROE BITE DRACULA
TO FIND OUT, COME BACK AND SEE THE NEXT EXCITING EPISODE
OF DRACULA AND MARILYN MONROE
```

Here's another run:

```
WHAT'S YOUR NAME? SUPERMAN
WHAT'S YOUR FRIEND'S NAME? KING KONG
IN 1 WORD, SAY SOMETHING YOU CAN DO TO YOUR FRIEND? TICKLE
HERE'S MY STORY....
ONCE UPON A TIME, THERE WAS A YOUNGSTER NAMED SUPERMAN
WHO HAD A FRIEND NAMED KING KONG
SUPERMAN WANTED TO TICKLE KING KONG
BUT KING KONG DIDN'T WANT TO TICKLE SUPERMAN
WILL SUPERMAN TICKLE KING KONG
WILL KING KONG TICKLE SUPERMAN
TO FIND OUT, COME BACK AND SEE THE NEXT EXCITING EPISODE
OF SUPERMAN AND KING KONG
```

Try it: put in your own name, the name of your friend, and something you'd like to do to your friend.

Contest

This program prints a certificate saying you won a contest:

```
10 INPUT "WHAT'S YOUR NAME";Y$
20 INPUT "WHAT'S YOUR FRIEND'S NAME";F$
30 INPUT "WHAT'S THE NAME OF ANOTHER FRIEND";A$
40 INPUT "NAME A COLOR";C$
50 INPUT "NAME A PLACE";P$
60 INPUT "NAME A FOOD";D$
70 INPUT "NAME AN OBJECT";J$
80 INPUT "NAME A PART OF THE BODY";B$
90 INPUT "NAME A STYLE OF COOKING (SUCH AS BAKED OR FRIED)";S$
100 PRINT
110 PRINT "CONGRATULATIONS ";Y$
120 PRINT "YOU'VE WON THE BEAUTY CONTEST, BECAUSE OF YOUR GORGEOUS ";B$
130 PRINT "YOUR PRIZE IS A ";C$;" ";J$
140 PRINT "PLUS A TRIP TO ";P$;" WITH YOUR FRIEND ";F$
150 PRINT "PLUS...AND THIS IS THE BEST PART OF ALL..."
160 PRINT "DINNER FOR THE TWO OF YOU AT ";A$;"'S NEW RESTAURANT"
170 PRINT "WHERE ";A$;" WILL GIVE YOU ALL THE ";S$;" ";D$;" YOU CAN EAT"
180 PRINT "CONGRATULATIONS ";Y$;"...TODAY'S YOUR LUCKY DAY..."
190 PRINT "NOW EVERYBODY WANTS TO KISS YOUR AWARD-WINNING ";B$
```

Here's a sample run:

```
WHAT'S YOUR NAME? LONG JOHN SILVER
WHAT'S YOUR FRIEND'S NAME? THE PARROT
WHAT'S THE NAME OF ANOTHER FRIEND? JIM
NAME A COLOR? GOLD
NAME A PLACE? TREASURE ISLAND
NAME A FOOD? RUM-SOAKED COCONUTS
NAME AN OBJECT? CHEST OF JEWELS
NAME A PART OF THE BODY? MISSING LEG
NAME A STYLE OF COOKING (SUCH AS BAKED OR FRIED)? BARBECUED

CONGRATULATIONS LONG JOHN SILVER
YOU'VE WON THE BEAUTY CONTEST, BECAUSE OF YOUR GORGEOUS MISSING LEG
YOUR PRIZE IS A GOLD CHEST OF JEWELS
PLUS A TRIP TO TREASURE ISLAND WITH YOUR FRIEND THE PARROT
PLUS...AND THIS IS THE BEST PART OF ALL...
DINNER FOR THE TWO OF YOU AT JIM'S NEW RESTAURANT
WHERE JIM WILL GIVE YOU ALL THE BARBECUED RUM-SOAKED COCONUTS YOU CAN EAT
CONGRATULATIONS LONG JOHN SILVER...TODAY'S YOUR LUCKY DAY...
NOW EVERYBODY WANTS TO KISS YOUR AWARD-WINNING MISSING LEG
```

This run describes the contest that brought Ronald Reagan to the White House:

```
WHAT'S YOUR NAME? RONNIE REAGAN
WHAT'S YOUR FRIEND'S NAME? NANCY
WHAT'S THE NAME OF ANOTHER FRIEND? ALICE
NAME A COLOR? RED-WHITE-AND-BLUE
NAME A PLACE? THE WHITE HOUSE
NAME A FOOD? JELLY BEANS
NAME AN OBJECT? COWBOY HAT
NAME A PART OF THE BODY? CHEEKS
NAME A STYLE OF COOKING (SUCH AS BAKED OR FRIED)? STEAMED

CONGRATULATIONS RONNIE REAGAN
YOU'VE WON THE BEAUTY CONTEST, BECAUSE OF YOUR GORGEOUS CHEEKS
YOUR PRIZE IS A RED-WHITE-AND-BLUE COWBOY HAT
PLUS A TRIP TO THE WHITE HOUSE WITH YOUR FRIEND NANCY
PLUS...AND THIS IS THE BEST PART OF ALL...
DINNER FOR THE TWO OF YOU AT ALICE'S NEW RESTAURANT
WHERE ALICE WILL GIVE YOU ALL THE STEAMED JELLY BEANS YOU CAN EAT
CONGRATULATIONS RONNIE REAGAN...TODAY'S YOUR LUCKY DAY...
NOW EVERYBODY WANTS TO KISS YOUR AWARD-WINNING CHEEKS
```

Bills

If you're a nasty bill collector, you'll love this program:

```
10 INPUT "WHAT IS THE CUSTOMER'S FIRST NAME";F$
20 INPUT "LAST NAME";L$
30 INPUT "STREET ADDRESS";A$
40 INPUT "CITY";C$
50 INPUT "STATE";S$
60 INPUT "ZIP CODE";Z$
70 PRINT
80 PRINT F$;" ";L$
90 PRINT A$
100 PRINT C$;" ";S$;" ";Z$
110 PRINT
120 PRINT "DEAR ";F$;","
130 PRINT "   YOU STILL HAVEN'T PAID THE BILL."
140 PRINT "IF YOU DON'T PAY IT SOON, ";F$;","
150 PRINT "I'LL COME VISIT YOU IN ";C$
160 PRINT "AND PERSONALLY SHOOT YOU."
170 PRINT "            YOURS TRULY,"
180 PRINT "            SURE-AS-SHOOTIN'"
190 PRINT "            YOUR CRAZY CREDITOR"
```

Can you figure out what that program does?

Numeric input

This program makes the computer predict your future:

```
10 PRINT "I PREDICT WHAT'LL HAPPEN TO YOU IN THE YEAR 2000!"
20 INPUT "IN WHAT YEAR WERE YOU BORN";Y
30 PRINT "IN THE YEAR 2000, YOU'LL TURN";2000-Y;"YEARS OLD."
```

Here's a sample run:

```
I PREDICT WHAT'LL HAPPEN TO YOU IN THE YEAR 2000!
IN WHAT YEAR WERE YOU BORN? 1962
IN THE YEAR 2000, YOU'LL TURN 38 YEARS OLD.
```

Suppose you're selling tickets to a play. Each ticket costs $2.79. (You decided $2.79 would be a nifty price, because the cast has 279 people.) This program finds the price of multiple tickets:

```
10 INPUT "HOW MANY TICKETS";T
20 PRINT "THE TOTAL PRICE IS $";T*2.79
```

This program tells you how much the "energy crisis" costs you, when you drive your car:

```
10 INPUT "HOW MANY MILES DO YOU WANT TO DRIVE";M
20 INPUT "HOW MANY PENNIES DOES A GALLON OF GAS COST";P
30 INPUT "HOW MANY MILES-PER-GALLON DOES YOUR CAR GET";R
40 PRINT "THE GAS FOR YOUR TRIP WILL COST YOU $";M*P/(R*100)
```

Here's a sample run:

```
HOW MANY MILES DO YOU WANT TO DRIVE? 400
HOW MANY PENNIES DOES A GALLON OF GAS COST? 95.9
HOW MANY MILES-PER-GALLON DOES YOUR CAR GET? 31
THE GAS FOR YOUR TRIP WILL COST YOU $ 12.3742
```

Conversion

This program converts feet to inches:

```
10 INPUT "HOW MANY FEET";F
20 PRINT F;"FEET =";F*12;"INCHES"
```

Here's a sample run:

```
HOW MANY FEET? 3
 3 FEET = 36 INCHES
```

Trying to convert to the metric system? This program converts inches to centimeters:

```
10 INPUT "HOW MANY INCHES";I
20 PRINT I;"INCHES =";I*2.54;"CENTIMETERS"
```

Nice day today, isn't it? This program converts the temperature from Celsius to Fahrenheit:

```
10 INPUT "HOW MANY DEGREES CELSIUS";C
20 PRINT C;"DEGREES CELSIUS =";C*1.8+32;"DEGREES FAHRENHEIT"
```

Here's a sample run:

```
HOW MANY DEGREES CELSIUS? 20
 20 DEGREES CELSIUS = 68 DEGREES FAHRENHEIT
```

See, you can write the *Guide* yourself! Just hunt through any old math or science book, find any old formula (such as F=C*1.8+32), and turn it into a program.

IF . . . THEN

The computer understands the words IF and THEN.

Therapist

Let's turn your computer into a therapist.

To make the computer ask the patient, "HOW ARE YOU?", begin the program like this:

```
10 INPUT "HOW ARE YOU";A$
```

That line makes the computer ask HOW ARE YOU and wait for the patient's answer, which is called A$.

If the patient feels FINE, let's make the computer say THAT'S GOOD. Here's how:

```
20 IF A$="FINE" THEN PRINT "THAT'S GOOD"
```

That line says that if the patient's answer (A$) is FINE, the computer will print THAT'S GOOD.

If the patient feels LOUSY instead, let's make the computer say TOO BAD. Here's how:

```
30 IF A$="LOUSY" THEN PRINT "TOO BAD"
```

Here's the entire program:

```
10 INPUT "HOW ARE YOU";A$
20 IF A$="FINE" THEN PRINT "THAT'S GOOD"
30 IF A$="LOUSY" THEN PRINT "TOO BAD"
```

When the patient types RUN, line 10 makes the computer ask HOW ARE YOU and wait for the patient's answer, which is called A$. If the patient's answer is FINE, line 20 makes the computer reply THAT'S GOOD. If the patient's answer is LOUSY, line 30 makes the computer reply TOO BAD.

Try running that program! Here's a sample run:

```
RUN
HOW ARE YOU? FINE
THAT'S GOOD
```

Here's another run:

```
RUN
HOW ARE YOU? LOUSY
TOO BAD
```

Underlying theory Whenever you say IF, you should also say THEN. For example, line 20 (which says IF) also says THEN. Similarly, line 30 (which says IF) says THEN.

Do *not* put a comma before THEN.

What comes between IF and THEN is called the **condition**. In line 20, the condition is:

```
A$="FINE"
```

If that condition is true (if A$ really does equal "FINE"), the computer does what comes after the word THEN, which is called the **consequence**, which is:

```
PRINT "THAT'S GOOD"
```

Increase the computer's vocabulary In that program, what happens if the patient says some word other than FINE or LOUSY?

For example, what happens if the patient says TERRIBLE? Since the program doesn't tell the computer how to react to TERRIBLE, the computer won't print any reaction at all. The computer will do just what it always does at the end of a program: it will say OK (or READY or a similar word).

Let's enhance the program, so that if the patient says TERRIBLE, the computer will say TOUGH TURKEY. Add the shaded line:

```
10 INPUT "HOW ARE YOU";A$
20 IF A$="FINE" THEN PRINT "THAT'S GOOD"
30 IF A$="LOUSY" THEN PRINT "TOO BAD"
40 IF A$="TERRIBLE" THEN PRINT "TOUGH TURKEY"
```

I feel the same way Let's make the computer end the conversation by saying I FEEL THE SAME WAY. Add the shaded line:

```
10 INPUT "HOW ARE YOU";A$
20 IF A$="FINE" THEN PRINT "THAT'S GOOD"
30 IF A$="LOUSY" THEN PRINT "TOO BAD"
40 IF A$="TERRIBLE" THEN PRINT "TOUGH TURKEY"
50 PRINT "I FEEL THE SAME WAY"
```

Since line 50 does *not* contain the word IF, the computer will *always* print I FEEL THE SAME WAY at the end of the conversation, regardless of what the patient says.

Here's a sample run:

```
RUN
HOW ARE YOU? FINE
THAT'S GOOD
I FEEL THE SAME WAY
```

Here's another:

```
RUN
HOW ARE YOU? TERRIBLE
TOUGH TURKEY
I FEEL THE SAME WAY
```

Another:

```
RUN
HOW ARE YOU? LONELY
I FEEL THE SAME WAY
```

Another:

```
RUN
HOW ARE YOU? I DON'T WANT TO TALK WITH YOU
I FEEL THE SAME WAY
```

Avoid monotony Having the computer always say I FEEL THE SAME WAY is monotonous. To make the program more interesting, let's make the computer say I FEEL THE SAME WAY only if the patient doesn't say FINE, LOUSY, or TERRIBLE. So if the patient says FINE, LOUSY, or TERRIBLE, let's prevent the computer from saying I FEEL THE SAME WAY.

Whenever you want to make the computer skip saying I FEEL THE SAME WAY, type the word END, like this:

```
10 INPUT "HOW ARE YOU";A$
20 IF A$="FINE" THEN PRINT "THAT'S GOOD": END
30 IF A$="LOUSY" THEN PRINT "TOO BAD": END
40 IF A$="TERRIBLE" THEN PRINT "TOUGH TURKEY": END
50 PRINT "I FEEL THE SAME WAY"
```

In that program, if the patient types FINE, LOUSY, or TERRIBLE, lines 20-40 make the computer print a two-word message and then END, without printing I FEEL THE SAME WAY. The only way the computer can reach line 50 (which prints I FEEL THE SAME WAY) is if the patient avoids FINE, LOUSY, and TERRIBLE.

Here's a sample run:

```
RUN
HOW ARE YOU? FINE
THAT'S GOOD
```

Here's another:

```
RUN
HOW ARE YOU? LONELY
I FEEL THE SAME WAY
```

Charge $50 After the computer's given the patient therapy, let's make the computer charge $50. Just add this line:

```
60 PRINT "I HOPE YOU ENJOYED YOUR THERAPY--NOW YOU OWE $50"
```

To make sure the computer always goes to that line and collects the $50, regardless of what the patient says, replace each END by GO TO 60. Altogether, the program looks like this:

```
10 INPUT "HOW ARE YOU";A$
20 IF A$="FINE" THEN PRINT "THAT'S GOOD": GO TO 60
30 IF A$="LOUSY" THEN PRINT "TOO BAD": GO TO 60
40 IF A$="TERRIBLE" THEN PRINT "TOUGH TURKEY": GO TO 60
50 PRINT "I FEEL THE SAME WAY"
60 PRINT "I HOPE YOU ENJOYED YOUR THERAPY--NOW YOU OWE $50"
```

Here's a sample run:

```
RUN
HOW ARE YOU? FINE
THAT'S GOOD
I HOPE YOU ENJOYED YOUR THERAPY--NOW YOU OWE $50
```

Here's another:

```
RUN
HOW ARE YOU? LONELY
I FEEL THE SAME WAY
I HOPE YOU ENJOYED YOUR THERAPY--NOW YOU OWE $50
```

In that program, try changing the strings to make the computer print smarter remarks, become a better therapist, and charge even more money.

Keywords

In that program, the only words the computer understands are INPUT, IF, THEN, PRINT, GO, and TO. Those words are called **keywords**.

Using just those keywords, you can write any program you wish! Here's why. . . .

Can a computer become President? To

become President of the United States, you need four basic skills.

First, you must be a good talker, so you can give effective speeches saying "Vote for me!", express your views, and make folks do what you want.

But even if you're a good talker, you're useless unless you're also a good listener. You must be able to listen to people's needs and ask, "What can I do to make you happy and get you to vote for me?"

But even if you're a good talker and listener, you're still useless unless you can make decisions. Should you give more money to poor people? Should you bomb the enemy? Which actions should you take, and under what conditions?

But even if you're a good talker and listener and decision maker, you still need one more trait to become President: you must be able to take the daily grind of politics. You must, again and again, shake hands, make compromises, and raise funds. You must have the patience to put up with the repetitive monotony of those chores.

So altogether, to become President you need to be a good talker and listener and decision maker and also have the patience to put up with monotonous repetition.

Those are exactly the four qualities the computer has! The word PRINT turns the computer into a good speech-maker: by using the word PRINT, you can make the computer write whatever speech you wish. The word INPUT turns the computer into a good listener: by using the word INPUT, you can make the computer ask humans lots of questions, to find out who the humans are and what they want. The words IF and THEN turn the computer into a decision maker: the computer can analyze the IF condition, determine whether that condition is true, and act accordingly. Finally, the words GO and TO enable the computer to perform loops, which the computer will repeat patiently.

So by using the words PRINT, INPUT, IF THEN, and GO TO, you can make the computer imitate any intellectual human activity. Those four magic phrases — PRINT, INPUT, IF THEN, and GO TO — are the only phrases you need, to write whatever program you wish!

Yes, you can make the computer imitate the President of the United States, do your company's payroll, compose a beautiful poem, play a perfect game of chess, contemplate the meaning of life, act as if it's falling in love, or do whatever other intellectual or emotional task you wish, by using just those four magic phrases. The only question is: how? *The Secret Guide to Computers* teaches you how, by showing you many examples of programs that do those remarkable things.

What programmers believe Yes, we programmers believe that all of life can be explained and programmed. We believe all of life can be reduced to just those four phrases: PRINT, INPUT, IF THEN, and GO TO. Programming is the ultimate act of scientific reductionism: programmers reduce all of life scientifically to just four phrases.

In addition to those keywords (PRINT, INPUT, IF, THEN, GO, and TO), the computer understands extra keywords also, such as END. Those extra keywords aren't strictly necessary: if they hadn't been invented, you could still write programs without them. But they make programming easier.

A programmer is a person who translates an ordinary English sentence (such as "act like the President" or "do the payroll") into a series of BASIC statements, using keywords such as PRINT, INPUT, IF THEN, GO TO, and END.

The mysteries of life Let's dig deeper into the mysteries of PRINT, INPUT, IF THEN, GO TO, and the extra keywords. The deeper we dig, the more you'll wonder: are *you* just a computer, made of flesh instead of wires? Can everything that *you* do be explained in terms of PRINT, INPUT, IF THEN, and GO TO?

By the time you finish *The Secret Guide to Computers*, you'll know!

Mary Poppins meets Frankenstein

To make the computer interrogate a human, have the computer ask:

```
ARE YOU MALE OR FEMALE?
```

If the human answers MALE, let's make the computer say:

```
SO IS FRANKENSTEIN
```

If the human answers FEMALE, let's make the computer say:

```
SO IS MARY POPPINS
```

Here's the program:

```
10 INPUT "ARE YOU MALE OR FEMALE";A$
20 IF A$="MALE" THEN PRINT "SO IS FRANKENSTEIN"
30 IF A$="FEMALE" THEN PRINT "SO IS MARY POPPINS"
```

Here's a sample run:

```
RUN
ARE YOU MALE OR FEMALE? MALE
SO IS FRANKENSTEIN
```

Here's another:

```
RUN
ARE YOU MALE OR FEMALE? FEMALE
SO IS MARY POPPINS
```

Neither MALE nor FEMALE?
What does that program do if the human says neither MALE nor FEMALE? What if the human says SUPER-MALE or MACHO or NOT SURE or BOTH or YES? In those cases, the program doesn't tell the computer how to reply, so the computer will make no reply at all.

Let's improve the program, so that if the human says neither MALE nor FEMALE the computer will reply —

```
PLEASE SAY MALE OR FEMALE
ARE YOU MALE OR FEMALE?
```

and force the human to answer the question correctly.

To do that, add this line —

```
40 PRINT "PLEASE SAY MALE OR FEMALE": GO TO 10
```

and put END at the end of lines 20 and 30, so the program looks like this:

```
10 INPUT "ARE YOU MALE OR FEMALE";A$
20 IF A$="MALE" THEN PRINT "SO IS FRANKENSTEIN": END
30 IF A$="FEMALE" THEN PRINT "SO IS MARY POPPINS": END
40 PRINT "PLEASE SAY MALE OR FEMALE": GO TO 10
```

Line 10 makes the computer ask "ARE YOU MALE OR FEMALE?" and wait for the human's answer, which is called A$. If the human's answer is MALE, line 20 makes the computer print SO IS FRANKENSTEIN and then end. If the human's answer is FEMALE, line 30 makes the computer print SO IS MARY POPPINS and then END. If the human's answer is neither MALE nor FEMALE, the computer skips over lines 20 and 30, so it comes to line 40, which makes it print PLEASE SAY MALE OR FEMALE and then go back to line 10, which forces the human to answer the question again.

Here's a sample run:

```
RUN
ARE YOU MALE OR FEMALE? MALE
SO IS FRANKENSTEIN
```

Here's another:

```
RUN
ARE YOU MALE OR FEMALE? FEMALE
SO IS MARY POPPINS
```

Another:

```
RUN
ARE YOU MALE OR FEMALE? MACHO
PLEASE SAY MALE OR FEMALE
ARE YOU MALE OR FEMALE? MALE
SO IS FRANKENSTEIN
```

Another:

```
RUN
ARE YOU MALE OR FEMALE? SUPER-MALE
PLEASE SAY MALE OR FEMALE
ARE YOU MALE OR FEMALE? NONE OF YOUR BUSINESS
PLEASE SAY MALE OR FEMALE
ARE YOU MALE OR FEMALE? MAIL
PLEASE SAY MALE OR FEMALE
ARE YOU MALE OR FEMALE? MALE
SO IS FRANKENSTEIN
```

In that program, if the human makes a typing error and answers neither MALE nor FEMALE, the computer arrives at line 40, which makes the computer gripe and tell the human to try again. So the purpose of line 40 is to react to errors. Line 40 is called an **error-handling routine** or an **error trap**. That's because an error's like a vicious monster, and line 40's purpose is to trap it.

Do you like Mary Poppins?
Let's extend the conversation. If the human says FEMALE, let's make the computer say SO IS MARY POPPINS and then ask "DO YOU LIKE HER?" If the human says YES, let's make the computer say:

```
I LIKE HER TOO--SHE IS MY MOTHER
```

If the human says NO, let's make the computer say:

```
NEITHER DO I--SHE STILL OWES ME A DIME
```

If the human says neither YES nor NO, let's make the computer say:

```
PLEASE SAY YES OR NO
DO YOU LIKE HER?
```

Here's the program:

```
10 INPUT "ARE YOU MALE OR FEMALE";A$
20 IF A$="MALE" THEN PRINT "SO IS FRANKENSTEIN": END
30 IF A$="FEMALE" THEN PRINT "SO IS MARY POPPINS": GO TO 100
40 PRINT "PLEASE SAY MALE OR FEMALE": GO TO 10

100 INPUT "DO YOU LIKE HER";B$
110 IF B$="YES" THEN PRINT "I LIKE HER TOO--SHE IS MY MOTHER
": END
120 IF B$="NO" THEN PRINT "NEITHER DO I--SHE STILL OWES ME A
 DIME": END
130 PRINT "PLEASE SAY YES OR NO": GO TO 100
```

Line 30 says: if the human's answer is FEMALE, print SO IS MARY POPPINS and then go to line 100, which asks "DO YOU LIKE HER?" Lines 110 and 120 make the computer react to the human's opinion of Mary Poppins. Line 130 is like line 40: it's an error trap.

Weird programs

The computer's abilities are limited only by your own imagination — and your weirdness. Here are some weird programs from weird minds. . . .

Friends Like a human, the computer wants to meet new friends. This program makes the computer show its true feelings:

```
10 INPUT "ARE YOU MY FRIEND";A$
20 IF A$="YES" THEN PRINT "THAT'S SWELL": END
30 IF A$="NO" THEN PRINT "GO JUMP IN A LAKE": END
40 PRINT "PLEASE SAY YES OR NO": GO TO 10
```

When you type RUN, the computer asks "ARE YOU MY FRIEND?" If you say YES, the computer says THAT'S SWELL. If you say NO, the computer says GO JUMP IN A LAKE.

Watch TV The most inventive programmers are kids. This program was written by a girl in the sixth grade:

```
10 INPUT "CAN I COME OVER TO YOUR HOUSE TO WATCH T.V.";A$
20 IF A$="YES" THEN PRINT "THANKS.  I'LL BE THERE AT 5 P.M.": END
30 IF A$="NO" THEN PRINT "HUMPH!  YOUR FEET SMELL, ANYWAY.": END
40 PRINT "PLEASE SAY YES OR NO": GO TO 10
```

When you type RUN, the computer asks to watch your TV. If you say YES, the computer promises to come to your house at 5. If you refuse, the computer insults your feet.

Honesty Another sixth-grade girl wrote this program, to test your honesty:

```
10 PRINT "FKGJDFGKJ*#K$JSLF*/#$()$&(IKJNHBGD52:?./KSDJK$E(EF$#/JIK(*"
20 PRINT "FASDFJKL:JFRFVFJUNJI*&()JNE$#SKI#(!SERF HHW NNWAZ MAME !!!"
30 PRINT "ZBB%%%%##)))))FESDFJK DSFE N.D.JJUJASD EHWLKD******"
40 INPUT "DO YOU UNDERSTAND WHAT I SAID";A$
50 IF A$="NO" THEN PRINT "SORRY TO HAVE BOTHERED YOU": END
60 IF A$="YES" THEN GO TO 100
70 PRINT "PLEASE SAY YES OR NO": GO TO 10

100 PRINT "SSFJSLFKDJFL++++4567345677839XSDWFEGF/#$&**()---==!!ZZXX"
110 PRINT "###EDFHTG NVFDF MKJKF ==+--*$&% #RHFS SESD DOPEKKKNJGFD DSBS"
120 INPUT "OKAY, WHAT DID I SAY";B$
130 PRINT "YOU ARE A LIAR, A LIAR, A BIG FAT LIAR!"
```

When you type RUN, lines 10-30 print nonsense. Then the computer asks whether you understand that stuff. *If you're honest* and answer NO, the computer will apologize. But *if you pretend that you understand the nonsense* and answer YES, the computer will print more nonsense, challenge you to translate it, wait for you to fake a translation, and then scold you for lying.

Daddy's always right A Daddy wrote a program for his five-year-old son, John.

When John runs the program and types his name, the computer asks "WHAT'S 2 AND 2?" If John answers 4, the computer says NO, 2 AND 2 IS 22. If he runs the program again and answers 22, the computer says NO, 2 AND 2 IS 4. No matter how many times he runs the program and how he answers the question, the computer says he's wrong. But when Daddy runs the program, the computer replies, YES, DADDY IS ALWAYS RIGHT.

Here's how Daddy programmed the computer:

```
10 INPUT "WHAT'S YOUR NAME";N$
20 INPUT "WHAT'S 2 AND 2";A
30 IF N$="DADDY" THEN PRINT "YES, DADDY IS ALWAYS RIGHT": END
40 IF A=4 THEN PRINT "NO, 2 AND 2 IS 22": END
50 PRINT "NO, 2 AND 2 IS 4"
```

Fancy relations

You can make the IF clause very fancy:

IF clause	Meaning
IF A$="MALE"	If A$ is "MALE"
IF A=4	If A is 4
IF A<4	If A is less than 4
IF A>4	If A is greater than 4
IF A<=4	If A is less than or equal to 4
IF A>=4	If A is greater than or equal to 4
IF A<>4	If A is not 4
IF A$<"MALE"	If A is a word that comes before "MALE" in the dictionary
IF A$>"MALE"	If A is a word that comes after "MALE" in the dictionary

In the IF statement, the symbols =, <, >, <=, >=, and <> are called **relations**.

When you write a relation, put the equal sign last:

Right	Wrong
<=	=<
>=	=>

To say "not equal to" say "less than or greater than", like this: < >.

OR

The computer understands the word OR. For example, here's how to say, "If X is either 7 or 8, print the word WONDERFUL":

```
IF X=7 OR X=8 THEN PRINT "WONDERFUL"
```

That example is composed of two conditions: the first condition is "X=7"; the second condition is "X=8". Those two conditions combine, to form "X=7 OR X=8", which is called a **compound condition**.

If you use the word OR, put it between two conditions.

Right: `IF X=7 OR X=8 THEN PRINT "WONDERFUL"` ("X=7" and "X=8" are conditions.)
Wrong: `IF X=7 OR 8 THEN PRINT "WONDERFUL"` ("8" is not a condition.)

AND

The computer understands the word AND. Here's how to say, "If P is more than 5 and less than 10, print TUNA FISH":

```
IF P>5 AND P<10 THEN PRINT "TUNA FISH"
```

Here's how to say, "If S is at least 60 and less than 65, print YOU ALMOST FAILED":

```
IF S>=60 AND S<65 THEN PRINT "YOU ALMOST FAILED"
```

Here's how to say, "If N is a number from 1 to 10, print THAT'S GOOD":

```
IF N>=1 AND N<=10 THEN PRINT "THAT'S GOOD"
```

ELSE

Here's how to say, "If A is less than 18, print MINOR; but if A is *not* less than 18, print ADULT":

```
IF A<18 THEN PRINT "MINOR" ELSE PRINT "ADULT"
```

That line says to either PRINT "MINOR" or ELSE PRINT "ADULT". If A is less than 18, the computer will PRINT "MINOR"; otherwise, the computer will PRINT "ADULT".

Here's how to say, "If A is less than 18, print MINOR and print YOUNG; if A is *not* less than 18, print ADULT and print OLD":

```
IF A<18 THEN PRINT "MINOR": PRINT "YOUNG" ELSE PRINT "ADULT": PRINT "OLD"
```

Primitive computers don't understand the word ELSE. To find out whether your computer is primitive, check the "Versions of BASIC" appendix.

DATA . . . READ

Let's make the computer print this message:

```
I LOVE MEAT
I LOVE POTATOES
I LOVE LETTUCE
I LOVE TOMATOES
I LOVE BUTTER
I LOVE CHEESE
I LOVE ONIONS
I LOVE PEAS
```

That message concerns this list of food: MEAT, POTATOES, LETTUCE, TOMATOES, BUTTER, CHEESE, ONIONS, PEAS. That list doesn't change: the computer continues to love those foods throughout the entire program.

A list that doesn't change is called <u>data</u>. So in the message about food, the **data** is MEAT, POTATOES, LETTUCE, TOMATOES, BUTTER, CHEESE, ONIONS, PEAS.

Whenever a problem involves data, put the data at the top of the program, like this:

```
10 DATA MEAT,POTATOES,LETTUCE,TOMATOES,BUTTER,CHEESE,ONIONS,PEAS
```

You must tell the computer to READ the DATA:

```
20 READ A$
```

Line 20 makes the computer read the first datum (MEAT) and call it A$. So A$ is MEAT.

Since A$ is MEAT, this line makes the computer print I LOVE MEAT:

```
30 PRINT "I LOVE ";A$
```

Hooray! We made the computer handle the first datum correctly: we made the computer print I LOVE MEAT. To make the computer handle the rest of the data (POTATOES, LETTUCE, etc.), tell the computer to READ the rest of the data: tell the computer to GO back to the READ statement. Since the READ statement is line 20, tell the computer to GO TO 20, like this:

```
40 GO TO 20
```

Line 40 makes the computer GO back TO line 20, which reads the next datum (POTATOES).

Altogether, the program looks like this:

```
10 DATA MEAT,POTATOES,LETTUCE,TOMATOES,BUTTER,CHEESE,ONIONS,PEAS
20 READ A$
30 PRINT "I LOVE ";A$
40 GO TO 20
```

Lines 20-40 form a **loop**. Like most loops, the loop's bottom line says GO TO. Since the loop's top line says READ, the loop is called a **READ loop**. The computer goes round and round the loop.

Each time the computer comes to line 20, it reads another datum. The first time it comes to line 20, it reads MEAT; the next time, it reads POTATOES; the next time, it reads LETTUCE; the next time, it reads TOMATOES; etc.

Line 30 makes the computer PRINT what it's read.

Altogether, the computer will print:

```
I LOVE MEAT
I LOVE POTATOES
I LOVE LETTUCE
I LOVE TOMATOES
I LOVE BUTTER
I LOVE CHEESE
I LOVE ONIONS
I LOVE PEAS
```

After the computer prints I LOVE PEAS, it comes to line 40 again, which makes it go back to line 20, so the computer tries to read even more data; but no more data remains! So the computer says:

```
OUT OF DATA
```

Then the computer stops.

Most practical computer programs involve data (a list that doesn't change). As a programmer, your job is to notice what the data is and begin your program by saying DATA. After you type the data, write the program's next line, which should say READ. Farther down in your program, you should say GO TO so that you create READ loop. Your program consists of two parts: the *DATA* and the *READ loop*.

In the DATA statement, you must put quotation marks around any string that contains a comma or colon. For example, if one of the foods is "HOT, JUICY, BIG, THICK, STEAKS" (which contains commas), you must put quotation marks around it.

Avoiding OUT OF DATA

When you run that sample program about food, the last three lines the computer prints are:

```
I LOVE ONIONS
I LOVE PEAS
OUT OF DATA
```

Instead of saying OUT OF DATA, let's make the computer say "I LOVE ALL THOSE FOODS", so that the last three lines look like this:

```
I LOVE ONIONS
I LOVE PEAS
I LOVE ALL THOSE FOODS
```

Here's how. . . .

Underneath the data, say DATA END:

```
15 DATA END
```

When the computer reads the DATA END, make the computer say I LOVE ALL THOSE FOODS and end:

```
20 READ A$: IF A$="END" THEN PRINT "I LOVE ALL THOSE FOODS": END
```

The DATA END underneath the data is called the **end mark**, because it marks the data's end. The routine that says —

```
        IF A$="END" THEN PRINT "I LOVE ALL THOSE FOODS": END
```

is called the **end routine**, because the computer does that routine at the end.

RESTORE

That program prints one copy of the computer's favorite foods. If you want the computer to print *many* copies, change line 20 to this:

```
20 READ A$: IF A$="END" THEN PRINT "I LOVE ALL THOSE FOODS": RESTORE: GO TO 20
```

The word RESTORE tells the computer to go back to the beginning of the data. The computer will print:

```
I LOVE MEAT
I LOVE POTATOES
I LOVE LETTUCE
I LOVE TOMATOES
I LOVE BUTTER
I LOVE CHEESE
I LOVE ONIONS
I LOVE PEAS
I LOVE ALL THOSE FOODS
I LOVE MEAT
I LOVE POTATOES
I LOVE LETTUCE
I LOVE TOMATOES
I LOVE BUTTER
I LOVE CHEESE
I LOVE ONIONS
I LOVE PEAS
I LOVE ALL THOSE FOODS
I LOVE MEAT
I LOVE POTATOES
etc.
```

The computer will print copies of what it likes again and again, forever, unless you abort the program.

Henry the Eighth

Let's make the computer print this nursery rhyme:

I love ice cream
I love red
I love ocean
I love bed
I love tall grass
I love to wed

I love candles
I love divorce
I love my kingdom
I love my horse
I love you
Of course, of course,
For I am Henry the Eighth!

If you own a jump rope, have fun: try to recite that poem while skipping rope!

This program makes the computer recite the poem repeatedly:

```
10 DATA ICE CREAM,RED,OCEAN,BED,TALL GRASS,TO WED
11 DATA CANDLES,DIVORCE,MY KINGDOM,MY HORSE,YOU
15 DATA END
20 READ A$: IF A$="END" THEN PRINT "OF COURSE, OF COURSE,": PRINT "FOR I AM HENR
Y THE EIGHTH!": PRINT: RESTORE: GO TO 20
30 PRINT "I LOVE ";A$
35 IF A$="TO WED" THEN PRINT
40 GO TO 20
```

Since the data's too long to fit on a single line, I've put part of the data in line 10 and the rest in line 11. Each line of data must begin with the word DATA. In each line, put commas between the items. Do *not* put a comma at the end of the line.

The program resembles the previous one. The only new line is 35, which makes the computer leave a blank line underneath "TO WED", to mark the bottom of the first verse.

Party

Let's throw a party! To make the party yummy, let's ask each guest to bring a kind of food that resembles the guest's name. For example, let's have Sal bring salad, Russ bring Russian dressing, Sue bring soup, Tom bring turkey, Winnie bring wine, Kay bring cake, and Al bring Alka-Seltzer.

Let's send all those people invitations, in this form:

DEAR _____
    person's name

    WE'RE THROWING A PARTY AT THE SECRET CLUBHOUSE TOMORROW AT NOON!

PLEASE BRING ___
          food

To make the computer print all the invitations, begin by feeding the computer the DATA:

```
10 DATA SAL,SALAD,RUSS,RUSSIAN DRESSING,SUE,SOUP,TOM,TURKEY
20 DATA WINNIE,WINE,KAY,CAKE,AL,ALKA-SELTZER
```

The data comes in pairs; the first pair consists of SAL and SALAD. Tell the computer to READ each pair of DATA:

```
30 READ P$,F$
```

Line 30 makes the computer read the first pair of data; so P$ is the first person (SAL), and F$ is his food (SALAD).

These lines print the letter:

```
40 PRINT "DEAR ";P$
50 PRINT "    WE'RE THROWING A PARTY AT THE SECRET CLUBHOUSE TOMORROW AT NOON!"
60 PRINT "PLEASE BRING ";F$
```

At the end of the letter, leave two blank lines, to make room for your signature:

```
70 PRINT
80 PRINT
```

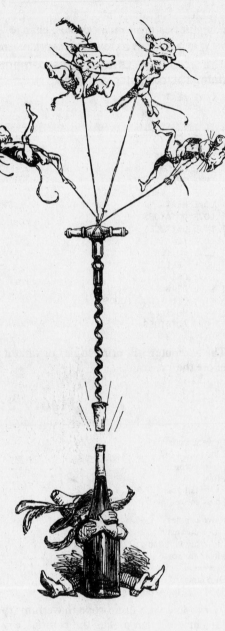

Then complete the READ loop, by making the computer go back to the beginning of the loop, to read the next pair:

```
90 GO TO 30
```

The computer will print a letter to each person, like this:

```
DEAR SAL
    WE'RE THROWING A PARTY AT THE SECRET CLUBHOUSE TOMORROW AT NOON!
PLEASE BRING SALAD


DEAR RUSS
    WE'RE THROWING A PARTY AT THE SECRET CLUBHOUSE TOMORROW AT NOON!
PLEASE BRING RUSSIAN DRESSING
```

etc.

After printing all the letters, the computer will say:

```
OUT OF DATA
```

Instead of saying OUT OF DATA, let's make the computer say:

```
I'VE FINISHED WRITING THE LETTERS
```

To do that, put END at the end of the data, *twice* —

```
25 DATA END,END
```

and say what to do when the computer reaches the END:

```
30 READ P$,F$: IF P$="END" THEN PRINT "I'VE FINISHED WRITING THE LETTERS": END
```

You need *two* ENDs at the end of the data, because the READ statement says to read two strings (P$ and F$).

Debts

Suppose these people owe you things:

Person	What the person owes
Bob	$537.29
Mike	a dime
Sue	2 golf balls
Harry	a steak dinner at Mario's
Mommy	a kiss

Let's remind those people of their debt, by writing them letters, in this form:

```
DEAR ____
     person's name

    I JUST WANT TO REMIND YOU...

THAT YOU STILL OWE ME ____
                       debt
```

Begin with the DATA:

```
10 DATA BOB,$537.29,MIKE,A DIME,SUE,2 GOLF BALLS
20 DATA HARRY,A STEAK DINNER AT MARIO'S,MOMMY,A KISS
```

The data comes in pairs; the first pair consists of BOB and $537.29. Tell the computer to READ each pair of DATA:

```
30 READ P$,D$
```

Line 30 makes the computer read the first pair of data; so P$ is the first person (BOB), and D$ is his debt ($537.29).

Here's the rest of the program:

```
40 PRINT "DEAR ";P$
50 PRINT "    I JUST WANT TO REMIND YOU..."
50 PRINT "THAT YOU STILL OWE ME ";D$
70 PRINT
80 PRINT
90 GO TO 30
```

The computer will print a letter to each person, like this:

```
DEAR BOB
    I JUST WANT TO REMIND YOU...
THAT YOU STILL OWE ME $537.29


DEAR MIKE
    I JUST WANT TO REMIND YOU...
THAT YOU STILL OWE ME A DIME
```

etc.

After printing all the letters, the computer will say:

```
OUT OF DATA
```

To prevent the computer from saying OUT OF DATA, add line 25 and retype line 30, as follows:

```
25 DATA END,END
30 READ P$,D$: IF P$="END" THEN PRINT "I'VE FINISHED WRITING
THE LETTERS": END
```

Diets

Suppose you're running a diet clinic and get these results:

Person	Weight before	Weight after
Joe	273 pounds	219 pounds
Mary	412 pounds	371 pounds
Bill	241 pounds	173 pounds
Sam	309 pounds	198 pounds

Here's how to make the computer print a nice report. . . .

Begin by feeding it the DATA:

```
10 DATA JOE,273,219,MARY,412,371,BILL,241,173,SAM,309,198
```

The DATA comes in triplets: the first triplet consists of JOE, 273, and 219. Tell the computer to READ each triplet of DATA:

```
20 READ N$,B,A
```

That line makes the computer read the first triplet of data; so N$ is the first person's name (JOE), B is his weight before (273), and A is his weight after (219). Since B and A stand for numbers instead of strings, they don't have any dollar signs.

These lines print the report about him:

```
30 PRINT N$;" WEIGHED";B;"POUNDS BEFORE ATTENDING THE DIET C
LINIC"
40 PRINT "BUT WEIGHED JUST";A;"POUNDS AFTERWARDS"
50 PRINT "THAT'S A LOSS OF";B-A;"POUNDS"
```

At the end of that report about him, leave a blank line:

```
60 PRINT
```

Then complete the READ loop, by making the computer go back to the loop's beginning:

```
70 GO TO 20
```

The computer will print:

```
JOE WEIGHED 273 POUNDS BEFORE ATTENDING THE DIET CLINIC
BUT WEIGHED JUST 219 POUNDS AFTERWARDS
THAT'S A LOSS OF 54 POUNDS

MARY WEIGHED 412 POUNDS BEFORE ATTENDING THE DIET CLINIC
BUT WEIGHED JUST 371 POUNDS AFTERWARDS
THAT'S A LOSS OF 41 POUNDS
```

etc.

At the end the computer will say OUT OF DATA. Instead, let's make it say:

```
COME TO OUR DIET CLINIC!
```

To do that, put END and two zeros at the end of the data —

```
15 DATA END,0,0
```

and say what to do when the computer reaches the END:

```
20 READ N$,B,A: IF N$="END" THEN PRINT "COME TO THE DIET CLI
NIC!": END
```

You need the two zeros after the END, because the READ statement says to read two numbers (B and A) after the string N$. If you omit the zeros, the computer will say OUT OF DATA. If you hate zeros, you can use other numbers instead; but most programmers prefer zeros.

French colors

Let's make the computer translate colors into French. For example, if the human says RED, we'll make the computer say the French equivalent, which is:

ROUGE

Altogether, a run will look like this:

```
RUN
WHICH COLOR INTERESTS YOU? RED
IN FRENCH, IT'S ROUGE
```

The program begins simply:

```
10 INPUT "WHICH COLOR INTERESTS YOU";C$
```

Next, we must make the computer translate the color into French. To do so, feed the computer this English-French dictionary:

English	French
white	blanc
yellow	jaune
orange	orange
red	rouge
green	vert
blue	bleu
brown	brun
black	noir

That dictionary becomes the data:

```
20 DATA WHITE,BLANC,YELLOW,JAUNE,ORANGE,ORANGE,RED,ROUGE
30 DATA GREEN,VERT,BLUE,BLEU,BROWN,BRUN,BLACK,NOIR
```

The data comes in pairs; the first pair consists of WHITE and BLANC. Tell the computer to READ each pair of DATA:

```
40 READ E$,F$
```

That line makes the computer read the first pair of data; so E$ is the first English color (WHITE), and F$ is its French equivalent (BLANC).

But that pair of data might be the *wrong pair*. For example, if the human requested RED, the human does *not* want the pair of WHITE and BLANC; instead, the human wants the pair of RED and ROUGE. Tell the computer that if the human's input (RED) doesn't match the English in the pair, go read another pair:

```
50 IF E$<>C$ THEN GO TO 40
```

That line says: if E$ (which is the English in the data) is not C$ (the color the human requested), go to 40 (which reads another pair).

Lines 40 and 50 form a loop. The computer goes round and round the loop, until it finds the pair of data that matches the human's request. Since the loop's purpose is to search for matching data, it's called a **search loop**.

After the computer's found the correct English-French pair, make the computer print the French:

```
60 PRINT "IN FRENCH, IT'S ";F$
```

Altogether, the program looks like this. . . .

Ask the human:	`10 INPUT "WHICH COLOR INTERESTS YOU";C$`
Use this dictionary:	`20 DATA WHITE,BLANC,YELLOW,JAUNE,ORANGE,ORANGE,RED,ROUGE`
	`30 DATA GREEN,VERT,BLUE,BLEU,BROWN,BRUN,BLACK,NOIR`
Look at the dictionary:	`40 READ E$,F$`
If not found, try again:	`50 IF E$<>C$ THEN GO TO 40`
Print the French:	`60 PRINT "IN FRENCH, IT'S ";F$`

Here's a sample run:

```
RUN
WHICH COLOR INTERESTS YOU? RED
IN FRENCH, IT'S ROUGE
```

Here's another:

```
RUN
WHICH COLOR INTERESTS YOU? BROWN
IN FRENCH, IT'S BRUN
```

Here's another:

```
RUN
WHICH COLOR INTERESTS YOU? PINK
OUT OF DATA
```

The computer says OUT OF DATA because it can't find PINK in the data.

Instead of saying OUT OF DATA, let's make the computer say I WASN'T TAUGHT THAT COLOR. To do that, put END at the end of the data; and when the computer reaches the END, make the computer say I WASN'T TAUGHT THAT COLOR:

```
10 INPUT "WHICH COLOR INTERESTS YOU";C$
20 DATA WHITE,BLANC,YELLOW,JAUNE,ORANGE,ORANGE,RED,ROUGE
30 DATA GREEN,VERT,BLUE,BLEU,BROWN,BRUN,BLACK,NOIR
35 DATA END,END
40 READ E$,F$: IF E$="END" THEN PRINT "I WASN'T TAUGHT THAT COLOR": END
50 IF E$<>C$ THEN GO TO 40
60 PRINT "IN FRENCH, IT'S ";F$
```

After line 60, the program just ends. Instead of letting the computer end, let's make it automatically rerun the program and translate another color. To do that, say GO TO and RESTORE:

```
10 INPUT "WHICH COLOR INTERESTS YOU";C$
20 DATA WHITE,BLANC,YELLOW,JAUNE,ORANGE,ORANGE,RED,ROUGE
30 DATA GREEN,VERT,BLUE,BLEU,BROWN,BRUN,BLACK,NOIR
35 DATA END,END
40 READ E$,F$: IF E$="END" THEN PRINT "I WASN'T TAUGHT THAT COLOR": GO TO 70
50 IF E$<>C$ THEN GO TO 40
60 PRINT "IN FRENCH, IT'S ";F$
70 RESTORE
80 GO TO 10
```

FOR . . . NEXT

Let's make the computer print every number from 1 to 100, like this:

```
1
2
3
4
5
6
7
etc.
100
```

To do that, type this line —

```
20    PRINT X
```

and also say that you want X to be every number from 1 to 100, like this:

```
10 FOR X = 1 TO 100
20    PRINT X
```

Whenever you write a program that contains the word FOR, you must say NEXT. So your program should look like this:

```
10 FOR X = 1 TO 100
20    PRINT X
30 NEXT X
```

That program works; it makes the computer print every number from 1 to 100.

Here's how it works. . . .

The computer begins at line 10, which says that you want X to be every number from 1 to 100. So X starts at 1.

Then the computer comes to line 20, which says to print X; so the computer prints:

```
1
```

Then the computer comes to line 30, which says to do the same thing for the next X, and for the next X, and for the next X; so the computer prints 2, and 3, and 4, and so on, all the way up to 100.

The computer prints many numbers, because the computer does line 20 many times (once for each X).

The computer does line 20 many times, because line 20 is between the words FOR and NEXT: it's underneath FOR, and above NEXT. **The computer repeats anything that's between the words FOR and NEXT.**

Most programmers get in the habit of indenting everything that comes between the words FOR and NEXT; so in that program, I indented the statement that says PRINT X. To make the indentation, you can hit the SPACE bar repeatedly.

In line 30, if you're too lazy to type the X, you can omit it and just type:

```
30 NEXT
```

When men meet women

Let's make the computer print these lyrics:

```
I SAW 2 MEN
MEET 2 WOMEN
TRA-LA-LA!

I SAW 3 MEN
MEET 3 WOMEN
TRA-LA-LA!

I SAW 4 MEN
MEET 4 WOMEN
TRA-LA-LA!

I SAW 5 MEN
MEET 5 WOMEN
TRA-LA-LA!

THEY ALL HAD A PARTY!
HA-HA-HA!
```

To do that, type these lines —

The first line of each verse:	`20    PRINT "I SAW";X;"MEN"`
The second line of each verse:	`30    PRINT "MEET";X;"WOMEN"`
The third line of each verse:	`40    PRINT "TRA-LA-LA!"`
Blank line under each verse:	`50    PRINT`

and make X be every number from 2 up to 5:

```
10 FOR X = 2 TO 5
20    PRINT "I SAW";X;"MEN"
30    PRINT "MEET";X;"WOMEN"
40    PRINT "TRA-LA-LA!"
50    PRINT
60 NEXT
```

At the end of the song, print the closing couplet:

```
10 FOR X = 2 TO 5
20    PRINT "I SAW";X;"MEN"
30    PRINT "MEET";X;"WOMEN"
40    PRINT "TRA-LA-LA!"
50    PRINT
60 NEXT
70 PRINT "THEY ALL HAD A PARTY!"
80 PRINT "HA-HA-HA!"
```

That program makes the computer print the entire song.

Here's an analysis:

The computer will do the indented lines repeatedly, for X=2, X=3, X=4, and X=5.	```10 FOR X = 2 TO 5```
	```20 PRINT "I SAW";X;"MEN"```
	```30 PRINT "MEET";X;"WOMEN"```
	```40 PRINT "TRA-LA-LA!"```
	```50 PRINT```
	```60 NEXT```

Then the computer will print this couplet once.	```70 PRINT "THEY ALL HAD A PARTY!"``` ```80 PRINT "HA-HA-HA!"```

Since the computer does lines 20-50 repeatedly, those lines form a loop. Here's the general rule: **the statements between FOR and NEXT form a loop.** The computer goes round and round the loop, for X=2, X=3, X=4, and X=5. Altogether, it goes around the loop 4 times, which is a finite number. Therefore, the loop is **finite**.

If you don't like the letter X, choose a different letter. For example, you can choose the letter I:

```
10 FOR I = 2 TO 5
20    PRINT "I SAW";I;"MEN"
30    PRINT "MEET";I;"WOMEN"
40    PRINT "TRA-LA-LA!"
50    PRINT
60 NEXT
70 PRINT "THEY ALL HAD A PARTY!"
80 PRINT "HA-HA-HA!"
```

When using the word FOR, most programmers prefer the letter I; most programmers say "FOR I" instead of "FOR X". Saying "FOR I" is an "old tradition". Following that tradition, the rest of this book says "FOR I" (instead of "FOR X"), except in situations where some other letter feels more natural.

Squares

To find the **square** of a number, multiply the number by itself. The square of 3 is "3 times 3", which is 9. The square of 4 is "4 times 4", which is 16.

Let's make the computer print the square of 3, 4, 5, etc., up to 100, like this:

```
THE SQUARE OF 3 IS 9
THE SQUARE OF 4 IS 16
THE SQUARE OF 5 IS 25
THE SQUARE OF 6 IS 36
THE SQUARE OF 7 IS 49
etc.
THE SQUARE OF 100 IS 10000
```

To do that, type this line —

```
20    PRINT "THE SQUARE OF";I;"IS";I*I
```

and make I be every number from 3 up to 100, like this:

```
10 FOR I = 3 TO 100
20    PRINT "THE SQUARE OF";I;"IS";I*I
30 NEXT
```

Secret meeting

This program prints 12 copies of the same message:

```
10 FOR I = 1 TO 12
20    PRINT "HUSH, HUSH!"
30    PRINT "  WE'RE HAVING A SECRET MEETING..."
40    PRINT "    IN THE COMPUTER ROOM..."
50    PRINT "       TONIGHT..."
60    PRINT "        AT 2 A.M."
70    PRINT "          WEAR A FUNNY HAT."
80    PRINT
90    PRINT
100 NEXT
```

Lines 80 and 90 leave blank lines at the end of each copy for your signature.

Midnight

This program makes the computer count to midnight:

```
10 FOR I = 1 TO 11
20    PRINT I
30 NEXT
40 PRINT "MIDNIGHT"
```

The computer will print:

```
1
2
3
4
5
6
7
8
9
10
11
MIDNIGHT
```

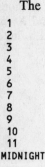

Let's put a semicolon at the end of line 20:

```
10 FOR I = 1 TO 11
20    PRINT I;
30 NEXT
40 PRINT "MIDNIGHT"
```

The semicolon makes the computer print each item on the same line, like this:

```
1 2 3 4 5 6 7 8 9 10 11 MIDNIGHT
```

If you want the computer to press the ENTER key before MIDNIGHT, insert a PRINT line:

```
10 FOR I = 1 TO 11
20    PRINT I;
30 NEXT
35 PRINT
40 PRINT "MIDNIGHT"
```

Line 35 makes the computer press the ENTER key just before MIDNIGHT, so the computer will print MIDNIGHT on a separate line, like this:

```
1 2 3 4 5 6 7 8 9 10 11
MIDNIGHT
```

In line 20, the semicolon means: do *not* press the ENTER key after I. Line 35 means: *do* press the ENTER key. So line 35 undoes line 20 and makes the computer press the ENTER key before MIDNIGHT.

Let's make the computer count to midnight 3 times, like this:

```
1 2 3 4 5 6 7 8 9 10 11
MIDNIGHT
1 2 3 4 5 6 7 8 9 10 11
MIDNIGHT
1 2 3 4 5 6 7 8 9 10 11
MIDNIGHT
```

To do that, put the entire program between the words FOR and NEXT:

```
5 FOR A = 1 TO 3
10    FOR I = 1 TO 11
20       PRINT I;
30    NEXT
35    PRINT
40    PRINT "MIDNIGHT"
50 NEXT
```

That version contains a loop inside a loop: the loop that says "FOR I" is inside the loop that says "FOR A". The A loop is called the **outer loop**; the I loop is called the **inner loop**. The inner loop's variable must differ from the outer loop's. Since we called the inner loop's variable "I", the outer loop's variable must *not* be called "I"; so I picked the letter A instead.

Programmers often think of the outer loop as a bird's nest, and the inner loop as an egg *inside the nest*. So programmers say the inner loop is **nested in** the outer loop; the inner loop is a **nested loop**.

Favorite color

This program plays a guessing game:

```
10 PRINT "I'LL GIVE YOU FIVE GUESSES...."
20 FOR I = 1 TO 5
30    INPUT "WHAT'S MY FAVORITE COLOR";G$
40    IF G$="PINK" THEN GO TO 100
50    PRINT "NO."
60 NEXT
70 PRINT "SORRY, YOUR FIVE GUESSES ARE UP! YOU LOSE."
80 END

100 PRINT "CONGRATULATIONS! YOU DISCOVERED MY FAVORITE COLOR."
110 PRINT "IT TOOK YOU";I;"GUESSES".
```

Line 10 warns the human that only five guesses are allowed. Line 20 makes the computer count from 1 to 5; to begin, I is 1. Line 30 asks the human to guess the computer's favorite color; the guess is called G$.

If the guess is PINK, the computer jumps from line 40 to line 100, prints CONGRATULATIONS, and tells how many guesses the human took. But if the guess is *not* PINK, the computer proceeds from line 40 to line 50, prints NO, and goes on to the next guess.

If the human guesses five times without success, the computer proceeds from line 60 to line 70 and prints SORRY . . . YOU LOSE.

For example, if the human's third guess is PINK, the computer prints:

```
CONGRATULATIONS! YOU DISCOVERED MY FAVORITE COLOR.
IT TOOK YOU 3 GUESSES.
```

If the human's very first guess is PINK, the computer prints:

```
CONGRATULATIONS! YOU DISCOVERED MY FAVORITE COLOR.
IT TOOK YOU 1 GUESSES.
```

Saying "1 GUESSES" is bad grammar but understandable.

Lines 20-60 form a loop. Line 20 says the loop will normally be done five times. The line after the loop, line 70, is the loop's **normal exit**. But if the human happens to input PINK, the computer jumps out of the loop early, to line 100, which is the loop's **abnormal exit**.

Finite pause

Have you ever met someone who acts romantic, then suddenly says something cruel that breaks the romance?

Let's make the computer act that way. For example, let's make the computer begin by crooning a romantic message:

```
10 PRINT "YOUR LUSCIOUS LIPS SMELL LIKE THE FINEST WINE"
```

Then let's make the computer pause, to give the human a chance to admire that romantic message and make the human wait in suspense for the next outburst of computer emotion. Here's how to make the computer pause:

```
20 FOR I = 1 TO 7000: NEXT
```

That line makes the computer pause, while it counts up to 7000. That line makes the computer mumble to itself, "I is 1, I is 2, I is 3, I is 4, . . . " without printing anything on the screen. While the computer is secretly and silently mumbling to itself up to 7000, the human has a chance to read and admire the romantic message printed by line 10.

Finally, let's make the computer analyze the meaning of lips smelling like wine:

```
30 PRINT "YOU MUST BE DRUNK"
```

So altogether, that program makes the computer print YOUR LUSCIOUS LIPS SMELL LIKE THE FINEST WINE, then pause, then say YOU MUST BE DRUNK.

In that program, line 20 makes the computer pause, by making the computer silently mumble up to 7000. The typical computer mumbles 1000 times per second. Since line 20 says to mumble 7000 times, that line takes 7 seconds altogether, and so it makes the computer pause for 7 seconds.

If you want the computer to pause for 12 seconds instead of 7, retype line 20 so it says to mumble 12000 times instead of 7000.

Although the *typical* computer mumbles 1000 times per second, *your* computer might mumble slightly faster or slower than that. Try the program on *your* computer, and notice how many seconds *your* computer pauses when doing 7000 mumbles. If your computer's typical, it pauses 7 seconds; if your computer mumbles quickly, it pauses *less* than 7 seconds; if your computer mumbles slowly, it pauses *more* than 7 seconds.

Warning: your computer mumbles more slowly in long programs than in short ones.

This program makes the computer print a famous joke:

```
10 PRINT "YOUR TEETH ARE LIKE STARS"
20 FOR I = 1 TO 7000: NEXT
30 PRINT "THEY COME OUT AT NIGHT"
```

Line 30 is the punch line. Line 20 makes the computer pause 7 seconds, before giving the punch line.

Experiment: invent your *own* joke, and make the computer pause before printing the punch line.

Eye test
This program makes the computer test how fast you can read:

```
10 CLS
20 PRINT "IF YOU CAN READ THIS, YOU READ QUICKLY"
30 FOR I = 1 TO 250: NEXT
40 CLS
```

Line 10 makes the computer clear the screen, so that the entire screen becomes blank. Line 20 makes the computer print:

```
IF YOU CAN READ THIS, YOU READ QUICKLY
```

Line 30 makes the computer pause for a quarter of a second (since 250 is a quarter of 1000). While the computer pauses, the message stays on the screen. Line 40 erases the screen, so the message stayed on the screen for just a quarter of a second. If you could read the message in a quarter of a second, you have very quick eyes!

I can't read that quickly. Can you? Try it! To make the eye test easier, allow yourself longer than a quarter of a second to read the message, by changing the 250 to a larger number.

Get together with your friends, and see how quickly they can read. Flash different messages on the screen by changing line 20. For example, try changing line 20 to this:

```
20 PRINT "MUMBLING MORONS MAKE MY MOM MISS MURDER MYSTERIES MONDAY MORNING"
```

If your friends can read all that in a quarter of a second, they probably belong in the Guinness Book of World Records.

To prevent your friends from cheating, make them close their eyes while you're typing the program. When you've finished typing the program, press the CLEAR key, so that the program becomes invisible. Then tell your friends to open their eyes and type RUN.

STEP
The FOR statement can be varied:

Statement	Meaning
FOR I = 5 TO 17 STEP .1	I will go from 5 to 17, counting by tenths. So I will be 5, then 5.1, then 5.2, etc., up to 17.
FOR I = 5 TO 17 STEP 3	I will be every third number from 5 to 17. So I will be 5, then 8, then 11, then 14, then 17.
FOR I = 17 TO 5 STEP -3	I will be every third number from 17 down to 5. So I will be 17, then 14, then 11, then 8, then 5.

To count down, you *must* use the word STEP. To count from 17 down to 5, give this instruction:

```
FOR I = 17 TO 5 STEP -1
```

This program prints a rocket countdown:

```
10 FOR I = 10 TO 1 STEP -1
20    PRINT I
30 NEXT
40 PRINT "BLAST OFF!"
```

The computer will print:

```
10
9
8
7
6
5
4
3
2
1
BLAST OFF!
```

This statement is tricky:

```
FOR I = 5 TO 16 STEP 3
```

It says to start I at 5, and keep adding 3 until it gets past 16. So I will be 5, then 8, then 11, then 14. I won't be 17, since 17 is past 16. The first value of I is 5; the last value is 14.

In the statement FOR I = 5 TO 16 STEP 3, the **first value** or **initial value** of I is 5, the **limit value** is 16, and the **step size** or **increment** is 3. The I is called the **counter** or **index** or **loop-control variable**. Although the limit value is 16, the **last value** or **terminal value** is 14.

Programmers usually say "FOR I", instead of "FOR X", because the letter I reminds them of the word **index**.

VARIABLES & CONSTANTS

A **numeric constant** is a simple number, such as:

```
0   1   2   8   43.7   -524.6   .003
```

Another example of a numeric constant is 1.3E5, which means, "take 1.3, and move its decimal point 5 places to the right".

A numeric constant does not contain any arithmetic. For example, since 7+1 contains arithmetic (+), it's *not* a numeric constant. 8 is a numeric constant, even though 7+1 isn't.

A **string constant** is a simple string, in quotation marks:

```
"I LOVE YOU"   "76 TROMBONES"   "GO AWAY!!!"   "XYPW EXR///746"
```

A **constant** is a numeric constant or a string constant:

```
0   8   -524.6   1.3E5   "I LOVE YOU"   "XYPW EXR///746"
```

A **variable** is something that stands for something else. If it stands for a string, it's called a **string variable** and ends with a dollar sign, like this:

```
A$   B$   Y$   Z$
```

If the variable stands for a number, it's called a **numeric variable** and lacks a dollar sign, like this:

```
A   B   Y   Z
```

So all these are variables:

```
A$   B$   Y$   Z$   A   B   Y   Z
```

Expressions

A **numeric expression** is a numeric constant (such as 8) or a numeric variable (such as A) or a combination of them, such as 8+Z, or 8*A, or Z*A, or 8*2, or 7+1, or even Z*A-(7+Z)/8+1.3E5*(-524.6+B).

A **string expression** is a string constant (such as "I LOVE YOU") or a string variable (such as A$) or a combination.

An **expression** is a numeric expression or a string expression.

Statements

At the end of a GO TO statement, the line number must be a numeric constant.

Right: `50 GO TO 100`	(100 is a numeric constant.)
Wrong: `50 GO TO N`	(N is not a numeric constant.)

The INPUT statement's prompt must be a string constant:

Right: `10 INPUT "WHAT IS YOUR NAME";N$`	("WHAT IS YOUR NAME" is a constant.)
Wrong: `10 INPUT Q$;N$`	(Q$ is not a constant.)

In a DATA statement, you must have constants.

Right: `10 DATA 8, 1.3E5`	(8 and 1.3E5 are constants.)
Wrong: `10 DATA 7+1, 1.3E5`	(7+1 is not a constant.)

In the DATA statement, if the constant is a string, you can omit the quotation marks (unless the string contains a comma or a colon).

Right: `10 DATA "JOE","MARY"`	
Also right: `10 DATA JOE,MARY`	

Here are the forms of the most popular BASIC statements:

General form	Example
`PRINT list of expressions`	`PRINT "THE TEMPERATURE IS";4+25;"DEGREES"`
`GO TO numeric constant`	`GO TO 10`
`END`	`END`
`STOP`	`STOP`
`variable = expression`	`X = 47+2`
`INPUT string constant ; variable`	`INPUT "WHAT IS YOUR NAME";N$`
`IF condition THEN list of statements`	`IF A>=18 THEN PRINT "YOU": PRINT "VOTE"`
`DATA list of constants`	`DATA JOE,273,219,MARY,412,371`
`READ list of variables`	`READ N$,B,A`
`RESTORE`	`RESTORE`

`FOR numeric variable =`
`    numeric expression TO`
`    numeric expression STEP`
`    numeric expression`
	`FOR I = 59+1 TO 100+N STEP 2+3`

`NEXT numeric variable`	`NEXT I`

LOOP TECHNIQUES

Here's a strange program:

```
10 A=5
20 A=3+A
30 PRINT A
```

Line 20 means: the new A is 3 plus the old A. So the new A is 3+5, which is 8. Line 30 prints:

```
8
```

Let's look at that program more closely. Line 10 puts 5 into box A:

When the computer sees line 20, it examines the equation's right side and sees the 3+A. Since A is 5, the 3+A is 3+5, which is 8. So line 20 says: A=8. The computer puts 8 into box A:

Line 30 prints 8.

Here's another weirdo:

```
10 B=6
20 B=B+1
30 PRINT B*2
```

Line 20 says the new B is "the old B plus 1". So the new B is 6+1, which is 7. Line 30 prints:

```
14
```

In that program, line 10 says B is 6; but line 20 increases B, by adding 1 to B; so B becomes 7. Programmers say that B has been **increased** or **incremented**. In line 20, the "1" is called the **increase** or the **increment**.

The opposite of "increment" is **decrement**:

```
10 J=500
20 J=J-1
30 PRINT J
```

Line 10 says J starts at 500. But line 20 says the new J is "the old J minus 1", so the new J is 500-1, which is 499. Line 30 prints:

```
499
```

In that program, J was **decreased** (or **decremented**). In line 20, the "1" is called the **decrease** (or **decrement**).

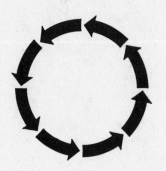

Counting

Suppose you want the computer to count, starting at 3, like this:

```
3
4
5
6
7
8
etc.
```

This program does it, by a special technique:

```
10 C=3
20 PRINT C
30 C=C+1
40 GO TO 20
```

In that program, C is called the **counter**, because it helps the computer count.

Line 10 says C starts at 3. Line 20 makes the computer print C, so the computer prints:

```
3
```

Line 30 increases C by adding 1 to it, so C becomes 4. Line 40 sends the computer back to line 20, which prints the new value of C:

```
4
```

Then the computer comes to line 30 again, which increases C again so C becomes 5. Line 40 sends the computer back to line 20 again, which prints:

```
5
```

The program's an infinite loop: the computer will print 3, 4, 5, 6, 7, 8, 9, 10, 11, 12, and so on, forever, unless you abort it.

General procedure Here's the general procedure for making the computer count:

1. Start C at some value (such as 3).
2. Use C. (For example, tell the computer to PRINT C.)
3. Increase C, by saying C=C+1.
4. GO back TO step 2.

Variations To read the printing more easily, put a semicolon at the end of the PRINT statement:

```
10 C=3
20 PRINT C;
30 C=C+1
40 GO TO 20
```

The semicolon makes the computer print horizontally:

```
3  4  5  6  7  8  etc.
```

This program makes the computer count, starting at 1:

```
10 C=1
20 PRINT C;
30 C=C+1
40 GO TO 20
```

The computer will print 1, 2, 3, 4, etc.

This program makes the computer count, starting at 0:

```
10 C=0
20 PRINT C;
30 C=C+1
40 GO TO 20
```

The computer will print 0, 1, 2, 3, 4, etc.

Quiz

Let's make the computer give this quiz:

What's the capital of Nevada?
What's the chemical symbol for iron?
What word means 'brother or sister'?
What was Beethoven's first name?
How many cups are in a quart?

To make the computer score the quiz, we must tell it the correct answers, which are:

Carson City
Fe
sibling
Ludwig
4

So the program contains this data:

```
10 DATA WHAT'S THE CAPITAL OF NEVADA,CARSON CITY
20 DATA WHAT'S THE CHEMICAL SYMBOL FOR IRON,FE
30 DATA WHAT WORD MEANS 'BROTHER OR SISTER',SIBLING
40 DATA WHAT WAS BEETHOVEN'S FIRST NAME,LUDWIG
50 DATA HOW MANY CUPS ARE IN A QUART,4
```

Tell the computer to READ the data:

```
100 READ Q$,A$
```

That line reads a pair of data: it reads a question (Q$) and the correct answer (A$).

Make the computer ask the question and wait for the human's response:

```
110 PRINT Q$;
120 INPUT "??";H$
```

Line 110 prints the question. Line 120 prints question marks after the question, and waits for the human to respond; the human's response is called H$.

Finally, evaluate the human's response. If the human's response (H$) is the correct answer (A$), make the computer say "CORRECT" and GO TO the next question:

```
130 IF H$=A$ THEN PRINT "CORRECT": GO TO 100
```

But if the human's response is wrong, make the computer say "NO" and reveal the correct answer:

```
140 PRINT "NO, THE ANSWER IS: ";A$: GO TO 100
```

Here's a sample run:

```
RUN
WHAT'S THE CAPITAL OF NEVADA??? LAS VEGAS
NO, THE ANSWER IS: CARSON CITY
WHAT'S THE CHEMICAL SYMBOL FOR IRON??? FE
CORRECT
WHAT WORD MEANS 'BROTHER OR SISTER'??? I GIVE UP
NO, THE ANSWER IS: SIBLING
WHAT WAS BEETHOVEN'S FIRST NAME??? LUDVIG
NO, THE ANSWER IS: LUDWIG
HOW MANY CUPS ARE IN A QUART??? 4
CORRECT
OUT OF DATA
```

To give a quiz about different topics, change the data in lines 10-50.

Avoid OUT OF DATA

Instead of making the computer say OUT OF DATA, let's make it say:

```
I HOPE YOU ENJOYED THE QUIZ
```

To do that, write an end mark and an end routine:

```
60 DATA END,END
100 READ Q$,A$: IF Q$="END" THEN PRINT "I HOPE YOU ENJOYED T
HE QUIZ": END
```

Count the correct answers

Let's make the computer count how many questions the human answered correctly. To do that, we need a counter. As usual, let's call it C:

```
5 C=0
10 DATA WHAT'S THE CAPITAL OF NEVADA,CARSON CITY
20 DATA WHAT'S THE CHEMICAL SYMBOL FOR IRON,FE
30 DATA WHAT WORD MEANS 'BROTHER OR SISTER',SIBLING
40 DATA WHAT WAS BEETHOVEN'S FIRST NAME,LUDWIG
50 DATA HOW MANY CUPS ARE IN A QUART,4
60 DATA END,END
100 READ Q$,A$: IF Q$="END" THEN PRINT "YOU ANSWERED";C;"OF
THE QUESTIONS CORRECTLY": PRINT "I HOPE YOU ENJOYED THE QUIZ
": END
110 PRINT Q$;
120 INPUT "??";H$
130 IF H$=A$ THEN PRINT "CORRECT": C=C+1: GO TO 100
140 PRINT "NO, THE ANSWER IS: ";A$: GO TO 100
```

At the beginning of the program, the human hasn't answered any questions correctly yet, so line 5 begins the counter at 0. Each time the human answers a question correctly, line 130 increases the counter. When the program ends, line 100 prints the counter, by printing a message such as:

```
YOU ANSWERED 2 OF THE QUESTIONS CORRECTLY
```

It would be nicer to print —

```
YOU ANSWERED 2 OF THE 5 QUESTIONS CORRECTLY
YOUR SCORE IS 40 %
```

or, if the quiz were changed to include 8 questions:

```
YOU ANSWERED 2 OF THE 8 QUESTIONS CORRECTLY
YOUR SCORE IS 25 %
```

To make the computer print such a message, we must make the computer count how many questions were asked. So we need another counter. Since we already used C to count the number of correct answers, let's use Q to count the number of questions asked. Like C, Q must start at 0; and we must increase Q, by adding 1 each time another question is asked:

```
5 C=0: Q=0
10 DATA WHAT'S THE CAPITAL OF NEVADA,CARSON CITY
20 DATA WHAT'S THE CHEMICAL SYMBOL FOR IRON,FE
30 DATA WHAT WORD MEANS 'BROTHER OR SISTER',SIBLING
40 DATA WHAT WAS BEETHOVEN'S FIRST NAME,LUDWIG
50 DATA HOW MANY CUPS ARE IN A QUART,4
60 DATA END,END
100 READ Q$,A$: IF Q$="END" THEN PRINT "YOU ANSWERED";C;"OF
THE";Q;"QUESTIONS CORRECTLY": PRINT "YOUR SCORE IS";C/Q*100;
"%": PRINT "I HOPE YOU ENJOYED THE QUIZ": END
110 PRINT Q$;
115 Q=Q+1
120 INPUT "??";H$
130 IF H$=A$ THEN PRINT "CORRECT": C=C+1: GO TO 100
140 PRINT "NO, THE ANSWER IS: ";A$: GO TO 100
```

Summing

Let's make the computer imitate an adding machine, so a run looks like this:

```
RUN
NOW THE SUM IS 0
WHAT NUMBER DO YOU WANT TO ADD TO THE SUM? 5
NOW THE SUM IS 5
WHAT NUMBER DO YOU WANT TO ADD TO THE SUM? 3
NOW THE SUM IS 8
WHAT NUMBER DO YOU WANT TO ADD TO THE SUM? 6.1
NOW THE SUM IS 14.1
WHAT NUMBER DO YOU WANT TO ADD TO THE SUM? -10
NOW THE SUM IS 4.1
etc.
```

Here's the program:

```
10 S=0
20 PRINT "NOW THE SUM IS";S
30 INPUT "WHAT NUMBER DO YOU WANT TO ADD TO THE SUM";X
40 S=S+X
50 GO TO 20
```

Line 10 starts the sum at 0. Line 20 prints the sum. Line 30 asks the human what number to add to the sum; the human's number is called X. Line 40 adds X to the sum, so the sum changes. Line 50 makes the computer go to line 20, which prints the new sum. Lines 20-50 form an infinite loop, which you must abort.

Here's the general procedure for making the computer find a sum:

1. Start S at 0.
2. Use S. (For example, tell the computer to PRINT S.)
3. Find out what number to add to S. (For example, let the human input an X.)
4. Increase S, by saying S = S + the number to be added.
5. GO back TO step 2.

Checking account

If your bank's nasty, it charges you 10¢ to process each good check that you write, and a $5 penalty for each check that bounces; and it pays no interest on the money you've deposited.

This program makes the computer imitate such a bank. . . .

Start the sum at 0:	`10 S=0`

Chat with the human:	`20 PRINT "YOUR CHECKING ACCOUNT CONTAINS";S`
	`30 INPUT "DEPOSIT OR WITHDRAW";A$`
	`40 IF A$="DEPOSIT" THEN GO TO 100`
	`50 IF A$="WITHDRAW" THEN GO TO 200`
	`60 PRINT "PLEASE SAY DEPOSIT OR WITHDRAW": GO TO 30`

Deposit some money:	`100 INPUT "HOW MUCH DO YOU WANT TO DEPOSIT";D`
	`110 S=S+D`
	`120 GO TO 20`

Withdraw some money:	`200 INPUT "HOW MUCH DO YOU WANT TO WITHDRAW";W`
	`210 W=W+.10`
	`220 IF W<=S THEN PRINT "OKAY": S=S-W: GO TO 20`
	`230 PRINT "THAT CHECK BOUNCED": S=S-5: GO TO 20`

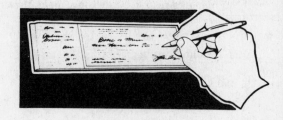

In that program, the total amount of money in the checking account is called the sum. Line 10 starts that sum at 0. Line 20 prints the sum. Line 30 asks whether the human wants to deposit or withdraw.

If the human says DEPOSIT, the computer goes from line 40 to line 100 (which asks how much to deposit), then to line 110 (which adds the deposit to the sum in the account), then back to line 20 (for the next transaction).

But if the human says WITHDRAW instead of DEPOSIT, the computer goes from line 50 to line 200 (which asks how much to withdraw), then to line 210 (which adds the 10¢ service charge to the withdrawal amount). Then the computer reaches line 220, which checks whether the sum S in the account is large enough to cover the withdrawal (W). If W< =S, the computer says OKAY and processes the check, by subtracting W from the sum in the account. If W>S instead, the computer says THAT CHECK BOUNCED and decreases the sum in the account by the $5 penalty.

How the program is nasty

That program is nasty to customers. For example, suppose you have $1 in your account, and you try to write a check for 95¢. Since 95¢ + the 10¢ service charge = $1.05, which is more than you have in your account, your check will bounce, and you'll be penalized $5. That makes your balance will become *negative* $4, and the bank will demand that *you* pay the *bank* $4 — just because you wrote a check for 95¢!

Another nuisance is when you leave town permanently and want to close your account. If your account contains $1, you can't get your dollar back! The most you can withdraw is 90¢, because 90¢ + the 10¢ service charge = $1.

That nasty program makes customers hate the bank — and hate the computer!

How to stop the nastiness

The bank should make the program friendlier. Here's how.

To stop accusing the customer of owing money, the bank should change any negative sum to 0:

```
15 IF S<0 THEN S=0
```

To make sure the computer goes to that line, the bank's program should say GO TO 15 instead of GO TO 20; so the bank should change line 230 to this:

```
230 PRINT "THAT CHECK BOUNCED": S=S-5: GO TO 15
```

Also, to be friendly, the bank should ignore the 10¢ service charge when deciding whether a check will clear. So the bank should eliminate line 210. On the other hand, if the check *does* clear, the bank should impose the 10¢ service charge afterwards, like this:

```
220 IF W<=S THEN PRINT "OKAY": S=S-W-.10: GO TO 15
```

So if the bank is kind, it will insert line 15, use the new version of line 230, eliminate line 210, and use the new version of line 220.

But some banks complain that those changes are *too* kind! For example, if a customer whose account contains just 1¢ writes a million-dollar check (which bounces), the new program charges him just 1¢ for the bad check; $5 might be more reasonable.

Moral: the hardest thing about programming is choosing your goal — deciding what you *want* the computer to do.

Series

Let's make the computer add together all the numbers from 7 to 100, so that the computer finds the sum of this series: 7+8+9+...+100. Here's how.

Start the Sum at 0:	`10 S=0`
Make I go from 7 to 100:	`20 FOR I = 7 TO 100`
Increase the Sum, by adding each I to it:	`30     S=S+I`
	`40 NEXT`
Print the final Sum (which is 5029):	`50 PRINT S`

Let's make the computer add together the *squares* of all the numbers from 7 to 100, so that the computer finds the sum of this series: (7 squared) + (8 squared) + (9 squared) + . . . + (100 squared). Here's how:

```
10 S=0
20 FOR I = 7 TO 100
30     S=S+I*I
40 NEXT
50 PRINT S
```

It's the same as the previous program, except that line 30 says to add I*I instead of I. Line 50 prints the final sum, which is 338259.

Data sums

This program adds together the numbers in the data:

```
10 S=0
20 DATA 5, 3, 6.1, etc.
30 DATA etc.
40 DATA etc.
50 DATA 0
60 READ X: IF X=0 THEN PRINT S: END
70 S=S+X
80 GO TO 60
```

Line 10 starts the sum at 0. Lines 20-40 contain the numbers to be added. The zero in line 50 is an end mark.

Line 60 reads an X from the data. If X=0, the end of the data's been reached, so we want the computer to print the sum (S) and end. But if the X it reads is *not* zero, the computer proceeds from line 60 to line 70, adds X to the sum, and goes from line 80 to line 60, which reads another X.

HELPFUL HINTS

DEBUGGING

If you write and run your own program, it probably won't work.

Your first reaction will be to blame the computer. Don't!

The probability is 99.99% that the fault is yours. Your program contains an error. An error is called a **bug**. Your next task is to **debug** the program, which means get the bugs out.

Bugs are common; top-notch programmers make errors all the time. If you write a program that works perfectly on the first run and doesn't need debugging, it's called a **gold-star program**, and means you should have tried writing a harder one instead!

It's easy to write a program that's almost completely correct, but hard to find the little bug that's fouling it up. Most of the time you spend at the computer will be devoted to debugging.

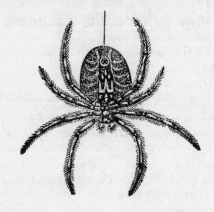

Debugging can be fun. Hunting for the bug is like going on a treasure hunt — or solving a murder mystery. Pretend you're Sherlock Holmes. Your mission: to find the bug and squish it! When you squish it, have fun: yell out, "Squish!"

How can you tell when a roomful of programmers is happy? Answer: when you hear continual cries of "Squish!"

To find a bug, use three techniques:

Inspect the program.
Trace the computer's thinking.
Shorten the program.

Here are the details. . . .

Inspect the program

Take a good, hard look at the program. If you stare hard enough, maybe you'll see the bug.

Ask the computer to help you. **Make the computer print the entire program.** To do that, type:

```
LIST
```

<u>**Popular typos**</u> Usually, the bug will turn out to be just a typing error, a **typo**. For example. . . .

Maybe you typed the letter O instead of a zero? Typed zero instead of the letter O?
Typed I instead of 1? Typed 1 instead of I?
Pressed the SHIFT key when you weren't supposed to? Forgot to press it?
Typed an extra letter? Omitted a letter?
Typed a line you thought you hadn't? Omitted a line?

<u>**Fix your strings**</u> You must put quotation marks around each string, and a dollar sign after each string variable:

```
Right:    A$="JERK"
Wrong:    A$=JERK
Wrong:    A="JERK"
```

<u>**Too much?**</u> Here are two reasons why the computer might print too much:

1. You forgot the insert the word END into your program.
2. You forgot to type NEW; so the computer is reprinting part of the previous program.

Trace the computer's thinking

If you've inspected the program thoroughly and *still* haven't found the bug, the next step is to **trace** the computer's thinking. **Pretend you are the computer. Do what your program says.** Do you find yourself printing the same wrong answers the computer printed? If so, why?

To help your analysis, **make the computer print everything it's thinking** while it's running your program. For example, suppose your program contains lines 10, 20, 30, and 40, and uses the variables B, C, and X$. Insert these lines into your program:

```
15 PRINT "I'M AT LINE 15.   THE VALUES ARE";B;C;X$
25 PRINT "I'M AT LINE 25.   THE VALUES ARE";B;C;X$
35 PRINT "I'M AT LINE 35.   THE VALUES ARE";B;C;X$
45 PRINT "I'M AT LINE 45.   THE VALUES ARE";B;C;X$
```

Then type the word RUN. The computer will run the program again; but lines 15, 25, 35, and 45 make the computer print everything it's thinking. Check what the computer prints. If the computer prints what you expect in lines 15 and 25, but prints strange values in line 35 (or doesn't even get to line 35), you know the bug occurs before line 35 but after line 25; so the bug must be in line 30.

If your program contains hundreds of lines, you might not have the patience to insert lines 15, 25, 35, 45, 55, 65, 75, etc. Here's a short cut. . . .

Halfway down your program, insert a line that says to print all the values. Then run your program. If the line you inserted prints the correct values, you know the bug lies underneath that line; but if the line prints *wrong* values (or if the computer never reaches that line), you know the bug lies *above* that line. In either case, you know which half of your program contains the bug. In that half of the program, insert more lines, until you finally zero in on the line that contains the bug.

Shorten the program

When all else fails, shorten the program.

Hunting for a bug in a program is like hunting for a needle in a haystack: the job is easier if the haystack is smaller. So make your program shorter: delete the last half of your program. Then run the shortened version. That way, you'll find out whether the first half of your program is working the way it's supposed to. When you've perfected the first half of your program, tack the second half back on.

Does your program contain **a statement whose meaning you're not completely sure of**? Check the meaning by reading a book or asking a friend; or **write a tiny experimental program that contains the statement**, and see what happens when you type RUN.

Hint: before you shorten your program (or write tiny experimental ones), **SAVE the original version**, even though it contains a bug. After you've played with the shorter versions, retrieve the original and fix it.

The easiest way to write a long, correct program is to write a short program first, debug it, then add a few more lines, debug them, add a few more lines, debug them, etc. In other words, start with a small program, perfect it, and then gradually add perfected extras so you *gradually* build a perfected masterpiece. If you try to compose a long program all at once — instead of building it from perfected pieces — you'll have nothing more than a master*mess* — full of bugs.

Moral: to build a large masterpiece, start with a *small* masterpiece. Putting it another way: to build a skyscraper, begin by laying a good foundation; double-check the foundation before you start adding the walls and the roof.

ERROR MESSAGES

If you type a command that the computer can't obey, the computer will gripe by printing an **error message**.

You can make 6 kinds of errors: syntax errors, numeric errors, printer errors, logic errors, disk errors, and advanced errors. Here are the most popular error messages printed by the IBM PC, in the order you'll probably encounter them.

Syntax errors

If you say PRIND instead of PRINT, the computer will say **SYNTAX ERROR**. That means the computer hasn't the faintest idea of what you're talking about!

If the computer says you have a SYNTAX ERROR, it's usually because you spelled a word wrong, or forgot a word, or used a word the computer doesn't understand. It can also result from wrong punctuation: check your commas, semicolons, and colons. It can also mean you typed a left parenthesis that doesn't have a corresponding right parenthesis, or vice versa.

It can also mean your DATA statement contains a string but your READ statement says to read a number instead. To fix that problem, change the READ statement by putting a dollar sign at the end of the variable's name.

Numeric errors

In a statement such as PRINT 5+2, the + is called the **operation**. The 5 and 2 are called the **operands**.

If you try to say PRINT 5+2 but forget to type the 2, the computer will say **MISSING OPERAND**.

The biggest number the computer can handle is about 1E38 (which means 1 followed by 38 zeros). If you try to go much higher, the computer will say **OVERFLOW**. For example, if you say 1E39, or you try to multiply together lots of big numbers, you'll get an OVERFLOW ERROR.

If you try to divide by zero, the computer will say **DIVISION BY ZERO**.

If you feed the computer a number that's inappropriate, the computer will say **ILLEGAL FUNCTION CALL**. For example, if you say DELETE 40, but your program doesn't contain any line whose number is 40, the computer will say ILLEGAL FUNCTION CALL.

Printer errors

If your printer runs out of paper, the computer will say **OUT OF PAPER**.

When the computer sends a message to a device (such as your printer), the computer waits for the device to respond to the message. If the computer has waited a long time without receiving any response from the device, the computer will give up waiting; it will say **DEVICE TIMEOUT**.

When you try using your printer, if the computer says DEVICE TIMEOUT it means the computer isn't receiving the proper feedback from your printer. That's because your printer isn't properly attached to the computer, or hasn't been turned on, or isn't in a state of being READY.

Logic errors

If you say GO TO 40 but there isn't a line 40 in your program, the computer will say **UNDEFINED LINE NUMBER**. The computer says UNDEFINED LINE NUMBER whenever you try to GO TO a missing line.

The computer handles two **types** of information: numbers and strings. If you feed the computer the wrong type of information — if you feed it a number when you should have fed it a string, or you feed it a string when you should have fed it a number — the computer will say **TYPE MISMATCH**.

When you feed the computer a string, you must put the string in quotation marks, and put a dollar sign after the string's variable. If you forget to type the string's quotation marks or dollar sign, the computer won't realize it's a string; the computer will think you're trying to type a number instead; and if a number would be inappropriate, the computer will say TYPE MISMATCH. So when the computer says TYPE MISMATCH, it usually means you forgot a quotation mark or a dollar sign.

Disk errors

To use the disks, you must invent a name for your program. If the name you invent is inappropriate, the computer will say **BAD FILE NAME**.

If you forget to put a disk into the disk drive, or you accidentally leave the disk drive's door open, the computer will say **DISK NOT READY**. If the disk's surface is scratched or otherwise damaged, the computer will say **DISK MEDIA ERROR**.

If the disk is write-protected by a write-protect tab (which stops you from writing onto the disk) and you nevertheless try to write information onto the disk, the computer will say **DISK WRITE PROTECT**. If you try to write information onto the disk but the disk doesn't have enough free space to hold the information, the computer will say **DISK FULL**.

The disk's **directory** is a place on the disk that remembers the names of all the disk's programs and files. If the directory is full, so that there's no more room to store names of programs, and you nevertheless try to put another program onto the disk, the computer will say **TOO MANY FILES**.

If you tell the computer to copy JOE from the disk to the RAM (by saying LOAD "JOE" or RUN "JOE"), but the computer can't find JOE on the disk, the computer will say **FILE NOT FOUND**.

Advanced errors

If you say READ, but the computer can't find any more DATA to read (because the computer has read all the DATA already), the computer will say **OUT OF DATA**.

Whenever you say FOR, you're supposed to say NEXT, and vice versa. If you say FOR without saying NEXT, the computer will say **FOR WITHOUT NEXT**. If you say NEXT without saying FOR, the computer will say **NEXT WITHOUT FOR**. If your program contains the words FOR and NEXT several times, but you accidentally have more FOR's than NEXT's or more NEXT's than FOR's, the computer will print one of those error messages, because the number of FOR's ought to equal the number of NEXT's.

If your computer doesn't have enough RAM to hold your information, it will say **OUT OF MEMORY**. Part of the RAM is used for handling strings; if that part isn't big enough to hold all your strings, the computer will say **OUT OF STRING SPACE**. If you get one of those error messages, shorten your program (by splitting it into several smaller programs).

The following commands make your life easier.

Renumbering

Suppose you've written a sloppy program, like this:

```
37 PRINT "SNARL"
68 PRINT "SMIRK"
91 GO TO 37
```

If you type —

```
RENUM
LIST
```

the computer will renumber your program, so that the lines are numbered 10, 20, and 30. The computer will say:

```
10 PRINT "SNARL"
20 PRINT "SMIRK"
30 GO TO 10
```

Notice that the computer even changed the "GO TO 37", so that it became "GO TO 10"!

If you type —

```
RENUM 500
LIST
```

the computer will renumber your program so that it begins at line 500. The computer will say:

```
500 PRINT "SNARL"
510 PRINT "SMIRK"
520 GO TO 500
```

Suppose you wrote a program that contained a line numbered 83, and you'd like that line to be called "line 500" instead. Here's how to start renumbering at line 83, so that line 83 becomes 500, and the next line becomes 600, and the line after *that* becomes 700, etc.:

```
RENUM 500,83,100
LIST
```

That command makes the computer renumber the program so that 500 is the new number for line 83, and the next lines are numbered 600, 700, 800, etc. (going up by 100's).

The RENUM command works on *most* computers. To find out about *your* computer, read the "Versions of BASIC" appendix.

The PAUSE key

Magicians often say, "The hand is quicker than the eye." The computer's the ultimate magician: the computer can print information on the screen much faster than you can read it.

When the computer is printing too fast for you to read, tap the PAUSE key. The computer will pause, to let you read what's on the screen.

When you've finished reading what's on the screen, and want the computer to stop pausing, tap the PAUSE key again. Then the computer will continue printing rapidly, where it left off.

If your eyes are as slow as mine, you'll need to use the PAUSE key often! You'll want the computer to pause when you're running a program that contains many PRINT statements, or if you're running a program that contains a PRINT statement in a loop, or if you're LISTing a long program.

The PAUSE key is on the Walter keyboard. To find out whether it's on *your* computer's keyboard, check the "Versions of BASIC" appendix.

Apostrophe

Occasionally, jot a note, to remind yourself what your program does and what the variables stand for. Slip the note into your program by putting an apostrophe before it:

```
10 'THIS PROGRAM IS ANOTHER DUMB EXAMPLE
20 'WRITTEN BY RUSSY-POO, A STUPID JERK
30 'IT WAS WRITTEN ON HALLOWEEN, UNDER A FULL MOON, SHADED BY HIS FANGS
40 C=40' BECAUSE RUSS HAS 40 COMPUTERS
50 H=23' BECAUSE 23 OF HIS COMPUTERS ARE HAUNTED
60 PRINT C-H' THAT IS HOW MANY COMPUTERS ARE UNHAUNTED AND SAFE FOR KIDS
```

When you type RUN, **the computer ignores everything that's to the right of an apostrophe.** So the computer ignores lines 10, 20, and 30; in lines 40 and 50 the computer ignores the "because . . . "; in line 60 the computer ignores the comments about being unhaunted. Since C is 40, and H is 23, line 60 makes the computer print:

17

Everything to the right of an apostrophe is called a **comment** (or **remark**). While the computer runs the program, it ignores the comments. But whenever you say LIST, the computer will LIST the entire program, including even the comments. Although the comments appear in the LIST, they don't affect the RUN.

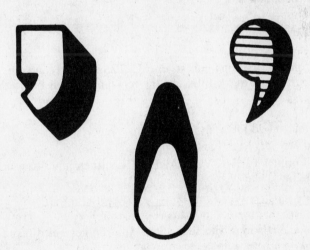

PRETTY OUTPUT

The leftmost part of the screen is called the first **zone**. To the right of that zone lies the second zone.

If your computer's fancy, it also has a third, fourth, and fifth zone; and each zone 16 characters wide, so the entire screen is 80 characters wide.

(If your computer's *not* so fancy, it might have fewer zones, or the zones might be narrower; and the screen might be less than 80 characters wide. To find out about *your* computer's peculiarities, read the "Versions of BASIC" appendix.)

A comma makes the computer jump to a new zone. Here's an example:

```
PRINT "SIN","KING"
```

The computer will print SIN and KING on the same line; but because of the comma before KING, the computer will print KING in the second zone, like this:

```
SIN             KING
```
first zone   second zone   third zone   fourth zone   fifth zone

To turn that example into a program, put a number in front of the line, like this:

```
10 PRINT "SIN","KING"
```

When you type RUN, the computer will print:

```
SIN             KING
```

This program does the same thing:

```
10 PRINT "SIN",
20 PRINT "KING"
```

Line 10 makes the computer print SIN and then jump to the next zone. Line 20 makes the computer print KING. The computer will print:

```
SIN             KING
```

This example's silly:

```
PRINT "LOVE","CRIES","OUT"
```

The computer will print LOVE in the first zone, CRIES in the second zone, and OUT in the third zone, like this:

```
LOVE            CRIES           OUT
```

This example's even sillier:

```
PRINT "LOVE","CRIES","OUT","TO","ME","AT","NIGHT"
```

The computer will print LOVE in the first zone, CRIES in the second, OUT in the third, TO in the fourth, ME in the fifth, and the remaining words below, like this:

```
LOVE            CRIES           OUT             TO              ME
AT              NIGHT
```

This example tells a bad joke:

```
PRINT "I THINK YOU ARE UGLY","I'M JOKING"
```

The computer will print I THINK YOU ARE UGLY, then jump to a new zone, then print I'M JOKING, like this:

```
I THINK YOU ARE UGLY          I'M JOKING
```
first zone   second zone   third zone   fourth zone   fifth zone

When you combine commas with semicolons, you can get weird results:

```
PRINT "EAT","ME";"AT";"BALLS","NO";"W"
```

That line contains commas and semicolons. A comma makes the computer jump to a new zone, but a semicolon does *not* make the computer jump. The computer will print EAT, then jump to a new zone, then print ME and AT and BALLS, then jump to a new zone, then print NO and W. Altogether, the computer will print:

```
EAT             MEATBALLS       NOW
```

Skipping a zone

You can make the computer skip over a zone:

```
PRINT "JOE"," ","LOVES SUE"
```

The computer will print JOE in the first zone, a blank space in the second zone, and LOVES SUE in the third zone, like this:

```
JOE                           LOVES SUE
```
⏜ first zone ⏜ second zone ⏜ third zone ⏜ fourth zone ⏜ fifth zone

You can type that example even more briefly, like this:

```
PRINT "JOE",,"LOVES SUE"
```

Loops

This program makes the computer greet you:

```
10 PRINT "HI",
20 GO TO 10
```

The computer will print HI many times. Each time will be in a new zone, like this:

```
HI          HI          HI          HI          HI
HI          HI          HI          HI          HI
HI          HI          HI          HI          HI
etc.
```

Tables

This program prints a list of words and their opposites:

```
10 PRINT "GOOD","BAD"
20 PRINT "BLACK","WHITE"
30 PRINT "GRANDPARENT","GRANDCHILD"
40 PRINT "HE","SHE"
```

Line 10 makes the computer print GOOD, then jump to the next zone, then print BAD. Altogether, the computer will print:

```
GOOD          BAD
BLACK         WHITE
GRANDPARENT   GRANDCHILD
HE            SHE
```

The first zone contains a column of words; the second zone contains the opposites. Altogether, the computer's printing looks like a table. So **whenever you want to make a table, use zones, by putting commas in your program.**

Let's make the computer print this table:

```
NUMBER        SQUARE
3             9
4             16
5             25
6             36
7             49
8             64
9             81
10            100
```

Here's the program:

```
10 PRINT "NUMBER","SQUARE"
20 FOR I = 3 TO 10
30     PRINT I,I*I
40 NEXT
```

Line 10 prints the word NUMBER at the top of the first column, and the word SQUARE at the top of the second. Line 20 says I goes from 3 to 10; to begin, I is 3. Line 30 makes the computer print:

```
3             9
```

Line 40 makes the computer do the same thing for the next I, and for the next I, and for the next; so the computer prints the whole table.

TAB

When the computer puts a line of information on your screen, the leftmost character in the line is said to be at **position 1**. The second character in the line is said to be at **position 2**.

This command makes the computer skip to position 6 and then print "HOT":

```
PRINT TAB(6)"HOT"
```

The computer will print:

```
     HOT
12345678
```

Here's a fancier example:

```
PRINT TAB(6)"HOT";TAB(13)"BUNS"
```

The computer will skip to the 6th position, then print "HOT", then skip to the 13th position, then print "BUNS":

```
     HOT    BUNS
12345678    13
```

Diagonal

This program prints a diagonal line:

```
10 FOR I = 1 TO 12
20     PRINT TAB(I)"*"
30 NEXT
```

Line 10 says to do the loop twelve times, so the computer does line 20 repeatedly. The first time the computer does line 20, the I is 1, so the computer prints an asterisk at position 1:

```
*
```

The next time, the I is 2, so the computer skips to position 2 and prints an asterisk:

```
 *
```

The next time, the I is 3, so the computer skips to position 3 and prints an asterisk:

```
  *
```

Altogether, the program makes the computer print this picture:

```
*
 *
  *
   *
    *
     *
      *
       *
        *
         *
          *
```

Calendar

Let's make the computer print a calendar for the whole year. We must begin by telling the computer how many days are in each month:

Month's name	Month's length
January	31
February	28 or 29
March	31
April	30
May	31
June	30
July	31
August	31
September	30
October	31
November	30
December	31

That list becomes our data:

```
10 DATA JANUARY,31,FEBRUARY,28,MARCH,31,APRIL,30
20 DATA MAY,31,JUNE,30,JULY,31,AUGUST,31
30 DATA SEPTEMBER,30,OCTOBER,31,NOVEMBER,30,DECEMBER,31
```

(For a leap year, change line 10.)

To make the computer look at that data, tell the computer to READ:

```
40 READ N$,L
```

That makes the computer read a month's Name and Length.

To read *all* the data, the computer should do line 40 twelve times. So put line 40 inside a loop, like this:

English	BASIC
Here are the months and their lengths.	`10 DATA JANUARY,31,FEBRUARY,28,MARCH,31,APRIL,30`
	`20 DATA MAY,31,JUNE,30,JULY,31,AUGUST,31`
	`30 DATA SEPTEMBER,30,OCTOBER,31,NOVEMBER,30,DECEMBER,31`
For each month,	`39 FOR M = 1 TO 12`
read its Name & Length,	`40     READ N$,L`
print its Name,	`50     PRINT N$`
print all its days,	`60     FOR D = 1 TO L`
	`70         PRINT D;`
	`80     NEXT`
and press the ENTER key	`90     PRINT`
twice at end of the month.	`91     PRINT`
	`100 NEXT`

When you run that program, the computer prints a calendar beginning like this:

```
JANUARY
 1  2  3  4  5  6  7  8  9  10  11  12  13  14  15  16  17  18  19  20
21 22 23 24 25 26 27 28 29  30  31

FEBRUARY
 1  2  3  4  5  6  7  8  9  10  11  12  13  14  15  16  17  18  19  20
21 22 23 24 25 26 27 28

MARCH
 1  2  3  4  5  6  7  8  9  10  11  12  13  14  15  16  17  18  19  20
21 22 23 24 25 26 27 28 29  30  31
```

Pretty weeks Although that program makes the computer print the right numbers for each month, it prints the numbers in the wrong places. Let's make the computer print at most 7 numbers in each row, so each is a week.

To print the numbers in the right places, use TAB:

```
70         PRINT TAB(T)D;
```

Line 70 will make the computer print each day in the right position . . . if we define T correctly. But how should we define T?

For Sunday, let's make T be 2, so that Sunday begins at position 2. For Monday, let's make T be 6, so that Monday begins at position 6. For Tuesday, let's make T be 10; for Wednesday, 14; Thursday, 18; Friday, 22; and Saturday, 26. So whenever a day's been printed, T should normally increase by 4 for the next day:

```
71         T=T+4
```

Saturday's the last day of the week; after Saturday, we must begin a new week. So if T has passed Saturday (which is 26), we want T to become 2 (for Sunday); and if there are more days left in the month, we want the computer to press the ENTER key (to start a new week):

```
72          IF T>26 THEN T=2: IF D<L THEN PRINT
```

Which year would you like a calendar for: 1993? 1994? 1995? This program makes a pretty calendar for 1993:

```
1 PRINT "CALENDAR FOR 1993"
2 PRINT
3 T=22
10 DATA JANUARY,31,FEBRUARY,28,MARCH,31,APRIL,30
20 DATA MAY,31,JUNE,30,JULY,31,AUGUST,31
30 DATA SEPTEMBER,30,OCTOBER,31,NOVEMBER,30,DECEMBER,31
39 FOR M = 1 TO 12
40      READ N$,L
50      PRINT N$
51      PRINT "  SUN MON TUE WED THU FRI SAT"
60      FOR D = 1 TO L
70          PRINT TAB(T)D;
71          T=T+4
72          IF T>26 THEN T=2: IF D<L THEN PRINT
80      NEXT
90      PRINT
91      PRINT
100 NEXT
```

Line 1 prints the heading. Line 2 puts a blank line underneath the heading. Since 1993 begins on a Friday, line 3 tells the computer to start T at 22 (which is the position for Friday). Line 51 prints the heading for each month; when you type that line, put 2 blank spaces before SUN.

The computer will print a calendar beginning like this:

```
CALENDAR FOR 1993

JANUARY
SUN MON TUE WED THU FRI SAT
                        1   2
 3   4   5   6   7   8   9
10  11  12  13  14  15  16
17  18  19  20  21  22  23
24  25  26  27  28  29  30
31

FEBRUARY
SUN MON TUE WED THU FRI SAT
     1   2   3   4   5   6
 7   8   9  10  11  12  13
14  15  16  17  18  19  20
21  22  23  24  25  26  27
28

MARCH
SUN MON TUE WED THU FRI SAT
     1   2   3   4   5   6
 7   8   9  10  11  12  13
14  15  16  17  18  19  20
21  22  23  24  25  26  27
28  29  30  31
```

Variations If you want a different year, change lines 1 and 3. For a leap year, change line 10.

If you want the calendar to be taller, insert extra blank lines. To do that, replace "PRINT" by "PRINT: PRINT: PRINT" in lines 2, 72, 90, and 91:

```
2 PRINT: PRINT: PRINT
72            IF T>26 THEN T=2: IF D<L THEN PRINT: PRINT: PRINT
90    PRINT: PRINT: PRINT
91    PRINT: PRINT: PRINT
```

If you want the calendar to look wider (or narrower), change the positions for Sunday, Monday, Tuesday, etc, by changing the T numbers (in lines 3, 51, 71, and 72).

LOCATE

The computer makes the screen show several lines of information. On the screen, the top line is called **line 1**; underneath it is **line 2**; then comes **line 3**; etc.

Each line consists of many characters. The leftmost character is at **position 1**; the next character is at **position 2**; etc.

On the screen, the computer will print wherever you wish.

For example, to make the computer print the word DROWN so that DROWN begins at line 3's 7th position, type this:

```
LOCATE 3,7: PRINT "DROWN"
```

The computer will print the word's first letter (D) at line 3's 7th position. The computer will print the rest of the word afterwards.

You'll see the first letter (D) at line 3's 7th position, the next letter (R) at the next position (line 3's 8th position), the next letter (O) at the next position (line 3's 9th position), etc.

Your computer

Most computers understand the word LOCATE, but *your* computer might be different. To find out about *your* computer, check the "Versions of BASIC" appendix.

PIXELS

The image on the computer's screen is called the **picture**. If you stare at the picture closely, you'll see the picture's composed of thousands of tiny rectangles. Each tiny rectangle is called a **picture's element**, or **pic's el**, or **pixel**, or **pel**.

Coordinates

The tiny rectangle in the screen's upper-left corner is called pixel (0,0); just to the right of it is pixel (1,0); then comes pixel (2,0); etc. Underneath pixel (0,0) is pixel (0,1). Here are the positions of the pixels:

pixel (0,0)	pixel (1,0)	pixel (2,0)	pixel (3,0)	pixel (4,0)	etc.
pixel (0,1)	pixel (1,1)	pixel (2,1)	pixel (3,1)	pixel (4,1)	etc.
pixel (0,2)	pixel (1,2)	pixel (2,2)	pixel (3,2)	pixel (4,2)	etc.
pixel (0,3)	pixel (1,3)	pixel (2,3)	pixel (3,3)	pixel (4,3)	etc.

Each pixel's name consists of two numbers in parentheses. The first number's called the **X coordinate**; the second number's called the **Y coordinate**. For example, if you're talking about pixel (4,3) its X coordinate is 4, and its Y coordinate is 3.

The X coordinate tells how far to the right the pixel is. The Y coordinate tells how far down. So **pixel (4,3) is the pixel that's 4 to the right and 3 down.**

On the computer, the Y coordinate measures how far *down*, not up! If you've had the misfortune of reading old-fashioned math books in which the Y coordinate measured how far up, you'll have to reverse your thinking!

How many pixels?

How many pixels are on the screen? The answer depends on which computer you have.

If your computer's typical, the X coordinate goes from 0 to 319, and the Y coordinate goes from 0 to 199. So on a typical computer, the pixel at the screen's lower right-hand corner is pixel (319,199); and the total number of pixels on the screen is "320 times 200" which is 64 thousand.

But *your* computer might not be "typical". Check the "Versions of BASIC" appendix.

Fundamental shapes

The computer can draw three fundamental shapes: dots, lines, and circles.

To make the computer draw a dot at pixel (100,100), say:

```
PLOT (100,100)
```

Though some computers understand the word PLOT, other computers require a different word instead, such as "DRAW" or "PSET". To find out which word *your* computer understands, check the "Versions of BASIC" appendix. For example, the appendix says that **if you have an IBM PC or clone, you must say "PSET" instead of "PLOT"**. The appendix also says that **if you have an IBM PC or clone, you must give a command such as "SCREEN 1" before giving any graphics commands**, so begin like this:

```
SCREEN 1
PSET (100,100)
```

To make the computer draw a line from pixel (0,0) to pixel (100,100), say:

```
LINE (0,0)-(100,100)
```

To make the computer draw a line from pixel (0,0) to pixel (100,100), and then draw a line from that pixel (100,100) to pixel (70,120), say:

```
LINE (0,0)-(100,100)
LINE -(70,120)
```

To make the computer draw a circle whose center is pixel (100,100) and whose radius is 50, say:

```
CIRCLE (100,100),50
```

The computer draws each shape in white, on a black background.

PAINT

After you've drawn an outline of a shape (by using dots, lines, and circles), you can fill in the middle of the shape, by telling the computer to PAINT the shape.

Here's how to PAINT a shape that you've drawn (such as a circle or a house). Find a pixel that's in the middle of the shape and that's still black; then tell the computer to PAINT, starting at that pixel. For example, if pixel (100,101) is inside the shape and is still black, say:

```
PAINT (100,101)
```

Colors

You can use these colors:

0. black	8. light black (gray)
1. blue	9. light blue
2. green	10. light green
3. cyan (greenish blue)	11. light cyan (aqua)
4. red	12. light red (pink)
5. magenta (purplish red)	13. light magenta
6. brown	14. light brown (yellow)
7. cream (yellowish white)	15. light cream (pure white)

Normally, the PLOT, LINE, CIRCLE, and PAINT commands draw in yellowish white (cream). If you prefer a different color, put a comma and the color's number at the end of the command. For example, if you want to draw a line from (0,0) to (100,0) in green (whose color number is 2), type this:

```
LINE (0,0)-(100,0),2
```

When you give a PAINT command, you must make its color the same as the color of the outline you're filling in.

If your screen is a TV or composite monitor (instead of an RGB monitor) or your computer is obsolescent (such as an Apple 2), you'll get the correct colors only when you draw horizontal lines and adjust the COLOR and TINT dials. When you draw vertical lines or diagonals or circles or dots, the colors will be slightly off.

Boxes

If you type —

```
LINE (0,0)-(100,100),2
```

the computer draws a line from pixel (0,0) to (100,100) using color 2.

If you put the letter B at the end of the LINE command, like this —

```
LINE (0,0)-(100,100),2,B
```

the computer will draw a box instead of a line. One corner of the box will be at pixel (0,0); the opposite corner will be at (100,100); and the box will be drawn using color 2.

If you put BF at the end of the LINE command, like this —

```
LINE (0,0)-(100,100),2,BF
```

the computer will draw a box and also fill it in, by painting its interior.

SOUNDS

To produce sounds, you can say BEEP, SOUND, or PLAY. BEEP appeals to business executives; SOUND appeals to doctors and engineers; and PLAY appeals to musicians.

I'll explain how the typical computer handles the words BEEP, SOUND, and PLAY; but check the "Versions of BASIC" appendix to find out whether *your* computer handles them differently.

BEEP

If you type —

```
BEEP
```

the typical computer will beep. Specifically, it will play a note whose frequency ("pitch") is 800 hertz, and it will play the note for a quarter of a second.

You can say BEEP in the middle of your program. For example, you can tell the computer to BEEP if a person enters wrong data.

Computerized weddings This program makes the computer act as a priest and perform a marriage ceremony:

```
10 INPUT "DO YOU TAKE THIS WOMAN TO BE YOUR LAWFUL WEDDED WIFE";A$
20 IF A$<>"I DO" THEN BEEP: PRINT "TRY AGAIN!": GO TO 10
30 INPUT "DO YOU TAKE THIS MAN TO BE YOUR LAWFUL WEDDED HUSBAND";A$
40 IF A$<>"I DO" THEN BEEP: PRINT "TRY AGAIN!": GO TO 30
50 PRINT "I NOW PRONOUNCE YOU HUSBAND AND WIFE."
```

Line 10 makes the computer ask the groom, "DO YOU TAKE THIS WOMAN TO BE YOUR LAWFUL WEDDED WIFE?" If the groom doesn't say "I DO", line 20 makes the computer beep, say "TRY AGAIN!", and repeat the question. Lines 30 and 40 do the same thing to the bride. Line 50 congratulates the couple for having answered correctly.

SOUND

If you type —

```
SOUND 440,18.2
```

the typical computer will produce a sound. In that command, the 440 is the frequency ("pitch"), measured in hertz (cycles per second); so the sound will be a musical note whose pitch is 440 hertz. (That note happens to be "the A above middle C").

If you replace the 440 by a higher number, the sound will have a higher pitch.

When you were a baby, you could probably hear up to 20000. As you get older, your hearing gets worse, and you can't hear such high notes. Today, the highest sound you can hear is probably somewhere around 14000.

To find out, give yourself a hearing test, by running this program:

```
10 INPUT "WHAT PITCH WOULD YOU LIKE ME TO PLAY";P
20 SOUND P,18.2
30 GO TO 10
```

When you run that program, begin by inputting a low pitch (such as 200). Then input a higher number, then an even higher number, until you finally pick a number so high you can't hear it. (When trying that test, put your ear close to the computer's speaker, which is in the computer's front left corner.) When you've picked a number too high for you to hear, try a slightly lower number. Keep trying different numbers, until you find the highest number you can hear.

Have a contest with your friends: find out which of your friends can hear best.

If you run that program every year, you'll see that your hearing gets gradually worse. For example, when I was 36 years old, the highest pitch I could hear was about 14500, but I can't hear that high anymore. How about *you*?

In those examples, the 18.2 makes the computer produce the sound for 1 second. If you want the sound to last longer — so that it lasts 2 seconds — replace the 18.2 by 18.2*2. For 10 seconds, say 18.2*10. (That's because the computer's metronome beats 18.2 times per second.)

PLAY

If you type —

```
PLAY "CDG#B-A"
```

the typical computer will play the note C, then D, then G sharp, then B flat, then A.

Octave The computer can play in seven octaves, numbered from 0 to 6. Octave 0 consists of very bass notes; octave 6 consists of very high-pitched notes. In each octave, the lowest note is a C: the notes in an octave are C, C#, D, D#, E, F, F#, G, G#, A, A#, and B.

"Middle C" is at the beginning of octave 2. Normally, the computer plays in octave 4. To make the computer switch to octave 3, type *the letter "O"* followed by a 3, like this:

```
PLAY "O3"
```

After giving that command, anything else you PLAY will be in octave 3, until you change octaves again.

Length Besides playing with pitches, you can also play with rhythms ("lengths" of the notes). Normally each note is a "quarter note". To make the computer switch to eighth notes (which are faster), type this:

```
PLAY "L8"
```

Besides using L8 for eighth notes, you can use L16 for sixteenth notes (which are even faster), L32 for thirty-second notes (which are super-fast), and L64 for sixty-fourth notes (which are super-super-fast). For long notes, you can use L2 (which gives a half note) or L1 (which gives a whole note).

You can use any length from L1 to L64. You can even use in-between lengths, such as L7 or L23 (though such rhythms are hard to stamp your foot to).

Dots If you put a period after a note, the computer will multiply the note's length by 1½.

For example, suppose you say:

```
PLAY "L8CE.D"
```

The C will be an 8th note, E will be 1½ times as long as an 8th note, and D will be an 8th note. Musicians call that E a **dotted eighth note**.

If you put *two* periods after a note (like this: E..), the computer will multiply the note's length by 1¾. Musicians say the note is **double dotted**.

If you put *three* periods after a note (like this: E...), the computer will multiply the note's length by 1⅞.

Pause To make the computer pause ("rest") for an eighth note, put a P8 into the music string.

Tempo Normally, the computer plays 120 quarter notes per minute; but you can change that tempo. To switch to 150 quarter notes per minute, say:

```
PLAY "T150"
```

You can switch to any tempo from 32 to 255. The 32 is very slow; 255 is very fast. In musical terms, 40=larghissimo, 50=largo, 63=larghetto, 65=grave, 68=lento, 71=adagio, 76=andantino, 92=andante, 114=moderato, 120=allegretto, 144=allegro, 168=vivace, 188=presto, and 208=prestissimo.

Combine them You can combine all those musical commands into a single PLAY statement. For example, to set the tempo to 150, the octave to 3, the length to 8 (which means an eighth note), and then play C and D, and then change the length to 4 and play E, type this:

```
PLAY "T150O3L8CDL4E"
```

PRINT USING

Suppose you want to add $12.47 to $1.03. The correct answer is $13.50. This almost works:

```
PRINT 12.47+1.03
```

It makes the computer print:

```
 13.5
```

But instead of 13.5, we should try to make the computer print 13.50.

This command forces the computer to print 13.50:

```
PRINT USING "##.##"; 12.47+1.03
```

The "##.##" is called the **picture** or **image** or **format**: it says to print two characters, then a decimal point, then two digits. The computer will print:

```
13.50
```

This command puts that answer into a sentence:

```
PRINT USING "YOU SPENT ##.## AT OUR STORE"; 12.47+1.03
```

The computer will print:

```
YOU SPENT 13.50 AT OUR STORE
```

Rounding

This program makes the computer divide 300 by 7 but round the answer to two decimal places:

```
PRINT USING "##.##"; 300/7
```

When the computer divides 300 by 7, it gets 42.8571, but the format rounds the answer to 42.86. The computer will print:

```
42.86
```

Multiple numbers

Every format (such as "###.##") is a string. You can replace the format by a string variable:

```
10 A$="###.##"
20 PRINT USING A$; 247.91
30 PRINT USING A$; 823
40 PRINT USING A$; 7
50 PRINT USING A$; -5
60 PRINT USING A$; -80.3
```

The computer will print:

```
247.91
823.00
  7.00
 -5.00
-80.30
```

When the computer prints that column of numbers, notice that the computer prints the decimal points underneath each other so that they line up. So **to make decimal points line up, say PRINT USING instead of just PRINT.**

To print those numbers *across* instead of down, say this:

```
PRINT USING "###.##"; 247.91,823,7,-5,-80.3
```

It makes the computer print 247.91, then 823.00, etc., like this:

```
247.91823.00  7.00 -5.00-80.30
```

Since the computer prints those numbers so close together, they're hard to read. To make the computer insert extra space between the numbers, widen the format by putting a fourth "#" before the decimal point:

```
PRINT USING "####.##"; 247.91,823,7,-5,-80.3
```

Then the computer will print:

```
 247.91 823.00   7.00  -5.00 -80.30
```

If you say —

```
PRINT USING "MY ## PALS DRANK ###.# PINTS OF GIN"; 24,983.5
```

the computer will print:

```
MY 24 PALS DRANK 983.5 PINTS OF GIN
```

Oversized numbers

Suppose you say:

```
PRINT USING "###.##"; 16238.7
```

The computer tries to print 16238.7 by using the format "###.##". But since that format allows just three digits before the decimal point, the format isn't large enough to fit 16238.7. So the computer must disobey the format. But the computer also prints a percent sign, which means, "Warning! I am disobeying you!" Altogether, the computer prints:

```
%16238.70
```

Final semicolon

At the end of the PRINT USING statement, you can put a semicolon:

```
10 PRINT USING "##.##"; 13.5;
20 PRINT "CREDIT"
```

Line 10 makes the computer print 13.50. The semicolon at the end of line 10 makes the computer print CREDIT on the same line, like this:

```
13.50CREDIT
```

Advanced formats

Suppose you're running a high-risk business. On Monday, your business runs badly: you *lose* $27,931.60, so your "profit" is *minus* $27,931.60. On Tuesday, your business does slightly better than break-even: your net profit for the day is $8.95.

Let's make the computer print the word PROFIT, then the amount of your profit (such as -$27,931.60 or $8.95), then the word HA (because you're cynical about how your business is going).

You can do that printing in several ways. Let's explore them. . . .

If you say —

```
10 A$="PROFIT#####.##HA"
20 PRINT USING A$; -27931.6
30 PRINT USING A$; 8.95
```

the computer will print:

```
PROFIT-27931.60HA
PROFIT    8.95HA
```

Comma If you change the format to "PROFIT###,###.##HA", the computer will insert a comma if the number is large:

```
PROFIT-27,931.60HA
PROFIT      8.95HA
```

Plus sign If you change the format to "PROFIT+#####.##HA", the computer will print a plus sign in front of any positive number:

```
PROFIT-27931.60HA
PROFIT    +8.95HA
```

Trailing minus To print a negative number, the computer normally prints a minus sign *before* the number. That's called a **leading minus**. You can make the computer put the minus sign *after* the number instead; that's called a **trailing minus**. For example, if you change the format to "PROFIT######.##-HA", the computer will print a

minus sign *after* a negative number (and no minus after a positive number), like this:

```
PROFIT27931.60-HA
PROFIT    8.95 HA
```

Dollar sign Normally, a format begins with ##. If you begin with $$ instead (like this: "PROFIT$$#####.##HA"), the computer will print a dollar sign before the digits:

```
PROFIT-$27931.60HA
PROFIT    $8.95HA
```

Check protection If you begin with ** (like this: "PROFIT**#####.##HA"), the computer will print asterisks before the number:

```
PROFIT*-27931.60HA
PROFIT******8.95HA
```

If you begin with **$ (like this: "PROFIT**$#####.##HA"), the computer will print asterisks and a dollar sign:

```
PROFIT*-$27931.60HA
PROFIT*****$8.95HA
```

When you're printing a paycheck, use the asterisks to prevent the employee from enlarging his salary. Since the asterisks protect the check from being altered, they're called **check protection**.

Combination You can combine several techniques into a single format. For example, you can combine the comma, the trailing minus, and the **$ (like this: "PROFIT**$##,###.##-HA"), so that the computer will print:

```
PROFIT**$27,931.60-HA
PROFIT*******$8.95 HA
```

E notation If you change the format to "PROFIT##.#####^^^^HA", the computer will print numbers by using E notation:

```
PROFIT-2.79316E+04HA
PROFIT 8.95000E+00HA
```

SUBS

SUBROUTINES

Here's a simple program:

```
10 PRINT "THE"
20 GO TO 1000
30 PRINT "DEAD"
40 END

1000 PRINT "BIRD"
1010 PRINT "IS"
1020 GO TO 30
```

It makes the computer print:

```
THE
BIRD
IS
DEAD
```

The program consists of two parts. The main part (lines 10-40) is called the **main routine**; the bottom part (lines 1000-1020) is called the **subroutine**. The bottom line of the main routine says END.

Line 20, which is in the main routine, makes the computer skip to the subroutine. Line 1020, in the subroutine, makes the computer return to the main routine.

To make the program more elegant, change lines 20 and 1020:

```
10 PRINT "THE"
20 GOSUB 1000
30 PRINT "DEAD"
40 END

1000 PRINT "BIRD"
1010 PRINT "IS"
1020 RETURN
```

The new line 20 says: GO to the SUBroutine that begins at line 1000. The new line 1020 says: RETURN to the main routine, where you left off. Like the old program, the new program prints:

```
THE
BIRD
IS
DEAD
```

GOSUB is like GO TO. The GOSUB 1000 means "GO TO line 1000, and remember where you came from"; so the computer goes to line 1000, while remembering that it came from line 20. In line 1020, the RETURN means "RETURN to where you came from"; so the computer returns to line 20, and then proceeds from line 20 to line 30, which prints the word "DEAD".

Bottom lines

The bottom line of a main routine should say END. The bottom line of a subroutine should say RETURN.

Yankee Doodle

This program prints the *original* version of Yankee Doodle:

Print the first verse:
```
10 PRINT "FATHER AND I WENT DOWN TO CAMP"
20 PRINT "ALONG WITH CAPTAIN GOODING,"
30 PRINT "AND THERE WE SAW THE MEN AND BOYS"
40 PRINT "AS THICK AS HASTY PUDDING."
```

Do the chorus, and then come back:
```
50 GOSUB 1000
```

Print the second verse:
```
60 PRINT "AND THERE WAS CAPTAIN WASHINGTON"
70 PRINT "UPON A SLAPPING STALLION,"
80 PRINT "A-GIVING ORDERS TO HIS MEN;"
90 PRINT "I GUESS THERE WERE A MILLION!"
```

Do the chorus, and then come back:
```
100 GOSUB 1000
```

Print the third verse:
```
110 PRINT "THE FLAMING RIBBONS IN HIS HAT,"
120 PRINT "THEY LOOKED SO TARNAL FINE, AH,"
130 PRINT "I WANTED POCKILY TO GET"
140 PRINT "TO GIVE TO MY JEMIMAH."
```

Do the chorus, and then come back:
```
150 GOSUB 1000
```

That's the end of the song:
```
160 END
```

Here's the chorus:
```
1000 PRINT
1010 PRINT "YANKEE DOODLE, KEEP IT UP."
1020 PRINT "YANKEE DOODLE DANDY,"
1030 PRINT "MIND THE MUSIC AND THE STEP,"
1040 PRINT "AND WITH THE GIRLS BE HANDY."
1050 PRINT
1060 RETURN
```

Lines 10-40 print the first verse. Lines 60-90 print the second. Lines 110-140 print the third.

At the end of each verse, the computer is told to "GOSUB 1000", which means go to line 1000, print the chorus (lines 1000-1050), and then RETURN to where it left off.

Lines 1000-1060, which print the chorus, are the subroutine. The verses (lines 10-160) are the main routine.

Lines 1000 and 1050 make the computer print a blank line at the beginning and end of the chorus.

The bottom line of the main routine is END. The bottom line of the subroutine is RETURN.

If you accidentally omit line 160 (which says END), the computer will proceed to do the subroutine an extra time, and then won't know where to RETURN. It will gripe, by saying:

```
RETURN BEFORE GOSUB
```

To avoid such gripes, the last line of a main routine should be END.

Love poem

This program prints a love poem:

```
10 PRINT "THE MOST BEAUTIFUL THING"
20 PRINT "IN THE WHOLE WIDE WORLD"
30 PRINT "IS..."
40 PRINT "LOVE!"
50 PRINT "THE OPPOSITE OF HATE IS"
60 PRINT "LOVE!"
70 PRINT "THE OPPOSITE OF WAR IS"
80 PRINT "LOVE!"
90 PRINT "THE OPPOSITE OF DESPAIR IS"
100 PRINT "LOVE!"
110 PRINT "AND WHEN I LOOK AT YOU,"
120 PRINT "I FEEL LOTS OF"
130 PRINT "LOVE!"
```

In that program, lines 40, 60, 80, 100, and 130 print the word LOVE. Let's make those lines print the word LOVE larger, like this:

Here's how:

```
10 PRINT "THE MOST BEAUTIFUL THING"
20 PRINT "IN THE WHOLE WIDE WORLD"
30 PRINT "IS..."
40 GOSUB 1000
50 PRINT "THE OPPOSITE OF HATE IS"
60 GOSUB 1000
70 PRINT "THE OPPOSITE OF WAR IS"
80 GOSUB 1000
90 PRINT "THE OPPOSITE OF DESPAIR IS"
100 GOSUB 1000
110 PRINT "AND WHEN I LOOK AT YOU,"
120 PRINT "I FEEL LOTS OF"
130 GOSUB 1000
140 END
```

Lines 1000-1070 are the subroutine

```
1000 PRINT "*            *        *           *     * * * * *"
1010 PRINT "*                 *   *       *       *       *"
1020 PRINT "*              *        *        *   *       * * *"
1030 PRINT "*                  *    *          * *       *"
1040 PRINT "* * * *          *              *       * * * *"
1050 PRINT
1060 PRINT
1070 RETURN
```

In that new version, lines 40, 60, 80, 100, and 130 say GOSUB 1000 instead of PRINT "LOVE!". The GOSUB 1000 means: do the subroutine that begins at line 1000. The subroutine prints the word LOVE in large letters.

Old lady

Here are the lyrics to a famous song:

There was an old lady who swallowed a fly,
But I don't know why she swallowed the fly.
Perhaps she'll die.

There was an old lady who swallowed a spider
That wiggled and jiggled and tickled inside her.
She swallowed the spider to catch the fly,
But I don't know why she swallowed the fly.
Perhaps she'll die.

There was an old lady who swallowed a bird.
Oh, how absurd! To swallow a bird!
She swallowed the bird to catch the spider
That wiggled and jiggled and tickled inside her.
She swallowed the spider to catch the fly,
But I don't know why she swallowed the fly.
Perhaps she'll die.

There was an old lady who swallowed a cat.
Imagine that! To swallow a cat!
She swallowed the cat to catch the bird.
She swallowed the bird to catch the spider
That wiggled and jiggled and tickled inside her.
She swallowed the spider to catch the fly,
But I don't know why she swallowed the fly.
Perhaps she'll die.

There was an old lady who swallowed a dog.
I swear on this log! She swallowed that dog!
She swallowed the dog to catch the cat.
She swallowed the cat to catch the bird.
She swallowed the bird to catch the spider
That wiggled and jiggled and tickled inside her.
She swallowed the spider to catch the fly,
But I don't know why she swallowed the fly.
Perhaps she'll die.

There was an old lady who swallowed a goat.
Including its coat, she swallowed that goat!
She swallowed the goat to catch the dog.
She swallowed the dog to catch the cat.
She swallowed the cat to catch the bird.
She swallowed the bird to catch the spider
That wiggled and jiggled and tickled inside her.
She swallowed the spider to catch the fly,
But I don't know why she swallowed the fly.
Perhaps she'll die.

There was an old lady who swallowed a cow.
I don't know how she swallowed that cow!
She swallowed the cow to catch the goat.
She swallowed the goat to catch the dog.
She swallowed the dog to catch the cat.
She swallowed the cat to catch the bird.
She swallowed the bird to catch the spider
That wiggled and jiggled and tickled inside her.
She swallowed the spider to catch the fly,
But I don't know why she swallowed the fly.
Perhaps she'll die.

There was an old lady who swallowed a horse,
And she died, of course!

This program prints the song:

```
10 A$="THERE WAS AN OLD LADY WHO SWALLOWED A "
20 PRINT A$;"FLY.": GOSUB 1070
30 PRINT A$;"SPIDER": GOSUB 1050
40 PRINT A$;"BIRD.": PRINT "OH, HOW ABSURD! TO SWALLOW A BIRD!": GOSUB 1040
50 PRINT A$;"CAT.": PRINT "IMAGINE THAT! TO SWALLOW A CAT!": GOSUB 1030
60 PRINT A$;"DOG.": PRINT "I SWEAR ON THIS LOG! SHE SWALLOWED THAT DOG!": GOSUB
1020
70 PRINT A$;"GOAT.": PRINT "INCLUDING ITS COAT, SHE SWALLOWED THAT GOAT!": GOSUB
1010
80 PRINT A$;"COW.": PRINT "I DON'T KNOW HOW SHE SWALLOWED THAT COW!": GOSUB 1000
90 PRINT A$;"HORSE,": PRINT "AND SHE DIED, OF COURSE!"
100 END

1000 PRINT "SHE SWALLOWED THE COW TO CATCH THE GOAT."
1010 PRINT "SHE SWALLOWED THE GOAT TO CATCH THE DOG."
1020 PRINT "SHE SWALLOWED THE DOG TO CATCH THE CAT."
1030 PRINT "SHE SWALLOWED THE CAT TO CATCH THE BIRD."
1040 PRINT "SHE SWALLOWED THE BIRD TO CATCH THE SPIDER"
1050 PRINT "THAT WIGGLED AND JIGGLED AND TICKLED INSIDE HER."
1060 PRINT "SHE SWALLOWED THE SPIDER TO CATCH THE FLY,"
1070 PRINT "BUT I DON'T KNOW WHY SHE SWALLOWED THE FLY."
1080 PRINT "PERHAPS SHE'LL DIE."
1090 PRINT
1100 RETURN
```

Lines 1000-1100 are a subroutine. That subroutine tells the whole story.

In line 20, the GOSUB says to do just *part* of the subroutine — the part that begins at line 1070. Line 30 says to do *more* of the subroutine — by beginning at line 1050. Lines 40, 50, 60, and 70 do progressively larger chunks of the subroutine. Line 80 is the climax: it says to do *all* of the subroutine.

Line 90 provides a humorous ending.

Nesting

One subroutine can lead to another:

Main routine:	```10 PRINT "MY"```
	```20 GOSUB 1000```
	```30 PRINT "NOSE"```
	```40 END```
Subroutine 1000:	```1000 PRINT "TOE"```
	```1010 PRINT "IS"```
	```1020 GOSUB 2000```
	```1030 PRINT "YOUR"```
	```1040 RETURN```
Subroutine 2000:	```2000 PRINT "STUCK"```
	```2010 PRINT "IN"```
	```2020 RETURN```

The program consists of three routines. The main routine ends with END; each subroutine ends with RETURN.

The main routine consists of lines 10, 20, 30, and 40. Let's see what those lines do.

Line 10 prints MY.

Line 20 makes the computer do subroutine 1000, which prints TOE, prints IS, does subroutine 2000 (STUCK and IN), and prints YOUR.

Line 30 prints NOSE.

Line 40 ends.

So altogether, the computer prints:

```
MY
TOE
IS
STUCK
IN
YOUR
NOSE
```

In that example, subroutine 2000 is **nested in** subroutine 1000.

Instead of being a single string, X$ can be a whole *list* of strings, like this:

$$X\$ = \begin{pmatrix} \text{"HATE"} \\ \text{"LOVE"} \\ \text{"KILL"} \\ \text{"KISS"} \\ \text{"WAR"} \\ \text{"PEACE"} \\ \text{"WHY"} \end{pmatrix}$$

Here's how to make X$ be that list of strings. . . .

Begin your program by saying:

```
10 DIM X$(7)
```

That says X$ will be a list of 7 strings. DIM means **dimension**; the line says the dimension of X$ is 7.

Next, tell the computer what strings are in X$. Type these lines:

```
20 X$(1)="HATE"
30 X$(2)="LOVE"
40 X$(3)="KILL"
50 X$(4)="KISS"
60 X$(5)="WAR"
70 X$(6)="PEACE"
80 X$(7)="WHY"
```

Line 20 says X$'s first string is HATE. Line 30 says X$'s second string is LOVE. The remaining lines define the other strings in X$.

If you'd like the computer to print all those strings, type this:

```
90 FOR I = 1 TO 7: PRINT X$(I): NEXT
```

That means: print all the strings in X$. The computer will print:

```
HATE
LOVE
KILL
KISS
WAR
PEACE
WHY
```

In that program, line 20 talks about X$(1). Instead of saying X$(1), math books say:

$$x_1$$

The "1" is called a **subscript**. Similarly, in line 30, which says X$(2)="LOVE", the number 2 is a subscript. Some programmers pronounce line 30 like this: "X string, subscripted by 2, is LOVE". Some programmers simply say: "X string 2 is LOVE".

In that program, X$ is called an **array** (or **matrix**). Definition: an **array** (or **matrix**) is a variable that has subscripts.

Subscripted DATA

That program said X$(1) is HATE, and X$(2) is LOVE, and so on. This program does the same thing, more briefly:

```
10 DIM X$(7)
20 DATA HATE,LOVE,KILL,KISS,WAR,PEACE,WHY
30 FOR I=1 TO 7: READ X$(I): NEXT
40 FOR I=1 TO 7: PRINT X$(I): NEXT
```

Line 10 says X$ will be a list of 7 strings. Line 20 contains a list of 7 strings. Line 30 makes the computer READ those strings and call them X$. Line 40 makes the computer print them.

In that program, the first three lines say:

```
DIM
```

```
DATA
FOR I
```

Most practical programs begin with those three lines.

Let's lengthen the program, so that the computer prints all this:

```
HATE
LOVE
KILL
KISS
WAR
PEACE
WHY

WHY HATE
WHY LOVE
WHY KILL
WHY KISS
WHY WAR
WHY PEACE
WHY WHY
```

That consists of two verses. The second verse resembles the first verse, except that each line of the second verse begins with WHY.

To make the computer print all that, just add these lines to the program:

```
50 PRINT
60 FOR I = 1 TO 7: PRINT "WHY ";X$(I): NEXT
```

Line 50 leaves a blank line between the first verse and the second verse. Line 60 prints the second verse. Line 60 resembles line 40 (which printed the first verse), except that line 60 prints "WHY " before each X$(I).

Let's add a third verse, which prints the words in reverse order:

```
WHY
PEACE
WAR
KISS
KILL
LOVE
HATE
```

Before printing that third verse, print a blank line:

```
70 PRINT
```

Then print the verse itself. To print the verse, you must print X$(7), then print X$(6), then print X$(5), etc. To do that, you could say:

```
80 PRINT X$(7)
90 PRINT X$(6)
100 PRINT X$(5)
etc.
```

But this way is shorter:

```
80 FOR I = 7 TO 1 STEP -1: PRINT X$(I): NEXT
```

Numeric arrays

Let's make Y be this list of six numbers: 100, 26, 94, 201, 8.3, and -7. To begin, tell the computer that Y will consist of six numbers:

```
10 DIM Y(6)
```

Next, tell the computer what the six numbers are:

```
20 DATA 100,26,94,201,8.3,-7
```

Make the computer READ all that data:

```
30 FOR I = 1 TO 6: READ Y(I): NEXT
```

To make the computer PRINT all that data, type this:

```
40 FOR I = 1 TO 6: PRINT Y(I): NEXT
```

If you want the computer to add those 6 numbers together and print their sum, say:

```
50 PRINT Y(1)+Y(2)+Y(3)+Y(4)+Y(5)+Y(6)
```

Strange example

Getting tired of X and Y? Then pick another letter! For example, you can play with Z:

Silly, useless program	What the program means
`10 DIM Z(5)`	Z will be a list of 5 numbers.
`20 FOR I = 2 TO 5`	
`30    Z(I)=I*100`	Z(2)=200. Z(3)=300. Z(4)=400. Z(5)=500.
`40 NEXT`	
`50 Z(1)=Z(2)-3`	Z(1) is 200-3, so Z(1) is 197.
`60 Z(3)=Z(1)-2`	Z(3) changes to 197-2, which is 195.
`70 FOR I = 1 TO 5: PRINT Z(I): NEXT`	Print Z(1), Z(2), Z(3), Z(4), and Z(5).

Line 70 prints:

```
197
200
195
400
500
```

Problems and solutions

Suppose you want to analyze 50 numbers. Begin your program by saying:

```
10 DIM X(50)
```

Then type the 50 numbers, as data, like this:

```
20 DATA etc.
30 DATA etc.
40 DATA etc.
```

Tell the computer to READ the data:

```
100 FOR I=1 TO 50: READ X(I): NEXT
```

After line 100, do one of the following, depending on which problem you want to solve. . . .

Print all the values of X Solution:

```
110 FOR I = 1 TO 50: PRINT X(I): NEXT
```

Print all the values of X, in reverse order Solution:

```
110 FOR I = 50 TO 1 STEP -1: PRINT X(I): NEXT
```

Print the sum of all the values of X In other words, print X(1)+X(2)+X(3)+ . . . +X(50). Solution: start the sum at 0 —

```
110 S=0
```

and then increase the sum, by adding each X(I) to it:

```
120 FOR I = 1 TO 50: S=S+X(I): NEXT
```

Finally, print the sum:

```
130 PRINT "THE SUM OF ALL THE NUMBERS IS";S
```

Find the average of X In other words, find the average of the 50 numbers. Solution: begin by finding the sum —

```
110 S=0
120 FOR I = 1 TO 50: S=S+X(I): NEXT
```

and then divide the sum by 50:

```
130 PRINT "THE AVERAGE IS";S/50
```

Find out whether any of the values of X is 79.4 In other words, find out whether 79.4 is a number in the list. Solution: if X(I) is 79.4, print "YES" —

```
110 FOR I = 1 TO 50
120    IF X(I)=79.4 THEN PRINT "YES, 79.4 IS IN THE LIST": END
130 NEXT
```

otherwise, print "NO":

```
140 PRINT "NO, 79.4 IS NOT IN THE LIST"
```

In X's list, count how often 79.4 appears
Solution: start the counter at zero —

```
110 C=0
```

and increase the counter each time you see the number 79.4:

```
120 FOR I = 1 TO 50
130    IF X(I)=79.4 THEN C=C+1
140 NEXT
```

Finally, print the counter:

```
150 PRINT "THE NUMBER 79.4 APPEARS";C;"TIMES"
```

Print all the values of X that are negative
In other words, print all the numbers that have minus signs. Solution: begin by announcing your purpose —

```
110 PRINT "HERE ARE THE VALUES THAT ARE NEGATIVE:"
```

and then print the values that are negative; in other words, print each X(I) that's less than 0:

```
120 FOR I = 1 TO 50
130    IF X(I)<0 THEN PRINT X(I)
140 NEXT
```

Print all the values of X that are "above average"
Solution: find the average, and call it A, like this —

```
110 S=0
120 FOR I = 1 TO 50: S=S+X(I): NEXT
130 A=S/50
```

then announce your purpose:

```
140 PRINT "THE FOLLOWING VALUES ARE ABOVE AVERAGE:"
```

Finally, print the values that are above average; in other words, print each X(I) that's greater than A:

```
150 FOR I = 1 TO 50
160    IF X(I)>A THEN PRINT X(I)
170 NEXT
```

Find the biggest value of X
In other words, find which of the 50 numbers is the biggest. Solution: let B stand for the biggest number. Begin by tentatively setting B equal to the first number —

```
110 B=X(1)
```

but if another number is bigger than that B, change B:

```
120 FOR I = 2 TO 50
130    IF X(I)>B THEN B=X(I)
140 NEXT
```

Afterwards, print B:

```
150 PRINT "THE BIGGEST NUMBER IN THE LIST IS";B
```

Find the smallest value of X
In other words, find which of the 50 numbers is the smallest. Solution: let S stand for the smallest number. Begin by tentatively setting S equal to the first number —

```
110 S=X(1)
```

but if another number is smaller than S, change S:

```
120 FOR I = 2 TO 50
130    IF X(I)<S THEN S=X(I)
140 NEXT
```

Afterwards, print S:

```
150 PRINT "THE SMALLEST NUMBER IN THE LIST IS";S
```

Check whether X's list is in strictly increasing order
In other words, find out whether the following statement is true: X(1) is a smaller number than X(2), which is a smaller number than X(3), which is a smaller number than X(4), etc. Solution: if X(I) is *not* smaller than X(I+1), print "NO" —

```
110 FOR I = 1 TO 49
120    IF X(I)>=X(I+1) THEN PRINT "NO, THE LIST IS NOT IN STRICTLY INCREASING OR
DER": END
130 NEXT
```

otherwise, print "YES":

```
140 PRINT "YES, THE LIST IS IN STRICTLY INCREASING ORDER"
```

Test yourself: look at those problems again, and see whether you can figure out the solutions *without peeking at the answers.*

Multiple arrays

Suppose your program involves three lists. Suppose the first list is called A$ and consists of 18 strings; the second list is called B and consists of 57 numbers; and the third list is called C$ and consists of just 3 strings. To say all that, begin your program with this statement:

```
10 DIM A$(18),B(57),C$(3)
```

Double subscripts

You can make X be a **table** of strings, like this:

$$X\$= \begin{pmatrix} \text{"DOG"} & \text{"CAT"} & \text{"MOUSE"} \\ \text{"HOTDOG"} & \text{"CATSUP"} & \text{"MOUSETARD"} \end{pmatrix}$$

Here's how to make X$ be that table....

Begin by saying:

```
10 DIM X$(2,3)
```

That says X$ will be a table having 2 rows and 3 columns.

Then tell the computer what strings are in X$. Type these lines:

```
20 X$(1,1)="DOG"
30 X$(1,2)="CAT"
40 X$(1,3)="MOUSE"
50 X$(2,1)="HOTDOG"
60 X$(2,2)="CATSUP"
70 X$(2,3)="MOUSETARD"
```

Line 20 says: the string in X$'s first row and first column is DOG. Line 30 says the string in X$'s first row and second column is CAT. The remaining lines define the other strings in X$.

If you'd like the computer to print all those strings, type this:

```
80 FOR I = 1 TO 2: FOR J = 1 TO 3: PRINT X$(I,J),: NEXT: PRINT: NEXT
```

That means: print all the strings in X$. The computer will print:

```
DOG          CAT          MOUSE
HOTDOG       CATSUP       MOUSETARD
```

In that program, X$ is called a **table** or **two-dimensional array** or **doubly subscripted array**.

Dog

Cat

Multiplication table

This program prints a multiplication table:

```
10 DIM X(10,4)
20 FOR I = 1 TO 10: FOR J = 1 TO 4: X(I,J)=I*J: NEXT: NEXT
30 FOR I = 1 TO 10: FOR J = 1 TO 4: PRINT X(I,J),: NEXT: PRINT: NEXT
```

Line 10 says X will be a table having 10 rows and 4 columns.

The middle of line 20 says X(I,J)=I*J. That means the number in row I and column J is I*J. For example, the number in row 3 and column 4 is 12.

The beginning of line 20 says "FOR I = 1 TO 10: FOR J = 1 TO 4", so that X(I,J)=I*J for *every* I and J, so *every* entry in the table is defined by multiplication.

Line 30 prints the whole table:

1	2	3	4
2	4	6	8
3	6	9	12
4	8	12	16
5	10	15	20
6	12	18	24
7	14	21	28
8	16	24	32
9	18	27	36
10	20	30	40

Instead of multiplication, you can have addition, subtraction, or division: just change line 20.

Most programmers follow this tradition: **the row's number is called I, and the column's number is called J**. Line 20 obeys that tradition. Notice I comes before J in the alphabet; I comes before J in X(I,J); and "FOR I" comes before "FOR J". If you follow the I-before-J tradition, you'll make fewer errors.

Mouse

Summing a table

Suppose you want to analyze this table:

32.7	19.4	31.6	85.1
-8	402	-61	0
5106	-.2	0	-1.1
36.9	.04	1	11
777	666	55.44	2
1.99	2.99	3.99	4.99
50	40	30	20
12	21	12	21
0	1000	2	500

Since the table has 9 rows and 4 columns, begin your program by saying:

```
10 DIM X(9,4)
```

Each row of the table becomes a row of the DATA:

```
11 DATA 32.7, 19.4, 31.6, 85.1
12 DATA -8, 402, -61, 0
13 DATA 5106, -.2, 0, -1.1
14 DATA 36.9, .04, 1, 11
15 DATA 777, 666, 55.44, 2
16 DATA 1.99, 2.99, 3.99, 4.99
17 DATA 50, 40, 30, 20
18 DATA 12, 21, 12, 21
19 DATA 0, 1000, 2, 500
```

Table

Make the computer READ the data:

```
20 FOR I = 1 TO 9: FOR J = 1 TO 4: READ X(I,J): NEXT: NEXT
```

To make the computer print the table, say this:

```
30 FOR I = 1 TO 9: FOR J = 1 TO 4: PRINT X(I,J),: NEXT: PRINT: NEXT
```

Here are some problems, with solutions. . . .

Find the sum of all the numbers in the table

Solution: start the sum at 0 —

```
100 S=0
```

and then increase the sum, by adding each X(I,J) to it:

```
110 FOR I = 1 TO 9: FOR J = 1 TO 4: S=S+X(I,J): NEXT: NEXT
```

Finally, print the sum:

```
120 PRINT "THE SUM OF ALL THE NUMBERS IS";S
```

The computer will print:

```
THE SUM OF ALL THE NUMBERS IS 8877.84
```

Find the sum of each row

In other words, make the computer print the sum of the numbers in the first row, then the sum of the numbers in the second row, then the sum of the numbers in the third row, etc. Solution: the general idea is —

```
100 FOR I = 1 TO 9
110      print the sum of row I
120 NEXT
```

Here are the details:

```
110 FOR I = 1 TO 9
110      S=0
111      FOR J = 1 TO 4: S=S+X(I,J): NEXT
112      PRINT "THE SUM OF ROW";I;"IS";S
120 NEXT
```

The computer will print:

```
THE SUM OF ROW 1 IS 168.8
THE SUM OF ROW 2 IS 333
THE SUM OF ROW 3 IS 5104.7
etc.
```

Find the sum of each column

In other words, make the computer print the sum of the numbers in the first column, then the sum of the numbers in the second column, then the sum of the numbers in the third column, etc. Solution: the general idea is —

```
100 FOR J = 1 TO 4
110      print the sum of column J
120 NEXT
```

Here are the details:

```
100 FOR J = 1 TO 4
110      S=0
111      FOR I = 1 TO 9: S=S+X(I,J): NEXT
112      PRINT "THE SUM OF COLUMN";J;"IS";S
120 NEXT
```

The computer will print:

```
THE SUM OF COLUMN 1 IS 6008.59
THE SUM OF COLUMN 2 IS 2151.23
THE SUM OF COLUMN 3 IS 75.03
THE SUM OF COLUMN 4 IS 642.99
```

In all the other examples, "FOR I" came before "FOR J"; but in this unusual example, "FOR I" comes *after* "FOR J".

FANCY CALCS

EXPONENTS

The computer understands exponents:

```
PRINT 4^3
```

That line makes the computer use the number 4, three times. The computer will multiply together those three 4's, like this: 4 times 4 times 4. Since "4 times 4 times 4" is 64, the computer will print:

```
64
```

The symbols +, -, *, /, and ^ are all called **operations**.

To solve a problem, the computer uses the three-step process taught in algebra and the "new math". For example, suppose you ask the computer to figure out 70-3^2+8/2*3. The computer will *not* begin by subtracting 3 from 70; instead, it will use the three-step process:

The problem is	70-3^2+8/2*3
Step 1: get rid of ^.	Now the problem is 70- 9 +8/2*3
Step 2: get rid of * and /.	Now the problem is 70- 9 + 12
Step 3: get rid of + and -.	The answer is 73

In each step, it looks from left to right. For example, in step 2, it sees / and gets rid of it before it sees *.

Although exponents are fun, the computer handles them slowly. For example, the computer handles 3^2 more slowly than it handles 3*3. So for speedy calculations, say 3*3 instead of 3^2.

Roots

What positive number, when multiplied by itself, gives 9? The answer is 3, because 3 times itself is 9.

3 **squared** is 9. 3 is called the **square root** of 9.

To make the computer deduce the square root of 9, type this:

```
PRINT SQR(9)
```

The computer will print 3.

When you tell the computer to PRINT SQR(9), make sure you put the parentheses around the 9.

The symbol SQR is called a **function**. The number in parentheses (9) is called the function's **input** (or **argument** or **parameter**). The answer, which is 3, is called the function's **output** (or **value**).

SQR(9) gives the same answer as 9^.5. Most computers handle SQR(9) more quickly than 9^.5.

Cube roots
What number, when multiplied by itself and then multiplied by itself *again*, gives 64? The answer is 4, because 4 times 4 times 4 is 64. The answer (4) is called the **cube root** of 64.

Here's how to make the computer find the cube root of 64:

```
PRINT 64^(1/3)
```

The computer will print 4.

EXP

The letter "e" stands for a special number, which is approximately 2.718281828459045. You can memorize that number easily, if you pair the digits:

2.7 18 28 18 28 45 90 45

That weird number is important in calculus, radioactivity, biological growth, and other areas of science. It's calculated by this formula:

$$e = 1 + \frac{1}{1} + \frac{1}{1*2} + \frac{1}{1*2*3} + \frac{1}{1*2*3*4} + \frac{1}{1*2*3*4*5} \cdots$$

Therefore:

$$e = 1 + 1 + \frac{1}{2} + \frac{1}{6} + \frac{1}{24} + \frac{1}{120} + \cdots$$

EXP(X) means e^X. For example, EXP(3) means e^3, which is e*e*e, which is:

2.718281828459045*2.718281828459045*2.718281828459045

EXP(4) means e^4, which is e*e*e*e. EXP(3.1) means $e^{3.1}$, which is more than e^3 but less than e^4.

Here's a practical application. Suppose you put $732 in a savings account, and the bank promises to give you 5% annual interest "compounded continuously". How much money will you have at the end of the year? The answer is 732*EXP(.05).

Logarithms

Here are some powers of 2:

X	2^X
1	2
2	4
3	8
4	16
5	32
6	64

To compute the logarithm-base-2 of a number, find the number in the right-hand column; the answer is in the left column. For example, the logarithm-base-2 of 32 is 5. The logarithm-base-2 of 15 is slightly less than 4.

The logarithm-base-2 of 64 is 6. That fact is written:

$\log_2 64$ is 6

It's also written:

$\frac{\log 64}{\log 2}$ is 6

To make the computer find the logarithm-base-2 of 64, say:

`PRINT LOG(64)/LOG(2)`

The computer will print 6.

Here are some powers of 10:

X	10^X
1	10
2	100
3	1000
4	10000
5	100000

The logarithm-base-10 of 100000 is 5. The logarithm-base-10 of 1001 is slightly more than 3.

The logarithm-base-10 of 10000 is 4. That fact is written:

$\log_{10} 10000$ is 4

It's also written:

$\frac{\log 10000}{\log 10}$ is 4

To make the computer do that calculation, say:

`PRINT LOG(10000)/LOG(10)`

The computer will print 4.

The logarithm-base-10 is called the **common logarithm**, and is the kind of logarithm used in high school and chemistry. So **if you're studying chemistry and your textbook tells you to find the logarithm of 10000, the textbook means the logarithm-base-10 of 10000, which is LOG(10000)/LOG(10)**.

What happens if you forget the base, and say just LOG(10000) instead of LOG(10000)/LOG(10)? If you say just LOG(10000), the computer will find the **natural logarithm** of 10000, which is $\log_e 10000$ (where e is 2.718281828459045), which isn't what your chemistry textbook wants.

The computer's notation resembles that of arithmetic and algebra, but beware of these contrasts. . . .

Multiplication

To make the computer multiply, you must type an asterisk:

Traditional notation	Computer notation
2n	2*N
5(n+m)	5*(N+M)
nm	N*M

Exponents

Put an exponent in parentheses, if it contains an operation:

Traditional notation	Computer notation
x^{n+2}	X^(N+2)
x^{3n}	X^(3*N)
$5^{2/3}$	5^(2/3)
2^{3^4}	2^(3^4)

Fractions

Put a fraction's numerator in parentheses, if it contains addition or subtraction:

Traditional notation	Computer notation
$\frac{a+b}{c}$	(A+B)/C
$\frac{k-20}{6}$	(K-20)/6

Put a denominator in parentheses, if it contains addition, subtraction, multiplication, or division:

Traditional notation	Computer notation
$\frac{5}{3+x}$	5/(3+X)
$\frac{5a^3}{4b}$	5*A^3/(4*B)

Mixed numbers

A **mixed number** is a number that contains a fraction. For example, 9½ is a mixed number. When you write a mixed number, put a plus sign before its fraction:

Traditional notation	Computer notation
9½	9+1/2

If you're using the mixed number in a further calculation, put the mixed number in parentheses:

Traditional notation	Computer notation
7-2¼	7-(2+1/4)

STRIPPING

Sometimes the computer prints *too* much information: you wish the computer would print less, to save yourself the agony of having to read excess information that's irrelevant to your needs. Whenever the computer prints too much information about a numerical answer, use ABS, INT, or SGN.

ABS removes any minus sign. For example, the ABS of -7.926 is 7.926. So if you say PRINT ABS(-7.926), the computer will print just 7.926.

INT removes any digits after the decimal point, and rounds the number down to an integer that's lower. For example, the INT of 7.926 is 7 (because 7 is an integer that's lower than 7.926); the INT of -7.926 is -8 (because -8 is lower than -7.926).

SGN removes all the digits and replaces them by a 1 — unless the number is 0. For example, the SGN of 7.926 is 1. The SGN of -7.926 is -1. The SGN of 0 is just 0.

ABS, INT, and SGN are all called **stripping functions** or **strippers** or **diet functions** or **diet pills**, because they strip away the number's excess fat and reveal just the fundamentals that interest you.

Here are more details about those three functions. . . .

ABS

To find the **absolute value** of a negative number, just omit the number's minus sign. For example, the absolute value of -7 is 7.

The absolute value of a positive number is the number itself. For example, the absolute value of 7 is 7.

To make the computer find the absolute value of -7, type this:

```
PRINT ABS(-7)
```

The computer will print:

```
7
```

Like SQR, ABS is a function: you must put parentheses after the ABS.

ABS helps you solve math and physics problems that involve "distance". For example, this program computes the distance between two numbers:

```
10 PRINT "I WILL FIND THE DISTANCE BETWEEN TWO NUMBERS."
20 INPUT "WHAT'S THE FIRST NUMBER";X
30 INPUT "WHAT'S THE SECOND NUMBER";Y
40 PRINT "THE DISTANCE BETWEEN THOSE NUMBERS IS";ABS(X-Y)
```

For example, if X is 4, and Y is 7, then the distance between those two numbers is ABS(4-7), which is ABS(-3), which is 3. If you reverse those two numbers, so that X is 7 and Y is 4, the distance between them is ABS(7-4), which is ABS(3), which is still 3.

INT

If you round 17.9 to an integer, what do you get?

If you round 17.9 to the *nearest* integer, you get 18. If you round 17.9 *down* to an integer, you get 17. If you round 17.9 *up* to an integer, you get 18.

To make the computer round 17.9 down to an integer, type this:

```
PRINT INT(17.9)
```

The computer will print:

```
17
```

Notice that INT rounds *down*. INT(17.9) tells the computer to round 17.9 *down* to an integer; the computer gets 17.

Like SQR and ABS, INT is a function: you must put parentheses after the INT.

If you give this command —

```
PRINT INT(-5.2)
```

what number will the computer print? Will it print -5? Or will it print -6 instead? Answer: the computer will print -6, because if today's temperature is -5.2 degrees, and you round the temperature *down*, the temperature becomes colder: -6 degrees. INT rounds *down*. INT(-5.2) is -6.

INT(54) is simply 54.

To explore further the mysteries of rounding, run this program:

```
10 INPUT "WHAT'S YOUR FAVORITE NUMBER";X
20 PRINT INT(X)
30 PRINT -INT(-X)
40 PRINT INT(X+.5)
```

In that program, line 10 asks you to type a number X. Line 20 prints your number rounded *down*; line 30 prints your number rounded *up*; and line 40 prints your number rounded to the *nearest* integer. For example, if you input 17.9, line 20 makes the computer print 17.9 rounded down (which is 17), line 30 makes the computer print 17.9 rounded up (which is 18), and line 40 makes the computer print 17.9 rounded to the nearest integer (which is 18).

Here's the rule: if X is a number, **INT(X) rounds X down; -INT(-X) rounds X up; INT(X+.5) rounds X to the nearest integer**.

Rounding down and rounding up are useful in the supermarket. . . .

Suppose some items are marked "30¢ each", and you have only two dollars. How many can you buy? Two dollars divided by 30¢ is 6.66667; rounding *down* to an integer, you can buy 6.

Suppose some items are marked "3 for a dollar", and you want to buy just one of them. How much will the supermarket charge you? One dollar divided by 3 is 33.3333¢; rounding *up* to an integer, you will be charged 34¢.

By using INT, you can do fancier kinds of rounding:

to round X to the nearest thousand,   ask for INT(X/1000+.5)*1000
to round X to the nearest thousandth, ask for INT(X/.001+.5)*.001

This program rounds a number, so that it will have just a *few* digits after the decimal point:

```
10 INPUT "WHAT'S YOUR FAVORITE NUMBER";X
20 INPUT "HOW MANY DIGITS WOULD YOU LIKE AFTER ITS DECIMAL POINT";D
30 B=10^-D
40 PRINT "YOUR NUMBER ROUNDED IS";INT(X/B+.5)*B
```

Here's a sample run:

```
WHAT'S YOUR FAVORITE NUMBER? 4.28631
HOW MANY DIGITS WOULD YOU LIKE AFTER ITS DECIMAL POINT? 2
YOUR NUMBER ROUNDED IS 4.29
```

SGN

If a number is negative, its **sign** is -1. For example, the sign of -546 is -1.
If a number is positive, its **sign** is +1. For example the sign of 8231 is +1.
The **sign** of 0 is 0.
The computer's abbreviation for "sign" is "SGN". So if you say —

```
PRINT SGN(-546)
```

the computer will print the sign of -546; it will print -1.
If you say —

```
PRINT SGN(8231)
```

the computer will print the sign of 8231; it will print 1.
If you say —

```
PRINT SGN(0)
```

the computer will print the sign of 0; it will print 0.

SGN is the opposite of ABS. Let's see what both functions do to -7.2. ABS removes the minus sign, but leaves the digits:

```
ABS(-7.2) is 7.2
```

SGN removes the digits, but leaves the minus sign:

```
SGN(-7.2) is -1
```

The Latin word for *sign* is **signum**. Most mathematicians prefer to talk in Latin — they say "signum" instead of "sign" — because the English word "sign" sounds too much like the trigonometry word "sine". So mathematicians call SGN the **signum function**.

RANDOM NUMBERS

Usually, the computer is predictable: it does exactly what you say. But sometimes, you want the computer to be *un*predictable.

For example, if you're going to play a game of cards with the computer and tell the computer to deal, you want the cards dealt to be unpredictable. If the cards were predictable — if you could figure out exactly which cards you and the computer would be dealt — the game would be boring.

In many other games too, you want the computer to be unpredictable, to "surprise" you. Without an element of surprise, the game would be boring.

Being unpredictable increases the pleasure you derive from games — and from art. To make the computer act artistic, and create a new *original* masterpiece that's a "work of art", you need a way to make the computer get a "flash of inspiration". Flashes of inspiration aren't predictable: they're surprises.

Here's how to make the computer act unpredictably. . . .

Random integers

This program makes the computer print an unpredictable number from 1 to 5:

```
10 RANDOMIZE
20 PRINT RND(5)
```

Unpredictable numbers are called **random** numbers. Line 10 tells the computer to make the numbers be *completely* unpredictable, *completely* random. Line 20 makes the computer print a random number from 1 to 5, so the computer will print. The computer's choice will be a surprise.

For example, when you type RUN, the computer might print 3. If you run the program a second time, the computer might print a different number (1 or 2 or 4 or 5), or it might print the same number (3). You can't predict which number the computer will print. The only thing you can be sure of is: the number will be from 1 to 5.

For YOUR computer, you'll probably have to write the program slightly differently. To find out your computer's peculiarities, check the "Versions of BASIC" appendix. For example, if you have an IBM PC or clone, that appendix tells you to say "RANDOMIZE TIMER" instead of just "RANDOMIZE", and to say 1+INT(RND*5) instead of just RND(5).

To make the computer print *many* such random numbers, say GO TO:

```
10 RANDOMIZE
20 PRINT RND(5)
30 GO TO 20
```

The computer will print many numbers, like this:

```
3
2
4
4
1
3
5
2
2
5
etc.
```

Each number will be 1 or 2 or 3 or 4 or 5. The order in which the computer prints them is unpredictable. The program's an infinite loop: it won't stop until you abort it. If you run the

program again, the pattern will be different; for example, it might be:

```
1
4
3
3
2
5
1
1
2
etc.
```

When you run that program, the numbers will fly up the screen faster than you can read. To make the numbers easier to read, make the computer print them *across* instead of down; make the computer print like this:

```
3 2 4 4 1 3 5 2 2 5 etc.
```

To do that, put a semicolon in the PRINT statement:

```
10 RANDOMIZE
20 PRINT RND(5);
30 GO TO 20
```

That program prints random numbers up to 5. To see random numbers up to 1000, say RND(1000):

```
10 RANDOMIZE
20 PRINT RND(1000);
30 GO TO 20
```

The computer will print something like this:

```
485 729 8 537 1000 13 1 842 842 156 1000 972
etc.
```

Guessing game

This program plays a guessing game:

```
10 RANDOMIZE
20 PRINT "I'M THINKING OF A NUMBER FROM 1 TO 100."
30 C=RND(100)
40 INPUT "WHAT DO YOU THINK MY NUMBER IS";G
50 IF G<C THEN PRINT "YOUR GUESS IS TOO LOW.": GO TO 40
60 IF G>C THEN PRINT "YOUR GUESS IS TOO HIGH.": GO TO 40
70 PRINT "CONGRATULATIONS!  YOU FOUND MY NUMBER!"
```

Line 20 makes the computer say:

```
I'M THINKING OF A NUMBER FROM 1 TO 100.
```

Line 30 makes the computer think of a random number from 1 to 100; the computer's number is called "C". Line 40 asks the human to guess the number; the guess is called "G".

If the guess is less than the computer's number, line 50 makes the computer say "YOUR GUESS IS TOO LOW" and then GO TO 40, which lets the human guess again. If the guess is *greater* than the computer's number, line 60 makes the computer say "YOUR GUESS IS TOO HIGH" and then GO TO 40.

When the human guesses correctly, the computer arrives at line 70, which prints:

```
CONGRATULATIONS!  YOU FOUND MY NUMBER!
```

Here's a sample run:

```
RUN
I'M THINKING OF A NUMBER FROM 1 TO 100.
WHAT DO YOU THINK MY NUMBER IS? 54
YOUR GUESS IS TOO LOW.
WHAT DO YOU THINK MY NUMBER IS? 73
YOUR GUESS IS TOO HIGH.
WHAT DO YOU THINK MY NUMBER IS? 62
YOUR GUESS IS TOO LOW.
WHAT DO YOU THINK MY NUMBER IS? 68
YOUR GUESS IS TOO LOW.
WHAT TO YOU THINK MY NUMBER IS? 70
YOUR GUESS IS TOO HIGH.
WHAT DO YOU THINK MY NUMBER IS? 69
CONGRATULATIONS!  YOU FOUND MY NUMBER!
```

Dice

This program makes the computer roll a pair of dice:

```
10 RANDOMIZE
20 PRINT "I'M ROLLING A PAIR OF DICE"
30 A=RND(6)
40 PRINT "ONE OF THE DICE SAYS";A
50 B=RND(6)
60 PRINT "THE OTHER SAYS";B
70 PRINT "THE TOTAL IS";A+B
```

Line 20 makes the computer say:

```
I'M ROLLING A PAIR OF DICE
```

Each of the dice has 6 sides. Lines 30 and 40 roll one of the dice, by picking a number from 1 to 6. Lines 50 and 60 roll the other. Line 70 prints the total.

Here's a sample run:

```
I'M ROLLING A PAIR OF DICE
ONE OF THE DICE SAYS 3
THE OTHER SAYS 5
THE TOTAL IS 8
```

Here's another run:

```
I'M ROLLING A PAIR OF DICE
ONE OF THE DICE SAYS 6
THE OTHER SAYS 4
THE TOTAL IS 10
```

Coin flipping

This program makes the computer flip a coin:

```
10 RANDOMIZE
20 IF RND(2)=1 THEN PRINT "HEADS" ELSE PRINT "TAILS"
```

RND(2) is a random number from 1 to 2; so it's either 1 or 2. If it's 1, line 20 makes the computer says HEADS; if it's 2 instead, line 20 makes the computer say TAILS.

Until you type RUN, you won't know which way the coin will flip; the choice is random. Each time you type RUN, the computer will flip the coin again; each time, the outcome is unpredictable.

(Warning: if your computer's too stupid to understand the word ELSE, you must retype line 20; the "Versions of BASIC" appendix explains how.)

Bets Let's permit the human to bet on whether the computer will say HEADS or TAILS. Here's how:

```
10 RANDOMIZE
15 INPUT "DO YOU WANT TO BET ON HEADS OR TAILS";B$
16 IF B$<>"HEADS" AND B$<>"TAILS" THEN PRINT "SAY HEADS OR TAILS": GO TO 15
20 IF RND(2)=1 THEN C$="HEADS" ELSE C$="TAILS"
30 PRINT "THE COIN SAYS ";C$
40 IF C$=B$ THEN PRINT "YOU WIN" ELSE PRINT "YOU LOSE"
```

Line 15 makes the computer ask:

```
DO YOU WANT TO BET ON HEADS OR TAILS?
```

Line 16 makes sure the human says HEADS or TAILS: if the human's answer isn't HEADS and isn't TAILS, the computer gripes. Lines 20 and 30 make the computer flip a coin. Line 40 determines whether the human won or lost the bet.

Here's a sample run:

```
DO YOU WANT TO BET ON HEADS OR TAILS? HEADS
THE COIN SAYS TAILS
YOU LOSE
```

Here's another:

```
DO YOU WANT TO BET ON HEADS OR TAILS? TAILS
THE COIN SAYS TAILS
YOU WIN
```

Here's another:

```
DO YOU WANT TO BET ON HEADS OR TAILS? TAILS
THE COIN SAYS HEADS
YOU LOSE
```

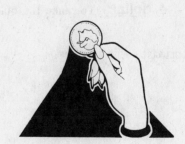

Money To make the program more fun, let the human use money when betting:

```
1 RANDOMIZE
2 S=100
3 PRINT "YOU HAVE";S;"DOLLARS"
10 INPUT "HOW MANY DOLLARS DO YOU WANT TO BET";B
11 IF B>S THEN PRINT "YOU DON'T HAVE THAT MUCH! YOU MUST BET LESS!": GO TO 10
12 IF B<0 THEN PRINT "YOU CAN'T BET LESS THAN NOTHING!": GO TO 10
13 IF B=0 THEN PRINT "I GUESS YOU DON'T WANT TO BET ANYMORE": GO TO 100
15 INPUT "DO YOU WANT TO BET ON HEADS OR TAILS";B$
16 IF B$<>"HEADS" AND B$<>"TAILS" THEN PRINT "SAY HEADS OR TAILS": GO TO 15
20 IF RND(2)=1 THEN C$="HEADS" ELSE C$="TAILS"
30 PRINT "THE COIN SAYS ";C$
40 IF C$=B$ THEN PRINT "YOU WIN";B;"DOLLARS": S=S+B: GO TO 3
50 PRINT "YOU LOSE";B;"DOLLARS": S=S-B: IF S>0 THEN GO TO 3
60 PRINT "YOU'RE BROKE!  TOO BAD!"
100 PRINT "THANKS FOR PLAYING WITH ME!  YOU WERE FUN TO PLAY WITH!"
110 PRINT "I HOPE YOU PLAY AGAIN SOMETIME"
```

Lines 2 and 3 make the computer say:

```
YOU HAVE 100 DOLLARS
```

Line 10 makes the computer ask:

```
HOW MANY DOLLARS DO YOU WANT TO BET?
```

Lines 11-13 make sure the bet is reasonable. Lines 15 and 16 get the human to bet on heads or tails. Lines 20 and 30 flip the coin. Lines 40 and 50 determine whether the human won or lost the bet, and then send the computer back to line 3 for another round (if the human isn't broke yet). Lines 60-110 say good-bye to the human.

Here's a sample run:

```
YOU HAVE 100 DOLLARS
HOW MANY DOLLARS DO YOU WANT TO BET? 120
YOU DON'T HAVE THAT MUCH!  YOU MUST BET LESS!
HOW MANY DOLLARS DO YOU WANT TO BET? 75
DO YOU WANT TO BET ON HEADS OR TAILS? HEADS
THE COIN SAYS TAILS
YOU LOSE 75 DOLLARS
YOU HAVE 25 DOLLARS
HOW MANY DOLLARS DO YOU WANT TO BET? 10
DO YOU WANT TO BET ON HEADS OR TAILS? TAILS
THE COIN SAYS TAILS
YOU WIN 10 DOLLARS
YOU HAVE 35 DOLLARS
HOW MANY DOLLARS DO YOU WANT TO BET? 35
DO YOU WANT TO BET ON HEADS OR TAILS? TAILS
THE COIN SAYS HEADS
YOU LOSE 35 DOLLARS
YOU'RE BROKE!  TOO BAD!
THANKS FOR PLAYING WITH ME!  YOU WERE FUN TO PLAY WITH!
I HOPE YOU PLAY AGAIN SOMETIME
```

Displaying all the dollars To make the output prettier, insert these lines:

```
3 PRINT
4 PRINT "YOU HAVE";S;"DOLLARS!  HERE THEY ARE:"
5 FOR I = 1 TO S
6     PRINT "$";
7 NEXT
8 PRINT
```

Now the run looks like this:

```
RUN

$$$$$$$$$$$$$$$$$$$$$$$$$$$$$$$$$$$$$$$$$$$$$$$$$$$$$$$$$$$$$$$$$$$$$$$$$$$$$$$$$$
$$$$$$$$$$$$$$$$$$$$$$$$$$
HOW MANY DOLLARS DO YOU WANT TO BET? 120
YOU DON'T HAVE THAT MUCH!  YOU MUST BET LESS!
HOW MANY DOLLARS DO YOU WANT TO BET? 75
DO YOU WANT TO BET ON HEADS OR TAILS? HEADS
THE COIN SAYS TAILS
YOU LOST 75 DOLLARS

YOU HAVE 25 DOLLARS!  HERE THEY ARE:
$$$$$$$$$$$$$$$$$$$$$$$$$$$
HOW MANY DOLLARS DO YOU WANT TO BET? 10
DO YOU WANT TO BET ON HEADS OR TAILS? TAILS
THE COIN SAYS TAILS
YOU WIN 10 DOLLARS

YOU HAVE 35 DOLLARS!  HERE THEY ARE:
$$$$$$$$$$$$$$$$$$$$$$$$$$$$$$$$$$$$$
HOW MANY DOLLARS DO YOU WANT TO BET? 35
DO YOU WANT TO BET ON HEADS OR TAILS? TAILS
THE COIN SAYS HEADS
YOU LOSE 35 DOLLARS
YOU'RE BROKE!  TOO BAD!
THANKS FOR PLAYING WITH ME!  YOU WERE FUN TO PLAY WITH!
I HOPE YOU PLAY AGAIN SOMETIME
```

Random decimals

You've seen that RND(5) is a random number from 1 to 5: it's 1 or 2 or 3 or 4 or 5. To get a random *decimal* between 0 and 1, say just RND instead of RND(5).

The decimal that RND produces is at least 0 and is less than 1, so it can be any decimal from 0.0000000 to 0.9999999. For example, the decimal might be 0.2845918.

Suppose you want the computer to *maybe* print LOVE. Here's how to make the probability of printing LOVE be 37 percent:

```
10 RANDOMIZE
20 IF RND<.37 THEN PRINT "LOVE"
```

Your friends

This program makes the computer reveal the secret desires of your friends:

```
10 RANDOMIZE
20 INPUT "TYPE THE NAME OF SOMEONE YOU LIKE...";N$
30 IF RND(3)=1 THEN PRINT N$;" WANTS TO TICKLE YOUR TOES" ELSE PRINT N$;" WANTS
YOU TO WIGGLE YOUR NOSE"
40 GO TO 20
```

Line 20 makes the computer ask:

```
TYPE THE NAME OF SOMEONE YOU LIKE...?
```

Suppose you say SUE. Then N$ is SUE. Line 30 makes the computer pick a random number up to 3. If the number is 1, the computer will say SUE WANTS TO TICKLE YOUR TOES; but if the number is 2 or 3 instead, the computer will say SUE WANTS YOU TO WIGGLE YOUR NOSE. Line 40 makes the computer go back to line 20 and analyze your other friends also.

In that program, the chance is only 1 out of 3 that the computer will say TICKLE YOUR TOES. The chance is 2 out of 3 that the computer will say WIGGLE YOUR NOSE instead.

Get together with your friends and run that program. For exciting results, take off your shoes, and put lipstick on your nose.

Daily horoscope

This program predicts what will happen to you today:

```
10 RANDOMIZE
20 PRINT "YOU WILL HAVE A ";
30 R=RND(5)
40 IF R=1 THEN PRINT "WONDERFUL";
50 IF R=2 THEN PRINT "BETTER-THAN-AVERAGE";
60 IF R=3 THEN PRINT "SO-SO";
70 IF R=4 THEN PRINT "WORSE-THAN-AVERAGE";
80 IF R=5 THEN PRINT "TERRIBLE";
90 PRINT " DAY TODAY"
```

The computer will say —

```
YOU WILL HAVE A WONDERFUL DAY TODAY
```

or —

```
YOU WILL HAVE A TERRIBLE DAY TODAY
```

or some in-between comment.

For inspiration, run that program when you get up in the morning.

CHARACTER CODES

Each character has a code number. For example, the code number for "A" is 65; the code number for "B" is 66; the code number for "C" is 67; etc.

Those code numbers form the **American Standard Code for Information Interchange**, which is abbreviated **ASCII**, which is pronounced "ass key". Programmers say, "the ASCII code number for A is 65".

If you say —

```
PRINT ASC("A")
```

the computer will print the ASCII code number for "A". It will print:

```
65
```

Similarly, if you say PRINT ASC("B"), the computer will print 66.

If you say —

```
PRINT CHR$(65)
```

the computer will print the CHaRacter whose code number is 65. It will print:

```
A
```

The code number for a capital "A" is 65, capital "B" is 66, capital "C" is 67, etc. The code number for a small "a" is 97, small "b" is 98, small "c" is 99, etc. The code number for the digit "0" is 48, the digit "1" is 49, the digit "2" is 50, etc.

Here's the complete list of code numbers, from 33 to 126:

Character:	!	"	#	$	%	&	'	(	)	*	+	,	-	.	/	0	1...9	:	;	<	=	>
Code #:	33	34	35	36	37	38	39	40	41	42	43	44	45	46	47	48	49...57	58	59	60	61	62

Character:	?	@	A	B...Z	[	\	]	^	_	`	a	b...z	{	|	}	~
Code #:	63	64	65	66...90	91	92	93	94	95	96	97	98...122	123	124	125	126

32 is the code number for a blank space. 127 is the code number for DELETE.

Notice that the code number for a quotation mark is 34. Here's how to make the computer print a quotation mark:

```
PRINT CHR$(34)
```

Suppose you want the computer to print:

```
SCHOLARS THINK "HAMLET" IS A GREAT PLAY
```

To make the computer print the quotation marks around "HAMLET", use CHR$(34), like this:

```
PRINT "SCHOLARS THINK ";CHR$(34);"HAMLET";CHR$(34);" IS A GREAT PLAY"
```

Control codes

On the typical computer's keyboard, you'll see a key marked CONTROL (or CTRL). That CONTROL key is near the left SHIFT key.

While you hold down the CONTROL key, you can tap the A key; that's called a **controlled A**. The code number for a controlled A is 1. Similarly, the code number for a controlled B is 2; a controlled C is 3; etc.

Holding down the CONTROL key subtracts 64 from the code number of the other key. For example, the A key is normally 65, so a controlled A is 65-64, which is 1. The B key is normally 66, so a controlled B is 66-64, which is 2.

You've seen that a controlled A has code 1, and a controlled B has code 2. Controlled @ has code 0. In fact, by using the CONTROL key, you can generate all the characters that have codes from 0 to 31.

Graphics codes

The code numbers from 128 up to 255 are used for graphics.

Explore

To explore your computer's ability to print both text and graphics, run this program:

```
10 FOR I = 33 TO 255
20     PRINT I;CHR$(I);"  ";
30 NEXT
```

The computer will print each number and its associated character, like this:

```
 33 !   34 "   35 #   36 $   etc.
```

When the computer finally reaches 128, it will start printing graphics characters.

In that program, you can try starting I at a number lower than 33. For example, you can try starting I at 5. But be careful: some of those low numbers will make your computer act very strangely!

On the Apple, do *not* say PRINT CHR$(4). The CHR$(4) might make your computer turn on the disk drive and start wrecking your disk!

If your computer is typical, you can make it beep by saying:

```
PRINT CHR$(7)
```

Printer codes

If you say —

```
PRINT "LOVE"
```

the computer will print LOVE on your screen. If you say —

```
LPRINT "LOVE"
```

the typical computer will print LOVE on paper (instead of your screen) by using a printer.

The most popular printers are manufactured by Epson. You can make an Epson printer do weird things on paper, by giving a special CHR$ command.

An Epson normally prints 10 characters per inch. You can change that:

Purpose	Command
print 17 characters per inch, so the characters are <u>condensed</u>	`LPRINT CHR$(15);`
cancel the condensed printing	`LPRINT CHR$(18);`
print 12 characters per inch, so the characters are <u>elite</u>	`LPRINT CHR$(27)"M";`
cancel the elite printing	`LPRINT CHR$(27)"P";`
print 5 characters per inch, so the characters are <u>enlarged</u>	`LPRINT CHR$(14);`
cancel the enlarged printing	`LPRINT CHR$(20);`
print with <u>proportional spacing</u>, so "m" is wider than "i"	`LPRINT CHR$(27)"p1";`
cancel the proportional spacing	`LPRINT CHR$(27)"p0";`

When an Epson finishes printing a line of characters, it normally jerks the paper up a sixth of an inch (so the next line of characters is a sixth of an inch below the first line, and the Epson prints six lines per inch). Computerists say, "The Epson normally **feeds** a sixth of an inch." You can change that amount:

Purpose	Command
feed 1/8 of an inch	`LPRINT CHR$(27)"0";`
feed about 1/10 of an inch (7/72 inch)	`LPRINT CHR$(27)"1";`
feed n/72 of an inch	`LPRINT CHR$(27)"A"CHR$(n);`
feed n/216 of an inch	`LPRINT CHR$(27)"3"CHR$(n);`
go back to normal: feed 1/6 of an inch	`LPRINT CHR$(27)"2";`

Here are some other fancy commands you can give:

Purpose	Command
beep for about a tenth of a second	`LPRINT CHR$(7);`
print italics	`LPRINT CHR$(27)"4";`
cancel the italics	`LPRINT CHR$(27)"5";`
print subscripts (tiny char. below line)	`LPRINT CHR$(27)"S1";`
print superscripts (tiny char. above line)	`LPRINT CHR$(27)"S0";`
cancel subscripts and superscripts	`LPRINT CHR$(27)"T";`
horizontal fill, so that "..." becomes "—"	`LPRINT CHR$(27)"E";`
cancel the horizontal fill	`LPRINT CHR$(27)"F";`
vertical fill, so that ":" becomes "⎮"	`LPRINT CHR$(27)"G";`
cancel the vertical fill	`LPRINT CHR$(27)"H";`
move to the top of the next page	`LPRINT CHR$(12);`
move to the right, to the next tab stop	`LPRINT CHR$(9);`
move left, to the previous character	`LPRINT CHR$(9);`
move left, all the way to the margin	`LPRINT CHR$(27)"<";`
make left margin be n characters wide	`LPRINT CHR$(27)"l"CHR$(n);`
make right margin be at position n	`LPRINT CHR$(27)"Q"CHR$(n);`
cancel all previous CHR$ commands	`LPRINT CHR$(27)"Q";`

Let's analyze the word "SMART".

Length

Since "SMART" has 5 characters in it, the **length** of "SMART" is 5. If you say —

```
PRINT LEN("SMART")
```

the computer will print the LENgth of "SMART"; it will print:

```
5
```

Left, right, middle

The left two characters of "SMART" are "SM". If you say —

```
PRINT LEFT$("SMART",2)
```

the computer will print:

```
SM
```

Try this program:

```
10 A$="SMART"
20 PRINT LEFT$(A$,2)
```

Line 10 says A$ is "SMART". Line 20 says to print the left 2 characters of A$, which are "SM". The computer will print:

```
SM
```

If A$ is "SMART", here are the consequences. . . .

LEN(A$) is the LENgth of A$. It is 5.
LEFT$(A$,2) is the LEFT 2 characters of A$. It is "SM".
RIGHT$(A$,2) is the RIGHT 2 characters of A$. It is "RT".
MID$(A$,2) is the MIDdle of A$, beginning at the 2nd character. It is "MART".
MID$(A$,2,3) begins at the 2nd character and includes 3 characters. It's "MAR".

<u>Changing the middle</u> You can change the middle of a string, like this:

```
10 A$="BUNKERS"
20 MID$(A$,2)="OWL"
30 PRINT A$
```

Line 10 says A$ is "BUNKERS". Line 20 changes the middle of A$ to "OWL"; the change begins at the 2nd character of A$. Line 30 prints:

```
BOWLERS
```

Here's a variation:

```
10 A$="BUNKERS"
20 MID$(A$,2)="AD AGENCY"
30 PRINT A$
```

Line 10 says A$ is "BUNKERS". Line 20 says to change the middle of A$, beginning at the 2nd character of A$. But "AD AGENCY" is too long to become part of "BUNKERS". The computer uses as much of "AD AGENCY" as will fit in "BUNKERS". The computer will print:

```
BAD AGE
```

Another variation:

```
10 A$="BUNKERS"
20 MID$(A$,2,1)="OWL"
30 PRINT A$
```

Line 10 says A$ is "BUNKERS". Line 20 says to change the middle of A$, beginning at the 2nd character of A$. But the ",1" makes the computer use just 1 letter from "OWL". Line 30 prints:

```
BONKERS
```

Adding strings

You can add strings together, to form a longer string:

```
10 A$="FAT"+"HER"
20 PRINT A$
```

Line 10 says A$ is "FATHER". Line 20 makes the computer print:

```
FATHER
```

Searching in a string

You can make the computer search in a string to find another string. To make the computer search IN the STRing "NEEDED" to find "ED", say:

```
PRINT INSTR("NEEDED","ED")
```

Since "ED" begins at the third character of "NEEDED", the computer will print:

```
3
```

If you say —

```
PRINT INSTR("NEEDED","EY")
```

the computer will search in the string "NEEDED" for "EY". Since "EY" is *not* in "NEEDED", the computer will print:

```
0
```

If you say —

```
PRINT INSTR(4,"NEEDED","ED")
```

the computer will hunt in the string "NEEDED" for "ED"; but the hunt will begin at the 4th character of "NEEDED". The computer finds the "ED" that begins at the 5th character of "NEEDED". The computer will print:

```
5
```

Clock

The typical computer has a built-in clock. To set the clock to 7 seconds after 1:45PM, type this:

```
TIME$="13:45:07"
```

To set the date to January 24, 1996, type this:

```
DATE$="01-24-1996"
```

Afterwards, whenever you want to find out the current time and date, type this:

```
PRINT TIME$
PRINT DATE$
```

If you say —

```
PRINT TIMER
```

the computer will tell you how many seconds have elapsed since midnight.

When you turn off the typical computer, it forgets the time and date. When you turn it on again, tell it the new time and date.

String-number conversion

This program converts a string to a number:

```
10 A$="72.6"
20 B=VAL(A$)
30 PRINT B+1
```

Line 10 says A$ is the string "72.6". Line 20 says B is the numeric VALue of A$, so B is the number 72.6. Line 30 prints:

```
73.6
```

VAL converts a string to a number. The opposite of VAL is STR$, which converts a number to a string. For example, STR$(-7.2) is the string "-7.2".

STR$(81.4) is the string " 81.4". Notice that in the string " 81.4", the 8 comes after a space (instead of coming after a minus sign).

Repeating characters

Suppose you love the letter B (because it stands for Big, Bold, and Beautiful) and want to print "BBBBBBBBBBBBBBBBBBBB". Here's a short-cut:

```
PRINT STRING$(20,"B")
```

That tells the computer to print a string of 20 B's.

Here's a different way to accomplish the same goal:

```
PRINT STRING$(20,66)
```

That tells the computer to print, 20 times, the character whose ASCII code number is 66.

STRING$ can make the computer repeat a single character, but not a whole word. So if you say STRING$(20,"BLOW"), the computer will *not* repeat the word "BLOW"; instead, the computer will repeat just the first character of "BLOW" (which is "B").

The study of triangles is called **trigonometry** — and the computer can do it for you!

For example, look at this triangle:

In that triangle, the left angle is 30°, the lower-right angle is 90°, and the longest side (the hypotenuse) is 1 inch long.

The side opposite the 30° angle is called the **sine** of 30°; the remaining side is called the **cosine** of 30°:

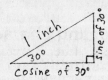

How long is the sine of 30°? How long is the cosine of 30°?

Since the longest side (the hypotenuse) is 1 inch long, and since the sine and the cosine are shorter sides, the sine and the cosine must each be shorter than 1 inch. So the lengths of the sine and cosine are each less than 1. But which decimals are they?

To find out, you can use a ruler. You'll discover that the sine is half an inch long, and the cosine is nearly seven-eighths of an inch long. But a faster and more accurate way to measure the sine and cosine is to let the computer do it! Yes, the computer can calculate triangles in its mind!

This program makes the computer measure the sine and cosine of 30°:

```
10 D=ATN(1)/45
20 PRINT SIN(30*D)
30 PRINT COS(30*D)
```

Line 10 is a special formula that defines D to mean "degrees". Line 20 prints the sine of 30 degrees; the computer will print:

```
.5
```

Line 30 prints the cosine of 30 degrees; the computer will print a decimal that's slightly less than .87.

The computer can measure the sine and cosine of *any* size angle. Try it! For example, to make the computer print the sine and cosine of a 33° angle, say:

```
10 D=ATN(1)/45
20 PRINT SIN(33*D)
30 PRINT COS(33*D)
```

If you choose an angle of -33° instead of 33°, the triangle will dip down instead of rising up, and so the sine will be a negative number instead of positive.

In lines 20 and 30, the "*D" is important: it tells the computer that you want the sine of 33 **degrees**. If you accidentally omit the "*D", the computer will print the sine of 33 **radians** instead. (A radian is larger than a degree. A radian is about 57.3 degrees. More precisely, a radian is 180/π degrees.)

Tangent

The sine divided by the cosine is called the **tangent**. For example, to find the tangent of 33°, divide the sine of 33° by the cosine of 33°.

To make the computer print the tangent of 33°, you could tell the computer to PRINT SIN(33*D)/COS(33*D). But to find the tangent more quickly and easily, just say PRINT TAN(33*D), by adding this line to your program:

```
40 PRINT TAN(33*D)
```

Arc functions

The opposite of the tangent is called the **arctangent**:

the tangent   of 30° is about .58
the arctangent of .58 is about 30°

Similarly, the opposite of the sine is called the **arcsine**, and the opposite of the cosine is called the **arccosine**.

This program prints the arctangent of .58, the arcsine of .5, and the arccosine of .87:

```
10 D=ATN(1)/45
20 PRINT ATN(.58)/D
30 X=.5: PRINT ATN(X/SQR(1-X*X))/D
40 X=.87: PRINT 90-ATN(X/SQR(1-X*X))/D
```

Line 10 is the special formula that defines "D" to be "degrees". Line 20 prints the arctangent of .58, in degrees. (If you omit the "/D", the computer will print the answer in radians instead of degrees.) Line 30 sets X equal to .5 and then prints its arcsine (by using a formula that combines ATN with SQR). Line 40 sets X equal to .87 and then prints its arccosine (by using a formula that combines 90 with ATN and SQR). The answer to each of the three problems is about 30 degrees.

TYPES OF NUMBERS

BASIC can handle three types of numbers: **integers**, **real numbers**, and **double-precision numbers**.

Generally speaking, an **integer** is a number that has no decimal point; a **real number** has a decimal point but no more that 7 digits; a **double-precision number** has a decimal point and more than 7 digits. For example, -27 is an integer, -27.51431 is a real number, and -27.514318 is a double-precision number.

Even though -27 is an integer, -27.0 is *not* an integer: it's a real number instead. -27.000000 is a double-precision number.

The highest permissible integer is 32767; the lowest permissible integer is -32768. If you try to type an integer higher than 32767 or lower than -32768, the computer will automatically add a decimal point at the end of the number, so that the number becomes real or double-precision. (The decimal point will appear in the computer's RAM but not necessarily on your screen.)

Any number that contains an E (such as 7E2) is real, even if the number contains no decimal point or contains more than 7 digits. To make such a number to be double-precision instead, type a D instead of an E (like this: 7D2).

Accuracy

The computer handles integers accurately. If you type a real number, the computer tries to handle it accurately, but sometimes makes slight mistakes with the 7th digit. If you type a double-precision number, the computer handles the first 16 digits accurately, but makes slight mistakes with the 17th digit.

Speed

The computer handles integers quickly, real numbers slowly, and double-precision numbers *very* slowly.

RAM consumption

When the computer handles numbers, it automatically compresses them so that the numbers consume very little RAM. Each integer consumes just 2 bytes of RAM, each real number consumes 4 bytes, and each double-precision number consumes 8 bytes.

For example, if your program says DIM X(50,20), the array X contains 50 rows of 20 numbers, making 1000 numbers altogether; and if each number is real (4 bytes), the entire array consumes 4000 bytes — theoretically. In practice, the array also contains a few extra bytes, for bureaucratic overhead. So the array contains slightly *more* than 4000 bytes — which is roughly 4K.

On most computers, BASIC is limited to 64K: if you buy extra RAM beyond 64K, BASIC ignores it. Most of that 64K is consumed by the lines of your program, the DOS, and BASIC itself, so only a few K are left for arrays.

Variables

An ordinary variable (such as X) stands for a real number. For example, you can say X=3.7, which makes X be the real number 3.7. If you say X=3, the computer will make X be 3.0 instead to make X be a real number.

You can create four kinds of variables. A simple variable (such as X) or a variable that ends in an exclamation point (such as X!) is a real; a variable that ends in a dollar sign (such as X$) is a string; a variable that ends in a percent sign (such as X%) is an integer; a variable that ends in a number sign (such as X#) is double-precision.

If you begin your program by saying —

```
1 DEFINT A-Z
```

all the simple variables (such as X) will be integers instead of reals.

What to do

Write your program simply, without worrying about which numbers and variables are integers, real numbers, and double-precision numbers. But after your program is finished and debugged, edit the program, by making the following changes, which improve the program's speed and accuracy.

All integers If your program doesn't involve any decimals or huge numbers, make line 1 say DEFINT A-Z. That will turn every variable into an integer, so that the program runs faster and consumes less RAM.

Mostly integers If your program involves just a *few* decimals or huge numbers, make line 1 say DEFINT A-Z, and put an exclamation point after every variable that stands for a decimal or huge number.

Extra accuracy If you want to perform one of the computations extra-accurately, put a number sign after all variables the computation involves (for example, say X# instead of X), and put at least 8 digits in each number (for example, say 2.4000000 instead of 2.4).

Before you make those changes, *check the "Versions of BASIC" appendix* to find out whether your computer is different.

INVENTING A PROGRAM

First, decide on your ultimate goal. Be optimistic. Maybe you'd like the computer to play the perfect game of chess? Or translate every English sentence into French?

Research the past

Chances are, whatever you want the computer to do, someone else has thought of the same idea already, and written a program for it.

Find out. Ask your friends. Ask the people in nearby schools, computer stores, computer centers, companies, libraries, and bookstores. Look through books and magazines. There are even books that list what programs have been written. Ask the company you bought your computer from.

Even if you don't find exactly the program you're looking for, you may find one that's close enough to be okay, or that will work with just a little fixing, or can serve as *part* of your program, or will at least give you a *clue* as to where to begin. In one of the textbooks or magazines, you'll probably find a discussion of the problem you're trying to solve, and the pros and cons of various solutions to it — some methods are faster than others.

Remember: if you keep your head in the sand, and don't look at what other people have done already, your programming effort may turn out to be a mere exercise useless to the rest of the world.

Simplify

All too often, programmers embark on huge projects and never get them done. Once you have an idea of what's been done before, and how hard your project seems to be, simplify it. Instead of making the computer play a perfect game of chess, how about settling for a game in which the computer plays unremarkably but at least doesn't cheat? Instead of translating every English sentence into French, how about translating just English colors? (We wrote that program already.) In other words, **pick a less ambitious, more realistic goal**, which if you achieve it, will make you feel good and will be a steppingstone to your ultimate goal.

Finding a bug in a program is like finding a needle in a haystack: removing the needle is easier if the haystack is small than if you wait until more hay's been piled on.

Specify the I/O

Make your new, simple goal more precise. That's called **specification**. One way to be specific is to **draw a picture, showing what your screen will look like if your program's running successfully**.

In that picture, find the lines typed by the computer. They become the PRINT statements in your program. Find the lines typed by the human: they become the INPUT statements. Now you can start writing your program: **write the PRINT and INPUT statements** on paper, with a pencil, and leave blank lines between them. You'll fill in the blanks later.

Suppose you want the computer to find the average of two numbers. Your picture will look like this:

```
RUN
WHAT'S THE FIRST NUMBER? number
WHAT'S THE SECOND NUMBER? number
THE AVERAGE IS number
```

Your program at this stage will be:

```
10 INPUT "WHAT'S THE FIRST NUMBER";A
20 INPUT "WHAT'S THE SECOND NUMBER";B
etc.
100 PRINT "THE AVERAGE IS";C
```

All you have left to do is figure out what the "etc." is. Here's the general method. . . .

Choose your statements

Suppose you didn't have a computer. Then how would you get the answer?

Would you have to use a mathematical formula? If so, put the formula into your program, but remember that the left side of the equation must have just one variable. For example, if you're trying to solve a problem about right triangles, you might have to use the Pythagorean formula $A^2+B^2=C^2$; but the left side of the equation must have just one variable, so your program must say $A=SQR(C^2-B^2)$, or $B=SQR(C^2-A^2)$, or $C=SQR(A^2+B^2)$, depending on whether you're trying to compute A, B, or C.

Would you have to use a memorized list, such as an English-French dictionary or the population of each state or the weight of each chemical element? If so, that list becomes your DATA, and you need to READ it. If it would be helpful to have the data numbered, so the first piece of data is called X(1), the next piece of data is called X(2), etc., use the DIM statement.

Subscripts are particularly useful if one long list of information will be referred to *several* times in the program.

Does your reasoning repeat? That means your program should have a loop. If you know how many times to repeat, say FOR . . . NEXT. If you're not sure how often, say GO TO. If the thing that's to be repeated isn't repeated immediately, but only after several other things have happened, call the repeated part a **subroutine**, put it at the *end* of your program (followed by RETURN), and say GOSUB whenever you want it done.

At some point in your reasoning, do you have to make a *decision*? Do you have to choose among several alternatives? The way to say "choose" is: IF . . . THEN. If you want the computer to make the choice arbitrarily, "by chance", rather than because of a reason, say: IF RND(2)=1 THEN.

Do you have to compare two things? The way to say "compare A with B" is: IF A=B THEN.

Write pseudocode

Some English teachers say that before you write a paper, you should make an outline. Some computer teachers give similar advice about writing programs.

The "outline" can look like a program in which some of the lines are written in plain English instead of computerese. For example, one statement in your outline might be:

```
130 A = the average of the twelve values of X
```

Such a statement, written in English instead of in computerese, is called **pseudocode**. Later, when you fill in the details, expand that pseudocode into the following:

```
130 S=0
131 FOR I = 1 TO 12
132    S=S+X(I)
133 NEXT
134 A=S/12
```

Organize yourself

Keep the program's over-all organization simple. That will make it easier for you to expand it and find bugs. Here is some folklore, handed down from generation to generation of programmers, that will simplify your organization. . . .

Use top-down programming. That means write a one-sentence description of your program; then expand that sentence to several sentences; then expand each of those sentences to several more sentences; and so on, until you can't expand any more. Then turn each of thse new sentences into lines of program. Your program will then be in the same order as the English sentences, and therefore organized the same way as an English-speaking mind.

A variation is to **use subroutines.** That means writing the essence of the program as a very short main routine; instead of filling in the grubby details immediately, replace each piece of grubbiness by the word GOSUB. After the main routine is written, write each subroutine. Your program will be like a good book: your main routine will move swiftly, and the annoying details will be relegated to the appendices at the back; the appendices are called **subroutines.** Keep each subroutine down to 50 lines; if it starts getting longer and grubbier, replace each piece of grubbiness by a GOSUB to *another* subroutine, written afterwards and having higher line numbers.

Avoid GO TO. It's hard for a human to understand a program that's a morass of GO TO statements. It's like trying to read a book where each paragraph says to turn to a different page! When you *must* say GO TO, try to go forward instead of backwards, and not go too far.

Divide your program into modules. A **module** is a bunch of consecutive lines forming a unit that cannot be "punctured"; in other words, there is no GO-TO-type statement outside the module that sends the computer to the module's middle; the only way the module can be activated is by starting with its top line. (If the module's particularly nice, the only way it can be deactivated is by arriving at its bottom line; in other words, there is no GO-TO-type statement in the module's middle that sends the computer outside the module.) If you used top-down programming, each module probably corresponds to one sentence in your program's description. Write that sentence at the top of the module, and put an apostrophe to the left of it.

Use variables

After you've written a few lines of your program, you may find that your reasoning "almost repeats"; several lines bear a strong resemblance to each other. You can't use GO TO or FOR . . . NEXT or GOSUB . . . RETURN unless the lines repeat exactly. To make the repetition complete, use a variable to represent the parts that are different.

For example, suppose your program contains these lines:

```
130 PRINT 29.3428+9.87627*SQR(5)
140 PRINT 29.3428+9.87627*SQR(7)
150 PRINT 29.3428+9.87627*SQR(9)
160 PRINT 29.3428+9.87627*SQR(11)
170 PRINT 29.3428+9.87627*SQR(13)
180 PRINT 29.3428+9.87627*SQR(15)
190 PRINT 29.3428+9.87627*SQR(17)
200 PRINT 29.3428+9.87627*SQR(19)
210 PRINT 29.3428+9.87627*SQR(21)
```

Each of those lines says PRINT 29.3428+9.87627*SQR(a number). The number keeps changing, so call it X. Lines 130-210 can be replaced by:

```
130 FOR X= 5 TO 21 STEP 2
140    PRINT 29.3428+9.87627*SQR(X)
150 NEXT
```

Here's a harder example to fix:

```
130 PRINT 29.3428+9.87627*SQR(5)
140 PRINT 29.3428+9.87627*SQR(97.3)
150 PRINT 29.3428+9.87627*SQR(8.62)
160 PRINT 29.3428+9.87627*SQR(.4)
170 PRINT 29.3428+9.87627*SQR(200)
180 PRINT 29.3428+9.87627*SQR(12)
190 PRINT 29.3428+9.87627*SQR(591)
200 PRINT 29.3428+9.87627*SQR(.2)
210 PRINT 29.2428+9.87627*SQR(100076)
```

Again, let's use X. Those nine lines can be combined like this:

```
130 DATA 5,97.3,8.62,.4,200,12,591,.2,100076
140 FOR I = 1 TO 9
150    READ X
160    PRINT 29.3428+9.87627*SQR(X)
170 NEXT
```

This one's even tougher:

```
130 PRINT 29.3428+9.87627*SQR(A)
140 PRINT 29.3428+9.87627*SQR(B)
150 PRINT 29.3428+9.87627*SQR(C)
160 PRINT 29.3428+9.87627*SQR(D)
170 PRINT 29.3428+9.87627*SQR(E)
180 PRINT 29.3428+9.87627*SQR(F)
190 PRINT 29.3428+9.87627*SQR(G)
200 PRINT 29.3428+9.87627*SQR(H)
210 PRINT 29.3428+9.87627*SQR(I)
```

Let's assume A, B, C, D, E, F, G, H, and I have been computed earlier in the program. The trick to shortening those lines is to change the names of the variables. Throughout the program, say X(1) instead of A, say X(2) instead of B, say X(3) instead of C, etc. Say DIM X(9) at the beginning of your program. Then lines 130-210 can be written:

```
130 FOR I=1 TO 9
140    PRINT 29.3428+9.87627*SQR(X(I))
150 NEXT
```

MAKE IT EFFICIENT

Your program should be **efficient**. That means it should use as little of the computer's time and memory as possible.

To use less of the computer's memory, make your DIMensions as small as possible. Try writing the program without any arrays at all; if that turns out to be terribly inconvenient, use the smallest and fewest arrays possible.

To use less of the computer's time, avoid having the computer do the same thing more than once.

These lines force the computer to compute SQR(8.2*N+7) three times:

```
50 PRINT SQR(8.3*N+7)+2
60 PRINT SQR(8.3*N+7)/9.1
70 PRINT 5-SQR(8.3*N+7)
```

You should change them to:

```
49 K=SQR(8.3*N+7)
50 PRINT K+2
60 PRINT K/9.1
70 PRINT 5-K
```

These lines force the computer to compute X^9+2 a hundred times:

```
50 FOR I = 1 TO 100
60     PRINT (X^9+2)/I
70 NEXT
```

You should change them to:

```
49 K=X^9+2
50 FOR I = 1 TO 100
60     PRINT K/I
70 NEXT
```

These lines force the computer to count to 100 twice:

```
50 S=0
60 FOR I = 1 TO 100
70     S=S+X(I)
80 NEXT
90 PRINT "THE SUM OF THE X'S IS";S
100 P=1
110 FOR I = 1 TO 100
120     P=P*X(I)
130 NEXT
140 PRINT "THE PRODUCT OF THE X'S IS";P
```

You should change them to:

```
50 S=0
51 P=1
60 FOR I = 1 TO 100
70     S=S+X(I)
71     P=P*X(I)
80 NEXT
90 PRINT "THE SUM OF THE X'S IS";S
140 PRINT "THE PRODUCT OF THE X'S IS";P
```

Here are more tricks for making your program run faster. . . .

Instead of exponents, use multiplication:

Slow	Faster
50 Y=X^2	50 Y=X*X

Combine statements, to form a single line:

Slow	Faster
50 A=3	50 A=3: B=7
60 B=7	

Warning: an IF statement cannot be combined with a later statement.

Cannot be combined
```
50 IF I<1 THEN GO TO 200
60 B=7
```

If a number contains a decimal point and is in a loop, turn the number into a variable:

Slow	Faster
	49 C=3.1
50 FOR I = 1 TO 900	50 FOR I = 1 TO 900
60 S=S+3.1/I	60 S=S+C/I
70 NEXT	70 NEXT

Omit the variable after NEXT (unless the FOR...NEXT loop contains another FOR...NEXT loop):

Slow	Faster
50 NEXT I	50 NEXT

If your program doesn't involve decimals or large numbers, put this statement at the beginning of your program:

```
1 DEFINT A-Z
```

If your program involves just a *few* decimals or large numbers, begin your program by saying DEFINT A-Z, and put an exclamation point after every variable that stands for a real number.

Alphabetizing

Suppose you want the computer to alphabetize a list of names. What's the best strategy?

Imagine trying to alphabetize the list yourself — each name is written on a file card, and you have to put the deck of cards in alphabetical order.

One strategy would be to compare the second card with the first, and swap them if necessary; then look at the third card, and swap if necessary; and so on to the end of the deck. A different strategy would be to put all the A's in one pile, all the B's in another, etc., and then sort each pile.

Which strategy is better? If the file has ten cards or less, the swap method is faster; if the file is very long, the 26-pile method is faster but requires space to lay out 26 piles.

Which method would make a more efficient program? That depends on how long the file is and whether your computer lacks fast parts or large memory.

Prime numbers

An integer is called **composite** if it's the product of two other integers. 35 is composite, because it's 5*7; 9 is composite, because it's 3*3; 12 is composite, because it's 2*6; 13 is *not* composite, and is therefore called **prime**. This program tells whether a number is prime or composite:

```
10 INPUT "WHAT'S YOUR FAVORITE POSITIVE INTEGER";N
20 FOR I = 1 TO N-1
30     FOR J = 1 TO N-1
40         IF N=I*J THEN PRINT N;"IS";I;"TIMES";J;"AND COMPOSITE": END
50     NEXT
60 NEXT
70 PRINT N;"IS PRIME"
```

Line 10 waits for you to type a number N. Line 40 checks whether N is the product of two other integers; if it is, the computer says N is composite.

How efficient is that program? Since it contains no arrays, it doesn't require much space in the memory. But if N turns out to be prime, line 40 is encountered once for every I and once for every J; altogether it's encountered $(N-1)^2$ times. If N is a large number, around a million, $(N-1)^2$ is around a trillion. To do line 40 a trillion times will take a typical microcomputer many years. In fact, if you say that your favorite number is 999983 (which is close to a million), the typical microcomputer will take about *200 years* before it comes to the conclusion that your number is prime! By the time the program finishes running, you'll be dead and so will your children! The program's very inefficient.

Some small improvements are possible; for example, I and J can start at 2 instead of 1. But so long as you have a loop inside a loop, the time will remain very large.

The following strategy requires just one loop: divide N by every integer less than it, to see whether the quotient is ever an integer. Here's the program:

```
10 INPUT "WHAT'S YOUR FAVORITE POSITIVE NUMBER";N
20 FOR I = 2 TO N-1
40     Q=N/I: IF Q=INT(Q) THEN PRINT N;"IS";I;"TIMES";Q;"AND COMPOSITE":END
60 NEXT
70 PRINT N;"IS PRIME"
```

Line 40 consists of two parts. The first part says to divide N by an integer (I); the quotient's called Q. The second part says that if Q is an integer, N is composite.

How efficient is our new program? If N turns out to be prime, line 40 is encountered once for every I; altogether it's encountered N-2 times. That's less than in the previous program, where it was encountered $(N-1)^2$ times. If N is about a million, our new program is nearly a million times faster than the previous one! To determine whether 999983 is prime, the new program takes a typical microcomputer about 3 hours instead of 200 years.

We can improve the program even further. If an N can't be divided by 2, it can't be divided by any even number; so after checking divisibility by 2, we have to check divisibility by just 3, 5, 7, . . . , N-2. Let's put that short-cut into our program, and also say that every N less than 4 is prime:

```
10 INPUT "WHAT'S YOUR FAVORITE NUMBER";N
11 IF N<4 THEN PRINT N;"IS PRIME":END
12 Q=N/2: IF Q=INT(Q) THEN PRINT N;"IS 2 TIMES";Q;"AND COMPOSITE": END
20 FOR I = 3 TO N-2 STEP 2
40     Q=N/I: IF Q=INT(Q) THEN PRINT N;"IS";I;"TIMES";Q;"AND COMPOSITE": END
60 NEXT
70 PRINT N;"IS PRIME"
```

Line 12 checks divisibility by 2; lines 20-60 check divisibility by 3, 5, 7, . . . , N-2. If N is prime, line 40 is encountered N/2 - 2 times, which is about half as often as in the previous program; so our new program takes about half as long to run. On a typical microcomputer, it takes about 1½ hours to handle 999983.

Our goal was to find a pair of integers whose product is N. If there is such a pair of integers, the smaller one will be no more than the square root of N, so we can restrict our hunt to the integers not exceeding the square root of N:

```
10 INPUT "WHAT'S YOUR FAVORITE NUMBER";N
11 IF N<4 THEN PRINT N;"IS PRIME":END
12 Q=N/2: IF Q=INT(Q) THEN PRINT N;"IS 2 TIMES";Q;"AND COMPOSITE": END
20 FOR I = 3 TO SQR(N)*1.00001 STEP 2
40     Q=N/I: IF Q=INT(Q) THEN PRINT N;"IS";I;"TIMES";Q;"AND COMPOSITE": END
60 NEXT
70 PRINT N;"IS PRIME"
```

The "1.00001" is to give a margin of safety, in case the computer rounds SQR(N) a bit down. If N is near a million, line 40 is encountered about 500 times, which is much less than the 500,000 times encountered in the previous program and the 1,000,000,000,000 times in the original. This program lets the typical microcomputer handle 999983 in about 6 seconds. That's much quicker than the earlier versions, which required 1½ hours, or 3 hours, or 200 years!

Moral: a few small changes in a program can make the computer take 6 seconds instead of 200 years.

The frightening thing about this example is that the first version we had was so terrible, but the only way to significantly improve it was to take a totally fresh approach. To be a successful programmer, you must always keep your mind open, and hunt for fresh ideas.

DON'T BE SILLY

After you've written a program, skim through it to see whether any of its lines are silly. Eliminate the silly lines, so that your program becomes briefer, simpler, and more pleasant.

In the following examples, I assume your program is numbered 10, 20, 30, 40, . . .

Don't tell the computer to GO TO the next line

For example, don't say:

```
30 GO TO 40
```

Omit it. The computer will go to line 40 anyway.

Here's another example of a GO TO that goes to the next line:

```
30 IF X<7 THEN GO TO 40
```

Omit it. The computer will go to line 40 anyway.

Here's another example of a GO TO that goes to the next line:

```
30 IF X<7 THEN PRINT "WOW" ELSE GO TO 40
```

Omit the "ELSE GO TO 40"; just say:

```
30 IF X<7 THEN PRINT "WOW"
```

Don't write an IF that skips over just one line

For example, don't write:

```
30 IF X<7 THEN GO TO 50
40 PRINT "WOW"
```

That line 30 is an IF that skips over just line 40. It's silly! Combine lines 30 and 40 into a single line:

```
30 IF X>=7 THEN PRINT "WOW"
```

Don't write an IF followed by its opposite

For example, don't write:

```
30 IF X<7 THEN PRINT "GEE"
40 IF X>=7 THEN PRINT "WOW"
```

Combine them into a single line:

```
30 IF X<7 THEN PRINT "GEE" ELSE PRINT "WOW"
```

(That combination works only on computers that understand the word ELSE.)

Here's another example of an IF followed by its opposite:

```
30 IF X<7 THEN GO TO 100
40 IF X>=7 THEN PRINT "WOW"
```

Remove the IF from line 40:

```
30 IF X<7 THEN GO TO 100
40 PRINT "WOW"
```

The new version does the same thing as the original, because the computer reaches the new 40 only if X is not less than 7.

Here's another IF followed by its opposite:

```
30 IF X<7 THEN GO TO 50
40 IF X>=7 THEN PRINT "WOW"
```

Applying the same technique as before, remove the IF from line 40:

```
30 IF X<7 THEN GO TO 50
40 PRINT "WOW"
```

But also notice that line 30 is an IF that skips over just one line; we've uncovered another piece of silliness! Applying more cosmetics, we get down to a single line:

```
30 IF X>=7 THEN PRINT "WOW"
```

Here's another IF followed by its opposites:

```
30 IF X<7 THEN GO TO 100
40 IF X=7 THEN GO TO 200
50 IF X>7 THEN PRINT "WOW"
```

Remove the last IF:

```
30 IF X<7 THEN GO TO 100
40 IF X=7 THEN GO TO 200
50 PRINT "WOW"
```

AVOID ROUND-OFF ERRORS

The computer cannot handle decimals accurately. If you say X=.1, the computer can't set X equal to .1 exactly; instead, it will set X equal to a number very, very close to .1. The reason for the slight inaccuracy is that the computer thinks in "binary", not decimals; and .1 can*not* be expressed in binary exactly.

Usually you won't see the slight inaccuracy: when you ask the computer to PRINT a number, the computer prints it rounded to six significant figures, and the inaccuracy is so small it doesn't show up in the rounded result. But **there are three situations in which the inaccuracy can be noticed:**

1. Telling the computer to do A-B, where A is almost equal to B, and the first several digits of A are the same as the first several digits of B. For example, if you ask a typical microcomputer to print 8.001-8, the computer will *not* print .001; instead it will print .000999451. The same thing happens if you do 8.001+(-8).

If you ask the typical microcomputer to print 987654.1-987654, it will print .125 instead of .1. The error can get magnified: if you ask the computer to multiply 987654.1-987654 by 1000, it will print .125*1000, which is 125, instead of .1*1000, which is 100. If you ask it to find the reciprocal of 987654.1-987654, it will print 1/.125, which is 8, instead of 1/.1, which is 10.

Those are the errors produced by a *typical* microcomputer. The errors produced by *your* computer might be slightly more or less. But even if your computer is a maxi that costs $10,000,000, it makes those same kinds of errors.

2. Saying "FOR X = A TO B STEP C", where C is a decimal and the loop will be done many times. For example:

```
10 FOR X = 1 TO 2 STEP .1
20     PRINT X
30 NEXT
```

Theoretically, the computer should print 1, 1.1, 1.2, 1.3, 1.4, 1.5, 1.6, 1.7, 1.8, 1.9, and 2. But that's not what actually happens. In line 10, the computer can't handle the decimal .1 accurately. The last few numbers the typical microcomputer thinks of are:

slightly more than 1.7
slightly more than 1.8
slightly more than 1.9

The computer does *not* think of the next number, slightly more than 2.0, because line 10 says not to go past 2. In line 20, the word PRINT makes the computer print the numbers rounded to six significant digits, so it prints:

```
1
1.1
1.2
1.3
1.4
1.5
1.6
1.7
1.8
1.9
```

It does not print 2.

If you want to compute 1 + 1.1 + 1.2 + 1.3 + 1.4 + 1.5 + 1.6 + 1.7 + 1.8 + 1.9 + 2, you might be tempted to write this program:

```
5 S=0
10 FOR X = 1 TO 2 STEP .1
20     S=S+X
30 NEXT
40 PRINT S
```

The computer will print a reasonable-looking answer: 14.5. But that "answer" is wrong, because the last number it added was slightly more than 1.9; it never added 2. The correct answer is 16.5.

One remedy is to change line 10 to this:

```
10 FOR X = 1 TO 2.05 STEP .1
```

The .05 after the 2 allows for the margin of error. The general strategy is to change —

```
10 FOR X = A TO B STEP C
```

to this:

```
10 FOR X = A TO B+C/2 STEP C
```

An alternative remedy is to replace —

```
10 FOR X = 1 TO 2 STEP .1
```

by this pair of lines:

```
10 FOR I = 10 TO 20
11     X= I/10
```

As I goes from 10 to 20, X will go from 1 to 2 in steps of .1. This remedy is the most accurate of all, since it eliminates decimals from line 10. But the division in line 11 makes the program very slow.

3. Asking the computer whether two numbers X and Y are equal. It's unwise to ask whether X is *exactly* equal to Y, since both X and Y have probably been affected by some slight error. Instead, ask the computer whether the difference between X and Y is much tinier than Y:

Bad   **Good**
IF X=Y THEN   IF ABS(X-Y)<=.000001*ABS(Y) THEN

The .000001 is requesting that the first six significant digits of X be the same as the first six significant digits of Y (except that the sixth significant digit might be off by one).

Why binary?

From those discussions, you might think computers should be made differently, and that they should use the decimal system instead of binary. There are two counterarguments.

First, binary arithmetic is faster.

Second, even if computers were using the decimal system, inaccuracy would still occur. To store the fraction 2/3 accurately by using the decimal system, the computer would have to store a decimal point followed by infinitely many 6's. That would require an infinite amount of space in memory, which is impossible (unless you know how to build an infinitely large computer?) So even in the decimal system, some fractions must be approximated instead of handled exactly.

Begin with the tiny

According to mathematicians, addition is supposed to obey these laws:

A+0 is exactly the same as A
A+B is exactly the same as B+A
A+-A is exactly the same as 0
(A+B)+C is exactly the same as A+(B+C)

On the computer, the first three laws hold, but the last does not. If A is a decimal tinier than C, the computer does (A+B)+C more accurately than A+(B+C). So **to add a list of numbers accurately, begin by adding together the tiniest decimals in the list.**

When you've written a program, **test** it: type RUN and see whether it works.

If the computer does *not* gripe, your tendency will be to say "Whoopee!" Don't cheer too loudly. **The answers the computer is printing may be wrong.** Even if its answers look reasonable, don't assume they're right: the computer's errors can be very subtle. Check some of its answers by doing them with a pencil.

Even if the answers the computer prints are correct, don't cheer. Maybe you were just lucky. Type different input, and see whether your program still works. Chances are, there's something you can input that will make your program go crazy or print a wrong answer. Your mission: to find input that will reveal the existence of a bug.

Try six kinds of input. . . .

Try simple input

Type in simple integers, like 2 and 10, so the computation is simple, and you can check the computer's answers easily.

Try input that increases

See how the computer's answer changes when the input changes from 2 to 1000.

Does the change in the computer's answer look reasonable? Does the computer's answer go up when it should go up, and down when it should go down? . . . and by a reasonable amount?

Try input testing each IF

For a program that says —

```
30 IF X<7 THEN GO TO 100
```

input an X less than 7 (to see whether line 100 works), then an X greater than 7 (to see whether line 40 works), then an X equal to 7 (to see whether you really want "<" instead of "< ="), then an X very close to 7, to check round-off error.

For a program that says —

```
30 IF A^2+B<C THEN GO TO 100
```

input an A, B, and C that make A^2+B less than C. Then try inputs that make A^2+B very close to C.

Try extreme input

What happens if you input:

a huge number, like 45392000000 or 1E35?
a tiny number, like .00000003954 or 1E-35?
a trivial number, like 0 or 1?
a typical number, like 45.13?
a negative number, like -52?

Find out.

If the input is supposed to be a string, what happens if you input AAAAA or ZZZZZ? If there are supposed to be two inputs, what happens if you input the same thing for each?

Try input making some lines act strange

If your program contains division, try input that will make the divisor be zero or a tiny decimal close to zero. If your program contains the square root of a quantity, try input that will make the quantity be negative. If your program says "FOR I=A TO B", try input that will make B be less than A, then equal to A. If your program mentions X(I), try input that will make I be zero or negative or greater than the DIM.

Try input that causes round-off error: for a program that says "A−B" or says "IF A=B THEN", try input that will make A almost equal B.

Try garbage

Many people hate computers because they often print wrong answers. A computer can print a wrong answer because its machinery is broken, or because a program has a bug. But **the main reason why computers print wrong answers is that the input is incorrect. Incorrect input is called <u>garbage</u>. It has several causes. . . .**

<u>The user's finger slips</u> Instead of 400, he inputs 4000. Instead of 27, he inputs 72. Trying to type .753, he leaves out the decimal point.

<u>The user got wrong information</u> He tries to input the temperature, but his thermometer is leaking. He tries to input the results of a questionnaire, but everybody who filled out his questionnaires lied.

<u>The instructions aren't clear</u> The program asks HOW FAR DID THE BALL FALL, and the user doesn't know whether to type the distance in feet or in meters.

Is time to be given in seconds or minutes? Are angles to be measured in degrees or radians?

If the program asks WHAT IS YOUR NAME, should the user type JOE SMITH or "SMITH,JOE" or just JOE?

Can the user input Y instead of YES?

Maybe the user isn't clear about whether to insert commas, quotation marks, and periods. If several items are to be typed, should they be typed on the same line or on separate lines? If your program asks HOW MANY BROTHERS AND SISTERS DO YOU HAVE, and the user has 2 brothers and 3 sisters, should he type 5 or "2,3" or "2 BROTHERS AND 3 SISTERS"?

For a quiz that asks WHO WAS THE FIRST U.S. PRESIDENT, what if the user answers GEORGE WASHINGTON or simply WASHINGTON or G. WASHINGTON or GENERAL GEORGE WASHINGTON or PRESIDENT WASHINGTON or MARTHA'S HUSBAND? Make the instructions clearer:

```
WHO WAS THE FIRST U.S. PRESIDENT (GIVE JUST HIS LAST NAME)?
```

<u>The user is trying to be funny or sabotage the computer</u> Instead of inputting his name, he types an obscene comment. When asked how many brothers and sisters he has, he says 275.

<u>Responsibility</u> It's your responsibility as a programmer to make sure that the directions for using your program are clear, and that the program rejects ridiculous input.

For example, if your program is supposed to print weekly paychecks, it should refuse to print checks for more than $10000. Your program should contain these lines:

```
20 INPUT "HOW MUCH MONEY DID THE EMPLOYEE EARN";E
30 IF E>10000 THEN PRINT E;"IS QUITE A BIG PAYCHECK! I DON'T BELIEVE YOU.": PRINT "PLEASE RETYPE YOUR REQUEST.": GO TO 20
```

Line 30 is called an **error trap** (or an **error-handling routine**). Your program should contain several, to prevent printing checks that are too small (2¢?) or negative or otherwise ridiculous ($200.73145?)

To see how your program reacts to input that's either garbage or unusual, **ask the person sitting next to you to run your program.** That person might input something you never thought of.

DOCUMENT IT

Write an explanation that helps other people understand your program. An explanation is called **documentation**; when you write an explanation, you're **documenting** the program.

You can write the documentation on a separate sheet of paper (to be put in the computer center's library), or you can make the computer print the documentation when the user types RUN or LIST.

A popular device is to begin the RUN by making the computer ask the user:

DO YOU NEED INSTRUCTIONS?

You need two kinds of documentation: how to use the program, and how the program was written.

How to use the program

Your explanation of how to use the program should include:

the program's name
how to get the program from the disk
the program's purpose
a list of other programs that must be combined with this program, to make a workable combination
the correct way to type the input and data (show an example)
the correct way to interpret the output
the program's limitations (input it can't handle, a list of error messages that might be printed, round-off error)
a list of bugs you haven't fixed yet

How the program was written

An explanation of how you wrote the program will help other programmers borrow your ideas, and help them expand your program to meet new situations. It should include:

your name
the date you finished it
the computer you wrote it for
the language you wrote it in (probably BASIC)
the name of the method you used ("solves quadratic equations by using the quadratic formula")
the name of the book or magazine where you found the method
the name of any program you borrowed ideas from
an informal explanation of how program works ("It loops until A>B, then computes the weather forecast.")
the purpose of each module
the meaning of each variable
the meaning of reaching a line (if the program says IF X<60 THEN GO TO 1000, say "Reaching line 1000 means the student flunked.")

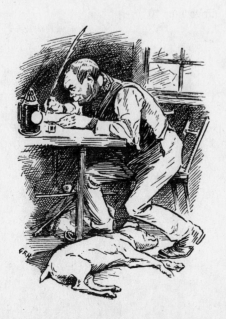

WEIRD FEATURES

FANCY INPUT

The typical INPUT statement looks like this:

```
10 INPUT "WHAT IS YOUR NAME";N$
```

It makes the computer ask "WHAT IS YOUR NAME?" then wait for you to answer to question. So when you run the program, the conversation looks like this:

```
WHAT IS YOUR NAME? MARIA
```

Notice that the computer automatically adds a question mark at the end of the question, and leaves a blank space after the question mark.

Omitting the question mark

If you want to omit the question mark and the blank space, replace the semicolon by a comma:

```
10 INPUT "WHAT IS YOUR NAME",N$
```

The computer will omit the question mark and the blank space, so the conversation will look like this:

```
WHAT IS YOUR NAMEMARIA
```

Here's a prettier example of how to use the comma:

```
10 INPUT "PLEASE TYPE YOUR NAME...",N$
```

The conversation will look like this:

```
PLEASE TYPE YOUR NAME...MARIA
```

Here's an even prettier example:

```
10 INPUT "TO BECOME A MOVIE STAR, TYPE YOUR NAME NEXT TO THE STARS***";N$
```

The conversation will look like this:

```
TO BECOME A MOVIE STAR, TYPE YOUR NAME NEXT TO THE STARS***MARIA
```

Omitting the prompt

The typical INPUT statement contains a question, such as "WHAT IS YOUR NAME". The question is called the **prompt**. If you wish, you can omit the prompt, like this:

```
10 INPUT N$
```

That line doesn't include a question, but the computer still prints a question mark followed by a blank space, so the conversation looks like this:

```
? MARIA
```

To make that example more practical, add a PRINT statement above line 10, like this:

```
9 PRINT "PLEASE TYPE YOUR NAME AFTER THE QUESTION MARK"
10 INPUT N$
```

That makes the conversation look like this:

```
PLEASE TYPE YOUR NAME AFTER THE QUESTION MARK
? MARIA
```

Adjacent printing

Here's a simple program:

```
10 INPUT "WHAT IS YOUR NAME";N$
20 PRINT "!!!WHAT A WONDERFUL NAME!!!"
```

It produces this conversation:

```
WHAT IS YOUR NAME? MARIA
!!!WHAT A WONDERFUL NAME!!!
```

To have more fun, insert a semicolon immediately after the word INPUT, like this:

```
10 INPUT;"WHAT IS YOUR NAME";N$
20 PRINT "!!!WHAT A WONDERFUL NAME!!!"
```

The conversation will begin normally:

```
WHAT IS YOUR NAME? MARIA
```

But when you press the ENTER key after MARY, the extra semicolon makes the computer print line 20 *next* to MARIA, like this:

```
WHAT IS YOUR NAME? MARIA!!!WHAT A WONDERFUL NAME!!!
```

To surprise your friends, run this program:

```
10 INPUT;"WHAT IS YOUR NAME";N$
20 PRINT N$;N$;N$
```

The program begins by asking:

```
WHAT IS YOUR NAME?
```

Suppose the person says MARIA, like this:

```
WHAT IS YOUR NAME? MARIA
```

When the person presses the ENTER key after MARIA, line 20 automatically prints MARIA three more times afterwards, like this:

```
WHAT IS YOUR NAME? MARIAMARIAMARIAMARIA
```

This program asks for your first name, then your last name:

```
10 INPUT;"WHAT IS YOUR FIRST NAME";F$
20 INPUT "   WHAT IS YOUR LAST NAME";L$
```

Line 10 makes the conversation begin like this:

```
WHAT IS YOUR FIRST NAME? MARIA
```

When you press the ENTER key after MARIA, the extra semicolon in line 10 makes line 20 appear on the same line, like this:

```
WHAT IS YOUR FIRST NAME? MARIA    WHAT IS YOUR LAST NAME?
```

If you answer WONG, the whole conversation looks like this:

```
WHAT IS YOUR FIRST NAME? MARIA    WHAT IS YOUR LAST NAME? YEE
```

Multiple input

This program asks for your name, age, and weight:

```
10 INPUT "NAME, AGE, WEIGHT";N$,A,W
```

When you run the program, the computer asks:

```
NAME, AGE, WEIGHT?
```

The computer waits for you to type your name, age, and weight. When you type them, put commas between them, like this:

```
NAME, AGE, WEIGHT? JOHN,25,148
```

If your name is "JOHN SMITH, JR.", and you want to input all that instead of just JOHN, you must put quotation marks around your name:

```
NAME, AGE, WEIGHT? "JOHN SMITH, JR.",25,148
```

Here's the rule: you must put quotation marks around any INPUT string that contains a comma.

LINE INPUT

If you say —

```
10 LINE INPUT "PLEASE TYPE YOUR NAME...";N$
```

the computer will say:

```
PLEASE TYPE YOUR NAME...
```

Then the computer will wait for you to type your name. You do *not* have to put quotation marks around your name, even if your name contains a comma. LINE INPUT means: the entire line that the person inputs will become the string, even if the line contains a comma.

Notice that the LINE INPUT statement does *not* make the computer automatically print a question mark. And notice that the variable must be a string (such as N$), not a number.

INPUT$

This program reveals private information about MARY:

```
10 PRINT "MARY SECRETLY WISHES TO KISS A COW"
```

Here's how to protect that program, so only people who know the "secret password" can run it. . . .

First, invent a secret password. Let's make it be "TUNA". Here's the program:

```
5 INPUT "WHAT'S THE SECRET PASSWORD";P$
10 IF P$="TUNA" THEN PRINT "MARY SECRETLY WISHES TO KISS A C
OW" ELSE PRINT "YOU ARE AN UNAUTHORIZED USER"
```

Line 5 asks the person to type the secret password. Whatever the person types is called P$. If the person types TUNA, line 10 makes the computer say:

```
MARY SECRETLY WISHES TO KISS A COW
```

But if the person does *not* type TUNA, the computer says "YOU ARE AN UNAUTHORIZED USER" and refuses to reveal Mary's secret desire.

This program's better:

```
5 PRINT "PLEASE TYPE THE SECRET PASSWORD"
6 P$=INPUT$(4)
10 IF P$="TUNA" THEN PRINT "MARY SECRETLY WISHES TO KISS A C
OW" ELSE PRINT "YOU ARE AN UNAUTHORIZED USER"
```

Line 5 makes the computer say:

```
PLEASE TYPE THE SECRET PASSWORD
```

Line 6 waits for the person to input 4 characters. The characters that the person inputs will become P$. For example, suppose the person types T, then U, then N, then A; then P$ will become TUNA and the computer will reveal Mary's secret.

While the person inputs the 4 characters, they won't appear on the screen; they'll be invisible. That's to prevent other people in the room from peeking at the screen and noticing the password.

After typing the 4 characters, the person does *not* have to press the ENTER key. As soon as the person types the 4th character, the computer makes P$ be the 4 characters that the person typed.

Broken computer This devilish program makes your computer pretend to be broken, so that whenever you press the W key your screen shows an F instead:

```
10 CLS
20 A$=INPUT$(1)
30 IF A$="W" THEN PRINT "F"; ELSE PRINT A$;
40 GO TO 20
```

Line 10 clears the screen (makes the screen go blank), so that your friends don't see the program. Line 20 waits for you to type 1 character. Line 30 says: if the character you typed was W, print an F on the screen instead; otherwise, print the character you typed. Line 40 makes the routine repeat, forever. For example, if you try to type "THE WEATHER IS WONDERFUL", you'll see this on the screen instead:

```
THE FEATHER IS FONDERFUL
```

For an even wilder time, tell the computer to change each "E" to "OOGA", by changing line 30 to this:

```
30 IF A$="E" THEN PRINT "OOGA"; ELSE PRINT A$;
```

Then if you try to type "WE ARE HERE", you'll see this on the screen instead:

```
WOOGA AROOGA HOOGAROOGA
```

Abridged literature This program gives you a choice of literature:

```
10 PRINT "WELCOME TO THE WORLD'S GREAT LITERATURE, ABRIDGED"
20 PRINT "WHICH KIND OF LITERATURE WOULD YOU LIKE?"
30 PRINT "N: NOVEL"
40 PRINT "P: POEM"
50 PRINT "PLEASE PRESS N OR P"
60 A$=INPUT$(1)
70 IF A$="N" THEN GO TO 100
80 IF A$="P" THEN GO TO 200
90 GO TO 50
100 PRINT "HE: I LOVE YOU"
110 PRINT "SHE: I'M PREGNANT"
120 PRINT "HE: LET'S GET MARRIED"
130 PRINT "SHE: LET'S GET DIVORCED"
140 PRINT "HE: LET'S GET BACK TOGETHER"
150 PRINT "SHE: TOO BAD YOU DIED IN THE WAR, BUT I'LL NEVER FORGET YOU!"
160 END
200 PRINT "NOSES"
210 PRINT "BLOWSES"
```

Lines 10-50 make the computer print:

```
WELCOME TO THE WORLD'S GREAT LITERATURE, ABRIDGED
WHICH KIND OF LITERATURE WOULD YOU LIKE?
N: NOVEL
P: POEM
PLEASE PRESS N OR P
```

Line 60 makes the computer wait for you to press a key. You do *not* have to press the ENTER key afterwards.

If you press the N key, line 70 sends the computer to line 100, which prints an abridged novel. If you press the P key instead, line 80 sends the computer to line 200, which prints an abridged poem.

If you press neither N nor P, the computer arrives at line 90, which sends the computer back to line 50, which reminds you to press N or P.

Instead of using the keyboard, you can input by using a **joystick** or **mouse**.

Joystick

A **joystick** is a stick that sticks up from a box. You can wiggle the stick in all four directions (left, right, forward, and back) and diagonally.

In line 100 of your program, if you want the computer to look at the joystick, say:

```
100 X=STICK(0): Y=STICK(1)
```

That line makes X become a number that indicates how far the joystick is being pulled to the right, and Y become a number that indicates how far the joystick is being pushed forward. To make the computer print X and Y on your screen, say:

```
110 PRINT X,Y
```

To make the computer look at the joystick again and again, repeatedly, create a loop, by adding this line:

```
120 GO TO 100
```

Then as you wiggle the joystick, you can watch the numbers on the screen change.

Besides printing the numbers X and Y on the screen, you can use the numbers X and Y in graphics statements (such as PLOT, LINE, and CIRCLE), so that the joystick controls the location of graphics shapes on the screen. You can also use the X and Y numbers in the SOUND statement, so that the joystick controls the pitch of musical sounds: moving the joystick will change the pitch.

Mouse

A **mouse** is a small box about the size of a pack of cigarettes. You can slide the mouse across your desk in all four directions (left, right, forward, and back) and diagonally.

Some versions of BASIC let your program contain commands to handle a mouse. Those commands are called **mouse commands**.

(GWBASIC and QBASIC do *not* let programs contain mouse commands. If you're using GWBASIC or QBASIC, skip ahead to the next page.)

If your computer's BASIC understands mouse commands, and you want the computer to look at the mouse in line 100 of your program, say this:

```
100 M=MOUSE(0): X=MOUSE(1): Y=MOUSE(2)
```

In that line, the "M=MOUSE(0)" makes the computer look at the mouse. The rest of the line makes X become a number that indicates how far the mouse was moved to the right, and Y become a number that indicates how far the mouse was moved forward. To make the computer print X and Y on your screen, say:

```
110 PRINT X,Y
```

To make the computer look at the mouse again and again repeatedly, create a loop by adding this line:

```
120 GO TO 100
```

Then as you move the mouse across your desk, you can watch the numbers on the screen change.

SWAP

Modern computers understand the word SWAP:

```
10 A=4: B=9
20 SWAP A,B
30 PRINT A;B
```

Line 10 says A is 4 and B is 9. Line 20 swaps A with B, so that A becomes 9, and B becomes 4. Line 30 prints:

```
 9 4
```

If your computer is old-fashioned and doesn't understand the word SWAP, replace line 20 by this:

```
20 S=A: A=B: B=S
```

That example swapped numbers. You can also swap strings:

```
10 A$="HORSE": B$="CART"
20 SWAP A$,B$
30 PRINT A$;" ";B$
```

Line 10 says A$ is "HORSE" and B$ is "CART". Line 20 swaps A$ with B$, so that A$ becomes "CART", and B$ becomes "HORSE". Line 30 puts the CART before the HORSE:

```
CART HORSE
```

If your computer doesn't understand SWAP, replace line 20 by this:

```
20 S$=A$: A$=B$: B$=S$
```

Don't forget the dollar signs!

Shuffling

Here are some cards:

Queen of Hearts
Jack of Diamonds
Ace of Spades
Joker
King of Clubs

Let's shuffle them, to put them into a random order.

To begin, put the list of cards into a DATA statement:

```
10 DATA QUEEN OF HEARTS,JACK OF DIAMONDS,ACE OF SPADES,JOKER,KING OF CLUBS
```

We have 5 cards:

```
20 N=5
```

Let the Queen of Hearts be called X$(1), the Jack of Diamonds be called X$(2), the Ace of Spades be called X$(3), the Joker be called X$(4), and the King of Clubs be called X$(5):

```
30 DIM X$(N)
40 FOR I = 1 TO N: READ X$(I): NEXT
```

Shuffle the cards, by using the following strategy. . . .

Swap the card N with a random card before it (or with itself); then swap card N-1 with a random card before it (or with itself); then swap card N-2 with a random card before it (or with itself); etc. Keep doing that, until you finally reach card 2, which you swap with a random card before it (or with itself). Here's the code:

```
50 RANDOMIZE
60 FOR I = N TO 2 STEP -1: SWAP X$(I),X$(RND(I)): NEXT
```

If your computer doesn't understand SWAP, replace "SWAP X$(I),X$(RND(I))" by this:

```
R=RND(I): S$=X$(I): X$(I)=X$(R): X$(R)=S$
```

If your computer doesn't understand the word RANDOMIZE, or doesn't understand that RND(I) is a random number from 1 to I, you must make further changes.

Finally, print the shuffled deck:

```
70 FOR I = 1 TO N: PRINT X$(I): NEXT
```

The computer will print something like this:

```
KING OF CLUBS
JOKER
JACK OF DIAMONDS
QUEEN OF HEARTS
ACE OF SPADES
```

To shuffle a larger deck, change just lines 10 and 20.

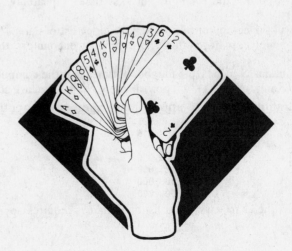

Sorting

Putting words in alphabetical order — or putting numbers in numerical order — is called **sorting**.

Short Three-Line Sort Here are a dozen names: Sue, Ann, Joe, Alice, Ted, Jill, Fred, Al, Sam, Pat, Sally, Moe. Let's make the computer alphabetize them (sort them).

To begin, put the list of names into a DATA statement:

```
10 DATA SUE,ANN,JOE,ALICE,TED,JILL,FRED,AL,SAM,PAT,SALLY,MOE
```

We have 12 names:

```
20 N=12
```

Let Sue be called X$(1), Ann be called X$(2), Joe be called X$(3), etc. Here's how:

```
30 DIM X$(N)
40 FOR I = 1 TO N: READ X$(I): NEXT
```

Alphabetize the names, by using the following strategy. . . .

Compare the first name against the second; if they're not in alphabetical order, swap them. Compare the second name against the third; if they're not in alphabetical order, swap them. Compare the third name against the fourth; if they're not in alphabetical order, swap them. Continue that process, until you finally compare the last two names. But each time you swap, you must start the whole process over again, to make sure the preceding names are still in alphabetical order. Here's the code:

```
50 FOR I = 1 TO N-1
60     IF X$(I)>X$(I+1) THEN SWAP X$(I),X$(I+1): GO TO 50
70 NEXT
```

Finally, print the alphabetized list:

```
80 FOR I = 1 TO N: PRINT X$(I): NEXT
```

The computer will print:

```
AL
ALICE
ANN
FRED
JILL
JOE
MOE
PAT
SALLY
SAM
SUE
TED
```

In that program, the sorting occurs in lines 50-70. Those three short lines are called the **Short Three-Line Sort**.

Those three lines form a loop. The part of the loop that the computer encounters the most often is the phrase "IF X$(I)>X$(I+1)". In fact, if you tell the computer to alphabetize a list of names that's long (several *hundred* names), the computer spends the *majority* of its time repeatedly handling "IF X$(I)>X$(I+1)".

How long will the computer take to handle a long list of names? The length of time depends mainly on how often the computer encounters the phrase "IF X$(I)>X$(I+1)".

If the list contains N names, the number of times that the computer encounters the phrase "IF X$(I)>X$(I+1)" is approximately $N^3/8$. Here are some examples:

N (number of names)	$N^3/8$ (approximate number of encounters)
10	125
12	216
20	1,000
40	8,000
100	125,000
1,000	125,000,000
10,000	125,000,000,000

For example, the chart says that a list of 12 names requires approximately 216 encounters.

The 216 is just an approximation: the exact number of encounters depends on which list of names you're trying to alphabetize. If the list is nearly in alphabetical order *already*, the number of encounters will be less than 216; if the list is in *reverse* alphabetical order, the number of encounters will be more than 216; but if the list is typical (not yet in any particular order), the number of encounters will be about 216. For the list that we tried (Sue, Ann, Joe, Alice, Ted, Jill, Fred, Al, Sam, Pat, Sally, Moe), the exact number of encounters happens to be 189, which is close to 216.

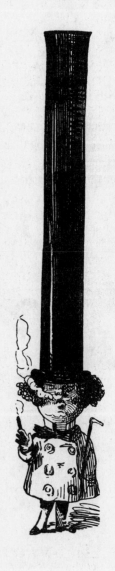

How long will your computer take to finish sorting? The length of time depends on which computer you have, how many names are in the list, and how long each name is. A typical microcomputer (handling a list of typical names) requires .01 seconds per encounter. Multiplying the number of encounters by .01 seconds, you get:

Number of names	Encounters ($N^3/8$)	Time	
10	125	1.25 secs	
12	216	2.16 secs	
20	1,000	10 secs	
40	8,000	80 secs = 1.3 minutes
100	125,000	1,250 secs = 20.8 minutes
1,000	125,000,000	1,250,000 secs = 14.4 days
10,000	125,000,000,000	1,250,000,000 secs = 39.6 years

Moral: never let a 70-year-old programmer alphabetize a list of 10,000 names by using the Short Three-Line Sort — because when the computer finishes running the program (39.6 years later), the programmer will probably be dead!

Fancy Three-Line Sort

In the Short Three-Line Sort, the end of line 60 says "GO TO 50". For an interesting experiment, replace the "GO TO 50" by "IF I>1 THEN I=I-1: GO TO 60", so that line 60 looks like this:

```
60    IF X$(I)>X$(I+1) THEN SWAP X$(I),X$(I+1): IF I>1 THEN I=I-1: GO TO 60
```

Even though that new, fancy version of line 60 is longer to type than the original, the computer handles it more quickly, because it tells the computer to GO TO line 60 instead of forcing the computer to go all the way back to line 50. The fancy version is called the **Fancy Three-Line Sort**.

If you feed the computer the Fancy Three-Line Sort (instead of the Short Three-Line Sort), the computer encounters the "IF X$(I) > X$(I+1)" less often: just $N^2/2$ times (instead of $N^3/8$).

Number of names	Encounters ($N^2/2$)	Time	
10	50	.50 secs	
12	72	.72 secs	
20	200	2 secs	
40	800	8 secs	
100	5,000	50 secs	
1,000	500,000	5,000 secs = 1.4 hours
10,000	50,000,000	500,000 secs = 5.8 days

Now you can hire the 70-year old programmer: to alphabetize 10,000 names, he'll need just 5.8 days instead of 39.6 years. By changing just the end of line 60, we saved almost 40 years of computer time — and the programmer's job!

Super-Fancy Three-Line Sort

To reduce the time even further, use the **Super-Fancy Three-Line Sort** instead, which is:

```
50 FOR I = 1 TO N-1
60    FOR J = 1 TO 1 STEP -1: IF X$(J)>X$(J+1) THEN SWAP X$(J),X$(J+1): NEXT
70 NEXT I
```

When typing the Super-Fancy Three-Line Sort, make sure you type line 60 correctly: you must put the IF on the same line as the NEXT. In line 70, make sure you put the "I" after NEXT; otherwise, the computer might think you mean NEXT J.

For the Super-Fancy Three-Line Sort, the number of times the computer encounters the phrase "IF X$(J) > X$(J+1)" is just $N^2/4$:

Number of names	Encounters ($N^2/4$)	Time	
10	25	.25 secs	
12	36	.36 secs	
20	100	1 secs	
40	400	4 secs	
100	2,500	25 secs	
1,000	250,000	2,500 secs = 41.7 minutes
10,000	25,000,000	250,000 secs = 2.9 days

Six-Line Sort

The **Six-Line Sort** reduces the time even further.

To construct the Six-Line Sort, begin with the Super-Fancy Three-Line Sort, but change each +1 to +D, and change each -1 to -D, so that you get:

```
50 FOR I = 1 TO N-D
60    FOR J = I TO 1 STEP -D: IF X$(J)>X$(J+D) THEN SWAP X$(J),X$(J+D): NEXT
70 NEXT I
```

D begins by being N —

```
42 D=N
```

but then decreases, so that it becomes a fifth of its original value:

```
44 D=INT(D/5)+1
```

After performing lines 50-70 for that D, check whether D is down to 1 yet; if it isn't, repeat the process:

```
75 IF D>1 THEN GO TO 44
```

So altogether, the complete Six-Line Sort looks like this:

```
42 D=N
44 D=INT(D/5)+1
50 FOR I = 1 TO N-D
60     FOR J = I TO 1 STEP -D: IF X$(J)>X$(J+D) THEN SWAP X$(J),X$(J+D): NEXT
70 NEXT I
75 IF D>1 THEN GO TO 44
```

For the Six-Line Sort, the number of times the computer encounters the phrase "IF X$(J)>X$(J+D)" is just $1.5*(N-1)^{(4/3)}$:

Number of names	Encounters	Time
10	28	.28 secs
12	37	.37 secs
20	76	.76 secs
40	198	1.98 secs
100	687	6.87 secs
1,000	14,980	149.80 secs = 2.5 minutes
10,000	323,122	3,231.22 secs = 53.9 minutes

Notice that the Six-Line Sort handles 10,000 names in 53.9 minutes. That's much faster than the Super-Fancy Three-Line Sort, which takes 2.9 days. But to handle just 10 names, the Six-Line Sort does *not* run faster than the Super-Fancy Three-Line Sort. So use the Six-Line Sort just for handling *long* lists of names.

To make the Six-Line Sort even faster, add this line:

```
1 DEFINT A-Z
```

That tells the computer that none of the variables stands for a decimal. By saying DEFINT A-Z, you enable the computer to run the program 20% faster, so that the timing looks like this:

Number of names	Time
10	.2 secs
12	.3 secs
20	.6 secs
40	1.6 secs
100	5.5 secs
1,000	120 secs = 2 minutes
10,000	2,580 secs = 43 minutes

We've sure come a long way! Our first attempt (the Short Three-Line Sort) took 39.6 years to alphabetize 10,000 names; our newest attempt (the Six-Line Sort with DEFINT) takes just 43 minutes.

If you try running those sorting methods on *your* computer, you'll find the timings are slightly different, since the exact timings depend on which computer you have, the length of each name, and how badly the names are out of order.

Famous sorts
Although I "invented" all those sorting methods, most of them are just slight improvements on methods that were developed by others. For example, the Super-Fancy Three-Line Sort is a slight improvement on the **Shuttle Sort**, which was invented by Shaw & Trimble in 1983. The Six-Line Sort is a slight improvement on the **Shell Sort**, which was invented by Donald Shell in 1959 and further developed by Hibbard & Boothroyd in 1963, Peterson & Russell in 1971, and Knuth in 1973.

Phone directory
Suppose you want to alphabetize this phone directory:

Name	Phone number
Mary Smith	277-8139
John Doe	513-9134
Russ Walter	666-2666
Information	555-1212

Just use one of the alphabetizing programs I showed you! Type the DATA like this:

```
10 DATA SMITH MARY 277-8139,DOE JOHN 513-9134
20 DATA WALTER RUSS 666-2666,INFORMATION 555-1212
```

The computer will print:

```
DOE JOHN 513-9134
INFORMATION 555-1212
SMITH MARY 277-8139
WALTER RUSS 666-2666
```

Sorting numbers
Suppose you want to put a list of numbers into increasing order. For example, if the numbers are 51, 4.257, -814, 62, and .2, let's make the computer print:

```
-814
 .2
4.257
51
62
```

To do that, just use one of the alphabetizing programs I showed you — but in the DATA statement, put the numbers instead of strings; and remove the dollar signs (say X instead of X$).

To put a list of numbers into *decreasing* order, begin by writing a program that puts them into *increasing* order, and then change line 60 from ">X" to "<X".

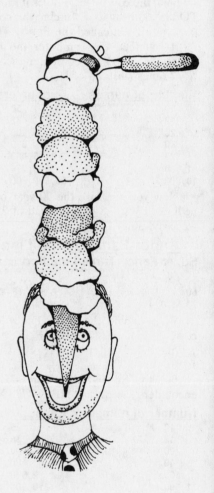

The computer understands the word "ON".

ON . . . GO TO

In your program, you can say:

```
50 ON N GO TO 80,100,20,350
```

That means: go to either 80, 100, 20, or 350; the decision depends on what N is. In other words:

If N is 1, go to 80.
If N is 2, go to 100.
If N is 3, go to 20.
If N is 4, go to 350.

In that example, if N is *not* 1, 2, 3, or 4, the computer will *not* go to line 80 or 100 or 20 or 350; instead, the computer will proceed to the line underneath line 50 (which is probably line 60).

Exception: if N is greater than 255 or a negative number (such as -1), the computer thinks you're crazy, and so the computer gripes at you instead of proceeding to line 60.

Another exception: if N is a decimal (such as 3.1), the computer treats N as if it were a whole number (3); so in that example, if N is 3.1, the computer will go to line 20.

Christmas Remember the Christmas carol called "The Twelve Days of Christmas"? The first three verses go like this:

```
ON THE FIRST DAY OF CHRISTMAS, MY TRUE LOVE SENT TO ME
A PARTRIDGE IN A PEAR TREE.

ON THE SECOND DAY OF CHRISTMAS, MY TRUE LOVE SENT TO ME
TWO TURTLE DOVES...AND
A PARTRIDGE IN A PEAR TREE.

ON THE THIRD DAY OF CHRISTMAS, MY TRUE LOVE SENT TO ME
THREE FRENCH HENS,
TWO TURTLE DOVES...AND
A PARTRIDGE IN A PEAR TREE.
```

This program prints the final verse:

```
10 PRINT "ON THE TWELFTH DAY OF CHRISTMAS, MY TRUE LOVE SENT TO ME"
20 PRINT "TWELVE DRUMMERS DRUMMING,"
30 PRINT "ELEVEN PIPERS PIPING,"
40 PRINT "TEN LORDS A-LEAPING,"
50 PRINT "NINE LADIES DANCING,"
60 PRINT "EIGHT MAIDS A-MILKING,"
70 PRINT "SEVEN SWANS A-SWIMMING,"
80 PRINT "SIX GEESE A-LAYING,"
90 PRINT "FIVE GO---OLD RINGS,"
100 PRINT "FOUR CALLING BIRDS,"
110 PRINT "THREE FRENCH HENS,"
120 PRINT "TWO TURTLE DOVES...AND"
130 PRINT "A PARTRIDGE IN A PEAR TREE."
```

This program prints all twelve verses:

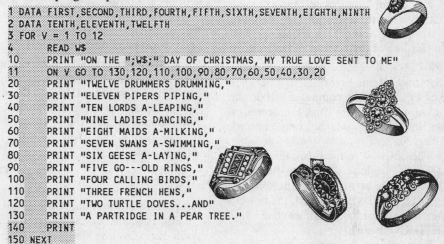

```
1 DATA FIRST,SECOND,THIRD,FOURTH,FIFTH,SIXTH,SEVENTH,EIGHTH,NINTH
2 DATA TENTH,ELEVENTH,TWELFTH
3 FOR V = 1 TO 12
4     READ W$
10    PRINT "ON THE ";W$;" DAY OF CHRISTMAS, MY TRUE LOVE SENT TO ME"
11    ON V GO TO 130,120,110,100,90,80,70,60,50,40,30,20
20    PRINT "TWELVE DRUMMERS DRUMMING,"
30    PRINT "ELEVEN PIPERS PIPING,"
40    PRINT "TEN LORDS A-LEAPING,"
50    PRINT "NINE LADIES DANCING,"
60    PRINT "EIGHT MAIDS A-MILKING,"
70    PRINT "SEVEN SWANS A-SWIMMING,"
80    PRINT "SIX GEESE A-LAYING,"
90    PRINT "FIVE GO---OLD RINGS,"
100   PRINT "FOUR CALLING BIRDS,"
110   PRINT "THREE FRENCH HENS,"
120   PRINT "TWO TURTLE DOVES...AND"
130   PRINT "A PARTRIDGE IN A PEAR TREE."
140   PRINT
150 NEXT
```

Lines 1 and 2 teach the computer how to spell the words "FIRST", "SECOND", "THIRD", etc. Line 3 makes the computer do lines 4 through 140, twelve times (once for each verse). Lines 4 and 10 look at the data and print the top line of the verse. Line 11 says:

If V is 1, go to line 130 (so the computer prints A PARTRIDGE IN A PEAR TREE).

If V is 2, go to line 120 (so the computer prints TWO TURTLE DOVES...AND A PARTRIDGE IN A PEAR TREE).

If V is 3, go to line 110 (so the computer prints THREE FRENCH HENS, TWO TURTLE DOVES...AND A PARTRIDGE IN A PEAR TREE).

And so on, for each verse.

ON . . . GOSUB

You can say:

```
50 ON N GOSUB 80,100,20,350
```

That means:

If N is 1, GOSUB 80.
If N is 2, GOSUB 100.
If N is 3, GOSUB 20.
If N is 4, GOSUB 350.

ON ERROR GO TO

If the computer finds an error while running your program, the computer wants to gripe. But instead of letting the computer gripe, you can force the computer to do something different.

For example, you can tell the computer, "If you find an error in lines 50-70, don't gripe; instead of griping, do the special routine that begins at line 1000." To tell the computer that, insert these lines:

```
49 ON ERROR GO TO 1000
71 ON ERROR GO TO 0
```

Lines 49 and 71 tell the computer, "If you find an error between lines 49 and 71, go to the special routine that begins at line 1000."

Invent your own special routine, so that it begins at line 1000 and continues onto lines 1010, 1020, etc.

The bottom line of your special routine should tell the computer where to go afterwards.

For example, suppose that after the routine is done, you want the computer to go back to line 30 (to try again). Just put this line at the bottom of the routine:

```
1090 RESUME 30
```

That way, if an error occurs between lines 49 and 71, the computer will do the routine in lines 1000-1080, then come to line 1090, which sends the computer back to line 30.

The special routine (in lines 1000-1090) is called an **error-handling routine** or an **error trap**. Its bottom line says RESUME. (By contrast, the bottom line of an ordinary subroutine says RETURN instead.)

To separate the main routine (lines 10-999) from the error-handing routine (lines 1000-1090), the bottom line of the main routine should say END, like this:

```
999 END
```

Instead of saying RESUME 30, which sends the computer back to line 30, you can send the computer back to any other line you wish. For example, you can say RESUME 80.

If you don't put any number after RESUME, the computer will go back to the line that contained the error.

If you say RESUME NEXT, the computer will go to the line *underneath* the line that contained the error. To make RESUME NEXT work properly, the line that contained the error should consists of just one statement (instead of statements separated by colons).

MEMORY CELLS

The computer's main memory consists of many **memory cells**. Each cell holds an integer from 0 to 255. For example, cell #7512 might hold the integer 17.

PEEK

To find out what number's in cell #7512, say:

```
PRINT PEEK(7512)
```

That makes the computer peek at cell #7512, find the number in that cell, and print that number on your screen. The number it prints will be an integer from 0 to 255. For example, it might be 17.

POKE

The memory contains two kinds of cells. One kind, called **ROM**, contains information permanently. The other kind, called **RAM**, contains information temporarily, and you can change that information. When you turn the computer on, each RAM cell contains a 0, but you can change the zeros to other numbers.

If you say —

```
POKE 7512,14
```

the computer will try to put the number 14 into cell #7512. If cell #7512 is in the RAM, the computer will succeed. If cell #7512 is in the ROM, the computer will give up, since the information in ROM cells is permanent and can't be changed.

To find out whether the computer successfully put the number 14 into cell #7512, say:

```
PRINT PEEK(7512)
```

If the computer prints 14, the computer successfully poked. If the computer prints a different number instead, the computer's POKE was unsuccessful, which means cell #7512 is in the ROM and therefore can't be changed.

When you turn the computer on, the ROM cells contain their permanent information, but the RAM cells are "blank"; each RAM cell contains 0. To change the numbers in the RAM cells, say POKE.

How RAM is used

Whenever you type a new program or command or data, the computer temporarily stores what you typed in the RAM.

For example, if you type the word CAB (because you're writing a program about taxicabs), the computer temporarily puts the ASCII code numbers for C, A, and B into RAM cells. Since C's ASCII code number is 67, A's is 65, and B's is 66, the computer puts the numbers 67, 65, and 66 into three RAM cells.

As you type more programs, commands, and data, the computer puts their ASCII code numbers into RAM cells. Into other RAM cells, the computer puts notes about what you and the computer are doing.

If you say to POKE a number into a RAM cell, beware: the computer might already be using that cell to hold an important note. The number you POKE into the cell will replace the computer's note. The computer will forget the note, get confused, and go crazy. If the RAM cell contained a note about your program, the computer might wreck your program; if the RAM cell contained a note about the disk drive, the computer might go so crazy that it will turn the drive on and wreck all the information on the disk!

So before you say POKE, find out which RAM cells the computer uses for which purposes — and as an extra precaution, remove your disk from the drive. Don't reinsert the disk until you've turned off the computer and started fresh again.

SEQUENTIAL DATA FILES

Here's a simple program:

```
10 PRINT "EAT"
20 PRINT 2+2
30 PRINT "EGGS"
```

It makes the computer print this message onto your screen:

```
EAT
4
EGGS
```

Instead of printing that message onto your screen, let's make the computer print the message onto your disk. Here's how. . . .

OPEN FOR OUTPUT

This program prints the message onto your disk, instead of onto your screen:

```
5 OPEN "SUE" FOR OUTPUT AS 1
10 PRINT#1, "EAT"
20 PRINT#1, 2+2
30 PRINT#1, "EGGS"
40 CLOSE
```

Lines 10-30 make the computer print the message onto your disk, instead of onto your screen. Each line says PRINT#1, which means: print onto the disk.

Line 5 is an introductory line that tells the computer *where* on the disk to print the message. Line 5 says: find a blank place on the disk, call it "SUE", and make "SUE" be file#1. So PRINT#1, will mean: print onto file#1, which is SUE.

Any program that says OPEN should also say CLOSE, so line 40 says CLOSE. The CLOSE line makes the computer put some "finishing touches" on SUE, so that SUE becomes a perfect, finished file.

When you RUN that program, the computer will automatically put onto the disk a file called "SUE" that contains this message:

```
EAT
4
EGGS
```

After running the program, if you want to see the names of all the files on the disk, type FILES (or DIRECTORY or CATALOG or whatever other word your computer uses). The computer will print the names of all the files — and one of the names it prints will be SUE.

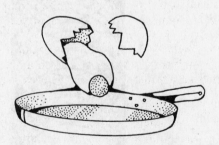

OPEN FOR INPUT

To see the message that's in SUE, run this program, which inputs from SUE and prints onto your screen:

```
5 OPEN "SUE" FOR INPUT AS 1
10 INPUT#1, A$
11 PRINT A$
20 INPUT#1, B
21 PRINT B
30 INPUT#1, C$
31 PRINT C$
40 CLOSE
```

Line 5 prepares the computer to input from SUE.

Line 10 inputs A$ from SUE, so A$ is EAT. Line 11 prints EAT onto your screen.

Line 20 inputs B from SUE, so B is 4. Line 21 prints 4 onto your screen.

Line 30 inputs C$ from SUE, so C$ is EGGS. Line 31 prints EGGS onto your screen. So altogether, on your screen you'll see:

```
EAT
4
EGGS
```

Line 40 tells the computer that you're done using SUE for a while (until you say OPEN again).

OPEN FOR APPEND

After you've put SUE onto the disk, so that SUE consists of EAT and 4 and EGGS, try running this program:

```
10 OPEN "SUE" FOR APPEND AS 1
20 PRINT#1, "GOOD MORNING!"
30 CLOSE
```

In line 10, the word APPEND tells the computer to keep adding onto SUE. So when the computer comes to line 20, it adds "GOOD MORNING" onto SUE, and SUE becomes this:

```
EAT
4
EGGS
GOOD MORNING!
```

Erasing

For your next experiment, try running this program:

```
10 OPEN "SUE" FOR OUTPUT AS 1
20 PRINT#1, "PICKLES ARE PLEASANT"
30 CLOSE
```

Since line 10 does *not* say APPEND, the computer will *not* keep adding onto SUE. Instead, the computer erases everything that's been in SUE. So when the computer finishes processing line 10, SUE's become blank.

Line 20 puts "PICKLES ARE PLEASANT" into SUE. So at the end of the program, SUE includes "PICKLES ARE PLEASANT"; but SUE does *not* include EAT and 4 and EGGS and "GOOD MORNING", which have all been erased.

Loops

This program lets you put the names of all your friends onto the disk:

```
10 OPEN "FRIENDS" FOR OUTPUT AS 1
20 PRINT "PLEASE TYPE A FRIEND'S NAME (OR THE WORD 'END')"
30 INPUT F$: IF F$="END" THEN CLOSE: END
40 PRINT#1, F$
50 GO TO 20
```

Line 10 makes the computer find a blank space on the disk and call it FRIENDS. Line 20 makes the computer print:

```
PLEASE TYPE A FRIEND'S NAME (OR THE WORD 'END')
```

Line 30 prints a question mark and waits for you to type something; whatever you type will be called F$. For example, if you type JOAN WILLIAMS, then F$ will be JOAN WILLIAMS, and line 40 prints the name JOAN WILLIAMS onto the disk.

Line 50 creates a loop, so that you can type as many names as you wish. (Remember to press the ENTER key after each name.)

When you've finished typing the names of all your friends, type the word END. Then the last part of line 30 will make the computer CLOSE the file and END the program.

This program makes the computer look at the FRIENDS file and copy all its names to your screen:

```
10 OPEN "FRIENDS" FOR INPUT AS 1
20 IF EOF(1) THEN PRINT "THOSE ARE ALL THE FRIENDS": CLOSE: END
30 INPUT#1, F$
40 PRINT F$
50 GO TO 20
```

Line 10 prepares the computer to input from the FRIENDS file. Line 20 is special; I'll explain it later. Line 30 makes the computer input a string from the file and call the string F$; so F$ becomes the name of one of your friends. Line 40 prints that friend's name onto your screen. Line 50 creates a loop, so that the names of *all* your friends are printed on the screen.

Eventually, the computer will reach the end of the file, and there won't be any more names to input from the file. Line 20 says: if the computer reaches the End Of the File and can't input any more names from it, the computer should print on your screen "THOSE ARE ALL THE FRIENDS", then CLOSE the file and END the program.

LOF

In the middle of your program, if you say PRINT LOF(1), the computer will tell you the Length Of the File: it will tell you how many bytes are in the file.

Multiple files

If you want the computer to handle two files simultaneously, use two OPEN statements. At the end of the first OPEN statement, say "AS 1"; at the end of the second OPEN statement, say "AS 2".

For the second file, say PRINT#2 instead of PRINT#1, say INPUT#2 instead of INPUT#1, say EOF(2) instead of EOF(1), and say LOF(2) instead of LOF(1).

How to CLOSE

The CLOSE statement closes all files. To be more specific, you can say CLOSE 1 (which closes just the first file) or CLOSE 2 (which closes just the second).

Whenever you're done using a file, CLOSE it immediately. When you say CLOSE, the computer puts finishing touches on the file that protect the file against damage.

Suppose that halfway through your program, you finish using file 2 but want to continue using file 1. Say CLOSE 2 there, and delay saying CLOSE 1 until later.

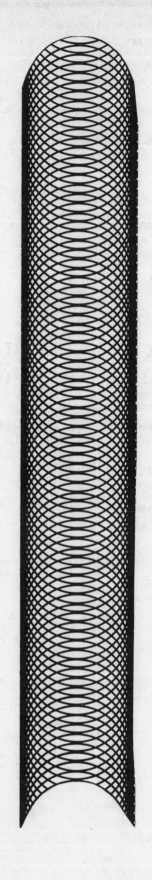

RANDOM ACCESS

On a disk, you can store two kinds of data files. The simple kind is called a **sequential-access** data file; the complicated kind is called a **random-access** (or **relative-access** or **direct-access**) data file. You've already learned how to create and retrieve a sequential-access file. Now let's look at random-access.

Though more complicated than sequential-access data files, **random-access** data files have an advantage: they let you skip around. In a sequential-access data file, you must look at the first item of data, then the second, then the third, etc. In a random-access data file, you can look at the seventh item of data, then skip directly to the tenth, then hop back to the third, then skip directly to the sixth, etc.

Each item is called a **record**. The number of characters (bytes) in the record is called the record's **length**. For example, if a record contains 30 characters, the record's length is 30. In a random-access file, all the records must have the same length as each other.

PUT

Let's create a random-access file called JIM. Let's make JIM's record length be 20, so that each record will contain 20 characters. Here's how:

```
5 OPEN "JIM" AS 1 LEN=20: FIELD 1, 20 AS X$
```

Let's make JIM's 7th record be "LOVE MAKES ME GIGGLE" (which contains 20 characters):

```
10 LSET X$="LOVE MAKES ME GIGGLE": PUT 1,7
```

Let's make JIM's 9th record be "PLEASE HOLD MY HAND":

```
20 LSET X$="PLEASE HOLD MY HAND": PUT 1,9
```

Since JIM's record length is supposed to be 20 characters but "PLEASE HOLD MY HAND" contains just 19 characters, the computer will automatically add a blank to the end of "PLEASE HOLD MY HAND".

Let's make JIM's 4th record be "I LOVE LUCY":

```
30 LSET X$="I LOVE LUCY": PUT 1,4
```

The computer will automatically add blanks to the end of "I LOVE LUCY".

To finish the program, say:

```
40 CLOSE
```

GET

This program makes the computer tell you JIM's 7th item:

```
5 OPEN "JIM" AS 1 LEN=20: FIELD 1, 20 AS X$
10 GET 1,7: PRINT X$
20 CLOSE
```

Multi-field records

If you want each record to be a *pair* of strings, begin like this:

```
5 OPEN "JIM" AS 1 LEN=34: FIELD 1, 30 AS X$, 4 AS Y$
10 LSET X$="LOVE MAKES ME GIGGLE": LSET Y$="WOW": PUT 1,7
etc.
```

Line 5 makes each record consist of two **fields**. The first field is a 30-character string called X$; the second field is a 4-character string called Y$.

Line 10 says to PUT into the 7th record this pair of strings: "LOVE MAKES ME GIGGLE" and "WOW".

LOC

While using a random-access file, if you say PRINT LOC(1), the computer tells you which record it just dealt with: it tells you the record LOCation. For example, if you say "PUT 1,7" or "GET 1,7" and then say PRINT LOC(1), the computer prints the number 7.

If you say "PUT 1" instead of "PUT 1,7", the computer will assume you mean "PUT 1,LOC(1)+1". If you say "GET 1", the computer will assume you mean "GET 1,LOC(1)+1".

End of the file

The EOF function doesn't work well for random-access files. To deal with the end of the file, use the following trick instead.

Suppose you say LEN=34, so that 34 bytes make a record. Since the number of bytes in the *entire* file is LOF(1), and 34 bytes make a record, the number of records in the file is LOF(1)/34. These lines print all the records:

```
100 FOR I = 1 TO LOF(1)/34
110     GET 1: PRINT X$;Y$
120 NEXT
```

Restrictions on FIELD variables

If you put a variable (such as X$) into a FIELD statement, you can*not* put it into an ordinary "=" statement: instead of saying X$="LOVE MAKES ME GIGGLE", you must say LSET X$="LOVE MAKES ME GIGGLE". You can*not* put the variable into an INPUT statement: instead of saying INPUT X$, you must say INPUT A$ and then LSET X$=A$.

Numerical data

On most computers, a random-access file must contain strings, not numbers. If you *want* to store numbers, you must turn them into strings.

To turn an integer into a string, use the function MKI$ (MaKe from Integer). It turns the integer into a 2-byte string, even if the integer is long. For example, to turn the integer 17999 into a 2-byte string called X$, say FIELD 1, 2 AS X$ and say LSET X$=MKI$(17999).

The function MKS$ (MaKe from Single-precision real) turns a real number into a 4-byte string. The function MKD$ (MaKe from Double-precision) turns a double-precision number into an 8-byte string.

Suppose you turn a number into a string (by using MKI$, MKS$, or MKD$), and PUT the string into a file, and later GET the string back from the file. You'll want to convert the string back to a number. Use the function CVI (ConVert to Integer) or CVS (ConVert to Single-precision) or CVD (ConVert to Double-precision). For example, if X$ is a 2-byte string that stands for an integer, you can make the computer print the integer by saying PRINT CVI(X$).

CREATE A DATABASE

The following program creates a database, in which you can store information about your friends & enemies, your business & bills, birthdays & appointments, desires & dreads, and whatever else bothers you. After storing the information in the database, you can peek at the information, change it, expand on it, delete it, or do whatever else strikes your fancy.

Chronological database

The program consists of a main routine and 7 subroutines:

The main routine

All variables will be integers.	`10 DEFINT A-Z`
Allow 100 topics & their data.	`20 DIM T$(100),D$(100)`
Number of topics starts at 0.	`30 N=0`
Ask the human for a topic.	`40 PRINT: PRINT "WHAT TOPIC INTERESTS YOU?": PRINT "(IF YOU'RE NOT SURE, TYPE A QUESTION MARK)": LINE INPUT T$`
Do what the human wishes.	`50 IF T$="?" THEN GOSUB 1000 ELSE GOSUB 2000`
Go to another topic.	`60 GO TO 40`

Subroutine 1000: tell the human what topics are in the database

If database is empty, say so.	`1000 IF N=0 THEN PRINT "I DON'T KNOW ANY TOPICS YET.": PRINT "MY MIND IS STILL BLANK.": PRINT "PLEASE TEACH ME A NEW TOPIC.": RETURN`
If not empty, list the topics.	`1010 PRINT "I KNOW ABOUT THESE TOPICS:": FOR I = 1 TO N: PRINT T$(I),: NEXT I: PRINT: PRINT "PICK ONE OF THOSE TOPICS, OR TEACH ME A NEW ONE."`
	`1020 RETURN`

Subroutine 2000: search through the database, to find the topic T$

Start searching.	`2000 FOR I = 1 TO N`
If the topic is found, do 3000.	`2010    IF T$=T$(I) THEN GOSUB 3000: RETURN`
If not found yet, try again.	`2020 NEXT`
If never found, do 4000.	`2030 GOSUB 4000`
	`2040 RETURN`

Subroutine 3000: the topic's in the database

Tell the human about the topic.	`3000 PRINT "HERE'S WHAT I KNOW ABOUT "T$":": PRINT D$(I)`
Ask whether to change the info.	`3010 INPUT "DO YOU WANT TO CHANGE THAT INFORMATION";A$`
If the human says yes, do 5000.	`3020 IF A$="YES" OR A$="Y" THEN GOSUB 5000`
	`3030 RETURN`

Subroutine 4000: the topic's not in the database

Say topic is not in database.	`4000 PRINT "I DON'T KNOW ANYTHING ABOUT "T$"."`
Request info about the topic.	`4010 PRINT: PRINT "TELL ME ABOUT "T$: PRINT "(IF YOU DON'T WANT TO TELL ME, TYPE THE LETTER X)": LINE INPUT D$`
If human wants, insert topic.	`4020 IF D$<>"X" THEN GOSUB 6000`
	`4030 RETURN`

Subroutine 5000: change the info

Agree to change the info.	`5000 PRINT "OKAY. I'VE ERASED THAT INFORMATION ABOUT "T$"."`
Request new info.	`5010 PRINT: PRINT "TYPE WHAT YOU WANT ME TO KNOW ABOUT "T$: PRINT "(IF YOU WANT ME TO FORGET "T$", TYPE THE LETTER X)": INPUT D$`
Change the info as requested.	`5020 IF D$="X" THEN GOSUB 7000 ELSE D$(I)=D$`
	`5030 RETURN`

Subroutine 6000: insert the topic into the database

Increase the number of topics.	`6000 N=N+1`
Append new topic & its data.	`6010 T$(N)=T$: D$(N)=D$`
	`6020 RETURN`

Subroutine 7000: delete the topic from the database

Replace that topic by topic #N.	`7000 T$(I)=T$(N): D$(I)=D$(N)`
Decrease the number of topics.	`7010 N=N-1`
	`7020 RETURN`

If your computer doesn't understand DEFINT, omit line 10. If your computer doesn't understand LINE INPUT, omit the word LINE from lines 40 and 4010.

The program stores the topics in **chronological order**: if you begin by feeding it information about SUE and then information about CAROL, it will let T$(1) be SUE and let T$(2) be CAROL.

Alphabetical database

Instead of chronological order, you might prefer **alphabetical order**.

For example, suppose you feed the computer information about SUE then CAROL then ZELDA then ALICE then JANE. Here's what the computer's memory would look like, in each kind of order:

Chronological order	Alphabetical order
SUE	ALICE
CAROL	CAROL
ZELDA	JANE
ALICE	SUE
JANE	ZELDA

Which is better: chronological order or alphabetical order?

Chronological order lets you quickly add a new name (just add it at the end of the list), but *finding* a name in the list is slow (since the list looks disorganized). Alphabetical order lets you find a name faster (since the list is alphabetized), but *adding* a new name to the alphabetized list is slow (since the only way to insert the new name is to make room for it by shoving other names out of the way).

So which is better?

Chronological order is the simplest to program and the fastest for INSERTING.
Alphabetical order is the fastest for FINDING information.

If you want to store the names in alphabetical order instead of chronological order, just change subroutines 2000, 6000, and 7000 to these:

Subroutine 2000A: search through the database, to find the topic T$

Create L and H.	`2000 L=0: H=N+1`
I is the average of L and H.	`2010 I=INT((L+H+1)/2)`
If I=H, do 4000.	`2020 IF I=H THEN GOSUB 4000: RETURN`
If the topic is found, do 3000.	`2030 IF T$=T$(I) THEN GOSUB 3000: RETURN`
Not found yet. Change H or L	`2040 IF T$<T$(I) THEN H=I ELSE L=I`
and try again to find topic!	`2050 GO TO 2010`

Subroutine 6000A: insert the topic into the database

Increase the number of topics.	`6000 N=N+1`
Move other topics out of way.	`6010 FOR J = N TO I+1 STEP -1: T$(J)=T$(J-1): D$(J)=D$(J-1): NEXT`
Insert new topic & its data.	`6020 T$(I)=T$: D$(I)=D$`
	`6030 RETURN`

Subroutine 7000A: delete the topic from the database

Decrease the number of topics.	`7000 N=N-1`
Close gap from deleted topic.	`7010 FOR J = 1 TO N: T$(J)=T$(J+1): D$(J)=D$(J+1): NEXT`
	`7020 RETURN`

Subroutine 2000A runs faster than chronological subroutine 2000, because searching through an alphabetical list is faster than searching through a chronological list. (To search through the alphabetical list super-quickly, subroutine 2000A uses a trick called **binary search**.)

Unfortunately, subroutines 6000A (which inserts) and 7000A (which deletes) run *slower* than chronological subroutines 6000 and 7000. To get the high speed of subroutine 2000A, you must accept the slowness of subroutines 6000A and 7000A.

You've seen that chronological order is fast for inserting and deleting but slow for searching, whereas alphabetical order is exactly the opposite: it's fast for searching but slow for inserting or deleting.

Tree-structured database

Instead of using chronological order or alphabetical order, advanced programmers use a **tree**. Like chronological order, a tree lets you insert and delete quickly. Like alphabetical order, a tree lets you search quickly also.

Poets say, "only God can make a tree." Does that mean advanced programmers are God?

To learn how to make a tree, begin by sketching a picture of a tree on paper. Since N is the alphabet's middle letter, begin by writing the letter N, and put two arrows underneath it:

The left arrow is called the **before-arrow**; it will point to the names that come alphabetically before N. The right arrow is called the **after-arrow**; it will point to the names that come alphabetically after N.

For example, suppose your first topic is SUE. Since SUE comes alphabetically after N, put SUE at the tip of N's after-arrow:

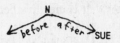

Suppose your next topic is CAROL. Since CAROL comes alphabetically before N, put CAROL at the tip of N's before-arrow:

Suppose your next topic is ZELDA. Since ZELDA comes after N, we'd like to put ZELDA at the tip of N's after-arrow; but SUE's already stolen that position. So compare ZELDA against SUE. Since ZELDA comes after SUE, put ZELDA at the tip of SUE's after-arrow:

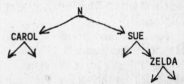

Suppose your next topic is ALICE. Since ALICE comes before N, look at the tip of N's before-arrow. Since CAROL's stolen that position, compare ALICE against CAROL; since ALICE comes before CAROL, put ALICE at the tip of CAROL's before-arrow:

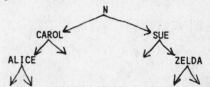

Suppose your next topic is JANE. Since JANE comes before N, look at the tip of N's before-arrow. Since CAROL's stolen that position, compare JANE against CAROL; since JANE comes after CAROL, put JANE at the tip of CAROL's after-arrow:

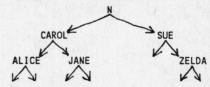

If the next few topics are FRED, then LOU, then RON, then BOB, the tree looks like this:

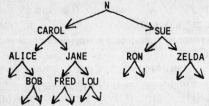

Look at the arrows that point down from N. N's before-arrow points to the group of names that come alphabetically before N (such as CAROL, ALICE, JANE, BOB, FRED, and LOU); N's after-arrow points to the group of names that come alphabetically after N (such as SUE, RON, and ZELDA). Similarly, CAROL's before-arrow points to the group of names that come alphabetically before CAROL (such as ALICE and BOB); CAROL's after-arrow points to the group of names that come alphabetically after CAROL (such as JANE, FRED, and LOU).

Programmers treat the tree as if it were a "family tree". CAROL is called the **parent** of ALICE and JANE, who are therefore called CAROL's **children**. CAROL is called the **ancestor** of ALICE, JANE, BOB, FRED, and LOU, who are therefore called CAROL's **descendants**. The arrows are called **pointers**.

To make the tree more useful, begin with "N !" instead of "N" (so you can choose "N" as a topic later), and number the topics in the order they appeared: since SUE was the first topic, put "1" in front of SUE; since CAROL was the second topic, put "2" in front of CAROL; since ZELDA was the third topic, put "3" in front of ZELDA, like this:

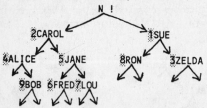

To describe the tree to the computer, store this table in the computer's memory:

Topic	Where the before-arrow points	Where the after-arrow points
0 N !	2	1
1 SUE	8	3
2 CAROL	4	5
3 ZELDA	0	0
4 ALICE	0	9
5 JANE	6	7
6 FRED	0	0
7 LOU	0	0
8 RON	0	0
9 BOB	0	0

That table **represents** the tree and is called the tree's **representation**.

The table's left column is in chronological order, but the other columns give information about alphabetizing. So a tree combines chronological order with alphabetical order: it combines the advantages of both. Adding a new topic to the tree is quick and easy (as in chronological order): just add the name to the bottom of the list, and adjust a few arrows. Using the tree to search for a topic is quick and easy (as in alphabetical order): just follow the arrows.

Like the alphabetical program, the program that creates and manipulates the tree uses the same subroutines 1000, 3000, 4000, and 5000 as the chronological program. To create the tree, change the main routine and subroutines 2000, 6000, and 7000. You must also add a new subroutine (8000). Here are those new routines:

The main routine T

All variables will be integers.	`10 DEFINT A-Z`
Allow 100 topics, data, etc.	`20 DIM T$(100),D$(100),P(100,2)`
Topic #0 is "N !".	`30 T$(0)="N !": P(0,1)=0: P(0,2)=0`
The number of real topics is 0.	`40 N=0`
Ask the human for a topic.	`50 PRINT: PRINT "WHAT TOPIC INTERESTS YOU?": PRINT "(IF YOU'RE NOT SURE, TYPE A QUESTION MARK)": LINE INPUT T$`
Do what the human wishes.	`60 IF T$="?" THEN GOSUB 1000 ELSE GOSUB 2000`
Go to another topic.	`70 GO TO 50`

Subroutine 2000T: search through the database, to find the topic T$

Starting at 0, hunt for T$.	`2000 I=0: GOSUB 8000`
If absent, do 4000, else 3000.	`2010 IF I=0 THEN GOSUB 4000 ELSE GOSUB 3000`
	`2020 RETURN`

Subroutine 6000T: insert the topic into the database

Increase the number of topics.	`6000 N=N+1`
Append new topic & its data.	`6010 T$(N)=T$: D$(N)=D$: P(N,1)=0: P(N,2)=0`
Make topic I1 point to it.	`6020 P(I1,J)=N`
	`6030 RETURN`

Subroutine 7000T: delete the topic from the database

Make topic I1 (which was pointing to the vanishing topic) point to the vanishing topic's left child instead.

`7000 P(I1,J)=P(I,1)`

A is the number of the vanishing topic. B is the number of the vanishing topic's right child.

`7010 A=I: B=P(I,2)`

If the vanishing topic has a right child, make something point to that child.

`7020 IF B>0 THEN T$=T$(B): I=I1: GOSUB 8000: P(I1,J)=B`

If the vanishing topic isn't topic N, move topic N to the gap left by the vanishing topic.

`7030 IF A<N THEN T$=T$(N): I=0: GOSUB 8000: P(I1,J)=A: T$(A)=T$: D$(A)=D$(N): P(A,1)=P(N,1): P(A,2)=P(N,2)`

Decrease the number of topics. `7040 N=N-1`

`7050 RETURN`

Subroutine 8000T

Starting at position I, hunt for T$ in the database. If T$ is missing from the database, make I be 0; otherwise make I be the position of T$. Find the topic that points to T$. Make I1 be that topic's position. If the arrow pointing to T$ points left, make J be 1; otherwise make J be 2. Here's how to do all that:

If the topic is found, return.	`8000 IF T$=T$(I) THEN RETURN`
Compute a tentative J.	`8010 IF T$<T$(I) THEN J=1 ELSE J=2`
Compute a tentative I1 and I.	`8020 I1=I: I=P(I,J)`
If pointer is not 0, hunt again.	`8030 IF I>0 THEN GO TO 8000`
	`8040 RETURN`

Disk-based database

All those database programs (chronological, alphabetical, and tree) put data into the RAM. When you turn off the power, the RAM forgets all the data!

This superior program puts the database onto a disk instead of into RAM:

The main routine D

Prepare the variables.	10 DEFINT A-Z: DIM PF$(2): Z$=MKI$(0)
Open the file and its fields.	20 OPEN "INFO" AS 1 LEN=128: FIELD 1, 44 AS TF$, 80 AS DF$, 2 AS PF$(1), 2 AS PF$(2)

Topics #1 and #2 are headers. Topic #2 should be "N !", and topic #1's left pointer should be N.

```
                    30 IF LOF(1)=0 THEN N=2: LSET TF$="N !": LSET PF$(1)=Z$: LSET PF$(2)=Z$: PUT 1,2 ELSE GET 1,1: N=CV
                    I(PF$(1))
```

Ask the human for a topic.	40 PRINT: PRINT "WHAT TOPIC INTERESTS YOU?": PRINT "(IF YOU'RE NOT SURE, TYPE A QUESTION MARK)": PRINT "(IF YOU WANT TO END, TYPE THE LETTER X)": LINE INPUT T$
If the human wishes, do 1000.	50 IF T$="?" THEN GOSUB 1000: GO TO 40
If the human wishes, end.	60 IF T$="X" THEN LSET PF$(1)=MKI$(N): PUT 1,1: CLOSE: END

Make TS$ resemble T$ but be 44 characters long (by adding blank spaces at the end).

```
                    70 LSET TF$=T$: TS$=TF$
```

Find the topic.	80 GOSUB 2000
Go to another topic.	90 GO TO 40

Subroutine 1000D: tell the human what topics are in the file

If just headers, say so.	1000 IF N=2 THEN PRINT "I DON'T KNOW ANY TOPICS YET.": PRINT "MY MIND IS STILL BLANK.": PRINT "PLEASE TEACH ME A NEW TOPIC.": RETURN
If file has topics, list them.	1010 PRINT "I KNOW ABOUT THESE TOPICS:": FOR I = 3 TO N: GET 1,I: PRINT TF$: NEXT: PRINT "PICK ONE OF THOSE TOPICS, OR TEACH ME A NEW ONE."
	1020 RETURN

Subroutine 2000D: search through the file, to find the topic TS$

Starting at 2, hunt for TS$.	2000 I=2: GOSUB 8000
If absent, do 4000, else 3000.	2010 IF I=0 THEN GOSUB 4000 ELSE GOSUB 3000
	2020 RETURN

Subroutine 3000D: the topic's in the file

Tell the human about the topic.	3000 PRINT "HERE'S WHAT I KNOW ABOUT "T$":": PRINT DF$
Ask whether to change the info.	3010 INPUT "DO YOU WANT TO CHANGE THAT INFORMATION";A$
If the human says yes, do 5000.	3020 IF A$="YES" OR A$="Y" THEN GOSUB 5000
	3030 RETURN

Subroutine 4000D: the topic's not in the file

Say topic is not in the file.	4000 PRINT "I DON'T KNOW ANYTHING ABOUT "T$"."
Request info about the topic.	4010 PRINT: PRINT "TELL ME ABOUT "T$: PRINT "(IF YOU DON'T WANT TO TELL ME, TYPE THE LETTER X)": LINE INPUT D$
If human wants, insert topic.	4020 IF D$<>"X" THEN GOSUB 6000
	4030 RETURN

Subroutine 5000D: change the info

Agree to change the info.	5000 PRINT "OKAY. I'VE ERASED THAT INFORMATION ABOUT "T$"."
Request new info.	5010 PRINT: PRINT "TYPE WHAT YOU WANT ME TO KNOW ABOUT "T$: PRINT "(IF YOU WANT ME TO FORGET "T$", TYPE THE LETTER X)": LINE INPUT D$
Change the info as requested.	5020 IF D$="X" THEN GOSUB 7000 ELSE LSET DF$=D$: PUT 1,I
	5030 RETURN

Subroutine 6000D: insert the topic into the file

Increase the number of topics.	6000 N=N+1
Let topic I1 point to topic N.	6010 LSET PF$(J)=MKI$(N): PUT 1,I1
Append the new topic, at N.	6020 LSET TF$=TS$: LSET DF$=D$: LSET PF$(1)=Z$: LSET PF$(2)=Z$: PUT 1,N
	6030 RETURN

Subroutine 7000D: delete the topic from the file

A is the number of the vanishing topic. P1 and P2 are the topic's pointers.

```
                    7000 A=I: P1=CVI(PF$(1)): P2=CVI(PF$(2))
```

Make topic I1 (which was pointing to the vanishing topic) point to the vanishing topic's left child instead.

```
                    7010 GET 1,I1: LSET PF$(J)=MKI$(P1): PUT 1,I1
```

If the vanishing topic has a right child, make something point to that child.

```
                    7020 IF P2>0 THEN GET 1,P2: TS$=TF$: I=I1: GOSUB 8000: LSET PF$(J)=MKI$(P2): PUT 1,I1
```

If the vanishing topic isn't topic N, move topic N to the gap left by the vanishing topic.

```
                    7030 IF A<N THEN GET 1,N: PUT 1,A: TS=TF$: I=2: GOSUB 8000: GET 1,I1: LSET PF$(J)=MKI$(A): PUT 1,I1
```

Decrease the number of topics.	7040 N=N-1
	7050 RETURN

Subroutine 8000D

Starting at position I, hunt for TS$ in the file. If TS$ is missing from the database, make I be 0; otherwise make I be the position of TS$.
Find the topic that points to TS$. Make I1 be that topic's position. If the arrow pointing to TS$ points left, make J be 1; otherwise make J be 2.
Here's how to do all that:

Start at position I.	8000 GET 1,I
If the topic is found, return.	8010 IF TS$=TF$ THEN RETURN
Compute a tentative J.	8020 IF TS$<TF$ THEN J=1 ELSE J=2
Compute a tentative I1 and I.	8030 I1=I: I=CVI(PF$(J))
If pointer not 0, hunt again.	8040 IF I>0 THEN GO TO 8000
	8050 RETURN

VERSIONS OF BASIC

IBM PC & CLONES

Here's how to use BASIC on the IBM PC. (The IBM PC Junior, IBM PC XT, IBM PC AT, IBM PS/1, IBM PS/2, and IBM Valuepoint are similar. So are the microcomputers that are called "IBM-compatible" or "IBM clones".)

The keyboard (page 324)

The original IBM PC contained 83 keys, placed like this:

F1	F2	Esc	! 1	@ 2	# 3	$ 4	% 5	^ 6	& 7	* 8	(9	) 0	_ -	+ =	Backsp	NumLock		ScrollLock
F3	F4	LeftTab Tab	Q	W	E	R	T	Y	U	I	O	P	{ [	}]		7 Home	8 ↑	9 PgUp	-
F5	F6	Ctrl	A	S	D	F	G	H	J	K	L	: ;	" '	~ `	Enter	4 ←	5	6 →
F7	F8	Shift	| \	Z	X	C	V	B	N	M	< ,	> .	? /	Shift	PrtSc *	1 End	2 ↓	3 PgDn
F9	F10	Alt				Space					CapsLock		0 Ins		. Del	+

In that diagram, I wrote the words "Shift", "Backsp", "Tab", and "Enter"; but if you look at the actual IBM PC keyboard, you'll see arrows on those keys instead. **The SHIFT key shows an arrow pointing up; the BACKSPACE key shows an arrow pointing to the left; the TAB key shows arrows crashing into walls; and the ENTER key shows an arrow that's bent.** IBM put arrows on those keys instead of words, to help people who don't read English.

In January 1986, IBM began selling a fancier keyboard, which contained 101 keys:

Esc		F1	F2	F3	F4		F5	F6	F7	F8		F9	F10	F11	F12		PrintScreen	ScrollLock	Pause

~ `	! 1	@ 2	# 3	$ 4	% 5	^ 6	& 7	* 8	(9	) 0	_ -	+ =	Backsp
LeftTab Tab	Q	W	E	R	T	Y	U	I	O	P	{ [	}]	| \
CapsLock	A	S	D	F	G	H	J	K	L	: ;	" '		Enter
Shift	Z	X	C	V	B	N	M	< ,	> .	? /			Shift
Ctrl		Alt		Space			Alt		Ctrl				

Insert	Home	PageUp
Delete	End	PageDown
	↑	
←	↓	→

NumLock	/	*	-
7 Home	8 ↑	9 PgUp	
4 ←	5	6 →	+
1 End	2 ↓	3 PgDn	
0 Ins		. Del	Enter

At first, that fancier keyboard was available just on an IBM computer called the **IBM RS**. Later, IBM made that keyboard available for the newest versions of the **IBM PC XT** and **IBM PC AT** and for the **IBM PS/2**. Today, IBM sells just that 101-key keyboard; it no longer sells the old 83-key keyboard.

Which keyboard does *your* computer have? If you have an 83-key keyboard, double-check to make sure you found the important keys correctly. . . .

The left SHIFT key is above the ALT key.
The right SHIFT key is above the CAPS LOCK key.
The BACKSPACE key is in the top row and left of the NUM LOCK key.
The TAB key is left of the Q.
The ENTER key is above the PRT SC key.

To type a number easily, use the keys in the top row of the main part of the keyboard. (For example, to type 4, press the key that has a 4 and a dollar sign.) Do *not* press the number keys on the right side of the keyboard: they produce numbers only if the NUM LOCK key is pressed beforehand, by you or the computer. If the NUM LOCK key was pressed to produce numbers, and you want to *stop* making those keys produce numbers, just tap the NUM LOCK key again.

Get started (page 325)

Start by obeying the instructions on pages 100 and 101. If you have a hard disk, those instructions make the computer say "C:\>". If you don't have a hard disk, those instructions make the computer say "A>" or "A:\>".

Versions of BASIC
Two popular versions of BASIC have been invented for the IBM PC.

The old version is called **GWBASIC**. (The GW stands for "gee whiz".) The new version is called **QBASIC**. (The Q stands for "quick".)

MS-DOS versions 5 & 6 include a pair of files that make the computer understand QBASIC. Those files are called "QBASIC.EXE" and "QBASIC.HLP".

Most older versions of MS-DOS include a file that makes the computer understand GWBASIC. That file is usually called "GWBASIC.EXE"; but some versions of MS-DOS call it "BASIC.COM" or "BASICA.COM" instead. Some versions of MS-DOS lack the file altogether and can't do BASIC.

Getting into QBASIC
If you're planning to use QBASIC (because you bought MS-DOS version 5 or 6), type "qbasic" after the C prompt, like this:

```
C:\>qbasic
```

The computer will say:

```
Welcome to MS-DOS QBasic
```

Press the Esc key, then the F6 key.

Instead of saying "OK", the computer will show a blinking line near the screen's bottom left corner.

Getting into GWBASIC
If you're planning to use GWBASIC (because you bought an old version of MS-DOS), here's what to do. . . .

If you have a hard disk, try typing:

```
C:\>gwbasic
```

If the computer gripes (by saying "Bad command or file name"), try typing:

```
C:\>basica
```

If the computer still gripes (by saying "Bad command or file name" again), try typing:

```
C:\>basic
```

If the computer still gripes (by saying "Bad command or file name" again), try saying "dos\gwbasic" or "dos\basica" or "dos\basic".

If you do *not* have a hard disk, find the floppy that contains GWBASIC.EXE or BASICA.COM or BASIC.COM. Insert that floppy into drive A and say "gwbasic" or "basica" or "basic".

When you get into GWBASIC successfully, the computer will say the word "Ok".

If the computer does *not* say the word "Ok", you probably used the wrong version of DOS. Make sure your version of DOS came from your computer's manufacturer. For example, if IBM built your computer, use IBM's PC-DOS, *not* a clone version of MS-DOS. If a clone company built your computer, use your clone's version of MS-DOS, *not* IBM's PC-DOS. Using the wrong version of DOS makes the computer print a strange message, the screen go crazy, or the keyboard stop working.

If you have an IBM PC Junior, buy the **BASIC cartridge** and put it into the left cartridge slot before you turn the computer on. (That cartridge makes the Junior understand CIRCLE, PAINT, PLAY, TIMER, and the BASIC words for disks.) If your Junior is attached to a monitor instead of a TV, type "width 80" after the computer says "Ok".

How to leave QBASIC
When you finish using QBASIC, say "File eXit" (by tapping the Alt key, then the F key, then the X key). If the computer asks "Save it now?", say "No" (by pressing N).

How to leave GWBASIC
When you finish using GWBASIC, type the word "system" (and press ENTER).

Math (page 326)

In QBASIC, when you give a command (such as PRINT 5+2), the answer appears at the bottom of the screen; after you examine the answer, press ENTER.

Three steps (page 328)

The way to program depends on whether you're using GWBASIC or QBASIC.

GWBASIC
In GWBASIC, if you're too lazy to type the word RUN, just press the F2 key, which makes the computer automatically type the word RUN for you and automatically press the ENTER key for you. On an PC Junior, press the Junior's Fn key before F2.

QBASIC
In QBASIC, here's how to program your computer.

First, say "File New" (by pressing the Alt key, then the F key, then the N key). If the computer asks "Save it now?", say "No" (by pressing the N key again).

Next, make sure the blinking underline is in the *top* part of the screen. (If the blinking underline is in the bottom part, move it to the top part by pressing the F6 key).

Then type your program. You do *not* have to type a number in front of each line; those numbers are optional. Instead of typing —

```
1 print "I love you"
2 print "you turn me on"
3 print "let's get married"
```

you can type:

```
print "I love you"
print "you turn me on"
print "let's get married"
```

Finally, say "Run" (by pressing the F5 key). At the bottom of the screen, the computer will print everything you requested; it will print:

```
I love you
you turn me on
let's get married
```

When you finish examining that printing, press the ENTER key.

Another example (page 329)

In QBASIC, do *not* type the word LIST, since the top part of the screen shows the list of your program already.

In GWBASIC, if you're too lazy to type the word LIST, just press the F1 key, which makes the computer automatically type the word LIST for you. Then press ENTER. On a PC Junior, press the Fn key before F1.

Correcting errors (page 330)

In QBASIC, if you mess up a line, do *not* retype it underneath. Instead, press the arrow keys to move to the first character you want to revise, then repeatedly press the DELETE (or Del) key until all the bad characters disappear, then type the characters you wish to insert, then press the down-arrow key.

What if computer gripes? (page 330)

If the computer gripes at you, press the ENTER key immediately.

After pressing the ENTER key, correct the error by retyping the line that the computer griped about.

Rearranging your program (page 331)

In QBASIC, the computer does *not* rearrange your program.

Here's how to make QBASIC erase a line. Move to that line (by pressing the arrow keys). Then, while holding down the Ctrl key, tap the Y key (which means "Yank out the line").

Here's how to make QBASIC insert a new line. Move to where you want the new line to begin. Then, while holding down the Ctrl key, tap the N key (which means "New line").

Ranges of lines (page 332)

QBASIC doesn't understand ranges of lines.

Arrow keys (page 332)

The DELETE key says "Del" on it. The INSERT key says "Ins" on it.

In QBASIC, do *not* press the INSERT key, and do *not* press the ENTER key at the end of your correction.

Clear the screen (page 333)

Your keyboard lacks a CLEAR key. To clear the screen, give the CLS command.

In GWBASIC, here's another way to clear the screen: while holding down the Ctrl key, tap the HOME key. (On a PC Junior do this instead: While pressing Ctrl, tap Fn then HOME.)

Print on paper (page 333)

There is no key marked "PRINT". To print a screen dump, do this instead: if your keyboard is modern (and has 101 keys), press the key marked "PRINT SCREEN". If your keyboard is old-fashioned (and has just 83 keys), press the PrtSc key *while holding down the SHIFT key*. If you have a PC Junior, press the Fn key then the PrtSc key.

Most computers lack an ECHO key. In QBASIC, you cannot echo. In GWBASIC, here's how to echo: press the PrtSc key *while holding down the Ctrl key*. To echo on the PC Junior, press the Fn key then the ECHO key.

In QBASIC, instead of saying LLIST do this: say "File Print" (by pressing Alt then F then P), then press ENTER.

GO TO (page 334)

The BREAK key is the last key in the top row. If your keyboard has 83 keys, the BREAK key says SCROLL LOCK on it; if your keyboard has 101 keys, the BREAK key says PAUSE on it.

The BREAK key works only if you simultaneously hold down the Ctrl key. So **to abort a program, do this: hold down the Ctrl key; and while you keep holding down the Ctrl key, tap the BREAK key.**

PC Junior Press the Fn key before pressing BREAK. You do *not* have the press the Ctrl key.

QBASIC Instead of typing this —

```
10 print "cat"
20 print "dog"
30 go to 10
```

you can type:

```
10 print "cat"
print "dog"
go to 10
```

Instead of using a number (such as 10), you can use a name (such as JOE), but you must put a colon after the name, like this:

```
joe: print "cat"
print "dog"
go to joe
```

After you abort a QBASIC program, pressing F5 makes the computer continue where it left off; pressing SHIFT with F5 makes the computer run the program from the beginning.

STOP (page 336)

In QBASIC, when the computer encounters the word STOP in a program, the computer stops running the program. Then it lists the program and highlights the line of your program that said STOP.

Save on disk (page 336)

Before using a blank disk, make sure the disk has been formatted. To learn how to format a disk, read my MS-DOS chapter.

In QBASIC, instead of typing SAVE "JOE", do this: say "File Save" (by pressing Alt then F then S), then type JOE (and press ENTER). QBASIC doesn't understand the word "FILES".

How to use other drives When you tell the computer to save JOE, the computer normally puts JOE into drive C's root directory (if you have a hard disk) or drive A's directory (if you have no hard disk). If you want the computer to put JOE into drive B instead, say "b:joe" instead of "joe".

To make GWBASIC print the names of all the programs in drive B, type this:

```
files "b:"
```

Exception: if you're using an obsolete version of DOS (version 1 or version 1.05 or version 1.1), you must type this instead:

```
files "b:*.*"
```

How to choose a name (page 337)

Your program's name can be short (such as JOE) or long: up to 8 characters. The name's first character must be a letter; the remaining characters should be letters or digits.

Load from disk (page 337)

In QBASIC, instead of typing LOAD "JOE", do this: say File Open (by pressing Alt then F then O), then type JOE (and press ENTER); if the computer asks "Save it now?", say "No" (by pressing N).

Edit the disk (page 337)

QBASIC doesn't understand RENAME at all. In GWBASIC, instead of saying RENAME "JOE" TO "FRED", say NAME "JOE.BAS" AS "FRED.BAS", to emphasize that JOE was written in BASIC.

Space on the disk (page 337)

QBASIC doesn't understand KILL at all. In GWBASIC, instead of saying KILL "JOE", say KILL "JOE.BAS".

Tapes (page 337)

Since practically everybody who buys an IBM PC uses disks instead of tapes, I won't bother explaining IBM's tape system.

FOR . . . NEXT (page 355)

To indent, you can hit the SPACE bar repeatedly. But to indent more easily, hit the TAB key (which is left of the Q key and has arrows on it).

In QBASIC, if you indent a line (by hitting the SPACE bar repeatedly, or by hitting the TAB key), the computer will assume you want to indent the line underneath also, and so the computer will automatically indent that line for you. If the computer indents a line that you don't want indented, erase the indentation by hitting the BACKSPACE key.

Renumbering (page 367)

QBASIC doesn't understand RENUM.

The PAUSE key (page 367)

If your keyboard has just 83 keys, it lacks a PAUSE key, so to pause do this instead: while holding down the Ctrl key, tap the NUM LOCK key. To make the PC Junior pause, press the Fn key then the PAUSE key.

To stop pausing, press the ENTER key.

Zones (page 368)

Your screen has five zones. Zones 1-4 are each 14 characters wide. Zone 5 is 24 characters wide.

How many pixels? (page 372)

IBM-compatible computers can handle several different **screen modes**:

Mode	Video card	Pixels	Colors
1	CGA (or EGA, MCGA, VGA)	320 by 200	4
2	CGA (or EGA, MCGA, VGA)	640 by 200	2
3	Hercules monochrome	720 by 348	2
4	Olivetti color	640 by 400	2
7	EGA (or VGA)	320 by 200	16
8	EGA (or VGA)	640 by 200	16
9	EGA (or VGA)	640 by 350	4 or 16
10	EGA mono (or VGA mono)	640 by 350	4
11	MCGA (or VGA)	640 by 480	2
12	VGA	640 by 480	16
13	MCGA (or VGA)	320 by 200	256

For example, here's what row 1 of that chart means:

To use mode 1, your video card must be CGA (or EGA or MCGA or VGA). That mode lets you use 320 values of X (numbered from 0 to 319). That mode lets you use 200 values of Y (numbered from 0 to 199). That mode lets the screen display 4 colors simultaneously.

Special mono modes Modes 3 and 10 require monochrome monitors; they do *not* work with color monitors. In mode 3, you have just 2 "colors": black and white.

Special color modes In mode 9, you usually get 16 colors, but you get just 4 colors if the video card is EGA having just 64K of video RAM.

Mode 4 requires a color video card made by Olivetti. That card is included in the AT&T 6300 computer.

Text mode There's also a "mode 0", which works on all computers and produces just text (no graphics).

Versions of BASIC QBASIC (which comes with DOS 5) understands all modes. GWBASIC understands less:

GWBASIC using DOS 1, 1.1, 2, 2.1, or 3 understands just modes 0, 1, and 2. GWBASIC using DOS 3.1 or 3.2 understands modes 0, 1, 2, and 3. GWBASIC using DOS 3.3 or 4 understands modes 0 through 10.

Which mode to choose If you're using QBASIC (which understands all modes), here's which mode to choose:

Video card	Which mode to choose
Hercules monochrome	3
Olivetti color	4
CGA color	1 (for many colors) or 2 (for many pixels)
EGA mono or VGA mono	10
EGA color	9
MCGA color	11 (for many pixels) or 13 (for many colors)
VGA color	12 (for many pixels) or 13 (for many colors)

For GWBASIC using DOS 3.3 or 4, use that same chart, but choose mode 9 instead of modes 11, 12, and 13.

For GWBASIC using DOS 3.1 or 3.2, use this chart instead:

Video card	Which mode to choose
Hercules monochrome	3
any other video card	1 (for many colors) or 2 (for many pixels)

How to change mode Before giving any commands about pixels, tell the computer which mode you want. For example, if you want mode 1, say:

screen 1

Whenever you finish using pixels, return to text mode by saying:

```
screen 0
width 80
```

The "width 80", which makes sure the screen will display 80 characters per line, is necessary only if you'd been using mode 1, 7, or 13.

PC Junior The PC Junior handles modes 0, 1, and 2. It also handles special versions of modes 3, 4, 5, and 6:

PC Junior mode	Pixels	Colors
3	160 by 200	16
4	320 by 200	4
5	320 by 200	16
6	640 by 200	4

Modes 5 and 6 require at least 128K of RAM and require that you give this command beforehand:

```
clear,,,32768
```

Fundamental shapes (page 372)

Say PSET instead of PLOT.

Colors (page 372)

In modes 4, 7, 8, and 12, you can choose from the 16 colors listed on page 372.

In mode 1, you must choose from these 4 colors instead:

0. black
1. cyan (greenish blue)
2. magenta (purplish red)
3. cream (yellowish white)

For example, if you type —

```
line (0,0)-(100,0),2
```

the computer will draw a line using color 2, which is magenta.

In modes 2, 3, and 11, you must choose from these 2 colors instead:

0. black
1. white

In mode 10, you have these 4 choices:

0. black
1. cream
2. blink
3. white

In mode 9, you can usually choose from the 16 colors mentioned on page 372; but if you're using mode 9 with an EGA card having just 64K of RAM, you're restricted to the 4 colors used in mode 1.

In mode 13, you can choose from the 16 colors listed on page 372 — and many more colors, too! Here's the spectrum:

```
  0 through   7: black, blue, green, cyan, red, magenta, brown, cream
  8 through  15: same colors as above, but lighter
 16 through  31: shades of gray (from dark to light)
 32 through  55: color blends (from blue to red to green to blue again)
 56 through  79: same color blends, but lighter
 80 through 103: same color blends, but even lighter
104 through 175: same as 32 through 103, but darker
176 through 247: same as 104 through 175, but even darker
248 through 255: black
```

Advanced commands (and page #)

PLAY (page 374). In the PLAY command, you can use the symbol ">" to mean "go up an octave", and you can use the symbol "<" to mean "go down an octave". For example, if you say —

```
play "g>cd<g"
```

the computer will play the note G, then go up an octave to play C and D in

that higher octave, then go down to the original octave to play G again. Exception: if you're using an obsolete version of DOS (version 1 or 1.05 or 1.1), the symbols ">" and "<" don't work.

The lowest note the computer can play (which is the C in octave 0) is called "note 1". The highest note the computer can play (which is the B in octave 6) is called "note 84". To make the computer play note 84, type this:

```
play "n84"
```

To make the computer play its lowest note (1), then its middle note (42), then its highest note (84), type this:

```
play "n1n42n84"
```

PC Junior. If you turn up the volume on your TV or monitor, and then say SOUND ON, you can make the Junior's three voices sing simultaneously, like this:

```
play "gab","efg","ccd"
```

While the first voice is singing "gab", the second voice sings "efg", and the third voice sings "ccd".

Random integers (388). Instead of saying just RANDOMIZE, say RANDOMIZE TIMER. Exception: if you're using GWBASIC with an obsolete version of DOS (version 1 or 1.05 or 1.1), you must say RANDOMIZE VAL(RIGHT$(TIME$,2)).

To get a random integer between 1 and 5, instead of saying RND(5), say 1+INT(RND*5).

Types of numbers (397). In GWBASIC, if your program involves trigonometry (SIN, COS, TAN, ATN) or exponents (^, SQR, EXP, LOG), and you want those computations done with double-precision accuracy, you must say "gwbasic/d" (instead of just "gwbasic"), or say "basica/d" (instead of just "basica").

In QBASIC, double-precision numbers can go higher than real numbers: the highest permissible double-precision number is about 1D308.

Accuracy (397). In QBASIC, if you type a double-precision number, the computer handles just the first 15 digits accurately.

Joystick (408). The coordinates of joystick A are STICK(0) and STICK(1). The coordinates of joystick B are STICK(2) and STICK(3).

When the computer comes to a line that mentions STICK(0), the computer looks at both joysticks and computes STICK(0), STICK(1), STICK(2), and STICK(3). If your program mentions STICK(1) or STICK(2) or STICK(3), without mentioning STICK(0), the computer won't look at the joysticks.

Mouse (408). Neither GWBASIC nor QBASIC is designed to control a mouse.

Peek (414). Your computer's memory is divided into segments. Each segment contains 64K of RAM or ROM.

Before saying PEEK or POKE, tell the computer which segment to use. For example, if you want the computer to use segment 3, begin your program by saying:

```
10 def seg=3
```

If you then say PRINT PEEK(50000), the computer will peek at the 50000th cell of segment 3. If you forget to say DEF SEG, or say just —

```
10 def seg
```

without putting a number afterwards, the computer will use its "favorite" segment.

Although you can play cute tricks by using the words PEEK and POKE, most IBM programmers avoid those words, for three reasons:

1. PEEK and POKE are awkward to use, because you must remember to say DEF SEG beforehand.

2. The PEEKs and POKEs that work on your computer system might not work on your friend's computer system, because different clones and DOS versions use different memory cells.

3. DOS and BASIC include many commands that are easier than PEEK and POKE and accomplish similar goals. To learn about them, browse through the DOS and BASIC manuals that came with your computer.

If you insist on fiddling with PEEKs and POKEs, read David Schneider's magazine article, which reveals the secrets of dozens of memory cells. Part 1 of his article is on pages 201-218 of the 11/12/85 issue of PC Magazine; part 2 is on pages 187-208 of the 11/26/85 issue. The articles are excerpted from the end of his book, called the *Handbook of BASIC for the IBM PC Revised and Expanded*, published by the Brady Book division of Simon & Schuster.

PUT (417). In GWBASIC, if you want the record length to be more than 128, you must warn the computer. For example, to warn the computer that you'll want a record length of 400, say "gwbasic/s:400" (instead of just "gwbasic"), or say "basica/s:400" (instead of just "basica").

Here's how to use BASIC on Apple's Mac Plus computer. (The 128K Mac, 512K Mac, Mac SE, Mac Classic, Mac LC, Mac 2, and other variants are similar.)

Microsoft BASIC (page 322)

When you buy the computer, make sure you also buy **Microsoft Quick BASIC**. It costs $65 and comes on two disks.

It works only on modern Macs (such as the Mac Plus, Mac SE, Mac SE/30, Mac Classic, Mac LC, Mac 2, Mac 2cx, Mac 2ci, Mac 2si, and Mac 2fx.) It does *not* work on older Macs (the 128K Mac, 512K Mac, and 512KE Mac), since they contain obsolete ROM chips.

Make sure you buy "Microsoft *Quick* BASIC", not just "Microsoft BASIC", which is obsolete.

Here's how to use Microsoft Quick BASIC. (I'll also explain how old "Microsoft BASIC" differs.)

The keyboard (page 324)

The keys are placed like this:

```
~   !   @   #   $   %   ^   &   *   (   )   _   +              Clr  =   /   *
`   1   2   3   4   5   6   7   8   9   0   -   =   Backsp

Tab  Q   W   E   R   T   Y   U   I   O   P   {   }            7   8   9   -
                                             [   ]

Caps  A   S   D   F   G   H   J   K   L   :   "   Return      4   5   6   +
                                         ;   '

Shift   Z   X   C   V   B   N   M   <   >   ?   Shift  ↑      1   2   3   Enter
                                    ,   .   /

Option Command      Space          |   ←   →   ↓            0       .
                                    \
```

To the left of the SPACE bar, you'll see the COMMAND key. In the diagram, I wrote the word "Command" on that key; but if you look at your actual Mac keyboard, you'll see a picture of a highway's cloverleaf on that key instead.

The keyboard contains a RETURN key and also an ENTER key. When you're using BASIC, those keys do the same thing as each other. You'll probably prefer the RETURN key, since your pinky can reach it more easily.

Get started (page 325)

To start using the Mac, read the chapter that explains the Mac Finder. Practice what's in that chapter, before you start playing with BASIC.

When you've practiced what's in that chapter, here's how to start using BASIC.

If you own an external hard drive, turn it on, and wait for the clicking to stop. Then turn on the Mac. Adjust the Mac's brightness knob, until you can read the screen. If the screen doesn't show a trash can, insert System Tools Disk #1, then eject it (by choosing Eject from the File menu).

Now your Mac screen shows the trash can, and your floppy-disk drive is empty. Insert the Microsoft Quick BASIC disk whose label says "Program". Then double-click the Program icon. (If you're using old Microsoft BASIC instead, insert the disk whose label says "Interpreter", then double-click the Microsoft BASIC icon.)

The disk contains two versions of BASIC. The **binary version** computes quickly: it's used by scientists who want blazing speed. The **decimal version** computes slowly but handles decimals with extra accuracy: it's used by accountants who are in no rush, but insist on never being off by a penny.

To choose the binary version, double-click the "Microsoft Quick BASIC (b)" icon. To choose the decimal version instead, double-click the "Microsoft Quick BASIC (d)" icon instead.

The icon will explode.

If you're using Microsoft Quick BASIC (instead of old Microsoft BASIC), and you don't have a hard disk or second floppy drive, the computer will tell you to swap disks 16 times. Obey the computer, and be patient!

Make the **command window** appear on the screen and be active. To do that, choose **Command** from the Windows menu, or use this short cut: while holding down the COMMAND key, type a period. (Old Microsoft BASIC permits an even shorter cut: just click the word "Command" at the bottom of the screen.)

Instead of saying OK, the computer shows a blinking vertical line.

How to quit Whenever you're done using BASIC, choose **Quit** from the File menu (or tap the Q key while holding down the COMMAND key).

Then the computer might say:

```
Current program is not saved. Do you
want to save it before proceeding?
Cancel   No   Yes
```

If the computer says that, click the word "No".

Then choose Shut Down from the Special menu. When the computer says "You may now switch off your Macintosh safely", turn off the Mac and then any external hard drive.

Math (page 326)

When you type a command (such as PRINT 5+2), the command appears at the bottom of the screen, in the command window. The computer prints the answer (7) at the top of the screen, in the **output window**.

Long commands on small screens (page 328)

Keep your commands short. If you type a command that's too long to fit on a line, the computer has difficulty handling it.

Three steps (page 328)

Programming your computer consists of three steps. . . .

Step 1: say NEW
But instead of typing the word NEW, choose **New** from the File menu. If you're lucky, you'll see horizontal stripes next to the word "List".

If you're unlucky, the computer will say:

```
Current program is not saved. Do you
want to save it before proceeding?
Cancel    No    Yes
```

Click the word "No". You'll see horizontal stripes next to the word "List".

Step 2: type your program
Whatever you type will appear underneath the word "Listing", in the **list window**. (Old Microsoft BASIC says "List" instead of "Listing".)

You do *not* have to type a number in front of each line; those numbers are optional. Instead of typing —

```
1 print "I love you"
2 print "you turn me on"
3 print "let's get married"
```

you can type:

```
print "I love you"
print "you turn me on"
print "let's get married"
```

Step 3: run the program
Instead of typing the word RUN and pressing ENTER, choose **Run Program** from the Run menu (or tap the R key while holding down the COMMAND key).

(Old Microsoft BASIC's Run menu says "Start" instead of "Run Program".)

The list window will disappear. The computer will print everything you requested; it will print:

```
I love you
you turn me on
let's get married
```

Then the list window will reappear, and you'll see your program in the window again.

Summary of those steps
Here's the rule: if you type a list of instructions in the list window, the computer won't obey those instructions until you choose Run Program (from the Run menu or by pressing COMMAND R).

Changing the list window
If your program's too long to fit in the list window, the window will show just *part* of your program. To see the rest of your program, use the window's scroll bars.

Clicking the window's zoom box makes the window expand, so that it consumes the entire screen. Clicking the zoom box again makes the window shrink back to its original size. (If your old Microsoft BASIC lacks a zoom box, double-click the word "List" instead.)

Clicking the close box makes the window disappear. To make the window reappear, choose **List** from the Windows menu (or tap the L key while holding down the COMMAND key).

Another example (page 329)

Do *not* type the word LIST. It's usually unnecessary, since the computer tries to *always* show the list of your program on the screen. If the computer ever fails to show the list on the screen, do *not* type the word LIST: instead, choose List from the Windows menu (or press COMMAND L).

Correcting errors (page 330)

If you mess up a line, do *not* retype it underneath. Instead, do the following. . . .

Point at the right edge of the rightmost character that you want to revise. Click once. Repeatedly press the key marked BACKSPACE or DELETE, until all the bad characters disappear. Then type the characters you wish to insert. When you've finished typing them, click underneath the entire program.

What if computer gripes? (page 330)

If you accidentally type PRIMT instead of PRINT, when you run the program the computer will gripe by saying:

```
Undefined subprogram
```

It will also put your program on the screen, and will draw a box around the line it griped about.

Click the word "OK", then revise the bad line.

Rearranging your program (page 331)

The computer does *not* rearrange your program! The computer does *not* put the lines in numerical order! If you type 80, the computer will *not* erase line 80!

How to erase a line
Point slightly left of the leftmost character in the line — so that you're pointing at the gap between the leftmost character and the window's left wall. Press the mouse's button; while you keep pressing the button, drag down one line, but without touching any characters. The line you want to erase will become black. Lift your finger off the button. Press the BACKSPACE key. The line will disappear. Click underneath the entire program.

How to insert a new line
Click at the right edge of the rightmost character of the line above. Press the RETURN key. You'll see a gap to put the new line in. Type the new line; do *not* press the RETURN key at the end of it. Click underneath the entire program.

Ranges of lines (page 332)

To list from line 30 to the end of your program, make the command window active (by clicking it or choosing Command from the Windows menu or pressing the COMMAND and period keys simultaneously). Then type:

```
list 30
```

The computer does *not* understand "LIST 30-80" or "LIST -80".

To delete lines 30 through 80, make the command window active and type:

```
delete 30-80
```

After you type that command (and press the RETURN key), make the list window active (by clicking it or choosing List from the Windows menu).

Arrow keys (page 332)

To insert some text between two characters, click at the gap between the two characters, then type the text.

To delete a group of characters, point at the left edge of the first character in the group, then drag to the right edge of the last character in the group. The characters you want to delete will turn black. Lift your finger off the mouse's button. Press the BACKSPACE key. The characters will disappear.

Clear the screen (page 333)

The CLEAR key doesn't work.

Print on paper (page 333)

Your keyboard lacks a PRINT key. Instead of pressing a PRINT key, press the CAPS LOCK key, so that it stays down; then hold down the SHIFT and COMMAND keys; while you keep holding down the SHIFT and COMMAND keys, tap the 4 key. The printer will print onto paper a copy of the entire screen. When the printer has finished, tap the CAPS LOCK key, so that it pops back up. That method works if your printer's an Imagewriter but *not* if it's a Laserwriter.

Your keyboard lacks an ECHO key.

Your computer understands LPRINT.

Although your computer understands LLIST (if typed in the command window), an easier way to list your program on paper is to make the list window active, then choose **Print** from the File menu, then click OK.

GO TO (page 334)

Instead of typing this —

```
10 print "cat"
20 print "dog"
30 go to 10
```

you can type:

```
10 print "cat"
print "dog"
go to 10
```

If you delete the 10 from the top line, the computer will gripe when it sees "go to 10".

Instead of using a number (such as 10), you can use a name (such as JOE), but you must put a colon after the name, like this:

```
joe: print "cat"
print "dog"
go to joe
```

To abort a program, choose **Stop** from the File menu, or tap the period key while holding down the COMMAND key. (Old Microsoft BASIC puts "Stop" in the Run menu instead of the File menu.)

After you've aborted a program, if you wish to see a LIST, make the list window active (by choosing List from the Windows menu, or pressing COMMAND with L).

How to single-step trace your program If a program runs faster than your eye can see or your mind can think, slow it down. To do that, instead of choosing Run Program from the Run menu, choose **Step** from the Run menu (or press COMMAND with T).

That makes the computer do just one line or subline of your program; then it will pause. When you choose Step again, the computer will do the next line or subline. Each time you choose Step, the computer will do one more line or subline. Each time the computer does a line, it also shows the program in the list window, and puts a box around the line it just did.

Love (page 334)

If a program involves a semicolon with a GO TO, begin the program by saying WIDTH 61, like this:

```
width 61
10 print "love";
go to 10
```

If you forget to say WIDTH 61, the computer will print just one line of love and then do nothing until you abort.

STOP (page 336)

When the computer encounters the word STOP in a program, the computer stops running the program. Then it lists the program and puts a box around the line of your program that said STOP.

Save on disk (page 336)

If you buy a blank disk and want to use it, you must initialize the disk. To learn how to do that, read the chapter that explains the Mac Finder.

After you initialize that disk, you should copy "Microsoft Quick BASIC (b)" and "System Folder" onto that disk, by dragging those icons to that disk. To learn how to do that, read the chapter that explains the Mac Finder.

You should *not* save programs on the original "Microsoft BASIC" disk. Instead, save your programs on a new disk that you turned into an easy-to-use BASIC disk.

So before you write programs to save, turn off the computer, insert a new easy-to-use BASIC disk, and then turn the computer back on.

Before typing SAVE "JOE" or FILES, make the command window active (by clicking it or choosing Command from the Windows menu or pressing the COMMAND and period keys simultaneously).

Here's a short cut: instead of activating the command window and then saying SAVE "JOE", just choose **Save** from the File menu and then type JOE (followed by RETURN).

How to choose a name (page 337)

Your program's name can be short (such as JOE) or long: up to 31 characters. Short names are better, because they can fit in small windows.

Load from disk (page 337)

Before saying LOAD "JOE" or RUN "JOE", activate the command window. Here's a short cut: instead of activating the command window and saying LOAD "JOE", just choose **Open** from the File menu and double-click JOE.

Edit the disk (page 337)

Instead of saying RENAME "JOE" TO "FRED", say NAME "JOE" AS "FRED".

Tapes (page 337)
Your computer can't handle tapes.

FOR . . . NEXT (page 355)
To indent, you can hit the SPACE bar repeatedly. But to indent more easily, hit the TAB key. Hitting the TAB key has the same effect as hitting the SPACE bar four times.

If you indent a line (by hitting the SPACE bar repeatedly, or by hitting the TAB key), the computer will assume you want to indent the line underneath also, and so the computer will automatically indent that line for you.

If the computer indents a line that you don't want indented, erase the indentation, by hitting the BACKSPACE key four times.

Renumbering (page 367)
Your computer doesn't understand RENUM.

The PAUSE key (page 367)
Your keyboard lacks a PAUSE key — but you don't need one. When you list a program, the listing automatically pauses when the list window is filled. While running a program, you can stop temporarily (by choosing Stop from the File menu or pressing CONTROL with a period), then continue where you left off by choosing **Continue** from the Run menu (or pressing CONTROL with G).

Old Microsoft BASIC understands Continue but not CONTROL with G.

Zones (page 368)
Your screen has 5 zones. Zones 1-4 are each 14 characters wide; zone 5 is 5 characters wide. Altogether, the screen is 61 characters wide.

Those measurements are for standard-size characters. Your computer can also produce characters that are extra-narrow or extra-wide.

Loops (page 369)
If a program involves zones with a GO TO, begin the program by saying WIDTH 61, like this:

```
width 60
10 print "hi",
go to 10
```

How many pixels? (page 372)
The X coordinate goes from 0 to 491. The Y coordinate goes from 0 to 297.

The high-numbered pixels hide behind the list and command windows. To see those pixels, put this line at the bottom of your program —

```
9999 go to 9999
```

That line creates an infinite loop, which keeps the output window on the screen. When you finish staring at the pixels in the output window, abort the program by choosing Stop from the File menu (or press COMMAND with period).

Fundamental shapes (page 372)
Say PSET instead of PLOT. The computer draws each shape in black, on a white background.

PAINT (page 372)
Your computer doesn't understand the word PAINT.

Colors (page 372)
The standard Mac displays just black and white: it can't display any other colors. The code number for white is 0; the code number for black is 1. (Any even number produces white; any odd number produces black.)

Advanced commands (and page #)
PLAY (page 374). Your computer doesn't understand the word PLAY.

Random integers (388). Instead of saying just RANDOMIZE, say RANDOMIZE TIMER. To get a random integer from 1 to 5, instead of saying RND(5), say 1+INT(RND*5).

Types of numbers (397). BASIC comes in two versions — binary and decimal — which you choose by clicking the appropriate icon.

Suppose you type a number containing a decimal point. If that number contains fewer than 7 digits, it's a real; if it contains more than 7 digits, it's double-precision; if it contains exactly 7 digits, the binary version treats it as a real, but the decimal version treats it as double-precision instead.

Accuracy (397). If you type a double-precision number, the binary version handles it to an accuracy of 15 to 16 digits, but the decimal version handles it to an accuracy of just 14 digits.

Variables (397). If a variable is simple (such as X), the binary version treats it as real, but the decimal version treats it as double-precision.

Joystick (408). Your computer doesn't use a joystick.

Here's how to use BASIC on the Apple 2c computer. (The Apple 2c+ and 2GS are similar.) I'll explain how the Apple 2, 2+, and 2e differ.

The keyboard (page 324)

On the Apple 2c, the keys are placed like this:

Reset	40	Keyboard

```
Esc  ! @ # $ % ^ & * ( )  - +  Delete
     1 2 3 4 5 6 7 8 9 0    =
Tab   Q W E R T Y U I O P { } |
                           [ ] \
Control A S D F G H J K L : "  Return
                         ; '
Shift   Z X C V B N M < > ?    Shift
                      , . /
CapsLock ~ OpenApple Space SolidApple ← → ↓ ↑
         `
```

The keys next to the SPACE bar are called the **Apple keys**. In the diagram, I wrote the words "Open Apple" and "Solid Apple" on those keys; but if you look at your actual Apple 2c keyboard, you'll see pictures of apples on those keys instead.

There's no BACKSPACE key.

To correct an error, press the left-arrow key, until you get back to where the error was. Then correct the error, by retyping. Then, if you wish, press the right-arrow key to move to the right.

Your computer has a key marked DELETE, but it doesn't work when you're using BASIC.

The ENTER key says RETURN on it.

Apple 2e The Apple 2e keyboard lacks a 40 key and a KEYBOARD key.

Apple 2 and 2+ The zero key is Swedish. The CONTROL key says CTRL on it. The letters are automatically capitalized. The keys are rearranged slightly. The following keys are missing: DELETE, TAB, CAPS LOCK, OPEN APPLE, SOLID APPLE, KEYBOARD, 40, down-arrow, up-arrow, left-bracket, right-bracket, backslash, and accent.

Get started (page 325)

Cut into the right side of your computer, you'll see a horizontal slot about 5 inches long. That slit's the entrance to the **built-in drive**.

At the center of the slit is a **door**, which is the same color as the keys on the keyboard. To open the door, push it to the left; then it will automatically pop up. To close the door, push it down. Practice opening and closing it.

Then open the door. Remove any disk from the built-in drive. Put the "System Utilities ProDOS disk" into the built-in drive; when inserting the disk, make sure the disk's label is on *top* of the disk, and make sure the disk's big oval cutout goes into the drive *before* the label does. After putting the disk into the drive, close the door.

The computer's green power switch is at the computer's rear, and has the numbers 0 and 1 on it. Flip the power switch on, by pressing the 1.

Turn on the TV or monitor.

If you're using a TV, turn it to channel 3 or 4. To switch the computer from channel 3 to channel 4 or back to channel 3, flip the channel-selection switch, which is on the box attached to the back of the computer. If the writing on the TV looks fuzzy, adjust the TV's fine tuning.

Adjust the screen's brightness and contrast.

The computer will put several messages onto the screen. Eventually, you'll see the **main menu**, which looks like this:

```
1. Copy files
2. Delete files
3. Rename files
4. Lock/unlock files
5. Duplicate a disk
6. Format a disk
7. Identify and catalog a disk
8. Advanced operations
9. Exit system utilities
```

Tap the 9 key, then tap the RETURN key twice.

You'll see this symbol on the screen, at the upper-left corner:

```
]
```

That symbol's called a **bracket**. It means everything's OK. **Your computer prints a bracket instead of the word OK.**

You can make the characters on your screen be either thin or fat. The screen is wide enough to hold 80 thin characters per line, or 40 fat characters. Fat characters are easier to read, so choose fat characters if your eyesight is poor, or if you're using a cheap TV (which is blurry) instead of a monitor.

To choose fat characters (40 per line), tap the ESC key, then the 4 key. To choose thin characters (80 per line), tap the ESC key, then the 8 key.

Apple 2, 2+, and 2e The disk drive and its slot are in a separate box (instead of being built into the right side of the computer). If you have *two* disk drives, begin by using disk drive #1, not disk drive #2.

Open the disk drive's door, by pulling the door out and up. Remove any disk from the drive. If you have a 2e, insert the "ProDOS User's Disk"; if you have a 2 or 2+, insert the "DOS 3.3 System Master Disk" instead. When inserting the disk, make sure the disk's label is on *top* of the disk, and make sure the disk's big oval cutout goes into the drive *before* the label does.

Close the door, by pushing it down and in.

Turn on the TV or monitor. If you're using a TV, turn it on to channel 33.

On the back of the computer, you'll see the computer's power switch, which is black. Flip it to the ON position.

Here's what happens next, *if you have a 2e:*

At the top of the screen, a message will appear briefly. If your 2e is old (manufactured before February 1985), the message says "Apple]["; if your 2e is new (or you've upgraded your old 2e), the message says "Apple 2e". Look at the message, to double-check whether your 2e is old or new.

If your 2e is old, it can't handle lower-case letters well, so you must type just capitals. To type capitals easily, press the CAPS LOCK key, and make sure the CAPS LOCK key stays down.

Your 2e will also print this menu:

```
YOUR OPTIONS ARE:
   ? - TUTOR: PRODOS EXPLANATION
   F - PRODOS FILER (UTILITIES)
   C - DOS <-> PRODOS CONVERSION
   S - DISPLAY SLOT ASSIGNMENTS
   T - DISPLAY/SET TIME
   B - APPLESOFT BASIC
```

Tap the B key.

Regardless of whether you have a 2, 2+, or 2e, you'll eventually see this symbol near the screen's left edge:

```
]
```

That symbol's called a **bracket**. It means everything's OK. Your computer prints a bracket instead of the word OK.

The characters are fat (40 per line). Your Apple might be able to make the characters thin (80 per line), but your Apple handles thin characters reliably only if your Apple is a *new* 2e that also contains an 80-column card. If you have that kind of Apple and want thin characters, say —

```
pr#3
```

and press the RETURN key.

Ranges of lines (page 332)

Instead of saying DELETE, say DEL. To delete lines 30 through 80, type this:

```
del 30,80
```

Arrow keys (page 332)

To edit line 30, first put line 30 onto the screen, by saying LIST 30. (Say LIST, not EDIT: your computer doesn't understand the word EDIT.)

On your computer, the cursor does *not* blink: it's a solid square that indicates where you'll be typing.

Your computer uses the Catholic method of editing, which uses the Catholic cross and its effect on bodies and souls. Here are the details. . . .

Tap the ESC key. A cross will appear in the middle of the cursor.

Move the cursor (including its cross) up to the line you want to edit, by pressing the up-arrow key repeatedly. Then tap the ESC key again, to get rid of the cross.

(The up-arrow key works only when you see a cross, because, according to Catholics, "to get to heaven you must follow the Cross". Most other keys are Temptations: they're effective only when you do *not* see a cross.)

Move the cursor to the part of the line you want to correct, by pressing the right-arrow key repeatedly.

Then make your corrections.

Replace To replace a character, move the cursor to the character you want to replace, then type the new character you want instead.

Delete To delete a group of characters, move the cursor to the first character in the group.

Create a cross (by tapping the ESC key), then move the cross across the group of characters (by pressing the right-arrow key), until you've passed the last character in the group. Then get rid of the cross (by tapping the ESC key again).

The characters that the cross passed over will go to heaven and disappear from their earthly existence. (Their bodies will remain on the screen, but their souls will departed so the characters won't affect any future LIST.)

Insert To insert extra characters, move the cursor to the place where you want the extra characters to begin appearing.

Then move the cursor up (by tapping the ESC key, then the up-arrow key, then the ESC key). Type the characters you want to insert. Then create a cross (by tapping the ESC key), and move the cross to where you want the extra characters to begin appearing (by tapping the down-arrow and left-arrow keys). Finally, get rid of the cross.

When you finish editing When you've finished correcting the line, press the right-arrow key repeatedly, until you get *past* the last character in the line. Then press the RETURN key. To see what happened to the line, LIST it.

Why bother? Because that Catholic method of editing is so long-winded, most programmers don't bother using it: instead, they type the entire line over!

Apple 2e The editing process is the same as for the 2c, with just two exceptions:

1. To begin the whole editing process, tap the ESC key, *then the left-arrow key*, then move the cursor up to the line you want to edit.

2. You see the cross only if your Apple 2e contains an 80-column card and you previously said PR#3. Otherwise, the cross is invisible: when the cross is at the cursor, the cursor covers up the cross, so that you can't see the cross (even though the cross is there).

Apple 2 and 2+ The method of editing is even more complicated, so don't bother! Just type the whole line over again.

Spaces after numbers (page 332)

Your computer does **not** automatically put spaces after numbers.

Spaces before numbers (page 333)

Your computer does **not** automatically put spaces before positive numbers.

For example, if you give this command —

```
print "the temperature is";4+25;"degrees"
```

the computer prints:

```
the temperature is29degrees
```

The computer does *not* automatically put a space before or after the 29.

To put spaces near the 29, put spaces in the strings nearby, like this:

```
print "the temperature is ";4+25;" degrees"
```

Multiple calculations (page 333)

If you give this command —

```
print 6+2;6-2
```

your computer will print the answer to 6+2 (which is 8) and also print the answer to 6-2 (which is 4), but won't put any spaces between the answers. Your computer will print:

```
84
```

To force your computer to put a space between the answers, replace the semicolon by a <u>space in quotation marks</u>, like this:

```
print 6+2" "6-2
```

That makes your computer print:

```
8 4
```

Clear the screen (page 333)

Your keyboard lacks a CLEAR key. Instead of pressing a CLEAR key, press the ESC key, then type an @ symbol. (To type the @ symbol, remember to press the SHIFT key.)

Your computer doesn't understand the CLS command. Instead of typing CLS, type the word HOME.

Print on paper (page 333)

Your keyboard doesn't have a PRINT key or ECHO key, and your computer doesn't understand LPRINT or LLIST. To print on paper, here's what to do instead. . . .

Make sure the printer is plugged in, turned on, and full of paper. Make sure any lights indicating POWER, READY, SELECT, and ON LINE are glowing.

To activate the printer, type this:

```
pr#1
```

That makes the computer use paper instead of your screen. After you type PR#1, everything you and the computer type will appear on paper instead of on the screen.

If you ever want to use your screen again, **you must deactivate the printer, by typing:**

```
pr#0
```

For example, to make the computer print just "I love you" on paper, you must activate the printer, then tell the computer to print "I love you", then deactivate the printer, like this:

```
pr#1
print "I love you"
pr#0
```

If a program prints on the screen but you want it to print on paper instead, activate the printer before you type RUN. Here's how:

```
pr#1
list
pr#0
```

In the middle of your program, one of the lines can say "pr#1". But if a line of your program simply says —

```
30 pr#1
```

the computer will get confused. Instead, say:

```
30 d$=chr$(4)
31 ?d$"pr#1"
```

To make line 60 deactivate the printer, say:

```
60 ?d$"pr#0"
```

For example, this program prints *two* poems. It prints "love is like a dove" on your screen, and prints "life is full of strife" on paper:

```
new
10 print "love"
20 print "is like a dove"
30 d$=chr$(4)
31 ?d$"pr#1"
40 print "life"
50 print "is full of strife"
60 ?d$"pr#0"
run
```

GO TO (page 334)

To abort a program, hold down the CONTROL key; and while you keep holding down the CONTROL key, tap the C key.

If the computer is printing on the screen faster than you can read, you can make the computer slow down. **To slow the printing, type this command:**

```
speed=0
```

For example, to make the computer LIST your program slowly, and also PRINT slowly when it runs your program, type this:

```
speed=0
list
run
```

To make the computer print quickly again, at full speed, type this command:

```
speed=255
```

SPEED=0 means slow; SPEED=255 means fast. For an intermediate speed, pick a number between 0 and 255.

Save on disk (page 336)

If you buy a blank disk and want your computer to use it, you must turn the blank disk into an Apple disk.

To do that, turn the computer off, make sure the built-in drive contains the "Systems Utilities ProDOS disk", close the door, then turn the computer back on.

The screen will eventually show you the main menu, which looks like this:

```
1.  Copy files
2.  Delete files
3.  Rename files
4.  Lock/unlock files
5.  Duplicate a disk
6.  Format a disk
7.  Identify and catalog a disk
8.  Advanced operations
9.  Exit system utilities
```

Tap the 6 key, then tap the RETURN key four times.

The computer will say:

```
Place the disk you wish to format in the built-in drive.
Press RETURN to continue.
```

Obey the computer: put the blank disk into the built-in drive, then press the RETURN key.

The computer will grunt several times loudly: hold your ears! 20 seconds later, the computer will say:

```
Format complete.
Press RETURN to continue, ESC to return to the main menu.
```

The blank disk has been turned into an Apple disk.

Press the ESC key. You'll see the main menu again. Tap the 9 key, then tap the RETURN key twice. Then tap the ESC key, followed by the 4 key (for fat characters) or the 8 key (for thin characters).

You can*not* copy a program onto the System Utilities ProDOS disk. Instead, copy your program onto a blank disk that you turned into an Apple disk.

Omit quotation marks.

```
Most computers:  SAVE "JOE"
Your computer:   save joe
```

Instead of saying FILES, say CATALOG or CAT. If you say CAT, the computer will print an abridged catalog.

How to use drive 2
The built-in drive is called **drive 1**. If you buy an extra drive, the extra is called the **external drive**; it's also called **drive 2**.

Normally, the computer uses drive 1. If you want it to use drive 2 instead, put a comma and a D2 at the end of the disk command. For example, to get a catalog of drive 2, say:

```
catalog,d2
```

To save JOE in drive 2, say:

```
save joe,d2
```

If you put a comma and D2 at the end of a command, the Apple assumes you're more interested in drive 2 than in drive 1. Therefore, it will automatically use drive 2 instead of drive 1 for all future commands. If you ever want to use drive 1 again, you must give a command that ends in a comma and D1.

How to copy an entire disk
To copy an entire disk, put the System Utilities ProDOS disk into the built-in drive. Turn the computer off, then on again. When you see the main menu, tap the 5 key, then tap the RETURN key three times.

The computer will say:

```
Place the source disk in the built-in drive.
Press RETURN to continue.
```

Obey the computer: into the built-in drive, put the disk you want to copy; then press the RETURN key.

The computer will say:

```
Place the destination disk into the built-in drive.
Press RETURN to continue.
```

Obey the computer: into the built-in drive, put a blank disk; then press the RETURN key twice.

The computer will turn the blank disk into an Apple disk. Then it will say, "Place the source disk into the built-in drive." Into the built-in drive, put the disk you want to copy; then press the RETURN key. Then it will say, "Place the destination disk into the built-in drive." Grab the blank disk that you had just turned into an Apple disk, and put it into the built-in drive; then press the RETURN key.

Seven more times, the computer will tell you to place the source disk and then the destination disk into the built-in drive. Obey the computer: swap the disks seven more pairs of times, and press the RETURN key after each time.

Finally, the computer will say:

```
Disk copy complete.
Press RETURN to continue, ESC to return to the main menu.
```

Press the ESC key. You'll see the main menu. Tap the 9 key, then the RETURN key twice, then say how wide you want the characters to be (by tapping ESC then 4, or ESC then 8).

How to create a quick-start disk
To create a quick-start disk (which helps start using BASIC faster), get a blank disk, and turn it into an Apple disk (by using the System Utilities ProDOS disk). Then get the main menu on the screen again, and make sure the System Utilities ProDOS disk is in the main drive. With the main menu still on the screen, tap the 1 key, tap the RETURN key four times, tap the down-arrow key six times, tap the right-arrow key, tap the down-arrow key again, tap the right-arrow key again, and tap the RETURN key.

The computer will say:

```
Place the destination disk in the built-in drive.
Press RETURN to continue.
```

Obey the computer: put the blank Apple disk into the built-in drive, then press the RETURN key. The computer will tell you to swap disks four more times. Finally, the computer will say:

```
Copying complete.
Press RETURN to continue, ESC to return to the main menu.
```

Press the ESC key. You'll see the main menu. Tap the 9 key, then the RETURN key twice, then say how wide you want the characters to be (by tapping ESC then 4, or ESC then 8).

You've created a quick-start disk. In the future, whenever you want to start using the computer quickly, put the quick-start disk into the drive (instead of the System Utilities ProDOS disk), and then turn on the computer. The computer will say:

```
PRODOS BASIC
]
```

Then just say how wide you want the characters to be (by tapping ESC then 4, or ESC then 8).

If you save a program on that disk, and call the program STARTUP (instead of JOE), the computer will automatically run that program whenever you start up the computer.

If you make the top two lines of that program say —

```
10 d$=chr$(4)
11 ?d$"pr#3"
```

the computer will automatically tap the ESC key and 8 key for you.

Apple 2e
To turn a blank disk into an Apple disk, turn the computer off, make sure drive 1 contains the ProDOS User's Disk, close the door, and turn the computer back on. The computer will say PRODOS USER'S DISK. Tap the F key; the computer will say FILER. Tap the V key; the computer will say VOLUME COMMANDS. Tap the F key; put the blank disk into drive 1; press the RETURN key three times; the computer will say FORMATTING. 25 seconds later, the computer will say FORMAT COMPLETE; the blank disk has been turned into an Apple disk. Press the ESC key twice, then the Q key, then the RETURN key.

To copy an entire disk, put the ProDOS User's Disk into drive 1. Turn the computer off, then on again. The computer will say PRODOS USER'S DISK. Tap the F key; the top of the screen will say FILER. Tap the V key; the top of the screen will say VOLUME COMMANDS. Tap the C key; grab the disk you want to copy, and put it in drive 1; put a blank disk in drive 2; press the RETURN key six times. When the computer finishes copying, press the ESC key twice, then the Q key, then the RETURN key.

Apple 2 and 2+ To turn a blank disk into an Apple disk, put the blank disk into drive 1 and then type:

```
NEW
10 PRINT "HELLO"
INIT HELLO
```

The drive's red light will glow for about 30 seconds. When it stops glowing, your blank disk is finally an Apple disk; it's called a "slave of a DOS 3.3 System Master". It's also a quick-start disk.

Your computer doesn't understand CAT: say CATALOG.

To copy an entire disk, put the DOS 3.3 System Master disk into drive 1. Type RUN COPYA and press the RETURN key. The computer will say APPLE DISKETTE DUPLICATION PROGRAM. Grab the disk you want to copy, and put it in drive 1; put a blank disk in drive 2; press the RETURN key five times. The computer will copy all information from drive 1's disk to the blank disk. (In the process, it will also turn the blank disk into an Apple disk.) Then the computer will ask DO YOU WANT TO MAKE ANOTHER COPY? If you don't, type an N and then press the RETURN key.

How to choose a name (page 337)

Your program's name can be short (such as JOE) or long: up to 15 characters. The name's first character must be a letter; the remaining characters must be letters, digits, or periods.

Load from disk (page 337)

Omit quotation marks.

Most computers	Your computer
LOAD "JOE"	load joe
RUN "JOE"	run joe

Edit the disk (page 337)

Instead of saying RENAME "JOE" TO "FRED", say:

```
rename joe,fred
```

Space on the disk (page 337)

To erase JOE from the disk, instead of saying KILL "JOE" say:

```
delete joe
```

Tapes (page 337)

The Apple 2c can't handle tapes.

Long variable names (page 340)

Variable names must be short. The name of a numeric variable must be just 1 or 2 characters; the name of a string variable must be just 1 or 2 characters followed by a dollar sign. If you try to make the variable's name longer than that, the computer will handle it unreliably.

If you want a variable name that's 2 characters long, avoid the following 2-character names, which have special meanings: TO, IF, ON, FN, GR, AT, OR.

INPUT (page 341)

In the INPUT statement, the computer's question is called the **prompt**. The prompt begins and ends with a quotation mark. On your computer, **the prompt should end with a question mark then a space then a quotation mark.** . . .

Most computers:	`10 INPUT "WHAT IS YOUR NAME";N$`
Your computer:	`10 input "What is your name? ";n$`

Usually, you can abort a program by tapping the C key while holding down the CONTROL key. But while the computer is doing an INPUT statement, that method won't work, unless you press the RETURN key afterwards.

Fancy relations (page 349)

Your computer can't handle the letter A followed by the word THEN. For example, it can't handle:

```
if x=a then print "wow"
```

To prevent the letter A from being next to THEN, reverse the equality —

```
if a=x then print "wow"
```

or use parentheses to separate the A from the THEN:

```
if (x=a) then print "wow"
```

ELSE (page 349)

Your computer doesn't understand the word ELSE.

FOR . . . NEXT (page 355)

If you indent the lines between FOR and NEXT, your computer ignores the indentation. When you LIST your program, you won't see any indentation. So **don't bother to indent**.

Renumbering (page 367)

Your computer doesn't understand RENUM.

The PAUSE key (page 367)

Your keyboard lacks a PAUSE key. To make the computer pause, hold down the CONTROL key; and while you keep holding down the CONTROL key, tap the S key.

To stop pausing, press the SPACE bar.

Apostrophe (page 367)

Instead of an apostrophe, type a colon followed by the word REM (which stands for "remark"). For example:

```
40 c=40: rem because Russ has 40 computers
```

Zones (page 368)

If you chose 80 characters per line (by tapping ESC and then 8), your screen has 5 zones, and each zone is 16 characters wide.

If you chose 40 characters per line (by tapping ESC and then 4), your screen has just 3 zones. The left zone is 16 characters wide; the middle zone is also 16 characters wide; the right zone is just 8 characters wide.

LOCATE (page 371)

Your computer doesn't understand the word LOCATE. To print "DROWN" beginning at line 3's 7th position, say this:

```
vtab 3: htab 7: print "DROWN"
```

Pixels (page 372)

Apple handles pixels differently from most other computers. Here are the details. . . .

Simple graphics
To use simple, low-resolution graphics, type:

```
gr
```

That makes the computer split the screen into two parts. The top part of your screen will be used for graphics. The bottom of your screen will *not* be used for graphics: instead, it will be used for non-graphics (which Apple calls "text").

When you type GR, the computer makes the top part of your screen (the graphics part) be entirely black.

Your next step is to choose a color to draw in. You can choose these colors:

```
0. black
1. magenta (purplish red)
2. dark blue
3. lavender (light purple)
4. dark green
5. gray
6. blue (light greenish blue)
7. light blue
8. brown
9. orange
10. gray
11. pink
12. green
13. yellow
14. aqua (light greenish blue)
15. white
```

You must also choose which pixel you want to color: the pixel's X and Y coordinates must each be from 0 to 39. For example, to make pixel (31,37) become pink, type this:

```
color=11: plot 31,37
```

To make pixel (5,9) and pixel (17,21) both become yellow, type this:

```
color=13: plot 5,9: plot 17,21
```

If the colors on your TV look wrong, adjust your TV's COLOR and TINT dials.

To draw a green horizontal line from pixel (4,19) to pixel (8,19), type this:

```
color=12: hlin 4,8 at 19
```

To draw a blue vertical line from pixel (4,20) to pixel (4,30), type this:

```
color=6: vlin 20,30 at 4
```

To print "welcome to the art museum" on the bottom part of the screen (which is for non-graphics), just say:

```
print "welcome to the art museum"
```

Whenever you want to stop using graphics, type:

```
text: home
```

That tells the computer to use the entire screen for non-graphics (TEXT).

You can put all those ideas into a program, like this:

```
10 home: gr
20 color=11: plot 31,37
30 color=13: plot 5,9: plot 17,21
40 color=12: hlin 4,8 at 19
50 color=6: vlin 20,30 at 4
60 print "welcome to the art museum"
70 for i = 1 TO 4000: next
80 text: home
```

Line 10 includes the word HOME, to make sure that the bottom part of the screen (for non-graphics) begins entirely black. Lines 20-50 draw a picture. Line 60 prints a caption. Line 70 makes the computer count to 4000: while the computer counts, you can admire the picture that the computer drew; if you want to admire the picture longer, change the 4000 to 10000. Line 80 returns the computer to its normal state, which is non-graphics.

In that program, lines 10, 70, and 80 are particularly important. **Every low-resolution graphics program should begin by saying "HOME: GR", and should end by saying "FOR I" and "TEXT: HOME".**

High-resolution graphics
High-resolution graphics differs from low-resolution graphics in the following ways . . .

For low-res, you say "GR". For high-res, you say "HGR: VTAB 21".

for low-res, you say "COLOR=" and choose a color from 0 to 15. For high-res, you say "HCOLOR=" and choose one of these high-res colors:

0. black			
1. usually green;	black	if X is even;	white if adjacent pixel isn't black
2. usually purple;	black	if X is odd;	white if adjacent pixel isn't black
3. usually white;	green	if X is odd	and adjacent pixel is black;
	purple	if X is even	and adjacent pixel is black
4. black			
5. usually orange;	black	if X is even;	white if adjacent pixel isn't black
6. usually blue;	black	if X is odd;	white if adjacent pixel isn't black
7. usually white;	orange	if X is odd	and adjacent pixel is black;
	blue	if X is even	and adjacent pixel is black

For low-res, you say "PLOT". For high-res, you say "HPLOT".

For low-res, the X coordinate and Y coordinate each go from 0 to 39. For high-res, the X coordinate goes from 0 to 279, and the Y coordinate goes from 0 to 159.

For low-res, you say "HLIN" to draw a horizontal line, and you say "VLIN" to draw a vertical line. For high-res, you can draw a line in *any* direction, by saying "HPLOT TO". For example, if you say —

```
hplot 250,140
hplot to 70.90
hplot to 180,114
```

the computer will plot the pixel (250,140), then draw a diagonal line from there to pixel (70,90), then draw a diagonal line from pixel (70,90) to pixel (180,114). You can combine those commands into a single command:

```
hplot 250,140 to 70,90 to 180,114
```

Here's a complete program:

```
Use high-res.      10 home: hgr: vtab 21
Draw green lines.  20 hcolor=1: hplot 250,140 to 70,90 to 180,114
Write a caption.   30 print "welcome to the art museum"
Pause.             40 for i = 1 to 4000: next
End the graphics.  50 text: home
```

Advanced commands (and page #)

BEEP (page 373). Instead of saying BEEP, say:

```
print chr$(7);
```

SOUND (373). Your computer doesn't understand the word SOUND.

PLAY (374). Your computer doesn't understand the word PLAY.

PRINT USING (374). Your computer doesn't understand PRINT USING.

Exponents (384). Your computer makes a mistake when handling exponents.

According to mathematicians and most other computers, -5^2 means "the negative of 5^2"; so it's -25. But the Apple makes the mistake of thinking that -5^2 means "the square of -5", which is 25.

If you say PRINT -5^2, the Apple will therefore print 25, which mathematicians consider to be wrong.

For another example, suppose you say:

```
10 x=5
20 print -x^2
```

The Apple mistakenly thinks that line 20 means "the square of -X", and therefore prints 25. (According to mathematicians and other computers, line 20 means "the negative of X^2", and so the answer ought to be -25.)

The Apple's mistake makes the Apple incorrectly handle several branches of mathematics. For example, the Apple incorrectly solves quadratic equations and incorrectly graphs upside-down parabolas — unless you *help* your Apple by typing parentheses.

To help your Apple, type parentheses whenever a minus sign is followed by an exponentiated number:

```
print -(5^2)
```

Another example:

```
10 x=5
20 print -(x^2)
```

Those parentheses make the Apple print the correct answer, which is -25.

Random integers (388). Omit the word RANDOMIZE. To get a random integer from 1 to 5, instead of saying RND(5), say 1+INT(RND(1)*5).

Random decimals (391). For a random decimal between 0 and 1, say RND(1) instead of just RND.

Left, right, middle (394). Your computer doesn't understand an equal sign after MID$.

Searching in a string (395). Your computer doesn't understand INSTR.

Clock (395). Your computer doesn't have a clock, and so it doesn't understand TIME$, TIMER, or DATE$.

String-number conversion (395). Your computer makes STR$(81.4) be the string "81.4", without a blank space.

Repeating characters (395). Your computer doesn't understand STRING$.

Types of numbers (397). You can't use double-precision. To create a real number, you can type as many digits as you wish, but the computer remembers just the first 10 digits accurately, and prints just the first 9 of them on your screen.

RAM consumption (397). Each real number consumes 5 bytes of RAM.

Variables (397). For integer variables, you can use the symbol % but not the word DEFINT.

Adjacent printing (407). You can't put a semicolon immediately after INPUT.

LINE INPUT (407). You can't say LINE INPUT.

INPUT$ (407). Instead of saying A$=INPUT$(1), say GET A$. Instead of saying —

```
6 P$=INPUT$(4)
```

say:

```
6 get p1$: get p2$: get p3$: get p4$: p$=p1$+p2$+p3$+p4$
```

Joystick (408). Say PDL instead of STICK. If you say PDL and then suddenly say PDL again, the computer won't compute the second PDL accurately. To improve the accuracy, make the computer pause before the second PDL, by inserting a FOR . . . NEXT loop:

```
100 x=pdl(0): for i = 1 TO 100: next: y=pdl(1)
```

Mouse (408). Your computer's version of BASIC is not designed to work with a mouse.

SWAP (409). Your computer doesn't understand SWAP, so use the alternative.

ON ERROR GO TO (414). Change ERROR to ERR, and change "ON ERROR GO TO 0" to "POKE 216,0".

You can say RESUME, but you cannot put a number or word after RESUME. You cannot say RESUME 30; you cannot say RESUME NEXT. Instead of saying RESUME 30, say "CALL 62248: GO TO 30".

POKE (414). Normally, the computer uses the whole screen. If you say —

```
poke 33,20
```

the computer will use just the left part of the screen. That part will be 20 characters wide. Whenever you try to type more than 20 characters on a line, the computer will put the excess characters underneath, as part of the line below. The rightmost part of the screen will be unused, and will act as a very wide right margin.

If you don't like a width of 20, choose a different width instead.

Problem: write a program that puts instructions on the screen and keeps the instructions there permanently, while the rest of the screen changes. Solution: turn on the computer, avoid saying POKE, write the instructions on the rightmost part of the screen (by giving ordinary PRINT statements with TAB or HTAB), and then say "POKE 33,20". That POKE prevents the computer from typing anything new on the rightmost part of the screen — but the instructions you typed there previously will remain.

Apple's LIST command is peculiar. To edit your program more easily, instead of saying just LIST, say:

```
poke 33,33
list
```

That makes the LIST be just 33 characters wide. That particular width — 3 characters — makes the LIST easier to edit.

OPEN FOR OUTPUT (415). This program prints "eat" and 4 and "eggs" onto a disk file called SUE:

```
5 d$=chr$(4): ?d$"open sue": ?d$"write sue"
10 print "eat"
20 print 2+2
30 print "eggs"
40 ?d$"close"
```

OPEN FOR INPUT (415). This program makes the computer read SUE and copy it to your screen:

```
5 d$=chr$(4): ?d$"open sue": ?d$"read sue"

10 input a$
11 print a$

20 input b
21 print b

30 input c$
31 print c$

40 ?d$"close"
```

OPEN FOR APPEND (415). This program makes the computer append "good morning!" to the end of SUE:

```
10 d$=chr$(4): ?d$"open sue": ?d$"append sue"
20 print "good morning!"
30 ?d$"close"
```

Loops (416). Your computer doesn't understand EOF(1). Instead of saying IF EOF(1) THEN GO TO 1000, put this line at the top of your program: ON ERR GO TO 1000.

LOF (416). Your computer doesn't understand LOF(1).

PUT (417). This program creates a random-access file called JIM whose record length is 21, and defines JIM's 7th, 9th, and 4th items:

```
5 d$=chr$(4): ?d$"open jim,l21"
10 ?d$"write jim,r" 7: print "love makes me giggle"
20 ?d$"write jim,r" 9: print "please hold my hand"
30 ?d$"write jim,r" 4: print "I love Lucy"
40 ?d$"close"
```

At the end of line 5, the L21 means Length 21. "LOVE MAKES ME GIGGLE" contains 20 characters but requires a record length of 21, because the RETURN key at the end of GIGGLE consumes 1 byte.

GET (417). This program makes the computer tell you JIM's 7th item:

```
5 d$=chr$(4): ?d$"open jim,l21"
10 ?d$"read jim,r" 7: input x$: print x$
20 ?d$"close"
```

LOC (417). Your computer doesn't understand LOC.

Numerical data (417). The computer lets you put numbers in the file. You do *not* have to convert the numbers to strings.

Here's how to use BASIC on the Commodore 64 computer. (The Commodore 64C and SX-64 are similar.) I'll explain how the Commodore 128, 128D, 16, Plus 4, Pet, Super Pet, CBM, and Vic-20 differ. The Amiga resembles the Apple Mac (explained on page 427).

The keyboard (page 324)

On the Commodore 64, the keys are placed like this:

←	! 1	" 2	# 3	$ 4	% 5	& 6	' 7	(8	) 9	0	+	-	£	Clr Home	Inst Del	F2 F1
Ctrl		Q	W	E	R	T	Y	U	I	O	P	@	*	↑	Restore	F4 F3
Run Stop	ShiftLock		A	S	D	F	G	H	J	K	L	[:	] ;	=	Return	F6 F5
Commodore	Shift		Z	X	C	V	B	N	M	< ,	> .	? /	Shift	↑ ↓	← →	F8 F7
					Space											

The key in the bottom left corner is called the **Commodore key**. In the diagram, I wrote the word "Commodore" on that key; but if you look at your actual Commodore 64 keyboard, you'll see a fancy C on that key instead.

The zero key is Swedish.

The computer capitalizes all letters automatically; so to type a capital letter, do *not* press the SHIFT key.

There is no CAPS key.

The BACKSPACE key is marked DEL (which stands for DELETE). So to backspace, make sure you hit the DEL key. Do *not* hit the keys that show left-arrows; the left arrow keys do *not* backspace correctly.

The ENTER key says RETURN on it.

Get started (page 325)

The computer's power switch is on the computer's right side. Flip that switch ON. Then turn on the TV or monitor.

If you're using a TV, turn it to channel 3 or 4. To switch the computer from channel 3 to channel 4 or back to channel 3, flip the computer's channel-selection switch, which is on the back of the computer. If the writing on the TV looks fuzzy, adjust the TV's fine tuning.

Adjust the screen's brightness and contrast.

When the computer's on and functioning correctly, **the computer will say READY** (instead of OK).

Commodore 128 and 128D Those computers resemble a Commodore Plus 4 until you say —

GO 64

which makes them imitate a Commodore 64 instead.

Math (page 326)

To type a plus sign, do *not* press the SHIFT key. (If you accidentally press the SHIFT key, you'll be typing a crucifix instead of a plus sign.)

Long commands on small screens (page 328)

A command can contain up to 80 characters. If you try to type more than 80 characters in a command, the computer will ignore the extra characters.

Colons (page 329)

Although you can put several statements on the same line, the total number of characters in the line must not be greater than 80.

Ranges of lines (page 332)

Your computer does <u>not</u> understand the word DELETE. To delete lines 30, 31, 32, 33, and 34, you can*not* type DELETE 30-34; instead, you must type:

```
30
31
32
33
34
```

Arrow keys (page 332)

To edit line 30, first put line 30 onto the screen, by saying LIST 30. (Say LIST, not EDIT: your computer doesn't understand the word EDIT.)

At the keyboard's lower-right corner, you'll see a pair of arrow keys. By pressing them with or without the SHIFT key, you can move the cursor in all four directions. Move the cursor to the part of line 30 you want to correct, then make your corrections.

To delete a character, move the cursor just past that character, then press the DELETE key. The DELETE key deletes the character to the left of the cursor.

To replace a character, move the cursor to the character you want to replace, then type the new character you want instead.

To insert an extra character in the middle of the line, move the cursor to where you want that character to appear, then tap the INST key *while holding down the SHIFT key*, then type the character you want to insert. (To insert *two* characters, you must tap the INST key with SHIFT, then type the first character, then tap the INST key with SHIFT again, then type the second character.)

When you've finished correcting the line, press the RETURN key, which tells the computer to take the corrections seriously.

After pressing the RETURN key, you might like to move the cursor to the bottom of the screen. If you'd like to do that, press the down-arrow key several times.

Hassle That editing procedure is easy, except for one hassle: under certain unusual conditions, the cursor keys and INST/DEL key don't work! Under those conditions, the cursor keys and INST/DEL keys print strange symbols on your screen instead of moving the cursor. If that happens to you, press the RETURN key and then try again to edit the line. If it happens again, press the RETURN key, then move the cursor to the bottom of the screen, and type the whole line over again.

I said the hassle occurs "under certain unusual conditions". Specifically, it occurs only if you begin an editing sequence (by pressing the cursor keys and INST/DEL key) when you're at the right-hand part of a line: the part that's to the right of an unmatched quotation mark or to the right of an inserted space (inserted by the INST key).

Clear the screen (page 333)

The CLEAR key is marked "CLR HOME". To clear the screen, hold down the SHIFT key; and while you keep holding down the SHIFT key, press the "CLR HOME" key.

Your computer does *not* understand CLS. To make line 10 clear the screen, type this instead:

```
10 PRINT "♥";
```

To make that heart, hold down the SHIFT key with the CLR HOME key.

Print on paper (page 333)

Your keyboard doesn't have a PRINT key or ECHO key, and your computer doesn't understand LPRINT or LLIST. To print on paper, here's what to do instead. . . .

Make sure the printer is plugged in, turned on, and full of paper. Make sure any lights indicating POWER, READY, SELECT, and ON LINE are glowing.

To activate the printer, type this:

```
OPEN 4,4: CMD 4
```

That makes the computer use paper instead of your screen. Henceforth, the computer will print all its answers on paper instead of on your screen.

If you ever want the computer to print on your screen again, **you must deactivate the printer, by typing:**

```
PRINT#4: CLOSE 4
```

For example, to make the computer print just "I LOVE YOU" on paper, you must activate the printer, then tell the computer to print "I LOVE YOU", then deactivate the printer, like this:

```
OPEN 4,4: CMD 4
PRINT "I LOVE YOU"
PRINT#4: CLOSE 4
```

If a program prints on the screen but you want it to print on paper instead, activate the printer before you type RUN. Here's how:

```
OPEN 4,4: CMD 4
RUN
PRINT#4: CLOSE 4
```

Here's a fancy program that prints *two* poems. It prints "LOVE IS LIKE A DOVE" on your screen, and prints "LIFE IS FULL OF STRIFE" on paper:

```
NEW
10 PRINT "LOVE"
20 PRINT "IS LIKE A DOVE"
30 OPEN 4,4: CMD 4
40 PRINT "LIFE"
50 PRINT "IS FULL OF STRIFE"
60 PRINT#4: CLOSE 4
RUN
```

To LIST your program on paper instead of on your screen, type this:

```
OPEN 4,4: CMD 4
LIST
PRINT#4: CLOSE 4
```

GO TO (page 334)

The BREAK key is marked "RUN STOP". So **to abort a program, press the "RUN STOP" key.**

If the computer is printing on the screen too quickly for you read, you can make the computer print more slowly. To slow the printing, hold down the CTRL key while the computer prints. The computer will print slowly, as long as you keep holding down the CTRL key. When you lift your finger from that key, the computer will print quickly again.

Save on disk (page 336)

When you flip the disk drive's power switch, you create an electrical surge that damages any disk inside the drive. So **before flipping the drive's power switch, make sure the drive is empty.**

So to turn on your computer system, first remove any disk from the drive; then flip on the drive's switch; then turn on the computer. Memorize that sequence: "disks out, drive on, computer on."

When you're done using the computer, follow this sequence: "disks out, computer off, drive off".

How to insert a disk To put a disk into the drive, first make sure the disk drive's red light is off. Then open the drive's door.

Insert the disk into the drive. When you insert it, make sure the disk's label is on *top* of the disk, and make sure the disk's big oval cutout goes into the drive *before* the label does. Close the drive's door.

How to turn a blank disk into a Commodore disk If you buy a blank disk and want your computer to use it, you must turn the blank disk into a Commodore disk.

To do that, insert the blank disk into the drive (and close the door). To name the disk ELIZABETH and give it ID number 00, type this:

```
OPEN 15,8,15,"N:ELIZABETH,00"
CLOSE 15
```

Each disk you create must have a different ID number. The ID number can be any number from 00 to 99 — or it can even be a pair of *letters*.

The drive's red light will glow for about 2 minutes. When the light stops glowing, your blank disk is finally a Commodore disk.

SAVE Instead of saying SAVE "JOE", say:

```
SAVE "JOE",8
```

FILES Instead of saying FILES, say:

```
LOAD "$",8
LIST
```

Watch the red light Whenever you give a disk command, the computer sends the command to the disk drive and immediately says READY. The word READY does *not* mean the drive's finished the command yet. The drive doesn't finish the command until the drive's red light stops glowing.

If you give a wrong disk command, the computer nevertheless sends it to the drive and says READY. But when the drive receives that command, the drive gripes by *blinking* its red light repeatedly. So a repeatedly blinking light means you made an error. A continually glowing light means your command is okay and the drive is obeying it. Here's the rule: "Blink is bad. Glow is good."

If you give a bad command and the light starts to blink, you must stop the blinking, by typing this:

```
OPEN 15,8,15,"I"
CLOSE 15
```

Commodore 16, Plus 4, Pet, Super Pet, and CBM
Turn a blank disk into a Commodore disk by saying HEADER "ELIZABETH",I00,D0. Save JOE by saying DSAVE "JOE". List the files on the disk by saying DIRECTORY (if you have a Commodore 16 or Plus 4) or CATALOG D0 (if you have a Pet, Super Pet, or CBM).

How to choose a name (page 337)
Your program's name can be short (such as JOE) or long: up to 16 characters.

Load from disk (page 337)
Instead of saying LOAD "JOE", say this:

```
LOAD "JOE",8
```

Instead of saying RUN "JOE", say this:

```
LOAD "JOE",8
RUN
```

Commodore 16, Plus 4, Pet, Super Pet, and CBM
Say DLOAD "JOE" instead of LOAD "JOE",8.

Edit the disk (page 337)
If you try to copy JOE onto a disk (by saying SAVE "JOE",8) and the disk *already* contains a program named JOE, the drive will gripe, by blinking its light. To avoid such griping, give this command instead:

```
SAVE "@:JOE",8
```

In that command, the at-sign followed by the colon tells the drive: save JOE, *even though the disk already contains a JOE*.

Instead of saying RENAME "JOE" TO "FRED", say:

```
OPEN 15,8,15,"R:FRED=JOE"
CLOSE 15
```

Commodore 16, Plus 4, Pet, Super Pet, and CBM
You *can* say RENAME "JOE" TO "FRED".

Space on the disk (page 337)
Instead of saying KILL "JOE", say:

```
OPEN 15,8,15,"S:JOE"
CLOSE 15
```

Commodore 16, Plus 4, Pet, Super Pet, and CBM
Say SCRATCH "JOE" instead.

Tapes (page 337)
To copy a program onto a tape, position the tape and notice the counter's number. Then type the word SAVE. At the end of that word, press the RETURN key.

Your computer will say:

```
PRESS RECORD & PLAY ON TAPE
```

Obey the computer: press the recorder's RECORD and PLAY buttons at the same time as each other.

The computer will say:

```
OK
SAVING
READY.
```

Then press the recorder's STOP button.

How to read a program from a tape. Put the tape into the recorder. (To do that, you might have to press the recorder's EJECT button.)

By using the REWIND, FAST FORWARD, PLAY, and STOP buttons (and the counter, if you have one), position the tape to the program's beginning (or slightly before). Then type the word LOAD. At the end of that word, press the RETURN key.

The computer will say:

```
PRESS PLAY ON TAPE
```

Obey the computer, by pressing the recorder's PLAY button.

The computer will say:

```
OK
SEARCHING
FOUND
LOADING
READY.
```

Then press the recorder's STOP button.

Type the word LIST or RUN; then press the RETURN key.

Long variable names (page 340)
Variable names must be short. The name of a numeric variable must be just 1 or 2 characters; the name of a string variable must be just 1 or 2 characters followed by a dollar sign. If you try to make the variable's name longer than that, the computer will handle it unreliably.

If you want a variable name that's 2 characters long, avoid the following 2-character names, which have special meanings: GO, TO, IF, ON, FN, TI, ST, OR.

INPUT (page 341)
Usually, you can abort a program by pressing the RUN STOP key. But while the computer is doing an INPUT statement, the RUN STOP key refuses to work, unless you simultaneously hold down the RESTORE key.

Test whether your Commodore 64 is old
Commodore has sold two versions of the Commodore 64. The old version has trouble handling the INPUT statement; the new version handles the INPUT statement correctly. Commodore switched to the new version around the beginning of 1984. Test whether your Commodore 64 is new or old, by running this program:

```
10 INPUT "ARE YOU THE HAPPIEST PERSON IN THE WHOLE WORLD";A$
20 PRINT "YOU SAID ";A$
```

When you run the program, and the computer asks "ARE YOU THE HAPPIEST PERSON IN THE WHOLE WORLD", answer YES. If your Commodore 64 is new and works correctly, it will reply:

```
YOU SAID YES
```

If your Commodore 64 is old, it will say this nonsense instead:

`YOU SAID ARE YOU THE HAPPIEST PERSON IN THE WHOLE WORLD? YES`

What to do if your Commodore 64 is old
In an INPUT statement, the computer's question is called the *prompt*. **An old Commodore 64 can't correctly handle a prompt longer than 38 characters.** For example, this line's prompt's too long for an old Commodore 64:

`10 INPUT "ARE YOU THE HAPPIEST PERSON IN THE WHOLE WORLD";A$`

To prevent the old Commodore 64 from printing nonsense, shorten the prompt to 38 characters or less, like this:

`10 INPUT "ARE YOU THE HAPPIEST PERSON";A$`

Better yet, eliminate the prompt altogether and replace it by a PRINT statement, like this:

`10 PRINT "ARE YOU THE HAPPIEST PERSON IN THE WHOLE WORLD?"`
`11 INPUT A$`

Many examples in this book contain prompts that are too long for an old Commodore 64 to handle. You must revise the examples or buy a newer computer.

Vic-20
If you have a Vic-20 computer, you must keep the INPUT statement's prompt short: no longer than 20 characters.

Pet, Super Pet, and CBM
The RESTORE key is missing. Instead of holding down the RUN STOP and RESTORE keys simultaneously, tap the RETURN key.

Once upon a time (page 342)
Reminder: some of the prompts are too long for an old Commodore 64 to handle, so you must revise them.

Numeric input (page 344)
If your Commodore 64 is old, shorten the prompts to 38 characters or less.

If you forget to shorten a prompt, when you run the program and input a number the computer will say:

`REDO FROM START`

Abort the program (by holding down the RUN STOP and RESTORE keys simultaneously), then shorten the prompt.

Therapist (page 345)
If you try to invent your own examples using IF . . . THEN, make sure each line of your program contains no more than 80 characters. You'll be tempted to make some of the IF . . . THEN lines be longer, but longer lines won't work.

ELSE (page 349)
Your computer doesn't understand the world ELSE.

DATA . . . READ (page 350)
If you invent your own list of data, remember that each line of your program must be short: no more than 80 characters!

FOR . . . NEXT (page 355)
If you indent the lines between FOR and NEXT, your computer ignores the indentation. When you LIST your program, you won't see any indentation. So **don't bother to indent.**

Renumbering (page 367)
Your computer doesn't understand the word RENUM.

The PAUSE key (page 367)
Your keyboard lacks a PAUSE key. Instead of pausing, you must either slow the computer down (by holding down the CTRL key) or abort (by pressing the STOP key).

After aborting a RUN, you can make the computer continue where it left off, by typing:

`CONT`

The word CONT will make the computer continue an aborted RUN, but will *not* make it continue an aborted LIST.

Pet, Super Pet, and CBM
The CTRL key is messing. Hold down the RVS key instead.

Apostrophe (page 367)
Instead of an apostrophe, type a colon followed by the word REM (which stands for "remark"). For example:

`40 C=40: REM BECAUSE RUSS HAS 40 COMPUTERS`

Zones (page 368)
Your screen has 4 zones. Each zone is 10 characters wide, so the entire screen is 40 characters wide.

TAB (page 370)
On other computers, the leftmost character in the line is said to be at position 1. But on your computer, **the leftmost character in the line is said to be at position 0** instead; after position 0 come positions 1, 2, 3, etc.

So on your computer, if you say TAB(0), you'll be going to the leftmost position; if you say TAB(1), you will *not* be going to the leftmost position.

LOCATE (page 371)
Your computer doesn't understand the word LOCATE. To make your computer move the cursor, use the following trick instead. . . .

In the middle of your program, write a PRINT statement that prints a string. (To do that, type a line number, followed by the word PRINT, followed by a quotation mark, followed by a string of characters, followed by another quotation mark.) But while you're in the middle of typing the string of characters, press a cursor-arrow key several times. When you press the cursor key, the cursor will *not* move immediately; instead, you'll see funny symbols in the middle of the string.

Later, when you RUN the program and the computer comes to that PRINT statement and sees those funny symbols, the computer will automatically move the cursor.

Here's the rule: while you're typing a string, if you try to move the cursor, the computer won't move the cursor until later when the program is running.

So to write a program that moves the cursor, tap the cursor-arrow keys in the middle of a string in a PRINT statement.

Pixels (page 372)
To make your computer easily handle pixels, you must insert a cartridge called **Simon's BASIC**, which costs extra. For details about how to use that cartridge, read the manual that comes with the cartridge.

Advanced commands (and page #)

Sounds (page 373). To make your computer easily produce sounds, you must buy the Simon's BASIC cartridge. For details about how to use that cartridge, read the manual that comes with the cartridge.

PRINT USING (374). Your computer doesn't understand PRINT USING.

Exponents (384). On the Commodore 64's keyboard, the exponent key is next to the RESTORE key and says "↑" instead of "^".

Random integers (388). Instead of saying RANDOMIZE, say R=RND(0). To get a random integer from 1 to 5, instead of saying RND(5), say 1+INT(RND(1)*5).

Commodore 16, Plus 4, and Pet. Say R=RND(-TI) instead of RANDOMIZE.

Random decimals (391). For a random decimal between 0 and 1, say RND(1) instead of just RND.

Left, right, middle (394). Your computer doesn't understand an equal sign after MID$.

Searching in a string (395). Your computer doesn't understand INSTR.

Clock (395). Your computer doesn't understand DATE$. It omits colons from the TIME$; so instead of saying TIME$="13:45:07", say TIME$="124507".

Repeating characters (395). Your computer doesn't understand STRING$.

Types of numbers (397). You can't use double-precision. To create a real number, you can type as many digits as you wish, but the computer remembers just the first 10 digits accurately, and prints just the first 9 of them on your screen.

RAM consumption (397). Each real number consumes 5 bytes of RAM.

Variables (397). For integer variables, you can use the symbol % but not the word DEFINT.

Omitting the question mark (406). In the INPUT statement, you can't replace the semicolon by a comma.

Adjacent printing (407). You can't put a semicolon immediately after INPUT.

LINE INPUT (407). You can't say LINE INPUT.

INPUT$ (407). Instead of saying ——

```
20 A$=INPUT$(1)
```

say:

```
20 GET A$: IF A$="" THEN GO TO 20
```

Instead of saying INPUT$(4), you must GET one character at a time.

Joystick (408). To make the computer look at joystick 1, say:

```
100 J=15-(PEEK(56321) AND 15)
```

If the joystick is pushed forward, J is 1. If the joystick is pulled back, J is 2. If the joystick is pushed to the left, J is 4. If the joystick is pushed to the right, J is 8.

Combined motions produce combined numbers. For example, if the joystick is pushed forward and to the left simultaneously, J is 1+4, which is 5.

If the joystick is untouched and centered, J is 0.

To make the computer look at joystick 2, say:

```
102 J2=15-(PEEK(56320) AND 15)
```

To see the numbers J and J2 on your screen continually, add these lines:

```
110 PRINT J,J2
120 GO TO 100
```

Mouse (408). Your computer doesn't use a mouse.

SWAP (409). Your computer doesn't understand SWAP, so use the alternative.

ON ERROR GO TO (414). Your computer doesn't understand ON ERROR GO TO.

POKE (414). Your computer can display 16 colors, which are numbered as follows: 0=black, 1=white, 2=red, 3=cyan, 4=purple, 5=green, 6=blue, 7=yellow, 8=orange, 9=brown, 10=light brown, 11=dark gray, 12=gray, 13=light green, 14=light blue, 15=light gray.

Normally, the characters on the screen are light blue (color 14). To choose a different character color, poke the color number into cell #646. For example, to create white characters, say:

```
POKE 646,1
```

Normally, the screen's background color is a deep blue (color 6). To choose a different background color, poke the color number into cell #53281. For example, to make the background be red, say:

```
POKE 53281,2
```

Normally, the border along the screen's edge is light blue (color 14). To choose a different border color, poke the color number into cell #53280. For example, to make the border be green, say:

```
POKE 53280,5
```

Vic-20. On a Vic-20 computer, colors 9 and 10 are pink, color 11 is light cyan, color 12 is light purple, and color 15 is light yellow. The border color number must be less than 8. To handle the border and background colors, don't use cells 53280 and 53281; instead compute (the color number of the background you want)*16+(the color number of the border you want)+8, then set C equal to that sum and say:

```
POKE 36879,C
```

If you omit the +8 from the formula for C, the characters will be inversed, so that you'll get light characters on a dark background, instead of dark characters on a light background.

OPEN FOR OUTPUT (415). This program prints EAT and 4 and EGGS onto a disk file called SUE:

```
5 OPEN 2,8,2,"SUE,S,W"
10 PRINT#2, "EAT"
20 PRINT#2, 2+2
30 PRINT#2, "EGGS"
40 CLOSE 2
```

Notice you must say PRINT#2, not PRINT#1. In line 5, the W tells the computer to Write SUE.

OPEN FOR INPUT (415). This program makes the computer Read SUE and copy it to your screen:

```
5 OPEN 2,8,2,"SUE,S,R"
10 INPUT#2, A$
11 PRINT A$
20 INPUT#2, B
21 PRINT B
30 INPUT#2, C$
31 PRINT C$
40 CLOSE 2
```

OPEN FOR APPEND (415). This program makes the computer Append "GOOD MORNING!" to the end of SUE:

```
10 OPEN 2,8,2,"SUE,S,A"
20 PRINT#2, "GOOD MORNING!"
30 CLOSE 2
```

Loops (416). Instead of saying EOF(1), say STAND64=64.

LOF (416). Your computer doesn't understand LOF.

Multiple files (416). The main file is called #2. The next file is called #3: say OPEN 3,8,3,"TOM,S,W". You can use #2, #3, #4, etc., up to #14. You cannot use #1.

How to CLOSE (416). After each CLOSE, you must put a number that says which file to CLOSE.

PUT (417). This program creates a random-access file called JIM whose record length is 20, and defines JIM's 7th, 9th, and 4th records:

```
5 OPEN 15,8,15: OPEN 2,8,2,"JIM,L,"+CHR$(20)
10 PRINT#15, "P"CHR$(2)CHR$(7)CHR$(0)CHR$(0): PRINT#2, "LOVE
MAKES ME GIGGLE";
20 PRINT#15, "P"CHR$(2)CHR$(9)CHR$(0)CHR$(0): PRINT#2, "PLEA
SE HOLD MY HAND";
30 PRINT#15, "P"CHR$(2)CHR$(4)CHR$(0)CHR$(0): PRINT#2, "I LO
VE LUCY";
40 CLOSE 2: CLOSE 15
```

GET (417). This program makes the computer tell you JIM's 7th item:

```
5 OPEN 15,8,15: OPEN 2,8,2,"JIM"
10 PRINT#15, "P"CHR$(2)CHR$(7)CHR$(0)CHR$(0): INPUT#2, X$: P
RINT X$
20 CLOSE 2: CLOSE 15
```

LOC (417). Your computer doesn't understand LOC.

Numerical data (417). The computer lets you put numbers in the file. You do *not* have to convert the numbers to strings.

Here's how to use BASIC on Tandy's Radio Shack TRS-80 Model 4 computer. (The Models 4D and 4P are similar.)

Microsoft BASIC (page 322)

Tandy's Radio Shack TRS-80 Model 4 computer can handle two versions of BASIC. The best version, called **Model 4 BASIC**, requires a disk called **Model 4 TRSDOS and BASIC Interpreter** and requires a drive to put it in. The alternative version, called **Model 3 BASIC**, is only for people who lack a disk drive or lost the disk called "Model 4 TRSDOS and BASIC Interpreter" or want to run obsolete "Model 3" software.

I'll assume you have the disk called "Model 4 TRSDOS and BASIC Interpreter" and a drive to put it in, so that you can run Model 4 BASIC.

Here's how to use Model 4 BASIC. . . .

The keyboard (page 324)

The keys are placed like this:

```
! " # $ % & ' ( )   * =
1 2 3 4 5 6 7 8 9 0 : -  Break

 Q W E R T Y U I O P `   Clear
                     a
Ctrl A S D F G H J K L +~  ±
                       ;^ Enter _

Shift Z X C V B N M <{ >} ?|  Shift ↑
                    ,[ .] /\
                         DelLn
     Space          Caps  ←    ↓ →
```

Exception: if you bought the computer before 1984, the Ctrl key, CLEAR key, and arrow keys are located differently.

The zero key is Swedish.

In that diagram, one of the keys looks like this:

```
<{
,[
```

If you tap that key, you'll be typing a comma. If you tap that key *while holding down the SHIFT key*, you'll be typing the symbol "<". If you tap that key *while holding down the CLEAR key*, you'll be typing the symbol "[". To type the remaining symbol on that key (the "{"), do this: hold down the CLEAR key; while you keep holding down the CLEAR key, hold down the SHIFT key; while holding down the CLEAR and SHIFT keys, tap the key that shows the "{".

The BACKSPACE key has a left-arrow on it; so if you tap the left-arrow key, the computer will erase the last character you typed. If you tap the left-arrow key *while holding down the SHIFT key*, the computer will erase the entire *line* you've been typing.

Get started (page 325)

When you flip the power switch, you create an electrical surge that damages any disks inside the computer. So **before flipping the power switch, remove any disks from the computer.**

Then flip on the computer's power switch, which is underneath the computer's right side. The red light on the bottom disk drive will turn on, then off.

Insert a disk that contains "Model 4 TRSDOS and BASIC Interpreter" into the bottom drive. When you insert it, make sure the disk's label is on *top* of the disk, and make sure the disk's big oval cutout goes into the drive *before* the label does. (The Model 4P is different: the disk drive's slot is vertical instead of horizontal and requires the disk's label to be on the disk's left side.) Close the drive's door.

On the far right side of the keyboard, you'll see an orange button. Press it.

The computer will say "Date". If the writing looks fuzzy, turn the brightness and contrast dials, which are underneath the computer's left side. Type the date. For example, if today is January 24, 1996, type 01/24/96 and then press the ENTER key.

The computer will say:

`TRSDOS Ready`

Type this word:

`basic`

Then press the ENTER key. After a brief pause, the computer will say:

`Ready`

Notice that **the computer says "Ready" instead of "OK".**

Whenever you're done using the computer, remove any disks from the drives, before you flip off the power.

What if computer gripes? (page 330)

If the computer gripes at you, press the ENTER key immediately.

After pressing the ENTER key, correct the error by retyping the line that the computer griped about.

Arrow keys (page 332)

To edit line 20, type:

`edit 20`

If the first character in line 20 is correct (and doesn't need to be edited), press the SPACE bar. If the second character in line 20 is correct also, press the SPACE bar again. Press the SPACE bar for each correct character. Each time you press the SPACE bar, the character that you said was correct appears on the screen.

When you get to the point where the next character on the screen would be *in*correct, press the D key instead of the SPACE bar. The D key means: delete the next character. Pressing the D key causes the next character to be surrounded by backslashes, which mean the character is being deleted.

To insert extra characters in the line, press the SPACE bar several times, until you get to where you want the characters to be inserted. Then press the I key (which tells the computer you want to insert). Then type the characters you want to insert. After typing them, tap the up-arrow key while holding down the SHIFT key.

When you've finished all the deletions and insertions for that line, press the ENTER key. That makes the screen show the remainder of the line (the right-hand part of the line), and tells the computer you've finished editing the line.

Clear the screen (page 333)

To clear the screen by using the CLEAR key, tap the CLEAR key *while holding down the SHIFT key.*

Print on paper (page 333)

Your keyboard lacks a PRINT key. Instead of pressing a PRINT key, tap the colon key (which is next to the zero key) *while holding down the CTRL key*.

Your keyboard lacks an ECHO key. Instead of pressing an ECHO key, type this:

```
system "link *do *pr"
```

To stop the echo, type this:

```
system "reset *do"
```

Save on disk (page 336)

If you buy a blank disk and want your computer to use it, you must turn the blank disk into a Radio Shack disk.

To do that, put the blank disk into the top drive. Type:

```
system
format 1 (q=n)
```

The computer will turn the blank disk into a Radio Shack disk. Then the computer will say "TRSDOS Ready".

Put Model 4 BASIC onto that disk, by typing:

```
backup :0 :1
```

The computer will ask whether you're sure; type the letter y. The computer will copy all information from the bottom disk to the top disk. Then the computer will say "TRSDOS Ready" again.

Tell the computer you want to use BASIC now, by typing:

```
basic
```

The computer will say "Ready".

FILES Instead of typing the word FILES, type this:

```
system "dir"
```

That makes the computer print a directory, showing the names of all the programs in all your disk drives.

How to use drive 1 The main drive is called **drive 0**. The other drive is called **drive 1**.

Normally, the computer uses drive 0. If you want JOE to be in drive 1 instead of drive 0, put a colon and a 1 after JOE, like this:

```
save "joe:1"
```

How to choose a name (page 337)

Your program's name can be short (such as JOE) or long: up to 8 characters. The name's first character must be a letter; the remaining characters should be letters or digits.

Tapes (page 337)

Model 4 BASIC doesn't use tapes.

FOR . . . NEXT (page 355)

To indent you can hit the SPACE bar repeatedly. But to indent more easily, hit the right-arrow key once.

The PAUSE key (page 367)

Your keyboard lacks a PAUSE key.

To make the computer pause, tap the @ key while holding down the SHIFT key. (Normally, pressing those keys makes the screen display an accent mark; but if you press those keys *while a program is running*, the computer will pause instead.)

To stop pausing, press the SPACE bar.

LOCATE (page 371)

Your computer doesn't understand the word LOCATE. Here's what to do instead . . .

Your computer considers the screen's top line to be **row 0**, and the line below it to be **row 1**. Your computer considers the row's leftmost character to be in **column 0**, and the next character to be in **column 1**.

To print the word DROWN, so that it begins at row 3 and column 7, type this:

```
print@(3,7), "drown"
```

Pixels (page 372)

To make Model 4 BASIC handle pixels, you must buy a graphics board. Read the instructions that come with the board.

Advanced commands (and page #)

BEEP (page 373). Your computer doesn't understand the word BEEP.

SOUND (373). If you type —

```
sound 4,10
```

the computer will produce a sound whose pitch is 4 and whose duration is 10.

The pitch can be any integer from 0 to 7: 0=D#, 1=E, 2=F, 3=F#, 4=G, 5=A, 6=A#, 7=B. The duration can be any integer from 0 to 31: 0 means half a second; 31 means about 15 seconds.

PLAY (374). Your computer doesn't understand the word PLAY.

Exponents (384). To make the symbol "^", tap the semicolon key while holding down the CLEAR key.

Random integers (388). Say RANDOM instead of RANDOMIZE.

Random decimals (391). For a random decimal between 0 and 1, say RND(0) instead of just RND.

Clock (395). To set the time to 13:45:07, say SYSTEM "TIME 13:45:07". To set the date to 01/24/1996, say SYSTEM "DATE 01/24/1996". Your computer doesn't understand TIMER.

Joystick versus mouse (408). Your computer doesn't use a joystick or mouse.

POKE (414). If you're using TRSDOS version 6.02, cell #2968 normally contains the number 95, which is the ASCII code number for an underline. That makes the cursor's shape be an underline.

To change the cursor's shape, POKE a different number into cell #2968. For example, to change the cursor's shape to the letter A (whose ASCII code number is 65), say:

```
poke 2968,65
```

To create a "feminist computer", turn the cursor into a female-sign (whose ASCII code number is 250), by saying:

```
poke 2968,250
```

Older versions of TRSDOS. Cell #2968 does that only in TRSDOS version 6.2. Instead of cell #2968, version 6.00 uses cell #3040; version 6.01 uses cell #3017.

When you turn on the computer, versions 6.00 and 6.01 begin by making the cursor be a double-underline (whose ASCII code is 176) instead of a single-underline.

OPEN FOR OUTPUT (415). Instead of saying OPEN "SUE" FOR OUTPUT AS 1, say OPEN "O",1,"SUE". In the quotation marks, be sure to put the letter O, not a zero.

OPEN FOR INPUT (415). Instead of saying OPEN "SUE" FOR INPUT AS 1, say OPEN "I",1,"SUE".

OPEN FOR APPEND (415). Instead of saying OPEN "SUE" FOR APPEND AS 1, say OPEN "E",1,"SUE". The "E" tells the computer to Extend the file.

LOF (416). Your computer doesn't understand the usual meaning of LOF(1).

PUT (417). Instead of saying OPEN "JIM" AS 1 LEN=20, say OPEN "R",1,"JIM",20.

End of the file (417). LOF(1) is the number of *records* in the file (instead of being the number of bytes).

TANDY COLOR COMPUTER

Here's how to use BASIC on Tandy's Radio Shack TRS-80 Color Computer 2. (The Color Computer 1, Color Computer 3, and Micro Color Computer are similar.)

Microsoft BASIC (page 322)

When you buy the Color Computer 2, make sure you get *extended* color BASIC, not *standard* color BASIC (which costs less but is crummy). The following comments apply to extended color BASIC.

The keyboard (page 324)

The keys are placed like this:

```
 !   "   #   $   %   &   '   (   )  Revrs  *   =
 1   2   3   4   5   6   7   8   9   0     :   -   Break

↑    Q   W   E   R   T   Y   U   I   O   P  Pause DelLn  ]
                                             @    ←     →

[    A   S   D   F   G   H   J   K   L   +
↓                                        ;   Enter      \
                                                      Clear

Shift    Z   X   C   V   B   N   M   <   >   ?        Shift
                                     ,   .   /

                    Space
```

The computer capitalizes all letters automatically; so to type a capital letter, do *not* press the SHIFT key.

There is no CAPS key.

The BACKSPACE key has a left-arrow on it; so if you tap the left-arrow key, the computer will erase the last character you typed. If you tap the left-arrow key *while holding down the SHIFT key*, the computer will erase the entire **line** you've been typing.

Get started (page 325)

Attach the computer to a TV. Turn on the computer's power, by pressing the POWER button, which is at the computer's rear. Turn on the TV, and turn it to channel 3 or 4. To switch the computer from channel 3 to channel 4 or back to channel 3, flip your computer's channel-selection switch, which is at the computer's rear. When the computer's on and functioning correctly, the computer will say OK.

Ranges of lines (page 332)

Say DEL instead of DELETE.

Arrow keys (page 332)

To edit line 20, type:

EDIT 20

If the first character in line 20 is correct (and doesn't need to be edited), press the SPACE bar. If the second character in line 20 is correct also, press the SPACE bar again. Press the SPACE bar for each correct character. Each time you press the SPACE bar, the character that you said was correct appears on the screen.

When you get to the point where the next character on the screen would be *in*correct, press the D key instead of the SPACE bar. The D key means: delete the next character. Pressing the D key prevents the next character from appearing on the screen.

To insert extra characters in the line, press the SPACE bar several times, until you get where you want the characters to be inserted. Then press the I key (which tells the computer you want to insert). Then type the characters you want to insert. After typing them, tap the up-arrow key while holding down the SHIFT key.

When you've finished all the deletions and insertions for that line, press the ENTER key. That makes the screen show the remainder of the line (the right-hand part of the line), and tells the computer you've finished editing the line.

Print on paper (page 333)

Your keyboard doesn't have a PRINT key or an ECHO key. Instead of saying "LPRINT" say "PRINT#-2,". For example, to print "I LOVE YOU" on paper, type this:

PRINT #-2, "I LOVE YOU"

Even though the computer doesn't understand "LPRINT", it *does* understand "LLIST".

Save on disk (page 336)

When you flip the disk drive's power switch, you create an electrical surge that damages any disk inside the drive. So **before flipping the drive's power switch, make sure the drive is empty.**

When you're done using the computer, remove any disk from the drive, before you flip off the power.

How to insert a disk
To put a disk into the drive, open the drive's door, then insert the disk into the drive. When you insert it, make sure the disk's label is on top of the disk, and make sure the disk's big oval cutout goes into the drive *before* the label does. Close the drive's door.

(Exception: if your drive was made before 1985, the drive's slit is vertical instead of horizontal, and the disk's label is on the left side of the disk instead of the top.)

How to turn a blank disk into a Radio Shack disk
If you buy a blank disk and want your computer to use it, you must turn the blank disk into a Radio Shack disk.

To do that, insert the blank disk into the drive (and close the door). Then type DSKINI0. (That last character is a zero, not the letter O.)

The disk drive's red light will glow for 40 seconds. When the light stops glowing, the computer will say OK.

FILES
Instead of saying FILES, say DIR (which stands for "directory").

How to use drive 1
The main drive is called **drive 0**. If you have an extra drive, that extra is called **drive 1**.

Normally, the computer uses drive 0. If you want JOE to be in drive 1 instead of drive 0, put a colon and a 1 after JOE, like this:

```
SAVE "JOE:1"
```

To make the computer print the names of all the programs in drive 1, type this:

```
DIR 1
```

How to choose a name (page 337)

Your program's name can be short (such as JOE) or long: up to 8 characters. the name's first character must be a letter; the remaining characters should be letters or digits.

Edit the disk (page 337)

Instead of saying RENAME "JOE" to "FRED", say RENAME "JOE/BAS" to "FRED/BAS", to emphasize that JOE was written in BASIC.

Space on the disk (page 337)

Instead of saying KILL "JOE", say KILL "JOE/BAS".

Tapes (page 337)

To copy a program onto a tape, position the tape and notice the counter's number. Then press the recorder's RECORD and PLAY buttons at the same time as each other. Type this:

```
CSAVE "A"
```

The computer will copy the program onto tape and then say OK. Press the recorder's STOP button.

How to read a program from a tape
Put the tape into the recorder. (To do that, you might have to press the recorder's EJECT button.)

Type the word CLOAD.

Press the recorder's REWIND button. When the tape is rewound, press the recorder's STOP button. Push the counter's button, so the counter becomes zero.

Press the recorder's FAST FORWARD button. Look at the counter. When the number on the counter is almost up to the number of the program's beginning, press the recorder's STOP button.

Press the recorder's PLAY button. The computer will search on the tape for the beginning of the program. When the computer reaches the beginning of the program, the computer will print an F.

Then the computer begins reading the program. When the computer finishes reading it, the computer will say OK.

Press the recorder's STOP button. Type the word LIST or RUN.

Long variable names (page 340)

Variable names must be short. The name of a numeric variable must be just 1 or 2 characters: the name of a string variable must be just 1 or 2 characters followed by a dollar sign. If you try to make the variable's name longer than that, the computer will handle it unreliably.

If you want a variable name that's 2 characters long, avoid the following 2-character names, which have special meanings: GO, TO, IF, ON, FN, OR.

INPUT (page 341)

For some of the programs that involve string input, **the computer will gripe about being "out of string space"**; the computer will say:

```
?OS ERROR
```

To stop the computer from griping, insert this statement:

```
1 CLEAR 1000
```

If the computer *still* says OS ERROR, raise 1000 to a higher number, like this:

```
1 CLEAR 2000
```

Keep raising, until the computer stops that gripe. On the other hand, if you raise *too* high, the computer will say —

```
?OM ERROR
```

That means you must go lower.

So **if the computer says "OS ERROR", you should raise the CLEAR number; if the computer says "OM ERROR", you should lower the CLEAR number.**

Here's why. . . .

Your program contains two kinds of strings: the strings that are known, and the strings that are unknown. For example, if you say —

```
10 G$="DOWN"
```

the G$ is known to be DOWN. If you say —

```
10 INPUT "WHAT IS YOUR NAME";N$
```

the N$ is unknown, because its value depends on what the human inputs.

Normally, the computer reserves enough memory space to hold just 200 unknown characters. If your program needs *more* characters than that — for example, if your program inputs 7 strings, each having 30 characters, so that the total number of characters is 210 — the computer will gripe, and say "out of string space error" (OS ERROR).

If you say —

```
1 CLEAR 1000
```

the computer will reserve enough space to hold 1000 unknown characters, instead of the normal quantity (which is just 200).

How much space can you reserve? That depends on how much memory you bought for your computer. If your computer has little memory, and you try to reserve more space than your computer has, the computer will give up, and say "out of memory error" (OM ERROR).

FOR . . . NEXT (page 355)

If you indent the lines between FOR and NEXT, your computer ignores the indentation. When you LIST your program, you won't see any indentations. So **don't bother to indent**.

The PAUSE key (page 367)

To make the computer pause, hold down the SHIFT key; and while you keep holding down the SHIFT key, tap the @ key.

To stop pausing, press the SPACE bar.

Zones (page 368)

Each zone is 16 characters wide. Your screen has just 2 zones, so your screen is 32 characters wide.

TAB (page 370)

On other computers, the leftmost character in the line is said to be at position 1. But on your computer, **the leftmost character in the line is said to be at position 0** instead; after position 0 come positions 1, 2, 3, etc.

So on your computer, if you say TAB(0), you'll be going to the leftmost position; if you say TAB(1), you will *not* be going to the leftmost position.

LOCATE (page 371)

Your computer doesn't understand the word LOCATE. Here's what to do instead . . .

Your computer considers the screen's top line to be **row 0**, and the line below it to be **row 1**. Your computer considers the row's leftmost character to be in **column 0**, and the next character to be in **column 1**.

To print the word DROWN, so that it begins at row 3 and column 7, type this:

```
PRINT@32* 3+7, "DROWN"
```

Pixels (page 372)

To use pixels, type these lines:

```
10 PMODE 4: PCLS: SCREEN 1
10000 GO TO 10000
```

Line 10 warns the computer that you want to use pixels. (In that line, the PMODE 4 makes the X coordinate go from 0 to 255 and the Y coordinate go from 0 to 191. The PCLS makes the graphic screen begin by being blank. The SCREEN 1 makes the computer show you the graphics instead of text.)

Line 10000, at the bottom of your program, makes the computer pause, so that you can admire whatever graphics have been drawn.

Between lines 10 and 10000, you can insert lines containing the following commands. . . .

To draw a dot at pixel (100,100), say PSET (100,100).

To draw a line from pixel (0,0) to pixel (100,100), say LINE (0,0)-(100,100),PSET.

To draw a box ("rectangle") that has a corner at pixel (0,0) and has an opposite corner at pixel (100,100), say LINE (0,0)-100,100),PSET,B.

To draw a box that has a corner at (0,0) and an opposite corner at (100,100), and also make the computer fill in the box (i.e., paint the box's interior), say LINE (0,0)-(100,100),PSET,BF.

Each of those commands contains the word PSET. To erase the shape that you drew, give the same command again, but replace the PSET by PRESET.

To draw a circle centered at pixel (100,100), and to make the circle's radius be 50, say CIRCLE (100,100),50. To erase that circle, say CIRCLE (100,100),50,0.

To paint the inside of any shape (such as a circle or a person), say PAINT and mention a point inside the shape. For example, to fill in an outline that has (101,101) inside it, say PAINT (101,101). To erase that paint (and also the shape itself), say PAINT (101,101),0.

To erase the entire drawing ("clear the screen"), say PCLS.

If you say SCREEN 0, the screen will stop showing graphics (and will show text instead), until you say SCREEN 1 (which brings back the graphics).

To get started experimenting with all those commands, run the following program; it draws a line from (0,0) to (100,100) and then draws a circle centered at pixel (100,100) and with radius 50:

```
10 PMODE 4: PCLS: SCREEN 1
20 LINE (0,0)-(100,100)
30 CIRCLE (100,100),50
10000 GO TO 10000
```

The computer draws the shapes in green, on a black background. After you've admired the pretty picture, abort the program by pressing the BREAK key.

Colors To get colors, line 10 must say PMODE 3 instead of PMODE 4.

After you've said PMODE 3, whenever the computer draws (or erases) a pixel, it does the same thing to the pixel next to it. Specifically, if you tell the computer to draw (or erase) a pixel whose X coordinate is even, the computer will do the same thing to the pixel at its right (whose X coordinate is odd). If you tell the computer to draw (or erase) a pixel whose X coordinate is odd, the computer will do the same thing to the pixel at its left (whose X coordinate is even).

After you've said PMODE 3, the computer normally draws red shapes on a green background. But if you don't like those colors, you can pick different colors instead.

To choose different colors, use these code numbers: 1=green, 2=yellow, 3=blue, and 4=red. For example, to draw yellow shapes on a blue background, say COLOR 2,3. the traditional place to say COLOR 2,3 is in line 10, like this:

```
10 PMODE 3: COLOR 2,3: PCLS: SCREEN 1
```

If you prefer, you can say COLOR 2,3 later in your program instead. If you say it later, the shapes at the beginning of your program will be unaffected by that COLOR statement. When you draw new shapes after giving that COLOR statement, the shapes that were already on the screen (in their old colors) remain unchanged; they keep their original colors.

When you say PRESET (in the middle of a dot or line or box command), the computer assumes you want the shape erased; to erase the shape, the computer redraws the shape by using the background color. If you recently changed the background color (by saying COLOR), the erasure will be done by using the new background color, which won't match the old background color.

If you say CIRCLE (100,100),50,2 the computer will draw the circle in yellow (because the 2 at the end of the CIRCLE command is the code number for yellow). Do *not* put a 0 at the end of the CIRCLE command, since 0 is not an acceptable color number. You must pick a number from 1 to 4.

If you say PAINT, you must say which pixel to start painting at; you must say which color paint to use; and you must remind the computer of what color the outline had that you're filling in. For example, if you want the computer to paint starting at pixel (101,101) — which is inside the outline — and you want the computer to use yellow paint (whose code number is 2), and the outline that you're filling in was drawn in blue (whose code number is 3), say PAINT (101,101),2,3.

Near the end of your program, if you say SCREEN 1,1, you'll see a "negative" of your picture. In the "negative", green becomes light blue (even though Radio Shack's manual incorrectly says it becomes "buff"), yellow becomes cyan (greenish blue), blue becomes magenta (purplish red), and red becomes orange. All future drawings (even by other programs) will be done using those "negative" colors, unless you tell the computer to return to a "positive", by saying SCREEN 1,0.

Advanced commands (and page #)

BEEP (page 373). Your computer doesn't understand the word BEEP.

SOUND (373). If you type —

```
SOUND 100,15
```

the computer will produce a sound whose pitch is 100. You can choose any pitch from 1 to 255.

In that example, the 15 makes the computer produce the sound for 1 second. If you want the sound to last longer — so that its lasts 2 seconds — replace the 15 by 15*2. For 10 seconds, say 15*10. (That's because your computer's metronome beats 15 times per second.)

PLAY (374). Your computer handles the PLAY command slightly differently than other computers.

Your computer can't play octaves 0 or 6: it plays just octaves 1 through 5. If you don't specify an octave, the computer will play in octave 2.

To create a dotted eighth note, put a dot after the 8 instead of after the note's name. For example, to make E be a dotted eighth note, say "L8.E".

If you say PLAY "T1", the computer will play 56 quarter notes per minute, which is very slow (largo). If you say PLAY "T2", the computer will play twice as fast: 112 quarter notes per minute (moderato). If you say PLAY "T3", the computer will play three times as fast: 168 quarter notes per minute (vivace). You can pick speeds up to PLAY "T255", which is ridiculously fast! If you don't specify a tempo, the computer will play at speed T2, which is 112 quarter notes per minute (moderato).

Normally, the computer plays at volume 15; but you can change the volume. To switch to volume 4 (which is lower, quieter), say:

```
PLAY "V4"
```

You can switch to any volume from 1 to 31.

If you try the bottom example in the main text, slow down the tempo: change T150 to T2.

Exponents (384). For exponents, the TRS-80 Color Computer 2 (with extended color BASIC) uses the symbol "↑" instead of "^".

Random integers (388). Omit the word RANDOMIZE.

Random decimals (391). For a random decimal between 0 and 1, say RND(0) instead of RND.

Clock (395). Your computer doesn't understand TIME$ or DATE$.

Here's how to use the TIMER function. First, reset the TIMER to zero, by saying TIMER=0. Later, whenever you say PRINT TIMER/60, the computer will tell you how many seconds ago the timer was reset.

Unfortunately, the TIMER lasts only 18 minutes; after 18 minutes, it resets itself to zero again.

Types of numbers (397). All variables are reals: you can't create integer variables or double-precision variables.

To create a real number, you can type as many digits as you wish, but the computer remembers just the first 10 digits accurately, and prints just the first 9 of them on your screen.

RAM consumption (397). Each real number consumes 5 bytes of RAM.

Omitting the question mark (406). In the INPUT statement, you can't replace the semicolon by a comma.

Adjacent printing (407). You can't put a semicolon immediately after INPUT.

INPUT$ (407). Instead of saying —

```
20 A$=INPUT$(1)
```

say:

```
20 A$=INKEY$: IF A$="" THEN GO TO 20
```

Instead of saying INPUT$(4), you must INKEY$ one character at a time.

Joystick (408). Say JOYSTK instead of STICK. The coordinates of the right joystick are JOYSTK(0) and JOYSTK(1). The coordinates of the left joystick are JOYSTK(2) and JOYSTK(3).

When the computer comes to a line that mentions JOYSTK(0), the computer looks at both joysticks and computes JOYSTK(0), JOYSTK(1), JOYSTK(2), and JOYSTK(3). If your program mentions JOYSTK(1) or JOYSTK(2) or JOYSTK(3), without mentioning JOYSTK(0), the computer won't look at the joysticks.

Mouse (408). Your computer's version of BASIC is not designed to work with a mouse.

SWAP (409). Your computer doesn't understand SWAP, so use the alternative.

ON ERROR GO TO (414). Your computer doesn't understand ON ERROR GO TO.

OPEN FOR OUTPUT (415). Instead of saying OPEN "SUE" FOR OUTPUT AS 1, say OPEN "O",1,"SUE". In the quotation marks, be sure to put the letter O, not a zero.

OPEN FOR INPUT (415). Instead of saying OPEN "SUE" FOR INPUT AS 1, say OPEN "I",1,"SUE".

OPEN FOR APPEND (415). Your computer doesn't understand APPEND.

LOF (416). Your computer doesn't understand the usual meaning of LOF(1).

PUT (417). Instead of saying OPEN "JIM" AS 1 LEN=20, say OPEN "D",1,"JIM",20.

End of the file (417). LOF(1) is the number of *records* in the file (instead of being the number of bytes).

Numerical data (417). Instead of using MKI$, MKS$, or MKD$, use MKN$. It MaKes a Number into a 5-byte string.

Instead of using CVI, CVS, or CVD, use CVN. It ConVerts a 5-byte string to a Number.

Here's how to use BASIC on other kinds of computers.

Tandy

On page 443, I explained how to use BASIC on the TRS-80 Model 4 (and Model 4D and Model 4P).

On page 445, I explained how to use BASIC on the TRS-80 Color Computer 2 (and Color Computer 1, Color Computer 3, and Micro Color Computer).

If your computer is numbered between 1000 and 5000 (such as the Tandy 1000, 1200, 1400, 2000, 3000, 4000, or 5000), it's an IBM PC clone (explained on page 422).

Here's how to use the TRS-80 Model 3. (Models 1, 2, 12, 16, 100, 102, 200, 6000, and Pocket Computers are similar.)

The keyboard. Similar to Color Computer. You cannot create the symbols "[", "]", and "\" by holding down the SHIFT key. To create the symbol "[", tap the up-arrow key. To switch to lower case, tap the zero key while holding down the SHIFT key.

Get started, if you don't have a disk. While holding down the BREAK key, flip on the power switch, which is underneath the computer's right side. The computer will say "Cass". If the writing looks fuzzy, turn the brightness and contrast dials, which are underneath the computer's left side. Press the ENTER key. The computer will say "Memory Size". Press ENTER again. The computer will say READY.

Get started, if you have a disk. Follow Model 4's procedure, with these exceptions. . . . The disk you insert contains "Model 3 TRSDOS" instead of "Model 4 TRSDOS". After you enter the date (and press the ENTER key), the computer will say "Enter Time". Type the time by using a 24-hour clock; for example, if the time is 1:45 PM, type 13:45:00 and press ENTER. The computer will say "How Many Files"; press ENTER. The computer will say "Memory Size"; press ENTER. Then the computer will say READY.

What if the computer gripes? Same as Model 4.

Arrow keys. Similar to Model 4. When you press the D key, the character will be surrounded by exclamation points instead of backslashes.

Print on paper. Your computer lacks a PRINT key. Instead of pressing a PRINT key, do the following: while depressing the down-arrow key and left SHIFT key simultaneously, tap the colon key.

Your computer lacks an ECHO key. If you're using a disk, you can turn the echo on by typing this —

```
CMD "Z","ON"
```

and turn the echo off by typing this:

```
CMD "Z","OFF"
```

Save on disk. Similar to Model 4. To make the computer print the names of all programs on disk 0, say:

```
CMD "D:0"
```

To make the computer print the names of all programs on disk 1, say:

```
CMD "D:1"
```

Do *not* say FILES or SYSTEM "DIR".

To turn a blank disk into a Radio Shack disk, do *not* say SYSTEM, etc. Instead, put the blank disk into the top drive, and then say:

```
CMD "S"
BACKUP :0 :1
```

The computer will ask, "Source Disk Master Password?" Type the word PASSWORD. The computer will copy all information from the bottom drive's disk to the blank disk. The computer will say "TRSDOS Ready". Type the word BASIC. The computer will say "How Many Files". Press the ENTER key. The computer will say "Memory Size". Press the ENTER key. The computer will say READY.

How to choose a name. Same as Model 4.

Tapes. Similar to Color Computer. The computer will say READY instead of OK, and will print a pair of asterisks instead of an F. The right asterisk flashes.

Long variable names. Same as Color Computer.

INPUT. Similar to Color Computer. If you're using a disk, the computer says "Out of string space" instead of "?OS ERROR", and says "Out of memory" instead of "?OM ERROR". If you don't say CLEAR, the computer reserves enough memory space to hold just 50 unknown characters.

FOR...NEXT. Same as Model 4.

Renumbering. To renumber, you must be using disks, and you must say NAME instead of RENUM.

PAUSE key. To pause (or stop pausing), tap the @ key while holding down the SHIFT key.

Zones. Each zone is 16 characters wide. Your screen has just 4 zones, so your screen is 64 characters wide.

TAB. Same as Color Computer.

LOCATE. Similar to Color Computer. Say 64 instead of 32.

Pixels. The X coordinate goes from 0 to 127. The Y coordinate goes from 0 to 47. Say SET instead of PLOT. Your computer doesn't understand LINE, CIRCLE, PAINT, or colors.

Sounds. Your computer can't produce sounds.

Exponents. Instead of typing the symbol "^", type the symbol "[", by pressing the up-arrow key.

Random integers, decimals. Same as Model 4.

Clock. To set the date to 01-24-1996, say:

```
POKE 16924,1: POKE 16923,24: POKE 16922,96
```

To set the time to 13:45:07, say:

```
POKE 16921,13: POKE 16920,45: POKE 16919,7
```

If you say PRINT TIME$, the computer will print both the date and time. Your computer doesn't understand TIMER.

POKE. Same as Model 4, but uses cell #16419 instead of #2968, and normally makes the cursor be a double-underline (ASCII 176) instead of a single-underline.

Omitting the question mark, adjacent printing, INPUT$. Same as Color Computer.

Joystick. Your computer doesn't use joysticks.

SWAP. Your computer doesn't understand SWAP, so use the alternative.

OPEN FOR OUTPUT, INPUT, APPEND, LOF, PUT, end of the file. Same as Model 4.

Laser 128

The Laser 128 computer imitates the Apple 2c (which is explained on page 431).

Franklin Ace

The Franklin Ace computer imitates the Apple 2+ (which is explained on page 431).

Coleco Adam

The Adam computer, manufactured by Coleco, resembles the Apple 2+ (which is explained on page 431). For a list of ways in which the Adam computer differs from the Apple 2+, get an earlier edition of *The Secret Guide to Computers* by phoning me at 617-666-2666.

Computers that use CP/M

The CP/M operating system is used by many old computers, such as the Kaypro 2, Kaypro 2X, Kaypro 4, Kaypro 10, and old relics manufactured by Osborne, Morrow, Cromemco, Vector, North Star, Xerox, and Zorba.

On CP/M computers, begin by learning **MBASIC** (which is also called **Microsoft BASIC** and **BASIC-80**), since that version of BASIC is the easiest to learn. It resembles Tandy Model 4 BASIC (which is explained on page 443). For more details, get an earlier edition of *The Secret Guide to Computers* by phoning me at 617-666-2666.

Atari, Texas Instruments, TimexSinclair

For details, get an earlier edition of *The Secret Guide to Computers* by phoning me at 617-666-2666.

DBASE

GET COMFORTABLE

DBASE is a programming language that lets you easily manipulate random-access files and databases. Invented by Wayne Ratliff, was published by **Ashton-Tate**, which sold over a million copies. In 1991, **Borland** bought Ashton-Tate, so now DBASE is published by Borland.

Versions of DBASE

The original version of DBASE was called **DBASE 2**. It ran on the IBM PC and also on computers using the CP/M operating system.

Then came an improvement called **DBASE 3**, then **DBASE 3+**, then **DBASE 4**, then **DBASE 4 version 1.1**, then **DBASE 4 version 1.5**, then **DBASE 4 version 2**, then **DBASE 5**. Those improvements run just on the IBM PC (and clones). Two versions of DBASE 5 are available: one for DOS, the other for Windows.

A company called **Fox Software** invented DBASE versions that run faster, contain extra features, and cost less! Microsoft bought Fox Software, so now Fox's versions are published by Microsoft.

Fox's versions of DBASE are called **FOXBASE** (which resembles DBASE 3), **FOXBASE+** (which resembles DBASE 3+), **FOXPRO** (which resembles DBASE 4), and **FOXPRO 2** (which goes beyond DBASE 4), **FOXPRO 2.5** (which goes even further), and **FOXPRO 2.6** (which goes even further).

Two versions of FOXPRO 2.6 are available: one for DOS, the other for Windows. A Mac version of FOXPRO 2.6 isn't available yet, but you can get a Mac version of FOXPRO 2.5.

Discount dealers sell each of those versions (FOXPRO 2.6 DOS, FOXPRO 2.6 Windows, and FOXPRO 2.5 Mac) for about $90, though that temporary low price will probably rise.

What's in this chapter

I'll explain how to use DBASE 4 version 1.5. (Newer versions of DBASE are similar.)

I'll also explain the differences in DBASE 3, DBASE 3+, DBASE 4 version 1.1, and FOXPRO 2. (Newer versions of FOXPRO are similar to FOXPRO 2.)

Hardware requirements

Fancy versions (such as DBASE 4, FOXBASE+, FOXPRO, and FOXPRO 2) require a hard disk. If you lack a hard disk, use DBASE 3 or 3+.

DBASE 4 requires 640K of RAM. FOXPRO and FOXPRO 2 require 512K. If you don't have so much RAM, use DBASE 3 or 3+, which require just 384K.

To use FOXPRO 2's *advanced* commands, you need at least 1½M of RAM and either a 386 or 486 CPU. To use FOXPRO 2 *easily*, you need a mouse.

Copy to the hard disk

When you buy DBASE 4 version 1.5, you get a big box that contains five manuals, four 1.2M floppies, and five 720K floppies. (If your disk drive needs 360K floppies instead, you can get them by mailing Borland $15 extra.)

Here's how to copy DBASE 4 version 1.5 onto your hard disk. (But if you're sharing the computer, ask your colleagues whether they did this step already!)

Turn on the computer without any floppy in drive A. When you see the C prompt, put the DBASE Install Disk into drive A. Type "a:". You'll see an A prompt. Type "install".

The computer will say "DBASE 4 Installation". Press ENTER twice.

The computer will say "Software Registration". Type your name and press ENTER. Type your company's name (if any) and press ENTER. Type your serial number, which is on the label of the 5¼-inch DBASE Install Disk. (If you remove that disk from the drive to peek at the serial number, put that disk back in the drive when you finish peeking.)

While holding down the Ctrl key, press the END key.

The computer will ask, "Do you wish to install caching?" To keep the installation procedure simple, press N.

When the computer tells you, insert the other DBASE disks, and press ENTER after each insertion.

The computer will say, "DBASE 4 can be run from any directory if your AUTOEXEC.BAT file contains the necessary information." To keep your AUTOEXEC.BAT file simple, press the Esc key.

The computer will say, "DBASE 4 will not run properly unless adequate file and buffer space is reserved." Press ENTER. The computer will make your CONFIG.SYS file says "files=99".

The computer will say, "The installation of DBASE 4 is complete." Press ENTER.

Turn off the computer so you can start fresh.

♦ Old versions DBASE 3 comes on three 360K disks. The first disk is the program itself; the second disk is a spare copy of the program, in case the first disk gets damaged; the third disk contains examples and utilities.

DBASE 3+ comes on seven 360K disks. Two disks contain the program itself, and the other five disks are supplementary.

Instead of copying DBASE 3 or 3+ to the hard disk, try using the procedures described in the next section.

DBASE 4 version 1.1 comes on ten 360K disks, which you install by using a procedure similar to DBASE version 1.5.

♦ FOXPRO 2 When you buy FOXPRO 2, you get a big box that contains nine manuals and four 1.2M disks.

Here's how to copy FOXPRO 2 onto your hard disk. (I assume you have a 386 or 486, at least 1½M of RAM, and a mouse. I assume you've practiced using the mouse with other software, such as Windows or Deluxe Paint.)

Turn on the computer without any floppy in drive A. When you see the C prompt, put FOXPRO Disk 1 into drive A. Type "a:install".

The computer will say, "Fox Software Product Installation". Press ENTER 6 times.

The computer will say, "Enter your FOXPRO Serial Number". Type the Serial Number (which came on a sheet of paper enclosed with the disks).

The computer will say, "Enter your FOXPRO Activation Key". Type the hidden Activation Key (which is hidden on the SECOND sheet of paper enclosed with the disks; do NOT type the DEMONSTRATION Activation Key).

The computer will say, "Please insert Disk #2". Insert FOXPRO Disk 2 into drive A, and press ENTER.

The computer will say, "Please insert Disk #3". Insert FOXPRO Disk 3 into drive A, and press ENTER three times.

The computer will say, "Programs To Install". Using the mouse, click the "Check All" button, then click the "Install" button.

The computer will say, "Please insert Disk #4". Insert FOXPRO Disk 4 into drive A, and press ENTER.

The computer will say, "Installation Complete". Press ENTER.

Turn off the computer so you can start fresh.

Start DBASE

To start using DBASE 4, turn on the computer without any floppy in drive A.

If you've put the DO.BAT file onto your hard disk (as I recommended in the MS-DOS chapter), type "do dbase". If you have *not* put DO.BAT onto your hard disk, you must type "cd dbase" and then "dbase".

(If you're using DBASE 4 version 1.0 or 1.1, the computer will say "This software is licensed". Press ENTER.)

The computer will say "DBASE 4 CONTROL CENTER". Press the Esc key. The computer will ask, "Are you sure?" Press the Y key.

At the screen's lower left corner, you'll see a period, which is called the **dot prompt**. After the dot prompt, you can type any DBASE command you wish.

Press the CAPS LOCK key, so any commands you type will be capitalized.

♦ <u>Old versions</u> Here's how to start using DBASE 3 and 3+.

Without putting any DBASE floppies into the drives, turn on the computer. Wait for a DOS prompt to appear.

Put DBASE System Disk 1 in drive A.

Make sure you see an A prompt. (If you're using a hard disk, do that by typing "a:" after the C prompt.)

Peculiarity: if you're using DBASE 3+ version 1.1 and nobody's ever used your System Disk 1 before, you must give it an "ID" by following the instructions in the "Getting Started" booklet that came with the disk.

Regardless of which version of DBASE 3+ you're using, your next step is to type "dbase" after the A prompt.

If the bottom of the screen says "Press ENTER to assent to the License Agreement", press ENTER. If the computer says "Insert System Disk 2", do so and press ENTER. If the bottom right corner of the screen says "Exit — Esc", press the Esc key.

At the screen's lower left corner, you'll see a period, which is the dot prompt. Press the CAPS LOCK key, so any commands you type will be capitalized.

If you have a hard disk, type "SET DEFAULT TO C". If you lack a hard disk, put a blank formatted disk in drive B and type "SET DEFAULT TO B".

♦ <u>FOXPRO 2</u> Here's how to start using FOXPRO 2.

Turn on the computer without any floppy in drive A.

When you see the C prompt, type "cd foxpro2". When you see the FOXPRO2 prompt, type "foxprox". (If you don't have enough RAM to run "foxprox", type "fox" instead.)

In the middle of the screen, you'll see a rectangle that has the word "Command" at the top of it. That rectangle is called the "Command Window". To move that rectangle to a different part of the screen, use the mouse: point at the word "Command", and drag it. To change the rectangle's size, point at the dot in the rectangle's bottom right corner, and drag it.

For best results, drag until the rectangle consumes most of the top third of the screen.

Press the CAPS LOCK key, so any commands you type will be capitalized.

Arithmetic

If you want the computer to print the answer to 5+2, say "? 5+2" after the dot prompt, so your screen looks like this:

. ? 5+2

The computer will print:

7

Notice that DBASE, like BASIC, uses a question mark to mean print. So "? 5+2" means: print 5+2. In DBASE, you *must* use the question mark; do *not* type the word PRINT.

DBASE, like BASIC, uses the symbols +, -, *, /, ^, E, and parentheses.

Unfortunately, DBASE gives the wrong answer to -5^2. According to mathematicians, -5^2 means "the negative of 5^2", which is "the negative of 25", which is -25. DBASE mistakenly thinks that -5^2 means "the square of -5" and therefore prints 25.

♦ <u>FOXPRO 2</u> You don't see a dot prompt. Just type:

? 5+2

Your typing will appear in the Command Window. At the end of your typing, when you press the ENTER key, the computer will print this answer at the screen's bottom:

7

Strings

DBASE, like BASIC, lets you use quotation marks to create strings. So if you say —

. ? "I LOVE YOU"

the computer will print:

I LOVE YOU

Multiple computations

You can print several computations on the same line. For example, if you say —

. ? 2+3,2-3,2*3,2/3

the computer will print:

    5   -1   6   0.67

QUIT

When you finish using DBASE, do *not* turn off the computer's power. Turning off the power will wreck the data files you've been working on.

Instead of turning off the power, say QUIT, so your screen looks like this:

. QUIT

That QUIT command makes the computer put the finishing touches on all your data files. Then the computer will stop using DBASE, and will say:

C:\>

After the "C:\>", you can give any DOS command, or turn off the power.

CREATE A DATA FILE

Let's create a data file about families in your neighborhood. Begin by saying:

. CREATE FAMILIES

That makes the computer create, on your disk, a data file named "FAMILIES.DBF". (The ".DBF" stands for "Data Base File".)

Complete the chart

Let's store each family's NAME, annual INCOME, and POPULATION (number of people in the family). Suppose the longest family NAME is Anagnostopoulos, the highest INCOME is 125000.00, and the largest POPULATION is 13 (because the family includes a mother, father, and 11 kids).

To prepare the computer to handle such data, feed the computer this chart:

Num	Field Name	Field Type	Width	Dec	Index
1	NAME	Character	15		N
2	INCOME	Numeric	9	2	N
3	POPULATION	Numeric	2	0	N

The second column says that for each family we're storing these **fields**: the family's NAME, INCOME, and POPULATION. The left column numbers those fields: 1, 2, and 3. The third column says that each family's NAME is a string of characters, and that each family's INCOME and POPULATION are numbers. The remaining columns say that each NAME can be up to 15 characters long (such as "Anagnostopoulos"), each INCOME can be up to 9 symbols long (such as 125000.00) and has 2 digits after the decimal point, each POPULATION can be up to 2 digits long (such as 13) and has no decimals, and No field is indexed.

As soon as you say CREATE FAMILIES (and press the ENTER key at the end of that line), the computer asks you to feed it that chart. To help you start, the computer puts this on the screen:

Num	Field Name	Field Type	Width	Dec	Index
1		Character			N

Just fill in all the other entries in the chart — and press the ENTER key after each entry. Here are the details....

Begin by typing NAME (by pressing the N key, then A, then M, then E). Press the ENTER key at the end of that entry.

Since the computer's already typed the next entry for you (Character), press the ENTER key again.

Type the next entry (15). Press ENTER.

Since the computer's already typed the next entry for you (N), press the ENTER key again.

Type the next entry (INCOME). Press ENTER.

Start typing the next entry (Numeric). As soon as you type the N of Numeric, the computer automatically types the "umeric" for you and presses the ENTER key for you.

Type the next entry (9); press ENTER. Type the next entry (2); press ENTER. Accept the N, by pressing ENTER again.

Type the next entry (POPULATION). Since POPULATION is so long, when you finish typing it the computer will automatically beep (to warn you not to make it even longer!) and press ENTER for you.

Type the next entry (N) and the next entry (2); press ENTER. Type the final entry (0). Since you've finished typing the entire table, tap the END key *while holding down the CONTROL key.*

♦ Old versions DBASE 3 and 3+ omit the Num and Index columns. DBASE 3 says Char/text instead of Character. When you tap the END key wwhile holding down the CONTROL key, DBASE 3+ says "Press ENTER to confirm"; DBASE 3 says "Hit RETURN to confirm"; obey those versions by pressing the ENTER/RETURN key.

♦ FOXPRO 2 Feed the computer this chart:

Name	Type	Width	Dec
NAME	Character	15	
INCOME	Numeric	9	2
POPULATION	Numeric	2	0

Begin by typing NAME. Press the TAB key at the end of that entry.

Since the computer's already typed the next entry for you (Character), press the TAB key again.

Type the next entry (15). Press TAB.

Type the next entry (INCOME). Press TAB.

Start typing the next entry (Numeric). As soon as you type the N of Numeric, the computer automatically types the "umeric" for you and presses the TAB key for you.

Type the next entry (9); press TAB. Type the next entry (2); press TAB. Type the next entry (POPULATION); press TAB. Type the next entry (N) and the next entry (2). The computer will automatically type the final 0.

Using the mouse, click the word "OK".

Input the data

The computer will ask:

Input data records now? (Y/N)

Tap the Y key, which means Yes.

On the screen, you'll see this:

NAME
INCOME
POPULATION

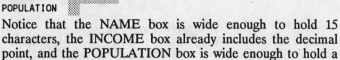

Notice that the NAME box is wide enough to hold 15 characters, the INCOME box already includes the decimal point, and the POPULATION box is wide enough to hold a 2-digit number.

Fill in the boxes. Here's how.

Type the first family's name (SMITH). As you type SMITH, you'll see it appear in the first box. When you finish typing SMITH, press ENTER.

Type family's income (24100.19). As you type 24100.19, you'll see it appear in the second box. When you type the decimal point, the number will automatically slide toward the right edge of the box, so that the decimal point you typed is at the same place as the decimal point that was already in the box. When you finish typing the number, the computer will automatically beep and move you to the third box.

Type the family's population (4). You'll see it appear in the third box.

When you press the ENTER key afterwards, the computer will record what you typed. Then the boxes will become blank again, so that you can enter a second family's data.

After entering the second family's data (and pressing the ENTER key if necessary), the screen will go blank again, so you can enter a third family's data.

Enter data for as many families as you wish.

When you've typed the data for the last family, and you're still looking at that data on the screen, tap the END key while holding down the CONTROL key.

The computer will display the dot prompt, so that you can give another DBASE command.

♦ FOXPRO 2 When you finish typing an entry (such as SMITH), you can press either the ENTER key or the TAB key.

In a numeric field (such as INCOME), you don't see the decimal point until you type it.

When you finish typing the first family's data, that data does NOT disappear from the screen; instead, the computer lets you type the second family's data underneath the first family's.

When you finish typing the last family's data, click the close box (which is the yellow square in the window's top left corner).

SEE YOUR DATA

After you've created a data file, you can say:

. LIST

That makes the computer list your file's information onto the screen, so the screen will look like this:

Record#	NAME	INCOME	POPULATION
1	SMITH	24100.19	4
2	ANAGNOSTOPOULOS	65143.26	5
3	SANCHEZ	50000.00	13
4	JONES	9873.00	2
5	SZCZEPANKIEWICZ	125000.00	4
6	SANTINI	-4130.15	4
7	WONG	15691.18	3

Notice that the Sanchez family has a high income (50000.00) but must split it among 13 people (mother, father, and 11 kids). The Jones family's population is just 2: a single mother and her baby. The Santini family's income is a negative number this year, because the family invested big money in the stock market and lost.

Choose your columns

You can make the computer omit some of the columns. If you say —

. LIST NAME,POPULATION

the computer will list the NAME and POPULATION columns but not the INCOME column; it will list this:

Record#	NAME	POPULATION
1	SMITH	4
2	ANAGNOSTOPOULOS	5
3	SANCHEZ	13
4	JONES	2
5	SZCZEPANKIEWICZ	4
6	SANTINI	4
7	WONG	3

If you say —

. LIST POPULATION,NAME

the computer will list the POPULATION column before the NAME column, like this:

Record#	POPULATION	NAME
1	4	SMITH
2	5	ANAGNOSTOPOULOS
3	13	SANCHEZ
4	2	JONES
5	4	SZCZEPANKIEWICZ
6	4	SANTINI
7	3	WONG

If you say —

. LIST OFF POPULATION,NAME

the computer will turn off the "Record#" column; it will list just this:

POPULATION	NAME
4	SMITH
5	ANAGNOSTOPOULOS
13	SANCHEZ
2	JONES
4	SZCZEPANKIEWICZ
4	SANTINI
3	WONG

For each family, let's compute the income *per person*. To do that, divide the family's income by the family's population. To display the income per person, and everything else, say —

```
. LIST NAME,INCOME,POPULATION,INCOME/POPULATION
```

The computer will list this:

```
Record#  NAME                INCOME POPULATION INCOME/POPULATION
     1   SMITH             24100.19       4            6025.05
     2   ANAGNOSTOPOULOS   65143.26       5           13028.65
     3   SANCHEZ           50000.00      13            3846.15
     4   JONES              9873.00       2            4936.50
     5   SZCZEPANKIEWICZ  125000.00       4           31250.00
     6   SANTINI           -4130.15       4           -1032.54
     7   WONG              15691.18       3            5230.39
```

LIST FOR

To list just the low-income families (earning under $10,000), say:

```
. LIST FOR INCOME<10000
```

The computer will list:

```
Record#  NAME                INCOME POPULATION
     4   JONES              9873.00       2
     6   SANTINI           -4130.15       4
```

To list just the high-income families (earning at least $50,000), say:

```
. LIST FOR INCOME>=50000
```

That means: list for INCOME greater than or equal to $50,000.

When you're comparing strings, an equal sign means "begins with". So to list every family whose NAME *begins with* "SAN", say:

```
. LIST FOR NAME="SAN"
```

The computer will list all data about SANCHEZ and SANTINI.

To list every family whose NAME does *not* begin with "SAN", say —

```
. LIST FOR NAME<>"SAN"
```

or, if you prefer, say:

```
. LIST FOR NAME#"SAN"
```

To list just the "SAN" families whose incomes are high, say:

```
. LIST FOR NAME="SAN" .AND. INCOME>=50000
```

That makes the computer list the data for SANCHEZ (whose income is 50000) but not SANTINI (whose income is -4130.15). Notice you must put periods around the word AND.

DBASE also understands the word OR, which you must surround with periods.

If you want to change DBASE, so that an equal sign between strings means "exactly equals" instead of "begins with", say:

```
. SET EXACT ON
```

The SET EXACT ON command remains in effect until you say QUIT or SET EXACT OFF.

♦ FOXPRO 2 You can omit the periods around AND and OR. For example, you can say either ".AND." or "AND"; the computer doesn't care.

LIST STRUCTURE

If you say —

```
. LIST STRUCTURE
```

the computer will say:

```
Field  Field name  Type       Width   Dec   Index
   1   NAME        Character     15                N
   2   INCOME      Numeric        9      2          N
   3   POPULATION  Numeric        2                 N
** Total **                      27
```

The computer will also say that the file contains 7 records, and it will say the date the file was last changed.

Compute the statistics

The computer can do statistics.

COUNT If you say —

```
. COUNT
```

the computer will count how many records are in the file. It will say:

```
7 records
```

SUM If you say —

```
. SUM
```

the computer will sum all the numbers in the file. It will say:

```
7 records summed
   INCOME POPULATION
285677.48         35
```

That means: the sum of all the incomes is $285,677.48, and the sum of all the populations is 35. So altogether, your entire neighborhood earns a total of $285,677.48, and the neighborhood's total population is 35.

AVERAGE If you say —

```
. AVERAGE
```

the computer will average all the numbers in the file. It will say:

```
7 records averaged
   INCOME POPULATION
 40811.07          5
```

That means the average family INCOME is $40,811.07, and the average family POPULATION is 5. (The average family population would be much lower if the Sanchez family didn't have 13 members.)

Restrictions After the word COUNT, SUM, or AVERAGE, you can add restrictions.

For example, if you want to find the average of just the SANCHEZ and SANTINI families, say:

```
. AVERAGE FOR NAME="SAN"
```

The computer will say:

```
2 records averaged
   INCOME    POPULATION
 22934.93          8.50
```

If you want to average just the incomes, and don't want to bother averaging the populations, say:

```
. AVERAGE INCOME FOR NAME="SAN"
```

♦ Old versions When you say AVERAGE FOR NAME="SAN", the average population is exactly 8.5, but DBASE 3 and 3+ make the computer shorten the answer and say just 8.

♦ FOXPRO 2 When you say AVERAGE FOR NAME="SAN", the average population is exactly 8.5, but the computer rounds the answer and says 9.

Print on paper

To print on paper, you can use several tricks.

The simplest is to tap the PRINT SCREEN key. (If your keyboard doesn't have a PRINT SCREEN key, press the PrtSc key while holding down the SHIFT key.) That makes the printer print a snapshot of what's on the screen.

Another way is to type:

```
. SET PRINT ON
```

Afterwards, anything that will appear on the screen will also appear on paper simultaneously. The SET PRINT ON command remains in effect until you say SET PRINT OFF.

To LIST on paper, you can say:

```
. SET PRINT ON
. LIST
. SET PRINT OFF
```

A faster way to LIST onto paper is to say:

```
. LIST TO PRINT
```

♦ Old versions If you say LIST TO PRINT while using DBASE 3+, the last line of the listing gets temporarily lost, in a part of RAM called the "buffer". That last line won't get transferred to paper until afterwards, when you give your next print-to-paper command, or when you say SET PRINT ON.

♦ FOXPRO 2 If you say SET PRINT ON, anything that will appear on the screen's bottom line will appear on paper simultaneously. (Saying SET PRINT ON will NOT make the paper show what's in the Command Window.)

Interrupt the computer

If the computer is doing something you don't like, and you want to stop the computer, press the ESCAPE key (which says "Esc" on it). That makes the computer abort what it was doing.

For example, suppose you say LIST, and the computer starts printing a long listing. If you get impatient and don't want to see the rest of the listing, press the ESCAPE key.

In some situations, when you press the ESCAPE key, the computer asks:

```
Cancel  Ignore  Suspend
```

Confirm that you want to cancel: press the C key.

After the computer aborts, it displays the dot prompt, so you can give another DBASE command.

In DBASE, as in IBM's BASIC and PC-DOS, you can make the computer pause by pressing the PAUSE key. (If your keyboard doesn't have a PAUSE key, tap the NUM LOCK key while holding down the CONTROL key.) To make the computer continue where it left off, press the SPACE bar.

If you say DISPLAY ALL instead of LIST, the computer will list the file but will automatically pause at the end of each screenful. At the end of each screenful, it will say, "Press any key to continue". When you press ENTER, the computer will continue on to the next screenful.

Short-cut: instead of saying DISPLAY ALL FOR NAME = "SAN", you can say DISPLAY FOR NAME = "SAN". Here's the rule: before the word FOR, you can omit ALL.

♦ Old versions Instead of saying "Cancel Ignore Suspend", DBASE 3+ says "Cancel, Ignore, or Suspend? (C, I, or S)"; DBASE 3 says "Terminate command file?", to which you respond by tapping the Y key.

Grab a particular record

To list just the 3rd record say:

```
. LIST RECORD 3
```

The computer will say:

```
Record#  NAME              INCOME POPULATION
      3  SANCHEZ         50000.00         13
```

Instead of saying LIST RECORD 3, you can say:

```
. GO 3
. DISPLAY
```

That makes the computer GO to record #3 and DISPLAY it. That pair of lines (GO 3 and DISPLAY) has exactly the same effect as saying LIST RECORD 3.

After you've gotten the record, you can use that record's NAME, INCOME, and POPULATION for further computations. For example, if you say —

```
. ? INCOME/20
```

the computer will print that record's INCOME divided by 20, which is:

```
2500
```

To go to record #1, which is the top record, you can say either GO 1 or GO TOP. If your file contains 7 records, and you want to go to record #7, which is the bottom record, you can say either GO 7 or GO BOTTOM. (After giving a GO command, remember to say DISPLAY.)

If you're lazy, you can usually omit the word GO. Instead of saying —

```
. GO 3
```

you can say just:

```
. 3
```

But you cannot omit the GO from "GO TOP" and "GO BOTTOM".

SKIP SKIP means "go to the next record".

For example, suppose you've been looking at record #3 (because you said GO 3 and DISPLAY), and you want to go to the next record, which is record #4. Just say:

```
. SKIP
. DISPLAY
```

If you say SKIP 2, the computer will skip ahead 2 records. For example, if you've been looking at record #4 and then say SKIP 2, the computer will go to record #6.

If you say SKIP -1, the computer will skip back to the previous record. For example, if you've been looking at record #6 and then say SKIP -1, the computer will go back to record #5.

LOCATE If you say —

```
. LOCATE FOR NAME="SAN"
. DISPLAY
```

the computer will start at the first record, and keep hunting until it finds a record whose NAME begins with "SAN". Then it will DISPLAY that record:

```
Record#  NAME              INCOME POPULATION
      3  SANCHEZ         50000.00         13
```

To find the next "SAN", say:

```
. CONTINUE
. DISPLAY
```

The computer will display:

```
Record#  NAME              INCOME POPULATION
      6  SANTINI         -4130.15         13
```

If you say CONTINUE again, the computer will continue hunting for SAN's. If the computer reaches the end of the file and still hasn't found another SAN, it will give up, and say:

End of LOCATE scope

♦ Old versions DBASE 3 and 3+ say just "End of LOCATE"; they omit the word "scope".

Attach fancy restrictions

If you say:

```
. GO 3
. DISPLAY
```

the computer will display just the 3rd record. If you say —

```
. GO 3
. DISPLAY NEXT 2
```

the computer will display 2 records (the 3rd and the 4th). If you say —

```
. GO 3
. DISPLAY NEXT 4
```

the computer will display 4 records (the 3rd, 4th, 5th, and 6th). If you say —

```
. GO 3
. DISPLAY REST
```

the computer will display the 3rd record and all the records that come after it. For example, if the data file contains 7 records, the computer will display the 3rd, 4th, 5th, 6th, and 7th records. (If your data file is long, the computer will pause at the end of each screenful, and wait for you to tell it to continue. If you don't want such pauses, say LIST instead of DISPLAY.)

If you say —

```
. GO 3
. DISPLAY WHILE INCOME<100000
```

the computer will start with the 3rd record, and continue displaying records as long as INCOME < 100000. Here are the details. . . .

The computer starts with the 3rd record, sees that its INCOME is less than 100000, and displays that record. Then the computer checks the 4th record, sees its INCOME is less than 100000, and displays that record. Then the computer checks the 5th record, sees its INCOME is *not* less than 100000, and refuses to display the 5th record. The computer stops there, and refuses to look at any more records. so the only records it displays are the 3rd and 4th.

Those four commands — DISPLAY and DISPLAY NEXT and DISPLAY REST and DISPLAY WHILE — are all affected by where you said to GO. Three different commands — DISPLAY ALL and DISPLAY RECORD and DISPLAY FOR — are unaffected by GO. Even if you said GO 3, a DISPLAY ALL will display the entire file, DISPLAY RECORD 2 will display record #2, and DISPLAY FOR INCOME<100000 will display *all* the records whose INCOMEs are less than 100000.

The words NEXT, REST, WHILE, ALL, RECORD, and FOR are called **restrictions**. You can attach a restriction to any DBASE command that scans data records. For example, you can add a restriction to DISPLAY, LIST, COUNT, SUM, AVERAGE, and LOCATE.

♦ Old versions DBASE 3 doesn't understand the word REST.

To revise your data, you can say EDIT, BROWSE, REPLACE, APPEND, INSERT, DELETE, or ZAP.

EDIT

To edit record #3, say —

```
. EDIT RECORD 3
```

or say —

```
. EDIT 3
```

or say:

```
. GO 3
. EDIT
```

The computer will display the 3rd record on the screen and let you edit it. While you edit, you can use the four arrow keys (to move around the screen), the BACKSPACE key (to erase the previous character), the DELETE key (to delete the current character), and the INSERT key (to switch from "replacing" to "inserting" and back to "replacing" again). DBASE handles those keys the same way as good word processors (such as Word Perfect, Q&A's word processor, and DOS 5's EDIT).

To erase all the data in a field, just move to that field (by using the arrow keys); then tap the Y key while holding down the CONTROL key.

After editing the 3rd record, if you press the PAGE DOWN key, the computer will let you edit the 4th record. If you press the PAGE DOWN key again, the computer will let you edit the 5th record. (Exception: if a record is too long to fit on the screen, pressing the PAGE DOWN key will get you to the next screenful of the same record.)

By pressing the PAGE UP key, you can return to earlier records. For example, if you've been editing the 5th record and then press the PAGE UP key, the computer will let you re-edit the 4th record.

When you've finished editing all the records you wish, tap the END key while holding down the CONTROL key. Then the computer will display the dot prompt, so you can type another DBASE command.

♦ FOXPRO 2 While you're editing the 3rd record, the screen also shows the 4th and 5th records. When you finishing editing the 3rd record, you can move to the 4th record by either pressing the PAGE DOWN key once or by pressing the down-arrow key several times.

When you finish editing all the records you wish, you can either press CONTROL with END or click the close box (the yellow square in the window's top left corner).

BROWSE

To see several records on the screen simultaneously, so you can edit them all at once, say:

```
. GO 1
. BROWSE
```

That makes the computer LIST the first several records in your file. The computer will let you use the arrow keys to move through the list and edit your data. To hop right to the next field, press the TAB key; to hop left to the previous field, press the TAB key *while holding down the SHIFT key*.

The computer will list as many records as can fit on the screen; to see the next screenful of records, press the PAGE DOWN key. The computer will list as many fields as can fit across the screen; to see other fields, tap the right-arrow key while holding down the CONTROL key.

When you've finished editing the data, tap the END key while holding down the CONTROL key.

♦ Old versions In DBASE 3 and 3+, the TAB key doesn't work. Instead, hop to the next field by pressing END; hop back to the previous field by pressing HOME.

♦ FOXPRO 2 The computer will list as many fields as fit across the window. To see other fields, press the TAB key several times.

The computer will list as many records as fit in the window. To see other records, press the PAGE DOWN key once or twice (or press the down-arrow key several times).

When you've finished editing the data, click the close box (or press CONTROL with END).

REPLACE

A more literary way to edit records is to type a sentence that begins with the word REPLACE.

For example, to change record #3's INCOME to $60,000, say:

```
. GO 3
. REPLACE INCOME WITH 60000
```

To increase record #5's INCOME by $700, say:

```
. GO 5
. REPLACE INCOME WITH INCOME+700
```

To increase *everybody's* INCOME by $700, say:

```
. REPLACE ALL INCOME WITH INCOME+700
```

To increase the INCOME of just families whose NAME begins with "SAN", say:

```
. REPLACE FOR NAME="SAN" INCOME WITH INCOME+700
```

APPEND

To add extra records, say:

```
. APPEND
```

The computer will display a blank record on the screen, and let you fill it in.

For example, if your data file contains 7 records, and you say APPEND, the computer will let you type record #8. When you finish typing it (and press the ENTER key at the end of the last field), the computer will let you type record #9, then record #10, etc.

When you've finished typing all the records you want to add, tap the END key while holding down the CONTROL key. Then the computer will display the dot prompt, so you can type another DBASE command.

♦ FOXPRO 2 When you've finished typing all the records you want to add, click the close box (or press CONTROL with END).

INSERT

To insert an extra record between record #3 and record #4, say:

```
. GO 3
. INSERT
```

The computer will display a blank record on your screen, and let you fill it in. When you finish filling it in, tap the END key while holding down the CONTROL key. The new record that you typed will become record #4; the old record #4 will become record #5; the old record #5 will become record #6; etc.

The computer will then display the dot prompt, so you can type another DBASE command.

♦ FOXPRO 2 When you finish filling in the record, click the close box (or press CONTROL with END).

DELETE

To delete records 3, 5, and 6, say:

```
. DELETE RECORD 3
. DELETE RECORD 5
. DELETE RECORD 6
. PACK
```

Here's why. When you give the DELETE commands, the computer makes notes about which records you want to delete. But it doesn't actually delete those records, until you say PACK.

When you say PACK, the computer finally deletes those records. It also renumbers all the other records, to fill the gaps left by the records you deleted.

Renumbering all the records takes a long time; so while the computer's doing a PACK, you should take your coffee break or lunch break. If you don't want to take a break yet, delay saying PACK until later. Say PACK at the end of the day, or when it's time to QUIT or to switch to a different file.

DELETE without PACK If you say to DELETE some records, but you haven't said PACK yet, what happens when you try to LIST the file? The listing will show an asterisk next to each record you said to delete. The asterisked records will disappear later, when you say PACK.

If you say —

```
. SET DELETED ON
```

the computer hides the asterisked records, so they don't appear in listings and don't affect the COUNT or SUM or AVERAGE. But although the asterisked records are hidden, they're still in the file, until you say PACK.

SET DELETED ON remains in effect until you say QUIT or SET DELETED OFF.

RECALL If you say DELETE RECORD 3 and then change your mind, you can get the record back by saying RECALL RECORD 3. But RECALL works only if you haven't said PACK yet.

Short cuts Instead of saying DELETE RECORD 3, you can say:

```
. GO 3
. DELETE
```

Here's another way to delete record 3: get that record onto your screen (by saying EDIT or BROWSE, and playing with the PAGE UP and PAGE DOWN keys); and while you're looking at that record, tap the U key while holding down the CONTROL key. (The U stands for Undo.)

To delete everybody whose name begins with "SAN", say:

```
. DELETE FOR NAME="SAN"
. PACK
```

ZAP

To delete *all* the records, instead of saying DELETE ALL and PACK, just say:

```
. ZAP
```

Then the computer asks whether you're sure; tap the Y key. Then the computer ZAPs the file, so that all the records are gone. But the computer will still remember how wide you wanted each field, so you can add new records without having to say CREATE.

You can switch to a different file. Here's how. . . .

USE

Suppose you create a DBASE file called FAMILIES.DBF, then create a DBASE file called FOODS.DBF. If you say LIST, the computer will assume you want to list the newest file (FOODS.DBF). If you want to list FAMILIES.DBF instead, say:

```
. USE FAMILIES
. LIST
```

Saying USE FAMILIES makes the computer switch its attention to FAMILIES.DBF, so that any future command you give (such as LIST or GO or DISPLAY) applies to FAMILIES.DBF. To switch to FOODS.DBF again, say USE FOODS.

If you QUIT using DBASE but return to DBASE later, the computer forgets which file you were using. Before saying LIST, say USE FAMILIES or USE FOODS.

DIR

To see a directory of all the files in your hard disk's DBASE folder, say:

```
. DIR *.*
```

To see a special directory of just your DBASE data files (which end in .DBF), say just:

```
. DIR
```

That makes the computer print a special directory showing each data file's name, *how many records it contains*, how many bytes it contains, and the date it was last changed.

COPY

Suppose you're using the FAMILIES.DBF file, and want to make a backup copy of it.

If you want the backup copy to be called FRED.DBF, say:

```
. COPY TO FRED
```

That makes FRED.DBF be an exact copy of the whole file.

If you want FRED.DBF to include just the records of families whose names begin with "SAN", say:

```
. COPY TO FRED FOR NAME="SAN"
```

If you want FRED.DBF to include every family's NAME and POPULATION but not the INCOME, say:

```
. COPY TO FRED FIELDS NAME,POPULATION
```

If you want FRED.DBF to include no records at all, but just have the same structure (the same lengths for all the fields), say:

```
. COPY STRUCTURE TO FRED
```

If you want FRED.DBF to contain all the records, but rearranged so that the NAMEs are in alphabetical order, say —

```
. SORT ON NAME TO FRED
```

If you want FRED.DBF to contain all the records, but rearranged so that the INCOMEs are in increasing order, say —

```
. SORT ON INCOME TO FRED
```

If you want FRED.DBF to contain all the records, but rearranged so that the INCOMEs are in decreasing order (from the largest to the smallest), say —

```
. SORT ON INCOME/D TO FRED
```

ERASE

If you ever want to erase FAMILIES.DBF, say:

```
. ERASE FAMILIES.DBF
```

♦ Hassle While you're in the middle of using FAMILIES.DBF, the computer will refuse to erase it. To stop using it (so you can erase it), tell the computer to use a different file instead (by giving a command such as USE FOODS), or just say —

```
.USE
```

which makes the computer use no file at all. Then you can say ERASE FAMILIES.DBF.

MODIFY STRUCTURE

When you said CREATE, you filled in a chart: for each field you chose a name (such as INCOME), type (such as Numeric), and width (such as 9).

If you later want to modify that chart, say:

```
. MODIFY STRUCTURE
```

The screen will again show the chart that you created. By using the arrow keys, you can move through the chart and modify it. You can change a field's name, type, width, or number of decimal places.

To delete a field altogether, move to that field, then tap the U key while holding down the CONTROL key. (The U stands for Undo.)

To insert an extra field, move to where you want the field to be, then tap the N key while holding down the CONTROL key. (The N stands for iNsert New.)

Change as many fields as you like.

When you've finished modifying the chart, tap the END key while holding down the CONTROL key. If the computer asks "Should data be COPIED from backup for all fields?", tap the Y key.

The computer will ask, "Are you sure you want to save these changes?" Tap the Y key.

The computer will revise your entire data file, so that the file matches the chart. For example, if you said to make a field wider, the computer will do so by adding extra spaces to your data; if you said to make a field narrower, the computer will do so by abridging your data.

To see what the computer did to your data file, say LIST.

♦ Hassle If you make the computer change names of fields, the computer can't reliably change anything else at the same time. So to make lots of changes, say MODIFY STRUCTURE and change names of fields; afterwards say MODIFY STRUCTURE again and make all the other changes you wish (widths, decimal places, types, deleted fields, and extra fields).

♦ Old versions After giving the MODIFY STRUCTURE command, DBASE 3 and 3+ make your disk contain two versions of your data file. For example, if you've been dealing with FAMILIES.DBF, your disk will contain a file called FAMILIES.DBF (which is the new, modified version), and your disk will also contain a file called FAMILIES.BAK (which is the previous unmodified version). FAMILIES.BAK is called the backup: use it only if you accidentally made a mistake when giving the MODIFY STRUCTURE command. To use FAMILIES.BAK, say:

```
. USE
. ERASE FAMILIES.DBF
. RENAME FAMILIES.BAK TO FAMILIES.DBF
. USE FAMILIES
```

♦ FOXPRO 2 To move through the chart quickly, use the mouse: click the part of the chart that interests you. To delete a field altogether, click that field then click the word "Delete". To insert an extra field, click where you want the field to be then click the word "Insert". When you finish modifying the chart, click the word "OK" then click the word "Yes". Like DBASE 3 and 3+, FOXPRO 2 creates a .BAK file; for details, read the paragraph above (entitled "Old versions").

INDEX FILES

Suppose you're using a file called FAMILIES.DBF. Let's play a trick, so that every time you say LIST or DISPLAY the NAMEs will appear in alphabetical order, to help you find a particular NAME very quickly.

Say:

```
. INDEX ON NAME TO FAMNAME
```

That makes the computer create a file called FAMNAME.NDX, which is an iNDeX file that helps the computer find each family's NAME.

Then if you say LIST, the computer will list the families in alphabetical order:

```
Record#  NAME             INCOME  POPULATION
    2  ANAGNOSTOPOULOS  65143.26          5
    4  JONES             9873.00          2
    3  SANCHEZ          50000.00         13
    6  SANTINI          -4130.15          4
    1  SMITH            24100.19          4
    5  SZCZEPANKIEWICZ 125000.00          4
    7  WONG             15691.18          3
```

In that file, the TOP is record #2: ANAGNOSTOPOULOS. So if you say —

```
. GO TOP
. DISPLAY
```

the computer will display:

```
Record#  NAME             INCOME  POPULATION
    2  ANAGNOSTOPOULOS  65143.26          5
```

Then if you say —

```
. SKIP
. DISPLAY
```

the computer will skip the next record in the alphabetized list, and display:

```
Record#  NAME     INCOME  POPULATION
    4  JONES    9873.00          2
```

In that alphabetized file, saying GO TOP has a different effect from saying GO 1. If you say GO TOP, you're going to the TOP record, which is ANAGNOSTOPOULOS; if you say GO 1, you're going to the record #1, which is SMITH.

If you want to add more records to the alphabetized list, say APPEND. As you type the extra records, the computer will automatically update the index file, so when you say LIST you'll see the entire data file — including even the new records — in alphabetical order.

♦ FOXPRO 2 When you say INDEX ON NAME TO FAMNAME, FOXPRO 2 creates an index file called FAMNAME.IDX (instead of FAMNAME.NDX).

How to find

To display the first record whose NAME begins with SAN, you can say:

```
. LOCATE FOR NAME="SAN"
. DISPLAY
```

To find that record faster, say this instead —

```
. SEEK "SAN"
. DISPLAY
```

or say:

```
. FIND SAN
. DISPLAY
```

The only difference between SEEK and FIND is that SEEK must be followed by quotation marks (or a variable), whereas FIND lets you omit the quotation marks.

SEEK and FIND tell the computer to find the record *immediately*, by using the index file.

By contrast, the word LOCATE makes the computer locate the record slowly, by searching through all the records in the whole data file, from beginning to end. If your data file is very long, you'll have to wait a long time for the computer to LOCATE the record! For example, if your data file contains 2,000 records, the LOCATE command takes about 25 times as long as the SEEK and FIND commands. **The main reason for creating an index file is so that you can use the words SEEK and FIND.**

Since the index file makes the computer list all the names in alphabetical order, all the SAN names are listed near each other. So after you've found the first SAN (by saying FIND SAN and DISPLAY), you can display the next one immediately, by saying:

```
. SKIP
. DISPLAY
```

Hassles

If you QUIT or switch to a different data file, and later try to return to FAMILIES.DBF by saying USE FAMILIES, you must remind the computer to look at the index file. Instead of saying just USE FAMILIES, say:

```
. USE FAMILIES INDEX FAMNAME
```

If you accidentally forget to say INDEX FAMNAME, the computer will forget to look at the index. If you then APPEND or DELETE some records, the computer won't update the index, and the index will be wrong. If you get into that jam, get out of it by saying —

```
. USE FAMILIES INDEX FAMNAME
. REINDEX
```

That makes the computer create the index all over again, correctly.

To see the names of all your index files (such as FAMNAME.NDX), say:

```
. DIR *.NDX
```

♦ FOXPRO 2 To see the names of all your index files (such as FAMNAME.IDX), say "DIR *.IDX".

Let's write a program so that whenever you say DO STATS, the computer will automatically print the SUM and AVERAGE of all the numbers in your data file. Here's how.

Begin by saying —

```
. MODIFY COMMAND STATS
```

That tells the computer you want to write a program called STATS.PRG.

Next, say what you want STATS to stand for. If you want STATS to stand for "the SUM followed by the AVERAGE", type:

```
SUM
AVERAGE
```

That pair of instructions (SUM and AVERAGE) is called the *program*. The computer does *not* put a dot prompt in front of the program lines.

While you're typing the program, you can edit it by using the arrow keys and all the other word-processing keys (DELETE, INSERT, PAGE UP, and PAGE DOWN).

To hop to the left margin, press the HOME key. To hop to the end of a line, press the END key.

To delete a line, move to that line, then tap the Y key while holding down the CONTROL key. (The Y stands for "Yank it out".) To insert an extra line between two other lines, move to where you want the extra line to begin, then tap the N key while holding down the CONTROL key. (The N stands for "iNsert New".)

When you've finished typing and editing the program, tap the END key while holding down the CONTROL key. That makes the computer put the entire program onto the disk. Then the screen will show a dot prompt.

If you want the computer to DO the STATS program you typed, say:

```
. DO STATS
```

Then the computer will print the SUM and AVERAGE of all the numbers in the current data file. For example, if you've been using the FAMILIES data file, the computer will print the SUM of the INCOMEs, SUM of the POPULATIONs, AVERAGE of the INCOMEs, and AVERAGE of the POPULATIONs. (If you haven't been using a data file, the computer will ask you which file to USE. If your data file doesn't contain any Numeric fields, the computer will gripe.)

If you ever want to revise that program, just say MODIFY COMMAND STATS again. The screen will show your program again and let you edit it. When you've finished editing it, tap the END key while holding down the CONTROL key. The new version of your program will be called STATS.PRG; the previous version of your program will still be on the disk but will be called STATS.BAK.

For another example, let's program the computer so that when you say DO SUPERDIR, the computer will print a superdirectory. Let's make the superdirectory include a directory of all your data files, followed by a directory of all your index files, followed by a directory of all your program files.

To make DO SUPERDIR accomplish all that, say:

```
. MODIFY COMMAND SUPERDIR
```

Then type this program —

```
DIR
DIR *.NDX
DIR *.PRG
```

End the program by tapping the END key while holding down the CONTROL key. From then on, whenever you say DO SUPERDIR, the computer will print a superdirectory.

Into a program, you can put any DBASE commands you wish. For example, your program can include a USE command (to switch to a different data file), an APPEND command (to let the user add extra records to the file), and a BROWSE command (to let the user browse through the entire file and edit it).

One of the lines in your program can even say DO a second program. When the computer encounters that line, the computer will DO the second program, then finish the original program.

Your program's bottom line can even say QUIT, so that when the computer finishes the program it will stop using DBASE.

♦ Old versions In DBASE 3 and 3+, here's how to hop to the left margin: tap the left-arrow key while holding down the CONTROL key. Here's how to hop to the end of the line: tap the right arrow key while holding down the CONTROL key.

♦ FOXPRO 2 Saying "MODIFY COMMAND STATS" makes the computer create a window called "STATS.PRG". In that window, type your program, like this:

```
SUM
AVERAGE
```

To insert an extra line, move to where you want the extra line to begin, then press ENTER. To delete a line, move to the beginning of that line, press SHIFT with down-arrow (so the line becomes brown), then press DELETE.

When you've finished typing and editing the program, click the close box then click "Yes".

In the SUPERDIR program, say "DIR *.IDX" instead of "DIR *.NDX".

TEXT

Let's program the computer so that whenever you say DO POEM, the computer will print this poem:

```
YOUR DATA FILES
ALL GIVE ME SMILES.
I FEEL SO LOW,
WHEN THEY MUST GO.
PLEASE DON'T ERASE
YOUR DATABASE!
        LOVE,
        YOUR COMPUTER
```

Here's how:

```
. MODIFY COMMAND POEM
? "YOUR DATA FILES"
? "ALL GIVE ME SMILES."
? "I FEEL SO LOW,"
? "WHEN THEY MUST GO."
? "PLEASE DON'T ERASE"
? "YOUR DATABASE!"
? "        LOVE,"
? "        YOUR COMPUTER"
```

But typing all those question marks and quotation marks is ridiculous! For a short-cut, type this instead:

```
. MODIFY COMMAND POEM
TEXT
YOUR DATA FILES
ALL GIVE ME SMILES.
I FEEL SO LOW,
WHEN THEY MUST GO.
PLEASE DON'T ERASE
YOUR DATABASE!
        LOVE,
        YOUR COMPUTER
ENDTEXT
```

The words TEXT and ENDTEXT tell the computer that everything between them should be printed as strings. To begin an indented passage (such as LOVE and YOUR COMPUTER), press the TAB key. Pressing the TAB key makes the computer indent the current line and all lines underneath, until you tell the computer to stop indenting (by pressing SHIFT with TAB).

♦ Old versions In DBASE 3 and 3+, pressing the TAB key makes the computer indent just 4 spaces (instead of 8). Pressing the TAB key makes the computer indent just the current line (not the lines underneath).

♦ FOXPRO 2 Pressing the TAB key makes the computer indent just 4 spaces (instead of 8). To tell the computer to stop indenting, press the BACKSPACE key.

Tricky output

Here are some commands you can put in your program, to produce tricky output.

To erase the screen, say:

```
CLEAR
```

If you say —

```
? "FAT"
?? "HER"
```

the double question mark makes the computer print HER on the same line as FAT. The computer will print:

```
FATHER
```

When using DBASE, the screen's top line is called *line 0*. Then come lines 1, 2, etc. In each line, the leftmost character is at *position 0*. Then come positions 1, 2, etc. To print the word DROWN beginning at line 3's 7th position, type this:

```
@3,7 SAY "DROWN"
```

SET HEADING OFF When you say LIST, DISPLAY, SUM, or AVERAGE, the computer prints data in columns and puts a heading at the top of each column. If you want the computer to omit the headings, say:

```
SET HEADING OFF
```

That command remains in effect until you say SET HEADING ON (or QUIT).

To invent your own customized heading, first get rid of the traditional headings (by saying SET HEADING OFF) and then print your own headings (by giving the "?" or "@SAY" commands).

SET TALK OFF While running your program, the computer prints messages telling you which records and numbers it's manipulating.

For example, if you say GO 3 and then SKIP 2, the computer prints a message saying it's skipping to record #5. If you say to COPY a file, the computer prints messages telling you how many records it's copied so far, until all the records are copied.

Those messages help DBASE programmers but confuse business executives who don't understand the messages' jargon. To stop the computer from printing those messages, say:

```
SET TALK OFF
```

That command remains in effect until you say SET TALK ON.

If you say SET TALK OFF, you'll have a hard time doing statistics: the simple COUNT, SUM, and AVERAGE commands don't work until you say SET TALK ON.

Variables

Like BASIC, DBASE lets you use variables easily. For example, if you say —

```
X=7-1
? X+3
```

the computer will print 9.

(While the computer performs X=7-1, the computer will also print a little message saying that X is 6, unless you say SET TALK OFF.)

A variable's name can be short (such as X) or longer. It can be up to 10 characters long (such as POPULATION). It can include underlines and digits (such as LOST_IN_86). It must begin with a letter. It cannot include blank spaces.

A variable can stand for either a number or a string. For example, if you say —

```
HUSBAND="TOM"
? HUSBAND
```

the computer will print TOM.

The computer handles two kinds of variables. A **field variable** stands for a field in a data file. For example, while you're using FAMILIES.DBF, you're using field variables called NAME, INCOME, and POPULATION. A **memory variable** is any variable that does *not* stand for a field. For example, if you say X=7-1, the X is a memory variable.

Suppose you're using FAMILIES.DBF, so INCOME is a field variable. to change a family's INCOME to 20000, do *not* say INCOME=20000. Instead, say:

```
REPLACE INCOME WITH 20000
```

Here's the rule: **to change the value of a memory variable, say "="; to change the value of a field variable, say "REPLACE".**

The computer will remember all your variables until you say CLEAR MEMORY (which erases the memory variables) or say to USE a different data file (which affects the field variables) or say CLEAR ALL (which erases *all* the variables and also makes the computer forget which file you were USEing).

The typical DBASE program begins by saying CLEAR ALL and ends by saying CLEAR ALL again, to make sure the variables from different programs don't interfere with each other.

STORE Instead of saying X=7-1, you can say STORE 7-1 TO X. Saying "STORE 7-1 TO X" has exactly the same effect as saying "X=7-1".

To make X, Y, and Z all be zero, say:

```
STORE 0 TO X,Y,Z
```

Statistics To make X be the SUM of all the INCOMEs in your data file, say:

```
SUM INCOME TO X
```

To make X be the SUM of all the INCOMEs and also make Y be the sum of all the POPULATIONs, say:

```
SUM INCOME, POPULATION TO X,Y
```

Similar commands work for COUNT and AVERAGE also. They all work even if you SET TALK OFF.

INPUT

Like BASIC, DBASE understands the word INPUT. If you say —

```
INPUT "HOW OLD ARE YOU? " TO AGE
```

the computer will ask —

```
HOW OLD ARE YOU?
```

and then wait for you to type a number. Whatever number you type will become the AGE.

The INPUT statement's variable must be a memory variable, not a field variable. For example, if you're using FAMILIES.DBF and want the person to input an INCOME (which is a field variable), you must *not* say INPUT "WHAT IS YOUR INCOME?" TO INCOME. Instead, input a memory variable called MINCOME, then copy it to a field by saying REPLACE, like this:

```
INPUT "WHAT IS YOUR INCOME? " TO MINCOME
REPLACE INCOME WITH MINCOME
```

ACCEPT

To input a string instead of a number, say ACCEPT instead of INPUT:

```
ACCEPT "WHAT IS YOUR FAVORITE FOOD? " TO FOOD
```

Underneath that ACCEPT statement, you might want to add this line:

```
FOOD=UPPER(FOOD)
```

It makes the computer convert the human's input to capital (upper-case) letters, in case the human forgot to press the CAPS LOCK key.

Like the INPUT statement, the ACCEPT statement takes a memory variable but *not* a field variable.

WAIT

This example says WAIT instead of ACCEPT:

```
WAIT "WHAT'S YOUR MIDDLE INITIAL? " TO INITIAL
? "CONGRATULATIONS!"
? "ACCORDING TO ASTROLOGY, THE FORCES OF THE UNIVERSE"
? "SHALL CAUSE WONDROUS JOYS TO BEFALL"
? "THOSE LUCKY PERSONS WHOSE EARTH-GIVEN NAMES ARE CENTERED"
? "AROUND THE LETTER",INITIAL
```

WAIT resembles ACCEPT. In that program, the first line makes the computer ask "WHAT'S YOUR MIDDLE INITIAL?" then wait for you to type a character. Whatever character you type will become the INITIAL. For example, if you type a Q, the Q will become the INITIAL.

If the line had said ACCEPT, the computer would have required you to press the ENTER key after the Q. But since the line said WAIT instead of ACCEPT, you do *not* have to press ENTER: as soon as you type the Q, the computer will know Q is the INITIAL (without waiting for ENTER) and will make the screen show this:

```
WHAT'S YOUR MIDDLE INITIAL? Q
CONGRATULATIONS! ACCORDING TO ASTROLOGY, THE FORCES OF THE UNIVERSE
SHALL CAUSE WONDROUS JOYS TO BEFALL
THOSE LUCKY PERSONS WHOSE EARTH-GIVEN NAMES ARE CENTERED
AROUND THE LETTER Q
```

WAIT is nicer than ACCEPT, because WAIT doesn't force you to press the ENTER key after answering the question. But alas, WAIT restricts you to typing just one character: you can use WAIT for a middle initial, but not for a whole name.

GET

Suppose you live in San Francisco with most of your friends, but a *few* of your friends live elsewhere. Run this program:

```
CLEAR ALL
CLEAR
SET TALK OFF
CITY="SAN FRANCISCO"
STATE="CA"
@10,25 SAY "WHAT IS YOUR CITY?" GET CITY
@11,25 SAY "WHAT IS YOUR STATE?" GET STATE
READ
```

```
? "I AM GLAD TO HEAR YOU LIVE IN THE KOOKY CITY OF",CITY
? "IN THE SEDUCTIVE STATE OF",STATE
SET TALK ON
CLEAR ALL
```

Like most DBASE programs, that program begins by saying CLEAR ALL (to avoid interference from other programs), CLEAR (to erase the screen), and SET TALK OFF (to avoid excessive messages).

The next pair of lines make CITY be "SAN FRANCISCO" and make STATE be "CA".

The next pair of lines put this message in the middle of your screen:

```
WHAT IS YOUR CITY? SAN FRANCISCO
WHAT IS YOUR STATE? CA
```

The READ statement lets you edit the data in the boxes, by using the arrow keys, ENTER key, and other word-processing keys. (If you want to erase an entire box, move to that box, then tap the Y key while holding down the CONTROL key.) You can edit the boxes however you like — for example, change SAN FRANCISCO to RENO, and change CA to NV — or do no editing at all, so that you still have SAN FRANCISCO and CA. When you've finished doing all the editing you wish, tap the END key while holding down the CONTROL key, or just move to the bottom box and tap the ENTER key.

If you changed SAN FRANCISCO to RENO and changed CA to NV, the next two lines in the program will print this, at the bottom of the screen:

```
I AM GLAD TO HEAR YOU LIVE IN THE KOOKY CITY OF RENO
IN THE SEDUCTIVE STATE OF NV
```

Like most DBASE programs, that program ends by putting the computer back to its normal state (SET TALK ON and CLEAR ALL).

To use the word GET, you should put it in an @ SAY command. Underneath the @ SAY GET commands, say READ.

If you forget to include the SAY "WHAT IS YOUR CITY?", and instead type just @10,25 GET CITY, the computer will omit the question but will still show the CITY box. If you forget to say READ, you'll still see boxes full of data, but you won't get a chance to edit what's in them.

By using GET and READ, you can edit any kind of variable. The variable can be a number or a string; it can be a memory variable or a field variable.

If it's a field variable, the computer automatically makes the box wide enough to hold the entire field; and when you edit the data in the box, the computer automatically updates your data file. (You do *not* have to say REPLACE.)

If it's a memory variable instead, your program must include a statement such as CITY="SAN FRANCISCO", which tells the computer how wide to make the box. To make the box even wider, put extra spaces after SAN FRANCISCO, like this:

```
CITY="SAN FRANCISCO          "
```

If the memory variable stands for a number instead of a string, the computer automatically makes the box wide enough to hold 10 digits before the decimal point — or even wider.

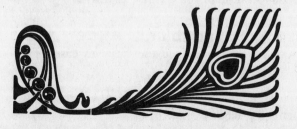

You can control the order in which the computer does your program's statements. Here's how. . . .

IF

Like BASIC and PASCAL, DBASE lets you use the words IF and ELSE. Write the IF statement like this:

```
IF AGE<18
        ? "MINOR"
        ? "YOUNG"
ELSE
        ? "ADULT"
        ? "OLD"
ENDIF
```

Whenever you say IF, you must also say ENDIF. To indent the lines in between, tap the TAB key. (The indentation is optional.)

Here's how to say, "If the NAME begins with SAN and the INCOME is at least 50000":

```
IF NAME="SAN" .AND. INCOME>=50000
```

Remember to put periods around the word AND. For strings, the symbol "=" means "begins with", unless you said SET EXACT ON.

DO WHILE

To create a loop, say DO WHILE. If you want the loop to be infinite, say DO WHILE .T., like this:

```
DO WHILE .T.
        ? "CAT"
        ? "DOG"
ENDDO
```

The computer will print CAT and DOG repeatedly, like this:

```
CAT
DOG
CAT
DOG
CAT
DOG
etc.
```

To abort the program, tap the Esc key (which stands for "Escape") and then the C key (which stands for "Cancel").

Any program that says DO WHILE must also say ENDDO. The computer will repeat all the lines between DO WHILE and ENDDO, to form a loop.

This program makes the computer print all the numbers from 1 to 10 and then print "WOW":

```
SET TALK OFF
X=1
DO WHILE X<=10
        ? X
        X=X+1
ENDDO
? "WOW"
SET TALK ON
```

The top line prevents the computer from printing excessive messages. The next line says X starts at 1. The lines between DO WHILE and ENDDO are done repeatedly, as long as X<=10. If X gets past 10, the computer refuses to do the loop again, and instead proceeds to the line underneath ENDDO, which makes the computer say WOW. The bottom of the program says SET TALK ON, to put the computer back to normal. Altogether, the computer prints:

```
1
2
3
4
5
6
7
8
9
10
WOW
```

In BASIC, you can create loops by giving commands such as "GO TO 10" and "FOR I = 1 TO 10...NEXT". Unfortunately, DBASE doesn't understand how to GO TO line 10 or how to do a FOR...NEXT loop. In DBASE, the only way to create a loop is to say DO WHILE...ENDDO.

In the middle of a WHILE loop, you can put a line saying LOOP or EXIT. If the computer encounters a line saying LOOP, the computer loops back (by jumping back to the WHILE loop's top line). If the computer encounters a line saying EXIT, the computer exits from the loop (by jumping ahead to the line underneath ENDDO).

RETURN

Instead of using the BASIC word END, DBASE uses the word RETURN.

While the computer is DOing your program, if the computer encounters a line that says RETURN, the computer will skip the rest of the program.

The ULTIMATE program

Congratulations! Now you know enough about DBASE so that you're ready to create the ULTIMATE program. This program lets you store and retrieve *any* information about *any* topic! Moreover, the program is so nicely designed that even a novice who knows nothing about DBASE can run the program and use its full power.

How the program acts After you've written the program, you can start using it by just typing:

```
. DO ULTIMATE
```

Then the computer starts running the ULTIMATE program, which makes the computer ask:

```
What topic interests you? (If unsure, type a question mark. To end, type an x.)
```

If you type just an x or a capital X, the computer stops running the program and displays the dot prompt.

If you type a question mark instead, the computer displays a list of all the topics it was fed previously. For example, those topics might include SHRUB, BUSH, QUAIL, BIRDBRAIN, MANHATTAN, SEX, THE MEANING OF LIFE, and STRANGE JOKES. Then the computer says:

```
Pick one of those topics, or teach me a new one.

What topic interests you? (If unsure, type a question mark. To end, type an x.)
```

If you type anything other than an x or an X or a question mark, the computer searches through its file, to see whether it's been fed that topic. If it finds the topic in the file, it reveals all it knows about the topic, and then lets you edit that data. If it does *not* find the topic in the file, it says so, and gives you an opportunity to teach it about the topic.

How to invent the program To make the computer do all that, so a novice can store and retrieve data easily, a professional (such as yourself!) must previously put three things onto the disk: the program itself (which is called ULTIMATE.PRG), a data file (called INFO.DBF), and an index file (called INFOTOP.NDX). Here's how. . . .

Data file Start by putting the data file INFO.DBF onto the disk. To do that, say:

`. CREATE INFO`

Then complete this chart:

Num	Field Name	Field Type	Width	Dec	Index
1	TOPIC	Character	25		N
2	DATA	Character	79		N

That allows each TOPIC to be 25 characters long, and the DATA about the topic to be 79 characters long.

After typing the chart, tap the END key while holding down the CONTROL key. Then tap the ENTER key. The computer will ask, "Input data records now?" Tap the N key.

Index file Next, put the index file INFOTOP.NDX onto the disk, by typing:

`. INDEX ON TOPIC TO INFOTOP`

That creates an index file called INFOTOP.NDX, which lets the computer find each TOPIC quickly.

The program itself Finally, put the program ULTIMATE.PRG onto the disk. To do that, begin by saying:

`. MODIFY COMMAND ULTIMATE`

Then type the program's introduction:

```
CLEAR ALL
CLEAR
SET TALK OFF
SET HEADING OFF
SET EXACT ON
SET DELETED ON
USE INFO INDEX INFOTOP
```

That introduction says to CLEAR ALL influences from previous programs, CLEAR the screen, SET the DBASE program so you have complete control over everything, and USE the INFO data file INDEXed by INFOTOP.

Then type the program's loop:

```
DO WHILE .T.
        ?
        ?"What topic interests you? "
        ?? "(If unsure, type a question mark. To end, type an x.)"
        ACCEPT TO DESIRE
        DESIRE=UPPER(DESIRE)
        CLEAR
        DO CASE
        CASE DESIRE="X"
                EXIT
        CASE DESIRE="?"
                GO TOP
                IF EOF()
                        ? "I don't know any topics yet. My mind is blank. "
                        ?? "Please teach me a new topic."
                ELSE
                        ? "I know about these topics:"
                        DISPLAY ALL OFF TOPIC
                        ? "Pick one of those topics, or teach me a new one."
                ENDIF
```

```
        CASE DESIRE=""
        OTHERWISE
            SEEK DESIRE
            IF FOUND()
                    ? "Here's what I know about",DESIRE+":"
                    @2,0 GET DATA
                    ? "You can edit that info now."
                    ? "(If you want me to forget about",DESIRE
                    ?? ", tap Y while holding down the CTRL key.)"
                    ? "When you're done, tap the ENTER key."
                    READ
                    CLEAR
                    IF DATA=""
                            DELETE
                    ENDIF
            ELSE
                    ? "I don't know anything about",DESIRE+"."
                    ? "Tell me about",DESIRE+"."
                    ? "(If you don't want to tell me, type an x.)"
                    ACCEPT TO NEWDATA
                    IF UPPER(NEWDATA)#"X"
                            APPEND BLANK
                            REPLACE TOPIC WITH DESIRE
                            REPLACE DATA WITH NEWDATA
                    ENDIF
            ENDIF
        ENDCASE
ENDDO
```

In that loop, each print statement uses small letters instead of capitals, so that the printing will look more sophisticated. (To create the small letters, just turn off the CAPS LOCK key, by tapping it.)

After saying ACCEPT TO DESIRE, the next statement says DESIRE=UPPER(DESIRE), which converts the user's desired topic to capital letters. That saves the user from worrying about whether to type REAGAN or Reagan or reagan: whichever of those the user types, the computer will convert it to REAGAN.

The DESIRE can be four kinds of things: it can be an X (which means the user wants to exit), a question mark (which means the user is confused and would like to see a list of topics), nothing at all (which means the user accidentally pressed the ENTER key an extra time), or a topic. The DO CASE statement tells the computer to handle those four cases: DESIRE="X", DESIRE="", and DESIRE=otherwise. Let's look at those four cases in more detail.

In the CASE where DESIRE="X", the computer lets the user EXIT from the DO WHILE loop.

In the CASE where DESIRE="?", the computer begins by checking whether the file contains any undeleted topics. Here's how. The lines GO TOP and IF EOF() tell the computer to GO to the TOP of the file and see if the TOP of the file is also the End Of the File. If the TOP of the file is also the End Of the File, the file doesn't contain any records yet (or all its records have been DELETED), so the computer will print "I don't know any topics yet. My mind is blank." If the computer's mind is *not* blank, the computer will say "I know about these topics" and will DISPLAY ALL of the TOPICS. The computer will display the topics themselves but will *not* display their record numbers, since the DISPLAY statement says to turn the record numbers OFF.

In the CASE where DESIRE="", the computer does nothing at all.

In the case where desire is OTHERWISE, the computer will hunt through all the topics in the file, to SEEK the user's DESIRE.

If the user's DESIRE is FOUND in the file, the computer is commanded to print "Here's what I know about",DESIRE+":". In that command, the word DESIRE is followed by a plus sign instead of a comma, to prevent the computer from leaving a blank space after DESIRE.

If the user's DESIRE is *not* FOUND in the file, the computer is commanded to print "I don't know anything about",DESIRE+".". Then the computer asks the user to type some NEWDATA about the topic. If the user does indeed type some useful NEWDATA (instead of just an X), the computer appends the NEWDATA to the end of the file. To do that, the computer first APPENDs a BLANK record, then puts the NEWDATA into that record by using REPLACE.

The remaining lines say ENDIF twice (to end the two IF statements) and ENDCASE (to end the DO CASE statement) and ENDDO (to end the DO WHILE statement).

At the bottom of the program, add these lines:

```
SET DELETED OFF
COUNT FOR DELETED() TO DELCOUNT
IF DELCOUNT>RECCOUNT()/4
        ? "Please wait, "
        ?? "while I compress your data."
        PACK
        ? "The compression is done."
ENDIF
SET EXACT OFF
SET HEADING ON
SET TALK ON
CLEAR ALL
```

The computer reaches those lines when the user chooses to EXIT from the DO WHILE loop (by saying the DESIRE is "X"). Those lines say to SET the computer back to normal and to CLEAR ALL interference from later programs.

One of those lines says to PACK the file. But if fewer than a quarter of the records have been marked for deletion, the program tells the computer not to bother PACKing.

Here's how the computer figures out whether to bother PACKing. The program says to COUNT how many records have been marked to be DELETED, and call that the DELCOUNT. The program says that IF the DELCOUNT is greater than the RECord COUNT divided by 4, then PACK.

After you've typed that entire program, tap the END key while holding down the CONTROL key. Then you're done: you've created the ULTIMATE data-management program!

Consequences Some parts of that program were hard to invent, but the program is super-easy to use. Try it!

Then challenge yourself: think of further improvements to the ULTIMATE program, to make the program even easier to use and even more powerful!

Such programs would be much harder to develop, if we were using BASIC, LOGO, PASCAL, C, COBOL or any other major computer language. That's why programmers love DBASE!

♦ Old versions DBASE 3 doesn't understand RECCOUNT(); instead of saying IF DELCOUNT>RECCOUNT()/4, say COUNT TO RECCOUNT and then IF DELCOUNT>RECCOUNT/4.

DBASE 3 doesn't understand the word FOUND. DBASE 3+ version 1.0 handles FOUND incorrectly if you deleted some records. For those versions of DBASE, instead of saying IF FOUND(), say IF .NOT. EOF().

PASCAL

Imagine that you're running for President against Calvin Coolidge. To win, you must pass Cal in the polls.

You must pass Cal. "Pass Cal" is the correct way to pronounce "PASCAL", the name of the computer language that programmers are falling in love with.

PASCAL is harder to learn than BASIC. But once you've learned PASCAL, you have amazing power: you can write fancy programs more easily in PASCAL than in BASIC because PASCAL helps organize your thinking; and your programs will run faster, too!

American teachers require kids to master LOGO in elementary school, BASIC in high school, and PASCAL in college. Gifted kids are given the opportunity to start BASIC and PASCAL even sooner — and so are kids in progressive schools.

Many high-school seniors take a PASCAL test given by the College Board. Seniors who pass can get "advanced placement" college credit and skip the college's first year of computer courses.

The nicest kinds of PASCAL are **Quick PASCAL** (published by Microsoft) and **Turbo PASCAL** (published by Borland). They're easy to understand, run quickly, and cost little.

Quick PASCAL runs on the IBM PC and lists for just $99. Discount dealers sell it for just $42.

Turbo PASCAL is available for the IBM PC, Mac, and computers using the CP/M operating system. The newest version of Turbo PASCAL for the IBM PC is **Turbo PASCAL 7**, which discount dealers sell for $99.

If you're on a tight budget, which should you buy — Quick PASCAL or Turbo PASCAL? Since they're very similar to each other, you'll probably buy Quick PASCAL because it costs less. Another advantage of Quick PASCAL is that it lets you edit your programs more easily than Turbo PASCAL. On the other hand, Turbo PASCAL runs your programs faster, consumes less RAM and disk space, comes with instruction manuals that are larger and more thorough, provides on-screen tutorials that are easier to use, understands better commands for advanced programming, and is the standard against which all other versions are judged. (Quick PASCAL was invented just to imitate Turbo PASCAL more cheaply.)

This chapter explains how to use Quick PASCAL and the most common versions of Turbo PASCAL (versions 4, 5.5, and 6).

If you have Turbo PASCAL 7, follow the instructions for Turbo PASCAL 6, which is similar. If you have Turbo PASCAL version 5, follow the instructions for version 5.5.

I'll comment on how other versions of PASCAL differ.

Copy to the hard disk

Quick PASCAL and Turbo PASCAL come on a pile of floppy disks. You should copy those disks to your hard disk. Here's how.

Quick PASCAL Turn on the computer without any floppy in drive A.

The original version of Quick PASCAL comes on five 5¼-inch floppy disks. When you see the C prompt, put the Quick PASCAL Setup/Utilities Disk in drive A and type "a:". The computer will display an A prompt. Type "setup". The computer will say "Microsoft Quick Pascal Setup Program".

Press ENTER twice. The computer will say "Easy Setup Menu". Type the letter I. Press ENTER four times.

Put the Quick PASCAL Program Disk in drive A, and press ENTER. Put the Quick PASCAL Advisor Disk in drive A, and press ENTER. Put the Quick PASCAL Libraries Disk in drive A, and press ENTER. Put the Quick PASCAL Express Disk in drive A; press ENTER twice.

Press R, so that the computer says "Setup Main Menu". Press X, so that you exit to DOS. You'll see an A prompt.

Turn off the computer, so you can start fresh.

Turbo PASCAL 4 Turn on the computer without any floppy in drive A.

After the C prompt, type "md turbo" (so you're making a subdirectory called TURBO). After the next C prompt, type "cd turbo" (so you're changing to the TURBO subdirectory).

Turbo PASCAL 4 comes on three floppy disks. Put one of those disks in drive A, and type "copy a:*.*" (which copies all the floppy's files onto the hard disk); follow the same procedure for the other two disks.

Turn off the computer, so you can start fresh.

Turbo PASCAL 5.5 and 6 Turn on the computer without any floppy in drive A.

Your Turbo PASCAL comes on four 5¼-inch floppy disks. When you see the C prompt, put the Install/Compiler disk in drive A, and type "a:install". The computer will say "Turbo PASCAL Installation Utility".

Press ENTER four times. You'll see "C:\TP". Press the BACKSPACE key, then type URBO so you see "C:\TURBO". At the end of the URBO, press ENTER.

Press the F9 key.

If you're using version 6, put the Turbo Vision/Tour disk in drive A, press ENTER, put the Help disk in drive A, press ENTER, put the BGI/Utilities disk in drive A, and press ENTER twice. (If you're using version 5.5, put the Tour/Online Help disk in drive A, press ENTER, put the OOP/Demos/BGI/Doc disk in drive A, press ENTER, put the Utilities/Misc disk in drive A, and press ENTER twice.)

You'll see an A prompt. Turn off the computer, so you can start fresh.

Start PASCAL

To start using PASCAL, turn on the computer without any floppy in drive A.

If you've put the DO.BAT file onto your hard disk (as I recommended in the MS-DOS chapter), your life is easy! Just type "do qp" to do Quick PASCAL; type "do turbo" to do Turbo PASCAL.

If you have *not* put DO.BAT onto your hard disk, your life is harder! You must type "cd qp" and then "qp" to do Quick PASCAL; you must type "cd turbo" and then "turbo" to do Turbo PASCAL.

Press the CAPS LOCK key, so the computer will automatically capitalize everything you type (and your typing will look like the examples in this chapter).

Here's what to do next.

Quick PASCAL You don't have to do anything!

Turbo PASCAL 4 Press the E key (which means "Edit"). Make sure the cursor is at a blank part of the screen. (If it's not, press the DELETE key several times.)

Turbo PASCAL 5.5 Press the F6 key (so the cursor moves to the bottom of the screen). Then press the F6 key *while holding down the Alt key* (so the bottom of the screen says "Output"). Then tap the F6 key without the Alt key (so the cursor moves to the top part of the screen).

Turbo PASCAL 6 Press F10 then W then the letter O (so the cursor moves to the bottom of the screen). Press F10 again then W then T. Press F6.

How to program

For example, type this PASCAL program:

```
BEGIN;
WRITELN('I WOULD LIKE TO KISS');
WRITELN('YOUR BOTTLE OF WINE');
END.
```

The program begins with the word BEGIN and ends with the word END. Every line ends with a semicolon, except that the bottom line ends with a period. The middle lines say WRITELN, which tells the computer to WRITE a LiNe.

Naming the program If you wish, you can put an extra line at the top of the program, to give the program a name. The name can be up to 8 letters long. For example, if you want to name the program WINE, you can begin the program by saying PROGRAM WINE, like this:

```
PROGRAM WINE;
BEGIN;
WRITELN('I WOULD LIKE TO KISS');
WRITELN('YOUR BOTTLE OF WINE');
END.
```

Colors If your screen can display colors, here's what you see. In Turbo PASCAL, the program is yellow. In Quick PASCAL, most of the program is white, but the keywords (PROGRAM, BEGIN, and END) turn purple and the strings ('I WOULD LIKE TO KISS' and 'YOUR BOTTLE OF WINE') turn light blue.

Run the program

When you finish typing the program, tell the computer to run it. Here's how. For Turbo PASCAL 4, press F10 then R. For Turbo PASCAL 5.5 & 6, press F10 then type RR. For Quick PASCAL, press F5; and if the computer asks "Rebuild?", press ENTER.

If you typed the program correctly, the computer will write:

```
I WOULD LIKE TO KISS
YOUR BOTTLE OF WINE
```

If you typed the program *in*correctly, the computer will say:

```
Error
```

(If you're using Quick PASCAL, then press ENTER.) The computer will put the cursor near your error. Correct the error (by using the arrow keys, DELETE key, and other word-processing keys), then tell the computer to run the program again.

After a good run After the computer has run the program successfully, do the following: for Quick PASCAL, press ENTER; for Turbo PASCAL 4, press ENTER then E; for Turbo PASCAL 5.5 and 6, you don't have to do anything!

You'll see the program again. If you wish, edit the program again and run the edited version.

♦ Other versions Some versions of PASCAL require you to say PROGRAM WINE at the top of the program; if you don't say PROGRAM WINE, those versions gripe.

Ancient versions require the top line to say this:

```
PROGRAM WINE(INPUT,OUTPUT);
```

Some Apple 2 and Mac versions automatically indent all lines between BEGIN and END and force you to omit the semicolon next to the word BEGIN.

Advanced editing

While typing and editing your program, you can edit faster by using these tricks. . . .

To delete a whole line, move to that line. Then tap the Y key (which means "Yank it out") while holding down the CONTROL key.

To insert an extra line in the middle of your program, move to where you want the extra line to begin. Press the ENTER key, then the up-arrow.

Here's how to delete or move a block of text. . . .

Turbo PASCAL 6 and Quick PASCAL Put the cursor at the block's beginning. Hold down the SHIFT key while moving to the block's end, so the entire block changes color.

Then say what you want to do to the block. If you want to delete the block, press the DELETE key for Quick PASCAL; press CONTROL with DELETE for Turbo PASCAL 6. If you want to move the block instead, press SHIFT with DELETE, then point where you want the block to appear and press SHIFT with INSERT.

Turbo PASCAL 4 and 5.5 Put the cursor at the block's beginning. Press CONTROL with K (which means "kommand"), then press B (which means "block").

Point at the character after the block's end. Press CONTROL with K, then press K (which means "klose"). The entire block changes color.

Then say what you want to do to the block. If you want to delete the block, press CONTROL K then Y ("which means "yank"). If you want to move the block instead, point where you want the block to appear and press CONTROL K then V (which means "visible").

Save your program

Here's how to copy your program onto the hard disk.

Quick PASCAL Press the Alt key. Say "File Save" by typing FS. If the computer says "File Name", type a name for the program (such as WINE) and press ENTER.

Turbo PASCAL 4 and 5.5 Press the F2 key. If the computer says "Rename", type a name for the program (such as WINE) and press ENTER.

Turbo PASCAL 6 Press the F2 key. If the computer says "Save file as", type a name for the program (such as WINE) and press ENTER.

Switch programs

Here's how to switch to other programs.

Quick PASCAL Press CONTROL with F4. If the computer asks "Do you want to save?", press N. The screen becomes blank. Press the Alt key.

If you want to invent a new program, say "File New" (by typing FN). If instead you want to retrieve a saved program, do this: say "File Open" (by typing FO), type the program's name (such as WINE), and press ENTER.

Turbo PASCAL 4 and 5.5 If you want to invent a new program, press F10 then type FN (which means File New). If instead you want to retrieve a saved program, do this: press F3 and ENTER; point at the program you want to use (by using the arrow keys and PAGE DOWN key) and press ENTER.

If the computer asks "Save?", press N.

Turbo PASCAL 6 Press Alt with F3. If the computer asks "Save?", press N.

If you want to invent a new program, press F10 then type FN (which means File New). If instead you want to retrieve a saved program, do this: press F3 and ENTER; point at the program you want to use (by using the arrow keys) and press ENTER.

Multiple writing

This program belongs in your bathroom:

```
BEGIN;
WRITELN('FAR','TIN','G');
END.
```

The computer will write FAR, TIN, and G all on the same line, like this:

```
FARTING
```

Exit

When you finish using PASCAL, here's how to return to the DOS prompt.

Quick PASCAL Press the Alt key. Say "File eXit" (by typing FX). If the computer asks "Do you want to save?", press N.

If you're using a fancy color monitor (such as VGA), you'll discover that Quick PASCAL has changed the monitor's colors. To reset the colors, turn the computer off and then back on.

Turbo PASCAL Press Alt with X. If the computer asks "Save?", press N.

EXE files

The computer can't really understand PASCAL. Whenever you tell the computer to run a PASCAL program, the computer secretly creates a second version of your program. The second version is written in **machine language** instead of PASCAL. (Machine language is the only language the computer really understands.) Then the computer runs the machine-language version of your program.

The program you typed (in PASCAL) is called the **source code**. The program the computer runs (in machine language) is called the **object code**.

When the computer is translating your program from PASCAL to machine language (from source code to object code), the computer is said to be **compiling** your program. Since Quick PASCAL and Turbo PASCAL make the computer compile your PASCAL programs, Quick PASCAL and Turbo PASCAL are called **PASCAL compilers**.

Example Suppose you type a PASCAL program, then tell the computer to save it on the hard disk and call it WINE. The computer will copy it to your hard disk's PASCAL subdirectory, where it will be called "WINE.PAS". The ".PAS" means "source code written in PASCAL".

When you tell the computer to run the WINE.PAS program, the computer translates it to machine language. The machine-language version (the object code) is called "WINE.EXE". The ".EXE" means "executable object code written in machine language".

If you're using Quick PASCAL, the computer automatically puts WINE.EXE in your disk's PASCAL subdirectory. If you're using Turbo PASCAL instead, the computer puts WINE.EXE in the RAM but not on disk — unless you give a special "Destination Disk" command.

After the computer has run your program and put WINE.EXE on disk, you can run the WINE.EXE machine-language program without using PASCAL. Here's how: quit PASCAL, then do a "cd" to the PASCAL subdirectory, then type "wine".

Experiment Try the following experiment. . . .

Step 1: type a PASCAL program.

Step 2: tell the computer to save the program and call it WINE. The computer will call your program WINE.PAS and copy it to PASCAL's subdirectory. (If you're using Turbo PASCAL, the computer will rename a previous WINE.PAS to WINE.BAK.)

Step 2½: if you're using Turbo PASCAL, say "Destination Disk". Here's how. Press F10 then C. If you see "Destination Memory" instead of "Destination Disk", press D. Then return to the editor (by pressing F6 for version 4, Esc for version 5.5).

Step 3: run the program. The computer will invent WINE.EXE (a machine-language version of WINE) and put it in PASCAL's subdirectory. Then the computer will run that machine-language program. (If you're using Quick PASCAL, the computer will also produce a WINE.QDB to help the Quick DeBugger.)

Step 4: exit from PASCAL, so you see the DOS prompt.

Step 5: notice that you can run WINE.EXE without using PASCAL. Specifically, go into PASCAL's subdirectory (by typing "cd \qp" for Quick PASCAL, or "cd \turbo" for Turbo PASCAL), then type "wine" (which runs the WINE.EXE program).

MATH

PASCAL distinguishes between **integers** and **real numbers**. Here's how PASCAL defines them. . . .

Integers

An **integer** contains no decimal point and no exponent.

Integer	Not an integer	Comment
-27	-27.0	An integer contains no decimal point.
50000	5E4	An integer contains no exponent.

Real numbers

A **real number** contains a decimal point or the letter E. For example, it can be 0.37 or 5.0 or 6E24. If it contains a decimal point, you should put digits before and after the decimal point.

Correct	Incorrect
0.37	.37
5.0	5.

♦ Other versions Old versions of PASCAL require you to put a decimal point in every real number; so instead of saying 6E24, you must say 6.0E24.

Arithmetic

Like BASIC, PASCAL lets you do arithmetic by using the symbols +, -, *, and /.

If you combine real numbers, the answer is real:

4.9+2.1 is the real number 7.0 (not 7)
5.0-5.0 is the real number 0.0 (not 0)

If you combine a real with an integer, the answer is still real:

3.5*2 is the real number 7.0 (not 7)
3/.5 is the real number 6.0 (not 6)

If you combine integers, the answer is an integer, *except for division*:

7+4 is the integer 11
7-4 is the integer 3
7*4 is the integer 28
7/4 is the real number 1.75

This program makes the computer do all that arithmetic:

```
BEGIN;
WRITELN(7+4);
WRITELN(7-4);
WRITELN(7*4);
WRITELN(7/4);
END.
```

The computer will write:

```
11
3
28
 1.7500000000E+00
```

(Quick PASCAL writes extra zeros, like this: 1.75000000000000E+0000.)

Let's try writing all those numbers on the same line:

```
BEGIN;
WRITELN(7+4,7-4,7*4,7/4);
END.
```

The computer will write:

11328 1.7500000000E+00

Like BASIC, PASCAL lets you use parentheses to indicate order of operations.

♦ Other versions Some versions of PASCAL automatically write blank spaces in front of integers.

Some versions of PASCAL write 1.75 instead of 1.7500000000E+00. Some Apple 2 and Mac versions automatically round the answer and write 1.8e+0.

Functions

PASCAL lets you use these functions:

Function	Meaning
ABS(-6)	the absolute value of -6; it's 6
SQR(3)	the square of 3; it's 9
SQRT(9)	the square root of 9; it's 3.0
SIN(2)	the sine of 2 radians
COS(2)	the cosine of 2 radians
ARCTAN(2)	the arctangent of 2, in radians
EXP(5)	e^5, where e is 2.71828182845904523536
LN(9)	the natural logarithm of 9; it's $\log_e 9$

The number in parentheses can be either an integer or a real. The computer's answer is usually a real (exception: for ABS and SQR, the computer's answer is an integer if the number in parentheses is an integer).

For example, this program computes the square root of 9:

```
BEGIN;
WRITELN(SQRT(9));
END.
```

The computer will write:

3.0000000000E+00

Don't confuse SQR with SQRT. The SQR means *square*; the SQRT means square *root*. To find the square of 3, say SQR(3) or 3*3. In BASIC, you could say 3^2; but in PASCAL, you can't use the symbol ^; use SQR instead.

To turn a real number into an integer, use these functions:

Function	Meaning	
ROUND(3.9)	3.9 rounded to the nearest integer;	it's 4
TRUNC(3.9)	3.9 truncated (by deleting the .9);	it's 3

♦ Other versions For UCSD PASCAL, say ATAN instead of ARCTAN.

If you're using UCSD PASCAL on an Apple and want to use the functions SQRT, SIN, COS, ATAN, EXP, and LN, you must insert this line immediately under the line that says PROGRAM:

```
USES TRANSCEND;
```

SIMPLE VARIABLES

You can use variables:

Program	Meaning
``` VAR ```	Here are the variables. . . .
``` FRED,MARTHA: INTEGER; ```	FRED & MARTHA integers;
``` JILL,TOM: REAL; ```	JILL & TOM are reals.
``` BEGIN; ```	Now let's begin the program.
``` FRED:=2; ```	FRED (an integer) is 2.
``` MARTHA:=4+5; ```	MARTHA (an integer) is 9.
``` JILL:=9.2; ```	JILL (a real) is 9.2.
``` TOM:=1.4+2.3; ```	TOM (a real) is 3.7.
``` WRITELN(FRED*MARTHA,JILL+TOM); ```	Write 18 and 1.2900000000E+01.

The top line says VAR. The word VAR doesn't have a semicolon after it; the lines underneath VAR are indented. The indentation is optional but a good habit. To indent easily, tap the TAB key.

For Quick PASCAL, the TAB key indents 8 spaces. For Turbo PASCAL, the TAB key indents just enough to get past the word above (VAR).

On the indented lines, say which variables are integers and which are reals.

Once you've indented a line, the computer automatically indents all the lines underneath it. If the computer automatically indents a line that you don't want to indent, here's how to undo the indentation: for Turbo PASCAL 5.5, press the BACKSPACE key once; for Turbo PASCAL 4, press the left-arrow key several times; for Quick PASCAL, tap the TAB key while holding down the SHIFT key.

In PASCAL, a variable's name can be as long as you like: the name can be FRED or WASHINGTON or even SUPERCALIFRAGILISTICEXPIALIDOCIOUS. The name can consists of letters and digits, but must begin with a letter.

In PASCAL, you must put a colon in front of the equal sign. . . .

Correct	Incorrect
``` FRED:=2; ```	``` FRED=2; ```

If you want to add a line saying PROGRAM WINE, put that line *above* the VAR line.

You can't set an integer variable equal to a real. For example, if you say —

```
VAR
    ANN: REAL;
    BILL: INTEGER;
BEGIN;
ANN:=3.9;
```

you can*not* then say:

```
BILL:=ANN;
```

Instead, you must say —

```
BILL:=ROUND(ANN);
```

or

```
BILL:=TRUNC(ANN);
```

♦ Other versions Some versions of PASCAL do **not** automatically indent the lines for you.

Old versions of PASCAL look at just the first 8 characters of a variable's name, and ignore the rest of the name.

READLN

Instead of saying INPUT, PASCAL says READLN.

```
VAR
    X: REAL;
BEGIN;
WRITELN('WHAT IS YOUR FAVORITE NUMBER?');
READLN(X);
WRITELN('ITS SQUARE ROOT IS',SQRT(X));
END.
```

When you run the program, the computer asks:

WHAT IS YOUR FAVORITE NUMBER?

Then the READLN(X) statement makes the computer wait for you to input a value of X. The computer expects you to input a real number; if you input an integer instead, the computer will automatically turn it into a real. For example, if you input 9, the computer will automatically turn it into 9.0 and will write:

ITS SQUARE ROOT IS 3.0000000000E+00

♦ Other versions For old versions of PASCAL, say READ instead of READLN.

IF

The computer can criticize your age:

```
VAR
   AGE: INTEGER;
BEGIN;
WRITELN('HOW OLD ARE YOU?');
READLN(AGE);
IF AGE<18 THEN
   BEGIN;
   WRITELN('YOU ARE STILL A MINOR.');
   WRITELN('AH, THE JOYS OF YOUTH!');
   END;
WRITELN('GLAD TO MEET YOU.');
END.
```

That program makes the computer ask:

```
HOW OLD ARE YOU?
```

If you input a number less than 18, the computer replies:

```
YOU ARE STILL A MINOR.
AH, THE JOYS OF YOUTH!
GLAD TO MEET YOU.
```

If you input a number that's at least 18, the computer says just this:

```
GLAD TO MEET YOU.
```

In that program, the line that says "IF" is a heading (the lines underneath it are indented), so do *not* put a semicolon at the end of that line!

ELSE

To make your program fancier, insert the shaded lines:

```
VAR
   AGE: INTEGER;
BEGIN;
WRITELN('HOW OLD ARE YOU');
READ(AGE);
IF AGE<18 THEN
   BEGIN;
   WRITELN('YOU ARE STILL A MINOR.');
   WRITELN('AH, THE JOYS OF YOUTH!');
   END
ELSE
   BEGIN;
   WRITELN('I AM GLAD TO HEAR YOU ARE AN ADULT!');
   WRITELN('NOW WE CAN HAVE SOME ADULT FUN!');
   END;
WRITELN('GLAD TO MEET YOU.');
END.
```

If your age is less than 18, the computer will say:

```
YOU ARE STILL A MINOR.
AH, THE JOYS OF YOUTH!
GLAD TO MEET YOU.
```

If your age is *not* less than 18, the computer will say:

```
GLAD TO HEAR YOU ARE AN ADULT!
NOW WE CAN HAVE SOME ADULT FUN!
GLAD TO MEET YOU.
```

In that program, the line that says "ELSE" is a heading, so do *not* put a semicolon after the "ELSE". **Immediately above the word ELSE, you'll see the word END; do <u>not</u> put a semicolon after that END.**

Symbols

Like BASIC, PASCAL uses these symbols in the IF line:

```
<      >      =      <=      >=      <>      AND      OR
```

In the IF line, the symbol for "equals" is "="; outside the IF line, the symbol for "equals" is ":=".

Instead of saying —

```
IF I=3 OR I=8 OR I=25 OR I=95 THEN
```

you can say:

```
IF I IN [3,8,25,95] THEN
```

That means "If I is in this set of numbers — 3,8,25,95 — then . . ."

LOOPS

To create a loop, say FOR or REPEAT or WHILE. Here's how to use those words.

FOR

Like BASIC, PASCAL uses the word FOR. This program makes the computer get drunk:

```
VAR
   I: INTEGER;
BEGIN;
FOR I := 7 TO 10 DO
   BEGIN;
   WRITELN('I DRANK ',I,' BOTTLES OF BEER');
   WRITELN('HOORAY!');
   END;
WRITELN('NOW I AM DEAD DRUNK');
END.
```

Since the FOR line is a heading, do *not* put a semicolon at the end of it. When you run the program, the computer will write:

```
I DRANK 7 BOTTLES OF BEER
HOORAY!
I DRANK 8 BOTTLES OF BEER
HOORAY!
I DRANK 9 BOTTLES OF BEER
HOORAY!
I DRANK 10 BOTTLES OF BEER
HOORAY!
NOW I AM DEAD DRUNK
```

If you want the computer to count backwards — from 10 down to 7 — change the FOR line to this:

```
FOR I := 10 DOWNTO 7 DO
```

REPEAT

This program plays a guessing game:

```
VAR
   GUESS: INTEGER;
BEGIN;
WRITELN('I AM THINKING OF A NUMBER FROM 1 TO 10');
REPEAT
     WRITELN('YOU HAVE NOT GUESSED MY NUMBER YET');
     WRITELN('WHAT IS MY NUMBER?');
     READLN(GUESS);
UNTIL GUESS=6;
WRITELN('CONGRATULATIONS! YOU GUESSED IT! MY NUMBER IS 6');
END.
```

The computer begins the game by saying:

```
I AM THINKING OF A NUMBER FROM 1 TO 10
```

Then the computer REPEATs the following procedure several times: it says YOU HAVE NOT GUESSED MY NUMBER YET, asks WHAT IS MY NUMBER, waits for the human to input a guess, and checks whether the human guessed 6. It repeats that procedure again and again, UNTIL the human finally guesses 6. Then the computer says:

```
CONGRATULATIONS! YOU GUESSED IT! MY NUMBER IS 6
```

In that program, the computer REPEATs the indented lines, UNTIL GUESS is 6.

If a program contains the word REPEAT, it must also contain the word UNTIL. The lines between REPEAT and UNTIL are done repeatedly. After each time, the computer checks whether to repeat again.

Since the REPEAT line's a heading, it has no semicolon.

Like an IF line, the UNTIL line can contain these symbols:

```
<    >    =    <=    >=    <>    AND    OR    IN
```

Here's another example. Let's make the computer start with the number 3 and keep doubling it, like this:

```
3
6
12
24
etc.
```

Let's make the computer keep doubling but not go over 1000. So altogether, let's make the computer write:

```
3
6
12
24
48
96
192
384
768
THOSE ARE ALL THE NUMBERS BELOW 1000
```

Here's the program:

```
VAR
   I: INTEGER;
BEGIN;
I:=3;                    Start I at 3.
REPEAT                   Repeat the indented lines until I> =1000.
     WRITELN(I);
     I:=I*2;
UNTIL I>=1000;
WRITELN('THOSE ARE ALL THE NUMBERS BELOW 1000');
END.
```

WHILE

The word WHILE resembles the word REPEAT. For example, the previous program (which doubled 3 repeatedly) can be rewritten to use WHILE:

```
VAR
   I: INTEGER;
BEGIN;
I:=3;                    Start I at 3.
WHILE I<1000 DO          If I<1000, do the indented lines, and repeat them
     BEGIN;              again and again, as long as I remains below 1000.
     WRITELN(I);
     I:=I*2;
     END;
WRITELN('THOSE ARE ALL THE NUMBERS BELOW 1000');
END.
```

The indented lines say to WRITELN(I) and then double I. The computer repeats those indented lines many times. Before each repetition, the computer checks to make sure I is still below 1000. When I passes 1000, the computer stops looping and proceeds to the next line, which writes THOSE ARE ALL THE NUMBERS BELOW 1000.

These two structures resemble each other:

Using REPEAT	Using WHILE
REPEAT	WHILE I<1000 DO
etc.	BEGIN;
UNTIL I>=1000;	etc.
	END;

Each of those structures makes the computer repeat the indented lines and check whether I is still below 1000. If you say REPEAT, the check is done at the loop's bottom, so the computer goes through the loop once before checking. If you say WHILE, the check is done at the loop's top, so the computer checks whether I<1000 before doing the loop the first time.

Every statement must end with a semicolon. You can put several statements on the same line:

Normal
```
A:=3;
B:=7.6;
WRITELN(A+B);
```

Alternative
```
A:=3; B:=7.6; WRITELN(A+B);
```

You can continue a statement on the next line:

Normal
```
A:=5-2+1;
```

Alternative
```
A:=
5-2
+1;
```

But do *not* divide a statement in the middle of a word, number, symbol, or string:

Normal	Okay	Wrong, because middle of word	Wrong, because middle of number	Wrong, because middle of symbol
`IF AGE>=18 THEN`	`IF AGE` `>=18 THEN`	`IF AG` `E>=18 THEN`	`IF AGE>=1` `8 THEN`	`IF AG>` `=18 THEN`

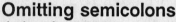

Omitting semicolons

You can omit the semicolon after BEGIN:

Normal
```
BEGIN;
```

Alternative
```
BEGIN
```

You can omit a semicolon, if the next word is END:

Normal
```
A:=3;
END;
```

Alternative
```
A:=3
END;
```

You can omit a semicolon, if the next word is UNTIL:

Normal
```
    I=*2;
UNTIL I>=1000;
```

Alternative
```
    I=I*2
UNTIL I>=1000;
```

Omitting BEGIN and END

If a heading heads *just one* indented line (besides BEGIN and END), you can put that indented line next to the heading (and omit the BEGIN and END).

Long way
```
FOR I := 1 TO 9 DO
    BEGIN;
    WRITELN(I);
    END;

WHILE A<100 DO
    BEGIN;
    A=A+7;
    END;

IF AGE>=65 THEN
    BEGIN;
    WRITELN('OLD');
    END;

IF WEIGHT>220 THEN
    BEGIN;
    WRITELN('FAT');
    END
ELSE
    BEGIN;
    WRITELN('OKAY');
    END;

REPEAT
    A:=A+7;
UNTIL A>100;
```

Short cut
```
FOR I := 1 TO 9 DO WRITELN(I);



WHILE A<100 DO A:=A+7;




IF AGE>=65 THEN WRITELN('OLD');




IF WEIGHT>220 THEN WRITELN('FAT') ELSE WRITELN('OKAY');







REPEAT A:=A+7 UNTIL A>100;
```

Comments

To put comments into your program, surround the comment by braces:

BASIC
```
10 'I HATE COMPUTERS
```

PASCAL
```
{I HATE COMPUTERS}
```

Do *not* put a semicolon after the comment.

If your screen can display colors, Quick PASCAL makes the comments and braces turn green.

♦ Other versions If your keyboard is old and lacks braces, use parentheses and asterisks instead:

```
(*I HATE COMPUTERS*)
```

GOTO

You can say GOTO.

```
LABEL 10;
BEGIN;
WRITELN('MY DOG');
GOTO 10;
WRITELN('NEVER');
10: WRITELN('DRINKS WHISKEY');
END.
```

The top line warns the computer that a future line will be labeled "line 10". The rest of the program makes the computer write MY DOG, then skip to line 10, which makes the computer write DRINKS WHISKEY. Altogether, the computer will write:

```
MY DOG
DRINKS WHISKEY
```

Do *not* put a space between GO and TO.

Here's another example:

```
LABEL 10;
BEGIN;
10: WRITELN('LOVE');
WRITELN('HATE');
GOTO 10;
END.
```

The computer will write LOVE and HATE repeatedly:

```
LOVE
HATE
LOVE
HATE
LOVE
HATE
etc.
```

To abort the program, tap the C key while holding down the CONTROL key. (For Quick PASCAL, then press ENTER.)

If your program contains lines numbered 10, 20, and 100, put this statement at the top of your program:

```
LABEL 10,20,100;
```

Put that statement at the very top of your program: the only statement that should go above it is the one saying PROGRAM. The PROGRAM and LABEL lines go above all other lines — even above VAR and BEGIN.

Each line number must be small: no higher than 9999.

In PASCAL, you'll rarely need to say GOTO. Instead, try using the words IF, ELSE, FOR, REPEAT, and WHILE.

♦ Other versions In UCSD PASCAL, if you want to say GOTO, you must say (*$G+*) at the top of your program:

```
(*$G+*)
PROGRAM SKIPPER;
LABEL 10;
etc.
```

Procedures

This program teases you, with the help of some insults:

```
PROGRAM INSULT;
BEGIN;
WRITELN('YOU ARE STUPID');
WRITELN('YOU ARE UGLY');
END;

{MAIN ROUTINE}
BEGIN;
WRITELN('WE ALL KNOW...');
INSULT;
WRITELN('...AND YET WE LOVE YOU');
END.
```

That program begins by defining INSULT to be this procedure:

```
WRITELN('YOU ARE STUPID');
WRITELN('YOU ARE UGLY');
```

The main routine makes the computer write 'WE ALL KNOW...', then do the INSULT procedure, then write '...AND YET WE LOVE YOU'; altogether, the computer will write:

```
WE ALL KNOW...
YOU ARE STUPID
YOU ARE UGLY
...AND YET WE LOVE YOU
```

The PROCEDURE, called INSULT, is a subroutine. In PASCAL, subroutines come *before* the main routine. (In BASIC, subroutines come *after* the main routine instead.)

Put a program's VAR above any procedures:

`VAR`	The program uses a variable,
`    I: INTEGER;`	called I, which is an integer.
`PROCEDURE DOUBLE;`	The subroutine is called DOUBLE.
`BEGIN;`	
`I:=2*I;`	The subroutine doubles the value of I
`WRITELN(I);`	and writes the new value of I.
`END;`	
`{MAIN ROUTINE}`	Here's the main routine. . . .
`BEGIN;`	
`I:=7;`	I starts at 7.
`DOUBLE;`	Do subroutine DOUBLE, which writes 14.
`DOUBLE;`	Do DOUBLE again, which writes 28.
`WRITELN(I+1);`	Write 29.
`END.`	

ADVANCED VARIABLES

You've seen that a variable can stand for a number. This section explains how to make a variable stand for a character, array, or string.

CHAR

A variable can stand for a character:

```
VAR
    ANN,JOAN: CHAR;    ANN and JOAN will each be a character.
BEGIN;
ANN:='U';              ANN is the character 'U'.
JOAN:='P';             JOAN is the character 'P'.
WRITELN(ANN,JOAN);     The computer will write 'U' and 'P'.
END.
```

The computer will write U and P like this:

```
UP
```

You can put a character variable after the word FOR:

```
VAR
    I: CHAR;
BEGIN;
FOR I := 'A' TO 'E' DO WRITELN(I);
END.
```

The computer will write:

```
A
B
C
D
E
```

ARRAY

Let's make X be this list of real numbers: 4.2, 71.6, 8.3, 92.6, 403.7, 1.4. Here's how:

```
VAR
    X: ARRAY [1..6] OF REAL;
BEGIN;
X[1]:=4.2;
X[2]:=71.6;
X[3]:=8.3;
X[4]:=92.6;
X[5]:=403.7;
X[6]:=1.4;
WRITELN(X[1]+X[2]+X[3]+X[4]+X[5]+X[6]);
END.
```

The computer will write the sum, 581.8.

Subscripts can be negative:

```
VAR
    Y: ARRAY [-2..3] OF REAL;
BEGIN;
Y[-2]:=400.1;
Y[-1]:=274.1;
Y[0]:=9.2;
Y[1]:=8.04;
Y[2]:=0.6;
Y[3]:=-5.0;
WRITELN(Y[-2]+Y[-1]+Y[0]+Y[1]+Y[2]+Y[3]);
END.
```

The computer will write the sum, 687.04.

Here's how to make Z be a table having 6 rows and 4 columns of reals:

```
VAR
    Z: ARRAY [1..6, 1..4] OF REAL;
```

The number in the 3rd row and 2nd column is called Z[3,2]. The entire first row of Z is called Z[1]; the second row is called Z[2]; etc. For example, if you say —

```
Z[5]:=Z[3];
```

the computer will look at the real numbers in the 3rd row of Z, and copy them into the 5th row. Suppose W is another array that has 6 rows and 4 columns; if you say —

```
W:=Z;
```

the computer will look at each real number in Z and copy it into W.

You can have many kinds of arrays: you can have an array of REAL, an array of INTEGER, and even an array of CHAR.

STRING

A variable can stand for a string:

```
VAR
    X: STRING;
BEGIN;
X:='I LOVE MY MOTH';
WRITELN(X,'ER');
END.
```

The computer will write 'I LOVE MY MOTH' and then 'ER', like this:

```
I LOVE MY MOTHER
```

You can make the computer read a string:

```
VAR
    X: STRING;
BEGIN;
WRITELN('WHAT IS YOUR NAME?');
READLN(X);
WRITELN('HELLO ',X,' THE BEAUTIFUL');
END.
```

When you run that program, the computer asks:

```
WHAT IS YOUR NAME?
```

Then the READLN(X) statement makes the computer wait for you to input a string. If you input the name MARILYN MONROE, the computer will write:

```
HELLO MARILYN MONROE THE BEAUTIFUL
```

♦ Other versions Instead of letting you say STRING, some versions of PASCAL require you to say STRING[80].

The oldest versions of PASCAL require you to say PACKED ARRAY [1..80] OF CHAR instead. Some of those old versions can't read or write the whole array string at once: instead you must create FOR loops that read and write one character at a time.

"C"

FUN

C is a computer language invented by Dennis Ritchie in 1972, while he was working for AT&T at Bell Labs. He called it "C" because it came after "B", which was an earlier language developed by a colleague.

Earlier chapters of *The Secret Guide to Computers* explained how to program in BASIC and PASCAL. C resembles those languages but has two advantages: C runs faster and consumes less RAM.

C has become the most popular language for creating advanced programs. The world's largest software companies have switched to C from assembly language:

Created using assembly lang.	Created using C
DBASE 2	DBASE 3, 3+, 4, and 5
Word Perfect 4.0, 4.1, and 4.2	Word Perfect 5, 5.1, and 6
1-2-3 release 1, 1A, 2, 2.01, 2.2, 2.3, 2.4	1-2-3 release 3, 3.1, 3.2, 3.3, 3.4

If you become an expert C programmer, you can help run those rich software companies and get rich yourself!

Before studying C, study BASIC and PASCAL, which are similar but easier.

Unlike BASIC and PASCAL, C lets you easily create a **pointer**, which is a note about which part of RAM to use. If you create the pointer incorrectly, C will use the wrong part of RAM — and erase whatever information had been there before. For example, C might erase the part of RAM used by DOS, so that DOS becomes confused and accidentally erases your disks!

A faulty pointer (which points to the wrong part of RAM) is called a **runaway pointer**, and it's a C programmer's greatest fear. Even if your innocent-looking program doesn't seem to mention pointers, a small error in your program might make C create a pointer that wrecks your computer. That's why many C programmers look thin and haggard and bite their nails. To keep your nails looking pretty, **make backup copies of your floppy and hard disks before trying to program in C.**

C is like a sports car with no brakes: it's fast, fun, slim, sleek, and dangerous. If you program in C, your friends will admire you and even whistle at you as you zoom along the freeway of computer heaven; but if you're not careful, your programs and disks will crash, and so will your career!

Versions of C

For the IBM PC, the nicest kinds of C are **Quick C** and **Turbo C**.

Quick C, published by Microsoft, lists for $99. You can buy it from discount dealers for just $59. Another way to get Quick C is to buy a combination package called **Quick C with Quick Assembler**. Discount dealers sell that combo for $139. Another combo is called the **Microsoft C** package: it contains Quick C and also an **optimizing** version of C (which produces programs that run faster). Discount dealers sell it for $293.

Turbo C is published by Borland. Although it's slightly harder to use than Quick C, many programmers prefer it because it runs much faster, consumes less RAM and disk space, comes with better instruction manuals, handles advanced topics more simply, and can be copied more easily onto your hard disk.

C++ You can buy a variant of C called **C++**. It's harder to learn than C. It lets you use an advanced technique called **object-oriented programming (OOP)**, in which you define "objects" and give those objects "properties".

To explore C++, get Microsoft's **Visual C++ for Windows** ($75) or Borland's **Turbo C++** ($67 for the DOS version, $74 for the Windows version). Those are the prices charged by discount dealers such as Computer Discount Warehouse (800-454-4CDW).

When you buy Turbo C++, you get a *free* copy of Turbo C, so you get *both* languages for a low total price!

Mac The best version of C for the Mac is **Think C**. It's published by the Lightspeed division of Symantec. You can get it for $165 from discount dealers such as Mac Connection.

Where to begin Since C++ is harder than C, begin by learning C. Here's how to use Quick C (version 2) and Turbo C (version 2).

Copy to the hard disk

Turbo C and Quick C come on floppy disks, which you should copy to your hard disk. Here's how.

Turn on the computer without any floppy in drive A. As I explained in the MS-DOS chapter, make sure your hard disk contains a CONFIG.SYS file saying "files=20" (or a bigger number) and "buffers=10" (or a bigger number).

Here's what to do next.

Turbo C Turbo C comes on six 5¼-inch floppy disks. When you see the C prompt, put the Turbo C Install/Help Disk in drive A and type "a:". The computer displays an A prompt.

Type "install". The computer says "Turbo C Installation Utility".

Press ENTER three times. The computer says "Turbo C Directory". Press the F9 key.

When the computer tells you, put the other Turbo C disks in drive A and press ENTER.

The computer says "Turbo C is now installed on your system." Ignore the computer's comments about PATH. Press ENTER.

Turn off the computer, so you can start fresh.

Quick C Quick C comes on ten 5¼-inch floppy disks. Put the Quick C Setup Disk in drive A and type "a:". The computer displays an A prompt.

Type "setup". The computer says "Microsoft Quick C Setup Program". Press ENTER ten times.

The computer asks, "Include in combined libraries?" The computer is asking whether you're planning to write programs that include graphics. Most C programs do *not* use graphics; most C courses do *not* discuss graphics; this chapter does *not* discuss graphics. Chapter 12 of the Quick C instruction manual *does* discuss graphics. If you plan to study and use graphics, press Y and ENTER, then Y again and ENTER (which makes the computer copy graphics commands to the hard disk); otherwise, press ENTER twice (so the computer doesn't bother copying graphics commands to the hard disk, and your hard disk won't be so full).

The computer asks, "Do you want to change any of the above options?" Press N and ENTER.

The computer asks, "Install Microsoft Mouse?" If you have a Microsoft Mouse (or clone), press ENTER; if you have no mouse or a different brand, press N then ENTER.

Press ENTER four more times. The computer asks again, "Do you want to change any of the above options?" Press N and ENTER.

Press ENTER eight more times. The computer asks again, "Do you want to change any of the above options?" Press N and ENTER.

Press ENTER again. When the computer tells you, put other Quick C disks in drive A press ENTER.

The computer says, "Press any key to start building combined libraries." Press ENTER twice. Ignore the computer's comments about "creating sample configuration files".

You'll see an A prompt. Type "copy con c:\qc2\qc2.bat" (and press ENTER at the end of that command). Underneath that command, type this:

```
set lib=\qc2\lib
set include=\qc2\include
cd bin
qc
cd \
```

Underneath all that, press the F6 key then ENTER.

Turn off the computer, so you can start fresh.

Start C

To start using C, turn on the computer without any floppy in drive A.

To do Turbo C, type "do tc". To do Quick C, type "do qc2".

(That "do" method works if you put the DO.BAT file onto your hard disk as I recommended in the MS-DOS chapter. If you have *not* put DO.BAT onto your hard disk, do Turbo C by typing "cd tc" and then "tc"; do Quick C by typing "cd qc2" and then "qc2".)

If you're using Turbo C, then press F10.

Type your program

For example, type this C program:

```
main(){
        puts("make your nose");
        puts("touch your toes");
        }
```

The program begins by saying "main()", which means: here comes the main program.

Do *not* capitalize the word "main". If you type "MAIN" instead of "main", the computer will gripe. **In C, you must type all commands by using lower-case letters, not capitals.**

After the "main()", the rest of the program is enclosed in braces: {}. Like PASCAL's "BEGIN" and "END", they mark the beginning and end of the program.

The lines between the braces are indented. To indent, tap the TAB key. The indentation is optional but helps other programmers understand your program.

Once you've indented a line, the computer automatically indents all the lines underneath it. (If the computer automatically indents a line that you don't want to indent, press the BACKSPACE key.)

The indented lines tell the computer to print two strings: "make your nose" and "touch your toes".

Notice that **C says "puts" instead of "print"**. (BASIC says PRINT; PASCAL says WRITELN; C says "puts" instead.) The command "puts" means: *put* the *s*tring onto your screen.

After "puts", you must put parentheses. (PASCAL's WRITELN requires parentheses also.)

Like BASIC, C makes you put each string in quotation marks.

Like PASCAL, C requires a semicolon at the end of each typical line. Here's the rule: **each line of C should end with a semicolon or brace**.

Run the program

When you finish typing the program, tell the computer to run it. Here's how: for Turbo C, press F10 then type RR; for Quick C, press F5 and if the computer asks "Rebuild?" press ENTER.

If you typed the program wrong, the computer will say ERRORS. (If you're using Turbo C, then press ENTER and F6.) Correct the error, then tell the computer to run the program again.

When the computer runs the program correctly, the computer prints:

```
make your nose
touch your toes
```

(If you're using Turbo C, that printing flashes on the screen too briefly for you to read; after the flash, press Alt with F5, which makes the printing reappear.)

After the computer's run the program successfully and you've read what the computer printed, press ENTER.

Manipulate your program

Here's how to manipulate your program.

Turbo C Turbo C lets you manipulate your program in the same way as Turbo PASCAL 5.5. For details, read the explanation of Turbo PASCAL 5.5 on pages 391-392. On those pages, read the sections entitled "Advanced editing", "Save your program", "Switch programs", and "Exit".

Quick C Quick C lets you manipulate your program in the same way as Quick PASCAL. For details, read the explanation of Quick PASCAL on pages 385-386. On those pages, read just the sections entitled "Advanced editing" and "Save your program".

Here's how to do further manipulations in Quick C. . . .

Save your program. To copy your program to the hard disk, press the Alt key then say "File Save" (by typing FS). If the computer says "File Name", type a name for the program (such as NOSE) and press ENTER. If you called the program "NOSE", the computer will put the program onto the hard disk as "NOSE.C". (It will be in the BIN subdirectory of the QC2 subdirectory.)

Erase the screen. To erase the screen so you can start writing a new program, press the Alt key then say "File New" (by typing FN). If the computer asks "Do you want to save?", press N.

Retrieve a program. To retrieve a saved program, press the Alt key then say "File Open" (by typing FO). Type the program's name (such as NOSE) and press ENTER. If the computer asks "Do you want to save?", press N.

Exit. When you finish using Quick C, here's how to return to the DOS prompt. Press the Alt key. Say "File eXit" (by typing FX). If the computer asks "Do you want to save?", press N.

Many versions

Suppose you write a program, save it as "NOSE", and then run it. Your hard disk will contain several versions of NOSE.

The first version, NOSE.C, is the program you typed. Turbo C puts NOSE.C in the TC subdirectory; Quick C puts NOSE.C in the BIN subdirectory of the QC2 subdirectory.

When you say to run, the computer automatically creates and runs NOSE.EXE, which is the Executable machine-language version of your program. After you quit C, you can run NOSE.EXE by typing "cd \tc" (for Turbo C) or "cd \qc2\bin" (for Quick C) and then typing "nose".

You can erase the version called NOSE.OBJ. The computer creates it just to help create NOSE.EXE.

Quick C creates three extra files (NOSE.MDT, NOSE.ILK, and NOSE.SYM), which you can erase.

\n

Here's a short cut. Instead of typing —

```
main(){
        puts("make your nose");
        puts("touch your toes");
}
```

you can type:

```
main(){
        puts("make your nose\ntouch your toes");
}
```

The symbol \n means: new line. It tells the computer to press the ENTER key. So puts("make your nose\ntouch your toes") tells the computer to print "make your nose", then press the ENTER key, then print "touch your toes". The computer will print:

```
make your nose
touch your toes
```

When you type the symbol \n, make sure you type a backslash: \. Do *not* type a division sign: /.

Printf

Instead of saying "puts", you can say "printf", like this:

```
main(){
        printf("I love her so");
        printf("up in the morning");
}
```

The command "printf" means: perform the *print* function. That program makes the computer print "I love her so" and "up in the morning" on the same line as each other, so the computer will print:

```
I love her soup in the morning
```

To force printf to press the ENTER key after "I love her so", say \n, like this:

```
main(){
        printf("I love her so\n");
        printf("up in the morning");
}
```

That makes the computer print:

```
I love her so
up in the morning
```

"Printf" differs from "puts" in two ways:

Printf doesn't make the computer press the ENTER key (unless you say \n).

Puts handles just strings. Printf is fancier: it can handle numbers also. Since printf is fancier, it requires more RAM than puts.

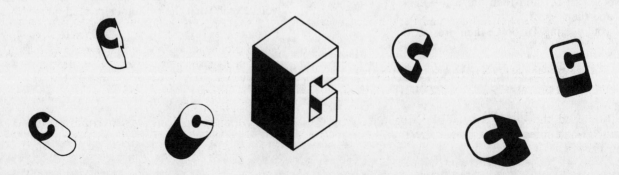

MATH

If you have 750 apples and buy 12 more, how many apples will you have altogether? This program prints the answer:

```
main(){
      printf("you will have %d apples",750+12);
      }
```

In the second line, the %d means: a bunch of digits. The computer will print "you will have", then a bunch of digits, then "apples". The "bunch of digits" will be the answer to 750+12. Altogether, the computer will print:

```
you will have 762 apples
```

In C, each printf line begins with a string (such as "you will have %d apples") and typically ends with a computation (such as 750+12). The computer automatically inserts the computation's answer into the string.

If you omit the words "you will have" and "apples", like this —

```
main(){
      printf("%d",750+12);
      }
```

the computer will print just the number 762. In that program, if you forget the "%d" or forget to say printf instead of puts, the computer will print wrong answers.

To print two answers on the same line, say %d twice:

```
main(){
      printf("%d %d", 21+4, 68+1);
      }
```

That program makes the computer print both answers:

```
25 69
```

The computer leaves a space between the answers because of the space between the %d's. If you omit the space between the %d's and say "%d%d" instead, the computer will print:

```
2569
```

Like BASIC and PASCAL, C lets you use the symbols +, -, *, /, parentheses, decimal points, and e notation. But if you're not careful, the computer will print wrong answers. Here's why. . . .

Integers versus double precision

C handles two types of numbers well.

One type of number is called an **integer** (or **int**). An int contains no decimal point and no e. For example, -27 and 30000 are ints.

The other type of number that C handles well is called a **double-precision number** (or a **double**). **A double contains a decimal point or an e.** For example, -27.0 and 3e4 are doubles. You can abbreviate: instead of writing "-27.0", you can write "-27.", and instead of writing "0.37" you can write ".37".

To print an int, say "%d" in the printf statement. **To print a double, say "%.15g"** instead. (The .15 makes the computer print 15 significant digits, and the g makes it use a general method of printing.)

Largest and tiniest numbers

The largest permissible int is 32767. The lowest is -32768.

If you feed the computer an int that's too large, the computer won't complain. Instead, the computer will print a wrong answer!

The largest permissible double is approximately 1.7e308. The tiniest is approximately 1.7e-308.

Tricky arithmetic

If you combine ints, the answer is an int. For example, 2+3 is this int: 5.

11/4 is this int: 2. (11/4 is *not* 2.75.)

If you combine doubles, the answer is a double. If you combine an int with a double, the answer is a double.

How much is 200*300? Theoretically, the answer should be this int: 60000. But since 60000 is too large to be an int, the computer will print a wrong answer. To make the computer multiply 200 by 300 correctly, ask for 200.0*300.0, like this:

```
main(){
      printf("%.15g",200.0*300.0);
      }
```

That program makes the computer get the correct answer, 60000.0. The computer won't bother printing the ".0"; it will print:

```
60000
```

Advanced math

The computer can do advanced math. For example, it can compute square roots. This program makes the computer print the square root of 9:

```
#include <math.h>
main(){
      printf("%.15g",sqrt(9.0));
      }
```

The computer will print 3.

Say sqrt(9.0) rather than sqrt(9), because the number you find the square root of should be double-precision, not an integer. If you make the mistake of saying sqrt(9), Turbo C and Quick C will print the correct answer but slowly; older versions of C will print a wrong answer.

That program's top line tells the computer to *include* a *math heading*. Begin that line by typing the symbol #, and end with the symbol > instead of a semicolon or brace. That line makes the computer use a file called MATH.H, which is in a subdirectory called INCLUDE, which is part of your C subdirectory. That MATH.H file tells the computer to make advanced-math answers be double-precision.

If you forget to say #include <math.h>, the computer will ignore MATH.H, think advanced-math answers are integers, and print wrong answers.

Besides sqrt, you can use other advanced math functions. All advanced-math functions require that you use double-precision numbers and say #include <math.h>. Here's a list of those advanced-math functions.

To handle exponents, you can use sqrt (square root), exp (exponential power of e), log (logarithm base e), and log10 (logarithm base 10). You can also use pow: for example, pow(3.0,2.0) is 3.0 raised to the 2.0 power.

For trigonometry, you can use sin (sine), cos (cosine), tan (tangent), asin (arcsin), acos (arccosine), atan (arctangent), sinh (sine hyperbolic), cosh (cosine hyperbolic), and tanh (tangent hyperbolic). You can also use atan2: for example, atan2(y,x) is the arctangent of y divided by x.

For absolute value, use fabs (floating absolute). For example, fabs(-2.3) is 2.3.

To round, use floor (which rounds down) or ceil (which stands for "ceiling" and rounds *up*). For example, floor(26.319) is 26.000, and ceil(26.319) is 27.000.

NUMERIC VARIABLES

Like BASIC, C lets you use variables. For example, you can say:

```
n=3;
```

A variable's name can be short (such as n) or long (such as town_population_in_1988). The name must begin with a letter. The name can contain letters, digits, and underlines, but not blank spaces. The computer looks at just the first eight characters and ignores the rest, so the computer considers town_population_in_1988 to be the same as town_pop.

At the top of your program, say what type of number the variable stands for. For example, if n and town_population_in_1988 will stand for numbers that are ints and mortgage_rate will stand for a double, begin your program by saying:

```
main(){
        int n,town_population_in_1988;
        double mortgage_rate;
```

Here's a short cut. Instead of beginning your program by saying —

```
main(){
        int n;
        n=3;
```

just say:

```
main(){
        int n=3;
```

If you're writing a program in which n starts at 3 and population_in_1988 starts at 21000, begin your program by saying:

```
main(){
        int n=3, population_in_1988=21000;
```

Increasing & decreasing

The symbol ++ means "increase". For example, ++n means "increase n". If you say —

```
main(){
        int n=3;
        ++n;
        printf("%d",n);
}
```

the n starts at 3 and increases to 4, so the computer prints 4.

Saying ++n gives the same answer as n=n+1, but the computer handles ++n faster.

The symbol ++ increases the number by 1, even if the number is a decimal. For example, if x is 17.4 and you say ++x, the x will become 18.4.

The opposite of ++ is --. The symbol -- means "decrease". For example, --n means "decrease n". Saying --n gives the same answer as n=n-1 but faster.

Strange short cuts

If you use the following short cuts, your programs will be briefer and run faster.

Instead of saying n=n+2, say n+=2, which means "n's increase is 2". Similarly, instead of saying n=n*3, say n*=3, which means "n's multiplier is 3".

Instead of saying ++n and then giving another command, say ++n in the middle of the other command. For example, instead of saying —

```
        ++n;
        j=7*n;
```

say:

```
        j=7*++n;
```

That's pronounced: "j is 7 times an increased n". So if n was 2, saying j=7*++n makes n become 3 and j become 21.

Notice that when you say j=7*++n, the computer increases n *before* computing j. If you say j=7*n++ instead, the computer increases n *after* computing j; so j=7*n++ has the same effect as saying:

```
        j=7*n;
        ++n;
```

How to input

This program predicts how old you'll be ten years from now:

Program	Meaning
| ```
main(){
    int age;
    printf("How old are you? ");
    scanf("%d",&age);
    printf("Ten years from now, you'll be %d years old.",age+10);
}
``` | The age is an integer.<br>Ask "How old are you? ".<br>Wait for person to input age.<br>Give result. |

Notice that in the scanf statement, you must say &age instead of age. (If you forget the symbol &, you'll have a runaway pointer — and a disaster!) Here's a sample run:

```
How old are you? 27
Ten years from now, you'll be 37 years old.
```

The next program converts feet to inches. It even handles decimals: it can convert 1.5 feet to 18.0 inches.

Program	Meaning
| ```
main(){
    double feet;
    printf("How many feet? ");
    scanf("%lf",&feet);
    printf("That makes %.15g inches.",feet*12.0);
}
``` | The number of feet is double-precision.<br>Ask "How many feet? ".<br>Wait for person to input how many feet.<br>Print the result. |

Notice that to input a double-precision number, the scanf statement must say "%lf", which means "long floating-point", which is a fancy way of saying "double precision".

Arrays

Like BASIC and PASCAL, C lets you create arrays. For example, if you want x to be a list of 3 double-precision numbers, begin your program by saying:

```
double x[3];
```

That says x will be a list of 3 double-precision numbers, called x[0], x[1], and x[2]. Notice that C starts counting at 0. (PASCAL starts counting at 1 instead; PASCAL would call those numbers x[1], x[2], and x[3].)

Here's a complete C program using that array:

```
main(){
    double x[3];
    x[0]=10.6;
    x[1]=3.2;
    x[2]=1.1;
    printf("%.15g",x[0]+x[1]+x[2]);
}
```

The computer will print the sum, 14.9.

Notice that if you say double x[3], you can refer to x[0], x[1], and x[2], but not x[3]. If you accidentally refer to x[3], you'll be creating a runaway pointer.

If you want x to be a table having 2 rows and 3 columns of double-precision numbers, begin your program by saying:

```
main(){
    double x[2][3];
```

Notice that C says x[2][3]. (PASCAL says x[2,3] instead.) In C, if you accidentally say x[2,3] instead of x[2][3], you'll have a runaway pointer.

Since C always starts counting at 0 (not 1), the number in the table's upper-left corner is called x[0][0].

CHARACTER VARIABLES

A variable can stand for a character. For example, suppose you're in school, take a test, and get an A on it. To proclaim your grade, write a program containing this line:

```
grade='A';
```

Here's the complete program:

Program	Meaning
`#include <stdio.h>`	INCLUDE the STanDard I/O Headers.
`main(){`	
`    char grade;`	The grade is a character.
`    grade='A';`	The grade is 'A'.
`    putchar(grade);`	Print the character that's the grade.
`}`	

The computer will print:

```
A
```

The usual way to print the grade is to say putchar(grade). To teach the computer what putchar means, say #include <stdio.h>.

Another way to print the grade is to say printf("%c",grade); the "%c" means "character".

To input a grade, say scanf("%c",&grade) or grade=getchar(). If you say scanf("%c",&grade), the user must press the ENTER key after entering the grade. If you say grade=getchar() instead, the user doesn't have to press ENTER. Like putchar, getchar requires you to say #include <stdio.h>.

Strings of characters

A variable can stand for a whole string of characters:

Program	Meaning
`main(){`	
`    char *torture;`	Torture is a whole string of characters.
`    torture="slice off your head";`	Here's torture.
`    puts(torture);`	Print the string that's torture.
`}`	

The computer will print:

```
slice off your head
```

That program begins by saying char *torture. The * means "string", so that char * means "character string". If you omit the *, torture will be just one character instead of a string of characters.

Put each string (such as "slice off your head") in double-quotes ("). Put a single character (such as 'A') in single-quotes (').

To print a string, say puts. To print a single character, say putchar.

The usual way to print the torture string is to say puts(torture). Another way is to say printf("%s",torture); the "%s" means "string".

Gets Here's how to input a string:

```
main(){
    char *name; name=(char *)malloc(41);
    printf("What is your name? ");
    gets(name);
    printf("I like the name %s",name);
}
```

Here's a sample run of that program:

```
What is your name? Maria Gonzales
I like the name Maria Gonzales
```

In that program, the most important line is "gets(name)". That tells the computer to *get* a *s*tring from the user; it lets the user input a name. Notice that to input a string instead of a number, you say "gets" instead of "scanf".

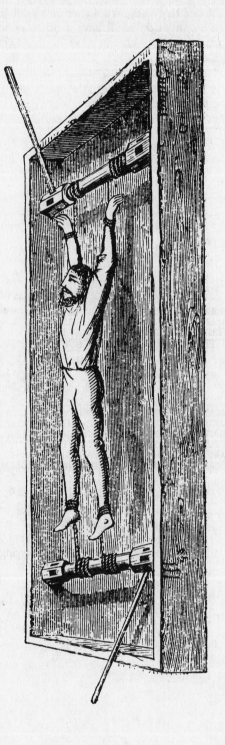

Malloc In that program, the top line says "name=(char *)malloc(41)". That warns the computer that the person's name might consume up to 41 characters in RAM (40 bytes for the name itself, plus 1 byte for the end-of-string marker). It makes the computer reserve 41 bytes of RAM for the name. The "malloc" means "*m*emory *alloc*ation". If you forget to say "name=(char *)malloc(41)", you'll have a runaway pointer.

To be extra safe, in case the person types an extra-long name, you might be better off saying malloc(51) or even malloc(81). Since most strings in most programs are less than 81 characters long, here's a rule of thumb: to be safe, say malloc(81) for each string.

In the program that says torture="slice off your head", you don't have to say torture=(char *)malloc(20), because when the computer sees "slice off your head" in your program, the computer automatically reserves 20 bytes of RAM to hold it. You need malloc just for variables that are input or that are built up by combining other variables.

Substrings If torture is "slice off your head", torture+1 means "torture without the first character"; it is "lice off your head". Similarly, torture+2 is "torture without the first 2 characters"; it is "ice off your head".

(Technically, torture+2 means "the string that begins 2 characters past the beginning of torture"; it's "the string whose starting memory address is 2 higher than torture's".)

For example:

Program	**Meaning**
`main(){`	
`    char *torture;`	Torture is a whole string of characters.
`    torture="slice off your head";`	Here's torture.
`    printf("%s",torture+2);`	Print "ice off your head".
`}`	

Here's how to make cool be torture+2, which is "ice off your head":

Program	**Meaning**
`main(){`	
`    char *torture,*cool;`	Torture and cool are strings.
`    torture="slice off your head";`	Here's torture.
`    cool=torture+2;`	Cool is "ice off your head".
`    printf("%s",cool);`	Print "ice off your head".
`}`	

Since cool uses the same part of RAM as torture, cool doesn't have to be malloc'ed.

Extracting a character from a string If torture is "slice off your head", *torture indicates the first character in torture; it is 's'. This program makes the computer print the 's':

Program	**Meaning**
`#include <stdio.h>`	Include the definition of putchar, etc.
`main(){`	
`    char *torture,hiss;`	Torture's a string. Hiss is a character.
`    torture="slice off your head";`	Here's torture.
`    hiss=*torture;`	Hiss is torture's first character, 's'.
`    putchar(hiss);`	Print 's'.
`}`	

If you want to print just torture's third character (which is the i), ask for *(torture+2), which means "the character in torture beyond the first 2"; or just ask for torture[2].

Suppose torture's a string, and you say cool=torture. If you change cool's third character to an x (by saying cool[2]='x'), you'll also be changing the third character of torture, since cool and torture share characters with each other and share the same part of RAM.

Like most computer languages, C lets you say "if", "while", "for", and "goto" and create comments and subroutines. Here's how....

If

If a person's age is less than 18, let's make the computer say "You are still a minor." Here's the fundamental line:

```
if (age<18) puts ("You are still a minor.");
```

Notice you must put parentheses after the word "if".

If a person's age is less than 18, let's make the computer say "You are still a minor." and also say "Ah, the joys of youth!" and "I wish I could be as young as you!" Here's how to say all that:

```
if (age<18){
        puts("You are still a minor.");
        puts("Ah, the joys of youth!");
        puts("I wish I could be as young as you!");
        }
```

Let's put that structure into a complete program:

```
main(){
        int age;
        printf("how old are you? ");
        scanf("%d",&age);
        if (age<18){
                puts("You are still a minor.");
                puts("Ah, the joys of youth!");
                puts("I wish I could be as young as you!");
                }
        else{
                puts("You are an adult.");
                puts("Now we can have some adult fun!");
                }
        puts("Glad to have met you.");
        }
```

If the person's age is less than 18, the computer will print "You are still a minor." and "Ah, the joys of youth!" and "I wish I could be as young as you!" If the person's age is *not* less than 18, the computer will print "You are an adult." and "Now we can have some adult fun!" Regardless of the person's age, the computer will end the conversation by saying "Glad to have met you."

The "if" statement uses this notation:

Notation	Meaning
if (age<18){	if age is less than 18
if (age<=18){	if age is less than or equal to 18
if (age==18){	if age is equal to 18
if (age!=18){	if age is not equal to 18
if (age<18 && weight>200){	if age<18 and weight>200
if (age<18 || weight>200){	if age<18 or weight>200

Look at that table carefully! Notice that in the "if" statement, you must use double symbols: you must say "==" instead of "=", say "&&" instead of "&", and say "||" instead of "|". If you accidentally use single symbols instead of double, the computer will print wrong answers.

Strings To put strings in an "if" statement, you must say "strcmp", which warns the computer to do a *string comparison*".

For example, suppose x and y are strings, and you want to test whether they're equal. Do *not* say "if (x==y)". Instead, say "if (strcmp(x,y)==0)", which means "if string comparison between x and y shows 0 difference between them".

To test whether x's string comes before y's in the dictionary, do *not* say "if (x<y)". Instead, say "if (strcmp(x,y)<0)".

While

Let's make the computer print the word "love" repeatedly, like this:

```
love love love love love love love love love love love etc.
love love love love love love love love love love love etc.
love love love love love love love love love love love etc.
etc.
```

This program does it:

```
main(){
        while (1) printf("love ");
        }
```

In that program, the "while (1)" means: do repeatedly. The computer will do printf("love") repeatedly, looping forever — or until you abort the program.

Let's make the computer start at 20 and keep counting, so the computer will print:

```
20 21 22 23 24 25 26 27 28 29 30 31 32 33 34 35 etc.
```

This program does it:

Program	Meaning
`main(){`	
`        int i=20;`	Start the integer i at 20.
`        while (1){`	Repeat these lines forever:
`                printf("%d ",i);`	print i
`                ++i;`	increase i
`                }`	
`        }`	

In that program, if you say "while (i<30)" instead of "while (1)", the computer will do the loop only while i remains less than 30; the computer will print just:

```
20 21 22 23 24 25 26 27 28 29
```

Instead of saying "while (i<30)", you can say "while (i<=29)".

For

Here's a more natural way to get that output of numbers from 20 to 29:

```
main(){
        int i;
        for (i=20; i<=29; ++i) printf("%d ",i);
        }
```

In that program, the "for (i=20; i<=29; ++i)" means "Do repeatedly. Start with i=20, and keep repeating as long as i<=29. At the end of each repetition, do ++i."

In that "for" statement, if you change the ++i to i+=3, the computer will increase i by 3 instead of by 1, so that the computer will print:

```
20 23 26 29
```

The "for" statement is quite flexible. You can even say "for (i=20; i<100; i*=2)", which makes i start at 20 and keep doubling, so the computer prints:

```
20 40 80
```

Like "if" and "while", the "for" statement can sit atop a group of indented lines that are in braces.

Goto

You can say "goto". For example, if you say "goto yummy", the computer will go to the line whose name is yummy:

```
main(){
        puts("my dog");
        goto yummy;
        puts("never");
        yummy: puts("drinks whiskey");
}
```

The computer will print:

```
my dog
drinks whiskey
```

Comments

To put a comment in your program, begin the comment with the symbol /* and end it with */. Here's an example:

```
/* The following program
is fishy */
main(){
        puts("Our funny God"); /* notice religious motif */
        puts("invented cod");  /* said by nasty flounder */
}
```

The computer will print just:

```
Our funny God
invented cod
```

Subroutines

Like PASCAL, C lets you invent subroutines and give them names. For example, here's how to invent a subroutine called "insult" and use it in the main routine:

Program | **Meaning**
```
main(){                       Here's main routine:
        puts("We all know..."); print "We all know..."
        insult();             do the insult
        puts("...but we love you"); print the ending
}
insult(){                     How to insult:
        puts("you are stupid"); print "you are stupid"
        puts("you are ugly");  print "you are ugly"
}
```

The computer will print:

```
We all know...
you are stupid
you are ugly
...but we love you
```

Like BASIC, C wants you to type the main routine first, then the definition of the subroutine (called "insult").

Whenever you write a subroutine's name, you must put parentheses afterwards, like this: insult(). Those parentheses tell the computer: insult's a subroutine, not a variable.

Here's another example:

Program | **Meaning**
```
main(){                       The main routine says
        laugh();              to laugh.
}
laugh(){                      Here's how to laugh:
        int i;                print "ha" 100 times.
        for (i=1; i<=100; ++i) printf("ha ");
}
```

The main routine says to laugh. The subroutine defines "laugh" to mean: print "ha " a hundred times. Notice that the "int i" is in the subroutine, not the main routine.

Let's create a more flexible subroutine, so that whenever the main routine says laugh(2), the computer will print "ha ha"; whenever the main routine says laugh(5), the computer will print "ha ha ha ha ha"; and so on. Here's how:

```
main(){
        puts("Here is a short laugh");
        laugh(2);
        puts("\nHere is a longer laugh");
        laugh(5);
}
laugh(int n){                 Here's how to laugh(n):
        int i;                print "ha", n times.
        for (i=1; i<=n; ++i) printf("ha ");
}
```

Average Let's define the "average" of a pair of integers, so that "average(3,7)" means the average of 3 and 7 (which is 5), and so a main routine saying "i=average(3,7)" makes i be 5.

This subroutine defines the "average" of all pairs of integers:

```
average(int a, int b){
        return ((a+b)/2);
}
```

The top line says, "Here's how to find the average of any two integers, a and b." The next line says, "Return to the main routine, with this answer: (a+b)/2."

Notice that the word "return" must be followed by parentheses.

Double-precision average Let's revise the subroutine, to make it handle double-precision numbers instead of integers, so a main routine saying "x=average(3.0,7.0)" makes x be 5.0.

Here's how:

```
double average(double a, double b){
        return ((a+b)/2.0);
}
```

The subroutine begins by saying "double average". That says the average will be a double-precision number. If you omit the word "double" and say just "average", the computer will make the average be an integer instead, because **the computer assumes all subroutine answers are integers, unless you specifically say "double" or "char" or some other alternative.**

So to get a double-precision answer, you must begin the subroutine by saying "double". You must also say "double" in the main routine:

```
main(){
        double x,average();
        x=average(3.0,7.0);
        printf("%.15g",x);
}
```

LOGO

TURTLE GRAPHICS

Like BASIC, **LOGO** is a computer language. LOGO is better than BASIC in three ways: by using LOGO, you can more easily create graphics, build "lists of lists", and design your *own* computer language (by adding your own words to LOGO). Let's see how!

I'll explain the best version of LOGO, then explain how other versions differ.

To start using LOGO, put the LOGO disk into the computer, then turn the computer on. The computer will say:

```
WELCOME TO LOGO
```

♦ Differences Some versions of LOGO come on tapes or ROM cartridges instead of disks. Some versions use a mouse and require you to point at a LOGO icon.

Most versions of LOGO don't understand small letters; they understand only capitals. If your computer has a CAPS LOCK key, make sure it's pressed down.

To start Commodore LOGO, say:

```
LOAD "LOGO",8
RUN
```

To start the disk version of Radio Shack Color LOGO, say:

```
LOADM "LOGO"
EXEC
```

After Radio Shack Color LOGO says "LOGO:", tap the R key.

To use a version of LOGO called "LOGO Writer", use the student disk that your teacher created from the master disk, or use the TRY ME disk. Before using the TRY ME disk on an IBM PC, do the following: insert the PC-DOS disk, turn on the computer, type the date and time, insert the TRY ME disk, then type —

```
A>logowrit
```

When you start using LOGO Writer, the top of the screen will say CONTENTS. To continue beyond that point, press the ENTER key.

Showing the turtle

To draw pictures, you move a turtle across the screen. To see the turtle, say **SHOWTURTLE**, like this:

```
SHOWTURTLE
```

SHOWTURTLE is all one word. Do *not* put a space between SHOW and TURTLE.

LOGO lets you abbreviate most words. The abbreviation for SHOWTURTLE is ST; so instead of typing SHOWTURTLE you can type just ST, like this:

```
ST
```

After you say SHOWTURTLE (or ST), you'll see a turtle in the center of your screen.

You can make the turtle either visible or invisible. To make it invisible, say **HIDETURTLE** (or HT). To make it visible again, say SHOWTURTLE (or ST) again.

♦ Differences Many versions of LOGO put a question mark on the screen and expect you to type a command after the question mark. For example, to say SHOWTURTLE, type SHOWTURTLE after the question mark, so your screen looks like this:

```
?SHOWTURTLE
```

Atari 800 LOGO shows a good picture of a turtle (including the turtle's head, feet, tail, and shell), but most other versions of LOGO show just the turtle's nose, which looks like an arrowhead.

LOGO Writer and Atari 800 LOGO require you to abbreviate. For example, they require you to say ST instead of SHOWTURTLE.

Rotating the turtle

The screen acts as a map of the turtle's desert. Since the desert's only occupant is the turtle, the turtle's the only thing you see on the screen.

Like most maps, the screen's a rectangle whose top edge is called north, bottom edge is south, right edge is east, and left edge is west.

When you start using LOGO, the turtle's at the screen's center. The turtle faces north and stares at the screen's top edge.

As on a compass, north is called 0 degrees, east is 90 degrees, south is 180 degrees, and west is 270 degrees. To make the turtle face east, say **SETHEADING 90** (or SETH 90).

When typing that command, you must press the SPACE bar before you type the 90. That command makes the turtle rotate, so that it faces east.

The turtle can rotate to any angle you wish. For example, to make the turtle face northeast, say SETHEADING 45.

You can choose any angle from 0 to 360. You can even choose decimals and negative numbers. Experiment!

Rotating to the right In LOGO, rotating clockwise is called "rotating to the right". To make the turtle rotate to the right, 90 degrees, say **RIGHT 90** (or RT 90).

For example, if the turtle is facing north, and you say RIGHT 90, the turtle will face east. Then if you say RIGHT 90 again, the turtle will turn clockwise 90 degrees more, so that the turtle will face south. If you say RIGHT 90 again, the turtle will face west. If you say RIGHT 90 again, the turtle will face north again.

Rotating to the left Rotating counterclockwise is called "rotating to the left". To make the turtle rotate to the left, 90 degrees, say **LEFT 90** (or LT 90).

♦ Differences The computer's RAM accurately handles decimals (such as 4.1 degrees), but the screen shows just an approximation of what's in the RAM. For most versions of LOGO, the screen shows the turtle's angle rounded to the nearest 15 degrees; Radio Shack Color LOGO shows the angle rounded to the nearest 45 degrees.

Moving the turtle

To make the turtle walk 50 steps in the direction it faces, say **FORWARD 50** (or **FD 50**).

For example, if the turtle faces east, and you say FORWARD 50, the turtle will walk 50 steps east. If you then say FORWARD 50 again, the turtle will walk 50 steps farther east.

To make the turtle retreat 50 steps *backwards*, say **BACK 50** (or **BK 50**). For example, if the turtle faces east and you say BACK 50, the turtle will retreat 50 steps backwards: the turtle will retreat to the west while still facing east.

The point at the screen's center is called **home**. That's where the turtle's life began. To make the turtle return to its home and its original heading (facing north), say **HOME**.

Setting the position

To make the turtle hop to the point whose coordinates are [30 70], say **SETPOS [30 70]**.

That makes the turtle hop to the point that's 30 steps east and 70 steps north of home. The turtle hops there regardless of where the turtle was before.

Hopping does *not* change the direction the turtle faces. For example, if the turtle faced south before hopping, the turtle still faces south after the hop, even if it's hopped north of where it started.

Instead of saying SETPOS [30 70], you can say **SETX 30** and then **SETY 70**, like this:

```
SETX 30
SETY 70
```

The SETX 30 makes the turtle hop across the screen horizontally east-west, until it reaches a point that's 30 steps further east than home was. The SETY 70 makes the turtle hop vertically north-south, until it reaches a point that's 70 steps further north than home was.

The screen's edge

When you try to move the turtle past the screen's edge, what happens? The answer depends on which kind of universe you create. You have three choices.

If you say **FENCE**, the computer erects a fence around the desert, so that the turtle can't move past the screen's edge. If you give the turtle a command that requires the turtle to go past the fence, the turtle gripes, refuses to do the command at all, and doesn't even walk up to the fence.

If you say **WINDOW** instead of FENCE, the computer lets the turtle wander off the screen, to locations you can't see. Your screen acts as a window, through which you see just *part* of the turtle's universe.

If you say **WRAP** (instead of WINDOW or FENCE), moving the turtle past the screen's edge makes the turtle take a quick trip around the world. For example, if the turtle travels west, past the screen's west edge, the turtle quickly travels around the world and returns from the east. If the turtle travels north, past the screen's top edge, the turtle quickly travels around the world (past the north and south poles) and returns from the south.

When you start using LOGO, you automatically begin with a WRAPped universe, but you can switch to a FENCE or WINDOW.

Leisure-time jogging

When the turtle isn't busy obeying your commands, how does it spend its leisure time? Normally, the turtle just sits still. But if you say **SETSP 30**, the turtle will spend all its leisure time jogging at speed 30, in whatever direction the turtle is facing.

For example, suppose the turtle is facing north, and you say SETSP 30. The turtle will jog north, at speed 30. The turtle will keep jogging north, until you give it another command. If you don't give another command soon, it will reach the edge of the screen, and its further fate depends on whether you said FENCE or WINDOW or WRAP.

While the turtle jogs, if you tell it to change direction (by saying SETHEADING or RIGHT or LEFT), it will continue jogging but in the new direction.

While the turtle jogs, if you tell it to walk (by saying FORWARD, BACK, SETPOS, SETX, or SETY), the turtle will walk where you said and then continue jogging from that new location.

To stop the jogging, say SETSP 0 (which sets the jogging speed to 0) or HOME (which makes the turtle go home and rest there).

♦ <u>Differences</u> Atari 800 LOGO understands SETSP, but most other versions of LOGO don't. Some versions of LOGO don't understand FENCE. LOGO Writer lacks SETSP, FENCE, WINDOW, WRAP, SETX, and SETY.

For MIT versions of LOGO (such as Krell LOGO, Terrapin Apple LOGO, and Commodore LOGO), change FENCE to NOWRAP, don't say WINDOW, and change SETPOS [30 70] to SETXY 30 70; if the second number in the SETXY command is negative, put that number in parentheses. Radio Shack Color LOGO resembles MIT versions but lacks some commands, such as SETXY.

Changing the pen

The turtle's belly has a ball-point pen sticking out of it. While the turtle moves, the pen scrapes along the ground and draws a line on the ground. That line's called the turtle's **trail**. It appears on your screen, since your screen's a map of what's on the ground. Even if you make the turtle invisible (by saying HIDETURTLE), you'll still see the turtle's trail.

If you say **PENUP** (or **PU**), the turtle lifts its pen from the ground, so that the pen stops drawing a trail. To put the pen back down on the ground again, say **PENDOWN** (or **PD**).

Creating colors

You can change the pen's ink to a different color. To switch to color #2, say **SETPC 2**. That makes the computer set the pencolor to 2.

Erasing

You can replace the pen by an eraser. To do that, say **PENERASE** (or **PE**). Then as the turtle moves, it erases any ink on the ground. For example, if you turn the turtle around and make it walk back along the trail it created, it will erase the trail.

The eraser scrapes across the ground until you lift it (by saying PENUP) or insert a pen instead (by saying PENDOWN).

Reversing colors

You can replace the pen by a reverser. To do that, say **PENREVERSE** (or **PX**). When you draw with the reverser on black ground, the ground becomes white, when you draw on white ground, the ground becomes black; when you draw on colored ground, the ground changes to the opposite color.

The reverser works until you lift it (by saying PENUP) or switch to a pen or eraser (by saying PENDOWN or PENERASE).

<u>Filling in the middle</u> After you draw a polygon (such as a triangle, rectangle, or octagon), you can fill in the middle. To do so, lift the pen (by saying PENUP), then move the turtle to somewhere in the middle of the polygon, then say PENDOWN, then say **FILL**. The FILL command makes the pen leak, until the ink fills the entire polygon.

♦ <u>Differences</u> Instead of saying SETPC, LOGO Writer and Atari 800 LOGO say SETC; MIT versions say PC.

Instead of PENERASE, Commodore LOGO says PC -1; Krell and Terrapin Apple LOGO say PC 0; Radio Shack Color LOGO says PC 3.

Instead of PENREVERSE, Krell and Terrapin Apple LOGO say PC 6. Commodore LOGO and Radio Shack Color LOGO lack the concept.

Apple's colors are numbered from 0 to 5; IBM's and the Color Computer's from 0 to 3, Commodore's and the Atari ST's from 0 to 15, and the Atari 800's from 0 to 127.

LOGO Writer, IBM LOGO, DR LOGO, and Atari ST LOGO understand FILL, but most other versions don't.

Changing the background

The desert sand is called the turtle's **background**. The sand appears a different color if you shine colored light at it. To make the sand appear to have color #1, say **SETBG 1**. That makes the computer set the background color to 1.

If you say **CLEAN**, a gust of wind blows all the sand around, so that the sand covers all the trails that the turtle made, and the screen is clean again: all that remains on the screen is the turtle itself.

To erase everything you did and "start over", you could say HOME (which makes the turtle return home and face north) and CLEAN (which erases the turtle's trails). But instead of saying HOME and then CLEAN, you can combine those two commands into this single command: **CLEARSCREEN** (or CS).

If you say **DOT [20 50]**, a drop of ink will fall from the sky and land on the point whose coordinates are [20 50], so that you see a dot of ink at that point.

♦ <u>Differences</u> For LOGO Writer, change CLEARSCREEN to CG (which means "Clear the Graphics"); to clear the graphics and the rest of the screen and make everything "fresh", say CT RG (which means "Clear the Text and Reset the Graphics". For MIT versions of LOGO, change CLEARSCREEN to DRAW, change CLEAN to CLEARSCREEN, and change SETBG to BG. LOGO Writer, MIT versions, and Atari 800 LOGO don't understand DOT.

Extra turtles

You can create several turtles, called turtle 0, turtle 1, turtle 2, turtle 3, etc. Normally, your commands are obeyed by just turtle 0.

To talk to turtle 1 instead, say **TELL 1**. That makes turtle 1 appear on the screen, and all your future commands will be obeyed by turtle 1 instead of turtle 0.

While turtle 1 obeys your commands and prances around, turtle 0 will sit quietly (unless you told it to jog, by saying SETSP 30).

To start talking to turtle 0 again, say TELL 0. To talk to turtle 2, say TELL 2. To talk to turtle 3, say TELL 3.

If you say TELL [0 1 2 3], you'll be talking to turtles 0, 1, 2, and 3 simultaneously. Any commands you give will be obeyed by all those turtles.

♦ <u>Differences</u> LOGO Writer, Commodore LOGO, and Atari 800 LOGO understand TELL, but most other versions of LOGO don't. LOGO Writer and Commodore LOGO hide turtles 1, 2, and 3, until you make them appear by typing ST.

In Commodore LOGO, TELL must be followed by a single number, not a list of numbers; and before saying TELL, you must feed the computer TELL's definition, by putting the Utilities Disk in the drive and typing:

READ "SPRITES

Put the quotation mark before SPRITES but not afterwards.

Graphics versus text

Usually, the top of the screen shows the map of the turtle's desert, and the bottom of the screen shows the commands you've been typing. For example, if you say SHOWTURTLE, the top of the screen shows the turtle, and the bottom of the screen shows what you typed: the word SHOWTURTLE.

If you want to devote the *entire* screen to the map, say **FULLSCREEN** (or FS). Then the map fills the entire screen, so that you see a larger portion of the desert. Since the entire screen shows the map instead of your typing, what you type will be invisible, until you return to the normal setup (by typing **MIXEDSCREEN** or MS) or devote the entire screen to your typing instead of a map (by saying **TEXTSCREEN** or TS).

♦ <u>Differences</u> For MIT versions, change MIXEDSCREEN to SPLITSCREEN, and don't use the abbreviations FS, MS, and TS. LOGO Writer always gives you a mixed screen and won't let you change to fullscreen or textscreen.

MATH

To make the computer print the answer to 5+2, say **PRINT 5+2** (or PR 5+2). The computer will print the answer:

7

Like BASIC, LOGO lets you use arithmetic symbols (+, -, *, and /), negative numbers, decimals, E notation, and parentheses.

♦ Differences For Apple LOGO 2, put a blank space before and after the symbol /. LOGO Writer puts its answers at the top of the screen and lacks E notation.

Square roots

SQRT 9 means "the square root of 9". So to print the square root of 9, type this:

PR SQRT 9

The computer will print the answer:

3

If you say —

PR SQRT 9+7

the computer will print the square root of 16, which is 4. If you leave extra spaces, like this —

PR SQRT 9 + 7

the computer will ignore the extra spaces: it will still print the square root of 16, which is 4. If you say —

PR (SQRT 9)+7

the computer will find the square root of 9, which is 3, and then add 7, so it will print 10.

♦ Differences LOGO Writer lacks SQRT.

Turtle numbers

To find out where the turtle is, say PR XCOR (which prints the X coordinate) and PR YCOR (which prints the Y coordinate).

To slide the turtle 20 steps farther east, say SETX XCOR+20. That says to increase the X coordinate by 20.

To slide the turtle 20 steps farther west instead, say SETX XCOR-20. To slide the turtle 20 steps north, say SETY YCOR+20. To slide the turtle 20 steps south, say SETY YCOR-20.

If you say PR HEADING, the computer will tell you which direction the turtle's facing. For example, if the turtle's facing east, the computer will print 90. The HEADING will always be a number between 0 and 360.

If you say PR TOWARDS [30 70], the computer will tell you which direction to turn the turtle, to make the turtle face the point [30 70]. The direction will be a number between 0 and 360. To actually turn the turtle in that direction, so that the turtle faces the point [30 70], say SETHEADING TOWARDS [30 70]. So to make the turtle "walk 10 steps towards the point [30 70]", say this:

SETHEADING TOWARDS [30 70]
FORWARD 10

To find out the color of the ink in the turtle's pen, say PR PENCOLOR (or PR PC); the computer will print the color's number. To find out the color of the background sand, say PR BACKGROUND (or PR BG).

To find out which turtle you're talking to, say PR WHO. The computer will print the turtle's number.

♦ Differences For MIT versions, change PENCOLOR to LAST TS, change BACKGROUND to ITEM 3 TS, and omit the brackets after TOWARDS. For LOGO Writer, change PENCOLOR to COLOR, change XCOR to FIRST POS, change YCOR to LAST POS, and don't say TOWARDS.

Random numbers

If you say PR RANDOM 5, the computer randomly chooses one of these 5 integers: 0, 1, 2, 3, 4. The computer prints the integer it chooses.

Rounding

If you say PR INT 3.9, the computer will convert 3.9 to an INTeger by omitting everything after the decimal point. The computer will print just 3.

If you say PR ROUND 3.9, the computer will ROUND 3.9 to the nearest integer, which is 4. The computer will print 4.

♦ Differences For MIT versions, change INT to INTEGER. LOGO Writer lacks INT and ROUND.

Fancy division

If you say PR 11/4, the computer will divide 11 by 4 and print the answer, which is 2.75.

If you say PR QUOTIENT 11 4, the computer will divide 11 by 4 but ignore what comes after the decimal point. The computer will print just 2.

If you say PR REMAINDER 11 4, the computer will divide 11 by 4, and realize that 4 goes into 11 "2 times, with a remainder of 3". The computer will print the remainder, 3.

♦ Differences LOGO Writer lacks QUOTIENT.

Trigonometry

To print the sine of 30 degrees, say PR SIN 30. To print the cosine of 30 degrees, say PR COS 30.

Since the tangent is "the sine divided by the cosine", you can print the tangent of 30 degrees by saying PR (SIN 30)/COS 30.

The opposite of tangent is arctangent. To print the arctangent of .58, say PR ARCTAN .58. That makes the computer print how many degrees are in the angle whose tangent is .58.

♦ Differences LOGO Writer and Atari 800 LOGO lack ARCTAN. For MIT versions, change ARCTAN .58 to ARCTAN .58 1.

To make the computer print the word LOVE, type this:

```
PR "LOVE
```

In LOGO, a quotation mark means: the word. So that whole line means:
PRint the word LOVE.

Make sure you put the quotation mark before LOVE, but do *not* put a
quotation mark afterwards! That line is pronounced: P R quotes LOVE.

When you press the ENTER key at the end of that line, the computer will print:

```
LOVE
```

Lists

To print a list of words, put the list in brackets, like this:

```
PR [MA CAN'T LOOK]
```

That tells the computer to print a list of three words. The first word is MA; the
second is CAN'T; the third is LOOK.

The computer will print the list but won't bother to print the brackets. The
computer will print just:

```
MA CAN'T LOOK
```

If you say **SHOW** instead of PR, the computer will print the brackets also, like
this:

```
[MA CAN'T LOOK]
```

The computer understands FIRST, LAST, and similar concepts:

Function	Meaning	Result
FIRST [MA CAN'T LOOK]	the list's first item	MA
LAST [MA CAN'T LOOK]	the list's last item	LOOK
ITEM 2 [MA CAN'T LOOK]	the list's 2nd item	CAN'T
COUNT [MA CAN'T LOOK]	how many items	3
BUTFIRST [MA CAN'T LOOK]	all but the first item	[CAN'T LOOK]
BUTLAST [MA CAN'T LOOK]	all but the last item	[MA CAN'T]
FPUT "WOW [MA CAN'T LOOK]	put WOW first	[WOW MA CAN'T LOOK]
LPUT "WOW [MA CAN'T LOOK]	put WOW last	[MA CAN'T LOOK WOW]
WORD "WOW "MA	combine words into long word	WOWMA
LIST "MA "CAN'T	combine words to form a list	[MA CAN'T]
SENTENCE [WOW MA] [CAN'T LOOK]	combine lists	[WOW MA CAN'T LOOK]

When you type those examples, begin each line by saying PR or SHOW. For
example, if you say —

```
SHOW BUTFIRST [MA CAN'T LOOK]
```

the computer will say:

```
[CAN'T LOOK]
```

You can abbreviate BUTFIRST to BF, BUTLAST to BL, and SENTENCE to
SE.

A word's a list of characters. For example, the word FUN is a list of three
characters (F, U, and N). So all the list concepts (such as FIRST, LAST, ITEM,
and COUNT) apply to words also. For example, if you say —

```
SHOW BUTFIRST "FUN
```

or —

```
PR BUTFIRST "FUN
```

the computer will say:

```
UN
```

Since FIRST [MA CAN'T LOOK] is MA, whose last character is A, the
computer knows that LAST FIRST [MA CAN'T LOOK] is A.

You can put lists inside lists. For example, since FIRST [[MA PA] CAN'T
LOOK] is [MA PA], whose last item is PA, the computer knows that LAST FIRST
[[MA PA] CAN'T LOOK] is PA.

◆ <u>Differences</u> MIT versions don't understand SHOW. For Commodore LOGO, change SHOW to
FPRINT.

Atari 800 LOGO doesn't understand ITEM. Version 1 of Terrapin Apple LOGO didn't understand
ITEM and COUNT. Version 1 of Apple LOGO could find an ITEM within a list of words but not
within a single word.

Multiple commands

You can put several LOGO commands on the same line. For example, you can say:

```
FD 50 RT 90
```

When you press the ENTER key at the end of that line, the turtle will go forward 50 and then turn right 90 degrees.

If you say —

```
PR 5+2 PR 30+9.1
```

the computer will print the answers on separate lines:

```
7
39.1
```

If you say —

```
PR [SKY IS BLUE] PR [SO ARE YOU]
```

the computer will print this poem:

```
SKY IS BLUE
SO ARE YOU
```

REPEAT

Let's make the turtle draw a square, so that each side is 50 steps long.

To do that, first make sure the turtle's pen is down, so that the turtle will draw as it moves. To make sure the pen's down, you can say PENDOWN (or PD).

To make the turtle draw the first side, say FORWARD 50 (or FD 50). Then tell the turtle to turn right 90 degrees, by saying RIGHT 90 or RT 90. Draw the second side, by saying FD 50 again. Then tell the turtle to turn right 90 degrees again, etc.

Altogether, these commands make the turtle draw all four sides of the square:

```
FD 50 RT 90 FD 50 RT 90 FD 50 RT 90 FD 50 RT 90
```

But instead of typing all that, you can type this short cut:

```
REPEAT 4 [FD 50 RT 90]
```

That makes the computer **REPEAT**, 4 times, the act of going forward 50 and turning right 90 degrees.

Let's make the computer print the word WOW, twenty times. Here's how:

```
REPEAT 20 [PR "WOW]
```

The computer will print the words on separate lines, like this:

```
WOW
WOW
WOW
etc.
```

Here's how to make the computer say FRANCE IS FUNNY, twenty times:

```
REPEAT 20 [PR [FRANCE IS FUNNY]]
```

Variables

You can **MAKE** a word stand for something. To make the word DRINKINGAGE stand for 21, type this:

```
MAKE "DRINKINGAGE 21
```

In that line, DRINKINGAGE is called the **variable** or the **name**; 21 is called **DRINKINGAGE's value** or **the thing that DRINKINGAGE stands for**.

After you type that line, you can say:

```
PR THING "DRINKINGAGE
```

That makes the computer print the THING that DRINKINGAGE stands for. The computer will print:

```
21
```

Instead of typing THING and then a quotation mark, you can type just a colon, like this:

```
PR :DRINKINGAGE
```

That means: PRint the thing that DRINKINGAGE stands for. It means: PRINT the value of DRINKINGAGE. The computer will print:

```
21
```

LOGO programmers have a nickname for the colon: they call it **dots**. So the statement —

```
PR :DRINKINGAGE
```

is pronounced: P R dots DRINKINGAGE.

Here's another example:

```
MAKE "MAGICNUMBER 7
PR :MAGICNUMBER+2
```

The first line makes the word MAGICNUMBER stand for 7. The next line says to print the value of the MAGICNUMBER, plus 2. The computer will print 9.

A word can stand for anything; it can even stand for a list. For example, you can say:

```
MAKE "STOOGES [MOE LARRY CURLEY]
PR COUNT :STOOGES
```

The first line says the word STOOGES stands for the list [MOE LARRY CURLEY]. The next line makes the computer print the COUNT of how many items are in that list; the computer will print:

```
3
```

Here's the rule: to *define* a word, say MAKE and type a quotation mark; to *use* the word's value, type a colon instead.

PROGRAMS

To teach the computer what the word SQUARE means, type this:

```
TO SQUARE
REPEAT 4 [FD 50 RT 90]
END
```

The first line means: here's how **TO** do a SQUARE. The next line gives the definition itself: repeat 4 times the act of going forward 50 steps and turning right 90 degrees. The bottom line of every definition says **END**.

Those three lines form the **definition** of SQUARE. They're also called the **program** for square, and the **procedure** for how to do a SQUARE.

After you type those three lines, the computer will know the meaning of SQUARE. So in the future, whenever you say —

```
SQUARE
```

the turtle will draw a square.

♦ Differences Before you type the word TO, LOGO Writer requires you to tap the F key while holding down the CONTROL key (on the IBM) or Open Apple key (on the Apple); Radio Shack Color LOGO requires you to tap the BREAK key, then tap the CLEAR key while holding down the SHIFT key, then tap the E key.

Many versions of LOGO automatically put the symbol ">" at the beginning of each line of the definition.

After you type the word END, some versions of LOGO require you to tap an extra key or two: for LOGO Writer, tap the F key while holding down the CONTROL key (IBM) or Open Apple key (Apple); for Commodore LOGO, tap the RUN STOP key; for Krell and Terrapin Apple LOGO, tap the C key while holding down the CONTROL key; for Radio Shack Color LOGO, tap the BREAK key then the R key.

Pinwheel

If you draw a square, then rotate 10 degrees, then draw another square, you get this:

Suppose you continue that process: draw a square, then rotate 10 degrees, then draw another square, then rotate 10 degrees again, then draw another square, then rotate 10 degrees again, etc. You'll get this pinwheel:

Let's define PINWHEEL to be that shape. Here's how:

```
TO PINWHEEL
REPEAT 36 [SQUARE RT 10]
END
```

Rebuke

Let's define REBUKE to be this message:

```
YOU LOOK TERRIF!
YOU DRESS SO SPIFF!
YOU ACT SO COOL!
YOU MAKE ME DROOL!

BUT YOU'RE A FOOL!
YOU'RE FAILING SCHOOL!
YOU'RE REALLY DUMB!
A FIRST - CLASS BUM!

SO GET YOUR MIND
OFF ITS BEHIND,
AND YOU WILL FIND
YOU'RE ONE - OF - A - KIND!
```

Here's how:

```
TO REBUKE
PR [YOU LOOK TERRIF!]
PR [YOU DRESS SO SPIFF!]
PR [YOU ACT SO COOL!]
PR [YOU MAKE ME DROOL!]
PR []
PR [BUT YOU'RE A FOOL!]
PR [YOU'RE FAILING SCHOOL!]
PR [YOU'RE REALLY DUMB!]
PR [A FIRST - CLASS BUM!]
PR []
PR [SO GET YOUR MIND]
PR [OFF ITS BEHIND,]
PR [AND YOU WILL FIND]
PR [YOU'RE ONE - OF - A - KIND!]
END
```

Then whenever you say —

```
REBUKE
```

the computer will print the poem. (To see the whole poem on the screen at once, say TEXTSCREEN before saying REBUKE.)

To have fun, say that poem out loud in a jive rap style, and clap your hands twice at the end of each line.

EDIT

After you've defined a word (such as REBUKE), you can EDIT that definition by saying —

```
EDIT "REBUKE
```

The computer will put your definition on the screen and let you edit that definition, by using the arrow keys and the other edit keys. When you've finished editing the definition, tap the ESCAPE key.

If you say EDIT [REBUKE PINWHEEL], the computer will put both definitions on the screen simultaneously and let you edit them both. When you've finished editing them, tap the ESCAPE key.

If you say just EDIT, the screen will show what you edited last time, so you can edit it again.

The abbreviation for EDIT is ED.

♦ Differences While editing, experiment! Try tapping the arrow keys, ENTER key, RETURN key, BACKSPACE key, DELETE key, INSERT key, CONTROL key, and any other edit keys on your keyboard. When using LOGO, those keys act the same as when using most word processors.

On old Apples that lack up-arrow, down-arrow, and DELETE keys, do this: to move up to the Previous line, tap the P key while holding down the CONTROL key; to delete the Next line, tap the N key while holding down the CONTROL key; to delete the character left of the cursor, tap the ESCAPE key; if you have Apple LOGO 1 and want to move Back to the left, tap the B key while holding down the CONTROL key.

For MIT versions, omit the quotation mark after EDIT.

Instead of tapping the ESCAPE key, do the following: for MIT versions and Apple LOGO 1, tap the C key while holding down the CONTROL key; for Apple LOGO 2, tap the A key while holding down the open-Apple key.

For LOGO Writer and Radio Shack Color LOGO, instead of saying EDIT, follow the procedure for saying TO.

Flexible definitions

Let's change the definition of SQUARE, to make it more flexible. Let's define SQUARE so that SQUARE 50 will be a square that's 50 steps long on each side, and SQUARE 100 will be a square that's 100 steps long on each side, and SQUARE 6 will be a square that's 6 steps long on each side, etc.

To do all that, edit the definition of SQUARE by saying:

```
EDIT "SQUARE
```

The computer will show our old definition of SQUARE:

```
TO SQUARE
REPEAT 4 [FD 50 RT 90]
END
```

Using the arrow keys, insert :SIDE after SQUARE, and change the 50 to :SIDE, so that the definition looks like this:

```
TO SQUARE
REPEAT 4 [FD :SIDE RT 90]
END
```

When you've finished the editing, press the ESCAPE key.

Then if you say —

```
SQUARE 100
```

the computer will look at the new definition of SQUARE, realize that :SIDE is 100, and do REPEAT 4 [FD 100 RT 90], which draws a square having 100 steps on each side.

After changing the definition of SQUARE in that way, you must always put a number after the word SQUARE. If you say SQUARE 100, the computer will draw a square whose side is 100; if you say SQUARE 6, the computer will draw a square whose side is 6; but if you say just SQUARE, the computer won't know how long to make the side and will gripe, by saying NOT ENOUGH INPUTS TO SQUARE.

After changing the definition of SQUARE, you must update the definition of PINWHEEL, so that it uses the new definition of SQUARE. Edit PINWHEEL so that it becomes:

```
TO PINWHEEL :SIDE
REPEAT 36 [SQUARE :SIDE RT 10]
END
```

Then if you say PINWHEEL 50, the computer will draw a normal pinwheel; if you say PINWHEEL 100, the computer will draw a pinwheel that's twice as long in each direction; if you say PINWHEEL 30, the computer will draw a pinwheel that's small.

Polygon

Let's define POLYGON so that POLYGON 5 40 will be a regular polygon having 5 sides, and each side will be 40 steps long.

Here's how:

```
TO POLYGON :N :SIDE
REPEAT :N [FD :SIDE RT 360/:N]
END
```

In that definition, :N is the number of sides (such as 5), and :SIDE is the length of each side (such as 40).

That definition will draw *any* regular polygon. For example, if you want a triangle so that each side is 60 steps long, say POLYGON 3 70. If you want an octagon so that each side is 20 steps long, say POLYGON 8 20.

If you pick a large number of sides (such as 36), the polygon will look almost like a circle. That's how you can make LOGO imitate a circle!

Star

Let's define STAR so that STAR 5 40 will be a 5-pointed star, and each side will be 40 steps long.

The definition is almost the same as POLYGON's:

```
TO STAR :N :SIDE
REPEAT :N [FD :SIDE RT 360/:N FD :SIDE LT 720/:N]
END
```

That definition makes the turtle start drawing a polygon, by drawing a polygon's first side (FD :SIDE), then turning right by the polygon's angle (RT 360/:N), then drawing the polygon's second side (FD :SIDE). But then the turtle veers sharply to the left (LT 720/:N). Repeating that procedure :N times produces a star:

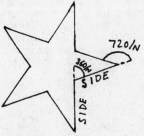

Choose as many points as you wish. For a 5-pointed star, say STAR 5 40. For a 6-pointed star (a "Jewish star"), say STAR 6 40. For an 8-pointed star that's smaller and has just 20 steps per side, say STAR 8 20.

Recursion

Here's a poem about LOGO lovers:

```
LOGO LOVERS LOOK LOVELY!
LINGERING LINES, LONGINGLY LEFT!
```

Let's program the computer so that when you say LOVERS, the computer will print that poem again and again, forever, like this:

```
LOGO LOVERS LOOK LOVELY!
LINGERING LINES, LONGINGLY LEFT!

LOGO LOVERS LOOK LOVELY!
LINGERING LINES, LONGINGLY LEFT!

LOGO LOVERS LOOK LOVELY!
LINGERING LINES, LONGINGLY LEFT!
```

etc.

Type this:

```
TO LOVERS
PR [LOGO LOVERS LOOK LOVELY!]
PR [LINGERING LINES, LONGINGLY LEFT!]
PR []
LOVERS
END
```

The three PR statements make the computer print the poem and a blank line underneath. The bottom line says END; but above the word END, I inserted the word LOVERS, which makes the computer do LOVERS again, so the computer again prints the poem and blank line and comes to the LOVERS line again, so the computer *again* prints the poem and blank line and comes to the LOVERS line again, etc. The program's an infinite loop.

After you type that definition of LOVERS, you can activate it by saying just LOVERS or — better yet — say TEXTSCREEN and then LOVERS.

To abort the program, press the BREAK key.

Notice I inserted the word LOVERS into the definition of LOVERS, so that LOVERS is defined in terms of itself. That's called a **self-referent** definition or **circular** definition or **recursive** definition. Using recursive definitions is called **recursion**. In LOGO, recursion's the usual way to create loops.

♦ <u>Differences</u> Atari 800 LOGO and Radio Shack Color LOGO let you abort by tapping the BREAK key, but most other versions of LOGO abort differently. For IBM LOGO, tap the BREAK key while holding down the CONTROL key. For LOGO Writer, tap the ESCAPE key. For Apple LOGO 2, tap the ESCAPE key while holding down the Open Apple key. For Apple LOGO 1, Atari ST LOGO, DR LOGO, and MIT versions, tap the G key while holding down the CONTROL key.

Countdown

Let's program the computer so that COUNTDOWN 10 will make the computer count down from 10, like this:

```
10
9
8
7
etc.
```

Here's the definition:

```
TO COUNTDOWN :N
PR :N
COUNTDOWN :N-1
END
```

To count down from a number N, that definition tells the computer to print the number N and then count down from N-1.

Unfortunately, that definition's an infinite loop! For example, if you say COUNTDOWN 10, that definition will make the computer print 10, 9, 8, 7, 6, 5, 4, 3, 2, 1, 0, -1, -2, -3, -4, etc., forever!

Let's edit that definition, to **STOP** the computer from printing negative numbers. Say:

```
EDIT "COUNTDOWN
```

Then use the arrow keys, to change the definition of COUNTDOWN to this:

```
TO COUNTDOWN :N
IF :N<0 [STOP]
PR :N
COUNTDOWN :N-1
END
```

♦ <u>Differences</u> For MIT versions, omit the brackets around STOP.

Squiral

Let's make the computer draw the first side of a square (by saying FD :SIDE), then turn right 90 degrees (by saying RT 90), then draw the second side — but make the second side shorter than the first! Then make the third side even shorter! Then make the fourth side even shorter!

The result will be a "shrinking square" whose fourth side doesn't meet the first side. It looks something like a square, but it spirals inward, becoming smaller. It's called a **squiral**.

To create an amazing squiral, feed the computer this definition:

```
TO SQUIRAL :SIDE
FD :SIDE
RT 90
SQUIRAL :SIDE-3
END
```

That program's an infinite loop. The side becomes smaller and smaller (decreasing by 3 each time), until finally the side becomes a negative number, which makes the turtle go wild and draw fascinating weird graphics on the screen.

Feed the computer that definition. Then for the most dramatic results, feed the computer this definition —

```
TO DRAMATICSQUIRAL
WRAP
PENREVERSE
FULLSCREEN
SQUIRAL 100
END
```

and type:

```
DRAMATICSQUIRAL
```

WORKSPACE

When you invent a definition, the computer puts it into a part of the RAM called the **workspace**. The workspace holds your definitions of names (such as MAKE "DRINKINGAGE 21) and your definitions of procedures (such as TO SQUARE do REPEAT 4 [FD 50 RT 90] then END).

Printouts

To see *all* those definitions on your screen, say TEXTSCREEN, so that the computer can use the entire screen for text; then say **POALL**, which means Print Out ALL. The computer will print out all the definitions. For example, if you defined the name DRINKINGAGE and then MAGICNUMBER, and then defined the procedure SQUARE :SIDE and then PINWHEEL :SIDE, the computer will print all those definitions, like this:

```
TO PINWHEEL :SIDE
REPEAT 36 [SQUARE :SIDE RT 10]
SQUARE
END

TO SQUARE :SIDE
REPEAT 4 [FD :SIDE RT 90]
END

MAKE "MAGICNUMBER 7
MAKE "DRINKINGAGE 21
```

The computer begins with the newest procedure (PINWHEEL), then any other procedures (such as SQUARE), then the newest name (MAGICNUMBER), then any other names (such as DRINKINGAGE).

If you don't want to see all that, you can ask for an abridgment. To see definitions of just the procedures (PINWHEEL and SQUARE), say **POPS**, which means Print Out ProcedureS. To see definitions of just the names (MAGICNUMBER and DRINKINGAGE), say **PONS**, which means Print Out NameS.

To see just the top line of each procedure, say **POTS**, which means Print out TopS or Print Out TitleS; the computer will print:

```
TO PINWHEEL :SIDE
TO SQUARE :SIDE
```

To see the definition of just the SQUARE procedure, say **PO "SQUARE**. That makes the computer print the definition of SQUARE :SIDE. To see that definition first, then the definition of PINWHEEL, say **PO [SQUARE PINWHEEL]**.

♦ Differences LOGO Writer doesn't understand any of those commands; instead, tap the F key while holding down the CONTROL or Open Apple key, then browse through all the procedures you created, by pressing the up-arrow and down-arrow keys.

For MIT versions, change POALL to PO ALL, change POPS to PO PROCEDURES, change PONS to PO NAMES, change POTS to PO TITLES, and change PO "SQUARE to PO SQUARE.

Erasing the definitions

If you no longer need the definitions you invented, you can erase them.

To ERase ALL the definitions, say **ERALL**. To ERase just the definitions of ProcedureS (such as PINWHEEL and SQUARE), say **ERPS**. To ERase just the definitions of NameS (such as MAGICNUMBER and DRINKINGAGE), say **ERNS**.

To **ERASE** just the definition of the PINWHEEL procedure, say:

```
ERASE "PINWHEEL
```

The abbreviation for ERASE is ER.

To ERase just the definition of the Name MAGICNUMBER, say **ERN "MAGICNUMBER**.

♦ Differences LOGO Writer doesn't understand any of those commands; instead, get onto the screen the procedures you want to erase, then erase them by holding down the DELETE or BACKSPACE key.

For MIT versions, change ERALL to ER ALL, change ERPS to ER PROCEDURES, change ERNS to ER NAMES, change ERASE "PINWHEEL to ERASE PINWHEEL, and change ERN to ERNAME.

Saving to disk

After you've *formatted* a blank disk (by using DOS or BASIC or some other method), you can put that disk into the drive and copy all your definitions onto the disk. Here's how.

Invent a filename (such as FRED) and say **SAVE "FRED**. On the disk, the computer will create a new file called FRED and copy all your definitions to FRED.

Later, whenever you want to use FRED, just say **LOAD "FRED**. The computer will go to the disk, find FRED, and copy FRED's definitions to the RAM, so you can use them.

To see a list of all the LOGO files on your disk, say **CATALOG**.

To delete FRED from the disk, say **ERASEFILE "FRED**.

♦ Differences For MIT versions, change LOAD to READ. For IBM LOGO, DR LOGO, and Atari ST LOGO, change CATALOG to DIR. For LOGO Writer, change ERASEFILE to ERPAGE, change LOAD to GETPAGE (or GP), change CATALOG to PR PAGELIST, and change SAVE "FRED to NAMEPAGE "FRED NEWPAGE (or NP "FRED NEWPAGE). For the Atari 800, change ERASEFILE to ERF, change "FRED to "D:FRED, and change CATALOG to CATALOG "D:.

FORTRAN

The most popular computer language is BASIC, which I explained earlier. Now you'll learn a different computer language, called **FORTRAN**.

Most maxicomputers and minicomputers understand both BASIC and FORTRAN. Some ideas are easier to express in BASIC; others are easier in FORTRAN.

Most scientists and engineers on large computers use FORTRAN, not BASIC.

IBM invented the first version of FORTRAN in 1957. Then came improvements, called **FORTRAN II, FORTRAN III,** and **FORTRAN IV.** The next version was called **FORTRAN 77** because it was invented in 1977. The newest version is called **FORTRAN 90** because it was invented in 1990.

Some computers use FORTRAN 77 or FORTRAN 90. Others still use FORTRAN IV or a slightly souped-up version of it (called **FORTRAN IV-EXTENDED** or **FORTRAN V** or **WATFOR** or **WATFIV** or **FORTRAN 10**).

This chapter explains the popular FORTRAN features that work on practically all computers.

Simple programs

Here's a FORTRAN program:

```
      PRINT 10
10    FORMAT (1X,'CHIPMUNKS ARE CHUBBY')
      PRINT 20
20    FORMAT (1X,'GOLDFISH GIGGLE')
      PRINT 10
      END
```

The top line says to print what's in line 10, so the computer will print CHIPMUNKS ARE CHUBBY. The next line says to print what's in line 20, so the computer will print GOLDFISH GIGGLE. The next line says to print what's in line 10, so the computer will print CHIPMUNKS ARE CHUBBY again. Altogether, the program makes the computer print:

```
CHIPMUNKS ARE CHUBBY
GOLDFISH GIGGLE
CHIPMUNKS ARE CHUBBY
```

Notice:

Each program line is indented 6 spaces, so it begins in the 7th position.
Each FORMAT begins with 1X.
Each string is enclosed in apostrophes.

You must number every line that's referred to. For example, you must number the FORMAT lines, since the PRINT lines refer to them. You don't have to number the PRINT lines.

The bottom line of every FORTRAN program must be END.

Different versions On PDP computers, say TYPE instead of PRINT. On CDC computers using TS FORTRAN, replace each apostrophe by an asterisk. On IBM computers, put STOP above END, so the bottom two lines of your program are:

```
      STOP
      END
```

How to type the program Ask the people in your computer center how to feed a FORTRAN program into the computer. On some computers, you must put an edit number in front of each line:

```
00100          PRINT 10
00110    10    FORMAT (1X,'CHIPMUNKS ARE CHUBBY')
00120          PRINT 20
00130    20    FORMAT (1X,'GOLDFISH GIGGLE')
00140          PRINT 10
00150          END
```

Some computers don't require you to indent each line. To indent quickly on PDP computers, hold down the CONTROL key, while you type the letter I.

Be brief Each line of your program must be brief: no more than 72 characters, including the spaces at the beginning of the line.

Carriage controls

The 1X at the beginning of each FORMAT is called the **carriage control**. It means: print the format normally.

For weirder printing, replace the 1X by '0' or '1' or '+':

```
      PRINT 10
10    FORMAT (1X,'NIFTY')
      PRINT 20
20    FORMAT ('0','SAL')
      END
```

In line 10, the 1X makes the computer print NIFTY normally. **In line 20, the zero-in-apostrophes make the computer leave a blank line, then print SAL.**

The computer will print:

```
NIFTY

SAL
```

Suppose you change the carriage control to '1':

```
      PRINT 10
10    FORMAT (1X,'NIFTY')
      PRINT 20
20    FORMAT ('1','SAL')
      END
```

If your terminal uses paper, **the '1' makes the computer print SAL on a new page**. If your terminal uses a screen instead of paper, the '1' makes the computer erase the screen before printing SAL.

Suppose you change the carriage control to '+':

```
      PRINT 10
10    FORMAT (1X,'NIFTY')
      PRINT 20
20    FORMAT ('+','SAL')
      END
```

If your terminal uses paper, **the '+' makes the computer print SAL in the same place as NIFTY**, like this:

```
NIFTY           SAL
```

If your terminal uses a screen instead, the computer will print NIFTY, but then the NIF will suddenly disappear, and you'll see SALTY.

To print the symbol θ, print 0 in the same place as -. To print the symbol ≠, print = in the same place as /. To print θ= /A, print 0=A in the same place as -/. If your terminal uses paper, the program prints θ≠A:

```
    PRINT 10
10  FORMAT (1X,'0=A')
    PRINT 20
20  FORMAT ('+','-/')
    END
```

Different versions
If you're using a Hazeltine terminal or CDC TS FORTRAN, the carriage controls won't work.

Fancy formats

In the format line, you can play fancy tricks.

Multiple fields
Examine this program:

```
    PRINT 10
10  FORMAT (1X,'JOHN','NY')
    END
```

The FORMAT consists of three **fields**: the first is the carriage control 1X, the second is 'JOHN', and the third is 'NY'. The computer will print JOHN and NY on the same line:

```
JOHNNY
```

Another example:

```
    PRINT
10  FORMAT (1X,'EAT A',8X,'MEATBALL')
    END
```

The computer will print EAT A, then 8 blank spaces, then MEATBALL:

```
EAT A       MEATBALL
```

This program does the same thing:

```
    PRINT 10
10  FORMAT (1X,'EAT A',T15,'MEATBALL')
    END
```

It makes the computer print EAT A, then Tab over to the 15th position on the line, and print MEATBALL. When the computer tabs to the 15th position, **it considers the carriage control to be the first "position"**; the E in EAT is the first character the computer will print, and the computer considers it to be the second "position"; the A in EAT is the second character the computer will print, and the computer considers it to be the third "position"; the M in MEATBALL is the 14th character the computer will print, since the T15 says it is the 15th "position".

Here's another program for meatball lovers:

```
    PRINT 10
10  FORMAT (1X,'EAT A',1X,'MEATBALL')
```

The computer will print EAT A, then 1 blank space, then MEATBALL:

```
EAT A MEATBALL
```

If you say X instead of 1X, the computer will gripe.

Multiple records
This program quotes Julius Caesar:

```
    PRINT 10
10  FORMAT (1X,'I CAME')
    PRINT 20
20  FORMAT (1X,'I SAW')
    PRINT 30
30  FORMAT (1X,'I CONQUERED')
    END
```

The computer will print:

```
I CAME
I SAW
I CONQUERED
```

This program does the same thing:

```
    PRINT 10
10  FORMAT (1X,'I CAME'/1X,'I SAW'/1X,'I CONQUERED')
    END
```

Line 10 consists of 3 **records**: the first is 1X,'I CAME'; the second is 1X,'I SAW'; the third is 1X,'I CONQUERED'. Each record begins with a carriage control; the records are separated by slashes. The computer will print each record on a separate line.

Example:

```
    PRINT 10
10  FORMAT (1X,'PLEASE'/1X,'NIBBLE'//1X,'MY'//////1X,'CHEESE')
    END
```

Line 10 makes the computer print several lines. The first line will say PLEASE. The next line will say NIBBLE. The next line will be blank. The next line will say MY. The next 4 lines will be blank. The last line will say CHEESE. So altogether, the computer will print:

```
PLEASE
NIBBLE

MY




CHEESE
```

Repeated formats
The computer can feel very depressed:

```
    PRINT 10
10  FORMAT (1X,'I FEEL ',3('DOWN'))
    END
```

Line 10 is an abbreviation for this format:

```
        1X,'I FEEL ','DOWN','DOWN','DOWN'
```

The computer will print:

```
I FEEL DOWNDOWNDOWN
```

Let's burp and pray:

```
    PRINT 10
10  FORMAT (1X,'JACK ',2('BURPS'/1X,'MARY '),'ALSO PRAYS')
    END
```

Line 10 is an abbreviation for this format:

```
        1X,'JACK ','BURPS'/1X,'MARY ','BURPS'/1X,'MARY ','ALSO PRAYS'
```

The computer will print:

```
JACK BURPS
MARY BURPS
MARY ALSO PRAYS
```

Double apostrophe
To make the computer print an apostrophe, use two apostrophes next to each other.

```
    PRINT 10
10  FORMAT (1X,'MOMMY ISN''T HERE')
    END
```

The computer will print:

```
MOMMY ISN'T HERE
```

Continuation

Some computers look at only the first 72 characters of each line of your program: if your line contains more than 72 characters, it won't work.

If you want to type a long statement, type just the first 72 characters. On the line below, type the remaining characters, beginning in the 7th print position; and in the 6th print position type a 6:

```
      PRINT 10
10    FORMAT (1X,'I LIKE ROSES IN MY TEA.'/1X,'THEY MAKE IT GLOW RED, LI
     6KE HOT BLOOD.')
      END
```

The computer will print:

```
I LIKE ROSES IN MY TEA.
THEY MAKE IT GLOW RED, LIKE HOT BLOOD.
```

A line that has a 6 in column 6 is called a **continuation line**, because it's a continuation of the line above it.

(I suggest you put a 6 in column 6, or a * in column 6, or a $ in column 6. In fact, you can put *any character* in column 6, except a zero. Choose your favorite character; the computer doesn't care.)

<u>**Different versions**</u> On PDP computers, put the 6 immediately after a controlled I, instead of in column 6:

```
10    FORMAT (1X,'I LIKE ROSES IN MY TEA.'/1X,'THEY MAKE IT GLOW RED, LI
     6KE HOT BLOOD.')
```

(I suggest you put a 6 after the controlled I. But you can put in *any non-zero digit*, instead of a 6.)

On CDC computers using TS FORTRAN, type a + instead of a 6, and put it immediately after the edit number, with no intervening spaces:

```
00120 10 FORMAT (1X,'I LIKE ROSES IN MY TEA.'/1X,'THEY MAKE IT GLOW RED, LI
00130+KE HOT BLOOD.')
```

GO TO

You can say GO TO:

```
10    PRINT 20
20    FORMAT (1X,'CAT')
      PRINT 30
30    FORMAT (1X,'DOG')
      GO TO 10
      END
```

The top line says to print what's in line 20, so the computer will print:

```
CAT
```

The next line says to print what's in line 30, so the computer will print:

```
DOG
```

The next line makes the computer go back to line 10. The computer will print CAT again, then DOG again, then jump back to line 10 again. . . . The computer will try to print the words CAT and DOG again and again, forever.

STOP

The computer understands the word STOP:

```
      PRINT 10
10    FORMAT (1X,'BUBBLE GUM')
      PRINT 20
20    FORMAT (1X,'SHAKESPEARE')
      STOP
      PRINT 30
30    FORMAT (1X,'DADA')
      END
```

The top line says to print what's in line 10, so the computer will print BUBBLE GUM. The next line says to print what's in line 20, so the computer will print SHAKESPEARE. The next line says STOP, so the computer will stop. It will never print DADA.

FORTRAN handles math rather well.

Integers versus real numbers

FORTRAN distinguishes between **integers** and **real numbers**. Here's how FORTRAN defines them. . . .

An **integer** contains no decimal point and no exponent.

Integer	Not an integer	Comment
-27	-27.0	An integer contains no decimal point.
50000	5E4	An integer contains no exponents.

A **real number** contains either a decimal point or the letter E.

Real number	Not a real number
-27.0	-27
2.35E8	235000000
5E4	50000

The largest permissible integer is different from the largest permissible real:

Computer	Largest integer	Largest real	Tiniest real
PDP-11 using FORTRAN IV	32767	1.7E38	2.9E-39
PDP-11 using FORTRAN IV-PLUS	2147483647	1.7E38	2.9E-39
PDP-10 or Honeywell	34359738367	1.7E38	2.9E-39
IBM mainframe	2147483647	7.2E75	5.4E-79
CDC	281474976710655	2.5E322	3.1E-294

Integers are also called **fixed-point numbers**. Real numbers are called **floating-point numbers**.

Variables

In BASIC, X can stand for a number, such as 3.7. The same is true in FORTRAN. A variable can be a letter (such as X) or a letter-followed-by-a-combination-of-letters-and-digits (such as FUN4U2).

The variable must be short: no more than 6 characters. AVERAGE is too long: say AVERAG instead.

If the variable begins with I, J, K, L, M, or N, it stands for an integer. If it begins with some other letter, it stands for a real number.

Using integer variables

Here's a simple example:

```
      JUNKY=-47
      PRINT 10, JUNKY
10    FORMAT (1X,I3)
      END
```

Since JUNKY begins with J, it stands for an integer. The first line says JUNKY stands for the integer -47. The second line says to print JUNKY, using line 10. Line 10 explains how to print JUNKY. **The I3 means: print it as an Integer having 3 characters.** The computer will print:

```
-47
```

If you change the I3 to I4, the computer will print JUNKY as an Integer having 4 characters. To print a total of 4 characters, the computer will print a blank space in front of -47, like this:

```
 -47
```

If you change to I5, the computer will print JUNKY as an Integer having 5 characters, by printing two blank spaces in front of -47:

```
  -47
```

If you change to I2, the computer will try to print JUNKY as an integer having 2 characters. But it's impossible to express -47 by using only 2 characters. The computer will obey the format and print 2 characters, but will make them asterisks:

```
**
```

Another example:

```
      NUM=31.9
      PRINT 10, NUM
10    FORMAT (1X,I4)
      END
```

Since NUM begins with N, it stands for an integer. The program's top line tries to make NUM stand for 31.9; but that's impossible, since 31.9 isn't an integer. The computer will omit the .9 and make NUM stand for the integer 31. The computer will print 31, using an I4 format:

```
 31
```

Example:

```
      JOE=-5.8
      PRINT 10, JOE
10    FORMAT (1X,I4)
      END
```

The computer will set JOE equal to the integer -5 and print it:

```
 -5
```

Example:

```
        JAIL=74
        KRIMNL=829
        PRINT 10, JAIL,KRIMNL
10      FORMAT (1X,I2,I3)
        END
```

Since JAIL begins with J, and KRIMNL begins with K, they're both integers. The computer will print JAIL and KRIMNL, using the format in line 10. The format says to print a 2-character integer, then a 3-character integer. The computer will print:

```
74829
```

If you change the format to (1X,I2,4X,I3), the computer will print a 2-character integer, then 4 blanks, then a 3-character integer:

```
74    829
```

If you change the format to —

```
10      FORMAT (1X,'JAIL NUMBER',1X,I2,1X,'CONTAINS CRIMINAL',1X,I3)
```

the computer will print JAIL NUMBER, then a blank, then a 2-character integer, then a blank, then CONTAINS CRIMINAL, then a blank, then a 3-character integer:

```
JAIL NUMBER 74 CONTAINS CRIMINAL 829
```

Example:

```
        J=43
        K=75
        L=96
        M=81
        N=24
        PRINT 10, J,K,L,M,N
10      FORMAT (1X,I2,I2,I2,I2,I2)
        END
```

The computer will print 43, then 75, then 96, then 81, then 24:

```
4375968124
```

You can write that format more briefly:

```
10      FORMAT (1X,5I2)
```

If you change the format to (1X,5I3), the computer will print each integer as 3 characters — a blank followed by two digits:

```
 43 75 96 81 24
```

If you change the format to (1X,I3), the computer will print only one integer per line:

```
 43
 75
 96
 81
 24
```

If you change the format to (1X,2I3), the computer will print 2 integers per line:

```
 43 75
 96 81
 24
```

If you change the format to (1X,'GOSH',I3,1X,'SUPERB',I3,1X,'JEEPERS'), the computer will print 2 integers per line:

```
GOSH 43 SUPERB 75 JEEPERS
GOSH 96 SUPERB 81 JEEPERS
GOSH 24 SUPERB
```

To be safe, use I14 format for integers. On most computers, I14 handles even the largest integers, and prints blank spaces between them.

Using real variables

The I format is only for integers. **For real numbers, use F or G format** instead.

F format The F format is easy to understand:

```
      RADIUS=-586.39
      PRINT 10, RADIUS
10    FORMAT (1X,F7.2)
      END
```

Since RADIUS doesn't begin with I, J, K, L, M, or N, it stands for a real number. The first line says RADIUS stands for the real number -586.39. The second line says to print RADIUS, using the format in line 10. **The F7.2 means: print it as a floating-point number having 7 characters, 2 of them after the decimal point**. The computer will print:

```
-586.39
```

If you change the F7.2 to a different format, the following chart shows what happens; in the chart, each ∎ represents a blank space:

Format	What the computer prints	Comment
F8.2	∎-586.39	To print 8 characters instead of 7, it prints a blank space at the beginning.
F8.3	-586.390	To print 3 characters after the decimal point instead of 2, it prints a zero at the end.
F8.1	∎∎-586.4	To print 1 character after the decimal point instead of 2, it rounds the .39 to 4.
F8.4	********	To print 4 characters after the decimal point, the computer would have to print -586.3900. Since that requires more than 8 characters, the computer complains by printing asterisks.

G format **To print a real number, the safest format is G14.6**, because G14.6 can handle *any* real number well, even if the number is very large or very tiny.

G14.6 prints 14 characters altogether, 6 of which are significant digits. Here are examples of numbers printed in G14.6 format:

```
∎-0.283941E-29
∎∎0.293027∎∎∎∎
∎∎∎5.34523∎∎∎∎
∎∎∎39.4539∎∎∎∎
∎∎∎47802.3∎∎∎∎
∎∎∎986327.∎∎∎∎
∎∎0.288341E+24
```

Example:

```
      PRUNES=17
      PRINT 10, PRUNES
10    FORMAT (1X,G14.6)
      END
```

Since PRUNES doesn't begin with I, J, K, L, M, or N, it stands for a real number. When the computer encounters the first line of the program, it will set PRUNES equal to the real number 17.0. It will print:

```
17.0000
```

The program will run faster if you change the top line to this:

```
      PRUNES=17.0
```

E format For real numbers, the usual formats are F and G, but another option is E.

If you say E14.6 instead of G14.6, the computer will print an E in the answer. Here are examples:

Using G14.6 format	Using E14.6 format
∎-0.283941E-29	∎-0.283941E-29
∎∎0.293027∎∎∎∎	∎∎0.293027E+00
∎∎∎5.34523∎∎∎∎	∎∎0.534523E+01
∎∎∎39.4539∎∎∎∎	∎∎0.394539E+02
∎∎∎47802.3∎∎∎∎	∎∎0.478023E+05
∎∎∎986327.∎∎∎∎	∎∎0.986327E+06
∎∎0.288341E+24	∎∎0.288341E+24

The G14.6 format is easier for a human to read than E14.6. But most programmers are stupid, don't know about G14.6, and use E14.6 instead.

P format FORTRAN's notation differs from BASIC.

If you ask the computer to print 288341000000000000000000.0 in FORTRAN by using G14.6 (or E14.6), the computer will normally print a 0 before the decimal point, like this: 0.288341E+24. In BASIC, the computer will print a non-zero digit before the decimal point, like this: 2.88341E+23.

If you're writing a program in FORTRAN, but you prefer BASIC's notation, ask for 1PG14.6 (or 1PE14.6). The 1P makes the computer imitate BASIC. But if a FORMAT contains 1PG, it must not contain F afterwards; this will print a wrong answer:

```
      FORMAT (1X,1PG14.6,F8.2)
               ↑         ↑
```
Here is P. The F afterwards
prints a wrong answer!

Operations

For addition, subtraction, multiplication, and division, FORTRAN uses the same symbols as BASIC.

```
      N=2*(3+1)
      S=7.3+2.1
      PRINT 10, N,S
10    FORMAT (1X,I14,G14.6)
      END
```

Since N is 8, and S is 9.4, the computer will print:

```
      8   9.40000
```

Exponents For exponents, FORTRAN uses a double star:

```
      J=7**2
      P=.5**3
      PRINT 10, J,P
10    FORMAT (1X,I14,G14.6)
      END
```

Since J is 7^2 (which is 49), and P is $.5^3$ (which is .125), the computer will print:

```
      49   0.125000
```

For negative exponents, you need parentheses. You must say 6.1**(-2), not 6.1**-2.

What type of answer? When you combine integers, the answer's an integer:

```
2+3     is 5
8-8     is 0
2*4     is 8
399/100 is 3 (not 3.99)
11/4    is 2 (not 2.75)
3/4     is 0 (not 0.75)
10**(-2) is 0 (not 0.01)
```

When you combine real numbers, the answer is real:

```
4.1+2.9      is 7.0 (not 7)
8.0-8.0      is 0.0 (not 0)
399.0/100.0  is 3.99
11.0/4.0     is 2.75
3.0/4.0      is .75
10.0**(-2.0) is .01
```

When you combine an integer with a real number, the answer is real:

3+2.0   is 5.0
399/100.0   is 3.99
11/4.0   is 2.75
3/4.0   is .75
10.0**(-2)   is .01

Compare these:

7/10*10   is 0   (because 7/10 is 0)
7/10*10.0   is 0.0 (because 0*10.0 is 0.0)
7/10.0*10   is 7.0 (because 7/10.0 is .7)

Example:

```
      JERK=20.0+30.9
      PRINT 10, JERK
10    FORMAT (1X,I14)
      END
```

Since JERK begins with J, it stands for an integer. Since 20.9+30.9 is 51.8, JERK stands for the integer 51. The computer will print:

        51

Another example:

```
      APPLE=37/10
      PRINT 10, APPLE
10    FORMAT (1X,G14.6)
      END
```

Since APPLE begins with A, it stands for a real number. Since 37/10 is 3, APPLE stands for the real number 3.0. The computer will print:

3.00000

Crimes that slow down the computer cop

If you commit one of these crimes, the computer will work slowly. . . .

little crime: use a real number
medium crime: mix reals with integers
big crime: use a real exponent

For example, the computer handles 2.0+2.0 slower than 2+2, because 2.0+2.0 is a little crime.

The bigger the crime, the slower the computer works. For example, the computer handles 2.1+7 (which is a medium crime) slower than 2.1+7.0 (which is just a *little* crime). Likewise, X=0 (a medium crime) gets handled slower than X=0.0 (a little crime).

5.1**2.0 is a big crime, since its exponent (2.0) is real. The computer handles it slower than 5.1**2, which is just a medium crime.

5**3.1 is a gigantic crime, since it's a medium crime and a big crime simultaneously. Because the crime's so gigantic, some computers refuse to handle it. Say 5.0**3.1 instead.

Advice about variables

FORTRAN, like BASIC, distinguishes variables, constants, and expressions:

X   is a variable
2.7   is not a variable; it's a **numeric constant**
'LOVE'   is not a variable; it's a **string constant**
X+Y   is not a variable; it's an **expression**

In a PRINT statement, some computers allow only variables. . . .

allowed: PRINT 10, X
not allowed: PRINT 10, 2.7   instead, say X=2.7 and PRINT 10, X
not allowed: PRINT 10, 'LOVE'   instead, say PRINT 10 and 10 FORMAT (1X,'LOVE')
not allowed: PRINT 10, X+Y   instead, say Z=X+Y and PRINT 10, Z

Other computers are more generous and allow anything. Find out about yours.

To help other humans understand your program, **use long variable names throughout your program**. Say RADIUS, not R; say AREA, not A; say VOLUME, not V; say SUM, not S; say TOTAL, not T. Because FORTRAN's variables are restricted to six characters, you might have to omit the last few syllables (*revolutions* becomes REVOLU) or the last few vowels (RVLTNS).

If you want a variable to be real, but its English name begins with I, J, K, L, M, or N, begin its FORTRAN name with an A (*mass* becomes AMAS; *length* becomes ALENGT or ALNGTH). If you want a variable to be an integer, but its English name doesn't begin with I, J, K, L, M, or N, begin its FORTRAN name with an I (*population* becomes IPOPUL) or misspell it (*count* becomes KOUNT) or choose a synonym (instead of *position*, say *location*, which is LOCATN).

PLEASANT I/O

You learned how to make the computer PRINT by using a FORMAT. Now you'll learn about PRINT's opposite (READ) and how to omit FORMATs altogether.

READ

The computer can READ.

```
      PRINT 10
10    FORMAT (1X,'TYPE SOME DIGITS')
      READ 20, N
20    FORMAT (I4)
      PRINT 30, N
30    FORMAT (1X,I4)
      END
```

When you run the program, here's what happens. . . .
The top two lines make the computer print:

```
TYPE SOME DIGITS
```

The word READ makes the computer wait for you to type something; it's like the BASIC word INPUT. The computer will wait for you to type the value of N, but line 20's FORMAT makes the computer read just the first 4 characters. For example, if you type —

```
-75198622
```

the computer will read just the first 4 characters, which are -751; it will ignore the 98622; so N will be -751. Line 30's FORMAT makes the computer print:

```
-751
```

Altogether, the run looks like this:

The computer says:	TYPE SOME DIGITS
You say:	-75198622
The computer replies:	-751

Hassles Line 30's FORMAT contains a carriage control 1X, but line 20's FORMAT omits the carriage control. **Put a carriage control in formats that PRINT, but not in formats that READ.**

On PDP computers, say ACCEPT instead of READ.

Blank spaces If you input a blank space, the computer treats it as a zero.

For example, suppose you input:

```
-3 28219
```

Because of the I4 format, the computer will read just the first 4 characters, which are -3 2; the blank space between the 3 and the 2 is treated as a zero, so N will be -302.

Suppose you input:

```
57
```

Because of the I4 format, the computer will read the 5, the 7, and two blanks. Since the blanks are treated as zeros, N will be 5700.

Suppose you input:

```
■■■9527
```

Because of the I4 format, the computer will read the three beginning blanks and the 9. Since the blanks are treated as zeros, N will be 0009, which is 9. Line 30 makes the computer print:

```
9
```

Multiple variables Suppose you write a program containing these lines:

```
      READ 20, L,M,N
20    FORMAT (I3,I4,2X,I2)
```

When you run that program, suppose you input:

```
58194138972824
```

The I3 format makes the first 3 characters (581) be L. The I4 format makes the next 4 characters (9413) be M. The 2X format makes the next 2 characters (89) be skipped over. The I2 format makes the next two characters (72) be N. The remaining characters (824) are ignored. So the line is split like this. . . .

Line you input:	581|94138|97|28|24
Fields in the FORMAT statement:	I3| I4 |2X|I2|
Variables in the READ statement:	L | M | |N|

Suppose you write a program containing these lines:

```
      READ 20, J,K,L,M,N
20    FORMAT (2I3)
```

The format says to read two 3-character integers on each line. Suppose you input:

```
78345692
85431684
46185327
```

J will be 783, and K will be 456. L will be 854, and M will be 316. N will be 461.

Real variables Here's how to input a real number:

```
      PRINT 10
10    FORMAT (1X,'TYPE SOME DIGITS')
      READ 20, P
20    FORMAT (F6.2)
      PRINT 30, P
30    FORMAT (1X,G14.6)
      END
```

The F6.2 format means: read 6 characters; if they don't contain the decimal point, insert it before the last 2 digits.

For example, suppose you input:

```
327514968
```

The computer reads the first 6 characters (327514). Since they don't contain the decimal point, the computer inserts it before the last 2 digits, so P is 3275.14. Line 30 prints:

```
3275.14
```

Suppose you input:

```
7.5423967
```

The computer reads the first 6 characters (7.5423). Since they already contain the decimal point, P is 7.5423. Line 30 says to print that number by using 6 significant digits, so the computer prints:

```
7.54230
```

Suppose you input:

```
497E3
```

The computer reads 6 characters (497E3, followed by a blank). Since blanks are treated as zeros, the computer gets 497E30. Since 497E30 doesn't contain the decimal point, the computer inserts it before the last 2 digits, so P is 4.97E30. Line 30 prints:

```
0.497000E+31
```

Omitting formats

Most computers let you omit numeric formats. This program works on most modern computers (such as computers having FORTRAN 77, PDP-20 computers, PDP-10 computers using FORTRAN 10, PDP-11 computers using FORTRAN IV-PLUS, CDC computers using FORTRAN IV-EXTENDED, and IBM computers using FORTRAN H-EXTENDED):

```
     PRINT 10
10   FORMAT (1X,'TYPE TWO INTEGERS')
     READ *, M,N
     ISUM=M+N
     PRINT *, ISUM
     END
```

On PDP computers, say TYPE instead of PRINT, and ACCEPT instead of READ.

The word READ is followed by an asterisk, instead of a FORMAT number. The last PRINT is followed by an asterisk also. **The asterisk makes the computer invent its own FORMAT**. To make the program add 241 and 82976, **input the numbers, separated by a comma:**

241,82976

The computer will notice the comma's location and automatically use an I3 format for 241, a 1X format to skip over the comma, and an I5 format for 82976. To print ISUM, the computer will use a safe format, such as I14 or I15.

By omitting formats, you gain two advantages:

1. You can write FORTRAN programs more quickly.

2. The person who inputs doesn't have to worry about whether his spacing matches the format. The computer invents a format that matches his input.

Different versions
On CDC computers using TS FORTRAN and on Honeywell computers, omit the asterisk after READ and PRINT:

```
     PRINT 10
10   FORMAT (1X,'TYPE THE NUMBERS')
     READ, M,N
     ISUM=M+N
     PRINT, ISUM
     END
```

On PDP-10 computers using F40 FORTRAN, and on PDP-11 computers using regular FORTRAN IV, you need FORMATs, but omit the number in the I format:

```
     TYPE 10
10   FORMAT (1X,'TYPE THE NUMBERS')
     ACCEPT 20, M,N
20   FORMAT (1X,2I)
     ISUM=M+N
     TYPE 30, ISUM
30   FORMAT (1X,I)
     END
```

Real numbers
You can use similar short cuts for real numbers.

LOGIC

You learned how to say GO TO and STOP. Taking those concepts further, let's see how to say IF and DO and give a *computed* GO TO.

IF

FORTRAN uses these clauses:

Clause	Meaning
IF (I .LT. 5)	If I is Less Than 5
IF (I .GT. 5)	If I is Greater Than 5
IF (I .LE. 5)	If I is Less than or Equal to 5
IF (I .GE. 5)	If I is Greater than or Equal to 5
IF (I .EQ. 5)	If I is EQual to 5
IF (I .NE. 5)	If I is Not Equal to 5

Notice that each **relational operator** (such as LT) must be enclosed in periods, and each **condition** (such as I .LT. 5) must be enclosed in parentheses.

By using those clauses, you can build statements:

Statement	Meaning
IF (I .LT. 5) J=3	If I is Less Than 5, let J=3
IF (I .LT. 5) GO TO 80	If I is Less Than 5, go to line 80.
IF (I .LT. 5) STOP	If I is Less Than 5, stop.
IF (I .LT. 5) PRINT 10, J	If I is Less Than 5, print J using line 10's FORMAT.

You can use the words AND and OR:

Idea	How to say it in FORTRAN
If I is 2 or 9 or 13	IF (I .EQ. 2 .OR. I .EQ. 9 .OR. I .EQ. 13)
If I is an integer from 1 to 8	IF (I .GE. 1 .AND. I .LE. 8)
If X<Y<Z	IF (X .LT. Y .AND. Y .LT. Z)
If A is less than both B and C	IF (A .LT. B .AND. A .LT. C)
If X negative or between 5 & 9	IF (X .LT. 0.0 .OR. X .GE. 5.0 .AND. X .LE. 9.0)

Take this test: cover the column that says "How to say it in FORTRAN". Try to translate each "Idea" into FORTRAN, then check your answers. If one of your answers is shorter than the correct answer, take the test again! For example, the following answer to the first idea is *wrong*:

```
IF (I .EQ. 2 .OR. 9 .OR. 13)
```

END IF FORTRAN 77 lets you say "END IF".

For example, here's how FORTRAN 77 lets you say, "If I is greater than 5, let J be 80 and let K be 90":

```
IF (I .GT. 5) THEN
    J=80
    K=90
END IF
```

Here's how FORTRAN 77 lets you say, "If I is greater than 5, let J be 80 and let K be 90; but if I is *not* greater than 5, let J be 30 and let K be 50":

```
IF (I .GT. 5) THEN
    J=80
    K=90
ELSE
    J=30
    K=50
END IF
```

Here's how FORTRAN 77 lets you say, "If I is greater than 5, let J be 80 and let K be 90; if I is *not* greater than 5, but I is greater than 2, let J be 81 and let K be 92; if I is not greater than 2, let J be 30 and let K be 50":

```
IF (I .GT. 5) THEN
    J=80
    K=90
ELSE IF (I .GT. 2) THEN
    J=81
    K=92
ELSE
    J=30
    K=50
END IF
```

Warning: to say "END IF", you must get FORTRAN 77. If you use FORTRAN IV instead, "END IF" doesn't work. I recommend that you get FORTRAN 77.

Three-way IF Here's a different kind of IF statement:

```
IF (X) 20,50,90
```

It means:

If X is a negative number, go to line 20.
If X is zero, go to line 50.
If X is a positive number, go to line 90.

That kind of IF statement is called a **three-way IF**, or an **arithmetic IF**. (To pronounce "arith*met*ic", put the accent on *met*.) The other kind of IF is called a **logical IF**.

Computed GO TO

In your program, you can say:

```
GO TO (80,100,20,350), I
```

That means: go to either 80, 100, 20, or 350, depending on what I is. More specifically, it means:

Go to line 80, if I is 1.
Go to line 100, if I is 2.
Go to line 20, if I is 3.
Go to line 350, if I is 4.
Proceed to the line underneath, if I is a different integer.

That FORTRAN statement is called a **computed GO TO**. It resembles this BASIC statement:

```
30 ON I GO TO 80,100,20,350
```

DO

This program prints the square of every number from 80 to 100, and then prints GET LOST:

BASIC	FORTRAN
10 FOR I = 80 TO 100	DO 30 I=80,100
20 PRINT I^2	J=I**2
	PRINT 20, J
	20 FORMAT (1X,I14)
30 NEXT I	30 CONTINUE
40 PRINT "GET LOST"	PRINT 40
	40 FORMAT (1X,'GET LOST')
	END

If you compare the BASIC with the FORTRAN, you'll notice FORTRAN uses the word DO instead of FOR, uses a comma instead of TO, and uses CONTINUE instead of NEXT. The statement **DO 30 I = 5,9** means: DO every line up through line 30, repeatedly, as I goes from 5 to 9. In BASIC, programmers indent every line between FOR and NEXT; in FORTRAN, programmers indent every line between DO and CONTINUE. In BASIC, the indented lines are called a **FOR...NEXT loop**; in FORTRAN, they're called a **DO loop**.

If you want the computer to print the square of every *fifth* number from 80 to 100, change the program's top line:

BASIC	FORTRAN
10 FOR I = 80 TO 100 STEP 5	DO 30 I=80,100,5

Restrictions

Restrictions In a DO statement, some computers allow only positive integer variables and constants:

Not allowed	Why	Say this instead
DO 10 X=1.0,5.0	reals are not allowed	DO 10 I=1,5
DO 10 X=17.3,98.5	reals are not allowed	DO 10 I=173,985
		X=I/10.0
DO 10 I=0,5	0 is not positive	DO 10 J=1,6
		I=J-1
DO 10 I=-3,5	-3 is not positive	DO 10 J=1,9
		I=J-4
DO 10 I=100,7,-1	-1 is not positive	DO 10 J=7,100
		I=107-J
DO 10 I=5,J+K	+ is not allowed	L=J+K
		DO 10 I=5,L

Other computers are more generous and allow anything. Find out about yours.

In the middle of a DO loop, don't change the value of the index. For example, if your DO loop begins with —

```
DO 10 I=1,100
```

don't insert this line in the middle of your loop:

```
I=14
```

It will confuse the computer.

Zero-trip DO loops

Zero-trip DO loops If you say —

```
DO 10 I=1,N
```

the computer will do up through line 10, N times. For example, if N is 73, the computer will do up through line 10, 73 times. If N is 2, the computer will do up through line 10, twice. If N is 1, the computer will do up through line 10, once.

What happens if N is less than 1? The answer depends on which version of FORTRAN you're using.

If you're using FORTRAN 77, the computer will skip the loop, and proceed to the line below line 10. But if you're using FORTRAN IV, the computer will do the loop once, as if N were 1.

FORTRAN 77 makes more sense; but alas, many computers still use FORTRAN IV.

A DO loop that FORTRAN 77 skips (because N is less than 1) is called a **zero-trip DO loop**, because the computer takes "zero trips through the loop" (instead of 1 trip or 2 trips or many trips).

Find out whether *your* computer's version of FORTRAN resembles FORTRAN 77 and permits zero-trip DO loops.

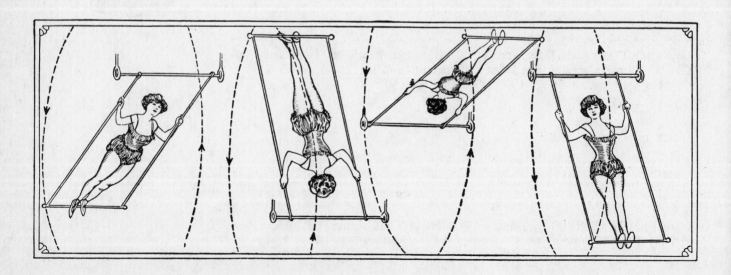

To handle lists, use these tricks. . . .

Subscripts

Like BASIC, FORTRAN permits subscripts:

```
      DIMENSION X(4)
      X(1)=.21
      X(2)=.3
      X(3)=1.08
      X(4)=5.0
      SUM=X(1)+X(2)+X(3)+X(4)
      PRINT 10, X,SUM
10    FORMAT (1X,G14.6)
      END
```

The top line says X will be a list of 4 numbers, called X(1), X(2), X(3), and X(4). Since X doesn't begin with I, J, K, L, M, or N, the 4 numbers will be real.

The PRINT statement makes the computer print the list and the SUM, like this:

```
0.210000
0.300000
1.08000
5.00000
6.59000
```

If you change the format to (1X,5G14.6), the computer will print all 5 numbers on the same line:

```
0.210000      0.300000      1.08000       5.00000       6.59000
```

You must say DIMENSION if your program uses subscripts, even if the subscripts are small. **Say DIMENSION at the very top of the program**. Make sure you say DIMENSION, not DIM or DIMENSIONS. The computer assumes all subscripts will be positive, so don't say X(0). If a subscript is zero or negative or larger than the DIMENSION statement says, the computer might not notice your error, and will print wrong answers without warning you.

If your program begins like this —

```
      DIMENSION A(6)
      READ 10, A
```

the computer will begin by reading 6 real numbers, which will become A(1), A(2), A(3), A(4), A(5), and A(6).

<u>Double subscripts</u> If you want T to be a table of numbers, and you want T to have 4 rows and 2 columns, begin your program by saying:

```
      DIMENSION T(4,2)
```

To print T, say:

```
      PRINT 10, T(1,1), T(1,2)
      PRINT 10, T(2,1), T(2,2)
      PRINT 10, T(3,1), T(3,2)
      PRINT 10, T(4,1), T(4,2)
10    FORMAT (1X,2G14.6)
```

If you say —

```
      PRINT 10, T
```

the computer will print the entire table T, but in an undesirable order: it will print T(1,1), T(2,1), T(3,1), and T(4,1), then T(1,2), T(2,2), T(3,2), and T(4,2). Similarly, "READ 5, T" makes the computer read T in an undesirable order.

Implied DO

This statement —

```
PRINT 10, X(3),X(4),X(5),X(6),X(7)
```

can be written more briefly, like this:

```
PRINT 10, (X(I), I=3,7)
```

It means: using line 10's format, print the value of X(I), for I = 3 to 7. The construction (X(I), I=3,7) is called an **implied DO loop**. Notice the parenthesis at the beginning, the parenthesis at the end, and the commas.

Here are other examples of implied DO loops:

Implied DO loop   **Meaning**
```
(X(I), I=100,120,5)   X(100),X(105),X(110),X(115),X(120)
(X(I),Y(I), I=3,7)    X(3),Y(3), X(4),Y(4), X(5),Y(5), X(6),Y(6), X(7),Y(7)
```

Calendar Here's a calendar:

```
 1  2  3  4  5  6  7
 8  9 10 11 12 13 14
15 16 17 18 19 20 21
22 23 24 25 26 27 28
29 30 31
```

This program prints it:

```
     PRINT 10, (I, I=1,31)
10   FORMAT (1X,I2,1X,I2,1X,I2,1X,I2,1X,I2,1X,I2,1X,I2)
     END
```

The program's top statement says to print every value of I, for I = 1 to 31. The FORMAT says to print 7 integers on each line, and separate the integers by spaces.

Since 1X followed by I2 is about the same as I3, you can write the FORMAT more briefly:

```
10   FORMAT (I3,I3,I3,I3,I3,I3,I3)
```

You can be even briefer:

```
10   FORMAT (7I3)
```

Tables If T is a table having 3 rows and 5 columns, these lines will print it in the correct order:

```
     PRINT 20, T(1,1), T(1,2), T(1,3), T(1,4), T(1,5)
     PRINT 20, T(2,1), T(2,2), T(2,3), T(2,4), T(2,5)
     PRINT 20, T(3,1), T(3,2), T(3,3), T(3,4), T(3,5)
20   FORMAT (1X,5G14.6)
```

This short cut does the same thing:

```
     PRINT 20, (T(1,J), J=1,5)
     PRINT 20, (T(2,J), J=1,5)
     PRINT 20, (T(3,J), J=1,5)
20   FORMAT (1X,5G14.6)
```

Here's a shorter cut:

```
     PRINT 20, ((T(I,J), J=1,5), I=1,3)
20   FORMAT (1X,5G14.6)
```

To read the table, say:

```
     READ 10, ((T(I,J), J=1,5), I=1,3)
```

DATA

This program shows FORTRAN's DATA statement, which differs from BASIC's:

Program	Meaning
`DATA X/8.7/, Y/1.4/, Z/9.0/`	X is 8.7, Y is 1.4, and Z is 9.0.
`X=100.6`	X changes to 100.6
`PRINT 10, X,Y,Z`	The computer will print:
`10    FORMAT (1X,3G14.6)`	100.600 1.40000 9.00000
`END`	

In that DATA statement, you must write 9.0, not 9: the number must be real, since Z is real.

The DATA statement resembles these three statements —

```
X=8.7
Y=1.4
Z=9.0
```

but is faster.

Here's another way to type the DATA statement:

```
DATA X,Y,Z/8.7,1.4,9.0/
```

It says X, Y, and Z are 8.7, 1.4, and 9.0 respectively.

Like the DIMENSION statement, the DATA statement belongs at the very top of the program. If you want both a DIMENSION statement and a DATA statement, put the DIMENSION statement first.

This DATA statement says A, B, C, D, and E are all 1.7, and X, Y, and Z are all 9.6:

```
DATA A,B,C,D,E,X,Y,Z/1.7,1.7,1.7,1.7,1.7,9.6,9.6,9.6/
```

Since the first 5 numbers are 1.7, and the next 3 numbers are 9.6, you can write more briefly:

```
DATA A,B,C,D,E,X,Y,Z/5*1.7,3*9.6/
```

Subscripted DATA   To make A be this list —

```
81.7
92.6
25.3
49.8
72.1
68.8
```

begin your program with these lines:

```
DIMENSION A(6)
DATA A/81.7,92.6,25.3,49.8,72.1,68.8/
```

To make T be this table —

```
8.4 9.7
5.1 6.8
2.5 7.2
6.3 9.8
```

begin your program with these lines:

```
DIMENSION T(4,2)
DATA T/8.4,5.1,2.5,6.3,9.7,6.8,7.2,9.8/
```

Notice you must list the entire first column, then the second.

String variables

This program works on most computers:

```
      N='UP'
      PRINT 10, N
10    FORMAT (1X,A2)
      END
```

The top line says N is the string 'UP'. The next line says to print N, using the format in line 10. **The A2 format means a 2-character string.** (The A is derived from the word Alphabet.) The computer will print:

```
UP
```

Different versions

Some computers allow apostrophes only in FORMAT, DATA, and CALL statements. (You'll learn about CALL statements later.) On such computers, the statement N='UP' is illegal. Instead say:

```
      DATA N/'UP'/
```

Restrictions

A string statement should look like an integer: it should begin with the letter I, J, K, L, M, or N. You can say N='UP' but shouldn't say X='UP'.

The string a variable stands for must be short. You can say N='UP' but not N='SUPERCALIFRAGILISTICEXPIALIDOCIOUS'. The longest permissible string depends on your computer:

Computer	Longest string allowed
PDP-11 (using FORTRAN IV)	2 characters
PDP-11 (using FORTRAN IV-PLUS), IBM	4 characters
PDP-10, PDP-20, Honeywell	5 characters
CDC	10 characters

Fancy examples

Examine this program:

```
      PRINT 10
10    FORMAT (1X,'DO YOU LIKE ME?')
      READ 20, IREPLY
20    FORMAT (A1)
      IF (IREPLY .EQ. 'Y') PRINT 30
30    FORMAT (1X,'I LIKE YOU TOO!')
      PRINT 40
40    FORMAT (1X,'SO LONG, BUSTER.')
      END
```

The first pair of lines make the computer print DO YOU LIKE ME? The next pair set IREPLY equal to the first letter the human types. If the human types YESIREE, the computer will set IREPLY equal to 'Y' and will therefore print:

```
I LIKE YOU TOO!
SO LONG, BUSTER.
```

But if the human types NOT AT ALL, the computer will set IREPLY equal to 'N' and will therefore print just:

```
SO LONG, BUSTER.
```

In that program, the string is called IREPLY instead of REPLY, to make it an integer.

Advanced example:

```
      DIMENSION NAME(25)
      PRINT 10
10    FORMAT (1X,'WHAT IS YOUR NAME?')
      READ 20, NAME
20    FORMAT (25A2)
      PRINT 30, NAME
30    FORMAT (1X,'I HATE ANYONE NAMED ',25A2)
      END
```

The top line says NAME will be a list of 25 elements. The next pair of lines print WHAT IS YOUR NAME? If the human answers —

```
BARTHOLOMEW HIERONYMOUS MCGILLICUDDY, M.D.
```

the format in line 20 sets NAME equal to 25 two-character strings:

NAME(1) is 'BA'	NAME(10) is 'YM'	NAME(19) is ', '
NAME(2) is 'RT'	NAME(11) is 'OU'	NAME(20) is 'M.'
NAME(3) is 'HO'	NAME(12) is 'S '	NAME(21) is 'D.'
NAME(4) is 'LO'	NAME(13) is 'MC'	NAME(22) is ' '
NAME(5) is 'ME'	NAME(14) is 'GI'	NAME(23) is ' '
NAME(6) is 'W '	NAME(15) is 'LL'	NAME(24) is ' '
NAME(7) is 'HI'	NAME(16) is 'IC'	NAME(25) is ' '
NAME(8) is 'ER'	NAME(17) is 'UD'	
NAME(9) is 'ON'	NAME(18) is 'DY'	

Format 30 prints:

```
I HATE ANYONE NAMED BARTHOLOMEW HIERONYMOUS MCGILLICUDDY, M.D.
```

To make that program run faster, use fewer strings. For example, if you have a CDC computer, each string can be as long as 10 characters, so you need only 5 strings to make 50 characters:

```
      DIMENSION NAME(5)
      PRINT 10
10    FORMAT (1X,'WHAT IS YOUR NAME?')
      READ 20, NAME
20    FORMAT (5A10)
      PRINT 30, NAME
30    FORMAT (1X,'I HATE ANYONE NAMED ',5A10)
      END
```

FORTRAN 77 strings

On computer having FORTRAN 77, and on IBM computers using WATFIV, you can request super-long strings:

```
      CHARACTER*50 NAME
      PRINT 10
10    FORMAT (1X,'WHAT IS YOUR NAME?')
      READ 20, NAME
20    FORMAT (A50)
      PRINT 30, NAME
30    FORMAT (1X,'I HATE ANYONE NAMED ',A50)
      END
```

The top line requests that NAME be a 50-character string. Like the DIMENSION statement, the CHARACTER statement must be put at the very top of the program, above even the DATA statements.

FUNCTIONS

To do advanced math, use FORTRAN's functions.

Square root

This program finds the square root of 9:

```
     A=SQRT(9.0)
     PRINT 10, A
10   FORMAT (1X,G14.6)
     END
```

The computer will print:

```
3.00000
```

In that program, you must say SQRT(9.0), not SQRT(9). If you say SQRT(9), the computer will either gripe or print a wrong answer.

The number in parentheses must be real. That's why you can say SQRT(9.0) but not SQRT(9). You can say SQRT(8.0+1.0) but not SQRT(8+1). You can say SQRT(X) but not SQRT(J).

Be careful when you translate from BASIC to FORTRAN: in BASIC, you say SQR; in FORTRAN, you say SQRT instead.

This program prints a table, showing the square root of 2.0, the square root of 3.0, the square root of 4.0, the square root of 5.0, etc.:

```
     X=2.0
10   Y=SQRT(X)
     PRINT 20, X,Y
20   FORMAT (1X,2G14.6)
     X=X+1.0
     GO TO 10
     END
```

The computer will print:

```
2.00000      1.41421
3.00000      1.73205
4.00000      2.00000
5.00000      2.23607
6.00000      2.44949
7.00000      2.64575
8.00000      2.82843
9.00000      3.00000
10.0000      3.16228
etc.
```

FLOAT

If you say FLOAT, the computer will create a FLOATing-point number (in other words, a real number), by using an integer. For example, FLOAT(3) is 3.0. If J is 7, then FLOAT(J) is 7.0.

The word FLOAT can help you solve the following problems. . . .

Find the square root of an integer J

Unfortunately, you aren't allowed to say SQRT(J), because what you take the square root of must be a real number. You can say SQRT(X) but not SQRT(J). *Solution:* say X=J, and then say SQRT(X). *Shorter solution:* say SQRT(FLOAT(J)).

Divide J by K accurately

Unfortunately, saying J/K gives an inaccurate answer, because when the computer divides integers it gives an integer answer, instead of an accurate real answer. *Solution:* say X=J, then Y=K, then X/Y. *Shorter solution:* say FLOAT(J)/FLOAT(K).

Random numbers

Here's how to set R equal to a random decimal between 0 and 1:

Computer	What to say
CDC	R=RANF(0)
PDP-10, PDP-11	R=RAN(0)
PDP-11	R=RAN(ISEED,ISEED2)

To randomize the random numbers on PDP-10 and PDP-20 computers, put these lines near the top of your program:

```
CALL TIME(ISEED,ISEED2)
CALL SETRAN(MOD(ISEED/2+ISEED2/2, 2147483648))
```

On other computers, randomizing is even more complicated; ask the people who run your computer center.

Maxima and minima

To find the maximum real number in a list, ask for AMAX1.

For example, AMAX1(4.7, 2.8, 41.6, 9.2, 82.3, 9.7) is 82.3. And AMIN1(4.7, 2.8, 41.6, 9.2, 82.3, 9.7) is the minimum, which is 2.8.

If the numbers in the list are integers, say MAX0 instead of AMAX1, and say MIN0 instead of AMIN1. When you type "MAX0" and "MIN0", make sure you end with a zero, not the letter "oh".

Absolute value

ABS(X) means the ABSolute value of X; in other words, X without its minus sign. For example:

```
ABS(-5.2) is 5.2
ABS(-7.0) is 7.0
ABS(9.3)  is 9.3
```

For integers, say IABS instead of ABS. For example, IABS(-7) is 7.

Remainder

When you divide 11 by 4, the remainder is 3:

$$4 \overline{)\, 11} \quad \begin{array}{c} 2 \\ -8 \\ \hline 3 \end{array} \text{ is the remainder}$$

If you ask for MOD(11,4) the computer will divide 11 by 4 and get the remainder, which is 3; so MOD(11,4) is 3.

Use MOD for integers; use AMOD for reals. For example, AMOD(11.0, 4.0) is 3.0.

Trigonometry

If your computer has FORTRAN 77, or your computer is an IBM having FORTRAN H-EXTENDED, or your computer is a PDP-11 having FORTRAN IV-PLUS, you can use these trigonometric functions:

Symbol	Meaning
SIN(X)	the SINe of X radians
COS(X)	the COSine of X radians
TAN(X)	the TANgent of X radians
ASIN(X)	the ArcSINe of X in radians; the number whose sine is X
ACOS(X)	the ArcCOSine of X in radians; the number whose cosine is X
ATAN(X)	the ArcTANgent of X in radians; the number whose tangent is X
SINH(X)	the SINe Hyperbolic of X
COSH(X)	the COSine Hyperbolic of X
TANH(X)	the TANgent Hyperbolic of X

If your computer is old-fashioned, it restricts you:

Old-fashioned system	Restriction
PDP-10, PDP-20	you can't say TAN(X)
CDC	you can't say SINH(X) or COSH(X)
other IBM computers	say ARSIN(X), not ASIN(X); say ARCOS(X), not ACOS(X)
FORTRAN IV computers	you can't say TAN(X), ASIN(X), ACOS(X), SINH(X), COSH(X)

You can replace X by any *real* number. For example, you can say SIN(4.0) but not SIN(4); you can say SIN(Y) but not SIN(J).

Be careful when you translate from BASIC to FORTRAN: in BASIC, you say ATN; in FORTRAN, you say ATAN instead.

You've seen that SIN(X) is the sine of X *radians*. But what's the sine of X *degrees*? On PDP-10 and PDP-20 computers, you can find the sine of X degrees by asking for SIND(X); and you can find the cosine of X degrees by asking for COSD(X).

ATAN2(Y,X) is about the same as ATAN(Y/X), but is faster, more accurate, and gives a useful answer even when X is zero or negative. ATAN2(Y,X) is the angle (in radians) of the line that goes through the origin and the point (X,Y).

Calculus

You can use these functions:

Function	Meaning
EXP(X)	e^X
ALOG(X)	$\log_e X$
ALOG10(X)	$\log_{10} X$

You can replace X by any real number, but not by an integer. Each of those functions produces a *real* answer, since none of them begins with I, J, K, L, M, or N.

The logarithm function is called ALOG instead of LOG, to avoid beginning with L. Be careful when you translate from BASIC to FORTRAN: in BASIC, you say LOG; in FORTRAN, you say ALOG instead.

EXOTIC FEATURES

Let's take off our handcuffs and go wild!

Let's go beyond integers and reals, to other kinds of numbers that are wilder: **double precision** and **complex**.

Let's go beyond standard functions and invent our *own* functions. Let's go beyond standard statements and invent our *own* statements, by using subroutines and comments. Let's go beyond the DATA statement and invent data *files*.

Here we go. . . .

Comments

If you type C instead of a line number, the computer will ignore the line.

```
      N=50+13
C  I HATE COMPUTERS!
      PRINT 10, N
10    FORMAT (1X,I14)
      END
```

The computer will ignore the Comment. The computer will print 63.

The C in FORTRAN is like the REMARK in BASIC: use it to document your program.

DOUBLE PRECISION

Some computers are more accurate than others:

Computer	Accuracy for real numbers
PDP-11, IBM	7 digits
PDP-10, PDP-20, Honeywell	8 digits
CDC	14 digits

For example, suppose you feed this program to a PDP-11 or IBM:

```
      A=5398.1642376236
      PRINT 10, A
10    FORMAT (1X,F15.10)
      END
```

Expect the first 7 digits the computer prints to be correct (5398.164), but the remaining digits it prints to be wrong: they arise from round-off error inside the computer.

A PDP-11 or IBM prints *some* numbers to an accuracy of 8 digits and others to an accuracy of just 6 digits, but 7 digits is typical.

For real numbers, I recommend you use a G14.6 format, because it's safe: it prints just the first 6 digits. If you want to see further digits that are probably correct, use these formats instead:

Computer	Format	What the format does
PDP-11, IBM	G15.7	prints the first 7 digits
PDP-10, PDP-20, Honeywell	G16.8	prints the first 8 digits
CDC	G22.14	prints the first 14 digits

You can obtain extra accuracy, by requesting **double precision**:

Computer	Accuracy for double precision	Format
PDP-11	14 digits	D22.14
PDP-10 (using KA), Honeywell	16 digits	D24.16
IBM	17 digits	D25.17
PDP-10 (using KI or KL), PDP-20	18 digits	D26.18
CDC	29 digits	D37.29

Each of these programs computes the square root of 6.3×10^8 on a PDP-11 computer:

Using reals

```
      A=SQRT(6.3E8)
      PRINT 10, A
10    FORMAT (1X,G15.7)
      END
```

Using double precision

```
      DOUBLE PRECISION A
      A=DSQRT(6.3D8)
      PRINT 10, A
10    FORMAT (1X,D22.14)
      END
```

The program on the left computes 7 digits. The program on the right computes 14. Comparing the programs, you'll notice four differences:

1. For double precision you must use **double precision numbers**. Instead of saying 6.3E8, say 6.3D8. The D means Double precision.

Real number	Double precision
6.3E8	6.3D8
29.6	29.6D0

                      ↑ this is a zero

2. For double precision, you must use **double precision functions**. Instead of saying SQRT, say DSQRT.

Real function	Double precision
SQRT	DSQRT
AMAX1	DMAX1
AMIN1	DMIN1
ABS	DABS
AMOD	DMOD
EXP	DEXP
ALOG	DLOG
ALOG10	DLOG10
SIN	DSIN
COS	DCOS
TAN	DTAN
ASIN	DASIN
ACOS	DACOS
ATAN	DATAN
ATAN2	DATAN2
SINH	DSINH
COSH	DCOSH
TANH	DTANH

3. For double precision, you must use **double precision variables**. Normally, the variable A would be real; to make it double precision instead, say:

```
DOUBLE PRECISION A
```

Normally, the variables LENGTH and MASS would be integers, and SPEED would be real; to make them all double precision, say:

```
DOUBLE PRECISION LENGTH,MASS,SPEED
```

Like the DIMENSION and CHARACTER statements, the DOUBLE PRECISION statement must be put at the very top of the program, above even the DATA statements. If you say —

```
IMPLICIT DOUBLE PRECISION(D)
```

every variable whose first letter is D will automatically be double precision; for example, DISTAN and DIAMET and DSIZE will automatically be double precision.

4. For double precision you must use **double precision formats**. Instead of a G format, use D22.14, or whichever D format is appropriate for your computer.

Expense Although double precision arithmetic is more precise than real arithmetic, it's also more expensive: it consumes more of the computer's time, and the numbers consume more of the computer's memory.

Combinations If you combine an integer or a real number with a double precision number, the answer will be double precision.

COMPLEX

In mathematics, the square root of -1 is called i. So i^2 is -1. The number i obeys most of the rules of algebra:

```
i+i  is 2i
2i+3i is 5i
(8+2i) + (7+3i) is 15+5i
(8+2i) * (7+3i) is 8*7 + 8*3i + 2i*7 + 2i*3i,
           which is 56 + 24i + 14i + 6i²,
           which is 56 + 24i + 14i + -6,
           which is 50 + 38i
```

The number i is neither positive nor negative nor zero; it's pictured instead as being above the real number line:

```
            i
-5 -4 -3 -2 -1  0  1  2  3  4  5
```

2i is further above the real number line: it's 2 units above 0. Another example: 5+2i is 2 units above 5.

A number that involves i is called **complex**. So 5+2i is complex. Its **real part** is 5, its **imaginary part** is 2, and its **conjugate** is 5-2i.

This program multiplies 8+2i by 7+3i and prints the correct answer, 50+38i:

```
     COMPLEX B
     B=(8.0, 2.0) * (7.0, 3.0)
     PRINT 10, B
10   FORMAT (1X,2G14.6)
     END
```

FORTRAN says (8.0, 2.0) instead of 8+2i. The decimal points and parentheses are required.

To make B complex instead of real, say COMPLEX B. Like the DIMENSION and CHARACTER and DOUBLE PRECISION statements, the COMPLEX statement must be put at the very top of the program, above even the DATA statements.

To print B, use the G14.6 format twice (once for the real part, and once for the imaginary part). The computer will print:

```
50.0000      38.0000
```

If you say IMPLICIT COMPLEX(C), every variable whose first letter is C will automatically be complex.

Although you can write 8+2i as (8.0, 2.0), you cannot write X+Yi as (X, Y); instead write CMPLX(X, Y).

Here's the rule: to build a complex number from variables instead of from constants, say CMPLX. The variables that the complex number is built from must be real.

If B is complex, you can use these functions:

Function	Meaning
CSQRT(B)	the complex number that's the square root of B
CSIN(B)	the complex number that's the sine of B
CCOS(B)	the complex number that's the cosine of B
CEXP(B)	the complex number that's e^B
CLOG(B)	the complex number that's log B
CABS(B)	the real number that's the absolute value of B
REAL(B)	the real number that's the real part of B
AIMAG(B)	the real number that's the imaginary part of B
CONJG(B)	the complex number that's the conjugate of B

This program finds the square root of -9 and prints the correct answer, 3i:

```
     COMPLEX B,Z
     B=-9
     Z=CSQRT(B)
     PRINT 10, Z
10   FORMAT (1X,2G14.6)
     END
```

Since the top line says B is complex, the second line makes B the complex number -9+0i. The next line makes Z the square root of -9+0i, which is 0+3i. The computer will print the 0 and the 3:

```
0.000000      3.00000
```

Since that program sets B equal to -9+0i, which FORTRAN writes as (-9.0, 0.0), you can shorten the program to this:

```
     COMPLEX Z
     Z=CSQRT( (-9.0, 0.0) )
     PRINT 10, Z
10   FORMAT (1X,2G14.6)
     END
```

Make sure the number inside CSQRT's parentheses is complex: you need the decimal points, comma, and parentheses.

When the computer combines a complex number with an integer, a real, or a double precision number, the result is complex.

Some computers limit your use of complex numbers, by restrictions such as:

"Don't say a complex number equals a double precision number."
"Don't combine a complex number with a double precision number."
"Don't raise a number to a complex power."
"Don't raise a complex number to a power, unless the power is an integer."

Find out whether *your* computer has those restrictions.

Subroutines

This program is a combination of two **routines**:

```
       PRINT 10
10     FORMAT (1X,'KIDS')
       CALL YUMMY
       PRINT 20
20     FORMAT (1X,'LOLLIPOPS')
       END

       SUBROUTINE YUMMY
       PRINT 10
10     FORMAT (1X,'SUCK')
       RETURN
       END
```

Each routine ends with the word END.

The first routine is called the **main routine**.

The second routine is called the **subroutine**, and begins with the word SUBROUTINE. I decided to name it YUMMY, so its top line says SUBROUTINE YUMMY.

Above the word SUBROUTINE, I put a blank line. That blank line is optional; it helps humans find where the subroutine begins.

In the main routine, the top pair of lines makes the computer print:

```
KIDS
```

The next line says CALL YUMMY, which makes the computer skip down to subroutine YUMMY. Subroutine YUMMY makes the computer print —

```
SUCK
```

and then RETURN to the main routine, which finishes by printing:

```
LOLLIPOPS
```

Altogether, the program prints:

```
KIDS
SUCK
LOLLIPOPS
```

Notice that line 10 in the main routine is different from line 10 in the subroutine. Similarly, an X in the main routine is different from one in the subroutine:

```
       X=3.4
       CALL FUNNY
       PRINT 10,X
10     FORMAT (1X,G14.6)
       END

       SUBROUTINE FUNNY
       X=925.1
       Y=X+1.0
       PRINT 10, Y
10     FORMAT (1X,G14.6)
       RETURN
       END
```

The computer will set the main routine's X equal to 3.4. Then it will call FUNNY. The X in FUNNY is 925.1, so Y is 926.1, and the computer will print:

```
   926.100
```

When the computer returns to the main routine, it will print the main routine's X, which is still:

```
   3.40000
```

Passing information between routines

To pass information from one routine to another, put the information in parentheses:

```
       A=5.2
       CALL LEMON(A)
       PRINT 10, A
10     FORMAT (1X,G14.6)
       END

       SUBROUTINE LEMON(X)
       PRINT 100, X
100    FORMAT (1X,G14.6)
       X=7.1
       RETURN
       END
```

The computer sets A equal to 5.2. Then it calls LEMON. **The A and X in parentheses mean: the main routine's A is the subroutine's X**, so the subroutine's X is 5.2. Line 100 prints:

```
   5.20000
```

The next line changes X to 7.1. When the computer returns to the main routine, the main routine's A is the subroutine's X, so the main routine's A is 7.1. Line 10 prints:

```
   7.10000
```

A harder example:

```
       P=2.1
       CALL JUNK(P)
       PRINT 10, P
10     FORMAT (1X,G14.6)
       END

       SUBROUTINE JUNK(P)
       P=3.0*P
       RETURN
       END
```

The computer sets P equal to 2.1 and then calls JUNK. **The P in parentheses means: the main routine's P is the subroutine's P**. The subroutine triples P, so P becomes 6.3. When the computer returns to the main routine, line 10 prints:

```
   6.30000
```

Another example:

```
       Q=1.4
       CALL FAT(5.0, Q+.3, R)
       PRINT 10, R
10     FORMAT (1X,G14.6)
       END

       SUBROUTINE FAT(X, Y, Z)
       Z=X+Y
       RETURN
       END
```

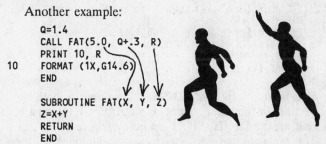

When the main routine calls FAT, the subroutine's X is 5.0; Y is Q+.3, which is 1.7; and Z is R, which is undefined. The subroutine sets Z equal to X+Y, which is 6.7. When the computer returns to the main routine, the main routine's R is the subroutine's Z, which is 6.7. Line 10 prints:

```
   6.70000
```

In that CALL, you must say 5.0, not 5, since X must be real. Saying 5 will confuse the computer and make it print a wrong answer.

Sum & average of a trio

This subroutine finds the sum and average of three real numbers — X, Y, and Z:

```
      SUBROUTINE STAT(X, Y, Z, SUM, AVERAG)
      SUM=X+Y+Z
      AVERAG=SUM/3.0
      RETURN
      END
```

This main routine uses STAT to find the sum and average of 8.1, 2.6, and 9.3:

```
      CALL STAT(8.1, 2.6, 9.3, SUM, AVERAG)
      PRINT 10, SUM,AVERAG
10    FORMAT (1X,2G14.6)
      END
```

This subroutine finds the sum and average of three *double precision* numbers:

```
      SUBROUTINE DSTAT(X, Y, Z, SUM, AVERAG)
      DOUBLE PRECISION X, Y, Z, SUM, AVERAG
      SUM=X+Y+Z
      AVERAG=SUM/3D0
      RETURN
      END
```

This main routine uses DSTAT to find the sum and average of π, e, and my phone number (6662666):

```
      DOUBLE PRECISION SUM, AVERAG
      CALL DSTAT(3.1415926535898D0, 2.7182818284590D0, 6662666D0, SUM,
     6AVERAG)
      PRINT 10, SUM, AVERAG
10    FORMAT (1X,2D22.14)
      END
```

You must say DOUBLE PRECISION in both the main routine and the subroutine.

Sum & average of a long list

This subroutine finds the sum and average of $X_1, X_2, X_3, \ldots, X_N$:

```
      SUBROUTINE STAT2(X, N, SUM, AVERAG)
      DIMENSION X(N)
      SUM=0.0
      DO 10 I=1,N
         SUM=SUM+X(I)
10    CONTINUE
      AVERAG=SUM/N
      RETURN
      END
```

This main routine uses STAT2 to find the sum and average of 8.4, 9.6, 20.1, 7.2, 91.5, and 3.6:

```
      DIMENSION X(6)
      DATA X/8.4,9.6,20.1,7.2,91.5,3.6/
      CALL STAT2(X, 6, SUM, AVERAG)
      PRINT 10, SUM,AVERAG
10    FORMAT (1X,2G14.6)
      END
```

You must put the DIMENSION statement in both the main routine and the subroutine. In the main routine, the DIMENSION must be a constant (6); in the subroutine, the DIMENSION can be a variable (N).

This main routine asks you to input some numbers, then prints their sum and average by using STAT2:

```
      DIMENSION X(100)
      PRINT 10
10    FORMAT (1X,'HOW MANY NUMBERS WOULD YOU LIKE TO GIVE ME?')
      READ *, N
      PRINT 20
20    FORMAT (1X,'TYPE THE NUMBERS')
      READ *, (X(I), I=1,N)
      CALL STAT(X, N, SUM, AVERAG)
      PRINT 10, SUM,AVERAG
10    FORMAT (1X,'THE SUM IS',G14.6,' AND THE AVERAGE IS',G14.6)
      END
```

That DIMENSION statement lets you input up to 100 numbers.

If a main routine says DIMENSION X(100), and X is passed between the main routine and the subroutine, the subroutine's DIMENSION statement must say no more than X(100): if the subroutine's DIMENSION statement says X(N), the N must be no more than 100.

Passing double subscripts

For *double* subscripts, the main routine's DIMENSION statement must be *exactly* the same as the subroutine's.

For example, suppose the main routine says DIMENSION X(25,4). Then the subroutine must say DIMENSION X(25,4) also. The subroutine must not say DIMENSION X(20,3). If the subroutine says DIMENSION X(M,N), the M must be exactly 25.

Famous subroutines

The **Scientific Subroutine Package (SSP)** is a collection of subroutines written by IBM that do statistics, calculus, equation-solving, and advanced math. The **Calcomp subroutines** make the computer operate a Calcomp plotter (a device that draws fancy shapes on paper, by using a felt-tip or ballpoint pen).

Most large computers store the SSP and Calcomp subroutines on disk permanently. Ask the people in your computer center how to combine your own main routines with those subroutines, and how to put your *own* library of subroutines onto the disk.

How to write a big program

If you and your friends want to write a big program together, divide the problem into a main routine and several subroutines, and have each person write one routine.

Although you'll need a group conference to decide what the SUBROUTINE and CALL statements will be, you don't have to agree on the names of variables, since the names of subroutine variables have nothing to do with the names of main-routine variables.

Your own functions

Instead of using functions such as SQRT and ABS, you can invent your *own* functions. Here's how to invent a function called F, and how to use the function you've invented:

```
    A=F(5.2)+1.0
    PRINT 10, A
10  FORMAT (1X,G14.6)
    END

    FUNCTION F(X)
    F=2.0*X
    RETURN
    END
```

The program consists of two routines. The first routine is the *main* routine. The second routine is the definition of the FUNCTION F. Each routine ends with the word END.

The main routine's top line requires the computer to find F(5.2), so the computer hunts for the definition of FUNCTION F. The definition says F is twice 5.2, which is 10.4. So A is 11.4. The computer will print:

```
11.40000
```

Like a subroutine, a function definition can be very long and have many variables in parentheses.

Naming your function
You can give your function the name F or G or any other name, such as MASS. If the function's name begins with I, J, K, L, M, or N, the computer will assume its value is an integer.

If you want the function MASS(X) to be double precision instead of an integer, begin your main routine by saying —

```
DOUBLE PRECISION MASS
```

and begin your function definition with this line:

```
DOUBLE PRECISION FUNCTION MASS(X)
```

Files

The computer can write its answers onto a data file:

```
    A=14.6+75.2
    WRITE(3,10) A
10  FORMAT (1X,G14.6)
    WRITE(7,20)
20  FORMAT (1X,'TINA, PLEASE TICKLE MY TUBA')
    END
```

Since A is 89.8, the second line makes the computer write 89.8 onto "file 3", using line 10's format. The next pair of lines make the computer write onto "file 7", using line 20's format; so the computer will write TINA, PLEASE TICKLE MY TUBA onto file 7.

Before running that program, tell the computer where to put files 3 and 7. You can make the computer put them on a disk, line printer, tape, terminal, or wherever else you please. Ask the people in your computer center how to tell the computer where to put the files.

If your program has many statements saying to write onto file 3, the computer will write many lines onto file 3, so the file will become long.

Use carriage controls only if the file is on a line printer or terminal.

If you say —

```
READ(4,30) X
```

the computer will read the value of X from file 4, using line 30's format. If you say file 4 is the card reader, the computer will wait for you to feed in a card; it you say file 4 is your terminal, the computer will wait for you to type on the terminal; if you say file 4 is on a tape or disk, the computer will assume you created the file before running the program.

For handling files, the word READ works even on PDP computers.

For PDP-10 and PDP-20 computers, here's how to make file 3 be on disk and named JOE. . . . Near the beginning of your program, say:

```
OPEN(UNIT=3, DEVICE='DSK', FILE='JOE.')
```

Near the end of your program, say:

```
CLOSE(UNIT=3)
```

COBOL

Like BASIC and PASCAL, **COBOL** is a computer language. "COBOL" is pronounced "koe ball" and stands for "COmmon Business Oriented Language".

COBOL solves *business* problems that involve *large* files of data, so COBOL's used mainly by *businesses* having *maxicomputers*. But today, you can use COBOL even on minicomputers and microcomputers.

In the "help wanted" section of your local newspaper, many ads that say "programmer wanted" are placed by businesses that have maxicomputers and use COBOL. To get a job through the "help wanted" section, a knowledge of COBOL will help you more than PASCAL or FORTRAN.

The first version of COBOL was called **COBOL 60**, because it was invented in 1960. Then came **COBOL 61**, **COBOL 65**, **COBOL 68**, **COBOL 74**, and **COBOL 85**. Today, most computers still use COBOL 74 or a variation of it. This chapter explains how to write COBOL programs that work on most computers.

During the 1960's and early 1970's, COBOL programmers used a style called "easy programming". Today, most COBOL programmers use a more sophisticated style, called **structured programming**. This chapter explains structured programming. Though it's harder to learn than easy programming, it will make your boss kiss you.

Simple programs

Every COBOL program is written as an outline. Here's a short outline; to turn it into a COBOL program, just fill in the blanks:

```
IDENTIFICATION DIVISION.
PROGRAM-ID.
        The program's name.
AUTHOR.
        Your name.

ENVIRONMENT DIVISION.
CONFIGURATION SECTION.
SOURCE-COMPUTER.
        The computer's name.
OBJECT-COMPUTER.
        The computer's name again.

DATA DIVISION.

PROCEDURE DIVISION.
MAIN-ROUTINE.
        What you want the computer to do.
        STOP RUN.
```

For example, here's a COBOL program I wrote:

Program	Reason
IDENTIFICATION DIVISION.	
PROGRAM-ID.	
HARRY.	The program's name is HARRY.
AUTHOR.	
RUSS WALTER.	My name is Russ Walter.
ENVIRONMENT DIVISION.	
CONFIGURATION SECTION.	
SOURCE-COMPUTER.	
DECSYSTEM-20.	My computer's a DECsystem-20.
OBJECT-COMPUTER.	
DECSYSTEM-20.	
DATA DIVISION.	
PROCEDURE DIVISION.	
MAIN-ROUTINE.	
DISPLAY "LIFE STINKS."	I want the computer to gripe.
STOP RUN.	

When I run that program, the computer will print:

```
LIFE STINKS
```

Every COBOL program consists of four parts. The first part of the program is called the IDENTIFICATION DIVISION: it includes the program's name and the programmer's name. The second part of the program is called the ENVIRONMENT DIVISION: it includes the computer's name. The third part of the program is called the DATA DIVISION; for a simple program, the DATA DIVISION is blank. The fourth part of the program is the PROCEDURE DIVISION: it says what you want the computer to do.

The order is important: the IDENTIFICATION DIVISION must come *first*, then the ENVIRONMENT DIVISION, then the DATA DIVISION, and finally the PROCEDURE DIVISION. So to become an expert COBOL programmer, you must memorize: "IDENTIFICATION, ENVIRONMENT, DATA, PROCEDURE".

To memorize that easily, memorize this easy sentence: "I enjoy data processing". In that sentence, the words begin with the letters "I E D P" — and so do the four COBOL divisions.

In the program, each blank that you fill is called a **paragraph**. In the first paragraph, write the program's name; in the next paragraph, write your *own* name; in the next two paragraphs, write the computer's name; and in the last paragraph, write what you want the computer to do. The first paragraph is called the PROGRAM-ID; the next paragraph is called the AUTHOR; the next two paragraphs are called the SOURCE-COMPUTER and the OBJECT-COMPUTER; and the last paragraph is called the MAIN-ROUTINE.

Each paragraph is indented. To indent on PDP and Eclipse computers, type a controlled I.

In COBOL, the only important punctuation mark is the period. When writing a simple program, **put a period at the end of each line**. COBOL never requires commas or semicolons.

Don't forget the hyphens! Put a hyphen in PROGRAM-ID, SOURCE-COMPUTER, OBJECT-COMPUTER, and MAIN-ROUTINE.

Use correct spacing.

```
Right:    DISPLAY "BURP".
Wrong:    DIS PLAY "BURP".
Wrong:    DISPLAY"BURP".
Wrong:    DISPLAY "BURP" .
```

In the paragraphs that are called SOURCE-COMPUTER and OBJECT-COMPUTER, you must type the computer's name correctly. Here are the correct names for some famous computers:

```
IBM-360.
IBM-370.
PDP-11.
DECSYSTEM-10.    (It means you have a PDP-10.)
DECSYSTEM-20.    (It means you have a PDP-20.)
ECLIPSE C300.
6600.            (It means you have a CDC 6600.)
```

Don't forget the hyphens!

Go ahead: try writing your *own* COBOL program. In the PROCEDURE DIVISION, remember to say DISPLAY:

```
BASIC:    10 PRINT "LIFE STINKS"
PASCAL:   WRITELN('LIFE STINKS');
COBOL:    DISPLAY "LIFE STINKS".
```

♦ <u>Old-fashioned computers</u> On IBM computers, instead of using quotation marks, you must use apostrophes.

```
Most computers:  DISPLAY "LIFE STINKS".
IBM computers:   DISPLAY 'LIFE STINKS'.
```

On IBM and CDC computers, you must indent the entire program, like this (each ■ represents a blank space):

```
⟨7 blanks⟩ ⟨8th column⟩
■■■■■■■IDENTIFICATION DIVISION.
■■■■■■■PROGRAM-ID.
■■■■■■■■■■■HARRY.
⟨7 blanks⟩⟨4 blanks⟩
⟨11 blanks⟩    ⟨12th column⟩
```

On those computers, each paragraph begins in column 12, and must not go farther to the right than column 72. (The computer ignores everything in columns 73-80.)

Abridgments

If you're lazy, you can omit the AUTHOR paragraph:

Complete IDENTIFICATION DIVISION
```
IDENTIFICATION DIVISION.
PROGRAM-ID.
      HARRY.
AUTHOR.
      RUSS WALTER.
```

Abridged version
```
IDENTIFICATION DIVISION.
PROGRAM-ID.
      HARRY.
```

If you're lazy, *and you're using a PDP-10, PDP-20, Eclipse, or IBM computer*, you can omit the CONFIGURATION SECTION, SOURCE-COMPUTER, and OBJECT-COMPUTER:

Complete ENVIRONMENT DIVISION
```
ENVIRONMENT DIVISION.
CONFIGURATION SECTION.
SOURCE-COMPUTER.
      The computer's name.
OBJECT-COMPUTER.
      The computer's name.
```

Abridged version
```
ENVIRONMENT DIVISION.
```

If you're *very* lazy, and you're using a PDP-10 or PDP-20 computer, you can abridge the program even further, so that the entire program looks like this:

```
IDENTIFICATION DIVISION.
PROCEDURE DIVISION.
      DISPLAY "LIFE STINKS".
      STOP RUN.
```

But if you're working for a big company, your employer will expect you to *not* be lazy: if you're lazy, you get fired!

Fancy displays

You've seen that every COBOL program consists of four divisions: IDENTIFICATION, ENVIRONMENT, DATA, and PROCEDURE. The most important division is the PROCEDURE DIVISION. Let's look at it more closely.

Here's a cute PROCEDURE DIVISION:

```
PROCEDURE DIVISION.
MAIN-ROUTINE.
      DISPLAY "BILLIE AND BONNIE".
      DISPLAY "BURP".
      STOP RUN.
```

It makes the computer display:

```
BILLIE AND BONNIE
BURP
```

Another example:

```
PROCEDURE DIVISION.
MAIN-ROUTINE.
      DISPLAY "FLU" "SHED".
      STOP RUN.
```

The computer will display FLU and SHED on the same line:

```
FLUSHED
```

PERFORM

Let's make the computer display "I LOVE YOU", then display "I HATE YOU" six times, then display "I AM CONFUSED", like this:

```
I LOVE YOU
I HATE YOU
I HATE YOU
I HATE YOU
I HATE YOU
I HATE YOU
I HATE YOU
I AM CONFUSED
```

Here's the PROCEDURE DIVISION:

```
PROCEDURE DIVISION.
MAIN-ROUTINE.
        DISPLAY "I LOVE YOU".
        PERFORM EXPRESS-THE-HATRED 6 TIMES.
        DISPLAY "I AM CONFUSED".
        STOP RUN.
EXPRESS-THE-HATRED.
        DISPLAY "I HATE YOU".
```

That PROCEDURE DIVISION consists of two paragraphs. The first paragraph is called the MAIN-ROUTINE. The second paragraph is called EXPRESS-THE-HATRED.

The computer obeys the first paragraph: it displays "I LOVE YOU", then performs the EXPRESS-THE-HATRED 6 times, then displays "I AM CONFUSED", and finally stops.

When you invent your own PROCEDURE DIVISION, the first paragraph should be called the MAIN-ROUTINE; for the other paragraphs underneath, invent whatever names you like (such as EXPRESS-THE-HATRED). A paragraph's name should be hyphenated, and should contain no more than 30 characters. (EXPRESS-THE-HATRED contains 18 characters, so it's okay.) The first paragraph is the main routine, the paragraphs underneath are subroutines. The bottom line of the main routine should say STOP RUN. In the middle of the main routine, you should say to PERFORM the subroutines.

In the example above, the main routine says to PERFORM the EXPRESS-THE-HATRED subroutine 6 times. If you'd like to see more hatred, say 100 times instead of 6:

```
        PERFORM EXPRESS-THE-HATRED 100 TIMES.
```

If you'd rather see just a *little* hatred, say just —

```
        PERFORM EXPRESS-THE-HATRED 1 TIMES.
```

or say just:

```
        PERFORM EXPRESS-THE-HATRED.
```

Let's make the computer display:

```
I KNOW THAT
YOU ARE DRIVING
ME CRAZY
YOU ARE DRIVING
ME CRAZY
YOU ARE DRIVING
ME CRAZY
YOU ARE DRIVING
ME CRAZY
YOU ARE DRIVING
ME CRAZY
AND YET I LOVE YOU
```

Here's the PROCEDURE DIVISION:

```
PROCEDURE DIVISION.
MAIN-ROUTINE.
        DISPLAY "I KNOW THAT".
        PERFORM ACT-AS-IF-GOING-INSANE 5 TIMES.
        DISPLAY "AND YET I LOVE YOU".
        STOP RUN.
ACT-AS-IF-GOING-INSANE.
        DISPLAY "YOU ARE DRIVING".
        DISPLAY "ME CRAZY".
```

Let's make the computer display:

```
THE ASTRONAUTS GO
UP
UP
UP
UP
UP
UP
UP
AND THEN THEY COME
DOWN
DOWN
DOWN
DOWN
DOWN
DOWN
DOWN
```

Here's the PROCEDURE DIVISION:

```
PROCEDURE DIVISION.
MAIN-ROUTINE.
        DISPLAY "THE ASTRONAUTS GO".
        PERFORM SHOW-THE-ASTRONAUTS-RISING 7 TIMES.
        DISPLAY "AND THEN THEY COME".
        PERFORM SHOW-THE-ASTRONAUTS-FALLING 7 TIMES.
        STOP RUN.
SHOW-THE-ASTRONAUTS-RISING.
        DISPLAY "UP".
SHOW-THE-ASTRONAUTS-FALLING.
        DISPLAY "DOWN".
```

Let's make the computer display:

```
YOU ARE VERY SWEET
HA-HA-HA!
HO-HO-HO!
YOU CANNOT BE BEAT
HA-HA-HA!
HO-HO-HO!
YOUR LIPS ARE LIKE WINE
HA-HA-HA!
HO-HO-HO!
BUT YOU SMELL LIKE TURPENTINE
HA-HA-HA!
HO-HO-HO!
YOU STINK!
```

Here's the PROCEDURE DIVISION:

```
PROCEDURE DIVISION.
MAIN-ROUTINE.
        DISPLAY "YOU ARE VERY SWEET".
        PERFORM LAUGH-A-LOT.
        DISPLAY "YOU CANNOT BE BEAT".
        PERFORM LAUGH-A-LOT.
        DISPLAY "YOUR LIPS ARE LIKE WINE".
        PERFORM LAUGH-A-LOT.
        DISPLAY "BUT YOU SMELL LIKE TURPENTINE".
        PERFORM LAUGH-A-LOT.
        DISPLAY "YOU STINK!".
        STOP RUN.
LAUGH-A-LOT.
        DISPLAY "HA-HA-HA!".
        DISPLAY "HO-HO-HO!".
```

VARIABLES

Like other languages, COBOL lets you use variables. The name of a variable can be a letter (like X or Y) or a hyphenated phrase (like NUMBER-OF-BULLIES-I-SQUIRTED). A hyphenated phrase can have up to 30 characters.

To use a variable, you must describe it in the data division, as in this example:

```
IDENTIFICATION DIVISION.
PROGRAM-ID.
        JUNK.
AUTHOR.
        RUSS WALTER.        Instead of "RUSS WALTER", write your own name.

ENVIRONMENT DIVISION.
CONFIGURATION SECTION.
SOURCE-COMPUTER.
        DECSYSTEM-20.       Instead of "DECSYSTEM-20", write your computer's name.
OBJECT-COMPUTER.
        DECSYSTEM-20.

DATA DIVISION.
WORKING-STORAGE SECTION.    In the DATA DIVISION, say WORKING-STORAGE SECTION.
01      K PICTURE IS XXX.

PROCEDURE DIVISION.
MAIN-ROUTINE.
        MOVE "HER" TO K.
        DISPLAY "PUS" K "S".
        STOP RUN.
```

In the DATA DIVISION's WORKING-STORAGE SECTION, the "01   K" says K is a variable. The PICTURE IS XXX says K is a string that has three characters; each X stands for a character. In the PROCEDURE DIVISION, the first sentence makes K become this 3-character string: "HER". The next sentence makes the computer display:

PUSHERS

When you type that program, make sure you **put a hyphen between WORKING and STORAGE**. If you forget the hyphen, the computer will act crazy, and will say that your program contains many, many errors.

Suppose you change the picture from XXX to XX, so that the DATA DIVISION and PROCEDURE DIVISION look like this:

```
DATA DIVISION
WORKING-STORAGE SECTION
01      K PICTURE IS XX.

PROCEDURE DIVISION.
MAIN-ROUTINE.
        MOVE "HER" TO K.
        DISPLAY "PUS" K "S".
        STOP RUN.
```

K will be a string having only two characters. When the computer tries to move "HER" to K, only the first two characters of "HER" will fit, so K will be "HE". The computer will display:

PUSHES

Suppose you change the picture to XXXX. K will have four characters. When the computer tries to move "HER" to K, it needs to move a fourth character also, so it moves a blank space at the end, which makes K be "HER ". The computer will display:

PUSHER S

This program shows how revolutionary politics lead to revolutionary clothing:

```
DATA DIVISION.
WORKING-STORAGE SECTION.
01      FIRST-PRESIDENT PICTURE IS XXXXXXXXXX.
01      CLEANING-METHOD PICTURE IS XXXX.

PROCEDURE DIVISION.
MAIN-ROUTINE.
        MOVE "WASHINGTON" TO FIRST-PRESIDENT.
        MOVE FIRST-PRESIDENT TO CLEANING-METHOD.
        DISPLAY CLEANING-METHOD " MY BLUE JEANS".
        STOP RUN.
```

Above the DATA DIVISION, write your own IDENTIFICATION DIVISION and ENVIRONMENT DIVISION. The DATA DIVISION says FIRST-PRESIDENT will be a string having ten characters, and CLEANING-METHOD will be a string having four. The first sentence of the MAIN-ROUTINE makes FIRST-PRESIDENT be "WASHINGTON". The next sentence tries to move "WASHINGTON" to CLEANING-METHOD; but because of CLEANING-METHOD's picture, the computer moves "WASH" instead. The computer will display:

```
WASH MY BLUE JEANS
```

To make sure you understand the word MOVE, examine this example:

```
DATA DIVISION.
WORKING-STORAGE SECTION.
01      C PICTURE IS XXX.
01      D PICTURE IS XXX.

PROCEDURE DIVISION.
MAIN-ROUTINE.
        MOVE "CAT" TO C.        C becomes "CAT".
        MOVE C TO D.            D becomes "CAT".
        DISPLAY C.              Since C is still "CAT", the computer displays "CAT".
        MOVE "HE" TO C.         C becomes "HE ".
        DISPLAY C "BLED".       The computer displays "HE BLED".
        STOP RUN.
```

COBOL allows abbreviations. You can say PIC instead of PICTURE IS, and X(7) instead of XXXXXXX.

Numeric variables

Let's make the computer add 53 and 4, and display the sum, 57. Here's how:

```
DATA DIVISION.
WORKING-STORAGE SECTION.
01      K PIC 99.

PROCEDURE DIVISION.
MAIN-ROUTINE.
        COMPUTE K = 53 + 4.
        DISPLAY K.
        STOP RUN.
```

The PIC 99 says K is a number having two digits. (Each 9 stands for a digit.) The MAIN-ROUTINE sets K equal to 53 + 4, which is 57. The computer will display:

```
57
```

In the COMPUTE statement, the equal sign and the plus sign must be surrounded by spaces.

```
Right:  COMPUTE K = 53 + 4.
Wrong:  COMPUTE K=53+4.
Wrong:  COMPUTE K = 53+4.
```

If you change the picture to 999, K will be a number having three digits. It will be 057 instead of 57. The computer will display:

```
057
```

(Exception: PDP-10 and PDP-20 computers are lazy; they don't bother to display the 0 at the left; they display just 57.)

If you change the picture to 9, K will be a number having only one digit. so K will not be 57. The computer will not display the correct sum.

Like FORTRAN, COBOL uses these operators:

Operator	Meaning
+	plus
-	minus
*	times
/	divided by
**	exponent

You must put a blank space before and after each operator:

Right	Wrong
53 + 4	53+4
7 ** 2	7**2
- J + 3	- J + 3

Like other computer languages, COBOL lets you use parentheses. Do *not* put a space after a left parenthesis:

Right

```
COMPUTE K = I * (- J + 3)
```
(no space) (spaces)

You can use these short cuts:

Sentence	Short cut
COMPUTE A = A + 7.	ADD 7 TO A.
COMPUTE B = B - 4.	SUBTRACT 4 FROM B.

Operators are allowed only in sentences that say COMPUTE, IF, UNTIL, or WHEN.

Allowed:	COMPUTE A = 2 * 3.
Not allowed:	DISPLAY 2 * 3.
Not allowed:	MOVE 2 * 3 TO A.
Not allowed:	ADD 2 * 3 TO A.

Decimals

You can use decimals:

```
DATA DIVISION.
WORKING-STORAGE SECTION.
01      K PIC 9999V99.

PROCEDURE DIVISION.
MAIN-ROUTINE.
        COMPUTE K = 2.208 + 4.109.
        DISPLAY K.
        STOP RUN.
```

The PIC 9999V99 says K is a number having four digits, followed by a decimal point, followed by two digits. (The V stands for the decimal point.) The MAIN-ROUTINE tries to set K equal to 2.208 + 4.109, which is 6.317; but because of K's picture, I will be 0006.31 instead. So the computer should display 0006.31.

PDP-10 and PDP-20 computers don't bother to display the zeros: they display 6.31. PDP-11, IBM, CDC, and Eclipse computers don't bother to display the decimal point: they display 000631.

You can change that program by saying ROUNDED:

```
        COMPUTE K ROUNDED = 2.208 + 4.109.
```

The computer will find the sum (6.317), and round it so K is 0006.32 instead of 0006.31.

If J's picture is 99, saying "COMPUTE J = 200 / 3" makes J be 66. Saying "COMPUTE J ROUNDED = 200 / 3" makes J be 67.

Which is better: saying "COMPUTE X = 4.9" or "MOVE 4.9 TO X"? You should usually say "MOVE 4.9 TO X", because the computer handles it more quickly. But MOVE cannot round; so if you want to round, say COMPUTE.

MOVE can do strange things:

```
DATA DIVISION.
WORKING-STORAGE SECTION.
01      L PIC 999V99.

PROCEDURE DIVISION.
MAIN-ROUTINE.
        MOVE 16725.048 TO L.
        DISPLAY L.
        STOP RUN.
```

L's picture makes the computer move the three digits just left of the decimal point and the two digits just right of it. L will be 725.04.

Negatives

You can use negative numbers:

```
DATA DIVISION.
WORKING-STORAGE SECTION.
01      K PIC S9999.

PROCEDURE DIVISION.
MAIN-ROUTINE.
        COMPUTE K = 100 - 367.
        DISPLAY K.
        STOP RUN.
```

In K's picture, the S stands for a sign (which can be plus or minus). K will be -0267. The computer should display -0267.

PDP-10 and PDP-20 computers don't bother to display the zero: they display -267. Some other computers display the minus sign on top of the right digit, like this: 0267. On many computers, the minus combines with the 7 and forms a P, like this: 026P.

If you omit the S from K's picture, K will be 0267 instead of -0267.

To find the negative of a power, use parentheses:

```
        COMPUTE A = - (3 ** 2).
```

If you omit the parentheses, the computer will get the wrong answer.

ACCEPT

Here's how to translate the BASIC word **INPUT** into PASCAL and COBOL.

```
BASIC:  INPUT K
PASCAL: READ(K);
COBOL:  ACCEPT K.
```

Let's look at a COBOL example:

```
DATA DIVISION.
WORKING-STORAGE SECTION.
01      K PIC XXX.

PROCEDURE DIVISION.
MAIN-ROUTINE.
        DISPLAY "THIS PROGRAM WANTS YOU TO TYPE SOMETHING".
        ACCEPT K.
        DISPLAY K.
        STOP RUN.
```

The computer displays:

```
THIS PROGRAM WANTS YOU TO TYPE SOMETHING
```

The statement ACCEPT K makes the computer wait for you to type something. If you type —

```
FIGHT
```

the computer will try to move "FIGHT" to K; but since K's picture is XXX, K will be "FIG". The computer will display:

```
FIG
```

If you type —

```
ME
```

the computer will try to move "ME" to K; since K's picture is XXX, K will be "ME ". The computer will display:

```
ME
```

Suppose a program says L PIC 999 and ACCEPT L. If you input —

```
4
```

a PDP-10 or PDP-20 computer will make L be 004, but an IBM or CDC computer will make L be 400.

Suppose a program says M PIC S9999V99 and ACCEPT M. If you want M to be -0034.27, here's what to input. . . .

```
On PDP-10 & PDP-20 computers: -0034.27 or -34.27
On IBM and CDC computers:       003427
```

Editing

The computer can edit the output:

```
DATA DIVISION.
WORKING-STORAGE SECTION.
01      K PIC XXXBXXX.

PROCEDURE DIVISION.
MAIN-ROUTINE.
        MOVE "HITHER" TO K.
        DISPLAY K.
        STOP RUN.
```

In K's picture, **B means a blank space**. So when the computer moves "HITHER", K becomes "HIT HER". The computer will display:

```
HIT HER
```

This program displays the Boston Computer Society's phone number:

```
DATA DIVISION.
WORKING-STORAGE SECTION.
01      PHONE-NUMBER PIC 999B9999.

PROCEDURE DIVISION.
MAIN-ROUTINE.
        MOVE 3678080 TO PHONE-NUMBER.
        DISPLAY PHONE-NUMBER.
        STOP RUN.
```

When the computer moves 3678080, PHONE-NUMBER becomes "367 8080". The computer will display:

```
367 8080
```

This program is of historical importance:

```
DATA DIVISION.
WORKING-STORAGE SECTION.
01      K PIC 9B9B9999.

PROCEDURE DIVISION.
MAIN-ROUTINE.
        COMPUTE K = 741775 + 1.
        DISPLAY "THE DECLARATION OF INDEPENDENCE WAS SIGNED ON " K.
        STOP RUN.
```

The computer will display:

```
THE DECLARATION OF INDEPENDENCE WAS SIGNED ON 7 4 1776
```

Using B to insert a blank is called **editing**. You've learned four kinds of variables:

Kind of variable	Symbols in picture
string	X
edited string	X B
number	9 V S
edited number	9 B Z , $ * . + - DB CR

You can use these pictures for editing numbers:

K's picture	Meaning	What K will be if you move 50320 to K	What K will be if you move 0 to K
B99999999	a blank then eight digits	" 00050320"	" 00000000"
ZZZZZZZZZ	blanks then digits	" 50320"	" "
$,$$$,$$$	put $ before the digits	" $50,320"	" "
*,***,***	stars instead of blanks	"***50,320"	"*********"

To edit decimals, put a decimal point in the picture.

K's picture	If you move 50320.6 to K	If you move .04 to K	If you move 0 to K
Z,ZZZ,ZZZ.ZZ	" 50,320.60"	" .04"	" "
$,$$$,$$$.$$	" $50,320.60"	" $.04"	" "
*,***,***.**	"***50,320.60"	"*********.04"	"*********.**"

With those pictures, if you move 0 to K the computer doesn't put any digits in K. To guarantee that K contains a digit, put 9 in the picture:

K's picture	If you move 50320.6 to K	If you move .04 to K	If you move 0 to K
Z,ZZZ,ZZ9.99	" 50,320.60"	" 0.04"	" 0.00"
$,$$$,$$9.99	" $50,320.60"	" $0.04"	" $0.00"
*,***,**9.99	"***50,320.60"	"*******0.04"	"*******0.00"

To edit negative numbers, use +, -, DB, or CR.

K's picture	Meaning	If you move -2.6 to K	If you move 2.6 to K
ZZZ.ZZ+	put - or + afterwards	" 2.60-"	" 2.60+"
ZZZ.ZZ-	put - or blank afterwards	" 2.60-"	" 2.60 "
ZZZ.ZZDB	if negative, put DB (for debit)	" 2.60DB"	" 2.60 "
ZZZ.ZZCR	if negative, put CR (for credit)	" 2.60CR"	" 2.60 "

For fancier pictures, replace the Z by $, *, or 9.

Here's how to put the sign before the digits:

K's picture	Meaning	If you move -2.6 to K	If you move 2.6 to K
+++.++	put - or + before digits	" -2.60"	" +2.60"
---.--	- or blank before digits	" -2.60"	" 2.60"

Here are the differences between numbers and edited numbers:

	Number	Edited number
how to put decimal point in the picture	V	.
how to put a sign in the picture	S	+, -, DB, or CR
how to fill up most of the picture	9	9, Z, $, *, +, or -
what the value should be	intermediate result in long calculation	the final answer to be displayed
If the value's called K, can you say ACCEPT K?	yes	no
If the value's called K, can you use K in further computations (such as COMPUTE L = K + 1)?	yes	no
What happens if you try to DISPLAY the value?	the "0", ".", and "-" might look wrong	displays correctly

DECIMAL-POINT IS COMMA

Some Europeans write commas instead of decimal points, and write decimal points instead of commas.

United States and England: 5,243,794.95
France and Italy: 5.243.794,95
Germany: 5 243 794,95

To write a COBOL program for a Frenchman, an Italian, or a German, make three changes. . . .

Change #1 Insert this line:

```
DECIMAL-POINT IS COMMA.
```

Put that line in a SPECIAL-NAMES paragraph, at the end of the ENVIRONMENT DIVISION's CONFIGURATION SECTION:

```
CONFIGURATION SECTION.
SOURCE-COMPUTER.
     The computer's name.
OBJECT-COMPUTER.
     The computer's name again.
SPECIAL-NAMES.
     DECIMAL-POINT IS COMMA.
```

Change #2 Type all numbers in French-Italian-German notation. So instead of typing —

```
MOVE 5243794.95 TO K
```

type:

```
MOVE 5243794,95 TO K
```

Change #3 Use French-Italian-German notation in pictures for *edited* numbers.

For a Frenchman or an Italian: K PIC Z.ZZZ.ZZZ,ZZ
For a German: K PIC ZBZZZBZZZ,ZZ

Those are the only changes Europeans make. They still put a period at the end of every sentence, and still use English COBOL words such as MOVE and DISPLAY.

American COBOL: DISPLAY "HELLO, STUPID".
French COBOL: DISPLAY "BONJOUR, BETE".
German COBOL: DISPLAY "GUTEN TAG, DUMMKOPF".

COBOL lets you do logic.

IF

Like other computer languages, COBOL uses the word IF:

BASIC	**PASCAL**	**COBOL**
`INPUT I`	`READ(I);`	`ACCEPT I.`
`IF I>5 THEN J=80: K=90`	`IF I>5 THEN`	`IF I > 5`
	`  BEGIN;`	`        MOVE 80 TO J`
	`  J:=80;`	`        MOVE 90 TO K.`
	`  K:=90;`	
	`  END;`	

COBOL also lets you say ELSE:

BASIC	**PASCAL**	**COBOL**
`INPUT I`	`READ(I);`	`ACCEPT I.`
`IF I>5 THEN J=80: K=90 ELSE J=30: K=50`	`IF I>5 THEN`	`IF I > 5`
	`  BEGIN;`	`        MOVE 80 TO J`
	`  J:=80;`	`        MOVE 90 TO K`
	`  K:=90;`	`ELSE`
	`  END`	`        MOVE 30 TO J`
	`ELSE`	`        MOVE 50 TO K.`
	`  BEGIN;`	
	`  J:=30;`	
	`  K:=50;`	
	`  END;`	

In COBOL, **when you write the IF statement, do not put a period at the end of every line; instead, put the period just at the end of the entire IF idea.**

Notice that I indented the word MOVE. The indentation is optional, but is a good habit. To indent on PDP and Eclipse computers, type a controlled I; to indent on IBM and CDC computers, press the space bar several times.

COBOL uses these IF lines:

IF line	Meaning
`IF I = 5`	If I is equal to 5
`IF I NOT = 5`	If I is not equal to 5
`IF I > 5`	If I is greater than 5
`IF I NOT > 5`	If I is not greater than 5
`IF I < 5`	If I is less than 5
`IF I NOT < 5`	IF I is not less than 5

You can use the words AND and OR and abbreviate:

IF line:	`IF J > 1 AND J < 100`
Abbreviation:	`IF J > 1 AND < 100`

IF line:	`IF K < -3 OR K = 6 OR K = 9 OR K = 12 OR K > 50`
Abbreviation:	`IF K < -3 OR = 6 OR 9 OR 12 OR > 50`

You can say this:

```
IF AGE < 13
        DISPLAY "CHILD"
ELSE IF AGE < 20
        DISPLAY "TEENAGER"
ELSE IF AGE < 40
        DISPLAY "YOUNG ADULT"
ELSE IF AGE < 60
        DISPLAY "MIDDLE-AGED"
ELSE
        DISPLAY "SENIOR CITIZEN".
```

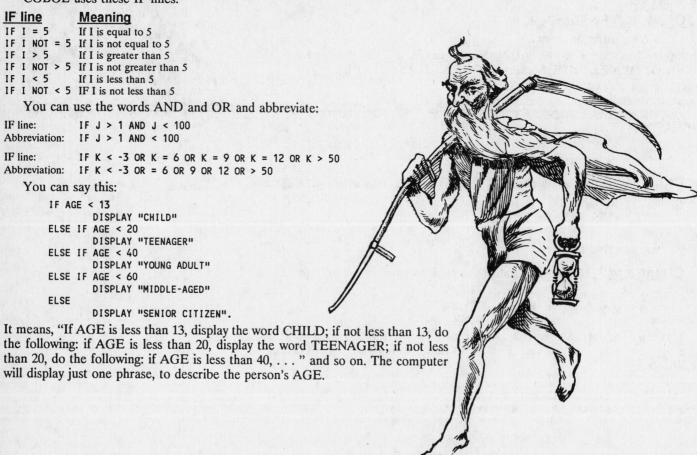

It means, "If AGE is less than 13, display the word CHILD; if not less than 13, do the following: if AGE is less than 20, display the word TEENAGER; if not less than 20, do the following: if AGE is less than 40, . . . " and so on. The computer will display just one phrase, to describe the person's AGE.

UNTIL

You can say UNTIL:

```
DATA DIVISION.
WORKING-STORAGE SECTION.
01      I PIC 999.

PROCEDURE DIVISION.
MAIN-ROUTINE.
        MOVE 5 TO I.
        PERFORM FIDDLE-WITH-I UNTIL I > 100.
        STOP RUN.
FIDDLE-WITH-I.
        DISPLAY I.
        COMPUTE I = I * 2.
```

The computer will perform FIDDLE-WITH-I repeatedly, until I > 100. The computer will display 5, 10, 20, 40, and 80. It will not display 160.

Here are the details. When the computer encounters PERFORM FIDDLE-WITH-I UNTIL I > 100, it checks whether I > 100. If I > 100, the computer proceeds to the next statement (the STOP RUN); but if I is *not* greater than 100, the computer performs FIDDLE-WITH-I and then re-executes the statement PERFORM FIDDLE-WITH-I UNTIL I > 100.

To translate a BASIC "FOR...NEXT loop" into COBOL, say "PERFORM":

BASIC	COBOL

```
10 FOR I = 5 TO 17        PROCEDURE DIVISION.
20     PRINT I            MAIN-ROUTINE.
30 NEXT I                         PERFORM DISPLAY-IT
                                          VARYING I FROM 5 BY 1 UNTIL I > 17.
                                  STOP RUN.
                          DISPLAY-IT.
                                  DISPLAY I.


10 FOR I = 5 TO 17 STEP 3 PROCEDURE DIVISION.
20     PRINT I            MAIN-ROUTINE.
30 NEXT I                         PERFORM DISPLAY-IT
                                          VARYING I FROM 5 BY 3 UNTIL I > 17.
                                  STOP RUN.
                          DISPLAY-IT.
                                  DISPLAY I.


10 FOR I = 5 TO 17        PROCEDURE DIVISION.
20     FOR J = 1 TO 3     MAIN-ROUTINE.
30         PRINT I,J              PERFORM DISPLAY-IT
40     NEXT J                             VARYING I FROM 5 BY 1 UNTIL I > 17
50 NEXT I                                 AFTER J FROM 1 BY 1 UNTIL J > 3.
                                  STOP RUN.
                          DISPLAY-IT.
                                  DISPLAY I J.
```

GO TO

Like other computer languages, COBOL lets you say GO TO. In COBOL, **put a space between GO and TO**. (In PASCAL, you do *not* put a space between GO and TO.)

For example, instead of saying STOP RUN, you can say GO TO MAIN-ROUTINE:

```
PROCEDURE DIVISION.
MAIN-ROUTINE.
        DISPLAY "WHEATIES".
        DISPLAY "ARE WONDERFUL".
        GO TO MAIN-ROUTINE.
```

The computer will display "WHEATIES" and "ARE WONDERFUL", repeatedly:

```
WHEATIES
ARE WONDERFUL
WHEATIES
ARE WONDERFUL
WHEATIES
ARE WONDERFUL
etc.
```

The main routine can consist of *two* paragraphs, called MAIN-ROUTINE-BEGINNING and MAIN-ROUTINE-LOOP:

```
PROCEDURE DIVISION.
MAIN-ROUTINE-BEGINNING.
       DISPLAY "PLEASE".
MAIN-ROUTINE-LOOP.
       DISPLAY "KISS".
       DISPLAY "ME".
       GO TO MAIN-ROUTINE-LOOP.
```

The computer will display PLEASE, then repeatedly display KISS and ME:

```
PLEASE
KISS
ME
KISS
ME
KISS
ME
etc.
```

The main routine can consist of *three* paragraphs, called MAIN-ROUTINE-BEGINNING, MAIN-ROUTINE-LOOP, and MAIN-ROUTINE-ENDING:

```
DATA DIVISION.
WORKING-STORAGE SECTION.
01      HUMAN-RESPONSE PIC XXX.

PROCEDURE DIVISION.
MAIN-ROUTINE-BEGINNING.
       DISPLAY "I WILL RECITE A SHORT POEM".
MAIN-ROUTINE-LOOP.
       DISPLAY " ".
       DISPLAY "YOUR NOSE".
       DISPLAY "BLOWS".
       DISPLAY " ".
       DISPLAY "WOULD YOU LIKE TO HEAR THE POEM AGAIN?".
       ACCEPT HUMAN-RESPONSE.
       IF HUMAN-RESPONSE = "YES"
               GO TO MAIN-ROUTINE=LOOP.
MAIN-ROUTINE-ENDING.
       DISPLAY "YOU HAVE BEEN A GREAT AUDIENCE".
       STOP RUN.
```

When you run that program, the computer says:

```
I WILL RECITE A SHORT POEM
```

Then it recites the program:

```
YOUR NOSE
BLOWS
```

Then it asks:

```
WOULD YOU LIKE TO HEAR THE POEM AGAIN?
```

If you answer YES, the computer repeats the poem, then asks whether you'd like to hear it a third time. If you answer YES again, the computer recites the poem a third time, then asks whether you'd like to hear it a *fourth* time. The computer recites the poem repeatedly, until you finally stop answering YES. Then the computer says —

```
YOU HAVE BEEN A GREAT AUDIENCE
```

and stops.

In that program, if you don't answer YES, the computer doesn't repeat the poem. So if you don't answer YES, the computer acts as if you said NO. The following version is an improvement; if you don't answer YES, and you don't say NO, the computer asks the question again:

```
DATA DIVISION.
WORKING-STORAGE SECTION.
01      HUMAN-RESPONSE PIC XXX.

PROCEDURE DIVISION.
MAIN-ROUTINE-BEGINNING.
       DISPLAY "I WILL RECITE A SHORT POEM".
MAIN-ROUTINE-LOOP.
       DISPLAY " ".
       DISPLAY "YOUR NOSE".
       DISPLAY "BLOWS".
       DISPLAY " ".
       PERFORM GET-HUMAN-RESPONSE.
       IF HUMAN-RESPONSE = "YES"
               GO TO MAIN-ROUTINE-LOOP.
MAIN-ROUTINE-ENDING.
       DISPLAY "YOU HAVE BEEN A GREAT AUDIENCE".
       STOP RUN.
GET-HUMAN-RESPONSE.
       DISPLAY "WOULD YOU LIKE TO HEAR THE POEM AGAIN?".
       ACCEPT HUMAN-RESPONSE.
       IF HUMAN-RESPONSE NOT = "YES" AND NOT = "NO"
               DISPLAY "PLEASE SAY YES OR NO!"
               GO TO GET-HUMAN-RESPONSE.
```

GO TO resembles PERFORM. Here's the difference between GO TO and PERFORM. . . .

To go to a *different routine*, say PERFORM.

To go to a different paragraph in the *same routine*, say GO TO.

For example, suppose you want to go from MAIN-ROUTINE-BEGINNING to FUNNY-SUBROUTINE; since you're going to a *different routine*, say PERFORM.

Suppose you want to go from MAIN-ROUTINE-BEGINNING to MAIN-ROUTINE-ENDING; since you're going to a different paragraph in the *same* routine, say GO TO.

THRU

Like the main routine, a subroutine can consist of several paragraphs. For example, subroutine FUNNY-FACE can consist of three paragraphs, called FUNNY-FACE-BEGINNING, FUNNY-FACE-LOOP, and FUNNY-FACE-ENDING. To make the computer do the entire subroutine, say:

```
PERFORM FUNNY-FACE-BEGINNING THRU FUNNY-FACE-ENDING.
```

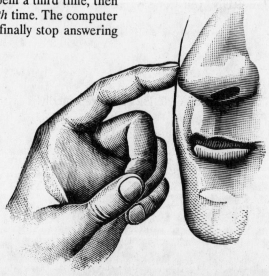

To manipulate a data file whose name is POEM, fill in the blanks:

```
IDENTIFICATION DIVISION.
PROGRAM-ID.
        The program's name.
AUTHOR
        Your name.

ENVIRONMENT DIVISION.
CONFIGURATION SECTION.
SOURCE-COMPUTER.
        The computer's name.
OBJECT-COMPUTER.
        The computer's name again.
INPUT-OUTPUT SECTION.
FILE-CONTROL.
        SELECT POEM-FILE ASSIGN TO the file's location.

DATA DIVISION.
FILE SECTION.
FD      POEM-FILE how the file is labeled.
01      POEM-LINE PIC a picture of a line of the file.
WORKING-STORAGE SECTION.
A description of each variable that's not in the file.

PROCEDURE DIVISION.
MAIN-ROUTINE.
        OPEN output or input POEM-FILE.
        What you want to do to the file.
        CLOSE POEM-FILE.
        STOP RUN.
```

The four divisions

Like every COBOL program, that outline consists of four divisions: the IDENTIFICATION DIVISION, the ENVIRONMENT DIVISION, the DATA DIVISION, and the PROCEDURE DIVISION. Let's look at each division.

IDENTIFICATION DIVISION The IDENTIFICATION DIVISION consists of two paragraphs: the PROGRAM-ID and the AUTHOR. For the PROGRAM-ID, fill in the program's name, *which must be different from the name of the file*. Since the name of the file is POEM, the name of the program must *not* be POEM. If you're lazy, you can omit the AUTHOR.

ENVIRONMENT DIVISION The ENVIRONMENT DIVISION consists of two sections: the CONFIGURATION SECTION and the INPUT-OUTPUT SECTION.

The CONFIGURATION SECTION consists of two paragraphs: the SOURCE-COMPUTER and the OBJECT-COMPUTER. On CDC and PDP-11 computers, the CONFIGURATION SECTION is required; but on IBM, Eclipse, PDP-10, and PDP-20 computers, the entire CONFIGURATION SECTION is optional, so you can abridge the ENVIRONMENT DIVISION:

```
ENVIRONMENT DIVISION.
INPUT-OUTPUT SECTION.
FILE-CONTROL.
        SELECT POEM-FILE ASSIGN TO the file's location.
```

The INPUT-OUTPUT SECTION consists of just one paragraph, which is the FILE-CONTROL. The FILE-CONTROL paragraph consists of a sentence that says SELECT, then the file's name (POEM-FILE), then ASSIGN TO, and finally a blank (which you must fill in, and which tells the file's location).

What do you put in that blank? The answer depends on the file's location. Is the file on a disk? On punched cards? Or on paper produced by the printer? **Here's what to put in the blank, for various computers:**

	Printer	**Card reader**	**Disk**
Eclipse	PRINTER	"$CDR"	"POEM"
CDC	OUTPUT	INPUT	POEM
PDP-11	"LP:"	"CR:"	"DK:"
PDP-10, PDP-20	LPT	CDR	DSK RECORDING MODE ASCII
IBM using OS	UT-S-POEM	UT-S-POEM	UT-S-POEM
IBM using DOS	SYS006-UR-1403-S	SYS005-UR-2540R-S	SYS020-UT-3330-S-POEM

DATA DIVISION
The DATA DIVISION consists of two sections: the FILE SECTION and the WORKING-STORAGE SECTION.

At the beginning of the FILE SECTION, say FD (which means "File Description"). To the right of the FD, say POEM-FILE, and then **fill in the blank, which tells how the file is labeled:**

Computer	**What to put in the blank**
CDC	LABEL RECORDS ARE OMITTED
PDP-11: disk	LABEL RECORDS ARE STANDARD VALUE OF ID "POEM"
PDP-11: printer or card reader	LABEL RECORDS ARE OMITTED
PDP-10, PDP-20	VALUE ID "POEM■■■■■"
IBM OS	LABEL RECORDS ARE STANDARD
IBM DOS: disk	LABEL RECORDS ARE STANDARD
IBM DOS: printer or card reader	LABEL RECORDS ARE OMITTED

On PDP-10 and PDP-20 computers, put enough blank spaces (■) after POEM so that the string has 9 characters. On Eclipse computers, do *not* fill in the blank; just say:

```
FD    POEM-FILE.
```

Underneath the line that says FD, you must say 01. The 01 line includes a picture of a line of the file. For example, if a line of the file is an 80-character string, the 01 line should say:

```
01    POEM-LINE PIC X(80).
```

The WORKING-STORAGE SECTION describes each variable that's not in the file.

PROCEDURE DIVISION
The PROCEDURE DIVISION's MAIN-ROUTINE should begin with the word OPEN, and end with the words CLOSE and STOP RUN.

In the OPEN statement, you can say either —

```
OPEN OUTPUT POEM-FILE.
```

or:

```
OPEN INPUT POEM-FILE.
```

If you say OPEN OUTPUT POEM-FILE, the computer will output to the POEM-FILE; so it will copy information from the RAM to the POEM-FILE. If you say OPEN INPUT POEM-FILE, the computer will input from the POEM-FILE; so it will copy information from the POEM-FILE to the RAM.

In the PROCEDURE DIVISION, when you fill in the blank about "what you want to do to the file", you must say either WRITE POEM-LINE or READ POEM-FILE. If the file is OPEN OUTPUT (which means you're copying from the RAM to the file), say WRITE POEM-LINE; if the file is OPEN INPUT (which means you're copying from the file to the RAM), say READ POEM-FILE.

Writing

Here's a poetic masterpiece:

```
CANDY IS DANDY
BUT LIKKER IS QUIKKER
```

It was composed by the famous poet Ogden Nash.

This program makes the computer write that masterpiece onto a disk, and make the masterpiece become a file named POEM:

Program   **Meaning**

```
IDENTIFICATION DIVISION.
PROGRAM-ID.
        CANDY.
```
This program is named CANDY.

```
ENVIRONMENT DIVISION.
CONFIGURATION SECTION.
SOURCE-COMPUTER.
        The computer's name.
OBJECT-COMPUTER.
        The computer's name again.
INPUT-OUTPUT SECTION.
FILE-CONTROL.
        SELECT POEM-FILE ASSIGN TO the file's location.
```
This program uses a file called POEM.

```
DATA DIVISION.
FILE SECTION.
FD      POEM-FILE how the file is labeled.
01      POEM-LINE PIC X(21).
```
Make each line have 21 characters, like this:
```
CANDY IS DANDY■■■■■■■
BUT LIKKER IS QUIKKER
```

```
PROCEDURE DIVISION.
MAIN-ROUTINE.
        OPEN OUTPUT POEM-FILE.
        MOVE "CANDY IS DANDY" TO POEM-LINE.
        WRITE POEM-LINE.
        MOVE "BUT LIKKER IS QUIKKER" TO POEM-LINE.
        WRITE POEM-LINE.
        CLOSE POEM-FILE.
        STOP RUN.
```
Prepare to output to POEM-FILE.
Make POEM-LINE be "CANDY IS DANDY■■■■■■■".
Copy that POEM-LINE to the file.
Make POEM-LINE become this new string: "BUT LIKKER IS QUIKKER".
Copy that new POEM-LINE to the file.
Finish using POEM-FILE.
Stop running this program.

That program doesn't require a WORKING-STORAGE SECTION, so I omitted it. Since I was lazy, I also omitted the AUTHOR paragraph.

When you run that program, the computer will create a file on disk. The file will be called POEM. It will contain this message:

```
CANDY IS DANDY■■■■■■■
BUT LIKKER IS QUIKKER
```

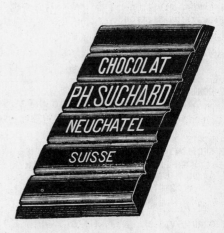

Reading

This program reads the file POEM, and displays it on your terminal:

```
IDENTIFICATION DIVISION.
PROGRAM-ID.
        READER.
```

The ENVIRONMENT DIVISION and DATA DIVISION are the same as the previous program's.

```
PROCEDURE DIVISION.
MAIN-ROUTINE-BEGINNING.
        OPEN INPUT POEM-FILE.
MAIN-ROUTINE-LOOP.
        READ POEM-FILE AT END GO TO MAIN-ROUTINE-ENDING.
        DISPLAY POEM-LINE.
        GO TO MAIN-ROUTINE-LOOP.
MAIN-ROUTINE-ENDING.
        DISPLAY "THAT WAS THE WHOLE POEM".
        CLOSE POEM-FILE.
        STOP RUN.
```
Find POEM on the disk, and prepare to input from it.

Read a line from POEM-FILE; if no more lines, go to next paragraph.
Display that line, so you see it on your screen.
Go back to read another line.

Display "THAT WAS THE WHOLE POEM" on your screen.
Finish using POEM-FILE.
Stop running this program.

In the MAIN-ROUTINE-LOOP, the first line means: try to READ a line from POEM-FILE; but if a line cannot be read (because the file has ended), go to MAIN-ROUTINE-ENDING instead.

The READ statement differs from the WRITE statement in two ways:

A WRITE statement mentions a LINE, but a READ statement mentions a FILE.
A READ statement must contain the words AT END.

Counting

This program reads a file called POEM, counts how many lines are in it, and displays the count:

```
IDENTIFICATION DIVISION.
PROGRAM-ID.
        COUNTS.
```

The ENVIRONMENT DIVISION is same as previous program's.

```
DATA DIVISION.
FILE SECTION.
FD      POEM-FILE how the file is labeled.
01      POEM-LINE PIC X(21).
WORKING-STORAGE SECTION.
01      COUNT-OF-HOW-MANY-LINES PIC 99.
```

Assume each POEM-LINE has 21 characters.

Assumes the count is a two-digit number, so assume POEM has less than 100 lines.

```
PROCEDURE DIVISION.
MAIN-ROUTINE-BEGINNING.
        OPEN INPUT POEM-FILE.
        MOVE 0 TO COUNT-OF-HOW-MANY-LINES.
MAIN-ROUTINE-LOOP.
        READ POEM-FILE AT END GO TO MAIN-ROUTINE-ENDING.
        ADD 1 TO COUNT-OF-HOW-MANY-LINES.
        GO TO MAIN-ROUTINE-LOOP.
MAIN-ROUTINE-ENDING.
        DISPLAY COUNT-OF-HOW-MANY-LINES.
        CLOSE POEM-FILE.
        STOP RUN.
```

Find POEM on the disk.
Start the count at 0.

Read a line from POEM-FILE.
Add 1 to the count.
Go read another line.
When all lines have been read,
display the count,
finish using POEM-FILE,
and stop running this program.

Copying

This program reads a file called POEM, and creates a copy of it; the copy is a file called POEM2:

```
IDENTIFICATION DIVISION.
PROGRAM-ID.
        COPIER.

ENVIRONMENT DIVISION.
CONFIGURATION SECTION.
SOURCE-COMPUTER.
        The computer's name.
OBJECT-COMPUTER.
        The computer's name again.
INPUT-OUTPUT SECTION.
FILE-CONTROL.
        SELECT POEM-FILE ASSIGN TO the location of POEM.
        SELECT POEM2-FILE ASSIGN TO the location of POEM-2.

DATA DIVISION.
FILE SECTION.
FD      POEM-FILE the labeling for POEM.
01      POEM-LINE PIC X(21).
FD      POEM2-FILE the labeling for POEM2.
01      POEM2-LINE PIC X(21).
```

```
PROCEDURE DIVISION.
MAIN-ROUTINE-BEGINNING.
        OPEN INPUT POEM-FILE.
        OPEN OUTPUT POEM2-FILE.
MAIN-ROUTINE-LOOP.
        READ POEM-FILE AT END GO TO MAIN-ROUTINE-ENDING.
        MOVE POEM-LINE TO POEM2-LINE.
        WRITE POEM2-LINE.
        GO TO MAIN-ROUTINE-LOOP.
MAIN-ROUTINE-ENDING.
        DISPLAY "THE FILE HAS BEEN COPIED".
        CLOSE POEM-FILE POEM2-FILE.
        STOP RUN.
```

Prepare to input from POEM-FILE,
and output to POEM2-FILE.
Do the following repeatedly:
read a line from POEM-FILE,
copy that line to POEM2-LINE,
and write POEM2-LINE to POEM2-FILE.

At the end,
display "THE FILE HAS BEEN COPIED" on the screen,
finish using the files,
and stop running this program.

Pictures

Suppose you're dealing with a file named JOE, and each line of JOE-FILE is a three-digit number. Should the line's picture be edited (JOE-LINE PIC ZZZ) or unedited (JOE-LINE PIC 999)?

When you read a file, the line's picture must be unedited and match the picture in the program that wrote the file.

When you write a file, ask yourself, "What will read it?" If the answer is "a COBOL program", the picture must be unedited. If the answer is "only a human", edit the picture.

Remember: if one program writes a file, and another program reads it, both programs must use the same picture. For example, if a program writes JACK-FILE and says JACK-LINE PIC S9999V99, the program that reads JACK-FILE must also say JACK-LINE PIC S9999V99.

Peculiarities

To write and read unedited numbers, the computer takes a short-cut: it omits decimal points, and locates the negative sign on top of the last digit. For example, instead of writing -0034.27 in JACK-FILE, the computer writes just 003427. When another program reads 003427 from the file, the S9999V99 picture tells the computer the 003427 means -0034.27.

After you WRITE a line, you cannot use the line again in the program. For example, after you say WRITE POEM-LINE, you should not say MOVE POEM-LINE TO K; it won't work.

Multiple widths

Let's make the computer compute the square of 12 and the square of 13 and write this file:

```
HERE ARE THE SQUARES:
144
169
THEY WERE REAL GROOVY
```

The top and bottom lines are long strings whose pictures are X(21). The other two lines are short numbers whose pictures are 999.

Here's the program:

```
IDENTIFICATION DIVISION.
PROGRAM-ID.
        SQUARE.

ENVIRONMENT DIVISION.
CONFIGURATION SECTION.
SOURCE-COMPUTER.
        The computer's name.
OBJECT-COMPUTER.
        The computer's name again.
INPUT-OUTPUT SECTION.
FILE-CONTROL.
        SELECT REPORT-FILE ASSIGN TO location of REPORT.
```

This program uses a file called REPORT.

```
DATA DIVISION.
FILE SECTION.
FD      REPORT-FILE the labeling for REPORT.
01      REPORT-LINE PIC X(21).
01      REPORT-LINE2 PIC 999.
```

REPORT-LINE is a 21-character string.
REPORT-LINE2 is a 3-digit number.

```
PROCEDURE DIVISION.
MAIN-ROUTINE.
        OPEN OUTPUT REPORT-FILE.
        MOVE "HERE ARE THE SQUARES:" TO REPORT-LINE.
        WRITE REPORT-LINE.
        COMPUTE REPORT-LINE2 = 12 * 12.
        WRITE REPORT-LINE2.
        COMPUTE REPORT-LINE2 = 13 * 13.
        WRITE REPORT-LINE2.
        MOVE "THEY WERE REAL GROOVY" TO REPORT-LINE.
        WRITE REPORT-LINE.
        CLOSE REPORT-FILE.
        STOP RUN.
```

Create a file named REPORT.
REPORT-LINE is "HERE ARE THE SQUARES:".
Write "HERE ARE THE SQUARES:".
REPORT-LINE2 is 144.
Write 144.
REPORT-LINE2 is 169.
Write 169.
REPORT-LINE is "THEY WERE REAL GROOVY".
Write "THEY WERE REAL GROOVY".
Finish using REPORT.
Stop running this program.

COBOL lets you create and manipulate advanced structures.

Group items

In the data division, you can say:

```
01      K.
        02      L PIC 999.
        02      M PIC 9.
        02      N PIC 99.
```

That means K is a combination of L, M, and N. If the procedure division says —

```
        MOVE 427 TO L.
        MOVE 8 TO M.
        MOVE 31 TO N.
```

then K will be "427831".

Since K is a combination of other variables, K is called a **group variable** or **group item**. L, M, and N are **elementary items**. Notice that K is the string "427831", not the number 427831. **A group item is always a string**. Since K is a string, not a number, you cannot say ADD 1 TO K, although you can say ADD 1 TO L or ADD 1 TO M or ADD 1 TO N.

Here's a group item, for a weight-reducing studio:

```
01      PERSONAL-INFO-ABOUT-CLIENT.
        02      CLIENT-NAME.
                03      FIRST-NAME PIC X(15).
                03      MIDDLE-INITIAL PIC X.
                03      LAST-NAME PIC X(20).
        02      CLIENT-SEX PIC X.              A person's sex is "M" or "F".
        02      CLIENT-AGE PIC 99.
        02      WEIGHT-PROGRESS.
                03      WEIGHT-WHEN-ENTERED-PROGRAM PIC 999.
                03      WEIGHT-THIS-WEEK PIC 999.
                03      NUMBER-OF-WEEKS-SO-FAR PIC 999.
```

PERSONAL-INFO-ABOUT-CLIENT is composed of CLIENT-NAME (which is composed of FIRST-NAME, MIDDLE-INITIAL, and LAST-NAME), CLIENT-SEX, and WEIGHT-PROGRESS (which is composed of WEIGHT-WHEN-ENTERED-PROGRAM, WEIGHT-THIS-WEEK, and NUMBER-OF-WEEKS-SO-FAR). So PERSONAL-INFO-ABOUT-CLIENT is composed of numbers and strings.

Altogether, PERSONAL-INFO-ABOUT-CLIENT contains 48 characters (15 + 1 + 20 + 1 + 2 + 3 + 3 + 3). The computer considers PERSONAL-INFO-ABOUT-CLIENT to be a string whose picture is X(48).

If you say L PIC X(48), you can move all the PERSONAL-INFO-ABOUT-CLIENT to L by saying:

```
        MOVE PERSONAL-INFO-ABOUT-CLIENT TO L.
```

To move the CLIENT-NAME to M, without moving the CLIENT-SEX, CLIENT-AGE, and WEIGHT-PROGRESS, say:

```
        MOVE CLIENT-NAME TO M.
```

To write lots of information to a file, make the file's LINE be a group item.

How to extract from a file Suppose you've already created a file whose name is EMPLOY; it's on disk or cards. Suppose the file contains information about employees. Suppose each line of the file contains 80 characters, as follows. Characters 1-40 are the employee's name. Characters 61-70 are the employee's home phone number, including the area code. The other characters (41-60 and 71-80) are miscellaneous information (such as the employee's age, sex, address, salary, kind of job, and number of years with the company).

Let's create a new file, called REPORT, on disk or on the printer's paper. Let's make REPORT contain just the employees' names and phone numbers, and omit the "miscellaneous information". Here's how:

```
IDENTIFICATION DIVISION.
PROGRAM-ID.
        PHONES.


ENVIRONMENT DIVISION.
CONFIGURATION SECTION.
SOURCE-COMPUTER.
        The computer's name.
OBJECT-COMPUTER.
        The computer's name again.
INPUT-OUTPUT SECTION.
FILE-CONTROL.
        SELECT EMPLOY-FILE ASSIGN TO location of EMPLOY.
        SELECT REPORT-FILE ASSIGN TO location of REPORT.
```

``
DATA DIVISION.
FILE SECTION.
FD   EMPLOY-FILE the labeling for EMPLOY.
01   EMPLOY-LINE.
      02   EMPLOYEE-NAME PIC X(40).
      02   FILLER PIC X(20).
      02   HOME-PHONE.
            03   AREA-CODE PIC 999.
            03   PHONE-EXCHANGE PIC 999.
            03   REST-OF-PHONE-NUMBER PIC 9999.
      02   FILLER PIC X(10).
FD   REPORT-FILE the labeling for REPORT.
01   REPORT-LINE.
      02   EMPLOYEE-NAME-REPORTED PIC X(40).
      02   HOME-PHONE-REPORTED.
            03   LEFT-PARENTHESIS PIC X.
            03   AREA-CODE-REPORTED PIC 999.
            03   RIGHT-PARENTHESIS PIC X.
            03   PHONE-EXCHANGE-REPORTED PIC B999.
            03   THE-DASH PIC X.
            03   REST-OF-PHONE-NUMBER-REPORTED PIC 9999.
``
	Throughout the DATA DIVISION, the special word "FILLER" stands for data the program won't use.
	
	Characters 1-40 are EMPLOYEE-NAME.
	Characters 41-60 are irrelevant.
	
	Characters 61-63 are AREA-CODE.
	Characters 64-66 are PHONE-EXCHANGE.
	Characters 67-70 are REST-OF-PHONE-NUMBER.
	Characters 71-80 are irrelevant.
	
	The PICs say HOME-PHONE looks like this —
	6176662666
	but make HOME-PHONE-REPORTED look like this:
	(617) 666-2666

``
PROCEDURE DIVISION.
MAIN-ROUTINE-BEGINNING.
      OPEN INPUT EMPLOY-FILE.
      OPEN OUTPUT REPORT-FILE.
MAIN-ROUTINE-LOOP.
      READ EMPLOY-FILE AT END GO TO MAIN-ROUTINE-ENDING.
      MOVE EMPLOYEE-NAME TO EMPLOYEE-NAME-REPORTED.
      MOVE "(" TO LEFT-PARENTHESIS.
      MOVE AREA-CODE TO AREA-CODE-REPORTED.
      MOVE ")" TO RIGHT-PARENTHESIS.
      MOVE PHONE-EXCHANGE TO PHONE-EXCHANGE-REPORTED.
      MOVE "-" TO THE-DASH.
      MOVE REST-OF-PHONE-NUMBER TO REST-OF-PHONE-NUMBER-REPORTED.
      WRITE REPORT-LINE.
      GO TO MAIN-ROUTINE-LOOP.
MAIN-ROUTINE-ENDING.
      CLOSE EMPLOY-FILE REPORT-FILE.
      STOP RUN.
``
	
	The MAIN-ROUTINE-LOOP
	reads a line from EMPLOY-FILE,
	copies data into each part of REPORT-LINE,
	
	and then writes REPORT-LINE.

SORT

Suppose CUSTOM is a disk file that contains information about your customers. Suppose each line of the file contains 80 characters, as follows. . . .

Characters 1-20: the customer's last name
Characters 21-80: other information about the customer

Alphabetical order
Here's how to put the file in alphabetical order, according to the customer's name:

```
IDENTIFICATION DIVISION.
PROGRAM-ID.
        ALPHA.

ENVIRONMENT DIVISION.
CONFIGURATION SECTION.
SOURCE-COMPUTER.
        The computer's name.
OBJECT-COMPUTER.
        The computer's name again.
INPUT-OUTPUT SECTION.
FILE-CONTROL.
        SELECT CUSTOM-FILE ASSIGN TO the location of CUSTOM.
        SELECT SORT-FILE ASSIGN TO the location of SORT.

DATA DIVISION.
FILE SECTION.
FD      CUSTOM-FILE the labeling for CUSTOM.
01      CUSTOM-LINE PIC X(80).
SD      SORT-FILE.
01      SORT-LINE.
        02      LAST-NAME PIC X(20).
        02      FILLER PIC X(60).

PROCEDURE DIVISION.
MAIN-ROUTINE.
        SORT SORT-FILE
                ASCENDING KEY LAST-NAME
                USING CUSTOM-FILE
                GIVING CUSTOM-FILE.
        STOP RUN.
```

Putting a file in order, by alphabetizing or any other method, is called **sorting**. To sort the CUSTOM-FILE, the computer has to create a temporary disk file called a SORT-FILE.

In the sentence that says SELECT SORT-FILE, here's what to put for "the location of SORT":

Computer	The location of SORT
Eclipse	"SORT"
CDC	SORT
PDP-10, PDP-20	DSK DSK DSK RECORDING MODE ASCII
IBM using OS	UT-S-POEM
IBM using DOS	SYS001-UT-3330-S-SORTWK1

In the DATA DIVISION's FILE SECTION, the SD means a Sort-file Description. In the PROCEDURE DIVISION, the SORT sentence makes the computer automatically open the CUSTOM-FILE, sort it, and close it.

In the SORT sentence, if you replace ASCENDING by DESCENDING, the computer will sort the file in reverse order, so the Z's come first and the A's come last.

You can make the program fancier, by inserting extra statements before and after the SORT statement. But since the SORT statement automatically tells the computer to open CUSTOM-FILE, the CUSTOM-FILE must not be open already. If you already said OPEN CUSTOM-FILE, you must say CLOSE CUSTOM-FILE before you give the SORT statement.

If you replace GIVING CUSTOM-FILE by GIVING REPORT-FILE, the computer won't change CUSTOM-FILE, but will create a REPORT-FILE containing the information sorted. For REPORT-FILE, you must type an FD and SELECT it. The computer will automatically open it, so it must not be open already.

Who bought the most?
Within each line of CUSTOM-FILE, suppose characters 51-57 tell how much the customer bought from you during the past year. Let's find out which customers bought the most.

Let's make the computer print the customer that bought the most, then the customer that bought the next most, etc. If two customers bought exactly the same amount, let's make the computer print their names in alphabetical order.

This program does it:

```
IDENTIFICATION DIVISION.
PROGRAM-ID.
        BIGBUY.
```

The ENVIRONMENT DIVISION is same as the previous program's.

```
DATA DIVISION.
FILE SECTION.
FD      CUSTOM-FILE the labeling for CUSTOM.
01      CUSTOM-LINE PIC X(80).
SD      SORT-FILE.
01      SORT-LINE.
        02      LAST-NAME PIC X(20).          characters 1-20
        02      FILLER PIC X(30).             characters 21-50
        02      AMOUNT-BOUGHT-DURING-YEAR PIC 99999V99.
        02      FILLER PIC X(23).

PROCEDURE DIVISION.
MAIN-ROUTINE.
        SORT SORT-FILE
                DESCENDING KEY AMOUNT-BOUGHT-DURING-YEAR
                ASCENDING KEY LAST-NAME
                USING CUSTOM-FILE
                GIVING CUSTOM-FILE.
        STOP RUN.
```

The SORT sentence says: sort the file so that AMOUNT-BOUGHT-DURING-YEAR is in DESCENDING order; in case of a tie, put LAST-NAME in ASCENDING order.

MERGE

Suppose OLDCUS and NEWCUS are files: OLDCUS describes your old customers, and NEWCUS describes your newer customers. In those files, each line contains 80 characters; characters 1-20 contain the customer's last name. Each file's already in alphabetical order, by customer's last name.

Let's combine the two files. In other words, let's create a "combination" file (on disk or printer paper), called ALLCUS, that contains *all* the customers; and let's make ALLCUS be in alphabetical order also. Here's how:

```
IDENTIFICATION DIVISION.
PROGRAM-ID.
        MERGER.


ENVIRONMENT DIVISION.
CONFIGURATION SECTION.
SOURCE-COMPUTER.
        The computer's name.
OBJECT-COMPUTER.
        The computer's name again.
INPUT-OUTPUT SECTION.
FILE-CONTROL.
        SELECT OLDCUS-FILE ASSIGN TO the location of OLDCUS.
        SELECT NEWCUS-FILE ASSIGN TO the location of NEWCUS.
        SELECT ALLCUS-FILE ASSIGN TO the location of ALLCUS.
        SELECT SORT-FILE ASSIGN TO the location of SORT.


DATA DIVISION.
FILE SECTION.
FD      OLDCUS-FILE the labeling for OLDCUS.
01      OLDCUS-LINE PIC X(80).
FD      NEWCUS-FILE the labeling for NEWCUS.
01      NEWCUS-LINE PIC X(80).
FD      ALLCUS-FILE the labeling for ALLCUS.
01      ALLCUS-LINE PIC X(80).
SD      SORT-FILE.
01      SORT-LINE.
        02      LAST-NAME PIC X(20).
        02      FILLER PIC X(60).


PROCEDURE DIVISION.
MAIN-ROUTINE.
        MERGE SORT-FILE
                ASCENDING KEY LAST-NAME
                USING OLDCUS-FILE NEWCUS-FILE
                GIVING ALLCUS-FILE.
        STOP RUN.
```

That program creates ALLCUS, which is a combination of OLDCUS and NEWCUS. To do that, the computer must create a SORT-FILE.

The word MERGE automatically opens and closes all the files involved. so do *not* say OPEN or CLOSE.

Warning: the word MERGE is in COBOL 74 but not in COBOL 68. So if your computer is old-fashioned and understands just COBOL 68, it doesn't understand the word MERGE.

If your computer understands the word MERGE, you can merge as many files as you like. For example, if you have files called CUS1, CUS2, CUS3, and CUS4, you can say:

```
MERGE SORT-FILE
        ASCENDING KEY LAST-NAME
        USING CUS1-FILE CUS2-FILE CUS3-FILE CUS4-FILE
        GIVING ALLCUS-FILE.
```

Before you MERGE, make sure that the files you're USING are already in alphabetical order.

Subscripts

Like other computer languages, COBOL lets you use subscripts.

For example, suppose your 4 favorite friends are SUE, JOE, TOM, and ANN. Let's make FAVORITE-FRIEND (1) be "SUE", FAVORITE-FRIEND (2) be "JOE", FAVORITE-FRIEND (3) be "TOM", and FAVORITE-FRIEND (4) be "ANN". Here's how:

```
DATA DIVISION.
WORKING-STORAGE SECTION.
01      FAVORITE-FRIEND-TABLE.
        02      FAVORITE-FRIEND OCCURS 4 TIMES PIC XXX.  You have 4 FAVORITE-FRIENDs; each has PIC XXX.

PROCEDURE DIVISION.
MAIN-ROUTINE.
        MOVE "SUE" TO FAVORITE-FRIEND (1).
        MOVE "JOE" TO FAVORITE-FRIEND (2).
        MOVE "TOM" TO FAVORITE-FRIEND (3).
        MOVE "ANN" TO FAVORITE-FRIEND (4).
        DISPLAY FAVORITE-FRIEND (1).
        DISPLAY FAVORITE-FRIEND (2).
        DISPLAY FAVORITE-FRIEND (3).
        DISPLAY FAVORITE-FRIEND (4).
        STOP RUN.
```

The computer will display:

```
SUE
JOE
TOM
ANN
```

When typing the program, remember to put a blank space before the subscript:

```
FAVORITE-FRIEND (1)
               ↑
            blank space
```

In COBOL, you say "OCCURS" instead of "DIMENSION":

```
BASIC:   DIM F(4)
FORTRAN: DIMENSION F(4)
PASCAL:  F: ARRAY [1..4]
COBOL:   F OCCURS 4 TIMES
```

The subscript can be a variable. For example, instead of saying —

```
DISPLAY FAVORITE-FRIEND (1).
DISPLAY FAVORITE-FRIEND (2).
DISPLAY FAVORITE-FRIEND (3).
DISPLAY FAVORITE-FRIEND (4).
```

you can say:

```
DISPLAY FAVORITE-FRIEND (I).
```

To do that, you must tell the computer that the I goes from 1 to 4. Here's how:

```
DATA DIVISION.
WORKING-STORAGE SECTION.
01      FAVORITE-FRIEND-TABLE.
        02      FAVORITE-FRIEND OCCURS 4 TIMES PIC XXX.
01      I PIC 9.                                         I is a one-digit number.

PROCEDURE DIVISION.
MAIN-ROUTINE.
        MOVE "SUE" TO FAVORITE-FRIEND (1).
        MOVE "JOE" TO FAVORITE-FRIEND (2).
        MOVE "TOM" TO FAVORITE-FRIEND (3).
        MOVE "ANN" TO FAVORITE-FRIEND (4).
        PERFORM SHOW-FRIENDSHIP
                VARYING I FROM 1 BY 1 UNTIL I > 4.       I will be 1, 2, 3, 4.
        STOP RUN.
SHOW-FRIENDSHIP.
        DISPLAY FAVORITE-FRIEND (I).                     I is the subscript.
```

To make the program run faster, say "COMP" at the end of the subscript's picture:

Computer	What to say		
PDP, Eclipse	01	I PIC 9 COMP.	
CDC	01	I PIC 9 COMP-1.	
IBM	01	I PIC 9 COMP SYNC.	

COMP stands for the word COMPUTATIONAL; SYNC stands for the word SYNCHRONIZED.

A subscript cannot contain an operation:

Okay: `FAVORITE-FRIEND (3)`

Wrong: `FAVORITE-FRIEND (2 + 1)`   The + is not allowed.

Here's how to make Y-TABLE be a table that has 4 rows and 6 columns:

```
01      Y-TABLE.
        02      Y-ROW OCCURS 4 TIMES.
                03      Y OCCURS 6 TIMES PIC XXX.
```

The entire table is called:

`Y-TABLE`

The first row of Y-TABLE is called:

`Y-ROW (1)`

The second row of Y-TABLE is called:

`Y-ROW (2)`

The entry in the 2nd row and 5th column of Y-TABLE is called:

`Y␣(2,␣5)`
  `spaces`

Test scores

Suppose you teach 25 students, you've given each student 4 tests, and you want to put the scores in a table.

You want the table to contain 25 rows (a row for each student). In each row, you want the student's first name, middle initial, last name, and 4 scores.

Here's how:

```
01      STUDENT-INFORMATION-TABLE.
        02      STUDENT-INFORMATION-ROW OCCURS 25 TIMES.
                03      FIRST-NAME PIC X(15).
                03      MIDDLE-INITIAL PIC X.
                03      LAST-NAME PIC X(20).
                03      TEST-SCORE OCCURS 4 TIMES PIC 999.
```

The entire table is called:

`STUDENT-INFORMATION-TABLE`

The table contains 25 rows. The first row is called:

`STUDENT-INFORMATION-ROW (1)`

The twelfth row is called:

`STUDENT-INFORMATION-ROW (12)`

The information in the twelfth row is called:

```
FIRST-NAME (12)
MIDDLE-INITIAL (12)
LAST-NAME (12)
TEST-SCORE (12, 1)
TEST-SCORE (12, 2)
TEST-SCORE (12, 3)
TEST-SCORE (12, 4)
```

EXTRA COMMENTS

Put extra comments in your program, to help your colleagues understand how the program works.

IDENTIFICATION DIVISION

The IDENTIFICATION DIVISION can include these paragraphs:

```
PROGRAM-ID.
AUTHOR.
INSTALLATION.
DATE-WRITTEN.
DATE-COMPILED.
SECURITY.
```

In each paragraph after the PROGRAM-ID, put whatever garbage you please. The computer ignores everything the IDENTIFICATION DIVISION says.

The IDENTIFICATION DIVISION helps the computer center's librarian classify your program. The librarian wants the INSTALLATION paragraph to contain the computer center's name and address, the DATE-WRITTEN paragraph to tell when you finished debugging the program, the DATE-COMPILED paragraph to tell when the computer translated the program from COBOL into machine language, and the SECURITY paragraph to tell who may look at the program and who must not.

If you put the wrong date in the date-compiled paragraph, don't worry: when you ask the computer to produce a **COBOL listing** of your program, the listing will automatically show the correct date instead.

Asterisks

The computer ignores any line that begins with an asterisk. So if you put this line in your program —

`*THIS IS A LOUSY PROGRAM`

— the computer will ignore the comment.

Create comments that explain how your program works. Put the comments near the bottom of the IDENTIFICATION DIVISION, near the top of the PROCEDURE DIVISION, and wherever your program looks confusing.

On PDP and Eclipse computers, put the asterisk at the far left; don't put any blank spaces before the asterisk. On IBM and CDC computers, put six blank spaces before the asterisk, so that the asterisk is in column 7.

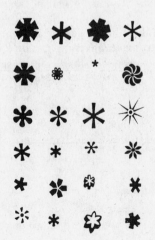

STRANGE TONGUES

You've already learned the most popular computer languages: BASIC, DBASE, PASCAL, C, LOGO, FORTRAN, and COBOL.

But those seven languages are just the tip of the iceberg. Programmers have invented *thousands* of others.

Here's a multilingual dictionary that lets you translate 15 languages. For example, it shows that BASIC says "DIM X(4)" but FORTRAN says "DIMENSION X(4)" instead.

```
BASIC    DIM X(4)                 FOR I = 5 TO 17                                      GOSUB 1000    GO TO 50
FORTRAN  DIMENSION X(4)           DO 10 I=5,17                                         CALL JOE      GO TO 50
PL/I     DECLARE X(4)             DO I = 5 TO 17                                       CALL JOE      GO TO GAIL

ALGOL    REAL ARRAY X[1:4]        FOR I := 5 STEP 1 UNTIL 17 DO                        JOE           GO TO GAIL
PASCAL   X: ARRAY[1..4] OF REAL   FOR I := 5 TO 17 DO                                  JOE           GOTO 50
MODULA   X: ARRAY[1..4] OF REAL   FOR I := 5 TO 17 DO                                  JOE           not available
ADA      X: ARRAY(1..4) OF FLOAT  FOR I IN 5..17 LOOP                                  JOE           GO TO GAIL

C        FLOAT X[4]               FOR (I=5; I<=17; ++I)                                JOE()         GOTO GAIL
EASY     PREPARE X(4)             LOOP I FROM 5 TO 17                                  JOE           SKIP TO GAIL
DBASE    DECLARE X[4]             not available                                       DO JOE        not available
COBOL    X OCCURS 4 TIMES         PERFORM SAM VARYING I FROM 5 BY 1 UNTIL I > 17       PERFORM JOE   GO TO GAIL

LOGO     DEFAR "X 4 1             not available                                        JOE           GO "GAIL
LISP     (ARRAY ((X (4) LIST)))   not available                                       (JOE)         (GO GAIL)
SNOBOL   X = ARRAY(4)             not available                                       JOE()         :(GAIL)
PILOT    DIM:#X(4)                not available                                        U:JOE         J:*GAIL
```

```
BASIC    IF X=4.3 THEN        INPUT K             J=K+2           PRINT K             'SILLY STUFF
FORTRAN  IF (X .EQ. 4.3)      READ *, K           J=K+2           PRINT *, K          C SILLY STUFF
PL/I     IF X=4.3 THEN        GET LIST(K)         J=K+2           PUT LIST(K)         /* SILLY STUFF */

ALGOL    IF X=4.3 THEN        READ(K)             J:=K+2          PRINT(K)            COMMENT  SILLY STUFF
PASCAL   IF X=4.3 THEN        READ(K)             J:=K+2          WRITELN(K)          {SILLY STUFF}
MODULA   IF X=4.3 THEN        READINTEGER(K)      J:=K+2          WRITEINTEGER(K,6)   (*SILLY STUFF*)
ADA      IF X=4.3 THEN        GET(K)              J:=K+2          PUT(K)              --SILLY STUFF

C        IF (X==4.3)          SCANF("%D,&K)       J=K+2           PRINTF("%D",K)      /* SILLY STUFF */
EASY     IF X=4.3             GET K               LET J=K+2       SAY K               'SILLY STUFF
DBASE    IF X=4.3             INPUT TO K          J=K+2           ? K                 &&SILLY STUFF
COBOL    IF X = 4.3           ACCEPT K            COMPUTE J = K + 2   DISPLAY K       *SILLY STUFF

LOGO     IF :X=4.3            MAKE "K READWORD    MAKE "J :K+2    PRINT :K            !SILLY STUFF
LISP     (COND ((EQUAL X 4.3) (SETQ K (READ))    (SETQ J (PLUS K 2))  K              ;SILLY STUFF
SNOBOL   EQ(X,4.3) :S(        K = INPUT           J = K + 2       OUTPUT = K          *SILLY STUFF
PILOT    (#X=4.3)             A:#K                C:#J=#K+2       T:#K                R:SILLY STUFF
```

The dictionary clumps the languages into groups. For example, look at the languages in the second group: ALGOL, PASCAL, MODULA, and ADA. Those four languages are almost identical to each other. For example, in each of them you say "J:=K+2".

The bottom group (LOGO, LISP, SNOBOL, and PILOT) differs wildly from the others. For example, look at how those four languages translate "IF X=4.3 THEN" and "J=K+2". They're called **radical languages**; the other eleven languages are called **mainstream**.

Two other radical languages are APL and FORTH. They're so weird that they won't fit in the chart!

Here's how to make the computer do 2+2 and print the answer (4), using each of those languages:

```
BASIC and LOGO   EASY     DBASE    APL    LISP          FORTH    SNOBOL              ALGOL           PASCAL            ADA
PRINT 2+2        SAY 2+2  ? 2+2    2+2    (PLUS 2 2)     2 2 + .      OUTPUT = 2 + 2   BEGIN           BEGIN             PROCEDURE HARRY IS
                                                                     END             PRINT(2+2);     WRITELN(2+2);     BEGIN
                                                                                     END             END.              PUT(2+2);
                                                                                                                       END;
```

```
FORTRAN      PILOT        C                    PL/I                                  MODULA                       COBOL
N=2+2        C:#N=2+2     MAIN(){              HARRY: PROCEDURE OPTIONS(MAIN);       MODULE HARRY;                IDENTIFICATION DIVISION.
PRINT *, N   T:#N            PRINTF("%D",2+2);        PUT LIST(2+2);                 FROM INOUT                   DATA DIVISION.
END                       }                          END;                             IMPORT WRITEINTEGER;       WORKING-STORAGE SECTION.
                                                                                     BEGIN                        01   N PIC 9.
                                                                                     WRITEINTEGER(2+2,6);         PROCEDURE DIVISION.
                                                                                     END HARRY.                   MAIN-ROUTINE.
                                                                                                                     ADD 2 2 GIVING N.
                                                                                                                     DISPLAY N.
                                                                                                                     STOP RUN.
```

Notice that APL's the briefest (just say 2+2), and COBOL's the most verbose (it requires 9 lines of typing).

Each of those 17 languages is flexible enough to program anything. Which language you choose is mainly a matter of personal taste.

Other languages are more specialized. For example, a language called "GPSS" is designed specifically to analyze how many employees to hire, to save your customers from waiting in long lines for service. DYNAMO analyzes social interactions inside your company and city and throughout the world; then it graphs your future. SPSS analyzes tables of numbers, by computing their averages, maxima, minima, standard deviations, and *hundreds* of other measurements used by statisticians. APT helps you run a factory by controlling "robots" that cut metal. PROLOG lets you store answers to your questions and act as an **expert system**. RPG spits out long business reports for executives who don't have enough time to program in COBOL.

The following table reveals more details about all those languages. Within each category ("mainstream", "radical", and "specialized"), the table lists the languages in chronological order.

Name	What the name stands for	Original use	Version 1 arose at	When	Names of new versions
Mainstream languages					
FORTRAN	FORmula TRANslating	sciences	IBM	1954-1957	FORTRAN 90, Lahey FORTRAN
ALGOL	ALGOrithmic Language	sciences	international	1957-1958	ALGOL W, ALGOL 68, BALGOL
COBOL	COmmon Business-Oriented Language	business	Defense Department	1959-1960	COBOL 85
BASIC	Beginners All-purp. Symbolic Instruc. Code	sciences	Dartmouth College	1963-1964	QBASIC, Visual BASIC
PL/I	Programming Language One	general	IBM	1963-1966	PL/I Optimizer, PL/C, ANSI PL/I
PASCAL	Blaise PASCAL	general	Switzerland	1968-1970	Turbo PASCAL, Quick PASCAL
MODULA	MODULAr programming	systems program'ng	Switzerland	1975	MODULA-2
C	C	systems program'ng	Bell Telephone Labs	1970-1977	Microsoft C, Turbo C, C++
ADA	ADA Lovelace	military equipment	France	1977-1980	ADA final version
DBASE	Data BASE	database manage'nt	Jet Prop'n Lab & Ashton-T.	1978-1980	DBASE 5, FOXPRO 2.6
EASY	EASY	general	Secret Guide	1972-1982	EASY
Radical languages					
LISP	LISt Processing	artificial intelligence	MIT	1958-1960	Common LISP
SNOBOL	StriNg-Oriented symBOlic Language	string processing	Bell Telephone Labs	1962-1963	SNOBOL 4B
APL	A Programming Language	sciences	Harvard & IBM	1956-1966	APLSV, APL PLUS
LOGO	LOGO	general	Bolt Beranek Newman	1967	LCSI LOGO, LOGO Writer
FORTH	FOuRTH-generation language	busin. & astronomy	Stanford Univ. & Mohasco	1963-1968	FORTH83, FIG-FORTH, MMS F.
PILOT	Programmed Inquiry, Learning, Or Teaching	tutoring kids	U. of Cal. at San Francisco	1968	Atari PILOT
Specialized languages					
APT	Automatically Programmed Tools	cutting metal	MIT	1952-1957	APT 77
DYNAMO	DYNAmic MOdels	simulation	MIT	1959	DYNAMO 3, STELLA
GPSS	General-Purpose Simulation System	simulation	IBM	1961	GPSS 5
RPG	Report Program Generator	business	IBM	1964	RPG 3
SPSS	Statistical Package for the Social Sciences	statistics	Stanford University	1965-1967	SPSS 5
PROLOG	PROgramming in LOGic	artificial intelligence	France	1972	Arity PROLOG, Turbo PROLOG

Of those 23 languages, 5 were invented in Europe (ALGOL, PASCAL, MODULA, ADA, and PROLOG). The others were invented in the United States.

5 were invented at IBM's research facilities (FORTRAN, PL/I, APL, GPSS, and RPG), 3 at MIT (LISP, APT, and DYNAMO), 2 at Stanford University (FORTH and SPSS), 2 by Professor Niklaus Wirth in Switzerland (PASCAL and MODULA), and 2 at Bell Telephone Labs (C and SNOBOL). The others were invented by geniuses elsewhere.

MAINSTREAM LANGUAGES

The first mainstream languages were **FORTRAN, ALGOL,** and **COBOL**. FORTRAN appealed to engineers, ALGOL to logicians, and COBOL to business executives. FORTRAN was invented by IBM, ALGOL by an international committee, and COBOL by a committee based at the Pentagon.

The other mainstream languages, which came later, were just slight improvements of FORTRAN, ALGOL, and COBOL.

For example, two professors at Dartmouth College combined FORTRAN with ALGOL, to form **BASIC**. It was designed for students, not professionals: it included just the *easiest* parts of FORTRAN and ALGOL. Students liked it because it was easy to learn, but professionals complained it lacked advanced features.

After inventing FORTRAN and further improvements (called FORTRAN II, FORTRAN III, FORTRAN IV, and FORTRAN V), IBM decided to invent the "ultimate" improvement: a language that would include all the important words of FORTRAN V and **ALGOL** and **COBOL**. At first, IBM called it "FORTRAN VI"; but since it included the best of everything and was the first *complete* language ever invented, IBM changed its name to **Programming Language One** (written as **PL/I**). IBM bragged about how PL/I was so eclectic, but most programmers considered it a confusing mishmash and continued using the original three languages (FORTRAN, ALGOL, and COBOL), which were pure and simple.

Among the folks who disliked PL/I was Niklaus Wirth, who preferred ALGOL. At a Swiss university, he invented an improved ALGOL and called it **PASCAL**. Then he invented a further improvement, called **MODULA**. ALGOL, PASCAL, and MODULA are all very similar to each other. He thinks MODULA's the best of the trio, but critics disagree. Today, PASCAL is still the most popular; hardly anybody uses the original ALGOL anymore, and MODULA is considered a controversial experiment.

While Wirth was developing and improving MODULA, other researchers were developing four competitors: C, ADA, DBASE, and EASY. Here's why.

Why C? Fancy languages, such as PL/I and MODULA, require lots of RAM. At Bell Telephone Labs, researchers needed a language small enough to fit in the tiny RAM of a minicomputer or microcomputer. They developed the ideal tiny language and called it **C**. Like PL/I, it borrows from FORTRAN, ALGOL, and COBOL; but it lacks PL/I's frills. It's "lean and mean" and runs very quickly.

Why ADA? The Department of Defense, which was happily using COBOL to run the military's bureaucracy, needed to invent a second kind of language, to control missiles and other military equipment. The Department held a contest to develop such a language and said it wanted the language to resemble PL/I, ALGOL, and PASCAL. (It didn't know about MODULA, which was still being developed.) The winner was a French company. The Department adopted that company's language and called it **ADA**. It resembled MODULA but included more commands — and therefore consumed more RAM and was more expensive. Critics complain that ADA, like PL/I, is too large and complex.

Why DBASE? Inspired by languages such as BASIC and PL/I, Wayne Ratliff invented **DBASE**. Like BASIC, DBASE is easy; like PL/I and PASCAL, DBASE creates loops by saying WHILE instead of GO TO. What makes DBASE unique is its new commands for manipulating databases. Of all the new mainstream languages (C, ADA, DBASE, and EASY), DBASE has become the greatest commercial success, and Wayne has become rich.

Why EASY? My own attempt to create the ideal language is called **EASY**. It's even easier to learn than BASIC, yet includes the power of languages such as PASCAL. But since I don't have the time to put EASY onto a computer, EASY's remained just an idea whose time should have come.

Dig in! Here are the inside secrets about all those mainstream languages. . . .

FORTRAN

During the early 1950's, the only available computer languages were specialized or awkward. FORTRAN was the first computer language good enough to be considered mainstream. ALGOL and COBOL came shortly afterwards. FORTRAN, ALGOL, and COBOL were so good that they made all earlier languages obsolete.

How FORTRAN developed In 1954, an IBM committee said it was planning a new computer language that would help engineers make the computer handle math formulas. The committee called the language **FORTRAN**, to emphasize that the language would be particularly good for TRANslating FORmulas into computer notation.

Those original plans for FORTRAN were modest. They did *not* allow long variable names, subroutines, long function definitions, double precision, complex numbers, or apostrophes.

According to the plans, a variable's name had to be short: just two letters. A function's definition had to fit on a single line. Instead of using apostrophes and writing 'PLEASE KISS ME', the programmers had to write 14HPLEASE KISS ME; the 14H meant a 14-character string.

The first working version of FORTRAN (1957) allowed longer variable names: up to 6 characters. FORTRAN II (1958) allowed subroutines and long function definitions. IBM experimented with FORTRAN III but never released it to the public. FORTRAN IV (1962) allowed double precision and complex numbers. Apostrophes around strings weren't allowed until later.

The original plans said you'd be able to add an integer to a real. That didn't work in FORTRAN I, FORTRAN II, and FORTRAN IV, but it works today.

The original plans said an IF statement would compare any two numbers. FORTRAN I and FORTRAN II required the second number to be zero, but FORTRAN IV removed that restriction.

IBM waged a campaign to convince everyone that FORTRAN was easier than previous methods of programming. IBM succeeded: FORTRAN became immediately popular. FORTRAN was easy enough so that, for the first time, engineers who weren't computer specialists could write programs.

Other manufacturers sold imitations of IBM's FORTRAN, but with modifications. The variety of modifications from all the manufacturers annoyed engineers, who wished manufacturers would all use a single, common version of FORTRAN. So the engineers turned to the **American National Standards Institute (ANSI)**, which is a non-profit group of engineers that sets standards. ("ANSI" is pronounced "an see". It sets standards for practically all equipment in your life. For example, ANSI sets the standard for screws: to tighten a screw, you turn it clockwise, not counterclockwise.)

In 1966, ANSI decided on a single version of FORTRAN IV to be used by all manufacturers. Thereafter, each manufacturer adhered to the ANSI standard but also added extra commands, to try to outclass the other manufacturers.

After several years had gone by, enough extra commands had been added by manufacturers so engineers asked ANSI to meet again and develop a common standard for those extras. ANSI finished developing the standard in 1977 and called it **FORTRAN 77**.

Today, each major manufacturer adheres to the standard for FORTRAN 77, so you can run FORTRAN 77 programs on most maxicomputers, minicomputers, and microcomputers. Each manufacturer adds extra commands beyond FORTRAN 77.

In 1984, an ANSI committee developed a "FORTRAN 88". 40 members of the committee approved it, but the other 2 members — IBM and DEC — refused to endorse it. In 1991, a variant called **FORTRAN 90** was finally approved by all.

FORTRAN's popularity
FORTRAN became popular immediately because it didn't have any serious competitors. Throughout the 1960's and 1970's, FORTRAN remained the most popular computer language among engineers, scientists, mathematicians, and college students. Colleges required all freshman computer-science majors to take FORTRAN.

But at the end of the 1970's, FORTRAN's popularity began to drop. Engineers switched to newer languages, such as BASIC (which is easier), PASCAL (more logical), and C (faster and more economical of RAM). Although FORTRAN 77 included extra commands to make FORTRAN resemble BASIC and PASCAL, those commands were "too little, too late": FORTRAN's new string commands weren't quite as good as BASIC's, and FORTRAN's new IF command wasn't quite as good as PASCAL's.

Now high-school kids are required to study BASIC, college kids are required to study PASCAL, professional programmers are required to study C, and hardly anybody studies FORTRAN. People who still program in FORTRAN are called "old-fashioned" by their colleagues.

But in some ways, FORTRAN's still better for engineering that BASIC, PASCAL, or C. For example, FORTRAN includes more commands for handling "complex numbers". FORTRAN programmers have developed libraries containing *thousands* of FORTRAN subroutines, which you can use in your own FORTRAN programs; such large libraries haven't been developed for BASIC, PASCAL, or C yet.

Although BASIC, PASCAL, and C work well on microcomputers and minicomputers, no *good* versions of those languages have been invented for IBM maxicomputers yet. The only language that lets you unleash an IBM maxicomputer's full power to solve engineering problems is FORTRAN.

ALGOL
In 1955, a committee in Germany began inventing a computer language. Though the committee spoke German, it decided the computer language should use English words instead, since English was the international language for science.

In 1957 those Germans invited Americans to join them. In 1958 other European countries joined also, to form an international committee, which proposed a new computer language, called "IAL" (International Algebraic Language).

The committee eventually changed the language's name to **ALGOL 58** (the ALGOrithmic Language invented in 1958), then created an improved version called **ALGOL 60**, then created a further revision called **ALGOL 60 Revised**, and disbanded. Today, programmers who mention "ALGOL" usually mean the committee's last report, ALGOL 60 Revised.

ALGOL differs from FORTRAN in many little ways. . . .

How to end a statement
At the end of each statement, FORTRAN requires you to press the ENTER key. ALGOL requires you to type a semicolon instead.

ALGOL's advantage: you can type many statements on the same line, by putting semicolons between the statements. ALGOL's disadvantage: those ugly semicolons are a nuisance to type and make your program look cluttered.

Integer variables
To tell the computer that a person's AGE is an integer (instead of a real number), FORTRAN requires you to put the letter I, J, K, L, M, or N before the variable's name, like this: IAGE. ALGOL requires you to insert a note saying "INTEGER AGE" at the top of your program instead.

ALGOL's advantage: you don't have to write unpronounceable gobbledygook such as "IAGE". ALGOL's disadvantage: whenever you create a new variable, ALGOL forces you to go back up to the top of your program and insert a line saying "INTEGER" or "REAL".

Assignment statements
In FORTRAN, you can say J=7. In ALGOL, you must insert a colon and say J:=7 instead.

To increase K by 1 in FORTRAN, you say K=K+1. In ALGOL, you say K:=K+1.

ALGOL's disadvantage: the colon is a nuisance to type. FORTRAN's disadvantage: according to the rules of algebra, it's impossible for K to equal K+1, and so the FORTRAN command K=K+1 looks like an impossibility.

ALGOL's beauty
ALGOL avoids FORTRAN's ugliness, in the following ways. . . .

In ALGOL, a variable's name can be practically as long as you like. In FORTRAN, a variable's name must be short: no more than 6 characters.

ALGOL lets you write 2 instead of 2.0, without affecting the computer's answer. In FORTRAN, if you write 1/2 instead of 1/2.0, you get 0 instead of .5; and if you write SQRT (9) instead of SQRT (9.0), you get nonsense.

ALGOL's IF statement is very flexible: it can include the words ELSE, BEGIN, and END, and it lets you insert as many statements as you want between BEGIN and END. ALGOL even lets you put an IF statement in the middle of an equation, like this: X:=2+(IF Y<5 THEN 8 ELSE 9). The IF statement in FORTRAN I, II, III, and IV was very limited; the IF statement in FORTRAN 77 copies some of ALGOL's power, but not yet all.

ALGOL's FOR statement is very flexible. To make X be 3.7, then be Y+6.2, then go from SQRT(Z) down to 5 in steps of .3, you can say "FOR X:=3.7, Y+6.2, SQRT(Z) STEP -.3 UNTIL 5 DO". FORTRAN's DO is more restrictive; some versions of FORTRAN even insist that the DO statement must not contain reals, must not contain negatives, and must not contain arithmetic operations.

At the beginning of a FORTRAN program, you can say DIMENSION X(20) but not DIMENSION X(N). ALGOL permits the "DIMENSION X(N)" concept; in ALGOL you say ARRAY X[1:N].

ALGOL's popularity

When ALGOL was invented, programmers loved it. Europeans began using ALGOL more than FORTRAN. The American computer association (called the **Association for Computing Machinery, ACM**) said all programs in its magazine would be in ALGOL.

But IBM refused to put ALGOL on its computers. Since most American programmers used IBM computers, most American programmers couldn't use ALGOL. That created a ridiculous situation: American programmers programmed in FORTRAN instead, but submitted ALGOL translations to the ACM's magazine, which published the programs in ALGOL, which the magazine's readers had to translate back to FORTRAN in order to run on IBM computers.

IBM computers eventually swept over Europe, so that even Europeans had to use FORTRAN instead of ALGOL.

In 1966 the ACM gave in and agreed to publish programs in FORTRAN. But since ALGOL was prettier, everybody continued to submit ALGOL versions anyway.

IBM gave in also and put ALGOL on its computers. But IBM's version of ALGOL was so limited and awkward that nobody took it seriously, and IBM stopped selling it and supporting it.

In 1972 Stanford University created ALGOL W, a better version that ran on IBM computers. But ALGOL W came too late: universities and businessmen had already grown tired of waiting for a good IBM ALGOL and had committed themselves to FORTRAN.

Critics blamed IBM for ALGOL's demise. But here's IBM's side of the story. . . .

IBM had invested 25 man-years to develop the first version of FORTRAN. By the time the ALGOL committee finished the report on ALGOL 60 Revised, IBM had also developed FORTRAN II and FORTRAN III and made plans for FORTRAN IV. IBM was proud of its FORTRANs and wanted to elaborate on them.

Moreover, IBM realized that **computers run FORTRAN programs more quickly than ALGOL.**

When asked why it didn't support ALGOL, IBM replied that the committee's description of ALGOL was incomplete. IBM was right; the ALGOL 60 Revised Report has three loopholes:

1. **The report doesn't say what words to use for input and output**, because the committee couldn't agree. So computers differ. If you want to transfer an ALGOL program from one computer to another, you must change all the input and output instructions.

2. **The report uses symbols such as ÷ and ∧, which aren't on most keyboards.** The report underlines keywords; most keyboards can't underline. To type ALGOL programs on a typical keyboard, you must substitute other symbols for ÷, ∧, and underlining. Here again, manufacturers differ. To transfer an ALGOL program to another manufacturer, you must change symbols.

3. **Some features of ALGOL are hard to teach to a computer.** Even today, no computer understands all of ALGOL. When a manufacturer says its computer "understands ALGOL", you must ask, *"Which* features of ALGOL?"

Attempts to improve ALGOL

Long after the original ALGOL committee wrote the ALGOL 60 Revised Report, two other ALGOL committees were formed.

One committee developed suggestions on how to do input and output, but its suggestions were largely ignored.

The other committee tried to invent a much fancier ALGOL. That committee wrote its preliminary report in 1968 and revised it in 1975. Called **ALGOL 68 Revised**, that weird report requires you to spell words backwards: to mark the end of the IF statement, you say FI; to mark the end of the DO statement, you say OD. The committee's decision was far from unanimous: several members refused to endorse the report.

ALGOL today

Few programmers still use ALGOL, but many use PASCAL (which is very similar to ALGOL 60 Revised) and BASIC (which is a compromise between ALGOL and FORTRAN).

COBOL

During the 1950's, several organizations developed languages to solve problems in business. The most popular business languages were IBM's COMMERCIAL TRANSLATOR (developed from 1957-1959), Honeywell's FACT (1959-1960), Sperry Rand's FLOW-MATIC (1954-1958), and the Air Force's AIMACO (1958).

In April 1959, a group of programmers and manufacturers met at the University of Pennsylvania and decided to develop a *single* business language for *all* computers. The group asked the Department of Defense to help sponsor the research.

The Department agreed, and so a follow-up meeting was held at the Pentagon in May. At that meeting, the group tentatively decided to call the new language "CBL" (for "Common Business Language") and created three committees.

The Short-Range Committee would meet immediately to develop a temporary language. A Medium-Range Committee would meet later to develop a more thoroughly thought-out language. Then a Long-Range Committee would develop the ultimate language.

The Short-Range Committee met immediately and created a language nice enough so that the Medium-Range and Long-Range Committees never bothered to meet.

The Short-Range Committee wanted a more pronounceable name for the language than "CBL". At a meeting in September 1969, the committee members proposed six names: "BUSY" (BUsiness SYstem), "BUSYL" (BUsiness SYstem Language), "INFOSYL" (INFOrmation SYstem Language), "DATASYL" (DATA SYstem Language), "COSYL" (COmmon SYstem Language), and "COCOSYL" (COmmon COmputer SYstem Language). The next day, a member of the committee suggested "COBOL" (COmmon Business-Oriented Language), and the rest of the committee agreed.

I wish they'd have kept the name "BUSY", because it's easier to pronounce and remember than "COBOL". Today, COBOL programmers are still known as "BUSY bodies".

From Sperry Rand's FLOW-MATIC, the new language (called "COBOL") borrowed two rules: begin each statement with an English verb, and put data descriptions in a different program division than procedures. From IBM's COMMERCIAL TRANSLATOR, COBOL borrowed group items (01 and 02), PICTURE symbols, fancy IF statements, and COMPUTE formulas.

Compromises

On some issues, the members of the committee couldn't agree, and so they had to compromise.

For example, some members wanted COBOL to let the programmers construct mathematical formulas by using these symbols:

$$+ \quad - \quad * \quad / \quad = \quad (\quad)$$

But other members of the committee disagreed: they argued that since COBOL is supposed to be for stupid businessmen who fear formulas, COBOL ought to use the words ADD, SUBTRACT, MULTIPLY, and DIVIDE instead. The committee compromised: when you write a COBOL program, you can use the words ADD, SUBTRACT, MULTIPLY, and DIVIDE; if you prefer, you can use a formula instead, but you must warn the computer by putting the word COMPUTE in front of the formula.

COBOL can handle short numbers. Can it handle long numbers also? How long? How many digits? The committee decided that COBOL would handle any number up to 18 digits long. The committee also decided that COBOL would handle any variable name up to 30 characters long. So the limits of COBOL are "18 and 30". Why did the committee pick those two numbers — "18 and 30" — instead of "16 and 32"? Answer: some manufacturers wanted "16 and 32" (because their computers were based on the numbers 16 and 32), but other manufacturers wanted other combinations (such as "24 and 236"); the committee, hunting for a compromise, chose "18 and 30", because *nobody* wanted it, and so it would give no manufacturer an unfair advantage over competitors. In other words, COBOL was designed to be equally terrible for everybody! That's politics!

COBOL's popularity

In 1960, the Department of Defense announced it would buy only computers that understand COBOL, unless a manufacturer can demonstrate why COBOL would not be helpful. In 1961, Westinghouse Electric Corp. made a similar announcement. Other companies followed. COBOL became the most popular computer language. Today it's still the most popular computer language for maxicomputers, though programmers on minicomputers and microcomputers have switched to newer languages.

Improvements

The original version of COBOL was finished in 1960 and called **COBOL 60**. Then came an improvement, called **COBOL 61**. The verb SORT and a "Report Writer" feature were added in 1962. Then came **COBOL 65**, **COBOL 68**, **COBOL 74**, AND **COBOL 85**.

COBOL's most obvious flaw

To write a COBOL program, you must put information about file labeling into the data division's FD command. Since file labeling describes the **environment**, not the **data**, COBOL should be changed, to put the labeling in the environment division instead. Jean Sammet, who headed some of the Short-Term Committee's subcommittees, admits her group goofed when it decided to put labeling in the data division. But alas, COBOL's too old to change now.

BASIC

The first version of BASIC was developed in 1963 and 1964 by a genius (John Kemeny) and his friend (Tom Kurtz).

How the genius grew up

John Kemeny is a Jew who was born in Hungary in 1926. In 1940 he and his parents fled from the Nazis and came to America. Although he knew hardly any English when he began high school in New York, he learned enough so that he graduated as the top student in the class. Four years later, he graduated from Princeton **summa cum laude** even though he had to spend 1½ of those years in the Army, where he helped solve equations for the atomic bomb.

Two years after his B.A., Princeton gave him a Ph.D. in mathematics *and* philosophy, because his thesis on symbolic logic combined both fields.

While working for the Ph.D., he was also Einstein's youngest assistant. He told Einstein he wanted to quit math and instead hand out leaflets for world peace. Einstein replied: handing out leaflets would waste his talents; the best way for him to help world peace would be to become a famous mathematician, so people would *listen* to him, as they had to Einstein. He took Einstein's advice and stayed with math.

After getting his Ph.D., he taught symbolic logic in Princeton's philosophy department. In 1953, most of Dartmouth College's math professors were retiring, so Dartmouth asked Kemeny to come to Dartmouth, chair the department, and "bring all your friends". He accepted the offer and brought his friends. That's how Dartmouth stole Princeton's math department.

At Dartmouth, Kemeny invented several new branches of mathematics. Then Kemeny's department got General Electric to sell Dartmouth a computer at 90% discount, in return for which his department had to invent programs for it and let General Electric use them. To write the programs, Kemeny invented his own little computer language in 1963 and showed it to his colleague Thomas Kurtz, who knew less about philosophy but more about computers. Kurtz added features from ALGOL and FORTRAN and called the combination "BASIC".

After inventing BASIC, Kemeny became bored and thought of quitting Dartmouth. Then Dartmouth asked him to become president of the college. He accepted.

Later, when the Three-Mile Island nuclear power plant almost exploded, President Jimmy Carter told Kemeny to head the investigation, because of Kemeny's reputation for profound philosophical and scientific impartiality. Kemeny's report was impartial — and sharply critical of the nuclear industry.

How BASIC compares with ALGOL and FORTRAN

BASIC is simpler than both ALGOL and FORTRAN in two ways:

1. In ALGOL and FORTRAN, you must tell the computer which variables are integers and which are reals. In ALGOL, you do that by saying INTEGER or REAL. In FORTRAN, you do that by choosing an appropriate first letter for the variable's name. **In BASIC, the computer assumes all variables are real**, unless you specifically say otherwise.

2. In ALGOL and FORTRAN, output is a hassle. In FORTRAN, you have to worry about FORMATs. In ALGOL, each computer handles output differently — and in most cases strangely. **BASIC's PRINT statement automatically invents a good format**.

Is BASIC closer to ALGOL than to FORTRAN? On the one hand, BASIC uses the ALGOL words FOR, STEP, and THEN and the ALGOL symbol ↑ (or ^). On the other hand, BASIC, uses the FORTRAN words RETURN and DIMENSION (abbreviated DIM); and BASIC's "FOR I = 1 TO 9 STEP 2" puts the step size at the *end* of the statement, like FORTRAN's "DO 30 I = 1,9,2" and unlike ALGOL's "FOR I:=1 STEP 2 UNTIL 9".

Why BASIC overshadows JOSS
BASIC is *not* the simplest computer language. **JOSS**, which was developed a year earlier by the RAND Corporation, is simpler to learn. But JOSS doesn't have string variables and doesn't name programs (you must give each program a number instead, and remember what the number was). Also, programs written in JOSS run more slowly and require more of the computer's memory than if written in BASIC.

A few programmers still use JOSS and three of its variants, which are called **AID, FOCAL**, and **MUMPS**. They all run on computers built by DEC. AID is used by high-school kids on PDP-8 computers, FOCAL by scientists on PDP-10 computers, and MUMPS by doctors designing databases of patient records on PDP-11 computers. Though MUMPS *does* have string variables and other modern features, it's gradually being replaced by newer database languages such as DBASE.

Six versions
Kemeny and Kurtz finished the original version of BASIC in May 1964. It included just these statements: PRINT, GO TO, IF...THEN, FOR...NEXT, DATA...READ, GOSUB...RETURN, DIM, LET (for commands such as LET X=3), REM (for REMarks and comments), DEF (to DEFine your own functions), and END.

In that version, the only punctuation allowed in the PRINT statement was the comma. The second version of BASIC (October 1964) added the semicolon.

The third version (1966) added the words INPUT, RESTORE, and MAT. (The word MAT helps you manipulate a "MATrix", which means an "array". Today, most versions of BASIC omit the word MAT, because its definition consumes too much RAM.)

In all those versions, you could use variables. For example, you could say LET X=3. A variable was a letter that stood for a number. The fourth version (1967) added a new concept: string variables (such as A$). That version also added TAB (to improve the printing), RANDOMIZE (to improve RND), and ON...GO TO.

The fifth version (1970) added data files (sequential access and random access).

The sixth version (1971) added PRINT USING and a sophisticated way to handle subroutines — a way so sophisticated that most microcomputers don't have it yet!

How BASIC became popular
During the 1960's and 1970's, Kemeny and Kurtz worked on BASIC with a fervor that was almost religious. They believed *every* college graduate should know how to program a computer, and be as literate in BASIC as in English. They convinced Dartmouth to spend as much on its computer as on the college library. They put computer terminals in practically every college building (even in the dorms), and let all the kids who lived in the town come onto the campus and join the fun. Altogether, the campus had about 300 terminals. Over 90% of all Dartmouth students used BASIC before they graduated.

Dartmouth trained high-school teachers how to use BASIC. Soon many colleges, high schools, and prep schools throughout New England had terminals connected to Dartmouth's computer via telephone.

General Electric, which built Dartmouth's computer, quit making computers and sold its computer factory to Honeywell. So today, Dartmouth's computer is called a "Honeywell".

Since Dartmouth's research on BASIC was partially funded by the National Science Foundation, BASIC was in the public domain. Other computer manufacturers could use it without having to worry about copyrights or patents.

DEC
The first company to copy Dartmouth's ideas was Digital Equipment Corporation (DEC).

DEC put BASIC and FOCAL on DEC's first popular minicomputer, the PDP-8. When DEC saw that programmers preferred BASIC, DEC stopped developing FOCAL and devoted all its energies to improving BASIC further.

DEC invented fancier minicomputers (the PDP-11 and Vax) and maxicomputers (the Decsystem-10 and Decsystem-20) and put BASIC on all of them. DEC's versions of BASIC were similar to Dartmouth's. Though the versions put on the PDP-8 were quite primitive (almost as bad as Dartmouth's first edition), the versions put on DEC's fancier computers were more sophisticated. Eventually, DEC put decent versions of BASIC even on the PDP-8.

DEC's best version of BASIC is **VAX BASIC**, which works only on VAX computers. DEC's second-best version of BASIC is **BASIC-PLUS-2**, which works on the VAX, the PDP-11, and the Decsystem-20. DEC's third-best version of BASIC is **BASIC-PLUS**, which works only on the PDP-11. DEC's other versions of BASIC aren't as fancy.

Hewlett-Packard
Soon after DEC started putting BASIC on its computers, Hewlett-Packard decided to do likewise: Hewlett-Packard put BASIC on the HP-2000 computer, and then put a better version of BASIC on the HP-300 computer.

Unfortunately, Hewlett-Packard's BASIC was more difficult to use than DEC's. On Hewlett-Packard computers, each time you used a string you had to write a "DIM statement" that warned the computer how long the string would be: the DIM statement had to say how many characters the string would contain.

Other major manufacturers
Most other manufacturers imitate the versions of BASIC invented by Dartmouth and DEC. Unfortunately, Data General, Wang, and IBM made the mistake of copying Hewlett-Packard instead.

That's how BASIC developed on maxicomputers and minicomputers.

How Microsoft BASIC arose
The first popular *micro*computer was the Altair 8800, which used a version of BASIC invented by a 20-year-old kid named Bill Gates. His version imitated DEC's.

The Altair computer was manufactured by a company called **Mits**. When Mits didn't treat Bill Gates fairly, he broke away from Mits and formed his own company, called **Microsoft**.

Bill Gates and his company, Microsoft, invented many versions of BASIC. The first was called **4K BASIC**, because it consumed only 4K of memory chips (RAM or ROM). Then came **8K BASIC**, which included a larger vocabulary. Then came **Extended BASIC**, which included an even larger vocabulary and consumed 14K. All those versions were intended for primitive microcomputers that used tapes instead of disks. Finally came **Disk BASIC**, which came on a disk and included all the commands for handling disks. His **Disk BASIC version 4** was further improved, to form **Disk BASIC version 5**, which is the version of BASIC still used on CP/M computers and on the Radio Shack model 4. It's also called **MBASIC** and **BASIC-80**.

All those versions of BASIC were written for computers that contained an 8080 or Z-80 CPU. Simultaneously, he wrote **6502 BASIC**, for Apple 2 and Commodore computers. The Apple 2 version of 6502 BASIC is called **Applesoft BASIC**; Commodore's version of 6502 BASIC is called **Commodore BASIC**.

Unfortunately, 6502 BASIC is rather primitive: it resembles his 8K BASIC. So if you're trying to learn advanced BASIC programming, you should *not* get an Apple 2e or 2c or Commodore 64!

After writing 6502 BASIC, Bill wrote an improved version of it, called **6809 BASIC**, which is available only for Radio Shack's Color Computer. Radio Shack calls it **Extended Color BASIC**.

Texas Instruments (TI) asked Bill to write a version of BASIC for TI computers. Bill said "yes". Then TI told Bill what kind of BASIC it wanted. Bill's company — Microsoft — found 90 ways in which TI's desires would contradict Microsoft's traditions. Microsoft convinced TI to change its mind and remove 80 of those 90 contradictions, but TI stood firm on the other 10. So TI BASIC (which is on the TI-990 and TI-99/4A computers) contradicts all other versions of Microsoft BASIC in 10 ways. For example, in TI BASIC, the INPUT statement uses a colon instead of a semicolon, and a multi-statement line uses a double colon (::) instead of a single colon. Because of those differences, TI's computers became unpopular, and TI stopped making them. Moral: if you contradict Bill, you'll die!

Bill later invented an amazingly wonderful version of BASIC, better than all the other versions that had been invented. He called it **GW BASIC** (which stands for "Gee-Whiz BASIC"). It runs only on the IBM PC and clones.

When you buy PC-DOS from IBM, you typically get GW BASIC at no extra charge. (IBM calls it **BASICA**.) When you buy MS-DOS for an IBM clone, the typical dealer includes GW BASIC at no extra charge, but ask!

Beyond GW BASIC
GW BASIC was the last version of BASIC that Bill developed personally. All further improvements and variations were done by his assistants at Microsoft.

Microsoft's newest variations are **Microsoft BASIC for the Mac**, **Amiga Microsoft BASIC** (for the Commodore's Amiga computer), **Quick BASIC** (for the IBM PC and clones), **QBASIC** (which you get instead of GWBASIC when you buy MS-DOS version 5 or 6), and **Visual BASIC** (which lets you easily create Windows-style programs that let the human use a mouse and pull-down menus). Those BASICs are slightly harder to learn how to use than GW BASIC; but once you understand them, you'll prefer them because they run faster and include a better editor, more words from ALGOL and PASCAL, and fancier output.

While developing those versions of BASIC, Microsoft added three new commands that are particularly exciting: SAY, END IF, and SUB.

The SAY command makes the computer talk, by using a voice synthesizer. for example, to make the computer's voice say "I love you", type this command:

```
SAY TRANSLATE$("I LOVE YOU")
```

That makes the computer translate "I love you" into phonetics and then say the phonetics. That command works on the Amiga, and I hope Microsoft will put it on other computers also.

The END IF and SUB commands give BASIC some of PASCAL's power. By using the END IF command, you can make the IF statement include many lines, like this:

```
IF AGE<18 THEN
        PRINT "YOU ARE STILL A MINOR."
        PRINT "AH, THE JOYS OF YOUTH!"
        PRINT "I WISH I COULD BE AS YOUNG AS YOU!"
END IF
```

By using the SUB command, you can give a subroutine a name, like this:

```
PRINT "WE ALL KNOW..."
CALL INSULT
PRINT "...AND YET WE LOVE YOU"

SUB INSULT STATIC
PRINT "YOU ARE STUPID"
PRINT "YOU ARE UGLY"
END SUB
```

Borland
Microsoft's main competitor for languages is **Borland**, which made **Turbo PASCAL**, **Turbo C**, and **Turbo BASIC**.

Turbo BASIC version 1.1 runs faster than Quick BASIC, is easier to understand, and includes almost as many commands. But Borland has stopped marketing Turbo BASIC, so that Borland can devote its energies to other Borland products that are more profitable (such as Turbo PASCAL, Turbo C, Quattro, and Paradox).

Divergences
GW BASIC, Microsoft BASIC for the Macintosh, Amiga Microsoft BASIC, Quick BASIC, and Turbo BASIC are all wonderful.

Over the years, several microcomputer manufacturers tried to invent their own versions of BASIC, to avoid paying royalties to Bill Gates. They were sorry!

For example, Radio Shack tried hiring somebody else to write Radio Shack's BASIC. That person quit in the middle of the job; Radio Shack's original BASIC was never completed. Nicknamed "Level 1 BASIC", it was a half-done mess. Radio Shack, like an obedient puppy dog, then went to Bill, who finally wrote a decent version of BASIC for Radio Shack; Bill's version was called "Level 2". Today, Radio Shack uses further improvements on Bill's Level 2 BASIC.

Apple's original attempt at BASIC was called "Apple Integer BASIC". It was written by Steve Wozniak and was terrible: it couldn't handle decimals, and it made the mistake of imitating Hewlett-Packard instead of DEC (because Steve had worked at Hewlett-Packard). Eventually, Steve wised up and hired Bill, who wrote Apple's better BASIC, called **Applesoft** (which means "Apple BASIC by Microsoft"). Applesoft was intended for tapes, not disks. Later, when Steve Wozniak wanted to add disks to the Apple computer, he made the mistake of not rehiring Bill — which is why Apple's disk system is worse than Radio Shack's.

At Atari, an executive who didn't want to hire Bill made the mistake of hiring the inventor of Apple's disastrous DOS. That guy's BASIC, which is called **Atari BASIC**, resembles Hewlett-Packard's BASIC. Like Apple's DOS, it looks pleasant at first glance but turns into a nightmare when you try to do any advanced programming. As a result, Atari's computers didn't become as popular as Atari hoped, and the executive who "didn't want to hire Bill" was fired. Atari finally hired Bill's company, which wrote **Atari Microsoft BASIC version 2**.

Two other microcomputer manufacturers — **North Star Computers** and APF — tried developing their own versions of BASIC, to avoid paying royalties to Bill. Since their versions of BASIC were lousy, they went out of business.

While DEC, Hewlett-Packard, Microsoft, and other companies were developing their own versions of BASIC, professors back at Dartmouth College were still tinkering with Dartmouth BASIC version 6. In 1976, Professor Steve Garland added more commands from ALGOL, PL/I, and PASCAL to Dartmouth BASIC. He called his version "Structured BASIC" or **SBASIC**.

One of BASIC's inventors, Professor Tom Kurtz, became chairman of an ANSI committee to standardize BASIC. His committee published two reports.

The 1977 report defined **ANSI Standard Minimal BASIC**, a minimal standard that all advertised versions of "BASIC" should live up to. That report was quite reasonable, and everybody agreed to abide by it. (Microsoft's old versions of BASIC were written before that report came out. Microsoft Disk BASIC version 5 was Microsoft's first version to obey that standard.)

In 1985, ANSI created a more ambitious report, to standardize the most advanced aspects of BASIC. The report said that the advanced aspects of BASIC should closely follow SBASIC and the other versions developed at Dartmouth. But Bill Gates, who invented Microsoft BASIC and was also one of the members of the committee, disliked some aspects of Dartmouth's BASIC and quit the committee. (He was particularly annoyed by the committee's desire to include Dartmouth's MAT commands, which consume lots of RAM and which hardly anybody uses.) He refused to follow the committee's recommendations.

That left two standards for advanced BASIC: the "official" standard, defined by the ANSI committee; and the "de facto" standard, which is Bill Gates' GW BASIC, the version of BASIC that most people use.

The two standards are quite different from each other. For example, in GW BASIC you say:

`10 INPUT "WHAT IS YOUR NAME"; A$`

In ANSI BASIC, you say this instead:

`10 INPUT PROMPT "WHAT IS YOUR NAME? ": A$`

Notice that in ANSI BASIC, you must insert the word PROMPT after INPUT, insert a questions mark and blank space before the second quotation mark, and type a colon instead of a semicolon.

Tom Kurtz (who chaired the ANSI committee) and John Kemeny (who invented BASIC with Tom Kurtz) put ANSI BASIC onto Dartmouth's computer. So ANSI BASIC became Dartmouth's seventh official version of BASIC.

Then Kurtz and Kemeny left Dartmouth and formed their own company, which invented **True BASIC**. It's a version of ANSI BASIC that runs on the IBM PC and the Apple Macintosh.

In some ways, True BASIC is slightly better than Microsoft's GW BASIC and Quick BASIC. In other ways, True BASIC is slightly worse. Since Microsoft's BASIC versions have become the de facto standard, and since True BASIC isn't *significantly* better, hardly anybody is switching from Microsoft BASIC to True BASIC.

Comparison chart

This chart compares the most popular versions of BASIC for microcomputers today:

	Video			Audio			Logic		
	USING	LINE	CIRCLE	SOUND	PLAY	SAY	ELSE	END IF	SUB
Commodore Amiga with Microsoft BASIC	✓	✓	✓	✓	✓		✓	✓	✓
IBM PC color with Visual BASIC 2 or 3 or QBASIC	✓	✓	✓	✓	✓		✓	✓	✓
Apple Macintosh with Quick BASIC	✓	✓	✓	✓			✓	✓	✓
IBM PC color GW BASIC, Commodore 128, or TRS-80 Color	✓	✓	✓	✓	✓				✓
Atari ST	✓	✓	✓	✓					✓
Atari XE (or XL) with Microsoft BASIC	✓	✓		✓					✓
IBM PC monochrome with GW BASIC	✓			✓	✓				✓
TRS-80 Model 3, 4, 4P, or 4D	✓								✓
Apple 2, 2+, 2e, 2c, 2c+, or 2GS	✓								
Commodore 64 or Vic-20									

It shows which versions of BASIC understand these 9 words: USING, LINE, CIRCLE, SOUND, PLAY, SAY, ELSE, END IF, and SUB.

The versions of BASIC at the top of the chart (Amiga BASIC, Visual BASIC, and QBASIC) are the best: they understand 8 of the 9 words. The versions of BASIC at the bottom of the chart (Commodore 64 BASIC & Vic-20 BASIC) are the worst: they understand none of the words.

Here's what those 9 words accomplish. The word USING (which you put immediately after the word PRINT) lets you control how many digits the computer will print after the decimal point. LINE makes the computer draw a diagonal line across the screen. CIRCLE makes the computer draw a circle as big as you wish. SOUND and PLAY make the computer create music. SAY makes the computer talk. ELSE and END IF let you create fancy IF statements. SUB lets you name subroutines.

Although the Commodore 128 and Radio Shack TRS-80 Color Computer are cheap, the chart shows their versions of BASIC are better than the Apple 2c's. If schools would have bought Commodore 128 and Radio Shack TRS-80 Color Computers instead of Apple 2c's, students would be better programmers!

PL/I

During the early 1960's, IBM sold two kinds of computers. One kind was for use by scientists; the other kind was for use by business bookkeepers. For the scientific kind of computer, the most popular language was FORTRAN. For the business kind of computer, the most popular language was COBOL.

In 1962, IBM secretly began working on a project to create a single, large computer that could be used by everybody: scientists and businesses. IBM called it the **IBM 360**, because it could handle the full circle of applications.

What language should the IBM 360 be programmed in? IBM decided to invent a single language that could be used for both science and business.

IBM's first attempt at such a language was "FORTRAN V". It ran all the FORTRAN IV programs but also included commands for handling strings and fields in data files. But IBM never announced FORTRAN V to the public; instead, in 1963 IBM began working on a dramatically more powerful language called "FORTRAN VI", which would resemble FORTRAN but be much more powerful and modern (and hence incompatible). It would also include *all* the important features of COBOL and ALGOL.

As work on FORTRAN VI progressed, IBM realized it would be so different from traditional FORTRAN that it should have a different name. In 1964, IBM changed the name to "NPL" (New Programming Language), since the language was intended to go with the IBM 360 and the rest of IBM's New Product Line.

When IBM discovered that the letters "NPL" already stood for the National Physics Laboratory in England, IBM changed the language's name to **Programming Language One (PL/I)**, to brag it was the first good programming language and all its predecessors were worth zero by comparison.

Troublesome timing

The committee that invented PL/I had a hard time. The committee consisted of just 6 official members (3 from IBM and 3 from a FORTRAN user group). A few friends of the committee attended also. The committee could meet only on weekends, and only in hotel rooms in New York State and California. The first meeting was in October 1963 (at the Motel-on-the-Mountain on the New York Thruway), and IBM insisted that the entire language design be finished by December. It was a rush job!

The committee didn't meet the deadline. It finished two months late, in February.

After the design was finished, the language still had to be put onto the computer. Since that took 2½ more years of programming and polishing, the language wasn't available for sale to IBM's customers until August 1966.

That was too late. It was *after* IBM had already begun shipping the IBM 360. The 360's customers continued using FORTRAN and COBOL, since PL/I wasn't available initially. After those customers bought, installed, and learned how to use FORTRAN and COBOL on the 360, they weren't willing to switch to PL/I. Switching was too much trouble.

Other troubles

PL/I was expensive to run. It required twice as much RAM as COBOL, four times as much RAM as FORTRAN. It ran slowly: it took 1½ times as long to compile as COBOL, twice as long as FORTRAN.

Another obstacle to PL/I's acceptance was lethargy: most programmers already knew FORTRAN and COBOL, were satisfied with those languages, and weren't willing to spend the time to learn something new.

Some programmers praise PL/I for being amazingly powerful. Others call it just a scheme by IBM to get people to buy more RAM. Others call it a disorganized mess, an "ugly kitchen sink of a language", thrown together by a committee that was in too much of a rush.

Since PL/I is such a large language, hardly anybody understands it all. As a typical harried PL/I programmer, you study just the part of the language you intend to use. But if you make a mistake, the computer might not gripe: instead, it might think you're trying to give a different PL/I command from a different part of the language that you never studied. So instead of griping, the computer will perform an instruction that wasn't what you meant.

Universities

Universities debated which language to teach freshman. For a while, the choice was between FORTRAN (the "standard"), ALGOL (the "pure and simple"), and PL/I (the "powerful").

In 1972, Cornell University developed a stripped-down version of PL/I for students. That version, called **PL/C**, is a compromise between PL/I's power and ALGOL's pure simplicity.

In 1975, The University of Toronto developed an even *more* stripped-down version of PL/I, and called it **SP/k**. Although it allows fewer statements than PL/C, it runs faster and prints messages that are even more helpful. SP/k comes in several sizes: the tiniest is SP/1; the largest is SP/8.

Stripped-down versions of PL/I remained popular in universities until about 1980, when they began to be replaced by PASCAL.

Microcomputers

Digital Research invented a tiny version of PL/I for microcomputers, and called it **PL/M**. Unfortunately, PL/M can't handle decimals. PL/M was popular during the late 1970's and early 1980's, but most PL/M programmers eventually switched to C.

Maxicomputers

PL/I is still used on large IBM computers, because it's the only language that includes enough commands to let programmers unleash IBM's full power.

Statements

PL/I uses many statements for input and output. The statement's meaning depends mainly on the statement's first word:

First word	What the computer will do
GET	input from a terminal or simple file
PUT	print on a terminal or simple file
OPEN	start using a file
CLOSE	stop using a file
READ	input from a file whose picture is unedited
WRITE	print on a file whose picture is unedited
DELETE	delete an item from a file
REWRITE	replace an item in a file
LOCATE	print a "based" variable onto a file
UNLOCK	let other programs use the file
FORMAT	use a certain form for spacing the input and output
DISPLAY	chat with operator who sits at computer's main terminal

These statements interrupt:

First word	What the computer will do
STOP	stop the program
EXIT	stop a task (in a program that involves several tasks)
HALT	interrupt the program; free the terminal to do other tasks
DELAY	pause for a certain number of milliseconds
WAIT	pause until other simultaneous routines finish their tasks

These statements handle conditions:

First word	What the computer will do
IF	if a certain condition occurs now, do certain statements
ON	if a certain condition occurs later, do certain statements
SIGNAL	pretend a condition such as OVERFLOW occurs
REVERT	cancel the ON statements

These statements handle variables:

First word	What the computer will do
DECLARE	make some variables be integers, other be reals, etc.
DEFAULT	assume all variables are integers, or a similar assumption
ALLOCATE	create a temporary variable
FREE	destroy a temporary variable and use its RAM otherwise

These statements handle general logic:

First word	What the computer will do
GO	go to a different line
CALL	go to a subroutine
RETURN	return from a subroutine to the main routine
ENTRY	skip the subroutine's previous lines; begin here instead
PROCEDURE	begin a program or subprogram
DO	begin a loop or compound statement
BEGIN	begin a block of statements
END	end program, subprog., loop, compound statem't, or block

Half of those statements are borrowed from FORTRAN, ALGOL, and COBOL.

from FORTRAN:	FORMAT, STOP, CALL, RETURN, DO
from ALGOL:	IF, GO, PROCEDURE, BEGIN, END
from COBOL:	OPEN, CLOSE, READ, WRITE, DISPLAY, EXIT

Like ALGOL, PL/I requires a semicolon at the end of each statement. Besides the statements listed above, you can also give an **assignment statement** (such as "N=5;"), a **null statement** (which consists of just a semicolon), and a **preprocessor statement** (which tells the computer how to create its own program).

PASCAL

In 1968, a European committee tried to invent an improved version of ALGOL. The majority of the committee agreed on a version called "ALGOL 68". It was strange: it even required you to spell some commands backwards.

A few members of the committee were dissidents who disagreed with the majority and thought ALGOL 68 was nuts. One of the dissidents, Niklaus Wirth, quit the committee and created his own version of ALGOL. He called his version **PASCAL**. Today, most computerists feel he was right and the majority of the committee was wrong, PASCAL is better than ALGOL 68.

He wrote PASCAL in Switzerland, for a CDC maxicomputer that used punched cards. His version of PASCAL couldn't handle video screens, couldn't handle random-access data files, and couldn't handle strings well. Those three limitations were corrected in later versions of PASCAL — especially the version invented at the University of California at San Diego (UCSD), which even includes LOGO-style commands that move a turtle.

Apple's PASCAL Apple Computer Company got permission to sell an Apple version of UCSD PASCAL. Apple ran full-page advertisements, bragging that the Apple 2 was the only popular microcomputer that could handle PASCAL.

For $495, Apple Computer Company sold the "Apple Language System", which included 4 disks containing PASCAL, 2 disks containing souped-up BASIC, and a card containing 16K of extra RAM. Many people spent the $495 for PASCAL but were disappointed. They expected that by spending $495, they'd be able to write programs more easily, but they discovered that PASCAL is *harder* to learn than BASIC.

PASCAL is helpful only if the program you're writing is very, very long. PASCAL helps you organize and dissect long programs more easily than BASIC. But the average Apple owner never writes long programs and never needs PASCAL.

Many customers felt "ripped off", since they had spent $495 and received no benefit in return. But maybe that's what "marketing" is all about.

PASCAL's popularity Many programmers who've been writing large FORTRAN programs for large computers are switching to PASCAL, because PASCAL helps organize large programs better, and because FORTRAN is archaic. Many programmers who've been using PL/I are switching to PASCAL, because PASCAL consumes less RAM than PL/I and fits in smaller computers.

Most colleges require freshman computer-science majors to take PASCAL.

Most high-school seniors who want to attend college take tests given by the College Entrance Examination Board. The most famous such test is the Scholastic Aptitude Test (SAT), but the board offers many others. One of the board's newest tests is the **Advanced Placement Test in Computer Science**; a high-school senior who scores high on that test can skip the first year of college computer-science courses and go immediately into college-sophomore courses. Since that test requires a knowledge of PASCAL, many high-school seniors are studying PASCAL.

Best versions The most powerful PASCAL for microcomputers is **Turbo PASCAL**, published by Borland. It's available for the IBM PC, Mac, and CP/M computers.

If you have a Mac, get either the Mac version of Turbo PASCAL or **Think PASCAL**. If you have an Apple 2e or 2c, get **Instant PASCAL** (which is much easier to use than the UCSD PASCAL that was sold under the name "Apple PASCAL").

If you have a Radio Shack TRS-80 model 3 or 4, get **PASCAL 80**, which costs $79.95 from New Classics Software (239 Fox Hill Rd., Denville, NJ 07834, phone 201-538-3131 days, 201-625-8838 evenings, ask for George Blank). If you're running a school, you'll love this deal: for just $279, you get the right to make unlimited copies of PASCAL 80 and use them throughout your school building.

MODULA

After Niklaus Wirth invented PASCAL, he began designing a more ambitious language, called **MODULA**.

He designed the first version of MODULA in 1975. In 1979 he designed an improvement called **MODULA-2**. When today's programmers discuss "MODULA", they mean MODULA-2.

MODULA-2 is very similar to PASCAL. Like PASCAL, MODULA-2 requires each program's main routing to begin with the word BEGIN; but MODULA-2 does *not* require you to say BEGIN after DO WHILE or IF THEN:

PASCAL
```
IF AGE<18 THEN
   BEGIN
   WRITELN('YOU ARE STILL A MINOR');
   WRITELN('AH, THE JOYS OF YOUTH');
   END
ELSE
   BEGIN
   WRITELN('GLAD YOU ARE AN ADULT');
   WRITELN('WE CAN HAVE ADULT FUN');
   END;
```

MODULA-2
```
IF AGE<18 THEN
   WRITESTRING("YOU ARE STILL A MINOR");
   WRITESTRING("AH, THE JOYS OF YOUTH");
ELSE
   WRITESTRING("GLAD YOU ARE AN ADULT");
   WRITESTRING("WE CAN HAVE ADULT FUN")
END;
```

That example shows four ways that MODULA-2 differs from PASCAL: MODULA-2 says WRITESTRING instead of WRITELN, uses regular quotation marks (") instead of apostrophes, lets you omit the word BEGIN after IF ELSE (and WHILE DO), and lets you omit the word END before ELSE.

Advanced programmers like MODULA-2 better than PASCAL because MODULA-2 includes extra commands for handling subroutines.

C

Many programmers are starting to use **C**.

How C arose In 1963 at England's Cambridge University and the University of London, researchers developed a "practical" version of ALGOL and called it the **Combined Programming Language (CPL)**. In 1967 at Cambridge University, Martin Richards invented a simpler, stripped-down version of CPL and called it **Basic CPL (BCPL)**. In 1970 at Bell Labs, Ken Thompson developed a version that was even more stripped-down and simpler; since it included just the most critical part of BCPL, he called it **B**.

Ken had stripped down the language *too* much. It no longer contained enough commands to do practical programming. In 1972, his colleague Dennis Ritchie added a few commands to B, to form a more extensive language. Since that language came after B, it was called **C**.

So C is a souped-up version of B, which is a stripped-down version of BCPL, which is a stripped-down version of CPL, which is a "practical" version of ALGOL.

Bell Labs invented an operating system called **Unix**. The original version of Unix was created by using B. The newest versions of Unix were created by using C instead, which is more powerful.

C's peculiarities Like B, C is a tiny language. It doesn't even include any words for input or output. When you buy C, you also get a **library** of routines that can be added to C. The library includes words for input and output (such as printf and scanf), math functions (such as sqrt), and other goodies. When you write a program in C, you can choose whichever parts of the library you need: the other parts of the library don't bother to stay in RAM. So if your program uses just a *few* of the library's functions, running it will consume very little RAM. It will consume less RAM than if the program were written in BASIC or PASCAL.

In BASIC, if you reserve 20 RAM locations for X (by saying DIM X(20)) and then say X(21)=3.7, the computer will gripe, because you haven't reserved a RAM location of X(21). If you use C instead, the computer will *not* gripe about that kind of error; instead, the computer will store the number 3.7 in the RAM location immediately after X(20), even if that location's already being used by another variable, such as Y. As a result, Y will get messed up. Moral: C programs run quickly and dangerously, because in C the computer never bothers to check your program's reasonableness.

In your program, which variables are integers, and which are real? BASIC assumes they're all real. FORTRAN and PL/I assume all variables beginning with I, J, K, L, M, and N are integers and the rest are real. ALGOL and PASCAL make no assumptions at all; they require you to write a declaration saying "integer" or "real" for each variable. C, by contrast, assumes all variables are integers, unless you specifically say otherwise.

ADA

In 1975, the U.S. Department of Defense decided it wanted a new kind of computer language, so the Department wrote a list of requirements the language would have to meet.

The original list of requirements was called the Strawman Requirements (1975). Then came improved versions, called Woodenman (1975), Tinman (1976), Ironman (1978), and finally Steelman (1979).

While the Department was moving from Strawman to Steelman, it also checked whether any existing computer language could meet such requirements. The Department concluded that no existing computer language came even close to meeting the requirements, and so a new language would indeed have to be invented. The Department also concluded that the new language would have to resemble PASCAL, ALGOL 68, or PL/I, but be better.

Contest In 1977, the Department held a contest, to see which software company could invent a language meeting such specifications (which were in the process of changing from Tinman to Ironman). 16 companies entered the contest.

The Department selected 4 semifinalists and paid them to continue their research for six more months. The semifinalists were CII-Honeywell-Bull (which is French and owned partly by Honeywell), Intermetrics (in Cambridge, Massachusetts), SRI International, and Softech.

In 1978, the semifinalists submitted improved designs, which were all souped-up versions of PASCAL (instead of ALGOL 68 or PL/I). To make the contest fair and prevent bribery, the judges weren't told which design belonged to which company. The 4 designs were called "Green", "Red", "Yellow", and "Blue".

Yellow and Blue lost. The winning designs were Green (designed by CII-Honeywell-Bull) and Red (designed by Intermetrics).

The Department paid the two winning companies to continue their research for one more year. In 1979, the winning companies submitted their improved versions. The winner was the Green language, designed by CII-Honeywell-Bull.

The Department decided that the Green language would be called **ADA** to honor Ada Lovelace, the woman who was the world's first programmer.

So ADA is a PASCAL-like language developed by a French company under contract to the U.S. Department of Defense.

Popularity

Will ADA become popular? Wait and see.

Many researchers are trying to make computers understand ADA. So far, the results are incomplete: you can buy disks containing *parts* of ADA, but the full version isn't on disk yet.

When full versions of ADA become available and programmers try using them, we'll know whether the language is a pleasure or a pain.

DBASE

DBASE was invented by Wayne Ratliff because he wanted to bet on which football teams would win the 1978 season. To bet wisely, he had to know how each team had scored in previous games, so every Monday he clipped pages of football scores from newspapers. Soon his whole room was covered with newspaper clippings. To reduce the clutter, he decided to write a data-management program to keep track of all the statistics.

He worked at the Jet Propulsion Laboratory (JPL). His coworkers had invented a data-management system called the **JPL Display and Information System (JPLDIS)**, which imitated IBM's **RETRIEVE**.

Unfortunately, RETRIEVE and JPLDIS both required maxicomputers. Working at home, he invented **VULCAN**, a stripped-down version of JPLDIS that was small enough to run on the CP/M microcomputer in his house. It was even good enough to let him compile football statistics — though by then he'd lost interest in football and was more interested in the theory of data management and business applications.

In 1979, he advertised his VULCAN data-management system in Byte Magazine. The mailman delivered so many orders to his house that he didn't have time to fill them all — especially since he still had a full-time job at JPL. He stopped advertising, to give himself a chance to catch up on filling the orders.

In 1980, the owners of Discount Software phoned him, visited his home, examined VULCAN, and offered to market it for him. He agreed.

Since "Discount Software" was the wrong name to market VULCAN under, Discount Software's owners — Hal Lashlee and George Tate — thought of marketing VULCAN under the name "Lashlee-Tate Software". But since the "Lashlee" part sounded too wimpy, they changed the name to *Ashton-Tate Software*.

Instead of selling the original version of VULCAN, Ashton-Tate Software decided to sell Wayne's further improvement, called **DBASE 2**. It ran faster, looked prettier on the screen, and was easier to use.

At Ashton-Tate, George Tate did most of the managing. Hal Lashlee was a silent partner who just contributed capital.

Advertisement

George Tate hired Hal Pawluck to write an ad for DBASE 2. Hal's ad was ingenious. It showed a photograph of a bilge pump (the kind of pump that removes water from a ship's bilge). The ad's headline said: "DBASE versus the Bilge Pump". The ad went on to say that most database systems are like bilge pumps: they suck!

That explicit ad appeared in *Infoworld*, which was a popular, concise weekly newspaper read by all computer experts. Suddenly, all experts knew that DBASE was the database-management system that claimed not to suck.

The ad generated just one serious complaint — from the company that manufactured the bilge pump!

George Tate offered to add a footnote, saying "*This* bilge pump does *not* suck". The pump manufacturer didn't like that either but stopped complaining.

Beyond DBASE 2

The original DBASE 2 ran on computers using the CP/M operating system. It worked well. When IBM began selling the IBM PC, Wayne invented an IBM PC version of DBASE 2, but it was buggy.

He created those early versions of DBASE by using assembly language. By using C instead, he finally created an IBM PC version that worked reliably and included extra commands. He called it **DBASE 3**.

DBASE 2 and DBASE 3 were sold as programming languages, but many people who wanted to use databases didn't want to learn programming and didn't want to hire a programmer. So Ashton-Tate created a new version, called **DBASE 3 PLUS**, which you can control by using menus instead of typing programming commands.

Unfortunately, the menus of DBASE 3 PLUS are hard to learn how to use. Also, the menus are incomplete: they don't let you tap the full power of DBASE 3 PLUS. So to use DBASE 3 PLUS well, you must learn how to program anyway.

In 1988, Ashton-Tate began shipping **DBASE 4**, which includes extra programming commands. Some of those commands were copied from a database language called **Structured Query Language (SQL)**, which IBM invented for mainframes. DBASE 4 also boasted better menus than DBASE 3 PLUS. Unfortunately, Ashton-Tate priced DBASE 4 high: $795 for the plain version, $1295 for the "developer's" version.

Over the years, Ashton-Tate became a stodgy bureaucracy. George Tate died, Wayne Ratliff quit, the company's list price for DBASE grew ridiculously high, and the company was callous to DBASE users.

In 1991, Borland bought Ashton-Tate. In 1994, Borland began selling **DBASE 5**. Discount dealers sell it for $529.

Dramatic improvements to DBASE have been created by other companies, who make clones of DBASE that outshine DBASE itself! The most popular clone is **FOXPRO 2.6**, which runs faster than DBASE, includes extra commands, and is marketed by Microsoft. Discount dealers have been selling it for just $94, but that temporary low price will probably rise.

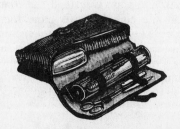

EASY

EASY is a language I developed several years ago. It combines the best features of all other languages. It's easy to learn, because it uses just these twelve keywords:

```
SAY & GET
LET

REPEAT & SKIP
HERE

IF & PICK
LOOP

PREPARE & DATA
HOW
```

Here's how to use them. . . .

SAY EASY uses the word SAY instead of BASIC's word PRINT, because SAY is briefer. If you want the computer to say the answer to 2+2, give this command:

```
SAY 2+2
```

The computer will say the answer:

```
4
```

Whenever the computer prints, it automatically prints a blank space afterwards but does *not* press the ENTER key. So if you run this program —

```
SAY "LOVE"
SAY "HATE"
```

the computer will say:

```
LOVE HATE
```

Here's a fancier example:

```
SAY "LOVE" AS 3 AT 20 15 TRIM !
```

The "AS 3" is a format: it makes the computer print just the first 3 letters of LOVE. The "AT 20 15" makes the computer begin printing LOVE at the screen's pixel whose X coordinate is 20 and whose Y coordinate is 15. The computer usually prints a blank space after everything, but the word TRIM suppresses that blank space. The exclamation point makes the computer press the ENTER key afterwards.

Here's another example:

```
SAY TO SCREEN PRINTER HARRY
```

It means that henceforth, whenever you give a SAY command, the computer will print the answer simultaneously onto your screen, onto your printer, and onto a disk file named HARRY. If you ever want to cancel that "SAY TO" command, give a "SAY TO" command that contradicts it.

GET EASY uses the word GET instead of BASIC's word INPUT, because GET is briefer. The command GET X makes the computer wait for you to input the value of X. Above the GET command, you typically put a SAY command that makes the computer ask a question.

You can make the GET command fancy, like this:

```
GET X AS 3 AT 20 15 WAIT 5
```

The "AS 3" tells the computer that X will be just 3 characters; the computer waits for you to type just 3 characters and doesn't require you to press the ENTER key afterwards. The "AT 20 15" makes the computer move to pixel 20 15 before your typing begins, so your input appears at that part of the screen. The "WAIT 5" makes the computer wait just 5 seconds for your response. If you reply within 5 seconds, the computer sets TIME equal to how many seconds you took. If you do *not* reply within the 5 seconds, the computer sets TIME equal to -1.

LET The LET statement resembles BASIC's. For example, you can say:

```
LET R=4
```

To let R be a random decimal, type:

```
LET R=RANDOM
```

To let R be a random integer from 1 to 6, type:

```
LET R=RANDOM TO 6
```

To let R be a random integer from -3 to 5, type:

```
LET R=RANDOM FROM -3 TO 5
```

REPEAT If you put the word REPEAT at the bottom of your program, the computer will repeat the entire program again and again, forming an infinite loop.

SKIP If you put the word SKIP in the middle of your program, the computer will skip the bottom part of the program. SKIP is like BASIC's END or STOP.

HERE In the middle of your program, you can say:

```
HERE IS FRED
```

An earlier line can say SKIP TO FRED. A later line can say REPEAT FROM FRED. The SKIP TO and REPEAT FROM are like BASIC's GO TO.

IF In your program, a line can say:

```
IF X<3
```

Underneath that line, you must put some indented lines, which the computer will do if X<3.

Suppose you give a student a test on which the score can be between 0 and 100. If the student's score is 100, let's make the computer say "PERFECT"; if the score is below 100 but at least 70, let's make the computer say the score and also say "OKAY THOUGH NOT PERFECT"; if the score is below 70, let's make the computer say "YOU FAILED". Here's how:

```
IF SCORE=100
  SAY "PERFECT"
IF SCORE<100 AND SCORE>=70
  SAY SCORE
  SAY "OKAY THOUGH NOT PERFECT"
IF SCORE<70
  SAY "YOU FAILED"
```

To shorten the program, use the words NOT and BUT:

```
IF SCORE=100
  SAY "PERFECT"
IF NOT BUT SCORE>=70
  SAY SCORE
  SAY "OKAY THOUGH NOT PERFECT"
IF NOT
  SAY "YOU FAILED"
```

The phrase "IF NOT" is like BASIC's ELSE. The phrase "IF NOT BUT" is like BASIC's ELSE IF.

PICK You can shorten that example even further, by telling the computer to pick just the first IF that's true:

```
PICK SCORE
  IF 100
    SAY "PERFECT"
  IF >=70
    SAY SCORE
    SAY "OKAY THOUGH NOT PERFECT"
  IF NOT
    SAY "YOU FAILED"
```

LOOP If you put the word LOOP above indented lines, the computer will do those lines repeatedly. For example, this program makes the computer say the words CAT and DOG repeatedly:

```
LOOP
    SAY "CAT"
    SAY "DOG"
```

This program makes the computer say 5, 8, 11, 14, and 17:

```
LOOP I FROM 5 BY 3 TO 17
    SAY I
```

That LOOP statement is like BASIC's "FOR I = 5 TO 17 STEP 3". If you omit the "BY 3", the computer will assume "BY 1". If you omit the "FROM 5", the computer will assume "FROM 1". If you omit the "TO 17", the computer will assume "to infinity".

To make the computer count down instead of up, insert the word DOWN, like this:

```
LOOP I FROM 17 DOWN BY 3 TO 5
```

PREPARE To do an unusual activity, you should PREPARE the computer for it. For example, if you want to use subscripted variables such as X(100), you should tell the computer:

```
PREPARE X(100)
```

In that example, PREPARE is like BASIC's DIM.

DATA EASY's DATA statement resembles BASIC's. But instead of saying READ X, say:

```
LET X=NEXT
```

HOW In EASY, you can give any command you wish, such as:

```
PRETEND YOU ARE HUMAN
```

If you give that command, you must also give an explanation that begins with the words:

```
HOW TO PRETEND YOU ARE HUMAN
```

Interrelated features In the middle of a loop, you can abort the loop. To skip out of the loop (and progress to the rest of the program), say SKIP LOOP. To hop back to the beginning of the loop (to do the next iteration of loop), say REPEAT LOOP.

Similarly, you can say SKIP IF (which makes the computer skip out of an IF) and REPEAT IF (which makes the computer repeat the IF statement, and thereby imitate PASCAL's WHILE).

Apostrophe Like BASIC, EASY uses an apostrophe to begin a comment. The computer ignores everything to the right of an apostrophe, unless the apostrophe is between quotation marks or in a DATA statement.

Comma If two statements begin with the same word, you can combine them into a single statement, by using a comma.

For example, instead of saying —

```
LET X=4
LET Y=7
```

you can say:

```
LET X=4, Y=7
```

Instead of saying —

```
PRETEND YOU ARE HUMAN
PRETEND GOD IS DEAD
```

you can say:

```
PRETEND YOU ARE HUMAN, GOD IS DEAD
```

More info I stopped working on EASY in 1982, but I expect to continue development again soon. To get on my mailing list of people who want more details and updated information about EASY, phone me at 617-666-2666 or send me a postcard.

RADICALS

Let's examine the radical languages, beginning with the oldest radical — the oldest hippie — LISP.

LISP

LISP is the only language made specifically to handle lists of concepts. It's the most popular language for research into artificial intelligence.

It's the father of LOGO, which is "oversimplified LISP" and the most popular language for young children. It inspired PROLOG, which is a LISP-like language that lets you make the computer imitate a wise expert and become an **expert system**.

Beginners in artificial intelligence love to play with LOGO and PROLOG, which are easier and more fun than LISP. But most professionals continue to use LISP because it's more powerful than its children.

The original version of LISP was called **LISP 1**. Then came an improvement, called **LISP 1.5** (because it wasn't different enough from LISP 1 to rate the title "LISP 2"). Then came a slight improvement on LISP 1.5, called **LISP 1.6**. The newest version of LISP is called **Common LISP**; it runs on maxicomputers, minicomputers, and microcomputers.

I'll explain "typical" LISP, which is halfway between LISP 1.6 and Common LISP.

Typical LISP uses these symbols:

BASIC	LISP	
5+2	(PLUS 5 2)	
5-2	(DIFFERENCE 5 2)	
5*2	(TIMES 5 2)	
5/2	(QUOTIENT 5 2)	
5^2	(EXPT 5 2)	
"LOVE"	'LOVE	Older versions say: (QUOTE LOVE)

If you want the computer to add 5 and 2, just type:

`(PLUS 5 2)`

When you press the ENTER key at the end of that line, the computer will print the answer. (You do *not* have to say PRINT or any other special word.) The computer will print:

`7`

If you type —

`(PLUS 1 3 1 1)`

the computer will add 1, 3, 1, and 1 and print:

`6`

If you type —

`(DIFFERENCE 7 (TIMES 2 3))`

the computer will find the difference between 7 and 2*3 and print:

`1`

If you type —

`'LOVE`

the computer will print:

`LOVE`

Notice that you must type an apostrophe before LOVE but must *not* type an apostrophe afterwards. The apostrophe is called a **single quotation mark** (or a **quote**).

You can put a quote in front of a word (such as 'LOVE) or in front of a parenthesized list of words, such as:

`'(LAUGH LOUDLY)`

That makes the computer print:

`(LAUGH LOUDLY)`

LISP 1, LISP 1.5, and LISP 1.6 don't understand the apostrophe. On those old versions of LISP, say (QUOTE LOVE) instead of 'LOVE, and say (QUOTE (LAUGH LOUDLY)) instead of '(LAUGH LOUDLY).

The theory of lists LISP can handle lists. Each list must begin and end with a parenthesis. Here's a list of numbers: (5 7 4 2). Here's a list of words: (LOVE HATE WAR PEACE DEATH).

Here's a list of numbers and words: (2 WOMEN KISS 7 MEN). That list has five items: 2, WOMEN, KISS, 7, and MEN.

Here's a list of four items: (HARRY LEMON (TICKLE MY TUBA TOMORROW AT TEN) RUSSIA). The first item is HARRY; the second is LEMON; the third is a list; the fourth is RUSSIA.

In a list, the first item is called the CAR, and the remainder of the list is called the CDR (pronounced "could er" or "cudder" or "coo der"). For example, the CAR of (SAILORS DRINK WHISKEY) is SAILORS, and the CDR is (DRINK WHISKEY).

To make the computer find the CAR of (SAILORS DRINK WHISKEY), type this:

`(CAR '(SAILORS DRINK WHISKEY))`

The computer will print:

`SAILORS`

If you type —

`(CDR '(SAILORS DRINK WHISKEY))`

the computer will print:

`(DRINK WHISKEY)`

If you type —

`(CAR (CDR '(SAILORS DRINK WHISKEY)))`

the computer will find the CAR of the CDR of (SAILORS DRINK WHISKEY). Since the CDR of (SAILORS DRINK WHISKEY) is (DRINK WHISKEY), whose CAR is DRINK, the computer will print:

`DRINK`

You can insert an extra item at the beginning of a list, to form a longer list. For example, you can insert MANY at the beginning of (SAILORS DRINK WHISKEY), to form (MANY SAILORS DRINK WHISKEY). To do that, tell the computer to CONStruct the longer list, by typing:

`(CONS 'MANY '(SAILORS DRINK WHISKEY))`

The computer will print:

`(MANY SAILORS DRINK WHISKEY)`

Notice that CONS is the opposite of CAR and CDR. The CONS combines MANY with (SAILORS DRINK WHISKEY) to form (MANY SAILORS DRINK WHISKEY). The CAR and CDR break down (MANY SAILORS DRINK WHISKEY), to form MANY and (SAILORS DRINK WHISKEY).

Variables To make X stand for the number 7, say:

```
(SETQ X 7)
```

Then if you say —

```
(PLUS X 2)
```

the computer will print 9.

To make Y stand for the word LOVE, say:

```
(SETQ Y 'LOVE)
```

Then if you say —

```
Y
```

the computer will say:

```
LOVE
```

To make STOOGES stand for the list (MOE LARRY CURLEY), say:

```
(SETQ STOOGES '(MOE LARRY CURLEY))
```

Then if you say —

```
STOOGES
```

the computer will say:

```
(MOE LARRY CURLEY)
```

To find the first of the STOOGES, say:

```
(CAR STOOGES)
```

The computer will say:

```
MOE
```

Your own functions You can define your own functions. For example, you can define (DOUBLE X) to be 2*X, by typing this:

```
(DEFUN DOUBLE (X)
        (TIMES 2 X)
)
```

Then if you say —

```
(DOUBLE 3)
```

the computer will print:

```
6
```

REPEAT Let's define REPEAT to be a function, so that (REPEAT 'LOVE 5) is (LOVE LOVE LOVE LOVE LOVE), and (REPEAT 'KISS 3) is (KISS KISS KISS), and (REPEAT 'KISS 0) is ().

If N is 0, we want (REPEAT X N) to be ().

If N is larger than 0, we want (REPEAT X N) to be a list of N X's. That's X followed by N-1 more X's. That's the CONS of X with a list of N-1 more X's. That's the CONS of X with (REPEAT X (DIFFERENCE N 1)). That's (CONS X (REPEAT X (DIFFERENCE N 1))). That's (CONS X (REPEAT X (SUB1 N))), since (SUB1 N) means N-1 in LISP.

You can define the answer to (REPEAT X N) as follows: if N is 0, the answer is (); if N is *not* 0, the answer is (CONS X (REPEAT X (SUB 1 N))). Here's how to type that definition:

```
(DEFUN REPEAT (X N)
        (COND
              ((ZEROP N) ())
              (T (CONS X (REPEAT X (SUB1 N))))
        )
)
```

The top line says you're going to DEfine a FUNction called REPEAT (X N). The next line says the answer depends on CONDitions. The next line gives one of those conditions: *if N is ZERO*, the answer is (). The next line says: *otherwise*, the value is (CONS X (REPEAT X (SUB1 N))). The next line closes the parentheses opened in the second line. The bottom line closes the parentheses opened in the top line.

Then if you type —

```
(REPEAT 'LOVE 5)
```

the computer will print:

```
(LOVE LOVE LOVE LOVE LOVE)
```

The definition is almost circular: the definition of REPEAT assumes you already know what REPEAT is. For example, (REPEAT 'KISS 3) is defined as the CONS of KISS with the following: (REPEAT 'KISS 2), which is defined as the CONS of KISS with the following: (REPEAT 'KISS 1), which is defined as the CONS of KISS with the following (REPEAT 'KISS 1), which is defined as the CONS of KISS with the following (REPEAT 'KISS 0), which is defined as ().

That kind of definition, which is almost circular, is called **recursive**. You can say "The definition of REPEAT is recursive", or "REPEAT is defined recursively", or "REPEAT is defined by recursion", or "REPEAT is defined by induction", or "REPEAT is a recursive function". LISP was the first popular language that allowed recursive definitions.

When the computer uses a recursive definition, the computer refers to the definition *repeatedly* before getting out of the circle. Since the computer repeats, it's performing a loop. In traditional BASIC and FORTRAN, the only way to make the computer perform a loop is to say GO TO or FOR or DO. Although LISP contains a go-to command, LISP programmers avoid it and write recursive definitions instead.

ITEM As another example of recursion, let's define the function ITEM so that (ITEM N X) is the Nth item in list X, and so that (ITEM 3 '(MANY SAILORS DRINK WHISKEY)) is the 3rd item of (MANY SAILORS DRINK WHISKEY), which is DRINK.

If N is 1, (ITEM N X) is the first item in X, which is the CAR of X, which is (CAR X).

If N is larger than 1, (ITEM N X) is the Nth item in X. That's the (N-1)th item in the CDR of X. That's (ITEM (SUB1 N) (CDR X)).

So define (ITEM N X) as follows: if N is 1, the answer is (CAR X); if N is not 1, the answer is (ITEM (SUB 1 N) (CDR X)). Here's what to type:

```
(DEFUN ITEM (N X)
        (COND
              ((ONEP N) (CAR X))
              (T (ITEM (SUB1 N) (CDR X)))
        )
)
```

If your computer doesn't understand (ONEP N), say (EQUAL 1 N) instead.

SNOBOL

SNOBOL lets you analyze strings more easily than any other language. It can handle numbers also.

Simple example
Here's a simple SNOBOL program:

```
A = -2
B = A + 10.6
C = "BODY TEMPERATURE IS 9" B
OUTPUT = "MY " C
END
```

When you type the program, indent each line except END. Indent *at least* one space; you can indent more spaces if you wish. Put spaces around the symbol =, the symbol +, and other operations.

The first line says A is the integer -2. The next line says B is the real number 8.6. The next line says C is the string "BODY TEMPERATURE IS 98.6". The next line makes the computer print:

```
BODY TEMPERATURE IS 98.6
```

In SNOBOL, a variable's name can be short (like A or B or C) or as long as you wish. The variable's name can even contain periods, like this:

```
NUMBER.OF.BULLIES.I.SQUIRTED
```

Looping
This program's a loop:

```
FRED    OUTPUT = "CAT"
        OUTPUT = "DOG" :(FRED)
END
```

The first line (whose name is FRED) makes the computer print:

```
CAT
```

The next line makes the computer print —

```
DOG
```

and then go to FRED. Altogether the computer will print:

```
CAT
DOG
CAT
DOG
CAT
DOG
etc.
```

Replacing
SNOBOL lets you easily replace one phrase by another.

```
X = "SIN ON A PIN WITH A DIN"
X "IN" = "UCK"
OUTPUT = X
END
```

The first line says X is the string "SIN ON A PIN WITH A DIN". The next line says: in X, replace the first "IN" by "UCK". So X becomes "SUCK ON A PIN WITH A DIN". The next line says the output is X, so the computer will print:

```
SUCK ON A PIN WITH A DIN
```

That program changed the *first* "IN" to "UCK". Here's how to change *every* "IN" to "UCK":

```
X = "SIN ON A PIN WITH A DIN"
X "IN" = "UCK"
X "IN" = "UCK"
X "IN" = "UCK"
OUTPUT = X
END
```

The first line says X is "SIN ON A PIN WITH A DIN". The second line replaces an "IN" by "UCK", so X becomes "SUCK ON A PIN WITH A DIN". The next line replaces another "IN" by "UCK", so X becomes "SUCK ON A PUCK WITH A DIN". The next line replaces another "IN", so X becomes "SUCK ON A PUCK WITH A DUCK", which the

next line prints.

This program does the same thing:

```
        X = "SIN ON A PIN WITH A DIN"
LOOP    X "IN" = "UCK" :S(LOOP)
        OUTPUT = X
END
```

The first line says X is "SIN ON A PIN WITH A DIN". The next line replaces "IN" successfully, so X becomes "SUCK ON A PIN WITH A DIN". At the end of the line, the :S(LOOP) means: if Successful, go to LOOP. So the computer goes back to LOOP. The computer replaces "IN" successfully again, so X becomes "SUCK ON A PUCK WITH A DIN", and the computer goes back to LOOP. The computer replaces "IN" successfully again, so X becomes "SUCK ON A PUCK WITH A DUCK", and the computer goes back to LOOP. The computer does not succeed. So the computer ignores the :S(LOOP) and proceeds instead to the next line, which prints:

```
SUCK ON A PUCK WITH A DUCK
```

Deleting
This program deletes the first "IN":

```
        X = "SIN ON A PIN WITH A DIN"
        X "IN" =
        OUTPUT = X
END
```

The second line says to replace an "IN" by nothing, so the "IN" gets deleted. X becomes "S ON A PIN WITH A DIN", which the computer will print.

This program deletes *every* "IN":

```
        X = "SIN ON A PIN WITH A DIN"
LOOP    X "IN" = :S(LOOP)
        OUTPUT = X
END
```

The computer will print:

```
S ON A P WITH A D
```

Counting
Let's count how often "IN" appears in "SIN ON A PIN WITH A DIN". To do that, delete each "IN"; but each time you delete one, increase the COUNT by 1:

```
        X = "SIN ON A PIN WITH A DIN"
        COUNT = 0
LOOP    X "IN" = :F(ENDING)
        COUNT = COUNT + 1 :(LOOP)
ENDING  OUTPUT = COUNT
END
```

The third line tries to delete an "IN": *if successful*, the computer proceeds to the next line, which increases the COUNT and goes back to LOOP; *if failing* (because no "IN" remains), the computer goes to ENDING, which prints the COUNT. The computer will print:

```
3
```

How SNOBOL developed
At MIT during the 1950's, Noam Chomsky invented a notation called **transformational-generative grammar**, which helps linguists analyze English and translate between English and other languages. His notation was nicknamed "linguist's algebra", because it helped linguists just as algebra helped scientists. (A decade later, he became famous for also starting the rebellion against the Vietnam War.)

Chomsky's notation was for pencil and paper. In 1957 and 1958, his colleague Victor Yngve developed a computerized version of Chomsky's notation: the computerized version was a language called **COMIT**. It was nicknamed "linguist's FORTRAN", because it helped linguists just as FORTRAN helped engineers.

COMIT manipulated strings of *words*. In 1962 at Bell Telephone Laboratories (Bell Labs), Chester Lee invented a variant called the **Symbolic Communication Language (SCL)**, which manipulated strings of *mathematical symbols* instead of words and helped mathematicians do abstract mathematics.

A team at Bell Labs decided to invent a language similar to SCL, but easier to learn and including features from COMIT. At first, they called their new language "SCL7", because it resembled SCL. Then they changed its name to "SEXI" (which stands for String EXpression Interpreter), but the management of Bell Labs didn't like sex. Then, as a joke, they named it SNOBOL, using the flimsy excuse that SNOBOL stands for StriNg-Oriented symBOlic Language.

Cynics jeered that SNOBOL didn't have "a snowball's chance in Hell". But the cynics were wrong, and SNOBOL became popular. It was used mainly for writing programs that translate between computer languages. (For example, you could write a SNOBOL program that translates FORTRAN into BASIC.)

Which is better: COMIT or SNOBOL? People who like Chomsky's notation (such as linguists) prefer COMIT. People who like algebra (such as scientists) prefer SNOBOL.

SNOBOL's supporters were more active than COMIT's: they produced SNOBOL 2, SNOBOL 3, SNOBOL 4, and SNOBOL 4B, taught SNOBOL to the newest computers, wrote many books about SNOBOL, and emphasized that SNOBOL can solve *any* problem about strings, even if the problem had nothing to do with linguistics. They won: most people use SNOBOL instead of COMIT, though COMIT might still make a comeback.

Today, most versions of SNOBOL are named after baseball pitching methods — such as FASBOL, SLOBOL, and SPITBOL. (SPITBOL stands for SPeedy ImplemenTation of snoBOL.)

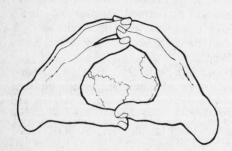

APL

APL lets you manipulate lists of numbers more easily than any other language. APL uses special characters that aren't on a normal keyboard.

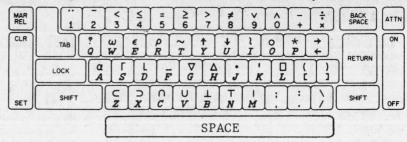

To compute 8+9, type this:

    8+9

Notice the line is indented. Whenever it's your turn to type, the computer automatically indents the line for you.

When you press the RETURN key at the end of that line, the computer will print the answer. (You don't have to say PRINT or any other special word.) The computer will print:

17

Scalar operators APL uses these **scalar operators**:

APL name	Symbol	Meaning
PLUS	A+B	add
identity	+B	same as just B
MINUS	A−B	subtract
negative	−B	negative
TIMES	A×B	multiply
signum	×B	1 if B>0; ¯1 if B<0; 0 if B=0
DIVIDE	A÷B	divide
reciprocal	÷B	1 divided by B
POWER	A∗B	A raised to the Bth power; A^B
exponential	∗B	e raised to the Bth power, where e is 2.718281828459045
LOG	A⍟B	logarithm, base A, of B
natural log	⍟B	logarithm, base e, of B
CEILING	⌈B	B rounded up to an integer
maximum	A⌈B	A or B, whichever is larger
FLOOR	⌊B	B rounded down to an integer
minimum	A⌊B	A or B, whichever is smaller
MAGNITUDE	|B	the absolute value of B
residue	A|B	the remainder when you divide A into B; so 4|19 is 3
FACTORIAL	!B	1 times 2 times 3 times 4 times . . . times B
combinations	A!B	how many A-element subsets you can form from a set of B
ROLL	?B	a random integer from 1 to B
deal	A?B	list of A random integers, each from 1 to B, no duplicates
PI TIMES	○B	π times B

circular A○B

sin B if A=1	arcsin B if A=¯1	square root of 1+B² if A= 4
cos B if A=2	arccos B if A=¯2	square root of 1-B² if A= 0
tan B if A=3	arctan B if A=¯3	square root of B²-1 if A= ¯4
sinh B if A=5	arcsinh B if A=¯5	
cosh B if A=6	arccosh B if A=¯6	
tanh B if A=7	arctanh B if A=¯7	

EQUAL	A=B	1 if A equals B;	otherwise 0
not equal	A≠B	1 if A is not equal to B;	otherwise 0
LESS	A<B	1 if A is less than B;	otherwise 0
less or equal	A≤B	1 if A is less than or equal to B;	otherwise 0
GREATER	A>B	1 if A is greater than B;	otherwise 0
gr. or equal	A≥B	1 if A is greater than or equal to B;	otherwise 0
AND	A∧B	1 if A and B are both 1;	otherwise 0
nand	A⍲B	1 if A and B are not both 1;	otherwise 0
OR	A∨B	1 if A or B is 1;	otherwise 0
nor	A⍱B	1 if neither A nor B is 1;	otherwise 0
NOT	~B	1 if B is 0;	otherwise 0

To make the symbol ⍟, type the symbol ∗, then press the BACKSPACE key, then type the symbol ○.

Order of operations

Order of operations Unlike all other popular languages, APL makes the computer do all calculations *from right to left*. For example, if you type —

```
2×3+5
```

the computer will start with 5, add 3 (to get 8), and then multiply by 2 (to get 16). The computer will print:

```
16
```

In BASIC and most other languages, the answer would be 11 instead.

If you type —

```
9-4-3
```

the computer will start with 3, subtract it from 4 (to get 1), and then subtract from 9 (to get 8). The computer will print:

```
8
```

In most other languages, the answer would be 2 instead.

You can use parentheses. Although 9-4-3 is 8, (9-4)-3 is 2.

Compare these examples:

```
-4+6 is ⁻10
⁻4+6 is 2
```

In both examples, the 4 is preceded by a negative sign; but in the second example, the negative sign is raised, to be as high as the 4. (To make the raised negative, tap the 2 key while holding down the SHIFT key. To make a regular negative, tap the + key while holding down the SHIFT key.) The first example makes the computer start with 6, add 4 (to get 10), and then negate it (to get ⁻10). The second example makes the computer start with 6 and add ⁻4, to get 2.

Double precision

Double precision APL is super-accurate. It does all calculations by using double precision.

Variables

Variables You can use variables:

```
X←3
X+2
```

The first line says X is 3. The second line makes the computer print X+2. The computer will print:

```
5
```

A variable's name can be long: up to 77 letters and digits. The name must begin with a letter.

Vectors

Vectors A variable can stand for a list of numbers:

```
Y←5 2 8
Y+1
```

The first line says Y is the **vector** 5 2 8. The next line makes the computer add 1 to each item and print:

```
6 3 9
```

This program prints the same answer:

```
5 2 8+1
```

The computer will print:

```
6 3 9
```

This program prints the same answer:

```
1+5 2 8
```

You can add a vector to another vector:

```
A←5 2.1 6
B←3 2.8 ⁻7
A+B
```

The computer will add 5 to 3, and 2.1 to 2.8, and 6 to ⁻7, and print:

```
8 4.9 ⁻1
```

This program prints the same answer:

```
5 2.1 6+3 2.8 ⁻7
```

This program prints the same answer:

```
A←5 2.1 6
B←3 2.8 ⁻7
C←A+B
C
```

Here's something different:

```
X←4 2 3
+/X
```

The first line says X is the vector 4 2 3. The next line makes the computer print the sum, 9.

This program prints the same answer:

```
Y←+/4 2 3
Y
```

You can combine many ideas on the same line, but remember that the computer goes from right to left:

```
219-1 4 3+6×+/5 1 3×2 4 7
```

The computer will start with 2 4 7, multiply it by 5 1 3 (to get 10 4 21), find the sum (which is 35), multiply by 6 (to get 210), add 1 4 3 (to get 211 214 213), and then subtract from 219 (to get 8 5 6). The computer will print:

```
8 5 6
```

Each of APL's scalar operators works like addition. Here are examples:

```
2 4 10×3 7 9     is 6 28 90
÷2 4 10          is .5 .25 .1
-2 4 10          is ⁻2 ⁻4 ⁻10
×/2 4 10         is 2×4×10, which is 80
-/9 5 3          is 9-5-3, which is 7 (since the computer works from right to left)
⌊/6.1 2.7 4.9    is 6.1⌊2.7⌊4.9, which is 2.7 (since ⌊ means minimum)
⌊6.1 2.7 4.9     is ⌊6.1 then ⌊2.7 then ⌊4.9, which is 6 2 4 (since ⌊ means floor)
```

Vector operators

Vector operators Here are **vector operators**; the examples assume V is 8 5 6:

APL name	Symbol	Value	Reason
SHAPE	ρV	3	V has 3 items
reshape	7ρV	8 5 6 8 5 6 8	make 7 items from V
REVERSE	ϕV	6 5 8	reverse V
rotate	1ϕV	5 6 8	rotate V, by beginning after the 1st item
GENERATE	ɩ3	1 2 3	count up to 3
index of	Vɩ5	2	in V, find 5; it's the 2nd item
TAKE	2↑V	8 5	the first 2 items from V
drop	2↓V	6	omit the first two items from V
SUBSCRIPT	V[2]	5	V's 2nd item
catenate	V,9 4	8 5 6 9 4	V followed by 9 4
COMPRESS	1 0 1/V	8 6	take part of V, using this pattern: take, omit, take
expand	1 0 0 1 1\V	8 0 0 5 6	insert zeros into V, using this pattern: item, 0, 0, item, item
GRADE UP	⍋V	2 3 1	here are V's numbers in increasing order: 5 (V's 2nd number), 6 (V's 3rd), 8 (V's 1st)
grade down	⍒V	1 3 2	here are V's numbers in decreasing order: 8 (V's 1st number), 6 (V's 3rd), 5 (V's 2nd)
DECODE	10⊥V	856	8, times 10, plus 5, times 10, plus 6
encode	10⊤856	8 5 6	opposite of decode
MEMBER	5∈V	1	search for 5 in V (1=found, 0=missing)

Love or hate?

Love or hate? Some programmers love APL, because its notation is brief. Other programmers hate it, because its notation is hard for a human to read. The haters are winning, and the percentage of programmers using APL is decreasing.

LOGO

LOGO began in 1967, during an evening at Dan Bobrow's home in Belmont, Massachusetts.

Dan had gotten his Ph.D. from MIT and was working for a company called **Bolt, Beranek, and Newman (BBN)**. In his living room were three of his colleagues from BBN (Wally Feurzeig, Cynthia Solomon, and Dick Grant) and an MIT professor: Seymour Papert.

BBN had tried to teach young kids how to program by using BBN's own language (TELCOMP), which was a variation of JOSS. BBN had asked Professor Seymour Papert for his opinion. The group was all gathered in Dan's house to hear Seymour's opinion.

Seymour chatted with the group, and the entire group agreed with Seymour on several points. First, TELCOMP was *not* a great language for kids. It placed too much emphasis on mathematical formulas. The group agreed that instead of struggling with math, the kids ought to have more fun by programming the computer to handle strings instead.

The group also agreed that the most sophisticated language for handling strings was LISP, but that LISP was too complex for kids.

The group concluded that a new, simplified LISP should be invented for kids, and that it should be called "LOGO".

That's how LOGO began. Professor Seymour Papert was the guiding light, and all the other members of the group gave helpful input during the conversation.

That night, after his guests left, Dan went to the terminal in his bedroom and started programming the computer to understand LOGO. Specifically, he wrote a LISP program that explained to the computer how to handle LOGO. That's how LOGO was born.

Work on LOGO continued. The three main researchers who continued improving LOGO were Seymour (the MIT guru), Wally (from BBN), and Cynthia (also from BBN). LOGO resembled LISP but required fewer parentheses.

After helping BBN for a year, Seymour returned to MIT. Cynthia and several other BBN folks worked with him at MIT's Artificial Intelligence Laboratory to improve LOGO.

Turtles At first, LOGO was as abstract and boring as most other computer languages. But in the spring of 1970, a strange creature walked into the LOGO lab. It was a big yellow mechanical turtle. It looked like "half a grapefruit on wheels" and had a pen in its belly:

wheel pen wheel

It also had a horn, feelers, and several other fancy attachments. To use it, you put paper all over the floor and then programmed it to roll across the paper. As it rolled, the pen in its belly drew pictures on the paper. The turtle was controlled remotely by a big computer programmed in LOGO.

Suddenly, LOGO became a fun language whose main purpose was to control the turtle. Kids watching the turtle screamed with delight and wanted to learn how to program it. LOGO became a favorite programming game for kids. Even kids who were just 7 years old started programming in LOGO. Those kids were barely old enough to read, but reading and writing were *not* prerequisites for learning how to program in LOGO. All the kids had to know was that "FD 3" made the turtle go forward 3 steps, and "RT 30" made the turtle turn to the right 30 degrees.

As for the rest of LOGO — all that abstract stuff about strings and numbers and LISP-like lists — the kids ignored it. They wanted to use just the commands "FD" and "RT" that moved the turtle.

The U.S. Government's National Science Foundation donated money, to help MIT improve LOGO further. Many kids came into the LOGO lab to play with the turtles.

The turtles were expensive, and so were the big computers that controlled them. To let more kids use LOGO, the first problem was to reduce the cost of the turtle and its controlling computer.

During the early 1970's, computer screens got dramatically cheaper. To save money, MIT stopped building mechanical turtles and instead bought cheap computer screens that showed pictures of turtles. Those pictures were called "mock turtles".

Cheaper computers The original version of LOGO was done on BBN's expensive weird computer (the MTS 940). Later versions were done on the PDP-1 (in 1968), the PDP-10 (in 1970), and finally on a cheaper computer: the PDP-11 minicomputer (in 1972).

At the end of the 1970's, companies such as Apple and Radio Shack began selling microcomputers, which were even cheaper. MIT wanted to put LOGO on microcomputers but ran out of money to pay for the research.

Texas Instruments (TI) came to the rescue. . . .

TI LOGO TI agreed to pay MIT to research how to put LOGO on TI's microcomputers (the TI-99/4 and the TI-99/4A).

TI and MIT thought the job would be easy, since MIT had already written a PASCAL program that made the computer understand LOGO, and since TI had already written a version of PASCAL for the CPU chip inside the TI-99/4. Initially, MIT was worried because the PASCAL program running on MIT's PDP-10 computer handled LOGO too slowly; but TI claimed TI's PASCAL was faster than the PDP-10's and that LOGO would therefore run fast enough on the TI.

TI was wrong. TI's PASCAL couldn't make LOGO run fast enough, and TI's PASCAL also required too much RAM. So TI had to take MIT's research (on the PDP-10) and laboriously translate it into TI's assembly language, by hand.

The hand translation went slower that TI expected. TI became impatient and took a short-cut: it omitted parts of LOGO, such as decimals. TI began selling its version of LOGO, which understood just integers.

MIT Apple LOGO After TI started selling its LOGO, the MIT group invented a version of LOGO for the Apple. The Apple version included decimals. But alas, the Apple version omitted "sprites" (which are animated creatures that carry objects across the screen) because Apple's hardware couldn't handle sprites fast enough. (TI's hardware was fancier and *did* handle sprites.)

MIT wanted to sell the Apple version to schools since more schools owned Apples than TI computers. But if MIT were to make lots of money from selling the Apple version, MIT might get into legal trouble, since MIT was supposed to be non-profit. And anyway, who "owned" LOGO? Possible contenders were:

MIT, which did most of the research
BBN, which trademarked the name "LOGO" and did the early research
Uncle Sam, whose National Science Foundation paid for much research
TI, which also paid for much research

Eventually, MIT solved the legal problems and sold the rights for "MIT Apple LOGO" to two companies: Krell and Terrapin.

Krell was strictly a marketing company. It sold MIT Apple LOGO to schools but made no attempt to improve LOGO further.

Terrapin, on the other hand, was a research organization that had built mechanical turtles for several years. Terrapin hired some MIT graduates to improve LOGO further.

LCSI versus competitors Back when MIT was asking its lawyers to determine who owned Apple LOGO, a group of MIT's faculty and students became impatient. The group, headed by Cynthia Solomon (one of the original inventors of LOGO), left MIT and formed a company called **LOGO Computer Systems Incorporated (LCSI)**. That company invented its own version of LOGO for the Apple.

LCSI became quite successful. Apple, IBM, Atari, and Microsoft all hired LCSI to write versions of LOGO. Commodore hired Terrapin instead.

Today, if you have an Apple 2c (or 2e or 2+), you can buy either the official Apple LOGO (sold by Apple Computer Inc. and created by LCSI), or "Terrapin LOGO for the Apple" (sold by Terrapin), or the original "MIT LOGO for the Apple" (sold by Krell).

Krell is becoming less popular. That leaves just two major players: Terrapin and LCSI. Generally speaking, LCSI's versions of LOGO are daring — LCSI tried wild experiments — while Terrapin's versions of LOGO are conservative — closer to the MIT original.

The two companies have different styles. Terrapin is small and friendly and charges very little. LCSI is large, charges more, and is often rude. Terrapin gives more help to customers on the phone than LCSI.

Recently, Terrapin has had financial difficulties and moved to Maine.

LOGO versus BASIC Most of LOGO's designers *hate* BASIC. They believe BASIC should be eliminated from schools altogether.

They believe LOGO is easier to learn than BASIC, and that LOGO encourages a kid to be more creative. They also believe that LOGO leads the kid to think in a more organized fashion than BASIC. They also argue that since LOGO is best for little kids, and since switching languages is difficult, the kids should continue using LOGO until they graduate from high school and should never use BASIC.

That argument is wrong. It ignores the fact that a knowledge of BASIC is *essential* to surviving in our computerized society. Today, most programs are still written in BASIC, not LOGO, because BASIC consumes less RAM and because BASIC's newest versions contain many practical features for business and science and graphics that LOGO lacks.

Another advantage of BASIC over LOGO is that LOGO suffers from awkward notation. For example, in BASIC you can type a formula such as —

A=B+C

but in LOGO you must type:

MAKE "A :B+:C

Notice how ugly the LOGO command looks! Notice you must put a quotation mark before the A but must *not* but a quotation mark afterwards! And look at those frightful colons! Anybody who thinks such notation is great for kids is a fool.

Extensible One of the nicest things about LOGO is that you can change it and turn it into your *own* language! That's because LOGO lets you invent your own commands and add them to the LOGO language. A language (such as LOGO) that lets you invent your own commands is called an **extensible language**. Although some earlier languages (such as LISP) were extensible also, LOGO is *more* extensible and more pleasant.

FORTH

Like LOGO, FORTH is extensible. But FORTH has two advantages over LOGO:

1. FORTH consumes less memory. You can easily run FORTH on a computer having just 8K of RAM.

2. FORTH runs faster. The computer handles FORTH almost as fast as assembly language.

Since FORTH is extensible and consumes so little of the computer's memory and time, professional programmers use it often. Famous programs written in FORTH include Easywriter (which is a word-processing program for the Apple and the IBM Personal Computer), Valdocs (which is the operating system for Epson's first computer), and Rapid File (an easy-to-learn data-management system developed by Miller Microcomputer Systems and sold by Ashton-Tate).

Unfortunately, the original versions of Easywriter and Valdocs contained many bugs, but that's because their programmers were careless.

In FORTH, if you want to add 2 and 3 (to get 5) you do *not* type 2+3. Instead, you must type:

```
2 3 +
```

The idea of putting the plus sign afterwards (instead of in the middle) is called **postfix notation**. The postfix notation (2 3 +) has two advantages over infix notation (2+3): the computer handles postfix notation faster, and you never need to use parentheses for "order of operations". On the other hand, postfix notation seems inhuman: it's hard for a human to read.

Like FORTH, Hewlett-Packard pocket calculators use postfix notation. So if you've already had experience with a Hewlett-Packard calculator, you'll find FORTH easy.

Postfix notation is the reverse of **prefix notation** (+ 2 3), which was invented around 1926 by the Polish mathematician Lukasiewicz. So postfix notation is often called **reverse Polish notation**.

Since FORTH is so difficult for a human to read, cynics call it "an inhuman Polish joke".

FORTH was invented by Chuck Moore, during his spare time while he worked at many schools and companies. He wanted to name it "FOURTH", because he considered it to be an ultra-modern "fourth-generation" language. Since he was using an old IBM 1130 minicomputer, which couldn't handle a name as long as "FOURTH", he omitted the letter "U".

PILOT

PILOT was invented at the San Francisco branch of the University of California, by John Starkweather in 1968. It's easier to learn than BASIC, but it's intended to be used by teachers instead of students. Teachers using PILOT can easily make the computer tutor students about history, geography, math, French, and other schoolbook subjects.

For example, suppose you're a teacher and want to make the computer chat with your students. Here's how to do it in BASIC, and more easily in PILOT:

BASIC program
```
10 PRINT "I AM A COMPUTER"
20 INPUT "DO YOU LIKE COMPUTERS";;A$
30 IF A$="YES" OR A$="YEAH" OR A$="YEP" OR A$="SURE" OR A$="SURELY" OR A$="I SUR
E DO" THEN PRINT "I LIKE YOU TOO" ELSE PRINT "TOUGH LUCK"
```

PILOT program	What the computer will do
T:I AM A COMPUTER	Type "I AM A COMPUTER".
T:DO YOU LIKE COMPUTERS?	Type "DO YOU LIKE COMPUTERS?"
A:	Accept the human's answer.
M:YE,SURE	Match. (See whether answer contains "YE" or "SURE".)
TY:I LIKE YOU TOO	If there was a match, type "I LIKE YOU TOO".
TN:TOUGH LUCK	If no match, type "TOUGH LUCK".

Notice that the PILOT program is briefer than BASIC.

Atari, Apple, and Radio Shack all sell versions of PILOT that include commands to handle graphics. Atari's version is the best, since it includes the fanciest graphics and music and even a LOGO-like turtle, and since it's also the easiest version to learn how to use.

Although PILOT is easier than BASIC, most teachers prefer to learn BASIC because BASIC is available on more computers, costs less, and accomplishes a greater variety of tasks. Hardly anybody uses PILOT.

For specialized applications, use a special language.

APT

If you use APT, the computer will help you cut metal.

Type an APT program that says how you want the metal cut. When you run the program, the computer will create a special instruction tape. If you feed that tape into a metal-cutting machine, the machine will cut metal as you said.

Let's write an APT program that makes the machine cut out the shaded area:

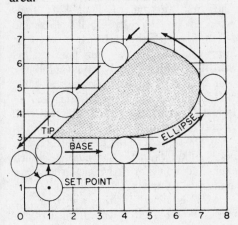

We'll make the machine move the cutter where the circles are.

Here's the program:

Program	What the computer will do
CUTTER/1	Use a cutter whose diameter is 1".
TOLER/.005	The tolerance of the cut is .005".
FEDRAT/80	Use a feedrate of 80" per minute.
HEAD/1	Use head 1.
MODE/1	Operate the tool in mode 1.
SPINDL/2400	Turn the spindle on, at 2400 rpm.
COOLNT/FLOOD	Turn the coolant on, at flood setting.
PT1=POINT/4,5	PT1 = the point whose coordinates are (4,5).
FROM/(SETPT=POINT/1,1)	SETPT = point (1,1). Start tool from SETPT.
INDIRP/(TIP=PIONT/1,3)	TIP = (1,3). Aim tool in direction of TIP.
BASE=LINE/TIP, AT ANGL, 0	BASE = line going through TIP at 0 degrees.
GOTO/BASE	Make the tool go to BASE.
TL RGT, GO RGT/BASE	With tool on right, go right along BASE.
GO FWD/(ELLIPS/CENTER, PT1, 3,2,0)	Go forward along ellipse whose center is PT1, semi-major axis is 3", semi-minor axis is 2", and major axis slants 0 degrees.
GO LFT/(LINE/2,4,1,3,), PAST, BASE	Go left along the line that joins (2,4) and (1,3), until you get past BASE.
GOTO/SETPT	Make the tool go to SETPT.
COOLNT/OFF	Turn the coolant off.
SPINDL/OFF	Turn the spindle off.
END	End use of the machine.
FINI	The program is finished.

DYNAMO

DYNAMO uses these symbols:

Symbol	Meaning
.J	a moment ago
.K	now
.JK	during the past moment
.KL	during the next moment
DT	how long "a moment" is

For example, suppose you want to explain to the computer how population depends on birth rate. If you let P be the population, BR be the birth rate, and DR be the death rate, here's what to say in DYNAMO:

```
P.K=P.J+DT*(BR.JK-DR.JK)
```

The equation says: Population now = Population before + (how long "a moment" is) times (Birth Rate during the past moment - Death Rate during the past moment).

World Dynamics The most famous DYNAMO program is the **World Dynamics Model**, which Jay Forrester programmed at MIT in 1970. His program has 117 equations that describe 112 variables about our world.

Here's how the program begins:

```
* WORLD DYNAMICS
L P.K=P.J+DT*(BR.JK-DR.JK)
N P=PI
C PI=1.65E9
R BR.KL=P.K*FIFGE(BRN,BRN1,SWT1,TIME.K)*BRFM.K*BRMM.K*BRCM.K*BRPM.K
etc.
```

The first line gives the program's title. The next line defines the Level of Population, in terms of Birth Rate and Death Rate.

The second equation defines the iNitial Population to be PI (Population Initial). The next equation defines the Constant PI to be 1.65e9, because the world's population was 1.65 billion in 1900.

The next equation says the Rate BR.KL (the Birth Rate during the next moment) is determined by the Population now and several other factors, such as the BRFM (Birth-Rate-from-Food Multiplier), the BRMM (Birth-Rate-from-Material Multiplier), the BRCM (Birth-Rate-from-Crowding Multiplier), and the BRPM (Birth-Rate-from-Pollution Multiplier). Each of those factors is defined in later equations.

When you run the program, the computer automatically solves all the equations simultaneously and draws graphs that show how the population, birth rate, etc. will change during this century and the next. Here are some of the results:

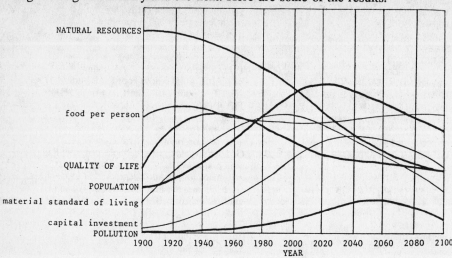

The graph shows the quality of life will decrease because of the overpopulation, pollution, and dwindling natural resources. Although the material standard of living will improve for a while, it too will eventually decrease, as will industrialization (capital investment).

Dwindling natural resources are the main problem. Suppose scientists suddenly make a new discovery that lets us reduce our usage of natural resources by 75%. Will our lives be better?

Here's what the computer predicted would happen, if the "new discovery" were made in 1970:

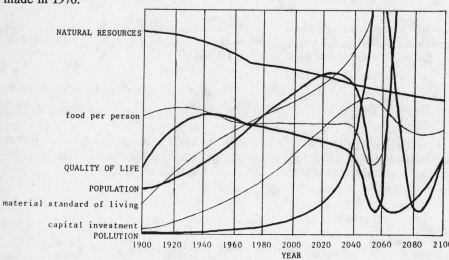

In that picture, you see the graph of natural resources changing sharply in 1970, because of the new scientific discovery. As a result, people live well, so that in 2030 the population is almost 4 times what it was in 1970. But the large population generates too much pollution; in 2030, the pollution is being created faster than it can dissipate. From 2040 to 2060, a pollution crisis occurs: the pollution increases until it is 40 times as great as in 1970; then most people on earth die, so that the world population in 2060 is a sixth of what it was in 2040. After the crisis, the few survivors create little pollution and enjoy a very high quality of life.

Forrester tried other experiments on the computer. To improve the quality of life, he tested the effect of requiring birth control, reducing pollution, and adopting other strategies. Each of them backfired. The graphs showed that the only way to maintain a high quality of life throughout the next century is to adopt a *combination* strategy now:

reduce natural resource usage by 75%
reduce pollution generation by 50%
reduce the birth rate by 30%
reduce capital-investment generation by 40%
reduce food production by 20%

Other popular applications

Although the World Dynamics Model is DYNAMO's most famous program, DYNAMO has also been applied to many other problems.

The first DYNAMO programs ever written were aimed at helping managers run companies. Just plug your policies about buying, selling, hiring, and firing into the program's equations; when you run the program, the computer draws a graph showing what will happen to your company during the coming months and years. If you don't like the computer's prediction, change your policies, put them into the equations, and see whether the computer's graphs are more optimistic.

How DYNAMO developed

The first version of DYNAMO was invented in 1959 by Phyllis Fox and Alexander Pugh III. It was an improvement on a language called **SIMPLE**, which had been invented the year before by Richard Bennett at MIT. "SIMPLE" stood for "Simulation of Industrial Management Problems with Lots of Equations".

In 1961 at MIT, Jay Forrester wrote a book called *Industrial Dynamics*, which explained how DYNAMO can help you manage a company.

MIT is near Boston, whose mayor from 1960 to 1967 was John Collins. When his term as mayor ended, he became a visiting professor at MIT.

His office happened to be next to Forrester's. He asked Forrester whether DYNAMO could solve the problems of managing a city. Forrester organized a conference of urban experts and got them to turn urban problems into 330 DYNAMO equations involving 310 variables. Forrester ran the program and made the computer graph the consequences.

The results were surprising. The graph showed that if you try to help the underemployed by giving them low-cost housing, job-training programs, and artificially-created jobs, here's what happens: as the city becomes better for the underemployed, more underemployed people move to the city; then the percentage of the city that is underemployed increases, and the city is worse than before the reforms were begun. In other words, socialist reform just backfires. Another example: free public transportation creates *more* traffic, because it encourages people to live farther from their jobs.

Instead, the graphs show the only long-term solution to the city's problems is to knock down slums, fund new "labor-intensive export" businesses (businesses that will hire many workers, occupy little land, and produce goods that can be sold outside the city), and let the underemployed fend for themselves in this new environment. Another surprise: any city-funded housing program makes matters *worse* — regardless of whether the housing is for the underemployed, the workers, or the rich — because additional housing means less space for industry and hence fewer jobs.

If you ever become a mayor or President, use the computer's recommendations cautiously: they'll improve the cities, but only by driving the underemployed out to the suburbs, which will worsen.

In 1970 Forrester created the World Dynamics Model to help "The Club of Rome", a private club of 75 people who try to save the world from ecological calamity.

GPSS

A **queue** is a line of people who are waiting. GPSS analyzes queues. For example, let's use GPSS to analyze the customers waiting in "Quickie Joe's Barbershop".

Joe's the only barber in the shop, and he spends exactly 7 minutes on each haircut. (That's why he's called "Quickie Joe".)

About once every 10 minutes, a new customer enters the barbershop. More precisely, the number of minutes before another customer enters is a random number between 5 and 15.

To make the computer imitate the barbershop and analyze what happens to the first 100 customers, type this program:

```
       SIMULATE
       GENERATE   10,5   A new customer comes every 10 minutes ± 5 minutes.
       QUEUE      JOEQ   He waits in the queue, called JOEQ.
       SEIZE      JOE    When his turn comes, he seizes JOE,
       DEPART     JOEQ   which means he leaves the JOEQ.
       ADVANCE    7      After 7 minutes go by,
       RELEASE    JOE    he releases JOE (so someone else can use JOE)
       TERMINATE  1      and leaves the shop.
       START      100    Do all that 100 times.
       END
```

Indent so that the word SIMULATE begins in column 8 (preceeded by 7 spaces) and the "10,5" begins in column 19.

When you run the program, the computer will tell you the following. . . .

Joe was working 68.5% of the time. The rest of the time, his shop was empty and he was waiting for customers.

There was never more than 1 customer waiting. "On the average", .04 customers were waiting.

There were 101 customers. (The 101st customer stopped the experiment.) 79 of them (78.2% of them) obtained Joe immediately and didn't have to wait.

The "average customer" had to wait in line .405 minutes. The "average not-immediately-served customer" had to wait in line 1.863 minutes.

How to make the program fancier

Below the RELEASE statement and above the TERMINATE statement, you can insert two extra statements:

```
       TABULATE   1
1      TABLE      M1,0,1,26
```

(Indent so that the 1 before TABLE is in column 2.) Those two statements make the computer add the following comments.

Of the 100 analyzed customers, the "average customer" spent 7.369 minutes in the shop (from when he walked in to when he walked out).

More precisely, 79 customers spend 7 minutes each, 9 customers spend 8 minutes each, 9 customers spend 9 minutes each, 2 customers spend 10 minutes each, and 1 customer had to spend 11 minutes.

The computer also prints the "standard deviation", "cumulative tables", and other statistical claptrap.

On your own computer, the numbers might be slightly different, depending on how the random numbers came out. To have more faith in the computer's averages, try 1000 customers instead of 100.

Alternative languages

For most problems about queues, GPSS is the easiest language to use. But if your problem is complex, you might have to use **SIMSCRIPT** (based on FORTRAN) or **SIMULA** (an elaboration of ALGOL) or **SIMPL/I** (an elaboration of PL/I).

RPG

RPG is the most popular language for IBM minicomputers, such as the IBM system/3, System/32, System/34, and System/36.

For example, suppose you have a file called MANHOURS, containing one punched card per employee:

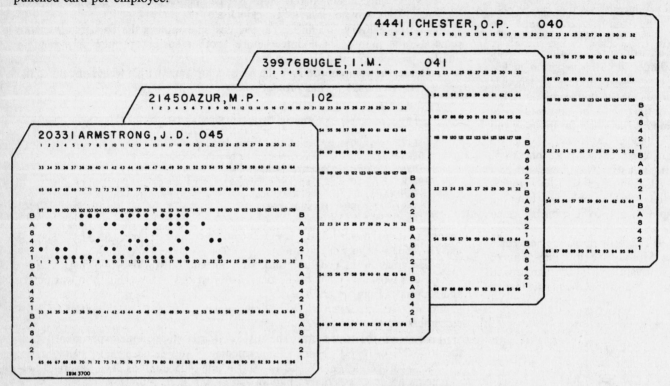

On each card, column 1-5 contain the employee's identification number, columns 6-20 contain his name, and columns 21-23 tell how many hours he worked. Let's make an IBM System/3 minicomputer print the whole file on the line printer, with extra spacing, and also print the total number of man-hours in the company, like this:

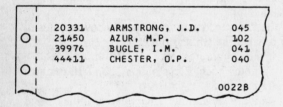

```
  20331     ARMSTRONG, J.D.     045
  21450     AZUR, M.P.          102
  39976     BUGLE, I.M.         041
  44411     CHESTER, O.P.       040

                               0022B
```

To write the program, fill out four forms.

The first form describes the controls and files, like COBOL's environment division. Here's how to fill it out:

IBM — International Business Machines Corporation — Form X21-9092, Printed in U.S.A.

RPG   CONTROL CARD AND FILE DESCRIPTION SPECIFICATIONS

Control Card Specifications (Line 01): `H  008  008`

File Description Specifications:

Line	Form Type	Filename	I/O/U/C		Record Length	Device
02	F	MANHOURS	IP		96	MFCU1
03	F	ADDLIST	O		96	PRINTER
04	F					

Line 01 says "008 008". That makes the computer reserve 8 kilobytes of memory for the program.

Line 02 describes the file MANHOURS. The "IP" means the file is for Input and is the Primary file. The "96" means each card in the file has 96 columns. The "MFCU1" means card reader #1.

Line 03 says "ADDLIST" will be the name of the Output file, which has 96 columns and will appear on the PRINTER.

The second form describes the input:

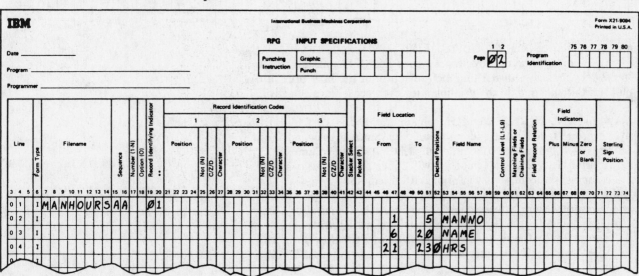

IBM — International Business Machines Corporation — Form X21-9094, Printed in U.S.A.

RPG   INPUT SPECIFICATIONS

Line	Form Type	Filename	Sequence	Record Identifying Indicator	From	To	Field Name
01	I	MANHOURS	AA	01			
02	I				1	5	MANNO
03	I				6	20	NAME
04	I				21	23	HRS

Line 01 says the file MANHOURS is unorganized ("AA"), reading a card from the file is called "activity #01". The remaining lines say that on each card, columns 1-5 contain MANNO, columns 6-20 contain NAME, and columns 21-23 contain HRS, which is a number having 0 digits after the decimal point.

The third form describes the calculations:

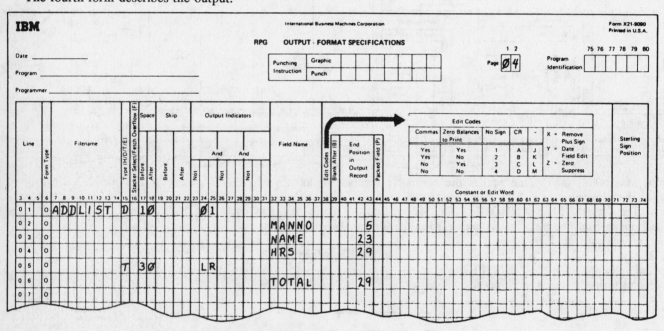

That form says: after each occurrence of activity #01, let HRS + TOTAL be the new TOTAL, which is a 5-digit number having 0 digits after the decimal point.

The fourth form describes the output:

That form explains how to print the file ADDLIST.

In line 01, the "D" means "here's how to print each line of Details". The "10 01" means "press the carriage return 1 time before you print the line, press it 0 times after you print the line, and do the printing after each occurrence of activity #01".

Line 02 says to print MANNO so it ends in column 5.

Line 03 says to print NAME so it ends in column 23. Since the second form said NAME requires 15 columns, the computer will print NAME in columns 9-23.

Line 04 says to print HRS so it ends in column 29. Since the second form said HRS requires 3 columns, the computer will print HRS in columns 27-29.

In line 05, the "T" means "here's how to print the Total". The "30" means "press the carriage return 3 times before you print the line, and 0 times after". The "LR" means "print it only after the last card's been read (Last Record)".

Line 06 says to print TOTAL so it ends in column 29. Since the third form said TOTAL requires 5 columns, the computer will print TOTAL in columns 25-29.

After you've filled out the four forms in longhand, type what you wrote. Here's the RPG program:

```
0101 H008  008
0102 FMANHOURSIP         96           MFCU1      } from the first form
0103 FADDLIST O          96           PRINTER
0201 IMANHOURSAA 01
0202 I                             1   5 MANNO   } from the second form
0203 I                             6  20 NAME
0204 I                            21 230HRS
0301 C   01     HRS      ADD  TOTAL    TOTAL  50 } from the third form
0401 OADDLIST D 10       01
0402 O                   MANNO      5
0403 O                   NAME      23            } from the fourth form
0404 O                   HRS       29
0405 O          T 30     LR
0406 O                   TOTAL     29
```

To do that in BASIC, FORTRAN, or traditional COBOL, you'd have to write a loop; you'd have to say GO TO, DO, or PERFORM. RPG makes the computer do loops automatically, without forcing you to specify how. The order in which you write statements is less important in RPG than in those other languages; you're less likely to err; RPG is more reliable.

But today, RPG is considered old-fashioned, since newer languages (such as DBASE) let you generate loops, totals, and reports even more easily than RPG. Moreover, DBASE costs less than RPG and can run on cheaper computers.

SPSS

The most popular computer language for statistics is **SPSS**, which stands for **Statistical Package for the Social Sciences**.

Simple example Suppose you survey 10 of your friends and ask each of them two questions:

1. In the next election, will you probably vote Republican or Democrat?
2. Are you male or female?

Maybe you can guess the answer to the second question by just looking at the person; but to be sure, you'd better ask.

Suppose nobody gives an unusual answer (such as Prohibitionist or Communist or Transsexual or Undecided). You think it would be cool to feed all the data into the computer. For example, if a person said "Republican Female", you'd feed the computer this line:

```
RF
```

If a person said "Democrat Male", you'd feed the computer this line:

```
DM
```

This SPSS program makes the computer analyze the data:

Program		Meaning
VARIABLE LIST	PARTY,SEX	Read each person's PARTY and SEX,
INPUT FORMAT	FIXED (2A1)	using this FORTRAN FORMAT: "2A1".
N OF CASES	10	There are 10 people.
INPUT MEDIUM	CARD	The data to read is on the "cards" below.
PRINT FORMATS	PARTY,SEX (A)	To print the PARTY and SEX, use "A" format.
CROSSTABS	TABLES=SEX BY PARTY	Print table showing how SEX relates to PARTY.
READ INPUT DATA		The data to read is on the following lines.
RF		
DM		
RM		
RM		
DF		the "data cards"
DM		
DF		
DF		
RM		
DF		
FINISH		The program is finished.

In the top line, the word PARTY begins in column 16. Most SPSS statements consist of a **control field** (columns 1-15) followed by a **specification field** (columns 16-80).

When you run the program, the computer will print this kind of table:

	R	D	ROW TOTAL
M	3 60.0% 75.0% 30.0%	2 40.0% 33.3% 20.0%	5 50.0%
F	1 20.0% 25.0% 10.0%	4 80.0% 66.7% 40.0%	5 50.0%
COLUMN TOTAL	4 40.0%	6 60.0%	10 100.0%

Look at the top number in each box. Those numbers say there were 3 male Republicans, 2 male Democrats, 1 female Republican, and 4 female Democrats. The first box says: the 3 male Republicans were 60% of the males, 75% of the Republicans, and 30% of the total population.

The computer prints the table in reverse-alphabetical order: "M" before "F", and "R" before "D". Each row is a SEX, and each column is a PARTY. In the program, if you change "SEX BY PARTY" to "PARTY BY SEX", each row will be a PARTY, and each column will be a SEX.

Fancy features

The CROSSTABS statement has **options**. Here are some of them.

option 3: don't print the row percentages (the 60.0%, 40.0%, 20.0%, and 80.0%)
option 4: don't print the column percentages (75.0%, 33.3%, 25.0%, and 66.7%)
option 5: don't print the total percentages (30.0%, 20.0%, 10.0% and 40.0%)

If you want options 3 and 5, insert this statement underneath the CROSSTABS statement:

```
OPTIONS      3,5
```

The CROSSTABS statement has **statistics**. Here are some of them:

1. chi-square, its degrees of freedom, and its level of significance
2. phi or Cramer's V
3. contingency coefficient
4. lambda, symmetric and asymmetric
5. uncertainty coefficient, symmetric and asymmetric
6. Kendall's tau b and its level of significance
7. Kendall's tau c and its level of significance
8. gamma
9. Somer's D

Those statistics are numbers that help you analyze the crosstab table. If you want statistics 1 and 8, insert this statement underneath the CROSSTABS and OPTIONS statements:

```
STATISTICS    1,8
```

It makes the computer print statistics 1 and 8 underneath the table. If you want the computer to print all 9 statistics, say:

```
STATISTICS    ALL
```

The CROSSTABS statement is called a **procedure**. Here are other procedures SPSS can handle:

```
AGGREGATE   ANOVA   BREAKDOWN   CANCORR   CONDESCRIPTIVE   DISCRIMINANT
FACTOR   FREQUENCIES   GUTTMAN SCALE   NONPAR CORR   ONEWAY   PARTIAL CORR
PEARSON CORR   REGRESSION   SCATTERGRAM   T-TEST   WRITE CASES
```

Each procedure has its own OPTIONS and STATISTICS.

SPSS includes many other kinds of statements:

```
ADD CASES  ADD DATA LIST  ADD SUBFILES  ADD VARIABLES  ALLOCATE  ASSIGN MISSING
COMMENT  COMPUTE  COUNT  DATA LIST  DELETE SUBFILES  DELETE VARS  DO REPEAT
DOCUMENT  EDIT  END REPEAT  FILE NAME  GET ARCHIVE  GET FILE  IF  KEEP VARS
LIST ARCHINFO  LIST CASES  LIST FILEINFO  MERGE FILES  MISSING VALUES  NUMBERED
PAGESIZE  PRINT BACK  RAW OUTPUT UNIT  READ MATRIX  RECODE  REORDER VARS
RUN NAME  RUN SUBFILES  SAMPLE  SAVE ARCHIVE  SAVE FILE  SELECT IF  SORT CASES
SUBFILE LIST  TASK NAME  VALUE LABELS  WEIGHT  WRITE FILEINFO
```

SPSS contains more statistical features than any other language. If you don't need quite so many features, use an easier language, such as STATPAK or DATATEXT.

PROLOG

In 1972, PROLOG was invented in France at the University of Marseilles. In 1981, a different version of PROLOG arose in Scotland at the University of Edinburgh. In 1986, **Turbo PROLOG** was created in California by Borland International (which also created Turbo PASCAL).

Those versions of PROLOG are called **Marseilles PROLOG**, **Edinburgh PROLOG**, and **Turbo PROLOG**.

Today, PROLOG programmers call Marseilles PROLOG the "old classic", Edinburgh PROLOG the "current standard", and Turbo PROLOG the "radical departure".

Turbo PROLOG has two advantages over its predecessors: it runs programs extra-fast, and it uses English words instead of weird symbols. On the other hand, it requires extra lines at the beginning of your program, to tell the computer which variables are strings.

The ideal PROLOG would be a compromise, incorporating the best features of Marseilles, Edinburgh, and Turbo. Here's how to use the ideal PROLOG, and how the various versions differ from it. . . .

Creating the database

PROLOG analyzes relationships. Suppose Alice loves tennis and sailing, Tom loves everything that Alice loves, and Tom also loves football (which Alice does *not* love). To feed all those facts to the computer, give these PROLOG commands:

```
loves(alice,tennis).
loves(alice,sailing).
loves(tom,X) if loves(alice,X).
loves(tom,football).
```

The top two lines say Alice loves tennis and sailing. In the third line, the "X" means "something", so that line says: Tom loves something if Alice loves it. The bottom line says Tom loves football.

When you type those lines, be careful about capitalization. You must capitalize variables (such as X). You must *not* capitalize specifics (such as tennis, sailing, football, alice, tom, and love).

At the end of each sentence, put a period.

That's how to program by using ideal PROLOG. Here's how other versions of PROLOG differ. . . .

For *Edinburgh PROLOG*, type the symbol ":-" instead of the word "if".

For *Marseilles PROLOG*, replace the period by a semicolon, and replace the word "if" by an arrow (->), which you must put in every line:

```
loves(alice,tennis)->;
loves(alice,sailing)->;
loves(tom,X) -> loves(alice,X);
loves(tom,football)->;
```

For *Turbo PROLOG*, you must add extra lines at the top of your program, to warn the computer that the person and sport are strings ("symbols"), and the word "loves" is a verb ("predicate") that relates a person to a sport:

```
domains
        person,sport=symbol
predicates
        loves(person,sport)
clauses
        loves(alice,tennis).
        loves(alice,sailing).
        loves(tom,X) if loves (alice,X).
        loves(tom,football).
```

(To indent, press the TAB key. To stop indenting, press the left-arrow key.) When you've typed all that, press the ESCape key and then the R key (which means Run).

Simple questions

After you've fed the database to the computer, you can ask the computer questions about it.

Does Alice love tennis? To ask the computer that question, type this:

```
loves(alice,tennis)?
```

The computer will answer:

```
yes
```

Does Alice love football? Ask this:

```
loves(alice,football)?
```

The computer will answer:

```
no
```

That's how the ideal PROLOG works. Other versions differ. *Marseilles PROLOG* is similar to the ideal PROLOG. *Turbo PROLOG* omits the question mark, says "true" instead of "yes", and says "false" instead of "no". *Edinburgh PROLOG* puts the question mark at the beginning of the sentence instead of the end, like this:

```
?-loves(alice,tennis).
```

Advanced questions

What does Alice love? Does Alice love something? Ask this:

```
loves(alice,X)?
```

The computer will answer:

```
X=tennis
X=sailing
2 solutions
```

What does Tom love? Does Tom love something? Ask:

```
loves(tom,X)?
```

The computer will answer:

```
X=tennis
X=sailing
X=football
3 solutions
```

Who loves tennis? Ask:

```
loves(X,tennis)?
```

The computer will answer:

```
X=alice
X=tom
2 solutions
```

Does anybody love hockey? Ask:

```
loves(X,hockey)?
```

The computer doesn't know of anybody who loves hockey, so the computer will answer:

```
no solution
```

Does Tom love something that Alice doesn't? Ask:

```
loves(tom,X) and not (loves(alice,X))?
```

The computer will answer:

```
X=football
1 solution
```

That's ideal PROLOG.

Turbo PROLOG is similar to ideal PROLOG. For *Marseilles PROLOG*, replace the word "and" by a blank space.

For *Edinburgh PROLOG*, replace the word "and" by a comma. After the computer finds a solution, type a semicolon, which tells the computer to find others; when the computer can't find any more solutions, it says "no" (which means "no more solutions") instead of printing a summary message such as "2 solutions".

PROLOG's popularity

After being invented in France, PROLOG quickly became popular throughout Europe.

Its main competitor was LISP, which was invented in the United States before PROLOG. Long after PROLOG's debut, Americans continued to use LISP and ignored PROLOG.

In the 1980's, the Japanese launched the Fifth Generation Project, which was an attempt to develop a more intelligent kind of computer. To develop that computer's software, the Japanese decided to use PROLOG instead of LISP, because PROLOG was non-American and therefore furthered the project's purpose, which was to one-up the Americans.

When American researchers heard that the Japanese chose PROLOG as a software weapon, the Americans got scared and decided to launch a counter-attack by learning PROLOG also.

When Borland — an American company — developed Turbo PROLOG, American researchers were thrilled, since Turbo PROLOG ran faster than any other PROLOG that had ever been invented. It ran faster on a cheap IBM PC than Japan's PROLOG ran on Japan's expensive maxicomputers! The money that Japan had spent on maxicomputers was wasted! The Americans giggled with glee.

Moral: though the Japanese can beat us in making hardware, we're still way ahead in software.

But wouldn't it be great if our countries could work together and *share* talents?

ASSEMBLER

NUMBER SYSTEMS

Most humans use the **decimal system**, which consists of ten digits (0, 1, 2, 3, 4, 5, 6, 7, 8, 9), because humans have ten fingers. The computer does not have fingers, so it prefers other number systems instead. Here they are. . . .

Binary

Look at these powers of 2:

$2^0 = 1$

$2^1 = 2$

$2^2 = 4$

$2^3 = 8$

$2^4 = 16$

$2^5 = 32$

$2^6 = 64$

Now try an experiment. Pick your favorite positive integer, and try to write it as a sum of powers of 2.

For example, suppose you pick 45; you can write it as $32+8+4+1$. Suppose you pick 74; you can write it as $64+8+2$. Suppose you pick 77. You can write it as $64+8+4+1$. *Every* positive integer can be written as a sum of powers of 2.

Let's put those examples in a table:

Original number	Written as sum of powers of 2	Does the sum contain . . . 64?	32?	16?	8?	4?	2?	1?
45	32+8+4+1	no	yes	no	yes	yes	no	yes
74	64+8+2	yes	no	no	yes	no	yes	no
77	64+8+4+1	yes	no	no	yes	yes	no	yes

To write those numbers in the **binary system**, replace "no" by 0 and "yes" by 1:

Decimal system	Binary system
45	0101101 (or simply 101101)
74	1001010
77	1001101

The **decimal system** uses the digits 0, 1, 2, 3, 4, 5, 6, 7, 8, and 9 and uses these columns:

thousands   hundreds   tens   units

For example, the decimal number 7105 means "7 thousands + 1 hundred + 0 tens + 5 units".

The **binary system** uses only the digits 0 and 1, and uses these columns:

sixty-fours   thirty-twos   sixteens   eights   fours   twos   units

For example, the binary number 1001101 means "1 sixty-four + 0 thirty-twos + 0 sixteens + 1 eight + 1 four + 0 twos + 1 unit". In other words, it means seventy-seven.

In elementary school, you were taught how to do arithmetic in the decimal system. You had to memorize the addition and multiplication tables:

DECIMAL ADDITION

	0	1	2	3	4	5	6	7	8	9
0	0	1	2	3	4	5	6	7	8	9
1	1	2	3	4	5	6	7	8	9	10
2	2	3	4	5	6	7	8	9	10	11
3	3	4	5	6	7	8	9	10	11	12
4	4	5	6	7	8	9	10	11	12	13
5	5	6	7	8	9	10	11	12	13	14
6	6	7	8	9	10	11	12	13	14	15
7	7	8	9	10	11	12	13	14	15	16
8	8	9	10	11	12	13	14	15	16	17
9	9	10	11	12	13	14	15	16	17	18

DECIMAL MULTIPLICATION

	0	1	2	3	4	5	6	7	8	9
0	0	0	0	0	0	0	0	0	0	0
1	0	1	2	3	4	5	6	7	8	9
2	0	2	4	6	8	10	12	14	16	18
3	0	3	6	9	12	15	18	21	24	27
4	0	4	8	12	16	20	24	28	32	36
5	0	5	10	15	20	25	30	35	40	45
6	0	6	12	18	24	30	36	42	48	54
7	0	7	14	21	28	35	42	49	56	63
8	0	8	16	24	32	40	48	56	64	72
9	0	9	18	27	36	45	54	63	72	81

In the binary system, the only digits are 0 and 1, so the tables are briefer:

BINARY ADDITION

	0	1
0	0	1
1	1	10 because two is written "10" in binary

BINARY MULTIPLICATION

	0	1
0	0	0
1	0	1

If society had adopted the binary system instead of the decimal system, you'd have been spared many hours of memorizing!

Usually, when you ask the computer to perform a computation, it converts your numbers from the decimal system to the binary system, performs the computation by using the binary addition and multiplication tables, and then converts the answer from the binary system to the decimal system, so you can read it. For example, if you ask the computer to print $45+74$, it will do this:

```
 45  converted to binary is    101101
+74  converted to binary is  +1001010
                             1110111  converted to decimal is 119
                                ↑
                             because 1+1=10
```

The conversion from decimal to binary and then back to decimal is slow. But the computation itself (in this case, addition) is quick, since the binary addition table is so simple. The only times the computer must convert is during input (decimal to binary) and output (binary to decimal). The rest of the execution is performed quickly, entirely in binary.

You know fractions can be written in the decimal system, by using these columns:

units   point   tenths   hundredths   thousandths

For example, $1\frac{5}{8}$ can be written as 1.625, which means "1 unit + 6 tenths + 2 hundredths + 5 thousandths".

To write fractions in the binary system, use these columns instead:

units   point   halves   fourths   eighths

For example, $1\frac{5}{8}$ is written in binary as 1.101, which means "1 unit + 1 half + 0 fourths + 1 eighth".

You know $\frac{1}{3}$ is written in the decimal system as 0.3333333 . . . , which unfortunately never terminates. In the binary system, the situation is no better: $\frac{1}{3}$ is written as 0.010101. . . . Since the computer stores only a finite number of digits, it cannot store $\frac{1}{3}$ accurately — it stores only an approximation.

A more distressing example is $\frac{1}{5}$. In the decimal system, it's .2, but in the binary system it's .0011001100110011. . . . So the computer can't handle $\frac{1}{5}$ accurately, even though a human can.

Most of today's microcomputers and minicomputers are inspired by a famous maxicomputer built by DEC and called the DECsystem-10 (or PDP-10). Though DEC doesn't sell the DECsystem-10 anymore, its influence lives on!

Suppose you run this BASIC program on a DECsystem-10 computer:

```
10 PRINT "MY FAVORITE NUMBER IS";4.001-4
20 END
```

The computer will try to convert 4.001 to binary. Unfortunately, it can't be converted exactly; the computer's binary approximation of it is slightly too small. The computer's final answer to 4.001-4 is therefore slightly less than the correct answer. Instead of printing MY FAVORITE NUMBER IS .001, the computer will print MY FAVORITE NUMBER IS .000999987.

If your computer isn't a DECsystem-10, its approximation will be slightly different. To test your computer's accuracy, try 4.0001-4, and 4.00001-4, and 4.000001-4, etc. You might be surprised at its answers.

Let's see how the DECsystem-10 handles this:

```
10 FOR X = 7 TO 193 STEP .1
20     PRINT X
30 NEXT X
40 END
```

The computer will convert 7 and 193 to binary accurately, but will convert .1 to binary only approximately; the approximation is slightly too large. The last few numbers it should print are 192.8, 192.9, and 193, but because of the approximation it will print slightly more than 192.8, then slightly more than 192.9, and then stop (since it is not allowed to print anything over 193).

There are only two binary digits: 0 and 1. A binary digit is called a bit. For example, .001100110011 is a binary approximation of $\frac{1}{5}$ that consists of twelve bits. A sixteen-bit approximation of $\frac{1}{5}$ would be .0011001100110011. A bit that is 1 is called **turned on**; a bit that is 0 is **turned off**. For example, in the expression 11001, three bits are turned on and two are off. We also say that three of the bits are **set** and two are **cleared**.

All information inside the computer is coded, in the form of bits:

Part of the computer	What a 1 bit is	What a 0 bit is
electric wire	high voltage	low voltage
punched paper tape	a hole in the tape	no hole in the tape
punched IBM card	a hole in the card	no hole in the card
magnetic drum	a magnetized area	a non-magnetized area
core memory	core magnetized clockwise	core magnetized counterclockwise
flashing light	the light is on	the light is off

For example, to represent 11 on part of a punched paper tape, the computer punches two holes close together. To represent 1101, the computer punches two holes close together, and then another hole farther away.

Octal

Octal is a shorthand notation for binary:

Octal	Meaning
0	000
1	001
2	010
3	011
4	100
5	101
6	110
7	111

Each octal digit stands for three bits. For example, the octal number 72 is short for this:

$$\underbrace{111}_{7}\underbrace{010}_{2}$$

To convert a binary integer to octal, divide the number into chunks of three bits, starting at the right. For example, here's how to convert 11110101 to octal:

$$\underbrace{11}_{3}\underbrace{110}_{6}\underbrace{101}_{5}$$

To convert a binary real number to octal, divide the number into chunks of three bits, starting at the decimal point and working in both directions:

$$\underbrace{10}_{2}\underbrace{100}_{4}\underbrace{001}_{1}.\underbrace{100}_{4}\underbrace{11}_{6}$$

Hexadecimal

Hexadecimal is another short-hand notation for binary:

Hexadecimal	Meaning
0	0000
1	0001
2	0010
3	0011
4	0100
5	0101
6	0110
7	0111
8	1000
9	1001
A	1010
B	1011
C	1100
D	1101
E	1110
F	1111

For example, the hexadecimal number 4F is short for this:

$$\underbrace{0100}_{4}\underbrace{1111}_{F}$$

To convert a binary number to hexadecimal, divide the number into chunks of 4 bits, starting at the decimal point and working in both directions:

$$\underbrace{110}_{6}\underbrace{1011}_{B}\underbrace{0100}_{4}.\underbrace{1111}_{F}\underbrace{111}_{E}$$

To store a character in a string, the computer uses a code.

ASCII

The most famous code is the **American Standard Code for Information Interchange (ASCII)**, which has 7 bits for each character. Here are examples:

Character	ASCII code	ASCII code in hexadec'l
space	0100000	20
!	0100001	21
"	0100010	22
#	0100011	23
$	0100100	24
%	0100101	25
&	0100110	26
'	0100111	27
(	0101000	28
)	0101001	29
*	0101010	2A
+	0101011	2B
,	0101100	2C
-	0101101	2D
.	0101110	2E
/	0101111	2F
0	0110000	30
1	0110001	31
2	0110010	32
etc.		
9	0111001	39
:	0111010	3A
;	0111011	3B
<	0111100	3C
=	0111101	3D
>	0111110	3E
?	0111111	3F
@	1000000	40
A	1000001	41
B	1000010	42
C	1000011	43
etc.		
Z	1011010	5A
[	1011011	5B
\	1011100	5C
]	1011101	5D
^	1011110	5E
_	1011111	5F

"ASCII" is pronounced "ass key".

Most terminals use 7-bit ASCII. Most microcomputers and the PDP-11 use an "8-bit ASCII" formed by putting a 0 before 7-bit ASCII.

PDP-8 computers use mainly a "6-bit ASCII" formed by eliminating 7-bit ASCII's leftmost bit, but they can also handle an "8-bit ASCII" formed by putting a 1 before 7-bit ASCII.

PDP-10 computers use mainly 7-bit ASCII but can also handle a "6-bit ASCII" formed by eliminating ASCII's second bit. For example, the 6-bit ASCII code for the symbol $ is 0 00100.

CDC computers use a special CDC 6-bit code.

EBCDIC

Instead of using ASCII, IBM mainframes use the **Extended Binary-Coded-Decimal Interchange Code (EBCDIC)**, which has 8 bits for each character. Here are examples:

Character	EBCDIC code in hexadecimal	Character	EBCDIC code in hexadecimal
space	40	A	C1
¢	4A	B	C2
<	4C	etc.	
(	4D	I	C9
+	4E	J	D1
|	4F	K	D2
&	50	etc.	
!	5A	R	D9
$	5B	S	E2
*	5C	T	E3
)	5D	etc.	
;	5E	Z	E9
¬	5F	0	F0
-	60	1	F1
/	61	etc.	
,	6B	9	F9
%	6C		
_	6D		
>	6E		
?	6F		
:	7A		
#	7B		
@	7C		
'	7D		
=	7E		
"	7F		

"EBCDIC" is pronounced "ebb sih Dick".

IBM 360 computers can also handle an "8-bit ASCII", formed by copying ASCII's first bit after the second bit. For example, the 8-bit ASCII code for the symbol $ is 01000100. But IBM 370 computers (which are newer than IBM 360 computers) don't bother with ASCII: they stick strictly with EBCDIC.

80-column IBM cards use **Hollerith code**, which resembles EBCDIC but has 12 bits instead of 8. 96-column IBM cards use a 6-bit code that's an abridgement of the Hollerith code.

Here's a program in BASIC:

```
10 IF "9"<"A" THEN 100
20 PRINT "CAT"
30 STOP
100 PRINT "DOG"
110 END
```

Which will the computer print: CAT or DOG? The answer depends on whether the computer uses ASCII or EBCDIC.

Suppose the computer uses 7-bit ASCII. Then the code for "9" is hexadecimal 39, and the code for "A" is hexadecimal 41. Since 39 is less than 41, the computer considers "9" to be less than "A", so the computer prints DOG.

But if the computer uses EBCDIC instead of ASCII, the code for "9" is hexadecimal F9, and the code for "A" is hexadecimal C1; since F9 is greater than C1, the computer considers "9" to be greater than "A", so the computer prints CAT.

Bytes

A **byte** usually means: eight bits. For example, here's a byte: 10001011.

For computers that use 7-bit ASCII, programmers sometimes define a byte to be 7 bits instead of 8. For computers that use 6-bit ASCII, programmers sometimes define a byte to be 6 bits. So if someone tries to sell you a computer whose memory can hold "16,000 bytes", he probably means 16,000 8-bit bytes, but might mean 7-bit bytes or 6-bit bytes.

Nibbles

A **nibble** is 4 bits. It's half of an 8-bit byte. Since a hexadecimal digit stands for 4 bits, **a hexadecimal digit stands for a nibble.**

SEXY ASSEMBLER

In this chapter, you'll learn the fundamental concepts of assembly language, quickly and easily.

Unfortunately, different CPU's have different assembly languages.

I've invented an assembly language that combines the best features of all the other assembly languages. My assembly language is called **SEXY ASS**, because it's a Simple, EXcellent, Yummy ASSembler.

After you study the mysteries of the SEXY ASS, you can easily get your rear in gear and become the dominant master of the assemblers sold for Apple, Radio Shack, IBM, DEC, etc. Mastering them will become so easy that you'll say, "Assembly language is a piece of cheesecake!"

Bytes in my ASS

Let's get a close-up view of the SEXY ASS. . . .

CPU registers The computer's guts consist of two main parts: the brain (which is called the **CPU**) and the **main memory** (which consists of RAM and ROM).

Inside the CPU are many electronic boxes, called **registers**. Each register holds several electrical signals; each signal is called a **bit**; so each register holds several bits. Each bit is either 1 or 0. A "1" represents a high voltage; a "0" represents a low voltage. If the bit is 1, the bit is said to be **high** or **on** or **set** or **true**; if the bit is 0, the bit is said to be **low** or **off** or **cleared** or **false**.

The CPU's most important register is called the **accumulator** (or A). In the SEXY ASS system, the accumulator consists of 8 bits, which is 1 byte. (Later, I'll explain how to make the CPU handle several bytes simultaneously; but the accumulator itself holds only 1 byte.)

Memory locations Like the CPU, the main memory consists of electronic boxes. The electronic boxes *in the CPU* are called **registers**, but the electronic boxes *in the main memory* are called **memory locations** instead. Because the main memory acts like a gigantic post office, the memory locations are also called **addresses**. In the SEXY ASS system, each memory location holds 1 byte. There are many *thousands* of memory locations; they're numbered 0, 1, 2, 3, etc.

Number systems When using SEXY ASS, you can type numbers in decimal, binary, or hexadecimal. (For SEXY ASS, octal isn't useful.) For example, the number "twelve" is written "12" in decimal, "1100" in binary, and "C" in hexadecimal. To indicate which number system you're using, **put a percent sign in front of each binary number, and put a dollar sign in front of each hexadecimal number.** For example, in SEXY ASS you can write the number "twelve" as either 12 or %1100 or $C. (In that respect, SEXY ASS copies the 6502 assembly language, which also uses the percent sign and the dollar sign.)

Most of the time, we'll be using hexadecimal, so let's quickly review what hexadecimal is all about. **To count in hexadecimal, just start counting as you learned in elementary school** ($1, $2, $3, $4, $5, $6, $7, $8, $9); **but after $9, you continue counting by using the letters of the alphabet** ($A, $B, $C, $D, $E, and $F). **After $F (which is fifteen), you say $10** (which means sixteen), then say $11 (which means seventeen), then $12, then $13, then $14, etc., until you reach $19; then come $1A, $1B, $1C, $1D, $1E, and $1F. Then come $20, $21, $22, etc., up to $29, then $2A, $2B, $2C, $2D, $2E, and $2F. Then comes $30. Eventually, you get up to $99, then $9A, $9B, $9C, $9D, $9E, and $9F. Then come $A0, $A1, $A2, etc., up to $AF. Then come $B0, $B1, $B2, etc., up to $BF. You continue that pattern, until you reach $FF. Get together with your friends, and try counting up to $FF. (Don't bother pronouncing the dollar signs.) Yes, you too can count like a pro!

Each hexadecimal digit represents 4 bits. Therefore, an 8-bit byte requires *two* hexadecimal digits. So a byte can be anything from $00 to $FF.

Main segment I said that the main memory consists of *thousands* of memory locations, numbered 0, 1, 2, etc. The most important part of the main memory is called the **main memory bank** or **main segment**: that part consists of 65,536 memory locations (64K), which are numbered from 0 to 65,535. Programmers usually number them in hexadecimal; the hexadecimal numbers go from $0000 from $FFFF. ($FFFF in hexadecimal is the same as 65.535 in decimal.) Later, I'll explain how to use other parts of the memory; but for now, let's restrict our attention to just 64K main segment.

How to copy a byte Here's a simple, one-line program, written in the SEXY ASS assembly language:

```
LOAD    $7000
```

It makes the computer copy one byte, from memory location $7000 to the accumulator. So after the computer obeys that instruction, the accumulator will contain the same data as the memory location. For example, if the memory location contains the byte %01001111 (which can also be written as $4F), so will the accumulator.

Notice the wide space before and after the word LOAD. To make the wide space, press the TAB key.

The word LOAD tells the computer to copy from a memory location to the accumulator. The opposite of the word LOAD is the word STORE: it tells the computer to copy from the accumulator to a memory location. For example, if you type —

```
STORE   $7000
```

the computer will copy a byte from the accumulator to memory location $7000.

Problem: write an assembly-language program that copies a byte from memory location $7000 to memory location $7001. Solution: you must do it in two steps. First, copy from memory location $7000 to the accumulator (by using the word LOAD); then copy from the accumulator to memory location $7001 (by using the word STORE). Here's the program:

```
LOAD    $7000
STORE   $7001
```

Arithmetic

If you say —

```
INC
```

the computer will **increment** (increase) the number in the accumulator, by adding 1 to it. For example, if the accumulator contains the number $25, and you then say INC, the accumulator will contain the number $26. For another example, if the accumulator contains the number $39, and you say INC, the accumulator will contain the number $3A (because, in hexadecimal, after 9 comes A).

Problem: write a program that increments the number that's in location $7000; for example, if location $7000 contains $25, the program should change that data, so that location $7000 contains $26 instead. Solution: copy the number from location $7000 to the accumulator, then increment the number, then copy it back to location $7000. . . .

```
LOAD    $7000
INC
STORE   $7000
```

That example illustrates the fundamental rule of assembly-language programming, which is: **to manipulate a memory location's data, copy the data to the accumulator, manipulate the accumulator, and then copy the revised data from the accumulator to memory.**

The opposite of INC is DEC: it **decrements** (decreases) the number in the accumulator, by subtracting 1 from it.

If you say —

```
ADD     $7000
```

the computer will change the number in the accumulator, by adding to it the number that was in memory location $7000. For example, if the accumulator had contained the number $16, and memory location $7000 had contained the number $43, the number in the accumulator will change and become the sum, $59. The number in memory location $7000 will remain unchanged: it will still be $43.

Problem: find the sum of the numbers in memory locations $7000, $7001, and $7002, and put that sum into location $7003. Solution: copy the number from memory location $7000 to the accumulator, then add to the accumulator the numbers from memory locations $7001 and $7002, so that the accumulator to memory location $7003. . . .

```
LOAD    $7000
ADD     $7001
ADD     $7002
STORE   $7003
```

The opposite of ADD is SUB, which means SUBtract. If you say SUB $7000, the computer will change the number in the accumulator, by subtracting from it the number in memory location $7000.

Immediate addressing

If you say —

```
LOAD    #$25
```

the computer will put the number $25 into the accumulator. The $25 is the data. In the instruction "LOAD #$25", the symbol "#" tells the computer that the $25 is the data instead of being a memory location.

If you were to omit the #, the computer would assume the $25 meant memory location $0025, and so the computer would copy data from memory location $0025 to the accumulator.

An instruction that contains the symbol # is said to be an **immediate** instruction; it is said to use **immediate** addressing. Such instructions are unusual.

The more usual kind of instruction, which does *not* use the symbol #, is called a **direct** instruction.

Problem: change the number in the accumulator, by adding $12 to it. Solution:

```
ADD     #$12
```

Problem: change the number in memory location $7000, by adding $12 to that number. Solution: copy the number from memory location $7000 to the accumulator, add $12 to it, and then copy the sum back to the memory location. . . .

```
LOAD    $7000
ADD     #$12
STORE   $7000
```

Problem: make the computer find the sum of $16 and $43, and put the sum into memory location $7000. Solution: put $16 into the accumulator, add $43 to it, and then copy from the accumulator to memory location $7000. . . .

```
LOAD    #$16
ADD     #$43
STORE   $7000
```

Video RAM

The video RAM is part of the computer's RAM, and holds a copy of what's on the screen.

For example, suppose you're running a program that analyzes taxicabs, and the screen (of your TV or monitor) shows information about various cabs. If the upper-left corner of the screen shows the word CAB, the video RAM contains the ASCII code numbers for the letters C, A, and B. Since the ASCII code number for C is 67 (which is $43), and the ASCII code number for A is 65 (which is $41), and the ASCII code number for B is 66 (which is $42), the video RAM contains $43, $41, and $42. The $43, $41, and $42 represent the word CAB.

Suppose that the video RAM begins at memory location $6000. If the screen's upper-left corner shows the word CAB, memory location $6000 contains the code for C (which is $43); the next memory location ($6001) contains the code for A (which is $41); and the next memory location ($6002) contains the code for B (which is $42).

Problem: assuming that the video RAM begins at location $6000, make the computer write the word CAB onto the screen's upper-left corner. Solution: write $43 into memory location $6000, write $41 into memory location $6001, and write $42 into memory location $6002. . . .

```
LOAD    #$43
STORE   $6000
LOAD    #$41
STORE   $6001
LOAD    #$42
STORE   $6002
```

The computer knows that $43 is the code number for "C". When you're writing that program, if you're too lazy to figure out the $43, you can simply write "C"; the computer will understand. So you can write the program like this:

```
LOAD    #"C"
STORE   $6000
LOAD    #"A"
STORE   $6001
LOAD    #"B"
STORE   $6002
```

That's the solution if the video RAM begins at memory location $6000. On *your* computer, the video RAM might begin at a different memory location instead. To find out about *your* computer's video RAM, look at the back of the technical manual that came with your computer. There you'll find a **memory map**: it shows which memory locations are used by the video RAM, which memory locations are used by other RAM, and which memory locations are used by the ROM.

Flags

The CPU contains **flags**. Here's how they work.

Carry flag A byte consists of 8 bits. The smallest number you can put into a byte is %00000000. The largest number you can put into a byte is %11111111, which in hexadecimal is $FF; in decimal, it's 255.

What happens if you try to go higher than %11111111? To find out, examine this program:

```
LOAD   #%10000001
ADD    #%10000010
```

In that program, the top line puts the binary number %10000001 into the accumulator. The next line tries to add %10000010 to the accumulator. But **the sum, which is %100000011, contains 9 bits instead of 8, and therefore can't fit into the accumulator.**

The computer splits that sum into two parts: the left bit (1) and the remaining bits (00000011). The left bit (1) is called the <u>carry bit</u>; the remaining bits (00000011) are called the **tail**. Since the tail contains 8 bits, it fits nicely into the accumulator; so the computer puts it into the accumulator. **The carry bit is put into a special place inside the CPU; that special place is called the <u>carry flag</u>.**

So that program makes the accumulator become 00000011, and makes the carry flag become 1.

Here's an easier program:

```
LOAD   #%1
ADD    #%10
```

The top line puts %1 into the accumulator; so the accumulator's 8 bits are %00000001. The bottom line adds %10 to the number in the accumulator; so the accumulator's 8 bits become %00000011. Since the numbers involved in that addition were so small, there was no need for a 9th bit — no need for a carry bit. To emphasize that no carry bit was required, the carry flag automatically becomes 0.

Here's the rule: if an arithmetic operation (such as ADD, SUB, INC, or DEC) gives a result that's too long to fit into 8 bits, the carry flag becomes 1; otherwise, the carry flag becomes 0.

Negatives The largest number you can fit into a byte is %11111111, which in decimal is 255. Suppose you try to add 1 to it. The sum is %100000000, which in decimal is 256. But since %100000000 contains 9 bits, it's too long to fit into a byte. So the computer sends the leftmost bit (the 1) to the carry flag, and puts the tail (the 00000000) into the accumulator. As a result, the accumulator contains 0.

So in assembly language, if you tell the computer to do %11111111+1 (which is 255+1), the accumulator says the answer is 0 (instead of 256).

In assembly language, %11111111+1 is 0. In other words, %11111111 solves the equation x+1=0.

According to high school algebra, the equation x+1=0 has this solution: x=-1. But we've seen that in the assembly language, the equation x+1=0 has the solution x=%11111111. Conclusion: in assembly language, -1 is the same as %11111111.

Now you know that -1 is the same as %11111111, which is 255. Yes, -1 is the same as 255. Similarly, -2 is the same as 254; -3 is the same as 253; -4 is the same as 252. Here's the general formula: -n is the same as 256-n. (That's because 256 is the same as 0.)

%11111111 is 255 and is also -1. Since -1 is a shorter name than 255, we say that %11111111 is *interpreted as* -1. Similarly, %11111110 is 254 and also -2; since -2 is a shorter name than 254, we say that %11111110 is interpreted as -2. At the other extreme, %00000010 is 2 and is also -254; since 2 is a shorter name than -254, we say that %11111110 is interpreted as 2. Here's the rule: if a number is "almost" 256, it's interpreted as a negative number; otherwise, it's interpreted as a positive number.

How high must a number be, in order to be "almost" 256, and therefore to be interpreted as a negative number? The answer is: if the number is at least 128, it's interpreted as a negative number. Putting it another way, if the number's leftmost bit is 1, it's interpreted as a negative number.

That strange train of reasoning leads to the following definition: **a <u>negative number</u> is a byte whose leftmost bit is 1**.

A byte's leftmost bit is therefore called the **negative bit** or the **sign bit**.

Flag register You've seen that the CPU contains a register called the **accumulator**. The CPU also contains a second register, called the **flag register**. In the SEXY ASS system, the flag register contains 8 bits (one byte). Each of the 8 bits in the flag register is called a **flag**; so the flag register contains 8 flags.

Each flag is a bit: it's either 1 or 0. If the flag is 1, the flag is said to be **up** or **raised** or **set**. If the flag is 0, the flag is said to be **down** or **lowered** or **cleared**.

One of the 8 flags is the carry flag: it's raised (becomes 1) whenever an arithmetic operation requires a 9th bit. (It's lowered whenever an arithmetic operation does *not* require a 9th bit.)

Another one of the flags is **the <u>negative flag</u>: it's raised whenever the number in the accumulator becomes negative**. For example, if the accumulator becomes %11111110 (which is -2), the negative flag is raised (i.e. the negative flag becomes 1). It's lowered whenever the number in the accumulator becomes *non*-negative.

Another one of the flags is **the <u>zero flag</u>: it's raised whenever the number in the accumulator becomes zero**. (It's lowered whenever the number in the accumulator becomes *non*-zero.)

Jumps

You can give each line of your program a name. For example, you can give a line the name FRED. To do so, put the name FRED at the beginning of the line, like this:

```
FRED    LOAD    $7000
```

The line's name (FRED) is at the left margin. The command itself (LOAD $7000) is indented by pressing the TAB key. In that line, FRED is called the **label**, LOAD is called the **operation** or **mnemonic**, and $7000 is called the **address**.

Languages such as BASIC let you say "GO TO". **In assembly language, you say "JUMP" instead of "GO TO".** For example, to make the computer GO TO the line named FRED, say:

```
    JUMP    FRED
```

The computer will obey: it will JUMP to the line named FRED.

You can say —

```
    JUMPN   FRED
```

That means: JUMP to FRED, if the Negative flag is raised. So the computer will JUMP to FRED if a negative number was recently put into the accumulator. (If a *non*-negative number was recently put into the accumulator, the computer will *not* jump to FRED.)

JUMPN means "JUMP if the Negative flag is raised." JUMPC means "JUMP if the Carry flag is raised." JUMPZ means "JUMP if the Zero flag is raised."

JUMPNL means "JUMP if the Negative flag is Lowered." JUMPCL means "JUMP if the Carry flag is Lowered." JUMPZL means "JUMP if the Zero flag is Lowered."

Problem: make the computer look at memory location $7000; if the number in that memory location is negative, make the computer jump to a line named FRED. Solution: copy the number from memory location $7000 to the accumulator, to influence the Negative flag; then JUMP if Negative. . . .

```
    LOAD    $7000
    JUMPN   FRED
```

Problem: make the computer look at memory location $7000. If the number in that memory location is negative, make the computer print a minus sign in the upper-left corner of the screen; if the number is positive instead, make the computer print a plus sign instead; if the number is zero, make the computer print a zero. Solution: copy the number from memory location $7000 to the accumulator (by saying LOAD); then analyze that number (by using JUMPN and JUMPZ); then LOAD the ASCII code number for either "+" or "-" or "0" into the accumulator (whichever is appropriate); finally copy that ASCII code number from the accumulator to the video RAM (by saying STORE). . . .

```
            LOAD    $7000
            JUMPN   NEGAT
            JUMPZ   ZERO
            LOAD    #"+"
            JUMP    DISPLAY
NEGAT       LOAD    #"-"
            JUMP    DISPLAY
ZERO        LOAD    #"0"
DISPLAY     STORE   $6000
```

Machine language

I've been explaining assembly language. **Machine language** resembles assembly language; what's the difference?

To find out, let's look at a machine language called **SEXY MACHO** (because it's a Simple, EXcellent, Yummy MACHine language Original).

SEXY MACHO resembles SEXY ASS; here are the major differences. . . .

In SEXY ASS assembly language, you use words such as LOAD, STORE, INC, DEC, ADD, SUB, and JUMP. Those words are called *operations* or *mnemonics*. In SEXY MACHO machine language, you replace those words by code numbers: the code number for LOAD is 1; the code number for STORE is 2; INC is 3; DEC is 4; ADD is 5; SUB is 6; and JUMP is 7. The code numbers are called the **operation codes** or **op codes**.

In SEXY ASS assembly language, the symbol "#" indicates immediate addressing; a lack of the symbol "#" indicates direct addressing instead. In SEXY MACHO machine language, you replace the symbol "#" by the code number 1; if you want direct addressing instead, you must use the code number 0.

In SEXY MACHO, all code numbers are hexadecimal.

For example, look at this SEXY ASS instruction:

```
    ADD     #$43
```

To translate that instruction into SEXY MACHO machine language, just replace each symbol by its code number. Since the code number for ADD is 5, and the code number for # is 1, the SEXY MACHO version of that line is:

5143

Let's translate STORE $7003 into SEXY MACHO machine language. Since the code for STORE is 2, and the code for direct addressing is 0, the SEXY MACHO version of that command is:

207003

In machine language, you can't use any words or symbols: you must use their code numbers instead. To translate a program from assembly language to machine language, you must look up the code number of each word or symbol.

An **assembler** is a program that makes the computer translate from assembly language to machine language.

The CPU understands only machine language: it understands only numbers. It does *not* understand assembly language: it does not understand words and symbols. **If you write a program in assembly language, you must buy an assembler, which translates your program from assembly language to machine language**, so that the computer can understand it.

Since assembly language uses English words (such as LOAD), assembly language seems more "human" than machine language (which uses code numbers). Since programmers are humans, programmers prefer assembly language over machine language. Therefore, the typical programmer writes in assembly language, and then uses an assembler to translate the program to machine language, which is the language that the CPU ultimately requires.

Here's how the typical assembly-language programmer works. First, the programmer types the assembly-language program and uses a word processor to help edit it. The word processor automatically puts the assembly-language program onto a disk. Next, the programmer uses the assembler to translate the assembly-language program into machine language. The assembler puts the machine-language version of the program onto the disk. So now the disk contains *two* versions of the program: the disk contains the original version (in assembly language) and also contains the translated version (in machine language). The original version (in assembly language) is called the **source code**; the translated version (in machine language) is called the **object code**. Finally, the programmer gives a command that makes the computer copy the machine-language version (the object code) from the disk to the RAM and run it.

Here's a tough question: how does the assembler translate "JUMP FRED" into machine language? Here's the answer. . . .

The assembler realizes that FRED is the name for a line in your program. The assembler hunts through your program, to find out which line is labeled FRED. When the assembler finds that line, it analyzes that line, to figure out where that line will be in the RAM after the program is translated into machine language and running. For example, suppose the line that's labeled FRED will become a machine-language line which, when the program is running, will be in the RAM at memory location $2053. Then "JUMP FRED" must be translated into this command: "jump to the machine-language line that's in the RAM at memory location $2053". So "JUMP FRED" really means:

        JUMP $2053

Since the code number for JUMP is 7, and the addressing isn't immediate (and therefore has code 0 instead of 1), the machine-language version of JUMP FRED is:

702053

System software

The computer's main memory consists of RAM and ROM. In a typical computer, the first few memory locations ($0000, $0001, $0002, etc.) are ROM: they permanently contain a program called the **bootstrap**, which is written in machine-language.

When you turn on the computer's power switch, the computer automatically runs the bootstrap program. If your computer uses disks, the bootstrap program makes the computer start reading information from the disk in the main drive. In fact, it makes the computer copy a machine-language program from the disk to the RAM. The machine-language program that it copies is called the **DOS**.

After the DOS has been copied to the RAM, the computer starts running the DOS program. The DOS program makes the computer print a message on the screen (such as "Welcome to CP/M" or "Welcome to MS-DOS") and print a symbol on the screen (such as "A>") and then wait for you to type a command.

That whole procedure is called **bootstrapping** (or **booting up**), because of the phrase "pull yourself up by your own bootstraps". By using the bootstrap program, the computer pulls itself up to new intellectual heights: it becomes a CP/M machine or an MS-DOS machine or an Apple DOS machine or a TRSDOS machine.

After booting up, you can start writing programs in BASIC. But how does the computer understand the BASIC words, such as PRINT, INPUT, IF, THEN, and GO TO? Here's how. . . .

While you're using BASIC, the computer is running a machine-language program, that makes the computer *seem* to understand BASIC. That machine-language program, which is in the computer's ROM or RAM, is called the **BASIC language processor** or **BASIC interpreter**. If your computer uses **Microsoft** BASIC, the BASIC interpreter is a machine-language program that was written by Microsoft Incorporated (a "corporation" that consists of Bill Gates and his pals).

How assemblers differ

In a microcomputer, the CPU is a single chip, called the **microprocessor**. The most popular microprocessors are the **8088**, the **68000**, and the **6502**.

The **8088**, designed by Intel, hides in the IBM PC and clones. (The plain version is called the 8088; a souped-up version, called the **80286**, is in the IBM PC AT.)

The **68000**, designed by Motorola, hides in the computers that rely on mice: the Apple Mac, Commodore Amiga, and Atari ST. (The plain version is called the 68000; a souped-up version, called the **68020**, is in the Mac 2; an even fancier version, called the **68030**, is in fancier Macs.)

The **6502**, designed by MOS Technology (which has become part of Commodore), hides in old-fashioned cheap computers: the Apple 2 family, the Commodore 64 & 128, and the Atari XL & XE.

Let's see how their assemblers differ from SEXY ASS.

Number systems SEXY ASS assumes all numbers are written in the decimal system, unless preceded by a dollar sign (which means hexadecimal) or percent sign (which means binary).

68000 and 6502 assemblers resemble SEXY ASS, except that they don't understand percent signs and binary notation. Some stripped-down 6502 assemblers don't understand the decimal system either: they require all numbers to be in hexadecimal.

The 8088 assembler comes in two versions.

The full version of the 8088 assembler is called the **Microsoft Macro ASseMbler (MASM)**. It lists for $150, but discount dealers sell it for just $83. It assumes all numbers are written in the decimal system, unless followed by an H (which means hexadecimal) or B (which means binary). For example, the number twelve can be written as 12 or as 0CH or as 1100B. It requires each number to begin with a digit: so to say twelve in hexadecimal, instead of saying CH you must say 0CH.

A stripped-down 8088 assembler, called the **DEBUG mini-assembler**, is part of DOS; so you get it at no extra charge when you buy DOS. It requires all numbers to be written in hexadecimal. For example, it requires the number twelve to be written as C. Do *not* put a dollar sign or H next to the C.

Accumulator Each microprocessor contains *several* accumulators, so you must say *which* accumulator to use. The main 8-bit accumulator is called "A" in the 6502, "AL" in the 8088, and "D0.B" in the 68000.

Labels SEXY ASS and the other full assemblers let you begin a line with a label, such as FRED. For the 8088 full assembler (MASM), add a colon after FRED. Mini-assemblers (such as 8088 DEBUG) don't understand labels.

Commands Here's how to translate from SEXY ASS to the popular assemblers:

Computer's action	SEXY ASS	6502	68000	8088 MASM
put 25 in accumulator	LOAD #$25	LDA #$25	MOVE.B #$25,D0	MOV AL,25H
copy location 7000 to acc.	LOAD $7000	LDA $7000	MOVE.B $7000,D0	MOV AL,[7000H]
copy acc. to location 7000	STORE $7000	STA $7000	MOVE.B D0,$7000	MOV [7000H],AL
add location 7000 to acc.	ADD $7000	ADC $7000	ADD.B $7000,D0	ADD AL,[7000H]
subtract loc. 7000 from acc.	SUB $7000	SBC $7000	SUB.B $7000,D0	SUB AL,[7000H]
increment accumulator	INC	ADC #$1	ADDQ.B #1,D0	INC AL
decrement accumulator	DEC	SBC #$1	SUBQ.B #1,D0	DEC AL
put character C in acc.	LOAD #"C"	LDA #'C	MOVE.B #'C',D0	MOV AL,"C"
jump to FRED	JUMP FRED	JMP FRED	JMP FRED	JMP FRED
jump if negative	JUMPN FRED	BMI FRED	BMI FRED	JS FRED
jump if carry	JUMPC FRED	BCS FRED	BCS FRED	JC FRED
jump if zero	JUMPZ FRED	BEQ FRED	BEQ FRED	JZ FRED
jump if negative lowered	JUMPNL FRED	BPL FRED	BPL FRED	JNS FRED
jump if carry lowered	JUMPCL FRED	BCC FRED	BCC FRED	JNC FRED
jump if zero lowered	JUMPZL FRED	BNE FRED	BNE FRED	JNZ FRED

Notice that in 6502 assembler, each mnemonic (such as LDA) is three characters long.

To refer to an ASCII character, SEXY ASS and 8088 MASM put the character in quotes, like this: "C". 68000 assembler uses apostrophes instead, like this: 'C'. 6502 assembler uses just a single apostrophe, like this: 'C.

Instead of saying "jump if", 6502 and 68000 programmers say "branch if" and use mnemonics that start with B instead of J. For example, they use mnemonics such as BMI (which means "Branch if MInus"), BCS ("Branch if Carry Set"), and BEQ ("Branch if EQual to zero").

To make the 68000 manipulate a byte, put ".B" after the mnemonic. (If you say ".W" instead, the computer will manipulate a 16-bit word instead of a byte. If you say ".L" instead, the computer will manipulate long data containing 32 bits. If you don't specify ".B" or ".W" or ".L", the assembler assumes you mean ".W".)

8088 assemblers require you to put each memory location in brackets. So whenever you refer to location 7000 hexadecimal, you put the 7000H in brackets, like this: [7000H].

DEBUG

When you buy PC-DOS for your IBM PC (or MS-DOS for your clone), you get a disk that contains many DOS files. One of the DOS files is called **DEBUG**. It helps you debug your software and hardware.

It lets you type special debugger commands. It also lets you type commands in assembly language.

How to start
Put the main DOS disk in drive A, then turn the computer on. Type the date and time.

Press the CAPS LOCK key, so that everything you type will be capitalized. If you're using PC-DOS instead of MS-DOS, put the disk marked "DOS Supplemental Programs" into drive A.

After the A prompt, type the word DEBUG, so your screen looks like this:

A>DEBUG

When you press the ENTER key after DEBUG, the computer will print a hyphen, like this:

-

After the hyphen, you can give any DEBUG command.

Registers
To see what's in the CPU registers, type an R after the hyphen, so your screen looks like this:

-R

When you press the ENTER key after the R, the computer will print:

AX=0000 BX=0000 CX=0000 DX=0000

That means the main registers (which are called AX, BX, CX, and DX) each contain hexadecimal 0000. Then the computer will tell you what's in the other registers, which are called SP, BP, SI, DI, DS, ES, SS, CS, IP, and FLAGS. Finally, the computer will print a hyphen, after which you can type another command.

Editing the registers To change what's in register BX, type RBX after the hyphen, so your screen looks like this:

-RBX

The computer will remind you of what's in register BX, by saying:

BX 0000

:

To change BX to hexadecimal 7251, type 7251 after the colon, so your screen looks like this:

:7251

That makes the computer put 7251 into register BX.

To see that the computer put 7251 into register BX, say:

```
-R
```

That makes the computer tell you what's in all the registers. It will begin by saying:

```
AX=0000  BX=7251  CX=0000  DX=0000
```

Experiment! Try putting different hexadecimal numbers into the registers! To be safe, use just the registers AX, BX, CX, and DX.

Segment registers
The computer's RAM is divided into **segments**. The **segment registers** (DS, ES, SS, and CS) tell the computer which segments to use.

Do *not* change the numbers in the segment registers! Changing them will make the computer use the wrong segments of the RAM and wreck your DOS and disks.

The CS register is called the **code segment** register. It tells the computer which RAM segment to put your programs in. For example, if the CS register contains the hexadecimal number 0E9F, the computer will put your programs in segment number 0E9F.

DEBUG's mini-assembler
To use assembly language, type A100 after the hyphen, so your screen looks like this:

```
-A100
```

The computer will print the code segment number, then a colon, then 0100. For example, if the code segment register contains the hexadecimal number 0E9F, the computer will print:

```
0E9F:0100
```

Now you can type an assembly-language program!

For example, suppose you want to move the hexadecimal number 2794 to register AX and move 8156 to BX. Here's the assembly-language program:

```
MOV AX,2794
MOV BX,8156
```

Type that program. As you type it, the computer will automatically put a segment number and memory location in front of each line, so your screen will look like this:

```
0E9F:0100 MOV AX,2794
0E9F:0103 MOV BX,8156
0E9F:0106
```

After the 0E9F:0106, press the ENTER key. The computer will stop using assembly language and will print a hyphen.

After the hyphen, type G=100 106, so your screen looks like this:

```
-G=100 106
```

That tells the computer to run your assembly-language program, going from location 100 to location 106, so the computer will start at location 100 and stop when it reaches memory location number 106.

After running the program, the computer will tell you what's in the registers. It will print:

```
AX=2794  BX=8156  CX=0000  DX=0000
```

It will also print the numbers in all the other registers.

Listing your program
To list your program, type U100 after the hyphen, so your screen looks like this:

```
-U100
```

The U stands for "Unassemble", which means "list". The computer will list your program, beginning at line 100. The computer will begin by saying:

```
0E9F:0100 B89427     MOV  AX,2794
0E9F:0103 BB5681     MOV  BX,8156
```

The top line consists of three parts. The left part (0E9F:0100) is the address in memory. The right part (MOV AX, 2794) is the assembly-language instruction beginning at that address.

The middle part (B89427) is the machine-language translation of MOV AX,2794. That middle part begins with B8, which is the machine-language translation of MOV AX. Then comes 9427, which is the machine-language translation of 2794; notice how machine language puts the digits in a different order than assembly language.

The machine-language version, B89427, occupies three bytes of RAM. The first byte (address 0100) contains the hexadecimal number B8; the next byte (address 0101) contains the hexadecimal number 94; the final byte (address 0102) contains the hexadecimal number 27.

So altogether, the machine-language version of MOV AX,2794 occupies addresses 0100, 0101, and 0102. That's why the next instruction (MOV BX,8156) begins at address 0103.

After the computer prints that analysis of your program, the computer will continue by printing an analysis of the next several bytes of memory also. Altogether, the computer will print an analysis of addresses up through 011F. What's in those addresses depends on which program your computer was running before you ran this one.

Editing your program
To edit line 0103, type:

```
-A103
```

Then type the assembly-language command you want for location 103.

When you finish the command and press the ENTER key, the computer will give you an opportunity to edit the next line (106). If you don't want to edit or create a line 106, press the ENTER key again.

After editing your program, list it (by typing U100), to make sure you edited correctly.

Arithmetic
This assembly-language program does arithmetic:

```
MOV AX,7
ADD AX,5
```

To feed that program to the computer, say A100 after the hyphen, then type the program, then press the ENTER key an extra time, then say G=100 106.

That program's top line moves the number 7 into the AX register. The next line adds 5 to the AX register, so the number in the AX register becomes twelve. In hexadecimal, twelve is written as C, so the computer will say:

```
AX=000C
```

The computer will also say what's in the other registers.

The opposite of ADD is SUB, which means subtract. For example, if you say —

```
SUB AX,3
```

the computer will subtract 3 from the number in the AX register, so the number in the AX register becomes smaller.

To add 1 to the number in the AX register, you can say:

```
ADD AX,1
```

For a short cut, say this instead:

```
INC AX
```

That tells the computer to INCrement the AX register, by adding 1.

To subtract 1 from the number in the AX register, you can say:

```
SUB AX,1
```

For a short cut, say this instead —

```
DEC AX
```

which means "DECrement the AX register".

Half registers

A register's left half is called the **high part**. The register's right half is called the **low part**.

For example, if the AX register contains 9273, the register's high part is 92, and the low part is 73.

The AX register's high part is called "A high" or AH. The AX register's low part is called "A low" or AL.

Suppose the AX register contains 9273 and you say:

```
MOV AH,41
```

The computer will make AX's high part be 41, so AX becomes 4173.

Copying to memory

Let's program the computer to put the hexadecimal number 52 into memory location 7000.

This command *almost* works:

```
MOV [7000],52
```

In that command, the brackets around the 7000 mean "memory location". That command says to move, into location 7000, the number 52.

Unfortunately, if you type that command, the computer will gripe, because the computer can't handle two numbers simultaneously (7000 and 52).

Instead, you split that complicated command into two simpler commands, each involving just one number. Instead of trying to move 52 directly into location 7000, first move 52 into a register (such as AL), then copy that register into location 7000, like this:

```
MOV AL,52
MOV [7000],AL
```

After running that program, you can prove the 52 got into location 7000, by typing:

```
-E7000
```

That makes the computer examine location 7000. The computer will find 52 there and print:

```
0E9F:7000 52.
```

That means: segment 0E9F's 7000th location contains 52.

If you change your mind and want it to contain 53 instead, type 53 after the period.

Next, press the ENTER key, which makes the computer print a hyphen, so you can give your next DEBUG command.

Interrupt 21

Here's how to write an assembly-language program that prints the letter C on the screen.

The ASCII code number for "C" is hexadecimal 43. Put 43 into the DL register:

```
0E9F:0100 MOV DL,43
```

The DOS code number for "screen output" is 2. Put 2 into the AH register:

```
0E9F:0102 MOV AH,2
```

To make the computer use the code numbers you put into the DL and AH registers, tell the computer to do DOS interrupt subroutine #21:

```
0E9F:0104 INT 21
```

So altogether, the program looks like this:

```
0E9F:0100 MOV DL,43
0E9F:0102 MOV AH,2
0E9F:0104 INT 21
0E9F:0106
```

To make the computer do that program, say G=100 106. The computer will obey the program, so your screen will say:

```
C
```

After running the program, the computer will tell you what's in all the registers. You'll see that DL has become 43 (because of line 100), AH has become 02 (because of line 102), and AL has become 43 (because INT 21 automatically makes the computer copy DL to AL). Then the computer will print a hyphen, so you can give another DEBUG command.

Instead of printing just C, let's make the computer print CCC. Here's how. Put the code numbers for "C" and "screen output" into the registers:

```
0E9F:0100 MOV DL,43
0E9F:0102 MOV AH,02
```

Then tell DOS to use those code numbers, three times:

```
0E9F:0104 INT 21
0E9F:0106 INT 21
0E9F:0108 INT 21
0E9F:010A
```

To run that program, say G=100 10A. The computer will print:

```
CCC
```

Jumps

Here's how to make the computer print C repeatedly, so that the entire screen gets filled with C's.

Put the code numbers for "C" and "screen output" into the registers:

```
0E9F:0100 MOV DL,43
0E9F:0102 MOV AH,02
```

In line 104, tell DOS to use those code numbers:

```
0E9F:0104 INT 21
```

To create a loop, jump back to line 104:

```
0E9F:0106 JMP 104
```

Altogether, the program looks like this:

```
0E9F:0100 MOV DL,43
0E9F:0102 MOV AH,03
0E9F:0104 INT 21
0E9F:0106 JMP 104
0E9F:0108
```

To run that program, say G=100 108. The computer will print C repeatedly, so the whole screen gets filled with C's. To abort the program, tap the BREAK key while holding down the CONTROL key.

Interrupt 20

I showed you this program, which makes the computer print the letter C:

```
0E9F:0100 MOV DL,43
0E9F:0102 MOV AH,2
0E9F:0104 INT 21
0E9F:0106
```

If you run that program by saying G=100 106, the computer will print C and then tell you what's in all the registers.

Instead of making the computer tell you what's in all the registers, let's make the computer say:

```
Program terminated normally
```

To do that, make the bottom line of your program say INT 20, like this:

```
0E9F:0100 MOV DL,43
0E9F:0102 MOV AH,2
0E9F:0104 INT 21
0E9F:0106 INT 20
0E9F:0108
```

The INT 20 makes the computer print "Program terminated normally" and then end, without printing a message about the registers.

To run the program, just say G=100. You do *not* have to say G=100 108, since the INT 20 ends the program before the computer reaches 108 anyway. The program makes the computer print:

```
C
Program terminated normally
```

Strings

This program makes the computer print the string "I LOVE YOU":

```
0E9F:0100 MOV DX,109
0E9F:0103 MOV AH,9
0E9F:0105 INT 21
0E9F:0107 INT 20
0E9F:0109 DB "I LOVE YOU$"
0E9F:0114
```

The bottom line contains the string to be printed: "I LOVE YOU$". Notice you must end the string with a dollar sign. In that line, the DB stands for Define Bytes.

Here's how the program works. The top line puts the string's line number (109) into DX. The next line puts 9, which is the code number for "string printing", into AH. The next line (INT 21) makes the computer use the line number and code number to do the printing. The next line (INT 20) makes the program print "Program terminated normally" and end.

When you run the program (by typing G=100), the computer will print:

```
I LOVE YOU
Program terminated normally
```

If you try to list the program by saying U100, the listing will look strange, because the computer can't list the DB line correctly. But even though the listing will look strange, the program will still run fine.

Saving your program

After you've created an assembly-language program, you can copy it onto a disk and save it. Here's how.

First, make sure the program ends by saying INT 20, so that the program terminates normally.

Next, invent a name for the program. The name should end in .COM. For example, to give your program the name LOVER.COM, type this:

```
-NLOVER.COM
```

Put 0 into register BX (by typing -RBX and then :0).

Put the program's length into register CS. For example, since the program above starts at line 0100 and ends at line 0114 (which is blank), the program's length is "0114 minus 0100", which is 14; so put 14 into register CX (by typing -RCX and then :14).

Finally, say -W, which makes the computer write the program onto the disk. The computer will say:

```
Writing 0014 bytes
```

Quitting

When you finish using DEBUG, tell the computer to quit, by typing a Q after the hyphen. When you press the ENTER key after the Q, the computer will quit using DEBUG and say:

```
A>
```

After quitting, you can give any DOS command you wish. If you used assembly language to create a program called LOVER.COM, you can run it by just typing:

```
A>LOVER
```

The computer will run the program and say:

```
I LOVE YOU
```

Then the computer will print "A>", so you can give another DOS command.

Notice that the computer doesn't bother to print a message saying "Program terminated normally". (It prints that message only when you're in the middle of using DEBUG.)

Now you know how to write assembly-language programs. Dive in! Write your own programs!

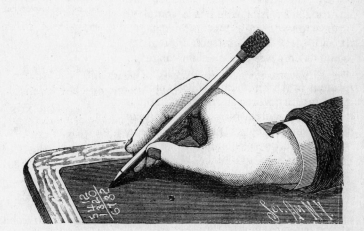

Let's peek inside the CPU and see what lurks within!

Program counter

Each CPU contains a special register called the **program counter**.

The program counter tells the CPU which line of your program to do next. For example, if the program counter contains the number 6 (written in binary), the CPU will do the line of your program that's stored in the 6th memory location.

More precisely, here's what happens if the program counter contains the number 6. . . .

A. The CPU moves the content of the 6th memory location to the CPU's **instruction register**. (That's called **fetching** the instruction.)

B. The CPU checks whether the instruction register contains a complete instruction written in machine language. If not — if the instruction register contains only *part* of a machine-language instruction — the CPU fetches the content of the 7th memory location also. (The instruction register is large enough to hold the content of memory locations 6 and 7 simultaneously.) If the instruction register still doesn't contain a complete instruction, the CPU fetches the content of the 8th memory location also. If the instruction register still doesn't contain a complete instruction, the CPU fetches the content of the 9th memory location also.

C. The CPU changes the number in the program counter. For example, if the CPU has fetched from the 6th and 7th memory locations, it makes the number in the program counter be 8; if the CPU has fetched from the 6th, 7th, and 8th memory locations, it makes the number in the program counter be 9. (That's called **updating the program counter.**)

D. The CPU figures out what the instruction means. (That's called **decoding** the instruction.)

E. The CPU obeys the instruction. (That's called **executing** the instruction.) If it's a "GO TO" type of instruction, the CPU makes the program counter contain the address of the memory location you want to go to.

After the CPU completes steps A, B, C, D, and E, it looks at the program counter and moves on to the next instruction. For example, if the program counter contains the number 9 now, the CPU does steps A, B, C, D, and E again, but by fetching, decoding, and executing the 9th memory location instead of the 6th.

The CPU repeats steps A, B, C, D, and E again and again; each time, the number in the program counter changes. Those five steps form a loop, called the **instruction cycle**.

Arithmetic/logic unit

The CPU contains two parts: the **control unit** (which is the boss) and the **arithmetic/logic unit (ALU)**. When the control unit comes to step D of the instruction cycle, and decides some arithmetic or logic needs to be done, it sends the problem to the ALU, which sends back the answer.

Here's what the ALU can do:

Name of operation	Example	Explanation
plus, added to, +	10001010 +10001001 100010011	add, but remember that 1+1 is 10 in binary
minus, subtract, -	10001010 -10001001 00000001	subtract, but remember 10-1 is 1 in binary
negative, -, the two's complement of	-10001010 01110110	*left of the rightmost 1,* do this: replace each 0 by 1, and each 1 by 0
not, ~,the complement of, the one's complement of	~10001010 01110101	replace each 0 by 1, and each 1 by 0
and, &, ^	10001010 ^10001001 10001000	put 1 wherever both original numbers had 1
or, inclusive or, v	10001010 v10001001 10001011	put 1 wherever some original number had 1
eXclusive OR, XOR, ⊻	10001010 ⊻10001001 00000011	put 1 wherever the original numbers differ

Also, the ALU can shift a register's bits. For example, suppose a register contains 10111001. The ALU can shift the bits toward the right:

before 10111001
after 01011100

It can shift the bits toward the left:

before 10111001
after 01110010

It can rotate the bits toward the right:

before 10111001
after 11011100

It can rotate the bits toward the left:

before 10111001
after 01110011

It can shift the bits toward the right **arithmetically**:

before 10111001
after 11011100

It can shift the bits toward the left arithmetically:

before 10111001
after 11110010

Doubling a number is the same as shifting it left arithmetically. For example, doubling six (to get twelve) is the same as shifting six left arithmetically:

six 00000110
twelve 00001100

Halving a number is the same as shifting it right arithmetically. For example, halving six (to get three) is the same as shifting six right arithmetically:

```
six      00000110
         MMMMMM
three    00000011
```

Halving negative six (to get negative three) is the same as shifting negative six right arithmetically:

```
negative six     11111010
                 MMMMMM
negative three   11111101
```

Using the ALU, the control unit can do operations such as:

A. Find the number in the 6th memory location, and move its negative to a register.
B. Change the number in a register, by adding to it the number in the 6th memory location.
C. Change the number in a register, by subtracting from it the number in the 6th memory location.

Most computers require each operation to have one source and one destination. In operations A, B, and C, the source is the 6th memory location; the destination is the register.

The control unit can*not* do a command such as "add together the number in the 6th memory location and the number in the 7th memory location, and put the sum in a register", because that operation would require two sources. Instead, you must give two shorter commands:

1. Move the number in the 6th memory location to the register.
2. Then add to that register the number in the 7th memory location.

Flags

The CPU contains a **flag register**, which comments on what the CPU is doing. In a typical CPU, the flag register has six bits, named as follows:

the Negative bit
the Zero bit
the Carry bit
the Overflow bit
the Priority bit
the Privilege bit

When the CPU performs an operation (such as addition, subtraction, shifting, rotating, or moving), the operation has a source and a destination. The number that goes into the destination is the operation's **result**. The CPU automatically analyzes that result.

Negative bit If the result is a negative number, the CPU turns on the **Negative bit**. In other words, it makes the Negative bit be 1. (If the result is a number that's *not* negative, the CPU makes the Negative bit be 0.)

Zero bit If the result is zero, the CPU turns on the **Zero bit**. In other words, it makes the Zero bit be 1.

Carry bit When the ALU computes the result, it also computes an extra bit, which becomes the **Carry bit**.

For example, here's how the ALU adds 7 and -4:

```
7 is                      00000111
-4 is                     11111100
binary addition gives    100000011
                          |      result
                         Carry
```

So the result is 3, and the Carry bit becomes 1.

Overflow bit If the ALU can't compute a result correctly, it turns on the **Overflow bit**.

For example, in elementary school you learned that 98+33 is 131; so in binary, the computation should look like this:

```
           128 64 32 16 8 4 2 1
98 is            1  1  0 0 0 1 0
33 is               1  0 0 0 0 1
the sum is   1  0  0  0 0 0 1 1, which is 131
```

But here's what an 8-bit ALU will do:

```
           sign 64 32 16 8 4 2 1
98 is         0  1  1  0  0 0 1 0
33 is         0  0  1  0  0 0 0 1
the sum is  0 1  0  0  0  0 0 1 1
            Carry      result
```

Unfortunately, the result's leftmost 1 is in the position marked **sign**, instead of the position marked 128; so the result looks like a negative number.

To warn you that the result is incorrect, the ALU turns on the Overflow bit. If you're programming in a language such as BASIC, the interpreter or compiler keeps checking whether the Overflow bit is on; when it finds that the bit's on, it prints the word OVERFLOW.

Priority bit While your program's running, it might be interrupted. Peripherals might interrupt, in order to input or output the data; the **real-time clock** might interrupt, to prevent you from hogging too much time, and to give another program a chance to run; and the computer's sensors might interrupt, when they sense that the computer is malfunctioning.

When something wants to interrupt your program, the CPU checks whether your program has priority, by checking the **Priority bit**. If the Priority bit is on, your program has priority and cannot be interrupted.

Privilege bit On a computer that's handling several programs at the same time, some operations are dangerous: if your program makes the computer do those operations, the other programs might be destroyed. Dangerous operations are called **privileged instructions**; to use them, you must be a **privileged user**.

When you walk up to a terminal attached to a large computer, and type HELLO or LOGIN, and type your user number, the operating system examines your user number to find out whether you are a privileged user. If you are, the operating system turns on the Privilege bit. When the CPU starts running your programs, **it refuses to do privileged instructions unless the Privilege bit is on**.

Microcomputers omit the Privilege bit, and can't prevent you from giving dangerous commands. But since the typical microcomputer has only one terminal, the only person your dangerous command can hurt is yourself.

Levels of priority & privilege

Some computers have *several* levels of priority and privilege.

If your priority level is "moderately high", your program is immune from most interruptions, but not from all of them. If your privilege level is "moderately high", you can order the CPU to do most of the privileged instructions, but not all of them.

To allow those fine distinctions, large computers devote *several* bits to explaining the priority level, and *several* bits to explaining the privilege level.

Where are the flags? The bits
in the flag register are called the **flags**. To emphasize that the flags comment on your program's status, people sometimes call them **status flags**.

In the CPU, the program counter is next to the flag register. Instead of viewing them as separate registers, some programmers consider them to be parts of a single big register, called the **program status word**.

Tests You can give a command
such as, "Test the 3rd memory location". The CPU will examine the number in the 3rd memory location. If that number is negative, the CPU will turn on the Negative bit; if that number is zero, the CPU will turn on the Zero bit.

You can give a command such as, "Test the difference between the number in the 3rd register and the number in the 4th". The CPU will adjust the flags according to whether the difference is negative or zero or carries or overflows.

Saying "if" The CPU uses the
flags when you give a command such as, "If the Negative bit is on, go do the instruction in memory location 6".

Speed

Computers are fast. To describe computer speeds, programmers use these words:

Word	Abbreviation	Meaning
millisecond	msec or ms	thousandth of a second; 10^{-3} seconds
microsecond	μsec or μs	millionth of a second; 10^{-6} seconds
nanosecond	nsec or ns	billionth of a second; 10^{-9} seconds
picosecond	psec or ps	trillionth of a second; 10^{-12} seconds

1000 picoseconds is a nanosecond; 1000 nanoseconds is a microsecond; 1000 microseconds is a millisecond; 1000 milliseconds is a second.

Earlier, I explained that the **instruction cycle** has five steps:

A. Fetch the instruction.
B. Fetch additional parts for the instruction.
C. Update the program counter.
D. Decode the instruction.
E. Execute the instruction.

The total time to complete the instruction cycle is about a microsecond. The exact time depends on the quality of the CPU, the quality of the main memory, and the difficulty of the instruction, but usually lies between .1 microseconds and 10 microseconds.

Here are 5 ways to make the computer act more quickly:

Method	Meaning
multiprocessing	The computer holds more than one CPU. (All the CPUs work simultaneously. They share the same main memory. The operating system decides which CPU works on which program. The collection of CPUs is called a **multiprocessor**.)
instruction lookahead	While the CPU is finishing an instruction cycle (by doing steps D and E), it simultaneously begins working on the next instruction cycle (steps A and B).
array processing	The CPU holds at least 16 ALUs. (All the ALUs work simultaneously. For example, when the control unit wants to solve 16 multiplication problems, it sends each problem to a separate ALU; the ALUs compute the products simultaneously. The collection of ALUs is called an **array processor**.)
parallel functional units	The ALU is divided into several functional units: an addition unit, a multiplication unit, a division unit, a shift unit, etc. All the units work simultaneously; while one unit is working on one problem, another unit is working on another.
pipeline architecture	The ALU (or each ALU functional unit) consists of a "first stage" and a "second stage". When the control unit sends a problem to the ALU, the problem enters the first stage, then leaves the first stage and enters the second stage. But while the problem is going through the second stage, a new problem starts going through the first stage. (Such an ALU is called a **pipeline processor**.)

Parity

Most large computers put an extra bit at the end of each memory location. For example, a memory location in the PDP-10 holds 36 bits, but the PDP-10 puts an extra bit at the end, making 37 bits altogether. The extra bit is called the **parity bit**.

If the number of ones in the memory location is even, the CPU turns the parity bit on. If the number of ones in the memory location is odd, the CPU turns the parity bit off.

For example, if the memory location contains these 36 bits —

000000000100010000001100000000000000

there are 4 ones, so the number of ones is even, so the CPU turns the parity bit on:

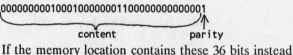

If the memory location contains these 36 bits instead —

000000000100010000001000000000000000

there are 3 ones, so the number of ones is odd, so the CPU turns the parity bit off:

000000000100010000001000000000000000

Whenever the CPU puts data into the main memory, it also puts in the parity bit. Whenever the CPU grabs data from the main memory, it checks whether the parity bit still matches the content.

If the parity bit doesn't match, the CPU knows there was an error, and tries once again to grab the content and the parity bit. If the parity bit disagrees with the content again, the CPU decides that the memory is broken, refuses to run your program, prints a message saying PARITY ERROR, and then sweeps through the whole memory, checking the parity bit of every location; if the CPU finds another parity error (in your program or anyone else's), the CPU shuts off the whole computer.

Cheap microcomputers (such as the Apple 2c and Commodore 64) lack parity bits, but the IBM PC has them.

UAL

Universal Assembly Language (UAL) is a notation I invented that makes programming in assembly language easier.

UAL uses these symbols:

Symbol	Meaning
M5	the number in the 5th memory location
R2	the number in the 2nd register
P	the number in the program counter
N	the Negative bit
Z	the Zero bit
C	the Carry bit
V	the oVerflow bit
PRIORITY	the PRIORITY bits
PRIVILEGE	the PRIVILEGE bits
F	the content of the entire flag register
F[5]	the 5th bit in the flag register
R2[5]	the 5th bit in R2
R2[LEFT]	the left half of R2; in other words, the left half of the data in the 2nd register
R2[RIGHT]	the right half of R2
M5 M6	long number whose left half is in 5th memory location, right half is in 6th location

Here are the UAL statements:

Statement	Meaning
R2=7	Let number in the 2nd register be 7 (by moving 7 into the 2nd register).
R2=M5	Copy the 5th memory location's contents into the 2nd register.
R2= = M5	Exchange R2 with M5. (Put 5th location's content into 2nd register and vice versa.)
R2=R2+M5	Change the integer in 2nd register, by adding to it the integer in 5th location.
R2=R2-M5	Change the integer in 2nd register, by subtracting the integer in 5th location.
R2=R2*M5	Change the integer in 2nd register, by multiplying it by integer in 5th location.
R2 REM R3=R2/M5	Change R2, by dividing it by the integer M5. Put division's remainder into R3.
R2=-M5	Let R2 be the negative of M5.
R2=NOT M5	Let R2 be the one's complement of M5.
R2=R2 AND M5	Change R2, by performing the AND operation.
R2=R2 OR M5	Change R2, by performing the OR operation.
R2=R2 XOR M5	Change R2, by performing the XOR operation.
SHIFTL R2	Shift left.
SHIFTR R2	Shift right.
SHIFTRA R2	Shift right arithmetically.
SHIFTR3 R2	Shift right, 3 times.
SHIFTR (R7) R2	Shift right, R7 times.
ROTATEL R2	Rotate left.
ROTATER R2	Rotate right.
TEST R2	Examine number in 2nd register, and adjust flag register's Negative and Zero bits.
TEST R2-R4	Examine the difference between R2 and R4, and adjust the flag register.
CONTINUE	No operation. Just continue on to the next instruction.
WAIT	Wait until an interrupt occurs.

IF R2<0, P=7 If the number in the 2nd register is negative, put 7 into the program counter.
IF R2<0, M5=3, P=7 If R2<0, do both of the following: let M5 be 3, and P be 7.

M5 can be written as M(5) or M(2+3). It can be written as M(R7), if R7 is 5 — in other words, if register 7 contains 5.

Addressing modes

Suppose you want the 2nd register to contain the number 6. You can accomplish that goal in one step, like this:

R2=6

Or you can accomplish it in two steps, like this:

M5=6
R2=M5

Or you can accomplish it in three steps, like this:

M5=6
M3=5
R2=M(M3)

Or you can accomplish it in an even weirder way:

M5=6
R3=1
R2=M(4+R3)

Each of those methods has a name. The first method (R2=6), which is the simplest, is called **immediate addressing**. The second method (R2=M5), which contains the letter M, is called **direct addressing**. The third method (R5=M(M3)), which contains the letter M twice, is called **indirect addressing**. The fourth method (R5=M(4+R3)), which contains the letter M and a plus sign, is called **indexed addressing**.

In each method, the 2nd register is the destination. In the last three methods, the 5th memory location is the source. In the fourth method, which involves R3, the 3rd register is called the **index register**, and R3 itself is called the **index**.

Each of those methods is called an **addressing mode**. So you've seen four addressing modes: immediate, direct, indirect, and indexed.

Program counter To handle the program counter, the computer uses other addressing modes instead.

For example, suppose P (the number in the program counter) is 2073, and you want to change it to 2077. You can accomplish that goal simply, like this:

P=2077

Or you can accomplish it in a weirder way, like this:

P=P+4

Or you can accomplish it in an even weirder way, like this:

R3=20
P=R3 77

The first method (P=2077), which is the simplest, is called **absolute addressing**.

The second method (P=P+4), which involves addition, is called **relative addressing**. The "+4" is the **offset**.

The third method (P=R3 77) is called **base-page addressing**. R3 (which is 20) is called the **page number** or **segment number**, and so the 3rd register is called the **page register** or **segment register**.

8088 DETAILS

The first **microprocessor** (CPU on a chip) was invented by Intel in 1971 and called the **Intel 4004**. Its accumulator was so short that it held just 4 bits! Later that year, Intel invented an improvement called the **Intel 8008**, whose accumulator held 8 bits. In 1973 Intel invented a further improvement, called the **Intel 8080**, which understood more op codes, contained more registers, handled more RAM (64K instead of 16K), and ran faster. Drunk on the glories of that 8080, Microsoft adopted the phone number VAT-8080, and the Boston Computer Society adopted the soberer phone number DOS-8080.

In 1978 Intel invented a further improvement, called the **8086**, which had a 16-bit accumulator and handled even more RAM & ROM (totalling 1 megabyte). Out of the 8086 came 16 wires (called the **data bus**), which transmitted 16 bits simultaneously from the accumulator to other computerized devices, such as RAM and disks. Since the 8086 had a 16-bit accumulator and 16-bit data bus, Intel called it a **16-bit CPU**.

But computerists complained that the 8086 was impractical, since nobody had developed RAM, disks, or other devices for the 16-bit data bus yet. So in 1979 Intel invented the **8088**, which understands the same machine language as the 8086 but has an 8-bit data bus. To transmit 16-bit data through the 8-bit bus, the 8088 sends 8 of the bits first, then sends the other 8 bits shortly afterwards. That technique of using a few wires (8) to imitate many (16) is called **multiplexing**.

When 16-bit data buses later became popular, Intel invented a slightly souped-up 8086, called the **80286** (nicknamed the **286**).

Then Intel invented a 32-bit version called the **80386** (nicknamed **386**). Intel has also invented a multiplexed version called the **386SX**, which understands the same machine language as the 386 but transmits 32-bit data through a 16-bit bus by sending 16 of the bits first and then sending the other 16. The letters "SX" mean "SiXteen-bit bus". The original 386, which has a 32-bit bus, is called the **386DX**; the letters "DX" mean "Double the siXteen-bit bus".

Then Intel invented a slightly souped-up 80386DX, called the **80486** (nicknamed **486**). It comes in two versions: the fancy version (called the **486DX**) includes a **math coprocessor**, which is circuitry that understands commands about advanced math; the stripped-down version (called the **486SX**) lacks a math coprocessor.

Here's how to use the 8088 and 8086. (The 286, 386, and 486 include the same features plus more.)

Registers

The CPU contains fourteen 16-bit registers: the **accumulator (AX)**, **base register (BX)**, **count register (CX)**, **data register (DX)**, **stack pointer** (which UAL calls **S** but Intel calls **SP**), **base pointer (BP)**, **source index (SI)**, **destination index (DI)**, **program counter** (which UAL calls **P** but Intel calls the **instruction pointer** or **IP**), **flag register** (which UAL calls **F**), **code segment (CS)**, **data segment (DS)**, **stack segment (SS)**, and **extra segment (ES)**.

In each of those registers, the sixteen bits are numbered from right to left, so the rightmost bit is called **bit 0** and the leftmost bit is called **bit fifteen**.

The AX register's low-numbered half (bits 0 through 7) is called **A low** (or **AL**). The AX register's high half (bits 8 through fifteen) is called **A high (AH)**.

In the flag register, bit 0 is the carry flag (which UAL calls **C**), bit 2 is for parity, bit 6 is the zero flag **(Z)**, bit 7 is the negative flag (which UAL calls **N** but Intel calls **sign** or **S**), bit eleven is the overflow flag **(V)**, bits 4, 8, 9, and ten are special (**auxiliary carry**, **trap**, **interrupts**, and **direction**), and the remaining bits are unused.

Memory locations

Each memory location contains a byte. In UAL, the 6th memory location is called **M6** or **M(6)**. The pair of bytes M7 M6 is called **memory word 6**, which UAL writes as **MW(6)**.

Instruction set

The next page shows the set of instructions that the 8088 understands. For each instruction, I've given the assembly-language mnemonic and its translation to UAL, where all numbers are hexadecimal.

The first line says that INC (which stands for INCrement) is the assembly-language mnemonic that means $x = x + 1$. For example, INC AL means $AL = AL + 1$.

The eighth line says that IMUL (which stands for Integer Multiply) is the assembly-language mnemonic that means $x = x*y$. For example, IMUL AX,BX means $AX = AX*BX$.

In most equations, you can replace the x and y by registers, half-registers, memory locations, numbers, or more exotic entities. To find out what you can replace x and y by, experiment!

For more details, read the manuals from Intel and Microsoft. They also explain how to modify an instruction's behavior by using flags, segment registers, other registers, and three **prefixes**: REPeat, SEGment, and LOCK.

Math

INCrement	x=x+1
DECrement	x=x-1
ADD	x=x+y
ADd Carry	x=x+y+C
SUBtract	x=x-y
SuBtract Borrow	x=x-y-C
MULtiply	x=x*y UNSIGNED
Integer MULtiply	x=x*y
DIVide	AX=AX/x UNSIGNED
Integer DIVide	AX=AX/x
NEGate	x=-x
Decimal Adjust Add	IF AL[RIGHT]>9, AL=AL+6
	IF AL[LEFT]>9, AL=AL+60
Decimal Adjust Subtr	IF AL[RIGHT]>9, AL=AL-6
	IF AL[LEFT]>9, AL=AL-60
Ascii Adjust Add	IF AL[RIGHT]>9, AL=AL+6, AH=AH+1
	AL[LEFT]=0
Ascii Adjust Subtract	IF AL[RIGHT]>9, AL=AL-6, AH=AH-1
	AL[LEFT]=0
Ascii Adjust Multiply	AH REM AL=AL/0A
Ascii Adjust Divide	AL=AL+(0A*AH)
	AH=0

Logic

AND	x=x AND y
OR	x=x OR y
XOR	x=x XOR y
CoMplement Carry	C=NOT C
SHift Left	SHIFTL(y) x
SHift Right	SHIFTR(y) x
Shift Arithmetic Right	SHIFTRA(y) x
ROtate Left	ROTATEL(y) x
ROtate Right	ROTATER(y) x
Rotate Carry Left	ROTATEL(y) C x
Rotate Carry Right	ROTATER(y) C x
CLear Carry	C=0
CLear Direction	DIRECTION=0
CLear Interrupts	INTERRUPTS=0
SeT Carry	C=1
SeT Direction	DIRECTION=1
SeT Interrupts	INTERRUPTS=1
TEST	TEST x AND y
CoMPare	TEST x-y
SCAn String Byte	TEST AL-M(DI); DI=DI+1-(2*DIRECTION)
SCAn String Word	TEST AX-MW(DI); DI=DI+2-(4*DIRECTION)
CoMPare String Byte	TEST M(SI)-M(DI)
	SI=SI+1-(2*DIRECTION)
	DI=DI+1-(2*DIRECTION)
CoMPare String Word	TEST MW(SI)-MW(DI)
	SI=SI+2-(4*DIRECTION)
	DI=DI+2-(4*DIRECTION)

Moving bytes

MOVe	x=y
Load AH from F	AH=F[RIGHT]
Store AH to F	F[RIGHT]=AH
Load register and DS	x=MW(y); DS=MW(y+2)
Load register and ES	x=MW(y); ES=MW(y+2)
LOaD String Byte	AL=M(SI); SI=SI+1-(2*DIRECTION)
LOaD String Word	AX=MW(SI); SI=SI+2-(4*DIRECTION)
STOre String Byte	M(DI)=AL; DI=DI+1-(2*DIRECTION)
STOre String Word	MW(DI)=AX; DI=DI+2-(4*DIRECTION)
MOVe String Byte	M(DI)=M(SI);
	DI=DI+1-(2*DIRECTION)
	SI=SI+1-(2*DIRECTION)
MOVe String Word	MW(DI)=MW(SI)
	DI=DI+2-(4*DIRECTION)
	SI=SI+2-(4*DIRECTION)
Convert Byte to Word	AH=-AL[7]
Convert Word to Dbl	DX=-AX[0F]
PUSH	S=S-2; MW(S)=x
PUSH F	S=S-2; MW(S)=F
POP	x=MW(S); S=S+2
POP F	F=MW(S); S=S+2
IN	x=PORT(y)
OUT	PORT(x)=y
ESCape	BUS=x
eXCHanGe	x= =y
XLATe	AL=M(BX+AL)
Load Effective Address	x=ADDRESS(y)

Program counter

JuMP	P=x
Jump if Zero	IF Z=1, P=x
Jump if Not Zero	IF Z=0, P=x
Jump if Sign	IF N=1, P=x
Jump if No Sign	IF N=0, P=x
Jump if Overflow	IF V=1, P=x
Jump if Not Overflow	IF V=0, P=x
Jump if Parity	IF PARITY=1, P=x
Jump if No Parity	IF PARITY=0, P=x
Jump if Below	IF C=1, P=x
Jump if Above or Eq	IF C=0, P=x
Jump if Below or Eq	IF C=1 OR Z=1, P=x
Jump if Above	IF C=0 AND Z=0, P=x
Jump if Greater or Eq	IF N=V, P=x
Jump if Less	IF N<>V, P=x
Jump if Greater	IF N=V AND Z=0, P=x
Jump if Less or Equal	IF N<>V OR Z=1, P=x
Jump if CX Zero	IF CX=0, P=x
LOOP	CX=CX-1; IF CX<>0, P=x
LOOP if Zero	CX=CX-1; IF CX<>0 AND Z=1, P=x
LOOP if Not Zero	CX=CX-1; IF CX<>0 AND Z=0, P=x
CALL	S=S-2; MW(S)=P; P=x
RETurn	P=MW(S); S=S+2
INTerrupt	S=S-6; MW(S)=P; MW(S+2)=CS; MW(S+4)=F
	P=MW(4*x); CS=MW(4*x+2)
	INTERRUPTS=0; TRAP=0
INTerrupt if Overflow	IF V=1, S=S-6, MW(S)=P, MW(S+2)=CS,
	MW(S+4)=F, P=MW(10), CS=MW(12),
	INTERRUPTS=0, TRAP=0
Interrupt RETurn	P=MW(S); CS=MW(S+2); F=MW(S+4); S=S+6
No OPeration	CONTINUE
HaLT	WAIT
WAIT	WAIT FOR COPROCESSOR

ΣΝDΝΟΤΣS

BACKGROUND

Computer experts know that when reading a computer book, the really interesting stuff is usually hidden in the back of the book, buried in the appendices, which are secret vaults full of fascinating treasures, hidden from the view of casual readers duped into assuming that the appendices contain "nothing important".

In this book, too, some of the most brilliant jewels are hidden in the appendices.

Here are the appendices. I hope you enjoy them. I was afraid to move them to the front of the book because some of them are tough, controversial. But so are computers!

Enjoy the final leg of your adventure.

REPAIRS

REDUCE YOUR RISKS

To reduce your need for computer repairs, remember the following tips.

Hot weather

If possible, avoid using the computer in hot weather.

When the room's temperature rises above 93 degrees, the fan inside the computer has trouble cooling the computer sufficiently. Wait until the weather is cooler (such as late at night), or buy an air conditioner, or buy a window fan to put on your desk and aim at the computer, or use the computer for just an hour at a time (so that the computer doesn't have a chance to overheat).

Another problem in the summer is electrical brownouts, where air conditioners in your house or community consume so much electricity that not enough voltage gets to your computer.

Transporting your computer

Some parts inside the computer are delicate. Don't bang or shake the computer!

If you need to move the computer to a different location, be gentle! And before moving the computer, make backups: copy everything important from the computer's hard disk onto floppy disks. For example, copy all the documents, database files, and spreadsheets you created, and also copy AUTOEXEC.BAT, CONFIG.SYS, and COMMAND.COM.

Transporting by hand If you must move the computer to a different desk or building, be *very gentle* when you pick up the computer, carry it, and plop it down. Be especially gentle when walking on stairs and through doorways.

Transporting by car If you're transporting your computer by car, put the computer in the *front* seat, put a blanket underneath the computer, and drive slowly (especially around curves and over bumps). Do *not* put the computer in the trunk, since the trunk has the least protection against bumps. If you have the original padded box that the computer came in, put the computer in it, since the box's padding is professionally designed to protect against bumps.

Transporting by air If you're transporting your computer by air, avoid checking the computer through the baggage department. The baggage handlers will treat the computer as if it were a football, and their "forward pass" will make you pissed.

Instead, try to carry the computer with you on the plane, if the computer's small enough to fit under your seat or in the overhead bin. If the whole computer won't fit, carry as much of the computer as *will* fit (the keyboard, the monitor, or the system unit?) and check the rest as baggage. If you *must* check the computer as baggage, use the original padded box that the computer came in, or else find a giant box and put *lots and lots and lots* of padding material in it.

When going through airport security, it's okay to let the security guards X-ray your computer and disks. Do *not* carry the computer and disks in your hands as you go through the metal detector, since the magnetic field might erase your disks. For best results, just tell the guards you have a computer and disks; instead of running the computer and disks through detection equipment, the guards will inspect your stuff personally. To make sure your computer doesn't contain a bomb, the guards might ask you to unscrew the computer or prove that it actually works. If your computer's a laptop and you need to prove it works, make sure you brought your batteries — and make sure the batteries are fully charged!

Since airport rules about baggage and security continually change, ask your airport for details before taking a trip.

Parking the head If your computer is ancient (an 8088 or an early-vintage 286), it might have come with a program called **SHIPDISK** or **PARK**. That program is *not* part of DOS; instead, the program comes on a floppy disk called **UTILITIES** or **DIAGNOSTICS**.

That program does an activity called **parking the head**: it moves the hard drive's head to the disk's innermost track, where there's no data. Then if the head accidentally bangs against the disk, it won't scrape off any data.

If your computer came with a SHIPDISK or PARK program, run it before you transport the computer. After your journey, when you turn the computer back on, the head automatically unparks itself and reads whatever data you wish.

If your computer did *not* come with a SHIPDISK or PARK program, don't worry about it. Modern disk drives park the head automatically whenever you turn the power off. For older disk drives, handling the computer gently is more important than parking the head. In any case, do *not* borrow a SHIPDISK or PARK program from a friend, since somebody else's program might assume the hard drive has a different number of tracks.

Repair shops use an extra-fancy PARK program: it tests the hard drive, determines how many tracks are on it, and then moves the head to the correct innermost track.

Saving your work

When you're typing lots of info into a word-processing program or spreadsheet, the stuff you've typed is in the computer's RAM. Every ten minutes, copy that info onto the hard disk, by giving the SAVE command. (To learn how to give the SAVE command, read my word-processing and spreadsheet chapters.)

That way, if the computer breaks down (or you make a boo-boo), the hard disk will contain a copy of most of your work, and you'll need to retype at most ten minutes worth.

Split into chapters If you're using a word-processing program to type a book, split the book into chapters. Make each chapter be a separate file. That way, if something goes wrong with the file, you've lost just one chapter instead of the whole book.

Disk space

Make sure your hard disk isn't full. Make sure your hard disk has at least 2 megabytes of unused space on it.

To find out how much unused space is on your hard disk, say:

```
c:\>dir
```

That makes the computer list the files in your root directory and also tell you how many bytes are free.

If the number of free bytes is less than 2,000,000, you have less than two megabytes of free space, and you're in a dangerous situation! Erase some files, so that the number of free bytes becomes more than 2,000,000.

If the number of free bytes is less than 2,000,000, some of your programs might act unreliably, because the programmers who wrote those programs were too lazy to check whether the programs would work on a hard disk that's so full. Some of those programs try to create temporary files on your hard disk; but if your hard disk is nearly full, the temporary files won't fit, and so the computer will gripe at you, act nuts, and seem broken.

If possible, erase enough unimportant files from your hard disk so that 5 megabytes are free. That ensures even the biggest temporary files will fit. It also helps DOS act faster, since DOS doesn't have to look so hard to find where your hard disk's free megabytes are.

Windows For Windows to run reasonably fast, at least 10 megabytes should be free, since Windows tries to create lots of temporary files.

Overly fancy software

Avoid buying and using software that adds many lines to your CONFIG.SYS and AUTOEXEC.BAT files. The longer and more complicated your CONFIG.SYS and AUTOEXEC.BAT files are, the greater the chance that something will go wrong with them, and your computer will refuse to boot up. Even if each line in your CONFIG.SYS and AUTOEXEC.BAT file looks fine, the lines may conflict with each other.

Keep your AUTOEXEC.BAT file simple, so that when you turn the computer on, the computer says:

```
c:\>
```

Do *not* make the computer automatically go into Windows or the DOS shell or a menu. Instead, get in the habit of manually typing "win" to go into Windows, "dosshell" to go into the DOS shell, a command such as "menu" to go into a menu, or a command such as "do wp" to go into Word Perfect (by using the DO.BAT trick I explained on page 130).

If you make the mistake of setting up your computer to automatically go into Windows, and Windows someday stops working properly, the computer won't boot at all. You'll be in a real mess!

Also, if the computer automatically goes into Windows, and you try to use Windows as a menu system to choose which non-Windows software to run, that non-Windows software will run slower and less reliably than if you ran the software directly without going through Windows.

Avoid compression If possible, avoid using programs such as **Stacker**, which attempts to squeeze extra megabytes of data onto your hard disk by using compression codes. Although such programs usually work, they're very delicate: if you accidentally erase those programs (or erase or modify the CONFIG.SYS file that mentions them), you won't be able to use *any* of the data on your hard disk!

Judging from the phone calls I receive, I get the impression that 90% of all the people who use Stacker are happy, and the other 10% lose all their data.

DOS 6 headaches

DOS 6 includes three routines that are dangerously unreliable: **Double Space**, **Smart Drive**, and **Mem Maker**. If you avoid those routines, DOS 6 is reliable; if you use those routines, DOS 6 can get quite nasty, which is why many companies have banned DOS 6!

Double Space Like Stacker, Double Space attempts to squeeze extra megabytes of data onto your hard disk by using compression codes. It has the same headaches.

Smart Drive To make your hard drive seem faster, the version of **Smart Drive** included with DOS 6 and Windows 3.1 tries to make RAM imitate your hard disk, so when you tell the computer to write to the hard disk the computer writes to RAM instead, which is faster. It writes to a part of the RAM called the **disk cache**.

Later, when you don't seem to be using the computer and seem to be just scratching your head wondering what to do next, Smart Drive copies the disk cache's contents to the hard disk. But what if you turn off the computer (or the computer's hardware or software malfunctions) before Smart Drive gets around to copying the disk cache's contents to the hard disk? Then the hard disk will contain less info than it's supposed to. When you restart the computer, Double Space will notice that info is missing from the hard disk; then Double Space will get confused and refuse to operate. Suddenly, your whole hard disk has become useless!

If you ignore my advice and decide to use Smart Drive anyway, get in the habit of waiting 10 seconds before turning your computer off. The 10-second wait makes Smart Drive realize you're doing nothing, so Smart Drive copies the disk cache's contents to the hard disk.

Another problem is that when Smart Drive suddenly decides to burst into action and write to your hard disk, it can interrupt the computer from handling any modem or fax transmissions that are in progress. Also, Smart Drive confuses the typical human, who doesn't understand why the hard-drive light goes on at strange times instead of when the human *said* to write to the hard disk.

Mem Maker Mem Maker tries to modify your CONFIG.SYS and AUTOEXEC.BAT files so specific programs get put into specific places in RAM. It works fine — until you buy an extra program that doesn't fit into the RAM-memory scheme created by Mem Maker. Then you must go through the hassle of telling Mem Maker to reanalyze the situation and put the programs into different places instead.

To avoid those hassles, avoid using Double Space, Smart Drive, and Mem Maker. Then DOS 6 works great!

DOS 6.2 In DOS 6.2, Microsoft improved Double Space, Smart Drive, and Mem Maker so that they cause problems less frequently and less severely. Nevertheless, those three routines can still cause the same kinds of problems, and I still recommend avoiding them.

After inventing DOS 6 and 6.2, Microsoft was sued by a company called **Stac Electronics**, which said Double Space contained routines that Microsoft illegally copied from Stacker. To duck the suit, Microsoft invented DOS 6.21 (which omits Double Space) and then DOS 6.22 (which replaces Double Space by a similar routine called **Disk Space** (and has the same problems).

GENERAL PRINCIPLES OF REPAIR

Here are the general principles you need to know, to repair a computer.

Ask

Ask for help. Instead of wasting many hours scratching your head about a computer problem, get help from your dealer, your computer's manufacturer, your software's publisher, your colleagues, your teachers, your friends, and me. You can phone me day or night, 24 hours, at 617-666-2666; I'm almost always in, and I sleep only lightly.

Most computers come with a one-year warranty. If your computer gives you trouble during that first year, make use of the warranty: get the free help you're entitled to from your dealer. If your "dealer" is a general-purpose department store that doesn't specialize in computers, the store might tell you to phone the computer's manufacturer.

For tough software questions, the dealer might tell you to phone the software's publisher.

Most computers come with a 30-day money-back guarantee. If the computer is giving you lots of headaches during the first 30 days, just return it!

Chuck

If the broken part is cheap, don't fix it: chuck it! For example, if one of the keys on your keyboard stops working, don't bother trying to fix that key; instead, buy a new keyboard. A new keyboard costs just $35. Fixing one key on a keyboard costs many hours of labor and is silly.

If a 10-megabyte hard disk stops working, and you can't fix the problem in an hour or so, just give up and buy a new hard disk, since 10-megabyte hard disks are obsolete anyway. Today, 10 megabytes aren't worth much; the price difference between a 30-megabyte drive and a 40-megabyte drive is about $10.

Observe

Read the screen. Often, the screen will display an error message that tells you what the problem is.

If the message flashes on the screen too briefly for you to read, try pressing the computer's PAUSE key as soon as the message appears. The PAUSE key makes the message stay on the screen for you to read. When you finish reading the message, press the ENTER key.

If you're having trouble with your printer, and your printer is modern enough to have a built-in screen, read the messages on that screen too.

Check the lights. Look at the blinking lights on the front of the computer and the front of the printer; see if the correct ones are glowing. Also notice whether the monitor's POWER light is glowing.

Check the switches. Check the ON-OFF switches for the computer, monitor, and printer: make sure they're all flipped on. If your computer equipment is plugged into a power strip, make sure the strip's ON-OFF switch is turned on.

Check the monitor's brightness and contrast knobs, to make sure they're turned to the normal (middle) position.

If you have a dot-matrix printer, make sure the paper is feeding correctly, and make sure you've put into the correct position the lever that lets you choose between tractor feed and friction feed.

Check the cables that run out of the computer. They run to the monitor, printer, keyboard, mouse, and wall. Make sure they're all plugged tightly into their sockets. To make *sure* they're plugged in tight, unplug them and then plug them back in again. (To be safe, turn the computer equipment off before fiddling with the cables.) Many monitor and printer problems are caused just by loose cables.

Make sure each cable is plugged into the correct socket. Examine the back of your computer, printer, monitor, and modem: if you see two sockets that look identical, try plugging the cable into the other socket. For example, the cable from your printer might fit into *two* identical sockets at the back of the computer (LPT1 and LPT2); the cable from your phone system might fit into *two* identical sockets at the back of your modem (LINE and PHONE); the cable from your monitor might fit into *two* identical sockets at the back of the computer (COLOR and MONOCHROME).

Strip

When analyzing a hardware problem, run no software except DOS and diagnostics. For example, if you're experiencing a problem while using a word-processing program, spreadsheet, database, game, Windows, or some other software, exit from whatever software you're in. Then turn off your printer, computer, and all your other equipment, so the RAM chips inside each device get erased and forget that software.

Then turn the computer back on. Try to make the screen say:

```
C:\>
```

If you succeed, your screen is working fine.

Then say "dir". If that makes the computer show you a directory of all the files in your hard disk's root directory, your hard disk is working fine.

Then turn on the printer and say "dir > prn". If that makes the computer copy the directory onto paper, your printer's working fine. (On some laser printers, such as the Hewlett Packard Laserjet 2, you need to manually eject the paper: press the printer's ON LINE button, then the FORM FEED button, then the ON LINE button again.)

If your computer, monitor, hard drive, and printer pass all those tests, your hardware is basically fine; and so the problem you were having was probably caused by software rather than hardware. For example, maybe you forgot to tell your software what kind of printer and monitor you bought.

If you wish to test your hardware more thoroughly, you can give additional DOS commands. Better yet, run **diagnostic software** such as **Check It** and **Norton Disk Doctor**. They test your computer and tell you what's wrong. To get Norton Disk Doctor, buy either the software collection called **Norton Utilities** or the software collection called **Norton Desktop for DOS**. The newest version of Norton Utilities, which is version 7, also includes diagnostic routines for checking your motherboard and other parts of your computer.

BOOTING PROBLEMS

Turning the computer on is called **booting**. When you turn the computer on, you might immediately experience one of these problems.

Lots of beeping

Problem When you turn the computer on, you just hear a very long beep or very many little beeps.

Cause The fault probably lies in your motherboard or power supply (AC/DC transformer). For example, the motherboard's circuitry might have a short or a break, or one of the chips might have become defective.

Cure Turn the computer off immediately, and take it in to a repair shop.

No video

Problem When you turn the computer on, the screen is entirely blank, so you don't even see the cursor.

Cause The fault probably lies in your monitor or its cables.

Cure Make sure the monitor is turned on, its contrast and brightness knobs are turned up, and its two cables (to the power and to the computer's video card) are both plugged in tight. (Those cables can easily come loose.)

If the monitor has a power-on light, check whether that light is glowing. If it doesn't glow, the monitor isn't getting any power (because the on-off button is in the wrong position, or the power cable is loose, or the monitor is broken). If the monitor is indeed broken, do *not* open the monitor, which contains high voltages even when turned off; instead, return the monitor to your dealer.

If you've fiddled with the knobs and cables and the power-on light is glowing but the screen is still blank, boot up the computer again, and look at the screen carefully: maybe a message *did* flash on the screen quickly?

If a message did appear, fix whatever problem the message talks about. (If the message was too fast for you to read, boot up again and quickly hit the PAUSE key as soon as the message appears, then press ENTER when you finish reading the message.) If the message appears but does *not* mention a problem, you're in the middle of a program that has crashed (stopped working), so the fault lies in software mentioned in CONFIG.SYS or AUTOEXEC.BAT or COMMAND.COM or some other software involved in booting; to explore further, put a DOS disk in drive A and reboot.

If absolutely no message appears on the screen during the booting process, so that the screen is entirely blank, check the lights on the computer (maybe the computer is turned off or broken) and recheck the cables that go to the monitor. If you still have no luck, the fault is probably in the video card inside the computer, though it might be on the motherboard or in the middle of the video cable that goes from the video card to the monitor. At this point, before you run out and buy new hardware, try swapping with a friend whose computer has the same kind of video as yours (for example, you both have VGA): try swapping monitors, then video cables, then video cards, while making notes about which combinations work, until you finally discover which piece of hardware is causing the failure. Then replace that hardware, and you're done!

SETUP

Problem When you turn the computer on, the computer gripes by printing a message such as "Invalid configuration specification: run SETUP."

Cause Your computer's CPU is fast. It's a 286, 386, 486, or Pentium. It's not an 8088.

Each fast computer contains a battery that feeds power to the CMOS RAM. That CMOS RAM tries to keep track of the date, time, how many megabytes of RAM you've bought, how you want the RAM used, what kind of video you bought, and what kind of disk drives you bought.

If the information in the CMOS RAM is wrong, the computer usually gripes during bootup by printing a message such as, "Invalid configuration specification: run SETUP."

Cure Try running the CMOS SETUP program, which asks you questions and then stores your answers to the CMOS RAM. To find out how to run that program, ask your dealer.

If your computer's CPU is an old 286, the CMOS SETUP program comes on a floppy disk. That disk is *not* in the set of MS-DOS disks; instead, the CMOS SETUP program comes on a separate utility disk.

If your computer is a newer 286 or a 386 or 486, the CMOS SETUP program does *not* come on a floppy disk. Instead, the CMOS SETUP program hides in a ROM chip inside your computer and is run when you hit a "special key" during the bootup's RAM test. That "special key" is usually either the DELETE key or the Esc key or the F1 key; to find out what the "special key" is on *your* computer, read your computer's manual or ask your dealer.

Once the CMOS SETUP program starts running, it asks you lots of questions. For each question, it also shows you what it guesses the answer is. (The computer's guesses are based on what information the computer was fed before.)

On a sheet of paper, jot down what the computer's guesses are. That sheet of paper will turn out to be *very* useful!

Some of those questions are easy to answer (such as the date and time).

A harder question is when the computer asks you to input your **hard-drive type number**. The answer is a code number from 1 to 47, which you must get from your dealer. (If your dealer doesn't know the answer, phone the computer's manufacturer. If the manufacturer doesn't know the answer, look inside the computer at the hard drive; stamped on the drive, you'll see the drive's manufacturer and model number; then phone the drive's manufacturer, tell the manufacturer which model number you bought, and ask for the corresponding hard-drive type number.) If the answer is 47, the computer then asks you technical questions about your drive; get the answers from your dealer (or drive's manufacturer).

If you don't know how to answer a question and can't reach your dealer for help, just move ahead to the next question. Leave intact the answer that the computer guessed.

After you've finished the questionnaire, the computer will automatically reboot. If the computer gripes again, either you answered the questions wrong or else the battery ran out — so that the computer forgot your answers!

In fact, the most popular reason why the computer asks you to run the CMOS SETUP program is that the battery ran out. (The battery usually lasts 1-4 years.) To solve the problem, first make sure you've jotted down the computer's guesses, then replace the battery, which is usually just to the left of the big power supply inside the computer. If you're lucky, the "battery" is actually a bunch of four AA flashlight batteries that you can buy in any hardware store. If you're unlucky, the battery is a round silver disk, made of lithium, like the battery in a digital watch: to get a replacement, see your dealer.

After replacing the battery, run the CMOS SETUP program again, and feed it the data that you jotted down.

That's the procedure. If you're ambitious, try it. If you're a beginner, save yourself the agony by just taking the whole computer to your dealer: let the dealer diddle with the CMOS SETUP program and batteries for you.

Whenever you upgrade your computer with a better disk drive or video card or extra RAM, you must run the CMOS SETUP program again to tell the computer what you bought.

AMIBIOS In many computers, the ROM BIOS chip is designed by **American Megatrends Inc. (AMI)**. AMI's design is called the **AMIBIOS** (pronounced "Amy buy us").

Here's how to use the 4/4/93 version of AMIBIOS. (Other versions are similar.)

When you turn the computer on, the screen briefly shows this message:

```
AMIBIOS (C)1993 American Megatrends Inc.
000000 KB OK
Hit <DEL> if you want to run SETUP
```

Then the number "000000 KB" increases, as the computer checks your RAM chips. While that number increases, try pressing your keyboard's DEL or DELETE key.

That makes the computer run the AMIBIOS CMOS SETUP program. The top of the screen will say:

```
AMIBIOS SETUP PROGRAM - BIOS SETUP UTILITIES
```

Underneath, you'll see this **main menu**:

```
STANDARD CMOS SETUP
ADVANCED CMOS SETUP
ADVANCED CHIPSET SETUP
AUTO CONFIGURATION WITH BIOS DEFAULTS
AUTO CONFIGURATION WITH POWER-ON DEFAULTS
CHANGE PASSWORD
AUTO DETECT HARD DISK
HARD DISK UTILITY
WRITE TO CMOS AND EXIT
DO NOT WRITE TO CMOS AND EXIT
```

The first and most popular choice, "STANDARD CMOS SETUP", is highlighted. Choose it (by pressing ENTER).

The computer will warn you by saying:

```
Improper use of Setup may cause problems!!!
```

Press ENTER again.

The computer will show you the info stored in the CMOS about the date, time, base memory, extended memory, hard drives, floppy drives, video card, and keyboard.

If that stored info is wrong, fix it! Here's how. . . .

By using the arrow keys on the keyboard, move the white box to the info that you want to fix. (Exception: you can't move the white box to the "base memory" or "extended memory".) Then change that info, by pressing the keyboard's PAGE UP or PAGE DOWN key several times, until the info is what you wish.

When you've finished examining and fixing that info, press the Esc key. You'll see the main menu again.

When you've finished using the main menu, you have two choices:

If you're UNSURE of yourself and wish you hadn't fiddled with the SETUP program, just turn off the computer's power! All your fiddling will be ignored, and the computer will act the same as before you fiddled.

On the other hand, if you're SURE of yourself and want the computer to take your fiddling seriously, press the F10 key then Y then ENTER. The computer will copy your desires to the CMOS and reboot.

Non-system disk

Problem The computer says "Non-system disk or disk error".

Cause The computer is having trouble finding the hidden system files. (If you're using MS-DOS, the hidden system files are called IO.SYS and MSDOS.SYS. If you're using PC-DOS instead, the hidden system files are called IBMIO.COM and IBMDOS.COM.)

Those hidden system files are supposed to be on your hard disk. One reason why you might get that error message is that those hidden system files are missing from your hard disk — because that disk is new and hasn't been formatted yet, or because when you formatted the disk you forgot to say "/s" at the end of the format command, or because you accidentally erased those files.

A more common reason for getting that error message is: you accidentally put a floppy disk into drive A! When the computer boots, it looks at that floppy disk instead of your hard disk, and gripes because it can't find those system files on your floppy disk.

Cure Remove any disk from drive A. Turn the computer off, wait until the computer quiets down, then turn the computer back on.

If the computer still says "Non-system disk or disk error", find the floppy disks that DOS came on and try again to install DOS onto your hard disk.

Command interpreter

Problem The computer says "Bad or missing command interpreter".

Cause The computer is having trouble finding and using your COMMAND.COM file. That file is supposed to be in your hard disk's root directory — unless your CONFIG.SYS file contains a "shell=" line that tells the computer to look elsewhere.

Probably you accidentally erased COMMAND.COM, or accidentally fiddled with your CONFIG.SYS file, or accidentally put a floppy disk in drive A (which makes the computer look for COMMAND.COM on your floppy disk instead of your hard disk), or your COMMAND.COM file came from a different version of DOS than your hidden files.

Cure Remove any disk from drive A, then try again to boot. If you get the same error, put into drive A the main floppy disk that DOS came on, and reboot again. (Make sure you use the original DOS floppy, not a copy. Make sure you use the same version of DOS as before; don't switch versions. If you're using DOS 4, insert the disk labeled "install". If you're using DOS 5 or 6, insert the disk lableled "setup". If a disk is labeled "DOS 5 *Upgrade*" instead of just "DOS 5", that disk isn't bootable; buy or borrow a disk labeled "DOS 5 — Setup".)

Then try to copy DOS onto your hard disk again.

If you had accidentally erased COMMAND.COM from your hard disk, you probably also erased CONFIG.SYS and AUTOEXEC.BAT, and you may need to reconstruct those files.

SHARE

Problem The computer says, "Warning — SHARE should be loaded for large media".

Cause You're using DOS 4, and it's installed incorrectly.

Cure Your best bet is to upgrade to DOS 5 or 6, which will make that message go away.

If you refuse to upgrade, here's another way to make sure that message disappears: put the SHARE.EXE program into your hard disk's root directory and also your hard disk's DOS directory.

(The SHARE.EXE program comes on the original DOS 4 floppy disks and is probably already in your hard disk's DOS directory. To copy it to the root directory, just give the copy command.)

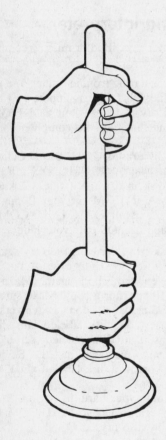

Your keyboard might seem broken. Here's what to do.

Wet keyboard

Problem You recently spilled water, coffee, soda, or some other drink into the keyboard, and now the computer refuses to react properly to your keyboard.

Cause The liquid in the keyboard is causing an electrical short-circuit.

Cure Turn off the computer. Turn the keyboard upside-down for a few minutes, in the hope that some of the liquid drips out. Then let the keyboard rest a few hours, until the remaining liquid in it dries. Try again to use the keyboard. It will probably work fine. If not, look for one of the symptoms below.

Dead keyboard

Problem When you press letters on the keyboard, those letters do *not* appear on the screen.

Cause Either the keyboard is improperly hooked up, or the computer is overheating, or you're running a frustrated program (which is ignoring what you type or waiting until a special event happens). For example, the program might be waiting for the printer to print, or the disk drive to manipulate a file, or the CPU to finish a computation, or your finger to hit a special key or give a special command.

Cure First, **try getting out of any program you've been running**: press the Esc key (which might let you escape from the program) or the F1 key (which might display a helpful message) or ENTER (which might move on to the next screenful of information) or Ctrl with C (which might abort the program) or Ctrl with Break. If the screen is unchanged and the computer still ignores your typing, reboot the computer; then watch the screen for error messages such as "301" (which means a defective keyboard), "201" (which means defective RAM chips), or "1701" (which means a defective hard drive).

If the keyboard seems to be "defective", it might just be unplugged from the computer. Make sure the cable from the keyboard is plugged *tightly* into the computer. To make sure it's tight, unplug it and then plug it back in again.

If you stand behind the original IBM PC (instead of a newer computer), you'll see two sockets that look identical. The left one (which usually has the word "Keyboard" and a "K" next to it) is for the keyboard cable; the other is for a cassette tape recorder (which nobody uses).

Underneath a keyboard built by a clone company, you might see a switch marked "XT - AT" (or simply "X - A"). Put that switch in the XT (or X) position if your computer is an IBM XT (or an original IBM PC or any computer containing an 8088 CPU). Put the switch in the AT (or A) position if your computer is an IBM AT (or any computer containing a 286, 386, or 486 CPU). If you don't see such a switch, make sure your keyboard was designed to work with your computer.

If fiddling with the cable and the XT-AT switch doesn't solve your problem, **reboot the computer and see what happens.** Maybe you'll get lucky.

Maybe some part of the computer is overheating. Here's how to find out. . . .

Turn the computer off. Leave it off for at least an hour, so it cools down.

Then turn the computer back on. Try to get to a C prompt. After the C prompt, type a letter (such as x) and notice whether the x appears on the screen. If the x appears, don't bother pressing the ENTER key afterwards; instead, walk away from the computer for two hours — leave the computer turned on — then come back two hours later and try typing another letter (such as y). If the y doesn't appear, you know that the computer "died" sometime after you typed x but before you typed y; and since during that time the computer was just sitting there doing nothing except being turned on and getting warmer, you know the problem was caused by overheating: some part inside the computer is failing as the internal temperature rises. That part could be a RAM chip, BIOS chip, or otherwise.

Since that part isn't tolerant enough of heat, it must be replaced: take the computer in for repair.

That kind of test — where you leave the computer on for several hours to see what happens as the computer warms up — is called **letting the computer cook**.

During the cooking, if smoke comes out of one of the computer's parts, that part is said to have **fried**. That same applies to humans: when a programmer's been working hard on a project for many hours and become too exhausted to think straight, the programmer says, "I'm **burnt out**. My brain is **fried**." Common solutions are sleep and pizza ("getting some z's & 'za").

When computers are manufactured, the last step in the assembly line is to leave the computer turned on a long time, to let the computer cook and make sure it still works when hot. A top-notch manufacturer leaves the computer on for 2 days (48 hours) or even 3 days (72 hours), while continually testing the computer to make sure no parts fail. That part of the assembly line is called **burning in** the computer; many top-notch manufacturers do **72-hour burn in**.

Sluggish key

<u>Problem</u> After pressing one of the keys, it doesn't pop back up fast enough.

<u>Cause</u> Probably there's dirt under the key. The "dirt" is probably dust or coagulated drinks (such as Coke or coffee).

<u>Cure</u> If *many* keys are sluggish, don't bother trying to fix them all. Just buy a new keyboard (for about $30).

If just one or two keys are sluggish, here's how to try fixing a sluggish key....

Take a paper clip, partly unravel it so it becomes a hook, then use that hook to pry the up the key, until the keycap pops off. Clean the part of the keyboard that was under that keycap: blow away the dust, and wipe away grime (such as coagulated drinks). With the keycap still off, turn on the computer, and try pressing the plunger that was under the keycap. If the plunger is still sluggish, you haven't cleaned it enough. (Don't try too hard: remember that a new keyboard costs just about $30.) When the plunger works fine, turn off the computer, put the keycap back on, and the key should work fine.

Caps

<u>Problem</u> While you're typing, each capital letter unexpectedly becomes small, and each small letter becomes capitalized.

<u>Cause</u> The SHIFT key or CAPS LOCK key is activated.

The culprit is usually the CAPS LOCK key. Probably you activated it by pressing it accidentally when you meant to press a nearby key instead. The CAPS LOCK key stays activated until you deactivate it by pressing it again.

<u>Cure</u> Press the CAPS LOCK key (again), then try typing some more, to see whether the problem has gone away.

If your keyboard is modern, its top right corner has a CAPS LOCK light. That light glows when the CAPS LOCK key is activated; the light stops glowing when the CAPS LOCK key is deactivated.

If pressing the CAPS LOCK key doesn't solve the problem, try jiggling the left and right SHIFT keys. (Maybe one of those SHIFT keys was accidentally stuck in the down position, because you spilled some soda that got into the keyboard and coagulated and made the SHIFT key too sticky to pop all the way back up.)

If playing with the CAPS LOCK and SHIFT keys doesn't immediately solve your problem, try typing a comma and notice what happens. If the screen shows the symbol "<" instead of a comma, your SHIFT key is activated. (The CAPS LOCK key has no effect on the comma key, since the CAPS LOCK key affects just letters, not punctuation.) If pressing the comma key makes the screen show a comma, your SHIFT key is *not* activated, and any problems you have must therefore be caused by the CAPS LOCK key instead.

Perhaps the CAPS LOCK key is being activated automatically by the program you're using. (For example, some programs automatically activate the CAPS LOCK key because they want your input to be capitalized.) To find out, exit from the program, reboot the computer, get to a C prompt, and try again to type. If the typing is displayed fine, the "problem" was probably caused by just the program you were using — perhaps on purpose.

In some old Leading Edge Model D computers, the ROM has a defect that occasionally misinterprets the signals from the CAPS LOCK and SHIFT keys. When that happens, just try tapping those keys until the display returns to normal.

If you're having trouble printing, the first thing to do is try this experiment. Turn off the computer and the printer (so you can start fresh). When the computer has become quiet, turn it back on; then turn the printer back on. Get out of Windows and any other software you're in, so you have a C prompt, like this:

```
C:\>
```

Then say "dir > prn" like this:

```
C:\>dir>prn
```

That's supposed to make the printer print a copy of your directory.

Another experment to try is this:

```
C:\>echo abcdefghijklmnopqrstuvwxyz>prn
```

That's supposed to make the printer print the alphabet.

If both of those experiments work fine, all your hardware is okay. Any remaining problem is probably just software: for example, you forgot to tell your program or Windows what kind of printer you bought, or you told it incorrectly.

If the experiments do *not* work fine, you're having a hardware problem: the problem lies in your printer, your computer, or the cable connecting them. Here are further details....

Incomplete characters

<u>Problem</u> Part of each character is missing. For example, for the letter "A" you see just the top part of the "A", or just the bottom part, or everything except the middle.

<u>Cause</u> You're probably using a 9-pin, 24-pin, ink-jet, or daisy-wheel printer, not a laser printer. Some of the pins (or ink jets or daisy petals) are not successfully putting ink onto the paper.

<u>Cure</u> If the bottom part of each character is missing, your printer probably uses a ribbon, and the ribbon is too high, so that the bottom pins miss hitting it. Push the ribbon down lower. Read the instructions that came with your printer and ribbon, to find out the correct way to thread the ribbon through your printer. If you're using a daisy-wheel printer, also check whether the daisy-wheel is inserted correctly: try removing it and then reinserting it.

If some other part of each character is missing, and you're using a 9-pin or 24-pin printer, probably one of the pins is broken or stuck. Look at the print head, where the pins are. See if one of the pins is missing or broken. If so, consider buying a new print head, but beware: since print heads are *not* available from discount dealers, you must pay full list price for the print head, and pay almost as much for it as discount dealers charge for a whole new printer!

Substitute characters

Problem When you tell the printer to print a word, it prints the correct number of characters but prints different letters of the alphabet instead. For example, instead of printing an "A", the printer prints a "B" or "C".

Cause In the cable going from the computer to the printer, some of the wires aren't working properly. The cable is probably loose or defective.

Cure Turn off the printer. Grab the cable that goes from the computer to the printer, unplug both ends of the cable, then plug both ends in again *tightly*. Try again to print. If you succeed, the cable was just loose: congratulations, you tightened it!

If unplugging and replugging the cable does *not* solve the problem, then the cable is *not* just loose: it's probably defective!

To *prove* that it's defective, borrow a cable from a friend and try again. If your friend's cable works with your computer and printer, your original cable was definitely the culprit.

Once you've convinced yourself that the problem is the cable, go to a store and buy a new cable. It costs about $8 from discount dealers (such as Staples).

It's cheaper to buy a new cable than to fix the old one.

If the new cable doesn't solve your problem, try a *third* cable, since many cables are defective!

If none of the three cables solves your problem, the problem is caused by defective circuitry in your printer or in your computer's parallel-printer port. Get together with a friend and try swapping printers, computers, and cables: make notes about which combinations work and which don't. You'll soon discover which computers, cables, and printers work correctly and which ones are defective.

Extra characters

Problem When using a program (such as a word-processing program), the printer prints a few extra characters at the top of each page.

Cause Those extra characters are special codes that the printer should *not* print. Those codes are supposed to tell the printer *how* to print. But your printer is misinterpreting those codes. That's because those codes were intended for a different kind of printer.

Cure Try again to tell your software which printer you bought.

To tell Windows which printer you bought, go to the program manager, then double-click the Main icon, then double-click the Control Panel icon, then double-click the Printers icon, then follow the prompts on the screen. To tell a non-Windows program which printer you bought, read the program's manual: look for the part of the manual that explains "printer installation & selection & setup".

Misaligned columns

Problem When printing a table of numbers or words, the columns wiggle: some of the words and numbers are printed slightly too far to the left or right, even though they looked perfectly aligned on the screen.

Cause You're trying to print by using a proportionally spaced font that doesn't match the screen's font.

Cure The simplest way to solve the problem is to **switch to a monospaced font**, such as Courier or Prestige Elite or Gothic or Lineprinter. Since those fonts are monospaced (each character is the same width as every other character), there are no surprises. To switch fonts while using Windows, use your mouse, drag across all the text whose font you wish to switch, then say which font you wish to switch to.

Unfortunately, monospaced fonts are ugly. If you insist on using proportionally spaced fonts, remember that when moving from column to column, you should **press the TAB key, not the SPACE bar**. (In proportionally spaced fonts, the SPACE bar creates a printed space that's too narrow: it's narrower than the space created by the typical digit or letter.)

If the TAB key doesn't make the columns your favorite width, customize how TAB key works by adjusting the TAB stops. (In most word-processing programs, you adjust the TAB stops by sliding them on the layout ruler.)

Normally, the computer tries to *justify* your text: it tries to make the right margin straight by inserting extra spaces between the words. But when you're printing a table, those extra spaces can wreck your column alignment. So when typing a table of numbers, do *not* tell the computer to justify your text: **turn justification OFF**.

Touching characters

Problem When printing on paper, some of the characters bump into each other, so that "cat" looks like "cat".

Cause The computer has fed the printer wrong information about how wide to make the characters and how much space to leave between them. That's because you told the computer wrong info about which printer you're going to use.

Cure Tell the computer again which printer you're going to use.

For example, suppose you plan to type a document by using your home computer's word-processing program, then copy the document onto a floppy disk, take the floppy disk to your office, and print a final draft on the *office's* printer. Since you'll be printing the final draft on the office's printer, tell your home computer that you'll be using the *office's* printer.

If you're using Windows, here's how: double-click the Main icon, double-click the Control Panel icon, double-click the Printer icon, click the Add button, then double-click the printer's name.

Margins

Problem On a sheet of paper, all the printing is too far to the left, or too far to the right, or too far up, or too far down.

Cause You forgot to tell the computer about the paper's size, margins, and feed, or you misfed the paper into the printer.

Cure Most computer software assumes the paper is 11 inches tall and 8½ inches wide (or slightly wider, if the paper has holes in its sides). The software also assumes that you want 1-inch margins on all four sides (top, bottom, left, and right).

If you told the software you have a dot-matrix printer, the software usually assumes you're using **pin-feed paper** (which has holes in the side); it's also called **continuous-feed paper**. For ink-jet and laser printers, the software typically assumes you're using **friction-feed paper** instead (which has no holes).

If those assumptions are not correct, tell the software. For example, give a "margin", "page size", or "feed" command to your word-processing software.

If you make a mistake about how tall the sheet of paper is, the computer will try to print too many or too few lines per page. The result is **creep**: on the first page, the printing begins correctly; but on the second page the printing is slightly too low or too high, and on the third page the printing is even more off.

To solve a creep problem, revise slightly what you tell the software about how tall the sheet of paper is. For example, **if the printing is fine on the first page but an inch too low on the second page, tell the software that each sheet of paper is an inch shorter.**

On pin-feed paper, the printer can print all the way from the very top of the paper to the very bottom. On friction-feed paper, the printer cannot print at the sheet's very top or very bottom (since the rollers can't grab the paper securely enough while printing there). So on friction-feed paper, the printable area is smaller, as if the paper were shorter. Telling the software wrong information about feed has the same effect as telling the software wrong information about the paper's height: you get creep.

So **to fix creep, revise what you tell the software about the paper's height or feed.** If the software doesn't let you talk about the paper's feed, kill the creep by revising what you say about the paper's height.

If you're using a dot-matrix printer that can handle both kinds of paper (pin-feed and friction-feed), **you'll solve most creep problems by choosing pin-feed paper.**

If all printing is too far to the left (or right), adjust what you tell the software about the left and right margins; or if you're using pin-feed paper in a dot-matrix printer with movable tractors, slide the tractors to the left or right (after loosening them by flipping their levers). For example, **if the printing is an inch too far to the right, slide the tractors an inch toward the right.**

INSUFFICIENT MEMORY

Here's the newest nuisance ever invented!

Problem When you try to install or run a new program (such as a game), the computer says "Insufficient memory", even though you bought several megabytes of RAM.

Cause Either the program requires even more megabytes of RAM than you bought, or too much of your RAM is being consumed by other purposes.

Cure First, find out how much RAM the program requires. If you're lucky, the "Insufficient memory" message will include a comment about how much RAM you need. For further details about how much RAM you need, read the program's "System Requirements" notice, which appears on the side or back of the box that the program came in. For even more details about how much RAM you need, read the beginning of the program's instruction manual: just before it explains how to install the program, it explains the detailed "System Requirements".

Notice not just how much RAM the program requires but also what *kind* of RAM. How much *conventional* RAM does it require? How much *extended (XMS)* RAM? How much *expanded (EMM)* RAM?

To find out how much RAM is in your computer at the moment, give the "mem" command, like this:

`c:\>mem`

That command tells you how much conventional, extended, and expanded RAM you have, and how much of each type is still available.

That command works just in DOS 4, 5, 6, and beyond. If you're stuck with an older DOS, say "chkdsk" instead of "mem". Unfortunately, "chkdsk" says just how much *conventional* RAM you have; it doesn't say how much *extended* or *expanded* RAM you have.

In most computers, the total amount of conventional RAM is 640K (where a **K** is 1024 bytes). **If you typed CONFIG.SYS and AUTOEXEC.BAT as I recommended on pages 118-123, about 619K of that conventional RAM will be free.**

If much *less* than 619K of your computer's conventional RAM is free, increase the conventional RAM by making your CONFIG.SYS and AUTOEXEC.BAT files resemble mine. Here are the fundamental techniques my CONFIG.SYS and AUTOEXEC.BAT files use, to increase the amount of conventional RAM:

In CONFIG.SYS, usually say "devicehigh=" instead of "device=".
In AUTOEXEC.BAT, usually say "Lh c:" instead of "c:".
In AUTOEXEC.BAT, delete any line mentioning SMARTDRV.EXE.
In CONFIG.SYS, say "buffers=40".
In CONFIG.SYS, say "dos=high,umb".
In CONFIG.SYS, mention HIMEM.SYS and EMM386.EXE.
In CONFIG.SYS and AUTOEXEC.BAT, delete any lines you don't need.

The amount of expanded RAM is 0, unless your CONFIG.SYS file contains a line mentioning "emm386.exe", and that line has the word "ram" in it (instead of "noems").

To use extended RAM, your CONFIG.SYS file must contain a line mentioning "himem.sys". You'll have more extended RAM available if you delete any line mentioning SMARTDRV.EXE and make sure your "emm386" line says "noems" instead of "ram". If you're still short of RAM, buy more RAM chips! To run modern Windows software well, get at least 8 megabytes of RAM altogether.

WINDOWS PROBLEMS

The main reason why Windows screws up is insufficient conventional RAM. Windows needs to have at least 565K of conventional RAM free, in order to run well. Unfortunately, companies such as Gateway and Dell ship computers having *less* than 565K of conventional RAM free. To find out how much conventional RAM you have free, say "mem".

To increase the amount of conventional free RAM, follow my suggestions on the previous page. You should also get rid of screen savers.

Windows wants 8M of RAM altogether. If your computer's total RAM is much less than 8M (for example, if you bought just 4M), get rid of the AUTOEXEC.BAT line that mentions SMARTDRV.EXE and change the number of buffers in CONFIG.SYS to 40. Exception: if you compressed your hard drive, you must keep SMARTDRV.EXE, in order to prevent your hard drive from seeming to slow.

Another source of Windows headaches is a full hard drive. Make sure your hard drive has at least 10M free. To check that, say "chkdsk" and look at the number of "bytes available on disk". If you have less than 10M free, erase the files you don't use.

Many other headaches can occur. Although Windows was supposed to make computer easier, it's had exactly the opposite effect. Much of my life is spent stuck on the phone answering questions about why Windows doesn't work properly. Those problems apply to Windows 3.1 and Windows 3.11. Theoretically, the next version of Windows (called **Windows 95**) should be better. That's the theory. I don't know the reality yet. Stay tuned!

OUR PAST

ANCIENT HISTORY

The first programmable computers were invented in the 1940's. Before then, people were stuck with the abacus, adding machine, and slide rule.

During the 1950's, 1960's, and 1970's, most computers used punched cards — whose history is weird. The cards were first used for *weaving tapestries*. Where the cards had holes, rods could move through the cards; those moving rods in turn made other rods move, which caused the threads to weave pictures. That machine was called the *Jacquard loom*.

Charles Babbage

Charles Babbage was a wild-eyed English mathematician who, in the 1800's, believed he could build a fancy computing machine. He convinced the British government to give him lots of money, then bilked the government for more. Many years later — and many British pounds later — he still hadn't finished his machine. So he dropped the idea and — can you believe this? — tried to build an even *fancier* machine. He didn't finish that one either. You might say his life was a failure that was expensive for the British government.

But Charlie (as I'll call him) is admired by all us computerniks (in spite of his face, which was even sterner than Beethoven's), because he was the first person to realize that a computing machine must be composed of an input device (he used a card reader), a memory (which he called "The Store"), a central processing unit (which he called "The Mill"), and an output device (he used a printer).

Lady Lovelace

Feminists will kill me if I don't mention Charlie's side-kick, Lady Lovelace. (No, she's not related to Linda.) She was one of Charlie's great admirers, but he never noticed her until she translated his stuff. And boy, it was impossible for him *not* to notice her translations. Her "footnotes" to the translation were three times as long as what she was translating!

She got very intense. She wrote to Charlie, "I am working very hard for you — like the Devil in fact (which perhaps I am)."

The two became love-birds, although he was old enough to be her father. (By the way, her father was Lord Byron, the poet. She was Lord Byron's only "official" daughter. His other daughters were illegitimate.) Some people argue that she was actually brighter than Charlie, despite Charlie's fame. She was better at explaining Charlie's machines and their implications than Charlie was. Some people have dubbed her, "the world's first programmer".

Stunning She stunned all the men she met. She was so bright and . . . a woman! Here's how the editor of *The Examiner* described her (note the pre-Women's-Lib language!):

"She was thoroughly original. Her genius, for genius she possessed, was not poetic, but metaphysical and mathematical. With an understanding thoroughly masculine in solidity, grasp, and firmness, Lady Lovelace had all the delicacies of the most refined female character. Her manners, tastes, and accomplishments were feminine in the nicest sense of the word; and the superficial observer would never have divined the strength and knowledge that lay hidden under the womanly graces. Proportionate to her distaste for the frivolous and commonplace was her enjoyment of true intellectual society. Eagerly she sought the acquaintance of all who were distinguished in science, art, and literature."

Mad Eventually, she went mad. Mattresses lined her room to prevent her from banging her head. Nevertheless, she died gruesomely, at the ripe young age of 36, the same age that her father croaked. (I guess premature death was popular in her Devilish family.)

Who's the heroine? I wish feminists would pick a different heroine than Lady Lovelace. She was *not* the most important woman in the history of computing.

Far more important were Grace Hopper and Jean Sammet. In the 1950's Grace Hopper invented the first programming languages, and she inspired many of us programmers until her recent death. Jean Sammet headed the main committee that invented COBOL; she's the world's top expert on the history of programming languages, and she's been president of the computer industry's main professional society, the ACM.

Lady Lovelace was second-string to Babbage. Grace Hopper and Jean Sammet were second-string to *nobody*.

But since Hopper and Sammet led less racy lives, journalists ignore them; and since Hopper was an Admiral in the Navy (bet you didn't know the Navy had lady Admirals!), she irked some of us doves. Nevertheless, whenever she stepped in front of an audience she got a standing ovation because all of us realize how crucial she was to the computer industry.

But I'm straying from my story. . . .

Herman Hollerith

The U.S. Bureau of the Census takes its census every ten years. To tabulate the results of the 1880 census, the Bureau took *7 years*: they didn't finish until 1887. When they contemplated the upcoming 1890 census, they got scared; at the rate America was growing, they figured that tallying the 1890 census would take 12 years. In other words, the results of the 1890 census wouldn't be ready until 1902. So they held a contest to see whether anyone could invent a faster way to tabulate the data.

The winner was Herman Hollerith. He was the first person to successfully use punched cards to process data.

Hermie (as I'll call him) was modest. When people asked him how he got the idea of using punched cards, he had two answers. One was, "Trains": he had watched a train's conductor punch the tickets. His other, more interesting answer was, "Chicken salad". After saying "Chicken salad", he'd pause for you to ask the obvious question, "*Why* chicken salad?" Then he'd tell his tale. . . .

One day, a girl saw him gulping down chicken salad. She said, "Oh, you like chicken salad? Come to my house. My mother makes excellent chicken salad." So he did. And her father was a head of the Census. (And he married the girl.)

By the way, Herman Hollerith hated one thing: spelling. In elementary school, he jumped out a second-story window, to avoid a spelling test.

In some versions of FORTRAN, every string must be preceded by the letter H. For example, instead of saying —

'DOG'

you must say:

3HDOG

The H is to honor Herman Hollerith.

Anyway, getting back to the story, in 1890 the Census used Hollerith's system, and used it again in 1900.

In 1910, the Census switched to a fancier system created by a Census Bureau employee, James Powers. Later, Powers quit his job and started his own company, which merged into Remington-Rand-Sperry-Univac. Meanwhile, Herman Hollerith's own company merged into IBM. That's how the first two computer companies began doing data processing.

World War II

The first programmable computers were invented in the 1940's because of World War II. They *could* have been invented sooner — most of the know-how was available several decades earlier — but you can't invent a computer unless you have big bucks for research. And the only organization that had big enough bucks was the Defense Department (which in those days was more honestly called the "War Department"). And the only event that was big enough to make the War Department spend that kind of money was World War II.

Of course, the Germans did the same thing. A German fellow, Konrad Zuse, built computers which in some ways surpassed the American ones. But since the Germans lost the war, you don't hear much about old Konrad anymore. Fortunately, throughout World War II the German military ignored what he was doing.

During the 1940's, most computers were invented at universities, usually funded by the War-Defense Department. Some of the most famous computers were the **Mark I** (at Harvard with help from IBM), the **ENIAC** and the **EDVAC** (both at the University of Pennsylvania), the **Whirlwind** (at the Massachusetts Institute of Technology, M.I.T.), and the **Ferranti Mark I** (at the University of Manchester, in England). Which of those computers deserves to be called "the first programmable computer"? The answer's up for grabs. Each of those machines had its own peculiar hang-ups and required years of debugging before working well.

Each of those computers was, as they say in the art world, a "signed original". No two of those computers were alike.

The first generation (1951-1958)

The first computer to be mass-produced was the UNIVAC I, in 1951. It was made by the same two guys (Eckert & Mauchly) who'd built the ENIAC and EDVAC at the University of Pennsylvania. (Mauchly was an instructor there, and Eckert was the graduate student who did the dirty work.) While others at the school were helping build the EDVAC, Eckert and Mauchly left and formed their own company, which invented and started building the UNIVAC. While building the UNIVAC, the Eckert-Mauchly company merged into Remington Rand (which later merged into Sperry-Rand, which later merged into Unisys).

The UNIVAC I was so important that historians call it the beginning of the "first generation". As for computers before UNIVAC — historians disparagingly call them the "zeroth generation".

So the first generation began in 1951. It lasted through 1958. Altogether, from 1951 to 1958, 46 of those UNIVACs were sold.

46 might not sound like many. But remember: in those days, computers were very expensive, and could do very little. Another reason why only 46 were sold is that newer models came out, such as the UNIVAC 1103, the UNIVAC 80, and the UNIVAC 90. But the biggest reason why only 46 of the UNIVAC I were sold is IBM.

The rise of IBM Although IBM didn't begin mass-marketing computers until 1953 — two years after UNIVAC — the IBM guys were much better salesmen, and soon practically everybody was buying from IBM. During the first generation, the hottest seller was the **IBM 650**. IBM sold hundreds and hundreds of them.

There were many smaller manufacturers too. People summarized the whole computer industry in one phrase: **IBM and the Seven Dwarfs**.

Who were the dwarfs? They kept changing. Companies rapidly entered the field — and rapidly left when they realized IBM had the upper hand. By the end of the first generation, IBM was getting 70% of the sales.

Primitive input and output During the first generation, there were no terminals. To program the UNIVAC I, you had to put the program onto magnetic tape (by using a non-computerized machine), feed that tape to the computer, and wait for the computer to vomit another magnetic tape, which you had to run through another machine to find out what the tape said.

One reason why the IBM 650 became more popular was that it could read cards instead of tapes. It really liked cards. In fact, the answers came out on cards. To transfer the answers from cards to paper, you had to run the cards through a separate non-computerized machine.

Memory At the beginning of the first generation, there was no RAM, no ROM, and no core. Instead, the UNIVAC's main memory was banks of liquid mercury, in which the bits were stored as ultrasonic sound waves. It worked slowly and serially, so the access time ranged from 40 to 400 microseconds per bit.

UNIVAC's manufacturer and IBM started playing around with a different kind of memory, called the Williams tube, which was faster (10 to 50 microseconds); but since it was less reliable, it didn't sell well.

In 1953, several manufacturers started selling computers that were much cheaper, because they used super-slow memory: it was a drum that rotated at 3600 rpm, giving an average access time of 17000 microseconds (17 milliseconds). (During the 1970's, some computers still used drums, but for *auxiliary* memory, not for *main* memory.) The most popular first generation computer, the IBM 650, was one of those cheap drum computers.

Core memory consists of tiny iron donuts strung on a grid of wires, whose electrical current magnetizes the donuts. That scheme was first conceived in 1950. The first working models were built in 1953 at M.I.T. and RCA, which argued with each other about who owned the patent. The courts decided in favor of M.I.T., so both RCA *and IBM* came out with core-memory computers. Core memory proved so popular that most computers used it through the 1970's, though in the 1980's RAM finally overshadowed it.

Languages During the first generation, computer programming improved a lot. During the early 1950's, all programs had to be written in **machine language**. In the middle 1950's, **assembly language** became available. By 1958, the end of the first generation, three major high-level languages had become available: **FORTRAN**, **ALGOL**, and **APT**.

Fancy programs Programmers tried to make computers play a decent game of chess. All the attempts failed. But at IBM, Arthur Samuel had some luck with checkers. He got his first checkers program working in 1952 and then continually improved it, to make it more and more sophisticated. In 1955, he rewrote it so that it learned from its own mistakes. In 1956, he demonstrated it on national TV. He kept working on it. Though it hadn't reached championship level yet, it was starting to look impressive.

Computer music scored its first big success in 1956, on the University of Illinois' ILLIAC computer. Hiller & Isaacson made the ILLIAC compose its own music in a style that sounded pre-Bach. In 1957, they made the program more flexible, so that it produced many styles of more modern music. The resulting mishmash composition was dubbed "The ILLIAC Suite" and put on a phonograph record.

In 1954, IBM wrote a program that translated simple sentences from Russian to English. Work on tackling harder sentences continued — with too much optimism.

The second generation (1959-1963)

Throughout the first generation, each CPU was composed of vacuum tubes. Back in 1948, Bell Telephone had invented the transistor, and everybody realized that transistors would be better than vacuum tubes; but putting transistors into computers posed many practical problems that weren't solved for many years.

Finally, **in 1959, computer companies started delivering transistorized computers. That year marked the beginning of the second generation.** Sales of vacuum-tube computers immediately stopped.

All second-generation computers used core memory.

IBM The *first* company to make transistors for computers was Philco, but the most *popular* second-generation computer turned out to be the **IBM 1401**, because it was business-oriented and cheap. IBM announced it in 1959 and began shipping it to customers in 1960.

Its core memory required 11½ microseconds per character. Each character consisted of 6 bits. The number of characters in the memory could range from 1.4K up to 16K. Most people rented the 1401 for about $8,000 per month, but you could spend anywhere from $4,000 to $12,000 per month, depending on how much memory you wanted, etc.

Altogether, IBM installed 14,000 of those machines.

IBM also installed 1,000 of a faster version, called the **1410**. It required only 4½ microseconds per character, had 10K to 80K, and rented for $8,000 to $18,000 per month, typically $11,000.

Altogether, IBM produced six kinds of computers. . . .

small business computers:	the 1401, 1410, 1440, and 1460
small scientific computers:	the 1620
medium-sized business computers:	the 7010
medium-sized scientific computers:	the 7040 and 7044
large business computers:	the 7070, 7074, and 7080
large scientific computers:	the 7090 and 7094

CDC Several employees left Remington-Rand-Sperry-Univac and formed their own company, called the Control Data Corporation (CDC). During the second generation, CDC produced popular scientific computers: the 1604, the 3600, and the 3800.

Software During the second generation, software improved tremendously.

The three major programming languages that had been invented during the first generation (FORTRAN, ALGOL, and APT) were significantly improved. Six new programming languages were invented: **COBOL**, **RPG**, **LISP**, **SNOBOL**, **DYNAMO**, and **GPSS**.

Programmers wrote advanced programs that answered questions about baseball, wrote poetry, tutored medical students, imitated three-person social interaction, controlled a mechanical hand, proved theorems in geometry, and solved indefinite integrals. The three most popular sorting methods were invented: the Shuffle Sort, the Shell Sort, and Quicksort.

Dawn of 3rd generation (1964-1967)

The third generation began with a big bang, in 1964. Here's what happened in 1964, 1965, 1966, and 1967. . . .

Families The first modern computer families were shipped. They were the **CDC 6600**, the **IBM 360**, and DEC's families (the **PDP-6**, **PDP-8**, and **PDP-10**).

Of those families, the CDC 6600 ran the fastest. The IBM 360 was the most flexible and was the only one that used integrated circuits. The PDP-6 and PDP-10 were the best for timesharing. The PDP-8 was the cheapest.

Here are the dates. CDC began shipping the CDC 6600 in 1964. IBM announced the IBM 360 in 1964 but didn't ship it until 1966. DEC began shipping the PDP-6 maxicomputer in 1964, the PDP-8 minicomputer in 1965, and the PDP-10 maxicomputer (a souped-up PDP-6) in 1967.

New languages IBM announced it would create **PL/I**, a new computer language combining FORTRAN, COBOL, ALGOL, and all other popular languages. It was designed especially for IBM's new computer, the 360. In 1966, IBM began delivering PL/I to customers.

Programmers invented the first successful languages for *beginners* using *terminals*. Those languages were **BASIC**, **JOSS**, and **APL**.

Dartmouth College invented the first version of BASIC in 1964, and significantly improved it in 1966 and 1967.

The RAND Corporation invented JOSS in 1964 for the JOHNNIAC computer, and put an improved version (JOSS II) on the PDP-6 in 1965. During the 1970's, three popular variants of JOSS arose: a souped-up version (called AID), a stripped-down version (FOCAL), and a business-oriented version (MUMPS).

IBM completed the first version of APL in 1965 and put it on an IBM 7090. IBM wrote a better version of APL in 1966 and put it on an IBM 360. IBM began shipping APL to customers in 1967.

Stanford University invented the most popular language for statistics: **SPSS**.

Artificial intelligence Researchers calling themselves "experts in artificial intelligence" taught the computer to chat in ordinary English. For example, Bertram Raphael made the computer learn from conversations, Daniel Bobrow made it use algebra to solve "story problems", The Systems Development Corporation made it know everything in an encyclopedia, General Electric made it answer military questions, Ross Quillian made it find underlying concepts, and Joe Weizenbaum made it act as a psychotherapist.

Also, Richard Greenblatt wrote the first decent chess program. It was good enough to play in championship tournaments against humans.

Era of boredom (1968-1974)

As you can see, the first, second, and third generations — up through 1967 — were exciting, full of action. But then, from 1968 to 1974, *nothing newsworthy happened*. That was the era of boredom.

During that era, progress was made, but it was gradual and predictable. Nothing dramatic happened.

Of course, nobody actually came out and said, "Life is boring." People phrased it more genteelly. For example, in September 1971 Robert Fenichel and Joe Weizenbaum wrote this introduction to *Scientific American*'s computer anthology:

"Partly because of the recent recession in the American economy, but more for reasons internal to the field, computer science has recently relaxed its pace. Work has not stopped, but that the current mood is one of consolidation can scarcely be doubted. Just a few years ago, computer science was moving so swiftly that even the professional journals were more archival than informative. This book could not then have been produced without great risk of misfocus. Today it's much easier to put the articles that constitute this book — even the most recent ones — into context."

Since the first generation had lasted eight years (1951-1958), and the second generation had lasted four years (1959-1963), people were expecting the third generation to last at most four years (1964-1967) and some kind of "fourth generation" to begin about 1968. But it never happened.

The only "major" announcement around then came in 1970, when IBM announced it would produce a new line of computers, called the **IBM 370**, which would make the IBM 360 obsolete. But to IBM's dismay, many computer centers decided to hang onto the old 360 instead of switching to the 370. The 370's advantage over the 360 was little, until several years later, when IBM started developing 370 software that wouldn't run on the 360.

Since the difference between the 370 and 360 was disappointingly small, not even IBM claimed that the 370 marked a fourth generation. Computer historians, desperate for something positive to say about the 370, called it the beginning of the "late third generation", as opposed to the 360, which belonged to the "early third generation".

The cruel fact is, in the entire history of computers, there was just one year all computer manufacturers acted together to produce something new. That year was 1959, when all manufacturers switched from vacuum tubes to transistors. Since 1959, we haven't had any consistency. For example, although the third generation began with a "big bang" in 1964, each manufacturer was banging on a different drum. IBM was proclaiming how great the IBM 360 would be because it would contain integrated circuits; but other manufacturers decided to ignore integrated circuits for several years, and concentrated on improving other aspects of the computer instead. For many years after the beginning of the third generation, CDC and DEC continued to use discrete transistors (a sign of the second generation) instead of integrated circuits.

<u>Why?</u> The era of boredom happened for three reasons:

1. The preceding years, 1964-1967, had been so successful that they were hard to improve on.

2. When the Vietnam War ended, the American economy had a recession, especially the computer industry, because it had depended on contracts from the Defense Department. In 1969, the recession hit bottom, and computer companies had to lay off many workers. In that year, General Electric gave up and sold its computer division to Honeywell. In 1971, RCA gave up too and sold its computer division to Remington-Rand-Sperry-Univac.

3. The world wasn't ready yet for "the era of personal computing", which began in 1975.

<u>Quiet changes</u> During the era of boredom, these changes occurred — quietly. . . .

In 1970, DEC began shipping the **PDP-11**. The PDP-8 and PDP-11 became the most popular minicomputers — far more popular than IBM's minicomputers. So in the field of minicomputers, IBM no longer had the upper hand.

BASIC became the most popular language for the PDP-8 and PDP-11 and most other minicomputers (except IBM's, which emphasized RPG). In high schools and business schools, most of the introductory courses used BASIC, instead of FORTRAN or COBOL.

Many businesses and high schools bought their own minicomputers, instead of renting time on neighbors' maxicomputers. The typical high-school computer class used a PDP-8. The richest high schools bought PDP-11's.

In universities, the social sciences started using computers — and heavily — to analyze statistics.

All new computer families used 8-bit bytes, so the length of each word was a multiple of 8 (such as 8, 16, 32, or 64). Most older computer families, invented before the era of boredom, had used 6-bit bytes, so the length of each word had been a multiple of 6: for example, the PDP-8 had a word of 12 bits; the PDP-10 , UNIVAC 1100, and General Electric-Honeywell computers had a word of 36 bits; and the CDC 6600 had a word of 60 bits. The IBM 360 was the first computer to use 8-bit bytes instead of 6-bit; during the era of boredom, all manufacturers copied that feature from IBM.

CRT terminals (TV-like screens attached to keyboards) got cheaper and cheaper, until they were finally as cheap as hard-copy terminals (which use paper). Most computer centers replaced hard-copy terminals by CRT terminals because CRT terminals were quicker, quieter, and could do fancy editing.

Use of keypunch machines decreased because many computer centers replaced cards by CRT terminals.

Interest in new computer languages died. Most computer managers decided to stick with the old classics (FORTRAN and COBOL), because switching to a progressive language (such as PL/I) would require too much time to retrain the programmers and rewrite all the old programs.

Programmers made two last-ditch attempts to improve ALGOL. The first attempt, called **ALGOL 68**, was too complicated to win popular appeal. The second attempt, called **PASCAL**, eventually gained more support.

Maxicomputers were given **virtual core** — disks that pretend to be core, in case you're trying to run a program that's too large to fit into core.

Memory chips got cheaper and cheaper, until they were finally cheaper than core. Most manufacturers replaced core by memory chips.

In 1971, **Intel** began shipping the first microprocessor (complete CPU on a chip). It was called the **4004** and had a word of just 4 bits. In 1972, Intel began shipping an improved version, the **8008**, whose word had 8 bits. In 1973, Intel began shipping an even better version, the **8080**.

MICRO HISTORY

In 1975, the first popular microcomputer was shipped. It was called the **Altair** and was built by a company called **MITS**. It cost just $395.

It was just a box that contained a CPU and very little RAM: just ¼ of a K!

It included no printer, no disk, no tape, no ROM, no screen, and not even a keyboard! The only way to communicate with the computer was to throw 25 switches and watch 36 blinking lights.

It didn't understand BASIC or any other high-level computer language. To learn how to throw the switches and watch the blinking lights, you had to take a course in "machine language".

You also had to take a course in electronics — because the $395 got you just a kit that you had to assemble yourself by using a soldering iron and reading electronics diagrams. Moreover, when you finished building the kit, you noticed some of the parts were missing or defective, so that you had to contact MITS for new parts.

That computer contained several empty slots to hold PC cards. Eventually, many companies invented PC cards to put into those slots. Those PC cards, which were expensive, let you insert extra RAM and attach a printer, tape recorder, disk drives, TV, and terminal (keyboard with either a screen or paper).

Bill Gates invented a way to make the Altair handle BASIC. He called his method **Microsoft BASIC**. He patterned it after DEC's BASIC; but he included extra features that exploited the Altair's ability to be "personal", and he eliminated features that would require too much RAM.

Gary Kildall invented a disk operating system that the Altair could use. He called that operating system **CP/M**.

Many companies built computers that imitated the Altair. Those imitations became more popular than the Altair itself. Eventually, the Altair's manufacturer (MITS) went out of business.

The computers that imitated the Altair were called **S-100 bus computers**, because they each used a Standard cable containing 100 wires.

In those days, the microcomputer industry was standardized. Each popular microcomputer used Microsoft BASIC, CP/M, and the S-100 bus. The microcomputer was just a box containing PC cards; it had no keyboard, no screen, and no disk drive. A cable went from the microcomputer to a terminal, which was priced separately. Another cable went from the microcomputer to a disk drive, which was also priced separately.

Built-in keyboards

In 1977, four companies began selling microcomputers that had built-in keyboards, so you didn't have to buy a terminal. Their computers became popular immediately. The four companies were Processor Technology, Apple, Commodore, and Radio Shack.

Processor Technology's computer was called the **Sol 20**, to honor Solomon Libes, an editor of Popular Electronics. Apple's computer was called the **Apple 2**, because it improved on the Apple 1, which had lacked a built-in keyboard. Commodore's computer was called the **Pet** (inspired by Pet Rocks). Radio Shack's computer was called the **TRS-80**, because it was manufactured by Tandy's Radio Shack and contained a Z-80 CPU.

For a fully assembled computer, Processor Technology charged $1850, Apple charged $970, Commodore charged $595 (but quickly raised the price to $795), and Radio Shack charged $599 (but soon lowered the price to $499).

Notice that Commodore and Radio Shack had the lowest prices. Also, the low prices from Commodore and Radio Shack *included* a monitor, whereas the prices from Processor Technology and Apple didn't. So Commodore and Radio Shack were the real "bargains".

In those days, "the lower the price, the more popular the computer". The cheapest and most popular computer was Radio Shack's. The second cheapest and second most popular was Commodore's Pet. The third cheapest and third most popular was the Apple 2. Processor Technology, after a brief fling of popularity, went bankrupt. The most expensive kind of microcomputer was the CP/M S-100 bus system, which was the oldest kind and therefore had accumulated the greatest quantity of business software.

Improvements

In 1978 and 1979, the three main companies (Apple, Commodore, and Radio Shack) improved their computers.

The improved Apple 2 was called the **Apple 2-plus**. The improved Commodore Pet was called the **Commodore Business Machine (CBM)**. The improved Radio Shack TRS-80 was called the **TRS-80 model 2**.

After announcing the Apple 2-plus, Apple Computer Company stopped selling the plain Apple 2.

Commodore continued selling its old computer (the Pet) to customers who couldn't afford the new version (the CBM), which cost more. Likewise, Radio Shack continued selling its model 1 to customers who couldn't afford the model 2.

Texas Instruments & Atari

In 1979, Texas Instruments (TI) and Atari entered the microcomputer marketplace and began selling low-priced computers.

TI's microcomputer was called the **TI 99/4**. Atari offered *two* microcomputers: the **Atari 400** and the **Atari 800**.

TI charged $1150. Atari charged $1000 for the regular model (the Atari 800) and $550 for the stripped-down model (the Atari 400).

TI's price included a color monitor. Atari's prices did *not* include a screen; you were to attach Atari's computers to your home's TV.

TI's computer was terrible, especially its keyboard. The Atari 800 computer was wonderful; reviewers were amazed at its easy-to-use keyboard, easy-to-use built-in editor, gorgeous color output on your TV, child-proofing (safe for little kids), and dazzling games, all at a wonderfully low price! It was cheaper than an Apple (whose price had by then risen to $1195) and yet was much *better* than an Apple.

From that description, you'd expect Atari 800 to become the world's best-selling computer, and the TI 99/4 to become an immediate flop. Indeed, that's what most computer experts hoped. And so did the TI 99/4's product manager: when he saw what a mess the TI 99/4 had become, he quit TI and went to work for Atari, where he became the product manager for the Atari 400 & 800!

But even though computer experts realized that TI's computer was junk, TI decided to market it very aggressively, in several ways. TI coaxed Milton Bradley and Scott Foresman to write lots of programs for the 99/4. It paid researchers at MIT to make the 99/4 understand LOGO (a computer language used by young children and very popular in elementary schools). It improved the keyboard just enough so that people would stop laughing at it; the version with the new keyboard was named the **99/4A**. TI paid Bill Cosby to praise the 99/4A and ran hundreds of TV ads showing Bill Cosby saying "wow". TI dramatically slashed the $1150 price to $650, then $150, and then finally to just $99.50! (To bring the price that low, TI had to exclude the color monitor from the price; instead, TI included a hookup to your home's color TV.)

By contrast, Atari did hardly anything to market or further improve the Atari 400 & 800. Instead, Atari concentrated on its other products: the big Atari game machines (which you find in video arcades) and the Atari VCS machine (which plays video games on your home TV).

The TI 99/4A therefore became more popular than the Atari 400 & 800 — even though the TI 99/4A was inherently worse.

Sinclair, Osborne, backlash

In 1980 and 1981, two important companies entered the microcomputer marketplace: Timex Sinclair (1980) and Osborne (1981).

The first complete computer selling for less than $200 was invented by a British chap named Clive Sinclair and manufactured by Timex. The original version was called the **ZX-80** (because it was invented in 1980, contained a Z-80 CPU, and was claimed to be "Xellent"); it sold for $199.95. In 1981, Clive Sinclair invented an improved version, called the **ZX-81**. Later, he and Timex invented further improvements, called the **ZX Spectrum** and the **Timex Sinclair 1000**. When TI dropped the price of the TI 99/4A to $99.50, Timex retaliated by dropping the list price of the Timex Sinclair 1000 to $49.95, so that the Timex Sinclair 1000 remained the cheapest complete computer.

In April 1981, Adam Osborne began the Osborne Computer Corp. and began selling the **Osborne 1** computer, designed by Lee Felsenstein (the inventor of Processor Technology's Sol 20 computer). The Osborne 1 computer included practically everything a business executive needed: its $1795 price included a keyboard, a monitor, a Z-80A CPU, a 64K RAM, two disk drives, CP/M, Microsoft BASIC, a second version of BASIC, the Wordstar word processor, and the Supercalc spreadsheet program. Moreover, it was the world's

first portable business computer: the entire computer system (including even the monitor and disk drives) was collapsible and turned itself into an easy-to-carry attaché case. (Many years later, Compaq copied Osborne's idea.)

While Timex Sinclair and Osborne were entering the marketplace, Radio Shack, Apple, and Commodore were introducing new computers of their own. Let's examine them. . . .

In 1980, Radio Shack began selling three new computers. The **TRS-80 model 3** replaced Radio Shack's cheapest computer (the model 1) and was almost as good as Radio Shack's fanciest computer (the model 2). The **TRS-80 Color Computer** drew pictures in color and cost less than the model 3. The **TRS-80 Pocket Computer** fit into your pocket, looked like a pocket calculator, and was built for Radio Shack by Sharp Electronics in Japan.

In 1980, Apple began selling the **Apple 3**. It was overpriced; and to make matters worse, the first Apple 3's that rolled off the assembly line were defective. Apple eventually lowered the price and fixed the defects; but since the Apple 3 had gotten off to such a bad start, computer consultants didn't trust it and told everybody to avoid it.

In 1981, Commodore began selling the **Vic-20**, which drew pictures in color and cost less than Radio Shack's Color Computer. In fact, the Vic-20 was the first computer that drew pictures in color for less than $300.

The Vic-20 originally sold for $299.95. When TI lowered the price of the TI 99/4A to $99.95, Commodore lowered the price of the Vic-20. At discount department stores (such as K Mart, Toys R Us, and Child World), you could buy the Vic-20 for just $85: it was still the cheapest computer that could handle color. (The Timex Sinclair 1000 was cheaper but handled only black-and-white.)

Moreover, the Vic-20 had standard Microsoft BASIC, whereas the Timex Sinclair 1000 and TI 99/4A did not; so the Vic-20 was the cheapest computer that had standard Microsoft BASIC. It was the cheapest computer that was pleasant to program.

Also, the Vic-20 had a nice keyboard, whereas the keyboards on the Timex Sinclair 1000 and TI 99/4A were pathetic.

The Vic-20 became immediately popular.

IBM PC

On August 12, 1981, IBM announced a new microcomputer, called the IBM Personal Computer (or IBM PC).

Although IBM had previously invented other microcomputers (the IBM 5100 and the IBM System 23 Datamaster), they'd been overpriced and nobody took them seriously — not even IBM. The IBM Personal Computer was IBM's first *serious* attempt to sell a microcomputer.

The IBM Personal Computer was a smashing success, because of its amazingly high quality and amazingly low price. It became the standard against which the rest of the microcomputer industry was judged.

CYCLES

Every 8 years, the country's mood about computers has changed. After 8 years of dramatic revolution, we switched to 8 years of subtle evolution, then back again.

Pivotal years

The pivotal years were 1943 (beginning the first revolution), 1951 (beginning the first period of *evolution*), 1959 (revolution), 1967 (evolution), 1975 (revolution), 1983 (evolution), and 1991 (revolution). Here are the details. . . .

Revolution From 1943 to 1950, researchers at universities were building the first true computers, which were big monsters. Each was custom-built; no two were alike.

Evolution In 1951, Sperry began selling the first mass-produced computer: the **UNIVAC I**. Sperry built 46 of them. During the 8-year era from 1951 to 1958, computers gradually became smaller and cheaper and acquired more software. That evolutionary era was called the **first generation**.

Revolution The next computer revolution began in 1959, when IBM began selling the **IBM 1401**, the first IBM computer to use transistors instead of vacuum tubes. During that eight-year revolution from 1959 to 1966, computerists polished FORTRAN and ALGOL (which had been begun earlier), invented 9 other major computer languages (COBOL, BASIC, PL/I, LISP, SNOBOL, APL, DYNAMO, GPSS, and RPG), and began developing FORTH and SPSS. They created many amazing programs for artificial intelligence, such as Weizenbaum's Eliza program, which made the computer imitate a therapist. During that same eight-year period, IBM invented the **IBM 360**: it was the first popular computer that used integrated circuits, and all of IBM's modern mainframes are based on it.

Evolution The years from 1967 to 1974 showed a gradual evolution. Computer prices continued to drop and quality continued to improve. DEC began selling PDP-10 and PDP-11 computers, which became the favorite computers among researchers in universities.

Revolution In 1975, MITS shipped the first popular microcomputer, the **Altair**, which launched the personal computer revolution. Soon Apple, Commodore, Tandy, and IBM began selling microcomputers also. Programmers developed lots of useful, fun software for them. The revolution climaxed at the end of 1982, when many Americans bought microcomputers as Christmas presents.

Evolution In January 1983, the cover of *Time* magazine declared that the 1982 "man of the year" was the personal computer. But consumers quickly tired of the personal-computer fad, chucked their Commodore Vic and Timex Sinclair computers into the closet, and shifted attention to less intellectual pursuits. Many computer companies went bankrupt. In 1983, Lotus announced **1-2-3**, but that was the computer industry's last major successful new product. After that, prices continued to fall and quality gradually increased, but no dramatic breakthroughs occurred. The computer industry became boring. During that time, if you were to ask "What fantastically great happened in the computer industry during the past year?" the answer was: "Not much".

Revolution In 1991, the computer industry became exciting again. Here's why. . . .

Part of that excitement came from revolutionary influences of the previous two years: in 1989 & 1990 the Berlin Wall fell, the Cold War ended, a new decade began, Microsoft finally invented a version of Windows that worked well (version 3.0), and Apple invented a color Mac that was affordable (the LC). In 1991, Microsoft put the finishing touches on Windows (version 3.1) and DOS (version 5).

In 1991 and 1992, a series of price wars made the cost of computers drop 45% per year instead of the customary 30%. Those lower prices made people spend *more* money on computers, because the ridiculously low prices for fancy stuff encouraged people to buy fancier computers: 486 instead of 286, Super VGA instead of plain VGA, 8M RAM instead of 1M, 200M hard drives instead of 40M.

The sudden popularity of Windows whetted the public's hunger for those muscle machines, since Windows requires lots of muscle to run well. That growing American muscle (bigger and bigger!) then made Windows practical enough to become desirable. All big software companies hastily converted their DOS and Mac software to Windows.

The challenge of doing that conversion forced them to rethink the twin questions of software wisdom: "What makes software easy to use?" and "What kinds of software power do users want?" Many creative solutions were invented to those questions.

During the 1992 Christmas season, fast CD-ROM drives finally became cheap enough to create a mass market: many American bought them, and CD-ROMs became the new standard way to distribute encyclopedias, directories, other major reference works, and software libraries (full of fonts and shareware). The attention given to CD-ROMs made customers think about the importance of sound, and many customers bought sound cards such as the Sound Blaster.

I'd tell you more about this computer revolution, but I'm stuck in the middle of it and must get back to my battle station.

When the revolution ends, historians will try to summarize it. They'll sit back in their easy chairs, smoke their pipe dreams, wax eloquent about their war stories, and gigglishly play Monday-morning quarterback, which is much funnier than calling the shots while the game's in progress.

Presidential politics

The 8-year computer cycle coincides with the American cycle of switching political parties. After years of Roosevelt & Truman, the presidential election of 1952 ushered in eight years of a Republican (Eisenhower); 1960 brought eight years of Democrats (Kennedy & Johnson); 1968, eight years of Republicans (Nixon & Ford).

1976 began another 16-year experience of "Democrat followed by Republicans"; but alas, the Democrat (Carter) got just 4 of those years, and the Republicans (Reagan and Bush) got the remaining 12. (Carter got just 4 of those years instead of 8 because he lost face in the middle of the Iran hostage crisis, oil crisis, and recession.)

1992 began another experience of "Democrat followed by Republicans". The Democrat was Clinton.

I wonder who will come after Clinton. If you're reading this book after Clinton has gone, please enter your time machine, go through a time warp, come back to *my* time, and tell me who Clinton's successor will be. I'm dying to know.

When Americans love liberals and revolution, they vote for Democrats; when Americans prefer conservative evolution, they vote for Republicans. As historian Krigsman remarked, "An excitable mood in the country causes a computer revolution, and the next year the Democrats grab power."

BECOME AN EXPERT

To become a computer expert, you need a computer, literature, and friends.

A computer to practice on

If possible, buy an IBM PC or clone. If you can't afford a full system, start by practicing DOS and BASIC on a one-floppy IBM PC clone with 256K of RAM and a monochrome monitor. Mail-order discount dealers sell that combination for about $200. So do many folks selling used computers. By saving your money, you can later add more RAM, a second disk drive, printer, and applications software.

To pay even less, ask your computer friends whether they want to get rid of any "used junky obsolete computers" for under $50, or ask them whether they can lend you a computer for a weekend. Swap: if they lend you an Apple for a weekend, bake them an apple pie.

Another way to save money is to join your friends for a group purchase. For example, if 9 of you each chip in $10, you can buy a $90 computer. Divide the 9 of you into 3 trios, and rotate the computer from trio to trio every day, so that you get to use the computer every third day.

Literature to read

Begin by reading *The Secret Guide to Computers*. Then read the manuals that came with your computer.

Find out what's new by subscribing to computer magazines or reading them in your town's library.

You can get computer books and magazines from the bookstore at your local college. You can also try your local branch of **Waldenbooks** or **B. Dalton Booksellers**, which are nationwide chains. A cheerier chain is **Borders**, whose salespeople are more knowledgeable. If you live near Denver, visit **Tattered Cover**, which is America's largest independent bookstore (303-322-7727).

To pay less, shop at discount chains such as **Staples** (which has a 20% discount on the few books it stocks) and **Comp USA** (which has big discounts on magazines and a 20% discount on all books). You can also get discounts of 10% to 31% from mail-order computer-book dealers such as **Business & Computer Bookstore** (Willow Grove PA, 215-657-8300, out-of-state 800-233-0233). If you live near Boston, go to Harvard Square in Cambridge to visit **Barillari Books** (20% discount on most books, 617-864-2400) and **Words Worth** (10% discount on all paperbacks, 617-354-5201).

The following big stores specialize in computer & technical books, and most are willing to ship all over the world. They usually charge full price:

Opamp Bookstore (Los Angeles, 213-464-4322)
Computer Literacy Bookshops (San Jose CA, 408-592-5775)
Stacey's Bookstore (San Francisco 415-421-4687, Palo Alto CA 415-326-0681)
Computer Book Works (New York City, 212-385-1616)
McGraw-Hill Bookstore (New York City, 212-997-1221)
Quantum Books (Cambridge MA, 617-494-5042)
Calgary Computer Books (Calgary Alberta Canada, 403-270-0952)

Since *The Secret Guide to Computers* is an underground book, you won't find it in stores that are "overground". To find out which nifty bookstores, computer stores, and consultants near you carry the *Secret Guide*, phone me at 617-666-2666, and I'll look up your ZIP code in my computer.

Friends to chat with

When you have a computer question, phone me at 617-666-2666. Another way to get help is to join a computer club.

The biggest and best computer club is the **Boston Computer Society (BCS)**, which has about 25,000 members, holds over 1,000 meetings per year, publishes many magazines and newsletters, and has hundreds of volunteers who give free phone help on technical topics. Regular membership costs $49. Pay just $32 if you're over 65, a teacher, or a full-time student. For free literature about membership, phone 617-290-5700.

If you live near New York, use a touch-tone phone to call **New York Personal Computer (NY PC)** at 212-LED-NYPC. You'll be talking to a computer using voice mail. The voices will guide you through verbal menus; you'll have lots of fun! The voices will also invite you to become a member for $35 per year and call Hy Bender at 212-829-5534 for more details.

If you live near Philadelphia, call the **Philadelphia Area Computer Society (PACS)** at 215-951-1255, 8AM-4PM weekdays. Membership costs $27 per year.

The biggest and best club for Macintosh computers is the **Berkeley Macintosh User Group (BMUG)**. It's based in Berkeley, California; but it's so good that it attracts members from all over the world. Join! Twice a year, you'll get a "newsletter" that's 400 pages long! Any day you have a question about Macs, you can get free technical help from the BMUG staff and volunteers, who answer their phones daily from 9:30AM to 5:30PM. Membership costs $25 for a half-year, $40 for a full year. To join, phone 510-549-2684 or 800-776-BMUG. Once you're a member, you can buy two huge BMUG books for $15 each:

"The BMUG Guide to Bulletin Boards and Beyond"
an excellent tutorial in how to use Mac communications software, 541 pages

"The BMUG Shareware Disk Catalog"
lists all the shareware you can buy from BMUG, 686 pages

Many other computer clubs have sprung up, all over the country! Ask your local computer store or high-school computer department about computer clubs in *your* home town; if there aren't any, start one yourself!

Americans living in Tokyo have started the **Tokyo PC Users Group**. Their newletter, written in English, is top-notch! If you're in Japan, phone (03) 3576-9783 (for a recorded message about membership) or write to Tokyo PC Club, Shibuya Post Restante, Shibuya, Tokyo 150 Japan.

If you take a computer course, get personal help by chatting with your teacher and classmates. To save money, sign up for the cheap courses given by your high school's "adult education" evening program and your local community college.

I occasionally travel around the world and give courses inexpensively or for free. Heads of the computer industry got their training from my courses. To join us, use the coupon on the back page.

LAND A COMPUTER JOB

To become a lawyer, you must graduate from law school and pass the Bar Exam. But to become a computer expert, there's no particular program you must graduate from, no particular exam to pass, and no particular piece of paper that "proves" you're an expert or even competent.

You can get a job in the computer industry even if you've never had any training. Your job will be sweeping the floor.

To become a top computer expert, you must study hard, day and night. Read lots of computer manuals, textbooks, guidebooks, magazines, newspapers, and newsletters. Practice using many kinds of computers, operating systems, languages, word-processing programs, spreadsheets, database systems, graphics packages, and telecommunications programs. Also explore the many educational programs for kids. Use many kinds of printers, disk drives, and modems. Study the human problems of dealing with computers. No matter how much you already know, learn more!

When I surveyed computer experts, I found that the average expert still spends two hours per day reading about computers, to fill holes in the expert's background and learn what happened in the computer industry that day! In addition to those two hours, the expert spends many more hours practicing what was read and swapping ideas by chatting with other computerists.

As a computer expert, you can choose your own hours, but they must be numerous: if your interest in computers lasts just from 9 AM to 5 PM, you'll never become a computer expert.

To break into the computer field, you can use six tools: college, home consulting, home programming, salesmanship, job expansion, and on-the-job training.

College

The most traditional way to get a computer job is to go to college and get a Ph.D. or M.A. in computer science. Unfortunately, that takes a lot of time.

Home consulting

The fastest way to break into the field is to keep your current job but spend your weekends and evenings helping your neighbors, friends, and colleagues learn about computers. Help them buy hardware and software. Then customize the software to meet their own personal needs. Then train them in how to use it all. Lots of folks want training in how to use DOS, Word Perfect, and other popular software.

At first, do it all for free. After you've become an experienced expert and developed a list of happy clients who will vouch for your brilliance, start requesting money from new clients. Start cheaply, at about $10 per hour, then gradually raise your rates over the next few years. Most computer consultants charge about $50 per hour, and some charge much more than that; but I suggest that you be gentler on your clients' pocketbooks! By charging little, you'll get more clients, they'll rack up more hours with you, and you won't need to spend lots of time and money on "advertising". For example, at $20 per hour you'll be very popular!

Home programming

You can write computer programs at home to sell to friends and software publishers, but make sure your programs serve a real need and don't duplicate what's already on the market. Be creative!

Salesmanship

For a quicker career path, learn enough about microcomputers to get a job selling them in a store. As a salesperson, you'll be helping people decide which hardware and software to buy; you'll be acting as a consultant.

The store will probably give you permission to take hardware, software, and literature home with you, so you can study and practice new computer techniques every evening and become brilliant. If you wish, you can even moonlight by helping your customers use the software they bought and designing your own customized programs for them.

After working in the store several months, you'll have the knowledge, experience, contacts, and reputation to establish yourself as an independent consultant. You can call your former customers and become their advisor, trainer, and programmer — or even set up your *own* store.

Job expansion

Another way to break into the field is to take a non-computer job and gradually enlarge its responsibilities, so that it involves computers.

For example, if you're a typist, urge your boss to let you use a word processor. If you're a clerk, ask permission to use spreadsheet and data-management programs to manage your work more efficiently. If you're a math teacher, ask the principal to let you teach a computer course or help run the school's computer club.

Keep your current job, but expand it to include new skills so you gradually become a computer expert.

On-the-job training

The final way to break into the field is to get a job in a computer company, as a janitor or clerk, and gradually move up by using the company's policy of free training for employees.

Phone me

Many companies phone me when they're looking for computer experts. If you think you're an expert and can demonstrate your expertise, I'll be glad to pass your name along to employers.

Occasionally, I even have job openings here at The Secret Guide to Computers. Feel free to ask. Although some of the jobs here are mundane, a nice fringe benefit is that you get to play with my 40 computers and oodles of software packages and take them home with you. You can also choose your own hours: work whenever you please! After you work here a few months and do your job well, I'll gladly give you an excellent reference that will help you get an even nicer job elsewhere.

If somebody's interested in hiring you to be a programmer or consultant, you must decide what rate to charge.

If this is your *first* such job, be humble and charge very little because your first job's main goal should *not* be money. Instead, your goal should be to gain experience, enhance your reputation, and find somebody you can use as a reference and who'll give you a good recommendation. Convince your first employer that you're the best bargain he ever got, so that he'll be wildly enthusiastic about you and give you a totally glowing recommendation when you go seek your second job.

If you can't find anyone willing to pay you, work for free, just so that you can put on your resume that you "helped computerize a company". After such an experience, you should easily find a second job that pays better.

Although your first computer job might pay little or nothing at all, it gets your foot in the computer industry's door. After your first job, your salary will rise rapidly because the most valuable attribute you can have in this field is *experience*.

Since experienced experts are in short supply, they get astronomical salaries. On the other hand, there's a *surplus* of "kids fresh out of college" who know nothing. So consider your first job to be an extremely valuable way to gain experience, even if the initial salary is low. When applying for your first job, remember that you're still unproven, and be thankful that your first employer is willing to take a risk on you.

Asking for a raise

After several months on the job, when you've thoroughly proved that you're worth much more than you're being paid, and your employer is thoroughly thrilled with your performance, gently ask your employer for a slight raise. If he declines, continue working at that job, but also keep your eyes open for a better alternative.

Negotiating a contract

The fundamental rule of contract negotiation is: never make a large commitment.

For example, suppose somebody offers to pay you $10,000 if you write a fancy program. Don't accept the offer; the commitment is too large. Instead, request $1,000 for writing a stripped-down version of the program.

After writing the stripped-down version, wait and see whether you get the $1,000; if you get it without any hassles, then agree to make the version slightly fancier, for a few thousand dollars more. That way, if you have an argument with your employer (which is common), you've lost only $1,000 of effort instead of $10,000.

Contract headaches

Arguments between programmers and employers are common, for six reasons. . . .

1. As a programmer, you'll probably make the mistake of underestimating the time for debugging the program, because you'll tend to be too optimistic about your own abilities.

2. Your employer won't be precise enough when he tells you what kind of program to write. You'll write a program that you *think* satisfies the employer's request and then discover that the employer really wanted something slightly different.

3. Your employer will forget to tell you about the various "strange cases" that the company must handle. They'll require extra "IF" statements in your program.

4. When the employer finally sees your program working, he'll suddenly think of extra things he'd like the program to do, and which will require extra programming effort from you.

5. When the program finally does everything that the employer expects, he'll want you to teach his staff how to use the program and the computer. If his staff has never dealt with computers before, the training period could be quite lengthy. He'll also want you to write a manual about the program, and to put the manual into the company's library.

6. After the company begins using the program, the employer will want you to make additional changes, and might even expect you to make them at no charge.

To minimize those six kinds of conflicts, be honest and kind to your employer. Explain to him that you're worried about those six kinds of conflicts, and that you'd like to chat about them *now*, before either you or he makes any commitments. Then make a small commitment for a small payment for a short time, and make sure that both you and the employer are happy with the way that small commitment worked out before attempting any larger commitments.

DEVELOP YOUR CAREER

Here are further tricks for developing your career.

Programmer

A **programmer** is a teacher: the programmer teaches the computer new tricks. For example, the programmer might teach the computer how to do the payroll. To do that, the programmer feeds the computer a list of instructions, that explain to the computer how to do the payroll. The list of instructions is called a **program**.

__Languages__ The program is written by using the very limited vocabulary that the computer understands already. Earlier in *The Secret Guide to Computers*, I explained a vocabulary called BASIC, which consists of words such as PRINT, INPUT, GO TO, IF, THEN, and STOP. That vocabulary — BASIC — is called a **computer language**. It's a small part of English. No computer understands the whole English language. The programmer's job is to translate an English sentence (such as "do the payroll") into language the computer understands (such as BASIC). So *the programmer is a translator*.

Some computers understand BASIC. Other computers understand a different vocabulary, called COBOL. For example, COBOL uses the words DISPLAY and WRITE instead of PRINT.

Before programming a computer, you must find out which language the computer understands. Does it understand BASIC? Or does it understand COBOL instead? Or does it understand a yet different language? The most popular languages are BASIC, COBOL, FORTRAN, and PASCAL; but there are also *thousands* of others. Your computer understands at least one of those languages; if you're lucky, your computer understands *several* of those languages.

When you apply for a programming job, the first question to ask the interviewer is: which languages does the company's computer understand? Or better yet, ask, "Which language do you want me to program in?" The interviewer will say "BASIC" or "COBOL" or some similar answer and then ask you, "Do you know that language?"

Most microcomputers use BASIC, DBASE, or C. Most minicomputers use BASIC, FORTRAN, COBOL, or C. Most maxicomputers use FORTRAN or COBOL. For all three sizes, PASCAL is another alternative.

Of those popular languages, BASIC is the easiest and the most fun. To become a programmer, begin by studying BASIC, then move on to the other languages, which are yukkier.

Since BASIC's so easy, saying you know BASIC is less prestigious than saying you know languages such as C. To get lots of prestige, learn *many* languages. To convince the interviewer you're brilliant, say that you know many languages well even if the job you're applying for needs just one language.

The most prestigious languages to know are assembly and machine languages, because they're the hardest. If you can convince the interviewer that you know assembly and machine languages, the interviewer will assume you're God and offer you a very high salary, even if the job doesn't require a knowledge of those languages.

__Specific computers__ Before going to the interview, learn about the specific computer the company uses. For example, if the company's computer is an IBM maxicomputer, study the IBM maxi's details. Study its operating system and its languages. If the job requires COBOL, study the particular dialect of COBOL used on the IBM maxi. Each computer has its own dialect of COBOL, its own dialect of BASIC, etc. Usually, the differences between dialects are small, but you must know them. For assembly and machine languages, the differences between dialects are much greater: the assembly language on an IBM PC is almost entirely different from the assembly language on an IBM maxi.

__Analysis versus coding__ The act of programming consists of two stages. In the first stage, analyze the problem to make it more specific. For example, suppose the problem is, "Program the computer to do the payroll". The first stage is to decide exactly how the company wants the payroll to be done. Should it be done weekly, bi-weekly, semi-monthly, or monthly? While computing the payroll checks, what other reports do you want the computer to generate? For example, do you want the computer to also print a report about the employees' attendance, and about how much money each department of the company is spending on salaries? Maybe one of the departments is over-budgeting. And what kind of paychecks do you want the computer to *refuse* to print? For example, if somebody in the company tries to make the computer print a paycheck for a ridiculous amount (such as $1,000,000 or ½¢), you want the computer to refuse (and perhaps signal an alarm).

That stage — analyzing a vague problem (such as "do the payroll") to make it more specific — is called **analysis**. A person who analyzes is called an **analyst** or, more prestigiously, a **systems analyst**. After analyzing the vague problem and transforming it into a series of smaller, more specific tasks, the analyst turns the problem over to a team of **coders**. Each coder takes one of the tasks and translates it into BASIC or COBOL or some other language.

If you're hired to be a "programmer", your first assignment will probably be as a coder. After you gain experience, you'll be promoted to a systems analyst.

The ideal systems analyst knows how to analyze a problem but also has prior experience as a coder. A systems analyst who knows how to both code and analyze is called a **programmer/analyst**. An analyst who doesn't know how to code — who doesn't know BASIC or COBOL — who merely knows how to break a big problem into a series of little ones — is paid less.

__Three kinds of programming__ Programming falls into three categories: **development**, **testing**, and **maintenance**. **Development** means inventing a new program. **Testing** means making sure the program works. **Maintenance** means making minor improvements to programs that were written long ago. (The "improvements" consist of eliminating errors that were discovered recently, or making the program conform to changed government regulations, or adding extra features so that the program produces extra reports or handles extra-special cases.) Development is more exciting than testing, which is more exciting than maintenance. So if you're a new programmer, the other programmers will probably "stick you" in the maintenance department, where you'll be part of the maintenance crew. Since your job will consist of "cleaning up" old programs, cruel programmers will call you a "computer janitor".

"Application program" versus a "system program"
Programs fall into two categories. The usual kinds of program is called an **application program**; it handles a specific application (such as "payroll" or "chess" or "send rocket to moon"). The other kind of program is called a **system program**; its only purpose is to help programmers write applications programs.

For example, hidden inside the computer is a program that makes the computer understand BASIC; that program explains to the computer what the words PRINT, INPUT, GO TO, IF, THEN, and STOP mean. That program (which is called the **BASIC language processor**) is an example of a system program.

Another system program is called the **operating system**. It tells the computer how to control the disks and printer and terminals. If the operating system is fancy, it even tells the computer how to handle many programmers at once.

Another system program, found on large computers, is the **editor**. It lets you edit programs written in languages such as COBOL and FORTRAN.

So system programs are tools, which help programmers write application programs. When you buy a computer, buy some system programs so you can create applications programs easily.

A person who invents system programs is called a **systems programmer**. To become a systems programmer, learn assembly language and machine language.

Creating a system program is very difficult; so a systems programmer usually gets paid more than an applications programmer.

The word "systems" is prestigious: it's used in the phrase "systems analyst" and in "systems programmer". In some companies, if your boss wants to praise you, the boss will put the word "systems" in front of your title even if your job has nothing to do with "systems".

How to learn programming
To be a good programmer, you need experience. You can't become a good programmer by just reading books and listening to lectures; you must *get your hands on a computer and practice*.

If you take a computer course, the books and lectures are much less valuable than the experience of using the school's computer. Spend lots of time in the computer center. Think of the course as just an excuse to get permission to use the school's computer. The quality of the lecture is less important than the quality of the school's computer center. The ideal computer center uses video terminals instead of punched cards; has a computer that can understand many languages; gives you *unlimited* use of the computer (no "extra charges"); is open 24 hours a day; has enough terminals so you don't have to wait in line for somebody else to finish; has a staff of "teaching assistants" who will answer your questions; has a rack full of easy-to-read manuals that explain how to use the computer; lets you borrow books and manuals, to take home with you; and has *several* kinds of computers, so that you get a broad range of experience. Before you enroll in a computer course, find out whether the school's computer center has those features.

Many computer schools are unnecessarily expensive. To save money, take fewer courses, and buy more books and magazines instead. Better yet, buy a computer yourself and keep it in your home! You can buy a used IBM XT clone for under $300, or a more primitive computer (such as a Radio Shack Color Computer) for under $100. Keep the computer a few months, practice writing BASIC programs on it and using some applications, then sell it to a friend for $70 less than you paid — so that using it cost you just $70 and gave you several *months* of education. That's a much better investment of your money than spending many hundreds of dollars on a computer course.

Another cheap way to get an education is to phone your town's board of education, and ask whether the town offers any adult-education courses in computers. Some towns offer adult-education computer courses for under $100.

For an even better deal, phone your town's board of education — or high school — and ask whether you can sit in the back of a high-school computer class. If you're an adult resident of the town, you might be able to sit in the back of the class for free. Your only "expense" will be the embarrassment of sitting in the same room as youngsters. After a day or two of feeling strange, you'll get used to it, and you'll get an excellent free education.

Community colleges offer low-cost courses that are decent. Explore the community colleges before sinking money into more expensive institutions that are over-priced.

Starting salary
For your first programming job, your salary will be somewhere between $18,000 and $25,000. The exact amount depends on which languages you know, how many programs you wrote previously, whether you have a college degree, whether you've had experience on the particular kind of computer the company uses, and whether you know the application area. (For example, if you're a programmer for an insurance company, it's helpful to know something about insurance.)

Degrees
A college degree ain't needed, but wow can it make you look smart! Try to get a degree in "computer science" or "management information systems".

"Computer science" emphasizes the underlying theory, systems programming, assembly language, PASCAL, FORTRAN, C, and applications to science. "Management information systems" emphasizes BASIC, COBOL, DBASE, and applications to business.

A major in "mathematics" that emphasizes computers is also acceptable.

Discrimination
If you're a woman or non-white or physically handicapped, you'll be pleased to know that the computer industry discriminates less than in other occupations. In fact, being a woman or non-white or physically handicapped works to your *advantage*, since many companies have affirmative-action programs.

On the other hand, discrimination *does* exist against older people. If you're over 40 and trying to get a job as an entry-level programmer, you'll have a tough time since the stereotypical programmer is "young, bright, and a fast thinker". If you're old, they'll assume you're "slow and sluggish".

Because of that unfair discrimination, if you're old you should probably try entering the computer industry through a different door: as a consultant, or a computer salesperson, or a computer-center manager, or a computer teacher. For those positions, your age works to your *advantage*, since those jobs require *wisdom*, and people will assume that since you're old, you're wise.

Shifting careers
If you're older, the best way to enter the computer field is to combine your new knowledge of computers with what you knew previously. If you already knew a lot about how to sell merchandise, get a job selling computers. If you already knew a lot about teaching, get a job teaching about computers — or helping teachers deal with computers. If you already knew a lot about real estate,

computerize your real estate office.

In other words, do *not* try to "hop" careers; instead, gradually *shift* your responsibilities so that they deal more with computers.

To get into the computer field safely, keep your current job but computerize it. For example, if you're already a math teacher, keep teaching math but convince your school to also let you teach a computer course, or at least incorporate computers into the math curriculum or help run the school's computer center. If you already work for a big company and your job bores you, try to transfer to a department that puts you in closer contact with the computer. After a year in such a transitional state, you can break into the computer field more easily since you can put the word "computer" somewhere on your resumé as "job experience".

If you're a college kid, write programs that help the professors, or help others during your summer vacations. Agree to write the programs for little or no pay. Your goal is *not* money: your goal is to put "experienced programmer" on your resumé.

Interviews

When applying for your first computer job, try to avoid the "personnel" office. The bureaucrats in that office will look at your resumé, see it includes too little experience, and trash it.

Instead, play the who-you-know game. Contact somebody who actually works with computers. Convince that person you're brighter than your resumé indicates. Prove you've learned so much (from reading, courses, and practice) that you can *quickly* conquer any task laid before you. If you impress that person enough, you might get the job even though your paper qualifications look too brief.

When you get an interview, be assertive. Ask the interviewer more questions than the interviewer asks you. Ask the interviewer about the company's computer, and about why the company doesn't have a different one instead. Ask the interviewer how the other people in the company feel about the computer center. Ask the same kinds of questions a data-processing manager would ask. That way, the interviewer will assume you have the potential to become a data-processing manager, and will hire you immediately. You'll also be showing you *care* enough about the company to ask questions. And you'll be showing you have a vibrant personality, and are not just "another vegetable who came through the door".

One of the strange things about applying for a programming job is that the interviewer will *not* ask to see a sample of your work. The interviewer doesn't have time to read your program. Even if the interviewer *did* have time to read your program, he couldn't be sure you wrote it yourself. Instead, the interviewer will just *chat* with you about your accomplishments. You must "talk smart". The best way is to know all the buzzwords of the computer industry — even if they don't really help you write programs.

During the interview, you'll probably be asked whether you know "structured programming". A **structured program** is a program that's well-organized. It consists of a short main routine and many subroutines. To write a structured program, avoid the words GO TO; instead, use words that involve subroutines:

LANGUAGE	Words that involve subroutines
BASIC	GOSUB and RETURN
FORTRAN	CALL, SUBROUTINE, and RETURN
PASCAL	PROCEDURE
COBOL	PERFORM

Later joys In your first job, your salary will be low, but don't worry about it. During your first job, you'll receive lots of training: you're getting a free education. After your training period is over, your salary will rise rapidly — especially if you do extra studying during evenings and weekends. Your *real* job is: to become brilliant.

After you've become brilliant and experienced, other companies will eagerly want to hire you. Your best strategy is to leave your current company and work elsewhere to gain new experiences. *Whenever you feel you're "coasting", and not learning anything new, it's time to move to a different job.* The "different job" can be in a new company — or in a different department of the same company.

By moving around — by gaining a wide variety of experiences — you can eventually become a qualified, wise consultant. And you'll feel like God.

Social contacts Being a programmer is not always glamorous. You'll spend many long hours staring at your screen and wondering why your program doesn't work. The job is intellectual, not social. But after you've become an expert coder, you get into "systems analysis" and "consulting" and "teaching" and "management", and interact with people more.

Software publishing To be a programmer, you do *not* have to work for a large company. Instead, you can sit home, write programs on your personal microcomputer, and sell them to software publishers, for a royalty. If the software publisher sells many copies of your program, you become rich. (On the other hand, if your program is *not* a "smash hit", you remain poor.)

Since your program might not become popular, do *not* rely on software publishing as a steady source of income. Instead, view it as a part-time activity which, if successful, will put some extra money in your pocket.

The most famous software publishers are Microsoft, Lotus, Word Perfect, Ashton-Tate, Borland, Software Publishing Corporation, Symantec, and Electronic Arts. There are many others. Browse through the ads in microcomputer magazines.

Software houses A company whose only goal is to produce software is called a **software house**. Software houses dealing with large computers typically hire full-time programmers and pay them fixed salaries. Software houses dealing with microcomputers sometimes pay royalties instead.

Management

Programming is fun for young kids. But as you get older, you'll tire of machines and want to deal with people instead. As you approach retirement, you'll want to help the younger generation relate to the computers you've mastered.

To be a successful manager, you need three skills: you must be technically competent; you must be wise; and you must know how to handle people.

You should know how to program. Know the strengths and weaknesses of each computer company, and be able to compare their products. Develop a philosophy about what makes a "good" computer center. Understand people's motives and channel them into constructive avenues.

Keep up to date. Read the latest books and periodicals about computers. Chat with other computer experts by phone and at conventions. If you live in New England and care about microcomputers, join the Boston Computer Society (101 First Ave., Suite 2, Waltham MA 02154, 617-290-5700).

When trying to run a computer center, you can easily make mistakes. For example, many computer centers put four-foot-high partitions between their programmers, to give the programmers "privacy"; unfortunately, the partitions are counter-productive: they're too low to block noise, and too high to permit helpful conversation with your neighbor.

When putting a computer center into a school, you must develop a *cadre* of hot-shot students who are bright, friendly, and outgoing, and who will help and encourage the other students to use the computer. If the hot-shots are *not* outgoing — if they become an elitist, snobbish club — the rest of the school will avoid the computer.

If you've hired "programming assistants" who help the programmers, don't let the programming assistants hide in an office or behind a desk. The programming assistants should walk up to the programmers at the computer keyboards and offer help.

In too many organizations, terminals are locked in the offices of prestigious people and aren't used. Let *everybody* share the terminals.

Too often, managers judge their own worth by the size of the computer center's budget: the bigger the budget, the more prestigious the manager. Remember that the sign of being a good manager is *not* having a big budget; the sign of a good manager is the ability to meet the company's needs on a *small* budget.

In computer jargon, a **word** is how many bits the CPU can handle simultaneously. For most microcomputers, a word is 8 bits (i.e., the CPU can handle 8 bits simultaneously); for most minicomputers, a word is 16 bits; for most maxicomputers, a word is 32 bits. A CPU having a big word is prestigious, but might not be cost-effective.

Too often, the head of the computer center decides who can use the computer. So the head of the computer center becomes powerful — and evil. To avoid concentrating so much power in the hands of one bureaucrat, use **distributed processing**: get several small computers instead of one big monster, and give each department its own small computer.

If you're a "microcomputer consultant" and honest, you'll tell your client to buy low-cost popular programs, instead of telling him to pay you to invent "customized" programs.

Sales

You can find three kinds of salesmen.

The "slick" kind knows "how to sell", but doesn't know any technical details about the computer he's selling. He doesn't know how to program, and doesn't know much about the computers sold by his competitors. All he knows is the "line" that his boss told him to give the customers. That kind of salesman usually resorts to off-color tactics, such as claiming that all computers sold by competitors are "toys".

The opposite kind of salesman is technical: he knows every detail about every computer manufactured, but can't give you any *practical* advice about which computer best meets *your* needs.

The best kind of salesman is a consultant. He asks a lot of questions about your particular needs, tells you which of his computers meets your needs best, and even tells you the *limitations* of his computer and why another, more expensive computer sold by a competitor might be better. He's an "honest Joe". He clinches the sale because you trust him, and because you know you won't have any unpleasant surprises after the sale. While selling you a computer, he teaches you a lot. He's a true friend.

A woman can sell computers more easily than a man. That's because most computer customers are men, and men are more attracted to women. It's also because, in our society, women are more "trusted" than men. But if you're a woman, say some technical buzzwords to convince the customer that you're technically competent. Otherwise, the customer will assume that since you're a woman, you must be a "dumb secretary".

Be an entrepreneur

How about starting a rental service, where people can rent microcomputers? How about starting a camp, where kids can spend the summer playing with computers? How about starting a computer set-up service, where you teach businesses how to start using microcomputers? How about writing easy manuals explaining the most popular software? Each of those ideas has been tried successfully; join the fun!

Learn to spell

If you don't spel gud, yur coleegs wil thinc yure an idiut.

Be especially careful with these words, which beginners often misspell:

Wrong	Right	Comments
COBAL	COBOL	"COBOL" means "COmmon Business-Oriented Language". "COBAL" is a co-ed who likes sex.
computor	computer	"Computer" is a machine or person that computes. "Computor" is a snobbish computer.
Dartmouth U.	Dartmouth College	"Dartmouth College" is where BASIC was invented. "Dartmouth U." exists only in utopia.
Epsom	Epson	"Epson" provides printers. "Epsom" provides salt.
hexidecimal	hexadecimal	"Hexadecimal" means "six and ten", or "sixteen". "Hexidecimal" is icky.
hobbiest	hobbyist	A "computer hobbyist" likes computers. A "computer hobbiest" is even more hobbier.
imput	input	"Input" is what the computer takes "in". "Imput" is said only by "im"beciles.
silicone	silicon	"Silicon" is what you put in an integrated circuit. "Silicone" is what you put in your breast.
softwear	software	"Software" is the opposite of "hardware". "Softwear" is a negligée.
TRS-232	RS-232	"RS-232" means "Recommended Standard #232". "TRS-232" means you worship Tandy's Radio Shack.
TSR-80	TRS-80	"TRS-80" stands for "Tandy's Radio Shack". "TSR-80" is a nut who says the alphabet backwards.

For the following words, choose your favorite spelling. . . .

Most computer experts write "disk", but some write "disc".
For "half a byte", humble programmers write "nibble", but snobbish programmers write "nybble".

COMPUTERIZE YOUR HOME

Back in 1970, computerists tried to predict what life would be like in 1990. Let's look at their predictions and see which ones came true.

The predictions appeared in Martin & Norman's *The Computerized Society* (published by Prentice-Hall in 1970), John Kemeny's *Man and the Computer* (published by Scribner's in 1972), and a prize-winning essay by G. Cuttle in 1969.

Work at home

Cuttle said, "It may be more economical for companies to subsidize home 'communications rooms' for their employees than renting expensive office space to commute to. Some establishments are already starting to provide computer terminals for the homes of senior staff. This is sensible when one considers the tendency for great ideas to materialize in the bath. Many of the better characteristics of the cottage industry may return, particularly in terms of personal freedom."

Martin and Norman said, "The first widespread use of home terminals will probably be sponsored by employers. Mothers who participate may be relieved of the boredom they feel when they are unable to leave their children."

Kemeny said, "Executives complain they rush into their offices and then spend half their time talking on the phone, which they could have done equally well at home. Office files will be kept in national computer networks, accessible from home. If the need for millions of people to rush in and out of the city every workday is removed, we'd be well on our way to solving urban problems. Perhaps the central city will become truly an information center where the machines are located but not the humans who use them. Since cities still would have a central location, they might expand their roles as entertainment centers and as places to live for those who insist on seeing a play or sports event in person rather than on TV."

What happened instead Personal computers have become so cheap that most homes contain them instead of terminals attached to timesharing services. Many executives work at home on personal computers during evenings and weekends but still prefer to meet face-to-face with other employees during the day.

Electronic shopping

Martin & Norman: "Instead of coming into a store, the consumer could scan a list of available goods and their prices at different shops on the home terminal, then use the terminal to order."

Kemeny: "For items costing over a dollar, cash transactions will totally disappear."

What happened instead Because banks charge merchants large fees to handle charge cards and fund transfers, merchants require cash for all purchases under $15. Most attempts to develop computerized shopping systems have failed because consumers want to see photographs of goods before buying them. TV shows such as *The Home Shopping Network* succeed because they let consumers view before buying.

Appliances

Cuttle: "Anyone who has any doubts about a computer's ability to cook breakfast has only to remember the average housewife's state of mind at 7AM to realize that preparing breakfast is a very mechanical task indeed. Many other household tasks are equally suitable for computers to invade. At present each piece of equipment needing such a computer has its own small one built in, but the logical development is to have a larger household computer tucked under the stairs. Circuits could be wired through the house so that each individual gadget could be plugged in."

Martin & Norman: "A family driving home after a few days away will phone home and key some digits on the Touch-Tone phone to switch on the heat or air conditioning unit. A woman before leaving for work will preprogram her kitchen equipment to cook a meal; she'll then phone at the appropriate time and have the meal prepared."

What happened instead Now that we have microwave ovens and gourmet frozen dinners, housewives (and househusbands!) can create dinner in less than five minutes without using a computer. Instead of being linked to a big household computer, each appliance contains its own fancy microprocessor (which controls the timing, temperature, etc.), since microprocessors have become so cheap.

Government

Cuttle: "The householder could readily ask the computer whether any legislation in progress affects his neighborhood or interests. He could have far easier access to his congressman than the present system permits. Conversely, he could be asked questions, and this might well be a better way to keep congressmen in touch with the feelings of their constituents."

What happened instead Not enough people have bought modems yet. Some communities have tried using two-way cable instead.

Newspapers

Kemeny: "Let's consider a system under which *The New York Times*, instead of publishing hundreds of thousands of copies, would store the same information in a computer tied to a national network, from which each reader could retrieve the items he wanted, in as much detail as he desired. Sitting at home, he could dial the computer network and ask for his personalized *New York Times*. The computer would remember which topics he normally reads and present stories on them a frame at a time. He could ask for more details. He'd have available at any moment, day or night, completely up-to-date information. The system would make sure he doesn't miss any news that concerns him. If *The New York Times* adopts this suggestion, it should change its motto to 'All the news that you see fit to read.'"

What happened instead On-line services, such as Compuserve, provide the complete text of daily newspapers around the country. Few people use those services, since they cost more than a traditional newspaper and work only while the reader sits by a phone jack.

Medicine

Cuttle: "Automatic diagnosis by computer could be a useful aid. Interrogation through a home terminal could pinpoint some everyday ailments. Much treatment can be carried out at home that today might necessitate hospital treatment. It may be far cheaper and pleasanter for the patient to have monitoring equipment brought to his home and connected through the terminal to a hospital computer."

What happened instead Many doctors and pharmacists use computers to double-check diagnoses and also warn of interactions between drugs. Diagnosis by computer-assisted tomography is widespread in hospitals. Many invalids stuck at home use beepers to call help when needed. Most patients trust neither computers nor doctors.

The whole family

Kemeny: "Father, if he brings his work home from the office, can use the terminal in place of a sizable office staff. Mother can do most of her shopping through a computer terminal. If by 1990 the roles of men and women have been completely reversed, the computer terminal will be equally happy to work out business problems for mother and to help father with his shopping and housework. Children will find the home terminal an immeasurable asset in doing homework; indeed the child of 1990 will find it impossible to conceive how the older generation managed to get through school without the help of a computer."

What happened instead The feminist revolution has encouraged role reversal. Kids use Apple computers mainly to play games, practice programming, do word processing, and run *Print Shop*.

TEACH YOUR KIDS

Here's how to introduce kids to computers.

Curriculum

Here's how to develop the curriculum.

When should kids start learning about computers? Programs have been developed even for kids in nursery school! For example, you can get "alphabet fun" programs: when the kid presses the A key, pictures of apples appear all over the screen; when the kid presses B, the screen is filled with bears; C generates cats, etc. To make the program fun, the pictures on the screen are **animated**; they dance!

Kids should start writing simple programs in BASIC when they're in the third grade. (The brightest kids can start even younger!) Before the third grade, the typical kid should learn how to run other people's programs (by typing the word RUN) and maybe should learn LOGO, which is a language for beginners that's easier than BASIC.

Which kids should take computer courses? *All* kids should be exposed to a computer. They should have the opportunity to press the buttons, type the word RUN, and do other fun things.

All kids should deal with the computer *before* entering high school. The introductory instruction should be broad: it should dip into BASIC programming, hardware jargon, application areas (such as word processing), and social effects.

The introduction is important for *all* kids, regardless of mathematical ability. Remember that most computer programming requires hardly any math.

Kids who are "slow" or who "hate school" should be included, since the computer often acts as a catalyst for making such students "turn on" to school. LOGO's been particularly effective at that.

If your school lacks enough computers to start an extensive program, the best compromise is to wheel the computers from classroom to classroom, so that each kid gets to spend at least a few minutes with the computer each semester.

Kids who want to go beyond introductory concepts should be allowed to join an after-school computer club.

Which language should kids learn to program in? More programs have been written in BASIC than in any other computer language. A person who doesn't understand BASIC is "out of touch" with reality and is a computer illiterate.

Every kid should learn BASIC before graduating from high school.

The youngest kids might also want to experiment with LOGO, which lets you draw pictures more easily than BASIC. The oldest kids might also want to experiment with PASCAL, which is more "sophisticated" than BASIC. But BASIC is the most "practical" language to learn, because it can handle a wider variety of applications than LOGO and PASCAL. (LOGO can't handle random-access files well; PASCAL can't handle output formats well.)

Another advantage of BASIC is that it comes free with most computers. LOGO and PASCAL cost extra.

What should a computer course emphasize? The course should emphasize hands-on programming with a wide variety of amusing applications.

The course should *not* be restricted to math and science. In fact, less than half the programming examples should involve math or science. Most of the examples should involve the arts, business, word processing, etc.

If the computer course is taught by a math teacher, the school's principal should make sure the teacher doesn't spend too much time talking about math.

In the "computer curriculum", how important are music and graphics?
Any computer for kids should play music and draw color graphics, because music and graphics create fun and maintain the kids' interest.

Any course on computer programming should discuss how to program music and graphics. Besides being fun, such a discussion emphasizes that computers are not "just for numbers", and also illustrates visually the effects of programming concepts such as FOR . . . NEXT loops.

In a computer course, what homework should be assigned?
The homework should be to write a computer program. To make that practical, the school must have enough computers to handle all the kids.

Although the teacher should assign some standard exercises, the kids should also be encouraged to invent their *own* programming projects.

In what order should computer topics be taught?
The course should begin with hands-on experience: the kids should write elementary programs (in BASIC or LOGO) and also run programs that others wrote.

As the course progresses and the programming examples become more complex, you should give the kids a breather by frequently inserting light-hearted topics such as video games, computer graphics, word processing, business software, kinds of hardware, computer companies, effects on society, and careers.

Educational applications

The computer can help teach many topics.

English
While trying to write a program, the kid learns the importance of punctuation: the kid learns to distinguish between colons, semicolons, commas, periods, parentheses, and brackets. The kid also learns the importance of spelling: if the kid misspells the word PRINT or INPUT, the computer gripes. The kid learns to handle long words, while wading through computer manuals.

Some kids "hate to write English compositions". The computer can change that attitude! If you let a kid use an easy word-processing program (such as Writing Assistant), the kid suddenly discovers that writing an English composition can be fun! The composition suddenly becomes "electronic"; it appears on the television screen! And revising the composition can be even *more* fun since the kid gets to use all the nifty "editing" keys on the keyboard. The whole experience becomes as much fun as a video game. A high-quality word processor also corrects the kid's spelling without forcing the kid to endlessly thumb through the dictionary; it even corrects the kid's grammar and style. Watching the computer correct the spelling, grammar, and style is educational and fun.

To make the kid understand why parts of speech (such as "nouns", "verbs", and "adjectives") are important, give the kid a computer program that writes sentences by choosing random nouns, random verbs, and random adjectives. Then tell the kid to invent his *own* nouns, verbs, and adjectives, feed them into the program, and watch what kind of sentences the program produces now.

Young kids enjoy a program called **Story Machine**. It gives you a list of nouns, verbs, adjectives, and other parts of speech that you can use to build a story. You type the story using any words on the list. As you type the story, the computer *automatically illustrates it!* For example, if you type, "The boy eats the apple," your screen will automatically show a picture of a boy eating an apple! If you type *several* sentences, to form a longer story, the computer will automatically illustrate the entire story and produce an animated cartoon of it! The program also criticizes your story's structure. For example, if you say "The boy eats the apple" but the boy isn't near the apple yet, the program will recommend that you insert a sentence such as "The boy runs to the apple" beforehand. The program comes on a $25 disk from Spinnaker Software (1 Kendall Square, Cambridge, MA 02139, phone 617-494-1200). To run the program, you need an Apple computer.

History
The computer can make history come "alive", by throwing the student into the middle of an historical situation. For example, a graduate of my intensive teacher-training institute wrote a program that says, "It's 1910. You're Kaiser Wilhelm. What are you going to do?" Then it gives you several choices. For example, it asks "Would you like to make a treaty with Russia?" If you answer "yes", the computer replies, "Russia breaks the treaty. *Now* what are you going to do?" No matter how you answer the questions, there are only two ways the program can end: either "You've plunged Europe into a World War" or "You've turned Germany into a second-rate country". After running that program several times, you get a real feeling for the terrible jam that the Kaiser was in, and you begin to pity him. Running the program is more dramatic than reading a book about the Kaiser's problems, because the program forces you to step into the Kaiser's shoes and react to his surroundings: you are there. When you finish running the program, you feel you've lived another life — the life of a 1910 Kaiser.

Such a program is called an historical **simulation**, since it makes the computer **simulate** (imitate) an historical event.

Current events
The best way to teach about current events is through simulation.

For example, when California's Governor Brown had trouble controlling medflies, teachers wrote programs that began by saying, "You're Governor Brown. What are you going to do?" (One of the programs was even called "Medfly Mania".)

The best way to encourage the student to analyze the conflict between Israel and the Arabs is to tell the student to run a program that begins by saying "You're Israel's Prime Minister" and then run a program that begins by saying "You're the PLO's leader, Yassir Arafat". By running both programs, the student learns to take both sides of the argument and understands the emotions of both leaders. Such programs could help warring nations understand each other enough to bring peace!

When Three-Mile Island almost exploded, teachers wrote a program that says "You're in the control room at Three-Mile Island". Your computer's screen shows a high-resolution color picture of the control room. Your goal is to make as much money as possible for the electric company, without blowing the place up. You can buy two versions of the program: one's called just "Three-Mile Island"; the other's called "Scram". To teach kids about Three-Mile Island, it's easier to buy the program than to get permission from parents to "take the kids on a field trip to Three-Mile Island" (which also requires that you sit on a bus while listening to 100 choruses of "100 bottles of beer on the wall" and worrying about kids who get lost at Three-Mile Island).

The best way to teach economics and politics is to give the student a program that says "You're running the country" and then asks the student to input an economic and political strategy. At the end of the program, the computer tells how many years the student lasted in office, how well the country fared, and how many people want to assassinate him.

The best way to learn anything is "by experience". Computer simulations let the student learn by "simulated experience", which condenses into a few minutes what would otherwise require many *years* of "natural experience".

Biology
The computer can do genetics calculations: it can compute the probabilities of having various kinds of offspring and predict how the characteristics of the population will shift over time.

The computer can handle taxonomy: it can classify different kinds of animals and plants. The computer asks you a series of questions about an organism and finally tells you the organism's name. One of the most popular programs is a game called "Animals", which lets the student teach the computer which questions to ask.

To teach ecology, a graduate of my teacher-training institute wrote a simulation program that begins by saying, "You're the game warden of New Jersey. What are you going to do?" For example, it asks how many weeks you want the deer-hunting season to last. If you make the hunting season too long, the hunters kill all the deer, and the deer-loving environmentalists hate you. On the other hand, if you make the deer-hunting season too *short*, the *hunters* hate you; moreover, the deer overpopulate, can't find enough to eat, and then die of starvation, whereupon *everybody* hates you. Your goal is to stay in office as long as possible.

Sex education
When Dartmouth College (which for centuries had been all-male and rowdy) suddenly became co-ed in 1971, its biology department realized the importance of teaching about birth control. The professors wrote a program that asks how old you are and which birth control method you wish to use this year. You have 9 choices, such as pill, diaphragm, IUD, condom, rhythm method, and "Providence".

After you type your choice, the computer computes the probabilities and may print (if you're unlucky) ***BOY*** or ***GIRL***. The computation is based, as in nature, on a combination of science and chance (random numbers). Then the computer asks your strategy for the next year.

The program continues until the computer finally prints ***MENOPAUSE***.

The program lets you explore how different strategies will result in different numbers of children. It's safer to experiment with the program than to experiment on your body. It's also faster. But maybe it's not as much fun!

How can programs that tutor, drill, and test students be made exciting?
The programs should use the same techniques that make video games exciting.

Specifically, the programs should include color graphics and animation, require the student to answer quickly, and display a running total of the student's points, so that each time the student answers a question correctly the score on the screen increases immediately.

At the end of the educational game, the computer shouldn't say "excellent" or "fair" or "poor". Instead, the computer should simply state the total number of points accumulated (which should be in the thousands) and then ask whether the student would like to try again, to increase the score.

If the student's score is exceptionally high, the computer should reward the student by giving lots of praise and by storing the student's name on the disk. If the student's score is low, no criticism should be given other than asking "Would you like to try again?"

Purchasing
When your school decides to buy computers, it will face these issues.

How many computers to buy
The more the better! Whatever the school can afford!

Stick to a single brand, or buy a variety?
The students should see a wide variety of computers, because each computer has its own strengths and weaknesses. The best business software is on the IBM PC, the best graphics and music software is on the Macintosh, and the best educational software is on the Apple 2GS.

The school should decide on a "main" brand of computer (to simplify the lectures about programming) but also buy samples of other brands (for demonstrations and for advanced students).

Best computer for teaching programming
The best versions of BASIC require a Commodore Amiga, IBM PC, or clone. For a lower-cost alternative, get Radio Shack Color Computer or a used Commodore 128. Their versions of BASIC are all far superior to the Apple 2's.

How to get free software
If you're a teacher, tell your hot-shot students to write the software for you. Your students will love the opportunity to work on a project that's useful. Tell the students that if their software is good you'll write them glowing recommendations saying that they computerized the school.

Many software publishers give educational discounts. Some publishers offer "site licenses", where you pay a large fee up front but then can make as many copies of the software as you wish, free.

The nicest publishers of business software offer "trial size" versions for $10 or even free. Nice trial-size versions let you try all the software's keystrokes and commands but require you to keep your documents and files brief — just long enough so that you can study and evaluate the software but short enough so that you'll eventually want to buy the full versions.

For example, trial-size versions of word processors restrict you to one-page documents; trial-size database programs restrict you to 15-record files. When you try to exceed those limits, the software makes the computer say, "Not available in trial size. Buy the full version."

Trial-size versions are nicknamed "crippled software". Software publishers often let you copy them free, so that you and your students and friends can run "software test drives" and "software taste tests".

Management

After buying computers, the school's administration must decide what to do with them.

Should you let kids play video games on the school's computers?
Give every kid the experience of briefly playing video games because they're fun, encourage speed and agility, reward self-improvement, create a positive attitude towards computers and technology, lead the kid to thinking about strategies and programming methods, and provide examples of the best programs ever invented.

But discourage kids from spending *excessive* time on games. Give game-players lower priority than other kids who want to use the computers. To do that, you can restrict game-playing to just a few of the computers or a few times of the day, or require game-players to leave whenever non-game-players want to use their computers.

By charging a small fee for game-playing, you can collect enough money to buy more computers.

Which room should contain the computers?
The safest place to put the computers is in the library. That reduces the chance of theft, encourages disks to be checked out like books, and makes sure the computer lab is run by a humanities-oriented librarian instead of a narrow-minded mathematician.

Most librarians know how to run audio-visual equipment and communicate with large databases and therefore *don't* fear technology. Since librarians enjoy the humanities (especially reading) and nevertheless are comfortable with scientific technology, librarians are the ideal choice for running a computer center that meets the needs of the *whole* school. And the library's the only place in the school where all the students and faculty can feel comfortable — except for the cafeteria.

Try moving some cheap computers into the cafeteria for students to use during lunch and study breaks. That will increase the computers' visibility and turn lunch into an intellectual affair. With adequate supervision, you can overcome the cafeteria's dangers (theft, food fights, and spilled drinks).

How can you supervise the computers cheaply?
You can get parents to volunteer. Many parents would love the opportunity to work in a computer environment, in the hope of entering a full-blown computer career later.

If the students in your school's computer club act responsibly, you can turn the club into a "Computer Service Organization" that helps teach the rest of the school about computers. The club's members can mention such service on their resumés, which will help them get into college.

Give a speech to all students: tell them that when they're using the computers they should help each other. Encourage teamwork.

Should you let students use the administration's computer?
The administration's computer handles the school's budget, payroll, schedules, attendance records, and report cards. Don't give students access to the disks containing that information.

But students *should* occasionally use the administration's computer (if the students use special "student disks" instead), because the students should see how a *big* computer operates. The brightest and most trustworthy students might even help the administration write some programs (though students shouldn't gain access to the real data).

AVOID DANGERS

How could computers change human society? The many good ways are obvious. Here are the bad ones.

Errors

Although the computer can have a mechanical breakdown, the usual reason for computer errors is *mental* breakdown — on the part of the people who run it. The usual computer blooper is caused by a programmer who writes an incorrect program, or a user who inputs a wrong number. If you want the computer to write a check for $10.00, but you forget to type the decimal point, the computer will nonchalantly write a check for $1000.

The biggest computer blooper ever made occurred at Cape Kennedy. A rocket rose majestically from its launch pad and headed toward Venus. Suddenly it began to wobble. It had to be destroyed after less than 5 minutes of flight. The loss was put at $18,500,000. What went wrong? After much head-scratching, the answer was finally found. In one of the lines of one of the programs, a programmer omitted a hyphen.

In one city's computer center, every inhabitant's vital statistics were put on cards. One lady in the town was 107, but the number 107 wouldn't fit on the card properly, because the space allotted for AGE was only two digits. The computer just examined the last two digits, which were 07, and assumed she was 7 years old. Since she was 7 and not going to school, the computer printed a truant notice. So city officials visited the home of the 107-year-old lady and demanded to see her mom.

A man in Germany received a bill from a computer requesting the payment of "zero deutschmark". He ignored it, but two weeks later the machine sent him a letter reminding him that he had not paid the sum of "zero deutschmark". Two weeks after that another and more strongly worded letter arrived. He still took no action other than photocopying the letters and gleefully showing them to his friends. But the computer persisted and eventually announced that it was referring his failure to pay to the company lawyers. So he telephoned the company. They explained to him there was a minor oversight in the program, assured him it was being corrected, but requested him to send a check for "zero deutschmark" to simplify the reconciliation. He duly made out a check for "0.0 DM." and mailed it. Two days later the check was returned to him from the bank with a polite (nonautomated) letter stating that the bank's computer was unable to process the check.

That last anecdote was from Martin and Norman's *The Computerized Society*. This is from *Time Magazine*:

> Rex Reed, writer and sometime actor, ordered a bed from a Manhattan department store. Three months passed. Then came the long anticipated announcement: the bed will be delivered on Friday.
>
> Reed waited all day. No bed. Having disposed of his other bed, he slept on the floor.
>
> Next day deliverers brought the bed but couldn't put it up. No screws.
>
> On Monday, men appeared with the screws. But they couldn't put in the mattresses. No slats. "That's not our department."
>
> Reed hired a carpenter to build them. The department store's slats finally arrived 15 weeks later.
>
> Undaunted, Reed went to the store to buy sheets. Two men came up and declared: "You're under arrest." Why? "You're using a stolen credit card. Rex Reed is dead." Great confusion. Reed flashed all his identity cards. The detectives apologized — and then tore up his store charge card. Why? "Our computer has been told that you are dead. And we cannot change this."

On a less humorous note, a woman died from freezing, because an errant computer thought she hadn't paid her utility bill.

Unemployment

Since the computer's a labor-saving device, it may make laborers unemployed. Clerks and other low-echelon white-collar workers might find themselves jobless and penniless.

The newspaper companies in New York City have realized they'd save money by hiring fewer printers and using computers instead. But the printers union, upset, cried "Breach of contract!" The companies and printers finally agreed to get the computers, hire no new printers, but retain the current ones until retirement.

The advent of computers doesn't have to mean a net loss of jobs. In fact, new ones are created. Not all computer-related jobs require abstract thinking: there's a need for mechanics, typists, secretaries, salesmen, editors, librarians, etc. There is a need for people to tell the programmers what kind of things to program. Running a computer center is a business, and there's a need for businessmen.

When computers do human work, will there be *enough* work left for us humans to do? Don't worry: when no work is necessary, humans have an amazing talent for inventing it. That's the purpose of Madison Avenue — to create new longings. Instead of significantly shortening the work week, Americans have always opted for a work week of nearly equal length but devoted to more luxurious ends. That's the gung-ho Protestant work ethic we're so famous for. Computers will change but not reduce our work.

. . . That's what will happen in the long run. But for the next decade or two, as society shifts to computers, many folks will be temporarily out of a job.

Quantification

Since the computer handles numbers easily, it encourages people to reduce problems to numbers. That's both good and bad. It's good because it forces people to be precise. It's bad because some people are starting to make quantification a goal in itself, forgetting that it's but a tool to other ends. Counting the words that Shakespeare wrote is of no value in itself: it must be put to some use. In both the humanities and the social sciences, I'm afraid the motto of the future will be, "If you can't think, count." Some cynics have remarked, "The problem with computers is that they make meaningless research possible."

Since only quantifiable problems can be computerized, there's a danger that, in a burst of computer enthusiasm, people will decide that unquantifiable problems aren't worth investigating, or that unquantifiable aspects of an otherwise quantifiable problem should be ignored. John Kemeny gives this example:

I've heard a story about the design of a new freeway in the City of Los Angeles.

At an open hearing, a number of voters complained bitterly that the freeway would go right through the midst of a part of the city heavily populated by blacks and would destroy the spirit of community they'd slowly and painfully built up. The voters' arguments were defeated by the simple statement that, according to an excellent computer, the proposed route was the best possible one.

Apparently none of them knew enough to ask how the computer had been instructed to evaluate the variety of possible routes. Was it asked only to consider the costs of building and acquiring property (in which case it would have found routing through a ghetto area highly advantageous), or was it also asked to take into account human suffering that a given route would cause?

Perhaps the voters would even have agreed it's not possible to measure human suffering in terms of dollars. But if we omit consideration of human suffering, then we're equating its cost to zero, which is certainly the worst of all procedures!

People are being reduced to numbers: telephone numbers, social security numbers, zip codes, etc. When you start treating another human as just a wrong telephone number, and hang up in his face, something is wrong.

Asocial behavior

The computer's a seductive toy. When you walk up to it, you expect to spend just a few minutes but wind up spending several hours instead. Whether catching bugs or playing Pac-Man, you'll probably while away lots of time. You may find yourself spending more time with the computer than with people. That can be dangerous. For the average American child, his mother is a television set. Will the computer replace T.V. as the national fixation?

Getting along with the computer is easy — perhaps *too* easy. Though it can gripe at you, it can't yell. If you don't like its behavior, you can turn it off. You can't do the same thing to people. Excessive time spent with the computer can leave you unprepared for the ambiguities and tensions of real life.

The computer replaces warmth by precision. Excessive time spent with it might inhibit your development as a loving individual.

Irresponsibility

Computerization is part of the oncoming technological bureaucracy. Like all bureaucracy, it encourages the individual to say, "Don't blame me — I can't change the bureaucracy." Only now the words will read, "Don't blame me — the computer did it."

When John Kemeny's sister asked a saleswoman whether a certain item was in stock, the woman said she couldn't answer, because the information was kept by a computer. The woman hadn't been able to answer questions about stock even before the computer came in — the computer was just a new scapegoat.

Computers will eventually be used to run governments and wars. The thought of someone saying, "I can't change that — that's the way the computer does it" is frightening.

Concentrated power

As computers amass more and more information about people, the computers will become centers of knowledge. The people who control them — the programmers, sociologists, generals, and politicians — will gain a lot of power. The thought of so much power being concentrated in the hands of a few is frightening. A handful of people, pressing the wrong buttons, could atom-bomb the earth.

Nobody should have complete control over a computer center. The power should be diversified. Sensitive data and programs should be protected by passwords and other devices, so that no single individual can get access to all of it.

Crime

The computer is the biggest tool in the kit of the white-collar criminal. All he has to do is insert a zero on a tape, and the computer will send him a paycheck for ten times the correct amount.

To catch such criminals, computers are programmed to do a lot of double-checking; but if the criminal evades the double-checks, he won't get caught. Police have a hard time tracking down computer criminals, because fingerprints and other traditional forms of evidence are irrelevant. Most computers have passwords to try to stop people from fooling around with sensitive data, but a bright programmer can devise various tricks to get around the passwords. The crudest is to bug the wires that go to the terminals. The cleverest is to slip extra lines into an innocent program, and get someone else to run it; the extra lines transfer money to the programmer's account.

Since you must be quite smart to be a computer criminal, if you're caught you're likely to be admired. The usual reaction of people is not — "What a terrible thing you've done!" — but rather — "Gee, you must be smart. Tell me, how did you do it?" A bright button-down computer criminal who steals $100,000 electronically usually gets a lighter sentence than the dude who must resort to a gun to get $1000. Is that justice?

Invaded privacy

Of all the harm computers can do, "invaded privacy" worries people the most. George Orwell, in his book *1984*, warned that someday "Big Brother will be watching you" via a computer. His prediction's already a reality: your whereabouts are constantly checked by computers owned by the FBI, the IRS, the military, credit-card companies, and mail-order houses. My brother once wrote an innocent letter asking for stamps. Instead of using his own name, he used the name of our dog, Rusty. Since then, we've received letters from many organizations, all addressed to "Mr. Rusty". Our dog's name sits in computers all across the country.

The information computers have stored about you may be misleading. If you never find out about the error, the consequences can haunt you the rest of your life. Examples:

A teacher saw one of the little boys in her class kiss another boy. She entered on his computerized school records, "displays homosexual tendencies".

According to computer records, a certain man had "three lawsuits against him". In fact, the first was a scare suit 30 years before, over a magazine subscription he had never ordered; the second had been withdrawn after a compromise over a disputed fee; the third case had been settled in his favor.

You have a right to see what information is stored about you, and change it if it's incorrect. For example, if a teacher or employer writes a "confidential recommendation" about you, you have a right to examine it, to prevent misleading statements from haunting you for life.

Even if the information stored about you is accurate, you have a right to prevent its dissemination to the world in general. No organization should store or disseminate information unjustifiably.

What is "justifiable"? Fearing "Big Brother", people don't want politicians to access personal information. On the other hand, fearing criminals, people want the police to have a free hand in sleuthing. How to give information to the police without giving it to politicians can be puzzling.

Outdated information should be obliterated. An individual shouldn't be haunted by his distant past; he should be given a chance to turn over a new leaf. Moreover, information 50 years old may be couched in words that have been redefined. To be a "leftist", for example, means something different in each decade.

Only facts should be stored, not opinions. It's okay to store that someone lives on Fifth Avenue, but not that he lives in a "nice neighborhood".

It's unfortunate that people feel a need for privacy. If the information stored about you is correct, why argue? But many people feel a need to be secretive, and I suppose people do have that right. It's sometimes called the right to be "let alone".

People don't want to feel their whole lives are on stage, recorded by a computer. It inhibits them from acting free and natural. Even if the computer doesn't store any damaging information about you, the mere *thought* that your every action is being recorded is damaging, because it makes you act more conservatively. You may be afraid of adopting a good but unusual lifestyle, because anything "different" about you will look bad on the computerized records used by banks, credit-card companies, insurance companies, and other conservative institutions. The harmful thing is not that Big Brother is watching, but that you *feel* he's watching. You are subjugated.

READ GOOD BOOKS

Begin by reading *The Secret Guide to Computers*.

Then read the hardware and software manuals that came with your computer. Although a beginner can't understand those manuals, *you'll* understand them — after you've mastered *The Secret Guide to Computers*!

Then read some of the books listed on the next page. For each topic, I've listed the two best books. If you read both books about the topic, you'll become an expert. For each book, I've listed the title, author, and publisher.

The typical book costs about $20. Publishers raise their prices every year. (I'm the only publisher whose prices move in the opposite direction.)

Details of popular microcomputers

repairing IBM clones: *Keeping Your PC Alive* by Boyce (New Riders Publishing)
The Complete PC Upgrade and Maintenance Guide by Minasi (Sybex)

MS-DOS: *DOS for Dummies* by Gookin (IDG)
Running MS-DOS by Wolverton (Microsoft)

Windows software: *More Windows for Dummies* by Rathbone (IDG)
Multimedia Madness by Wodaski (Sams)

Mac: *Macs for Dummies* by Pogue (IDG)
The Macintosh Bible by Naiman (Goldstein & Blair)

classic computers: *Apple 2 User's Guide* by Poole et al (Osborne/McGraw-Hill)
A Guide to Programming the Commodore Comp'rs by Presley (Lawrenceville)

The computer's subculture

subculture's history: *Fire in the Valley* by Freiberger & Swaine (Osborne/McGraw-Hill)
Hackers by Levy (Anchor/Doubleday)

biographies of Bill Gates: *Hard Drive* by Wallace & Erickson (Wiley)
Gates by Manes & Andrews (Doubleday)

subculture's fun facts: *The Naked Computer* by Rochester & Gantz (Morrow)
The New Hacker's Dictionary by Raymond (MIT Press)

on-line services: *Cruising America Online* by Gardner & Beatty (Prima)
Internet for Windows: AOL Edition by Gardner & Beatty & Sauer (Prima)

Programming

BASIC: *BASIC & the Personal Computer* by Dwyer & Critchfield (Addison-Wesley)
A Guide to Programming: IBM Personal Computer by Presley (Lawrenceville)

DBASE: *Everyman's Database Primer* by Byers (Ashton-Tate/Borland)
DBASE 2 for the Programmer by Dinerstein (Scott Foresman)

PASCAL: *Introduction to PASCAL* by Zaks (Sybex)
Oh! Pascal! by Cooper & Clancy (Norton)

C: *The C Programming Language* by Kernighan & Ritchie (Prentice-Hall)
The C Primer by Hancock & Krieger (McGraw-Hill)

LOGO: *LOGO for the Apple* by Abelson (McGraw-Hill)
Mindstorms by Papert (Basic Books)

FORTRAN: *FORTRAN 77 for Humans* by Page & Didday (West)
The Elements of FORTRAN Style by Kreitzberg & Shneiderman (Harcourt)

COBOL: *A Simplified Guide to Structured COBOL Prog'ing* by McCracken (Wiley)
Structured ANS COBOL by Murach & Noll (2 volumes, Mike Murach)

assembler for IBM PC: *Assembly Language Primer for the IBM PC&XT* by Lafore (Plume/New American Library)
Peter Norton's Assembly Language Book for the IBM PC by Norton & Socha (Brady/Prentice-Hall)

assembler for mainframes: *Assembly Language Programming* by Tuggle (Science Research Associates)
Systems Programming by Donovan (McGraw-Hill)

surveys of languages: *Introduction to Programming Languages* by Peterson (Prentice-Hall)
Programming Languages by Tucker (McGraw-Hill)

ADA: *Introduction to ADA* by Price (Prentice-Hall)
Programming in ADA by Wegner (Prentice-Hall)

FORTH: *Starting FORTH* by Brodie (Prentice-Hall)
FORTH Fundamentals Volume 1 by McCabe (Dilithium)

string-handling languages: *LISP* by Winston & Horn (Addison-Wesley)
The SNOBOL4 Programming Language by Griswold & Poage & Polonsky (Prentice-Hall)

numeric languages: *Statistical Package for the Social Sciences* by Nie et al (McGraw-Hill)
APL an Interactive Approach by Gilman & Rose (Wiley)

Thank you for reading *The Secret Guide to Computers*. If you have any questions about what you've read, phone me at (617) 666-2666, day or night.

Editions

You've been reading the 20th edition. I've been revising the *Guide* for over 20 years:

Edition	Copyrt.	Format	Total pages, $		How typed	What it praised	New tutorials it included
edition 0	1972	pamphlet	17 pages	free	typewriter	HP-2000	BASIC
edition 1	1972	pamphlet	12 pages	free	typewriter	DEC-10	DEC computers
edition 2	1972	pamphlet	20 pages	free	typewriter	DEC-10	FORTRAN
edition 3	1972	pamphlet	32 pages	$1	typewriter	DEC-10	data files
edition 4	1973	2 pamphlets	63 pages	$2	typewriter	DEC-10	ALGOL
edition 5	1973	booklet	73 pages	$2	typewriter	DEC-10	graphics
edition 6	1974	3 booklets	260 pages	$5.20	typewriter	DEC-10	artificial intelligence, numerical analysis
editions 7-9	1976-1979	6 booklets	410 pages	$16.25	typewriter	TRS-80 model 1	hardware, micros, COBOL, language survey
edition 10	1980-1982	8 booklets	696 pages	$29.60	typewriter	TRS-80 model 3	discount dealers, video graphics, PASCAL
edition 11	1984	2 books	750 pages	$28	TRS-80 model 3	IBM PC	IBM PC, word processing
edition 12	1986-1987	3 books	909 pages	$24	TRS-80 model 3	clones by Leading Edge	DOS, WordPer., 1-2-3, DBASE, C, LOGO, 8088
edition 13	1988	3 books	909 pages	$24	TRS-80 model 3	clones by Swan	Q&A
edition 14	1990	reference	607 2-col.	$15	Word Perfect 5.0	clones by Gateway	Mac, Excel, Quattro
edition 15	1991	reference	607 2-col.	$15	Word Perfect 5.1	clones by Gateway	Windows, Ami Pro, advanced Word Perfect
edition 16	1992	reference	607 2-col.	$15	Word Perfect 5.1	clones by Micro Express	DOS 5, Quattro Pro
edition 17	1993	reference	607 2-col.	$15	Word Perfect 5.1	clones by VTech	Mac System 7, Microsoft Word, Excel 4, repairs
edition 18	1993	reference	607 2-col.	$15	Word Perfect 5.1	clones by VTech	DOS 6
edition 19	1994	reference	639 2-col.	$15	Word Perfect 5.1	clones by VTech	Pentium, multimedia computers, DOS 6.2
edition 20	1995	reference	639 2-col.	$15	Word Perfect 5.1	clones by Quantex	Microsoft Word 6, Terminal, AMIBIOS

To get on the mailing list for a *free* brochure about the 21st edition, use the coupon on page 639, or just send me a postcard with your name, address, and the words "send 21st edition info".

Let's meet

I hope to meet you someday. If you ever visit the Boston area, drop in, say hello, and browse through my computer library. My heavy workload prevents me from chatting long, but at least we can grin.

If you like, join one of my blitz courses, where we cover everything worth knowing about computers in one intensive weekend. I give the course in many cities and charge just $2.50 per hour.

I can also visit your home town and give a course to you and your friends privately. If you have lots of friends, the cost per person can get quite cheap.

For more information about what I can do for you at little or no charge, phone me at (617) 666-2666 or mail the coupon on the back page.

How to give a course

After you practice using computers and become a computer expert, why not give your *own* courses? You too can become a guru. Here are some suggestions.

When giving a course, you won't have enough time to cover every detail, so don't even try. Tell the students that the details can be found in *The Secret Guide to Computers* and the manuals that come with their computers.

Instead of grinding through details, have fun! **Demonstrate** hardware and software that the audience hasn't seen, **argue cheerily** about computer hassles, **let the audience ask lots of questions**, and give the audience **hands-on experience aided by tutors**.

Here are some of the lines I use to liven up my classes and loosen up my students. Feel free to copy them.

"Hi, I'm Russ. I'm supposed to turn all of you into computer experts by five o'clock. I'll try."

"In this course, I'm your slave. Anything you want, you get."

"If you're a boring group, we'll follow the curriculum. If you're interesting, you'll ask lots of questions and we'll dig into the good stuff."

"Don't bother taking notes. If God wanted you to be a Xerox machine, He would have made you look that way. So just relax. If you forget what I say, phone me anytime, and I'll repeat it all back to you."

"There's no attendance requirement. Leave whenever you wish. If we hit a topic that bores you, that's a good time to go to the bathroom, get some munchies, or take a walk in the fresh air. Better yet, play with the computers at the back of the room, so you become super-smart. The tutors will get you any software you wish."

When you're planning to teach a course, phone me for free help with curriculum, dramatics, and tricks of the trade.

Your first course might have some rough edges, because you haven't had experience yet in giving demonstrations, fielding audience questions, and dramatically varying the pace so that your audience stays awake. So for your first course, play safe: charge as little as possible, so everybody in the audience feels the course was a "good deal" and a "wonderful bargain" and nobody feels "ripped off". For that first course your goal should *not* be money: instead, your goal should be to gain experience and a good reputation.

No matter how great you think you are, your audience will tire of you eventually. To keep your audience awake, offer variety by including your friends as part of your act.

Good luck. Try hard. You can cast a spell over the audience. Courses change lives.

Your source of free help,
At your service,
Your computer butler,

Russ

(617) 666-2666

NUMERIC ANALYSIS

ERRORS

Computers make mathematical errors. Here's why.

Twin problems that confuse the computer

Look at this pair of problems. . . .

Problem 1: solve the equation $x^2 - 4x + 4 = 0$.
Problem 2: solve the equation $x^2 - 4x + 3.9999999 = 0$.

Those two problems resemble each other. The only difference is that where the second problem says 3.9999999, the first problem says 4. But the correct solutions to the problems are quite different from each other:

The correct solution to problem 1 is "$x = 2$".
The correct solution to problem 2 is "$x = 1.9996838$ or $x = 2.0003162$".

Unfortunately, problem 1 looks so similar to problem 2 that the computer can hardly tell the difference. **Some computers treat 3.9999999 as if it were 4.** If you ask such a computer to solve problem 2, it will solve problem 1 instead, and its answer to problem 2 will therefore be wrong.

Here's another pair of problems. . . .

Problem 3: solve the equation $(x-1)*(x-2)*(x-3)*(x-4)*...*(x-20) = 0$.

Problem 4: solve the equation $(x-1)*(x-2)*(x-3)*(x-4)*...*(x-20) -2^{-23}*x^{19} = 0$.

Those two problems resemble each other. In fact, if you "expand the polynomial", you'll see that problem 3 can be rewritten like this:

$x^{20} - 210x^{19} + ... = 0.$

Problem 4 can be rewritten like this:

$x^{20} - (210+2^{-23})x^{19} + ... = 0.$

So problem 4 differs from problem 3 just by saying $210+2^{-23}$ instead of 210. Since 2^{-23} is a tiny number (approximately .0000001), some computers can't tell the difference between 210 and $210+2^{-23}$, can't distinguish problem 4 from problem 3, and say the same answer to problem 4 as to problem 3. But the *correct* solutions to the two problems are different:

The correct solution to problem 3 is "$x=1$ or $x=2$ or $x=3$ or $x=4$ or ... or $x=20$".

The correct solution to problem 4 is "$x=1.000$ or $x=2.000$ or $x=3.000$ or $x=4.000$ or $x=5.000$ or $x=6.000$ or $x=7.000$ or $x=8.007$ or $x=8.917$ or $x=10.095\pm.644i$ or $x=11.794\pm1.652i$ or $x=13.992\pm1.519i$ or $x=16.731\pm2.813i$ or $x=19.502\pm1.940i$ or $x=20.847$". (i denotes the square root of -1.)

Here's one more case. . . .

Problem 5: solve the simultaneous equations "$913x+659y=254$ and $780x+563y=217$".
Problem 6: solve the simultaneous equations "$913x+659y=254$ and $780x+563y=216.999$".

Although the problems are almost identical (so that some computers can't distinguish them from each other), the correct solutions are quite different:

The correct solution to problem 5 is "$x=1$ and $y=-1$".
The correct solution to problem 6 is "$x=.341$ and $y=-.087$".

That last case of "confusing twins" leads to this fascinating paradox. . . . Suppose you tell your friendly computer to "guess" an x and y to solve problem 5:

$913x + 659y = 254$
$780x + 563y = 217$

If the computer guesses "$x=.999$ and $y=-1.001$", it finds:

$913x + 659y = 252.428$
$780x + 563y = 215.757$

But if the computer guesses "$x=.341$ and $y=-.087$" instead, it finds:

$913x + 659y = 254$
$780x + 563y = 216.999$, which is about 217

The computer therefore deduces that its second guess is almost perfect and much better than its first guess. But — here's the paradox — the second guess is *not*

better than the first guess; the *first* guess is better, because the correct solution is "$x=1$ and $y=-1$", which is closer to the *first* guess.

Reduce round-off error

By the laws of mathematics, $5+.14+.14+.14$ should be the same as $.14+.14+.14+5$. But a calculator that holds just two significant digits gives different answers:

5+.14+.14+.14	.14+.14+.14+5
5.0	.14
+.14	+.14
5.1	.28
+.14	+.14
5.2	.42
+.14	+5.0
5.3	5.4

Since the correct answer is 5.42, the calculation on the right is more accurate. The general rule is: **when adding a list of numbers, you'll get more accuracy if you begin with the numbers closest to 0**. The rule is valid even on a top-quality computer, although the computer's inaccuracies are not so obvious.

By the laws of mathematics, $(3\frac{1}{5} - 3\frac{1}{7})*70$ is 4:

$3\frac{1}{5} = 3\frac{7}{35}$

$-3\frac{1}{7} = 3\frac{5}{35}$

$\frac{2}{35} * 70 = 4$

But if we try that calculation on our two-digit calculator, we get a totally different answer:

$3\frac{1}{5} = 3+.2 = 3.2$

$-3\frac{1}{7} = 3+.14 = 3.1$

$.1 * 70 = 7.0$

The general warning is: **when you subtract two numbers that are almost equal (like $3\frac{1}{5}$ and $3\frac{1}{7}$), few of the digits in your answer will be correct.** The warning is valid even on a top-quality computer, although the computer's inaccuracies are not so obvious.

ESTIMATES

The computer can estimate an answer.

Connecting the dots

Suppose you're given the value of y when x is 1, 2, 3, 4, and 5:

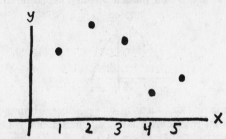

Suppose you'd like to make an "intelligent guess" as to the value of y when x is 1.5, 3.01, 100, -400, and other values. Guessing y for an in-between x (such as 1.5 and 3.01) is called **interpolation**; guessing y for a very large x or a very small x (such as 100 and -400) is called **extrapolation**.

One way to guess is to connect the points with line segments:

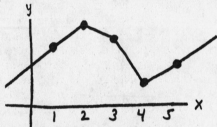

That's called **piecewise linear** estimation.

You get a much smoother picture by using a **cubic spline**:

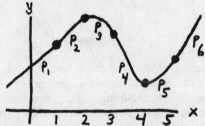

P_1 and P_6 are parts of straight lines. P_2, P_3, P_4, and P_5 are parts of four different cubics (third-degree polynomials), chosen so that, at the point where P_i meets P_{i+1}, P_i has the same **derivative** and **second derivative** as P_{i+1}. (The term "derivative" is defined by calculus.)

Least-square line

Suppose you're given these **approximate** values of y:

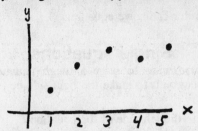

To estimate y for other values of x, you could use piecewise linear estimation or a cubic spline. But notice the points lie almost on a straight line:

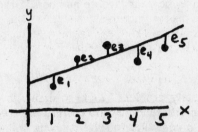

The points aren't exactly on that line; the errors in the y values are e_1, e_2, e_3, e_4, and e_5. The line's **squared error** is $e_1^2 + e_2^2 + e_3^2 + e_4^2 + e_5^2$. This line has a larger squared error:

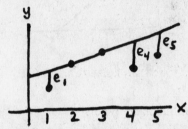

The line having the smallest squared error is called the **least-square line**, and is considered to be the line that best approximates the data.

SOLVE EQUATIONS

The computer can solve equations.

Single equations

Suppose you want to solve a tough equation, such as $2^x + x^3 = 20$. Rewrite it to make the right side be 0:

$2^x + x^3 - 20 = 0$

Let $f(x)$ denote the left side of the equation:

$f(x)$ is $2^x + x^3 - 20$

So the equation you want to solve is $f(x) = 0$. Here's a way to solve it — called the **secant method**. . . .

Let x_1 and x_2 be your favorite numbers. Graph $f(x_1)$ and $f(x_2)$:

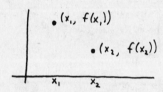

Let x_3 be where the line connecting those points hits the x axis:

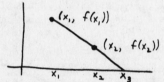

Graph $f(x_3)$; it's probably close to 0:

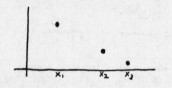

Connect the x_2 point to the x_3 point, to find x_4:

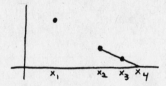

Connect the x_3 point to the x_4 point, to find x_5:

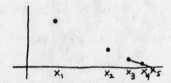

Probably you'll get closer and closer to the point where $f(x)$ is 0.

A different method, called **Muller's method**, uses parabolas instead of straight lines. . . .

Let x_1, x_2, and x_3 be your three favorite numbers. A common choice is -.5, .5, and 0. Graph $f(x_1)$, $f(x_2)$, and $f(x_3)$:

Draw the parabola that passes through those points:

The parabola hits the x axis at two points (although the points might be what mathematicians call "imaginary"). Let x_4 be at one of those points. For best results, choose the point that's closer to the origin:

Graph $f(x_4)$:

Draw a parabola through the x_2, x_3, and x_4 points, to find x_5:

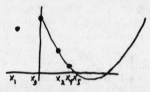

Probably you'll get closer to the place where $f(x)$ is 0.

Usually, Muller's method moves toward the solution more rapidly than the secant method. It can even find complex, "non-real" solutions, since the x value where the parabola hits the x axis might be of the form $a + bi$, where i denotes the square root of -1. (If you're interested in just solutions that are real, pretend b is 0.)

Using either the secant method or Muller's, suppose you finally find a solution of the equation $2^x + x^3 - 20 = 0$. Let s_1 denote that solution. To hunt for additional solutions, try solving this equation:

$$\frac{2^x + x^3 - 20}{x - s_1} = 0$$

If you find a solution of that new equation, call it s_2, and solve this equation:

$$\frac{2^x + x^3 - 20}{(x - s_1)(x - s_2)} = 0$$

If that produces a solution s_3, solve

$$\frac{2^x + x^3 - 20}{(x - s_1)(x - s_2)(x - s_3)} = 0$$

to find s_4. The solutions s_1, s_2, s_3, s_4, etc., are all solutions of the original equation.

The round-off error will be less if $|s_1| < |s_2| < |s_3| < |s_4| < \ldots$. So when you hunt for solutions, begin by trying to find the solutions closest to zero. That's why, when Muller's parabola hits the x axis in two points, you should pick the point that's closer to zero. And that's why a common choice for x_1, x_2, and x_3 is numbers near zero.

Simultaneous equations

Try to solve these simultaneous linear equations:

$$8x + y - z = 8$$
$$2x + y + 9z = 12$$
$$x - 7y + 2z = -4$$

An obvious way is **Gauss-Jordan elimination**. Eliminate the first coefficient:

$$x + \tfrac{1}{8}y - \tfrac{1}{8}z = 1 \quad \text{(I multiplied by } \tfrac{1}{8}\text{)}$$
$$2x + y + 9z = 12$$
$$x - 7y + 2z = -4$$

Eliminate everything below it:

$$x + \tfrac{1}{8}y - \tfrac{1}{8}z = 1$$
$$\tfrac{3}{4}y + \tfrac{37}{4}z = 10 \quad \text{(I subtracted twice the first row)}$$
$$-\tfrac{57}{8}y + \tfrac{17}{8}z = -5 \quad \text{(I subtracted the first row)}$$

Eliminate the first coefficient in the second row:

$$x + \tfrac{1}{8}y - \tfrac{1}{8}z = 1$$
$$y + \tfrac{37}{3}z = \tfrac{40}{3} \quad \text{(I multiplied by } \tfrac{4}{3}\text{)}$$
$$-\tfrac{57}{8}y + \tfrac{17}{8}z = -5$$

Eliminate everything above and below it:

$$x \quad\; - \tfrac{5}{3}z = -\tfrac{2}{3} \quad \text{(I subtracted } \tfrac{1}{8} \text{ times the second row)}$$
$$y + \tfrac{37}{3}z = \tfrac{40}{3}$$
$$90z = 90 \quad \text{(I added } \tfrac{57}{8} \text{ times the second row)}$$

Eliminate the first coefficient in the third row:

$$x \quad\; - \tfrac{5}{3}z = -\tfrac{2}{3}$$
$$y + \tfrac{37}{3}z = \tfrac{40}{3}$$
$$z = 1 \quad \text{(I multiplied by } \tfrac{1}{90}\text{)}$$

Eliminate everything above it:

$$x \qquad = 1 \quad \text{(I added } \tfrac{5}{3} \text{ times the third row)}$$
$$y \qquad = 1 \quad \text{(I subtracted } \tfrac{37}{3} \text{ times the third row)}$$
$$z = 1$$

That's the solution. (It's depressing that so much computation was needed, to get such a simple solution!)

In that example, I pivoted on the first coefficient of the first equation, then the first coefficient of the second equation, and finally the first coefficient of the third equation. To reduce the computer's round-off error, it's better at each stage to pivot on the coefficient that has the largest absolute value, relative to the coefficients in its row. For example, at this stage —

$$x + \tfrac{1}{8}y - \tfrac{1}{8}z = 1$$
$$\tfrac{3}{4}y + \tfrac{37}{4}z = 10$$
$$-\tfrac{57}{8}y + \tfrac{17}{8}z = -5$$

it would have been better to pivot on $-\tfrac{57}{8}$ than on $\tfrac{3}{4}$, since $\tfrac{57}{8}$ divided by $\tfrac{17}{8}$ is bigger than $\tfrac{3}{4}$ divided by $\tfrac{37}{4}$.

Now let's go back to the original equations —

$$8x + y - z = 8$$
$$2x + y + 9z = 12$$
$$x - 7y + 2z = -4$$

and solve them by a different method, called **Gauss-Seidel iteration**. In each equation, find the variable whose coefficient has the largest absolute value, and put that variable on one side:

$$x = -\tfrac{1}{8}y + \tfrac{1}{8}z + 1$$
$$z = -\tfrac{2}{9}x - \tfrac{1}{9}y + \tfrac{4}{3}$$
$$y = \tfrac{1}{7}x + \tfrac{2}{7}z + \tfrac{4}{7}$$

Begin by guessing that x, y, and z are all 0, then improve the guesses by using those equations. Here are the calculations, to three decimal places:

$$x = 0$$
$$y = 0$$
$$z = 0$$
$$x = -\tfrac{1}{8}y + \tfrac{1}{8}z + 1 = 1.000$$
$$y = \tfrac{1}{7}x + \tfrac{2}{7}z + \tfrac{4}{7} = .714$$
$$z = -\tfrac{2}{9}x - \tfrac{1}{9}y + \tfrac{4}{3} = 1.032$$
$$x = -\tfrac{1}{8}y + \tfrac{1}{8}z + 1 = 1.041$$
$$y = \tfrac{1}{7}x + \tfrac{2}{7}z + \tfrac{4}{7} = 1.014$$
$$z = -\tfrac{2}{9}x - \tfrac{1}{9}y + \tfrac{4}{3} = .990$$
$$x = -\tfrac{1}{8}y + \tfrac{1}{8}z + 1 = .997$$
$$y = \tfrac{1}{7}x + \tfrac{2}{7}z + \tfrac{4}{7} = .996$$
$$z = -\tfrac{2}{9}x - \tfrac{1}{9}y + \tfrac{4}{3} = 1.002$$
$$x = -\tfrac{1}{8}y + \tfrac{1}{8}z + 1 = 1.001$$
$$y = \tfrac{1}{7}x + \tfrac{2}{7}z + \tfrac{4}{7} = 1.000$$
$$z = -\tfrac{2}{9}x - \tfrac{1}{9}y + \tfrac{4}{3} = 1.000$$
$$x = -\tfrac{1}{8}y + \tfrac{1}{8}z + 1 = 1.000$$
$$y = \tfrac{1}{7}x + \tfrac{2}{7}z + \tfrac{4}{7} = 1.000$$
$$z = -\tfrac{2}{9}x - \tfrac{1}{9}y + \tfrac{4}{3} = 1.000$$

In the example, x and y and z gradually approach the correct solutions.

Is Gauss-Seidel iteration better or worse than Gauss-Jordan elimination?

A disadvantage of Gauss-Seidel iteration is: it doesn't guarantee you'll approach the correct solution. If you follow the advice about pivoting on the coefficient that has the largest relative absolute value, you stand a better chance of approaching the correct solution, but there's no guarantee.

On the other hand, if Gauss-Seidel iteration *does* approach a solution, the solution will have less round-off error than with Gauss-Jordan elimination.

INDEX

VENDOR PHONE BOOK

Vendor	State	Phone	Comment	Page
American Computer Exchange	GA	800-786-0717, 404-250-0050	broker of used computers	21
Apple	CA	800-776-2333, 408-996-1010	get free catalog by phoning 800-795-1000	11, 81, 605
Artisoft	AZ	800-TINY-RAM, 602-293-4000	makes Lantastic; tech 602-293-6363	277
Berkeley Macintosh User Group	CA	800-776-BMUG, 510-549-2684	gives Mac help, by phone	608
Borland	CA	800-336-6464, 408-461-9000	tech support for DBASE: 408-431-9060	63, 450
Boston Computer Exchange	MA	800-262-6399, 617-542-4414	broker of used computers	21
Boston Computer Society	MA	617-290-5700	largest computer club	608
Brøderbund	CA	800-521-6263, 415-492-3500	makes Print Shop; tech 415-382-4750	64
Comp USA	TX	800-COMP-USA, 214-702-0055	chain of computer superstores	11, 20, 80
Dell	TX	800-BUY-DELL	makes computers; ask for a free catalog	11, 79
Egghead Discount Software	WA	800-EGG-HEAD	chain of software stores	21
EPS Technologies	SD	800-447-0921, 605-966-5586	makes fancy notebook computers, cheap	13, 77
Expotech Computers	IL	800-215-3976	to reach Tim, press 3 then TIM then #	77
Gateway 2000	SD	800-LAD-2000, 605-232-2000	the biggest mail-order clone maker	11, 74
Harmony Computers	NY	800-441-1144, 718-692-3232	printers, software, etc.	21, 44
Insight	AZ	800-998-8028, 602-902-1176	low prices on hard drives, etc.	20, 34, 38, 40
Lotus	MA	800-872-3387, 617-577-8500	tech support for 1-2-3: 800-223-1662	61, 63, 157, 158, 220, 221, 235
Mac Connection	NH	800-800-4444, 603-446-4444	mainly software, helpful	20
Microsoft	WA	800-426-9400, 206-882-8080	for tech support, phone 206-454-2030	64
Midwest Micro	OH	800-423-8215, 513-368-2309	notebook computers, modems, printers	13, 20, 44, 56, 80
National Computer Exchange	NY	800-NACOMEX, 212-614-0700	broker of used computers	21
Novell	UT	800-453-1267, 801-379-5900	the most popular networking software	63, 276
NY PC	NY	212-533-NYPC	New York's computer club	608
PC Connection	NH	800-800-0004, 603-446-0004	mainly software, helpful	20
Philadelphia Area Comp. Soc.	PA	215-951-1255	Philadelphia's computer club	608
Quantex	NJ	800-836-0566, 908-563-4166	sells tower & Pentium computers cheap	12, 73
Seagate Technology	CA	800-468-3472, 408-438-6550	biggest manufacturer of hard drives	37
Secret Guide to Computers	MA	617-666-2666	publishes this book	1
Symantec	CA	800-441-7234, 408-253-9600	tech support about Q&A: 408-252-5700	61, 64, 157, 173, 207, 208, 172
USA Flex	IL	800-USA-FLEX, 708-351-7172	monitors, printers, etc.	20, 40, 44
Western Digital	CA	800-832-4778, 714-863-0102	makes hard drives & controllers	37
Word Perfect Corporation	UT	800-451-5151, 801-225-5000	tech support: 800-541-5096, 801-222-9010	60, 63, 157, 183
Zeos	MN	800-554-7172, 612-633-6163	makes 386 & 486 computers	80

MENUS & ICONS

Word Perfect

The Word Perfect index is on page 186.

BASIC

The BASIC index is on pages 322-323.

DBASE

PASCAL

C

LOGO

FORTRAN

COBOL

EASY

LISP

8088 Assembler

For each topic, this index tells the page number where the discussion begins; read the next few pages also.
To find a PASCAL command, look up "PASCAL summary", which in turn will lead you to the specific command.

You'll want more copies of *The Secret Guide to Computers* for yourself and your friends. The books make great presents for Christmas, birthdays, graduations, and celebrations.

To get books or free brochures, you can use the coupon on this page. Photocopy it for your friends.

Money-back guarantee

If you're not sure whether to order a book, go ahead: you can return unused books anytime for a 100% refund.

Walk in

If you're in the Boston area, you can pick up the books personally. Phone 617-666-2666 for directions and a guaranteed pickup time.

Phone & purchase orders

You can order by phoning 617-666-2666 (or using a purchase order) if you're employed by an established computer company, bookstore, school, government agency, or public utility or if you bought at least 10 books from us before. Give us your address *and phone number*. We'll ship the books with a bill, due in 30 days.

Other countries

We accept all checks, money orders, and cash from all countries. Pay in U.S. dollars or the equivalent amount of foreign currency. We convert foreign currency and send you change.

Though we accept all checks, you'll get faster processing by sending cash or an international postal money order (from Canada denominated in U.S. dollars) or a foreign check (from any country) denominated in U.S. dollars and having a U.S. or Canadian city printed somewhere on the check.

Review copies

If you write reviews for magazines, run a big computer department, teach many computer students, or plan to introduce the book to at least 100 people, phone 617-666-2666 to request a complimentary book for review.

Special services

To find out about our special services, read page 9 of *The Secret Guide to Computers*.

- - - CUT OUT THIS COUPON - - -

Books with discounts

The Secret Guide to Computers lists for $15. To pay less, team up with your friends.

20% discount if you order at least   2 books: pay just $12 per book.
40% discount if you order at least   4 books: pay just $9 per book.
60% discount if you order at least   60 books: pay just $6 per book.
67% discount if you order at least 666 books; pay just $4.95 per book.

Because of those discounts, don't order 3 books (order 4 instead); don't order 40-59 books (order 60 instead); don't order 550-665 books (order 666 instead).

How many books do you want? _____ Write their *total* cost here: $ _____

Free brochures

Free brochures on the following topics will be available soon. Get on our mailing list now, by marking the brochures you want:
- ☐ **how you can get the next edition of The Secret Guide to Computers**
- ☐ **how you can get The Secret Guide to Tricky Living**
- ☐ **how you can get Secret Videotapes**
- ☐ **how you can get a 2-day Blitz Course taught by Russ in many cities**
- ☐ **how you can get Secret Brochures about us to give your friends**

Address

Print the name and address where you want the goods sent:

Tax?

Usually, we don't have to charge sales tax. But *if the person ordering or receiving the book is in Massachusetts*, we must typically charge 5% sales tax:

Price	$15	$24	$36	$45	$54	$63	$72	$360
Tax	$0.75	$1.20	$1.80	$2.25	$2.70	$3.15	$3.60	$18

If in Massachusetts, write the tax here ($_____), unless you're tax-exempt (give us your tax-exempt number) or resell the book (give us your Massachusetts resale number) or take a course requiring the book (name the school and course).

Shipping

We ship all over the world. We charge *nothing* for standard shipping. If you pay extra, we'll use extra-fast shipping methods. Mark the shipping method you prefer:

☐ **Standard shipping** usually takes 1 week to ZIP codes below 27000, 2 weeks to the rest of the USA, 4 weeks to Canada & Mexico, 6 weeks to other countries. We usually ship by post office Surface Book Rate. We charge nothing.

☐ **UPS** usually takes 2 days to ZIP codes below 27000, 1 week to the rest of the USA. You must order at least 2 books, be in the 48 states or DC, and give a street address (not just a PO Box, APO, or FPO). We charge $2 to ship a box holding up to 4 books, $4 to ship a box holding up to 10 books. If you're ordering over 10 books, we charge just $6 total, even if your order is huge.

☐ **Air** usually takes 2 days to USA (Priority Mail), 3 weeks to other countries (post office Air Book). We charge $2 per book to USA, $4 per book to Canada&Mexico, $14 per book to other countries.

Final steps

If the books are a gift to a friend, include a greeting card or note for us to give your friend. On the back of this coupon, please write comments (pro or con) about the *Guide*. Send check made out to *The Secret Guide to Computers*, money order, or cash. Mail to Russ Walter, 22 Ashland St. (Floor 2), Somerville, MA 02144-3202.

You'll want more copies of *The Secret Guide to Computers* for yourself and your friends. The books make great presents for Christmas, birthdays, graduations, and celebrations.

To get books or free brochures, you can use the coupon on this page. Photocopy it for your friends.

Money-back guarantee

If you're not sure whether to order a book, go ahead: you can return unused books anytime for a 100% refund.

Walk in

If you're in the Boston area, you can pick up the books personally. Phone 617-666-2666 for directions and a guaranteed pickup time.

Phone & purchase orders

You can order by phoning 617-666-2666 (or using a purchase order) if you're employed by an established computer company, bookstore, school, government agency, or public utility or if you bought at least 10 books from us before. Give us your address *and phone number*. We'll ship the books with a bill, due in 30 days.

Other countries

We accept all checks, money orders, and cash from all countries. Pay in U.S. dollars or the equivalent amount of foreign currency. We convert foreign currency and send you change.

Though we accept all checks, you'll get faster processing by sending cash or an international postal money order (from Canada denominated in U.S. dollars) or a foreign check (from any country) denominated in U.S. dollars and having a U.S. or Canadian city printed somewhere on the check.

Review copies

If you write reviews for magazines, run a big computer department, teach many computer students, or plan to introduce the book to at least 100 people, phone 617-666-2666 to request a complimentary book for review.

Special services

To find out about our special services, read page 9 of *The Secret Guide to Computers*.

CUT OUT THIS COUPON

Books with discounts

The Secret Guide to Computers lists for $15. To pay less, team up with your friends.

20% discount if you order at least   2 books: pay just $12 per book.
40% discount if you order at least   4 books: pay just $9 per book.
60% discount if you order at least 60 books: pay just $6 per book.
67% discount if you order at least 666 books; pay just $4.95 per book.

Because of those discounts, don't order 3 books (order 4 instead); don't order 40-59 books (order 60 instead); don't order 550-665 books (order 666 instead).

How many books do you want? _____ Write their *total* cost here: $ _____

Free brochures

Free brochures on the following topics will be available soon. Get on our mailing list now, by marking the brochures you want:

☐ **how you can get the next edition of The Secret Guide to Computers**
☐ **how you can get The Secret Guide to Tricky Living**
☐ **how you can get Secret Videotapes**
☐ **how you can get a 2-day Blitz Course taught by Russ in many cities**
☐ **how you can get Secret Brochures about us to give your friends**

Address

Print the name and address where you want the goods sent:

Tax?

Usually, we don't have to charge sales tax. But *if the person ordering or receiving the book is in Massachusetts*, we must typically charge 5% sales tax:

Price	$15	$24	$36	$45	$54	$63	$72	$360
Tax	$0.75	$1.20	$1.80	$2.25	$2.70	$3.15	$3.60	$18

If in Massachusetts, write the tax here ($ _____), unless you're tax-exempt (give us your tax-exempt number) or resell the book (give us your Massachusetts resale number) or take a course requiring the book (name the school and course).

Shipping

We ship all over the world. We charge *nothing* for standard shipping. If you pay extra, we'll use extra-fast shipping methods. Mark the shipping method you prefer:

☐ **Standard shipping** usually takes 1 week to ZIP codes below 27000, 2 weeks to the rest of the USA, 4 weeks to Canada & Mexico, 6 weeks to other countries. We usually ship by post office Surface Book Rate. We charge nothing.

☐ **UPS** usually takes 2 days to ZIP codes below 27000, 1 week to the rest of the USA. You must order at least 2 books, be in the 48 states or DC, and give a street address (not just a PO Box, APO, or FPO). We charge $2 to ship a box holding up to 4 books, $4 to ship a box holding up to 10 books. If you're ordering over 10 books, we charge just $6 total, even if your order is huge.

☐ **Air** usually takes 2 days to USA (Priority Mail), 3 weeks to other countries (post office Air Book). We charge $2 per book to USA, $4 per book to Canada&Mexico, $14 per book to other countries.

Final steps

If the books are a gift to a friend, include a greeting card or note for us to give your friend. On the back of this coupon, please write comments (pro or con) about the *Guide*. Send check made out to *The Secret Guide to Computers*, money order, or cash. Mail to Russ Walter, 22 Ashland St. (Floor 2), Somerville, MA 02144-3202.